VRIO

"VALUE. RARITY. IMITABILITY. ORGANIZATION."

What Is It?

This book is not just a list of concepts, models, and theories. It is the first undergraduate textbook to introduce a **theory-based, multi-chapter organizing framework** to add additional structure to the field of strategic management.

"VRIO" is a mechanism that integrates two existing theoretical frameworks: the positioning perspective and the resource-based view. It is the primary tool for accomplishing internal analysis. It stands for four questions one must ask about a resource or capability to determine its competitive potential:

1. **The Question of Value:** Does a resource enable a firm to exploit an environmental opportunity, and/or neutralize an environmental threat?

2. **The Question of Rarity:** Is a resource currently controlled by only a small number of competing firms?

3. **The Question of Imitability:** Do firms without a resource face a cost disadvantage in obtaining or developing it?

4. **The Question of Organization:** Are a firm's other policies and procedures organized to support the exploitation of its valuable, rare, and costly-to-imitate resources?

What's the Benefit of the VRIO Framework?

The VRIO framework is the organizational foundation of the text. **It creates a decision-making framework for students** to use in analyzing case and business situations.

Students tend to view concepts, models, and theories (in all of their coursework) as fragmented and disconnected. Strategy is no exception. This view encourages rote memorization, not real understanding. VRIO, by serving as a consistent framework, connects ideas together. This encourages real understanding, not memorization.

This understanding enables students to better analyze business cases and situations—the goal of the course.

The VRIO framework makes it possible to discuss the formulation and implementation of a strategy simultaneously, within each chapter.

Because the VRIO framework provides a simple integrative structure, we are actually able to address issues in this book that are largely ignored elsewhere—including discussions of vertical integration, outsourcing, real options logic, and mergers and acquisitions, to name just a few.

O t h e r   B e n e f i t s

Element	Description	Benefit	Example
Chapter Opening Cases	We have chosen firms that are familiar to most students. Opening cases focus on iTunes' success in the music download industry, how Ryanair has become the lowest cost airline in the world, how Victoria's Secret differentiated its products, how ESPN has diversified its operations, and so forth.	By having cases tightly linked to the material, students can develop strategic analysis skills by studying firms familiar to them.	2–3
Full Length Cases	This book contains selective, part-ending cases that underscore the concepts in each part. This provides a tight link to the chapter concepts to reinforce understanding of recent research. These are 1) decision oriented, 2) recent, 3) student-recognized companies, and 4) cases where the data are only partly analyzed.	Provides a tight link to chapter concepts, facilitating students' ability to apply text ideas to case analysis.	PC 1-1– PC 1-12
Strategy in Depth	For professors and students interested in understanding the full intellectual underpinnings of the field, we have included an optional Strategy in Depth feature in every chapter. Knowledge in strategic management continues to evolve rapidly, in ways that are well beyond what is normally included in introductory texts.	Customize your course as desired to provide enrichment material for advanced students.	288
Research Made Relevant	The Research Made Relevant feature highlights very current research findings related to some of the strategic topics discussed in that chapter.	Shows students the evolving nature of strategy.	49
Challenge Questions	These might be of an ethical or moral nature, forcing students to apply concepts across chapters, apply concepts to themselves, or extend chapter ideas in creative ways.	Requires students to think critically.	245
Problem Set	Problem Set asks students to apply theories and tools from the chapter. These often require calculations. They can be thought of as homework assignments. If students struggle with these problems they might have trouble with the more complex cases. These problem sets are largely diagnostic in character.	Sharpens quantitative skills, and provides a bridge between chapter material and case analysis.	128–129
Ethics and Strategy	Highlights some of the most important dilemmas faced by firms when creating and implementing strategies.	Helps students make better ethical decisions as managers.	210
Strategy in the Emerging Enterprise	Growing number of graduates work for small and medium-sized firms. This feature presents an extended example, in each chapter, of the unique strategic problems facing those employed in small and medium-sized firms.	This feature highlights the unique challenges of doing strategic analysis in emerging enterprises, and small and medium-sized firms.	22

EDITION

4

Strategic Management and Competitive Advantage

CONCEPTS AND CASES

Jay B. Barney

The Ohio State University

William S. Hesterly

The University of Utah

PEARSON

Boston   Columbus   Indianapolis   New York   San Francisco   Upper Saddle River
Amsterdam   Cape Town   Dubai   London   Madrid   Milan   Munich   Paris   Montreal   Toronto
Delhi   Mexico City   Sao Paulo   Sydney   Hong Kong   Seoul   Singapore   Taipei   Tokyo

Editorial Director: Sally Yagan
Editor in Chief: Eric Svendsen
Senior Acquisitions Editor: Kim Norbuta
Director of Editorial Services: Ashley Santora
Editorial Project Manager: Claudia Fernandes
Editorial Assistant: Carter Anderson
Director of Marketing: Patrice Lumumba Jones
Senior Marketing Manager: Nikki Ayana Jones
Marketing Assistant: Ian Gold
Senior Managing Editor: Judy Leale
Production Project Manager: Ann Pulido
Senior Operations Supervisor: Arnold Vila
Operations Specialist: Cathleen Petersen
Creative Director: Blair Brown
Senior Art Director/Design Supervisor:
 Janet Slowik

Interior Designer: Wanda Espana
Cover Designer: Karen Quigley
Cover Illustration: Gary Hovland
Illustrator (Interior): Gary Hovland
Manager, Rights and Permissions:
 Hessa Albader
Media Project Manager: Lisa Rinaldi
Editorial Media Project Manager:
 Denise Vaughn
Full-Service Project Management:
 PreMediaGlobal, Inc.
Composition: PreMediaGlobal, Inc.
Printer/Binder: R. R. Donnelley/Willard
Cover Printer: Lehigh-Phoenix
 Color/Hagerstown
Text Font: Palatino 10/12

Credits and acknowledgments borrowed from other sources and reproduced, with permission, in this textbook appear on appropriate page within text.

Microsoft® and Windows® are registered trademarks of the Microsoft Corporation in the U.S.A. and other countries. Screen shots and icons reprinted with permission from the Microsoft Corporation. This book is not sponsored or endorsed by or affiliated with the Microsoft Corporation.

Library of Congress Cataloging-in-Publication Data
Barney, Jay B.
 Strategic management and competitive advantage : concepts and cases / Jay B. Barney, William S. Hesterly.—4th ed.
  p. cm.
 Includes bibliographical references and index.
 ISBN 978-0-13-255550-0 (alk. paper)
 1. Strategic planning—Case studies.   2. Business planning—Case studies.   3. Industrial management—Case studies.   4. Competition—Case studies.   I.   Hesterly, William S.   II.   Title.

 HD30.28.B36834 2012
 658.4'012—dc22

                                                                        2011014817

10 9 8 7 6 5 4 3 2 1

ISBN 10:   0-13-255550-6
ISBN 13: 978-0-13-255550-0

This book is dedicated to my expanding family: my wife, Kim; our children, Lindsay, Kristian, and Erin; their spouses, Ryan, Amy, and Dave; and most of all, our eight grandchildren, Isaac, Dylanie, Audrey, Chloe, Lucas, Royal, Lincoln, and Nolan. They all help me remember that no success could compensate for failure in the home.

Jay B. Barney
Columbus, Ohio

This book is for my family who has taught me life's greatest lessons about what matters most. To my wife, Denise; my sons, Drew, Ian, Austin, and Alex; my daughters, Lindsay and Jessica (and their husbands, Matt and John); and grandchildren, Ellie, Owen, Emerson, Cade, and Elizabeth.

William Hesterly
Salt Lake City, Utah

Brief Contents

Contents

Part 1: THE TOOLS of STRATEGIC ANALYSIS

Part 2: BUSINESS-LEVEL STRATEGIES

CHAPTER 5   Product Differentiation   130

End-of-Part 2 Cases

Part 3: CORPORATE STRATEGIES

End-of-Part 3 Cases

Appendix: Analyzing Cases and Preparing for Class Discussions   343

Preface

The first thing you will notice as you look through this edition of our book is that it continues to be much shorter than most textbooks on strategic management. There is not the usual "later edition" increase in number of pages and bulk. We're strong proponents of the philosophy that, often, less is more. The general tendency is for textbooks to get longer and longer as authors make sure that their books leave out nothing that is in other books. We take a different approach. Our guiding principle in deciding what to include is: "Does this concept help students analyze cases and real business situations?" For many concepts we considered, the answer is no. But, where the answer is yes, the concept is in the book.

New to this Edition

This edition features several new and updated cases, including:

- Pfizer and the Challenges of the Global Pharmaceutical Industry
- Wal-Mart Stores, Inc., in 2010
- True Religion Brand Jeans and the Premium Jeans Industry
- JetBlue Airways: Managing Growth
- Nucor in 2010
- Danaher Corporation
- LVMH: Managing the Multi-Brand Conglomerate
- McDonald's and KFC: Recipes for Success in China

VRIO Framework and Other Hallmark Features

One thing that has not changed in the fourth edition is that we continue to have a point of view about the field of strategic management. In planning for this book, we recalled our own educational experience and the textbooks that did and didn't work for us then. Those few that stood out as the best did not merely cover all of the different topics in a field of study. They provided a framework that we could carry around in our heads, and they helped us to see what we were studying as an integrated whole rather than a disjointed sequence of loosely related subjects. This text continues to be integrated around the VRIO framework. As those of you familiar with the resource-based theory of strategy recognize, the VRIO framework addresses the central questions around gaining and sustaining competitive advantage. The VRIO logic of competitive advantage is applied in every chapter. It is simple enough to understand and teach yet broad enough to apply to a wide variety of cases and business settings.

Our consistent use of the VRIO framework does not mean that any of the concepts fundamental to a strategy course are missing. We still have all of the core ideas and theories that are essential to a strategy course. Ideas such as the five forces framework, value chain analysis, generic strategies, and corporate strategy are all in the book. Because the VRIO framework provides a single integrative structure, we are able to address issues in this book that are largely ignored elsewhere—including discussions of vertical integration, outsourcing, real options logic, and mergers and acquisitions, to name a few.

We also have designed flexibility into the book. Each chapter has four short sections that present specific issues in more depth. These sections allow instructors to adapt the book to the particular needs of their students. "Strategy in Depth" examines the intellectual foundations that are behind the way managers think about and practice strategy today. "Strategy in the Emerging Enterprise" presents examples of strategic challenges faced by new and emerging enterprises. "Ethics and Strategy" delves into some of the ethical dilemmas that managers face as they confront strategic decisions. "Research Made Relevant" includes recent research related to the topics in that chapter.

We have also included cases—including many new cases in this edition—that provide students an opportunity to apply the ideas they learn to business situations. The cases include a variety of contexts, such as entrepreneurial, service, manufacturing, and international settings. The power of the VRIO framework is that it applies across all of these settings. Applying the VRIO framework to many topics and cases throughout the book leads to real understanding instead of rote memorization. The end result is that students will find that they have the tools they need to do strategic analysis. Nothing more. Nothing less.

Supplements

At the Instructor Resource Center, at www.pearsonhighered.com/irc, instructors can access a variety of print, digital, and presentation resources available with this text in downloadable format. Registration is simple and gives you immediate access to new titles and new editions. As a registered faculty member, you can download resource files and receive immediate access to and instructions for installing course management content on your campus server. In case you ever need assistance, our dedicated technical support team is ready to help with the media supplements that accompany this text. Visit http://247 .pearsoned.custhelp.com for answers to frequently asked questions and toll-free user support phone numbers.

The following supplements are available for download to adopting instructors:

- Instructor's Manual
- Case Teaching Notes
- Test Item File
- TestGen® Computerized Test Bank
- PowerPoint Slides

Videos on DVD

Exciting and high-quality video clips help deliver engaging topics to the classroom to help students better understand the concepts explained in the textbook. Please contact your local representative to receive a copy of the DVD.

Acknowledgments

Obviously, a book like this is not written in isolation. We owe a debt of gratitude to all those at Prentice Hall who have supported its development. In particular, we want to thank Eric Svendsen, Editor-in-Chief; Kim Norbuta, Senior Acquisitions Editor; Claudia Fernandes, Editorial Project Manager; Nikki Ayana Jones, Marketing Manager; Judy Leale, Senior Managing Editor; Ann Pulido, Production Project Manager; and Janet Slowik, Art Director.

Many people were involved in reviewing drafts of each edition's manuscript. Their efforts undoubtedly improved the manuscript dramatically. Their efforts are largely unsung, but very much appreciated.

Thank you to these professors who participated in manuscript reviews:

Yusaf Akbar—Southern New Hampshire University

Joseph D. Botana II—Lakeland College

Pam Braden—West Virginia University at Parkersburg

Erick PC Chang—Arkansas State University

Mustafa Colak—Temple University

Ron Eggers—Barton College

Michael Frandsen—Albion College

Swapnil Garg—University of Florida

Michele Gee—University of Wisconsin, Parkside

Peter Goulet—University of Northern Iowa

Rebecca Guidice—University of Nevada Las Vegas

Laura Hart—Lynn University, College of Business & Management

Tom Hewett—Kaplan University

Phyllis Holland—Valdosta State University

Paul Howard—Penn State University

Richard Insinga—St. John Fisher College

Homer Johnson—Loyola University Chicago

Marilyn Kaplan—University of Texas at Dallas

Joseph Leonard—Miami University

Paul Maxwell—St. Thomas University, Miami

Stephen Mayer—Niagara University

Richard Nemanick—Saint Louis University

Hossein Noorian—Wentworth Institute of Technology

Ralph Parrish—University of Central Oklahoma

Raman Patel—Robert Morris College

Jiten Ruparel—Otterbein College

Roy Simerly—East Carolina University

Sally Sledge—Christopher Newport University

David Stahl—Montclair State University

David Stephens—Utah State University

Philip Stoeberl—Saint Louis University

Ram Subramanian—Grand Valley State University

William W. Topper—Curry College

Thomas Turk—Chapman University

Henry Ulrich—Central Connecticut State soon to be UCONN

Floyd Willoughby—Oakland University

Author Biographies

JAY B. BARNEY

Jay Barney is Chase Chair for Excellence in Corporate Strategy at the Max M. Fisher College of Business, The Ohio State University. He received his Ph.D. from Yale and has held faculty appointments at UCLA and Texas A&M. Jay has published over 100 journal articles and books; has served on the editorial boards of *Academy of Management Review, Strategic Management Journal*, and *Organization Science;* and has served as an associate editor of *The Journal of Management*, senior editor at *Organization Science*, and currently serves as co-editor at the *Strategic Entrepreneurship Journal*. He has received honorary doctorate degrees from the University of Lund (Sweden), the Copenhagen Business School (Denmark), and the Universidad Pontificia Comillas (Spain), and has been elected to the Academy of Management Fellows and Strategic Management Society Fellows. He currently holds honorary visiting professor positions at Waikato University (New Zealand), Sun Yat-Sen University (China), and Peking University (China). He has also consulted for a wide variety of public and private organizations, including Hewlett-Packard, Texas Instruments, Arco, Koch Industries Inc., and Nationwide Insurance, focusing on implementing large-scale organizational change and strategic analysis. He has received teaching awards at UCLA, Texas A&M, and Ohio State. Jay served as assistant program chair and program chair, chair elect, and chair of the Business Policy and Strategy Division. In 2005, he received the Irwin Outstanding Educator Award for the BPS Division of the Academy of Management; and in 2010 he won the Academy's Scholarly Contribution to Management Award. In 2008, he was elected as the President-elect of the Strategic Management Society, where he currently serves as president.

WILLIAM S. HESTERLY

William Hesterly is the Associate Dean for Faculty and Research as well as the Dumke Family Endowed Presidential Chair in Management in the David Eccles School of Business, University of Utah. After studying at Louisiana State University, he received bachelors, and masters degrees from Brigham Young University and a Ph.D. from the University of California, Los Angeles. Professor Hesterly has been recognized multiple times as the outstanding teacher in the MBA Program at the David Eccles School of Business and he has also been the recipient of the Student's Choice Award. He has taught in a variety of executive programs for both large and small companies. Professor Hesterly's research on organizational economics, vertical integration, organizational forms, and entrepreneurial networks has appeared in top journals including the *Academy of Management Review, Organization Science, Strategic Management Journal, Journal of Management*, and the *Journal of Economic Behavior and Organization*. Currently, he is studying the sources of value creation in firms and also the determinants of who captures the value from a firm's competitive advantage. Recent papers in this area have appeared in the *Academy of Management Review* and *Managerial and Decision Economics*. Professor Hesterly's research was recognized with the Western Academy of Management's Ascendant Scholar Award in 1999. Dr. Hesterly has also received best paper awards from the Western Academy of Management and the Academy of Management. Dr. Hesterly has served on the editorial boards of *Strategic Organization, Organization Science,* and the *Journal of Management*. He has served as Department Chair and also as Vice-President and President of the faculty at the David Eccles School of Business at the University of Utah.

1 THE TOOLS of STRATEGIC ANALYSIS

What Is Strategy and the Strategic Management Process?

After reading this chapter, you should be able to:

1. Define strategy.

2. Describe the strategic management process.

3. Define competitive advantage and explain its relationship to economic value creation.

4. Describe two different measures of competitive advantage.

5. Explain the difference between emergent and intended strategies.

6. Discuss the importance of understanding a firm's strategy even if you are not a senior manager in a firm.

The Music Download Industry

It all began with Napster—uploading digital music files and then sharing them with others on the Web. Nothing could be easier. Hard drives around the world began to fill with vast music libraries, all for free. There was only one little problem: It turned out that such downloading was illegal.

Not that this stopped illegal downloads. Indeed, even today there are 40 illegal music downloads for every legal one. Not surprisingly, the music industry continues to sue those engaging in this practice; over 12,000 such lawsuits have been filed around the world so far.

But declaring some music downloads illegal only created a new market, with new competitive opportunities: the legal download market. After just a few years, iTunes has emerged as a clear winner in this legal download market. In 2006, iTunes had over 88 percent of the legal download market. In 2008, iTunes surpassed Best Buy and Wal-Mart to become the largest music seller in the United States. The second most successful firm in the online music market—eMusic—has less than 10 percent of the market. Other contenders, including Amazon's digital music store and MusicPass (owned by Sony BMG), have less than 5 percent of the market.

So, why has iTunes been so successful? iTunes is a division of Apple and understanding iTunes' success begins by recognizing the link between the iTunes Web site and iPod, Apple's incredibly successful MP3 portable music player. The iPod is generally recognized as one of the simplest, most elegant music listening devices ever created. Efforts to imitate iPod's simple interface and software have, according to most reviewers, simply failed. So Apple began with a great music-playing product, the iPod.

Apple made it easy to link the iPod to its iTunes Web site. Even technological neophytes can download songs from iTunes to their iPods in just a few minutes. Of course, to make this transfer as seamless as possible, Apple developed proprietary software—called FairPlay. This software restricts the use of music downloaded from iTunes to iPod MP3 players. That means once you start downloading music from iTunes to your iPod, you are unlikely to change to another music Web site because you would have to download and pay for the music a second time.

Pretty clever. Build a great player—the iPod—develop proprietary download software—iTunes—and you have built-in customer loyalty. It is also pretty profitable. As the number of iPod or iTunes users continued to grow, more and more music producers were willing to sign agreements to let Apple distribute their music through

iTunes. The result was Apple's dominance of the legal music download industry.

So, can anyone catch iTunes? Several firms are trying.

Some people think that the future of the music download industry is going to depend on the extent to which restrictions on the use of downloaded music are eliminated. These restrictions are created by the digital rights management (DRM) software that is "wrapped" around each song downloaded from iTunes. Initially, music companies insisted on DRM protection, to ensure that they were compensated for the use of their music. But now Apple's proprietary DRM system seems to be one reason that iTunes has been able to create and sustain a huge advantage in the music download industry.

Enter Amazon. In 2007, Amazon.com announced that it would start selling music without DRM restrictions on its online music store. As important, most of the big music companies signed up to sell music on Amazon. Shortly thereafter, SonyBMG, eMusic, and Rhapsody all announced the creation of non-DRM music download sites. Would legal downloads without use restrictions begin to erode iTunes' huge advantage?

It's early days, but so far iTunes' competitive advantage seems to be secure. Of course, Apple did not ignore this potential competitive threat. Almost immediately, it began to sell non-DRM music downloads on iTunes, albeit at a price higher than its DRM-restricted downloads. As important, Apple continued to invest in its MP3 player and related technologies. First there was the iPhone, then more advanced iPods that played videos and games. Now some iPod models have the same "soft touch" interface system as Apple's iPhone. All this has made iPods and related products more

Morgan Lane Photography/Shutterstock

attractive than competing MP3 players, and people who buy Apple MP3 players are more likely to download music from iTunes than any other Web site. So Apple matched the non-DRM offer and simultaneously reinforced its perceived hardware advantages—essentially implementing many of the same strategies that enabled it to gain its advantages in the music download industry in the first place.

But competition in this industry continues to evolve. What's next? Watch for Nokia and other cellphone manufacturers!

Sources: E. Smith (2006). "Can anybody catch iTunes?" *The Wall Street Journal*, November 27, pp. R1 +; J. Chaffin and A. van Duyn (2006). "Universal backs free music rival to iTunes." August 29, www.ft.com/cms/s; P. Thurrott and K. Furman (2004). "Illegal music downloads jump despite RIAA legal action." January 22, www.connectedhomemag.com. David Kravets (2007). "Like Amazon's DRM-free music downloads? Thank Apple," wired.com/ entertainment/music/news/2007/09; Peter Kafka (2008). "iTunes competitors: We're number 2, we're number 2," *Silicon Alley Insider*, www. alleyinsider.com/ 2008/3; Peter Kafka (2008). "How are those DRM-free MP3s selling?" *Silicon Alley Insider*, www.alleyinsider.com/2008/3.

Figuring out how iTunes has come to dominate the music download industry and what competitors can do about it will go a long way in determining a firm's performance in this industry. The process by which these kinds of questions are answered is the strategic management process; the answer a firm develops for these questions is a firm's strategy.

Strategy and the Strategic Management Process

Although most can agree that a firm's ability to survive and prosper depends on choosing and implementing a good strategy, there is less agreement about what a strategy is, and even less agreement about what constitutes a good strategy. Indeed, there are almost as many different definitions of these concepts as there are books written about them.

Defining Strategy

In this book, a firm's **strategy** is defined as its theory about how to gain competitive advantages.[1] A good strategy is a strategy that actually generates such advantages. Apple's *theory* of how to gain a competitive advantage in the music download-for-a-fee business is to link the music download business with particular MP3 players. Amazon's eMusic's and Sony BMG's theory is that users will want to have no restrictions on the use of downloaded music.

Each of these theories of how to gain competitive advantages in the music download-for-a-fee business—like all theories—is based on a set of assumptions and hypotheses about the way competition in this industry is likely to evolve, and how that evolution can be exploited to earn a profit. The greater the extent to which these assumptions and hypotheses accurately reflect how competition in this industry actually evolves, the more likely it is that a firm will gain a competitive advantage from implementing its strategies. If these assumptions and hypotheses turn out not to be accurate, then a firm's strategies are not likely to be a source of competitive advantage.

But here is the challenge. It is usually very difficult to predict how competition in an industry will evolve, and so it is rarely possible to know for sure that a firm is choosing the right strategy. This is why a firm's strategy is almost always a theory: It's a firm's best bet about how competition is going to evolve, and how that evolution can be exploited for competitive advantage.

The Strategic Management Process

Although it is usually difficult to know for sure that a firm is pursuing the best strategy, it is possible to reduce the likelihood that mistakes are being made. The best way to do this is for a firm to choose its strategy carefully and systematically and to follow the strategic management process. The **strategic management process** is a sequential set of analyses and choices that can increase the likelihood that a firm will choose a good strategy; that is, a strategy that generates competitive advantages. An example of the strategic management process is presented in Figure 1.1. Not surprisingly, this book is organized around this strategic management process.

A Firm's Mission

The strategic management process begins when a firm defines its mission. A firm's **mission** is its long-term purpose. Missions define both what a firm aspires to be in

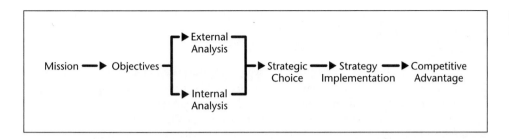

Figure 1.1   The Strategic Management Process

the long run and what it wants to avoid in the meantime. Missions are often written down in the form of **mission statements**. Table 1.1 contains examples of several mission statements taken from well-known firms.

Some Missions May Not Affect Firm Performance.   As shown in Table 1.1, most mission statements incorporate common elements. For example, many define the businesses within which a firm will operate—automobiles for Ford; computer hardware, software, and services for IBM; or it can be very simple like how a firm will compete in those businesses—doing everything direct at Dell. Many even define the core values that a firm espouses—the "soul of Dell" and Anheuser-Busch's values, for examples.

Indeed, mission statements often contain so many common elements that some have questioned whether having a mission statement even creates value for a firm.[2] Moreover, even if a mission statement does say something unique about a company, if that mission statement does not influence behavior throughout an organization, it is unlikely to have much impact on a firm's actions. After all, Enron's 1999 annual report includes the following statement of values:

> *Integrity: We work with customers and prospects openly, honestly, and sincerely. When we say we will do something, we will do it; when we say we cannot or will not do something, then we won't do it.*[3]

This statement was published at exactly the same time that senior management at Enron was engaging in activities that ultimately defrauded investors, partners, and Enron's own employees, and that landed some Enron executives in jail.[4]

Some Missions Can Improve Firm Performance.   Despite these caveats, research has identified some firms whose sense of purpose and mission permeates all that they do. Some of these **visionary firms**, or firms whose mission is central to all they do, have been compiled by Jim Collins and Jerry I. Porras in their book *Built to Last*, and are presented in Table 1.2.[5] One interesting thing to note about visionary firms is their long-term profitability. From 1926 through 1995, an investment of $1 in one of these firms would have increased in value to $6,536. That same dollar invested in an average firm over this same time period would have been worth $415 in 1995.

These visionary firms earned substantially higher returns than average firms even though many of their mission statements suggest that profit maximizing, although an important corporate objective, is not their primary reason for existence. Consider what Jim Burke, a former Chief Executive Officer (CEO) at Johnson & Johnson (J&J; one of the visionary firms identified in Table 1.2), says about the relationship between profits and his firm's mission and mission statement:

> *All our management is geared to profit on a day-to-day basis. That's part of the business of being in business. But too often, in this and other businesses, people are inclined to think, "We'd better do this because if we don't, it's going to show up on*

Johnson & Johnson

Our Credo

We believe our first responsibility is to the doctors, nurses and patients, to mothers and fathers and all others who use our products and services. In meeting their needs everything we do must be of high quality. We must constantly strive to reduce our costs in order to maintain reasonable prices. Customers' orders must be serviced promptly and accurately. Our suppliers and distributors must have an opportunity to make a fair profit.

We are responsible to our employees, the men and women who work with us through-out the world. Everyone must be considered as an individual. We must respect their dignity and recognize their merit. They must have a sense of security in their jobs. Compensation must be fair and adequate, and working conditions clean, orderly and safe. We must be mindful of ways to help our employees fulfill their family responsibil-ities. Employees must feel free to make suggestions and complaints. There must be equal opportunity for employment, development and advancement for those qualified. We must provide competent management, and their actions must be just and ethical.

We are responsible to the communities in which we live and work and to the world community as well. We must be good citizens—support good works and charities and bear our fair share of taxes. We must encourage civic improve-ments and better health and education. We must maintain in good order the prop-erty we are privileged to use, protecting the environment and natural resources.

Our final responsibility is to our stockholders. Business must make a sound profit. We must experiment with new ideas. Research must be carried on, innovative pro-grams developed and mistakes paid for. New equipment must be purchased, new facilities provided and new products launched. Reserves must be created to provide for adverse times. When we operate according to these principles, the stockholders should realize a fair return.

Dell

Dell is building its technology, its business, and its communities through direct rela-tionships with our customers, our employees, and our neighbors. Through this process, we are committed to bringing value to customers and adding value to our company, our neighborhoods, our communities, and our world through diversity, environmental and global citizenship initiatives.

The core elements of the "soul of Dell":

Customers: We believe in creating loyal customers by providing a superior expe-rience at a great value.

The Dell Team: We believe our continued success lies in teamwork and in the opportunity each team member has to learn, develop, and grow.

Direct Relationships: We believe in being direct in all we do.

Global Citizenship: We believe in participating responsibly in the global marketplace.

Winning: We have a passion for winning in everything we do.

IBM

At IBM, we strive to lead in the invention, development, and manufacture of the industry's most advanced information technologies, including computer systems, software, storage systems, and microelectronics. We translate these advanced technologies into value for customers through our professional solutions, services, and consulting businesses worldwide.

Sources: © Johnson & Johnson; Used with permission of Dell Computer Corporation; Used with permission of IBM.

the figures over the short-term." [Our mission] allows them to say, "Wait a minute. I don't have to do that." The management has told me that they're ... interested in me operating under this set of principles.[6]

Some Missions Can Hurt Firm Performance.   Although some firms have used their missions to develop strategies that create significant competitive advantages, missions can hurt a firm's performance as well. For example, sometimes a firm's mission will be very inwardly focused and defined only with reference to the personal values and priorities of its founders or top managers, independent of whether those values and priorities are consistent with the economic realities facing a firm. Strategies derived from such missions or visions are not likely to be a source of competitive advantage.

For example, Ben & Jerry's Ice Cream was founded in 1977 by Ben Cohen and Jerry Greenfield, both as a way to produce super-premium ice cream and as a way to create an organization based on the values of the 1960s' counterculture. This strong sense of mission led Ben & Jerry's to adopt some very unusual human resource and other policies. Among these policies, the company adopted a compensation system whereby the highest paid firm employee could earn no more than five times the income of the lowest paid firm employee. Later, this ratio was adjusted to seven to one. However, even at this level, such a compensation policy made it very difficult to acquire the senior management talent needed to ensure the growth and profitability of the firm without grossly overpaying the lowest paid employees in the firm. When a new CEO was appointed to the firm in 1995, his $250,000 salary violated this compensation policy.

Indeed, though the frozen dessert market rapidly consolidated through the late 1990s, Ben & Jerry's Ice Cream remained an independent firm, partly because of Cohen's and Greenfield's commitment to maintaining the social values that their firm embodied. Lacking access to the broad distribution network and managerial talent that would have been available if Ben & Jerry's had merged with another firm, the company's growth and profitability lagged. Finally, in April 2000, Ben & Jerry's Ice Cream was acquired by Unilever. The 66 percent premium finally earned by Ben & Jerry's stockholders in April 2000 had been delayed for

TABLE 1.2 A Sample of Visionary Firms

3M	Hewlett-Packard	Nordstrom
American Express	IBM	Philip Morris
Boeing	Johnson & Johnson	Procter & Gamble
Citicorp	Marriott	Sony
Ford	Merck	Wal-Mart
General Electric	Motorola	Walt Disney

Source: J. C. Collins and J. I. Porras. *Built to last: successful habits of visionary companies.* New York: Harper Collins Publishers, Inc. ©1994 James C. Collins and Jerry I. Porras. Reprinted with permission by Jim Collins.

several years. In this sense, Cohen's and Greenfield's commitment to a set of personal values and priorities was at least partly inconsistent with the economic realities of the frozen dessert market in the United States.[7]

Obviously, because a firm's mission can help, hurt, or have no impact on its performance, missions by themselves do not necessarily lead a firm to choose and implement strategies that generate competitive advantages. Indeed, as suggested in Figure 1.1, while defining a firm's mission is an important step in the strategic management process, it is only the first step in that process.

Objectives

Whereas a firm's mission is a broad statement of its purpose and values, its **objectives** are specific measurable targets a firm can use to evaluate the extent to which it is realizing its mission. Consider, for example, 3M's mission statement in Table 1.3. This statement emphasizes the importance of finding innovative products and producing high returns for shareholders. However, it is also possible to link specific objectives to each of the elements of this mission statement. This is also done in Table 1.3. For example, for the Investor Mission, possible objectives might include: growth in earnings per share averaging 10 percent or better per year, a return on employed capital of 27 percent or better, at least 30 percent of sales from products that are no more than four years old, and so forth.

High-quality objectives are tightly connected to elements of a firm's mission and are relatively easy to measure and track over time. Low-quality objectives either do not exist or are not connected to elements of a firm's mission, are not quantitative, or are difficult to measure or difficult to track over time. Obviously, low-quality objectives cannot be used by management to evaluate how well a mission is being realized. Indeed, one indication that a firm is not that serious about realizing part of its mission statement is when there are no objectives, or only low-quality objectives, associated with that part of the mission.

External and Internal Analysis

The next two phases of the strategic management process—external analysis and internal analysis—occur more or less simultaneously. By conducting an **external analysis**, a firm identifies the critical threats and opportunities in its competitive environment. It also examines how competition in this environment is likely to evolve and what implications that evolution has for the threats and opportunities a firm is facing. A considerable literature on techniques for and approaches to conducting external analysis has evolved over the past several years. This literature is the primary subject matter of Chapter 2 of this book.

Whereas external analysis focuses on the environmental threats and opportunities facing a firm, **internal analysis** helps a firm identify its organizational strengths and weaknesses. It also helps a firm understand which of its resources and capabilities are likely to be sources of competitive advantage and which are less likely to be sources of such advantages. Finally, internal analysis can be used by firms to identify those areas of its organization that require improvement and change. As with external analysis, a considerable literature on techniques for and approaches to conducting internal analysis has evolved over the past several years. This literature is the primary subject matter of Chapter 3 of this book.

Strategic Choice

Armed with a mission, objectives, and completed external and internal analyses, a firm is ready to make its strategic choices. That is, a firm is ready to choose its "theory of how to gain competitive advantage."

TABLE 1.3 3M's Value Statement

Our Values:

Act with uncompromising honesty and integrity in everything we do.

Satisfy our customers with innovative technology and superior quality, value and service.

Provide our investors with an attractive return through sustainable, global growth.

Respect our social and physical environment around the world.

Value and develop our employees' diverse talents, initiative and leadership.

Earn the admiration of all those associated with 3M worldwide.

Source: Courtesy of 3M Company.

As suggested in Abrahams (1995), these values could be expanded to include specific objectives:

Satisfy our customers with superior quality and value:

- Providing the highest quality products and services consistent with our customers' requirements and preferences.
- Making every aspect of every transaction a satisfying experience for our customers.
- Finding innovative ways to make life easier and better for our customers.

Providing investors an attractive return through sustained, high-quality growth:

Our goals are:

- Growth in earnings per share averaging 10 percent a year or better.
- A return on capital employed of 27 percent or better.
- A return on stockholders' equity of between 20 and 25 percent.
- At least 30 percent of our sales each year from products new in the last four years.

Respecting our social and physical environment:

- Complying with all laws and meeting or exceeding regulations.
- Keeping customers, employees, investors and the public informed about our operations.
- Developing products and processes that have a minimal impact on the environment.
- Staying attuned to the changing needs and preferences of our customers, employees and society.
- Uncompromising honesty and integrity in every aspect of our operations.

Being a company that employees are proud to be a part of:

- Respecting the dignity and worth of individuals.
- Encouraging individual initiative and innovation in an atmosphere characterized by flexibility, cooperation and trust.
- Challenging individual capabilities.
- Valuing human diversity and providing equal opportunity for development.

Source: J. Abrahams (1995). *The mission statement book.* Berkeley, CA: TenSpeedPress, pp. 400–402.

The strategic choices available to firms fall into two large categories: business-level strategies and corporate-level strategies. **Business-level strategies** are actions firms take to gain competitive advantages in a single market or industry. These strategies are the topic of Part 2 of this book. The two most common business-level strategies are cost leadership (Chapter 4) and product differentiation (Chapter 5).

Corporate-level strategies are actions firms take to gain competitive advantages by operating in multiple markets or industries simultaneously. These strategies are the topic of Part 3 of this book. Common corporate-level strategies include vertical integration strategies (Chapter 6), diversification strategies (Chapters 7 and 8), strategic alliance strategies (Chapter 9), merger and acquisition strategies (Chapter 10), and global strategies (Chapter 11).

Obviously, the details of choosing specific strategies can be quite complex, and a discussion of these details will be delayed until later in the book. However, the underlying logic of strategic choice is not complex. Based on the strategic management process, the objective when making a strategic choice is to choose a strategy that (1) supports the firm's mission, (2) is consistent with a firm's objectives, (3) exploits opportunities in a firm's environment with a firm's strengths, and (4) neutralizes threats in a firm's environment while avoiding a firm's weaknesses. Assuming that this strategy is implemented—the last step of the strategic management process—a strategy that meets these four criteria is very likely to be a source of competitive advantage for a firm.

Strategy Implementation

Of course, simply choosing a strategy means nothing if that strategy is not implemented. **Strategy implementation** occurs when a firm adopts organizational policies and practices that are consistent with its strategy. Three specific organizational policies and practices are particularly important in implementing a strategy: a firm's formal organizational structure, its formal and informal management control systems, and its employee compensation policies. A firm that adopts an organizational structure, management controls, and compensation policy that are consistent with and reinforce its strategies is more likely to be able to implement those strategies than a firm that adopts an organizational structure, management controls, and compensation policy that are inconsistent with its strategies. Specific organizational structures, management controls, and compensation policies used to implement the business-level strategies of cost leadership and product differentiation are discussed in Chapters 4 and 5. How organizational structure, management controls, and compensation can be used to implement corporate-level strategies, including vertical integration, strategic alliance, merger and acquisition, and global strategies, is discussed in Chapters 6, 9, 10, and 11, respectively. However, there is so much information about implementing diversification strategies that an entire chapter, Chapter 8, is dedicated to the discussion of how this corporate-level strategy is implemented.

What Is Competitive Advantage?

Of course, the ultimate objective of the strategic management process is to enable a firm to choose and implement a strategy that generates a competitive advantage. But what is a competitive advantage? In general, a firm has a **competitive advantage** when it is able to create more economic value than rival firms. **Economic value** is simply the difference between the perceived benefits gained by a customer that purchases a firm's products or services and the full economic cost of these products or services. Thus, the size of a firm's competitive advantage is the difference between the economic value a firm is able to create and the economic value its rivals are able to create.[8]

Consider the two firms presented in Figure 1.2. Both these firms compete in the same market for the same customers. However, Firm I generates $180 of economic value each time it sells a product or service, whereas Firm II generates $150 of economic value each time it sells a product or service. Because Firm I generates more economic value each time it sells a product or service, it has a competitive advantage

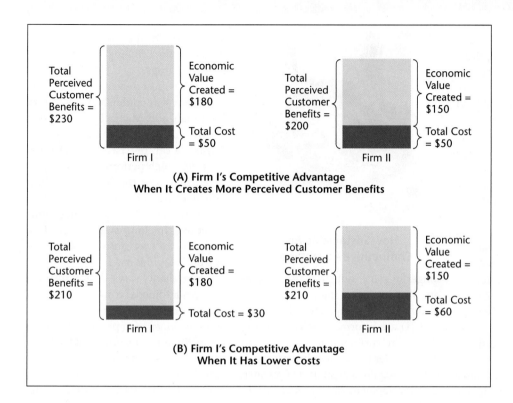

Figure 1.2 The Sources of a Firm's Competitive Advantage

over Firm II. The size of this competitive advantage is equal to the difference in the economic value these two firms create, in this case, $30 ($180 − $150 = $30).

However, as shown in the figure, Firm I's advantage may come from different sources. For example, it might be the case that Firm I creates greater perceived benefits for its customers than Firm II. In panel A of the figure, Firm I creates perceived customer benefits worth $230, whereas Firm II creates perceived customer benefits worth only $200. Thus, even though both firms' costs are the same (equal to $50 per unit sold), Firm I creates more economic value ($230 − $50 = $180) than Firm II ($200 − $50 = $150). Indeed, it is possible for Firm I, in this situation, to have higher costs than Firm II and still create more economic value than Firm II if these higher costs are offset by Firm I's ability to create greater perceived benefits for its customers.

Alternatively, as shown in panel B of the figure, these two firms may create the same level of perceived customer benefit (equal to $210 in this example) but have different costs. If Firm I's costs per unit are only $30, it will generate $180 worth of economic value ($210 − $30 = $180). If Firm II's costs are $60, it will generate only $150 of economic value ($210 − $60 = $150). Indeed, it might be possible for Firm I to create a lower level of perceived benefits for its customers than Firm II and still create more economic value than Firm II, as long as its disadvantage in perceived customer benefits is more than offset by its cost advantage.

A firm's competitive advantage can be temporary or sustained. As summarized in Figure 1.3, a **temporary competitive advantage** is a competitive advantage that lasts for a very short period of time. A **sustained competitive advantage**, in contrast, can last much longer. How long sustained competitive advantages can last is discussed in the Research Made Relevant feature. Firms that create the same economic value as their rivals experience **competitive parity**. Finally, firms that generate less economic value than their rivals have a **competitive disadvantage**. Not surprisingly, competitive disadvantages can be either temporary or sustained, depending on the duration of the disadvantage.

For some time, economists have been interested in how long firms are able to sustain competitive advantages. Traditional economic theory predicts that such advantages should be short-lived in highly competitive markets. This theory suggests that any competitive advantages gained by a particular firm will quickly be identified and imitated by other firms, ensuring competitive parity in the long run. However, in real life, competitive advantages often last longer than traditional economic theory predicts.

One of the first scholars to examine this issue was Dennis Mueller. Mueller divided a sample of 472 firms into eight categories, depending on their level of performance in 1949. He then examined the impact of a firm's initial performance on its subsequent performance. The traditional economic hypothesis was that all firms in the sample would converge on an average level of performance. This did not occur. Indeed, firms that were performing well in an earlier time period tended to perform well in later time periods, and firms that performed poorly in an earlier time period tended to perform poorly in later time periods as well.

Geoffrey Waring followed up on Mueller's work by explaining why competitive advantages seem to persist

How Sustainable Are Competitive Advantages?

longer in some industries than in others. Waring found that, among other factors, firms that operate in industries that (1) are informationally complex, (2) require customers to know a great deal in order to use an industry's products, (3) require a great deal of research and development, and (4) have significant economies of scale are more likely to have sustained competitive advantages compared to firms that operate in industries without these attributes.

Peter Roberts studied the persistence of profitability in one particular industry—the U.S. pharmaceutical industry. Roberts found that not only can firms sustain competitive advantages in this industry, but that the ability to do so is almost entirely

attributable to the firms' capacity to innovate by bringing out new and powerful drugs.

The most recent work in this tradition was published by Anita McGahan and Michael Porter. They showed that both high and low performance can persist for some time. Persistent high performance is related to attributes of the industry within which a firm operates and the corporation within which a business unit functions. In contrast, persistent low performance was caused by attributes of a business unit itself.

In many ways, the difference between traditional economics research and strategic management research is that the former attempts to explain why competitive advantages should not persist, whereas the latter attempts to explain when they can. Thus far, most empirical research suggests that firms, in at least some settings, can sustain competitive advantages.

Sources: D. C. Mueller (1977). "The persistence of profits above the norm." *Economica*, 44, pp. 369–380; P. W. Roberts (1999). "Product innovation, product-market competition, and persistent profitability in the U.S. pharmaceutical industry." *Strategic Management Journal*, 20, pp. 655–670; G. F. Waring (1996). "Industry differences in the persistence of firm-specific returns." *The American Economic Review*, 86, pp. 1253–1265; A. McGahan and M. Porter (2003). "The emergence and sustainability of abnormal profits." *Strategic Organization*, 1(1), pp. 79–108.

Competitive Advantage		**Competitive Parity**	**Competitive Disadvantage**	
When a firm creates more economic value than its rivals		When a firm creates the same economic value as its rivals	When a firm creates less economic value than its rivals	

Temporary Competitive Advantages	**Sustained Competitive Advantages**		**Temporary Competitive Disadvantages**	**Sustained Competitive Disadvantages**
Competitive advantages that last a short time	Competitive advantages that last a long time		Competitive disadvantages that last a short time	Competitive disadvantages that last a long time

Figure 1.3 Types of Competitive Advantage

The Strategic Management Process, Revisited

With this description of the strategic management process now complete, it is possible to redraw the process, as depicted in Figure 1.1, to incorporate the various options a firm faces as it chooses and implements its strategy. This is done in Figure 1.4. Figure 1.4 is the organizing framework that will be used throughout this book.

Measuring Competitive Advantage

A firm has a *competitive advantage* when it creates more economic value than its rivals. *Economic value* is the difference between the perceived customer benefits associated with buying a firm's products or services and the cost of producing and selling these products or services. These are deceptively simple definitions. However, these concepts are not always easy to measure directly. For example, the benefits of a firm's products or services are always a matter of customer perception, and perceptions are not easy to measure. Also, the total costs associated with producing a particular product or service may not always be easy to identify or associate with a particular product or service. Despite the very real challenges associated with measuring a firm's competitive advantage, two approaches have emerged. The first estimates a firm's competitive advantage by examining its accounting performance; the second examines the firm's economic performance. These approaches are discussed in the following sections.

Accounting Measures of Competitive Advantage

A firm's **accounting performance** is a measure of its competitive advantage calculated by using information from a firm's published profit and loss and balance sheet statements. A firm's profit and loss and balance sheet statements, in turn, are typically created using widely accepted accounting standards and principles. The application of these standards and principles makes it possible to compare the accounting performance of one firm to the accounting performance of other firms, even if those firms are not in the same industry. However, to the extent that these

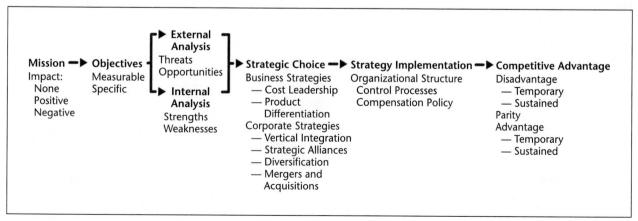

Figure 1.4   Organizing Framework

TABLE 1.4 Common Ratios to Measure a Firm's Accounting Performance

Ratio	Calculation	Interpretation
Profitability Ratios		
1. ROA	$\dfrac{\text{profit after taxes}}{\text{total assets}}$	A measure of return on total investment in a firm. Larger is usually better.
2. ROE	$\dfrac{\text{profit after taxes}}{\text{total stockholder's equity}}$	A measure of return on total equity investment in a firm. Larger is usually better.
3. Gross profit margin	$\dfrac{\text{sales} - \text{cost of goods sold}}{\text{sales}}$	A measure of sales available to cover operating expenses and still generate a profit. Larger is usually better.
4. Earnings per share (EPS)	$\dfrac{\text{profits (after taxes)} - \text{preferred stock dividends}}{\text{number of shares of common stock outstanding}}$	A measure of profit available to owners of common stock. Larger is usually better.
5. Price earnings ratio (p/e)	$\dfrac{\text{current market price/share}}{\text{after-tax earnings/share}}$	A measure of anticipated firm performance—a high p/e ratio tends to indicate that the stock market anticipates strong future performance. Larger is usually better.
6. Cash flow per share	$\dfrac{\text{after-tax profit} + \text{depreciation}}{\text{number of common shares stock outstanding}}$	A measure of funds available to fund activities above current level of costs. Larger is usually better.
Liquidity Ratios		
1. Current ratio	$\dfrac{\text{current assets}}{\text{current liabilities}}$	A measure of the ability of a firm to cover its current liabilities with assets that can be converted into cash in the short term. Recommended in the range of 2 to 3.
2. Quick ratio	$\dfrac{\text{current assets} - \text{inventory}}{\text{current liabilities}}$	A measure of the ability of a firm to meet its short-term obligations without selling off its current inventory. A ratio of 1 is thought to be acceptable in many industries.
Leverage Ratios		
1. Debt to assets	$\dfrac{\text{total debt}}{\text{total assets}}$	A measure of the extent to which debt has financed a firm's business activities. The higher, the greater the risk of bankruptcy.
2. Debt to equity	$\dfrac{\text{total debt}}{\text{total equity}}$	A measure of the use of debt versus equity to finance a firm's business activities. Generally recommended less than 1.
3. Times interest earned	$\dfrac{\text{profit before interest and taxes}}{\text{total interest charges}}$	A measure of how much a firm's profits can decline and still meet its interest obligations. Should be well above 1.

Activity Ratios		
1. Inventory turnover	$\dfrac{sales}{inventory}$	A measure of the speed with which a firm's inventory is turning over.
2. Accounts receivable turnover	$\dfrac{annual\ credit\ sales}{accounts\ receivable}$	A measure of the average time it takes a firm to collect on credit sales.
3. Average collection period	$\dfrac{accounts\ receivable}{average\ daily\ sales}$	A measure of the time it takes a firm to receive payment after a sale has been made.

standards and principles are not applied in generating a firm's accounting statements, or to the extent that different firms use different accounting standards and principles in generating their statements, it can be difficult to compare the accounting performance of firms. As described in the Global Perspectives feature, these issues can be particularly challenging when comparing the performance of firms in different countries around the world.

One way to use a firm's accounting statements to measure its competitive advantage is through the use of accounting ratios. **Accounting ratios** are simply numbers taken from a firm's financial statements that are manipulated in ways that describe various aspects of a firm's performance. Some of the most common accounting ratios that can be used to characterize a firm's performance are presented in Table 1.4. These measures of firm accounting performance can be grouped into four categories: (1) **profitability ratios**, or ratios with some measure of profit in the numerator and some measure of firm size or assets in the denominator; (2) **liquidity ratios**, or ratios that focus on the ability of a firm to meet its short-term financial obligations; (3) **leverage ratios**, or ratios that focus on the level of a firm's financial flexibility, including its ability to obtain more debt; and (4) **activity ratios**, or ratios that focus on the level of activity in a firm's business.

Of course, these ratios, by themselves, say very little about a firm. To determine how a firm is performing, its accounting ratios must be compared with some standard. In general, that standard is the average of accounting ratios of other firms in the same industry. Using ratio analysis, a firm earns **above average accounting performance** when its performance is greater than the industry average. Such firms typically have competitive advantages, sustained or otherwise. A firm earns **average accounting performance** when its performance is equal to the industry average. These firms generally enjoy only competitive parity. A firm earns **below average accounting performance** when its performance is less than the industry average. These firms generally experience competitive disadvantages.

Consider, for example, the performance of Apple Computer. Apple's financial statements for 2007 and 2008 are presented in Table 1.5. Losses in this table would be presented in parentheses. Several ratio measures of accounting performance are calculated for Apple in these two years in Table 1.6.

Apple's sales increased dramatically from 2007 to 2008, from just over $24 billion to just under $32.5 billion. However, some profitability accounting ratios suggest that its profitability dropped somewhat during this same time period, from a return on total assets (ROA) of 0.138 to 0.122, and from a return on equity (ROE) of 0.241 to 0.230. On the other hand, Apple's gross profit margin increased from 0.340 to 0.343. So its sales went up, its overall profitability went

TABLE 1.5 Apple Computer's Financial Statements for 2007 and 2008 (numbers in millions of dollars)

	2007	2008
Net sales	24,006	32,479
Cost of goods sold	15,852	21,334
Gross margin	8,154	11,145
Selling, general and administrative expenses	2,963	3,761
Research and development expenses	782	1,109
Total operating expenses	3,745	4,870
Operating income (loss)	4,409	6,275
Total income (loss), before taxes	5,008	6,895
Provision for (benefit from) income taxes	1,512	2,061
Net income, after taxes	3,496	4,834
Inventories	346	509
Total current assets	21,956	34,690
Total assets	25,347	39,572
Total current liabilities	9,280	14,092
Total debt	10,815	18,542
Total shareholders' equity	14,532	21,030

down a little, but its gross profit margin went up a little. This pattern could reflect several changes in Apple's business. For example, perhaps Apple was selling more products, but at lower margins, in 2008 compared to 2007. This would explain the lower ROA and ROE, but would not explain the increased gross profit margin. Alternatively, maybe some of Apple's operating expenses increased at a rate greater than the increase in its sales revenues. However, a quick look at Table 1.5 suggests that Apple's operating expenses increased at about the same rate as its sales. The explanation of the slightly lower ROA and ROE numbers in 2008 doesn't have to do with revenues and costs, but rather has to do with increases in Apple's total assets and its total shareholders' equity. Both of these balance sheet numbers increased at a rate faster than Apple's sales increased, leading to slightly lower ROA and ROE numbers for 2008 compared to 2007.

On the other hand, Apple's liquidity and leverage ratios remain largely unchanged over these two years. With current and quick ratios well over two, it's pretty clear that Apple has enough cash on hand to respond to any short-term financial needs. And its leverage ratios suggest that it still has some opportunities to borrow money for long-term investments should the need arise.

Overall, the information in Tables 1.5 and 1.6 suggests that Apple Computer, in 2007 and 2008, is, financially speaking, very healthy.

TABLE 1.6 Some Accounting Ratios for Apple Computer in 2007 and 2008

	2007	2008
ROA	0.138	0.122
ROE	0.241	0.230
Gross profit margin	0.340	0.343
Current ratio	2.37	2.46
Quick ratio	2.33	2.43
Debt to assets	0.427	0.469
Debt to equity	0.744	0.882

Economic Measures of Competitive Advantage

The great advantage of accounting measures of competitive advantage is that they are relatively easy to compute. All publicly traded firms must make their accounting statements available to the public. Even privately owned firms will typically release some information about their accounting performance. From these statements, it is quite easy to calculate various accounting ratios. One can learn a lot about a firm's competitive position by comparing these ratios to industry averages.

However, accounting measures of competitive advantage have at least one significant limitation. Earlier, economic profit was defined as the difference between the perceived benefit associated with purchasing a firm's products or services and the cost of producing and selling that product or service. However, one important component of cost typically is not included in most accounting measures of competitive advantage—the cost of the capital a firm employs to produce and sell its products. The **cost of capital** is the rate of return that a firm promises to pay its suppliers of capital to induce them to invest in the firm. Once these investments are made, a firm can use this capital to produce and sell products and services. However, a firm must provide the promised return to its sources of capital if it expects to obtain more investment capital in the future. **Economic measures of competitive advantage** compare a firm's level of return to its cost of capital instead of to the average level of return in the industry.

Generally, there are two broad categories of sources of capital: **debt** (capital from banks and bondholders) and **equity** (capital from individuals and institutions that purchase a firm's stock). The **cost of debt** is equal to the interest that a firm must pay its debt holders (adjusted for taxes) in order to induce those debt holders to lend money to a firm. The **cost of equity** is equal to the rate of return a firm must promise its equity holders in order to induce these individuals and institutions to invest in a firm. A firm's **weighted average cost of capital (WACC)** is simply the percentage of a firm's total capital, which is debt times the cost of debt, plus the percentage of a firm's total capital; that is, equity times the cost of equity. A simple approach to measuring a firm's WACC is described in the Strategy in Depth feature.

Conceptually, a firm's cost of capital is the level of performance a firm must attain if it is to satisfy the economic objectives of two of its critical stakeholders: debt holders and equity holders. A firm that earns above its cost of capital is likely to be able to attract additional capital, because debt holders and equity holders will scramble to make additional funds available for this firm. Such a firm is said to be earning **above normal economic performance** and will be able to use its access to cheap capital to grow and expand its business. A firm that earns its cost of capital is said to have **normal economic performance**. This level of performance is said to be "normal" because this is the level of performance that most of a firm's equity and debt holders expect. Firms that have normal economic performance are able to gain access to the capital they need to survive, although they are not prospering. Growth opportunities may be somewhat limited for these firms. In general, firms with competitive parity usually have normal economic performance. A firm that earns less than its cost of capital is in the process of liquidating. **Below normal economic performance** implies that a firm's debt and equity holders will be looking for alternative ways to invest their money, someplace where they can earn at least what they expect to

Strategy in Depth

A firm's WACC can be an important benchmark against which to compare a firm's performance. However, calculating this number can sometimes be tricky. Fortunately, it is possible to obtain all the information needed to calculate a firm's WACC—at least for publicly traded firms—from information published in outlets such as Moody's, Standard and Poor's, Dun and Bradstreet, and Value Line. These publications are in every major business school library in the world and are also available online.

To calculate a firm's WACC, five pieces of information are required: (1) a firm's debt rating, (2) its marginal tax rate, (3) its Beta, (4) the risk-free and market rates of return in the years a firm's WACC is being calculated, and (5) information about a firm's capital structure.

Typically, a firm's debt rating will be presented in the form of a series of letters—for example, AA or BBB+. Think of these ratings as grades for a firm's riskiness: an "A" is less risky than an "AA," which is less risky than a "BBB+," and so forth. At any given point in time, a firm with a given debt rating has a market-determined interest. Suppose that the market-determined interest rate for a firm with a BBB debt rating is 7.5 percent. This is a firm's before-tax cost of debt. However, because interest payments are tax deductible in the United States, this before-tax cost of debt has to be adjusted for the tax savings a firm has from using debt. If a firm is reasonably large, then it will almost certainly have to pay the

Estimating a Firm's Weighted Average Cost of Capital

largest marginal tax rate, which in the United States has been 39 percent. So, the after-tax cost of debt in this example is $(1 - 0.39)(7.5)$, or 4.58 percent.

A firm's *Beta* is a measure of how highly correlated the price of a firm's equity is to the overall stock market. Betas are published for most publicly traded firms. The *risk-free rate of return* is the rate the U.S. federal government has to pay on its long-term bonds to get investors to buy these bonds, and the market rate of return is the return investors would obtain if they purchased one share of each of the stocks traded on public exchanges. Historically, this risk-free rate of return has been low—around 3 percent. The *market rate of return* has averaged around 8.5 percent in the United States. Using these numbers, and assuming that a firm's Beta is equal to 1.2, the cost of a firm's equity capital can be estimated using the Capital Asset Pricing Model (CAPM) as follows:

Cost of Equity = Risk Free Rate of Return + (Market Rate of Return − Risk Free Rate of Return) Beta

For our example, this equation is:

$$9.6 = 3.0 + (8.5 - 3.0)1.2$$

Because firms do not gain tax advantages from using equity capital, the before- and after-tax cost of equity is the same.

To calculate a firm's WACC, simply multiple the percentage of a firm's total capital; that is, debt times the after-tax cost of debt, and add it to the percentage of a firm's total capital; that is, equity times the cost of equity. If a firm has total assets of $5 million and stockholders' equity of $4 million, then it must have debt with a market value of $1 million. The WACC for this hypothetical firm thus becomes:

$$
\begin{aligned}
\text{WACC} &= (\text{Stockholders' Equity}/\text{Total} \\
&\quad \text{Assets}) \text{ Cost of Equity} + \\
&\quad (\text{Debt}/\text{Total Assets}) \text{ After-} \\
&\quad \text{Tax Cost of Debt} \\
&= 4/5(9.6) + 1/5(4.58) \\
&= 7.68 + 0.916 \\
&= 8.59
\end{aligned}
$$

Obviously, firms can have a much more complicated capital structure than this hypothetical example. Moreover, the taxes a firm pays can be quite complicated to calculate. There are also some problems in using the CAPM to calculate a firm's cost of equity. However, even with these caveats, this approach usually gives a reasonable approximation to a firm's weighted average cost of capital.

earn; that is, normal economic performance. Unless a firm with below normal performance changes, its long-term viability will come into question. Obviously, firms that have a competitive disadvantage generally have below normal economic performance.

Measuring a firm's performance relative to its cost of capital has several advantages for strategic analysis. Foremost among these is the notion that a firm that earns at least its cost of capital is satisfying two of its most important stakeholders—debt holders and equity holders. Despite the advantages of comparing a firm's performance to its cost of capital, this approach has some important limitations as well.

For example, it can sometimes be difficult to calculate a firm's cost of capital. This is especially true if a firm is **privately held**—that is, if it has stock that is not traded on public stock markets or if it is a division of a larger company. In these situations, it may be necessary to use accounting ratios to measure a firm's performance.

Moreover, some have suggested that although accounting measures of competitive advantage understate the importance of a firm's equity and debt holders in evaluating a firm's performance, economic measures of competitive advantage exaggerate the importance of these two particular stakeholders, often to the disadvantage of other stakeholders in a firm. These issues are discussed in more detail in the Ethics and Strategy feature.

The Relationship Between Economic and Accounting Performance Measures

The correlation between economic and accounting measures of competitive advantage is high. That is, firms that perform well using one of these measures usually perform well using the other. Conversely, firms that do poorly using one of these measures normally do poorly using the other. Thus, the relationships among competitive advantage, accounting performance, and economic performance depicted in Figure 1.5 generally hold.

However, it is possible for a firm to have above average accounting performance and simultaneously have below normal economic performance. This could happen, for example, when a firm is not earning its cost of capital but has above industry average accounting performance. Also, it is possible for a firm to have below average accounting performance and above normal economic performance. This could happen when a firm has a very low cost of capital and is earning at a rate in excess of this cost, but still below the industry average.

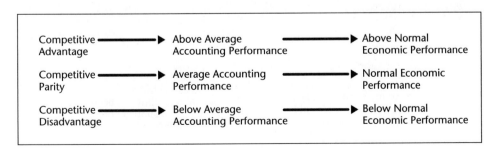

Figure 1.5 Competitive Advantage and Firm Performance

Emergent Versus Intended Strategies

The simplest way of thinking about a firm's strategy is to assume that firms choose and implement their strategies exactly as described by the strategic management process in Figure 1.1. That is, they begin with a well-defined mission and objectives, they engage in external and internal analyses, they make their strategic choices, and then they implement their strategies. And there is no doubt that this describes the process for choosing and implementing a strategy in many firms.

For example, FedEx, the world leader in the overnight delivery business, entered this industry with a very well-developed theory about how to gain competitive advantages in this business. Indeed, Fred Smith, the founder of FedEx (originally known as Federal Express), first articulated this theory as a student in a term paper for an undergraduate business class at Yale University. Legend has it that he received only a "C" on the paper, but the company that was founded on the theory of competitive advantage in the overnight delivery business developed in that paper has done extremely well. Founded in 1971, FedEx had 2008 sales just under $38 billion and profits of over $1.125 billion.[9]

Other firms have also begun operations with a well-defined, well-formed strategy, but have found it necessary to modify this strategy so much once it is actually implemented in the marketplace that it bears little resemblance to the theory with which the firm started. **Emergent strategies** are theories of how to gain competitive advantage in an industry that emerge over time or that have been radically reshaped once they are initially implemented.[10] The relationship between a firm's intended and emergent strategies is depicted in Figure 1.6.

Several well-known firms have strategies that are at least partly emergent. For example, J&J was originally a supplier of antiseptic gauze and medical plasters. It had no consumer business at all. Then, in response to complaints about irritation caused by some of its medical plasters, J&J began enclosing a small packet of talcum powder with each of the medical plasters it sold. Soon customers were asking to purchase the talcum powder by itself, and the company introduced "Johnson's Toilet and Baby Powder." Later, an employee invented a ready-to-use bandage for his wife. It seems she often cut herself while using knives in the

Figure 1.6 Mintzberg's Analysis of the Relationship Between Intended and Realized Strategies

Source: Reprinted from "Strategy formation in an adhocracy," by H. Mintzberg and A. McHugh, published in *Administrative Science Quarterly, 30*, No. 2, June 1985, by permission of Administrative Science Quarterly. Copyright © 1985 by Administrative Science Quarterly.

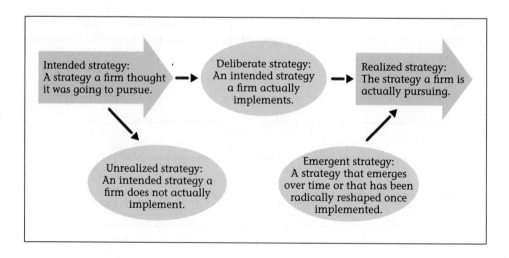

Ethics and Strategy

Considerable debate exists about the role of a firm's equity and debt holders versus its other stakeholders in defining and measuring a firm's performance. These other stakeholders include a firm's suppliers, its customers, its employees, and the communities within which it does business. Like equity and debt holders, these other stakeholders make investments in a firm. They, too, expect some compensation for making these investments.

On the one hand, some argue that if a firm maximizes the wealth of its equity holders, it will automatically satisfy all of its other stakeholders. This view of the firm depends on what is called the *residual claimants* view of equity holders. This view is that equity holders only receive payment on their investment in a firm after all legitimate claims by a firm's other stakeholders are satisfied. Thus, a firm's equity holders, in this view, only receive payment on their investments after the firm's employees are compensated, its suppliers are paid, its customers are satisfied, and its obligations to the communities within which it does business have been met. By maximizing returns to its equity holders, a firm is ensuring that its other stakeholders are fully compensated for investing in a firm.

Stockholders Versus Stakeholders

On the other hand, some argue that the interests of equity holders and a firm's other stakeholders often collide, and that a firm that maximizes the wealth of its equity holders does not necessarily satisfy its other stakeholders. For example, whereas a firm's customers may want it to sell higher-quality products at lower prices, a firm's equity holders may want it to sell low-quality products at higher prices; this obviously would increase the amount of money left over to pay off a firm's equity holders. Also, whereas a firm's employees may want it to adopt policies that lead to steady performance over long periods of time—because this will lead to stable employment—a firm's

equity holders may be more interested in its maximizing its short-term profitability, even if this hurts employment stability. The interests of equity holders and the broader community may also clash, especially when it is very costly for a firm to engage in environmentally friendly behaviors that could reduce its short-term performance.

This debate manifests itself in a variety of ways. For example, many groups that oppose the globalization of the U.S. economy do so on the basis that firms make production, marketing, and other strategic choices in ways that maximize profits for equity holders, often to the detriment of a firm's other stakeholders. These people are concerned about the effects of globalization on workers, on the environment, and on the cultures in the developing economies where global firms sometimes locate their manufacturing and other operations. Managers in global firms respond by saying that they have a responsibility to maximize the wealth of their equity holders. Given the passions that surround this debate, it is unlikely that these issues will be resolved soon.

Sources: T. Copeland, T. Koller, and J. Murrin (1995). *Valuation: Measuring and managing the value of companies.* New York: Wiley; L. Donaldson (1990). "The ethereal hand: Organizational economics and management theory." *Academy of Review*, 15, pp. 369–381.

kitchen. When J&J marketing managers learned of this invention, they decided to introduce it into the marketplace. J&J's Band-Aid products have since become the largest selling brand category at J&J. Overall, J&J's intended strategy was to compete in the medical products market, but its emergent consumer products strategies now generate over 40 percent of total corporate sales.

Another firm with what turns out to be an emergent strategy is the Marriott Corporation. Marriott was originally in the restaurant business. In the late 1930s, Marriott owned and operated eight restaurants. However, one of these restaurants was close to a Washington, D.C., airport. Managers at this restaurant noticed that airline passengers would come into the restaurant to purchase food to eat on their

Strategy in the Emerging Enterprise

Every entrepreneur—and would-be entrepreneur—is familiar with the drill: If you want to receive financial support for your idea, you need to write a business plan. Business plans are typically 25 to 30 pages long. Most begin with an Executive Summary; then move quickly to describing an entrepreneur's business idea, why customers will be interested in this idea, how much it will cost to realize this idea; and usually end with a series of charts that project a firm's cash flows over the next five years.

Of course, because these business ideas are often new and untried, no one—including the entrepreneur—really knows if customers will like the idea well enough to buy from this firm. No one really knows how much it will cost to build these products or produce these services—they've never been built or produced before. And, certainly, no one really knows what a firm's cash flows will look like over the next five years or so. Indeed, it is not unusual for entrepreneurs to constantly revise their business plan to reflect new information they have obtained about their business idea and its viability. It is not even unusual for entrepreneurs to fundamentally revise their central business idea as they begin to pursue it in earnest.

Emergent Strategies and Entrepreneurship

The truth is, most decisions about whether to create an entrepreneurial firm take place under conditions of high uncertainty and high unpredictability. In this setting, the ability to adjust on the fly, to be flexible, and to recast a business idea in ways that are more consistent with customer interests may be a central determinant of a firm's ultimate success. This, of course, suggests that emergent strategies are likely to be very important for entrepreneurial firms.

This view of entrepreneurship is different from the popular stereotype. In the popular view, entrepreneurs are assumed to be hit by a "blinding rush of insight" about a previously unexploited market opportunity. In reality, entrepreneurs are more likely to experience a series of smaller insights about market opportunities. But typically, these periods of insight will be preceded by periods of disappointment, as an entrepreneur discovers that what he or she thought was a new and complete business model is, in fact, either not new or not complete or both. In the popular view, entrepreneurship is all about creativity, about being able to see opportunities others cannot see. In reality, entrepreneurship may be more about tenacity than creativity, because entrepreneurs build their firms step-by-step out of the uncertainty and unpredictability that plague their decision making. In the popular view, entrepreneurs can envision their success well before it occurs. In reality, although entrepreneurs may dream about financial and other forms of success, they usually do not know the exact path they will take, nor what success will actually look like, until after they have arrived.

Sources: S. Alvarez and J. Barney (2005). "How do entrepreneurs organize firms under conditions of uncertainty?" *Journal of Management*, 31 (5), pp. 776–793; S. Alvarez and J. Barney (2004). "Organizing rent generation and appropriation: Toward a theory of the entrepreneurial firm," *Journal of Business Venturing*, 19, pp. 621–636; W. Gartner (1988). "Who is the entrepreneur? is the wrong question." *American Journal of Small Business*, 12, pp. 11–32; S. Sarasvathy (2001). "Causation and effectuation: Toward a theoretical shift from economic inevitability to entrepreneurial contingency." *Academy of Management Review*, 26, pp. 243–264.

trip. J. Willard Marriott, the founder of the Marriott Corporation, noticed this trend and negotiated a deal with Eastern Airlines whereby Marriott's restaurant would deliver prepackaged lunches directly to Eastern's planes. This arrangement was later extended to include American Airlines. Over time, providing food service to airlines became a major business segment for Marriott. Although Marriott's initial intended strategy was to operate in the restaurant business, it became engaged in the emergent food service business at over 100 airports throughout the world.[11]

Some firms have almost entirely emergent strategies. PEZ Candy, Inc., for example, manufactures and sells small plastic candy dispensers with cartoon and movie character heads, along with candy refills. This privately held firm has made few efforts to speed its growth, yet demand for current and older PEZ products continues to grow. In the 1990s, PEZ doubled the size of its manufacturing operation to keep up with demand. Old PEZ dispensers have become something of a collector's item. Several national conferences on PEZ collecting have been held, and some rare PEZ dispensers were once auctioned at Christie's. This demand has enabled PEZ to raise its prices without increases in advertising, sales personnel, and movie tie-ins so typical in the candy industry.[12]

Of course, one might argue that emergent strategies are only important when a firm fails to implement the strategic management process effectively. After all, if this process is implemented effectively, then would it ever be necessary to fundamentally alter the strategies that a firm has chosen?

In reality, it will often be the case that at the time a firm chooses its strategies, some of the information needed to complete the strategic management process may simply not be available. As suggested earlier, in this setting a firm simply has to make its "best bet" about how competition in an industry is likely to emerge. In such a situation, a firm's ability to change its strategies quickly to respond to emergent trends in an industry may be as important a source of competitive advantage as the ability to complete the strategic management process. For all these reasons, emergent strategies may be particularly important for entrepreneurial firms, as described in the Strategy in the Emerging Enterprise feature.

Why You Need to Know About Strategy

At first glance, it may not be obvious why students would need to know about strategy and the strategic management process. After all, the process of choosing and implementing a strategy is normally the responsibility of senior managers in a firm, and most students are unlikely to be senior managers in large corporations until many years after graduation. Why study strategy and the strategic management process now?

In fact, there are at least three very compelling reasons why it is important to study strategy and the strategic management process now. First, it can give you the tools you need to evaluate the strategies of firms that may employ you. We have already seen how a firm's strategy can have a huge impact on its competitive advantage. Your career opportunities in a firm are largely determined by that firm's competitive advantage. Thus, in choosing a place to begin or continue your career, understanding a firm's theory of how it is going to gain a competitive advantage can be essential in evaluating the career opportunities in a firm. Firms with strategies that are unlikely to be a source of competitive advantage will rarely provide the same career opportunities as firms with strategies that do generate such advantages. Being able to distinguish between these types of strategies can be very important in your career choices.

Second, once you are working for a firm, understanding that firm's strategies, and your role in implementing those strategies, can be very important for your personal success. It will often be the case that expectations of how you perform your function in a firm will change, depending on the strategies a firm is pursuing. For example, as we will see in Part 2 of this book, the accounting function plays a very different role in a firm pursuing a cost leadership strategy versus a product differentiation strategy. Marketing and manufacturing also play very different roles in these two types of strategies. Your effectiveness in a firm can be reduced by doing accounting, marketing, and manufacturing as if your firm were pursuing a cost leadership strategy when it is actually pursuing a product differentiation strategy.

Finally, although it is true that strategic choices are generally limited to very experienced senior managers in large organizations, in smaller and entrepreneurial firms many employees end up being involved in the strategic management process. If you choose to work for one of these smaller or entrepreneurial firms—even if it is not right after graduation—you could very easily find yourself to be part of the strategic management team, implementing the strategic management process and choosing which strategies this firm should implement. In this setting, a familiarity with the essential concepts that underlie the choice and implementation of a strategy may turn out to be very helpful.

Summary

A firm's strategy is its theory of how to gain competitive advantages. These theories, like all theories, are based on assumptions and hypotheses about how competition in an industry is likely to evolve. When those assumptions and hypotheses are consistent with the actual evolution of competition in an industry, a firm's strategy is more likely to be able to generate a competitive advantage.

One way that a firm can choose its strategies is through the strategic management process. This process is a set of analyses and decisions that increase the likelihood that a firm will be able to choose a "good" strategy, that is, a strategy that will lead to a competitive advantage.

The strategic management process begins when a firm identifies its mission, or its long-term purpose. This mission is often written down in the form of a mission statement. Mission statements, by themselves, can have no impact on performance, enhance a firm's performance, or hurt a firm's performance. Objectives are measurable milestones firms use to evaluate whether they are accomplishing their missions. External and internal analyses are the processes through which a firm identifies its environmental threats and opportunities and organizational strengths and weaknesses. Armed with these analyses, it is possible for a firm to engage in strategic choice. Strategies can be classified into two categories: business-level strategies (including cost leadership and product differentiation) and corporate-level strategies (including vertical integration, strategic alliances, diversification, and mergers and acquisitions). Strategy implementation follows strategic choice and involves choosing organizational structures, management control policies, and compensation schemes that support a firm's strategies.

The ultimate objective of the strategic management process is the realization of competitive advantage. A firm has a competitive advantage if it is creating more economic value than its rivals. Economic value is defined as the difference between the perceived customer benefits from purchasing a product or service from a firm and the total economic cost of developing and selling that product or service. Competitive advantages can be temporary or sustained. Competitive parity exists when a firm creates the same economic value as its rivals. A competitive disadvantage exists when a firm creates less economic value than its rivals, and it can be either temporary or sustained.

Two popular measures of a firm's competitive advantage are accounting performance and economic performance. Accounting performance measures competitive advantage using various ratios calculated from a firm's profit and loss and balance sheet statements. A firm's accounting performance is compared with the average level of accounting performance in a firm's industry. Economic performance compares a firm's level of return to its cost of capital. A firm's cost of capital is the rate of return it had to promise to pay to its debt and equity investors to induce them to invest in the firm.

Although many firms use the strategic management process to choose and implement strategies, not all strategies are chosen this way. Some strategies emerge over time, as firms respond to unanticipated changes in the structure of competition in an industry.

Students need to understand strategy and the strategic management process for at least three reasons. First, it can help in deciding where to work. Second, once you have a job it can help you to be successful in that job. Finally, if you have a job in a small or entrepreneurial firm you may become involved in strategy and the strategic management process from the very beginning.

Challenge Questions

1. Some firms publicize their corporate mission statements by including them in annual reports, on company letterheads, and in corporate advertising. What, if anything, does this practice say about the ability of these mission statements to be sources of sustained competitive advantage for a firm? Why?

2. Little empirical evidence indicates that having a formal, written mission statement improves a firm's performance. Yet many firms spend a great deal of time and money developing mission statements. Why?

3. Is it possible to distinguish between an emergent strategy and an ad hoc rationalization of a firm's past decisions? Explain.

4. Both external and internal analyses are important in the strategic management process. Is the order in which these analyses are conducted important? If yes, which should come first: external analysis or internal analysis? If the order is not important, why not?

5. Will a firm that has a sustained competitive disadvantage necessarily go out of business? What about a firm with below average accounting performance over a long period of time? Or a firm with below normal economic performance over a long period of time?

6. Can more than one firm have a competitive advantage in an industry at the same time? Is it possible for a firm to simultaneously have a competitive advantage and a competitive disadvantage?

Problem Set

1. Write objectives for each of the following mission statements.
(a) We will be a leader in pharmaceutical innovation.
(b) Customer satisfaction is our primary goal.
(c) We promise on-time delivery.
(d) Product quality is our first priority.

2. Rewrite each of the following objectives to make them more helpful in guiding a firm's strategic management process.
(a) We will introduce five new drugs.
(b) We will understand our customers' needs.
(c) Almost all of our products will be delivered on time.
(d) The number of defects in our products will fall.

3. Do firms with the following financial results have below normal, normal, or above normal economic performance?
(a) ROA = 14.3%, WACC = 12.8%
(b) ROA = 4.3%, WACC = 6.7%
(c) ROA = 6.5%, WACC = 9.2%
(d) ROA = 8.3%, WACC = 8.3%

4. Do these same firms have below average, average, or above average accounting performance?
(a) ROA = 14.3%, Industry Avg. ROA = 15.2%
(b) ROA = 4.3%, Industry Avg. ROA = 4.1%
(c) ROA = 6.5%, Industry Avg. ROA = 6.1%
(d) ROA = 8.3%, Industry Avg. ROA = 9.4%

5. Is it possible for a firm to simultaneously earn above normal economic returns and below average accounting returns? What about below normal economic returns and above average accounting returns? Why or why not? If this can occur, which measure of performance is more reliable: economic performance or accounting performance? Explain.

6. Examine the following corporate Web sites and determine if the strategies pursued by these firms were emergent, deliberate, or both emergent and deliberate. Justify your answer with facts from the Web sites.
(a) www.walmart.com
(b) www.ibm.com
(c) www.homedepot.com
(d) www.cardinal.com

7. Using the information provided, calculate this firm's ROA, ROE, gross profit margin, and quick ratio. If this firm's WACC is 6.6 percent and the average firm in its industry has an ROA of 8 percent, is this firm earning above or below normal economic performance and above or below average accounting performance?

Net sales	6,134	Operating cash	3,226	Net other operating assets	916
Cost of goods sold	(4,438)	Accounts receivable	681	Total assets	5,161
Selling, general administrative expenses	(996)	Inventories	20	Net current liabilities	1,549
		Other current assets	0	Long-term debt	300
Other expenses	(341)	Total current assets	3,927	Deferred income taxes	208
Interest income	72	Gross properties, plant, equipment	729	Preferred stock	0
Interest expense	(47)			Retained earnings	0
Provision for taxes	(75)	Accumulated depreciation	(411)	Common stock	3,104
Other income	245	Book value of fixed assets	318	Other liabilities	0
Net income	554	Goodwill	0	Total liabilities and equity	5,161

End Notes

1. This approach to defining strategy was first suggested in Drucker, P. (1994). "The theory of business." *Harvard Business Review, 75,* September–October, pp. 95–105.
2. This approach to defining strategy was first suggested in Drucker, P. (1994). "The theory of business." *Harvard Business Review, 75,* September–October, pp. 95–105.
3. See www.enron.com.
4. See Emshwiller, J., D. Solomon, and R. Smith. (2004). "Lay is indicted for his role in Enron collapse." *The Wall Street Journal,* July 8, pp. A1+; Gilmartin, R. (2005). "They fought the law." *BusinessWeek,* January 10, pp. 82–83.
5. These performance results were presented originally in Collins, J. C., and J. I. Porras. (1997). *Built to last: successful habits of visionary companies.* New York: HarperCollins.
6. Quoted in Collins, J. C., and J. I. Porras. (1997). *Built to last: successful habits of visionary companies,* New York: HarperCollins.
7. See Theroux, J., and J. Hurstak. (1993). "Ben & Jerry's Homemade Ice Cream Inc.: keeping the mission(s) alive." Harvard Business School Case No. 9-392-025; Applebaum, A. (2000). "Smartmoney.com: Unilever feels hungry, buys Ben & Jerry's." *The Wall Street Journal,* April 13, pp. B1+.
8. This definition of competitive advantage has a long history in the field of strategic management. For example, it is closely related to the definitions provided in Barney (1986, 1991) and Porter (1985). It is also consistent with the value-based approach described in Peteraf (2001), Brandenburger, and Stuart (1999), and Besanko, Dranove, and Shanley (2000). For more discussion on this definition, see Peteraf and Barney (2004).
9. FedEx's history is described in Trimble, V. (1993). *Overnight success: Federal Express and Frederick Smith, its renegade creator.* New York: Crown.
10. Mintzberg, H. (1978). "Patterns in strategy formulation." *Management Science,* 24(9), pp. 934–948; and Mintzberg, H. (1985). "Of strategies, deliberate and emergent." *Strategic Management Journal,* 6(3), pp. 257–272. Mintzberg has been most influential in expanding the study of strategy to include emergent strategies.
11. The J&J and Marriott emergent strategy stories can be found in Collins, J. C., and J. I. Porras. (1997). *Built to last: successful habits of visionary companies.* New York: HarperCollins.
12. See McCarthy, M. J. (1993). "The PEZ fancy is hard to explain, let alone justify." *The Wall Street Journal,* March 10, p. A1, for a discussion of PEZ's surprising emergent strategy.

Evaluating a Firm's External Environment

After reading this chapter, you should be able to:

1. Describe the dimensions of the general environment facing a firm and how this environment can affect a firm's opportunities and threats.

2. Describe how the structure-conduct-performance (S-C-P) model suggests that industry structure can influence a firm's competitive choices.

3. Describe the "five forces model of industry attractiveness" and indicators of when each of these forces will improve or reduce the attractiveness of an industry.

4. Describe how rivals and substitutes differ.

5. Discuss the role of complements in analyzing competition within an industry.

6. Describe four generic industry structures and specific strategic opportunities in those industries.

7. Describe the impact of tariffs, quotas, and other nontariff barriers to entry on the cost of entry into new geographic markets.

Competing College?

On August 1, 2006, a new athletic stadium in Glendale, Arizona, opened. With 63,400 permanent seats, expandable to 73,000, this stadium was the first to have both a retractable roof and a retractable grass field. Weighing 18.9 billion pounds, the grass field is transported 741 feet at 1/8 mile per hour outside the stadium's wall so that it can soak up the Arizona sunshine and provide a healthy and safe playing surface for professional and college football players. Since opening, the stadium has hosted numerous NFL and college games, including a BCS National Championship game and Super Bowl XLII. An impressive architectural sight—described by many as an alien space ship landing on the desert—the stadium is the state of the art in providing fans and players a great sporting venue. Indeed, there is only one thing unusual about this stadium—its name. It is called the University of Phoenix Stadium.[1]

Now, having a football stadium associated with a university is not that unusual in the United States. Many large and small colleges and universities in the United States have football stadiums on campus, and some of them bear the name of the school or the state within which the school resides—Ohio State University has, for example, the 105,000-seat Ohio Stadium; the University of Michigan has

the 110,000-seat Michigan Stadium; the University of Texas has the 94,000-seat Texas Memorial Stadium.

However, unlike these other universities, the University of Phoenix has no football team. It has no cheerleaders, no mascot, no overpaid coach. Indeed, it has no campus, in the traditional sense of a single location where most of its students attend class. Instead, the University of Phoenix is a private university, founded in 1976, with more than 330,000 students attending classes in 194 locations in 39 U.S. states, Puerto Rico, District of Columbia, Netherlands, Canada, and Mexico. Its students can major in over 100 different degree programs, many of which can be completed entirely online. Just like United Airline's investment in the United Center in Chicago, and Chase's investment in Chase Ball Park in Arizona, the University of Phoenix signed on as a sponsor to the new stadium in Glendale to advertise its brand to potential consumers.

The University of Phoenix is one of an increasing number of new entrants into higher education. According to its founder, Dr. John Sperling, the University of Phoenix entered into this industry to meet the growing demand for higher education opportunities for working adults. Committed to removing the barriers that have prevented working adults from completing their education, the University of Phoenix

has been the fastest growing university in the United States virtually from its founding.[2]

Competition seems to have come to the higher education industry. And it's not just restricted to new entrants like the University of Phoenix. After almost two centuries of gentle competition among universities confined almost entirely to the athletic field, universities and colleges now find themselves competing for the best students with attractive financial packages, luxurious on-campus health clubs, and state-of-the-art computing facilities. Universities now compete to hire the best-known, most widely published professors, who then compete with each other for research grants from the government and various nongovernmental organizations. University and college development officers compete to gain the favor of potential donors—people who can help build a university or college's endowment, which, in turn, can be used to fund programs for faculty, staff, and students.

Indeed, competition in the higher education industry has never been more intense. University presidents are now held responsible to the Trustees, for the development and implementation of strategies designed to give their schools a competitive advantage. This is the case even though most colleges and universities in the United States are not-for-profit organizations. But, just because these organizations are not trying to maximize their economic profit does not mean that they are not competing in a very competitive industry.[3]

The strategic management process described in Chapter 1 suggested that one of the critical determinants of a firm's strategies is the threats and opportunities in its competitive environment. If a firm understands these threats and opportunities, it is one step closer to being able to choose and implement a "good strategy"; that is, a strategy that leads to competitive advantage.

There are clearly both new threats—like new entrants including the University of Phoenix—and new opportunities in higher education.

However, it is not enough to recognize that it is important to understand the threats and opportunities in a firm's competitive environment. A set of tools that managers can apply to systematically complete this external analysis as part of the strategic management process is also required. These tools must be rooted in a strong theoretical base, so that managers know that they have not been developed in an arbitrary way. Fortunately, such tools exist and will be described in this chapter.

Understanding a Firm's General Environment

Any analysis of the threats and opportunities facing a firm must begin with an understanding of the general environment within which a firm operates. This **general environment** consists of broad trends in the context within which a firm operates that can have an impact on a firm's strategic choices. As depicted in Figure 2.1, the general environment consists of six interrelated elements: technological change, demographic trends, cultural trends, the economic climate, legal and political conditions, and specific international events. Each of these elements of the general environment is discussed in this section.

In 1899, Charles H. Duell, commissioner of the U.S. patent office, said, "Everything that can be invented has been invented."[4] He was wrong. Technological changes over the past few years have had significant impacts on the ways firms do business and on the products and services they sell. These impacts

Figure 2.1 The General Environment Facing Firms

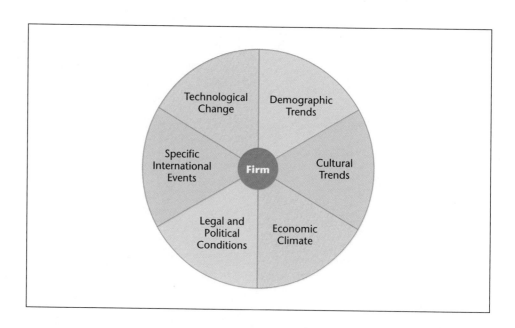

have been most obvious for technologies that build on digital information—computers, the Internet, cell phones, and so forth. Many of us routinely use digital products or services that did not exist just a few years ago—including TiVo. However, rapid technological innovation has not been restricted to digital technologies. Biotechnology has also made rapid progress over the past 10 years. New kinds of medicines are now being created. As important, biotechnology holds the promise of developing entirely new ways of both preventing and treating disease.[5]

Technological change creates both opportunity, as firms begin to explore how to use technology to create new products and services, and threats, as technological change forces firms to rethink their technological strategies. Indeed, in Chapter 1, we saw how one technological innovation—downloading digital music from the Internet—has changed competition in the music industry.[6]

A second element of the general environment facing firms is demographic trends. **Demographics** is the distribution of individuals in a society in terms of age, sex, marital status, income, ethnicity, and other personal attributes that may determine buying patterns. Understanding this basic information about a population can help a firm determine whether its products or services will appeal to customers and how many potential customers for these products or services it might have.

Some demographic trends are very well known. For example, everyone has heard of the "baby boomers"—those who were born shortly after World War II. This large population has had an impact on the strategies of many firms, especially as the boomers have grown older and have had more disposable income. However, other demographic groups have also had an impact on firm strategies. This is especially true in the automobile industry. For example, minivans were invented to meet the demands of "soccer moms"—women who live in the suburbs and have young children. The 3-series BMW seems to have been designed for "Yuppies"—the young, urban, and upwardly mobile adults of the 1970s and 1980s—whereas the Jeep Liberty and Nissan Xterra seem to have been designed for the so-called Generation Y—young men and women currently in their twenties and either just out of college or anticipating graduation shortly.

In the United States, an important demographic trend over the past 20 years has been the growth of the Hispanic population. In 1990, the percentage of the U.S. population that was African American was greater than the percentage that was Hispanic. However, by 2000, people of Latin descent outnumbered African Americans. By 2010, it is expected that Hispanics will constitute almost 15 percent of the U.S. population, whereas the percentage of African Americans will remain constant at less than 8 percent. These trends are particularly notable in the South and Southwest. For example, 36 percent of children under 18 in Houston are Hispanic, 39 percent in Miami and San Diego, 53 percent in Los Angeles, and 61 percent in San Antonio.[7]

Of course, firms are aware of this growing population and its buying power. Indeed, Hispanic disposable income in the United States jumped 29 percent, to $652 billion, from 2001 to 2003. In response, firms have begun marketing directly to the U.S. Hispanic population. In one year, Procter & Gamble spent $90 million marketing directly to Spanish-speaking customers. Procter & Gamble has also formed a 65-person bilingual team to manage the marketing of products to Hispanics. Indeed, Procter & Gamble expects that the Hispanic population will be the cornerstone of its sales growth in North America.[8]

Firms can try to exploit their understanding of a particular demographic segment of the population to create a competitive advantage—as Procter &

Gamble is doing with the U.S. Hispanic population—but focusing on too narrow a demographic segment can limit demand for a firm's products. The WB, the alternative television network created by Time Warner in 1995, faced this dilemma. Initially, the WB found success in producing shows for teens—classics such as *Dawson's Creek* and *Buffy the Vampire Slayer*. However, in 2003, the WB saw an 11 percent drop in viewership and a $25 million drop in advertising revenues. Although it did not leave its traditional demographic behind, the WB began producing some programs intended to appeal to older viewers. Ultimately, the WB merged with UPN to form a new network, the CW network. CW is a joint venture between CBS (owner of UPN) and Time Warner (owner of the WB).[9]

A third element of a firm's general environment is cultural trends. **Culture** is the values, beliefs, and norms that guide behavior in a society. These values, beliefs, and norms define what is "right and wrong" in a society, what is acceptable and unacceptable, what is fashionable and unfashionable. Failure to understand changes in culture, or differences between cultures, can have a very large impact on the ability of a firm to gain a competitive advantage.

This becomes most obvious when firms operate in multiple countries simultaneously. Even seemingly small differences in culture can have an impact. For example, advertisements in the United States that end with a person putting their index finger and thumb together mean that a product is "okay"; in Brazil, the same symbol is vulgar and offensive. Ads in the United States that have a bride dressed in white may be very confusing to the Chinese, because in China, white is the traditional color worn at funerals. In Germany, women typically purchase their own engagement rings, whereas in the United States, men purchase engagement rings for their fiancées. And what might be appropriate ways to treat women colleagues in Japan or France would land most men in U.S. firms in serious trouble. Understanding the cultural context within which a firm operates is important in evaluating the ability of a firm to generate competitive advantages.[10]

A fourth element of a firm's general environment is the current economic climate. The **economic climate** is the overall health of the economic systems within which a firm operates. The health of the economy varies over time in a distinct pattern: Periods of relative prosperity, when demand for goods and services is high and unemployment is low, are followed by periods of relatively low prosperity, when demand for goods and services is low and unemployment is high. When activity in an economy is relatively low, the economy is said to be in **recession**. A severe recession that lasts for several years is known as a **depression**. This alternating pattern of prosperity followed by recession, followed by prosperity, is called the **business cycle**.

Throughout the 1990s, the world, and especially the United States, enjoyed a period of sustained economic growth. Some observers even speculated that the government had become so skilled at managing demand in the economy through adjusting interest rates that a period of recession did not necessarily have to follow a period of sustained economic growth. Of course, the business cycle has reared its ugly head twice since the 1990s—first with the technology bubble-burst around 2001 and, more recently, in the credit crunch in 2008. Most observers now agree that although government policy can have a significant impact on the frequency and size of economic downturns, these policies are unlikely to be able prevent these downturns altogether.

A fifth element of a firm's general environment is **legal and political conditions**. The legal and political dimensions of an organization's general environment are the laws and the legal system's impact on business, together with the general nature of the relationship between government and business. These laws and the relationship between business and government can vary significantly around the world. For example, in Japan, business and the government are generally seen as having a consistently close and cooperative relationship. Indeed, some have observed that one reason that the Japanese economy has been growing so slowly over the last decade has been the government's reluctance to impose economic restructuring that would hurt the performance of some Japanese firms—especially the largest Japanese banks. In the United States, however, the quality of the relationship between business and the government tends to vary over time. In some administrations, rigorous antitrust regulation and tough environmental standards—both seen as inconsistent with the interests of business—dominate. In other administrations, antitrust regulation is less rigorous and the imposition of environmental standards is delayed, suggesting a more business-friendly perspective.

A final attribute of a firm's general environment is **specific international events**. These include events such as civil wars, political coups, terrorism, wars between countries, famines, and country or regional economic recessions. All of these specific events can have an enormous impact on the ability of a firm's strategies to generate competitive advantage.

Of course, one of the most important of these specific events to have occurred over the past several decades was the terrorist attacks on New York City and Washington, D.C., on September 11, 2001. Beyond the tragic loss of life, these attacks had important business implications as well. For example, it took over five years for airline demand to return to pre–September 11 levels. Insurance companies had to pay out billions of dollars in unanticipated claims as a result of the attacks. Defense contractors saw demand for their products soar as the United States and some of its allies began waging war in Afghanistan and then Iraq.

A firm's general environment defines the broad contextual background within which it operates. Understanding this general environment can help a firm identify some of the threats and opportunities it faces. However, this general environment often has an impact on a firm's threats and opportunities through its impact on a firm's more local environment. Thus, while analyzing a firm's general environment is an important step in any application of the strategic management process, this general analysis must be accompanied by an analysis of a firm's more local environment if the threats and opportunities facing a firm are to be fully understood. The next section discusses specific tools for analyzing a firm's local environment and the theoretical perspectives from which these tools have been derived.

The Structure-Conduct-Performance Model of Firm Performance

In the 1930s, a group of economists began developing an approach for understanding the relationship among a firm's environment, behavior, and performance. The original objective of this work was to describe conditions under which competition in an industry would *not* develop. Understanding when competition was not developing in an industry assisted government regulators in identifying industries where competition-enhancing regulations should be implemented.[11]

Ethics and Strategy

One of the basic tenets of economic theory is that society is better off when industries are very competitive. Industries are very competitive when there are large numbers of firms operating in an industry, when the products and services that these firms sell are similar to each other, and when it is not very costly for firms to enter into or exit these industries. Indeed, as is described in more detail in the Strategy in Depth feature, these industries are said to be *perfectly competitive.*

The reasons that society is better off when industries are perfectly competitive are well known. In such industries, firms must constantly strive to keep their costs low, their quality high, and, when appropriate, innovate if they are to even survive. Low costs, high quality, and appropriate innovation are generally consistent with the interests of a firm's customers, and thus consistent with society's overall welfare.

Indeed, concern for **social welfare**, or the overall good of society, is the primary reason the S-C-P model was developed. This model was to be used to identify industries where perfect competition was not occurring, and thus where social welfare was not being maximized. With these industries identified, the government could then engage in activities to increase the

Is a Firm Gaining a Competitive Advantage Good for Society?

competitiveness of these industries, thereby increasing social welfare.

Strategic management scholars turned the S-C-P model upside down by using it to describe industries where firms could gain competitive advantages and attain above-average performance. However, some have asked that if strategic management is all about creating and exploiting competitive imperfections in industries, is strategic management also all about reducing the overall good of society for advantages to be gained by a few firms? It is not surprising that individuals who are more interested in improving society than improving the

performance of a few firms question the moral legitimacy of the field of strategic management.

However, there is another view about strategic management and social welfare. The S-C-P model assumes that any competitive advantages a firm has in an industry must hurt society. The alternative view is that at least some of the competitive advantages exist because a firm addresses customer needs more effectively than its competitors. From this perspective, competitive advantages are not bad for social welfare; they are actually good for social welfare.

Of course, both perspectives can be true. For example, a firm such as Microsoft has engaged in activities that at least some courts have concluded are inconsistent with social welfare. However, Microsoft also sells applications software that is routinely ranked among the best in the industry, an action that is consistent with meeting customer needs in ways that maximize social welfare.

Sources: J. B. Barney (1986). "Types of competition and the theory of strategy." *Academy of Management Review,* 11, pp. 791–800; H. Demsetz (1973). "Industry structure, market rivalry, and public policy." *Journal of Law and Economics,* 16, pp. 1–9; M. Porter (1981). "The contribution of industrial organization to strategic management." *Academy of Management Review,* 6, pp. 609–620.

The theoretical framework that developed out of this effort became known as the **structure-conduct-performance (S-C-P) model**; it is summarized in Figure 2.2. The term **structure** in this model refers to industry structure, measured by such factors as the number of competitors in an industry, the heterogeneity of products in an industry, the cost of entry and exit in an industry, and so forth. **Conduct** refers to the strategies that firms in an industry implement. **Performance** in the S-C-P model has two meanings: (1) the performance of individual firms and (2) the performance of the economy as a whole. Although both definitions of performance in the S-C-P model are important, as suggested in Chapter 1, the strategic management process is much more focused on the performance of individual firms than on the performance of the economy as a whole. That said, the

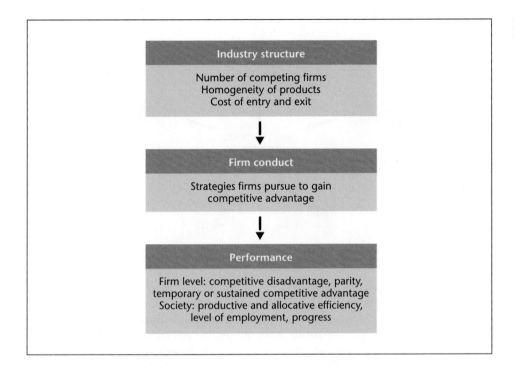

Figure 2.2 The Structure-Conduct-Performance Model

relationship between these two types of performance can sometimes be complex, as described in the Ethics and Strategy feature.

The logic that links industry structure to conduct and performance is well known. Attributes of the industry structure within which a firm operates define the range of options and constraints facing a firm. In some industries, firms have very few options and face many constraints. In general, firms in these industries can only gain competitive parity. In this setting, industry structure completely determines both firm conduct and long-run firm performance.

However, in other, less competitive industries, firms face fewer constraints and a greater range of conduct options. Some of these options may enable them to obtain competitive advantages. However, even when firms have more conduct options, industry structure still constrains the range of options. Moreover, as will be shown in more detail later in this chapter, industry structure also has an impact on how long firms can expect to maintain their competitive advantages in the face of increased competition.

The Five Forces Model of Environmental Threats

As a theoretical framework, the S-C-P model has proven to be very useful in informing both research and government policy. However, the model can sometimes be awkward to use to identify threats in a firm's local environment. Fortunately, several scholars have developed models of environmental threats based on the S-C-P model that are highly applicable in identifying threats facing a particular firm. The most influential of these models was developed by Professor Michael Porter and is known as the "five forces framework."[12] The **five forces framework** identifies the five most common threats faced by firms in their local competitive environments and the conditions under which these threats are more

Figure 2.3   Five Forces Model
of Environmental Threats

Source: Adapted with the permission of The Free Press, a division of Simon & Schuster Adult Publishing Group, from *Competitive Strategy: Techniques for Analyzing Industries and Competitors* by Michael E. Porter. Copyright © 1980, 1998 by The Free Press. All rights reserved.

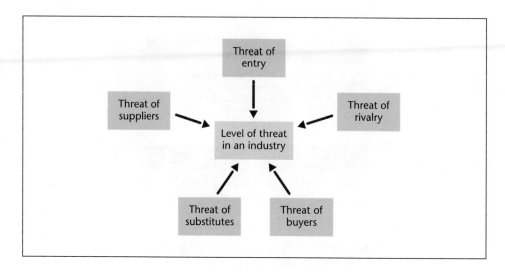

or less likely to be present. The relationship between the S-C-P model and the five forces framework is discussed in the Strategy in Depth feature.

To a firm seeking competitive advantages, an **environmental threat** is any individual, group, or organization outside a firm that seeks to reduce the level of that firm's performance. Threats increase a firm's costs, decrease a firm's revenues, or in other ways reduce a firm's performance. In S-C-P terms, environmental threats are forces that tend to increase the competitiveness of an industry and force firm performance to competitive parity level. The five common environmental threats identified in the five forces framework are: (1) the threat of entry, (2) the threat of rivalry, (3) the threat of substitutes, (4) the threat of suppliers, and (5) the threat of buyers. The five forces framework is summarized in Figure 2.3.

The Threat of Entry

The first environmental threat identified in the five forces framework is the threat of new entry. **New entrants** are firms that have either recently started operating in an industry or that threaten to begin operations in an industry soon. For Amazon.com, Barnes & Noble.com and Borders.com are new entrants to the online book-ordering business. Amazon largely invented this way of selling books, and both Barnes & Noble and Borders later followed with their entry into this market, even though both these firms already operated in the traditional book sales industry. For ESPN in the television sports industry, the Fox Sports Regional Network is a new entrant. The Fox Sports Regional Network consists of several regional sports channels that broadcast both national and regional sporting events, sports news shows, and sports entertainment shows—including *The Best Damn Sports Show Period*.[13]

According to the S-C-P model, new entrants are motivated to enter into an industry by the superior profits that some incumbent firms in that industry may be earning. Firms seeking these high profits enter the industry, thereby increasing the level of industry competition and reducing the performance of incumbent firms. With the absence of any barriers, entry will continue as long as any firms in the industry are earning competitive advantages, and entry will cease when all incumbent firms are earning competitive parity.

The extent to which new entry acts as a threat to an incumbent firm's performance depends on the cost of entry. If the cost of entry into an industry is

Strategy in Depth

The relationship between the five forces framework and the S-C-P model turns on the relationship between the threats identified in the framework and the nature of competition in an industry. When all five threats are very high, competition in an industry begins to approach what economists call *perfect competition*. When all five threats are very low, competition in an industry begins to approach what economists call a *monopoly*. Between perfect competition and monopoly, economists have identified two other types of competition in an industry—*monopolistic competition* and *oligopoly*—where the five threats identified in the framework are moderately high. These four types of competition, and the expected performance of firms in these different industries, are summarized in the table below.

Industries are **perfectly competitive** when there are large numbers of competing firms, the products being sold are homogeneous with respect to cost and product attributes, and entry and exit costs are very low. An example of a perfectly competitive industry is the spot market for crude oil. Firms

The Five Forces Framework and the S-C-P Model

in perfectly competitive industries can expect to earn only competitive parity.

In **monopolistically competitive industries**, there are large numbers of competing firms and low-cost entry into and exit from the industry. However, unlike the case of perfect competition, products in these industries are not homogeneous with respect to costs or product attributes. Examples of monopolistically competitive industries include toothpaste, shampoo, golf balls, and automobiles. Firms in such industries can earn competitive advantages.

Oligopolies are characterized by a small number of competing firms, by homogeneous products, and by high entry and exit costs. Examples of oligopolistic industries include the U.S. automobile and steel industries in the 1950s and the U.S. breakfast cereal market today. Currently, the top four producers of breakfast cereal account for about 90 percent of the breakfast cereal sold in the United States. Firms in such industries can earn competitive advantages.

Finally, **monopolistic industries** consist of only a single firm. Entry into this type of industry is very costly. There are few examples of purely monopolistic industries. Historically, for example, the U.S. Post Office had a monopoly on home mail delivery. However, this monopoly has been challenged in small-package delivery by FedEx, larger-package delivery by UPS, and in mail delivery by e-mail. Monopolists can generate competitive advantages—although they are sometimes managed very inefficiently.

Source: J. Barney (2007). *Gaining and sustaining competitive advantage*, 3rd ed. Upper Saddle River, NJ: Pearson Higher Education.

Types of Competition and Expected Firm Performance

Type of Competition	Attributes	Examples	Expected Firm Performance
Perfect competition	Large number of firms Homogeneous products Low-cost entry and exit	Stock market Crude oil	Competitive parity
Monopolistic competition	Large number of firms Heterogeneous products Low-cost entry and exit	Toothpaste Shampoo Golf balls Automobiles	Competitive advantage
Oligopoly	Small number of firms Homogenous products Costly entry and exit	U.S. steel and autos in the 1950s U.S. breakfast cereal	Competitive advantage
Monopoly	One firm Costly entry	Home mail delivery	Competitive advantage

TABLE 2.1 Barriers to Entry into an Industry	
	1. Economies of scale
	2. Product differentiation
	3. Cost advantages independent of scale
	4. Government regulation of entry

greater than the potential profits a new entrant could obtain by entering, then entry will not be forthcoming, and new entrants are not a threat to incumbent firms. However, if the cost of entry is lower than the return from entry, entry will occur until the profits derived from entry are less than the costs of entry.

The threat of entry depends on the cost of entry, and the cost of entry, in turn, depends on the existence and "height" of barriers to entry. **Barriers to entry** are attributes of an industry's structure that increase the cost of entry. The greater the cost of entry, the greater the height of these barriers. When there are significant barriers to entry, potential entrants will not enter into an industry even if incumbent firms are earning competitive advantages.

Four important barriers to entry have been identified in the S-C-P and strategy literatures. These four barriers, listed in Table 2.1, are (1) economies of scale, (2) product differentiation, (3) cost advantages independent of scale, and (4) government regulation of entry.[14]

Economies of Scale as a Barrier to Entry

Economies of scale exist in an industry when a firm's costs fall as a function of its volume of production. **Diseconomies of scale** exist when a firm's costs rise as a function of its volume of production. The relationship among economies of scale, diseconomies of scale, and a firm's volume of production is summarized in Figure 2.4. As a firm's volume of production increases, its costs begin to fall. This is a manifestation of economies of scale. However, at some point a firm's volume of production becomes too large and its costs begin to rise. This is a manifestation of diseconomies of scale. For economies of scale to act as a barrier to entry, the relationship between the volume of production and firm costs must have the shape of

Figure 2.4   Economies of Scale and the Cost of Production

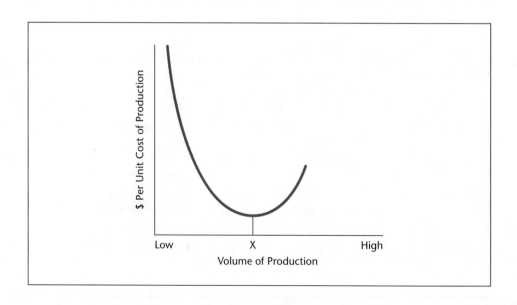

the line in Figure 2.4. This curve suggests that any deviation, positive or negative, from an optimal level of production (point X in Figure 2.4) will lead a firm to experience much higher costs of production.

To see how economies of scale can act as a barrier to entry, consider the following scenario. Imagine an industry with the following attributes: The industry has five incumbent firms (each firm has only one plant); the optimal level of production in each of these plants is 4,000 units (X = 4,000 units); total demand for the output of this industry is fixed at 22,000 units; the economies-of-scale curve is as depicted in Figure 2.4; and products in this industry are very homogeneous. Total demand in this industry (22,000 units) is greater than total supply (5 × 4,000 units = 20,000). Everyone knows that, when demand is greater than supply, prices go up. This means that the five incumbent firms in this industry will have high levels of profit. The S-C-P model suggests that, absent barriers, these superior profits should motivate entry.

However, look at the entry decision from the point of view of potential entrants. Certainly, incumbent firms are earning superior profits, but potential entrants face an unsavory choice. On the one hand, new entrants could enter the industry with an optimally efficient plant and produce 4,000 units. However, this form of entry will lead industry supply to rise to 24,000 units (20,000 + 4,000). Suddenly, supply will be greater than demand (24,000 > 22,000), and all the firms in the industry, including the new entrant, will earn negative profits. On the other hand, the new entrant might enter the industry with a plant of smaller-than-optimal size (e.g., 1,000 units). This kind of entry leaves total industry demand larger than industry supply (22,000 > 21,000). However, the new entrant faces a serious cost disadvantage in this case because it does not produce at the low-cost position on the economies-of-scale curve. Faced with these bleak alternatives, the potential entrant simply does not enter even though incumbent firms are earning positive profits.

Of course, potential entrants have other options besides entering at the efficient scale and losing money or entering at an inefficient scale and losing money. For example, potential entrants can attempt to expand the total size of the market (i.e., increase total demand from 22,000 to 24,000 units or more) and enter at the optimal size. Potential entrants can also attempt to develop new production technology, shift the economies-of-scale curve to the left (thereby reducing the optimal plant size), and enter. Or, potential entrants may try to make their products seem very special to their customers, enabling them to charge higher prices to offset higher production costs associated with a smaller-than-optimal plant.[15]

Any of these actions may enable a firm to enter an industry. However, these actions are costly. If the cost of engaging in these "barrier-busting" activities is greater than the return from entry, entry will not occur, even if incumbent firms are earning positive profits.

Historically, economies of scale acted as a barrier to entry into the worldwide steel market. To fully exploit economies of scale, traditional steel plants had to be very large. If new entrants into the steel market had built these efficient and large steel-manufacturing plants, they would have had the effect of increasing the steel supply over the demand for steel, and the outcome would have been reduced profits for both new entrants and incumbent firms. This discouraged new entry. However, in the 1970s, the development of alternative mini-mill technology shifted the economies-of-scale curve to the left by making smaller plants very efficient in addressing some segments of the steel market. This shift had the effect of decreasing barriers to entry into the steel industry. Recent entrants, including Nucor Steel and Chaparral Steel, now have significant cost advantages over firms still using outdated, less efficient production technology.[16]

Product Differentiation as a Barrier to Entry

Product differentiation means that incumbent firms possess brand identification and customer loyalty that potential entrants do not. Brand identification and customer loyalty serve as entry barriers because new entrants not only have to absorb the standard costs associated with starting production in a new industry; they also have to absorb the costs associated with overcoming incumbent firms' differentiation advantages. If the cost of overcoming these advantages is greater than the potential return from entering an industry, entry will not occur, even if incumbent firms are earning positive profits.

Numerous examples exist of industries in which product differentiation tends to act as a barrier to entry. In the brewing industry, for example, substantial investments by Budweiser, Miller, and Coors (among other incumbent firms) in advertising (will we ever forget the Budweiser frogs?) and brand recognition have made large-scale entry into the U.S. brewing industry very costly.[17] Indeed, rather than attempting to enter the U.S. market, InBev, a large brewer headquartered in Belgium, decided to purchase Anheuser Busch.[18]

E. & J. Gallo Winery, a U.S. winemaker, faced product differentiation barriers to entry in its efforts to sell Gallo wine in the French market. The market for wine in France is huge—the French consume 16.1 gallons of wine per person per year, for a total consumption of over 400 million cases of wine, whereas U.S. consumers drink only 1.8 gallons of wine per person per year, for a total consumption of less than 200 million cases. Despite this difference, intense loyalties to local French vineyards have made it very difficult for Gallo to break into the huge French market—a market where American wines are still given as "gag gifts" and only American theme restaurants carry U.S. wines on their menus. Gallo is attempting to overcome this product differentiation advantage of French wineries by emphasizing its California roots—roots that many French consider to be exotic—and downplaying the fact that it is a U.S. company, corporate origins that are less attractive to many French consumers.[19]

Cost Advantages Independent of Scale as Barriers to Entry

In addition to the barriers that have been cited, incumbent firms may have a whole range of cost advantages, independent of economies of scale, compared to new entrants. These cost advantages can act to deter entry, because new entrants will find themselves at a cost disadvantage vis-à-vis incumbent firms with these cost advantages. New entrants can engage in activities to overcome the cost advantages of incumbent firms, but as the cost of overcoming them increases, the economic profit potential from entry is reduced. In some settings, incumbent firms enjoying cost advantages, independent of scale, can earn superior profits and still not be threatened by new entry because the cost of overcoming those advantages can be prohibitive. Examples of these cost advantages, independent of scale, are presented in Table 2.2; they include (1) proprietary technology, (2) managerial know-how, (3) favorable access to raw materials, and (4) learning-curve cost advantages.

Proprietary Technology.   In some industries, **proprietary** (i.e., secret or patented) **technology** gives incumbent firms important cost advantages over potential entrants. To enter these industries, potential entrants must develop their own substitute technologies or run the risks of copying another firm's patented technologies. Both of these activities can be costly. Numerous firms in a wide variety of industries have discovered the sometimes substantial economic costs associated with violating another firm's patented proprietary technology. For

TABLE 2.2 Sources of Cost Advantage, Independent of Scale, That Can Act as Barriers to Entry

Proprietary technology. When incumbent firms have secret or patented technology that reduces their costs below the costs of potential entrants, potential entrants must develop substitute technologies to compete. The cost of developing this technology can act as a barrier to entry.

Managerial know-how. When incumbent firms have taken-for-granted knowledge, skills, and information that take years to develop and that is not possessed by potential entrants. The cost of developing this know-how can act as a barrier to entry.

Favorable access to raw materials. When incumbent firms have low-cost access to critical raw materials not enjoyed by potential entrants. The cost of gaining similar access can act as a barrier to entry.

Learning-curve cost advantages. When the cumulative volume of production of incumbent firms gives them cost advantages not enjoyed by potential entrants. These cost disadvantages of potential entrants can act as a barrier to entry.

example, in the 1990s Eastman Kodak had to pay Polaroid $910 million and Intel had to pay Digital $700 million for violating patents. More recently, Roche Holding had to pay Igen International $505 million and Genentech had to pay City of Hope National Medical Center $500 million for violating patents. Eolas had to pay $521 million for infringing a Microsoft patent, and Gateway had to pay $250 million for violating an Intergraph patent.

Indeed, in the United States at least 20 firms have had to pay some other firm over $100 million for violating the other firm's patents. And this does not include the numerous patent infringement suits that are settled out of court, suits that involve literally billions of dollars exchanging hands. Obviously, if an industry has several firms with proprietary technologies, these technologies can substantially increase the cost of entry into that industry.[20]

The number of patent infringement suits filed in the United States has increased every year for the past 15 years. The number of such suits in 1991 was 1,171; the number in 2004 (the last year for which complete data are available) was 3,075. Since 1994, the median damage award in a patent infringement suit has been $8 million. Currently, 60 percent of the patent infringement suits filed lead to financial compensation. Patent suits are distributed across numerous industries, including electronic equipment (14.6 percent), chemicals (14 percent), measuring instruments (13.4 percent), computer equipment (12.2 percent), and business services (9.8 percent).[21]

Managerial Know-How. Even more important than technology per se as a barrier to entry is the managerial know-how built up by incumbent firms over their history.[22] **Managerial know-how** is the often-taken-for-granted knowledge and information that are needed to compete in an industry on a day-to-day basis.[23] Know-how includes information that it has taken years, sometimes decades, for a firm to accumulate that enables it to interact with customers and suppliers, to be innovative and creative, to manufacture quality products, and so forth. Typically, new entrants will not have access to this know-now, and it will often be costly for them to build it quickly.

One industry where this kind of know-how is a very important barrier to entry is the pharmaceutical industry. Success in this industry depends on having high-quality research and development skills. The development of world-class research and development skills—the know-how—takes decades to accumulate. New entrants face enormous cost disadvantages for decades as they attempt to develop these abilities, and thus entry into the pharmaceutical industry has been quite limited.[24]

Favorable Access to Raw Materials.   Incumbent firms may also have cost advantages, compared to new entrants, based on favorable access to raw materials. If, for example, only a few sources of high-quality iron ore are available in a specific geographic region, steel firms that have access to these sources may have a cost advantage over those that must ship their ore in from distant sources.[25]

Learning-Curve Cost Advantages.   It has been shown that in certain industries (such as airplane manufacturing) the cost of production falls with the cumulative volume of production. Over time, as incumbent firms gain experience in manufacturing, their costs fall below those of potential entrants. Potential entrants, in this context, must endure substantially higher costs while they gain experience, and thus they may not enter the industry despite the superior profits being earned by incumbent firms. These learning-curve economies are discussed in more detail in Chapter 4.

Government Policy as a Barrier to Entry

Governments, for their own reasons, may decide to increase the cost of entry into an industry. This occurs most frequently when a firm operates as a government-regulated monopoly. In this setting, the government has concluded that it is in a better position to ensure that specific products or services are made available to the population at reasonable prices than competitive market forces. Industries such as electric power generation and elementary and secondary education have been (and to some extent, continue to be) protected from competitive entry by government restrictions on entry.

Although the government has acted to restrict competitive entry in many industries in the past, the number of such industries and the level of this entry restriction have both fallen dramatically over the past several years. Indeed, in the United States, deregulation in the electric power generation industry has been occurring at a rapid pace. And although the bankruptcy of Enron may delay the relaxing of government-imposed barriers to entry into the power generation industry, most observers agree that these restrictions will continue to be less important in the future. Entry is even occurring in the primary and secondary school industry with the creation of "charter schools"—schools that provide educational alternatives to traditional public school systems.

The Threat of Rivalry

New entrants are an important threat to the ability of firms to maintain or improve their level of performance, but they are not the only threat in a firm's environment. A second environmental threat in the five forces framework is **rivalry**—the intensity of competition among a firm's direct competitors. Both Barnes & Noble.com and Borders.com have become rivals of Amazon.com. CBS, NBC, Fox, USA Networks, and TNN—to name a few—are all rivals of ESPN.

Rivalry threatens firms by reducing their economic profits. High levels of rivalry are indicated by such actions as frequent price cutting by firms in an

1. Large number of competing firms that are roughly the same size
2. Slow industry growth
3. Lack of product differentiation
4. Capacity added in large increments

TABLE 2.3 Attributes of an Industry That Increase the Threat of Rivalry

industry (e.g., price discounts in the airline industry), frequent introduction of new products by firms in an industry (e.g., continuous product introductions in consumer electronics), intense advertising campaigns (e.g., Pepsi versus Coke advertising), and rapid competitive actions and reactions in an industry (e.g., competing airlines quickly matching the discounts of other airlines).

Some of the attributes of an industry that are likely to generate high levels of rivalry are listed in Table 2.3. First, rivalry tends to be high when there are numerous firms in an industry and these firms tend to be roughly the same size. Such is the case in the laptop personal computer industry. Worldwide, over 120 firms have entered the laptop computer market, and no one firm dominates in market share. Since the early 1990s, prices in the laptop market have been declining 25 to 30 percent a year. Profit margins for laptop personal computer firms that used to be in the 10 to 13 percent range have rapidly fallen to 3 to 4 percent.[26]

Second, rivalry tends to be high when industry growth is slow. When industry growth is slow, firms seeking to increase their sales must acquire market share from established competitors. This tends to increase rivalry. Intense price rivalry emerged in the U.S. fast-food industry—with 99-cent Whoppers at Burger King and "dollar menus" at Wendy's and McDonald's—when the growth in this industry declined.[27]

Third, rivalry tends to be high when firms are unable to differentiate their products in an industry. When product differentiation is not a viable strategic option, firms are often forced to compete only on the basis of price. Intense price competition is typical of high-rivalry industries. In the airline industry, for example, intense competition on longer routes—such as between Los Angeles and New York and Los Angeles and Chicago—has kept prices on these routes down. These routes have relatively few product differentiation options. However, by creating hub-and-spoke systems, certain airlines (American, United, Delta) have been able to develop regions of the United States where they are the dominant carrier. These hub-and-spoke systems enable airlines to partially differentiate their products geographically, thus reducing the level of rivalry in segments of this industry.[28]

Finally, rivalry tends to be high when production capacity is added in large increments. If, in order to obtain economies of scale, production capacity must be added in large increments, an industry is likely to experience periods of oversupply after new capacity comes on line. This overcapacity often leads to price cuts. Much of the growing rivalry in the commercial jet industry between Boeing and AirBus can be traced to the large manufacturing capacity additions made by AirBus when it entered the industry.[29]

The Threat of Substitutes

A third environmental threat in the five forces framework is substitutes. The products or services provided by a firm's rivals meet approximately the same customer needs in the same ways as the products or services provided by the firm itself. **Substitutes** meet approximately the same customer needs, but do so in different ways. Close substitutes for Amazon.com include Barnes & Noble and Borders bookstores. Television is a somewhat more distant substitute for Amazon, because the popularity of television comedies, dramas, and documentaries dampens demand for books. Substitutes for ESPN include sports magazines, sports pages in the newspapers, and actually attending sporting events.

Substitutes place a ceiling on the prices firms in an industry can charge and on the profits firms in an industry can earn. In the extreme, substitutes can ultimately replace an industry's products and services. This happens when a substitute is clearly superior to previous products. Examples include electronic calculators as substitutes for slide rules and mechanical calculators, electronic watch movements as substitutes for pin–lever mechanical watch movements, and compact discs as substitutes for long-playing (LP) records (although some audiophiles continue to argue for the sonic superiority of LPs). An open question remains about the extent to which online downloading of music will replace compact discs.

Substitutes are playing an increasingly important role in reducing the profit potential in a variety of industries. For example, in the legal profession private mediation and arbitration services are becoming viable substitutes for lawyers. Computerized texts are becoming viable substitutes for printed books in the publishing industry. Television news programs, especially services such as CNN, are very threatening substitutes for weekly newsmagazines, including *Time* and *Newsweek*. In Europe, so-called superstores are threatening smaller food shops. Minor league baseball teams are partial substitutes for major league teams. Cable television is a substitute for broadcast television. Groups of "Big Box" retailers are substitutes for traditional shopping centers. Private mail delivery systems (such as those in the Netherlands and Australia) are substitutes for government postal services. Home financial planning software is a partial substitute for professional financial planners.[30]

The Threat of Powerful Suppliers

A fourth environmental threat in the five forces framework is suppliers. **Suppliers** make a wide variety of raw materials, labor, and other critical assets available to firms. Suppliers can threaten the performance of firms in an industry by increasing the price of their supplies or by reducing the quality of those supplies. Any profits that were being earned in an industry can be transferred to suppliers in this way. For Amazon, book publishers and, more recently, book authors are critical suppliers, along with the employees that provide programming and logistics capabilities to Amazon. Critical suppliers for ESPN include sports leagues—such as the NFL and the NHL—as well as the TV personalities that staff ESPN television shows.

Some supplier attributes that can lead to high levels of threat are listed in Table 2.4. First, a firm's suppliers are a greater threat if the *suppliers'* industry is

TABLE 2.4 Indicators of the Threat of Suppliers in an Industry

1. Suppliers' industry is dominated by small number of firms.
2. Suppliers sell unique or highly differentiated products.
3. Suppliers are *not* threatened by substitutes.
4. Suppliers threaten forward vertical integration.
5. Firms are *not* important customers for suppliers.

dominated by a small number of firms. In this setting, a firm has little choice but to purchase supplies from these firms. These few firms thus have enormous flexibility to charge high prices, to reduce quality, or in other ways to squeeze the profits of the firms to which they sell. Much of Microsoft's power in the software industry reflects its dominance in the operating system market, where Windows Vista remains the de facto standard for most personal computers. For now, at least, if a company wants to sell personal computers, it is going to need to interact with Microsoft. It will be interesting to see if Linux-based PCs become more powerful, thereby limiting some of Microsoft's power as a supplier.

Conversely, when a firm has the option of purchasing from a large number of suppliers, suppliers have less power to threaten a firm's profits. For example, as the number of lawyers in the United States has increased over the years (up 40 percent since 1981, currently over 1 million), lawyers and law firms have been forced to begin competing for work. Some corporate clients have forced law firms to reduce their hourly fees and to handle repetitive simple legal tasks for low flat fees.[31]

Second, suppliers are a greater threat when what they supply is unique or highly differentiated. There was only one Michael Jordan, as a basketball player, as a spokesperson, and as a celebrity (but *not* as a baseball player). Jordan's unique status gave him enormous bargaining power as a supplier and enabled him to extract much of the economic profit that would otherwise have been earned by the Chicago Bulls and Nike. Currently, there is only one LeBron James. In the same way, Intel's unique ability to develop, manufacture, and sell microprocessors gives it significant bargaining power as a supplier in the personal computer industry.

The uniqueness of suppliers can operate in almost any industry. For example, in the highly competitive world of television talk shows, some guests, as suppliers, can gain surprising fame for their unique characteristics. For example, one woman was a guest on eight talk shows. Her claim to fame: She was the tenth wife of a gay, con-man bigamist. Talk show hosts can also exercise significant power as suppliers. King World, the distributor of the *Oprah* talk show, has depended on *Oprah* for as much as 40 percent of its revenues. This, of course, has given the show's host, Oprah Winfrey, significant leverage in negotiating with King World.[32]

Third, suppliers are a greater threat to firms in an industry when suppliers are *not* threatened by substitutes. When there are no effective substitutes, suppliers can take advantage of their position to extract economic profits from firms they supply. Both Intel (in microprocessors) and Microsoft (in PC operating systems) have been accused of exploiting their unique product positions to extract profits from customers.

When there are substitutes for supplies, supplier power is checked. In the metal can industry, for example, steel cans are threatened by aluminum and plastic containers as substitutes. In order to continue to sell to can manufacturers, steel companies have had to keep their prices lower than would otherwise have been the case. In this way, the potential power of the steel companies is checked by the existence of substitute products.[33]

Fourth, suppliers are a greater threat to firms when they can credibly threaten to enter into and begin competing in a firm's industry. This is called **forward vertical integration**; in this situation, suppliers cease to be suppliers only and become suppliers *and* rivals. The threat of forward vertical integration is partially a function of barriers to entry into an industry. When an industry has high barriers to entry, suppliers face significant costs of forward vertical integration, and thus forward integration is not as serious a threat to the profits of incumbent firms. (Vertical integration is discussed in detail in Chapter 6.)

Finally, suppliers are a threat to firms when firms are *not* an important part of suppliers' business. Steel companies, for example, are not too concerned with losing the business of a sculptor or of a small construction company. However, they are very concerned about losing the business of the major can manufacturers, major white-goods manufacturers (i.e., manufacturers of refrigerators, washing machines, dryers, and so forth), and automobile companies. Steel companies, as suppliers, are likely to be very accommodating and willing to reduce prices and increase quality for can manufacturers, white-goods manufacturers, and auto companies. Smaller, "less important" customers, however, are likely to be subject to greater price increases, lower-quality service, and lower-quality products.

The Threat of Powerful Buyers

The final environmental threat in the five forces framework is buyers. **Buyers** purchase a firm's products or services. Whereas powerful suppliers act to increase a firm's costs, powerful buyers act to decrease a firm's revenues. Amazon.com's buyers include all those who purchase books online as well as those who purchase advertising space on Amazon's Web site. ESPN's buyers include all those who watch sports on television as well as those who purchase advertising space on the network. Some of the important indicators of the threat of buyers are listed in Table 2.5.

First, if a firm has only one buyer, or a small number of buyers, these buyers can be very threatening. Firms that sell a significant amount of their output to the U.S. Department of Defense recognize the influence of this buyer on their operations. Reductions in defense spending have forced defense companies to try even harder to reduce costs and increase quality to satisfy government demands. All these actions reduce the economic profits of these defense-oriented companies.[34] Firms that sell to large retail chains have also found it difficult to maintain high levels of profitability. Powerful retail firms—such as Wal-Mart and Home Depot—can make significant and complex logistical and other demands on their suppliers and, if suppliers fail to meet these demands, buyers can "fire" their suppliers. These demands can have the effect of reducing the profits of suppliers.

Second, if the products or services that are being sold to buyers are standard and not differentiated, then the threat of buyers can be greater. For example, farmers sell a very standard product. It is very difficult to differentiate products such as wheat, corn, or tomatoes (although this can be done to some extent through the development of new strains of crops, the timing of harvests, pesticide-free crops, and so forth). In general, wholesale grocers and food brokers can always find alternative suppliers of basic food products. These numerous alternative suppliers increase the threat of buyers and force farmers to keep their prices and profits low. If any one farmer attempts to raise prices, wholesale grocers and food brokers simply purchase their supplies from some other farmer.

TABLE 2.5 Indicators of the Threat of Buyers in an Industry

1. Number of buyers is small.
2. Products sold to buyers are undifferentiated and standard.
3. Products sold to buyers are a significant percentage of a buyer's final costs.
4. Buyers are *not* earning significant economic profits.
5. Buyers threaten backward vertical integration.

Third, buyers are likely to be more of a threat when the supplies they purchase are a significant portion of the costs of their final products. In this context, buyers are likely to be very concerned about the costs of their supplies and constantly on the lookout for cheaper alternatives. For example, in the canned food industry, the cost of the can itself can constitute up to 40 percent of a product's final price. Not surprisingly, firms such as Campbell Soup Company are very concerned about keeping the price of the cans they purchase as low as possible.[35]

Fourth, buyers are likely to be more of a threat when they are *not* earning significant economic profits. In these circumstances, buyers are likely to be very sensitive to costs and insist on the lowest possible cost and the highest possible quality from suppliers. This effect can be exacerbated when the profits suppliers earn are greater than the profits buyers earn. In this setting, a buyer would have a strong incentive to enter into its supplier's business to capture some of the economic profits being earned by the supplier. This strategy of **backward vertical integration** is discussed in more detail in Chapter 6.

Finally, buyers are more of a threat to firms in an industry when they have the ability to vertically integrate backward. In this case, buyers become both buyers and rivals and lock in a certain percentage of an industry's sales. The extent to which buyers represent a threat to vertically integrate, in turn, depends on the barriers to entry that are not in place in an industry. If there are significant barriers to entry, buyers may not be able to engage in backward vertical integration, and their threat to firms is reduced.

The Five Forces Model and Average Industry Performance

The five forces model has three important implications for managers seeking to choose and implement strategies. First, this model describes the most common sources of local environmental threat in industries. These are the threat of entry, the threat of rivalry, the threat of substitutes, the threat of suppliers, and the threat of buyers. Second, this model can be used to characterize the overall level of threat in an industry. Finally, because the overall level of threat in an industry is, according to S-C-P logic, related to the average level of performance of a firm in an industry, the five forces model can also be used to anticipate the average level of performance of firms in an industry.

Of course, it will rarely be the case that all five forces in an industry will be equally threatening at the same time. This can sometimes complicate the anticipation of the average level of firm performance in an industry. Consider, for example, the four industries in Table 2.6. It is easy to anticipate the average level of performance of firms in the first two industries: In Industry I, this performance will be

	Industry I	Industry II	Industry III	Industry IV
Threat of entry	High	Low	High	Low
Threat of rivalry	High	Low	Low	High
Threat of substitutes	High	Low	High	Low
Threat of powerful suppliers	High	Low	Low	High
Threat of powerful buyers	High	Low	High	Low
Expected average firm performance	Low	High	Mixed	Mixed

TABLE 2.6 Estimating the Level of Average Performance in an Industry

low; in Industry II, this performance will be high; however, in Industries III and IV it is somewhat more complicated. In these mixed situations, the real question to ask in anticipating the average performance of firms in an industry is, "Are one or more threats in this industry powerful enough to appropriate most of the profits that firms in this industry might generate?" If the answer to this question is yes, then the anticipated average level of performance will be low. If the answer is no, then the anticipated performance will be high.

Even more fundamentally, the five forces framework can be used only to anticipate the average level of firm performance in an industry. This is acceptable if a firm's industry is the primary determinant of its overall performance. However, as described in the Research Made Relevant feature, research suggests that the industry a firm operates in is far from the only determinant of its performance.

Another Environmental Force: Complementors

Recently, Professors Adam Brandenburger and Barry Nalebuff have suggested that another force needs to be added to Porter's five forces framework.[36] These authors distinguish between competitors and what they call a firm's *complementors*. If you were the Chief Executive Officer of a firm, the following is how you could tell the difference between your competitors and your complementors: Another firm is a **competitor** if your customers value your product less when they have the other firm's product than when they have your product alone. Rivals, new entrants, and substitutes are all examples of competitors. In contrast, another firm is a **complementor** if your customers value your product more when they have this other firm's product than when they have your product alone.

Consider, for example, the relationship between producers of television programming and cable television companies. The value of these firms' products partially depends on the existence of one another. Television producers need outlets for their programming. The growth in the number of channels on cable television provides more of these outlets and thus increases the value of these production firms. Cable television companies can continue to add channels, but those channels need content. So, the value of cable television companies depends partly on the existence of television production firms. Because the value of program-producing companies is greater when cable television firms exist and because the value of cable television companies is greater when program-producing companies exist, these types of firms are complements.

Brandenburger and Nalebuff go on to argue that an important difference between complementors and competitors is that a firm's complementors help to increase the size of a firm's market, whereas a firm's competitors divide this market among a set of firms. Based on this logic, these authors suggest that, although it is usually the case that a firm will want to discourage the entry of competitors into its market, it will usually want to encourage the entry of complementors. Returning to the television producers/cable television example, television producers will actually want cable television companies to grow and prosper and constantly add new channels, and cable television firms will want television show producers to grow and constantly create new and innovative programming. If the growth of either of these businesses slows, it hurts the growth of the other.

Of course, the same firm can be a complementor for one firm and a competitor for another. For example, the invention of satellite television and increased popularity of DirecTV and the Dish Network represent a competitive challenge to cable television companies. That is, DirecTV and, say, Time Warner Cable are

Research Made Relevant

For some time now, scholars have been interested in the relative impact of the attributes of the industry within which a firm operates and the attributes of the firm itself on its performance. The first work in this area was published by Richard Schmalansee. Using a single year's worth of data, Schmalansee estimated the variance in the performance of firms that was attributable to the industries within which firms operated versus other sources of performance variance. Schmalansee's conclusion was that approximately 20 percent of the variance in firm performance was explained by the industry within which a firm operated—a conclusion consistent with the S-C-P model and its emphasis on industry as a primary determinant of a firm's performance.

Richard Rumelt identified some weaknesses in Schmalansee's research. Most important of these was that Schmalansee had only one year's worth of data with which to examine the effects of industry and firm attributes on firm performance. Rumelt was able to use four years' worth of data, which allowed him to distinguish between stable and transient industry and firm effects on firm performance.

The Impact of Industry and Firm Characteristics on Firm Performance

Rumelt's results were consistent with Schmalansee's in one sense: Rumelt also found that about 16 percent of the variance in firm performance was due to industry effects, versus Schmalansee's 20 percent. However, only about half of this industry effect was stable. The rest represented year-to-year fluctuations in the business conditions in an industry. This result is broadly inconsistent with the S-C-P model.

Rumelt also examined the impact of firm attributes on firm performance and found that over 80 percent of the variance in firm performance was due

to these firm attributes, but that over half of this 80 percent (46.38 percent) was due to stable firm effects. The importance of stable firm differences in explaining differences in firm performance is also inconsistent with the S-C-P framework. These results are consistent with another model of firm performance called the *Resource-Based View*, which will be described in Chapter 3.

Since Rumelt's research, efforts to identify the factors that explain variance in firm performance have accelerated. At least nine articles addressing this issue have been published in the literature. One of the most recent of these suggests that, while the impact of the industry, the corporation, and the business on business unit performance can vary across industries and across corporations, overall, business unit effects are larger than either corporate or industry effects.

Sources: R. P. Rumelt (1991). "How much does industry matter?" *Strategic Management Journal*, 12, pp. 167–185; R. Schmalansee (1985). "Do markets differ much?" *American Economic Review*, 75, pp. 341–351; V. F. Misangyi, H. Elms, T. Greckhamer, and J. A. Lepine (2006). "A new perspective on a fundamental debate: A multi-level approach to industry, corporate, and business unit effects." *Strategic Management Journal*, 27(6), pp. 571–590.

competitors. However, DirecTV and television production companies are complementors to each other. In deciding whether to encourage the entry of new complementors, a firm has to weigh the extra value these new complementors will create against the competitive impact of this entry on a firm's current complementors.

It is also the case that a single firm can be both a competitor and a complementor to the same firm. This is very common in industries where it is important to create technological standards. Without standards for, say, the size of a CD, how information on a CD will be stored, how this information will be read, and so forth, consumers will often be unwilling to purchase a CD player. With standards in place, however, sales of a particular technology can soar. To develop technology standards, firms must be willing to cooperate. This cooperation means that, with respect to the technology standard, these firms are complementors. And indeed, when these firms act as complementors, their actions have the effect of increasing the total size of the market. However, once these firms cooperate to establish standards, they begin to compete to try to obtain as much of the market they jointly created as possible. In this sense, these firms are also competitors.

Understanding when firms in an industry should behave as complementors and when they should behave as competitors is sometimes very difficult. It is even more difficult for a firm that has interacted with other firms in its industry as a competitor to change its organizational structure, formal and informal control systems, and compensation policy and start interacting with these firms as a complementor, at least for some purposes. Learning to manage what Brandenburger and Nalebuff call the "Jekyll and Hyde" dilemma associated with competitors and complementors can distinguish excellent from average firms.

Industry Structure and Environmental Opportunities

Identifying environmental threats is only half the task in accomplishing an external analysis. Such an analysis must also identify opportunities. Fortunately, the same S-C-P logic that made it possible to develop tools for the analysis of environmental threats can also be used to develop tools for the analysis of environmental opportunities. However, instead of identifying the threats that are common in most industries, opportunity analysis begins by identifying several generic industry structures and then describing the strategic opportunities that are available in each of these different kinds of industries.[37]

Of course, there are many different generic industry structures. However, four are very common and will be the focus of opportunity analysis in this book: (1) fragmented industries, (2) emerging industries, (3) mature industries, and (4) declining industries. A fifth industry structure—international industries—will be discussed later in the chapter. The kinds of opportunities typically associated with these industry structures are presented in Table 2.7.

Opportunities in Fragmented Industries: Consolidation

Fragmented industries are industries in which a large number of small or medium-sized firms operate and no small set of firms has dominant market share or creates dominant technologies. Most service industries, including retailing, fabrics, and commercial printing, to name just a few, are fragmented industries.

TABLE 2.7 Industry Structure and Environmental Opportunities

Industry Structure	Opportunities
Fragmented industry	Consolidation
Emerging industry	First-mover advantages
Mature industry	Product refinement
	Investment in service quality
	Process innovation
Declining industry	Leadership
	Niche
	Harvest
	Divestment

Industries can be fragmented for a wide variety of reasons. For example, the fragmented industry may have few barriers to entry, thereby encouraging numerous small firms to enter. The industry may have few, if any, economies of scale, and even some important diseconomies of scale, thus encouraging firms to remain small. Also, close local control over enterprises in an industry may be necessary—for example, local movie houses and local restaurants—to ensure quality and to minimize losses from theft.

The major opportunity facing firms in fragmented industries is the implementation of strategies that begin to consolidate the industry into a smaller number of firms. Firms that are successful in implementing this **consolidation strategy** can become industry leaders and obtain benefits from this kind of effort, if they exist.

Consolidation can occur in several ways. For example, an incumbent firm may discover new economies of scale in an industry. In the highly fragmented funeral home industry, Service Corporation International (SCI) found that the development of a chain of funeral homes gave it advantages in acquiring key supplies (coffins) and in the allocation of scarce resources (morticians and hearses). By acquiring numerous previously independent funeral homes, SCI was able to substantially reduce its costs and gain higher levels of economic performance.[38]

Incumbent firms sometimes adopt new ownership structures to help consolidate an industry. Kampgrounds of America (KOA) uses franchise agreements with local operators to provide camping facilities to travelers in the fragmented private campgrounds industry. KOA provides local operators with professional training, technical skills, and access to its brand-name reputation. Local operators, in return, provide KOA with local managers who are intensely interested in the financial and operational success of their campgrounds. Similar franchise agreements have been instrumental in the consolidation of other fragmented industries, including fast food (McDonald's), muffler repair (Midas), and motels (La Quinta, Holiday Inn, Howard Johnson's).[39]

The benefits of implementing a consolidation strategy in a fragmented industry turn on the advantages larger firms in such industries gain from their larger market share. As will be discussed in Chapter 4, firms with large market share can have important cost advantages. Large market share can also help a firm differentiate its products.

Opportunities in Emerging Industries: First-Mover Advantages

Emerging industries are newly created or newly re-created industries formed by technological innovations, changes in demand, the emergence of new customer needs, and so forth. Over the past 30 years, the world economy has been flooded by emerging industries, including the microprocessor industry, the personal computer industry, the medical imaging industry, and the biotechnology industry, to name a few. Firms in emerging industries face a unique set of opportunities, the exploitation of which can be a source of superior performance for some time for some firms.

The opportunities that face firms in emerging industries fall into the general category of first-mover advantages. **First-mover advantages** are advantages that come to firms that make important strategic and technological decisions early in the development of an industry. In emerging industries, many of the rules of the game and standard operating procedures for competing and succeeding have yet to be established. First-moving firms can sometimes help establish the rules of the game and create an industry's structure in ways that are uniquely beneficial to them.

In general, first-mover advantages can arise from three primary sources: (1) technological leadership, (2) preemption of strategically valuable assets, and (3) the creation of customer-switching costs.[40]

First-Mover Advantages and Technological Leadership

Firms that make early investments in particular technologies in an industry are implementing a **technological leadership strategy**. Such strategies can generate two advantages in emerging industries. First, firms that have implemented these strategies may obtain a low-cost position based on their greater cumulative volume of production with a particular technology. These cost advantages have had important competitive implications in such diverse industries as the manufacture of titanium dioxide by DuPont and Procter & Gamble's competitive advantage in disposable diapers.[41]

Second, firms that make early investments in a technology may obtain patent protections that enhance their performance.[42] Xerox's patents on the xerography process and General Electric's patent on Edison's original lightbulb design were important for these firms' success when these two industries were emerging.[43] However, although there are some exceptions (e.g., the pharmaceutical industry and specialty chemicals), patents, per se, seem to provide relatively small profit opportunities for first-moving firms in most emerging industries. One group of researchers found that imitators can duplicate first movers' patent-based advantages for about 65 percent of the first mover's costs.[44] These researchers also found that 60 percent of all patents are imitated within four years of being granted—without legally violating patent rights obtained by first movers. As we will discuss in detail in Chapter 3, patents are rarely a source of sustained competitive advantage for firms, even in emerging industries.

First-Mover Advantages and Preemption of Strategically Valuable Assets

First movers that invest only in technology usually do not obtain sustained competitive advantages. However, first movers that move to tie up strategically valuable resources in an industry before their full value is widely understood can gain sustained competitive advantages. **Strategically valuable assets** are resources required to successfully compete in an industry. Firms that are able to acquire these resources have, in effect, erected formidable barriers to imitation in an industry. Some strategically valuable assets that can be acquired in this way include access to raw materials, particularly favorable geographic locations, and particularly valuable product market positions.

When an oil company such as Royal Dutch Shell (because of its superior exploration skills) acquires leases with greater development potential than was expected by its competition, the company is gaining access to raw materials in a way that is likely to generate sustained competitive advantages. When Wal-Mart opens stores in medium-sized cities before the arrival of its competition, Wal-Mart is making it difficult for the competition to enter into this market. And, when breakfast cereal companies expand their product lines to include all possible combinations of wheat, oats, bran, corn, and sugar, they, too, are using a first-mover advantage to deter entry.[45]

First-Mover Advantages and Creating Customer-Switching Costs

Firms can also gain first-mover advantages in an emerging industry by creating customer-switching costs. **Customer-switching costs** exist when customers make investments in order to use a firm's particular products or services. These investments tie customers to a particular firm and make it more difficult for customers to begin purchasing from other firms.[46] Such switching costs are important factors in industries as diverse as applications software for personal computers, prescription pharmaceuticals, and groceries.[47]

In applications software for personal computers, users make significant investments to learn how to use a particular software package. Once computer users have learned how to operate particular software, they are unlikely to switch to new software, even if that new software system is superior to what they currently use. Such a switch would require learning the new software and determining how it is similar to and different from the old software. For these reasons, some computer users will continue to use outdated software, even though new software performs much better.

Similar switching costs can exist in some segments of the prescription pharmaceutical industry. Once medical doctors become familiar with a particular drug, its applications, and side effects, they are sometimes reluctant to change to a new drug, even if that new drug promises to be more effective than the older, more familiar one. Trying the new drug requires learning about its properties and side effects. Even if the new drug has received government approvals, its use requires doctors to be willing to "experiment" with the health of their patients. Given these issues, many physicians are unwilling to rapidly adopt new drug therapies. This is one reason that pharmaceutical firms spend so much time and money using their sales forces to educate their physician customers. This kind of education is necessary if a doctor is going to be willing to switch from an old drug to a new one.

Customer-switching costs can even play a role in the grocery store industry. Each grocery store has a particular layout of products. Once customers learn where different products in a particular store are located, they are not likely to change stores, because they would then have to relearn the location of products. Many customers want to avoid the time and frustration associated with wandering around a new store looking for some obscure product. Indeed, the cost of switching stores may be large enough to enable some grocery stores to charge higher prices than would be the case without customer-switching costs.

First-Mover Disadvantages

Of course, the advantages of first moving in emerging industries must be balanced against the risks associated with exploiting this opportunity. Emerging industries are characterized by a great deal of uncertainty. When first-moving firms are making critical strategic decisions, it may not be at all clear what the right decisions are. In such highly uncertain settings, a reasonable strategic alternative to first moving may be retaining flexibility. Where first-moving firms attempt to resolve the uncertainty they face by making decisions early and then trying to influence the evolution of an emerging industry, they use flexibility to resolve this uncertainty by delaying decisions until the economically correct path is clear and then moving quickly to take advantage of that path.

Opportunities in Mature Industries: Product Refinement, Service, and Process Innovation

Emerging industries are often formed by the creation of new products or technologies that radically alter the rules of the game in an industry. However, over time, as these new ways of doing business become widely understood, as technologies diffuse through competitors, and as the rate of innovation in new products and technologies drops, an industry begins to enter the mature phase of its development. As described in the Strategy in the Emerging Enterprise feature, this change in the nature of a firm's industry can be difficult to recognize and can create both strategic and operational problems for a firm.

Common characteristics of **mature industries** include (1) slowing growth in total industry demand, (2) the development of experienced repeat customers, (3) a slowdown in increases in production capacity, (4) a slowdown in the introduction of new products or services, (5) an increase in the amount of international competition, and (6) an overall reduction in the profitability of firms in the industry.[48]

The fast-food industry in the United States has matured over the past 10 to 15 years. In the 1960s, the United States had only three large national fast-food chains: McDonald's, Burger King, and Dairy Queen. Through the 1980s, all three of these chains grew rapidly, although the rate of growth at McDonald's outstripped the growth rate of the other two firms. During this time period, however, other fast-food chains also entered the market. These included some national chains, such as Kentucky Fried Chicken, Wendy's, and Taco Bell, and some strong regional chains, such as Jack in the Box and In and Out Burger. By the early 1990s, growth in this industry had slowed considerably. McDonald's announced that it was having difficulty finding locations for new McDonald's that did not impinge on the sales of already existing McDonald's. Except for non–U.S. operations, where competition in the fast-food industry is not as mature, the profitability of most U.S. fast-food companies did not grow as much in the 1990s as it did in the 1960s through the 1980s. Indeed, by 2002, all the major fast-food chains were either not making very much money, or, like McDonald's, actually losing money.[49]

Opportunities for firms in mature industries typically shift from the development of new technologies and products in an emerging industry to a greater emphasis on refining a firm's current products, an emphasis on increasing the quality of service, and a focus on reducing manufacturing costs and increased quality through process innovations.

Refining Current Products

In mature industries, such as home detergents, motor oil, and kitchen appliances, few, if any, major technological breakthroughs are likely. However, this does not mean that innovation is not occurring in these industries. Innovation in these industries focuses on extending and improving current products and technologies. In home detergents, innovation recently has focused on changes in packaging and on selling more highly concentrated detergents. In motor oil, packaging changes (from fiber foil cans to plastic containers), additives that keep oil cleaner longer, and oil formulated to operate in four-cylinder engines are recent examples of this kind of innovation. In kitchen appliances, recent improvements include the availability of refrigerators with crushed ice and water through the door, commercial-grade stoves for home use, and dishwashers that automatically adjust the cleaning cycle depending on how dirty the dishes are.[50]

Emphasis on Service

When firms in an industry have only limited ability to invest in radical new technologies and products, efforts to differentiate products often turn toward the quality of customer service. A firm that is able to develop a reputation for high-quality customer service may be able to obtain superior performance even though its products are not highly differentiated.

Strategy in the Emerging Enterprise

It began with a 5,000-word e-mail sent by Steve Balmer, CEO of Microsoft, to all 57,000 employees. Whereas previous e-mails from Microsoft founder Bill Gates—including one in 1995 calling on the firm to learn how to "ride the wave of the Internet"—inspired the firm to move on to conquer more technological challenges, Balmer's e-mail focused on Microsoft's current state and called on the firm to become more focused and efficient. Balmer also announced that Microsoft would cut its costs by $1 billion during the next fiscal year. One observer described it as the kind of e-mail you would expect to read at Procter & Gamble, not at Microsoft.

Then the other shoe dropped. In a surprise move, Balmer announced that Microsoft would distribute a large portion of its $56 billion cash reserve in the form of a special dividend to stockholders. In what is believed to be the largest such cash dispersion ever, Microsoft distributed $32 billion to its stockholders and used an additional $30 billion to buy back stock. Bill Gates received a $3.2 billion cash dividend. These changes meant that Microsoft's capital structure was more similar to, say, Procter & Gamble's than to an entrepreneurial, high-flying software company.

What happened at Microsoft? Did Microsoft's management conclude that the PC software industry was no longer emerging, but had matured to the point that Microsoft

Microsoft Grows Up

would have to alter some of its traditional strategies? Most observers believe that Balmer's e-mail, and the decision to reduce its cash reserves, signaled that Microsoft had come to this conclusion. In fact, although most of Microsoft's core businesses—its Windows operating systems, its PC applications software, and its server software—are still growing at the rate of about $3 billion a year, if they were growing at historical rates these businesses would be generating $7 billion in new revenues each year. Moreover, Microsoft's new businesses—video games, Internet services, business software, and software for phones and handheld computers—are adding less than $1 billion in new revenues each year. That is, growth in Microsoft's new businesses is not offsetting slower growth in its traditional businesses.

Other indicators of the growing maturity of the PC software industry,

and Microsoft's strategic changes, also exist. For example, during 2003 and 2004, Microsoft resolved most of the outstanding antitrust litigation it was facing, abandoned its employee stock option plan in favor of a stock-based compensation scheme popular with slower-growth firms, improved its systems for receiving and acting on feedback from customers, and improved the quality of its relationships with some of its major rivals, including Sun Microsystems, Inc. These are all the actions of a firm that recognizes that the rapid growth opportunities that existed in the software industry when Microsoft was a new company do not exist anymore.

At this point, Microsoft has to choose whether it is going to jump-start its growth through a series of large acquisitions or accept the lower growth rates in its core markets. As described in the opening case for Chapter 10, it made a significant, but ultimately unsuccessful, effort to acquire Yahoo in an attempt to jump-start its growth in online services, a strong indicator that Microsoft, while acknowledging slower growth in its core, has not completely abandoned the idea of growing quickly in some parts of its business.

Sources: J. Greene (2004). "Microsoft's midlife crisis." *BusinessWeek*, April 19, 2004, pp. 88 +; R. Guth and S. Thurm (2004). "Microsoft to dole out its cash hoard." *The Wall Street Journal*, Wednesday, July 21, 2004, pp. A1 +; S. Hamm (2004). "Microsoft's worst enemy: Success." *BusinessWeek*, July 19, 2004, p. 33; www.microsoft.com/billgates/speeches/2006/00-15transition.asp.

This emphasis on service has become very important in a wide variety of industries. For example, in the convenience food industry, one of the major reasons for slower growth in the fast-food segment has been growth in the so-called "casual dining" segment. This segment includes restaurants such as Chili's and Applebee's. The food sold at fast-food restaurants and casual dining restaurants overlaps—they both sell burgers, soft drinks, salads, chicken, desserts, and so forth—although many consumers believe that the quality of food is superior in the casual dining restaurants. In addition to any perceived differences in the food, however, the level of service in the two kinds of establishments varies significantly. At fast-food restaurants, food is handed to consumers on a tray; in casual dining restaurants, wait staff actually bring food to consumers on a plate. This level of service is one reason that casual dining is growing in popularity.[51]

Process Innovation

A firm's **processes** are the activities it engages in to design, produce, and sell its products or services. **Process innovation**, then, is a firm's effort to refine and improve its current processes. Several authors have studied the relationship between process innovation, product innovation, and the maturity of an industry.[52] This work suggests that, in the early stages of industry development, product innovation is very important. However, over time product innovation becomes less important, and process innovations designed to reduce manufacturing costs, increase product quality, and streamline management become more important. In mature industries, firms can often gain an advantage by manufacturing the same product as competitors, but at a lower cost. Alternatively, firms can manufacture a product that is perceived to be of higher quality and do so at a competitive cost. Process innovations facilitate both the reduction of costs and the increase in quality.

The role of process innovation in more mature industries is perhaps best exemplified by the improvement in quality in U.S. automobiles. In the 1980s, Japanese firms such as Nissan, Toyota, and Honda sold cars that were of significantly higher quality than those produced by U.S. firms General Motors, Ford, and Chrysler. In the face of that competitive disadvantage, the U.S. firms engaged in numerous process reforms to improve the quality of their cars. In the 1980s, U.S. manufacturers were cited for car body panels that did not fit well, bumpers that were hung crookedly on cars, and the wrong engines being placed in cars. Today, the differences in quality between newly manufactured U.S. and Japanese automobiles are very small. Indeed, one well-known judge of initial manufacturing quality—J. D. Powers—now focuses on items such as the quality of a car's cup holders and the maximum distance at which a car's keyless entry system still works to establish quality rankings. The really significant quality issues of the 1980s are virtually gone.[53]

Opportunities in Declining Industries: Leadership, Niche, Harvest, and Divestment

A **declining industry** is an industry that has experienced an absolute decline in unit sales over a sustained period of time.[54] Obviously, firms in a declining industry face more threats than opportunities. Rivalry in a declining industry is likely to be very high, as is the threat of buyers, suppliers, and substitutes. However, even though threats are significant, firms do have opportunities they can exploit. The major strategic opportunities that firms in this kind of industry face are leadership, niche, harvest, and divestment.

Market Leadership

An industry in decline is often characterized by overcapacity in manufacturing, distribution, and so forth. Reduced demand often means that firms in a declining industry will have to endure a significant shakeout period until overcapacity is reduced and capacity is brought in line with demand. After the shakeout, a smaller number of lean and focused firms may enjoy a relatively benign environment with few threats and several opportunities. If the industry structure that is likely to exist after a shakeout is quite attractive, firms in an industry before the shakeout may have an incentive to weather the storm of decline—to survive until the situation improves to the point that they can begin to earn higher profits.

If a firm has decided to wait out the storm of decline in hopes of better environmental conditions in the future, it should consider various steps to increase its chances of survival. Most important of these is that a firm must establish itself as a **market leader** in the pre-shakeout industry, most typically by becoming the firm with the largest market share in that industry. The purpose of becoming a market leader is *not* to facilitate tacit collusion (see Chapter 9) or to obtain lower costs from economies of scale (see Chapter 6). Rather, in a declining industry the leader's objective should be to try to facilitate the exit of firms that are not likely to survive a shakeout, thereby obtaining a more favorable competitive environment as quickly as possible.

Market leaders in declining industries can facilitate exit in a variety of ways, including purchasing and then deemphasizing competitors' product lines, purchasing and retiring competitors' manufacturing capacity, manufacturing spare parts for competitors' product lines, and sending unambiguous signals of their intention to stay in an industry and remain a dominant firm. For example, overcapacity problems in the European petrochemical industry were partially resolved when Imperial Chemical Industries (ICI) traded its polyethylene plants to British Petroleum for BP's polyvinylchloride (PVC) plants. In this case, both firms were able to close some excess capacity in specific markets (polyethylene and PVC), while sending clear signals of their intention to remain in these markets.[55]

Market Niche

A firm in a declining industry following a leadership strategy attempts to facilitate exit by other firms, but a firm following a **niche strategy** in a declining industry reduces its scope of operations and focuses on narrow segments of the declining industry. If only a few firms choose a particular niche, then these firms may have a favorable competitive setting, even though the industry as a whole is facing shrinking demand.

Two firms that used the niche approach in a declining market are GTE Sylvania and General Electric (GE) in the vacuum tube industry. The invention of the transistor followed by the semiconductor just about destroyed demand for vacuum tubes in new products. GTE Sylvania and GE rapidly recognized that new product sales in vacuum tubes were drying up. In response, these firms began specializing in supplying *replacement* vacuum tubes to the consumer and military markets. To earn high profits, these firms had to refocus their sales efforts and scale down their sales and manufacturing staffs. Over time, as fewer and fewer firms manufactured vacuum tubes, GTE Sylvania and GE were able to charge very high prices for replacement parts.[56]

Harvest

Leadership and niche strategies, though differing along several dimensions, have one attribute in common: Firms that implement these strategies intend to remain in the industry despite its decline. Firms pursuing a **harvest strategy** in a declining industry do not expect to remain in the industry over the long term. Instead, they engage in a long, systematic, phased withdrawal, extracting as much value as possible during the withdrawal period.

The extraction of value during the implementation of a harvest strategy presumes that there is some value to harvest. Thus, firms that implement this strategy must ordinarily have enjoyed at least some profits at some time in their history, before the industry began declining. Firms can implement a harvest strategy by reducing the range of products they sell, reducing their distribution network, eliminating less profitable customers, reducing product quality, reducing service quality, deferring maintenance and equipment repair, and so forth. In the end, after a period of harvesting in a declining industry, firms can either sell their operations (to a market leader) or simply cease operations.

In principle, the harvest opportunity sounds simple, but in practice it presents some significant management challenges. The movement toward a harvest strategy often means that some of the characteristics of a business that have long been a source of pride to managers may have to be abandoned. Thus, where prior to harvest a firm may have specialized in high-quality service, quality products, and excellent customer value, during the harvest period service quality may fall, product quality may deteriorate, and prices may rise. These changes may be difficult for managers to accept, and higher turnover may be the result. It is also difficult to hire quality managers into a harvesting business, because such individuals are likely to seek greater opportunities elsewhere.

For these reasons, few firms explicitly announce a harvest strategy. However, examples can be found. GE seems to be following a harvest strategy in the electric turbine business. Also, United States Steel and the International Steel Group seem to be following this strategy in certain segments of the steel market.[57]

Divestment

The final opportunity facing firms in a declining industry is divestment. Like a harvest strategy, the objective of **divestment** is to extract a firm from a declining industry. However, unlike harvest, divestment occurs quickly, often soon after a pattern of decline has been established. Firms without established competitive advantages may find divestment a superior option to harvest, because they have few competitive advantages they can exploit through harvesting.

In the 1980s, GE used this rapid divestment approach to virtually abandon the consumer electronics business. Total demand in this business was more or less stable during the 1980s, but competition (mainly from Asian manufacturers) increased substantially. Rather than remain in this business, GE sold most of its consumer electronics operations and used the capital to enter into the medical imaging industry, where this firm has found an environment more conducive to superior performance.[58]

In the defense business, divestment is the stated strategy of General Dynamics, at least in some of its business segments. General Dynamics' managers recognized early on that the changing defense industry could not support all the incumbent firms. When General Dynamics concluded that it could not remain a leader in some of its businesses, it decided to divest those and concentrate on a few remaining businesses. Since 1991, General Dynamics has sold businesses worth over $2.83 billion, including its missile systems business, its Cessna aircraft division, and its tactical aircraft division (maker of the very successful F-16 aircraft and partner in the development of the next generation of fighter aircraft, the F-22). These divestitures have left General Dynamics in just three businesses: armored tanks, nuclear submarines, and space launch vehicles. During this time, the market price of General Dynamics stock has returned almost $4.5 billion to its investors, has seen its stock go from $25 per share to a high of $110 per share, and has provided a total return to stockholders of 555 percent.[59]

Of course, not all divestments are caused by industry decline. Sometimes firms divest certain operations to focus their efforts on remaining operations, sometimes they divest to raise capital, and sometimes they divest to simplify operations. These types of divestments reflect a firm's diversification strategy and are explored in detail in Chapter 11.

Summary

The strategic management process requires that a firm engage in an analysis of threats and opportunities in its competitive environment before a strategic choice can be made. This analysis begins with an understanding of the firm's general environment. This general environment has six components: technological change, demographic trends, cultural trends, economic climate, legal and political conditions, and specific international events. Although some of these components of the general environment can affect a firm directly, more frequently they affect a firm through their impact on its local environment.

The S-C-P model is a theoretical framework that enables the analysis of a firm's local environment and that links the structure of the industry within which a firm operates, its strategic alternatives, and firm performance. In this model, *structure* is defined as industry structure and includes those attributes of a firm's industry that constrain a firm's strategic alternatives and performance. *Conduct* is defined as a firm's strategies. *Performance* refers either to the performance of a firm in an industry or the performance of the entire economy—although the former definition of performance is more important for most strategic management purposes.

The S-C-P model can be used to develop tools for analyzing threats in a firm's competitive environment. The most influential of these tools is called the "five forces framework." The five forces are: the threat of entry, the threat of rivalry, the threat of substitutes, the threat of suppliers, and the threat of buyers. The threat of entry depends on the existence and "height" of barriers to entry. Common barriers to entry include economies of scale, product differentiation, cost advantages independent of scale, and government regulation. The threat of rivalry depends on the number and competitiveness of firms in an industry. The threat of rivalry is high in an industry when there are large numbers of competing firms, competing firms are roughly the same size and have the same influence, growth in an industry is slow, there is no product differentiation, and productive capacity is added in large increments. The threat of substitutes depends on how close substitute products and services are—in performance and cost—to products and services in an industry. Whereas rivals all meet the same customer needs in approximately the same way, substitutes meet the same customer needs, but do so in very different ways. The threat of suppliers in an industry depends on the number and distinctiveness of the products suppliers provide to an industry. The threat of suppliers increases when a supplier's industry is dominated by a few firms, when suppliers sell unique or highly differentiated products, when suppliers are not threatened by substitutes, when suppliers threaten forward vertical integration, and when firms are not important customers for suppliers. Finally, the threat of buyers depends on the number and size of an industry's customers. The threat of buyers is greater when the number of buyers is small, products sold to buyers are undifferentiated and standard, products sold to buyers are a significant percentage of a buyer's final costs, buyers are not earning significant profits, and buyers threaten backward vertical integration. Taken together, the level of these threats in an industry can be used to determine the expected average performance of firms in an industry.

One force in a firm's environment not included within the five forces framework is complementors. Where competitors (including rivals, new entrants, and substitutes) compete with a firm to divide profits in a market, complementors increase the total size of the market. If you are a CEO of a firm, you know that another firm is a complementor when the value of your products to your customers is higher in combination with this other firm's products than when customers use your products alone. Where firms have strong incentives to reduce the entry of competitors, they can sometimes have strong incentives to increase the entry of complementors.

The S-C-P model can also be used to develop tools for analyzing strategic opportunities in an industry. This is done by identifying generic industry structures and the strategic opportunities available in these different kinds of industries. Four common industry structures are fragmented industries, emerging industries, mature industries, and declining industries. The primary opportunity in fragmented industries is consolidation. In emerging industries, the most important opportunity is first-mover advantages from technological leadership, preemption of strategically valuable assets, or creation of customer-switching costs. In mature industries, the primary opportunities are product refinement, service, and process innovation. In declining industries, opportunities include market leadership, niche, harvest, and divestment.

Challenge Questions

1. Your former college roommate calls you and asks to borrow $10,000 so that he can open a pizza restaurant in his hometown. In justifying this request, he argues that there must be significant demand for pizza and other fast food in his hometown because there are lots of such restaurants already there and three or four new ones are opening each month. He also argues that demand for convenience food will continue to increase, and he points to the large number of firms that now sell frozen dinners in grocery stores. Will you lend him the money? Why or why not?

2. According to the five forces model, one potential threat in an industry is buyers. Yet unless buyers are satisfied, they are likely to look for satisfaction elsewhere. Can the fact that buyers can be threats be reconciled with the need to satisfy buyers?

3. Government policies can have a significant impact on the average profitability of firms in an industry. Government, however, is not included as a potential threat in the five forces model. Should the model be expanded to include government (to make a "six forces" model)? Why or why not?

4. How would you add complementors to the five forces model? In particular, if an industry has large numbers of complementors, does that make it more attractive, less attractive, or does it have no impact on the industry's attractiveness? Justify your answer.

5. Opportunities analysis seems to suggest that strategic opportunities are available in almost any industry, including declining ones. If that is true, is it fair to say that there is really no such thing as an unattractive industry? If yes, what implications does this have for the five forces model? If no, describe an industry that has no opportunities.

6. Is the evolution of industry structure from an emerging industry to a mature industry to a declining industry inevitable? Why or why not?

Problem Set

1. Perform a five forces analysis on the following two industries:

The Pharmaceutical Industry

The pharmaceutical industry consists of firms that develop, patent, and distribute drugs. Although this industry does not have significant production economies, it does have important economies in research and development. Product differentiation exists as well, because firms often sell branded products. Firms compete in research and development. However, once a product is developed and patented, competition is significantly reduced. Recently, the increased availability of generic, nonbranded drugs has threatened the profitability of some drug lines. Once an effective drug is developed, few, if any, alternatives to that drug usually are available. Drugs are manufactured from commodity chemicals that are available from numerous suppliers. Major customers include doctors and patients. Recently, increased costs have led the federal government and insurance companies to pressure drug companies to reduce their prices.

The Textile Industry

The textile industry consists of firms that manufacture and distribute fabrics for use in clothing, furniture, carpeting, and so forth. Several firms have invested heavily in sophisticated manufacturing technology, and many lower-cost firms located in Asia have begun fabric production. Textiles are not branded products. Recently, tariffs on some imported textiles have been implemented. The industry has numerous firms; the largest have less than 10 percent market share. Traditional fabric materials (such as cotton and wool) have recently been threatened by the development of alternative chemical-based materials (such as nylon and rayon), although many textile companies have begun manufacturing with these new materials as well. Most raw materials are widely available, although some synthetic products periodically may be in short supply. There are numerous textile customers, but textile costs are usually a large percentage of their final product's total costs. Many users shop around the world for the lowest textile prices.

2. Perform an opportunities analysis on the following industries.
(a) The U.S. airline industry
(b) The U.S. beer industry
(c) The U.S. property and casualty insurance industry
(d) The worldwide portable digital media (e.g., flash drives) industry
(e) The worldwide small package overnight delivery industry

3. For each of the following firms identify at least two competitors (rivals, new entrants, or substitutes) and two complementors.
(a) Yahoo!
(b) Microsoft
(c) Dell
(d) Boeing
(e) McDonald's

End Notes

1. www.universityofphoenixstadium.com. Accessed June 17, 2009.
2. www.upxnewsroom.com/facts. Accessed June 17, 2009.
3. DeFraja, G., and E. Iossa (2002). "Competition among universities and the emergence of the elite institution." *Bulletin of Economic Research*, 54(3), pp. 275–293; Gate, Denise S. (2001). *The competition for top undergraduates by America's colleges and universities*. The Center. http://the center.ufl.edu.
4. See (2003). *The big book of business quotations*. New York: Basic Books, p. 209.
5. See Weintraub, A. (2004). "Repairing the engines of life." *BusinessWeek*, May 24, 2004, pp. 99 + for a discussion of recent developments in biotechnology research and the business challenges they have created.
6. See the opening case in Chapter 1.
7. See Grow, B. (2004). "Hispanic nation." *BusinessWeek*, March 15, 2004, pp. 59 +.
8. Ibid.
9. Barnes, B. (2004). "The WB grows up." *The Wall Street Journal*, July 19, 2004, pp. B1 +; money.cnn.com/2006/01/24/news/companies/cbs_warner. Accessed February 2007.
10. These and other cultural differences are described in Rugman, A., and R. Hodgetts (1995). *International business*. New York: McGraw-Hill. A discussion of the dimensions along which country cultures can vary is presented in a later chapter.
11. Early contributors to the structure-conduct-performance model include Mason, E. S. (1939). "Price and production policies of large scale enterprises." *American Economic Review*, 29, pp. 61–74; and Bain, J. S. (1956). *Barriers to new competition*. Cambridge, MA: Harvard University Press. The major developments in this framework are summarized in Bain, J. S. (1968). *Industrial organization*. New York: John Wiley & Sons, Inc.; and Scherer, F. M. (1980). *Industrial market structure and economic performance*. Boston: Houghton Mifflin. The links between this framework and work in strategic management are discussed by Porter, M. E. (1981a). "The contribution of industrial organization to strategic management." *Academy of Management Review*, 6, pp. 609–620; and Barney, J. B. (1986c). "Types of competition and the theory of strategy: Toward an integrative framework." *Academy of Management Review*, 1, pp. 791–800.
12. The five forces framework is described in detail in Porter, M. E. (1979). "How competitive forces shape strategy." *Harvard Business Review*, March–April, pp. 137–156; and Porter, M. E. (1980). *Competitive strategy*. New York: Free Press.
13. In 2005, ESPN also entered the college sports cable business with the introduction of the ESPN-U channel. See http://sports.espn.go.com/espntv.
14. These barriers were originally proposed by Bain, J. S. (1968). *Industrial organization*. New York: John Wiley & Sons, Inc.; and Porter, M. E. (1980). *Competitive strategy*. New York: Free Press. It is actually possible to estimate the "height" of barriers to entry in an industry by comparing the cost of entry into an industry with barriers and the cost of entry into that industry if barriers did not exist. The difference between these costs is the "height" of the barriers to entry.
15. Another alternative would be for a firm to own and operate more than one plant. If there are economies of scope in this industry, a firm might be able to enter and earn above-normal profits. An economy of scope exists when the value of operating in two businesses simultaneously is greater than the value of operating in these two businesses separately. The concept of economy of scope is explored in more detail in Part 3 of this book.
16. See Ghemawat, P., and H. J. Stander III (1992). "Nucor at a crossroads." Harvard Business School Case No. 9-793-039.
17. See Montgomery, C. A., and B. Wernerfelt (1991). "Sources of superior performance: Market share versus industry effects in the U.S. brewing industry." *Management Science*, 37, pp. 954–959.
18. A. R. Sorkin and M. Merced (2008). "Brewer bids $46 billion for Anheuser-Busch." *New York Times*, June 12, 2008.
19. Stecklow, S. (1999). "Gallo woos French, but don't expect Bordeaux by the jug." *The Wall Street Journal*, March 26, pp. A1 +.
20. See www.bustpatents.com/awards.html. Accessed February 2007.
21. See www.pwc.com/images/us/eng/about/svcs/advisor for a very informative report written by PWC about patents and patent violators. Accessed February 2007.
22. See Kogut, B., and U. Zander. (1992). "Knowledge of the firm, combinative capabilities, and the replication of technology." *Organization Science*, 3, pp. 383–397; and Dierickx, I., and K. Cool. (1989). "Asset stock accumulation and sustainability of competitive advantage." *Management Science*, 35, pp. 1504–1511. Both emphasize the importance of know-how as a barrier to entry into an industry. More generally, intangible resources are seen as particularly important sources of sustained competitive advantage. This will be discussed in more detail in Chapter 5.
23. See Polanyi, M. (1962). *Personal knowledge: Towards a post-critical philosophy*. London: Routledge & Kegan Paul; and Itami, H. (1987). *Mobilizing invisible assets*. Cambridge, MA: Harvard University Press.

24. See Henderson, R., and I. Cockburn. (1994). "Measuring competence: Exploring firm effects in pharmaceutical research." *Strategic Management Journal*, 15, pp. 361–374.

25. See Scherer, F. M. (1980). *Industrial market structure and economic performance*. Boston: Houghton Mifflin.

26. See Saporito, B. (1992). "Why the price wars never end." *Fortune*, March 23, pp. 68–78; and Allen, M., and M. Siconolfi. (1993). "Dell Computer drops planned share offering." *The Wall Street Journal*, February 25, p. A3.

27. Chartier, John. (2002). "Burger battles." CNN/Money, http://money.cnn.com, December 11.

28. See Ghemawat, P., and A. McGahan. (1995). "The U.S. airline industry in 1995." Harvard Business School Case No. 9-795-113.

29. Labich, K. (1992). "Airbus takes off." *Fortune*, June 1, pp. 102–108.

30. See Pollock, E. J. (1993). "Mediation firms alter the legal landscape." *The Wall Street Journal*, March 22, p. B1; Cox, M. (1993). "Electronic campus: Technology threatens to shatter the world of college textbooks." *The Wall Street Journal*, June 1, p. A1; Reilly, P. M. (1993). "At a crossroads: The instant-new age leaves *Time* magazine searching for a mission." *The Wall Street Journal*, May 12, p. A1; Rohwedder, C. (1993). "Europe's smaller food shops face finis." *The Wall Street Journal*, May 12, p. B1; Fatsis, S. (1995). "Major leagues keep minors at a distance." *The Wall Street Journal*, November 8, pp. B1 +; Norton, E., and G. Stern. (1995). "Steel and aluminum vie over every ounce in a car's construction." *The Wall Street Journal*, May 9, pp. A1 +; Paré, T. P. (1995). "Why the banks lined up against Gates." *Fortune*, May 29, p. 18; "Hitting the mail on the head." *The Economist*, April 30, 1994, pp. 69–70; Pacelle, M. (1996). "'Big Boxes' by discounters are booming." *The Wall Street Journal*, January 17, p. A2; and Pope, K., and L. Cauley (1998). "In battle for TV ads, cable is now the enemy." *The Wall Street Journal*, May 6, pp. B1 +.

31. Tully, S. (1992). "How to cut those #$%* legal costs." *Fortune*, September 21, pp. 119–124.

32. Jensen, E. (1993). "Tales are oft told as TV talk shows fill up airtime." *The Wall Street Journal*, May 25, p. A1; Jensen, E. (1995). "King World ponders life without Oprah." *The Wall Street Journal*, September 26, p. B1.

33. See DeWitt, W. (1997). "Crown Cork & Seal/Carnaud Metalbox." Harvard Business School Case No. 9-296-019.

34. Perry, N. J. (1993). "What's next for the defense industry." *Fortune*, February 22, pp. 94–100.

35. See "Crown Cork and Seal in 1989." Harvard Business School Case No. 5-395-224.

36. See Brandenburger, A., and B. Nalebuff (1996). *Co-opetition*. New York: Doubleday.

37. This approach to studying opportunities was also first suggested in Porter, M. E. (1980). *Competitive strategy*. New York: Free Press.

38. Jacob, R. (1992). "Service Corp. International: Acquisitions done the right way." *Fortune*, November 16, p. 96.

39. Porter, M. E. (1980). *Competitive strategy*. New York: Free Press.

40. For the definitive discussion of first-mover advantages, see Lieberman, M., and C. Montgomery. (1988). "First-mover advantages." *Strategic Management Journal*, 9, pp. 41–58.

41. See Ghemawat, P. (1991). *Commitment*. New York: Free Press.

42. See Gilbert, R. J., and D. M. Newbery. (1982). "Preemptive patenting and the persistence of monopoly." *American Economic Review*, 72(3), pp. 514–526.

43. See Bresnahan, T. F. (1985). "Post-entry competition in the plain paper copier market." *American Economic Review*, 85, pp. 15–19, for a discussion of Xerox's patents; and Bright, A. A. (1949). *The electric lamp industry*. New York: Macmillan, for a discussion of General Electric's patents.

44. See Mansfield, E., M. Schwartz, and S. Wagner. (1981). "Imitation costs and patents: An empirical study." *Economic Journal*, 91, pp. 907–918.

45. See Main, O. W. (1955). *The Canadian nickel industry.* Toronto: University of Toronto Press, for a discussion of asset preemption in the oil and gas industry; Ghemawat, P. (1986). "Wal-Mart store's discount operations." Harvard Business School Case No. 9-387-018, for Wal-Mart's preemption strategy; Schmalansee, R. (1978). "Entry deterrence in the ready-to-eat breakfast cereal industry." *Bell Journal of Economics*, 9(2), pp. 305–327; and Robinson, W. T., and C. Fornell. (1985). "Sources of market pioneer advantages in consumer goods industries." *Journal of Marketing Research*, 22(3), pp. 305–307, for a discussion of preemption in the breakfast cereal industry. In this latter case, the preempted valuable asset is shelf space in grocery stores.

46. Klemperer, P. (1986). "Markets with consumer switching costs." Doctoral thesis, Graduate School of Business, Stanford University; and Wernerfelt, B. (1986). "A special case of dynamic pricing policy." *Management Science*, 32, pp. 1562–1566.

47. See Gross, N. (1995). "The technology paradox." *BusinessWeek*, March 6, pp. 691–719; Bond, R. S., and D. F. Lean. (1977). *Sales, promotion, and product differentiation in two prescription drug markets*. Washington, D.C.: U.S. Federal Trade Commission; Montgomery, D. B. (1975). "New product distribution: An analysis of supermarket buyer decision." *Journal of Marketing Research*, 12, pp. 255–264; Ries, A., and J. Trout. (1986). *Marketing warfare*. New York: McGraw-Hill; and Davidson, J. H. (1976). "Why most new consumer brands fail." *Harvard Business Review*, 54, March–April, pp. 117–122, for a discussion of switching costs in these industries.

48. Porter, M. E. (1980). *Competitive strategy*. New York: Free Press.

49. Gibson, R. (1991). "McDonald's insiders increase their sales of company's stock." *The Wall Street Journal*, June 14, p. A1; and Chartier, J. (2002). "Burger Battles." CNN/Money, http://money.cnn.com, December 11. McDonald's lost money for only one quarter. It has since repositioned itself with nice upscale fast foods and has returned to profitability.

50. Descriptions of these product refinements can be found in Demetrakakes, P. (1994). "Household-chemical makers concentrate on downsizing." *Packaging*, 39(1), p. 41; Reda, S. (1995). "Motor oil: Hands-on approach." *Stores*, 77(5), pp. 48–49; and Quinn, J. (1995). "KitchenAid." *Incentive*, 169(5), pp. 46–47.

51. Chartier, J. (2002). "Burger Battles." CNN/Money, http://money.cnn.com, December 11.

52. See Hayes, R. H., and S. G. Wheelwright. (1979). "The Dynamics of process-product life cycles." *Harvard Business Review*, March–April, p. 127.

53. See www.jdpowers.com.

54. See Porter, M. E. (1980). *Competitive strategy*. New York: Free Press; and Harrigan, K. R. (1980). *Strategies for declining businesses*. Lexington, MA: Lexington Books.

55. See Aguilar, F. J., J. L. Bower, and B. Gomes-Casseres. (1985). "Restructuring European petrochemicals: Imperial Chemical Industries, P.L.C." Harvard Business School Case No. 9-385-203.

56. See Harrigan, K. R. (1980). *Strategies for declining businesses*. Lexington, MA: Lexington Books.

57. See Klebnikov, P. (1991). "The powerhouse." *Forbes*, September 2, pp. 46–52; and Rosenbloom, R. S., and C. Christensen. (1990). "Continuous casting investments at USX corporation." Harvard Business School Case No. 9-391-121.

58. Finn, E. A. (1987). "General Eclectic." *Forbes*, March 23, pp. 74–80.

59. See Smith, L. (1993). "Can defense pain be turned to gain?" *Fortune*, February 8, pp. 84–96; Perry, N. J. (1993). "What's next for the defense industry?" *Fortune*, February 22, pp. 94–100; and Dial, J., and K. J. Murphy. (1995). "Incentive, downsizing, and value creation at General Dynamics." *Journal of Financial Economics*, 37, pp. 261–314.

3

Evaluating a Firm's Internal Capabilities

LEARNING OBJECTIVES

After reading this chapter, you should be able to:

1. Describe the critical assumptions of the resource-based view.

2. Describe four types of resources and capabilities.

3. Apply the VRIO framework to identify the competitive implications of a firm's resources and capabilities.

4. Apply value chain analysis to identify a firm's valuable resources and capabilities.

5. Describe the kinds of resources and capabilities that are likely to be costly to imitate.

6. Describe how a firm uses its structure, formal and informal control processes, and compensation policy to exploit its resources.

7. Discuss how the decision of whether to imitate a firm with a competitive advantage affects the competitive dynamics in an industry.

Has eBay Lost Its Way?

On January 23, 2008, Meg Whitman—the high-profile CEO of eBay—announced her retirement. During her 10 years as CEO, Whitman transformed eBay from a modestly profitable online auction site to a diversified e-commerce giant, with net income up 53 percent to $531 million on revenues that increased 27 percent to $2.2 billion in the fourth quarter of 2007. Not bad numbers to go out on for Whitman.

However, the story at eBay is actually a bit more complicated than these simple numbers suggest. Most of eBay's recent growth comes from businesses that eBay purchased—PayPal, the online payment system, and Skype, the free Internet telephone service. In fact, eBay's core online auction service has remained quite stable over the past few years. The number of active eBay users has remained constant for almost a year, at around 83 million. New product listings on the site have only increased 4 percent, and the number of companies selling products on eBay at fixed prices has actually declined.

What has happened to the core business at eBay? First, in an attempt to increase the firm's overall profitability, Whitman increased the fees that sellers are charged for using the auction service. This

drove many sellers to look for alternative venues.

Second, competition emerged. For example, despite eBay's substantial head start, both in terms of auction software and its number of users, Amazon.com has become an increasingly attractive alternative to eBay for online auctions. Many users find Amazon's online auction system to be easier—and cheaper—to use. eBay only recently began upgrading is auction system to offer services currently available on Amazon—including new search software that enables shoppers to look at product photos instead of long lists of thumbnail product descriptions.

In addition to alternative online auction services like Yahoo, other Web sites that compete with eBay have also emerged—including the online classified ad site called Craig's List. Instead of trying to buy and sell products through an auction, many users prefer the simplicity of buying and selling on Craig's List.

Maybe part of eBay's challenge with its online auction business has been its efforts to expand beyond its core auction business. With two major acquisitions in three years—PayPal in October of 2002 and Skype in October of 2005—eBay's management has had to focus much of its effort on integrating these companies with

eBay. All this was complicated when, two years after acquiring Skype for $2.5 billion, eBay wrote off $1.43 billion of this investment—essentially acknowledging that it had significantly overpaid for Skype.

In any case, eBay's new CEO—John Donahoe—will have to find some way to revitalize eBay's core auction business. Once eBay's central product around which all of its other services were organized, the online auction service faces the real threat of becoming a mature, slow growth, and low-profit business for eBay.

Source: Catherin Holahan (2008). "eBay's new tough love CEO." *Business Week*, February 4, pp. 58–59.

goldenangel/Shutterstock

Bay has historically been the leader in online auctions. But this position now seems to be at risk. Just how sustainable was eBay's original advantage in the auction market?

The Resource-Based View of the Firm

In Chapter 2, we saw that it was possible to take some theoretical models developed in economics—specifically the structure-conduct-performance (S-C-P) model—and apply them to develop tools for analyzing a firm's external threats and opportunities. The same is true for analyzing a firm's internal strengths and weaknesses. However, whereas the tools described in Chapter 2 were based on the S-C-P model, the tools described in this chapter are based on the **resource-based view (RBV)** of the firm. The RBV is a model of firm performance that focuses on the resources and capabilities controlled by a firm as sources of competitive advantage.[1]

What Are Resources and Capabilities?

Resources in the RBV are defined as the tangible and intangible assets that a firm controls that it can use to conceive and implement its strategies. Examples of resources include a firm's factories (a tangible asset), its products (a tangible asset), its reputation among customers (an intangible asset), and teamwork among its managers (an intangible asset). eBay's tangible assets include its Web site and associated software. Its intangible assets include its brand name in the auction business.

Capabilities are a subset of a firm's resources and are defined as the tangible and intangible assets that enable a firm to take full advantage of the other resources it controls. That is, capabilities alone do not enable a firm to conceive and implement its strategies, but they enable a firm to use other resources to conceive and implement such strategies. Examples of capabilities might include a firm's marketing skills and teamwork and cooperation among its managers. At eBay, the cooperation among software developers and marketing people that made it possible for eBay to dominate the online action market is an example of a capability.

A firm's resources and capabilities can be classified into four broad categories: financial resources, physical resources, individual resources, and organizational resources. **Financial resources** include all the money, from whatever source, that firms use to conceive and implement strategies. These financial resources include cash from entrepreneurs, equity holders, bondholders, and banks. **Retained earnings**, or the profit that a firm made earlier in its history and invests in itself, are also an important type of financial resource.

Physical resources include all the physical technology used in a firm. This includes a firm's plant and equipment, its geographic location, and its access to raw materials. Specific examples of plant and equipment that are part of a firm's physical resources are a firm's computer hardware and software technology, robots used in manufacturing, and automated warehouses. Geographic location, as a type of physical resource, is important for firms as diverse as Wal-Mart (with its operations in rural markets generating, on average, higher returns than its operations in more competitive urban markets) and L. L. Bean (a catalogue retail firm that believes that its rural Maine location helps its employees identify with the outdoor lifestyle of many of its customers).[2]

Human resources include the training, experience, judgment, intelligence, relationships, and insight of *individual* managers and workers in a firm.[3] The importance of the human resources of well-known entrepreneurs such as Bill Gates (Microsoft) and Steve Jobs (currently at Apple) is broadly understood. However, valuable human resources are not limited to just entrepreneurs or senior managers. Each employee at a firm like Southwest Airlines is seen as essential for the overall success of the firm. Whether it is the willingness of the gate agent to joke with the harried traveler, or a baggage handler hustling to get a passenger's bag into a plane, or even a pilot's decision to fly in a way that saves fuel—all of these human resources are part of the resource base that has enabled Southwest to gain competitive advantages in the very competitive U.S. airline industry.[4]

Whereas human resources are an attribute of single individuals, **organizational resources** are an attribute of groups of individuals. Organizational resources include a firm's formal reporting structure; its formal and informal planning, controlling, and coordinating systems; its culture and reputation; and informal relations among groups within a firm and between a firm and those in its environment. At Southwest Airlines, relationships among individual resources are an important organizational resource. For example, it is not unusual to see the pilots at Southwest helping to load the bags on an airplane to ensure that the plane leaves on time. This kind of cooperation and dedication shows up in an intense loyalty between Southwest employees and the firm—a loyalty that manifests itself in low employee turnover and high employee productivity, even though over 80 percent of Southwest's workforce is unionized.

Critical Assumptions of the Resource-Based View

The RBV rests on two fundamental assumptions about the resources and capabilities that firms may control. First, different firms may possess different bundles of resources and capabilities, even if they are competing in the same industry. This is the assumption of firm **resource heterogeneity**. Resource heterogeneity implies that for a given business activity, some firms may be more skilled in accomplishing this activity than other firms. In manufacturing, for example, Toyota continues to be more skilled than, say, General Motors. In product design, Apple continues to be more skilled than, say, IBM. In motorcycles, Harley Davidson's reputation for big, bad, and loud rides separates it from its competitors.

Second, some of these resource and capability differences among firms may be long lasting, because it may be very costly for firms without certain resources and capabilities to develop or acquire them. This is the assumption of **resource immobility**. For example, Toyota has had its advantage in manufacturing for at least 30 years. Apple has had product design advantages over IBM since Apple was founded in the 1980s. And eBay has been able to retain its brand reputation since the beginning of the online auction industry. It is not that GM, IBM, and eBay's competitors are unaware of their disadvantages. Indeed, some of these firms—notably GM and IBM—have made progress in addressing their disadvantages. However, despite these efforts, Toyota, Apple, and, to a lesser extent, eBay continue to enjoy advantages over their competition.

Taken together, these two assumptions make it possible to explain why some firms outperform other firms, even if these firms are all competing in the same industry. If a firm possesses valuable resources and capabilities that few other firms possess, and if these other firms find it too costly to imitate these resources and capabilities, the firm that possesses these tangible and intangible assets can gain a sustained competitive advantage. The economic logic that underlies the RBV is described in more detail in the Strategy in Depth feature.

The theoretical roots of the resource-based view can be traced to research done by David Ricardo in 1817. Interestingly, Ricardo was not even studying the profitability of firms; he was interested in the economic consequences of owning more or less fertile farm land.

Unlike many other inputs into the production process, the total supply of land is relatively fixed and cannot be significantly increased in response to higher demand and prices. Such inputs are said to be **inelastic in supply**, because their quantity of supply is fixed and does not respond to price increases. In these settings, it is possible for those who own higher-quality inputs to gain competitive advantages.

Ricardo's argument concerning land as a productive input is summarized in Figure 3.1. Imagine that there are many parcels of land suitable for growing wheat. Also, suppose that the fertility of these different parcels varies from high fertility (low costs of production) to low fertility (high costs of production). It seems obvious that when the market price for wheat is low, it will only pay farmers with the most fertile land to grow wheat. Only these farmers will have costs low enough to make money when the market price for wheat is low. As the market price for

Ricardian Economics and the Resource-Based View

wheat increases, then farmers with progressively less fertile land will be able to use it to grow wheat. These observations lead to the market supply curve in panel A of Figure 3.1: As prices (P) go up, supply (S) also goes up. At some point on this supply curve, supply will equal demand (D). This point determines the market price for wheat, given supply and demand. This price is called P^* in the figure.

Now consider the situation facing two different kinds of farmers. Ricardo assumed that both these farmers follow traditional economic logic by producing a quantity (q) such that their marginal cost (MC) equals their marginal revenue (MR); that is, they

produce enough wheat so that the cost of producing the last bushel of wheat equals the revenue they will get from selling that last bushel. However, this decision for the farm with less fertile land (in panel B of the figure) generates revenues that exactly equal the average total cost (ATC) of the only capital this farmer is assumed to employ, the cost of his land. In contrast, the farmer with more fertile land (in panel C of the figure) has an average total cost (ATC) less than the market-determined price, and thus is able to earn an above-normal economic profit. This is because at the market-determined price, P^*, MC equals ATC for the farmer with less fertile land, whereas MC is greater than ATC for the farmer with more fertile land.

In traditional economic analysis, the profit earned by the farmer with more fertile land should lead other farmers to enter into this market, that is, to obtain some land and produce wheat. However, all the land that can be used to produce wheat in a way that generates at least a normal return given the market price P^* is already in production. In particular, no more very fertile land is available, and fertile land (by assumption) cannot be created. This is what is meant by land being inelastic in supply. Thus, the farmer

The VRIO Framework

Armed with the RBV, it is possible to develop a set of tools for analyzing all the different resources and capabilities a firm might possess and the potential of each of these to generate competitive advantages. In this way, it will be possible to identify a firm's internal strengths and its internal weaknesses. The primary tool for accomplishing this internal analysis is called the VRIO framework.[5] The acronym, *VRIO*, in **VRIO framework** stands for four questions one must ask about a resource or capability to determine its competitive potential: the question

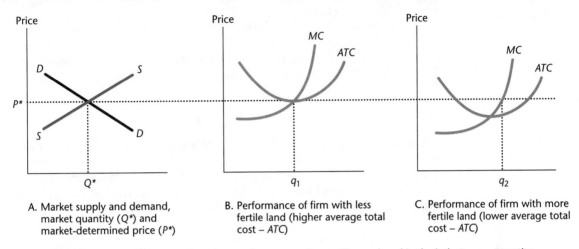

A. Market supply and demand, market quantity (Q*) and market-determined price (P*)

B. Performance of firm with less fertile land (higher average total cost – ATC)

C. Performance of firm with more fertile land (lower average total cost – ATC)

MC = marginal costs, ATC = average total costs, Q = aggregate quantity produced in the industry, q = quantity produced by each firm in the industry

Figure 3.1   The Economics of Land with Different Levels of Fertility

with more fertile land and lower production costs has a sustained competitive advantage over those farmers with less fertile land and higher production costs. Therefore, the farmer with the more fertile land is able to earn an above-normal economic profit.

Of course, at least two events can threaten this sustained competitive advantage. First, market demand may shift down and to the left. This would force farmers with less fertile land to cease production and would also

reduce the profit of those with more fertile land. If demand shifted far enough, this profit might disappear altogether.

Second, farmers with less fertile land may discover low-cost ways of increasing their land's fertility, thereby reducing the competitive advantage of farmers with more fertile land. For example, farmers with less fertile land may be able to use inexpensive fertilizers to increase their land's fertility. The existence of such low-cost fertilizers suggests that, although *land* may be in

fixed supply, *fertility* may not be. If enough farmers can increase the fertility of their land, then the profits originally earned by the farmers with the more fertile land will disappear.

Of course, what the RBV does is recognize that land is not the only productive input that is inelastic in supply, and that farmers are not the only firms that benefit from having such resources at their disposal.

Source: D. Ricardo (1817). *Principles of political economy and taxation.* London: J. Murray.

of **Value**, the question of **Rarity**, the question of **Imitability**, and the question of **Organization**. These four questions are summarized in Table 3.1.

The Question of Value

The **question of value** is: "Do resources and capabilities enable a firm to exploit an external opportunity or neutralize an external threat?" If a firm answers this question with a "yes," then its resources and capabilities are valuable and can be considered *strengths*. If a firm answers this question with a "no," its resources and

1. *The Question of Value.* Does a resource enable a firm to exploit an environmental opportunity and/or neutralize an environmental threat?
2. *The Question of Rarity.* Is a resource currently controlled by only a small number of competing firms?
3. *The Question of Imitability.* Do firms without a resource face a cost disadvantage in obtaining or developing it?
4. *The Question of Organization.* Are a firm's other policies and procedures organized to support the exploitation of its valuable, rare, and costly-to-imitate resources?

capabilities are *weaknesses*. There is nothing inherently valuable about a firm's resources and capabilities. Rather, they are only valuable to the extent that they enable a firm to enhance its competitive position. Sometimes, the same resources and capabilities can be strengths in one market and weaknesses in another. The Global Perspectives feature discusses this issue in more detail.

Valuable Resources and Firm Performance

Sometimes it is difficult to know for sure whether a firm's resources and capabilities really enable it to exploit its external opportunities or neutralize its external threats. Sometimes this requires detailed operational information that may not be readily available. Other times, the full impact of a firm's resources and capabilities on its external opportunities and threats may not be known for some time.

One way to track the impact of a firm's resources and capabilities on its opportunities and threats is to examine the impact of using these resources and capabilities on a firm's revenues and costs. In general, firms that use their resources and capabilities to exploit opportunities or neutralize threats will see an increase in their net revenues, or a decrease in their net costs, or both, compared to the situation in which they were not using these resources and capabilities to exploit opportunities or neutralize threats. That is, the value of these resources and capabilities will generally manifest itself in either higher revenues or lower costs or both, once a firm starts using them to exploit opportunities or neutralize threats.

Applying the Question of Value

For many firms, the answer to the question of value has been "yes." That is, many firms have resources and capabilities that are used to exploit opportunities and neutralize threats, and the use of these resources and capabilities enables these firms to increase their net revenues or decrease their net costs. For example, Sony has a great deal of experience in designing, manufacturing, and selling miniaturized electronic technology. Sony has used these resources and capabilities to exploit opportunities, including video games, digital cameras, computers and peripherals, handheld computers, home video and audio, portable audio, and car audio. 3M has used its resources and capabilities in substrates, coatings, and adhesives, along with an organizational culture that rewards risk-taking and creativity, to exploit opportunities in office products, including invisible tape and Post-It notes. Sony's and 3M's resources and capabilities—including their specific technological skills and their creative organizational cultures—have made it possible for these firms to respond to, and even create, new opportunities.[6]

Unfortunately, for other firms the answer to the question of value appears to be "no." The merger of AOL and Time Warner was supposed create a new kind of

Strategy in the Emerging Enterprise

Entrepreneurial firms, like all other firms, must be able to answer "yes" to the question of value. That is, decisions by entrepreneurs to organize a firm to exploit an opportunity must increase revenues or reduce costs beyond what would be the case if they did not choose to organize a firm to exploit an opportunity.

However, entrepreneurs often find it difficult to answer the question of value before they actually organize a firm and try to exploit an opportunity. This is because the impact of exploiting an opportunity on a firm's revenues and costs often cannot be known, with certainty, before that opportunity is exploited.

Despite these challenges, entrepreneurs often are required to not only estimate the value of any opportunities they are thinking about exploiting, but to do so in some detail and in a written form. Projections about how organizing a firm to exploit an opportunity will affect a firm's revenues and costs are often the centerpiece of an entrepreneur's **business plan**—a document that summarizes how an entrepreneur will organize a firm to exploit an opportunity, along with the economic implications of exploiting that opportunity.

Two schools of thought exist as to the value of entrepreneurs writing business plans. On the one hand, some authors argue that writing a business plan is likely to be helpful for entrepreneurs, because it forces them to be

Are Business Plans Good for Entrepreneurs?

explicit about their assumptions, exposes those assumptions to others for critique and analysis, and helps entrepreneurs focus their efforts on building a new organization and exploiting an opportunity. On the other hand, other authors argue that writing a business plan may actually hurt an entrepreneur's performance, because writing such a plan may divert an entrepreneur's attention from more important activities, may give entrepreneurs the illusion that they have more control of their business than they actually do, and may lead to decision-making errors.

Research supports both points of view. Scott Shane and Frederic Delmar have shown that writing a business plan significantly enhances the probability that an entrepreneurial firm will survive. In contrast, Amar Bhide shows that most entrepreneurs go through

many different business plans before they land on one that describes a business opportunity that they actually support. For Bhide, writing the business plan is, at best, a means of helping to create a new opportunity. Because most business plans are abandoned soon after they are written, writing business plans has limited value.

One way to resolve the conflicts among these scholars is to accept that writing a business plan may be very useful in some settings and not so useful in others. In particular, when it is possible for entrepreneurs to collect sufficient information about a potential market opportunity so as to be able to describe the probability of different outcomes associated with exploiting that opportunity—a setting described as *risky* in the entrepreneurship literature—business planning can be very helpful. However, when such information cannot be collected—a setting described as *uncertain* in the entrepreneurship literature—then writing a business plan would be of only limited value, and its disadvantages might outweigh any advantages it might create.

Sources: S. Shane and F. Delmar (2004). "Planning for the market: Business planning before marketing and the continuation of organizing efforts." *Journal of Business Venturing,* 19, pp. 767–785; A. Bhide (2000). *The origin and evolution of new businesses.* New York: Oxford; R. H. Knight (1921). *Risk, uncertainty, and profit.* Chicago: University of Chicago Press; S. Alvarez and J. Barney (2006). "Discovery and creation: Alternative theories in the field of entrepreneurship." *Strategic Entrepreneurship Journal,* 1(1), pp. 11–26.

entertainment and media company; it is now widely recognized that Time Warner has been unable to marshal the resources necessary to create economic value. Time Warner wrote-off $90 billion in value in 2002; its stock price has been at record lows, and there have been rumors that it will be broken up. Ironically, many of the segments of this diverse media conglomerate continue to create value. However, the company as a whole has not realized the synergies that it was expected to generate when it was created. Put differently, these synergies—as resources and capabilities—are apparently not valuable.[7]

Using Value-Chain Analysis to Identify Potentially Valuable Resources and Capabilities

One way to identify potentially valuable resources and capabilities controlled by a firm is to study that firm's value chain. A firm's **value chain** is the set of business activities in which it engages to develop, produce, and market its products or services. Each step in a firm's value chain requires the application and integration of different resources and capabilities. Because different firms may make different choices about which value-chain activities they will engage in, they can end up developing different sets of resources and capabilities. This can be the case even if these firms are all operating in the same industry. These choices can have implications for a firm's strategies, and, as described in the Ethics and Strategy feature, they can also have implications for society more generally.

Consider, for example, the oil industry. Figure 3.2 provides a simplified list of all the business activities that must be completed if crude oil is to be turned into consumer products, such as gasoline. These activities include exploring for crude oil, drilling for crude oil, pumping crude oil, shipping crude oil, buying crude oil, refining crude oil, selling refined products to distributors, shipping refined products, and selling refined products to final customers.

Different firms may make different choices about which of these stages in the oil industry they want to operate. Thus, the firms in the oil industry may have very different resources and capabilities. For example, exploring for crude oil is very expensive and requires substantial financial resources. It also requires access to land (a physical resource), the application of substantial scientific and technical knowledge (individual resources), and an organizational commitment to risk-taking and exploration (organizational resources). Firms that operate in this stage of the oil business are likely to have very different resources and capabilities than those that,

Figure 3.2 A Simplified Value Chain of Activities of Oil-Based Refined Products such as Gasoline and Motor Oil

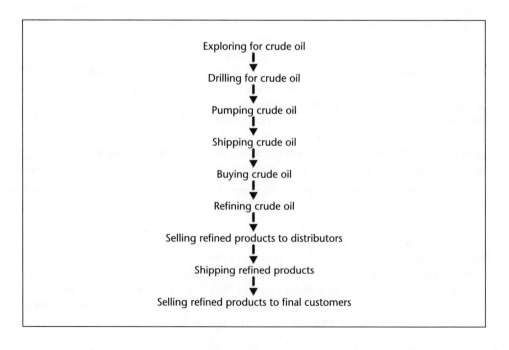

Exploring for crude oil

Drilling for crude oil

Pumping crude oil

Shipping crude oil

Buying crude oil

Refining crude oil

Selling refined products to distributors

Shipping refined products

Selling refined products to final customers

Ethics and Strategy

Strategic management adopts the perspective of a firm's owners in discussing how to gain and sustain competitive advantages. Even when adopting a stakeholder perspective (see the Ethics and Strategy feature in Chapter 1), how a firm can improve its performance and increase the wealth of its owners still takes center stage.

However, an exclusive focus on the performance of a firm and the wealth of its owners can sometimes have broader effects—on society and on the environment—that are not fully recognized. Economists call these broader effects "externalities," because they are external to the core issue in economics and strategic management of how firms can maximize their performance. They are external to this issue because firms generally do not bear the full costs of the externalities their profit-maximizing behavior creates.

Externalities can take many forms. The most obvious of these has to do with pollution and the environment. If, for example, in the process of maximizing its performance a firm engages in activities that pollute the environment, the impact of that pollution is an externality. Such pollution reduces our quality of life and hurts the environment, but the firm creating this pollution often does not bear the full costs of doing so.

Other externalities have to do with a firm's impact on the public's health. For example, when tobacco companies maximize their profits by selling tobacco to children, they are also creating a public health externality. Getting children hooked on tobacco early on might be good for the

Externalities and the Broader Consequences of Profit Maximization

bottom line of a tobacco company, but it increases the chances of these children developing lung cancer, emphysema, heart disease, and the other ailments associated with tobacco. Obviously, these individuals absorb most of the adverse consequences of these diseases, but society suffers as well from the high health care costs that are engendered.

Put differently, while adopting a simple profit-maximizing perspective in choosing and implementing strategies can have positive impacts for a firm, its owners, and its stakeholders, it can also have negative consequences for society as a whole. Two broad solutions to this problem of externalities have been proposed. First, governments can take on the responsibility of directly monitoring and regulating the behavior of firms in areas where these kinds of externalities are likely to develop. Second, governments can use lawsuits and regulations to ensure that firms directly bear more

of the costs of any externalities their behavior might generate. Once these externalities are "internalized," it is then a matter of self-interest for firms not to engage in activities that generate negative externalities.

Consumers can sometimes also help internalize the externalities generated by a firm's behavior by adjusting their consumption patterns to buy products or services only from companies that do not generate negative externalities. Consumers can even be more proactive and let firms know which of their strategies are particularly troubling. For example, many consumers united to boycott firms with operations in South Africa when South Africa was still implementing a policy of apartheid. Ultimately, this pressure not only changed the strategies of many firms; it also helped change South Africa's domestic policies. More recently, consumer pressures on pharmaceutical companies forced these firms to make their AIDS drugs more accessible in less developed countries in Africa; similar pressures forced Nike to adjust the wages and working conditions of the individuals who manufacture Nike's shoes. To the extent that sufficient demand for "socially responsible firms" exists in the marketplace, it may make profit-maximizing sense for a firm to engage in socially responsible behavior by reducing the extent to which its actions generate negative externalities.

Sources: "AIDS in Africa." *British Medical Journal*, June 1, p. 456; J. S. Friedman (2003). "Paying for apartheid." *Nation*, June 6, pp. 7 +; L. Lee (2000). "Can Nike still do it?" *BusinessWeek*, February 21, pp. 121 +.

for example, sell refined oil products to final customers. To be successful in the retail stage of this industry, a firm needs retail outlets (such as stores and gas stations), which are costly to build and require both financial and physical resources. These outlets, in turn, need to be staffed by salespeople—individual resources—and marketing these products to customers through advertisements and other means can require a commitment to creativity—an organizational resource.

However, even firms that operate in the same set of value-chain activities in an industry may approach these activities very differently, and therefore may develop very different resources and capabilities associated with these activities. For example, two firms may sell refined oil products to final customers. However, one of these firms may sell only through retail outlets it owns, whereas the second may sell only through retail outlets it does not own. The first firm's financial and physical resources are likely to be very different from the second firm's, although these two firms may have similar individual and organizational resources.

Studying a firm's value chain forces us to think about firm resources and capabilities in a disaggregated way. Although it is possible to characterize a firm's resources and capabilities more broadly, it is usually more helpful to think about how each of the activities a firm engages in affects its financial, physical, individual, and organizational resources. With this understanding, it is possible to begin to recognize potential sources of competitive advantage for a firm in a much more detailed way.

Because this type of analysis can be so helpful in identifying the financial, physical, individual, and organizational resources and capabilities controlled by a firm, several generic value chains for identifying them have been developed. The first, proposed by the management-consulting firm McKinsey and Company, is presented in Figure 3.3.[8] This relatively simple model suggests that the creation of value almost always involves six distinct activities: technology development, product design, manufacturing, marketing, distribution, and service. Firms can develop distinctive capabilities in any one or any combination of these activities.

Michael E. Porter has developed a second generic value chain.[9] This value chain, presented in Figure 3.4, divides value-creating activities into two large categories: primary activities and support activities. Primary activities include inbound logistics (purchasing, inventory, and so forth), production, outbound logistics (warehousing and distribution), sales and marketing, and service (dealer support and customer service). Support activities include infrastructure (planning, finance, information services, legal), technology development (research and development, product design), and human resource management and development. Primary activities are directly associated with the manufacture and

Technology development	Product design	Manufacturing	Marketing	Distribution	Service
Source	Function	Integration	Prices	Channels	Warranty Speed
Sophistication	Physical	Raw materials	Advertising/	Integration	Captive/independent
Patents	characteristics	Capacity	promotion	Inventory	Prices
Product/process	Aesthetics	Location	Sales force	Warehousing	
choices	Quality	Procurement	Package	Transport	
		Parts production	Brand		
		Assembly			

Figure 3.3   The Generic Value Chain Developed by McKinsey and Company

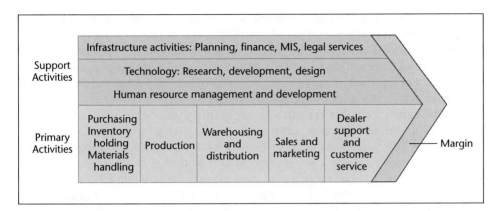

Figure 3.4 The Generic Value Chain Developed by Porter

Source: Reprinted with permission of The Free Press, a Division of Simon and Schuster Adult Publishing Group, from *Competitive Advantage: Creating and Sustaining Superior Performance* by Michael E. Porter. Copyright ©1985, 1998 by Michael E. Porter. All rights reserved.

distribution of a product. Support activities assist a firm in accomplishing its primary activities. As with the McKinsey value chain, a firm can develop strengths or weaknesses in any one or in any combination of the activities listed in Porter's value chain. These activities, and how they are linked to one another, point to the kinds of resources and capabilities a firm is likely to have developed.

The Question of Rarity

Understanding the value of a firm's resources and capabilities is an important first consideration in understanding a firm's internal strengths and weaknesses. However, if a particular resource or capability is controlled by numerous competing firms, then that resource is unlikely to be a source of competitive advantage for any one of them. Instead, valuable but common (i.e., not rare) resources and capabilities are sources of competitive parity. Only when a resource is not controlled by numerous other firms is it likely to be a source of competitive advantage. These observations lead to the **question of rarity**: "How many competing firms already possess particular valuable resources and capabilities?"

Consider, for example, competition among television sports channels. All the major networks broadcast sports. In addition, several sports-only cable channels are available, including the best-known all-sports channel, ESPN. Several years ago, ESPN began televising what were then called alternative sports—skateboarding, snowboarding, mountain biking, and so forth. The surprising popularity of these programs led ESPN to package them into an annual competition called the "X-Games." "X" stands for "extreme," and ESPN has definitely gone to the extreme in including sports in the X-Games. The X-Games now include sports such as sky-surfing, competitive high diving, competitive bungee cord jumping, and so forth. ESPN broadcasts both a summer X-Games and a winter X-Games. No other sports outlet has yet made such a commitment to so-called extreme sports, and it has paid handsome dividends for ESPN—extreme sports have very low-cost broadcast rights and draw a fairly large audience. This commitment to extreme sports has been a source of at least a temporary competitive advantage for ESPN.

Of course, not all of a firm's resources and capabilities have to be valuable and rare. Indeed, most firms have a resource base that is composed primarily of valuable but common resources and capabilities. These resources cannot be sources of even temporary competitive advantage, but are essential if a firm is to gain competitive parity. Under conditions of competitive parity, although no one firm gains a competitive advantage, firms do increase their probability of survival.

Consider, for example, a telephone system as a resource or capability. Because telephone systems are widely available, and because virtually all organizations have access to telephone systems, these systems are not rare, and thus are not a source of competitive advantage. However, firms that do not possess a telephone system are likely to give their competitors an important advantage and place themselves at a competitive disadvantage.

How rare a valuable resource or capability must be in order to have the potential for generating a competitive advantage varies from situation to situation. It is not difficult to see that, if a firm's valuable resources and capabilities are absolutely unique among a set of current and potential competitors, they can generate a competitive advantage. However, it may be possible for a small number of firms in an industry to possess a particular valuable resource or capability and still obtain a competitive advantage. In general, as long as the number of firms that possess a particular valuable resource or capability is less than the number of firms needed to generate perfect competition dynamics in an industry, that resource or capability can be considered rare and a potential source of competitive advantage.

The Question of Imitability

Firms with valuable and rare resources are often strategic innovators, because they are able to conceive and engage in strategies that other firms cannot because they lack the relevant resources and capabilities. These firms may gain the first-mover advantages discussed in Chapter 2.

Valuable and rare organizational resources, however, can be sources of sustained competitive advantage only if firms that do not possess them face a cost disadvantage in obtaining or developing them, compared to firms that already possess them. These kinds of resources are **imperfectly imitable**.[10] These observations lead to the **question of imitability**: "Do firms without a resource or capability face a cost disadvantage in obtaining or developing it compared to firms that already possess it?"

Imagine an industry with five essentially identical firms. Each of these firms manufactures the same products, uses the same raw materials, and sells the products to the same customers through the same distribution channels. It is not hard to see that firms in this kind of industry will have normal economic performance. Now, suppose that one of these firms, for whatever reason, discovers or develops a heretofore unrecognized valuable resource and uses that resource either to exploit an external opportunity or to neutralize an external threat. Obviously, this firm will gain a competitive advantage over the others.

This firm's competitors can respond to this competitive advantage in at least two ways. First, they can ignore the success of this one firm and continue as before. This action, of course, will put them at a competitive disadvantage. Second, these firms can attempt to understand why this one firm is able to be successful and then duplicate its resources to implement a similar strategy. If competitors have no cost disadvantages in acquiring or developing the needed resources, then this imitative approach will generate competitive parity in the industry.

Sometimes, however, for reasons that will be discussed later, competing firms may face an important cost disadvantage in duplicating a successful firm's valuable resources. If this is the case, this one innovative firm may gain a **sustained competitive advantage**—an advantage that is not competed away through strategic imitation. Firms that possess and exploit costly-to-imitate, rare, and valuable resources in choosing and implementing their strategies may enjoy a period of sustained competitive advantage.[11]

For example, other sports networks have observed the success of ESPN's X-Games and are beginning to broadcast similar competitions. NBC, for example, has developed its own version of the X-Games, called the "Gravity Games," and even the Olympics now include sports that were previously perceived as being "too extreme" for this mainline sports competition. Several Fox sports channels broadcast programs that feature extreme sports, and at least one new cable channel (Fuel) broadcasts only extreme sports. Whether these efforts will be able to attract the competitors that the X-Games attract, whether winners at these other competitions will gain as much status in their sports as do winners of the X-Games, and whether these other competitions and programs will gain the reputation among viewers enjoyed by ESPN will go a long way to determining whether ESPN's competitive advantage in extreme sports is temporary or sustained.[12]

Forms of Imitation: Direct Duplication and Substitution

In general, imitation occurs in one of two ways: **direct duplication** or **substitution**. Imitating firms can attempt to directly duplicate the resources possessed by the firm with a competitive advantage. Thus, NBC sponsoring an alternative extreme games competition can be thought of as an effort to directly duplicate the resources that enabled ESPN's X-Games to be successful. If the cost of this direct duplication is too high, then a firm with these resources and capabilities may obtain a sustained competitive advantage. If this cost is not too high, then any competitive advantages in this setting will be temporary.

Imitating firms can also attempt to substitute other resources for a costly to imitate resource possessed by a firm with a competitive advantage. Extreme sports shows and an extreme sports cable channel are potential substitutes for ESPN's X-Games strategy. These shows appeal to much the same audience as the X-Games, but they do not require the same resources as an X-Games strategy requires (i.e., because they are not competitions, they do not require the network to bring together a large number of athletes all at once). If substitute resources exist, and if imitating firms do not face a cost disadvantage in obtaining them, then the competitive advantage of other firms will be temporary. However, if these resources have no substitutes, or if the cost of acquiring these substitutes is greater than the cost of obtaining the original resources, then competitive advantages can be sustained.

Why Might It Be Costly to Imitate Another Firm's Resources or Capabilities?

A number of authors have studied why it might be costly for one firm to imitate the resources and capabilities of another. Four sources of costly imitation have been noted.[13] They are summarized in Table 3.2 and discussed in the following text.

Unique Historical Conditions.   It may be the case that a firm was able to acquire or develop its resources and capabilities in a low-cost manner because of its unique historical conditions. The ability of firms to acquire, develop, and use resources often depends on their place in time and space. Once time and history pass, firms that do not have space-and-time-dependent resources face a significant cost disadvantage in obtaining and developing them, because doing so would require them to re-create history.[14]

TABLE 3.2 Sources of Costly Imitation

Unique Historical Conditions. When a firm gains low-cost access to resources because of its place in time and space, other firms may find these resources to be costly to imitate. Both first-mover advantages and path dependence can create unique historical conditions.

Causal Ambiguity. When competitors cannot tell, for sure, what enables a firm to gain an advantage, that advantage may be costly to imitate. Sources of causal ambiguity include when competitive advantages are based on "taken-for-granted" resources and capabilities, when multiple non-testable hypotheses exist about why a firm has a competitive advantage, and when a firm's advantages are based on complex sets of interrelated capabilities.

Social Complexity. When the resources and capabilities a firm uses to gain a competitive advantage involve interpersonal relationships, trust, culture, and other social resources that are costly to imitate in the short term.

Patents. Only a source of sustained competitive advantage in a few industries, including pharmaceuticals and specialty chemicals.

ESPN's early commitment to extreme sports is an example of these unique historical conditions. The status and reputation of the X-Games were created because ESPN happened to be the first major sports outlet that took these competitions seriously. The X-Games became the most important competition in many of these extreme sports. Indeed, for snowboarders, winning a gold medal in the X-Games is almost as important—if not more important—as winning a gold medal in the Winter Olympics. Other sports outlets that hope to be able to compete with the X-Games will have to overcome both the status of ESPN as "the worldwide leader in sports" and its historical advantage in extreme sports. Overcoming these advantages is likely to be very costly, making competitive threats from direct duplication, at least, less significant.

Of course, firms can also act to increase the costliness of imitating the resources and capabilities they control. ESPN is doing this by expanding its coverage of extreme sports and by engaging in a "grassroots" marketing campaign that engages young "extreme athletes" in local competitions. The purpose of these efforts is clear: to keep ESPN's status as the most important source of extreme sports competitions intact.[15]

Unique historical circumstances can give a firm a sustained competitive advantage in at least two ways. First, it may be that a particular firm was the first in an industry to recognize and exploit an opportunity, and being first gave the firm one or more of the first-mover advantages discussed in Chapter 2. Thus, although in principle other firms in an industry could have exploited an opportunity, that only one firm did so makes it more costly for other firms to imitate the original firm.

A second way that history can have an impact on a firm builds on the concept of **path dependence**.[16] A process is said to be path dependent when events early in the evolution of a process have significant effects on subsequent events. In the evolution of competitive advantage, path dependence suggests that a firm may gain a competitive advantage in the current period based on the acquisition and development of resources in earlier periods. In these earlier periods, it is often not clear what the full future value of particular resources will be. Because of this uncertainty, firms are able to acquire or develop these resources for less than what will turn out to be their full value. However, once the full value of these resources is revealed, other firms seeking to acquire or develop these resources will need to pay their full known value, which (in general) will be greater than the costs incurred by the firm that acquired or developed these resources in some earlier period. The cost of acquiring both duplicate and substitute resources would rise once their full value became known.

Consider, for example, a firm that purchased land for ranching some time ago and discovered a rich supply of oil on this land in the current period. The difference between the value of this land as a supplier of oil (high) and the value of this land for ranching (low) is a source of competitive advantage for this firm. Moreover, other firms attempting to acquire this or adjacent land will now have to pay for the full value of the land in its use as a supply of oil (high), and thus will be at a cost disadvantage compared to the firm that acquired it some time ago for ranching.

Causal Ambiguity. A second reason why a firm's resources and capabilities may be costly to imitate is that imitating firms may not understand the relationship between the resources and capabilities controlled by a firm and that firm's competitive advantage. In other words, the relationship between firm resources and capabilities and competitive advantage may be **causally ambiguous**.

At first, it seems unlikely that causal ambiguity about the sources of competitive advantage for a firm would ever exist. Managers in a firm seem likely to understand the sources of their own competitive advantage. If managers in one firm understand the relationship between resources and competitive advantage, then it seems likely that managers in other firms would also be able to discover these relationships and thus would have a clear understanding of which resources and capabilities they should duplicate or seek substitutes for. If there are no other sources of cost disadvantage for imitating firms, imitation should lead to competitive parity and normal economic performance.[17]

However, it is not always the case that managers in a particular firm will fully understand the relationship between the resources and capabilities they control and competitive advantage. This lack of understanding could occur for at least three reasons. First, it may be that the resources and capabilities that generate competitive advantage are so taken for granted, so much a part of the day-to-day experience of managers in a firm, that these managers are unaware of them.[18] Organizational resources and capabilities such as teamwork among top managers, organizational culture, relationships among other employees, and relationships with customers and suppliers may be almost "invisible" to managers in a firm.[19] If managers in firms that have such capabilities do not understand their relationship to competitive advantage, managers in other firms face significant challenges in understanding which resources they should imitate.

Second, managers may have multiple hypotheses about which resources and capabilities enable their firm to gain a competitive advantage, but they may be unable to evaluate which of these resources and capabilities, alone or in combination, actually create the competitive advantage. For example, if one asks successful entrepreneurs what enabled them to be successful, they are likely to reply with several hypotheses, such as "hard work, willingness to take risks, and a high-quality top management team." However, if one asks what happened to unsuccessful entrepreneurs, they, too, are likely to suggest that their firms were characterized by "hard work, willingness to take risks, and a high-quality top management team." It may be the case that "hard work, willingness to take risks, and a high-quality top management team" are important resources and capabilities for entrepreneurial firm success, but other factors may also play a role. Without rigorous experiments, it is difficult to establish which of these resources have a causal relationship with competitive advantage and which do not.

Finally, it may be that not just a few resources and capabilities enable a firm to gain a competitive advantage, but that literally thousands of these organizational attributes, bundled together, generate these advantages. When the resources and capabilities that generate competitive advantage are complex networks of relationships between individuals, groups, and technology, imitation can be costly.

Whenever the sources of competitive advantage are widely diffused across people, locations, and processes in a firm, those sources will be costly to imitate. Perhaps the best example of such a resource is knowledge itself. To the extent that valuable knowledge about a firm's products, processes, customers, and so on is widely diffused throughout an organization, competitors will have difficulty imitating that knowledge, and it can be a source of sustained competitive advantage.[20]

Social Complexity.   A third reason that a firm's resources and capabilities may be costly to imitate is that they may be socially complex phenomena, beyond the ability of firms to systematically manage and influence. When competitive advantages are based on such complex social phenomena, the ability of other firms to imitate these resources and capabilities, either through direct duplication or substitution, is significantly constrained. Efforts to influence these kinds of phenomena are likely to be much more costly than they would be if these phenomena developed in a natural way over time in a firm.[21]

A wide variety of firm resources and capabilities may be **socially complex**. Examples include the interpersonal relations among managers in a firm, a firm's culture, and a firm's reputation among suppliers and customers.[22] Notice that in most of these cases it is possible to specify how these socially complex resources add value to a firm. Thus, there is little or no causal ambiguity surrounding the link between these firm resources and capabilities and competitive advantage. However, understanding that an organizational culture with certain attributes or quality relations among managers can improve a firm's efficiency and effectiveness does not necessarily imply that firms lacking these attributes can engage in systematic efforts to create them, or that low-cost substitutes for them exist. For the time being, such social engineering may be beyond the abilities of most firms. At the very least, such social engineering is likely to be much more costly than it would be if socially complex resources evolved naturally within a firm.[23]

It is interesting to note that firms seeking to imitate complex physical technology often do not face the cost disadvantages of imitating complex social phenomena. A great deal of physical technology (machine tools, robots, and so forth) can be purchased in supply markets. Even when a firm develops its own unique physical technology, reverse engineering tends to diffuse this technology among competing firms in a low-cost manner. Indeed, the costs of imitating a successful physical technology are often lower than the costs of developing a new technology.[24]

Although physical technology is usually not costly to imitate, the application of this technology in a firm is likely to call for a wide variety of socially complex organizational resources and capabilities. These organizational resources may be costly to imitate, and, if they are valuable and rare, the combination of physical and socially complex resources may be a source of sustained competitive advantage.

The importance of socially complex resources and capabilities for firm performance has been studied in detail in the field of strategic human resource management, as described in the Research Made Relevant feature.

Patents.   At first glance, it might appear that a firm's patents would make it very costly for competitors to imitate its products.[25] Patents do have this effect in some industries. For example, patents in the pharmaceutical and specialty chemical industry effectively foreclose other firms from marketing the same products until a firm's patents expire. As suggested in Chapter 2, patents can raise the cost of imitation in a variety of other industries as well.

However, from another point of view a firm's patents may decrease, rather than increase, the costs of imitation. When a firm files for patent protection, it is forced to reveal a significant amount of information about its product. Governments require this information to ensure that the technology in question is patentable. By obtaining a patent, a firm may provide important information to competitors about how to imitate its technology.

Moreover, most technological developments in an industry are diffused throughout firms in that industry in a relatively brief period of time, even if the technology in question is patented, because patented technology is not immune from low-cost imitation. Patents may restrict direct duplication for a time, but they may actually increase the chances of substitution by functionally equivalent technologies.[26]

The Question of Organization

A firm's potential for competitive advantage depends on the value, rarity, and imitability of its resources and capabilities. However, to fully realize this potential, a firm must be organized to exploit its resources and capabilities. These observations lead to the **question of organization**: "Is a firm organized to exploit the full competitive potential of its resources and capabilities?"

Numerous components of a firm's organization are relevant to the question of organization, including its formal reporting structure, its formal and informal management control systems, and its compensation policies. A firm's **formal reporting structure** is a description of whom in the organization reports to whom; it is often embodied in a firm's **organizational chart**. **Management control systems** include a range of formal and informal mechanisms to ensure that managers are behaving in ways consistent with a firm's strategies. **Formal management controls** include a firm's budgeting and reporting activities that keep people higher up in a firm's organizational chart informed about the actions taken by people lower down in a firm's organizational chart. **Informal management controls** might include a firm's culture and the willingness of employees to monitor each others' behavior. **Compensation policies** are the ways that firms pay employees. Such policies create incentives for employees to behave in certain ways.

These components of a firm's organization are often called **complementary resources and capabilities**, because they have limited ability to generate competitive advantage in isolation. However, in combination with other resources and capabilities they can enable a firm to realize its full potential for competitive advantage.[27]

For example, it has already been suggested that ESPN may have a sustained competitive advantage in the extreme sports segment of the sports broadcasting industry. However, if ESPN's management had not taken advantage of its

Research Made Relevant

Most empirical tests of the RBV have focused on the extent to which history, causal ambiguity, and social complexity have an impact on the ability of firms to gain and sustain competitive advantages. Among the most important of these tests has been research that examines the extent to which human resource practices that are likely to generate socially complex resources and capabilities are related to firm performance. This area of research is known as *strategic human resources management.*

The first of these tests was conducted as part of a larger study of efficient low-cost manufacturing in the worldwide automobile industry. A group of researchers from Massachusetts Institute of Technology developed rigorous measures of the cost and quality of over 70 manufacturing plants that assembled mid-size sedans around the world. They discovered that at the time of their study only six of these plants had simultaneous low costs and high-quality manufacturing—a position that obviously would give these plants a competitive advantage in the marketplace.

In trying to understand what distinguished these six plants from the

Strategic Human Resource Management Research

others in the sample, the researchers found that, not surprisingly, these six plants had the most modern and up-to-date manufacturing technology. However, so did many of the less effective plants. What distinguished these effective plants was not their manufacturing technology, per se, but their human resource (HR) practices. These six plants all implemented a bundle of such practices that included participative decision making, quality circles, and an emphasis on team production. One of the results of these efforts—and another distinguishing feature of these

six plants—was a high level of employee loyalty and commitment to a plant, as well as the belief that plant managers would treat employees fairly. These socially complex resources and capabilities are the types of resources that the RBV suggests should be sources of sustained competitive advantage.

Later work has followed up on this approach and has examined the impact of HR practices on firm performance outside the manufacturing arena. Using a variety of measures of firm performance and several different measures of HR practices, the results of this research continue to be very consistent with RBV logic. That is, firms that are able to use HR practices to develop socially complex human and organizational resources are able to gain competitive advantages over firms that do not engage in such practices.

Sources: J. P. Womack, D. I. Jones, and D. Roos (1990). *The machine that changed the world.* New York: Rawson; M. Huselid (1995). "The impact of human resource management practices on turnover, productivity, and corporate financial performance." *Academy of Management Journal,* 38, pp. 635–672; J. B. Barney and P. Wright (1998). "On becoming a strategic partner." *Human Resource Management,* 37, pp. 31–46.

opportunities in extreme sports by expanding coverage, ensuring that the best competitors come to ESPN competitions, adding additional competitions, and changing up older competitions, then its potential for competitive advantage would not have been fully realized. Of course, the reason that ESPN has done all these things is because it has an appropriate organizational structure, management controls, and employee compensation policies. By themselves, these attributes of ESPN's organization could not be a source of competitive advantage; however, they were essential for ESPN to realize its full competitive advantage potential.

Having an appropriate organization in place has enabled ESPN to realize the full competitive advantage potential of its other resources and capabilities. Having an inappropriate organization in place prevented Xerox from taking full advantage of some of its most critical valuable, rare, and costly-to-imitate resources and capabilities.

Through the 1960s and early 1970s, Xerox invested in a series of very innovative technology development research efforts. It managed these efforts by creating a stand-alone research center in Palo Alto, California (Palo Alto Research Center [PARC]), and staffing it with a large group of highly creative and innovative scientists and engineers. Left to their own devices, these scientists and engineers at Xerox PARC developed an amazing array of technological innovations: the personal computer, the "mouse," Windows-type software, the laser printer, the "paperless office," Ethernet, and so forth. In retrospect, it is clear that the market potential of these technologies was enormous. Moreover, because they were developed at Xerox PARC, they were rare. Xerox might have been able to gain some important first-mover advantages if the organization had been able to translate these technologies into products, thereby increasing the cost to other firms of imitating these technologies.

Xerox possessed the resources and capabilities, but it did not have an organization in place to take advantage of them. No structure existed whereby Xerox PARC innovations could become known to managers at Xerox. Indeed, most Xerox managers—even many senior managers—were unaware of these technological developments through the mid-1970s. Once they finally became aware of them, very few of the technologies survived Xerox's highly bureaucratic product development process, a process whereby product development projects were divided into hundreds of minute tasks and progress in each task was reviewed by dozens of large committees. Even innovations that survived the product development process were not exploited by Xerox managers, because management compensation at Xerox depended almost exclusively on maximizing current revenue. Short-term profitability was relatively less important in compensation calculations, and the development of markets for future sales and profitability was essentially irrelevant. Xerox's formal reporting structure, its explicit management control systems, and its compensation policies were all inconsistent with exploiting the valuable, rare, and costly-to-imitate resources it had developed. Not surprisingly, the company failed to exploit any of its potential sources of sustained competitive advantage.[28]

Applying the VRIO Framework

The questions of value, rarity, imitability, and organization can be brought together into a single framework to understand the return potential associated with exploiting any of a firm's resources or capabilities. This is done in Table 3.3. The relationship of the VRIO framework to strengths and weaknesses is presented in Table 3.4.

If a resource or capability controlled by a firm is not valuable, it will not enable a firm to choose or implement strategies that exploit environmental opportunities or neutralize environmental threats. Organizing to exploit this resource will increase a firm's costs or decrease its revenues. These types of resources are weaknesses. Firms will either have to fix these weaknesses or avoid using them when choosing and implementing strategies. If firms do exploit these kinds of resources and capabilities, they can expect to put themselves at a competitive disadvantage compared to those that either do not possess these nonvaluable resources or do not use them in conceiving and implementing strategies.

If a resource or capability is valuable but not rare, exploitation of this resource in conceiving and implementing strategies will generate competitive parity. Exploiting these types of resources will generally not create competitive

TABLE 3.3 The VRIO
Framework

Is a resource or capability:				
Valuable?	**Rare?**	**Costly to imitate?**	**Exploited by organization?**	**Competitive implications**
No	—	—	No	Competitive disadvantage
Yes	No	—	↑	Competitive parity
Yes	Yes	No	↕	Temporary competitive advantage
Yes	Yes	Yes	Yes	Sustained competitive advantage

advantages, but failure to exploit them can put a firm at a competitive disadvantage. In this sense, valuable-but-not-rare resources can be thought of as organizational strengths.

If a resource or capability is valuable and rare but not costly to imitate, exploiting this resource will generate a temporary competitive advantage for a firm. A firm that exploits this kind of resource is, in an important sense, gaining a first-mover advantage, because it is the first firm that is able to exploit a particular resource. However, once competing firms observe this competitive advantage, they will be able to acquire or develop the resources needed to implement this strategy through direct duplication or substitution at no cost disadvantage, compared to the first-moving firm. Over time, any competitive advantage that the first mover obtained would be competed away as other firms imitate the resources needed to compete. Consequently, this type of resource or capability can be thought of as an organizational strength and as a **distinctive competence**.

If a resource or capability is valuable, rare, and costly to imitate, exploiting it will generate a sustained competitive advantage. In this case, competing firms face a significant cost disadvantage in imitating a successful firm's resources and capabilities. As suggested earlier, this competitive advantage may reflect the unique history of the successful firm, causal ambiguity about which resources to imitate, the socially complex nature of these resources and capabilities, or any patent advantages a firm might possess. In any case, attempts to compete away the advantages of firms that exploit these resources will not generate competitive advantage, or even

TABLE 3.4 The Relationship
Between the VRIO Framework
and Organizational Strengths
and Weaknesses

Is a resource or capability:				
Valuable?	**Rare?**	**Costly to imitate?**	**Exploited by organization?**	**Strength or weakness**
No	—	—	No	Weakness
Yes	No	—	↑	Strength
Yes	Yes	No	↕	Strength and distinctive competence
Yes	Yes	Yes	Yes	Strength and sustainable distinctive competence

competitive parity, for imitating firms. Even if these firms are able to acquire or develop the resources or capabilities in question, the very high costs of doing so would put them at a competitive disadvantage. These kinds of resources and capabilities are organizational strengths and **sustainable distinctive competencies**.

The question of organization operates as an adjustment factor in the VRIO framework. For example, if a firm has a valuable, rare, and costly-to-imitate resource and capability but fails to organize itself to take full advantage of this resource, some of its potential competitive advantage could be lost (this is the Xerox example). Extremely poor organization, in this case, could actually lead a firm that has the potential for competitive advantage to gain only competitive parity or competitive disadvantages.

Applying the VRIO Framework to Southwest Airlines

To examine how the VRIO framework can be applied in analyzing real strategic situations, consider the competitive position of Southwest Airlines. Southwest Airlines has been the only consistently profitable airline in the United States over the past 30 years. While many U.S. airlines have gone in and out of bankruptcy, Southwest has remained profitable. How has it been able to gain this competitive advantage?

Potential sources of this competitive advantage fall into the two big categories: Operational choices Southwest has made and Southwest's approach to managing its people. On the operational side, Southwest has chosen to fly only a single type of aircraft (Boeing 737), only flies into smaller airports, has avoided complicated hub-and-spoke route systems, and, instead, flies a point-to-point system. On the people-management side, despite being highly unionized, Southwest has been able to develop a sense of commitment and loyalty among its employees. It is not unusual to see Southwest employees go well beyond their narrowly defined job responsibilities, helping out in whatever way is necessary to get a plane off the ground safely and on time. Which of these—operational choices or Southwest's approach to managing its people—are more likely to be a source of sustained competitive advantage?

Southwest's Operational Choices and Competitive Advantage

Consider first Southwest's operational choices. First, do these operational choices reduce Southwest's costs or increase the willingness of its customers to pay—that is, are these operational choices valuable? It can be shown most of Southwest's operational choices have the effect of reducing its costs. For example, by flying only one type of airliner, Southwest is able to reduce the cost of training its maintenance staff, reduce its spare parts inventory, and reduce the time its planes are being repaired. By flying into smaller airports, Southwest reduces the fees it would otherwise have to pay to land at larger airports. Its point-to-point system of routes avoids the costs associated with establishing large hub-and-spoke systems. Overall, these operational choices are valuable.

Second, are these operational choices rare? For most of its history, Southwest's operational choices have been rare. Only recently have large incumbent airlines and smaller new entrants begun to implement similar operational choices.

Third, are these operational choices costly to imitate? Several incumbent airline firms have set up subsidiaries designed to emulate most of Southwest's operational choices. For example, Continental created the Continental Lite division, United created the Ted division, and Delta created the Song division. All of these divisions chose a single type of airplane to fly, flew into smaller airports, adopted a point-to-point route structure, and so forth.

In addition to these incumbent airlines, many new entrants into the airline industry—both in the United States and elsewhere—have adopted similar operational choices as Southwest. In the United States, these new entrants include AirTran Airlines, Allegiant Airlines, JetBlue, Skybus Airlines, Spirit Airlines, and Virgin American Airlines.

Thus, while Southwest's operational choices are valuable and have been rare, they are apparently not costly to imitate. This is not surprising since these operational choices have few of the attributes of resources or capabilities that are costly to imitate. They do not derive from a firm's unique history, they are not path dependent, they are not causally ambiguous, and they are not socially complex.

Finally, is Southwest organized to fully exploit its operational choices? Most observers agree that Southwest's structure, management controls, and compensation policies are consistent with its operational choices.

Taken together, this analysis of Southwest's operational choices suggests that they are valuable, have been rare, but are not costly to imitate. While Southwest is organized to exploit these opportunities, they are likely to be only a source of temporary competitive advantage for Southwest.

Southwest's People-Management and Competitive Advantage

A similar VRIO analysis can be conducted for Southwest's approach to people management. First, is this approach valuable; that is, does it reduce Southwest's costs or increase the willingness of its customers to pay?

Employee commitment and loyalty at Southwest is one explanation of why Southwest is able to get higher levels of employee productivity than most other U.S. airlines. This increased productivity shows up in numerous ways. For example, the average turnaround time for Southwest flights is around 18 minutes. The average turnaround time for the average U.S. airline is 45 minutes. Southwest Airline employees are simply more effective in unloading and loading luggage, fueling, and catering their airplanes than employees in other airlines. This means that Southwest Airlines airplanes are on the ground for less time and in the air more time than its competitors. Of course, an airplane is only making money if it is in the air. This seemingly simple idea is worth hundreds of millions of dollars in lower costs to Southwest.

Has such loyalty and teamwork been rare in the U.S. airline industry? Over the past 15 years, the U.S. airline industry has been wracked by employment strife. Many airlines have had to cut employment, reduce wages, and in other ways strain their relationship with their employees. Overall, in comparison to incumbent airlines, the relationship that Southwest enjoys with its employees has been rare.

Is this relationship costly to imitate? Certainly, relationships between an airline and its employees have many of the attributes that should make them costly to imitate. They emerge over time; they are path dependent, causally ambiguous, and socially complex. It is reasonable to expect that incumbent airlines, airlines that already have strained relationships with their employees, would have difficulty imitating the relationship Southwest enjoys with its employees. Thus, in comparison to incumbent airlines, Southwest's approach to managing its people is probably valuable, rare, and costly to imitate. Assuming it is organized appropriately (and this seems to be the case), this would mean that—relative to incumbent airlines—Southwest has a sustained competitive advantage.

The situation may be somewhat different for new entrants into the U.S. airline industry. These airlines may not have a history of strained employee relationships. As new firms, they may be able to develop more valuable employee relationships from the very beginning. This suggests that, relative to new entrants, Southwest's approach to people management may be valuable and rare, but not costly to imitate. Again, assuming Southwest is organized appropriately, relative to new entrants into the U.S. airline industry, Southwest's people management capabilities may be a source of only a temporary competitive advantage.

Imitation and Competitive Dynamics in an Industry

Suppose a firm in an industry has conducted an analysis of its resources and capabilities, concludes that it possesses some valuable, rare, and costly-to-imitate resources and capabilities, and uses these to choose a strategy that it implements with the appropriate organizational structure, formal and informal management controls, and compensation policies. The RBV suggests that this firm will gain a competitive advantage even if it is operating in what a five forces analysis (see Chapter 2) would suggest is a very unattractive industry. Examples of firms that have competitive advantages in unattractive industries include Southwest Airlines, Nucor Steel, Wal-Mart, and Dell, to name a few.

Given that a particular firm in an industry has a competitive advantage, how should other firms respond? Decisions made by other firms given the strategic choices of a particular firm define the nature of the **competitive dynamics** that exist in an industry. In general, other firms in an industry can respond to the advantages of a competitor in one of three ways. First, they can choose to limit their response. For example, when Airbus decided to build a super-jumbo airliner designed to dominate international travel for the next 30 years, Boeing limited its responses to redesigning some aspects of two of its existing planes, the 777 and the 747. Second, they can choose to alter some of their business tactics. For example, when Southwest Airlines began operating out of Philadelphia's airport and charged very low airfares, US Airways—the airline that used to dominate the Philadelphia market—lowered its fares as well. Finally, they can choose to alter their strategy—their theory of how to gain competitive advantage (see Chapter 1). For example, when Dell's direct and Internet-based approach to selling personal computers became dominant, Gateway decided to abandon its retail stores in favor of a direct and Internet-based approach.[29] A firm's responses determine the structure of the competitive dynamics in an industry.

Not Responding to Another Firm's Competitive Advantage

A firm might not respond to another firm's competitive advantage for at least three reasons. First, this firm might have its own competitive advantage. By responding to another firm's competitive advantage, it might destroy, or at least compromise, its own sources of competitive advantage. For example, digital timekeeping has made accurate watches available to most consumers at reasonable prices. Firms such as Casio have a competitive advantage in this market because of its miniaturization and electronic capabilities. Indeed, Casio's market share and performance in the watch business continue to climb. How should Rolex—a manufacturer of very expensive, non-electronic watches—respond to Casio? Rolex's decision has been: *Not at all.* Rolex appeals to a very different market segment than Casio. Should Rolex change its strategies—even if it replaced its mechanical self-winding design with the technologically superior digital design—it could easily compromise its competitive advantage in its own niche market.[30] In general, when a firm already possesses its own sources of competitive advantage, it will not respond to different sources of competitive advantage controlled by another firm.

Second, a firm may not respond to another firm's competitive advantage because it does not have the resources and capabilities to do so. A firm with insufficient or inappropriate resources and capabilities—be they physical, financial, human, or organizational—typically will not be able to imitate a successful firm's resources either through direct duplication or substitution. This may very well be the case with US Airways and Southwest Airlines. It may simply be beyond the ability of US Airways to imitate Southwest's managerial resources and capabilities. In this setting, US Airways is likely to find itself at a sustained competitive disadvantage.[31]

Finally, a firm may not respond to the advantages of a competitor because it is trying to reduce the level of rivalry in an industry. Any actions a firm takes that have the effect of reducing the level of rivalry in an industry and that also do not require firms in an industry to directly communicate or negotiate with each other can be thought of as **tacit cooperation**. Explicit cooperation, where firms do directly communicate and negotiate with each other, is discussed in detail in Chapter 9's analysis of strategic alliances.

Reducing the level of rivalry in an industry can benefit all firms operating in that industry. This decision can have the effect of reducing the quantity of goods and services provided in an industry to below the competitive level, actions that will have the effect of increasing the prices of these goods or services. When tacit cooperation has the effect of reducing supply and increasing prices, it is known as **tacit collusion**. Tacit collusion can be illegal in some settings. However, firms can also tacitly cooperate along other dimensions besides quantity and price. These actions can also benefit all the firms in an industry and typically are not illegal.[32]

For example, it may be that firms can tacitly agree not to invest in certain kinds of research and development. Some forms of research and development are very expensive, and although these investments might end up generating products or services that could benefit customers, firms might still prefer to avoid the expense and risk. Firms can also tacitly agree not to market their products in certain ways. For example, before regulations compelled them to do so, most tobacco companies had already decided not to put cigarette vending machines in locations usually frequented by children, even though these machines could have generated significant revenues. Also, firms can tacitly cooperate by agreeing not to engage in certain manufacturing practices, such as outsourcing to developing countries and engaging in environmentally unsound practices.

All of these actions can have the effect of reducing the level of rivalry in an industry. And reducing the level of rivalry can have the effect of increasing the average level of performance for a firm in an industry. However, tacit cooperative relationships among firms are sometimes difficult to maintain. Typically, in order for tacit cooperation to work, an industry must have the structural attributes described in Table 3.5. First, the industry must have relatively few firms. Informally communicating and coordinating strategies among a few firms is difficult enough; it is even more difficult when the industry has a large number of firms. For this reason, tacit cooperation is a viable strategy only when an industry is an oligopoly (see Chapter 2).

Second, firms in this industry must be homogeneous with respect to the products they sell and their cost structure. Having heterogeneous products makes it too easy for a firm to "cheat" on its tacitly cooperative agreements by modifying its products, and heterogeneous cost means that the optimal level of output for a particular firm may be very different from the level agreed to through tacit cooperation.

1. Small number of competing firms
2. Homogeneous products and costs
3. Market-share leader
4. High barriers to entry

TABLE 3.5 Attributes of Industry Structure That Facilitate the Development of Tacit Cooperation

In this setting, a firm might have a strong incentive to increase its output and upset cooperative agreements.

Third, an industry typically has to have at least one strong market-share leader if firms are going to tacitly cooperate. This would be a relatively large firm that has established an example of the kind of behavior that will be mutually beneficial in the industry, and other firms in the industry sometimes fall into line with this example. Indeed, it is often the market-share leader that will choose not to respond to the competitive actions of another firm in the industry in order to maintain cooperative relations.

Finally, the maintenance of tacit cooperation in an industry almost always requires the existence of high barriers to entry. If tacit cooperation is successful, the average performance of firms in an industry will improve. However, this higher level of performance can induce other firms to enter into this industry (see Chapter 2). Such entry will increase the number of firms in an industry and make it very difficult to maintain tacitly cooperative relationships. Thus, it must be very costly for new firms to enter into an industry for those in that industry to maintain their tacit cooperation. The higher these costs, the higher the barriers to entry.

Changing Tactics in Response to Another Firm's Competitive Advantage

Tactics are the specific actions a firm takes to implement its strategies. Examples of tactics include decisions firms make about various attributes of their products—including size, shape, color, and price—specific advertising approaches adopted by a firm, and specific sales and marketing efforts. Generally, firms change their tactics much more frequently than they change their strategies.[33]

When competing firms are pursuing approximately the same strategies, the competitive advantages that any one firm might enjoy at a given point in time are most likely due to the tactics that that firm is pursuing. In this setting, it is not unusual for competing firms to change their tactics by imitating the tactics of the firm with an advantage in order to reduce that firm's advantage. Although changing one's tactics in this manner will only generate competitive parity, this is usually better than the competitive disadvantage these firms were experiencing.

Several industries provide excellent examples of these kinds of tactical interactions. In consumer goods, for example, if one company increases its sales by adding a "lemon scent" to laundry detergent, then lemon scents start showing up in everyone's laundry detergent. If Coke starts selling a soft drink with half the sugar and half the carbs of regular Coke, can Pepsi's low-sugar/low-carb product be far behind? And when Delta Airlines cuts it airfares, can American and United be far behind? Not surprisingly, these kinds of tactical changes, because they initially may be valuable and rare, are seldom costly to imitate, and thus are typically only sources of temporary competitive advantage.

Sometimes, rather than simply imitating the tactics of a firm with a competitive advantage, a firm at a disadvantage may "leapfrog" its competitors by developing an entirely new set of tactics. Procter & Gamble engaged in this strategy when it introduced its laundry detergent, Tide, in a new, concentrated formula. This new formulation required new manufacturing and packaging equipment—the smaller box could not be filled in the current manufacturing lines in the industry—which meant that Tide's competitors had to take more time in imitating the concentrated laundry detergent tactic than other tactics pursued in this industry. Nevertheless, within just a few weeks other firms in this market were introducing their own versions of concentrated laundry detergent.

Indeed, some firms can become so skilled at innovating new products and other tactics that this innovative capability can be a source of sustained competitive advantage. Consider, for example, the performance of Sony. Most observers agree that Sony possesses some special management and coordination skills that enable it to conceive, design, and manufacture high-quality miniaturized consumer electronics. However, virtually every time Sony brings out a new miniaturized product several of its competitors quickly duplicate that product through reverse engineering, thereby reducing Sony's technological advantage. In what way can Sony's socially complex miniaturization resources and capabilities be a source of sustained competitive advantage when most of Sony's products are quickly imitated through direct duplication?

After Sony introduces each new product, it experiences a rapid increase in profits attributable to the new product's unique features. This increase, however, leads other firms to reverse-engineer the Sony product and introduce their own versions. Increased competition results in a reduction in the profits associated with a new product. Thus, at the level of individual products, Sony apparently enjoys only temporary competitive advantages. However, looking at the total returns earned by Sony across all of its new products over time makes clear the source of Sony's sustained competitive advantage: By exploiting its resources and capabilities in miniaturization, Sony is able to constantly introduce new and exciting personal electronics products. No single product generates a sustained competitive advantage, but, over time, across several such product introductions, Sony's resource and capability advantages lead to sustained competitive advantages.[34]

Changing Strategies in Response to Another Firm's Competitive Advantage

Finally, firms sometimes respond to another firm's competitive advantage by changing their strategies. Obviously, this does not occur very often, and it typically only occurs when another firm's strategies usurp a firm's competitive advantage. In this setting, a firm will not be able to gain even competitive parity if it maintains its strategy, even if it implements that strategy very effectively.

Changes in consumer tastes, in population demographics, and in the laws that govern a business can all have the effect of rendering what once was a valuable strategy as valueless. However, the most frequent impact is changes in technology. For example, no matter how well-made a mechanical calculator is, it is simply inferior to an electronic calculator. No matter how efficient the telegraph was in its day, it is an inferior technology to the telephone. And no matter how quickly one's fingers can move the beads on an abacus, an electronic cash register is a better way of keeping track of sales and making change in a store.

When firms change their strategies, they must proceed through the entire strategic management process, as described in Chapter 1. However, these firms will often have difficulty abandoning their traditional strategies. For most firms, their strategy helps define what they do and who they are. Changing its strategy often requires a firm to change its identity and its purposes. These are difficult changes to make, and many firms wait to change their strategy until absolutely forced to do so by disastrous financial results. By then, these firms not only have to change their strategy—with all that implies—they have to do so in the face of significant financial pressures.

The ability of virtually all strategies to generate competitive advantages typically expires, sooner or later. In general, it is much better for a firm to change its strategy before that strategy is no longer viable. In this way, a firm can make a planned move to a new strategy that maintains whatever resources and capabilities it still possesses while it develops the new resources and capabilities it will need to compete in the future.

Implications of the Resource-Based View

The RBV and the VRIO framework can be applied to individual firms to understand whether these firms will gain competitive advantages, how sustainable these competitive advantages are likely to be, and what the sources of these competitive advantages are. In this way, the RBV and the VRIO framework can be understood as important complements to the threats and opportunities analyses described in Chapter 2.

However, beyond what these frameworks can say about the competitive performance of a particular firm, the RBV has some broader implications for managers seeking to gain competitive advantages. Some of these broader implications are listed in Table 3.6 and discussed in the following section.

TABLE 3.6 Broader Implications of the Resource-Based View

1. The responsibility for competitive advantage in a firm:
   Competitive advantage is every employee's responsibility.
2. Competitive parity and competitive advantage:
   If all a firm does is what its competition does, it can gain only competitive parity. In gaining competitive advantage, it is better for a firm to exploit its own valuable, rare, and costly-to-imitate resources than to imitate the valuable and rare resources of a competitor.
3. Difficult to implement strategies:
   As long as the cost of strategy implementation is less than the value of strategy implementation, the relative cost of implementing a strategy is more important for competitive advantage than the absolute cost of implementing a strategy.
   Firms can systematically overestimate and underestimate their uniqueness.
4. Socially complex resources:
   Not only can employee empowerment, organizational culture, and teamwork be valuable; they can also be sources of sustained competitive advantage.
5. The role of the organization:
   Organization should support the use of valuable, rare, and costly-to-imitate resources. If conflicts between these attributes of a firm arise, change the organization.

Where Does the Responsibility for Competitive Advantage in a Firm Reside?

First, the RBV suggests that competitive advantages can be found in several of the different resources and capabilities controlled by the firm. These resources and capabilities are not limited to those that are controlled directly by a firm's senior managers. Thus, the responsibility for creating, nurturing, and exploiting valuable, rare, and costly-to-imitate resources and capabilities for competitive advantage is not restricted to senior managers, but falls on every employee in a firm. Therefore, employees should go beyond defining their jobs in functional terms and instead define their jobs in competitive and economic terms.

Consider a simple example. In a recent visit to a very successful automobile manufacturing plant, the plant manager was asked to describe his job responsibilities. He said, "My job is to manage this plant in order to help the firm make and sell the best cars in the world." In response to a similar question, the person in charge of the manufacturing line said, "My job is to manage this manufacturing line in order to help the firm make and sell the best cars in the world." A janitor was also asked to describe his job responsibilities. Although he had not been present in the two earlier interviews, the janitor responded, "My job is to keep this facility clean in order to help the firm make and sell the best cars in the world."

Which of these three employees is most likely to be a source of sustained competitive advantage for this firm? Certainly, the plant manager and the manufacturing line manager *should* define their jobs in terms of helping the firm make and sell the best cars in the world. However, it is unlikely that their responses to this question would be any different than the responses of other senior managers at other manufacturing plants around the world. Put differently, although the definition of these two managers' jobs in terms of enabling the firm to make and sell the best cars in the world is valuable, it is unlikely to be rare, and thus it is likely to be a source of competitive parity, not competitive advantage. However, a janitor who defines her job as helping the firm make and sell the best cars in the world instead of simply to clean the facility is, most would agree, quite unusual. Because it is rare, it might be a source of at least a temporary competitive advantage.[35]

The value created by one janitor defining her job in competitive terms rather than functional terms is not huge, but suppose that all the employees in this plant defined their jobs in these terms. Suddenly, the value that might be created could be substantial. Moreover, the organizational culture and tradition in a firm that would lead employees to define their jobs in this way is likely to be costly for other firms to imitate. Thus, if this approach to defining job responsibilities is broadly diffused in a particular plant, it seems likely to be valuable, rare, and costly to imitate, and thus a source of sustained competitive advantage, assuming the firm is organized to take advantage of this unusual resource.

In the end, it is clear that competitive advantage is too important to remain the sole property of senior management. To the extent that employees throughout an organization are empowered to develop and exploit valuable, rare, and costly-to-imitate resources and capabilities in the accomplishment of their job responsibilities, a firm may actually be able to gain sustained competitive advantages.

Competitive Parity and Competitive Advantage

Second, the RBV suggests that, if all a firm does is create value in the same way as its competitors, the best performance it can ever expect to gain is competitive parity. To do better than competitive parity, firms must engage in valuable and rare activities. They must do things to create economic value that other firms have not even thought of, let alone implemented.

This is especially critical for firms that find themselves at a competitive disadvantage. Such a firm certainly should examine its more successful competition, understand what has made this competition so successful, and, where imitation is very low cost, imitate the successful actions of its competitors. In this sense, benchmarking a firm's performance against the performance of its competitors can be extremely important.

However, if this is all that a firm does, it can only expect to gain competitive parity. Gaining competitive advantage depends on a firm discovering its own unique resources and capabilities and how they can be used in choosing and implementing strategies. For a firm seeking competitive advantage, it is better to be excellent in how it develops and exploits its own unique resources and capabilities than it is to be excellent in how it imitates the resources and capabilities of other firms.

This does not imply that firms must always be first movers to gain competitive advantages. Some firms develop valuable, rare, and costly-to-imitate resources and capabilities in being efficient second movers—that is, in rapidly imitating and improving on the product and technological innovations of other firms. Rather than suggesting that firms must always be first movers, the RBV suggests that, in order to gain competitive advantages, firms must implement strategies that rely on valuable, rare, and costly-to-imitate resources and capabilities, whatever those strategies or resources might be.

Difficult-to-Implement Strategies

Third, as firms contemplate different strategic options, they often ask how difficult and costly it will be to implement different strategies. As long as the cost of implementing a strategy is less than the value that a strategy creates, the RBV suggests that the critical question facing firms is not "Is a strategy easy to implement or not?" but rather "Is this strategy easier for us to implement than it is for our competitors to implement?" Firms that already possess the valuable, rare, and costly-to-imitate resources needed to implement a strategy will, in general, find it easier (i.e., less costly) to implement a strategy than firms that first have to develop the required resources and then implement the proposed strategy. For firms that already possess a resource, strategy implementation can be natural and swift.

In understanding the relative costs of implementing a strategy, firms can make two errors. First, they can overestimate the uniqueness of the resources they control. Although every firm's history is unique and no two management teams are exactly the same, this does not always mean that a firm's resources and capabilities will be rare. Firms with similar histories operating in similar industries will often develop similar capabilities. If a firm overestimates the rarity of its resources and capabilities, it can overestimate its ability to generate competitive advantages.

For example, when asked what their most critical sources of competitive advantage are, many firms will cite the quality of their top management team, the quality of their technology, and their commitment to excellence in all that they do. When pushed about their competitors, these same firms will admit that they too have high-quality top management teams, high-quality technology, and a commitment to excellence in all that they do. Although these three attributes can be sources of competitive parity, they cannot be sources of competitive advantage.

Second, firms can sometimes underestimate their uniqueness and thus underestimate the extent to which the strategies they pursue can be sources of sustained competitive advantage. When firms possess valuable, rare, and costly-to-imitate resources, strategy implementation can be relatively easy. In this context, it seems reasonable to expect that other firms will be able to quickly imitate this "easy-to-implement" strategy. Of course, this is not the case if these resources controlled by a firm are, in fact, rare and costly to imitate.

In general, firms must take great care not to overestimate or underestimate their uniqueness. An accurate assessment of the value, rarity, and imitability of a firm's resources is necessary to develop an accurate understanding of the relative costs of implementing a firm's strategies, and thus the ability of those strategies to generate competitive advantages. Often, firms must employ outside assistance in helping them describe the rarity and imitability of their resources, even though managers in firms will generally be much more familiar with the resources controlled by a firm than outsiders. However, outsiders can provide a measure of objectivity in evaluating the uniqueness of a firm.

Socially Complex Resources

Over the past several decades, much has been written about the importance of employee empowerment, organizational culture, and teamwork for firm performance. Most of this work suggests that firms that empower employees, that have an enabling culture, and that encourage teamwork will, on average, make better strategic choices and implement them more efficiently than firms without these organizational attributes. Using the language of the RBV, most of this work has suggested that employee empowerment, organizational culture, and teamwork, at least in some settings, are economically valuable.[36]

Resource-based logic acknowledges the importance of the value of these organizational attributes. However, it also suggests that these socially complex resources and capabilities can be rare and costly to imitate—and it is these attributes that make it possible for socially complex resources and capabilities to be sources of sustained competitive advantage. Put differently, the RBV actually extends and broadens traditional analyses of the socially complex attributes of firms. Not only can these attributes be valuable, but they can also be rare and costly to imitate, and thus sources of sustained competitive advantage.

The Role of Organization

Finally, resource-based logic suggests that an organization's structure, control systems, and compensation policies should support and enable a firm's efforts to fully exploit the valuable, rare, and costly-to-imitate resources and capabilities it controls. These attributes of organization, by themselves, are usually not sources of sustained competitive advantage.

These observations suggest that if there is a conflict between the resources a firm controls and that firm's organization, the organization should be changed. However, it is often the case that once a firm's structure, control systems, and compensation policies are put in place they tend to remain, regardless of whether they are consistent with a firm's underlying resources and capabilities. In such settings, a firm will not be able to realize the full competitive potential of its underlying resource base. To the extent that a firm's resources and capabilities are continuously evolving, its organizational structure, control systems, and compensation policies must also evolve. For these attributes of organization to evolve, managers must be aware of their link with a firm's resources and capabilities and of organizational alternatives.

Summary

The RBV is an economic theory that suggests that firm performance is a function of the types of resources and capabilities controlled by firms. Resources are the tangible and intangible assets a firm uses to conceive and implement its strategies. Capabilities are a subset of resources that enable a firm to take advantage of its other resources. Resources and capabilities can be categorized into financial, physical, human, and organizational resources categories.

The RBV makes two assumptions about resources and capabilities: the assumption of resource heterogeneity (that some resources and capabilities may be heterogeneously distributed across competing firms) and the assumption of resource immobility (that this heterogeneity may be long lasting). These two assumptions can be used to describe conditions under which firms will gain competitive advantages by exploiting their resources.

A tool for analyzing a firm's internal strengths and weaknesses can be derived from the RBV. Called the VRIO framework, this tool asks four questions about a firm's resources and capabilities in order to evaluate their competitive potential. These questions are the question of value, the question of rarity, the question of imitability, and the question of organization.

A firm's resources and capabilities are valuable when they enable it to exploit external opportunities or neutralize external threats. Such valuable resources and capabilities are a firm's strengths. Resources and capabilities that are not valuable are a firm's weaknesses. Using valuable resources to exploit external opportunities or neutralize external threats will have the effect of increasing a firm's net revenues or decreasing its net costs.

One way to identify a firm's valuable resources and capabilities is by examining its value chain. A firm's value chain is the list of business activities it engages in to develop, produce, and sell its products or services. Different stages in this value chain require different resources and capabilities, and differences in value-chain choices across firms can lead to important differences among the resources and capabilities controlled by different companies. Two generic value chains have been developed, one by McKinsey and Company and another by Michael Porter.

Valuable and common (i.e., not rare) resources and capabilities can be a source of competitive parity. Failure to invest in such resources can create a competitive disadvantage for a firm. Valuable and rare resources can be a source of at least a temporary competitive advantage. There are fewer firms able to control such a resource and still exploit it as a source of at least temporary competitive advantage than there are firms that will generate perfect competition dynamics in an industry.

Valuable, rare, and costly-to-imitate resources and capabilities can be a source of sustained competitive advantage. Imitation can occur through direct duplication or through substitution. A firm's resources and capabilities may be costly to imitate for at least four reasons: unique historical circumstances, causal ambiguity, socially complex resources and capabilities, and patents.

To take full advantage of the potential of its resources and capabilities, a firm must be appropriately organized. A firm's organization consists of its formal reporting structure, its formal and informal control processes, and its compensation policy. These are complementary resources in that they are rarely sources of competitive advantage on their own.

The VRIO framework can be used to identify the competitive implications of a firm's resources and capabilities—whether they are a source of competitive disadvantage, competitive parity, temporary competitive advantage, or sustained competitive advantage—and the extent to which these resources and capabilities are strengths or weaknesses.

When a firm faces a competitor that has a sustained competitive advantage, the firm's options are not to respond, to change its tactics, or to change its strategies. A firm may choose not to respond in this setting for at least three reasons. First, a response might weaken its own sources of sustained competitive advantage. Second, a firm may not have the resources required to respond. Third, a firm may be trying to create or maintain tacit cooperation within an industry.

The RBV has a series of broader managerial implications as well. For example, resource-based logic suggests that competitive advantage is every employee's responsibility. It also suggests that if all a firm does is what its competition does, it can gain only competitive parity, and that in gaining competitive advantage it is better for a firm to exploit its own valuable, rare, and costly-to-imitate resources than to imitate the valuable and rare resources of a competitor. Also, resource-based logic implies that as long as the cost of strategy implementation is less than the value of strategy implementation, the relative cost of implementing a strategy is more important for competitive advantage than the absolute cost of implementing a strategy. It also implies that firms can systematically overestimate and underestimate their uniqueness. With regard to a firm's resources and capabilities, resource-based logic suggests that not only can employee empowerment, organizational culture, and teamwork be valuable; they can also be sources of sustained competitive advantage. Also, if conflicts arise between a firm's valuable, rare, and costly-to-imitate resources and its organization, the organization should be changed.

Challenge Questions

1. Which of the following approaches to strategy formulation is more likely to generate economic profits: (a) evaluating external opportunities and threats and then developing resources and capabilities to exploit these opportunities and neutralize these threats or (b) evaluating internal resources and capabilities and then searching for industries where they can be exploited? Explain your answer.

2. Which firm will have a higher level of economic performance: (a) a firm with valuable, rare, and costly-to-imitate resources and capabilities operating in a very attractive industry or (b) a firm with valuable, rare, and costly-to-imitate resources and capabilities operating in a very unattractive industry? Assume both these firms are appropriately organized. Explain your answer.

3. Which is more critical to sustaining human life—water or diamonds? Why do firms that provide water to customers generally earn lower economic performance than firms that provide diamonds?

4. Will a firm currently experiencing competitive parity be able to gain sustained competitive advantages by studying another firm that is currently experiencing sustained competitive advantages? Why or why not?

5. Your former college roommate calls you and asks to borrow $10,000 so that he can open a pizza restaurant in his hometown. He acknowledges that there is a high degree of rivalry in this market, that the cost of entry is low, and that there are numerous substitutes for pizza, but he believes that his pizza restaurant will have some sustained competitive advantages. For example, he is going to have sawdust on his floor, a variety of imported beers, and a late-night delivery service. Will you lend him the money? Why or why not?

6. In the text, it is suggested that Boeing did not respond to Airbus's announcement of the development of a super-jumbo aircraft. Assuming this aircraft will give Airbus a competitive advantage in the segment of the airliner business that supplies airplanes for long international flights, why did Boeing not respond?

(a) Does it have its own competitive advantage that it does not want to abandon?

(b) Does it not have the resources and capabilities needed to respond?

(c) Is it trying to reduce the level of rivalry in this industry?

7. Which firm is more likely to be successful in exploiting its sources of sustained competitive advantage in its home market than in a highly competitive, nondomestic market: (a) a firm from a less competitive home country or (b) a firm from a more competitive home country? Why?

Problem Set

1. Apply the VRIO framework in the following settings. Will the actions described be a source of competitive disadvantage, parity, temporary advantage, or sustained competitive advantage? Explain your answers.

(a) Procter & Gamble introduces new, smaller packaging for its Tide laundry detergent.

(b) American Airlines announces a five percent across-the-board reduction in airfares.

(c) The Korean automobile firm Hyundai announces a 10-year, 100,000 mile warranty on its cars.

(d) Microsoft makes it easier to transfer data and information from Microsoft Word to Microsoft Excel.

(e) Merck is able to coordinate the work of its chemists and biologists in the development of new drugs.

(f) Ford patents a new kind of brake pad for its cars.

(g) Ashland Chemical, a specialty chemical company, patents a new chemical.

(h) The New York Yankees sign All-Star pitcher Randy Johnson to a long-term contract.

(i) Michael Dell uses the money he has made from Dell to purchase the Dallas Cowboys football team.

(j) Ted Turner uses the money he has made from his broadcasting empire to purchase the Atlanta Braves baseball team.

2. Identify three firms you might want to work for. Using the VRIO framework, evaluate the extent to which the resources and capabilities of these firms give them the potential to realize competitive disadvantages, parity, temporary advantages, or sustained advantages. What implications, if any, does this analysis have for the company you might want to work for?

3. You have been assigned to estimate the present value of a potential construction project for your company. How would you use the VRIO framework to construct the cash-flow analysis that is a part of any present-value calculation?

End Notes

1. The term *"the resource-based view"* was coined by Wernerfelt, B. (1984). "A resource-based view of the firm." *Strategic Management Journal*, 5, pp. 171–180. Some important early contributors to this theory include Rumelt, R. P. (1984). "Toward a strategic theory of the firm." In R. Lamb (ed.), *Competitive strategic management* (pp. 556–570). Upper Saddle River, NJ: Prentice Hall; and Barney, J. B. (1986). "Strategic factor markets: Expectations, luck and business strategy." *Management Science*, 32, pp. 1512–1514. A second wave of important early resource-based theoretical work includes Barney, J. B. (1991). "Firm resources and sustained competitive advantage." *Journal of Management*, 7, pp. 49–64; Dierickx, I., and K. Cool. (1989). "Asset stock accumulation and sustainability of competitive advantage." *Management Science*, 35, pp. 1504–1511; Conner, K. R. (1991). "A historical comparison of resource-based theory and five schools of thought within industrial organization economics: Do we have a new theory of the firm?" *Journal of Management*, 17(1), pp. 121–154; and Peteraf, M. A. (1993). "The cornerstones of competitive advantage: A resource-based view." *Strategic Management Journal*, 14, pp. 179–191. A review of much of this early theoretical literature can be found in Mahoney, J. T., and J. R. Pandian. (1992). "The resource-based view within the conversation of strategic management." *Strategic Management Journal*, 13, pp. 363–380. The theoretical perspective has also spawned a growing body of empirical work, including Brush, T. H., and K. W. Artz. (1999). "Toward a contingent resource-based theory." *Strategic Management Journal*, 20, pp. 223–250; A. Marcus and D. Geffen. (1998). "The dialectics of competency acquisition." *Strategic Management Journal*, 19, pp. 1145–1168; Brush, T. H., P. Bromiley, and M. Hendrickx. (1999). "The relative influence of industry and corporation on business segment performance." *Strategic Management Journal*, 20, pp. 519–547; Yeoh, P.-L., and K. Roth. (1999). "An empirical analysis of sustained advantage in the U.S. pharmaceutical industry." *Strategic Management Journal*, 20, pp. 637–653; Roberts, P. (1999). "Product innovation, product-market competition and persistent profitability in the U.S. pharmaceutical industry." *Strategic Management Journal*, 20, pp. 655–670; Gulati, R. (1999). "Network location and learning." *Strategic Management Journal*, 20, pp. 397–420; Lorenzoni, G., and A. Lipparini. (1999). "The leveraging of interfirm relationships as a distinctive organizational capability." *Strategic Management Journal*, 20, pp. 317–338; Majumdar, S. (1998). "On the utilization of resources." *Strategic Management Journal*, 19(9), pp. 809–831; Makadok, R. (1997). "Do inter-firm differences in capabilities affect strategic pricing dynamics?" *Academy of Management Proceedings '97*, pp. 30–34; Silverman, B. S., J. A. Nickerson, and J. Freeman. (1997). "Profitability, transactional alignment, and organizational mortality in the U.S. trucking industry." *Strategic Management Journal*, 18 (Summer special issue), pp. 31–52; Powell, T. C., and A. Dent-Micallef. (1997). "Information technology as competitive advantage." *Strategic Management Journal*, 18(5), pp. 375–405; Miller, D., and J. Shamsie. (1996). "The Resource-Based View of the firm in two environments." *Academy of Management Journal*, 39(3), pp. 519–543; and Maijoor, S., and A. Van Witteloostuijn. (1996). "An empirical test of the resource-based theory." *Strategic Management Journal*, 17, pp. 549–569; Barnett, W. P., H. R. Greve, and D. Y. Park. (1994). "An evolutionary model of

organizational performance." *Strategic Management Journal*, 15 (Winter special issue), pp. 11–28; Levinthal, D., and J. Myatt. (1994). "Co-evolution of capabilities and industry: The evolution of mutual fund processing." *Strategic Management Journal*, 17, pp. 45–62; Henderson, R., and I. Cockburn. (1994). "Measuring competence? Exploring firm effects in pharmaceutical research." *Strategic Management Journal*, 15, pp. 63–84; Pisano, G. P. (1994). "Knowledge, integration, and the locus of learning: An empirical analysis of process development." *Strategic Management Journal*, 15, pp. 85–100; and Zajac, E. J., and J. D. Westphal. (1994). "The costs and benefits of managerial incentives and monitoring in large U.S. corporations: When is more not better?" *Strategic Management Journal*, 15, pp. 121–142.
2. Ghemawat, P. (1986). "Wal-Mart stores' discount operations." Harvard Business School Case No. 9-387-018, on Wal-Mart; Kupfer, A. (1991). "The champion of cheap clones." *Fortune*, September 23, pp. 115–120; and Holder, D. (1989). "L. L. Bean, Inc.—1974." Harvard Business School Case No. 9-676-014, on L. L. Bean. Some of Wal-Mart's more recent moves, especially its international acquisitions, are described in Laing, J. R. (1999). "Blimey! Wal-Mart." *Barron's*, 79, p. 14. L. L. Bean's lethargic performance in the 1990s, together with its turnaround plan, is described in Symonds, W. (1998). "Paddling harder at L. L. Bean." *BusinessWeek*, December 7, p. 72.
3. For an early discussion of the importance of human capital in firms, see Becker, G. S. (1964). *Human capital.* New York: Columbia University Press.
4. Heskett, J. L., and R. H. Hallowell. (1993). "Southwest Airlines: 1993 (A)." Harvard Business School Case No. 9-695-023.
5. See Barney, J. (1991). "Firm resources and sustained competitive advantage." *Journal of Management*, 17, pp. 99–120.
6. See Schlender, B. R. (1992). "How Sony keeps the magic going." *Fortune*, February 24, pp. 75–84; and (1999). "The weakling kicks back." *The Economist*, July 3, p. 46, for a discussion at Sony. See Krogh, L., J. Praeger, D. Sorenson, and J. Tomlinson. (1988). "How 3M evaluates its R&D programs." *Research Technology Management*, 31, pp. 10–14.
7. Anders, G. (2002). "AOL's true believers." *Fast Company*, July pp. 96 +. In a recent *The Wall Street Journal* article, managers of AOL Time Warner admitted they are no longer seeking synergies across their businesses. See Karnitschnig, M. (2006). "That's All, Folks: After years of pushing synergy, Time Warner, Inc. says enough." *The Wall Street Journal*, June 2, A1+.
8. See Grant, R. M. (1991). *Contemporary strategy analysis.* Cambridge, MA: Basil Blackwell.
9. Porter, M. E. (1987). *Competitive advantage.* New York: Free Press.
10. Lipman, S., and R. Rumelt. (1982). "Uncertain imitability: An analysis of interfirm differences in efficiency under competition." *Bell Journal of Economics*, 13, pp. 418–438; Barney, J. B. (1986). "Strategic factor markets: Expectations, luck and business strategy." *Management Science*, 32, pp. 1512–1514; and Barney, J. B. (1986). "Organizational culture: Can it be a source of sustained competitive advantage?" *Academy of Management Review*, 11, pp. 656–665.
11. Note that the definition of sustained competitive advantage presented here, though different, is consistent with the definition given in

Chapter 1. In particular, a firm that enjoys a competitive advantage for a long period of time (the Chapter 1 definition) does not have its advantage competed away through imitation (the Chapter 3 definition).

12. See Breen, B. (2003). "What's selling in America." *Fast Company*, January, pp. 80 +.

13. These explanations of costly imitation were first developed by Dierickx, I., and K. Cool. (1989). "Asset stock accumulation and sustainability of competitive advantage." *Management Science*, 35, pp. 1504–1511; Barney, J. B. (1991). "Firm resources and sustained competitive advantage." *Journal of Management*, 7, pp. 49–64; Mahoney, J. T., and J. R. Pandian. (1992). "The resource-based view within the conversation of strategic management." *Strategic Management Journal*, 13, pp. 363–380; and Peteraf, M. A. (1993). "The cornerstones of competitive advantage: A resource-based view." *Strategic Management Journal*, 14, pp. 179–191.

14. Dierickx, I., and K. Cool. (1989). "Asset stock accumulation and sustainability of competitive advantage." *Management Science*, 35, pp. 1504–1511. In economics, the role of history in determining competitive outcomes was first examined by Arthur, W. B. (1989). "Competing technologies, increasing returns, and lock-in by historical events." *Economic Journal*, 99, pp. 116–131.

15. See Breen, B. (2003). "What's selling in America." *Fast Company*, January, pp. 80 +.

16. This term was first suggested by Arthur, W. B. (1989). "Competing technologies, increasing returns, and lock-in by historical events." *Economic Journal*, 99, pp. 116–131. A good example of path dependence is the development of Silicon Valley and the important role that Stanford University and a few early firms played in creating the network of organizations that has since become the center of much of the electronics business. See Alley, J. (1997). "The heart of Silicon Valley." *Fortune*, July 7, pp. 86 +.

17. Reed, R., and R. J. DeFillippi. (1990). "Causal ambiguity, barriers to imitation, and sustainable competitive advantage." *Academy of Management Review*, 15(1), pp. 88–102, suggest that causal ambiguity about the sources of a firm's competitive advantage need only exist among a firm's competitors for it to be a source of sustained competitive advantage. Managers in a firm, they argue, may fully understand the sources of their advantage. However, in a world where employees freely and frequently move from firm to firm, such special insights into the sources of a firm's competitive advantage would not remain proprietary for very long. For this reason, for causal ambiguity to be a source of sustained competitive advantage, both the firm trying to gain such an advantage and those trying to imitate it must face similar levels of causal ambiguity. Indeed, Wal-Mart recently sued Amazon for trying to steal some of its secrets by hiring employees away from Wal-Mart. See Nelson, E. (1998). "Wal-Mart accuses Amazon. com of stealing its secrets in lawsuit." *The Wall Street Journal*, October 19, p. B10. For a discussion of how difficult it is to maintain secrets, especially in a world of the World Wide Web, see Farnham, A. (1997). "How safe are your secrets?" *Fortune*, September 8, pp. 114 +. The international dimensions of the challenges associated with maintaining secrets are discussed in Robinson, E. (1998). "China spies target corporate America." *Fortune*, March 30, pp. 118 +.

18. Itami, H. (1987). *Mobilizing invisible assets*. Cambridge, MA: Harvard University Press.

19. See Barney, J. B., and B. Tyler. (1990). "The attributes of top management teams and sustained competitive advantage." In M. Lawless and L. Gomez-Mejia (eds.), *Managing the high technology firm* (pp. 33–48). Greenwich, CT: JAI Press, on teamwork in top management teams; Barney, J. B. (1986). "Organizational culture: Can it be a source of sustained competitive advantage?" *Academy of Management Review*, 11, pp. 656–665, on organizational culture; Henderson, R. M., and I. Cockburn. (1994). "Measuring competence? Exploring firm effects in pharmaceutical research." *Strategic Management Journal*, 15, pp. 63–84, on relationships among employees; and Dyer, J. H., and H. Singh. (1998). "The relational view: Cooperative strategy and sources of interorganizational competitive advantage." *Academy of Management Review*, 23(4), pp. 660–679, on relationships with suppliers and customers.

20. For a discussion of knowledge as a source of competitive advantage in the popular business press, see Stewart, T. (1995). "Getting real about brain power." *Fortune*, November 27, pp. 201 +; Stewart, T. (1995). "Mapping corporate knowledge." *Fortune*, October 30, pp. 209 +. For the academic version of this same issue, see Simonin, B. L. (1999). "Ambiguity and the process of knowledge transfer in

strategic alliances." *Strategic Management Journal*, 20(7), pp. 595–623; Spender, J. C. (1996). "Making knowledge the basis of a dynamic theory of the firm." *Strategic Management Journal*, 17 (Winter special issue), pp. 109–122; Hatfield, D. D., J. P. Liebeskind, and T. C. Opler. (1996). "The effects of corporate restructuring on aggregate industry specialization." *Strategic Management Journal*, 17, pp. 55–72; and Grant, R. M. (1996). "Toward a knowledge-based theory of the firm." *Strategic Management Journal*, 17 (Winter special issue), pp. 109–122.

21. Porras, J., and P. O. Berg. (1978). "The impact of organizational development." *Academy of Management Review*, 3, pp. 249–266, have done one of the few empirical studies on whether or not systematic efforts to change socially complex resources are effective. They found that such efforts are usually not effective. Although this study is getting older, it is unlikely that current change methods will be any more effective than the methods examined by these authors.

22. See Hambrick, D. (1987). "Top management teams: Key to strategic success." *California Management Review*, 30, pp. 88–108, on top management teams; Barney, J. B. (1986). "Organizational culture: Can it be a source of sustained competitive advantage?" *Academy of Management Review*, 11, pp. 656–665, on culture; Porter, M. E. (1980). *Competitive strategy*. New York: Free Press; and Klein, B., and K. Leffler. (1981). "The role of market forces in assuring contractual performance." *Journal of Political Economy*, 89, pp. 615–641, on relations with customers.

23. See Harris, L. C., and E. Ogbonna. (1999). "Developing a market oriented culture: A critical evaluation." *Journal of Management Studies*, 36(2), pp. 177–196.

24. Lieberman, M. B. (1987). "The learning curve, diffusion, and competitive strategy." *Strategic Management Journal*, 8, pp. 441–452, has a very good analysis of the cost of imitation in the chemical industry. See also Lieberman, M. B., and D. B. Montgomery. (1988). "First-mover advantages." *Strategic Management Journal*, 9, pp. 41–58.

25. Rumelt, R. P. (1984). "Toward a strategic theory of the firm." In R. Lamb (ed.), *Competitive strategic management* (pp. 556–570). Upper Saddle River, NJ: Prentice Hall, among others, cites patents as a source of costly imitation.

26. Significant debate surrounds the patentability of different kinds of products. For example, although typefaces are not patentable (and cannot be copyrighted), the process for displaying typefaces may be. See Thurm, S. (1998). "Copy this typeface? Court ruling counsels caution." *The Wall Street Journal*, July 15, pp. B1 +.

27. For an insightful discussion of these complementary resources, see Amit, R., and P. J. H. Schoemaker. (1993). "Strategic assets and organizational rent." *Strategic Management Journal*, 14(1), pp. 33–45.

28. See Kearns, D. T., and D. A. Nadler. (1992). *Prophets in the dark*. New York: HarperCollins; and Smith, D. K., and R. C. Alexander. (1988). *Fumbling the future*. New York: William Morrow.

29. (2004). "Gateway will close remaining retail stores." *The Wall Street Journal*, April 2, p. B2; Michaels, D. (2004). "AA Airbus, picturing huge jet was easy; building it was hard." *The Wall Street Journal*, May 27, pp. A1 +; Zeller, W., A. Michael, and L. Woellert. (2004). "The airline debate over cheap seats." *The Wall Street Journal*, May 24, pp. A1 +.

30. (2004). "Casio." *Marketing*, May 6, p. 95; Weisul, K. (2003). "When time is money—and art." *BusinessWeek*, July 21, p. 86.

31. That said, there have been some "cracks" in Southwest's capabilities armor lately. Its CEO suddenly resigned, and its level of profitability dropped precipitously in 2004. Whether these are indicators that Southwest's core strengths are being dissipated or there are short-term problems is not yet known. However, Southwest's stumbling would give US Airways some hope. Trottman, M., S. McCartney, and J. Lublin. (2004). "Southwest's CEO abruptly quits 'draining job.' " *The Wall Street Journal*, July 16, pp. A1 +.

32. One should consult a lawyer before getting involved in these forms of tacit cooperation.

33. This aspect of the competitive dynamics in an industry is discussed in Smith, K. G., C. M. Grimm, and M. J. Gannon. (1992). *Dynamics of competitive strategy*. Newberry Park, CA: Sage.

34. Schlender, B. R. (1992). "How Sony keeps the magic going." *Fortune*, February 24, pp. 75–84.

35. Personal communication.

36. See, for example, Peters, T., and R. Waterman. (1982). *In search of excellence*. New York: Harper Collins; Collins, J., and J. Porras. (1994). *Built to last*. New York: Harper Business; Collins, J. (2001). *Good to great*. New York: Harper Collins; and Bennis, W. G., and R. Townsend. (2006). *Reinventing leadership*. New York: Harper Collins.

PART 1 CASES

Case 1–1: Pfizer and the Challenges of the Global Pharmaceutical Industry*

Introduction—Pfizer

In the beginning of 2007 Jeffrey Kindler, Pfizer's new chairman, pondered over the company's stagnating performance. Growth had slowed down recently and the company could not achieve its annual goals. Having just joined the company, Kindler still had to spend time to learn about the pharmaceutical industry and Pfizer's strategic position. His previous leadership of McDonald's had proven to be a success story. Now the switch to Pfizer proved to be a challenge as Pfizer's shareholders continued to be disappointed with the company's recent developments.

Not only had revenues declined but also the blockbuster drug called "Lipitor" was losing its momentum. Lipitor is a cholesterol-lowering drug that had contributed US$13 billion in sales. This comprised 40% to total company's profit. In December 2006, Pfizer faced a setback in developing "Torcetrapib" which should have been the "blockbuster" successor for Lipitor. The research program for "Torcetrapib" was stopped due to significant concerns regarding human safety. Drastic side-effects had risen unexpectedly resulting in financial investment losses for Pfizer.

The general changes and industry developments worried many pharmaceutical managers. One area of concern was the role and influence of pharmaceutical firms on price setting. In 2005 the German government demanded price reductions across the board for all types of drugs. For example, the German government wanted to reimburse the medical expenses of Lipitor patients up to a certain amount. If the price of Lipitor was further reduced by 38%, then German patients could receive full reimbursement for their purchase cost. Previously, the German government had already negotiated the lowest possible price for Lipitor. This dual step price reduction had a drastic effect on the potential earnings of Pfizer.

Price pressures existed not only in Germany. On the 1st of January 2005, the Pharmaceutical Price Regulation Scheme ("PPRS") came into effect in the United Kingdom. The PPRS's goal was to set profit boundaries on all types of medicines. Kindler's colleague Tom Mckillop, the CEO of AstraZeneca, spoke of an "Extortion like" situation.[1] Felix Raeber, head of European media relations for Novartis referred to a situation where the pharmaceutical companies were "without control."[2]

In addition, managers were also worried about the public recognition and evaluation of the activities of pharmaceutical firms. Normally the efforts of drug companies to develop new medicines were accepted favorably by the general public. However, pharmaceutical firms had a negative image during the previous few years. A survey in the US showed that only 14% of the respondents had a very positive impression of the pharmaceutical industry. Fifty percent of the respondents had a bad impression. This implied the pharmaceutical industry had a reputation similar to oil and tobacco companies. Historically, the pharmaceutical industry had been one of the most profitable and high margin industries for many years. Could the industry continue to sustain such trends given ongoing changes?

*This case was written by Dr. Phillip Nell,[1] Center for Strategic Management and Globalization at Copenhagen Business School and Dr. Björn Ambos,[2] Institute for International Marketing and Management at Wirtschaftsuniversität Wien. It is intended to be used as the basis for class discussion rather than to illustrate either effective or ineffective handling of a management situation. The case was compiled from published sources and generalised experience.

[1] Dr. Phillip C. Nell is Assistant Professor at the Center for Strategic Management and Globalization at Copenhagen Business School.

[2] Dr. Björn Ambos is Professor and head of the Institute for International Marketing and Management at Wirtschaftsuniversität Wien.

Exhibit 1   Development of Total Expenditures on Health Per Capita in USD Purchasing Power Parity

	1960	1970	1980	1990	2000	2001	2002	2003
North America	136	326	928	2.245	3.546	3.826	4.093	4.355
Europe	69	202	641	1.165	1.934	2.075	2.253	2.409
Japan	30	149	580	1.116	1.967	2.082	2.138	2.249
Asia/Pacific	94	232	455	887	1.594	1.725	1.842	1.949
Latin America	—	—	—	306	506	548	578	608
OECD average	79	214	639	1.180	1.961	2.106	2.275	2.427

Source: OECD Health Data 2006.

The Pharmaceutical Industry

Global health expenses increased steadily during the last decades. In 2003, the average per capita spending on health care in OECD countries amounted to US$2,400. (Refer to Exhibit 1.) The health expense measured as a proportion of gross domestic product rose from 7.8% in 1997 to 8.8% in 2003.

Currently, medicines comprised 18% of global health expenses with a tendency to increase in the near future. The reasons for this were numerous. First, the proportional increase of the ageing population in most countries led to a larger demand of medicinal usage (Exhibit 2). Second, there was a need to develop innovative and expensive medicines during the last few decades especially for new strains of diseases such as cancer and AIDS which had previously no cure. In this case, differences among countries could be observed due to differences in consumption patterns, medicine prices as well as income levels. (See Exhibit 3.)

During recent years medication expenditures had risen faster than total health spending. The global medicine market amounted to US$643 billion in 2006. (See Exhibit 4 below.) The medicine product market was segmented based on various categories depending on the chemical composition, safety and frequency of usage. The first category was whether a prescription was required. Prescription drugs can only be given out by doctors and pharmacies.

Exhibit 2   Share of Elderly People (≥65) of the Total Population in %

	1960	2003
UK	12	16
US	9	12
Italy	9	19
Japan	6	19
OECD	9	14

Source: OECD Health at a Glance, OECD Indicators 2005.

Exhibit 3   Per Capita Expenditures on Pharmaceutical Products in USD for Selected Countries

Land	Per capita expenditures on pharmaceutical products in USD purchasing power parity in 2003
US	728
France	606
Germany	436
Italy	498
Sweden	340
Poland	225
Mexico	125
Turkey	112

Source: OECD Health at a Glance, OECD Indicators 2005.

The second category was called over-the-counter-drugs or "OTC." These are medicines purchased without a prescription. This category also includes food supplements and vitamins. The latter were not classified as medicines and were sold in pharmacies and, in the US, in supermarkets. The OTC-market was comparable to the consumer goods markets.[3] In the prescription drug market, a distinction was drawn between generics and branded drugs. A generic (multiple generics) was a medicine that had the same active agents as a branded drug. In other words, a generic was a copy of branded drug that patent had expired. Generics are marketed only the after the patent expires.

Health systems in Europe and in the US were fundamentally different. In the US, there was no public health insurance to reimburse patients for the costs of medicines completely or partly. The large majority of the Americans were, therefore, privately insured. The US government seldom got involved with price regulation. Consequently, the US market offers the highest prices worldwide and was by far the most important market for the pharmaceutical industry.

In most European countries there was compulsory health insurance supported by the state and accessible for the whole population. A large portion of the drug expenses were paid by the state. In 2001, the share of public

Exhibit 4   Development of the Global Pharmaceutical Market

Year	1998	1999	2000	2001	2002	2003	2004	2005	2006	2007	2008
Total global sales (in US$ billions ex-manufacture price)	298	334	362	387	427	498	559	601	643	712	775
Growth rate (in % at a constant US$)		14.5	11.7	11.8	10.6	10.4	8.0	6.8	7.1	6.4	5.3

Source: IMS Health (2009).

spending to total spending added up to 72% on average in OECD countries. The other 28% of the expenditures were funded privately by private insurance or by patients. This average, however, did not show the significant disparities between some countries. In addition, there were considerable differences relating to the share of public and private financing sources within medicine expenditures (Exhibit 5). On average 60% of medication expenses in OECD countries were financed publicly.

Based on this, the national health systems were the basic principal payer for medicines in Europe. Considering the increasing health care spending and tight national budgets, the European governments were considerably more active

Exhibit 5   Public and Private Spending on Pharmaceuticals Per Country in % of Total Spending

	Public spending	Private spending
US	21%	79%
Canada	38%	62%
Switzerland	66%	34%
Norway	59%	41%
Iceland	58%	42%
UK	64%	36%
Sweden	70%	30%
Spain	74%	26%
Slovakia	83%	17%
Portugal	66%	34%
Poland	41%	59%
Netherlands	57%	43%
Luxembourg	83%	17%
Italy	49%	51%
Ireland	86%	14%
Hungary	63%	37%
Greece	74%	26%
Germany	75%	25%
France	67%	33%
Finland	54%	46%
Denmark	49%	51%
Czech Republic	77%	23%
Belgium	45%	55%
Austria	70%	30%

Source: OECD Health Data 2006.

in price regulation. To achieve this, the governments used various measures. One of these measures was setting fixed prices in negotiations between the state and the manufacturer. This involved lengthy price and reimbursement negotiations which could delay product launch significantly.

Governments could also set prices by so-called "referencing." The price of drugs were adjusted to the prices of other countries. Also "internal referencing" was employed where products with similar therapeutic effect were grouped together and a relatively lower all-in price is determined for every group. The reimbursement system was then aligned so that the patient must pay for the drug himself if the drug price was higher than the reference price. Other measures taken by governments were "all-in price markdowns" that were demanded from all manufacturers and the limitation on profit margins for certain products such as the PPRS system in the UK.

Despite the mechanism of "referencing," the different price regulation schemes led to considerable price differences within the European markets. For products that entered the market in Europe in 2000, a price range of 30% over and under the EU average price existed. This price control, combined with the free transportation of goods within the EU, resulted in parallel imports during the previous years. This led to forgone profits of approximately three to four billion Euros for the pharmaceuticals industry.

Governments influenced not only the price, but also the demand through the reimbursement system of their respective health care institutions/authorities. Patients often could only get their medicine expenses repaid if the drug was recognized as reimbursable by their national health care system. Many countries established so-called positive lists where all products on the list were reimbursed, negative lists where all products on the list were not reimbursed, or both. When a prescription drug was not reimbursed, the demand for this drug was automatically limited. Premium prices and the reimbursement of costs were mostly achieved by medicines that brought therapeutic advantages: "First-in-class products" and highly innovative biotechnology products are examples of such medicines.

In most health care systems, doctors were relatively free to determine the treatment and medication. Usually they could choose between different substances and between branded medicines versus generics. While many EU countries fostered the prescription of generics which were bioequivalent to the branded drugs, doctors could still often intervene and push through the choice for the branded drug. Therefore, in some countries doctors could only mention the active ingredient in the prescription and not the brand name.

When choosing medication, doctors tended to be extremely loyal and frequently choose one particular product that they felt provided a positive feedback for their patients. Often, these were the branded drugs. The market power of expensive branded drugs was sustained by the fact that in most countries there were no defined regulations on cost cutting or preferences for generics (such as the above-mentioned rule to prescribe only active ingredients), and that neither patients nor doctors themselves had to pay for the branded drug as these were subsidized by the governments in Europe. Usually, however, doctors become sensitive to price increases when the patient himself had to bear a large part of the costs.

The marketing activities of pharmaceutical companies were focused on the doctors, who served as key decision makers. Approximately 70% of the total administrative and marketing costs were spent on direct contact with doctors. This was roughly US$13,000 per year per doctor. Sales representatives were the main communication channel between pharmaceutical firms and doctors. Therefore, many firms had invested extensively in the number and training of their sales personnel. Meanwhile there were signs of "over marketing." Doctors were complaining about the numerous and extensive sales pitches by sales representatives. Many firms, however, did not want to reduce their sales force unless the competition did the same. The firms were trapped in a "marketing and sales arms-race" as phrased in the magazine *The Economist*. Most market participants were aware of the

substantial effect this had on their profitability due to the high overhead, administrative and marketing costs for pharmaceuticals firms. Such expenses were twice the research expenditures. It was also claimed that corrupt practices were sometimes used in order successfully bring selective products into the market.

The role of patients in the buying process had increased over time. Traditionally doctors were the only information source for patients, even though they spent less and less time with their patients. This was related to the increasing trend of self-medication. For pharmaceutical firms this development was dangerous, because in Europe all direct marketing targeted at patients was prohibited.

Another trend was the rise of alternative and complementary medicines and treatments. In Africa, Asia and Latin America, traditional medicine played an important role in health care. In Western markets, many of these treatments were scientifically controversial where the medical effects were unclear or the side effects relatively strong or unforeseeable. In the largest European markets, the US and Japan, alternative medicines were often used as complementary therapy to a more conventional treatment. The additional costs were often paid by patients themselves.

Development of Drugs and the Patenting Process

The pharmaceuticals industry was, similar to the oil industry, a "self-liquidating" industry. Both had to continually develop new products, i.e. locate oil- and gas fields to fill their pipelines. Both involved long gestation periods of development before a product was launched. In the pharmaceuticals industry, the product development phase took around 10 to 15 years and there were signs that the "simple discoveries" had been made by the 2000s (Exhibit 6).

The development process started with identifying a "goal" in the human body; for example, a protein against which the medicine can act. Then, the different chemical properties within the formula (preparations) were tested

Exhibit 6 Duration of Research and Development Phases (in years per time period)			
Time Period	**Pre-clinical Test Phase**	**Clinical Test Phase**	**Patent Approval Phase**
1963–1969	2.6	3.1	2.4
1970–1979	2.4	7.1	2.1
1980–1989	2.3	9.0	2.8
1990–1999	3.8	8.6	1.8

Source: DiMasi (2001:292).

Exhibit 7   Broad Overview of the Research and Development Process

Development of a potential medicine	5000–10000 Active Ingredients	
		Laboratory and animal testing
Pre-clinical tests	250 Active Ingredients	
Approved as test preparation		
Clinical tests	5 Active Ingredients	Phase I—20–100 human test subjects
		Phase II—100–500 human test subjects
		Phase III—1000–5000 human test subjects
Approved as a new medicine		
Marketing		Ongoing tests on the effectiveness, side effects and product safety

and continually modified to achieve the maximum effective treatment with minimal side effects. In this phase up to 10,000 preparations were tested and evaluated. If the preliminary results were promising, then a patent was registered to avoid potential competition for the preparation in advance.

These "New Chemical Entities" (NCE) were subsequently subjected to pre-clinical testing and to a certain extent tested on animals. The objective was to research the toxic effects such as toxicity, carcinogenicity or reproductive effects. In addition, the biological effectiveness of the NCE was strenuously tested.

The preclinical test results were subsequently evaluated by health authorities. If the safety and the effectiveness of the preparation could be ascertained by the previous tests then permission was given for further (clinical) tests. In the US the regulatory agency was the FDA (Food and Drug Administration). This was comparable to agencies in European countries, i.e. at a European level (European Drug Agency). A European patent was only required for some areas and consisted of a bundle of national patents. On average only 5 out of 10000 preparations make it to the clinical tests which were then designated as "Investigational New Drug." The clinical tests were then divided into different phases depending on the country.

If these clinical tests in Phases I to II were positive in terms of human effectiveness and had no side effects, then a new medicine was approved for marketing. However, the pharmaceuticals firms were required, even after market launch, to carry out continuous tests in order to exclude long term or rare side effects. The health agencies could call

for additional investigations and tests, change markings and labeling or, possibly, take the medicine off the market even after initial authorization.

The success rate for a new medicine product launch was approximately one out of 5,000–10,000 substances (Exhibit 7). The process also involved considerable costs. In 1975, the average R&D costs for one new drug were estimated at roughly €150 million. By 1987 R&D costs amounted to approximately €344 million. This further increased by 2000 to €870 million (see Exhibit 8). This implied that only around one third of all medicines actually generated revenues that exceeded the research and development costs.

In general, most large pharmaceutical firms had a centralized R&D unit. This hardly changed for several years. Recently the importance of the "new sciences" like biotechnology, genetics, Pharmaco Genomics and Proteomics had increased leading to a growing trend of "personalized medication." The "one drug fits all" policy,

Exhibit 8   R&D Expenses of the Pharmaceuticals Industry in Europe, Japan and the US in Billion EUR at 2006 Exchange Rates

Year	R&D spending
1990	15.9
1995	25.8
2000	48.5
2004	51.6

Source: EFPIA 2006.

which previously characterized large blockbusters, could potentially expire. Medicines for specific patient groups had become more numerous, supported by further developments in the research process. For example there were iterative test processes using imaging methods. These were processes that had little to do with the traditional R&D of the large pharmaceutical firms. Universities and smaller biotechnology firms increasingly ranked higher in innovations than the large pharmaceutical firms. As a result GlaxoSmithKline reacted some years previously and initiated a decentralization process in order to have more flexibility at the research front. It was possible that this trend could continue for the foreseeable future.

In order to provide pharmaceutical firms with an incentive to further invest in the research of new medicines despite high costs, a patent system was developed. Patents were the exclusive right to use an invention. A patent on a medicine gave the patent holder the right to prohibit others to produce, offer or use the medicine commercially. This right was in most countries limited to 20 years. Only in exceptional situations could governments use the right, regardless of the patent, to produce a medicine and make it available to patients without the consent of the patent holder ("compulsory licensing").

Although patents offered a certain protection, the so-called "between-patent" competition posed a dangerous threat to existing pharmaceutical firms. Between-patent competition arose between branded products in the same "Disease Class." Such a therapeutic area comprised drugs that had either the same chemical structure or used the same pharmacological "mode of action" against a disorder. Drugs from the same therapeutic area were, therefore,

relatively good substitutes even when the drug was still under patent protection. Most firms researched very similar medicines at the same time. An innovation that led a branded drug and with a new therapeutic area was called a "breakthrough drug" (or first-in-class). New medicines in existing therapeutic areas were "follow-ons." Pfizer's Viagra, for example, was a breakthrough drug when it was launched on the market in 1998. Pfizer profited from a monopoly position and patent protection until 2003 when Bayer introduced a similar product in the same therapy class (Levitra). The times that a breakthrough product existed on the market without any competition were decreasing. First-in-class products which were authorized in the 70s survived on the market for approximately 8 years without follow-on. For products authorized between 1995 and 1998, this time period was only 1.8 years.

In addition the days of excessive high profit margins were over even though "follow-ons" brought only limited therapeutic advantages as governments became more cost-conscious. Even in the US market, which offered 50% profit margins for many pharmaceutical firms, there were signs that the free pricing policy had ended.

The special situation of the market combined with patent laws had caused most firms to earn gigantic revenues with only a few products. Products that generated more than US$1 billion in revenues were called "blockbusters."

Firms tried to make maximum use of the patent protection. New globally standardized products were, therefore, registered for a patent in concerted action worldwide and brought into the market simultaneously (Exhibit 9).

When patent protection ended, generics entered the competition. Often, the generics manufacturers made use

---

Exhibit 9   Top 10 Blockbusters 2005

Product	Firm	Therapeutic Area	Revenue 2005 in billion USD
Lipitor	Pfizer	Cardiovascular	12.9
Plavix	Sanofi-aventis/BMS	Cardiovascular	5.9
Nexium	AstraZeneca	Gastrointestinal	5.7
Seretide/Advair	GlaxoSmithKline	Respiratory	5.6
Zocor	Merck & Co	Cardiovascular	5.3
Norvasc	Pfizer	Cardiovascular	5.0
Zyprexa	Eli Lilly	Nervous system	4.7
Risperdal	J&J	Nervous system	4.0
Ogastro/Prevacid	Abbott/Takeda	Gastrointestinal	4.0
Effexor	Wyeth	Nervous system	3.8

Source: IMS Health (2006).

of the scientific progress since the development of an old preparation. Consequently, generics could be significantly superior to the originally branded products in effectiveness and side effects. Generics were generally named after the international non-proprietary name of the active ingredient, with the addition of the manufacturer name. Competition for blockbusters was, therefore, extremely high. In the US for example, BMS's diabetes product called Glucophage lost patent protection in 2002. During the previous few years 19 generics competitors entered the market. Market share of the branded product fell rapidly by around 90% in a short span of time.

In contrast to the innovative branded products, generics clearly had a lower profit margin as manufacturers could forego a large part of the expensive development and test phases. These had a positive effect on the cost structure (see Exhibit 10). Therefore, many governments had taken steps to improve the market position of generics to profit from the much lower prices. The share of generics in the total drug market was very different. In the US the number of generics prescriptions exceeded those for branded products for the first time in 2005.

In European countries as well as in Japan, generic drug markets were often still underdeveloped and offered large growth potentials. In the meantime most countries—even outside of Europe—had initiated or implemented measures that gave preference to generics. However, not only the actions of the national health authorities drove the growth of generics' share. Many doctors and patients now had more confidence in generics. The growth of the generics business was estimated at approximately 20% which was higher than the expected growth rate of 5% to −8% on average for the total medicine market.

The competitive pressure for the imminent generics led brand manufacturers to increasingly implement Life Cycle Strategies. The goal was to either increase the time a branded product had on the market without competition from generics; to increase the revenue a product generated under patent protection; or to minimize the loss of revenue to competing generics. Pharmaceutical firms started developing these strategies 6 to 8 years before the expiration of the patent. Around $\frac{1}{3}$ of all medicines, that were in Phase III of the clinical tests in the US, did not contain entirely new chemical entities. This means that they were already sold on the market in a some other form.

A more recent strategy was to bring authorized generic versions on the market. These could be marketed by the original branded drug manufacturer; by the firm's internal generics division or by a generics firm that received an exclusive license for this. In case of licensing, the product was usually produced by the manufacturer to utilize full capacity. Marketing and distribution however was done by the licensee. The producer received, in addition to the licensing fee, a share of the profit. This strategy was particularly useful if generics firms had already contested the patent protection successfully. Instead of costly patent law disputes, this cooperative strategy was a fast and acceptable solution for both sides. When Pfizer's US patent on Zithromax, an oral antibiotic, lost patent protection in 2005, Pfizer's own generics division brought an authorized generic on the market. At the same time, three other firms started with generics for Zithromax. After only seven weeks, the market for the branded drug collapsed and 90% of all prescribed drugs were generics. Nevertheless, Pfizer was able to achieve a 49% market share with its own generic.

The Supply Chain

From manufacturing to consumption by the patient, a medicine went through a number of steps.

Production

Fine chemicals were the production base for most medicines. Branded products made up between ten to fifteen percent of the medicine price. Generic products comprised about 25% to 30% of the medicine price. Half of this global medicine market was manufactured by the pharmaceutical firms themselves; whereas the other half was produced by firms from the fine chemicals industry. These fine chemicals consisted of standard practice or customized molecules

Exhibit 10   Costs Per Category in % of Revenues for 2005

Firm	R&D Costs	Cost of Sales
Pfizer	15	17
GSK	14	22
Sanofi-aventis	15	26
Novartis	15	28
J&J	12	28
AstraZeneca	14	22
Merck & Co	17	23
Abbott	8	48
BMS	14	31
Wyeth	15	29
Eli Lilly	21	24
Teva[1]	7	53
Sandoz[1]	9	61
IVAX[1]	6	58

Source: Company annual report.
1) Teva, Sandoz and Ivax are primarily generics manufacturers.

and active agents that were prepared for further processing into the final medicine in pill, fluid or gaseous form. The fine chemicals could be seen as mass-production items or raw materials that could normally be produced by various firms in high quality. As a result, there were many potential suppliers. No chemical firm had been able to achieve a dominant market position and the market to date remains highly fragmented. The pharmaceuticals industry was by far the largest buyer of fine chemicals and a substantial percentage of chemical firms' revenues often depended on a few pharmaceutical customers. Medicine manufacturers, on their part, must guarantee high product quality. To produce a specific medicine, every factory needed exactly defined processes and a permission that was checked regularly. If health institutions assessed that there were variations in the areas of quality, safety and effectiveness, then product authorization could be withdrawn immediately.

Distribution and Pricing

Wholesalers and pharmacies ensured that the products reach the patients. In this area, there were large differences between the US and the European markets. In most European markets maximum mark ups for pharmacies and wholesalers were set by the health authorities. In the US, there was considerably more flexibility. On average, the medicine manufacturer received around 60% of the sales price, the wholesaler around 7% and the pharmacy about 20%. (See Exhibit 11.) The wholesalers bought directly from the drug manufacturers and distributed the product further to hospitals and pharmacies. To carry out his function, the wholesalers needed a license and were required to conform to certain criteria, e.g. keep a safety stock, so that

they could deliver within a short time. Moreover, they often had to cover a whole region—and guarantee the integrity of the drug.

Around 94% of the medicine provided in the EU was undertaken by wholesalers. Nevertheless, a multichannel system dominated Europe, in which a product could be sold by multiple wholesalers. Large pharmacy chains, specialized pharmacies and mail order pharmacies could to some extent buy the medicines directly from the (medicine) manufacturer as well. The growing importance of chains and mail order houses in Europe led to an increasing trend to bypass the distributor. Hence, in February 2005, Pfizer announced that it would deliver directly to pharmacies, to fight parallel imports.

Price pressure on the wholesalers had risen over the previous years resulting in tighter competition. The net profit margins were decreasing and averaged around 0.7 to 0.8% of sales price. A reason for this was increasing packaging, delivery, and transportation costs that could be attributed to the rising oil and fuel prices. Another reason was the trend of medicine manufacturers to establish Just-In-Time production systems which limited the wholesalers' opportunities to profit from efficient ware-house management. As a result, the industry both in the US and Europe had undergone substantial consolidation over the last decades. In the EU-15 countries, the number of wholesalers declined from 600 in 1990 to around 150 in 2004. In US market the three largest wholesalers control approximately 90% of the market.

Pricing was more critical for generic manufacturers because they are traded in larger mass volumes. In particular, the competitive environment in generics for each of the respective therapeutic areas played a major role. In addition, the ability of the wholesaler to support the manufacturer in

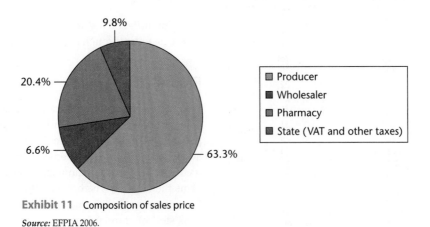

Exhibit 11   Composition of sales price
Source: EFPIA 2006.

revenue or volume growth as well as the prevention of parallel imports further affected the price levels for generic drugs. Many distributors had added activities to their core business, for example, services in the areas of market data gathering and processing or packaging. For the manufacturers, distributors increasingly offered marketing and advertising support activities as well as support in the area of logistics, which was necessary in the clinical tests, or in product launches. Some distributors had even vertically integrated, both downstream and upstream, and had taken over production and pharmacy functions. This strategy, however, was disliked by national health authorities and was highly restricted.

The significance of pharmacies varied from country to country. Prescription drugs were generally only available through pharmacies. But the influence of pharmacists on the choice of drug or the brand was dependent on the respective legal environment. Principally, the decision on which medicine was consumed by patients was made by the prescribing doctor. In many countries, however, the pharmacist was allowed to replace the original prescribed branded product with a preparation that contained the same active agents. Pharmacies usually bought medicines directly from wholesalers and even this was strongly regulated in all countries. In most European countries, for example, only pharmacists could operate pharmacies. The number of pharmacies that could be owned by a single owner was limited. A license was required. Over the last years, however, there had been tendencies to lighten this regulation.

Competition among Pharmaceutical Firms

In comparison to other industries, the pharmaceuticals industry was highly fragmented. Over the previous few years there has been a tendency for firms to consolidate. In 1988 the top ten pharmaceutical firms had a market share of around 25%; whereas, in 1996 the same group held around 33% of the market. As more mergers and consolidations occurred, it was reported that by 2006 the market share of the top pharmaceutical firms improved to 43.3%.

All top ten firms were research-oriented companies (Exhibit 12). Only Sanofi-aventis and Novartis included a large generics domain into their activities. Others were also active in the OTC market, diagnostics, and in non-medical consumer goods. Overall, most firms were highly vertically integrated compared to other industries and carried out R&D, production, marketing and distribution activities. Some experts, therefore, claimed that these firms should focus more on their specific core competences, such as R&D or marketing & sales, make use of contract research and independent development firms as well as incorporating freelance marketing organizations into their business.

Pfizer was the undisputed market leader. Its core business consisted of 86% prescription drugs for humans. The division "Consumer Health Care" which included personal hygiene and OTC-products (approximately 8% of total revenues or US$4 billion) was sold to Johnson & Johnson in June 2006 for US$16.6 billion. Four percent of

Exhibit 12   Top 10 Pharmaceutical Firms 2006

Company	Origin	2006 Revenue (in billion US$)	Growth 2005–2006 (in %)	Average Annual Growth 2001–2005
Pfizer	USA	46.1	−0.7	4.8
GlaxoSmithKline	UK	37.0	5.5	5.0
Sanofi-aventis	France	31.1	1.4	11.2
Novartis	Switzerland	31.6	6.1	14.1
Johnson & Johnson	USA	27.3	1.2	9.2
AstraZeneca	UK	26.7	11.2	7.0
Merck & Co	USA	25.0	4.9	4.1
Roche	Switzerland	23.5	16.1	13.5
Abbott	USA	17.6	6.4	10.7
Amgen	USA	16.1	20.6	30.2
Total Top 10		282.1	5.7	8.8

Source: IMS Health 2006.

Exhibit 13   Size and Development of R&D Spending for Selected Industries

Industry	R&D spending in % of revenue 2004
Pharmaceutical industry and Biotechnology	15.3
Software and Computer Services	10.7
IT Hardware	8.6
Automotive	4.3
Electronics and Electrical Equipment	5.6
Chemicals Industry	3.7
Food Industry	1.8
Telecommunication	1.5
Average of all industries	3.8

Source: EFPIA 2006.

Exhibit 14   Number of Developed New Molecular Entities (NMEs) and Biotechnology Products Between 1997 and 2004

Year	Number of new NMEs
1990	36
1991	51
1992	43
1993	40
1994	40
1995	41
1996	36
1997	46
1998	37
1999	41
2000	32
2001	31
2002	28
2003	26
2004	25

Source: EFPIA 2006.

Pfizer's revenue was generated by the division "Animal Health Business." Pfizer was most active in the cardiovascular diseases and metabolism diseases therapeutic areas. Close to half of the company's total revenues were generated from prescription drugs. In the meantime, Pfizer had divested its generics business which had been previously integrated into the company after the acquisition of Pharmacia in 2004. Instead, it had bought some smaller biotechnology firms. The patents for its second and third best blockbusters, namely, Zoloft and Norvasc expired at end of 2006 and 2007 respectively.

GlaxoSmithKline (GSK) was somewhat more differentiated. The pharmaceuticals division was responsible for 86% of the revenues. The remaining 14% was contributed by the consumer goods and OTC division. Therapeutic focus concentrated on respiratory diseases (27% of revenue), nervous system diseases (17.2%) and antiviral drugs (13.9%). GSK is currently expanding in the vaccine business (7.4% of revenues in 2005) and is broadening its biotechnology base by acquiring several smaller firms. For two of the top five products, new generics had recently appeared on the market. In the OTC market, GSK was presently number 3 worldwide.

Sanofi-aventis was a firm that emerged from the merger between Sanofi-Synthélabo. This was the result of earlier multi-mergers between Hoechst and Rhône-Poulenc and Aventis. Sanofi-aventis was dominated by its pharmaceuticals division (92% of revenues). The remainder was generated by the vaccine business. The firm was active in seven different therapeutic areas. The pharmaceuticals division included a generics department, which covered only 14 European countries. In March 2006, around 25% of the Czech generics manufacturer Zentive, a leading firm in Central-Eastern Europe, was bought. Together with Merck &

Co., Sanofi-aventis operated a Joint-Venture in Europe in the OTC and the vaccine products.

Novartis' business was divided into three main segments, namely: Branded products (innovative prescription drugs that contributed 63% of revenues in 2005) and generics, which represented 15% of the revenues and were marketed under the name Sandoz. Both were grouped together in the pharmaceuticals division. The third branch was the Consumer Health Care division that consisted of the OTC business, animal products, baby food, food supplements and contact lenses. During the previous years Novartis expanded primarily through acquisitions such as Sandoz (the Slovak manufacturer LEK in 2002), the generics business of AstraZeneca (2004), the German firm Hexal (2005), Eon Labs (2005) and Chiron (2006) for the vaccine and diagnostic branches. The Consumer Health Care division was also restructured by the purchase of the foods business as well as the Consumer Health division of Bristol-Myers Squibb (2004). At the same time, however, the dietary products division and further food divisions were sold off.

Johnson & Johnson (J&J) was a highly differentiated conglomerate and was highly decentralized. The pharmaceuticals division contributed only around 44% of the revenues. About 18% of total revenues were generated by the Consumer division which encompassed the OTC products, food products and supplements, skin care, and children's products. Within the pharmaceutical division, the therapy focus was on nervous system disorders, anti-inflammatory drugs and hormone treatments. J&J had bought firms for

Exhibit 15   Share of the Top 5 Products in the Total Revenue in Percent

Firm	Product 1	Product 2	Product 3	Product 4	Product 5
Eli Lilly	29	9	8	7	7
Wyeth	18	9	8	6	5
BMS	20	12	5	5	4
Roche	12	6	6	5	5
Merck & Co	20	14	14	14	3
AstraZeneca	19	12	7	7	5
J&J	7	7	5	3	3
Novartis	11	7	4	4	3
Sanofi-aventis	8	7	6	6	6
GSK	14	3	3	3	3
Pfizer	24	9	6	3	3

Source: Company annual reports 2005.

all its business areas over the last years. In the OTC market, J&J was the global market leader.

AstraZeneca operated only one division: pharmaceuticals. The five main therapeutic areas were gastrointestinal diseases (27% of total revenues), cardiovascular (23%), neuroscience (17%), oncology (16.5%) and respiratory diseases (12%). In the beginning of 2006 AstraZeneca acquired the biotech firm KuDOS.

The US firm **Merck & Co** had long been considered as the largest pharmaceuticals firm globally. The firm still suffered the consequences of the premature market withdrawal of the arthritis product Vioxx in 2004. Vioxx was launched in 1999. Merck sold over US$2.5 billion worth of this arthritis drug in 2003 alone. Ongoing tests, however, showed a heightened risk of a heart attack for Vioxx, which led to the immediate withdrawal of the license. Because of this, Merck became a takeover target on the stock market with its stock price dropping almost 30% on the day of the announcement. By 2008, two more important products would lose patent protection. Merck operated almost exclusively in the area of prescription drugs (95% of revenues). Merck was the only top ten firm that had not been involved in the large horizontal merger over the last 15 years. In 2004, Merck sold its 50% stake in a European Joint-Venture of non-prescription pharmaceuticals to its partner J&J.

Roche's pharmaceuticals division contributed 77% to total revenues. The most important division for the company was the diagnostics area. However, a large part of the sales (about 1/3) originated from the consolidated majority stake in the US biotech firm Ganentech and the Japanese firm Chugai. Roche was the market leader in oncology with 40% of revenues based on anti-cancer medicines. 15% of total revenue was contributed by virology and 8% by

transplant pharmaceuticals. In 2004 Roche sold off the Consumer Health division to Bayer. Acquisitions were made in the area of biotechnology. Novartis owned one third stake in Roche.

The US firm **Abbott** realized 61% of its revenues from the pharmaceuticals division. The remaining revenues were contributed by the diagnostics and the food products. Abbott owned 50% of TAP pharmaceuticals, a Joint-Venture with the Japanese firm Takea. During the last years Abbott made some acquisitions, mainly to strengthen the area of medical devices (stents) and diagnostics.

Bristol-Myers Squibb (BMS): almost 80% of the total revenues was generated by the pharmaceuticals division. BMS had a strong presence in the field of cardiology, virology and oncology. In the future BMS wanted to specialize even further in "Specialty Products." In 2004, the adult nutritional division was sold to Novartis. In addition the Consumer Medicines Business was divested in 2005. The expiry of the patent for a blockbuster Pravachol in 2006 combined with the difficult market conditions resulted in weaker financial results for BMS. Another burden for the company was the lost patent law suit against a Canadian generics firm for the blockbuster drug Plavix.

Pfizer's Future Strategy

Kindler announced a radical change in strategy that would encompass multiple divisions and Pfizer's corporate culture: He was quoted in an article as commenting: "There are no longer sacred cows."[4] This was very uncommon for the hitherto profitable industry.

In January 2007, he announced that 10,000 employees would be dismissed. This was around 1/10 of Pfizer's total employees. One fifth of the sales force in the US and in Europe had to go. Five research centers and several factories were closed down. Research was reorganized. Instead of globally dispersed "Centers of Excellence," research activities were structured around five therapeutic areas (e.g. Cancer, Diabetes). In the future Pfizer had to minimize losses in research and development costs resulting from the delayed identification of potential long lasting side effects such as in the case of Torcetrapib. To achieve this, Kindler wanted to integrate General Electric's "fast falling" policy. In addition, Kindler aimed to encourage his "traditionally isolated" researchers to do more external collaboration. He had already ordered that Pfizer's research initiatives (often referred to as the "pipeline") be broadcasted via the internet to provide the public and competitors with relevant information to foster focused collaboration or acquisitions. Finally, Kindler demanded a paradigm shift regarding the product portfolio: "We need to be as effective at selling a large number of US$500 million drugs as we are at selling drugs with multi-billion dollar sales."[5]

Would all this help Pfizer? Would collaborative research and streamlining Pfizer's existing operations prove effective? The stock market appeared to be skeptical. In contrast to normal financial market reactions to similar corporate announcements, Pfizer's stock price fell after the announcement of employee cuts.

Bibliography

1. Annual Reports of the pharmaceutical firms mentioned in the text.
2. DiMasi, Joseph A. (2001): "New drug development in the United States from 1963 to 1999." In: *Clinical Pharmacology & Therapeutics*, 69/5 (May 2001), 286–296.
3. EFPIA (2006): "The pharmaceutical industry in figures. 2006 editor." European Federation of Pharmaceutical Industries and Associations, www.efpia.org
4. IMS Health (2009): "Global Pharmaceutical Sales, 1999–2008." Top-Line Industry Data—Global.
5. Organization for Economic Cooperation and Development (2005): "Health at a glance. OECD-indicators 2005."
6. Organization for Economic Cooperation and Development (2006): OECD Health Data 2006.
7. *The Economist* (2007), Billion dollar pills. The Economist Newspaper Limited, London 2007, January 27, 2007.

Endnotes

1. Quoted directly from the article "Billion Dollar Pills" in *The Economist*, January 27, 2007.
2. Ibid.
3. Note to reader: The OTC market will not be further discussed within the parameters of this case study. The focus of this case is primarily on prescription drugs.
4. Quoted directly from the article "Billion Dollar Pills" in *The Economist*, January 27, 2007.
5. Ibid.

Case 1-2: Wal-Mart Stores, Inc., in 2010*

As recently as 1979, Wal-Mart had been a regional retailer little known outside the South with only 229 discount stores compared to the industry leader Kmart's 1,891 stores. In less than 25 years, Wal-Mart had risen to become the largest U.S. corporation in sales. With over $405 billion in revenues (see Exhibits 1 and 2), Wal-Mart had far eclipsed Kmart, whose sales had fallen to a fraction of Wal-Mart's. Yet another measure of Wal-Mart's dominance was that it accounted for approximately 45 percent of general merchandise, 30 percent of health and beauty aids, and 29 percent of non-food grocery sales[1] in the United States. *Forbes* put Wal-Mart's success into perspective:

> With 3,550 stores in the U.S. and 1,000 Supercenters to be added in the next five years, all that's left for Wal-Mart is mop-up. It already sells more toys than Toys "R" Us, more clothes than the Gap and Limited combined and more food than Kroger. If it were its own economy, Wal-Mart Stores would rank 30th in the world, right behind Saudi Arabia. Growing at 11 percent a year, Wal-Mart would hit half a trillion dollars in sales by early in the next decade.[2]

Despite its remarkable record of success, though, Wal-Mart was not without challenges. Many observers believed that the company would find it increasingly difficult to sustain its remarkable record of growth (see Exhibit 3). Wal-Mart faced a maturing market in its core business that would not likely see the growth rates it had previously enjoyed. Growth in same-store sales had declined for five consecutive quarters in 2009 and 2010, while other major retailers—Target, Costco, Kroger, Safeway, and Best Buy—all enjoyed superior same-store growth over the previous five years. Many investors believed that Wal-Mart had reached a point of saturation with its stores. Supercenters had provided significant growth for Wal-Mart, but it was not clear how long they could deliver the company's customary growth rates. The company added new stores at a prodigious rate, but the new stores often cannibalized sales from nearby Wal-Mart stores. Wal-Mart faced problems in other business areas as well. The Wal-Mart–owned Sam's Club warehouse stores had not measured up to Costco, its leading competitor. International operations were another challenge for Wal-Mart. Faced with slowing growth domestically, it had tried to capitalize on international opportunities. These international efforts, however, had met with only mixed success at best.

Wal-Mart was also a target for critics who attacked its record on social issues.[3] Wal-Mart had been blamed for pushing production from the United States to low-wage overseas producers. Some claimed that Wal-Mart had almost single-handedly depressed wage growth in the U.S. economy. For many, Wal-Mart had become a symbol of capitalism that had run out of control. Indeed, *Time* magazine asked, "Will Wal-Mart Steal Christmas?"[4] Much of the criticism directed at Wal-Mart did not go beyond angry rhetoric. In many cases, however, Wal-Mart had faced stiff community opposition to building new stores.

With such challenges, some investment analysts questioned whether it was even possible for a company like Wal-Mart, with over $400 billion in sales, to sustain its accustomed high growth rates. To do so, Wal-Mart would have to address a number of challenges such as maturing markets, competition in discount retailing from both traditional competitors and specialty retailers, aggressive efforts by competitors to imitate Wal-Mart's products and processes, and international expansion. Indeed, some believed that Wal-Mart would need to find new business if it were to continue its historic success.

The Discount Retail Industry

General retailing in the United States evolved dramatically during the twentieth century. Before 1950, general retailing most often took the form of Main Street department stores. These stores typically sold a wide variety of general merchandise. Department stores were also different from other retailers in that they emphasized service and credit. Before World War II, few stores allowed customers to take goods directly from shelves. Instead, sales clerks served customers at store counters. Not until the 1950s did self-help department stores begin to spread. Discount retail stores also began to emerge in the late 1950s. Discount retailers emphasized low prices and generally offered less service, credit, and return privileges. Their growth was spawned by the repeal of fair trade laws in many states. Many states

---

* This case was prepared by William Hesterly for the purpose of classroom discussion.

Exhibit 1   Wal-Mart Stores, Inc., Income Statement, 2006–2010

Year Ended:	1/31/10	1/31/09 *Reclass 1/31/10	1/31/08 *Reclass 1/31/10	1/31/07 *Restated 1/31/09	1/31/06 *Restated 1/31/07
Net Sales	$405,046	$401,087	$373,821	$344,759	$308,945
Other Income	3,168	3,287	3,202	3,609	3,156
Rental Income	—	—	—	—	—
Total Revenue	408,214	404,374	377,023	348,368	312,101
Cost of Sales	304,657	304,056	284,137	263,979	237,649
Operating, Selling, General and Admin.	79,607	77,520	70,934	63,892	55,739
Total Operating Expense	384,264	381,576	355,071	327,871	293,388
Operating Income	23,950	22,798	21,952	20,497	18,713
Debt Interest	(1,787)	(1,896)	(1,863)	(1,549)	(1,171)
Capital Lease Exp.	(278)	(288)	(240)	(260)	(249)
Interest Income	181	284	309	280	242
Net Income Before Taxes	22,066	20,898	20,158	18,968	17,535
Provision for Income Taxes	7,139	7,145	6,889	6,354	5,803
Net Income After Taxes	14,927	13,753	13,269	12,614	11,732
Minority Interest	(513)	(499)	(406)	(425)	(324)
Net Income Before Extra. Items	14,414	13,254	12,863	12,189	11,408
Income (Loss) from Discontinued Operations	(79)	146	(132)	(905)	(177)
Accounting Change	—	—	—	—	—
Net Income Attributable to Wal-Mart Stores, Inc.	14,335	13,400	12,731	11,284	11,231
Income Available to Com Excl ExtraOrd	14,414	13,254	12,863	12,189	11,408
Income Available to Com Incl ExtraOrd	14,335	13,400	12,731	11,284	11,231
Basic Weighted Average Shares	3,866	3,939	4,066	4,164	4,183
Basic EPS Excluding ExtraOrdinary Items	3.73	3.36	3.16	2.93	2.73
Basic EPS Including ExtraOrdinary Items	3.71	3.40	3.13	2.71	2.68
Dilution Adjustment	—	—	—	—	0.00
Diluted Net Income	14,335	13,400	12,731	11,284	11,231
Diluted Weighted Average Shares	3,877	3,951	4,072	4,168	4,188
Diluted EPS Excluding ExtraOrd Items	3.72	3.35	3.16	2.92	2.72
Diluted EPS Including ExtraOrd Items	3.70	3.39	3.13	2.71	2.68
DPS–Common Stock	1	0.950	0.880	0.670	0.60
Gross Dividends–Common Stock	4,271	3,746	3,586	2,802	2,511

Figures from annual income statement. Figures in millions except shares outstanding. Figures in parentheses are losses.

Exhibit 2   Wal-Mart Stores, Inc., Balance Sheet 2006–2010

Year Ended:	1/31/10	1/31/09	1/31/08 *Reclass 1/31/09	1/31/07 *Restated 1/31/08	1/31/06 *Reclass 1/31/07
Cash/Equivalents	$7,907	$7,275	$5,492	$7,767	$6,193
Receivables	4,144	3,905	3,642	2,840	2,575
Inv. Replac. Cost	—	—	—	—	—
LIFO Reserve	—	—	—	—	—
Inventories	33,160	34,511	35,159	33,685	31,910
Prepaid Expenses and Other	2,980	3,063	2,760	2,690	2,468
Recoverable Cost	—	—	—	—	—
Current Assets of Discontinued Operations	140	195	967	—	679
Total Current Assets	**48,331**	**48,949**	**48,020**	**46,982**	**43,825**
Land	22,591	19,852	19,879	18,612	16,174
Building	77,452	73,810	72,141	64,052	55,206
Fixtures	35,450	29,851	28,026	25,168	22,413
Trans. Equipment	2,355	2,307	2,210	1,966	1,744
Depreciation	(38,304)	(32,964)	(28,531)	(24,408)	(20,937)
Net Leases	—	—	—	—	—
Capital Leases	5,669	5,341	5,736	5,392	5,392
Amortization	(2,906)	(2,544)	(2,594)	(2,342)	(2,127)
Goodwill	16,126	15,260	15,879	13,759	12,097
Other Assets	3,942	3,567	2,748	2,406	2,516
Assets Discont.	—	—	—	—	1,884
Total Assets	**170,706**	**163,429**	**163,514**	**151,587**	**138,187**
Commercial Paper	523	1,506	5,040	2,570	3,754
Accounts Payable	30,451	28,849	30,344	28,484	25,101
Accrued Liabilities	18,734	18,112	15,725	14,675	13,274
Accrued Income Taxes	1,365	677	1,000	706	1,340
Cur. Port. LT Debt	4,050	5,848	5,913	5,428	4,595
Cur. Port. Cap Lse	346	315	316	285	284
Short Term Debt	—	—	—	—	—
Current Liabilities of Discontinued Oper	92	83	140	—	477
Total Current Liabilities	**55,561**	**55,390**	**58,478**	**52,148**	**48,825**
Long Term Debt	33,231	31,349	29,799	27,222	26,429
Capital Leases	3,170	3,200	3,603	3,513	3,667
Total Long Term Debt	**36,401**	**34,549**	**33,402**	**30,735**	**30,096**
Liabs. Discont.	—	—	—	—	129
Deferred Income Taxes and Other	5,508	6,014	5,087	4,971	4,501
Noncontrolling Interest	2,180	1,794	1,939	2,160	1,465
Redeemable Noncontrolling Interest	307	397	—	—	—
Total Liabilities	**99,957**	**98,144**	**98,906**	**90,014**	**85,016**
Common Stock	378	393	397	413	417
Paid in Capital	3,803	3,920	3,028	2,834	2,596
Retained Erngs.	66,638	63,660	57,319	55,818	49,105
Other Comprehen.	(70)	(2,688)	3,864	2,508	1,053
Trans. Adjust.	—	—	—	—	—
Total Equity	**70,749**	**65,285**	**64,608**	**61,573**	**53,171**
Total Liabilities & Shareholders' Equity	**170,706**	**163,429**	**163,514**	**151,587**	**138,187**

Exhibit 3   Wal-Mart Stores, Inc., Performance by Segment, 2008–2010

Growth Net Sales

| (Dollar amounts in millions) | Fiscal Years Ended January 31, | | | | | | | |
| | 2010 | | | 2009 | | | 2008 | |
	Net sales	Percent of total	Percent increase	Net sales	Percent of total	Percent increase	Net sales	Percent of total
Walmart U.S.	$258,229	63.8%	1.1%	$255,348	63.7%	6.9%	$238,915	63.9%
International	100,107	24.7%	1.3%	98,840	24.6%	9.1%	90,570	24.2%
Sam's Club	46,710	11.5%	−0.4%	46,899	11.7%	5.8%	44,336	11.9%
Net Sales	$405,046	100.0%	10.0%	$401,087	100.0%	7.3%	$373,821	100.0%

Comparable Store Sales

| | Fiscal Years Ended January 31, | | |
	2010	2009	2008
Walmart U.S.	−0.7%	3.2%	1.0%
Sam's Club	−1.4%	4.9%	4.9%
Total U.S.	−0.8%	3.5%	1.6%

Source: Annual Report

had passed such laws during the Depression to protect local grocers from chains such as the Atlantic & Pacific Company. The laws fixed prices so that local merchants could not be undercut on price. The repeal of these laws freed discounters to offer prices below the manufacturer's suggested retail price.

Among discount retailers, there were both general and specialty chains. General chains carried a wide assortment of hard and soft goods. Specialty retailers, on the other hand, focused on a fairly narrow range of goods such as office products or sporting goods. Specialty discount retailers such as Office Depot, Home Depot, Staples, Best Buy, and Lowe's began to enjoy widespread success in the 1980s. One result of the emergence of both general and specialty discount retailers was the decline of some of the best-known traditional retailers. Moderate-priced general retailers such as Sears and JCPenney had seen their market share decline in response to the rise of discount stores.

A number of factors explained why discount retailers had enjoyed such success at the expense of general old-line retailers. Consumers' greater concern for value, broadly defined, was perhaps most central. Value in the industry was not precisely defined but involved price, service, quality, and convenience. One example of this value orientation

was in apparel. Consumers who once shunned the private-label clothing lines found in discount stores as a source of stigma were increasingly buying labels offered by Kmart, Target, and Wal-Mart. According to one estimate, discount stores were enjoying double-digit growth in apparel while clothing sales in department stores had decreased since the 1990s.

Another aspect of consumers' concern for value involved price. Retail consumers were less reliant on established brand names in a wide variety of goods and showed a greater willingness to purchase the private-label brands of firms such as JCPenney, Sears, Kmart, and Wal-Mart. Convenience had also taken on greater importance for customers. As demographics shifted to include more working mothers and longer workweeks, many American workers placed a greater emphasis on fast, efficient shopping trips. More consumers desired "one-stop shopping" where a broad range of goods were available in one store, to minimize the time they spent shopping. This trend accelerated in the previous decade with the spread of supercenters. Supercenters, which combined traditional discount retail stores with supermarkets under one roof, grew to more than $100 billion in sales by 2001 and blurred some of the traditional lines in retailing.

Larger firms had an advantage in discount retailing. The proportion of retail sales that went to multi-store chains had risen dramatically since the 1970s. The number of retail business failures had risen markedly in the mid-1990s. Most of these failures were individual stores and small chains, but some discount chains such as Venture, Bradlee, and Caldor had filed for bankruptcy. Large size enabled firms to spread their overhead costs over more stores. Larger firms were also able to distribute their advertising costs over a broader base. Perhaps the greatest advantage of size, however, was in relationships with suppliers. Increased size led to savings in negotiating price reductions, but it also helped in other important ways. Suppliers were more likely to engage in arrangements with large store chains such as cooperative advertising and electronic data interchange (EDI) links.

The Internet posed an increasing threat to discount retailers as more people became comfortable with shopping online. By 2008, the number of Internet users had increased dramatically over the nearly 37 million users just over a decade earlier. Some estimates placed the number of Internet users at over 70 percent of the population by 2008. Internet shopping was appealing because of the convenience and selection available, but perhaps the most attractive aspect was the competitive pricing. Some Internet retailers were able to offer steep discounts because of lower overhead costs. Additionally, customers were able to quickly compare prices between different Internet retailers. By 2008, at least most, if not all, major retailers sold goods via the Internet.

Large discount retailers such as Wal-Mart derived considerable purchasing clout with suppliers because of their immense size. Even many of the company's largest suppliers gained a high proportion of their sales from Wal-Mart (see Exhibit 4). Suppliers with over $1 billion in sales such as Newell, Fruit of the Loom, Sunbeam, and Fieldcrest Cannon received over 15 percent of their sales from Wal-Mart. Many of these large manufacturers also sold a

Exhibit 4   Proportion of Sales That Suppliers Receive from Wal-Mart

For better or for worse Company/business	Revenues		Operating Margins*[%]	Price	
	Latest 12 months [$mil]	From Wal- Mart* [%]		12-month change [%]	recent
Newell/housewares, home furnishings	$2,498	15%	20.7%	17%	27½
Fruit of the Loom/apparel	2,478	16	17.0	3	25¼
Rubbermaid/plastic and rubber products	2,329	15	20.3	−10	29
Springs Industries/finished fabrics, home furnishings	2,333	12	10.9	10	43½
Westpoint Stevens/linens, home furnishings	1,651	10	13	43	19½
Sunbeam/household appliances	1,202	31	14.7	−33	16½
Fieldcrest Cannon/linens, home furnishings	1,095	18	9.4	−13	18½
First Brands/household products	1,053	12	15.0	38	51½
Coleman/recreational gear	942	10+	14.7	12	38
Huffy/recreational gear	685	10+	4.6	−11	10½
Roadmaster Industries/recreational gear	675	28	8.0	−37	2½
Paragon Trade Brands/diapers	519	15	12.7	90	25
Playtex Products/personal care products	471	15	28.8	10	8½
Ekco Group/housewares	278	10+	13.6	−2	6½
Royal Appliance Manufacturing/vacuum cleaners	270	23	7.0	−19	3½
Crown Crafts/textiles, home furnishings	214	15	12.3	−34	9½
Armor All Products/polishes, protectants	204	20	20.5	−23	15½
Toastmaster/home appliances	187	30	7.3	−38	4
Windmere/personal care products	185	18	10.6	−4	8
National Presto Industries/home appliances	123	35	19.8	3	42½
Empire of Carolina/toys	119	17	5.5	−11	10
General Housewares/household products	117	18	10.6	−32	9½
Safety 1st/child safety products	70	38	16.9	−50	13½
National Picture & Frame/frames, mirrors	61	36	14.2	−3	9½
Ohio Art/toys	43	20	5.9	48	49

*Based on latest fiscal year disclosure.
Sources: Value line and database services via one sources information service; company disclosures, analysis.

substantial proportion of their output to Kmart, Target, and other discount retailers. Wal-Mart's purchasing clout was considerable, though, even compared to other large retailers. For example, Wal-Mart accounted for over 28 percent of Dial's sales, and it was estimated that it would have double sales to its next seven largest customers to replace the sales made to Wal-Mart.[5] Frequently, smaller manufacturers were even more reliant on the large discount retailers such as Wal-Mart. For example, Wal-Mart accounted for as much as 50 percent of revenues for many smaller suppliers.

Private-label goods offered by discount stores had become much more important in the recent years and presented new challenges in supplier relationships. Managing private labels required a high level of coordination between designers and manufacturers (who were often foreign). Investment in systems that could track production and inventory were also necessary.

Technology investments in sophisticated inventory management systems, state-of-the-art distribution centers, and other aspects of logistics were seen as critically important for all discount retailers. Discount retailers were spending large sums of money on computer and telecommunications technology in order to lower their costs in these areas. The widespread use of Universal Product Codes (UPC) allowed retailers to more accurately track inventories for shopkeeping units (SKUs) and better match inventory to demand. Discount retailers also used EDI to shorten the distribution cycle. EDI involved the electronic transmission of sales and inventory data from the registers and computers of discounters directly to suppliers' computers. Often, replenishment of inventories was triggered without human intervention. Thus, EDI removed the need for several intermediate steps in procurement such as data entry by the discounter, ordering by purchasers, data entry by the supplier, and even some production scheduling by supplier managers. Wal-Mart was also pushing the adoption of radio frequency identification (RFID), a new technology for tracking and identifying products. RFID promised to eliminate the need for employees to scan UPC codes and would also dramatically reduce shrinkage, another term for shoplifting and employee pilferage. Suppliers anticipated that RFID would be costly to implement, but the benefits for Wal-Mart were estimated to be as high as $8 billion in labor savings and $2 billion in reducing shrinkage.

Another important aspect of managing inventory was accurate forecasting. Having the right quantity of products in the correct stores was essential to success. Stories of retailers having an abundance of snow sleds in Florida stores while stores in other areas with heavy snowfall had none were common examples of the challenges in managing inventory. Discounters used variables such as past store sales, the presence of competition, variation in seasonal demand, and year-to-year calendar changes to arrive at their forecasts.

Point-of-sale (POS) scanning enabled retailers to gain information for any purchase on the dollar amount of the purchase, category of merchandise, color, vendor, and SKU number. POS scanning, while valuable in managing inventory, was also seen as a potentially significant marketing tool. Databases of such information offered retailers the potential to "micromarket" to their customers. Upscale department stores had used the POS database marketing more extensively than discounters. Wal-Mart, however, had used such information extensively. For example, POS data showed that customers who purchased children's videos typically bought more than one. Based on this finding, Wal-Mart emphasized placing other children's videos near displays of hot-selling videos.

Competitors

Competition in discount retailing came from both general and specialty discount stores. Among the general discount retailers, Wal-Mart was the largest, followed by Target and Kmart. Kmart had approximately 10 times more sales than the next largest retailers Dollar General and ShopKo. The most formidable specialty discount retailers included office supply chains such as Office Depot with over $15 billion in sales and Staples with approximately $19 billion, Toys "R" Us with over $11 billion, Best Buy in electronics with approximately $40 billion. In warehouse clubs, Costco and Sam's Club dominated. Costco was the leader with over $71 billion in sales in 2007, followed by Sam's Warehouse Club with $44 billion in revenue the same year. BJ's Wholesale Club followed far behind at $9 billion in sales.

Once Wal-Mart's largest competitor, Kmart, had experienced a long slide in performance. Kmart operated approximately 1,300 stores at the beginning of 2010 and had sales of $17.2 billion in 2008, down from $36 billion just six years earlier. Traditionally, Kmart's discount philosophy had differed from Wal-Mart's. Kmart discount centers sought to price close to, but not necessarily lower than, Wal-Mart's everyday low prices (EDLP). More emphasis was placed on sale items at Kmart. Pricing strategy revolved around several key items that were advertised in Kmart's 73 million advertising circulars distributed in newspapers each Sunday. These items were priced sharply lower than competitors' prices. The effective implementation of this strategy had been impeded by Kmart's difficulty in keeping shelves stocked with sale items and by Wal-Mart's willingness to match Kmart's sale prices. An attempt to imitate Wal-Mart's everyday low pricing strategy failed to deliver sales growth; at the same time, it squeezed margins, so Kmart returned to its traditional pricing strategy in 2003.

Performance at Kmart had suffered dramatically in the 1990s. It experienced losses of over $300 million from 1993 to 1995 and by 1995 had seen its debt rating fall below investment grade. Various attempts to revitalize the company had fallen short of restoring profitability. A restructuring that closed over 200 stores in the mid-1990s and shuttered another 600 stores in 2002–2003 did not result in profitability in any year from 2001 to 2004. Sales per square foot dropped to $212 in 2002, which was down from $236 a year earlier. By 2004, there was some indication that all the restructuring might have eventually paid off as Kmart reported profitability in the first three quarters of the year. It was still plagued, however, by declining same-store sales. Some suggested that Kmart's primary goal was to serve as a cash cow for ESL Investments, Inc., and its founder Eddie Lampert. Assisted by $3.8 billion in accumulated tax credits, Kmart had generated over $2 billion in positive cash flow in the first three quarters of 2004. The presumption was cash would be used to fund other investments by ESL.[6] In 2005, Lampert orchestrated the merger of Kmart with the traditional retail icon Sears and became part of Sears Holdings.

Kmart sought to follow Wal-Mart's pattern in many of its activities. The company expressed a commitment to building a strong culture that emphasized performance, teamwork, and respect for individuals who, borrowing from Wal-Mart, were referred to as associates. Establishing such a culture was particularly challenging in the midst of workforce reductions that had taken Kmart from 373,000 employees in 1990 to 307,000 at the end of 1995, and then an even more precipitous drop to 158,000 in 2004. Kmart had also adopted Wal-Mart departmental structure within stores. Another area in which Kmart emulated Wal-Mart was in offering larger income potential to store managers. Each store manager's bonus was linked to an index of customer satisfaction. Kmart had also sought to close the gap between it and Wal-Mart in technology and distribution. The company made large information technology investments in the mid-1990s.

Kmart's strategy focused on three major initiatives. First, it defined itself as "the store of the neighborhood." Ethnic groups such as Asians and African Americans were a particular focus of Kmart's neighborhood strategy. Individual store managers were given greater autonomy to customize their merchandise assortments to suit local community needs. A second emphasis in Kmart's strategy was on exclusive branded products. Its most prominent brands included Martha Stewart in home products, Jaclyn Smith in women's apparel, and Route 66 in men's and women's apparel. The "top sellers" program also focused on improving sales and in-stock positions for each of the store's top 300 selling items. Additionally, with further testing of the "store of the future" prototype, significant improvements in the customer shopping experience were expected. The third prong in Kmart's strategy was to further rationalize its operations. Kmart intended to focus more on higher-performing products and to continue to eliminate under-performing SKUs and reallocate shelf space to more profitable items. The company claimed that it had significantly improved the inventory management practices around forecasting and replenishment that had plagued it so often in the past. These practices were particularly critical to a focus on highly advertised products.

Target, Wal-Mart's other large national competitor, was owned by Target Corporation, formerly Dayton Hudson Corporation, based in Minneapolis, Minnesota. In 2009, Target's 1,752 stores accounted for $65.4 billion in sales and $2.5 billion in profits. Target was considered an "upscale discounter." The median income of Target shoppers was considerably higher than its two main competitors, and 50 percent of its customers had completed college.[7] Target attracted a more affluent clientele through a more trendy and upscale product mix and through a store ambience that differed from most discounters in aspects such as wider aisles and brighter lighting. The company also emphasized design much more in its products and had partnered with a number of designers to develop products across a broad range of apparel and housewares. Target had also introduced a proprietary credit card, the Target Guest Card, to differentiate it from other discounters. The conventional wisdom in the industry suggested that pricing at Target was generally not as low as Wal-Mart but was lower than middle-market department stores such as JCPenney and Mervyn's. As with Wal-Mart and Kmart, supercenters were also high on Target's list of strategic priorities. The supercenters, named Super Targets, had opened in many cities and the company planned to aggressively grow in this area. Promotions were an important part of Target's marketing approach. Each week, over 100 million Target advertising circulars were distributed in Sunday newspapers. Holiday promotions were also emphasized at Target. Like Kmart, Target had traditionally focused much of its effort on metropolitan areas. Early in the decade, over half of its stores were in 30 metropolitan markets. Target's philanthropic activities gave it greater visibility. Each year, the company gave 5 percent of its pretax earnings to not-for-profit organizations. St. Jude Children's Research Hospital and local schools were perhaps Target's highest philanthropic priorities.

Wal-Mart's History

Wal-Mart was started in 1962 by Sam Walton. The discount retail industry was then in its infancy. A couple of regional firms had experimented with discount retailing, but that year three major retail firms joined Wal-Mart in entering the discount industry. Kresge Corporation started Kmart, Dayton Hudson began Target, and the venerable F. W. Woolworth initiated Woolco. Sam Walton had been the most successful franchisee in the Ben Franklin variety store chain, but discount stores threatened the success of his 18 stores. Walton was convinced that discount retailing would have a bright future even though most in the industry were highly skeptical of the concept. Indeed, Walton was quickly rebuffed in his efforts to convince Ben Franklin and others to provide financial backing for his proposed venture into discounting. With no major chains willing to back him, Walton risked his home and all his property to secure financing for the first Wal-Mart in Rogers, Arkansas.

Of the four new ventures in discount retailing started that year, Wal-Mart seemed the least likely to succeed. Most Wal-Mart stores were in northwestern Arkansas and adjacent areas of Oklahoma, Missouri, and Kansas. Walton had started his retailing career with Ben Franklin in small towns because his wife Helen did not want to live in any city with a population of over 10,000 people. He had chosen northwestern Arkansas as a base because it allowed him to take advantage of the quail-hunting season in four states. Wal-Mart was, in Sam Walton's words, "underfinanced and undercapitalized"[8] in the beginning. Nevertheless, Walton sought to grow Wal-Mart as fast as he could, because he feared new competitors would preempt growth opportunities if Wal-Mart did not open stores in new towns. After five years, Wal-Mart had 19 stores and sales of $9 million. In contrast, Kmart had 250 stores and $800 million in sales.

Walton retained many of the practices regarding customer service and satisfaction that he had learned in the variety stores business. The central focus of Wal-Mart, however, was on price. Walton sought to make Wal-Mart the low-priced provider of any product it sold. As Walton said,

> What we were obsessed with was keeping our prices below everybody else's. Our dedication to that idea was total. Everybody worked like crazy to keep the expenses down. We didn't have systems. We didn't have ordering programs. We didn't have a basic merchandise assortment. We certainly didn't have any sort of computers. In fact, when I look at it today, I realize that so much of what we did in the beginning was really poorly done. But we managed to sell our merchandise as low as we possibly could and that kept us right-side up for the first ten years. . . . The idea was simple: when customers thought of Wal-Mart, they should think of low prices and satisfaction guaranteed. They could be pretty sure they wouldn't find it any cheaper anywhere else, and if they didn't like it, they could bring it back.[9]

By 1970, Wal-Mart had expanded to 30 stores in the small towns of Arkansas, Missouri, and Oklahoma. Sam Walton, however, was personally several million dollars in debt. For Wal-Mart to expand beyond its small region required an infusion of capital beyond what the Walton family could provide. Walton thus decided to offer Wal-Mart stock publicly. The initial public offering yielded nearly $5 million in capital. By the early 1990s, 100 shares of that initial stock offering would increase in value from $1,650 to over $3,000,000.

The other problem that plagued Wal-Mart in its early years was finding a way to keep its costs down. Large vendors were reluctant to call on Wal-Mart and, when they did do business with the company, they would dictate the price and quantity of what they sold. Walton described the situation as, "I don't mind saying that we were the victims of a good bit of arrogance from a lot of vendors in those days. They didn't need us, and they acted that way."[10] Another problem that contributed to high costs was distribution. Distributors did not service Wal-Mart with the same care that they did its larger competitors. Walton saw that "the only alternative was to build our own warehouse so we could buy in volume at attractive prices and store the merchandise."[11]

Wal-Mart increased from 32 stores in 1970 to 859 stores 15 years later. For much of that time, Wal-Mart retained its small-town focus. Over half its stores were in towns with populations of under 25,000. Because of its small-town operations, Wal-Mart was not highly visible to many others in the retail industry. By 1985, though, that had changed. *Forbes* named Sam Walton the richest man in America. Furthermore, Wal-Mart had begun to expand from its small-town base in the South and had established a strong presence in several large cities. By the 1990s, it had spread throughout the United States in both large cities and small towns.

Wal-Mart in 2010

By the beginning of 2010, Wal-Mart's activities had spread beyond its historical roots in domestic discount centers. The number of domestic discount centers had declined to 750 from a high 1,995 in 1996. Many discount centers had been converted to supercenters, which had increased by approximately six times in the previous 10 years, to 2,843 stores. Wal-Mart Supercenters combined full-line supermarkets and discount centers into one store. Wal-Mart also operated 607 Sam's Clubs, which were warehouse membership clubs. In 1999, Wal-Mart opened its first Neighborhood Markets, which were supermarkets, and it had 181 in operation by 2010.

Operations

From its beginning, Wal-Mart had focused on EDLP. EDLP saved on advertising costs and on labor costs since employees did not have to rearrange stock before and after sales. The company changed its traditional slogan, "Always the Lowest Price," in the 1990s to "Always Low Prices. *Always.*" In late 2007, Wal-Mart changed its tagline to "Save Money, Live Better." Despite the changes in slogan, however, Wal-Mart continued to price goods lower than its competitors (see Exhibit 5). When faced with a decline in profits in the late 1990s, Wal-Mart considered raising margins.[12] Instead of pricing 7 to 8 percent below competitors, some managers believed that pricing only about 6 percent below would raise gross margins without jeopardizing sales. Some managers and board members, however, were skeptical that price hikes would work at Wal-Mart. They reasoned that Wal-Mart's culture and identity were so closely attached to low prices that broad price increases would clash with the company's bedrock beliefs. Another concern was that competitors might seize any opportunity to narrow the gap with Wal-Mart. While the reason was unclear, it appeared that some narrowing on price was occurring by 2008. One study showed that the price gap between Wal-Mart and Kroger had shrunk to 7.5 percent in 2007 from 15 percent a few years earlier.[13] Some analysts worried that many shoppers would switch to other retailers as the gap narrowed.

Wal-Mart's low prices were at least partly due to its aggressive use of technology. Wal-Mart had pioneered the use of technology in retail operations for many years and still possessed significant advantages over its competitors. It was the leader in forging EDI links with suppliers. Its Retail Link technology gave over 3,200 vendors POS data and authorization to replace inventory for over 3,000 stores.[14] The fine-tuning of its Retail Link system allowed Wal-Mart to reduce inventory by 25 percent of SKUs while

Exhibit 5   Comparison of Prices at Wal-Mart, Kmart, and Target, Nov. 2008

Item	Wal-Mart	Kmart	Target
Oral B Pulsar ProHealth Toothbrush	5.97	6.19	4.74
Crest ProHealth Toothpaste 6 oz	3.62	3.99	3.79
Pantene Pro V 2-in-1 25.4 oz	5.88	7.79	5.29
Head & Shoulders Classic 14.2 oz	4.72	5.49	4.89
Edge Shave Gel 7 oz	2.27	2.79	1.89
Schick Extreme 3 8 pk	9.97	11.99	9.99
Gillette Mach 3 Disposable 3 pk	6.12	6.99	5.59
1-a-Day Women's Vitamins 100 tab	6.87	8.49	6.89
1-a-Day Energy Vitamins 50 tab	7.87	8.49	6.89
Bausch & Lomb ReNu	6.97	8.29	6.19
Advil Liquigel 40 tablets	6.48	7.29	5.34
Prestone Extended Life Antifreeze 1 gal	9.00	14.49	9.04
Penzoil Motor Oil 5W-30 1 qt	3.57	3.49	3.29
Armour All Glass Wipes 25	4.24	4.29	4.24
TopFlite D2 Straight Golf Balls 15	14.95	15.99	14.99
Perfect Pullup	77.00	99.99	99.99
Coleman Quickbed Queen	19.88	24.99	24.99
Crayola Colored Pencils 12 ct	1.88	2.59	1.99
Scott Double-Sided Tape	2.97	3.19	2.99

Some prices are sale prices.

still increasing sales in the mid-1990s. Competitors traditionally faced high costs in developing a proprietary EDI system to rival Wal-Mart's. Connecting seamlessly with a large number of suppliers was a daunting task given the complexity and cost of dealing with a large variety of computer and information systems. A recent trend, however, was the emergence of intermediaries who provided EDI links between purchasers and suppliers. With the intermediaries, retailers could simply send all their EDI data to one source, and various manufacturers could also reduce their difficulties in connecting with a large number of buyers by using one intermediary for transactions with many customers. Such intermediaries also made EDI a more feasible alternative for smaller retailers, who lacked the scale necessary to implement their own EDI systems. In August 2002, Wal-Mart informed suppliers that they would be required to do EDI exchanges over the Internet using AS2, a software package from Isoft Corp. Competitors had responded to Wal-Mart's advantage in logistics and EDI by forming cooperative exchanges, but, despite their efforts, a large gap remained between Wal-Mart and its competitors.[15] As a result, Wal-Mart possessed a substantial advantage in information about supply and demand, which reduced both the number of items that were either overstocked or out of stock.

November 2003 was also notable for another Wal-Mart technological initiative. It announced plans to implement RFID to all products by January 2005, a goal that had still not been realized by 2010. RFID, as its name implies, involves the use of tags that transmit radio signals. It had the potential to track inventory more precisely than traditional methods and to eventually reduce much of the labor involved in activities such as manually scanning bar codes for incoming goods. Some analysts estimated that Wal-Mart's cost savings from RFID could run as high $8 billion.[16] Some information technology observers suggested that Wal-Mart had only experienced lukewarm results from RFID as many suppliers struggled to comply with the company's demands. Wal-Mart focused its RFID implementation efforts on tagging pallets for Sam's Club stores and promotional displays in Wal-Marts. Reportedly, some Sam's Club suppliers were warned they would be assessed a stiff fine for every pallet that was not tagged with RFID, but by 2009 the fines had been reduced to just 12 cents a pallett.

Technology was only one area where Wal-Mart exploited advantages through its relationships with suppliers. Wal-Mart's clout was clearly evident in the payment terms it had with its suppliers. Suppliers frequently offered 2 percent discounts to customers who paid their bills within 15 days. Wal-Mart typically paid its bills at close to 30 days from the time of purchase but still usually received a 2 percent discount on the gross amount of an invoice rather than the net amount.[17] Several suppliers had attributed performance problems to Wal-Mart's actions. Rubbermaid, for example, experienced higher raw materials costs in the 1990s that Wal-Mart did not allow it to pass along in the form of higher prices. At the same time, Wal-Mart gave more shelf space to Rubbermaid's lower-cost competitors. As a result, Rubbermaid's profits dropped by 30 percent and it was forced to cut its workforce by over 1,000 employees.[18] Besides pushing for low prices, the large discounters also required suppliers to pick up an increasing amount of inventory and merchandising costs. Wal-Mart required large suppliers such as Procter & Gamble to place large contingents of employees at its Bentonville, Arkansas, headquarters in order to service its account.

Although several companies such as Rubbermaid and the pickle vendor Vlasic had experienced dramatic downfalls largely through being squeezed by Wal-Mart, other companies suggested that their relationship with Wal-Mart had made them much more efficient.[19] Some critics suggested, however, that these extreme efficiency pressures had driven many suppliers to move production from the United States to nations such as China that had much lower wages. Wal-Mart set standards for all of its suppliers in areas such as child labor and safety. A 2001 audit, however, revealed that as many as one-third of Wal-Mart's international suppliers were in "serious violation" of the standards.[20] Wal-Mart pursued steps to help suppliers address the violations, but it was unclear how successful these efforts were.

A *Fast Company* article on Wal-Mart interviewed several former suppliers of the company and concluded that "To a person, all those interviewed credit Wal-Mart with a fundamental integrity in its dealings that's unusual in the world of consumer goods, retailing, and groceries. Wal-Mart does not cheat its suppliers, it keeps its word, it pays its bills briskly. 'They are tough people but very honest; they treat you honestly,' says Peter Campanella, a former Corning manager."[21]

At the heart of Wal-Mart's success was its distribution system. To a large extent, it had been born out of the necessity of servicing so many stores in small towns while trying to maintain low prices. Wal-Mart used distribution centers to achieve efficiencies in logistics. Initially, distribution centers were large facilities—the first were 72,000 square feet—that served 80–100 Wal-Mart stores within a 250-mile radius. Newer distribution centers were considerably larger than the early ones and in some cases served a wider geographical radius. Over 85 percent of Wal-Mart's products were distributed through distribution centers, in contrast to only 50 percent for Kmart. As a result, Wal-Mart had far more distribution centers than any of its competitors. Cross-docking was a particularly important practice of these centers.[22] In cross-docking, goods were delivered to distribution centers and often simply loaded from one dock to another or even from one truck to another without ever sitting in inventory. Cross-docking reduced Wal-Mart's cost of sales by 2 to 3 percent compared to competitors. Cross-docking was receiving a great deal of attention among retailers with most attempting to implement it for a greater proportion of goods. It was extremely difficult to manage, however, because of the close coordination and timing required between the store, manufacturer, and warehouse. As one supplier noted, "Everyone from the forklift driver on up to me, the CEO, knew we had to deliver on time. Not 10 minutes late. And not 45 minutes early, either . . . . The message came through clearly: You have this 30-second delivery window. Either you're there or you're out."[23] Because of the close coordination needed, cross-docking required an information system that effectively linked stores, warehouses, and manufacturers. Most major retailers were finding it difficult to duplicate Wal-Mart's success at cross-docking.

Wal-Mart's focus on logistics manifested itself in other ways. Before 2006, the company essentially employed two distribution networks, one for general merchandise and one for groceries. The company created High Velocity Distribution Centers in 2006 that distributed both grocery and general merchandise goods that needed more frequent replenishment. Wal-Mart's logistics system also included a fleet of over 2,000 company-owned trucks. It was able to routinely ship goods from distribution centers to stores within 48 hours of receiving an order. Store shelves were replenished twice a week on average in contrast to the industry average of once every two weeks.[24]

Wal-Mart stores typically included many departments in areas such as soft goods/domestics, hard goods, stationery and candy, pharmaceuticals, records and electronics, sporting goods, toys, shoes, and jewelry. The selection of products varied from one region to another. Department managers and in some cases associates (or employees) had the authority to change prices in response to competitors. This was in stark contrast to the traditional practice of many chains where prices were centrally set at a company's headquarters. Wal-Mart's use of technology was particularly useful in determining the mix of goods in each store. The company used historical selling data and complex models that included many variables such as local demographics to decide what items should be placed in each store.

Unlike many of its competitors, Wal-Mart had no regional offices until 2006. Instead, regional vice presidents maintained their offices at company headquarters in Bentonville, Arkansas. The absence of regional offices was estimated to save Wal-Mart as much as 1 percent of sales. Regional managers visited stores from Monday to Thursday of each week. Each Saturday at 7:30 A.M., regional vice presidents and a few hundred other managers and employees met with the firm's top managers to discuss the previous week's results and discuss different directions for the next week. Regional managers then conveyed information from the meeting to managers in the field via the videoconferencing links that were present in each store. In 2006, Wal-Mart shifted this policy by requiring many of its 27 regional managers to live in the areas they supervised.

Aside from Wal-Mart's impact on suppliers, it was frequently criticized for its employment practices, which critics characterized as being low in both wages and benefits. Charles Fishman acknowledged that Wal-Mart saved customers $30 billion on groceries alone and possibly as much as $150 billion overall when its effect on competitor pricing was considered, but he estimated that while Wal-Mart created 125,000 jobs in 2005, it destroyed 127,500.[25] Others agreed that Wal-Mart's employment and supplier practices resulted in negative externalities on employees, communities, and taxpayers. Harvard professor Pankaj Ghemawat responded to Fishman by calculating that—based on Fishman's numbers—Wal-Mart created customer savings ranging from $12 million to $60 million for each job lost.[26] He also argued that, since Wal-Mart operated more heavily in lower-income areas of the poorest one-third of United States, low-income customers were much more likely to benefit from Wal-Mart's lower prices. Another criticism of Wal-Mart was that it consistently drove small local retailers out of business when it introduced new stores in small towns and that employees in such rural areas were increasingly at the mercy of Wal-Mart, essentially redistributing wealth from these areas to Bentonville. Jack and Suzy Welch defended Wal-Mart by pointing out that employees in these areas were better off after a Wal-Mart opened:

> In most small towns the storeowner drove the best car, lived in the fanciest house, and belonged to the country club. Meanwhile, employees weren't exactly sharing the wealth. They rarely had life insurance or health benefits and certainly did not receive much in the way of training or big salaries. And few of these storeowners had plans for growth or expansion. . . a killer for employees seeking life-changing careers.[27]

Sam's Club

A notable exception to Wal-Mart's dominance in discount retailing was in the warehouse club segment. Despite significant

Exhibit 6   Costco Versus Sam's Club

	Costco	Sam's Club
Year founded	1983	1983
U.S. revenues (year ended Aug. 31, 2003)	$34.4 billion	$32.9 billion (est.)
Presidents (or equivalents, since founding)	one	seven
Membership cardholders	42 million	46 million
Members' average salary	$95,333	N.A.
Annual membership fees	$45	$30–35
Average transaction	$94	$78
Average sales per square foot	$797	$497
Starting hourly wage	$10	N.A.
Employee turnover per year	23%	45% (Wal-Mart)
Private label (as % of sales)	15%	10%

Source: Heylar, John. "The only company Wal-Mart fears." *Fortune*, November 24, 2003.

efforts by Wal-Mart's Sam's Club, Costco was the established leader. Sam's Club had far more stores than Costco—607 to 425—yet, Costco still reported far more sales—$71.4 billion versus $47 billion. Costco stores averaged considerably more revenue per store than Sam's Club (see Exhibit 6).

To the casual observer, Costco and Sam's Clubs appeared to be very similar. Both charged small membership fees, and both were "warehouse" stores that sold goods from pallets. The goods were often packaged or bundled into larger quantities than typical retailers offered. Beneath these similarities, however, were important differences. Costco focused on more upscale small business owners and consumers while Sam's, following Wal-Mart's pattern, had positioned itself more to the mass middle market. Relative to Costco, Sam's was also concentrated more in smaller cities.

Consistent with its more upscale strategy, Costco stocked more luxury and premium-branded items than Sam's Club had traditionally done. This changed somewhat when Sam's began to stock more high-end merchandise after the 1990s, but some questioned whether or not its typical customers demanded such items. A Costco executive pointed to the differences between Costco and Sam's customers by describing a scene where a Sam's customer responded to a $39 price on a Ralph Lauren Polo shirt by saying, "Can you imagine? Who in their right mind would buy a T-shirt for $39?" Despite the focus on pricier goods, Costco still focused intensely on managing costs and keeping prices down. Costco set a goal of 10 percent margins and capped markups at 14 percent (compared to the usual 40 percent markup by department stores). Managers were discouraged from exceeding the margin goals.

Some analysts claimed that Sam's Club's lackluster performance was a result of a copycat strategy. Costco was the first of the two competitors to sell fresh meat, produce, and gasoline and to introduce a premium private label for many goods. In each case, Sam's followed suit two to four years later.

> *"By looking at what Costco did and trying to emulate it, Sam's didn't carve out its own unique strategy," says Michael Clayman, editor of the trade newsletter Warehouse Club Focus. And at least one of the "me too" moves made things worse. Soon after Costco and Price Club merged in 1993, Sam's bulked up by purchasing Pace warehouse clubs from Kmart. Many of the 91 stores were marginal operations in marginal locations. Analysts say that Sam's Club management became distracted as it tried to integrate the Pace stores into its system.[28]*

To close the gap against Costco, Wal-Mart in 2003 started to integrate the activities of Sam's Club and Wal-Mart more. Buyers for the two coordinated their efforts to get better prices from suppliers.

Culture

Perhaps the most distinctive aspect of Wal-Mart was its culture. To a large extent, Wal-Mart's culture was an extension of Sam Walton's philosophy and was rooted in the early experiences and practices of Wal-Mart. The Wal-Mart culture emphasized values such as thriftiness, hard work, innovation, and continuous improvement. As Sam Walton wrote,

> *Because wherever we've been, we've always tried to instill in our folks the idea that we at Wal-Mart have our own way of doing things. It may be different and it may take some folks a while to adjust to it at first. But it's straight and honest and basically pretty*

simple to figure it out if you want to. And whether or not other folks want to accommodate us, we pretty much stick to what we believe in because it's proven to be very, very successful.[29]

Wal-Mart's thriftiness was consistent with its obsession with controlling costs. One observer joked that "the Wal-Mart folks stay at Mo 3, where they don't even leave the light on for you."[30] This was not, however, far from the truth. Sam Walton told of early buying trips to New York where several Wal-Mart managers shared the same hotel room and walked everywhere they went rather than use taxis. One of the early managers described how these early trips taught managers to work hard and keep costs low:

> *From the very beginning, Sam was always trying to instill in us that you just didn't go to New York and roll with the flow. We always walked everywhere. We never took cabs. And Sam had an equation for the trips: expenses should never exceed 1 percent of our purchases, so we would all crowd in these little hotel rooms somewhere down around Madison Square Garden. . . . We never finished up until about twelve-thirty at night, and we'd all go out for a beer except Mr. Walton. He'd say, "I'll meet you at breakfast at six o'clock." And we'd say, "Mr. Walton, there's no reason to meet that early. We can't even get into the buildings that early." And he'd just say, "We'll find something to do."*[31]

The roots of Wal-Mart's emphasis on innovation and continuous improvement can also be seen in Sam Walton's example. Walton's drive for achievement was evident early in life. He achieved the rank of Eagle Scout earlier than anyone previously had in the state of Missouri. Later, in high school, he quarterbacked the undefeated state champion football team and played guard on the undefeated state champion basketball team while serving as student body president. This same drive was evident in Walton's early retailing efforts. He studied other retailers by spending time in their stores, asking endless questions, and taking notes about various store practices. Walton was quick to borrow a new idea if he thought it would increase sales and profits. When, in his early days at Ben Franklin, Walton read about two variety stores in Minnesota that were using self-service, he immediately took an all-night bus ride to visit the stores. Upon his return from Minnesota, he converted one of his stores to self-service, which, at the time, was only the third variety store in the United States to do so. Later, he was one of the first to see the potential of discount retailing.

Walton also emphasized always looking for ways to improve. Wal-Mart managers were encouraged to critique their own operations. Managers met regularly to discuss their store operations. Lessons learned in one store were quickly spread to other stores. Wal-Mart managers also carefully analyzed the activities of their competitors and tried to borrow practices that worked well. Sam Walton stressed the importance of observing what other firms did well rather than what they did wrong. Another way in which Wal-Mart had focused on improvement from its earliest days was in information and measurement. Long before Wal-Mart had any computers, Sam Walton would personally enter measures on several variables for each store into a ledger he carried with him. Information technology enabled Wal-Mart to extend this emphasis on information and measurement.

International Operations

Wal-Mart's entry into the international retail arena had been somewhat recent. As late as 1992, Wal-Mart's entire international operations consisted of only 162,535 square feet of retail space in Mexico. Although it was the company's fastest-growing division—going from about $59 billion in sales in 2006 to over $100 billion in 2010—Wal-Mart's performance in international markets had been mixed or as *Forbes* put it, "Overseas, Wal-Mart has won some—and lost a lot."[32] Over 80 percent of Wal-Mart's international revenue came from only three countries: Canada, Mexico, and the United Kingdom.

Wal-Mart had tried a variety of approaches and faced a diverse set of challenges in the different countries they entered. Entry into international markets had ranged from greenfield development to franchising, joint ventures, and acquisitions. Each country that Wal-Mart had entered had presented new and unique challenges. In China, Wal-Mart had to deal with a backward supply chain. It had to negotiate a Japanese environment that was hostile to large chains and protective of its small retailers. Strong foreign competitors were the problem in Brazil and Argentina. Labor unions had plagued Wal-Mart's entry into Germany along with unforeseen difficulties in integrating acquisitions. Mistakes in choosing store locations had hampered the company in South Korea and Hong Kong.

Wal-Mart approached international operations with much the same philosophy they had used in the United States. "We're still very young at this, we're still learning,"[33] stated John Menzer, chief executive of Wal-Mart International. Menzer's approach was to have country presidents make decisions. His thinking was that it would facilitate the faster implementation of decisions. Each country president made decisions regarding his own sourcing, merchandising, and real estate. Menzer concluded, "Over time all you really have is speed. I think that's our most important asset."[34]

In most countries, entrenched competitors responded vigorously to Wal-Mart's entry. For example, Tesco, the United Kingdom's biggest grocer, responded by opening supercenters. In China, Lianhua and Huilan, the two largest retailers, merged in 2003 into one state-owned entity named the Bailan Group. Wal-Mart was also not alone among major international retailers in seeking new growth in South America and Asia. One international competitor, the French retailer Carrefour, was already the leading retailer in Brazil and Argentina. Carrefour expanded into China in the late 1990s with a hypermarket in Shanghai. In Asia, Makro, a Dutch wholesale club retailer, was the regional leader. Both of the European firms were viewed as able, experienced competitors. The Japanese retailer, Yaohan, moved its headquarters from Tokyo to Hong Kong with the aim of becoming the world's largest retailer. Helped by the close relationship between Chairman Kazuo Wada and Mao's successor Deng Xiaoping, Yaohan was the first foreign retail firm to receive a license to operate in China and planned to open over 1,000 stores there. Like Wal-Mart, these international firms were motivated to expand internationally by slowing down growth in their own domestic markets. Some analysts feared that the pace of expansion by these major retailers was faster than the rate of growth in the market and could result in a price war. Like Wal-Mart, these competitors had also found difficulty in moving into international markets and adapting to local differences. Both Carrefour and Makro had experienced visible failures in their international efforts. Folkert Schukken, chairman of Makro, noted this challenge: "We have trouble selling the same toilet paper in Belgium and Holland." The chairman of Carrefour, Daniel Bernard, agreed, "If people think that going international is a solution to their problems at home, they will learn by spilling their blood. Global retailing demands a huge investment and gives no guarantee of a return."[35]

Wal-Mart planned for aggressive growth in its international operations for 2011. The company planned to add more than 600 units during 2011. Most of the new stores were projected to be organic growth rather than acquisitions. The company anticipated approximately $13–15 billion in new investment in 2011 with 33 percent of it focusing on international growth. In 2010, 31 percent of Wal-Mart's capital expenditures were spent on international operations.

Looking Ahead

Wal-Mart CEO Mike Duke, who had only recently succeeded Lee Scott Jr. as the top executive at Wal-Mart, faced the daunting challenge of achieving the company's expected growth rates despite its enormous size. A 5 percent organic growth rate would require the firm to add the equivalent of a firm ranking 125 in the *Fortune* 500 each year. Could Wal-Mart deliver that kind of growth in metropolitan markets with innovative new formats and by accelerating growth internationally? Or would the company need to either make a more dramatic strategy change or adjust its aspirations?

End Notes

1. Standard and Poor's Industry Surveys. *Retailing*, February 1998.
2. Upbin, B. "Wall-to-wall Wal-Mart." *Forbes*, April 12, 2004.
3. Nordlinger, J. (2004). "The new colossus: Wal-Mart is America's store, and the world's and its enemies are sadly behind." *National Review*, April 19, 2004.
4. Ibid.
5. Fishman, C. (2003). "The Wal-Mart you don't know." *Fast Company*, December 2003.
6. Berner, R. (2004). "The next Warren Buffett?" *BusinessWeek*, November 22, 2004.
7. Standard and Poor's Industry Surveys. (1998). *Retailing: General*, February 5, 1998.
8. Walton, S. (with J. Huey). (1993). *Sam Walton: Made in America*. New York: Doubleday, p. 63.
9. Ibid., pp. 64–65. 10. Ibid., p. 66.
10. Ibid., p. 66.
11. (1982). *Forbes*, August 16, p. 43.
12. Pulliam, S. (1996). "Wal-Mart considers raising prices, drawing praise from analysts, but concern from board." *Wall Street Journal*, March 8, 1996, p. C2.
13. Bianco, A. (2007). "Wal-Mart's midlife crisis." *BusinessWeek*, April 30, 2007.
14. Standard and Poor's Industry Surveys. (1998). *Retailing: General*, February 5, 1998.
15. Useem, J. (2003). "America's most admired companies." *Fortune*, February 18, 2003.
16. Boyle, M. (2003). *Fortune*, November 10, 2003, p. 46.

17. Schifrin, M. (1996). "The big squeeze." *Forbes*, March 11, 1996.
18. Ibid.
19. Fishman, C. (2003). "The Wal-Mart you don't know." *Fast Company*, December 2003.
20. Wal-Mart Web site.
21. Fishman, C. (2003). "The Wal-Mart you don't know." *Fast Company*, December 2003, p. 73.
22. Stalk, G., P. Evans, and L. E. Schulman. (1992). "Competing on capabilities: The new rules of corporate strategy." *Harvard Business Review*, March/April 1992, pp. 57–58.
23. Fishman, C. (2003). "The Wal-Mart you don't know." *Fast Company*, December 2003, p. 73.
24. Stalk G., P. Evans, and L. E. Schulman. (1992). "Competing on capabilities: The new rules of corporate strategy." *Harvard Business Review*, March/April 1992, pp. 57–58.
25. Fishman, C. (2006). "Wal-Mart and the decent society: Who knew that shopping was so important." *Academy of Management Perspectives*, August 2006.
26. Ghemawat, P. (2006). "Business, society, and the 'Wal-Mart effect." *Academy of Management Perspectives*, August 2006.
27. Welch, J., and S. Welch. (2006). "What's right about Wal-Mart." *BusinessWeek*, May 1, 2006, p. 112.
28. Helyar, J. (2003). "The only company Wal-Mart fears." *Fortune*, November 24, 2003, p. 158.
29. Walton, S. (with J. Huey). (1993). *Sam Walton: Made in America*. New York: Doubleday, p. 85.
30. Loeb, M. (1994). "Editor's desk: The secret of two successes." *Fortune*, May 2, 1994.
31. Walton, S. (with J. Huey). (1993). *Sam Walton: Made in America*. New York: Doubleday, p. 84.
32. Upbin, B. (2004). "Wall-to-wall Wal-Mart." *Forbes*, April 12, 2004.
33. Ibid.
34. Ibid.
35. Rapoport, C. (1995). "Retailers go global." *Fortune*, February 20, 1995.

Case 1-3: Harlequin Enterprises: The Mira Decision*[1]

IVEY | Ivey Publishing

Richard Ivey School of Business
The University of Western Ontario

During June 1993, Harlequin management was deciding whether or not to launch MIRA, a new line of single-title women's fiction novels. With the increased popularity of single-title women's fiction, Harlequin's leading position as the world's largest romance publisher was being threatened. While Harlequin was the dominant and very profitable producer of *series* romance novels, research indicated that many customers were reading as many *single-title* romance and women's fiction books as series romances. Facing a steady loss of share in a growing total women's fiction market, Harlequin convened a task force in December 1992 to study the possibility of relaunching a single-title women's fiction program. Donna Hayes, vice-president of direct marketing, stated:

> Industry trends reveal that demand for single-title women's fiction continues to grow while demand for series romance remains stable. Our strengths lie in series romance... by any account, launching MIRA (single-title) will still be a challenge for us. How do we successfully launch a single-title women's fiction program?

Tentatively named "MIRA," Harlequin's proposed single-title program would focus exclusively on women's

* Ken Mark prepared this case under the supervision of Professors Rod White and Mary Crossan solely to provide material for class discussion. The authors do not intend to illustrate either effective or ineffective handling of a managerial situation. The authors may have disguised certain names and other identifying information to protect confidentiality.

Ivey Management Services prohibits any form of reproduction, storage or transmittal without its written permission. This material is not covered under authorization from CanCopy or any reproduction rights organization. To order copies or request permission to reproduce materials, contact Ivey Publishing, Ivey Management Services, c/o Richard Ivey School of Business, The University of Western Ontario, London, Ontario, Canada, N6A 3K7; phone (519) 661-3208; fax (519) 661-3882; e-mail cases@ivey.uwo.ca. One-time permission to reproduce granted by Ivey Management Services on February 9, 2007.

fiction. Management hoped MIRA's launch would provide the opportunity to continue Harlequin's history of strong revenue growth.

Hayes, leader of the MIRA team, knew this was a significant decision for Harlequin. Several years earlier an attempt at single-title publishing—Worldwide Library—had failed. Before going to her executive group for approval, Hayes thought about the decisions the company faced if it wished to enter single-title women's fiction publishing: What were the growth and profitability implications if Harlequin broadened its scope from series romance to single-title women's fiction? What fundamental changes would have to be made to Harlequin's current business model? Did the company have the necessary resources and capabilities to succeed in this new arena? If the company proceeds, how should it go about launching MIRA?

The Publishing Industry[2]

Apart from educational material, traditional single-title book publishing was typically a high-risk venture. Each book was a new product with all the risks attendant on any new product introduction. The risks varied with the author's reputation, the subject matter, and thus the predictability of the market's response. Among the numerous decisions facing the publisher were selecting manuscripts out of the thousands submitted each year, deciding how many copies to print, and deciding how to promote the book.

Insiders judged one key to success in publishing was the creative genius needed to identify good young authors among the hundreds of would-be writers, and then publish and develop them through their careers. Years ago, Sol Stein of Stein and Day Publishers had commented, "Most successful publishers are creative editors at heart and contribute more than risk capital and marketing expertise to the books they publish. If a publisher does not add value to what he publishes, he's a printer, not a publisher."

Traditional single-title publishers allowed distributors 50 percent margins (from which the retailer's margin would come).[3] Some other typical costs included royalty payments of more than 12 percent, warehouse and handling costs of 4 percent, and selling expenses at 5.5 percent. Advertising generally required 6 percent and printing costs[4] required another 12 percent. The remainder was earnings before indirect overhead. Typically, indirect overhead accounted for two percent of the retail price of a book. Because of author advances, pre-publication, promotion, and fixed costs of printing, break-even volumes were significant. And if the publisher failed to sell enough books, the losses could be substantial. Harlequin's core business, series romance fiction, was significantly different from traditional single-title publishing.

Harlequin Enterprises Limited

The word *romance* and the name Harlequin had become synonymous over the last half-century. Founded in 1949, Harlequin began applying its revolutionary approach to publishing—a packaged, consumer-goods strategy—in 1968 shortly after acquiring the publishing business of U.K.-based Mills & Boon. Each book was part of an identifiable product line, consistently delivering the expected benefit to the consumer. With a growth rate of 25 percent per year during the 1970s, Harlequin became the world's largest publisher of women's series romance fiction. It was during this time that Torstar, a newspaper publisher, acquired all of Harlequin Enterprises Ltd.

Over the years, many book publishers had attempted to enter Harlequin's segment of the industry. All had eventually withdrawn. Only once had Harlequin's dominance in series romance fiction been seriously challenged. The "romance wars" began in 1980 when Harlequin took over U.S. distribution of its series products from Simon & Schuster (S&S), a large single-title publisher with established paperback distribution. Subsequently, S&S began publishing series romance fiction under the Silhouette imprint. After several years, a truce was negotiated between Harlequin and S&S. Harlequin acquired Silhouette, S&S's series romance business, and S&S got a 20-year deal as Harlequin's sole U.S. distributor for series fiction.

During the late 1980s and early 1990s, growth in the series market slowed. Harlequin was able to maintain revenues by publishing longer and more expensive series products and generally raising prices. However, as shown in Exhibit 1, global unit volume was no longer growing.

Harlequin's Target Market and Products

Harlequin books were sold in more than 100 international markets in more than 23 languages around the world. Along with romance fiction, Harlequin participated in the series mystery and male action-adventure markets under its Worldwide Library and Gold Eagle imprints. Harlequin had an estimated 20 million readers in North America and 50 million readers around the world.

With a median age of 41, the Harlequin's romance series reader was likely to be married, well educated, and working outside the home. More than half of Harlequin readers spent at least three hours reading per week. Harlequin series readers were brand loyal; a survey indicated four out of five readers would continue to buy Harlequin books in the next year. Larry Heisey, Harlequin's former chief executive officer and chairman, expanded on the value of Harlequin's products: "I think our books are so popular because they provide relaxation and escape.... We get many letters from people who tell us how much these books mean to them."

While Harlequin had advertised its series product on television, current marketing efforts centered on print media. Harlequin advertised in leading women's magazines such as *Cosmopolitan, Glamour, Redbook,* and *Good Housekeeping,* and general interest magazines such as *People*. The print advertisement usually featured one of Harlequin's series products and also promoted the company's brands.

Romance Series Product: Well Defined and Consistent

Under the Harlequin and Silhouette brands, Harlequin published 13 different series with 64 titles each month. Each series was distinctly positioned, featuring a particular genre (e.g., historical romances) or level of explicitness. Isabel Swift, editorial director of Silhouette, described the different types of series books published by Harlequin:

Our different lines deliver different promises to our readers. For example, Harlequin Temptation's tagline is sassy, sexy, and seductive, promising that each story

Exhibit 1	Total Unit Sales (in $000s)					
Year	**1988**	**1989**	**1990**	**1991**	**1992**	**1993**
Operating Revenue	344,574	326,539	348,358	357,013	417,884	443,825
Operating Profit	48,142	56,217	57,769	52,385	61,842	62,589
Total Unit Sales	202	191	196	193	205	199

Exhibit 2 Harlequin/ Silhouette Series Positioning Scales

Source: Company files.

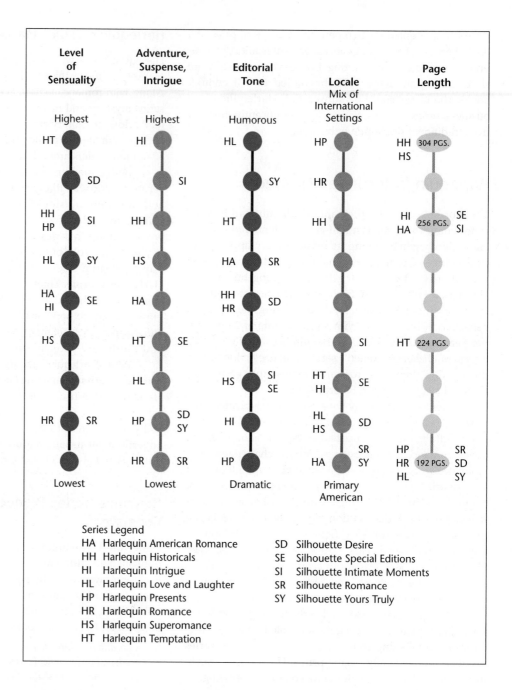

Series Legend
HA	Harlequin American Romance	SD	Silhouette Desire
HH	Harlequin Historicals	SE	Silhouette Special Editions
HI	Harlequin Intrigue	SI	Silhouette Intimate Moments
HL	Harlequin Love and Laughter	SR	Silhouette Romance
HP	Harlequin Presents	SY	Silhouette Yours Truly
HR	Harlequin Romance		
HS	Harlequin Superomance		
HT	Harlequin Temptation		

will deliver a sexy, fun, contemporary romance between one man and one woman, whereas the Silhouette Romance title, in comparison, is a tender read within a framework of more traditional values.

Overall, the product portfolio offered a wide variety of stories to capture readers' interests. For the positioning of Harlequin's series, see Exhibit 2. Sold in more than a dozen countries. Harlequin had the ability to publish series books worldwide. The average retail price of a Harlequin series novel was $4.40,[5] significantly less than the $7 retail price for the typical single-title paperback novel, and much less than the $15 to $25 for longer, hardcover titles by best-selling authors.

Harlequin's series romance product was fundamentally different from that of traditional single-title publishers: content, length, artwork size, basic formats, and print were all well defined to ensure a consistent product. Each book was not a new product, but rather an addition to a clearly defined product line. Unlike single-title books, Harlequin's series products had a common format. They

Exhibit 3   Typical Harlequin Series Romance Products

Source: Company files.

measured 105 millimeters by 168 millimeters and fit neatly into specially designed racks located primarily in super-markets and drugstores. Most product lines were 192 to 256 pages in length; some were up to 304 pages in length. Cover designs differed slightly by product line and country, but the look and feel was similar (see Exhibit 3).

Harlequin provided prospective series romance authors with plot, style, and book length guidelines. However, crafting the stories still demanded skill and work. As David Galloway, chief executive officer of Torstar, Harlequin's parent company, and the former head of Harlequin observed:

> The books are quite simply good stories. If they weren't, we wouldn't be getting the repeat purchases we do. A lot of writers think they can dash off a Harlequin, but they can't. We've had submissions from

> Ph.D.'s in English who can certainly write but they can't tell a story.

To ensure a consistent product emerged, Harlequin's editors assessed many elements, including plot, story line, main character(s), setting, percentage of romance in the plot, level of realism, level of fantasy, sensuality, social and/or individual problems, happy ending, and reading impact. Even though many different authors contributed to series romance, Harlequin's editors ensured a consistent finished product, satisfying the needs of their loyal series romance readers. The consequences of this uniformity were significant. The reader was buying a Harlequin novel, and advertising promoted the Harlequin brands rather than a particular book or author.

Bookstores were not the primary channel for series romance novels. Most retail purchases were made at supermarkets or drugstores and increasingly mass merchandisers like Wal-Mart. But many avid Harlequin readers got the product delivered to their home every month through Harlequin's direct mail service. The standardized size and format made warehousing and distribution more efficient. In addition, the product's consistency enabled standing order distribution to retail. As Pam Laycock, director of new product development, explained:

> A major contributor to our success as a series publisher is our standing order distribution. Each series is distributed to a retail location in a predetermined configuration—for example in a series where we publish four titles per month, a retailer may take six copies per title and this level of distribution is generally agreed upon and maintained for the entire year. This approach enables us to more accurately predict monthly print quantities and achieve significant print cost effectiveness.

Orders (and sales) for conventional single-title books were not as predictable. Another significant difference was that series romance books were part of Harlequin's standing order distribution plan. And more like magazines, they were displayed on retail shelves for four weeks. Harlequin's distributors then removed and returned any unsold books, and replaced them with the next month's offerings. By comparison, single-title books were typically displayed at retail from 6 to 12 months or more.

Harlequin's series romance business did not generate or even encourage best-sellers. "Best-sellers (in series romance) would ruin our system," a Harlequin insider stated. "Our objective is consistency in volume. We have no winners and no losers." Unsold books could be returned to the publisher for credit. A consequence of Harlequin's even and predictable sales was that order regulation and returns could be more easily optimized to maximize the contribution to profits.

A comparison of Harlequin's series business model and the operations of traditional "one-off" publishers is presented in Exhibit 4.

With a consistent quality product, standing orders, predictable retail traffic patterns, and the ability to produce and deliver books at low costs, Harlequin had achieved great success. Harlequin's series romance business had consistently earned a return on sales of 15 percent. As shown in Exhibit 5, this figure compared favorably with larger traditional publishers.

Loriana Sacilotto, director of retail marketing, explained why Harlequin outperformed other traditional single-title publishers:

> There are a variety of reasons why other publishers do not achieve the same margins we enjoy. The main reason is that they are broad in their publishing focus whereas we focus on women's fiction. They don't have the same reader recognition, trust and relationships. We invest in it.

Harlequin Business System

The Global Author–Editor Team. Harlequin had established a strong level of reader trust and brand equity by consistently delivering quality content. Editors in three acquisition centers in Toronto, New York, and London were responsible for working closely with 1,300-plus authors to develop and publish more than 1,000 new titles annually. In

---

Exhibit 4   Comparing Harlequin's Series Business Model and a Traditional Publisher's

	Harlequin Series	Single-Title Publisher
Editorial	Emphasizes consistency within established guidelines	Requires separate judgment on potential consumer demand for each manuscript
Rights	Uses standardized contract	Can be a complex process, involving subrights, hard/soft deals, advances, and tying up authors for future books
Author Management	Less dependent on specific authors	Vulnerable to key authors changing publisher
Production	Uses consistent format with focus on efficiency	Emphasizes package, size, and format—cost control secondary
Marketing	Builds the imprint/series	Builds each title/author
Distribution	Supermarkets, drugstores, mass merchandisers, big-box bookstores. Large direct mail	Bookstores (all types) Book clubs and mass merchandisers
Selling	Emphasizes servicing, rack placement, and order regulation	Cover, in-store placement, critical reviews, special promotional tactics (e.g., author signings)
Order Regulation/ Information Systems	Utilizes very sophisticated shipping and returns handling procedures	Historically has not received much attention, and hence, is not as sophisticated

Exhibit 5   Comparison of Harlequin's Performance with Traditional Publishers—1993 (in millions of dollars)

	Harlequin[a]	Simon & Schuster[b]	Harper/Avon[c]
Sales Revenue	417.8	1,929.0	1,210.4
Operating Profit	61.8	218.4	160.8
Identifiable Assets	319.2	2,875.8	2,528.0
R.O.S.	14.8%	11.3%	13.2%
R.O.I.A.	19.4%	7.6%	6.4%

[a] Canadian dollars   [b] U.S. dollars (Cdn$1.20 = US$1)   [c] Australian dollars (Cdn$0.80 = AUD$1)

addition to the work of its regular writers, Harlequin received approximately 30,000 unsolicited manuscripts per year. Typically, about 100 of these were accepted in any given year.

Series authors received royalties of 13 percent of retail book price. Harlequin's typical series authors had more than 100,000 of each of their books distributed worldwide.

Harlequin's series romance product focused solely on front-list sales. In the publishing world, *front-list* sales refers to the first print runs of a book supporting its initial market launch. *Back-list* refers to books reprinted and reissued years after the book's initial run (often to support an author's subsequent books). Harlequin's series romance novels—unlike a traditional publisher's single-title books—were not available on back-list. However, Harlequin retained these rights.

Printing was a highly competitive business and Harlequin subcontracted its requirements. Costs per series book were typically $0.44 per book compared to the competitors' average costs of $0.88 per single-title soft cover book.

Distribution, Selling, and Promotion.   With its standing orders, Harlequin's distribution costs per book were $0.18, with selling expenses at an average of $0.09 per book. Because it was the dominant player in series romance, Harlequin had relatively low advertising and promotion costs—about $0.22 per book.

In Canada, Harlequin had its own distribution. Elsewhere in the world, independent distributors were employed. In the United States, Pocketbooks, the sales division of Simon & Schuster, a large traditional publisher, handled Harlequin's series romance books. Supermarkets, drugstores, discount department stores, and mass merchandisers accounted for 70 percent of North American retail sales. Specialty big-box bookstores like Barnes and Noble and other chains and independent bookstores accounted for the remainder of retail sales. Globally, Harlequin's products were in over 250,000 retail outlets. Eighty thousand of these outlets were in North America; almost 50,000 of these were supermarkets and drugstores. Harlequin's series products were in 70 percent of supermarkets, but only 55 percent of bookstores. In Europe, kiosks and tobacconists accounted for the largest proportion of retail outlets.

The direct channel handled direct-to-reader book sales. Harlequin's "Reader Service" book club was an important source of sales and profits. Investing in advertising to acquire readers, this direct mail operation offered frequent Harlequin readers the possibility of purchasing every book the company published, delivered right to their doorstep. In the United States, six books were sold through the book club for every 10 sold at retail. Furthermore, a book sold through the book club yielded Harlequin the full cover price, whereas a book sold at retail netted the company approximately half the retail price, and required advertising, distribution costs, and the acceptance of returns from retailers.

Rise of Single-Title Romance

The proliferation of titles and authors during the "Romance Wars" had resulted in the emergence of single-titles as a significant factor in the women's romance fiction market. Exhibit 6 provides the sales breakdown for romance novels.

Exhibit 6   Romance Novel Sales in North America (millions of units)

	1985	1986	1987	1988	1989	1990
Harlequin series romance	77	79	80	82	83	85
Other romance series publishers	12	12	13	13	14	14
Single-title romance books by other publishers	72	79	86	94	102	112
Total romance books	**161**	**170**	**179**	**189**	**199**	**211**

Exhibit 7   Range of Worldwide Titles (1987)

Book Title	Type/Genre	Unit Sales Data	Harlequin Series Author?
Longest Pleasure	Romance	304,000	Yes
Quarantine	Horror	62,000	No
Eve of Regression	Psychological Thriller	55,000	No
War Moon	Suspense	72,000	No
Illusion	Psychological Suspense	35,000	No
Dream Escape	Romance	297,000	Yes
Alien Planet	Science Fiction	71,000	No

In an attempt to capitalize on readers' growing appetite for single-titles, Harlequin launched Worldwide Library in 1986, its first single-title publishing program. This move also gave Harlequin's more accomplished series authors another outlet. Laycock commented:

> Several authors who began their writing careers with Harlequin writing series romance wanted broader opportunities—opportunities that they saw in the single-title women's fiction publishing arena. Prior to the launch of Worldwide Library, Harlequin didn't have publishing opportunities to meet the desires of these authors. As a result, authors would seek out competitive publishers to support their single-title works.

Exhibit 8   Monthly Single-Title Romance Output Analysis North American Market

Single-Title Romance by Category	1985	1989	1991
Contemporary	2	6	12
Historical	22	37	43
Regency	6	8	17
Total	**30**	**51**	**72**
By Publisher			
Zebra (Kensington Publishing)	5	15	21
Bantam/Dell	2	2	8
Diamond	0	0	4
Harper Paperbacks	0	0	3
Avon	4	5	6
Jove	2	2	4
Leisure Books	3	3	5
NAL/Signet	6	7	8
Pocket Books (Simon & Schuster)	1	6	3
Ballantine/Fawcett, Onyx, SMP	4	7	7
Warner Books/Popular Library	3	4	3
Total	**30**	**51**	**72**

Source: Company files.

By 1988, Worldwide was shut down as a result of several problems. "Worldwide could never decide if it was a romance program, a women's fiction program, or a general fiction program," a Harlequin insider commented. Exhibit 7 illustrates a list of typical titles published at Worldwide.

With the shutdown of Worldwide Library, popular authors moved to other publishers. As shown in Exhibit 8, other publishers continued to exploit the popularity of single-title romance novels.

Eager to find ways to grow its publishing business, Harlequin's management reexamined the publishing market. A broader analysis revealed that although Harlequin's series romance had captured well over 80 percent of the North American series romance market by 1990, Harlequin's estimated share of the North American *women's fiction* market was only about 5 percent. Exhibit 9 provides a breakdown of the women's fiction market.

There was substantial overlap in the readership of series romance fiction and other fiction. Mark Mailman, vice president of market research and analysis, added:

> One compelling reason to get into single-title publishing is that when we look at our research on customers, they're reading 20 Harlequin books and 20 single-title books from other publishers. We have an opportunity to take a greater share of that market.

Harlequin's Single-Title Task Force

Faced with slow or no growth in series romance, a Harlequin task force convened in 1992 to study the feasibility of launching a new women's fiction single-title program. To begin, they examined why Worldwide had failed and concluded that overall lack of success was attributable to: editorial parameters that were too broad; less than optimal North American retail distribution; very

Exhibit 9   North American Women's Fiction Market Size Estimate, 1993 (as a percentage of overall segment sizes in US$ millions)

	General Fiction	Romance	Mystery	Sci-Fi	Total Fiction
Total Segment Size	2,222	1,220	353	476	4,271
Estimated Women's Fiction Share of Segment	60%	100%	60%	38%	69%

few Worldwide titles distributed through the direct-to-reader channel; global support for the program was not timely and universal; and the selection of authors and titles was unsuccessful. The task force report stated:

> In the past few years, sell-through efficiencies in the supermarket channels are not as great as the sell-through efficiencies in both mass merchandisers and bookstores. The more efficient retailer knew that the consumer was spending her discretionary reading dollar to buy a diversity of romantic reads, including those that had previously been thought of as mainstream.
>
> Since a single-title strategy requires a single-title solicitation from the sales force and more expensive single-title packaging, two of Harlequin's strategic lynchpins of our earlier decades have to be rethought (for single-title): standing order program and same format production. However, Harlequin can still capitalize on its global base and its ability to distribute widely to points of purchase that women visit on a regular basis.

MIRA Launch Decision

The task force was preparing its recommendation for MIRA, Harlequin's proposed women's fiction single-title program. The addition of single titles would make a welcome contribution to overhead costs. Currently, indirect overhead costs per series novel were $0.09 per book. Because infrastructure was already in place, it was estimated that MIRA novels would not incur additional indirect overhead costs. Printing costs for single-titles were expected to be $0.71 per book (350 pages on average). Estimated advertising and promotional costs for new single-titles were 6 percent of (the higher) retail price.

Author Management

In the single-title market, authors were categorized into three groups, based on their sales potential: brand new, mid-list, and best-seller (see Exhibit 10). Depending on the author group royalties, sales, and promotional support varied. Best-selling authors were expected to sell more than a million books. Publishers were known to sign established authors for up to a five-book contract with large multimillion dollar advances. It had not been determined whether MIRA should follow suit. In addition to author advances, typical royalties per MIRA-type book were estimated to be 13 percent of the $6.75 retail price.

Exhibit 10   General Industry Contract Terms for Fiction Category by Author Group

	Brand-New Author	Mid-List Author	Best-Selling Author
Advance	$10,000 to $30,000	$80,000 to $200,000	$1 million to $5 million
Royalties	5% to 13%	8% to 15%	10% to 17%
Overseas Publishing Schedule	Within 18 months	Within 12 months	Simultaneous
Overseas Publishing Markets	Major markets	All markets	All markets
Minimum Distribution	30,000 to 80,000	100,000 to 400,000	>1 million
Promotional Support per book	Possibly some support (up to $50,000)	Support ($100,000)	Very strong support (more than $300,000)

Sources: Industry sources and casewriter estimates.

A Different Format

Women's fiction books were expected to have many differences from well-defined series romance books. Unlike series romance, topics would cover a broader range of segments including general fiction, science fiction, and mystery. Women's fiction books would be longer in length: 100,000 to 400,000 words compared with a series romance book length of 75,000 words. Naturally, book sizes would be bigger in terms of page length: from 250 to 400 pages versus a norm of 192 to 304 pages for series romance.

Distribution

Harlequin had a strong distribution network for its series romances through supermarkets, drugstores, and discount department stores. Single-title women's fiction novels required more mainstream distribution focusing on retail bookstores. In addition, standing order distribution, a hallmark of Harlequin's series romance business model, would have to be abandoned in favor of relying on orders generated by the distributor's sales force for single-titles.

Success in the United States would be key for MIRA, and in this market, Harlequin relied upon Simon and Schuster's sales force. Since S&S was a major single-title publisher, Harlequin did not know how much support MIRA would be afforded. Harlequin was considering offering better margins to the distributors than those it offered for series romance distribution. Expenses for single-title distribution were expected to be $0.27 per book.

MIRA books would rely more heavily upon distribution through bookstores when distributed through the same channels as the series product. Retailers would be encouraged to shelve MIRA books separately from the series offering. The more intensive selling effort for single titles would require 4 percent of the single title retail price. The new single-title program planned to offer $3.38 in margin to the distribution channel for single-title books (50 percent of the typical retail price of $6.75) versus $2.42 for series books (45 percent of the $4.40 suggested retail price).

Acquiring Single-Title Rights

Harlequin subsidiaries in some countries were already buying rights to publish single titles. By launching MIRA Harlequin could negotiate better global-author deals. The task force report added: "By acquiring mainstream titles through a central acquiring office, the collective clout of Harlequin could create the likelihood of better-selling mainstream titles marketed by all countries in the global enterprise."

Harlequin's author and editor relationships remained strong, so much so that many series authors were enthusiastic about maintaining a long-term relationship with a trusted editor as they pursued their break-out mainstream book. With MIRA, these authors could remain loyal to Harlequin.

How Best to Proceed

There were many issues to be resolved prior to any launch of MIRA. Most pressing was the question of whether Harlequin had the resources and capabilities to succeed in its new women's fiction segment. Certainly there were elements of its series business model that could be transferred to the broader women's fiction market. But what were the gaps? What else did Harlequin need?

Hayes had several options if MIRA was launched. Several established best-selling authors had begun their writing careers with Harlequin and had moved on to writing single-title books. These authors had established reputations. Harlequin could approach one or more of these authors to sign with MIRA/Harlequin. Such an arrangement would involve a multi-book contract and substantial advances. While risky, this approach would ensure that MIRA's launch attracted attention.

A different, seemingly less risky alternative was to tap into Harlequin's extensive back-list collection and reissue a selection of novels by current best-selling authors currently signed with rival single-title publishers. The physical size of the book and page length could be extended to 250 pages from 192 by adjusting format. In addition, a new, MIRA-branded cover could be produced to repackage the books. Coincident with the launch of this back-list, Harlequin's editors would cultivate and develop existing series authors, encouraging them to write single-title books for MIRA.

Returning to the strategic dilemma that Harlequin faced, Swift commented on the challenge of successfully launching MIRA:

> Our biggest challenge is the requirement to publish on a title-by-title basis. Every new book will have to stand on its own, with its own cover, a new marketing plan and possibly even an author tour. Can we as a company develop the flexibility to remain nimble? How patient should we be in waiting for success? Given Worldwide's poor results, how should we approach this challenge?

End Notes

1. To protect confidentiality, all financial information within this case study has been disguised.
2. This section is adapted from the Richard Ivey School of Business case # 9A87M002. Harlequin Enterprises Limited—1979, Peter Killing.
3. All amounts are a percentage of the suggested retail price.
4. Numbers are for the typical paperback. Hardcover books cost more to produce, but as a percentage of its higher retail price, printing costs were roughly the same proportion.
5. All amounts in Canadian dollars unless otherwise specified.

Case 1–4: True Religion Brand Jeans and the Premium Jeans Industry: Cyclical Downturn or Secular Slowdown?

August 27, 2010 (San Francisco—Reuters.) The words sounded ominous, especially coming from a jeans brand: "We are basically at the end of the denim dominance." But the co-founder of Guess, Maurice Marciano, who broke the news to analysts in an earnings conference call this week, said the change would mean more sales, not less. The fashion cycle is turning yet again, and next spring it's spinning toward a greater emphasis on other fabrics. Khaki, corduroy, and twill pants are expected to knock premium denim off of its pedestal and inspire fickle consumers to shop. Guess' pronouncement rattled the nerves of investors—already concerned about inventory levels and a conservative outlook—who sent shares down more than 7 percent the next morning. Shares of premium denim brand True Religion shed 7 percent from the beginning of the week.[1]

True Religion Brand Jeans

Founded in 2002 by Jeff and Kym Lubell, True Religion had become the second largest premium denim brand in the United States by 2010. The line sold through upscale department stores like Nordstrom, Neiman-Marcus, Bergdorf Goodman, Bloomingdales, and Saks Fifth Avenue as well in about 800 trendy boutiques in the United States. Despite the company's historically strong financial performance, the stock had a chart like a roller coaster. Investors worried that premium jeans, jeans priced over $100 per pair, would go the way of go-go boots as fickle "fashionistas" moved on to the next fashion trend. Moreover, the recent economic weakness accompanied by enormous improvements in bargain-priced jeans' fabric, fit, and styling raised the specter of consumers "trading down" from expensive brands to stalwarts like Levi's, Lee, and Gap jeans.

After years of skyrocketing sales, the premium jeans industry experienced its first slowdown in 2007 with sales down by about –5 percent. Although the premium jeans industry seemed to defy economic weakness with sales up by an estimated 17 percent in 2008, the industry saw revenues slump an estimated –8 percent to about $1.6 billion at retail in 2009 (see Exhibit 1). Upscale department stores and boutiques alike struggled in 2009. Premium industry bellwether Nordstrom reported over a –12 percent drop in same-store sales in 2008 and more than a –7 percent decline in comparable store sales in 2009 in its full-line department stores. Neiman-Marcus, Bergdorf Goodman, and Saks also reported major declines in same-store sales in 2009. In April 2009 alone, Neiman-Marcus reported a –27 percent drop in same-store sales for its namesake stores as well as for subsidiary Bergdorf Goodman. Similarly, Saks saw same-store sales plummet by –32 percent in the month.[2]

Upscale department stores experienced a significant improvement in same-store sales against easy comparisons in 2010. Nevertheless, premium denim sales remained "soft" in the pricey retail outlets. Retail buyers reportedly remained cautious—keeping inventory levels tight—and retailers increased their focus on store brand merchandise in order to boost profit margins. At the same time, a 2009 consumer survey by McKinsey and Company suggested that many Americans had traded down to less expensive products during the recession and had no intention of trading back up to premium goods after the economy recovered. Some analysts estimated that up to 70 percent of luxury brand sales and 50 percent of the growth in the luxury market was derived from the so-called aspirational shoppers prior to the recession.[3] Aspirational shoppers—middle-class consumers with luxury tastes—had household incomes between $75,000 and $150,000. Easy credit and rising home prices fueled spending and made the aspirational shopper the target of many brand marketing campaigns in the heady days before the housing bubble burst and unemployment surged to post-Great Depression highs.

Prior to the recession, many premium denim labels defined themselves as "aspirational brands"—expensive but not as pricey as couture brands who charged thousands for each piece of clothing. Numerous press articles declared the death of the aspirational shopper and a new "bargain hunting is cool" zeitgeist that would survive after the economy rebounded. In addition to weak demand, premium denim labels experienced cost pressures as cotton prices hit a post–Civil War high in 2010. At the same time, consumers had begun to shy away from embellished and distressed fashion jeans in favor of so-called clean styles that could last for several years. The trend toward wardrobe staples meant that it was increasingly difficult for premium labels to demonstrate their "value" to the consumer as it was harder to differentiate a plain, dark blue pair of expensive jeans from a less expensive basic jean. In an interview with Reuters, industry analyst Eric Beder said, "Premium denim slows

Exhibit 1   2009 Selected Financials—Jeans Companies ($ in thousands except per share amounts & betas)

	Buckle	Guess	Joe's	Levi's	Liz Claiborne	People's Liberation	True Religion	VF Corp
Sales	$898,287	$2,128,466[a]	$80,116	$4,105,766[c]	$3,011,859	$35,635	$311,001	$7,220,286[g]
Gross Profit	400,668	941,487	39,785	1,973,405	1,397,750	17,245	195,562	3,195,164
Gross Margin	44.6%	44.2%	49.7%	48.1%	46.4%	48.4%	62.9%	44.3%
Operating Profit	$199,462	$358,816	$8,523	$378,088	−$334,584	−$442	$77,597	$736,817
Operating Margin	22.2%	16.9%	10.6%	9.2%	−11.1%	−1.2%	25.0%	10.2%
Interest Expense	$0	$2,176	$388[b]	$148,718	$65,100	$208[e]	$0	−$85,902
Net Income	127,303	242,761	24,520	151,875	−305,410	484	47,332	461,271
EPS (fully diluted)	$2.73	$2.61		NA	−$3.26	$0.01	$1.92	$4.13
Shares Outstanding	46,381	91,592	61,121	NA	93,880	36,022	24,659	
Cash	$158,027	$502,062	$13,195	$270,804	$20,372	$2,734	$110,479	$731,549
Accounts Receivable	6,911	289,638	1,731	552,252	263,508	94	27,217	776,140
Inventory	88,187	246,197	22,887	451,272	319,713	2,732	34,502	958,639
Total Assets	488,903	1,539,175	79,624	2,989,381	1,605,903	8,990	229,806	6,470,657
Accounts Payable	$24,364	$195,075	$13,590	$198,220	$144,942	$3,455	$11,717	$373,186
Total Debt	0	90,055	0	1,860,265	658,151	0	0	1,187,126
Shareholders Equity	354,259	1,026,343	61,506	−333,119	219,879	4,711	197,854	3,813,285
Depreciation	$25,135	$56,521	$536	$84,603	$163,564	$536	$6,492	$153,707
Capital Expenditures	50,561	82,286	873	82,938	65,332	873	20,082	85,859
Company Owned Stores	401	711	6	414	240[d]	5	73	28[h]
Licensed Stores	0	775	0	1,500	0	0	0	0
Beta (as of 12/22/10)	0.82	1.78	1.74	NA	2.47	1.42	1.77	0.97
Share Price (12/22/10)	$37.78	$48.17	1.58	NA	$7.53	$0.14	$23.01	$86.75
Denim Sales as % of Total	43%	30%	97%	84%	50%	NA	13%	NA
Comparable Store Sales Change	7.8%	−4.5%	NA	NA	−16.2%	NA	NA[f]	NA

(a) Includes $ 97.4 million in licensing royalties. Denim estimate Source Reuters: Analysis-Garmentos Proclaim the End of Denim Dominance by Alexandria Sage http://www.reuters.com

(b) Interest on recourse accounts receivable sold to Factor, cash advances on inventory, and to maintain open Letters of Credit. Interest rate on accounts receivable assigned to Factor was 3.50% per month on 11/30/2009 or 0.25 + the Chase Prime Rate. Note receivables are sold to the Factor at 85% of face value. Pg. 79 JOEZ 10K 2009. Denim sales as a percentage of total sales source: Marc Crossman CEO, Company Press Release.

(c) Includes $82.9 million in licensing royalties. Operating income includes $5.2 million restructuring charge Denim percentage author's estimates.

(d) Lucky Brand stores only. Liz Claiborne owned 458 specially retail stores and 363 outlet stores. Sales of Lucky Brand were $439.6 million-down 7.8% in 2009. Source Page 52, Liz Claiborne 2009 10K Denim as a percentage of Lucky Brand total sales source: WWD "Denim in Depth: New Lucky Brand CEO Seeks Sharper Focus" 5/20/10 accessed 12/23/10. http://WWW.WWd.com/WWd-publications/WWd-denim-in depth/2010-05-19/#/article/markets-news/new-lucky-brand-ceo-seeks-sharper-focus-3080889?navSection=issues&navld=3080751.

(e) Interest expense on factored receivables and inventory borrowings.

(f) Denim sales as a percentage of total sales for True Religion-Bonita Austin's estimate. TRLG did not release full-year comparable store sales gains for 2009. Comparable store sales were up 22% in 4Q:09.

(g) Includes $77.2 million in licensing/royalty income.

(h) 7 for All Mankind stores only. VF Corp owns and operates 757 stores worldwide with 681 of them monobrand stores dedicated to sales of Vans, The North Face, 7 for All Mankind, Nautica, Lucy Lee, and Wrangler.

down when the trend goes basic. How do you recognize its premium? How much differentiation is there in that pair of $189 jeans compared to a $79 pair when they are just dark and straight?"[4]

The combination of the consumer's tight pocketbook and the shift toward basic styles constrained the brands' ability to pass on the raw material price increases to their customers. Notably, one of the most expensive denim lines,

Rock & Republic, declared bankruptcy in April 2010. Moreover, several jeans makers reported disappointing sales and earnings in the first nine months of 2010 and lowered their full-year forecasts.

The True Religion brand had weathered the economic storm relatively well. Fueled by the expansion of the number of company-owned retail stores, True Religion's revenues jumped 30 percent per year on average accompanied by a

28 percent average annual increase in earnings per share from 2006 to 2009. However, the company reported surprisingly disappointing third-quarter sales and profits and cut its full-year forecast in 2010. While sales rose 16 percent in the first nine months of 2010, earnings per share plunged—18 percent in the period. Growth in company-owned stores and international markets was robust in 2010, but the company's domestic wholesale jeans business was quite weak for the second straight year as department-store accounts and boutique stores continued to cut back on orders.

Recent changes in the competitive landscape raised questions about the relevance of the True Religion brand as brands targeted to women over 40, and women with "curvy figures" gained strength. Women over 40 spent more and had more spending power than younger consumers. While "curvy women" received attention from the likes of Gap and Levi's, premium denim makers mainly ignored them. Jeff Lubell so far had kept the brand on track and on the cutting edge of denim fashion. True Religion's sweet spot was the very young, very slim, and fashion-forward woman. Until 2009, the company offered its products only up to a misses size 8, while the average American woman was two sizes larger at a misses size 12. The line's focus on the very young and very slim consumer created an opportunity for brands such as Not Your Daughter's (NYDJ) Jeans with its famous tummy tuck line to carve out a potentially sizeable niche of the premium market. It was not clear how well True Religion would fare if fashion jeans remained out of favor. Given the average American woman had seven pairs of jeans in her closet in 2009, would she shop for new premium jeans if her jeans remained fashionable for years rather than for a few seasons?[5] More to the point, would she turn to True Religion brand rather than less fashion-oriented lines like 7 For All Mankind or Joe's Jeans?

Lubell's goal was to boost worldwide revenues to $1 billion from $311 million in 2009. In order to hit this target, True Religion had to diversify away from denim into other apparel and related categories. Could Lubell persuade consumers to view True Religion as a diversified "lifestyle brand" like Ralph Lauren or would the line remain predominantly a denim jeans label? Given the shifts in the market, did Lubell have to achieve lifestyle brand status for True Religion merely to survive over the next few years? While non-denim sales stood to about a quarter of unit sales in company-owned stores in 2009, other retailers largely remained uninterested in the company's offerings outside of the jeans category. As a result, non-denim revenues came in at an estimated 13 percent of revenues in 2010.

The firm's management expected retail store expansion to be the company's major growth engine in the future. Nearly all of True Religion's important competitors had similar plans and long-term growth strategies. Would retail store expansions by the likes of 7 For All Mankind keep True Religion from obtaining the most productive retail sites for its stores? How did the unexpected resignation of company President Michael Buckley in May 2010 impact True Religion's long-term strategy? True Religion had hired industry-veteran Mike Egeck (former CEO of 7 For All Mankind) as Buckley's replacement in June, but Egeck had yet to make any public comments about his plans for the business.

In the meantime, VF Corporation snapped up the assets out of bankruptcy of trendsetter Rock & Republic in mid-2010. A private equity group led by former Reebok President Paul Fireman purchased a stake in Hudson jeans for $30 million in 2010. In addition, Star Capital purchased a majority stake in J Brand premium jeans for about $50 million. Private equity investors were attracted to the sector due to the high profits and returns the larger established brands earned. All of these investments in the sector increased the likelihood that competition would become fiercer as the smaller brands had more financial flexibility to aggressively fight for market share.

Could True Religion successfully navigate the changes in broad industry trends, the shifts in the competitive landscape, and a possible consumer move-away from denim? Would True Religion survive all of its challenges and emerge as a powerful $1 billion brand or would the brand fade as many others had in the volatile apparel market over the years? Investors had many questions about the long-term viability of the company.

A Brief Recap of the Recent History of the U.S. Denim Market

Calvin Klein popularized the concept of premium jeans in the late 1970s. The designer burst onto the jeans scene with shockingly high prices, a skin-tight fit, and a controversial advertising campaign featuring a very young Brooke Shields. As Brooke Shields confided to U.S. consumers that nothing came between her and her "Calvins," the $35 per pair jeans flew off store shelves. At the time, mainstream Lee and Wrangler blue jeans retailed for about $12 per pair on average. Suddenly, jeans were no longer functional wardrobe staples. They were sexy fashion statements. The jeans craze peaked in 1981 when retail sales jumped to a record $6 billion and 520 million pairs.[6] As designer jeans fell out of favor, and the prime 14–24-year-old jeans-buying cohort aged, domestic annual jeans sales slid to 416 million pairs by 1985.

Following a protracted decline in the 1980s, the market surpassed its earlier peak and hit annual sales of 511 million pairs in 1995. Denim jeans unit sales grew at a strong 7–10 percent per year from 1990 to 1996. Then in 1997, the denim market experienced a sharp slowdown in growth that lasted until the end of 1999—rising just 3 percent per year on average. For some industry players the slowdown meant disaster. Levi Strauss saw its sales plunge over 13 percent in 1998, almost 14 percent in 1999, and nearly 10 percent in 2000. U.S. textile giants, Cone, Swift, and Burlington, cut prices and idled production lines—all victims of a denim glut at retail caused by a shift in fashion trends.

The introduction of new stretch fabrics and widespread acceptance of "casual Friday" and other office "dress down" days stimulated demand for khakis, carpenter, and cargo pants and cut into denim demand in the late 1990s. Casual wear for work became so socially acceptable during the "dot-com bubble" that even staid Wall Street firms permitted employees to wear "golf casual" rather than formal business attire to work on Fridays in spring and summer. Nevertheless, even as demand for basic five-pocket denim jeans suffered from the shift in consumer preferences in casual wear in the late 1990s, demand for women's fashion jeans grew. Angelo La Grega, president of VF Corporation's Mass Market Denim Division, noted in a 1997 interview with *Women's Wear Daily* (*WWD*), "The business is moving from pure commodity to fashion basics."[7] The primary reason for the resurgence in demand for fashion jeans was the availability of denim jeans in exciting new washes and finishes.

"Distressed" and "dirty" denim hit retail shelves in spring 2000. The new distressed jeans tapped into consumers' taste for vintage denim. Distressed, dirty jeans were already "broken in," wrinkled, stained, and looked as if the owner had worn them for years. The Italian jeans maker Diesel had pushed dirty denim for several seasons before it gained approval from other designers. A few designers like Kenneth Cole also experimented with the new stretch denim, a cotton denim that incorporated 2 percent Lycra spandex to improve wearing comfort.[8]

Against that backdrop, Jerome Dahan and Michael Glasser introduced their 7 For All Mankind premium denim line to a consumer market hungry for fashion innovations. The new denim label would fuel the hottest upscale denim market since the late 1970s, and eventually would spark product improvements at every price point in the jeans spectrum. Aspiring as well as established designers would introduce literally hundreds of denim labels in the new decade as they answered the siren call of high growth and high profit margins. Retailers eagerly snapped up new offerings as their customers demanded the latest hot jeans. The premium denim market, defined as jeans retailing for $100 or more, would jump from a dollar market share of about 1 percent in 2000 to about 12 percent or an estimated $1.6 billion in retail sales in 2009.[9] Premium denim's hold on the $8.3 billion women's jeans market was greater as 75 percent of premium denim sales were made to women—putting the product's dollar share at an estimated 15 percent of the women's segment.[10]

According to *WWD*, the premium segment drove the women's denim market to double-digit growth from 2001 to 2005, but total denim sales fell about 5 percent in 2007 as the premium market softened. Sales of jeans priced above $60 per pair fell about 18 percent in 2007—causing some industry observers to predict that a "shake out" was in the making. Indeed, Michael Buckley, then president of True Religion brand jeans, said on a November 2008 conference call with investors, "I think what we've seen over the last probably year to year and a half is a consolidation in brands where there [were] 20 brands . . . and then it was 10, and now it is five or six brands that you really see front and center in most of the major accounts . . . premium denim overall open-to-buy might only be going up slightly, but they're giving more dollars to fewer brands." Jeff Rudes, founder and designer of J Brand Jeans, commented in a 2010 interview for the Sundance Channel documentary *Dirty Denim*, "In 2006 it got narrower and in 2007 it got even narrower and then in 2008 it was about the brands that were . . . doing well at retail. [They] were the only ones that survived."[11]

In 2008, premium denim sales jumped 18 percent even as the U.S. economy weakened and most apparel categories struggled to maintain the 2007 sales levels. The overall denim market eked out about a 2 percent rise in revenues in 2008. However, the cutback in consumer spending hit the premium denim segment in 2009, which saw sales fall an estimated −8 percent. The first nine months of 2010 were difficult ones for many premium denim labels as department-store sales stayed weak for the category. Along with the new frugality forced upon consumers as housing prices plunged, there remained the possibility that consumers permanently would eschew paying $100–$200 per pair for a part of their wardrobes that until recently had been regarded as comfortable casual wear. After all, American women paid a mere $23.44 per pair on average for jeans in 2009.[12] Was the market still "rich & skinny"—like denim guru Michael Glasser's premium brand—or had it become more like Cheap Monday, the Swedish line of mid-priced jeans?

Competitive Landscape

Despite weak category sales and reports of an ongoing industry shakeout, the premium denim market remained crowded. With an estimated $800 million in manufacturer's sales, the top four premium jeans brands held an estimated combined 75–80 percent share of the market in 2009—up from an estimated combined share of 65–68 percent in 2007. The largest premium denim brand, 7 For all Mankind, had slightly less than two times the market share of the number two player in the premium segment. The remaining 20–25 percent of the market was split between dozens of denim labels. Retailers constantly were on the lookout for the next hot brand as premium denim buyers were fickle. In a recent Cotton, Inc., survey of premium denim consumers, 84 percent of those surveyed indicated they were willing to try a new brand.[13] In fact, jeans designers launched new brands even in the depths of the recession and downturn in the market. Current/Elliott, "the most refreshing denim line to come out of LA's jeans scene in a long, long time" according to a *Vogue* magazine article, launched in 2008, gained traction in upscale department stores as the new "it-jeans." CJ by Cookie Johnson, launched in summer 2009, also got play from the same retailers. The line was a collaborative effort between Cookie Johnson (wife of basketball star Magic Johnson) and Michael Glasser (founder of 7 for All Mankind and Citizens of Humanity) designed for "curvy women of all sizes." CJ by Cookie Johnson claimed to be the jeans "made with just a little bit of self-esteem."

As Exhibit 2 shows, a December 2010 Internet survey of the six major U.S. upscale department stores and nine prominent boutiques revealed that each carried about 21 different brands of premium jeans on average. However, some retailers sold many more brands. Notably, trend-setting California-based Revolve Clothing offered 55 different brands of premium women's jeans and 34 denim labels for men. In total, the retailer offered 75 unique brands of premium denim. Similarly, Nordstrom sold 45 brands of women's premium jeans and 18 men's premium denim lines. Overall, the upscale retailer offered 63 unique brands of premium denim to shoppers.

Exhibit 2   Number of Women's Premium Brands Sold by Type of Retailer; Six Upscale Department Stores and Nine Boutiques Sampled

	December 2010	
	Total	**Avg/Store**
Department Store	66	20.5
Boutique Store	94	20.9
Total Brands Carried	126	
Brands Carried in Both Types of Retail Stores	34	

Source: Bonita Austin's calculations.

While a handful of jeans brands dominated the premium space in 2010, the market remained highly competitive. New brands entered the space frequently and grabbed shelf space as upscale retailers continued to try to differentiate their stores from their rivals' stores through product offerings and a fashion "point of view." Established large brands had to fend off the advances of upstarts and smaller brands as jeans lines attempted to segment the premium market and carve out their own niches. The high margins and returns of the larger players along with low capital requirements enticed new "jeaners" or denim specialists to enter the segment. As denim designer Mik Serfontaine stated in a 2010 interview for the Sundance Channel documentary *Dirty Denim*, "Make up some samples and take it to the trade show—you're in business."[14] Moreover, established fashion designers such as Donna Karen and Helmut Lang could knock out a few jeans styles and get shelf space on the strength of their broad apparel lines. While these designers might not pose a serious threat to the big premium brands, if industry growth remained low after the economy rebounded, the premium denim labels would have to deal with them as every market share point would be important.

Exhibit 3 shows the top 16 women's premium jeans brands by "e-shelf space" or Internet shelf space devoted to them by the six major upscale department stores and nine boutiques in December 2010. No other brands held more than a 2 percent share of the available shelf space in either type of retail outlet. J Brand and NYDJ both appeared poised to gain market share and break into the ranks of the large brands. J Brand, now majority owned by Star Capital, had been an up-and-comer prior to the recession. NYDJ commanded more e-shelf space than any other women's premium brand in upscale department stores—including industry leader 7 for All Mankind. Note 7 for All Mankind, Citizens of Humanity, True Religion, and Joe's Jeans along with Diesel, AG Jeans, and Rock & Republic each had a substantial position in the men's premium market.

Nevertheless, NYDJ had appeared from nowhere in previous years. The line was targeted at women over 40 and utilized the company's patented lift tuck technology. The jeans were designed to make women look a full size smaller by holding in their stomachs (the tummy tuck) and lifting their derrières (the lift). The company's pitch to customers included the following; "Here's to our Lift Technology that will make you look a full size smaller. Here's to defying gravity with denim. Here's to jeans that will never let you down. Here's to NYDJ."[15] The appeal apparently resonated with retailers and consumers alike as the company reportedly had sales "approaching $80 million" in 2008.[16]

Exhibit 3   Top Women's Premium Jeans e-Shelf Space Percentage of Available Space on Sites by Brand Selected Department Stores and Jeans Boutiques

	eShelf Space Share		
	Department Stores	**Boutique Stores**	**Total**
7 for all Mankind	12.5%	11.0%	11.3%
AG Jeans	2.1	3.4	2.9
Citizens of Humanity	9.0	11.5	10.5
CJ by Cookie Johnson	3.1	0.0	1.0
Current/Elliot	6.1	3.6	4.4
Genetic Denim	1.8	2.8	2.4
Hudson	4.6	2.2	3.0
J Brand	11.3	5.7	7.5
James Jeans	1.7	2.1	1.9
Joe's Jeans	3.8	8.3	6.7
Not Your Daughter's Jeans	13.5	0.1	4.5
Paige Premium	5.5	6.2	5.9
Rock & Republic	1.3	2.5	2.1
Siwy	0.2	3.3	2.2
True Religion	4.2	5.3	4.9
William Rast	0.7	2.6	1.9
Total for Selected Brands	81.4%	70.6%	73.1%

Source: Barneys.Com; Bergdorfgoodman.com; Bloomingdales.com; NiemanMarcus.com; Nordstrom.com; Saks.com http://stores.intuitwebsites.com/ TMcKnight/stores.html; couturecandy.com; jules-boutique.com; nationaljeancompany.com; net-a-porter.com; www.poshboutique.com; revolveclothing.com; shopbop.com; and http://store.solutionsdenim.com. Websites Accessed 12/20/10–12/28/10.

The premium jeans market was characterized by its first ever round of price cuts between 2008 and 2010 as jeans lines tried to stimulate demand. Premium denim prices overall fell 10–15 percent over the period. Designers used several tactics to attempt to maintain their premium positioning, while also attracting price conscious consumers. Industry leader 7 For All Mankind shifted more of its product mix away from jeans priced over $200 to jeans priced under $200. A recent survey of the brand's Web site showed 81 percent of the line's jeans priced under $200, while pre-recession levels stood at 70 percent. Notably, Nordstrom did not offer any 7 for All Mankind Jeans priced above $200 at the end of 2010.

True Religion Brand Jeans sold about 45 percent of its line at price points under $200 in 2010. For the first time in three years, True Religion's average selling point in its full-line stores dropped below $200 per pair in 2009. The company's average selling price was $213 per pair for women's and $217 per pair for men's jeans in 2007. Its average selling price per pair dropped about –3 percent to $207 for women's jeans and –7 percent to $202 per pair for men's jeans in 2008. Prices fell an additional –5 percent in 2009 to $196 for women jeans and $192 for men's jeans. True Religion's absolute price points were higher in company-owned stores than in other retail stores, but the price changes were representative of the trends in entire jeans

business over the period. Rock & Republic, known for jeans priced at $250 and up, launched two lower-priced lines called the "Recession Collection" and "Plain Wrap."

Capitalizing on the staying power of so-called skinny jeans, every major premium denim brand launched "jeggings" in 2009. The product was essentially a denim legging and many retailed at substantially lower price points than skinny jeans—giving denim lines both a new fashion twist and a lower entry price for cost-conscious consumers. While many women simply did not look good in either skinny jeans or leggings, the jegging was a bit more forgiving to those without the ideal figures for the skin-tight look. The typical jegging was made of knit-fabric with 25–50 percent stretch compared to 2 to 5 percent stretch for denim. Unlike a legging, the jegging featured a zipper, a waistband, and pockets. The fashion item looked like a "super skinny jean" and stretched like a legging but never sagged like leggings.

Manufacturing Process and Supply Chain

One bale of cotton can be made into 215 pairs of men's jeans or 250 pairs of women's jeans, according to the National Cotton Council.[17] At 480 pounds per bale and a 2010 average world cotton price of about $0.99 per pound, raw cotton accounted for an estimated $1.91 per pair of women's jeans. How did less than $2 per pair of cotton result in jeans that retailed for $100–$350 per pair?

Premium jeans ranged from traditional 100 percent cotton denim jeans to jeans made from stretch denim—a combination of cotton and spandex—to jeans made from denim fabric composed of cotton and small amounts of polyester. Nevertheless, cotton was the major raw material for premium jeans. The top five cotton-producing nations were China, India, the United States, Pakistan, and Brazil in 2010. The big five accounted for 79 percent of the world's cotton supply, according to the U.S. Department of Agriculture. China alone produced 26 percent of the world's supply of cotton in 2010. Number two producer, India, supplied 23 percent of the world's cotton. At number three in the world, the United States produced about 18 million 480-pound bales of cotton or 16 percent of the world's supply.[18]

Cotton prices had been in a long-term decline as worldwide production costs fell with farm technology and farming practice improvements. After hitting their lowest levels in over 30 years in 2001, cotton prices rebounded in 2002 only to slump for another four years. Prices rose slightly over 10 percent in 2007 and about 14 percent in 2008.[19] As a result of the "worst global consumption contraction in 65 years," cotton prices fell by −12 percent on average in 2009. Unusually low stockpiles, heavy rains and flooding in China and Pakistan, and export restrictions in India reduced the cotton supply and pushed prices up to a 140-year high in 2010. Calendar year prices were up by 60 percent on average through November to nearly $1.00 per pound, but prices surged to over $1.60 per pound in December 2010. According to the University of Georgia agricultural service, cotton prices were expected to soften somewhat in 2011 due to increased crop production but were likely to remain at historically high levels.[20]

Many U.S. cotton farmers, "ginners," and merchants banded together into cooperatives and trade associations in order to try to maximize their bargaining power. About half of the domestic annual cotton supply fell under the control of four large cooperatives—Calcot, Plains Cotton Cooperative Association, Staplcotn, and Cotton Growers Cooperative. The four cooperatives were linked through membership in Amcot, an international sales agency representing 30,000 cotton growers. While not uncommon in developing countries, only one of the U.S. cooperatives was vertically integrated into fabric production, the Plains Cotton Cooperative Association (PCCA). The cooperative, through its American Cotton Growers division, produced about 38 million yards of denim fabric or about 27 percent of the 141 million yards of domestically produced denim in 2009. In 2009, PCCA purchased the assets of a jeans manufacturer and formed a new

company to produce fashion jeans in Guatemala. The company, Denimatrix, used PCCA's denim fabric and had a 60–90-day shorter production cycle than its competitors in the Far East.

U.S. denim producers dominated worldwide production and exports of the fabric for many years but had been surpassed by China due to its favorable production costs. U.S. production had declined for years as manufacturers closed American mills and relocated capacity to lower-cost countries. North Carolina–based Cone Mills, known as the "King of Denim," was the world's largest producer of denim fabric for most of its 117-year existence. While the company remained a major player in the industry, Cone struggled against low-cost international competition and the phaseout of U.S. denim fabric quotas. The company was known for its ability to produce high-quality denim and had been the sole supplier of denim for Levi's for nearly 40 years. Established in 1891 by the Cone brothers, Cone Denim was a subsidiary of the publicly traded International Textile Group in 2010. Massive restructuring efforts and a focus on high-valued added materials allowed the company's denim division to turn a profit in 2009 and remain profitable in the first nine months of 2010. While Cone was unable to completely recoup higher cotton prices with denim price hikes in 2010, the company planned to gradually pass on its higher input costs to customers.

Some premium jeans companies like True Religion preferred to source denim fabric from U.S. suppliers like Cone's famous White Oak mill because their designers felt the fabric was superior in quality and gave their jeans "authenticity" associated with being made in the United States. Other premium jeans makers swore by Japanese and Italian denim fabric. At any rate, denim fabric makers like Cone and privately held Swift Denim had low margins and little bargaining power. As it had been for most of the decade, the issue for U.S. denim makers in 2010 was survival in the face of intense competition from foreign competitors.

In jeans made of stretch denim, cotton content typically ranged from 95 to 99 percent, with spandex making up the rest of the fiber in the stretch denim fabric. The incorporation of spandex into cotton denim allowed women's jeans to be form fitting, but comfortable due to the "give" of the spandex fibers. The use of "stretch" in premium jeans was limited by spandex's inability to withstand harsher finishing treatments like bleaching as well as the lack of rigidity of high spandex content denim and its relative lack of durability.

Each pair of jeans used about 1.5 yards of denim fabric. While basic denim went for $2–$3 per yard, premium denim typically sold for about $7 per yard but could wholesale at as much as $15 per yard. Some designers experimented with denim woven with cotton and alternative fibers like linen and cashmere, which could push up cost per pair significantly. Denim with cashmere fibers wholesaled at about $23 per yard—putting the fabric cost per pair at about $35. However, the usual fabric cost per pair was around $11. Upscale jeans companies did not own their own manufacturing capacity, rather they used contract manufacturers to cut and sew the fabric into jeans. There were thousands of cut and sew operations around the world, but the U.S. premium brands all used U.S. manufacturers. The premium denim companies liked the shorter lead times and lower shipping costs as well as the high-quality control they got by using domestic suppliers. In addition, they felt U.S. consumers wanted and expected their expensive jeans to be "made in America"—the inventor of blue jeans. Manufacturing costs came in at about $10 per pair with another $2 per pair spent on shipping.

The contract manufacturing model worked well for denim designers, but it created an opportunity for jeans cut and sew operators to forward vertically integrate into jeans design and marketing. Drawing on its experience in manufacturing denim, Grupo Denim launched Vintage Revolution premium jeans in fall 2010. The Mexican company was vertically integrated into pattern design, manufacturing, and finishing. Grupo Denim hired premium denim veteran, Michael Press, as CEO. Press previously served as the president of Earnest Sewn and vice president for Paige Premium. Vintage Revolution debuted in 400 major department and specialty stores in the United States. Vintage Revolution jeans retailed for $118–$140 per pair as Grupo Denim had a significant cost advantage compared to other premium jeans marketers and chose to pass on some of its savings to consumers.

Garments went from the factory to denim laundries, which were responsible for the all-important finishing process. Many jeans designers hung their shingles out in Los Angeles due to the prevalence of laundries in the LA area. "Raw" jeans underwent a variety of labor-intensive finishing processes including special washes, sand blasting, painting, bleaching, ripping, tearing, the addition of whiskers, the application of resins, baking, and pocket embroidery. One popular process, stonewashing, literally involved putting jeans in huge washers full of pumice stones in order to break the denim fibers down and make them softer. One pair of jeans could undergo 15 different treatments before achieving the desired "look."

The finishing process added about $12 per pair to the cost of a pair of premium jeans.[21] However, some washes could run to $16 per pair or even much higher. In the documentary, *Dirty Denim*, Chip Foster points out a pair of jeans with a $25 wash made to give the appearance of having been worn extensively.[22] According to the designer and co-owner of Chip N Pepper Jeans, it would take approximately six years of wear to get the same look provided by the expensive wash.

While it was possible for the jeans companies to backward vertically integrate into the finishing end of production, very few U.S. designers had opted to do so as it generally fell out of the area of management expertise and required meaningful capital investment. One notable exception was Adriano Goldschmeid, founder of AG Jeans. Goldschmeid had owned his own "wash house" since 2004. Moreover, different laundries had developed distinctive skills with different types of finishes. LA's washhouses were known for their high levels of technical skill and innovation. As industry growth slowed, more denim companies might opt for the ownership of denim laundries despite the barriers to entry. The wash and other finishing treatments had become increasingly important in differentiating the features of premium denim lines, and thus the keeping of finishing details proprietary was critical to success. Washhouses typically did not work exclusively for one premium denim customer. While the designers endeavored to keep details about fit and finish secret, it was extremely difficult to do so given the nature of the denim laundries and their processes.

Once the jeans were finished, the jeans designer companies applied a markup of about two times to the wholesale cost of each pair before shipping them to retailers. The jeans designers paid sales commissions, inventory holding, labor, marketing, and administrative costs out of their markups. Retailers marked each pair of premium jeans up 2.0 times to 2.5 times their cost. Through this markup process, the designers and their retail partners captured the lion's share of the profits in the industry.

Premium denim designers and retailers alike for the first time faced the challenge of passing on increased raw material prices to the final consumer. The favorable cotton price environment coupled with the strong demand for premium denim made denim prices largely a non-issue prior to the recession. Questions about premium denim's ability to maintain high price points had surfaced for the first time in 2009. Given the four- to six-month order lead times on most apparel items, the companies had not yet felt the brunt of the third- and fourth-quarter 2010 spike in cotton prices. As Ilse Metchek, president of the California Fashion Association, noted in a September 2010 interview with CNNMoney.com, "Add $2 to that $10 T-shirt next year."[23] Some jeans companies planned to raise prices in 2011 to offset their increased costs. Eric Wiseman, CEO of VF Corporation, said in the same CNNMoney.com interview, "Clearly, price increases will be part of the formula for protecting our gross margins in 2011." Would consumers accept the price increases or stay away from premium denim in 2011?

Lifestyle Brands and the Diesel Model

The ultimate in product differentiation, many companies attempt to create so-called lifestyle brands that transcend product category and inspire deep consumer loyalty. Four of the five best selling premium denim companies were attempting to transform their denim labels into lifestyle brands in 2010. Once thought to be the key to continued high growth, "lifestyle brand status" might have become critical to survival.

In the 2007 Touchstone movie *Wild Hogs*, the character Dudley Frank (played by William H. Macy) proudly declares: "I got a tat." He pulls down his black leather jacket to reveal a multicolored version of the Apple corporate logo tattooed on his right shoulder. Dudley Frank, a computer programmer, identifies so closely with the Apple brand and its core values, he chooses to have it etched into his skin.[24]

Only a handful of companies have been able to establish such a strong association with a particular way of living that their brands symbolize the core values embodied in that lifestyle—Ralph Lauren, Harley-Davidson, Nike, Apple, Abercrombie & Fitch, Diesel, and a few others. Examples of failed attempts to transform regular brands into lifestyle brands abound such as McDonalds, Starbucks, Microsoft, and Uggs.

The appeal of the lifestyle brand is threefold—potential for sales growth, brand premiums (high margins), and protection from downturns in product cycles. Developing a strong emotional bond with consumers that goes beyond product functionality can allow a company to go beyond using mere line extensions to generate growth. Lifestyle brands have the potential to move into a whole host of related product categories. In some cases, a brand can be used as a growth platform even in product categories that are seemingly unrelated to its original market due to the strength of the brand's identity with its associated lifestyle. Harley-Davidson, the motorcycle manufacturer, successfully extended its brand to a wide variety of product categories including clothing, footwear, eyewear, jewelry, Christmas ornaments, trucks, and wine bottle stoppers among others.

The creation of a strong sense of identity with a brand by consumers also has the potential to let a company charge a premium for its products as relative prices can be less important than the consumer's relationship with the brand. In addition, diversifying into related product categories such as footwear for an apparel label can help protect a brand from downturns related to changes in fashion trends—thus, reducing risk in the volatile fashion business. The measure of success in creating a lifestyle brand is the degree to which revenues and profits are diversified away from the original product line.

Within the domestic premium denim market, three of the top four premium denim companies were attempting to do just that—create lifestyle brands that would allow them to move outside of the denim business. All three—7 For All Mankind, True Religion, and Joe's Jeans—were attempting to emulate the Diesel brand model. Although the brand's roots were in the denim market, only about 35 percent of Diesel's revenues are derived from denim sales in 2010. Sales of products as diverse as wine, cars, fragrances, sunglasses, shoes, and watches as well as non-denim apparel generate the remaining 65 percent of revenues.[25] In addition to product diversification, the company was forward vertically integrated into wholly company-owned and partly owned (with distributor partners) retail stores around the world. It also operated a Web site that both promotes the Diesel lifestyle and sells products. The company's motto, [Diesel] "For Successful Living," and its Web site's invitation to consumers to join "the cult" highlight the strong linkage between the brand and its customers.

Founded in 1978 by Renzo Rosso and Adriano Goldschmeid, the Italian denim company sells through 5,000 distribution points in 80 countries including 300 Diesel brand stores. With 50 stores in the United States in 2010, the *Wall Street Journal* put the privately held company's worldwide sales at $1.81 billion.[26]

At the same time, premium denim juggernaut, 7 For All Mankind, planned to take its store count from 10 in the United States in 2008 to 100 worldwide by the end of 2012. There were 22 domestic and 46 international 7 For All Mankind stores at the end of 2010. True Religion expected its U.S. store base to go from 89 in December 2010 to 100 full-priced stores and 20 outlets in the longer term. Joe's Jeans operated 15 stores in the United States in 2010. It also expects to expand its U.S. retail footprint over the next few years. All of these new monobrand stores would be located in A plus and A shopping malls and lifestyle shopping centers around the United States.

In a March 2008 interview with *WWD*, Diesel's Steve Birkhold said: "It will take these brands a long time to get to what Diesel already has, which is the full lifestyle, You can't go from being a flat denim brand with a huge wholesale distribution to being a lifestyle denim brand with a niche retail distribution unless you have the product engine to fuel it. That's where I think Diesel is differentiated."[27]

7 For All Mankind and the Premium Denim Market

The premium denim market was populated with fanciful brand names and was characterized by all the melodrama of the best television soap operas. Chip 'n Pepper, Citizens of Humanity, Earnest Sewn, True Religion, Joe's Jeans, Rock & Republic, People's Liberation, Paige Premium, Antik, and NYDJ were some of the premium denim labels launched on the heels of 7 For All Mankind's successful debut. "Seven," as it was affectionately referred to in the fashion press, was the brainchild of L.A. designer Jerome Dahan and salesman Michael Glasser.

Dahan was the head designer for Lucky Jeans and a former designer for Guess jeans. Glasser started the sportswear brand Democracy in 1990. The two men approached Peter Koral, owner of California sportswear maker L'Koral, in 2000 with the idea of launching a new jeans line at the nearly unheard of price points of $100–$160 per pair. In contrast, the average price paid for jeans in the U.S. market was just under $21. Over half of the jeans sold in the United States that year retailed for under $20 per pair. "Designer" denim had been all but dead for nearly 20 years. Nevertheless, Koral agreed to provide financial backing to the venture in return for a 50 percent ownership stake in the line.

For the first time in denim's history, designers turned their attention to creating a pair of jeans whose function was to flatter and enhance women's figures rather than to serve as durable casual wear or a skin-tight spot to paste a designer name for those fortunate enough to both afford it and carry it off. Jerome Dahan deconstructed the basic five-pocket jean and re-engineered it with an eye toward enhancing and flattering women's bodies. He added a distinctive stitching design to the back pockets of Sevens, so consumers could easily identify the product, and be identified with it. Dahan used a stylish bootcut coupled with a low rise, slim fit, high-quality denim, and subtle detailing to create a one-of-a-kind silhouette. One twenty-something woman commented in a 2003 *Boston Herald* industry article, "I remember when Seven jeans would pay for themselves because when you went out you'd look so good that guys would buy you drinks."[28] As Charles Lessor, the former CFO of competitor True Religion Brand Jeans noted succinctly in the same article, "It's all about the butt."[29] Sevens made a woman's derriere look great, and women rushed to stores to buy them. Celebrity trendsetters like Cameron Diaz were photographed wearing Sevens in everyday life. The line's popularity exploded, and it generated an unprecedented $13 million in first year sales accompanied by $2 million in net profits. Two years later in 2003, the brand did $80 million in sales before jumping to $130 million in revenues in 2004.

The brand's success did not go unnoticed. Los Angeles became the denim capital of the world despite the fact that North Carolina–based mega-brands Lee and Wrangler's operations were far from the glitz of the City of Angels, and brand leader Levi's was headquartered in San Francisco. There was a veritable volcanic eruption in the number of premium denim brands between 2001 and 2003. According to STS Market Research, consumers purchased 297 denim brands in 2001. That number jumped to 350 in 2002 and 438 in 2003—a 47 percent increase in two years, accounting for a third of all apparel brands purchased in the United States.[30] The new brands mimicked the Seven model of in-house design, outsourcing production and finishing, using the highest-quality denim, and selling to trendy upscale boutiques and high-end department stores.

Below the surface at 7 For All Mankind, things were not going well between the partners. Jerome Dahan and Michael Glasser left Seven and filed a $20 million lawsuit against Peter Koral in 2002. The lawsuit accused Koral of using profits from Seven to prop up his knitwear business and failing to live up to the partners' oral agreement to establish Seven as a separate entity once sales hit $12 million. Koral claimed he plowed all the profits back into the brand. Further, he maintained that his partners gave up their share of the company by leaving to start a competing product line. A judge awarded the two men $55.5 million in September 2004, $50 million for the combined 50 percent share of Seven, and $5.5 million in profits from 2001 and 2002.

With $20 million in net profits on $60 million in sales in their second year of business, it is no wonder that Dahan and Glasser immediately applied their expertise to creating another premium denim brand. The two started Citizens of Humanity in 2002 using the same general business model that had served them so well with 7 For All Mankind. Glasser focused his merchandising and marketing efforts on the same accounts he did business with at Seven like Nordstrom, Barney's, and Neiman-Marcus. Dahan updated his designs and added new washes and detailing.

Citizens had an even bigger first year than Seven due to soaring demand for high-priced denim. In 2003, the line generated $23 million in sales. Sales leapt to $80 million reportedly accompanied a whopping $35 million in profits in 2005. The brand sold in 35 countries with about 90 percent of its revenues coming from the sale of women's jeans. Dahan bought out his partner in 2005, and then sold 66 percent of Citizens to the Boston venture capital firm, Berkshire Partners in 2006. According to press accounts, the majority stake in the privately held firm fetched $250–$300 million or

3.8–4.5 times estimated 2006 sales of $100 million. With the backing of Berkshire Partners, Citizens purchased GoldSign Jeans from Adriano Goldschmeid along with his denim laundry in 2007 for an undisclosed sum.

In March 2005, Peter Koral sold 50 percent of 7 For All Mankind to the investment bank Bear Sterns. Although specific terms of the deal were not disclosed, Koral confirmed publicly that Bear Sterns paid $75–$100 million for its stake in the firm. The brand had sales of about $200 million in 2004 so the deal was valued at 0.75 times to 1.0 times sales. The buzz on Wall Street was that the line had the potential to morph into a large global lifestyle brand. Denim giant, VF Corporation, picked up all of 7 For All Mankind in mid-2007 for a cool $775 million. The maker of Lee, Wrangler, and Rustler jeans pegged 2007 sales of the number one premium denim brand at about $300 million, valuing the brand at nearly 2.6 times sales.

VF Corporation and 7 For All Mankind

VF Corporation was the world's largest apparel company with 2009 revenues of $7.2 billion. The company began in 1899 as a glove and mitten manufacturer, but diversified into women's silk lingerie in 1914. The company retained the initials "VF" after dropping the Vanity Fair moniker following the acquisition of Lee jeans in 1969. Lee was one of the oldest apparel brands in the United States, having been established in 1899 (about 25 years after Levi Strauss). VF went on to acquire Wrangler and Rustler as part of its friendly acquisition of Blue Bell in 1986. In 2007, VF Corporation acquired 7 For All Mankind, the leading premium denim brand in the United States.

VF Corporation adopted a new corporate strategy in 2004. Its vision was to "grow by building leading lifestyle brands that excite consumers around the world."[31] In other words, the company wanted to transform itself into a global lifestyle apparel company with 60 percent of revenues being derived from lifestyle brands by 2015. As part of that initiative, it sought to stay on top of the apparel market by combining design and science to create value-added products for consumers. According to company statements, "innovation is about much more than delivering a new product, fabric, or style. . . . Innovation is a holistic process, one that touches every aspect of our enterprise—branding, supply chain management, global expansion, even our corporate citizenship initiatives."[32] Management saw growth in lifestyle brands, an increase in company-owned stores, and international expansion as keys to longer-term success. In particular, VF Corporation planned to double the number of company-owned stores and increase its product mix to 60 percent lifestyle brands by 2015.

VF had massive global operation in which it managed 400 million units and 500,000 stockkeeping units (SKUs) across 30 brands in nearly every country in the world in 2009. Unlike many of its competitors, VF used a mix of 30 company-owned and -operated manufacturing facilities, and 1,600 contract manufacturers. As is noted in VF's 2009 10K filing, company-owned facilities in the Western Hemisphere generally delivered lower-cost product, but contractor-sourced goods offered more flexibility and shorter lead times. As a result, VF balanced the need for lower manufacturing costs with the ability to hold lower inventories, resulting from the use of contractors. In addition to global sourcing of raw materials and manufacturing, the company used "best of class" technology to manage its resources. Best of class technology extended to inventory management at the retail level. VF employed a point-of-sale inventory management system that allowed it to gather daily sales information down to the individual store and SKU level (size, style, and color detail). The company believed that this point-of-sale inventory system gave it an advantage over its less sophisticated competitors. Its 10 largest customers accounted for 27 percent of 2009 sales and were all located in the United States.

The company's brands were organized into "coalitions" including jeanswear, outdoor, imagewear, sportswear, and contemporary. The jeanswear coalition was made up of the so-called heritage brands Lee, Wrangler, and Rustler. VF management felt the jeanswear and imagewear (licensed and work apparel) coalitions would likely generate strong profits and cash flow with low-single digit growth in the longer term. The outdoor, sportswear, and contemporary coalitions were to be the growth engines of VF in management's view. These lifestyle brand groups were expected to grow at a mid-single digit to low-double digit rate in the long term.

Seven For All Mankind was placed into the newly created contemporary group in August 2007, which also included the recently acquired Lucy, a women's activewear company. When acquired in August 2007, Lucy's domestic sales accounted for 75 percent. By the end of 2009, international revenues had jumped to about one-third of brand sales. While some of the increase was due to VF Corporation's aggressive expansion in international markets, the U.S. business had suffered due to the recession and slumping premium denim industry sales. 7 For All Mankind's large share of the premium segment made it difficult for the brand to outperform the category. Prices dropped as Seven increased its emphasis on lower-priced items in order to stimulate demand. Before the recession, about 30 percent of sales were derived from jeans priced above $200 per pair. In late 2010, only 19 percent of Seven's women's jeans carried a price tag above $200, and more than a third of the women's line was priced below $175 per pair. Moreover, 70 percent of Seven's women's jeans were heavily discounted on its e-commerce site at year-end 2010. Some items regularly priced at $155 per pair were discounted to $89–$99 per pair. A late December store check of a Utah Costco store revealed 7 For All Mankind women's jeans regularly priced at $155 were offered at $109 per pair.

A strong competitor in all of its markets, the North Carolina–based VF Corporation spent $329 million on advertising and promotions in 2009. The company possessed a formidable stable of brands including The North Face, Nautica, Vans, Reef, and Majestic. As of September 2009, the company had $732 million in cash and $1.1 billion in total debt. Shareholder's equity stood at $3.8 billion.

Rock & Republic Goes to VF Corporation in Late 2010

VF announced it had picked up the assets of rival premium denim label Rock & Republic out of bankruptcy in December 2010. The deal was expected to close in spring 2011. Details of the deal were not disclosed, but the assets were valued at about $57 million in the California bankruptcy filing. Notably, VF did not retain the services of the brand's flamboyant founder, Michael Ball.

According to company press, Rock & Republic "transcends the denim world with its luxe yet edgy approach to fashion." Its first collection "mixed an edgy, rebellious style with sophistication," which "inspires music and fashion industries alike." The company paired with Victoria Beckham (Posh Spice) to create signature jeans marketed under the Rock & Republic brand name, but the relationship soured and was dissolved. Co-founded by Michael Ball and Andrea Bernholtz in 2002, Rock & Republic retailed its premium denim jeans for $186–$330 per pair. The privately held company had become something of a force in the premium denim market by appealing to the fickle tastes of the most fashion forward, affluent young consumers. Rock & Republic was all about trendy and fast. Nevertheless, the company moved in sync with the rest of the premium denim segment away from embellished jeans to cleaner and less provocative styling, and raised its waistlines in 2007. Company co-founder Andrea Bernholtz commented to WWD, "It's [the rise is] just not as low as it was before with everything hanging out. It's that quarter of an inch between sexy and slutty."[33]

Rock & Republic reportedly did $2.4 million in sales in 2002, and around $23 million in 2004. Michael Ball claimed the company did over $100 million in sales in 2006. The outspoken Ball said he had a plan that would allow Rock & Republic to "literally dominate our market in the next fifteen years."[34] Ball's plan revolved around transforming Rock & Republic into a full-line lifestyle brand including shoes, eyewear, and retail store ownership.

While it was easy to dismiss the outspoken Michael Ball as an insignificant player in the denim market, Rock & Republic's success with the fashion-forward consumer had other companies looking over their shoulders. The jeans featured a distinctive, stylized "R" on each back pocket, high quality denim, and a flattering fit. The brand commanded even higher price points than True Religion, and consumers appeared willing to pay them. As Ball told the *Daily News Record* in a 2006 interview, "If you want Rock, you have to pay top dollar—you have to pay to be in the VIP section."[35] Michael Ball's view of the brand's cache may ultimately have been its downfall.

There were several questions for VF Corporation's premium denim competitors. Would the addition of VF Corporation's financial resources allow Seven and Rock & Republic to extend the company's already large market share lead in the category? Was Seven's recent decline completely related to slumping industry sales or had the brand lost some of its cache? Could the Rock & Republic sensibility add to Seven's presence in the fashion-forward segment of the market or would the trend toward basic, clean styles mean Rock's heyday was over? If VF Corporation pursued an aggressive store expansion plan with both lines, would the company snap up the best locations, leaving competing brands only less productive sites for their own retail stores? Was there room for more than one denim-based lifestyle brand in the United States?

Joe's Jeans

Moroccan-born Joe Dahan (no relation to Jerome Dahan of 7 For All Mankind and Citizens fame) entered the fashion business with a line of men's formal wear and dress shirts in 1986 that rang up $8 million in sales when Joe was just 17 years old.[36] From 1996 to 2001, Dahan was the head designer for Azteca Productions, a private label manufacturer of sportswear and denim. Dahan entered the premium denim market in 2001 with five styles of fashion jeans under the Joe's Jeans brand. The products retailed for $124 to $155 per pair. In March 2001, Innovo Group purchased the rights to the Joe's Jeans brand from Azteca and moved into the premium denim market. Innovo later changed its name to Joe's Jeans and trades on the NASDAQ market under the JOEZ symbol.

Joe's Jeans emphasized fit rather than the hottest trend. As Dahan said in a 2005 interview, "We've always been about clean, even when the market was embellished. We're not about fast or trendy."[37] Joe's Jeans aficionados sang the praises of the line claiming the jeans had an "insanely good fit." Joe Dahan's attention to fit paid off with first year sales coming in at $9.1 million. The line retailed at tony department stores like Barney's New York, Nordstrom, Bloomingdale's, and Macy's as well as boutiques catering to affluent shoppers. Nordstrom, Bloomingdale's, and Macy's together accounted for 47 percent of 2009 sales. Total sales rang up at more than $80 million in 2009.

Like its competitors, Joe's outsourced production and sales in order to attempt to keep capital investment and manufacturing costs low. Additionally, Joe's outsourced packing, order picking, and warehousing. Nevertheless, the line's gross margin was only 50 percent in 2009 compared to 63 percent for True Religion in the same period. Similarly, Joe's operating margin was only about 11 percent in 2009 compared to True Religion's 2009 operating margin of 25 percent.

After several years of financial difficulty, Joe's made some important management changes. The company's CFO, Marc Crossman, became CEO in January 2006. Crossman was an investment banker who focused the company on developing and exploiting opportunities for the licensed Joe's Jeans brand and closed its unprofitable private label business. In August 2007, Joe's added Hamish Sandhu as CFO. Joe Dahan remained on board as the company's creative director and designer as well as a major shareholder. Later that year, Joe's Jeans acquired the Joe's Jeans brand from Joe Dahan. As part of the deal, Joe's agreed to pay Dahan 11.33 percent of annual gross profits as long as gross profits fell between $11.25 million and $22.5 million. Dahan's payout would fall to 3 percent of gross profits when they exceeded $22.5 million up to $31.5 million. Dahan's payout scale declined further as gross profit rose beyond $31.5 million. Dahan received an estimated payout of just under $800,000 in 2009. The agreement was in force through 2017 and provided Dahan with a substantial financial incentive to help the company be successful. However, it was unclear if Dahan planned to stay with the company after 2017.

Crossman and his team specifically worked on boosting gross margin through more effective outsourcing relationships with an increased number of contract manufacturers, improving the existing account penetration, increasing distribution in the Midwest, and re-entering international markets. Joe's moved to expand into retail through company-owned stores. The company owned 15 stores as of August 2010 and planned to open three more before the end of fiscal 2010. Crossman and Dahan also expanded successfully the Joe's Jeans line into related apparel categories. In 2009, non-jeans items accounted for a mere 3 percent of sales.

On the strength of its unisex woven shirts (called The Shirt) and its jeggings, non-jeans items jumped to 16 percent of sales in the first nine months of 2010. Despite the challenging environment for premium denim, Joe's reported a 36 percent jump in sales accompanied by a 27 percent increase in gross profits in the first nine months of 2010. Gross margin fell primarily due to the shift in product mix of non-jeans products. Overall profits fell sharply (−26 percent) for the period as Joe's incurred significantly higher expenses related to the addition of distribution facilities and headcount to support the business's larger size.

Cash flow from operations was −$5.5 million compared to $5.3 million in the same period the year before. Given the management's plan to increase the number of company-owned stores over the next few years, Joe's negative cash flow raised questions for investors. Would the company be able to fund its expansion plans via internal cash flow or be forced to consider a stock or debt offering? Joe's Jeans' balance sheet was solid with no debt and $64 million in shareholder's equity. Long-term operating leases committed the company to $37.5 million in payments for the next four years. With a beta of 1.65 and a recent stock price of just $1.62 per share, a stock offering was likely to prove expensive. However, it was unclear whether a debt offering would be feasible for the small company over the next year or so. There seemed to be an appetite for investing in the sector by private equity groups as evidenced by the recent investments in J Brand and Hudson, but both companies were smaller than Joe's. Back in 2008, Falcon Head Capital purchased a 50 percent stake in NYDJ for $50 million (also a smaller company than Joe's). VF Corporation or Diesel might be interested in acquiring Joe's down the road, as both companies had recently made acquisitions. However, Dahan might balk at selling his namesake company rather than continuing to build the brand without being hampered by the goals of a corporate parent.

With wholesale sales up 27 percent and company-owned store revenues up 173 percent, Joe's brand appeared to be quite strong. Same-store sales increased 23.5 percent in the third quarter—indicating the business was very strong and was not just benefiting from the addition of new stores. Joe's Jeans positioning seemed to be working in its favor, as did the line's relatively affordable prices. The line's average women's jeans price point in December 2010 was $163—far below True Religion's average of $196 per pair.

Levi Strauss

Levi Strauss invented the denim jean in 1874. The company's iconic 501 five-pocket jean still remains the brand leader in the global denim market. Nevertheless, the company struggled to combat upstart premium denim labels in this decade. The $4.1 billion company remained largely unsuccessful in its attempts to penetrate the luxury denim segment in 2010. Part of the problem stemmed from the company's eight-year battle to turn around its operations. From 1997 to 2005, Levi Strauss experienced a dramatic drop in sales from $6.9 billion to $4.1 billion. The company focused on stabilizing sales and profits, paying down debt, and later on regaining momentum in its basic denim business. For the first time in its history, Levi's was forced reinvent itself as a company. In order to be competitive, Levi's had to shutter nearly all of its worldwide manufacturing facilities and to mainly replay on outsourced finished goods produced by independent contractors.

The company appeared to be back on track from 2005 to 2007 with sales rising about 2 percent per year on average to $4.3 billion. Operating profits excluding restructuring charges increased by about 4 percent per year to $655 million in 2007. Revenues were flat in 2008 and operating profits fell about −19 percent due to increased expenses associated with the company's retail store expansion plan and investments in global information technology infrastructure. Results for 2009 were weaker, with revenues down by about −7 percent accompanied by a −28 percent drop in operating profit due to economic weakness in Europe and the United States as well as a stronger dollar. Things looked up for Levi's in the first nine months of 2010 due to favorable currency trends, the acquisition of retail stores, and growth in the Levi's brand. Levi's brand products accounted for 81 percent of company revenues in the first nine months of 2010. Total revenues were up about 7 percent in the period. The company's gross margin improved as a higher percentage of revenues came from retail stores, which carry significantly higher gross margins than wholesale goods. Operating margin fell though as advertising and promotional expenses jumped by 39 percent to $222 million, as the company spent more to drive the sales of Levi's and Dockers brands worldwide.

Levi's growth strategy outlined in the 2009 10K included five initiatives—build on brands' leadership in jeans and khakis, diversify and transform the wholesale business, accelerate through dedicated company-owned stores, increase operational efficiency, and capitalize on the company's global footprint. The company intended to focus on growth through innovation and "premiumization." Levi's management felt the company could use its brand heritage and design and marketing expertise to lead innovation in the jeans category. As part of this initiative, Levi's intended to target underserved segments of the market—especially women's jeans and "attractive price segments." Management had identified a greater focus on more premium categories as a priority back in 2007.

Levi's launched a major campaign with newly designed jeans for women in August 2010. The new product line, dubbed Levi's Curve ID, featured three different fits for women with different body types. According to a company press release, Levi's worked with scientists to analyze 60,000 body scans of women in 13 different countries to understand body types and fit problems especially the hip to seat placement.[38] The result was jeans in "the slight curve—to celebrate straight figures," "the demi curve—to fit even proportions," and "the bold curve—to honor genuine curves." Levi's claimed its new line would fit 80 percent of women. The company planned to launch Levi's Extreme Curve, which would fit an additional 16 percent of women, in late 2010 or early 2011. As part of its consumer research, Levi's found 54 percent of women try on 10 pairs of jeans to find one pair they would buy; 87 percent of women wish they could find jeans that fit better, and 67 percent of women feel jeans are designed for women with "ideal" bodies (not theirs). The new line retailed for $102–$121 per pair—far below most premium denim lines but well-above the traditional Levi's price points.

Changing consumer perceptions of a brand found in such disparate retail locations as Wal-Mart and Barney's New York had proved to be a difficult task in the past. Nevertheless, the Levi's brand had incredible name recognition and a reputation for quality. Moreover, the company had re-engineered its products and increased its fashion quotient throughout the decade. Even so, questions about the company's prospects remained. With the improvements in design and fabric quality, could Levi's build a leadership position in the premium sector? Would Levi's scientific approach to fit resonate with women tired of trying on so many pairs of jeans to find one that fit properly? On the one hand, the weak U.S. economy could cause consumers to take another look at the more reasonably priced Levi's line now that its design team had updated the fit and finishing details on the line. According to Cotton Inc.'s 2009 Lifestyle Monitor, 55 percent of women cited fit as the single most important determinant of jeans selection.[39] On the other hand, the brand's strong identity as a durable, reliable, and authentic vintage product could keep it from ever converting consumers interested in the cache of premium denim labels. Premium denim buyers placed more emphasis on style (36 percent) than fit (31 percent) in selecting jeans to buy.[40]

True Religion Brand Jeans

Jeff Lubell had struck out on two occasions previously in his attempt to shift from textile salesman to independent jeans designer. He and his wife launched two jeans labels in the late 1990s—Bella Dahl and Jeffri Jeans—and lost both after running out of cash. Events turned ugly when Bella Dahl, Inc., could not keep up with payments to its factor and had to file for bankruptcy in late 2000. Several lawsuits later, Jeff Lubell was on his own with no assets or ownership in his jeans creations. In 2002, the Lubells launched a new premium denim line, True Religion Brand Jeans. Lubell registered his new line's trademarks in his name and formed a holding company that he owned and controlled called Guru Denim. Things would turn out differently this time for the 46-year-old Los Angeles resident.

The brand hit store shelves in December 2002 with five styles of women's jeans available in five different "washes" under the True Religion label. (Sevens were only available in two basic styles at the time.) The corporate logo appeared on every tag and featured a fat, smiling Buddha strumming a guitar. According to a November 2002 *WWD* article, "True Religion has an 'evolutionary' mannish styling." *WWD* interviewed Lubell for the article and quoted him as saying "there are a lot of women who love to wear their boyfriend's jeans or husband's jeans. This plays off of that." The jeans had one of the lowest rises on the market and some of the highest prices. Lubell created "buzz" for the line by sending celebrity trendsetters free pairs of jeans with the hope they would appear in photos in the popular press wearing jeans with True Religion's signature horseshoe-shaped back pocket stitching. The strategy worked, and the line's sales took off. First year sales came in at $2.4 million and jumped to $27.7 million in 2004.

The popularity of "distressed," "destroyed," and "embellished" jeans had helped drive growth in the premium denim segment for years. The Joey Destroyed model had been one of True Religion's best selling products. The jeans model featured pre-washed denim that had been artfully aged and ripped so that most of the front of the left thigh was made up of strings rather than solid fabric. The designers added in a ripped left knee and extensive tearing on the front of the right thigh to complete the destroyed look (an extreme version of distressing). Embellished jeans also had been very popular for a number of years in the early part of this decade. So-called embellishments ranged from elaborate embroidery to the addition of sparkly crystals and metallic threads. True Religion marketed women's jeans with intricate embroidery on the back pockets like the Miss Groovy, Buddha, Fairy Girl, Godiva, and Geisha Girl designs. All of these popular "looks" required a substantial amount of additional labor to produce relative to basic denim looks. They all commanded a significant premium to the more basic models in the True Religion portfolio with prices starting well above $200 per pair. Some True Religion models went for over $500 per pair at retail.

In 2008, premium denim designers responded to the mood of the times and moved away from elaborate finishing details back to more basic styles as consumers became interested in styles that would stay fashionable for years rather than for a season. True Religion followed suit and emphasized the lower-priced, more basic items in its lineup. Nevertheless, the brand remained one of the highest priced on the market with an average selling point of $196 for women's jeans and $192 for men's jeans in 2009. The company had not been as successful historically in the basic end of the premium market as had Seven and Citizens. Indeed, True Religion's wholesale sales plummeted –20 percent during 2009 and –16 percent in the first nine months of 2010.

The company relied on Jeff Lubell's fashion sense and ability to spot the right trends to sell the "hottest" jean styles. Lubell had an impressive track record, but True Religion's sales to the wholesale off-price channel had become worryingly large by 2009. The company used off-price retailers such as Nordstrom Rack as well as its own outlet stores to sell slow-moving and obsolete inventory. Sales to the off-price channel accounted for nearly one-third of U.S. wholesale sales in 2009. Most likely, the magnitude of sale of slow-moving inventory had more to do with the economic weakness than with Lubell's ability to develop appealing jeans styles.

Investors worried that if the new consumer distaste for conspicuous consumption lingered after the U.S. economy rebounded, the company would not be able to differentiate its product and demonstrate its "value" to consumers. The brand had been built on fashion not on fit and classic styling. If fashion were no longer the key determinant of brand selection by consumers, would True Religion survive? Moreover, if price points came down significantly in the category, could True Religion change its mindset and its cost structure enough to compete and maintain high-profit margins and returns? Evidently, Rock & Republic had not been able to do so and had ended up in bankruptcy.

Recent changes at industry trendsetter Diesel also raised questions about the viability of True Religion's and other premium denim lines' approach to design. Traditionally, the premium denim brands relied on one or two designers to create the next "hot" look and drive consumer demand. That's what made Diesel's new design philosophy so interesting and unusual. Renzo Russo decided to redefine the role of Diesel's creative director. Rather than the traditional all-powerful designer who "pushed" his vision to consumers, Diesel now employed a creative director whose job was to spot broad trends in society and translate them into a "look" for the Diesel line that fit what consumers were looking for at the time. He did not draw or make samples nor was his name closely associated with the brand. Moreover, Diesel's creative director reported to the head of marketing rather than directly to the CEO. As Russo told the *Wall Street Journal* in a late December 2010 interview, "[Designers] think they are idols . . . The consumer doesn't care [about the designer]. They just want to see the right product at the right moment."[41] Russo tapped a fashion magazine editor as Diesel's creative director and shifted the firm's emphasis squarely to product development—away from design.

True Religion's Strategy

The company's initial strategy was to emphasize distribution through upscale department stores and boutiques and outsource every function except design and marketing to third parties. By the end of 2005, True Religion jeans sold in about 600 specialty stores and boutique doors as well as about 200 upscale department store doors through Nordstrom, Neiman-Marcus, Saks Fifth Avenue, Barney's, Henri Bendel, Bergdorf Goodman, Bloomingdale's, and Marshall Fields. By September 2010, the company sold its line through six major department-store accounts (due to consolidation in the retail channel) and about 800 boutiques in the United States.

By late 2006, True Religion's focus had shifted away from selling products wholesale to selling its products through company-owned stores. True Religion management, under then President Michael Buckley, had started to vertically integrate into retail for several reasons. First, the company had faced resistance from retailers when it tried to diversify away from denim jeans into adjacent clothing categories such as sportswear. Big retailers viewed True Religion as a denim label—not as an apparel brand. Owning its own stores allowed True Religion to introduce a broader range of apparel to its customers. Management hoped that the sell-through figures from company-owned stores on non-denim items would convince its retail accounts to carry the full line of True Religion apparel. Diversifying into other apparel categories and related product lines was absolutely critical to achieving management's goal of creating a lifestyle brand. In its full-priced company-owned stores, non-denim items had increased from 10 percent of unit sales to 26 percent of unit sales by September 2010. Non-denim items only accounted for an estimated 13 percent of dollar sales, as the company largely had been unable to convince its retail accounts to carry its non-denim items. The firm's non-denim items carried lower price points than its jeans.

Second, the margins in the company-owned stores were even higher than True Religion's very high denim margins as the company captured the retail markup as well as its traditional wholesale markup. Management estimated that retail store gross margin would come in at 75 percent and "four-wall contribution margin" would be about 40 percent as the company captured the benefits of the typical retail markup on its products as well as the existing wholesale margin. Management's prediction turned out to be an accurate one, as gross margin for the consumer direct segment (company-owned stores and e-commerce) leapt to nearly 77 percent in 2008 before dipping to 74 percent in 2009. The consumer direct segment's operating margin was 37 percent in 2008 and about 35 percent in 2009.

True Religion's total gross margin was about 53 percent in 2006 but rose to almost 63 percent by year-end 2009 as the consumer direct segment grew in importance. Operating margin came in at 29 percent in 2006 but was down to 25 percent by the end of 2009. The combination of heavy spending behind the rapid store-rollout program, weak sales in the 15 original True Religion stores, and a $30 million drop in wholesale revenues pushed margins down. Sales to major department-store accounts fell (−15 percent) and sales to boutique customers fell even more sharply as the premium denim category suffered from economic weakness in the United States.

Third, company-owned outlet stores gave True Religion a place to sell seconds, irregulars, and slow-moving merchandise. Without these outlet stores, True Religion brand products could surface in any type of discount outlet—potentially damaging the brand's premium positioning. Prior to 2007, True Religion jeans appeared in Filene's Basement, Costco, Century 21, and similar outlets on occasion.

Fourth, retail industry mergers and bankruptcies periodically caused manufacturers to miss sales and earnings forecasts. Using company-owned stores helped reduce the firm's dependence on retailers and reduced the risk of major disruptions in sales. Company-owned stores and e-commerce accounted for 41 percent of revenues in 2009 compared to 17 percent in 2007. In total, True Religion owned 70 stores in the United States at year-end 2009 and 89 stores as of September 30, 2010. Over time, management planned to open 100 stores in the United States. Nevertheless, the company still relied heavily on one major account, Nordstrom, for a significant portion of its sales. In 2005, Nordstrom and Neiman-Marcus together accounted for 11 percent of net sales. In 2009, Nordstrom alone accounted for 15.2 percent of net sales.

Given the recent results, it was difficult to characterize True Religion's retail strategy as completely successful at meeting management's goals. However, one thing was

Exhibit 4   True Religion Brand Jeans Operating Segments ($ in thousands)

				First Nine Months	
Net Sales	**2007**	**2008**	**2009**	**2009**	**2010**
U.S. Consumer Direct	$29,268	$75,314	$129,029	$83,885	$126,611
U.S. Wholesale	111,390	153,235	123,203	91,621	76,748
International	31,728	40,044	54,479	39,862	45,564
Other [a]	870	1,407	4,289	2,795	3,884
Total	$173,256	$270,000	$311,001	$218,163	$252,807
Gross Profit					
U.S. Consumer Direct	$22,380	$57,669	$95,276	$62,129	$92,323
U.S. Wholesale	60,007	78,670	65,882	49,862	39,904
International	15,498	19,255	30,115	22,067	24,106
Other	870	1,407	4,289	2,795	3,884
Total	$98,755	$157,001	$195,562	$136,853	$160,217
Operating Profit					
U.S. Consumer Direct	$11,875	$27,810	$44,766	$27,354	$41,214
U.S. Wholesale	36,405	47,452	30,763	24,511	9,209
International	14,718	16,761	25,167	18,792	13,711
Other [b]	−15,856	−23,147	−23,099	−16,943	−20,402
Total	$47,142	$68,876	$77,597	$53,714	$43,732
Assets					
U.S. Consumer Direct	$10,167	$36,603	$55,763	$58,491	$63,272
U.S. Wholesale	41,248	43,030	31,159	33,616	46,057
International	6,519	8,362	16,897	11,309	29,038
Other	55,324	78,457	125,987	109,329	134,734
Total	$113,258	$166,452	$229,806	$212,745	$273,101

(a) Licensing revenues generated by royalty agreements.
(b) Unallocated corporate.

Sources: True Religion Apparel Inc. 10K-2007, 2008, 2009. 10Q September 2010. All figures are actuals unless noted otherwise.

clear. The True Religion brand had grown in the U.S. market as a result of the retail strategy. Adjusting for retail markup, True Religion's total U.S. sales in manufacturer's dollars had grown at an estimated 21 percent per year between 2007 and 2009. Three questions remained with regard to the company's focus on company-owned stores. Would True Religion's major competitors bid up the cost of retail space in so-called "A" locations or create scarcity in desirable locations as they all tried to expand their retail footprints? Was a target of 100 company-owned stores in the United States an appropriate number or was there potential for more stores? What would happen to the retail business if True Religion management was not successful in restarting the domestic growth of the wholesale business? In other words, were the stores viable without a strong and growing wholesale brand?

Along with forward vertical integration into retail, True Religion's management team decided to staff an in-house sales force. The sales function formerly was handled by third party independent sales reps. Prior to 2007, reps received a 10 percent commission on sales to specialty shops and boutiques in the United States. The firm's major U.S. distributor, L'Atelier, exclusively sold the product to upscale department stores, receiving a 7 percent commission in the process. L'Atelier's owner, Jana Rangel, had 15 years experience successfully positioning and branding denim lines AG-Adriano Goldschmied, Ya Ya, Earl Jeans, and Paul Gaultier jeans. With her help, several denim lines went from a start-up position to sales in the $30–$40 million range. True Religion successfully renegotiated terms with L'Atelier in 2007. L'Atelier's commissions dropped to 4 percent for department stores and 8 percent for specialty boutiques. True Religion ended its relationship with Rangel and L'Atelier as of December 31, 2010. Management felt that having its own sales force would enhance the firm's relationships with important retail accounts and allow it to improve customer service.

Similarly, True Religion changed its distribution strategy in international markets in 2008 and 2009. The company's original model was one that used exclusive third-party distributors to gain access to upscale retailers in foreign markets. Beginning in 2008, the company moved to a combination of in-house sales forces and strategic alliances with distributors. True Religion originally sold its products to outside distributors at a 25 percent discount to wholesale. The distributors then sold the product line to retailers. The strategy worked very well for True Religion for a number of years. It was especially successful in the Japanese market, which accounted for a whopping 29 percent of net revenues in 2005.

True Religion's brand positioning as a "Made in the USA" product based on a unique combination of a Wild West cowboy heritage paired with a California-hippie-bohemian image played well in the Japanese market where affluent consumers paid top-dollar for American icons like vintage Levis. Unlike many jeans manufacturers, True Religion purchased the majority of its denim from an American supplier, Cone Mills. Like most other premium denim brands, True Religion relied upon U.S. manufacturers a to produce its jeans and LA washhouses to finish them. Management felt the "authenticity" of an American made jean played well in both the domestic market and in many international markets. Eric Beder, an analyst with Brean Murray, told the *LA Times* in 2009, "In the US, people care that their jeans are manufactured here. To consumers outside the US, it's crucial...In order to be considered a real premium brand, you need to have the Made in the USA label on it."[42] True Religion off shored production of non-denim items such as hoodies and T-shirts, where country of origin was not important to consumers.

An enormous disappointment in Japanese sales in 2006 prompted management to reconsider the distributor model. Full-year sales to Japan plunged 50 percent and the company fought accusations from the financial press that it had "stuffed" the Japanese retail trade with product in the back half of 2005 in order to meet aggressive sales forecasts. Management's analysis of the retail distribution for the brand in Japan suggested that the company needed to pull back and eliminate marginal accounts in order to preserve the brand's exclusive image. As a result, management decided to switch from the distributor model to a company-owned subsidiary in some countries such as Japan in order to better control the brand's retail placement and image.

In addition to establishing in-country sales forces in some markets, True Religion announced in July 2010 that it had formed a joint venture with its German distributor UNIFA. The joint venture took over the wholesale distribution of True Religion products in Germany, Austria, Switzerland, The Netherlands, Belgium, and Luxembourg as well as a company-owned store in Germany in August. Jeff Lubell stated, "We established the joint venture to expand our wholesale business in each of these countries and to roll out branded retail stores in the territory."[43] True Religion owned 60 percent of the joint venture, which was managed by UNIFA. Prior to the deal, UNIFA was True Religion's largest international distributor.

At the end of 2009, international sales stood at about $55 million or 18 percent of sales and 32 percent of operating profits. With over a 46 percent operating margin in 2009, the international division was by far the company's most profitable business. After falling from about $46 million in sales in 2005 to $32 million in 2007, the international business regained its momentum as Japanese sales rebounded and the company gained share in Europe.

Management Changes

The company named denim industry veteran Michael Buckley to the newly created post of president in April 2006. Buckley was president and CEO of Ben Sherman's North American business from 2001 to 2005. Prior to 2001, Buckley served as a vice president of denim giant Diesel USA for four years. He was to be responsible for day-to-day operations, including retail expansion, licensing, sourcing, and production. Jeff Lubell would remain in his post of chairman and CEO but devote more of his time to product design. Lubell commented to *WWD*, "Now I feel like I have a true partner and associate to help build the company and realize my vision of becoming a $1-billion brand."[44]

In August 2006, the company tapped Levi Strauss Europe designer Ziahaad Wells to be its design director. The following March, True Religion named Peter Collins as CFO. Pete Collins was the former corporate controller for Nordstrom. Collins managed a staff of 100 and was an expert on compliance with Sarbanes-Oxley requirements. In addition, Pete Collins had valuable accounting experience in international operations. He reported to Michael Buckley in his new position at True Religion. In January 2010, True

Exhibit 5   True Religion Brand Jeans Selected Financials ($ in thousands except per share amounts)

	2007	2008	2009	First Nine Months 2009	First Nine Months 2010
Revenues	$173,256	$270,000	$311,001	$218,163	$252,807
Cost of Goods Sold	74,429	112,999	115,439	81,310	92,590
Gross Profit	$98,827	$157,001	$195,562	$136,853	$160,217
Gross Margin	57.0%	58.1%	62.9%	62.7%	63.4%
Selling, General & Administrative Exp.	51,685	88,125	117,965	83,139	116,485
Operating Profit	47,142	68,876	77,597	53,714	43,732
Operating Margin	27.2%	25.5%	25.0%	24.6%	17.3%
Other Expense (Income)	−1803	−1065	−169	−94	−205
Pretax Profit	48,945	69,941	77,766	53,808	43,937
Taxes	21,100	25,570	30,434	21,111	16,137
Tax Rate	43.1%	36.6%	39.1%	39.2%	36.7%
Net Income	$27,845	$44,371	$47,332	$32,697	$27,800
Redeemable Noncontrolling Interest	0	0	0	0	0
Net Income Attributable to True Religion	$27,845	$44,371	$47,332	$32,697	$27,708
Net Margin	16.1%	164.4%	15.2%	15.0%	11.0%
Earnings Per Share (Diluted)	$1.16	$1.83	$1.92	$1.35	$1.12
Average Shares Outstanding (Diluted)	23,949	24,270	24,659	24,146	24,807
Selected Balance Sheet Figures					
Cash & Short-Term Investments	$34,031	$62,095	$110,479	$93,681	$127,718
Accounts Receivable	27,898	33,103	27,217	28,546	27,036
Inventory	20,771	25,828	34,502	37,835	51,565
Propterty, Plant & Equipment	11,579	28,006	39,693	38,284	46,089
Total Assets	113,258	166,452	229,806	212,745	273,101
Accounts Payable	$9,597	$10,633	$11,717	$15,310	$17,605
Total Debit	0	0	0	0	0
Shareholders' Equity	95,247	142,250	197,854	180,101	231,162
Total Liabilities & Equity	229,806	166,452	229,806	212,745	273,101
Rent Expense	$3,700	$9,300	$16,200	$11,600	$17,200
Capital Expenditures	8,765	18,187	20,082	15,636	12,986
Number of Company–Owned Stores	15	42	73	66	89

Sources: True Religion 10Ks 2007-2009, 10Q September 2010.

Religion added Lynn Koplin as COO. Koplin was formerly president of Tommy Bahama's women's division.

True Religion's financial performance generally was strong between 2006 and first quarter 2009. The company was well on its way to establishing 100 company-owned stores in the United States. The True Religion brand appeared strong at the number two position in the U.S. market. Then, in May 2010, Michael Buckley abruptly resigned from the company. Two days before his resignation, Buckley sold over 193,000 shares of stock. The company offered no explanation for Buckley's resignation and promptly replaced him with Mike Egeck about two weeks later. Egeck had served as the CEO of 7 For All Mankind. Four months later, True Religion reported disappointing sales and earnings and lowered its full-year 2010 forecast. The timing of Buckley's departure and the speed at which he was replaced suggested that Lubell was aware that Buckley planned to leave—or had forced him out. As chairman and CEO, Lubell had an enormous amount of influence with the company's board of directors.

The company's strategic initiatives under Buckley were outlined in its 2009 10K. The initiatives were to continue to develop trendsetting styles, grow the consumer direct business by adding company-owned stores, increase True Religion's international presence, improve the U.S. wholesale business by changing to an in-house salesforce, and reduce the company's sales to the wholesale off-price channel. Would these initiatives change under the new company president Mike Egeck?

End Notes

1. Sage, A. (2010). "Analysis: Garmentos proclaim the end of denim dominance." *Reuters Business & Financial News*, August 27, 2010.
2. Neiman-Marcus Sees Same-Store Sales Drop Nearly 25%. *Dallas Morning News*, May 7, 2009. www.dallasnews.com. Accessed December 31, 2010.
3. Klara, R. (November 7, 2010). The "Aspirational" Consumer: R.I.P. Brandweek.com. Accessed December 31, 2010.
4. Sage, A. (2010). "Analysis: Garmentos proclaim the end of denim dominance." *Reuters Business & Financial News*, August 27, 2010.
5. Cotton Incorporated Supply Chain Insights: Price Is Not Premium in Jeans. June 2009. www.cottoninc.com. Accessed November 15, 2010.
6. A comfortable fit: Levi Strauss has prospered by combining Maverick marketing with gentle style of management. Company profile. *The Economist* (U.S.), June 22, 1991. Retrieved from High Beam.
7. Ozzard, J. (1997). "Shortening the denim pipeline (inventory management)." *Women's Wear Daily*, May 8, 1997.
8. Knight, M. (1999). "Hot new jeans will be down and dirty at MAGIC; for spring 2000, light washes are re-creating that old, friendly, worn blue denim look." *Daily News Record*, May 23, 1999.
9. A Generation in Blue Jeans. *Chicago Tribune*, July 6, 2010.
10. Premium Denim: From Deadwood to Hollywood. *The Apparel Analyst*, 2006, no. 3, pp. 12–13.
11. Keeve, D. "Dirty denim episode 4: The crash." Sundance Channel Documentary. http://www.sundancechannel.com/digital-shorts/#/theme/64930111001/64569579001. Accessed December 30, 2010.
12. Miller, L. "How much did you pay for those jeans?" *Fashion Matters*. http://blog.newsok.com/FashionMatters/2009/07/14/how-much-did-you-pay-for-those-jeans. Accessed December 31, 2010.
13. Premium Denim: Fit To Be Tried. Cotton Inc. Press Release. September 12, 2005.
14. Keeve, D. "Dirty denim introduction.: Sundance Channel Documentary. http://www.sundancechannel.com/digital-shorts/#/theme/64930111001/64683988001. Accessed December 30, 2010.
15. Not Your Daughter's Jeans—About Us. http://www.nydj.com/#/footer/about-us/. Accessed December 30, 2010.
16. Belgum, D. (2008). "Not your daughter's jeans sells 50 percent stake for $100 million." *California Apparel News*, September 25, 2008.
17. http://www.diesel.com/info/history.php. Accessed December 2008.
18. World Cotton Supply and Demand. National Cotton Council of America. http://www.cotton.org/econ/cropinfo/supply-demand.cfm. Accessed December 30, 2010.
19. Monthly Cotton Prices 1975 to November 2008. National Cotton Council of America.
20. Cotton Economic Situation and Outlook for 2011. University of Georgia Extension Service. December 20, 2010. www.farms.com. Accessed January 4, 2011.
21. Park, E. (2004). "What price perfection?" *The Record* (Bergen County, NJ), September 2, 2004.
22. Keeve, D. "Dirty denim episode 2: The wash." Sundance Channel Documentary. http://www.sundancechannel.com/digital-shorts/#/theme/64930111001/64571005001. Accessed December 30, 2010.
23. Kavilantz, P. (September 9, 2010). "Cotton shortage: Pricey t-shirts and jeans." CNNMoney.com. http://money.cnn.com/2010/09/09/news/economy/cotton_shortage_could_inflate_clothing_prices/index.htm. Accessed January 4, 2011.
24. blog.wired.com/cultofmac/2007/03/William_h_macy.html. Accessed December 2008.
25. Passariello, C. (2010). "Ditching designers to sell clothes." *Wall Street Journal*, March 5, 2010.

26. Ibid.
27. Tucker, R. (2008). "Some brands balk at Invista's XFIT fee plan." *Womens Wear Daily*, August 7, 2008.
28. Radsken, J. (2003). "Fashion: Jeans splicing; express knockoffs do a number on Seven's fans." *Boston Herald*, August 14, 2003.
29. Ibid.
30. Tuner, D. (2005). "Understanding the EPS/HVI advantage in a world without quota." EPS Conference Presentation (Singapore), April 20, 2005.
31. http://www.vfc.com/about/vision-values. Accessed December 2008.
32. http://www.vfc.com/about/innovation. Accessed December 2008.
33. Harmon, A. (2007). "Blue blood: The Dahan brothers reflect on the highs and lows of developing their denim lines (Occupation Overview)." *Daily News Record*, October 15, 2007.
34. Lipke, D. (2005). "Blue notes: Dispatches from the denim market (Label Chip N Pepper)." *Daily News Record*, November 7, 2005.
35. Ibid.
36. McGuiness, D. (2006). "Predicting the denim fallout: Trends and forecast." *Women's Wear Daily*, February 9, 2006.
37. Lipke, D. (2005). "Blue notes: Dispatches from the denim market (Label Chip N Pepper)." *Daily News Record*, November 7, 2005.
38. Levi's to Launch Curve ID, the Jeans That Fit All Body Types. Company Press Release. August 30, 2010.
39. Cotton Incorporated Supply Chain Insights: Price Is Not Premium in Jeans. June 2009. www.cottoninc.com. Accessed November 15, 2010.
40. Cotton Incorporated Supply Chain Insights: Price Is Not Premium in Jeans. June 2009. www.cottoninc.com. Accessed November 15, 2010.
41. Passariello, C. (2010). "Ditching designers to sell clothes." *Wall Street Journal*, March 5, 2010.
42. White, R. (2009). "In L.A. pricey denim jumps off the racks." *LA Times*, May 27, 2009.
43. True Religion Apparel and UNIFA Premium Enter into a Joint Venture. True Religion Company Press Release. July 26, 2010.
44. Tschorn, A. (2006). "True Religion taps Michael Buckley: Former head of Ben Sherman's U.S. business appointed president of denim label, True Religion Apparel Inc." *Daily News Record*, April 17, 2006.

2 BUSINESS-LEVEL STRATEGIES

Cost Leadership

After reading this chapter, you should be able to:

1. Define cost leadership.

2. Identify six reasons firms can differ in their costs.

3. Identify four reasons economies of scale can exist and four reasons diseconomies of scale can exist.

4. Explain the relationship between cost advantages due to learning-curve economies and a firm's market share, as well as the limitations of this logic.

5. Identify how cost leadership helps neutralize each of the major threats in an industry.

6. Identify the bases of cost leadership that are more likely to be rare and costly to imitate.

7. Explain how firms use a functional organizational structure to implement business-level strategies, such as cost leadership.

8. Describe the formal and informal management controls and compensation policies firms use to implement cost leadership strategies.

The World's Lowest-Cost Airline

Everyone's heard of low-cost airlines—Southwest, AirTran, and JetBlue, for example. But have you heard of the world's lowest-cost airline? This airline currently gives 25 percent of its seats away for free. Its goal is to double that within a couple of years. And yet, from 2007 to 2008, its revenues jumped 21 percent to €2.7 billion, while its net income increased 20 percent to €480.9 million. And this in spite of unprecedented increases in jet fuel prices during this same time period!

The name of this airline is Ryanair. Headquartered in Dublin, Ireland, Ryanair flies short flights throughout Western Europe. In 1985, Ryanair's founders started a small airline to fly between Ireland and England. For six years, this airline barely broke even. Then, in 1991, Michael O'Leary—current CEO at Ryanair—was brought on board. O'Leary traveled to the United States and studied the most successful low-cost airline in the world at that time—Southwest Airlines. O'Leary became convinced that, once European airspace was deregulated, an airline that adopted Southwest's model of quick turnarounds, no frills, no business class, flying into smaller regional airports, and using only a single kind of aircraft could be extremely successful. Prices in the European air market were fully deregulated in 1997.

Since then, Ryanair has become an even lower-cost airline than Southwest. For example, like Southwest, Ryanair only flies a single type of aircraft—a Boeing 737–800. However, to save on the cost of its airplanes, Ryanair orders them without window shades and with seats that do not recline. This saves several hundred thousand dollars per plane and also reduces ongoing maintenance costs. Both Southwest and Ryanair try to make it easy for consumers to order tickets online, thereby avoiding the costs of call centers and travel agents. However, just 59 percent of Southwest's tickets are sold online; 98 percent of Ryanair's tickets are sold online.

This focus on low costs allows Ryanair to have the lowest prices possible for a seat on its airplanes. The average fare on Southwest is $92; the average fare on Ryanair is $53. But, even at those low prices, Ryanair is still able to earn comfortable margins.

However, those net margins don't come just from Ryanair's low costs. They also reflect the fact that the fare you pay Ryanair includes only the seat and virtually no other services. If you want any other services, you have to pay extra for them. For example, you want to check bags? It will cost $9.95 per bag. You want a snack on the airplane? It will cost you $5.50. For that, you get a not-very-tasty hot dog. You want a bottle of water? It will cost you $3.50. You want a blanket or pillow—they cost $2.50 each.

In addition, flight attendants will sell you all sorts of extras to keep you occupied during your flight. These include scratch-card games, perfume, digital cameras ($137.50), and MP3 players ($165). During 2007, Ryanair began offering in-flight mobile telephone service. Not only did this enable passengers to call their friends and family, Ryanair also used this service to introduce mobile gambling on its planes. Now, on your way from London to Paris, you can play blackjack, poker, and slot machines.

Finally, to further increase revenues, Ryanair sells space on its planes to advertisers. When your seat tray is up, you may see an ad for a cell phone from Vodaphone. When the tray is down, you may see an ad from Hertz.

All of these actions enable Ryanair to keep its profits up while keeping its fares as low as possible. And the results of this strategy have been impressive—from near bankruptcy in 1991, Ryanair is now the largest international airline—transporting over 49 million passengers in 2008.

Of course, this success did not happen without some controversy. For example, in October 2006, Ryanair was chosen as the most disliked European

Tupungato/Shutterstock

airline in a poll of some 4,000 readers of TripAdvisor, a British Web site for frequent travelers. Ryanair's response: These frequent travelers usually have their companies pay for their travel. If they had to pay for their own tickets, they would prefer Ryanair. Also, Ryanair's strong anti-union stance has caused it political problems in many of the union-dominated countries where it flies. Finally, Ryanair has been criticized for some of its lax security and safety procedures, for how it treats disabled passengers, and for the cleanliness of its planes.

However, if you want to fly from London to Barcelona for $60 round trip, it's hard to beat Ryanair.

Source: K. Capell (2006). "Wal-Mart with wings." *BusinessWeek,* November 27, pp. 44–46; www//en.wikipedia.org/wiki/Ryanair; and Peter Arnold, Inc.

Ryanair has been profitable in an industry—the airline industry—that has historically been populated by bankrupt firms. It does this by implementing an aggressive low-cost strategy.

What Is Business-Level Strategy?

Part 1 of this book introduced you to the basic tools required to conduct a strategic analysis: tools for analyzing external threats and opportunities (in Chapter 2) and tools for analyzing internal strengths and weaknesses (in Chapter 3). Once you have completed these two analyses, it is possible to begin making strategic choices. As explained in Chapter 1, strategic choices fall into two large categories: business strategies and corporate strategies. **Business-level strategies** are actions firms take to gain competitive advantages in a single market or industry. **Corporate-level strategies** are actions firms take to gain competitive advantages by operating in multiple markets or industries simultaneously.

The two business-level strategies discussed in this book are cost leadership (this chapter) and product differentiation (Chapter 5). The importance of these two business-level strategies is so widely recognized that they are often called **generic business strategies**.

What Is Cost Leadership?

A firm that chooses a **cost leadership business strategy** focuses on gaining advantages by reducing its costs to below those of all its competitors. This does not mean that this firm abandons other business or corporate strategies. Indeed, a single-minded focus on *just* reducing costs can lead a firm to make low-cost products that no one wants to buy. However, a firm pursuing a cost leadership strategy focuses much of its effort on keeping its costs low.

Numerous firms have pursued cost leadership strategies. Ryanair clearly follows this strategy in the airline industry, Timex and Casio in the watch industry, and BIC in the disposable pen and razor market. All these firms advertise their products. However, these advertisements tend to emphasize reliability and low prices—the kinds of product attributes that are usually emphasized by firms pursuing cost leadership strategies.

In automobiles, Hyundai has implemented a cost leadership strategy with its emphasis on low-priced cars for basic transportation. Like Ryanair, Timex, Casio, and BIC, Hyundai spends a significant amount of money advertising its products, but its advertisements tend to emphasize its sporty styling and high gas mileage. Hyundai is positioned as a fun and inexpensive car, not a high-performance sports car or a luxurious status symbol. Hyundai's ability to sell these fun and inexpensive automobiles depends on its design choices (keep it simple) and its low manufacturing costs.[1]

Sources of Cost Advantages

An individual firm may have a cost advantage over its competitors for a number of reasons. Cost advantages are possible even when competing firms produce similar products. Some of the most important of these sources of cost advantage are listed in Table 4.1 and discussed in this section.

TABLE 4.1 Important Sources of Cost Advantages for Firms

Size Differences and Economies of Scale

One of the most widely cited sources of cost advantages for a firm is its size. When there are significant economies of scale in manufacturing, marketing, distribution, service, or other functions of a business, larger firms (up to some point) have a cost advantage over smaller firms. The concept of economies of scale was first defined in Chapter 2. **Economies of scale** are said to exist when the increase in firm size (measured in terms of volume of production) is associated with lower costs (measured in terms of average costs per unit of production), as depicted in Figure 4.1. As the volume of production in a firm increases, the average cost per unit decreases until some optimal volume of production (point X) is reached, after which the average costs per unit of production begin to rise because of **diseconomies of scale** (a concept discussed in more detail later in this chapter).

If the relationship between volume of production and average costs per unit of production depicted in Figure 4.1 holds, and if a firm in an industry has the largest volume of production (but not greater than the optimal level, X), then that firm will have a cost advantage in that industry. Increasing the volume of production can reduce a firm's costs for several reasons. Some of the most important of these reasons are summarized in Table 4.2 and discussed in the following text.

Volume of Production and Specialized Machines.   When a firm has high levels of production, it is often able to purchase and use specialized manufacturing tools that cannot be kept in operation in small firms. Manufacturing managers at BIC

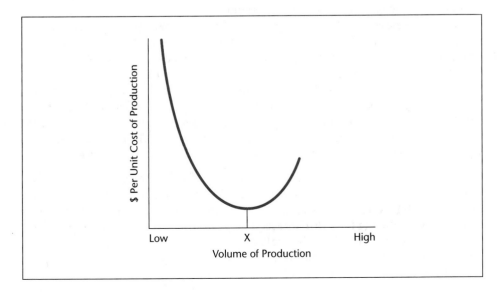

Figure 4.1 Economies of Scale

TABLE 4.2 Why Higher Volumes of Production in a Firm Can Lead to Lower Costs

With higher production volume . . .
1. firms can use specialized machines . . .
2. firms can build larger plants . . .
3. firms can increase employee specialization . . .
4. firms can spread overhead costs across more units produced . . .
. . . which can lower per-unit production costs.

Corporation, for example, have emphasized this important advantage of high volumes of production. A former director of manufacturing at BIC once observed:

> We are in the automation business. Because of our large volume, one tenth of 1 cent in savings turns out to be enormous. . . . One advantage of the high-volume business is that you can get the best equipment and amortize it entirely over a short period of time (4 to 5 months). I'm always looking for new equipment. If I see a cost-savings machine, I can buy it. I'm not constrained by money.[2]

Only firms with BIC's level of production in the pen industry have the ability to reduce their costs in this manner.

Volume of Production and the Cost of Plant and Equipment. High volumes of production may also enable a firm to build larger manufacturing operations. In some industries, the cost of building these manufacturing operations per unit of production is lower than the cost of building smaller manufacturing operations per unit of production. Thus, large-volume firms, other factors being equal, will be able to build lower-per-unit-cost manufacturing operations and will have lower average costs of production.

The link between volume of production and the cost of building manufacturing operations is particularly important in industries characterized by **process manufacturing**—chemical, oil refining, paper and pulp manufacturing, and so forth. Because of the physical geometry of process manufacturing facilities, the costs of constructing a processing plant with increased capacity can be expected to rise as the two-thirds power of a plant's capacity. This is because the area of the surface of some three-dimensional containers (such as spheres and cylinders) increases at a slower rate than the volume of these containers. Thus, larger containers hold greater volumes and require less material per unit volume for the outside skins of these containers. Up to some point, increases in capacity come at a less-than-proportionate rise in the cost of building this capacity.[3]

For example, it might cost a firm $100 to build a plant with a capacity of 1,000 units, for a per-unit average cost of $0.01. But, assuming that the "two-thirds rule" applies, it might cost a firm $465 to build a plant with a capacity of 10,000 units ($465 = 10,000^{2/3}$), for a per-unit average cost of $0.0046. The difference between $0.01 per unit and $0.0046 per unit represents a cost advantage for a large firm.

Volume of Production and Employee Specialization. High volumes of production are also associated with high levels of employee specialization. As workers specialize in accomplishing a narrow task, they can become more and more efficient at this task, thereby reducing their firm's costs. This reasoning applies both in specialized manufacturing tasks (such as the highly specialized manufacturing functions in an assembly line) and in specialized management functions (such as the highly specialized managerial functions of accounting, finance, and sales).

Smaller firms often do not possess the volume of production needed to justify this level of employee specialization. With smaller volumes of production, highly specialized employees may not have enough work to keep them busy an entire workday. This low volume of production is one reason why smaller firms often have employees that perform multiple business functions and often use outside contract employees and part-time workers to accomplish highly specialized functions, such as accounting, taxes, and human resource management.

Volume of Production and Overhead Costs.   A firm with high volumes of production has the luxury of spreading its overhead costs over more units and thereby reducing the overhead costs per unit. Suppose, in a particular industry, that the operation of a variety of accounting, control, and research and development functions, regardless of a firm's size, is $100,000. Clearly, a firm that manufactures 1,000 units is imposing a cost of $100 per unit to cover overhead expenses. However, a firm that manufactures 10,000 units is imposing a cost of $10 per unit to cover overhead. Again, the larger-volume firm's average per-unit costs are lower than the small-volume firm's average per-unit cost.

Size Differences and Diseconomies of Scale

Just as economies of scale can generate cost advantages for larger firms, important diseconomies of scale can actually increase costs if firms grow too large. As Figure 4.1 shows, if the volume of production rises beyond some optimal point (point X in the figure), this can actually lead to an increase in per-unit costs. If other firms in an industry have grown beyond the optimal firm size, a smaller firm (with a level of production closer to the optimal) may obtain a cost advantage even when all firms in the industry are producing very similar products. Some important sources of diseconomies of scale for a firm are listed in Table 4.3 and discussed in this section.

Physical Limits to Efficient Size.   Applying the two-thirds rule to the construction of manufacturing facilities seems to imply, for some industries at least, that larger is always better. However, there are some important physical limitations to the size of some manufacturing processes. Engineers have found, for example, that cement kilns develop unstable internal aerodynamics at capacities of above 7 million barrels per year. Others have suggested that scaling up nuclear reactors from small installations to huge facilities generates forces and physical processes that, though nondetectable in smaller facilities, can become significant in larger operations. These physical limitations on manufacturing processes reflect the underlying physics and engineering in a manufacturing process and suggest when the cost curve in Figure 4.1 will begin to rise.[4]

Managerial Diseconomies.   Although the underlying physics and engineering in a manufacturing process have an important impact on a firm's costs, managerial diseconomies are perhaps an even more important cause of these cost increases.

When the volume of production gets too large . . .

1. physical limits to efficient size . . .
2. managerial diseconomies . . .
3. worker de-motivation . . .
4. distance to markets and suppliers . . .

. . . can increase per-unit costs.

TABLE 4.3 Major Sources of Diseconomies of Scale

As a firm increases in size, it often increases in complexity, and the ability of managers to control and operate it efficiently becomes limited.

One well-known example of a manufacturing plant that grew too large and thus became inefficient is Crown, Cork and Seal's can-manufacturing plant in Philadelphia. Through the early part of this century, this Philadelphia facility handled as many as 75 different can-manufacturing lines. The most efficient plants in the industry, however, were running from 10 to 15 lines simultaneously. The huge Philadelphia facility was simply too large to operate efficiently and was characterized by large numbers of breakdowns, a high percentage of idle lines, and poor-quality products.[5]

Worker De-Motivation.   A third source of diseconomies of scale depends on the relationship between firm size, employee specialization, and employee motivation. It has already been suggested that one of the advantages of increased volumes of production is that it allows workers to specialize in smaller and more narrowly defined production tasks. With specialization, workers become more and more efficient at the particular task facing them.

However, a significant stream of research suggests that these types of very specialized jobs can be unmotivating for employees. Based on motivational theories taken from social psychology, this work suggests that as workers are removed further from the complete product that is the end result of a manufacturing process, the role that a worker's job plays in the overall manufacturing process becomes more and more obscure. As workers become mere "cogs in a manufacturing machine," worker motivation wanes, and productivity and quality can both suffer.[6]

Distance to Markets and Suppliers.   A final source of diseconomies of scale can be the distance between a large manufacturing facility and where the goods in question are to be sold or where essential raw materials are purchased. Any reductions in cost attributable to the exploitation of economies of scale in manufacturing may be more than offset by large transportation costs associated with moving supplies and products to and from the manufacturing facility. Firms that build highly efficient plants without recognizing these significant transportation costs may put themselves at a competitive disadvantage compared to firms with slightly less efficient plants that are located closer to suppliers and key markets.

Experience Differences and Learning-Curve Economies

A third possible source of cost advantages for firms in a particular business depends on their different cumulative levels of production. In some circumstances, firms with the greatest experience in manufacturing a product or service will have the lowest costs in an industry and thus will have a cost-based advantage. The link between cumulative volumes of production and cost has been formalized in the concept of the **learning curve**. The relationship between cumulative volumes of production and per unit costs is graphically represented in Figure 4.2.

The Learning Curve and Economies of Scale.   As depicted in Figure 4.2, the learning curve is very similar to the concept of economies of scale. However, there are two important differences. First, whereas economies of scale focus on the relationship between the volume of production at a given point in time and average unit costs, the learning curve focuses on the relationship between the *cumulative* volume of production—that is, how much a firm has produced over time—and average unit costs. Second, where diseconomies of scale are presumed to exist if a firm gets too large, there is no corresponding increase in costs in the learning-curve model as

Second, even if a location is not unique, once its value is revealed, acquisition of that location is not likely to generate economic profits. Thus, for example, although being located in Silicon Valley provides access to some important low-cost productive inputs for electronics firms, firms that moved to this location after its value was revealed have substantially higher costs than firms that moved there before its full value was revealed. These higher costs effectively reduce the economic profit that otherwise could have been generated. Referring to the discussion in Chapter 3, these arguments suggest that gaining differential access to productive inputs in a way that generates economic profits may reflect a firm's unique path through history.

Technological software is also likely to be difficult to duplicate and often can be a source of sustained competitive advantage. As suggested in Chapter 3, the values, beliefs, culture, and teamwork that constitute this software are socially complex and may be immune from competitive duplication. Firms with cost advantages rooted in these socially complex resources incorporate cost savings in every aspect of their organization; they constantly focus on improving the quality and cost of their operations, and they have employees who are firmly committed to, and understand, what it takes to be a cost leader. Other firms may talk about low costs; these firms live cost leadership. Ryanair, Dell, Wal-Mart, and Southwest are all examples of such firms. If there are few firms in an industry with these kinds of beliefs and commitments, then they can gain a sustained competitive advantage from their cost advantage.

Substitutes for Sources of Cost Advantage

In an important sense, all of the sources of cost advantage listed in this chapter are at least partial substitutes for each other. Thus, for example, one firm may reduce its cost through exploiting economies of scale in large-scale production, and a competing firm may reduce its costs through exploiting learning-curve economies and large cumulative volume of production. If these different activities have similar effects on a firm's cost position, and if they are equally costly to implement, then they are strategic substitutes for each other.

Because of the substitute effects of different sources of cost advantage, it is not unusual for firms pursuing cost leadership to simultaneously pursue *all* the cost-reduction activities discussed in this chapter. Implemention of this *bundle* of cost-reducing activities may have few substitutes. If duplicating this bundle of activities is also rare and difficult, then a firm may be able to gain a sustained competitive advantage from doing so.

Several of the other strategies discussed in later chapters can also have the effect of reducing a firm's costs and thus may be substitutes for the sources of cost reduction discussed in this chapter. For example, one common motivation for firms implementing strategic alliance strategies is to exploit economies of scale in combination with other firms. Thus, a strategic alliance that reduces a firm's costs may be a substitute for a firm exploiting economies of scale on its own to reduce its costs. As is discussed in more detail in Chapter 8, many of the strategic alliances among aluminum mining and smelting companies are motivated by realizing economies of scale and cost reduction. Also, corporate diversification strategies often enable firms to exploit economies of scale across different businesses within which they operate. In this setting, each of these businesses—treated separately—may have scale disadvantages, but collectively their scale creates the same low-cost position as that of an individual firm that fully exploits economies of scale to reduce costs in a single business (see Chapter 9).

Baseball in the United States has a problem. Most observers agree that it is better for fans if there is competitive balance in the league—that is, if, at the beginning of the year, the fans of several teams believe that their team has a chance to go to the World Series and win it all. However, the economic reality of competition in baseball is that only a small number of financially successful teams in large cities—the New York Yankees, the Los Angeles Dodgers, the Chicago Cubs, the California Angels—have the resources necessary to compete for a spot in the World Series year after year. So-called "small-market teams," such as the Pittsburgh Pirates or the Milwaukee Brewers, may be able to compete every once in a while, but these exceptions prove the general rule—teams from large markets usually win the World Series.

And then there is Oakland and the Oakland A's. Oakland (with a population of just over 400,000) is the smallest—and least glamorous—of the three cities in the San Francisco Bay Area, the other two being San Francisco and San Jose. The A's play in an outdated stadium to an average crowd of 26,038 fans—ranking nineteenth among the 30 major league baseball teams in the United States. In 2008, the A's player payroll was $48 million, about one-fifth of the Yankees' player payroll.

Despite these liabilities, from 1999 to 2008, the A's either won their division or placed second in all but two years. Over this period, the A's won 57 percent of their games, second only to the Yankees, who won 60 percent of their games over this same period. And, the team made money!

What is the "secret" to the A's success? Their general manager, William Lamar Beane, says that it has to do with three factors: how players are evaluated, making sure that every personnel decision in the organization is consistent

The Oakland A's: Inventing a New Way to Play Competitive Baseball

with this approach to evaluation, and ensuring that all personnel decisions are thought of as business decisions.

The criteria used by the A's to evaluate players are easy enough to state. For batters, the A's focus on on-base percentage (i.e., how often a batter reaches base) and total bases (a measure of the ability of a batter to hit for power); that is, they focus on the ability of players to get on base and score. For pitchers, the A's focus on the percentage of first pitches that are strikes and the quality of a pitcher's fast ball. First-pitch strikes and throwing a good fast ball are correlated with keeping runners off base. Thus, not surprisingly, the A's criteria for evaluating pitchers are the reverse of their criteria for evaluating hitters.

Although these evaluation criteria are easy to state, getting the entire organization to apply them consistently in scouting, choosing, developing, and managing players is much more difficult. Almost every baseball player and fan has his or her own favorite way to evaluate players. However, if you want to work in the A's organization, you must be willing to let go of your personal favorite and evaluate players the A's way. The result is that players that come through the A's farm system—the minor leagues where younger players are developed

until they are ready to play in the major leagues—learn a single way of playing baseball instead of learning a new approach to the game every time they change managers or coaches. One of the implications of this consistency has been that the A's farm system has been among the most productive in baseball.

This consistent farm system enables the A's to treat personnel decisions—including decisions about whether they should re-sign a star player or let him go to another team—as business decisions. The A's simply do not have the resources necessary to play the personnel game the same way as the Los Angeles Dodgers or the New York Yankees. When these teams need a particular kind of player, they go and sign one. Oakland has to rely more on its farm system. But because its farm system performs so well, the A's can let so-called "superstars" go to other teams, knowing that they are likely to have a younger—and cheaper—player in the minor leagues, just waiting for the chance to play in "the show"—the players' nickname for the major leagues. This allows the A's to keep their payroll costs down and remain profitable, despite relatively small crowds, while still fielding a team that competes virtually every year for the right to play in the World Series.

Of course, an important question becomes: How sustainable is the A's competitive advantage? The evaluation criteria themselves are not a source of sustained competitive advantage. However, the socially complex nature of how these criteria are consistently applied throughout the A's organization may be a source of sustained competitive advantage in enabling the A's to gain the differential access to low-cost productive inputs—in this case, baseball players.

Sources: K. Hammonds (2003). "How to play Beane ball." *Fast Company*, May, pp. 84 +; M. Lewis (2003). *Moneyball*. New York: Norton; A. McGahan, J. F. McGuire, and J. Kou (1997). "The baseball strike." Harvard Business School Case No. 9-796-059.

Organizing to Implement Cost Leadership

As with all strategies, firms seeking to implement cost leadership strategies must adopt an organizational structure, management controls, and compensation policies that reinforce this strategy. Some key issues associated with using these organizing tools to implement cost leadership are summarized in Table 4.6.

Organizational Structure in Implementing Cost Leadership

As suggested in Table 4.6, firms implementing cost leadership strategies will generally adopt what is known as a **functional organizational structure**.[21] An example of a functional organization structure is presented in Figure 4.4. Indeed, this functional organizational structure is the structure used to implement all business-level strategies a firm might pursue, although this structure is modified when used to implement these different strategies.

In a functional structure, each of the major business functions is managed by a **functional manager**. For example, if manufacturing, marketing, finance, accounting, and sales are all included within a functional organization, then a manufacturing manager leads that function, a marketing manager leads that function, a finance manager leads that function, and so forth. In a functional organizational structure, all these functional managers report to one person. This person has many different titles—including *president, CEO, chair,* or *founder.* However, for purposes of this discussion, this person will be called the **chief executive officer (CEO)**.

The CEO in a functional organization has a unique status. Everyone else in this company is a functional specialist. The manufacturing people manufacture, the marketing people market, the finance people finance, and so forth. Indeed, only one person in the functional organization has to have a multifunctional perspective—the CEO. This role is so important that sometimes the functional organization is called a **U-form structure**, where the "U" stands for "unitary"—because there is only one person in this organization that has a broad, multifunctional corporate perspective.

When used to implement a cost leadership strategy, this U-form structure is kept as simple as possible. As suggested in Table 4.6, firms implementing cost leadership strategies will have relatively few layers in their reporting structure.

Organization structure: Functional structure with

1. Few layers in the reporting structure
2. Simple reporting relationships
3. Small corporate staff
4. Focus on narrow range of business functions

Management control systems

1. Tight cost control systems
2. Quantitative cost goals
3. Close supervision of labor, raw material, inventory, and other costs
4. A cost leadership philosophy

Compensation policies

1. Reward for cost reduction
2. Incentives for all employees to be involved in cost reduction

TABLE 4.6 Organizing to Realize the Full Potential of Cost Leadership Strategies

Figure 4.4 An Example of
the U-form Organizational
Structure

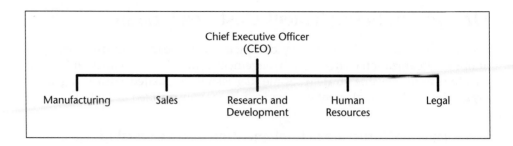

Complicated reporting structures, including **matrix structures** where one employee reports to two or more people, are usually avoided.[22] Corporate staff in these organizations is kept small. Such firms do not operate in a wide range of business functions, but instead operate only in those few business functions where they have valuable, rare, and costly-to-imitate resources and capabilities.

One excellent example of a firm pursuing a cost leadership strategy is Nucor Steel. A leader in the mini-mill industry, Nucor has only five layers in its reporting structure, compared to 12 to 15 in its major higher-cost competitors. Most operating decisions at Nucor are delegated to plant managers, who have full profit-and-loss responsibility for their operations. Corporate staff at Nucor is small and focuses its efforts on accounting for revenues and costs and on exploring new manufacturing processes to further reduce Nucor's operating expenses and expand its business opportunities. Nucor's former president, Ken Iverson, believed that Nucor does only two things well: build plants efficiently and run them effectively. Thus, Nucor focuses its efforts in these areas and subcontracts many of its other business functions, including the purchase of its raw materials, to outside vendors.[23]

Responsibilities of the CEO in a Functional Organization

The CEO in a U-form organization has two basic responsibilities: (1) to formulate the strategy of the firm and (2) to coordinate the activities of the functional specialists in the firm to facilitate the implementation of this strategy. In the special case of a cost leadership strategy, the CEO must decide on which bases such a strategy should be founded—including any of those listed in Table 4.1—and then coordinate functions within a firm to make sure that the economic potential of this strategy is fully realized.

Strategy Formulation.   The CEO in a U-form organization engages in strategy formulation by applying the strategic management process described in Chapter 1. A CEO establishes the firm's mission and associated objectives, evaluates environmental threats and opportunities, understands the firm's strengths and weaknesses, and then chooses one or more of the business and corporate strategies discussed in this book. In the case of a cost leadership strategy, the application of the strategic management process must lead a CEO to conclude that the best chance for achieving a firm's mission is for that firm to adopt a cost leadership business-level strategy.

Although the responsibility for strategy formulation in a U-form organization ultimately rests with the CEO, this individual needs to draw on the insights, analysis, and involvement of functional managers throughout the firm. CEOs who fail to involve functional managers in strategy formulation run several risks. First, strategic choices made in isolation from functional managers may be made without complete information. Second, limiting the involvement of functional managers in strategy formulation can limit their understanding of, and commitment to, the chosen strategy. This can severely limit their ability, and willingness, to implement any strategy—including cost leadership—that is chosen.[24]

Coordinating Functions for Strategy Implementation.   Even the best formulated strategy is competitively irrelevant if it is not implemented. And the only way that strategies can be effectively implemented is if all the functions within a firm are aligned in a way consistent with this strategy.

For example, compare two firms pursuing a cost leadership strategy. All but one of the first firm's functions—marketing—are aligned with this cost leadership strategy. All of the second firm's functions—including marketing—are aligned with this cost leadership strategy. Because marketing is not aligned with the first firm's cost leadership strategy, this firm is likely to advertise products that it does not sell. That is, this firm might advertise its products on the basis of their style and performance, but sell products that are reliable (but not stylish) and inexpensive (but not high performers). A firm that markets products it does not actually sell is likely to disappoint its customers. In contrast, the second firm that has all of its functions—including marketing—aligned with its chosen strategy is more likely to advertise products it actually sells and thus is less likely to disappoint its customers. In the long run, it seems reasonable to expect this second firm to outperform the first, at least with respect to implementing a cost leadership strategy.

Of course, alignment is required of all of a firm's functional areas, not just marketing. Also, misalignment can emerge in any of a firm's functional areas. Some common misalignments between a firm's cost leadership strategy and its functional activities are listed in Table 4.7.

Management Controls in Implementing Cost Leadership

As suggested in Table 4.6, cost leadership firms are typically characterized by very tight cost-control systems; frequent and detailed cost-control reports; an emphasis on quantitative cost goals and targets; and close supervision of labor, raw materials, inventory, and other costs. Again, Nucor Steel is an example of a cost leadership firm that has implemented these kinds of control systems. At Nucor, groups of employees are given weekly cost and productivity improvement goals. Groups

	When Function Is *Aligned* with Cost Leadership Strategies	**When Function Is *Misaligned* with Cost Leadership Strategies**
Manufacturing	Lean, low cost, good quality	Inefficient, high cost, poor quality
Marketing	Emphasize value, reliability, and price	Emphasize style and performance
Research and Development	Focus on product extensions and process improvements	Focus on radical new technologies and products
Finance	Focus on low cost and stable financial structure	Focus on nontraditional financial instruments
Accounting	Collect cost data and adopt conservative accounting principles	Collect no-cost data and adopt very aggressive accounting principles
Sales	Focus on value, reliability, and low price	Focus on style and performance and high price

TABLE 4.7 Common Misalignments Between Business Functions and a Cost Leadership Strategy

that meet or exceed these goals receive extra compensation. Plant managers are held responsible for cost and profit performance. A plant manager who does not meet corporate performance expectations cannot expect a long career at Nucor. Similar group-oriented cost-reduction systems are in place at some of Nucor's major competitors, including Chaparral Steel.[25]

Less formal management control systems also drive a cost-reduction philosophy at cost leadership firms. For example, although Wal-Mart is one of the most successful retail operations in the world, its Arkansas headquarters is plain and simple. Indeed, some have suggested that Wal-Mart's headquarters looks like a warehouse. Its style of interior decoration was once described as "early bus station." Wal-Mart even involves its customers in reducing costs by asking them to "help keep your costs low" by returning shopping carts to the designated areas in Wal-Mart's parking lots.[26]

Compensation Policies and Implementing Cost Leadership Strategies

As suggested in Table 4.6, compensation in cost leadership firms is usually tied directly to cost-reducing efforts. Such firms often provide incentives for employees to work together to reduce costs and increase or maintain quality, and they expect *every* employee to take responsibility for both costs and quality. For example, an important expense for retail stores like Wal-Mart is "shrinkage"—a nice way of saying people steal stuff. About half the shrinkage in most stores comes from employees stealing their own companies' products.

Wal-Mart used to have a serious problem with shrinkage. Among other solutions (including hiring "greeters" whose real job is to discourage shoplifters), Wal-Mart developed a compensation scheme that took half the cost savings created by reduced shrinkage and shared it with employees in the form of a bonus. With this incentive in place, Wal-Mart's shrinkage problems dropped significantly.

Summary

Firms producing essentially the same products can have different costs for several reasons. Some of the most important of these are: (1) size differences and economies of scale, (2) size differences and diseconomies of scale, (3) experience differences and learning-curve economies, (4) differential access to productive inputs, and (5) technological advantages independent of scale. In addition, firms competing in the same industry can make policy choices about the kinds of products and services to sell that can have an important impact on their relative cost position. Cost leadership in an industry can be valuable by assisting a firm in reducing the threat of each of the five forces in an industry outlined in Chapter 2.

Each of the sources of cost advantage discussed in this chapter can be a source of sustained competitive advantage if it is rare and costly to imitate. Overall, learning-curve economies, differential access to productive inputs, and technological "software" are more likely to be rare than other sources of cost advantage. Differential access to productive inputs and technological "software" is more likely to be costly to imitate—either through direct duplication or through substitution—than the other sources of cost advantage. Thus, differential access to productive inputs and technological "software" will often be more likely to be a source of sustained competitive advantage than cost advantages based on other sources.

Of course, to realize the full potential of these competitive advantages, a firm must be organized appropriately. Organizing to implement a strategy always involves a firm's organizational structure, its management control systems, and its compensation policies. The organizational structure used to implement cost leadership—and other business strategies—is called a *functional,* or *U-form,* structure. The CEO is the only person in this structure who has a corporate perspective. The CEO has two responsibilities: to formulate a firm's strategy and to implement it by coordinating functions within a firm. Ensuring that a firm's functions are aligned with its strategy is essential to successful strategy implementation.

When used to implement a cost leadership strategy, the U-form structure generally has few layers, simple reporting relationships, and a small corporate staff. It focuses on a narrow range of business functions. The management control systems used to implement these strategies generally include tight cost controls; quantitative cost goals; close supervision of labor, raw materials, inventory, and other costs; and a cost leadership culture and mentality. Finally, compensation policies in these firms typically reward cost reduction and provide incentives for everyone in the organization to be part of the cost-reduction effort.

Challenge Questions

1. Ryanair, Wal-Mart, Timex, Casio, and Hyundai are all cited as examples of firms pursuing cost leadership strategies, but these firms make substantial investments in advertising, which seems more likely to be associated with a product differentiation strategy. Are these firms really pursuing a cost leadership strategy, or are they pursuing a product differentiation strategy by emphasizing their lower costs?

2. When economies of scale exist, firms with large volumes of production will have lower costs than those with smaller volumes of production. The realization of these economies of scale, however, is far from automatic. What actions can firms take to ensure that they realize whatever economies of sale are created by their volume of production?

3. Firms engage in an activity called "forward pricing" when they establish, during the early stages of the learning curve, a price for their products that is lower than their actual costs, in anticipation of lower costs later on, after significant learning has occurred. Under what conditions, if any, does forward pricing make sense? What risks, if any, do firms engaging in forward pricing face?

4. One way of thinking about organizing to implement cost leadership strategies is that firms that pursue this strategy should be highly centralized, have high levels of direct supervision, and keep employee wages to an absolute minimum. Another approach is to decentralize decision-making authority—to ensure that individuals who know the most about reducing costs make decisions about how to reduce costs. This, in turn, would imply less direct supervision and somewhat higher levels of employee wages. Why is this? Which of these two approaches seems more reasonable? Under what conditions would these different approaches make more or less sense?

Problem Set

1. The economies of scale curve in Figure 4.1 can be represented algebraically in the following equation:

$$\text{Average costs} = a + bQ + cQ^2$$

where Q is the quantity produced by a firm and a, b, and c are coefficients that are estimated from industry data. For example, it has been shown that the economies of scale curve for U.S. savings and loans is:

$$\text{Average costs} = 2.38 - .615A + .54A^2$$

where A is a savings and loan's total assets. Using this equation, what is the optimal size of a savings and loan? (Hint: Plug in different values of A and calculate average costs. The lowest possible average cost is the optimal size for a savings and loan.)

2. The learning curve depicted in Figure 4.2 can be represented algebraically by the following equation:

$$\text{Average time to produce } x \text{ units} = ax^{-\beta}$$

where x is the total number of units produced by a firm in its history, a is the amount of time it took a firm to produce its first unit, and β is a coefficient that describes the rate of learning in a firm.

Suppose it takes a team of workers 45 hours to assemble its first product ($a = 45$) and 40.5 hours to assemble the second. When a firm doubles its production (in this case, from one to two units) and cuts its production time (in this case, from 45 hours to 40.5 hours), learning is said to have occurred (in this case, a 40.5/45, or 90 percent, learning curve). The β for a 90 percent learning curve is 0.3219. Thus, this firm's learning curve is:

$$\text{Average time to produce } x \text{ units} = 45x^{-0.3219}$$

What is the average amount of time it will take this firm to produce six products? (Hint: Simply plug "6" in for x in the equation and solve.) What is the total time it took this firm to produce these six products? (Hint: Simply multiply the number of units produced, 6, by the average time it will take to produce these six products.) What is the average time it will take this firm to produce five products? What is the total time it will take this firm to produce five products? So, what is the total time it will take this firm to produce its sixth product? (Hint: Subtract the total time needed to produce five products from the total time needed to produce six products.)

Suppose a new firm is going to start producing these same products. Assuming this new firm does not learn anything from established firms, what will its cost disadvantage be when it assembles its first product? (Hint: Compare the costs of the experienced firm's sixth product with the cost of the new firm's first product.)

End Notes

1. Weiner, S. (1987). "The road most traveled." *Forbes*, October 19, pp. 60–64.
2. Christensen, C. R., N. A. Berg, and M. S. Salter. (1980). *Policy formulation and administration: A casebook of senior management problems in business*, 8th ed. Homewood, IL: Irwin, p. 163.
3. Scherer, F. M. (1980). *Industrial market structure and economic performance*. Boston: Houghton Mifflin; Moore, F. T. (1959). "Economies of scale: Some statistical evidence." *Quarterly Journal of Economics*, 73, pp. 232–245; and Lau, L. J., and S. Tamura. (1972). "Economies of scale, technical progress, and the nonhomothetic leontief production function." *Journal of Political Economy*, 80, pp. 1167–1187.
4. Scherer, F. M. (1980). *Industrial market structure and economic performance*. Boston: Houghton Mifflin; and Perrow, C. (1984). *Normal accidents: Living with high-risk technologies*. New York: Basic Books.
5. Hamermesh, R. G., and R. S. Rosenbloom. (1989). "Crown Cork and Seal Co., Inc." Harvard Business School Case No. 9-388-096.
6. See Hackman, J. R., and G. R. Oldham. (1980). *Work redesign*. Reading, MA: Addison-Wesley.
7. This relationship was first noticed in 1925 by the commander of Wright-Patterson Air Force Base in Dayton, Ohio.
8. Learning curves have been estimated for numerous industries. Boston Consulting Group. (1970). "Perspectives on experience." Boston: BCG, presents learning curves for over 20 industries while Lieberman, M. (1984). "The learning curve and pricing in the chemical processing industries." *Rand Journal of Economics*, 15, pp. 213–228, estimates learning curves for 37 chemical products.
9. See Henderson, B. (1974). *The experience curve reviewed III—How does it work?* Boston: Boston Consulting Group; and Boston Consulting Group. (1970). "Perspectives on experience." Boston: BCG.
10. Hall, G., and S. Howell. (1985). "The experience curve from the economist's perspective." *Strategic Management Journal*, 6, pp. 197–212.
11. Hill, C. W. L. (1988). "Differentiation versus low-cost or differentiation and low-cost: A contingency framework." *Academy of Management Review*, 13(3), pp. 401–412.
12. See Ghemawat, P., and H. J. Stander III. (1992). "Nucor at a crossroads." Harvard Business School Case No. 9-793-039 on technology in steel manufacturing and cost advantages; Shaffer, R. A. (1995). "Intel as conquistador." *Forbes*, February 27, p. 130 on technology in semiconductor manufacturing and cost advantages; Monteverde, K., and D. Teece. (1982). "Supplier switching costs and vertical integration in the automobile industry." *Rand Journal of Economics*, 13(1), pp. 206–213; and McCormick, J., and N. Stone. (1990). "From national champion to global competitor: An interview with Thomson's Alain Gomez." *Harvard Business Review*, May/June, pp. 126–135 on technology in consumer electronic manufacturing and cost advantages.
13. Schultz, E. (1989). "Climbing high with discount brokers." *Fortune*, Fall (special issue), pp. 219–223.
14. Schonfeld, E. (1998). "Can computers cure health care?" *Fortune*, March 30, pp. 111 +.
15. Ibid.
16. See Meyer, M. W., and L. B. Zucker. (1989). *Permanently failing organizations*. Newbury Park, CA: Sage.
17. Staw, B. M. (1981). "The escalation of commitment to a course of action." *Academy of Management Review*, 6, pp. 577–587.
18. Hesterly, W. S. (1989). *Top management succession as a determinant of firm performance and de-escalation: An agency problem.* Unpublished doctoral dissertation, University of California, Los Angeles.
19. Barney, J. B. (1986). "Organizational culture: Can it be a source of sustained competitive advantage?" *Academy of Management Review*, 11, pp. 656–665.
20. See Spence, A. M. (1981). "The learning curve and competition." *Bell Journal of Economics*, 12, pp. 49–70, on why learning needs to be proprietary; Mansfield, E. (1985). "How rapidly does new industrial technology leak out?" *Journal of Industrial Economics*, 34(2), pp. 217–223; Lieberman, M. B. (1982). *The learning-curve, pricing and market structure in the chemical processing industries.* Unpublished doctoral dissertation, Harvard University; Lieberman, M. B. (1987). "The learning curve, diffusion, and competitive strategy." *Strategic Management Journal*, 8, pp. 441–452 on why it usually is not proprietary.
21. Williamson, O. (1975). *Markets and hierarchies*. New York: Free Press.
22. Davis, S. M., and P. R. Lawrence. (1977). *Matrix*. Reading, MA: Addison-Wesley.
23. See Ghemawat, P., and H. J. Stander III. (1992). "Nucor at a crossroads." Harvard Business School Case No. 9-793-039.
24. See Floyd, S. W., and B. Woldridge. (1992). "Middle management involvement in strategy and its association with strategic type: A research note." *Strategic Management Journal*, 13, pp. 153–167.
25. Ibid.
26. Walton, S. (1992). *Sam Walton, Made in America: My story*. New York: Doubleday.

5

Product Differentiation

Who Is Victoria, and What Is Her Secret?

Sexy. Glamorous. Mysterious. Victoria's Secret is the world's leading specialty retailer of lingerie and beauty products. With 2007 sales of almost $6.1 billion, Victoria's Secret sells its mix of sexy lingerie, prestige fragrances, and fashion-inspired collections through over 1,000 retail stores and the almost 400 million catalogues it distributes each year.

But all this glamour and success leaves the two central questions about this firm unanswered: "Who is Victoria?" and "What is her secret?"

It turns out that Victoria is a retired fashion model who lives in an up-and-coming fashionable district in London. She has a committed relationship and is thinking about starting a family. However, these maternal instincts are balanced by Victoria's adventurous and sexy side. She loves good food, classical music, and great wine. She travels frequently and is as much at home in New York, Paris, and Los Angeles as she is in London. Her fashion tastes are edgy enough to never be boring, but practical enough to never be extreme. Her lingerie is an essential part of her wardrobe. Sexy and alluring, but never cheap, trashy, or vulgar, Victoria's lingerie is the perfect complement to her overall lifestyle. Most important, while Victoria knows she is beautiful and sexy, she also knows that it is her brains, not her looks, that have enabled her to succeed in life.

This is who Victoria is. This is the woman that Victoria's Secret's designers design for, the woman Victoria's Secret marketers create advertising for, and the woman to whom all Victoria's Secret sales associates are trained to sell.

And this is her secret—Victoria doesn't really exist. Or, more precisely, the number of real women in the entire world who are like Victoria is very small—no more than a handful. So why would a company like Victoria's Secret organize all of its design, marketing, and sales efforts around meeting the lingerie needs of a woman who, for all practical purposes, doesn't really exist?

Victoria's Secret knows how few of its actual customers are like Victoria. However, it is convinced that many of its customers would like to be treated as if they were Victoria, if only for a few hours, when they come into a Victoria's Secret store. Victoria's Secret is not just selling lingerie; it is selling an opportunity, almost a fantasy, to be like Victoria—to live in an exciting and sexy city, to travel the world, to have refined, yet edgy, tastes. To buy and wear Victoria's Secret lingerie is—if only for a moment or two—an opportunity to experience life as Victoria experiences it.

Practically speaking, building an entire company around meeting the needs of a customer who does not actually exist creates some interesting problems. You can't just call Victoria on the phone and ask her about trends in her lifestyle; you can't form a focus group of people like Victoria and ask them to evaluate new lines of lingerie. In a sense, not only has Victoria's Secret invented Victoria; it also had to invent Victoria's lifestyle—and the lingerie, fragrances, and accessories that go along with that lifestyle. And as long as the lifestyle that it invents for Victoria is desirable to but just beyond the reach of its actual customers, Victoria's Secret will continue to be able to sell a romantic fantasy—along with its bras and panties.

Stephen Coburn/Shutterstock

Sources: www.limitedbrands.com; www.victoriassecret.com; and Corbis/Bettmann.

Victoria's Secret uses the fictional character "Victoria" to help implement its product differentiation strategy. As successful as this effort is, however, this is only one of many ways that firms can try to differentiate their products.

What Is Product Differentiation?

Whereas Wal-Mart exemplifies a firm pursuing a cost leadership strategy, Victoria's Secret exemplifies a firm pursuing a product differentiation strategy. **Product differentiation** is a business strategy whereby firms attempt to gain a competitive advantage by increasing the perceived value of their products or services relative to the perceived value of other firms' products or services. These other firms can be rivals or firms that provide substitute products or services. By increasing the perceived value of its products or services, a firm will be able to charge a higher price than it would otherwise. This higher price can increase a firm's revenues and generate competitive advantages.

A firm's attempts to create differences in the relative perceived value of its products or services often are made by altering the objective properties of those products or services. Rolex attempts to differentiate its watches from Timex and Casio watches by manufacturing them with solid gold cases. Mercedes attempts to differentiate its cars from Hyundai's cars through sophisticated engineering and high performance. Victoria's Secret attempts to differentiate its shopping experience from Wal-Mart, and other retailers, through the merchandise it sells and the way it sells it.

Although firms often alter the objective properties of their products or services in order to implement a product differentiation strategy, the existence of product differentiation, in the end, is *always* a matter of customer perception. Products sold by two different firms may be very similar, but if customers believe the first is more valuable than the second, then the first product has a differentiation advantage.

In the world of "craft" or "microbrewery" beers, for example, the consumers' image of how a beer is brewed may be very different from how it is actually brewed. Boston Beer Company, for example, sells Samuel Adams Beer. Customers can tour the Boston Beer Company, where they will see a small row of fermenting tanks and two 10-barrel kettles being tended by a brewmaster wearing rubber boots. However, Samuel Adams Beer was not actually brewed in this small factory. Instead, it was, for much of its history, brewed—in 200-barrel steel tanks—in Cincinnati, Ohio, by the Hudepohl-Schoenling Brewing Company, a contract brewing firm that also manufactures Hudy Bold Beer and Little Kings Cream Ale. Maui Beer Company's Aloha Lager brand was brewed in Portland, Oregon, and Pete's Wicked Ale (a craft beer that claims it is brewed "one batch at a time. Carefully.") was brewed in batches of 400 barrels each by Stroh Brewery Company, makers of Old Milwaukee Beer. However, the more consumers believe there are important differences between these "craft" beers and more traditional brews—despite many of their common manufacturing methods—the more willing they will be to pay more for a craft beer. This willingness to pay more suggests that an important "perceptual" basis of product differentiation exists for these craft beers.[1] If products or services are *perceived* as being different in a way that is valued by consumers, then product differentiation exists.

Just as perceptions can create product differentiation between products that are essentially identical, the lack of perceived differences between products with very different characteristics can prevent product differentiation. For example, consumers with an untrained palate may not be able to distinguish between two different wines, even though expert wine tasters would be very much aware of their differences. Those who are not aware of these differences, even if they exist, will not be willing to pay more for one wine over the other. In this sense, for these consumers at least, these two wines, though different, are not differentiated.

Product differentiation is always a matter of customer perceptions, but firms can take a variety of actions to influence these perceptions. These actions can be thought of as different bases of product differentiation.

Bases of Product Differentiation

A large number of authors, drawing on both theory and empirical research, have developed lists of ways firms can differentiate their products or services.[2] Some of these are listed in Table 5.1. Although the purpose of all these bases of product differentiation is to create the perception that a firm's products or services are unusually valuable, different bases of product differentiation attempt to accomplish this objective in different ways. For example, the first four bases of product differentiation listed in Table 5.1 attempt to create this perception by focusing directly on the attributes of the products or services a firm sells. The second three attempt to create this perception by developing a relationship between a firm and its customers. The last five attempt to create this perception through linkages within and between firms. Of course, these bases of product differentiation are not mutually exclusive. Indeed, firms will often attempt to differentiate their products or services along multiple dimensions simultaneously. An empirical method for identifying ways that firms have differentiated their products is discussed in the Research Made Relevant feature.

Focusing on the Attributes of a Firm's Products or Services

The first group of bases of product differentiation identified in Table 5.1 focuses on the attributes of a firm's products or services.

TABLE 5.1 Ways Firms Can Differentiate Their Products

To differentiate its products, a firm can focus directly on the attributes of its products or services:

1. Product features
2. Product complexity
3. Timing of product introduction
4. Location

or, on relationships between itself and its customers:
5. Product customization
6. Consumer marketing
7. Product reputation

or, on linkages within or between firms:
8. Linkages among functions within a firm
9. Linkages with other firms
10. Product mix
11. Distribution channels
12. Service and support

Sources: M. E. Porter. (1980). *Competitive strategy.* New York: Free Press; R. E. Caves and P. Williamson. (1985). "What is product differentiation, really?" *Journal of Industrial Economics,* 34, pp. 113–132.

Product Features.   The most obvious way that firms can try to differentiate their products is by altering the features of the products they sell. One industry in which firms are constantly modifying product features to attempt to differentiate their products is the automobile industry. Chrysler, for example, introduced the "cab forward" design to try to give its cars a distinctive look, whereas Audi went with a more radical flowing and curved design to differentiate its cars. For emergency situations, General Motors (GM) introduced the "On Star" system, which instantly connects drivers to GM operators 24 hours a day, while Mercedes-Benz continued to develop its "crumple zone" system to ensure passenger safety in a crash. In body construction, General Motors continues to develop its "uni-body" construction system, whereby different parts of a car are welded to each other rather than built on a single frame, while Jaguar introduced a 100 percent aluminum body to help differentiate its top-of-the-line model from other luxury cars. Mazda continues to tinker with the motor and suspension of its sporty Miata, while Nissan introduced the 370 Z—a continuation of the famous 240 Z line—and Porsche changed from air-cooled to water-cooled engines in its 911 series of sports cars. All these—and many more—changes in the attributes of automobiles are examples of firms trying to differentiate their products by altering product features.

Product Complexity.   Product complexity can be thought of as a special case of altering a product's features to create product differentiation. In a given industry, product complexity can vary significantly. The BIC "crystal pen," for example, has only a handful of parts, whereas a Cross or a Mont Blanc pen has many more parts. To the extent that these differences in product complexity convince consumers that the products of some firms are more valuable than the products of other firms, product complexity can be a basis of product differentiation.

Timing of Product Introduction.   Introducing a product at the right time can also help create product differentiation. As suggested in Chapter 2, in some industry settings (e.g., in emerging industries) *the* critical issue is to be a first mover—to introduce a new product before all other firms. Being first in emerging industries can enable a firm to set important technological standards, preempt strategically valuable assets, and develop customer-switching costs. These first-mover advantages can create a perception among customers that the products or services of the first-moving firm are somehow more valuable than the products or services of other firms.[3]

Timing-based product differentiation, however, does not depend only on being a first mover. Sometimes, a firm can be a later mover in an industry but introduce products or services at just the right time and thereby gain a competitive advantage. This can happen when the ultimate success of a product or service depends on the availability of complementary products or technologies. For example, the domination of Microsoft's MS-DOS operating system, and thus ultimately the domination of Windows, was only possible because IBM introduced its version of the personal computer. Without the IBM PC, it would have been difficult for any operating system—including MS-DOS—to have such a large market presence.[4]

Location.   The physical location of a firm can also be a source of product differentiation.[5] Consider, for example, Disney's operations in Orlando, Florida. Beginning with The Magic Kingdom and EPCOT Center, Disney built a world-class destination resort in Orlando. Over the years, Disney has added numerous attractions to its core entertainment activities, including MGM Studios, over 11,000 Disney-owned hotel rooms, a $100 million sports center, an automobile racing track, an after-hours entertainment district, and most recently, a $1 billion

Of all the possible bases of product differentiation that might exist in a particular market, how does one pinpoint those that have actually been used? Research in strategic management and marketing has shown that the bases of product differentiation can be identified using multiple regression analysis to estimate what are called **hedonic prices**. A hedonic price is that part of the price of a product or service that is attributable to a particular characteristic of that product or service.

The logic behind hedonic prices is straightforward. If customers are willing to spend more for a product with a particular attribute than they are willing to spend for that same product without that attribute, then that attribute differentiates the first product from the second. That is, this attribute is a basis of product differentiation in this market.

Consider, for example, the price of used cars. The market price of a used car can be determined through the use of a variety of used car buying guides. These guides typically establish the base price of a used car. This base price typically includes product features that are common to almost all cars—a radio, a standard engine, a heater/defroster. Because these product attributes are

**Discovering the Bases
of Product Differentiation**

common to virtually all cars, they are not a basis for product differentiation.

However, in addition to these common features, the base price of an automobile is adjusted based on some less common features—a high-end stereo system, a larger engine, air-conditioning. How much the base price of the car is adjusted when these features are added—$300 for a high-end stereo, $500 for a larger engine, $200 for air-conditioning—are the hedonic prices of these product attributes. These product attributes differentiate well-equipped cars from less-well-equipped cars and, because consumers are willing to pay more for

well-equipped cars, can be thought of as bases of product differentiation in this market.

Multiple regression techniques are used to estimate these hedonic prices in the following way. For our simple car example, the following regression equation is estimated:

$$Price = a_1 + b_1(Stereo) + b_2(Engine) + b_3(AC)$$

where *Price* is the retail price of cars, *Stereo* is a variable describing whether a car has a high-end stereo, *Engine* is a variable describing whether a car has a large engine, and *AC* is a variable describing whether or not a car has air-conditioning. If the hedonic prices for these features are those suggested earlier, the results of running this regression analysis would be:

$$Price = \$7,800 + \$300(Stereo) + \$500(Engine) + \$200(AC)$$

where $7,800 is the base price of this type of used car.

Source: D. Hay and D. Morris. (1979). *Industrial economics: Theory and evidence.* Oxford: Oxford University Press; K. Cowling and J. Cubbin (1971). "Price, quality, and advertising competition." *Economica,* 38, pp. 378–394.

theme park called "The Animal Kingdom"—all in and around Orlando. Now, families can travel from around the world to Orlando, knowing that in a single location they can enjoy a full range of Disney adventures.[6]

Focusing on the Relationship Between a Firm and Its Customers
The second group of bases of product differentiation identified in Table 5.1 focuses on relationships between a firm and its customers.

Product Customization.   Products can also be differentiated by the extent to which they are customized for particular customer applications. Product customization is an important basis for product differentiation in a wide variety of industries, from enterprise software to bicycles.

Enterprise software is software that is designed to support all of a firm's critical business functions, including human resources, payroll, customer service, sales, quality control, and so forth. Major competitors in this industry include Oracle and SAP. However, although these firms sell basic software packages, most firms find it necessary to customize these basic packages to meet their specific business needs. The ability to build complex software packages that can also be customized to meet the specific needs of a particular customer is an important basis of product differentiation in this marketplace.

In the bicycle industry, consumers can spend as little as $50 on a bicycle, and as much as—well, almost as much as they want on a bicycle, easily in excess of $10,000. High-end bicycles use, of course, the very best components, such as brakes and gears. But what really distinguishes these bicycles is their customized fit. Once a serious rider becomes accustomed to a particular bicycle, it is very difficult for that rider to switch to alternative suppliers.

Consumer Marketing.   Differential emphasis on consumer marketing has been a basis for product differentiation in a wide variety of industries. Through advertising and other consumer marketing efforts, firms attempt to alter the perceptions of current and potential customers, whether or not specific attributes of a firm's products or services are actually altered.

For example, in the soft drink industry, Mountain Dew—a product of PepsiCo—was originally marketed as a fruity, lightly carbonated drink that tasted "as light as a morning dew in the mountains." However, beginning in the late 1990s Mountain Dew's marketing efforts changed dramatically. "As light as a morning dew in the mountains" became "Do the Dew," and Mountain Dew focused its marketing efforts on young, mostly male, extreme-sports–oriented consumers. Young men riding snowboards, roller blades, mountain bikes, and skateboards—mostly upside down—became central to most Mountain Dew commercials. Mountain Dew became a sponsor of a wide variety of extreme sports contests and an important sponsor of the X Games on ESPN. And will we ever forget the confrontation between the young Dew enthusiast and a big horn sheep over a can of Mountain Dew in a meadow? Note that this radical repositioning of Mountain Dew depended entirely on changes in consumer marketing. The features of the underlying product were not changed.

Reputation.   Perhaps the most important relationship between a firm and its customers depends on a firm's reputation in its marketplace. Indeed, a firm's **reputation** is really no more than a socially complex relationship between a firm and its customers. Once developed, a firm's reputation can last a long time, even if the basis for that reputation no longer exists.[7]

A firm that has tried to exploit its reputation for cutting-edge entertainment is MTV, a division of Viacom, Inc. Although several well-known video artists—including Madonna—have had their videos banned from MTV, it has still been able to develop a reputation for risk-taking on television. MTV believes that its viewers have come to expect the unexpected in MTV programming. One of the first efforts to exploit, and reinforce, this reputation for risk-taking was *Beavis and Butthead*, an animated series starring two teenage boys with serious social and emotional development problems. More recently, MTV exploited its reputation by inventing an entirely new genre of television—"reality TV"—through its *Real World* and *House Rules* programs. Not only are these shows cheap to produce, they build on the reputation that MTV has for providing entertainment that is a little risky, a little sexy, and a little controversial. Indeed, MTV has been so successful in providing this kind of entertainment that it had to form an entirely new cable station—MTV 2—to actually show music videos.[8]

Focusing on Links Within and Between Firms

The third group of bases of product differentiation identified in Table 5.1 focuses on links within and between firms.

Linkages Between Functions.   A less obvious but still important way in which a firm can attempt to differentiate its products is through linking different functions within the firm. For example, research in the pharmaceutical industry suggests that firms vary in the extent to which they are able to integrate different scientific specialties—such as genetics, biology, chemistry, and pharmacology—to develop new drugs. Firms that are able to form effective multidisciplinary teams to explore new drug categories have what some have called an **architectural competence**, that is, the ability to use organizational structure to facilitate coordination among scientific disciplines to conduct research. Firms that have this competence are able to more effectively pursue product differentiation strategies—by introducing new and powerful drugs—than those that do not have this competence. And in the pharmaceutical industry, where firms that introduce such drugs can experience very large positive returns, the ability to coordinate across functions is an important source of competitive advantage.[9]

Links with Other Firms.   Another basis of product differentiation is linkages with other firms. Here, instead of differentiating products or services on the basis of linkages between functions within a single firm or linkages between different products, differentiation is based on explicit linkages between one firm's products and the products or services of other firms.

This form of product differentiation has increased in popularity over the last several years. For example, with the growth in popularity of stock car racing in the United States, more and more corporations are looking to link their products or services with famous names and cars in NASCAR. Firms such as Kodak, Gatorade, McDonald's, Home Depot, The Cartoon Network, True Value, and Pfizer (manufacturers of Viagra) have all been major sponsors of NASCAR teams. In one year, the Coca-Cola Corporation filled orders for over 200,000 NASCAR-themed vending machines. Visa struggled to keep up with demand for its NASCAR affinity cards, and over 1 million NASCAR Barbies were sold by Mattel—generating revenues of about $50 million. Notice that none of these firms sells products for automobiles. Rather, these firms seek to associate themselves with NASCAR because of the sport's popularity.[10]

In general, linkages between firms that differentiate their products are examples of cooperative strategic alliance strategies. The conditions under which cooperative strategic alliances create value and are sources of sustained competitive advantage are discussed in detail in Chapter 9.

Product Mix.   One of the outcomes of links among functions within a firm and links between firms can be changes in the mix of products a firm brings to the market. This mix of products or services can be a source of product differentiation, especially when (1) those products or services are technologically linked or (2) when a single set of customers purchases several of a firm's products or services.

For example, technological interconnectivity is an extremely important selling point in the information technology business, and thus an important basis of potential product differentiation. However, seamless interconnectivity—where Company A's computers talk to Company B's computers across Company C's data line merging a database created by Company D's software with a database created by Company E's software to be used in a calling center that operates with Company F's technology—has been extremely difficult to realize. For this reason, some information technology firms try to realize the goal of interconnectivity by adjusting their product mix, that is, by selling a bundle of products whose interconnectivity they can control and guarantee to customers. This goal of selling a bundle of interconnected technologies can influence a firm's research and development, strategic alliance, and merger and acquisition strategies, because all these activities can influence the set of products a firm brings to market.

Shopping malls are an example of the second kind of linkage among a mix of products—where products have a common set of customers. Many customers prefer to go to one location, to shop at several stores at once, rather than travel to a series of locations to shop. This one-stop shopping reduces travel time and helps turn shopping into a social experience. Mall development companies have recognized that the value of several stores brought together in a particular location is greater than the value of those stores if they were isolated, and they have invested to help create this mix of retail shopping opportunities.[11]

Distribution Channels.   Linkages within and between firms can also have an impact on how a firm chooses to distribute its products, and distribution channels can be a basis of product differentiation. For example, in the soft drink industry Coca-Cola, PepsiCo, and 7-Up all distribute their drinks through a network of independent and company-owned bottlers. These firms manufacture key ingredients for their soft drinks and ship these ingredients to local bottlers, who add carbonated water, package the drinks in bottles or cans, and distribute the final product to soft drink outlets in a given geographic area. Each local bottler has exclusive rights to distribute a particular brand in a geographic location.

Canada Dry has adopted a completely different distribution network. Instead of relying on local bottlers, Canada Dry packages its soft drinks in several locations and then ships them directly to wholesale grocers, who distribute the product to local grocery stores, convenience stores, and other retail outlets.

One of the consequences of these alternative distribution strategies is that Canada Dry has a relatively strong presence in grocery stores but a relatively small presence in soft drink vending machines. The vending machine market is dominated by Coca-Cola and PepsiCo. These two firms have local distributors that maintain and stock vending machines. Canada Dry has no local distributors and is able to get its products into vending machines only when they are purchased by local Coca-Cola or Pepsi distributors. These local distributors are likely to purchase and stock Canada Dry products such as Canada Dry ginger ale, but they are contractually prohibited from purchasing Canada Dry's various cola products.[12]

Service and Support.   Finally, products have been differentiated by the level of service and support associated with them. Some firms in the home appliance market, including General Electric, have not developed their own service and support network and instead rely on a network of independent service and support operations throughout the United States. Other firms in the same industry, including Sears, have developed their own service and support networks.[13]

Product Differentiation and Creativity

The bases of product differentiation listed in Table 5.1 indicate a broad range of ways in which firms can differentiate their products and services. In the end, however, any effort to list all possible ways to differentiate products and services is doomed to failure. Product differentiation is ultimately an expression of the creativity of individuals and groups within firms. It is limited only by the opportunities that exist, or that can be created, in a particular industry and by the willingness and ability of firms to creatively explore ways to take advantage of those opportunities. It is not unreasonable to expect that the day some academic researcher claims to have developed the definitive list of bases of product differentiation, some creative engineer, marketing specialist, or manager will think of yet another way to differentiate his or her product.

The Value of Product Differentiation

V R I O

In order to have the potential for generating competitive advantages, the bases of product differentiation upon which a firm competes must be valuable. The market conditions under which product differentiation can be valuable are discussed in the Strategy in Depth feature. More generally, in order to be valuable, bases of product differentiation must enable a firm to neutralize its threats and/or exploit its opportunities.

Product Differentiation and Environmental Threats

Successful product differentiation helps a firm respond to each of the environmental threats identified in the five forces framework. For example, product differentiation helps reduce the threat of new entry by forcing potential entrants to an industry to absorb not only the standard costs of beginning business, but also the additional costs associated with overcoming incumbent firms' product differentiation advantages. The relationship between product differentiation and new entry has already been discussed in Chapter 2.

Product differentiation reduces the threat of rivalry, because each firm in an industry attempts to carve out its own unique product niche. Rivalry is not reduced to zero, because these products still compete with one another for a common set of customers, but it is somewhat attenuated because the customers each firm seeks are different. For example, both a Rolls Royce and a Hyundai satisfy the same basic consumer need—transportation—but it is unlikely that potential customers of Rolls Royce will also be interested in purchasing a Hyundai or vice versa.

Product differentiation also helps firms reduce the threat of substitutes by making a firm's current products appear more attractive than substitute products. For example, fresh food can be thought of as a substitute for frozen processed foods. In order to make its frozen processed foods more attractive than fresh foods, products such as Stouffer's and Swanson are marketed heavily through television advertisements, newspaper ads, point-of-purchase displays, and coupons.

Product differentiation can also reduce the threat of powerful suppliers. Powerful suppliers can raise the prices of the products or services they provide. Often, these increased supply costs must be passed on to a firm's customers in the form of higher prices if a firm's profit margin is not to deteriorate. A firm without a highly differentiated product may find it difficult to pass its increased costs on to customers, because these customers will have numerous other ways to purchase

Strategy in Depth

The two classic treatments of the relationship between product differentiation and firm value, developed independently and published at approximately the same time, are by Edward Chamberlin and Joan Robinson.

Both Chamberlin and Robinson examine product differentiation and firm performance relative to perfect competition. As explained in Chapter 2, under perfect competition, it is assumed that there are numerous firms in an industry, each controlling a small proportion of the market, and the products or services sold by these firms are assumed to be identical. Under these conditions, firms face a horizontal demand curve (because they have no control over the price of the products they sell), and they maximize their economic performance by producing and selling output such that marginal revenue equals marginal costs. The maximum economic performance a firm in a perfectly competitive market can obtain, assuming no cost differences across firms, is normal economic performance.

When firms sell differentiated products, they gain some ability to adjust their prices. A firm can sell its output at very high prices and produce relatively smaller amounts of output, or it can sell its output at very low prices and produce relatively greater

The Economics of Product Differentiation

amounts of output. These trade-offs between price and quantity produced suggest that firms selling differentiated products face a downward-sloping demand curve, rather than the horizontal demand curve for firms in a perfectly competitive market. Firms selling differentiated products and facing a downward-sloping demand curve are in an industry structure described by Chamberlin as **monopolistic competition**. It is as if, within the market niche defined by a firm's differentiated product, a firm possesses a monopoly.

Firms in monopolistically competitive markets still maximize their economic profit by producing and selling a quantity of products such that

marginal revenue equals marginal cost. The price that firms can charge at this optimal point depends on the demand they face for their differentiated product. If demand is large, then the price that can be charged is greater; if demand is low, then the price that can be charged is lower. However, if a firm's average total cost is below the price it can charge (i.e., if average total cost is less than the demand-determined price), then a firm selling a differentiated product can earn an above-normal economic profit.

Consider the example presented in Figure 5.1. Several curves are relevant in this figure. First, note that a firm in this industry faces downward-sloping demand (D). This means that the industry is not perfectly competitive and that a firm has some control over the prices it will charge for its products. Also, the marginal-revenue curve (MR) is downward sloping and everywhere lower than the demand curve. Marginal revenue is downward sloping because in order to sell additional levels of output of a single product, a firm must be willing to lower its price. The marginal-revenue curve is lower than the demand curve because this lower price applies to all the products sold by a firm, not just to any additional products the firm sells. The marginal-cost curve (MC) is upward sloping,

similar products or services from a firm's competitors. However, a firm with a highly differentiated product may have loyal customers or customers who are unable to purchase similar products or services from other firms. These types of customers are more likely to accept increased prices. Thus, a powerful supplier may be able to raise its prices, but, up to some point, these increases will not reduce the profitability of a firm selling a highly differentiated product.

Finally, product differentiation can reduce the threat of powerful buyers. When a firm sells a highly differentiated product, it enjoys a "quasi-monopoly" in that segment of the market. Buyers interested in purchasing this particular product must buy it from a particular firm. Any potential buyer power is reduced by the ability of a firm to withhold highly valued products or services from a buyer.

indicating that in order to produce additional outputs a firm must accept additional costs. The average-total-cost curve (*ATC*) can have a variety of shapes, depending on the economies of scale, the cost of productive inputs, and other cost phenomena described in Chapter 4.

These four curves (demand, marginal revenue, marginal cost, and average total cost) can be used to determine the level of economic profit for a firm under monopolistic competition. To maximize profit, the firm produces an amount (Q_e) such that marginal costs equal marginal revenues. To determine the price of a firm's output at this level of production, a vertical line is drawn from the point where marginal costs equal marginal revenues. This line will intersect with the demand curve. Where this vertical line intersects demand, a horizontal line is drawn to the vertical (price) axis to determine the price a firm can charge. In the figure, this price is P_e. At the point P_e, average total cost is less than the price. The

total revenue obtained by the firm in this situation (price × quantity) is indicated by the shaded area in the figure. The economic profit portion of this total revenue is indicated by the crosshatched section of the shaded portion of the figure. Because this crosshatched section is above average total costs in the figure, it represents a competitive advantage. If this section was below average total costs, it would represent a competitive disadvantage.

Chamberlin and Robinson go on to discuss the impact of entry into the market niche defined by a firm's differentiated product. As discussed in Chapter 2, a basic assumption of S-C-P models is that the existence of

above-normal economic performance motivates entry into an industry or into a market niche within an industry. In monopolistically competitive industries, such entry means that the demand curve facing incumbent firms shifts downward and to the left. This implies that an incumbent firm's customers will buy less of its output if it maintains its prices or (equivalently) that a firm will have to lower its prices to maintain its current volume of sales. In the long run, entry into this market niche can lead to a situation where the price of goods or services sold when a firm produces output such that marginal cost equals marginal revenue is exactly equal to that firm's average total cost. At this point, a firm earns zero economic profits even if it still sells a differentiated product.

Sources: E. H. Chamberlin. (1933). *The economics of monopolistic competition.* Cambridge, MA: MIT Press; J. Robinson. (1934). "What is perfect competition?" *Quarterly Journal of Economics,* 49, pp. 104–120.

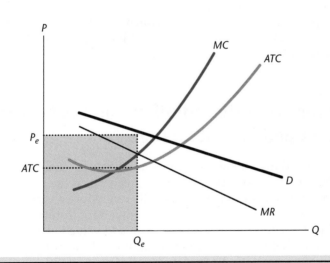

Figure 5.1   Product Differentiation and Firm Performance: The Analysis of Monopolistic Competition

Product Differentiation and Environmental Opportunities

Product differentiation can also help a firm take advantage of environmental opportunities. For example, in fragmented industries firms can use product differentiation strategies to help consolidate a market. In the office-paper industry, Xerox has used its brand name to become the leading seller of paper for office copy machines and printers. Arguing that its paper is specially manufactured to avoid jamming in its own copy machines, Xerox was able to brand what had been a commodity product and facilitate the consolidation of what had been a very fragmented industry.[14]

The role of product differentiation in emerging industries was discussed in Chapter 2. By being a first mover in these industries, firms can gain product differentiation advantages based on perceived technological leadership, preemption of strategically valuable assets, and buyer loyalty due to high switching costs.

In mature industries, product differentiation efforts often switch from attempts to introduce radically new technologies to product refinement as a basis of product differentiation. For example, in the mature retail gasoline market firms attempt to differentiate their products by selling slightly modified gasoline (cleaner-burning gasoline, gasoline that cleans fuel injectors, and so forth) and by altering the product mix (linking gasoline sales with convenience stores). In mature markets, it is sometimes difficult to find ways to actually refine a product or service. In such settings, firms can sometimes be tempted to exaggerate the extent to which they have refined and improved their products or services. The implications of these exaggerations are discussed in the Ethics and Strategy feature.

Product differentiation can also be an important strategic option in a declining industry. Product-differentiating firms may be able to become leaders in this kind of industry (based on their reputation, unique product attributes, or some other product differentiation basis). Alternatively, highly differentiated firms may be able to discover a viable market niche that will enable them to survive despite the overall decline in the market.

Finally, the decision to implement a product differentiation strategy can have a significant impact on how a firm acts in a global industry. For example, several firms in the retail clothing industry with important product differentiation advantages in their home markets are beginning to enter into the U.S. retail clothing market. These firms include Sweden's H & M Hennes & Mauritz AB, with its emphasis on "cheap chic"; the Dutch firm Mexx (a division of Liz Claiborne); the Spanish company Zara (a division of Inditex SA); and the French sportswear company Lacoste (a division of Devanlay SA).[15]

Product Differentiation and Sustained Competitive Advantage

Product differentiation strategies add value by enabling firms to charge prices for their products or services that are greater than their average total cost. Firms that implement this strategy successfully can reduce a variety of environmental threats and exploit a variety of environmental opportunities. However, as discussed in Chapter 3, the ability of a strategy to add value to a firm must be linked with rare and costly-to-imitate organizational strengths in order to generate a sustained competitive advantage. Each of the bases of product differentiation listed earlier in this chapter varies with respect to how likely it is to be rare and costly to imitate.

Rare Bases for Product Differentiation

The concept of product differentiation generally assumes that the number of firms that have been able to differentiate their products in a particular way is, at some point in time, smaller than the number of firms needed to generate perfect competition dynamics. Indeed, the reason that highly differentiated firms can charge a price for their product that is greater than average total cost is because these firms are using a basis for product differentiation that few competing firms are also using.

Ultimately, the rarity of a product differentiation strategy depends on the ability of individual firms to be creative in finding new ways to differentiate

Ethics and Strategy

One of the most common ways to try to differentiate a product is to make claims about that product's performance. In general, high-performance products command a price premium over low-performance products. However, the potential price advantages enjoyed by high-performance products can sometimes lead firms to make claims about their products that, at the least, strain credibility, and at the most, simply lie about what their products can do.

Some of these claims are easily dismissed as harmless exaggerations. Few people actually believe that using a particular type of whitening toothpaste is going to make your in-laws like you or that not wearing a particular type of deodorant is going to cause patrons in a bar to collapse when you lift your arms in victory after a foosball game. These exaggerations are harmless and present few ethical challenges.

However, in the field of health care, exaggerated product performance claims can have serious consequences. This can happen when a patient takes a medication with exaggerated performance claims in lieu of a medication with more modest, although accurate, performance claims. A history of false medical performance claims in the United States led to the formation of the Food and Drug Administration (FDA), a federal regulatory agency charged with evaluating the efficacy of drugs before they are marketed. Historically, the FDA has adopted the

Product Claims and the Ethical Dilemmas in Health Care

"gold standard" of drug approval—not only must a drug demonstrate that it does what it claims, it must also demonstrate that it does not do any significant harm to the patient. Patients can be confident that drugs that pass the FDA approval process meet the highest standards in the world.

However, this "gold standard" of approval creates important ethical dilemmas—mostly stemming from the time it takes a drug to pass FDA inspections. This process can take between five and seven years. During FDA trials, patients who might otherwise benefit from a drug are not allowed to use it because it has not yet received FDA approval. Thus, although the FDA approval process may work very well for people who may need a drug sometime in the future, it works less well for those who need a drug right now.

A growing suspicion among some consumers that the FDA process may prevent effective drugs from being marketed has helped feed the growth of alternative treatments—usually based on some herbal or more natural formula. Such treatments are careful to note that their claims—everything from regrowing hair to losing weight to enhancing athletic performance to quitting smoking—have not been tested by the FDA. And yet, these claims are still made.

Some of these performance claims seem at least reasonable. For example, it is now widely accepted that ephedra does behave as an amphetamine and thus is likely to enhance strength and athletic performance. Others—including those that claim that a mixture of herbs can actually increase the size of male genitals—seem farfetched, at best. Indeed, a recent analysis of herbal treatments making this claim found no ingredients that could have this effect, but did find an unacceptably high concentration of bacteria from animal feces that can cause serious stomach disorders. Firms that sell products on the basis of exaggerated and unsubstantiated claims face their own ethical dilemmas. And, without the FDA to ensure product safety and efficacy, the adage *caveat emptor*—let the buyer beware—seems like good advice.

Sources: J. Angwin. (2003). "Some 'enlargement pills' pack impurities." *The Wall Street Journal*, April 8, p. B1; G. Pisano. (1991). "Nucleon, Inc." Harvard Business School Case No. 9-692-041.

their products. As suggested earlier, highly creative firms will be able to discover or create new ways to do this. These kinds of firms will always be one step ahead of the competition, because rival firms will often be trying to imitate these firms' last product differentiation moves while creative firms are working on their next one.

The Imitability of Product Differentiation

Valuable and rare bases of product differentiation must be costly to imitate if they are to be sources of sustained competitive advantage. Both direct duplication and substitution, as approaches to imitation, are important in understanding the ability of product differentiation to generate competitive advantages.

Direct Duplication of Product Differentiation

As discussed in Chapter 4, firms that successfully implement a cost leadership strategy can choose whether they want to reveal this strategic choice to their competition by adjusting their prices. If they keep their prices high—despite their cost advantages—the existence of those cost advantages may not be revealed to competitors. Of course, other firms—such as Wal-Mart—that are confident that their cost advantages cannot be duplicated at low cost are willing to reveal their cost advantage through charging lower prices for their products or services.

Firms pursuing product differentiation strategies usually do not have this option. More often than not, the act of selling a highly differentiated product or service reveals the basis upon which a firm is trying to differentiate its products. In fact, most firms go to great lengths to let their customers know how they are differentiating their products, and in the process of informing potential customers they also inform their competitors. Indeed, if competitors are not sure how a firm is differentiating its product, all they need to do is purchase that product themselves. Their own experience with the product—its features and other attributes—will tell them all they need to know about this firm's product differentiation strategy.

Knowing how a firm is differentiating its products, however, does not necessarily mean that competitors will be able to duplicate the strategy at low cost. The ability to duplicate a valuable and rare product differentiation strategy depends on the basis upon which a firm is differentiating its products. As suggested in Table 5.2, some bases of product differentiation—including the use of product features—are almost always easy to duplicate. Others—including product mix, links with other firms, product customization, product complexity, and consumer marketing—can sometimes be costly to duplicate. Finally, still other bases of product differentiation—including links between functions, timing, location, reputation, distribution channels, and service and support—are usually costly to duplicate.

How costly it is to duplicate a particular basis of product differentiation depends on the kinds of resources and capabilities that basis uses. When those resources and capabilities are acquired in unique historical settings, when there is some uncertainty about how to build these resources and capabilities, or when these resources and capabilities are socially complex in nature, then product differentiation strategies that exploit these kinds of resources and capabilities will be costly to imitate. These strategies can be a source of sustained competitive advantage for a firm. However, when a product differentiation strategy exploits resources and capabilities that do not possess these attributes, then those strategies are likely to be less costly to duplicate, and even if they are valuable and rare, will only be sources of temporary competitive advantage.

Bases of Product Differentiation That Are Easy to Duplicate.   The one basis of product differentiation in Table 5.2 that is identified as almost always being easy to duplicate is product features. The irony is that product features are by far the most popular way for firms to try to differentiate their products. Rarely do product

	History	Uncertainty	Social Complexity
Low-cost duplication usually possible			
1. Product features	—	—	—
May be costly to duplicate			
2. Product mix	*	*	*
3. Links with other firms	*	—	**
4. Product customization	*	—	**
5. Product complexity	*	—	*
6. Consumer marketing	—	**	—
Usually costly to duplicate			
7. Links between functions	*	*	**
8. Timing	***	*	—
9. Location	***	—	—
10. Reputation	***	**	***
11. Distribution channels	**	*	**
12. Service and support	*	*	**

— = Not likely to be a source of costly duplication,   * = Somewhat likely to be a source of costly duplication,
** = Likely to be a source of costly duplication,   *** = Very likely to be a source of costly duplication

TABLE 5.2 Bases of Product Differentiation and the Cost of Duplication

features, by themselves, enable a firm to gain sustained competitive advantages from a product differentiation strategy.

For example, virtually every one of the product features used in the automobile industry to differentiate the products of different automobile companies has been duplicated. Chrysler's "cab forward" design has been incorporated into the design of many manufacturers. The curved, sporty styling of the Audi has surfaced in cars manufactured by Lexus and General Motors. GM's "On Star" system has been duplicated by Mercedes. Mercedes' crumple-zone technology has become the industry standard, as has GM's uni-body construction method. Indeed, only the Mazda Miata, Nissan 370 Z, and the Porsche 911 have remained unduplicated—and this has little to do with the product features of these cars and much more to do with their reputation.

The only time product features, per se, can be a source of sustained competitive advantage for a firm is when those features are protected by patents. However, as was discussed in Chapters 2 and 3, even patents provide only limited protection from direct duplication, except in very unusual settings.

Although product features, by themselves, are usually not a source of sustained competitive advantage, they can be a source of a temporary competitive advantage. During the period of time when a firm has a temporary competitive advantage from implementing a product differentiation strategy based on product features, it may be able to attract new customers. Once these customers try the product, they may discover other features of a firm's products that make them attractive. If these other features are costly to duplicate, then they can be a source of sustained competitive advantage, even though the features that originally attracted a customer to a firm's products will often be rapidly duplicated by competitors.

Bases of Product Differentiation That May Be Costly to Duplicate.   Some bases of product differentiation may be costly to duplicate, at least in some circumstances. The first of these, listed in Table 5.2, is product mix.

Duplicating the features of another firm's products is usually not difficult. However, if that firm brings a series of products to market, if each of these products has unique features, and most important, if the products are highly integrated with each other, then this mix of products may be costly to duplicate. Certainly, the technological integration of the mix of information technology products sold by IBM and other firms has been relatively difficult to duplicate for firms that do not manufacture all these products themselves.

However, when this basis of a product mix advantage is a common customer, then duplication is often less difficult. Thus, although having a mall that brings several stores together in a single place is a source of competitive advantage over stand-alone stores, it is not a competitive advantage over other malls that provide the same service. Because there continue to be opportunities to build such malls, the fact that malls make it easier for a common set of customers to shop does not give any one mall a sustained competitive advantage.

Links with other firms may also be costly to duplicate, especially when those links depend on socially complex relationships. The extent to which interfirm links can provide sources of sustained competitive advantage is discussed in more detail in Chapter 9.

In the same way, product customization and product complexity are often easy-to-duplicate bases of product differentiation. However, sometimes the ability of a firm to customize its products for one of its customers depends on the close relationships it has developed with those customers. Product customization of this sort depends on the willingness of a firm to share often-proprietary details about its operations, products, research and development, or other characteristics with a supplying firm. Willingness to share this kind of information, in turn, depends on the ability of each firm to trust and rely on the other. The firm opening its operations to a supplier must trust that that supplier will not make this information broadly available to competing firms. The firm supplying customized products must trust that its customer will not take unfair advantage of it. If two firms have developed these kinds of socially complex relationships, and few other firms have them, then links with other firms will be costly to duplicate and a source of sustained competitive advantage.

The product customization seen in both enterprise software and in high-end customized bicycles has these socially complex features. In a real sense, when these products are purchased, a relationship with a supplier is being established— a relationship that is likely to last a long period of time. Once this relationship is established, partners are likely to be unwilling to abandon it, unless, of course, a party to the exchange tries to take unfair advantage of another party to that exchange. This possibility is discussed in detail in Chapter 9.

Finally, consumer marketing, though a very common form of product differentiation, is often easy to duplicate. Thus, whereas Mountain Dew has established itself as the "extreme games" drink, other drinks, including Gatorade, have also begun to tap into this market segment. Of course, every once in a while an advertising campaign or slogan, a point-of-purchase display, or some other attribute of a consumer marketing campaign will unexpectedly catch on and create greater-than-expected product awareness. In beer, marketing campaigns such as "Tastes great, less filling," "Why ask why?," the "Budweiser Frogs," and "What's Up?" have had these unusual effects. If a firm, in relation with its various consumer marketing agencies, is systematically able to develop these superior consumer marketing campaigns, then it may be able to obtain a sustained competitive advantage. However, if such campaigns are unpredictable and largely a matter of a firm's good luck, they cannot be expected to be a source of sustained competitive advantage.

Bases of Product Differentiation That Are Usually Costly to Duplicate.   The remaining bases of product differentiation listed in Table 5.2 are usually costly to duplicate. Firms that differentiate their products on these bases may be able to obtain sustained competitive advantages.

Linkages across functions within a single firm are usually a costly-to-duplicate basis of product differentiation. Whereas linkages with other firms can be either easy or costly to duplicate, depending on the nature of the relationship that exists between firms, linkages across functions within a single firm usually require socially complex, trusting relations. There are numerous built-in conflicts between functions and divisions within a single firm. Organizations that have a history and culture that support cooperative relations among conflicting divisions may be able to set aside functional and divisional conflicts to cooperate in delivering a differentiated product to the market. However, firms with a history of conflict across functional and divisional boundaries face a significant, and costly, challenge in altering these socially complex, historical patterns.

Indeed, the research on architectural competence in pharmaceutical firms suggests that not only do some firms possess this competence, but that other firms do not. Moreover, despite the significant advantages that accrue to firms with this competence, firms without this competence have, on average, been unable to develop it. All this suggests that such a competence, if it is also rare, is likely to be costly to duplicate and thus a source of sustained competitive advantage.

Timing is also a difficult-to-duplicate basis of product differentiation. As suggested in Chapter 3, it is difficult (if not impossible) to re-create a firm's unique history. If that history endows a firm with special resources and capabilities it can use to differentiate its products, this product differentiation strategy can be a source of sustained competitive advantage. Rivals of a firm with such a timing-based product differentiation advantage may need to seek alternative ways to differentiate their products. Thus, it is not surprising that universities that compete with the oldest universities in the country find alternative ways to differentiate themselves—through their size, the quality of the extramural sports, through their diversity—rather than relying on their age.

Location is often a difficult-to-duplicate basis of product differentiation. This is especially the case when a firm's location is unique. For example, research on the hotel preferences of business travelers suggests that location is a major determinant of the decision to stay in a hotel. Hotels that are convenient to both major transportation and commercial centers in a city are preferred, other things being equal, to hotels in other types of locations. Indeed, location has been shown to be a more important decision criterion for business travelers than price. If only a few hotels in a city have these prime locations, and if no further hotel development is possible, then hotels with these locations can gain sustained competitive advantages.

Of all the bases of product differentiation listed in this chapter, perhaps none is more difficult to duplicate than a firm's reputation. As suggested earlier, a firm's reputation is actually a socially complex relationship between a firm and its customers, based on years of experience, commitment, and trust. Reputations are not built quickly, nor can they be bought and sold. Rather, they can only be developed over time by consistent investment in the relationship between a firm and its customers. A firm with a positive reputation can enjoy a significant competitive advantage, whereas a firm with a negative reputation, or no reputation, may have to invest significant amounts over long periods of time to match the differentiated firm.

Distribution channels can also be a costly-to-duplicate basis of product differentiation, for at least two reasons. First, relations between a firm and its distribution channels are often socially complex and thus costly to duplicate. Second, the supply of distribution channels may be limited. Firms that already have access to these channels may be able to use them, but firms that do not have such access may be forced to create their own or develop new channels. Creating new channels, or developing entirely new means of distribution, can be difficult and costly undertakings.[16] These costs are one of the primary motivations under-lying many international joint ventures (see Chapter 9).

Finally, level of service and support can be a costly-to-duplicate basis of product differentiation. In most industries, it is usually not too costly to provide a minimum level of service and support. In home electronics, this minimum level of service can be provided by a network of independent electronic repair shops. In automobiles, this level of service can be provided by service facilities associated with dealerships. In fast foods, this level of service can be provided by a minimum level of employee training.

However, moving beyond this minimum level of service and support can be difficult for at least two reasons. First, increasing the quality of service and sup-port may involve substantial amounts of costly training. McDonald's has created a sophisticated training facility (Hamburger University) to maintain its unusually high level of service in fast foods. General Electric has invested heavily in training for service and support over the last several years. Many Japanese automakers spent millions on training employees to help support auto dealerships, before they opened U.S. manufacturing facilities.[17]

More important than the direct costs of the training needed to provide high-quality service and support, these bases of product differentiation often reflect the attitude of a firm and its employees toward customers. In many firms throughout the world, the customer has become "the bad guy." This is, in many ways, understandable. Employees tend to interact with their customers less fre-quently than they interact with other employees. When they do interact with cus-tomers, they are often the recipients of complaints directed at the firm. In these settings, hostility toward the customer can develop. Such hostility is, of course, inconsistent with a product differentiation strategy based on customer service and support.

In the end, high levels of customer service and support are based on socially complex relations between firms and customers. Firms that have conflicts with their customers may face some difficulty duplicating the high levels of service and support provided by competing firms.

Substitutes for Product Differentiation

The bases of product differentiation outlined in this chapter vary in how rare they are likely to be and in how difficult they are to duplicate. However, the ability of the bases of product differentiation to generate a sustained competitive advantage also depends on whether low-cost substitutes exist.

Substitutes for bases of product differentiation can take two forms. First, many of the bases of product differentiation listed in Table 5.1 can be partial substitutes for each other. For example, product features, product customization, and product complexity are all very similar bases of product differentiation and thus can act as substitutes for each other. A particular firm may try to develop a competitive advan-tage by differentiating its products on the basis of product customization only to find that its customization advantages are reduced as another firm alters the fea-tures of its products. In a similar way, linkages between functions, linkages between firms, and product mix, as bases of product differentiation, can also be substitutes for each other. IBM links its sales, service, and consulting functions to differentiate itself in the computer market. Other computer firms, however, may develop close relationships with computer service companies and consulting firms to close this product differentiation advantage. Given that different bases of product differentiation are often partial substitutes for each other, it is not surprising that firms pursue these multiple bases of product differentiation simultaneously.

Second, other strategies discussed throughout this book can be substitutes for many of the bases of product differentiation listed in Table 5.1. One firm may try to gain a competitive advantage through adjusting its product mix, and another firm may substitute strategic alliances to create the same type of product differentiation. For example, Southwest Airline's continued emphasis on friendly, on-time, low-cost service and United Airlines' emphasis on its links to Lufthansa and other worldwide airlines through the Star Alliance can both be seen as product differentiation efforts that are at least partial substitutes.[18]

In contrast, some of the other bases of product differentiation discussed in this chapter have few obvious close substitutes. These include timing, location, distribution channels, and service and support. To the extent that these bases of product differentiation are also valuable, rare, and difficult to duplicate, they may be sources of sustained competitive advantage.

Organizing to Implement Product Differentiation

V R I O

As was suggested in Chapter 3, the ability to implement a strategy depends on the adjustment of a firm's structure, its management controls, and its compensation policies to be consistent with that strategy. Whereas strategy implementation for firms adopting a cost leadership strategy focuses on reducing a firm's costs and increasing its efficiency, strategy implementation for a firm adopting a product differentiation strategy must focus on innovation, creativity, and product performance. Whereas cost-leading firms are all about customer value, product-differentiating firms are all about style. How the need for style is reflected in a firm's structure, controls, and compensation policies is summarized in Table 5.3.

TABLE 5.3 Organizing to Implement Product Differentiation Strategies

Organizational Structure:

1. Cross-divisional/cross-functional product development teams
2. Complex matrix structures
3. Isolated pockets of intense creative efforts: Skunk works

Management Control Systems:

1. Broad decision-making guidelines
2. Managerial freedom within guidelines
3. A policy of experimentation

Compensation Policies:

1. Rewards for risk-taking, not punishment for failures
2. Rewards for creative flair
3. Multidimensional performance measurement

Organizational Structure and Implementing Product Differentiation

Both cost leadership and product differentiation strategies are implemented through the use of a functional, or U-form, organizational structure. However, whereas the U-form structure used to implement a cost leadership strategy has few layers, simple reporting relationships, a small corporate staff, and a focus on only a few business functions, the U-form structure for a firm implementing a product differentiation strategy can be somewhat more complex. For example, these firms often use temporary cross-divisional *and* cross-functional teams to manage the development and implementation of new, innovative, and highly differentiated products. These teams bring individuals from different businesses and different functional areas together to cooperate on a particular new product or service.

One firm that has used these cross-divisional and cross-functional teams effectively is the British advertising agency WPP. WPP owns several very large advertising agencies, several public relations firms, several market research companies, and so forth. Each of these businesses operates relatively independently in most areas. However, the corporation has identified a few markets where cross-divisional and cross-functional collaboration is important. One of these is the health care market. To exploit opportunities in the health care market, WPP, the corporation, forms teams of advertising specialists, market research specialists, public relations specialists, and so on, drawn from each of the businesses it owns. The resulting cross-divisional teams are given the responsibility of developing new and highly differentiated approaches to developing marketing strategies for their clients in the health care industry.[19]

The creation of cross-divisional or cross-functional teams often implies that a firm has implemented some form of matrix structure. As suggested in Chapter 4, a **matrix structure** exists when individuals in a firm have two or more "bosses" simultaneously. Thus, for example, if a person from one of WPP's advertising agencies is assigned temporarily to a cross-divisional team, that person has two bosses: the head of the temporary team and the boss back in the advertising agency. Managing two bosses simultaneously can be very challenging, especially when they have conflicting interests. And as we will see in Chapter 8, the interests of these multiple bosses *will* often conflict.

A particularly important form of the cross-divisional or cross-functional team exists when this team is relieved of all other responsibilities in the firm and focuses all its attention on developing a new innovative product or service. The best-known example of this approach to developing a differentiated product occurred at the Lockheed Corporation during the 1950s and 1960s when small groups of engineers were put on very focused teams to develop sophisticated and top secret military aircraft. These teams would have a section of the Lockheed facility dedicated to their efforts and designated as off-limits to almost all other employees. The joke was that these intensive creative efforts were so engaging that members of these teams actually would forget to shower—hence, the name "**skunk works**." Skunk works have been used by numerous firms to focus the creative energy required to develop and introduce highly differentiated products.[20]

Management Controls and Implementing Product Differentiation

The first two management controls helpful for implementing product differentiation listed in Table 5.3—broad decision-making guidelines and managerial freedom within those guidelines—often go together, even though they sound somewhat contradictory. These potential contradictions are discussed in the Strategy in the

Strategy in the Emerging Enterprise

In the 1950s, a well-known economist named Joseph Schumpeter suggested that only very large and profitable companies have the resources necessary to invest in creating new and highly innovative products and services. His conclusion suggested that the social evils caused by economic power being concentrated in the hands of a relatively few large and powerful organizations was simply the price society had to pay for innovations that could benefit consumers.

The economic history of the past 30 years or so suggests that one of Schumpeter's key assumptions—that only large firms can afford to be innovative—is wrong. Indeed, over this time period it is clear that a great deal of innovation has occurred through the creation of entrepreneurial firms. Firms such as Dell, Microsoft, Intel, Apple, Home Depot, Cisco, Gateway, Sun, Office Depot, Nike, Oracle, PeopleSoft, Foot Locker, Amazon.com, and Starbucks have all been sources of major innovations in their industries, and all were begun as entrepreneurial ventures in the past 35 years. Indeed, given the impact of these and other entrepreneurial ventures on the worldwide economy during this time period, it is possible to call the past 30 years the "era of the entrepreneur."

What is it about entrepreneurial firms that enables them to develop

Can Only Small Firms Be Innovative?

innovations that sometimes come to dominate a market? Some scholars have suggested that the small size and lack of resources that characterize entrepreneurial start-ups, far from limiting their innovativeness, actually facilitate innovation.

For example, entrepreneurial firms have relatively little to lose when engaging in innovation. If the market accepts their innovation, great; if it doesn't, they can move on to the next innovation. Established firms, however, may have a significant stake in an older technology, an older distribution system, or an older type of customer. Established firms may be unwilling to cannibalize the sales of their current products for new and innovative products.

Moreover, small entrepreneurial firms have relatively few bureaucratic controls. Information and ideas flow

freely in these organizations. Such information flow tends to facilitate innovation. Larger firms, in contrast, have usually installed numerous bureaucratic controls that impede cross-functional communication, and thus slow innovation.

Indeed, some have even argued that the types of people who are attracted to small entrepreneurial firms tend to be more innovative than those who are attracted to larger, more stable companies. People who are comfortable with risk-seeking and creativity may be attracted to an entrepreneurial firm, whereas those who are less comfortable with risk-seeking and creativity may be attracted to larger, more stable firms.

Whatever the reasons, many large firms have come to realize that they cannot afford to be "out-innovated" and "outmaneuvered" by entrepreneurial start-ups. In response, larger firms have begun to adopt policies and procedures that try to create the kind of innovativeness and creativity one often sees in entrepreneurial firms. Some firms—such as 3M (see Table 5.4)—have been quite successful in this effort. Others have been less successful.

Sources: C. Christensen. (1997). *The innovator's dilemma.* Boston: Harvard Business School Press; J. Schumpeter. (1942). *Capitalism, socialism, and democracy.* New York: Harper and Rowe; T. Zenger and E. Rasmusen. (1990). "Diseconomies of scale in employment contracts." *Journal of Law, Economics, and Organization,* 6, pp. 65–98.

Emerging Enterprise feature. Managing these contradictions is one of the central challenges of firms looking to implement product differentiation strategies.

Broad decision-making guidelines help bring order to what otherwise might be a chaotic decision-making process. When managers have no constraints in their decision making, they can make decisions that are disconnected from each other and inconsistent with a firm's overall mission and objectives. This results in decisions that are either not implemented or not implemented well.

TABLE 5.4 Guiding Innovative Principles at 3M*

1. **Vision.** Declare the importance of innovation; make it part of the company's self-image.

   "Our efforts to encourage and support innovation are proof that we really do intend to achieve our vision of ourselves . . . that we intend to become what we want to be . . . as a business and as creative individuals."

2. **Foresight.** Find out where technologies and markets are going. Identify articulated and unarticulated needs of customers.

   "If you are working on a next-generation medical imaging device, you'll probably talk to radiologists, but you might also sit down with people who enhance images from interplanetary space probes."

3. **Stretch goals.** Set goals that will make you and the organization stretch to make quantum improvements. Although many projects are pursued, place your biggest bets on those that change the basis of competition and redefine the industry.

   "We have a number of stretch goals at 3M. The first states that we will drive 30 percent of all sales from products introduced in the past 4 years. . . . To establish a sense of urgency, we've recently added another goal, which is that we want 10 percent of our sales to come from products that have been in the market for just 1 year. . . . Innovation is time sensitive . . . you need to move quickly."

4. **Empowerment.** Hire good people and trust them, delegate responsibilities, provide slack resources, and get out of the way. Be tolerant of initiative and the mistakes that occur because of that initiative.

   "William McKnight [a former chairman of 3M] came up with one way to institutionalize a tolerance of individual effort. He said that all technical employees could devote 15 percent of their time to a project of their own invention. In other words, they could manage themselves for 15 percent of the time. . . . The number is not so important as the message, which is this: The system has some slack in it. If you have a good idea, and the commitment to squirrel away time to work on it and the raw nerve to skirt your lab manager's expressed desires, then go for it.

   "Put another way, we want to institutionalize a bit of rebellion in our labs. We can't
   have all our people off totally on their own . . . we do believe in discipline . . . but at the same time 3M management encourages a healthy disrespect for 3M management. This is not the sort of thing we publicize in our annual report, but the stories we tell—with relish—are frequently about 3Mers who have circumvented their supervisors and succeeded.*

   "We also recognize that when you let people follow their own lead . . . everyone doesn't wind up at the same place. You can't ask people to have unique visions and march in lockstep. Some people are very precise, detail-oriented people . . . and others are fuzzy thinkers and visionaries . . . and this is exactly what we want."

5. **Communications.** Open, extensive exchanges according to ground rules in forums that are present for sharing ideas and where networking is each individual's responsibility. Multiple methods for sharing information are necessary.

   "When innovators communicate with each other, you can leverage their discoveries. This is critically important because it allows companies to get the maximum return on their substantial investments in new technologies. It also acts as a stimulus to further innovation. Indeed, we believe that the ability to combine and transfer technologies is as important as the original discovery of a technology."

6. **Rewards and recognition.** Emphasize individual recognition more than monetary rewards through peer recognition and by choice of managerial or technical promotion routes. "Innovation is an intensely human activity."

   "I've laid out six elements of 3M's corporate culture that contribute to a tradition of innovation: vision, foresight, stretch goals, empowerment, communication, and recognition. . . . The list is . . . too orderly. Innovation at 3M is anything but orderly. It is sensible, in that our efforts are directed at reaching our goals, but the organization . . . and the process . . . and sometimes the people can be chaotic. We are managing in chaos, and this is the right way to manage if you want innovation. It's been said that the competition never knows what we are going to come up with next. The fact is, neither do we."

*As expressed by W. Coyne. (1996). *Building a tradition of innovation.* The Fifth U.K. Innovation Lecture, Department of Trade and Industry, London. Cited in Van de Ven et al. (1999), pp. 198–200.

However, if these decision-making guidelines become too narrow, they can stifle creativity within a firm. As was suggested earlier, a firm's ability to differentiate its products is limited only by its creativity. Thus, decision guidelines must be narrow enough to ensure that the decisions made are consistent with a firm's mission and objectives. Yet, these guidelines also must be broad enough so that managerial creativity is not destroyed. In well-managed firms implementing product differentiation strategies, as long as managerial decisions fall within the broad decision-making guidelines in a firm, managers have the right—in fact, are expected—to make creative decisions.

A firm that has worked hard to reach this balance between chaos and control is 3M. In an effort to provide guiding principles that define the range of acceptable decisions at 3M, its senior managers have developed a set of innovating principles. These are presented in Table 5.4 and define the boundaries of innovative chaos at 3M. Within these boundaries, managers and engineers are expected to be creative and innovative in developing highly differentiated products and services.[21]

Another firm that has managed this tension well is British Airways (BA). BA has extensive training programs to teach its flight attendants how to provide world-class service, especially for its business-class customers. This training constitutes standard operating procedures that give purpose and structure to BA's efforts to provide a differentiated service in the highly competitive airline industry. Interestingly, however, BA also trains its flight attendants in when to violate these standard policies and procedures. By recognizing that no set of management controls can ever anticipate all the special situations that can occur when providing service to customers, BA empowers its employees to meet specific customer needs. This enables BA to have both a clearly defined product differentiation strategy and the flexibility to adjust this strategy as the situation dictates.[22]

Firms can also facilitate the implementation of a product differentiation strategy by adopting a **policy of experimentation**. Such a policy exists when firms are committed to engaging in several related product differentiation efforts simultaneously. That these product differentiation efforts are related suggests that a firm has some vision about how a particular market is likely to unfold over time. However, that there are several of these product differentiation efforts occurring simultaneously suggests that a firm is not overly committed to a particular narrow vision about how a market is going to evolve. Rather, several different experiments facilitate the exploration of different futures in a marketplace. Indeed, successful experiments can actually help define the future evolution of a marketplace.

Consider, for example, Charles Schwab, the innovative discount broker. In the face of increased competition from full-service and Internet-based brokerage firms, Schwab engaged in a series of experiments to discover the next generation of products it could offer to its customers and the different ways it could differentiate those products. Schwab investigated software for simplifying online mutual fund selection, online futures trading, and online company research. It also formed an exploratory alliance with Goldman Sachs to evaluate the possibility of enabling Schwab customers to trade in initial public offerings. Not all of Schwab's experiments led to the introduction of highly differentiated products. For example, based on some experimental investments, Schwab decided not to enter the credit card market. However, by experimenting with a range of possible product differentiation moves, it was able to develop a range of new products for the fast-changing financial services industry.[23]

Compensation Policies and Implementing Product Differentiation Strategies

The compensation policies used to implement product differentiation listed in Table 5.3 very much complement the organizational structure and managerial controls listed in that table. For example, a policy of experimentation has little impact on the ability of a firm to implement product differentiation strategies if every time an innovative experiment fails individuals are punished for taking risks. Thus, compensation policies that reward risk-taking and celebrate a creative flair help to enable a firm to implement its product differentiation strategy.

Consider, for example, Nordstrom. Nordstrom is a department store that celebrates the risk-taking and creative flair of its associates as they try to satisfy their customers' needs. The story is often told of a Nordstrom sales associate who allowed a customer to return a set of tires to the store because she wasn't satisfied with them. What makes this story interesting—whether or not it is true—is that Nordstrom doesn't sell tires. But this sales associate felt empowered to make what was obviously a risky decision, and this decision is celebrated within Nordstrom as an example of the kind of service that Nordstrom's customers should expect.

The last compensation policy listed in Table 5.3 is multidimensional performance measurement. In implementing a cost leadership strategy, compensation should focus on providing appropriate incentives for managers and employees to reduce costs. Various forms of cash payments, stock, and stock options can all be tied to the attainment of specific cost goals, and thus can be used to create incentives for realizing cost advantages. Similar techniques can be used to create incentives for helping a firm implement its product differentiation advantage. However, because the implementation of a product differentiation strategy generally involves the integration of multiple business functions, often through the use of product development teams, compensation schemes designed to help implement this strategy must generally recognize its multi-functional character.

Thus, rather than focusing only on a single dimension of performance, these firms often examine employee performance along multiple dimensions simultaneously. Examples of such dimensions include not only a product's sales and profitability, but customer satisfaction, an employee's willingness to cooperate with other businesses and functions within a firm, an employee's ability to effectively facilitate cross-divisional and cross-functional teams, and an employee's ability to engage in creative decision making.

Can Firms Implement Product Differentiation and Cost Leadership Simultaneously?

The arguments developed in Chapter 4 and in this chapter suggest that cost leadership and product differentiation business strategies, under certain conditions, can both create sustained competitive advantages. Given the beneficial impact of both strategies on a firm's competitive position, an important question becomes: Can a single firm simultaneously implement both strategies? After all, if each separately can improve a firm's performance, wouldn't it be better for a firm to implement both?

No: These Strategies Cannot Be Implemented Simultaneously

A quick comparison of the organizational requirements for the successful implementation of cost leadership strategies and product differentiation strategies presented in Table 5.5 summarizes one perspective on the question of whether these strategies can be implemented simultaneously. In this view, the organizational requirements of these strategies are essentially contradictory. Cost leadership requires simple reporting relationships, whereas product differentiation requires cross-divisional/cross-functional linkages. Cost leadership requires intense labor supervision, whereas product differentiation requires less intense supervision of creative employees. Cost leadership requires rewards for cost reduction, whereas product differentiation requires rewards for creative flair. It is reasonable to ask "Can a single firm combine these multiple contradictory skills and abilities?"

Some have argued that firms attempting to implement both strategies will end up doing neither well. This logic leads to the curve pictured in Figure 5.2. This figure suggests that there are often only two ways to earn superior economic performance within a single industry: (1) by selling high-priced products and gaining small market share (product differentiation) or (2) by selling low-priced products and gaining large market share (cost leadership). Firms that do not make this choice of strategies (medium price, medium market share) or that attempt to implement both strategies will fail. These firms are said to be "stuck in the middle."[24]

TABLE 5.5 The Organizational Requirements for Implementing Cost Leadership and Product Differentiation Strategies

Cost leadership	Product differentiation
Organizational structure	**Organizational structure**
1. Few layers in the reporting structure	1. Cross-divisional/cross-functional product development teams
2. Simple reporting relationships	2. Willingness to explore new structures to exploit new opportunities
3. Small corporate staff	3. Isolated pockets of intense creative efforts
4. Focus on narrow range of business functions	
Management control systems	**Management control systems**
1. Tight cost-control systems	1. Broad decision-making guidelines
2. Quantitative cost goals	2. Managerial freedom within guidelines
3. Close supervision of labor, raw material, inventory, and other costs	3. Policy of experimentation
4. A cost leadership philosophy	
Compensation policies	**Compensation policies**
1. Reward for cost reduction	1. Rewards for risk-taking, not punishment for failures
2. Incentives for all employees to be involved in cost reduction	2. Rewards for creative flair
	3. Multidimensional performance measurement

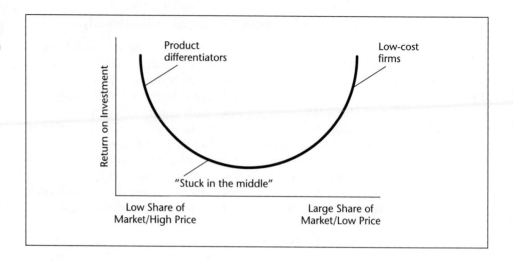

Yes: These Strategies Can Be Implemented Simultaneously

More recent work contradicts assertions about being "stuck in the middle." This work suggests that firms that are successful in both cost leadership and product differentiation can often expect to gain a sustained competitive advantage. This advantage reflects at least two processes.

Differentiation, Market Share, and Low-Cost Leadership

Firms able to successfully differentiate their products and services are likely to see an increase in their volume of sales. This is especially the case if the basis of product differentiation is attractive to a large number of potential customers. Thus, product differentiation can lead to increased volumes of sales. It has already been established (in Chapter 4) that an increased volume of sales can lead to economies of scale, learning, and other forms of cost reduction. So, successful product differentiation can, in turn, lead to cost reductions and a cost leadership position.[25]

This is the situation that best describes McDonald's. McDonald's has traditionally followed a product differentiation strategy, emphasizing cleanliness, consistency, and fun in its fast-food outlets. Over time, McDonald's has used its differentiated product to become the market share leader in the fast-food industry. This market position has enabled it to reduce its costs, so that it is now the cost leader in fast foods as well. Thus, McDonald's level of profitability depends both on its product differentiation strategy and its low-cost strategy. Either one of these two strategies by itself would be difficult to overcome; together they give McDonald's a very costly-to-imitate competitive advantage.[26]

Managing Organizational Contradictions

Product differentiation can lead to high market share and low costs. It may also be the case that some firms develop special skills in managing the contradictions that are part of simultaneously implementing low-cost and product differentiation strategies. Some recent research on automobile manufacturing helps describe these special skills.[27] Traditional thinking in automotive manufacturing was that plants could either reduce manufacturing costs by speeding up the assembly line or increase the quality of the cars they made by slowing the line, emphasizing team-based production, and so forth. In general, it was thought that plants could not simultaneously build low-cost/high-quality (i.e., low-cost *and* highly differentiated) automobiles.

Several researchers at the Massachusetts Institute of Technology examined this traditional wisdom. They began by developing rigorous measures of the cost and quality performance of automobile plants and then applied these measures to over 70 auto plants throughout the world that assembled mid-size sedans. What they discovered was six plants in the entire world that had, at the time this research was done, very low costs *and* very high quality.[28]

In examining what made these six plants different from other auto plants, the researchers focused on a broad range of manufacturing policies, management practices, and cultural variables. Three important findings emerged. First, these six plants had the best manufacturing technology hardware available—robots, laser-guided paint machines, and so forth. However, because many of the plants in the study had these same technologies, manufacturing technology by itself was not enough to make these six plants special. In addition, policies and procedures at these plants implemented a range of highly participative, group-oriented management techniques, including participative management, team production, and total quality management. As important, employees in these plants had a sense of loyalty and commitment toward the plant they worked for—a belief that they would be treated fairly by their plant managers.

What this research shows is that firms *can* simultaneously implement cost leadership and product differentiation strategies if they learn how to manage the contradictions inherent in these two strategies. The management of these contradictions, in turn, depends on socially complex relations among employees, between employees and the technology they use, and between employees and the firm for which they work. These relations are not only valuable (because they enable a firm to implement cost leadership and differentiation strategies) but also socially complex and thus likely to be costly to imitate and a source of sustained competitive advantage.

Recently, many scholars have backed away from the original "stuck in the middle" arguments and now suggest that low-cost firms must have competitive levels of product differentiation to survive, and that product differentiation firms must have competitive levels of cost to survive.[29] For example, the fashion design company Versace—the ultimate product differentiating firm—has recently hired a new CEO and controller to help control its costs.[30]

Summary

Product differentiation exists when customers perceive a particular firm's products to be more valuable than other firms' products. Although differentiation can have several bases, it is, in the end, always a matter of customer perception. Bases of product differentiation include: (1) attributes of the products or services a firm sells (including product features, product complexity, the timing of product introduction, and location); (2) relations between a firm and its customers (including product customization, consumer marketing, and reputation); and (3) links within and between firms (including links between functions, links with other firms, a firm's product mix, its distribution system, and its level of service and support). However, in the end, product differentiation is limited only by the creativity of a firm's managers.

Product differentiation is valuable to the extent that it enables a firm to set its prices higher than what it would otherwise be able to. Each of the bases of product differentiation identified can be used to neutralize environmental threats and exploit environmental opportunities. The rarity and imitability of bases of product differentiation vary. Highly imitable bases of product differentiation include product features. Somewhat imitable bases include product mix, links with other firms, product customization, and consumer marketing. Costly to-imitate bases of product differentiation include linking business functions, timing, location, reputation, and service and support.

The implementation of a product differentiation strategy involves management of organizational structure, management controls, and compensation policies. Structurally, it is not unusual for firms implementing product differentiation strategies to use cross-divisional and cross-functional teams, together with teams that are focused exclusively on a particular product differentiation effort, so-called "skunk works." Managerial controls that provide free managerial decision making within broad decision-making guidelines can be helpful in implementing product differentiation strategies, as is a policy of experimentation. Finally, compensation policies that tolerate risk-taking and a creative flair and that measure employee performance along multiple dimensions simultaneously can also be helpful in implementing product differentiation strategies.

A variety of organizational attributes is required to successfully implement a product differentiation strategy. Some have argued that contradictions between these organizational characteristics and those required to implement a cost leadership strategy mean that firms that attempt to do both will perform poorly. More recent research has noted the relationship between product differentiation, market share, and low costs and has observed that some firms have learned to manage the contradictions between cost leadership and product differentiation.

Challenge Questions

1. Although cost leadership is perhaps less relevant for firms pursuing product differentiation, costs are not totally irrelevant. What advice about costs would you give a firm pursuing a product differentiation strategy?

2. Product features are often the focus of product differentiation efforts. Yet product features are among the easiest-to-imitate bases of product differentiation and thus among the least likely bases of product differentiation to be a source of sustained competitive advantage. Does this seem paradoxical to you? If no, why not? If yes, how can you resolve this paradox?

3. What are the strengths and weaknesses of using regression analysis and hedonic prices to describe the bases of product differentiation?

4. Chamberlin used the term "monopolistic competition" to describe firms pursuing a product differentiation strategy in a competitive industry. However, it is usually the case that firms that operate in monopolies are less efficient and less competitive than those that operate in more competitive settings (see Chapter 3). Does this same problem exist for firms operating in a "monopolistic competition" context? Why or why not?

5. Implementing a product differentiation strategy seems to require just the right mix of control and creativity. How do you know if a firm has the right mix? Is it possible to evaluate this mix before problems associated with being out of balance manifest themselves? If yes, how? If no, why not?

6. A firm with a highly differentiated product can increase the volume of its sales. Increased sales volumes can enable a firm to reduce its costs. High volumes with low costs can lead a firm to have very high profits, some of which the firm can use to invest in further differentiating its products. What advice would you give a firm whose competition is enjoying this product differentiation and cost leadership advantage?

Problem Set

1. For each of the listed products, describe at least two ways they are differentiated.
(a) Ben & Jerry's ice cream
(b) The Hummer H2
(c) The X-Games
(d) The Pussycat Dolls
(e) The movies *Animal House* and *Caddyshack*
(f) Frederick's of Hollywood
(g) Taco Bell

2. Which, if any, of the bases of product differentiation in question #1 are likely to be sources of sustained competitive advantage? Why?

3. Suppose you obtained the following regression results, where the starred (*) coefficients are statistically significant. What could you say about the bases of product differentiation in this market? (Hint: A regression coefficient is statistically significant when it is so large that its effect is very unlikely to have emerged by chance.)

$$\text{House Price} = \$125,000^* + \$15,000^* \text{ (More than three bedrooms)}$$
$$+ \$18,000^* \text{ (More than 3,500 square feet)}$$
$$+ \$150 \text{ (Has plumbing)} + \$180 \text{ (Has lawn)}$$
$$+ \$17,000^* \text{ (Lot larger than 1/2 acre)}$$

How much would you expect to pay for a four-bedroom, 3,800-square-foot house on a one-acre lot? How much for a four-bedroom, 2,700-square-foot house on a quarter-acre lot?

Do these results say anything about the sustainability of competitive advantages in this market?

4. Which of the following management controls and compensation policies is consistent with implementing cost leadership? With product differentiation? With both cost leadership and product differentiation? With neither cost leadership nor product differentiation?

(a) Firm-wide stock options

(b) Compensation that rewards each function separately for meeting its own objectives

(c) A detailed financial budget plan

(d) A document that describes, in detail, how the innovation process will unfold in a firm

(e) A policy that reduces the compensation of a manager who introduces a product that fails in the market

(f) A policy that reduces the compensation of a manager who introduces several products that fail in the market

(g) The creation of a purchasing council to discuss how different business units can reduce their costs

5. Identify three industries or markets that have the volume–profit relationship described in Figure 5.2. Which firms in this industry are implementing cost leadership strategies? Which are implementing product differentiation strategies? Are any firms "stuck in the middle"? If yes, which ones? If no, why not? Are any firms implementing both cost leadership and product differentiation strategies? If yes, which ones? If no, why not?

End Notes

1. See Ono, Y. (1996). "Who really makes that cute little beer? You'd be surprised." *Wall Street Journal*, April 15, pp. A1 +. Since this 1996 article, some of these craft beer companies have changed the way they manufacture the beers to be more consistent with the image they are trying to project.
2. See Porter, M. E. (1980). *Competitive strategy*. New York: Free Press; and Caves, R. E., and P. Williamson. (1985). "What is product differentiation, really?" *Journal of Industrial Organization Economics*, 34, pp. 113–132.
3. Lieberman, M. B., and D. B. Montgomery. (1988). "First-mover advantages." *Strategic Management Journal*, 9, pp. 41–58.
4. Carroll, P. (1993). *Big blues: The unmaking of IBM*. New York: Crown Publishers.
5. These ideas were first developed in Hotelling, H. (1929). "Stability in competition." *Economic Journal*, 39, pp. 41–57; and Ricardo, D. (1817). *Principles of political economy and taxation*. London: J. Murray.
6. See Gunther, M. (1998). "Disney's Call of the Wild." *Fortune*, April 13, pp. 120–124.
7. The idea of reputation is explained in Klein, B., and K. Leffler. (1981). "The role of market forces in assuring contractual performance." *Journal of Political Economy*, 89, pp. 615–641.
8. See Robichaux M. (1995). "It's a book! A T-shirt! A toy! No, just MTV trying to be Disney." *Wall Street Journal*, February 8, pp. A1 +.
9. See Henderson, R., and I. Cockburn. (1994). "Measuring competence? Exploring firm effects in pharmaceutical research." *Strategic Management Journal*, 15, pp. 63–84.
10. See Johnson, R. (1999). "Speed sells." *Fortune*, April 12, pp. 56–70. In fact, NASCAR fans either love or hate Jeff Gordon.
11. Kotler, P. (1986). *Principles of marketing*. Upper Saddle River, NJ: Prentice Hall.
12. Porter, M. E., and R. Wayland. (1991). "Coca-Cola vs. Pepsi-Cola and the soft drink industry." Harvard Business School Case No. 9-391-179.
13. Ghemawat, P. (1993). "Sears, Roebuck and Company: The merchandise group." Harvard Business School Case No. 9-794-039.
14. Welsh, J. (1998). "Office-paper firms pursue elusive goal: Brand loyalty." *The Wall Street Journal*, September 21, p. B6.
15. See White, E., and K. Palmer. (2003). "U.S. retailing 101." *The Wall Street Journal*, August 12, pp. B1 +.
16. See Hennart, J. F. (1988). "A transaction cost theory of equity joint ventures." *Strategic Management Journal*, 9, pp. 361–374.
17. Deutsch, C. H. (1991). "How is it done? For a small fee. . ." *New York Times*, October 27, p. 25; and Armstrong, L. (1991). "Services: The customer as 'Honored Guest.'" *BusinessWeek*, October 25, p. 104.
18. See Yoffie, D. (1994). "Swissair's alliances (A)." Harvard Business School Case No. 9-794-152.
19. "WPP—Integrating icons." Harvard Business School Case No. 9-396-249.
20. Orosz, J. J. (2002). "Big funds need a 'Skunk Works' to stir ideas." *Chronicle of Philanthropy*, June 27, p. 47.
21. Van de Ven, A., D. Polley, R. Garud, and S. Venkatraman. (1999). *The innovation journey*. New York: Oxford, pp. 198–200.
22. Prokesch, S. (1995). "Competing on customer service: An interview with British Airways' Sir Colin Marshall." *Harvard Business Review*, November–December, p. 101. Now if they wouldn't lose our luggage at Heathrow, they would be a great airline.
23. Position, L. L. (1999). "David S. Pottruck." *BusinessWeek*, September 27, EB 51.
24. Porter, M. E. (1980). *Competitive strategy*. New York: Free Press.
25. Hill, C. W. L. (1988). "Differentiation versus low cost or differentiation and low cost: A contingency framework." *Academy of Management Review*, 13(3), pp. 401–412.
26. Gibson, R. (1995). "Food: At McDonald's, new recipes for buns, eggs." *The Wall Street Journal*, June 13, p. B1.
27. Originally discussed in the Research Made Relevant feature in Chapter 3.
28. Womack, J. P., D. I. Jones, and D. Roos. (1990). *The machine that changed the world*. New York: Rawson.
29. Porter, M. E. (1985). *Competitive advantage*. New York: Free Press.
30. Agins, T., and A. Galloni. (2003). "Facing a squeeze, Versace struggles to trim the fat." *The Wall Street Journal*, September 30, pp. A1 +.

Case 2-1 JetBlue Airways: Managing Growth

It was May 11, 2007, and David Barger finally had a moment to take in the view from his office window at JetBlue Airways' modest corporate headquarters in Forest Hills, New York. Less than 24 hours earlier, Barger, previously president and COO of JetBlue, was named the airline's CEO. JetBlue's board promoted Barger to the CEO role in the wake of a highly publicized operational crisis in February that led to the cancellation of over 1,100 JetBlue flights and adversely affected the travel plans of thousands of passengers. Though numerous interviews and meetings during the past day allowed Barger to outline his vision for the airline, he realized that he needed to move quickly in implementing that vision to maintain the confidence of customers, employees, and shareholders.

Just a few miles outside Barger's window was John Fitzgerald Kennedy (JFK) Airport, where JetBlue began operations as a low-cost carrier (LCC) in 2000 and by the beginning of 2007, held a 30% share of domestic departures. Looking beyond the construction site for JetBlue's new Terminal 5—an $800 million state-of-the-art facility that was scheduled to open in the fall of 2008 and would offer 26 gates and a wide range of passenger amenities—Barger noticed one JetBlue plane, a 100-seat Embraer 190 (E190), taking off. Immediately following it was another JetBlue plane, a 150-seat Airbus 320 (A320). Wrapping up some email responses, Barger was pleased to see other JetBlue planes—some E190s and some A320s—take to the air over the next fifteen minutes. He could not help but appreciate this setting as an appropriate backdrop for some critical short-term decisions that the airline needed to make.

In late 2005, JetBlue added the E190 to its fleet, which was then composed exclusively of 85 A320s. This decision was a break with the traditional practice of many LCCs of limiting their fleets to one type of aircraft to streamline operations and reduce costs. JetBlue was in the

simultaneously advantageous and risky position of being the launch customer for the E190. By the end of 2006, JetBlue had 23 E190s in its fleet of 119 planes.

By late 2006 JetBlue, like other airlines, faced softening demand and higher costs due to increasing fuel prices. Barger played a large role in the airline's decision at the end of 2006 to slow its rate of growth by reducing its purchase commitments for new planes.

In light of the operational challenges faced by JetBlue in February 2007, as well as the unabated rise in fuel costs (Exhibit 1), Barger realized that the airline would need to take further steps to slow its rate of growth. Though convinced JetBlue needed to decrease plane deliveries once again, Barger was not certain as to how these reductions should be distributed across E190s and A320s. The E190 was a promising plane that presented interesting growth opportunities and challenges for JetBlue. At the same time, the A320 was a proven plane that served as the basis for JetBlue's operations over the past six years and the company had developed a high level of comfort with it. Given the current pressures facing JetBlue and the industry, Barger knew this decision would not be easy.

LCCs and the Airline Industry

The airline industry in 2006 included two groups of competitors: legacy carriers and LCCs Most of the best-known U.S. airlines, such as United or American Airlines, were legacy carriers, so called because of their long histories reaching back, in some cases, as far as the 1920s. One part of this legacy was the "hub and spoke" system that characterized the operations of these companies. In this system, airlines created large "hubs" at specific airports where thousands of passengers were shuttled every day to connecting flights (the "spokes"). The "hub and spoke" was pioneered by Delta Air Lines in 1955;[1] it became increasingly useful to airlines in the turbulent years after airline deregulation in 1978 as a means to keep their costs low and protect their market share. By centralizing the transfer of passengers during long journeys across the country, such structures allowed passengers to travel between numerous destinations without changing

Professors Robert S. Huckman and Gary P. Pisano prepared this case with the assistance of Global Research Group Research Associate Mark Rennella. HBS cases are developed solely as the basis for class discussion. Cases are not intended to serve as endorsements, sources of primary data, or illustrations of effective or ineffective management.

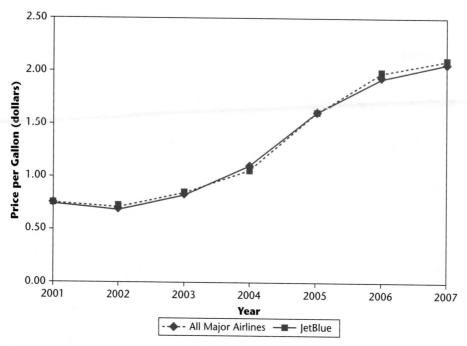

Exhibit 1   Average Fuel Prices for U.S. Domestic Commercial Air Travel, 2001 to 2007

Note: Figures for 2007 are estimated.

Source: U.S. Department of Transportation, Research and Innovative Technology Administration website (http://www.transtats.bts.gov/fuel.asp?pn=1), accessed August 9, 2008.

airlines. Some carriers also used hubs to dominate geographical segments of the market, as did Delta in Atlanta's Hartsfield International Airport. Despite the advantages of the hub-and-spoke model, this kind of centralization proved challenging if weather, maintenance problems, and air traffic delays interfered with flight schedules.

Emerging in Texas in the late 1960s, Southwest Airlines offered an alternative business model of air transportation. In contrast to the hub-and-spoke model, Southwest took passengers direct (i.e., "point to point") between cities that were often less than 500 miles apart and, wherever possible, used secondary airports serving major metropolitan areas. Attracting passengers who would have otherwise traveled by car or bus, Southwest was able to maintain high levels of plane utilization, thereby keeping its operating costs low enough to support its discounted fares. A key component of Southwest's ability to manage costs was its reliance on a single type of plane—the Boeing 737. Over time, Southwest's ground and flight personnel became very familiar with the 737; this decreased the airline's average turnaround time between landing a plane and putting it back into the air. This efficiency, combined with the shrewd use of fuel hedges, buoyed Southwest's profits.

Attempts by competitors to mimic Southwest's LCC model typically were unsuccessful, as demonstrated by the infamous rise and fall of no-frills People Express Airlines during the 1980s and the short-lived attempts of several major airlines—including Continental Airlines, Delta Air Lines, and United Airlines—to create LCC subsidiaries during the 1990s. By 2006, Southwest was firmly established as the only consistently profitable airline in an industry rocked by deregulation, fare wars, overcapacity, and the terrorist attacks of September 11, 2001. Specifically, Southwest was the only airline in America to show a profit for each year since 1973 up to 2005. Exhibit 2 provides a comparison of Southwest, JetBlue, and selected major carriers in 2005.

After September 11, the airline industry experienced more troubles. Domestic airline yields (computed by dividing passenger revenues by revenue passenger miles) dropped almost 20% in the aftermath of the attack and remained below pre-attack levels until 2005. As of October 2006, five major U.S. airlines, including US Airways Group, were operating under Chapter 11 bankruptcy protection.[2]

JetBlue: A Short History

JetBlue was founded by David Neeleman in 1999 after he had already established a strong record as a leader in the airline industry. Neeleman previously was Executive Vice

Exhibit 2   2005 Financial and Operational Results for Selected Carriers

	Continental	Delta	Southwest	JetBlue	American[a]	United[b]
Operating Revenues ($ millions)	$11,208	$16,191	$7,584	$1,701	$20,657	$17,304
Operating Expenses ($ millions)	11,247	18,192	6,764	1,653	21,008	17,529
Operating Profit (Loss) ($ millions)	(39)	(2,001)	820	48	(351)	(225)
Net Income (Loss) ($ millions)	(68)	(3,836)	548	(20)	(892)	(21,036)
Earnings (Loss) per Share	(0.96)	(23.75)	0.70	(0.13)	(5.21)[f]	
Wages, Benefits, etc (millions)	$2,649	$5,058	$2,702	$428	$6,173	$4,014
Fuel/Oil ($ millions)	2,443	4,271	$1,342	$438	5,080	4,032
Passengers (thousands)[c]	44,939	118,856	77,693	14,729		67,000
Revenue Passenger Miles (millions)[d]	71,261	119,954	60,223	20,200	138,374	114,272
Available Seat Miles (millions)	89,647	156,659	85,172	23,703	176,112	140,300
Passenger Load Factor[e]	79.5%	76.5%	70.7%	85.2%	78.6%	81.4%
Breakeven Load Factor		87.0%		86.1%		82.8%
Employment	42,200	55,700	91,729	6,797	88,400[g]	57,000
Fleet	356	649	445	92	699	460

Source: Compiled from 10-K and Annual Reports for Selected Carriers, 2005.

[a]American is a subsidiary of the AMR Corporation, which also owns regional carrier American Eagle.
[b]United is a subsidiary of UAL Corporation.
[c]Revenue passengers measured by each flight segment flown.
[d]The number of scheduled miles flown by revenue passengers.
[e]Revenue passenger miles divided by available seat miles.
[f]Loss per share for AMR Corporation.
[g]For the AMR Corporation.

President of Morris Air, an airline based in his home state of Utah and modeled after Southwest Airlines. In 1993, at the age of 34, Neeleman sold Morris Air to Southwest for $129 million in stock.[3]

JetBlue entered the market by connecting large, typically northeastern, U.S. cities (e.g., New York) with warmer cities in the southeast (e.g., Ft. Lauderdale, Florida). Starting with just 10 airplanes in 2000, the company achieved major-airline status in 2004 by exceeding $1 billion in annual revenue. As JetBlue's CEO, Neeleman planned from the beginning to make the airline a "growth company" and set ambitious annual goals that were largely met. These included consistent, quarterly profitability during each of the airline's first five years. In 2005, JetBlue became the ninth-largest passenger carrier in the United States.[4] Exhibit 3 provides information on financial performance and selected operating statistics for JetBlue from 2003 to 2006. By 2011, the company planned to have 290 planes in service.

JetBlue was often compared to Southwest Airlines—where Neeleman had spent a short tenure in the 1990s—due to its emphasis on low fares and its decision to eschew the hub-and-spoke architecture of legacy airlines. Consistent with Southwest's decision to limit its aircraft fleet to a single

type of plane, JetBlue's fleet was comprised entirely of A320s. The A320 was introduced by Airbus in 1988 and had rapidly become one of the most popular planes in commercial use.[a] Its maximum capacity (162 passengers[b]) and range (2,700 nautical miles, or approximately 3,100 miles) made it capable of serving a variety of medium- and long-haul routes, and it did so with relatively high fuel efficiency. By using the A320 as its sole aircraft type, JetBlue was able to standardize its training and servicing processes around the aircraft and also gained flexibility in scheduling and capacity management.

Despite some similarities, JetBlue differed from Southwest in several ways. Southwest focused on customers whose priority was low-cost, on-time performance. There were no frills, not even seat assignments.

---

[a] Between the launch of the A320 and the end of 2006, Airbus had received orders for more than 2,932 of these aircraft; as of the end of 2006, 1,633 of these planes had been delivered. This significant and growing backlog, together with A320s ubiquity across airlines and regions, created a vibrant secondary market for A320s.

[b] Between 2005 and 2007, JetBlue removed two rows of seats (i.e., 12 seats) from the standard 162-seat A320 configuration to create several rows with additional legroom.

Exhibit 3   JetBlue Financial and Operating Summary, 2003–2006

	2006	2005	2004	2003
Selected Financial Data (in millions)				
Operating revenues	$2,363	$1,701	$1,265	$998
Salaries, wages and benefits	553	428	337	267
Aircraft fuel	752	488	255	147
Total operating expenses	2,236	1,653	1,154	831
Operating income	127	48	111	167
Net income (loss)	(1)	(20)	46	103
Cash and cash equivalents	10	6	19	103
Short-term investments	689	478	431	505
Other current assets				
Total current assets	927	635	514	746
Total other assets				
Total assets	4,843	3,892	2,797	2,186
Total current liabilities	854	676	488	370
Total long-term debt	2,626	2,103	1,396	1,012
Total other liabilities				
Total liabilities	3,891	2,981	2,043	1,515
Total shareholders' equity	952	911	754	671
Total liabilities and shareholders' equity	4,843	3,892	2,797	2,186
Selected Operating Statistics				
Average fare	$119.93	$110.03	$103.49	$107.09
Flights	159,152	112,009	90,532	66,920
Average flight length (miles)	1,186	1,358	1,339	1,272
Revenue passengers (thousands)	18,565	14,729	11,783	9,012
Revenue passenger miles (millions)	23,320	20,200	15,730	11,527
Available seat miles (ASMs) (millions)	28,594	23,703	18,911	13,639
Passenger load factor	81.6%	85.20%	83.20%	84.50%
Breakeven load factor	81.4%	86.10%	77.90%	72.60%
Operating revenue per ASM (cents)	8.26	7.18	6.69	7.32
Operating expense per ASM (cents)	7.82	6.98	6.1	6.09
Operating expense per ASM, excluding fuel (cents)	5.19	4.92	4.75	5.01
Employees (FTEs)	9,515	8,326	6,601	5,012
Pilots	1,545	1,253	897	684
Fleet (average number of operating aircraft)	106.5	77.5	60.6	44
Cities served	50	34	26	21

Source: Adapted from JetBlue Corporation Annual Reports.

JetBlue offered fares up to 65% lower than legacy competitors but added comfort features such as assigned seating, leather upholstery and satellite TV on individual screens in every seat.[5] A key operating principle for JetBlue was that flight cancellations should be avoided at all costs. As such, JetBlue was routinely a top performing airline in terms of flight completion, though success on that dimension came at the expense of performance in terms of on-time arrivals. In contrast to Southwest, JetBlue flew significantly more long-haul flights (i.e., flights longer than 500 miles) and offered numerous overnight "red eye" flights from California to eastern cities. Exhibit 4 provides data on the routes served by JetBlue as of late 2005.

Exhibit 4   Routes Served by JetBlue as of November 2005

Airport	City	Airport	City	Distance (Miles)	Average Passengers/ Flight	A320 Round Trips/Day	Revenue Available Seat-Mile (Cents)
BOS	Boston, MA	DEN	Denver, CO	1,751	111.82	1	4.18
BOS	Boston, MA	FLL	Fort Lauderdale, FL	1,240	130.54	4	6.49
BOS	Boston, MA	LGB	Long Beach, CA	2,599	129.66	2	4.25
BOS	Boston, MA	MCO	Orlando, FL	1,124	121.91	4	5.97
BOS	Boston, MA	OAK	Oakland, CA	2,690	125.33	2	3.89
BOS	Boston, MA	RSW	Fort Myers, FL	1,252	127.19	1	7.01
BOS	Boston, MA	TPA	Tampa, FL	1,187	122.86	2	5.62
FLL	Fort Lauderdale, FL	IAD	Washington, DC	904	130.57	2	8.76
FLL	Fort Lauderdale, FL	LGA	New York, NY	1,079	132.86	7	7.55
FLL	Fort Lauderdale, FL	LGB	Long Beach, CA	2,326	131.54	1	4.51
IAD	Washington, DC	LGB	Long Beach, CA	2,275	134.43	4	5.01
IAD	Washington, DC	OAK	Oakland, CA	2,405	132.15	2	4.50
IAD	Washington, DC	SMF	Sacramento, CA	2,355	99.67	1	2.89
JFK	New York, NY	BQN	Aguadilla, PR	1,582	135.01	1	6.31
JFK	New York, NY	BTV	Burlington, VT	267	129.78	3	16.22
JFK	New York, NY	BUF	Buffalo, NY	301	126.72	7	16.91
JFK	New York, NY	DEN	Denver, CO	1,623	123.90	2	5.45
JFK	New York, NY	FLL	Fort Lauderdale, FL	1,072	136.97	10	8.12
JFK	New York, NY	LAS	Las Vegas, NV	2,246	131.39	4	5.18
JFK	New York, NY	LGB	Long Beach, CA	2,462	140.89	7	5.07
JFK	New York, NY	MCO	Orlando, FL	947	137.85	9	8.95
JFK	New York, NY	MSY	New Orleans, LA	1,183	136.59	1	7.72
JFK	New York, NY	NAS	Nassau, BS	1,100	112.98	1	8.16
JFK	New York, NY	OAK	Oakland, CA	2,572	132.21	5	4.25
JFK	New York, NY	ONT	Ontario, CA	2,427	139.27	2	4.86
JFK	New York, NY	PBI	West Palm Beach, FL	1,031	136.01	7	8.57
JFK	New York, NY	PHX	Phoenix, AZ	2,151	123.67	1	4.31
JFK	New York, NY	ROC	Rochester, NY	264	123.61	4	17.18
JFK	New York, NY	RSW	Fort Myers, FL	1,077	131.27	6	7.78
JFK	New York, NY	SAN	San Diego, CA	2,443	132.30	2	4.46
JFK	New York, NY	SDO	Santo Domingo, DO	1,555	101.18	1	3.88
JFK	New York, NY	SEA	Seattle, WA	2,418	139.46	1	4.77
JFK	New York, NY	SJC	San Jose, CA	2,566	127.75	2	3.99
JFK	New York, NY	SJU	San Juan, PR	1,603	130.25	3	6.42
JFK	New York, NY	SLC	Salt Lake City, UT	1,986	128.61	1	4.80
JFK	New York, NY	SMF	Sacramento, CA	2,518	130.93	1	4.30
JFK	New York, NY	STI	Santiago, DO	1,476	109.47	1	4.78
JFK	New York, NY	SYR	Syracuse, NY	209	133.14	3	20.65
JFK	New York, NY	TPA	Tampa, FL	1,008	137.27	7	7.94
LGB	Long Beach, CA	LAS	Las Vegas, NV	231	133.14	2	20.31
LGB	Long Beach, CA	OAK	Oakland, CA	354	126.40	6	13.75
LGB	Long Beach, CA	SLC	Salt Lake City, UT	590	129.53	1	10.48

Note: During 2005, the typical JetBlue A320 had 156 available seats.

Source: Company documents.

JetBlue supported its lower fares by providing customers with incentives to reserve and purchase tickets via the company's web site. To support customers who wanted to make reservations over the phone, the company set up a corps of reservations agents,[c] most of whom worked part-time from their homes. Given the flexibility offered to these part-time employees, JetBlue was able to run its reservations function at significantly lower cost relative to other airlines.

Despite JetBlue's success in gaining share along its existing routes, Neeleman and his colleagues realized the need to consider new markets as a source of growth. They decided that the largest growth opportunity existed in connecting the large cities already served by JetBlue to medium-sized cities that were currently served by regional airlines affiliated with legacy carriers.[d]

Regional airlines tended to serve medium- and small-sized markets with regional jets (RJs) that had capacity of no more than 76 seats. To a large degree, these size limits were dictated by the demands of the Air Line Pilots Association (ALPA).[e] ALPA's demands concerning the size of RJs helped to shape the relationship between regional airlines and major airlines. To ensure that regional airlines would not encroach upon the routes flown by the larger legacy airlines, pilots unions demanded the inclusion of "scope clauses" in their contracts. These clauses limited the number and seating capacity of the flights that regional airlines could fly. After 2001, the demand for smaller regional routes expanded as many airlines cut longer routes as a way to reduce costs. Since that time, regional carriers had become quite profitable.[6] One source of this profitability was financial support from their affiliated legacy airlines in the form of profit margin guarantees and coverage of key expense items (e.g., insurance, fuel and landing fees). This support helpd ensure that regional airlines provided a steady flow of passengers to fill the seats on the longer-haul routes of their affiliated legacy carriers. Exhibit 5 provides data on passenger emplanements and fleet size for mainline and regional airlines.

Because its employees were not unionized and it did not have an affiliation with a legacy carrier, JetBlue did not face limitations on the size of the planes that it could use to serve routes traditionally served by RJs. Nevertheless, JetBlue—like other LCCs—had not entered these markets in any significant way due to concerns that they would not generate enough traffic to fill the larger jets (e.g., the A320 or Boeing 737) that served as the mainstay of the LCCs fleets.

Unwilling to forego the opportunity to serve regional markets, JetBlue decided to consider whether it could profitably enter such markets using a mid-sized aircraft. After looking at seven airplanes ranging from a capacity of 68 passengers (the CRJ-700) to 117 passengers (Airbus A318), JetBlue decided that the Embraer's E190—a new airplane for which JetBlue would serve as the launch customer—represented its best option for efficiently serving medium-sized markets while offering passengers a more comfortable flight than they would receive on the typical RJ. In 2003, JetBlue signed a deal with Embraer for the purchase of 101 E190s (for delivery through 2011) and options to purchase up to 100 additional E190s between 2011 and 2016.

The E190

When JetBlue agreed to become the launch customer for the E190 in 2003, the airplane existed only on paper and was planned as Embraer's largest plan to date. This gave JetBlue the opportunity to play a significant role in designing the interior of the aircraft to improve passenger comfort. Exhibits 6a and 6b provide pictures of the interiors of the A320 and E190, respectively. Exhibit 7 presents a comparison of various features of the two planes.

JetBlue projected that the E190 could be operated at a cost per available seat-mile (CASM) that was 12% *greater* than that for an A320 and 34% *less* than that for a typical RJ. Because of its greater range and seating capacity relative to RJs (see Exhibit 8), the E190 could target a wider range of profitable destinations. Rob Maruster, senior vice president of customer service, claimed, "If we decided to open a focus city in Kansas City tomorrow, we could probably serve every market in the U.S. with the E190. That's an incredibly powerful corporate weapon."

The E190 increased the range of choices available to JetBlue passengers by feeding customers to connecting A320 flights at "focus cities," such as New York. For example, a customer flying on an E190 from Portland, Maine, to JFK could connect with an A320 flight to Oakland, California.

---

[c] By 2007, JetBlue employed roughly 2,000 reservations agents.

[d] For example, American Eagle was the regional affiliate of American Airlines, and Northwest Airlink was the regional affiliate of Northwest Airlnes.

[e] As of the summer of 2006, the maximum RJ seating capacity that ALPA agreed upon was 76, up from the limit of 50 that most airlines had abided by for years. Only US Airways had a higher limit, which was agreed upon with the ALPA as the airline was emerging from bankruptcy protection and merging with America West Airlines in September of 2006. A US Airways executive explained that its regional feeder airlines could now fly "'anything below an E-190,'" which meant a fixed number of 90-seater aircraft. See Mary Kirby, "Drawing the Line," *Flight International*, May 16, 2006, via LexisNexis, accessed January 31, 2007.

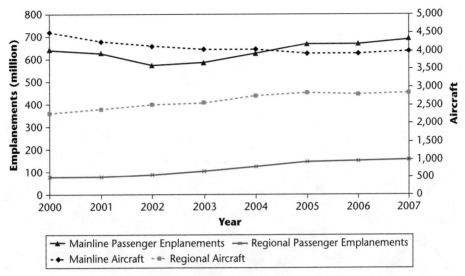

Exhibit 5   Passenger Emplanements and Aircraft for Mainline and Regional Airlines, 2000 to 2007

Source: Federal Aviation Administration, *FAA Aerospace Forecast, 2008–2025.*

Exhibit 6a   Photograph of the A320 Interior, Rear to Front

Source: http://www.airliners.net/usephotos/, accessed July 31, 2008

Exhibit 6b   Photograph of the E190 Interior, Front to Rear

Source: Company document.

Exhibit 7   Comparison of Airbus A320 and Embraer 190

	Airbus A320	Embraer 190
Seats	150[a]	100
Seat configuration	25 rows (3-and-3 layout)	25 rows (2-and-2 layout)
Seat pitch	34–36 inches	32–33 inches
Seat width	17.8 inches	18.25 inches
Cabin height	7 feet, 1 inch	6 feet, 7 inches
Bathrooms	3	2
Length	123 feet, 3 inches	118 feet, 11 inches
Wingspan	111 feet, 10 inches	94 feet, 3 inches
Range	2,700 nautical miles (~3,100 miles)	2,100 nautical miles (~2,400 miles)
Estimated acquisition cost per plane	$50–60 million	$30–40 million

Source: Adapted from http://www.jetblue.com/about/whyyoulllike/about_whyairbusstats.html and http://www.jetblue.com/about/whyyoulllike/about_whyembraerstats.html, accessed August, 2007.

[a]Initially, JetBlue's A320s were equipped with the standard 162 seats offered by Airbus. Between 2005 and 2007, JetBlue decreased the number of seats on its A320 on two occasions. First was the reduction from 162 to 156 seats by removing one row of seats from each plane. Later, a second row of seats was removed, reducing capacity to 150 seats. Federal Aviation Administration (FAA) regulations required the staffing of one flight attendant per 50 seats on an aircraft.

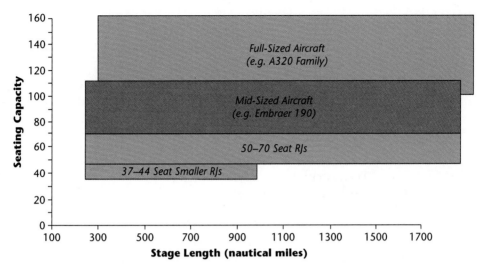

Exhibit 8 Range and Seating Capacity of the E-190 and Selected RJs

Source: Company documents.

Prior to the introduction of the E190, this Portland customer could not have considered JetBlue as an option. Of course, A320s could feed into E190 flights as well, resulting in higher loads and improved economics for JetBlue. Transfers at focus cities would also improve the utilization of existing airport facilities, thus increasing productivity and reducing downtime for airport crewmembers. This synergy between the E190 and A320 enabled JetBlue to run E190s at an average daily utilization of 10 to 11 hours a day, significantly more than the average of 8 hours per day for RJs. In 2004, JetBlue flew its A320s an average of 13.4 hours a day.

Ramping UP

The initial plans for integrating the E190 were ambitious. After taking on seven E190s in the last two months of 2005, JetBlue took delivery of 16 additional E190s in 2006 and planned to take on another 18 in 2007. Maruster noted that, because that number of passengers required for a flight to meet the typical "breakeven" load of 75-to-80 percent was much lower on the E190 than the A320, the new plane made it easier for JetBlue to introduce service in new markets. In fact, a key assumption in JetBlue's planning was that it would add an average of one new city-pair market with the delivery of each E190. See Exhibit 9 for data on the routes served by JetBlue as of April 2007.

Tom Anderson senior vice president of Fleet Programs, explained: "We wanted to get to efficient scale quickly. With any new airplane type in your fleet, in general,

you need to get to 40 or 50 airplanes before you benefit from economies of scale."

Successful integration of the E190 into the fleet also provided some extra advantages over competitors. According to Barger, JetBlue was buying E190s "as fast as Embraer could make them," Neeleman added, "Embraer is somewhat limited in its production capacity—it was able to build about ten planes a month and that was split between several models—E170s, E175s, E190s, and E195s. To go bigger than that, Embraer would have to build a whole other facility."

While taking delivery of new E190s, JetBlue also continued its purchases of A320s. The A320 had proven to be an extremely reliable plane around which JetBlue had standardized its operations. Furthermore, the wide adoption and popularity of the A320 across airlines—combined with the relatively standard formats for the plane—provided significant flexibility with respect to firm orders and options for additional planes. In comparison, the E190 was a newer plane with many aspects that were customized to the specific needs of each of the relatively small number of airlines that had already adopted it.

Though individual pilot could theoretically be trained to fly both the A320 and the E190, simultaneous dual certification was practically infeasible. Certification depended on the number of flights a pilot had flown on a given aircraft type within the prior month. As a result, it was simply not possible for a pilot to obtain enough flights as an E190 captain and enough as an A320 captain during a single month to retain dual certification in the following month. Shifting

Exhibit 9 Routes Served by JetBlue as of April 2007

Airport	City	Airport	City	Distance (Miles)	Average Passengers/ Flight	A320 Round Trips/Day	E190 Round Trips/Day	Revenue/ Available Seat-Mile (Cents)
BOS	Boston, MA	AUS	Austin, TX	1,695	71.88		1	6.51
BOS	Boston, MA	BUF	Buffalo, NY	895	59.36		3	9.33
BOS	Boston, MA	CMH	Columbus, OH	639	59.47		1	6.53
BOS	Boston, MA	DEN	Denver, CO	1,751	101.88	1		5.11
BOS	Boston, MA	FLL	Fort Laud., FL	1,240	132.35	2		8.60
BOS	Boston, MA	IAD	Washington, DC	413	72.14		5	14.06
BOS	Boston, MA	LAS	Las Vegas, NY	2,378	114.19	1		4.36
BOS	Boston, MA	LGB	Long Beach, CA	2,599	130.21	3		5.84
BOS	Boston, MA	MCO	Orlando, FL	1,124	125.75	4		8.99
BOS	Boston, MA	OAK	Oakland, CA	2,690	128.72	2		5.75
BOS	Boston, MA	PBI	W Palm Bch, FL	1,200	126.83	1		8.85
BOS	Boston, MA	PHX	Phoenix, AZ	2,297	92.41	1		3.44
BOS	Boston, MA	PIT	Pittsburgh, PA	495	55.16		2	8.42
BOS	Boston, MA	RDU	Raleigh, NC	612	62.16		1	9.99
BOS	Boston, MA	RIC	Richmond, VA	474	61.81		2	10.79
BOS	Boston, MA	RSW	Fort Myers, FL	1,252	119.26	2		8.63
BOS	Boston, MA	SEA	Seattle, WA	2,492	116.33	1		5.15
BOS	Boston, MA	SJC	San Jose, CA	2,685	126.16	1		5.38
BOS	Boston, MA	TPA	Tampa, FL	1,187	102.66	1	1	8.47
EWR	Newark, NJ	PBI	W Palm Bch, FL	1,027	131.41	1		9.97
EWR	Newark, NJ	RSW	Fort Myers, FL	1,071	122.44	1		8.37
FLL	Fort Laud., FL	EWR	Newark, NJ	1,068	130.61	4		9.55
FLL	Fort Laud., FL	IAD	Washington, DC	904	123.54	2		8.81
FLL	Fort Laud., FL	LGA	New York, NY	1,079	134.46	5		9.78
FLL	Fort Laud., FL	LGB	Long Beach, CA	2,326	124.39	1		5.29
FLL	Fort Laud., FL	OAK	Oakland, CA	2,574	102.20	1		3.76
FLL	Fort Laud., FL	SWF	Newburgh, NY	1,122	113.94	2		7.01
IAD	Washington, DC	LAS	Las Vegas, NV	2,063	107.85	1		3.99
IAD	Washington, DC	LGB	Long Beach, CA	2,275	128.23	4		6.05
IAD	Washington, DC	OAK	Oakland, CA	2,405	125.03	3		5.80
IAD	Washington, DC	SAN	San Diego, CA	2,251	113.34	1		4.90
JFK	New York, NY	AUS	Austin, TX	1,519	78.00		3	7.63
JFK	New York, NY	BNA	Nashville, TN	765	68.37		3	8.30
JFK	New York, NY	BOS	Boston, MA	187	81.71	5	3	21.22
JFK	New York, NY	BQN	Aguadilla, PR	1,582	134.08	2		7.36
JFK	New York, NY	BTV	Burlington, VT	267	117.47	4		17.31
JFK	New York, NY	BUF	Buffalo, NY	301	119.75	8	1	19.72
JFK	New York, NY	BUR	Burbank, CA	2,462	132.48	5		6.66
JFK	New York, NY	CLT	Charlotte, NC	541	76.19	1	4	12.60
JFK	New York, NY	CMH	Columbus, OH	482	60.00		3	8.13
JFK	New York, NY	CUN	Cancun, MX	1,559	117.82	2		8.18
JFK	New York, NY	DEN	Denver, CO	1,623	120.35	2		6.58
JFK	New York, NY	FLL	Fort Laud., FL	1,072	131.96	10		9.36
JFK	New York, NY	HOU	Houston, TX	1,428	90.45		3	4.22

Exhibit 9   Routes Served by JetBlue as of April 2007 (*continued*)

Airport	City	Airport	City	Distance (Miles)	Average Passengers/ Flight	A320 Round Trips/Day	E190 Round Trips/Day	Revenue/ Available Seat-Mile (Cents)
JFK	New York, NY	IAD	Washington, DC	228	65.54		5	14.63
JFK	New York, NY	JAX	Jacksonville, FL	831	103.59	3		8.57
JFK	New York, NY	LAS	Las Vegas, NV	2,246	129.64	6		6.59
JFK	New York, NY	LGB	Long Beach, CA	2,462	135.83	6		6.63
JFK	New York, NY	MCO	Orlando, FL	947	132.96	11		9.84
JFK	New York, NY	MSY	New Orleans, LA	1,183	124.78	2		8.81
JFK	New York, NY	NAS	Nassau, BS	1,100	123.28	2		9.35
JFK	New York, NY	OAK	Oakland, CA	2,572	132.32	4		6.12
JFK	New York, NY	ONT	Ontario, CA	2,427	133.57	1		6.28
JFK	New York, NY	ORD	Chicago, IL	739	89.63	2	3	6.10
JFK	New York, NY	PBI	West Palm Bch, FL	1,031	128.83	5	1	9.53
JFK	New York, NY	PDX	Portland, OR	2,450	120.88	1		5.35
JFK	New York, NY	PHX	Phoenix, AZ	2,151	122.27	2		5.76
JFK	New York, NY	PIT	Pittsburgh, PA	339	61.07		4	11.84
JFK	New York, NY	PSE	Ponce, PR	1,623	126.02	1		6.24
JFK	New York, NY	PWM	Portland, ME	274	93.60	3	1	16.77
JFK	New York, NY	RDU	Raleigh, NC	427	70.95		5	14.17
JFK	New York, NY	RIC	Richmond, VA	288	67.54		4	15.84
JFK	New York, NY	ROC	Rochester, NY	264	113.34	5		18.77
JFK	New York, NY	RSW	Fort Myers, FL	1,077	124.63	4		8.53
JFK	New York, NY	SAN	San Diego, CA	2,443	130.05	3		5.72
JFK	New York, NY	SEA	Seattle, WA	2,418	132.64	2		6.17
JFK	New York, NY	SJC	San Jose, CA	2,566	129.02	2		5.77
JFK	New York, NY	SJU	San Juan, PR	1,603	129.13	4		7.20
JFK	New York, NY	SLC	Salt Lake City, UT	1,986	128.68	1		6.25
JFK	New York, NY	SMF	Sacramento, CA	2,518	121.78	1		5.18
JFK	New York, NY	SRQ	Sarasota, FL	1,044	130.11	1		9.66
JFK	New York, NY	STI	Santiago, DO	1,476	128.39	1		8.07
JFK	New York, NY	SYR	Syracuse, NY	209	119.50	3	1	21.55
JFK	New York, NY	TPA	Tampa, FL	1,008	131.62	6		9.09
JFK	New York, NY	TUS	Tucson, AZ	2,134	101.24	1		4.28
LGB	Long Beach, CA	LAS	Las Vegas, NV	231	113.43	6		21.39
LGB	Long Beach, CA	OAK	Oakland, CA	354	113.24	5		14.64
LGB	Long Beach, CA	ORD	Chicago, IL	1,734	126.93	2		4.74
LGB	Long Beach, CA	SLC	Salt Lake City, UT	590	121.94	2		11.61
LGB	Long Beach, CA	SMF	Sacramento, CA	388	89.32	2		9.20
MCO	Orlando, FL	BON	Aguadilla, PR	1,131	114.15	1		7.37
MCO	Orlando, FL	EWR	Newark, NJ	940	123.72	4		9.67
MCO	Orlando, FL	LGA	New York, NY	953	129.42	11		9.65
MCO	Orlando, FL	SJU	San Juan, PR	1,191	126.48	2		8.01
MCO	Orlando, FL	SWF	Newburgh, NY	992	125.17	2		8.24
MCO	Orlando, FL	SYR	Syracuse, NY	1,056	129.50	1		9.09
PBI	West Palm Bch, FL	LGA	New York, NY	1,038	127.47	1		9.62

Note: As of April 2007, the typical JetBlue A320 had 156 available seats and each E190 had 100 available seats.
Source: Company documents.

from one plane to another thus required a period of non-revenue "training" flying that was simply too expensive for the airline to subsidize. As a result, most JetBlue pilots were only trained to fly one of the two plane types.

In addition to training, the introduction of the E190 brought changes in pilot compensation. An E190 captain (i.e., pilot in command) received hourly pay that was lower than that for an A320 captain but higher than that for an A320 first officer (i.e., co-pilot). Anderson explained that JetBlue had to manage pilot expectations with respect to these changes. He observed.

> The way you get the pilots comfortable with this sort of quasi-regional jet being introduced into our fleet is you keep taking deliveries of A320s at the same rate and creating A320 captain jobs that are the top of the pyramid—the highest paying pilot jobs in the company. So from a career-path perspective, pilots would not feel that we slowed down A320 deliveries to make room for the E190. We'd have a lot of unhappy, highly influential employees. So we had to keep the status quo with the A320 deliveries.

Long-Haul vs. Short-Haul Routes

After some debate over the best initial market for the E190, JetBlue decided to introduce the plane in November 2005 on select flights between New York and Boston. Though both cities represented major markets with busy airports, JetBlue already had well-established operations in each city. Although the short-haul routes to be served by the E190 promised an increase in JetBlue's revenues (Exhibit 10), they also brought increased costs, as more frequent flights required E190s to spend more time on the ground than A320s for taxiing, loading, and unloading between flights.

Reactions to the E190

Pilots

An additional problem with the introduction or short-haul routes was that most E190 pilots would be at a disadvantage in accumulating flying hours (and increasing their seniority) vis-à-vis pilots of the long-haul A320. Pilots accumulated flying hours only for time spent in the air; any time spent on the ground because of bad weather or congested air traffic (which could be acute on routes connecting busy airports like Boston and New York) was not included in their block accumulation of hours. Seniority was important not only in terms of raising pilots' compensation per flight hour but also in terms of providing them with greater say over their number of flight hours per month.[f]

These changes were concerning to many JetBlue pilots. Scott Green, vice president of Flight Operations, described the initial reaction of many pilots to the adoption of the E190: "If it ain't broke, don't fix it. We're doing well financially with the A320, so why on earth would we put our company at risk by doing this?"

Employees

In addition to requiring changes to JetBlue's airport infrastructure (e.g., lowering the height of its current jetways to accommodate a smaller plane), the E190 posed challenges for the airline's personnel who had grown accustomed to the A320.

Steven Predmore, vice president and chief safety officer, described how seemingly innocuous variations in the design of the two planes resulted in unexpected changes for employees. He noted innovation of using non-skid flooring on the cargo bins of the E190 (versus the bare floors found on the A320). This was adopted as a safety feature to prevent baggage handlers from slipping on the floor of the cargo bin while loading and unloading bags under rainy or snowy conditions. With respect to the non-skid flooring, Predmore noted:

> From a health and safety standpoint, it seems to be a good thing. But the loading procedure established with the A320 was to slide bags along the floor of the bins. Well now we couldn't slide bags. This not only increased loading time, but also increased the potential for strains and back sprains as handlers had to lift bags they previously would have slid.

Vicky Stennes, vice president of Inflight Services added that flight attendants also had to make a significant adjustment to the E190. Though the ratio of available seats to flight attendants was the same (i.e., 50 to 1) for both the A320 and E190, the latter plane had smaller galleys from which to serve customers. Further, the shorter duration of E190 flights provided less time for each attendant to provide the high-level of service to which JetBlue passengers had become accustomed.

For those employees involved with servicing and maintaining JetBlue's aircraft, the adoption of the E190 created additional operating complexity. Because the A320 and E190 were different sizes and their engines, avionics, and other major components were manufactured by different

---

[f]In contrast, the seniority of flight attendants was not determined by hours spent in flight.

Exhibit 10   Average Number of Daily JetBlue Roundtrips by City-Pair Distance and Year

City-Pair Distance	2005	2006	2007
<500 miles	27	57	78
500–1,000 miles	12	22	50
1,000–1,500 miles	49	55	67
1,500–2,000 miles	10	17	21
2,000–2,500 miles	34	40	40
>2,500 miles	16	17	19
Total	148	208	275

Source: Company documents.

companies, there were few opportunities to standardize parts and servicing procedures across the two types of aircraft. Given the volume of E190 flights either originating or arriving at JFK, JetBlue decided to invest in maintenance capabilities (i.e., equipment and staff) for the E190 at that airport. However, investing in similar capabilities at other airports—smaller JetBlue focus cities and other destinations—was not economically justifiable. Further, the novelty of the E190 meant that there were few opportunities to outsource or share with other carriers the maintenance responsibilities for E190s at airports other than JFK.

Customers

The E190 required changes in behavior and expectations for JetBlue's existing customers. For example, overhead storage bins on the E190 were smaller than those on the A320, causing many passengers to be surprised and disappointed when they were told that they would need to check their luggage at the gate. Maruster reflected on the impact of this and related differences between the two planes, "So now we had to tell customers to do two different things. If it's the first plane, you do this. If it's the other plane, you do that. Those kind of differences were a bit concerning to me."

Beyond the airline's existing customers, the short-haul routes that JetBlue introduced with the E190 brought new customers with new expectations. JetBlue had grown as an airline geared toward personal and leisure travel, determined to overcome delays and technical problems to get passengers to their destinations. Passengers flying from New York to vacation spots in Florida, for example, were usually not following a tight schedule. This was not the case, however, for the business travelers who would fly

short-haul routes on the E190. David Ramage, vice president of technical operations, described the attitude of these business travelers: "I've got to be in Boston by 8:00, and if I'm not, there are serious consequences." Ian Deason, director of alliances and partnerships, added, "With business customers, you get one chance. If they are not satisfied the first time, it's hard to get them back."

The short-haul routes attracted other passengers that tested the limits of JetBlue's "get-to-the-destination-at-all-costs" culture. One such test occurred during on New Year's Eve in 2005. A 6:00 p.m. E190 flight from Boston to New York was filled with revelers who were planning to spend the evening in New York and return the next morning. Mechanical problems combined with bad weather resulted in a long delay. As usual, JetBlue was determined to get its passengers in the air, but the flight crew did not communicate how long the delay was expected to last. After a while, flight attendants soon had to soothe angry passengers. One passenger's complaint captured the feeling or many: "If you had cancelled me I would have been happier. I would have gotten off the plane and *driven* to New York."

These were new kinds of demands that Mike Barger and others involved in training JetBlue employees now had to face. He noted:

> Our "secret sauce" historically has been that when something goes wrong, you buy a pizza and give somebody a hug, and everything's great. As for the business customers, they do not want a slice of pizza. Instead, they are thinking, "I've got a meeting in the city." The "a-ha moment" from a training perspective was that we did not prepare our customer-facing people to deal with the passenger who says, "I don't want a pizza. In fact, go get my bag off the airplane!"

Complex Intangibles

Drawing on his experience at one of the legacy airlines, Maruster reflected on another issue that arose from adding a new plane into JetBlue's operating system:

> When you start adding complexity, you start to lose your ability to track it and put your finger on it. When I was at another airline, we got rid of a sub-fleet of 12 airplanes that was sitting out there all by itself, requiring different processes and training. We really didn't have a strong financial case for getting rid of this fleet; everybody just knew we had to do it.

The high standards of service and reliability JetBlue had set in the past increased the frustrations of working through the integration of the E190. Neeleman noted:

> We wanted the plane to work, and we wanted to make sure that it worked every time. When you launch an airplane, there's this process of flying it and figuring out why this thing broke, particularly when the plane is so new. Does it need to be re-engineered? Does the software need to be re-written? Does this clamp need to be replaced? Moreover, why did this clamp fail? Well, it wasn't strong enough. Why wasn't it strong enough? Well, because it's a new plane.

Applying the Brakes

On a crisp autumn evening in 2006, Barger held a meeting with several members of JetBlue's management team, and others from a key banking advisor, over dinner at Il Corso in New York City. The goal of the meeting was to discuss options for financing the future growth of the airline. Mark Powers, senior vice president and treasurer, presented data on the cash flow implications of the airline's prior and planned aircraft purchases and growth over the next several years.

Though Powers presented several slides, he spent the majority of his time discussing only one of them—a picture showing the cash flows associated with acquisition of each new airplane. Powers recalled.

> That slide showed a much longer path to breaking even on a cash basis than most of us in that room ever assumed. When you took the cash flow picture for the average plane acquisition and multiplied it by the number of planes we were acquiring each year, it was clear that, if we stayed on the current course, we would grow ourselves to death.

By the end of the dinner, it was clear that the data and analysis presented by Powers—combined with rapidly increasing fuel prices—dictated that JetBlue slow its rate of growth significantly. To that end, within several months of

the dinner, JetBlue announced that it would decrease the rate at which it took delivery of new airplanes and redouble efforts to sell used aircraft. With respect to new aircraft, the company reduced its planned deliveries of A320s from 17 to 12 for both 2007 and 2008. For E190s, planned deliveries decreased from 18 to 10 for both 2007 and 2008. Exhibit 11 provides JetBlue's actual and expected fleet size from 2000 to 2011 under its original and revised assumptions about annual plane deliveries. At the time JetBlue announced these reductions, the airline noted that its plan was to slow the annual rate of growth in available seat miles (ASMs) for the airline from 18–20% to 14–17%.[7]

JetBlue's pilots were arguably impacted more than any other department by the decision to slow growth. Reducing aircraft purchases, explained Scott Green, "hurts the pilot group unlike any other work group, because your whole seniority and income ability is tied to the number of airplanes that we take."

The Valentine's Day Crisis

On February 14, 2007, JetBlue faced the beginning of what then-CEO Neeleman would later refer to as "the worst operational week in JetBlue's seven year history."[8] JetBlue's flights from JFK were heavily booked on that particular Wednesday, as many customers in northeastern states hoped to get a head start on travel for the upcoming President's Day weekend. The weather forecast for JFK predicted early snow turning to rain. Despite the fact that the snow lingered longer than expected, JetBlue continued to board flights at JFK and have them taxi to their runways in anticipation of the expected changeover to rain.

Unfortunately, the snow turned to freezing rain, creating, "ice pellet" conditions under which the FAA prohibited domestic flights from taking off. Because planes were still able to land at JFK under these conditions, the planes on the tarmac were left without gates to which they could return. The result was that several JetBlue planes were stranded on the tarmac at JFK, with nine spending at least 6 hours each waiting for gates.[9] Beyond the disgruntled passengers on these flights, the inability of JetBlue planes to leave JFK wreaked havoc on the entire JetBlue system as planes and flight crews were increasingly out of position and unable to make scheduled flights. Over the course of the six-day event over 1,100 flights were cancelled in total—approximately 40% of JetBlue's operations. In total, more than 131,000 JetBlue customers were affected by cancellations, delays, or diversions during the period.[10]

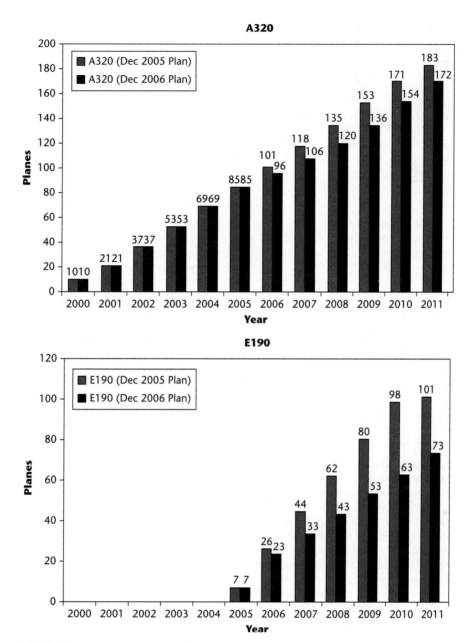

Exhibit 11 JetBlue Fleet by Plane Type, December 2005 Plan vs. December 2006 Plan

Note: Figures for 2006 forward are based on planned deliveries.
Source: JetBlue Annual Reports.

The crisis exposed the informal patchwork of operating systems that had emerged since JetBlue's founding but had not previously created significant problems for the airline. In response to the crisis, JetBlue took several steps to shore up its operations in the areas of reservations staffing, airport staffing (e.g., the credentialing of corporate staff at Forest Hills to staff selected operations positions at JFK (on an emergency basis), and information systems. Most importantly, the crisis highlighted the need to reconsider JetBlue's long-standing operating principle of not canceling flights.

The crisis prompted Neeleman, on February 20, to introduce JetBlue's Customer Bill of Rights. The Bill of Rights, which was the first of its kind among U.S. airlines and was retroactively applied to those affected by the February

JetBlue Airways Customer Bill of Rights

Above all else, JetBlue Airways is dedicated to bringing humanity back to air travel. We strive to make every part of your experience as simple and as pleasant as possible. Unfortunately, there are times when things do not go as planned. If you're inconvenienced as a result, we think it is important that you know exactly what you can expect from us. That's why we created our Customer Bill of Rights. These Rights will always be subject to the highest level of safety and security for our customers and crewmembers.

INFORMATION

JetBlue will notify customers of the following:
- Delays prior to scheduled departure
- Cancellations and their cause
- Diversions and their cause

CANCELLATIONS

All customers whose flight is cancelled by JetBlue will, at the customer's option, receive a full refund or re-accommodation on a future JetBlue flight at no additional charge or fare. If JetBlue cancels a flight within 12 hours of scheduled departure and the cancellation is due to a *Controllable Irregularity*, JetBlue will also provide the customer with a Voucher valid for future travel on JetBlue in the amount paid by the customer for the roundtrip.

DEPARTURE DELAYS

1. Customers whose flight is delayed prior to scheduled departure for 1-1:59 hours due to a *Controllable Irregularity* are entitled to a $25 Voucher good for future travel on JetBlue.
2. Customers whose flight is delayed prior to scheduled departure for 2-3:59 hours due to a *Controllable Irregularity* are entitled to a $50 Voucher good for future travel on JetBlue.
3. Customers whose flight is delayed prior to scheduled departure for 4-5:59 hours due to a *Controllable Irregularity* are entitled to a Voucher good for future travel on JetBlue in the amount paid by the customer for the oneway trip.
4. Customers whose flight is delayed prior to scheduled departure for 6 or more hours due to a *Controllable Irregularity* are entitled to a Voucher good for future travel on JetBlue in the amount paid by the customer for the roundtrip.

OVERBOOKINGS (As defined in JetBlue's Contract of Carriage)

Customers who are involuntarily denied boarding shall receive $1,000.

ONBOARD GROUND DELAYS

For customers who experience an onboard Ground Delay for more than 5 hours, JetBlue will take necessary action so that customers may deplane. JetBlue will also provide customers experiencing an onboard Ground Delay with food and drink, access to restrooms and, as necessary, medical treatment.

Arrivals:

1. Customers who experience an onboard Ground Delay on Arrival for 30-59 minutes after scheduled arrival time are entitled to a $25 Voucher good for future travel on JetBlue.
2. Customers who experience an onboard Ground Delay on Arrival for 1-1:59 hours after scheduled arrival time are entitled to a $100 Voucher good for future travel on JetBlue.
3. Customers who experience an onboard Ground Delay on Arrival for 2-2:59 hours after scheduled arrival time are entitled to a Voucher good for future travel on JetBlue in the amount paid by the customer for the oneway trip.
4. Customers who experience an onboard Ground Delay on Arrival for 3 or more hours after scheduled arrival time are entitled to a Voucher good for future travel on JetBlue in the amount paid by the customer for the roundtrip.

Departures:

1. Customers who experience an onboard Ground Delay on Departure for 3-3:59 hours are entitled to a $100 Voucher good for future travel on JetBlue.
2. Customers who experience an onboard Ground Delay on Departure for 4 or more hours are entitled to a Voucher good for future travel on JetBlue in the amount paid by the customer for the roundtrip.

JetBlue Airways
Forest Hills Support Center
118-29 Queens Blvd
Forest Hills, NY 11375

1-800-JETBLUE   1-800-538-2583   jetblue.com

*These Rights are subject to JetBlue's Contract of Carriage and, as applicable, the operational control of the flight crew, and apply to only JetBlue operated flights.
This document is representative of what is reflected in JetBlue's Contract of Carriage, the legal binding document between JetBlue and it's customers.

Exhibit 12   JetBlue Customer Bill of Rights
Source: http://www.jetblue.com/p/about/ourcompany/promise/Bill_Of_Rights.pdf, accessed April 2007.

crisis, delineated JetBlue's responsibilities to its customers in the following areas: information-sharing, cancellations, departure delays, overbookings, and onboard ground delays for arrivals and departures (Exhibit 12). Prior to the crisis, *BusinessWeek* had compiled its list of top performing companies with respect to customer service, placing JetBlue in the fourth spot. When the list appeared in the March 5 issue of the magazine, however, the cover showed JetBlue's name scratched off the list with title "Customer Service Champs . . . and One Extraordinary Stumble."

At multiple points during February and March, the provisions of the company's Bill of Rights were tested by weather conditions in the eastern U.S. On those occasions, the airline moved proactively to cancel flights. In early March, JetBlue introduced Russ Chew, former COO of the FAA, as the airline's new COO with Barger retaining the title of president. In May, Neeleman announced his resignation as CEO, and Barger was named as his successor.

Moving Forward

Though disappointed by the crisis itself, Barger was pleased with the manner in which the airline had moved swiftly to shore up its operating procedures in the three subsequent months. As the immediate stress of crisis recovery began to subside, however, Barger found himself facing an equally perplexing issue related to JetBlue's capacity. Despite the steps taken to slow JetBlue's rate of aircraft deliveries in late 2006, it was clear—particularly in light of rapidly increasing fuel costs—that the airline needed to curtail further its capacity growth.

While the exact magnitude of the necessary reductions in capacity growth was still being determined, Barger realized that the cuts would be significant. What was not clear was how much of the capacity reduction should come from the E190 fleet versus that of the A320. Barger saw the E190 as a unique plane that JetBlue could use as an engine for future growth. At the same time, the A320 was a proven aircraft around which JetBlue had standardized its training and operating activities over the past seven years. Ultimately, Barger knew that neither Embraer nor Airbus would be pleased with any future reductions or deferrals sought by JetBlue. While the need for slower capacity growth was clear, the best path for achieving was less certain.

Endnotes

1. Delta Air Lines, "Delta Through the Decades," Delta Air Lines Company web site, http://www.delta.com/about_delta/corporate_information/delta_stats_facts_/ delta_through_the_decades/index.jsp, accessed February 7, 2007.
2. This section draws from Jim Corridore, "Airlines," Industry Surveys, *Standard & Poor's Industry Surveys,* November 23, 2006, via NetAdvantage, accessed November 15, 2006.
3. Steve Huettel, "Soaring Ahead," *St. Petersburg Times,* accessed via Factiva, December 12, 2006.
4. JetBlue, December 31, 2005 10-K (Forrest Hills JetBlue, 2005), p. 1, via Thomson Research accessed January 2007.
5. Susan Carey, "Balancing Act: Amid JetBlue's Rapid Ascent, CEO Adopts Big Rivals' Traits," *Wall Street Journal,* August 25, 2005, accessed via Factiva, December 19, 2006.
6. Brian Nelson, "Worst Has Yet to Come for Regional Airlines," *Morningstar Column,* October 16, 2006, via LexisNexis, accessed January 31, 2007.
7. JetBlue Airways, "JetBlue Adjusts Fleet Delivery Plan Through 2016," company press release, December 4, 2006.
8. David Neeleman, "An Apology from David Neeleman," JetBlue Company Web site, http://www.jetblue.com/about/ourcompany/apology/index.html, accessed March 2007.
9. Jeff Bailey, "JetBlue Cancels More Flights, Leading to Passenger Discord," *The New York Times,* February 18, 2007, via Factiva, accessed September 2007.
10. JetBlue Airways Conference Call to Announce Details of Customer Bill of Rights Program, February 20, 2007, accessed via Thomson Financial, April 2007.

Case 2-2: Nucor in 2010*

Twenty years ago when the United States was liquidating its historic manufacturing businesses, like steel, Nucor fought against the trend, found success, and became a model for the second millennium. But as 2010 came to a close, the United States' recovery from what some referred to as the second Depression remained in doubt. Prices for scrap metal rose drastically, prices for steel products fluctuated unpredictably, and a Chinese steel company, Anshan Iron & Steel, stood poised to enter the U.S. market, where two foreign-owned firms already hold the first and fifth places in steel production. Nucor had survived the crash of 2008 and the depression of 2009 better than most, but could it get back on the growth track of the last 20 years?

Nucor faced unique challenges in the United States, with increased costs of scrap metal driven by the voracious appetite of China, balance of trade challenges with China, rising energy costs, and climate change-related financial risk associated with proposed U.S. legislation. Would U.S. industry yield technical leadership to government-controlled steel companies in China and companies in India, Russia, and other developing countries? The industry was consolidating and global competition was stiff with countries with low labor costs and government subsidies. Would U.S. steel manufacturing slide into decline as had England, the birthplace of steel production, in the 1960s and 1970s? The challenges facing the company in the last quarter of 2010 had never been greater, but Nucor remained confident that its conservative financial strength, unique team-based culture, and vertically integrated and diversified strategy would allow it to prosper.

Background

Surprisingly rock-solid Nucor emerged from two blue-sky failures. First was Nuclear Consultants, a company formed after World War II to ride the wave of growth coming in "nuclear" technology. When this did not happen, the Nuclear Corporation of America moved on to the "conglomerate" trend popular at the time. Nuclear Corporation acquired various "high-tech" businesses such as radiation

sensors, semiconductors, rare earths, and air-conditioning equipment. However, the company still lost money and a fourth reorganization in 1966 put 40-year-old Ken Iverson in charge. The building of Nucor began.

Ken Iverson had joined the Navy after high school in 1943 and had been transferred from officer training school to Cornell's Aeronautical Engineering Program. On graduation, he selected mechanical engineering/metallurgy for a master's degree to avoid the long drafting apprenticeship in aeronautical engineering. His college work with an electron microscope earned him a job with International Harvester. After five years in their laboratory, his boss, and mentor, prodded him to expand his vision by going with a smaller company.

Over the next 10 years, Iverson worked for four small metal companies, gaining technical knowledge and increasing his exposure to other business functions. He enjoyed working with the presidents of these small companies and admired their ability to achieve outstanding results. Nuclear Corporation, after failing to buy the company Iverson worked for, hired him as a consultant to find them another metal business to buy. In 1962, the firm bought a small joist plant in South Carolina that Iverson found, on the condition that he run it.

Over the next four years, Iverson built up the Vulcraft division as Nuclear Corporation struggled. The president, David Thomas, was described as a great promoter and salesman but a weak manager. A partner with Bear Stearns actually made a personal loan to the company to keep it going. In 1965, when the company was on the edge of bankruptcy, Iverson, who headed the only successful division, was named president and moved the company's headquarters to Charlotte, North Carolina. He immediately began getting rid of the esoteric, but unprofitable, high-tech divisions and concentrated on the steel joist business he found successful. They built more joist plants and in 1968 began building their first steel mill in South Carolina to "make steel cheaper than they were buying from importers." By 1984 Nucor had six joist plants and four steel mills, using the new "mini-mill" technology.

The original owner of Vulcraft, Sanborn Chase, was known at Vulcraft as "a scientific genius." He had been a man of great compassion who understood the atmosphere necessary for people to self-motivate. Chase, an engineer

*This case study was prepared by Frank C. Barnes, Belk College of Business, University of North Carolina, Charlotte, and Beverly B. Tyler, College of Management, North Carolina State University.

Exhibit 1   Thomson Financial Annual Ratios Report on Nucor

Nucor Corp.   **Symbol: (C000003357)**

http://www.nucor.com   CUSIP: 670346105   **Price 8/30/2010 Shrs Out (th) Mkt Cap (th)**
Exchange: NYSE   DCN: N953250000   36.67   315,125   11,738,416
Country: USA   ISIN: US6703461052
DJ Sector: Basic Materials   **PE Ratio   Tot Ret 1Yr   Beta**
DJ Industry: Steel   79.26   −8.98   0.96
Company Status: Active

Profitability Ratios	12/31/09	12/31/08	12/31/07	12/31/06	12/31/05
Return on assets	−1.48	16.19	17.00	23.75	20.10
Return on invested capital	−1.76	19.91	22.04	31.34	26.81
Cash flow to sales	4.98	10.86	12.88	15.83	14.01
Cost of goods sold to sales	93.11	80.56	78.56	74.02	76.45
Gross profit margin	1.83	17.12	18.86	23.51	20.59
Operating profit margin	−1.29	13.95	15.38	19.49	16.71
Pretax margin	−2.96	13.12	15.35	19.75	16.75
Net margin	−2.62	7.74	8.87	11.92	10.32

Asset Utilization Ratios	12/31/09	12/31/08	12/31/07	12/31/06	12/31/05
Asset turnover	0.89	1.71	1.69	1.87	1.78
Inventory turnover	5.60	9.51	9.51	10.47	8.89
Capital expend PCT total assets	2.81	10.37	6.60	4.74	5.40
Capital expend PCT sales	3.49	4.31	3.14	2.29	2.61

Leverage Ratios	12/31/09	12/31/08	12/31/07	12/31/06	12/31/05
Total debt PCT common equity	42.78	42.09	44.46	19.11	21.58
LT debt PCT common equity	41.68	38.92	44.01	19.11	21.55
LT debt PCT total capital	28.88	27.21	29.41	15.41	17.09
Equity PCT total capital	69.30	69.90	66.83	80.61	79.31
Total debt PCT total assets	25.15	24.05	23.13	11.70	12.94
Common equity PCT total assets	58.79	57.15	52.03	61.20	59.95
Total capital PCT total assets	84.83	81.75	77.86	75.93	75.59
Dividend payout	#N/A	35.94	49.33	32.87	16.01
Cash dividend coverage ratio	1.26	3.91	2.94	4.04	8.48
Working cap PCT total capital	37.09	40.05	45.63	53.87	52.18

Liquidity Ratios	12/31/09	12/31/08	12/31/07	12/31/06	12/31/05
Quick ratio	2.74	1.93	2.02	2.26	2.27
Current ratio	4.22	3.45	3.21	3.22	3.24
Cash and EQT PCT current assets	43.27	36.81	31.07	46.98	45.13
Receivables PCT current assets	21.54	19.21	31.77	23.04	24.82
Accounts receivable days	38.24	21.91	29.58	25.83	28.36
Inventories days held	65.18	38.39	38.40	34.87	41.06

Currency: USD
Source: ThomsonFinancial

by training, invented a number of things in diverse fields. He also established the incentive programs for which Nucor later became known. With only one plant, he was still able to operate in a "decentralized" manner. Before his death in 1960, while still in his 40s, the company was studying the building of a steel mill using the newly developed mini-mill technology. His widow ran the company until it was sold to Nucor in 1962.

Dave Aycock met Ken Iverson when Nuclear purchased Vulcraft, and they worked together closely for the next year and a half. With his office located in Phoenix, at the corporate headquarters, he was responsible for all the joist operations and was given the task of planning and building a new joist plant in Texas. In late 1963, he was transferred to Norfolk, where he lived for the next 13 years and managed a number of Nucor's joist plants. Then in 1977 he was named the manager of the Darlington, South Carolina, steel plant. In 1984, Aycock became Nucor's president and chief operating officer, while Iverson became chairman and chief executive officer.

Exhibit 2   Global Steel Statistics—2010

Country	Jan	Feb	Mar	Apr	May	Jun	Jul	Aug	Sep	Oct	Nov	Dec	Total
Austria	524	503	592	632	659	636	581	0	0	0	0	0	0
Belgium	623	540	680	708	815	710	650	0	0	0	0	0	0
Bulgaria	65	58	64	65	64	58	65	0	0	0	0	0	0
Czech Republic	412	419	489	476	461	464	394	0	0	0	0	0	0
Finland	349	318	363	289	291	340	332	0	0	0	0	0	0
France	1,136	1,127	1,476	1,451	1,573	1,457	1,450	0	0	0	0	0	0
Germany	3,497	3,399	4,021	3,883	4,073	3,857	3,492	0	0	0	0	0	0
Greece	64	148	171	132	215	210	190	0	0	0	0	0	0
Hungary	125	121	139	149	165	149	150	0	0	0	0	0	0
Italy	1,876	2,164	2,377	2,352	2,471	2,264	2,200	0	0	0	0	0	0
Latvia	0	0	0	0	0	0	0	0	0	0	0	0	0
Luxembourg	228	209	252	221	274	175	180	0	0	0	0	0	0
The Netherlands	578	492	465	441	604	559	532	0	0	0	0	0	0
Poland	603	536	696	775	827	660	680	0	0	0	0	0	0
Portugal	0	0	0	0	0	0	0	0	0	0	0	0	0
Romania	250	225	250	310	350	360	370	0	0	0	0	0	0
Slovakia	340	366	442	430	460	394	276	0	0	0	0	0	0
Slovenia	47	47	51	48	55	52	55	0	0	0	0	0	0
Spain	1,358	1,343	1,581	1,541	1,646	1,433	1,100	0	0	0	0	0	0
Sweden	390	382	430	452	439	448	281	0	0	0	0	0	0
United Kingdom	984	763	813	899	894	793	782	0	0	0	0	0	0
Other E.U. (27)	170	154	195	166	173	162	165	0	0	0	0	0	0
Total–European Union (27)	13,619	13,314	15,548	15,419	16,509	15,180	13,926	0	0	0	0	0	0
Albania	0	0	0	0	0	0	0	0	0	0	0	0	0
Bosnia and Herzegovina	46	48	64	53	53	48	47	0	0	0	0	0	0
Croatia	6	5	4	5	5	3	3	0	0	0	0	0	0
Macedonia	10	11	30	30	30	20	35	0	0	0	0	0	0
Norway	60	37	43	45	50	52	20	0	0	0	0	0	0
Serbia	136	136	82	61	83	155	93	0	0	0	0	0	0
Switzerland	99	110	121	91	121	120	65	0	0	0	0	0	0
Turkey	2,059	1,821	2,194	2,402	2,526	2,495	2,376	0	0	0	0	0	0
Total–other Europe	2,416	2,168	2,538	2,686	2,868	2,893	2,639	0	0	0	0	0	0
Azerbaijan	0	0	0	0	0	0	0	0	0	0	0	0	0
Byelorussia	170	202	216	217	241	236	222	0	0	0	0	0	0
Kazakhstan	400	274	305	307	492	405	412	0	0	0	0	0	0
Moldova	15	38	47	50	56	0	0	0	0	0	0	0	0
Russia	5,190	4,952	5,588	5,640	5,885	5,430	5,595	0	0	0	0	0	0
Ukraine	2,726	2,343	2,995	2,974	2,850	2,470	2,406	0	0	0	0	0	0
Uzbekistan	52	58	62	60	62	60	65	0	0	0	0	0	0
Total–C.I.S. (6)	8,553	7,867	9,213	9,248	9,586	8,601	8,700	0	0	0	0	0	0
Canada	1,000	1,050	1,150	1,100	1,135	1,030	975	0	0	0	0	0	0
Cuba	24	25	25	25	25	25	25	0	0	0	0	0	0
Dominican Republic	0	0	0	0	0	0	0	0	0	0	0	0	0
El Salvador	6	5	7	7	7	5	5	0	0	0	0	0	0
Guatemala	22	20	25	25	25	22	22	0	0	0	0	0	0
Mexico	1,300	1,300	1,466	1,389	1,484	1,336	1,380	0	0	0	0	0	0
Trinidad and Tobago	51	46	55	55	54	57	60	0	0	0	0	0	0
United States	6,234	6,243	7,112	6,955	7,264	7,090	6,699	0	0	0	0	0	0
Total–North America	8,637	8,689	9,841	9,557	9,993	9,565	9,166	0	0	0	0	0	0

Exhibit 2   Global Steel Statistics—2010 (*continued*)

Country	Jan	Feb	Mar	Apr	May	Jun	Jul	Aug	Sep	Oct	Nov	Dec	Total
Argentina	337	381	443	428	438	421	437	0	0	0	0	0	0
Brazil	2,751	2,446	2,829	2,707	2,856	2,850	2,950	0	0	0	0	0	0
Chile	133	120	0	0	0	50	50	0	0	0	0	0	0
Colombia	61	55	85	85	90	95	100	0	0	0	0	0	0
Ecuador	16	15	20	20	20	30	30	0	0	0	0	0	0
Paraguay	5	5	7	7	7	6	6	0	0	0	0	0	0
Peru	72	65	75	75	80	70	75	0	0	0	0	0	0
Uruguay	6	5	7	7	7	6	6	0	0	0	0	0	0
Venezuela	316	285	200	195	200	105	110	0	0	0	0	0	0
Total–South America	3,697	3,376	3,665	3,524	3,698	3,633	3,764	0	0	0	0	0	0
Algeria	35	35	40	40	45	40	45	0	0	0	0	0	0
D.R. Congo (former Zaire)	0	0	0	0	0	0	0	0	0	0	0	0	0
Egypt	508	449	498	523	553	513	557	0	0	0	0	0	0
Ghana	0	0	0	0	0	0	0	0	0	0	0	0	0
Kenya	0	0	0	0	0	0	0	0	0	0	0	0	0
Libya	60	57	71	70	65	67	70	0	0	0	0	0	0
Mauritania	0	0	0	0	0	0	0	0	0	0	0	0	0
Morocco	41	39	59	52	58	14	8	0	0	0	0	0	0
Nigeria	0	0	0	0	0	0	0	0	0	0	0	0	0
South Africa	710	640	710	690	715	690	720	0	0	0	0	0	0
Tunisia	0	0	0	0	0	0	0	0	0	0	0	0	0
Uganda	0	0	0	0	0	0	0	0	0	0	0	0	0
Zimbabwe	0	0	0	0	0	0	0	0	0	0	0	0	0
Total–Africa	1,354	1,220	1,378	1,375	1,436	1,324	1,401	0	0	0	0	0	0
Iran	947	1,000	935	1,033	1,027	1,000	857	0	0	0	0	0	0
Israel	0	0	0	0	0	0	0	0	0	0	0	0	0
Jordan	0	0	0	0	0	0	0	0	0	0	0	0	0
Qatar	160	150	170	165	178	165	160	0	0	0	0	0	0
Saudi Arabia	471	440	419	468	444	410	400	0	0	0	0	0	0
Syria	0	0	0	0	0	0	0	0	0	0	0	0	0
United Arab Emirates	0	0	0	0	0	0	0	0	0	0	0	0	0
Total–Middle East	1,578	1,591	1,524	1,665	1,650	1,575	1,417	0	0	0	0	0	0
China	52,535	50,357	54,968	55,403	56,143	53,766	51,743	0	0	0	0	0	0
India	5,430	5,125	5,532	5,350	5,530	5,462	5,750	0	0	0	0	0	0
Indonesia	0	0	0	0	0	0	0	0	0	0	0	0	0
Japan	8,724	8,445	9,341	8,987	9,724	9,356	9,222	0	0	0	0	0	0
North Korea	0	0	0	0	0	0	0	0	0	0	0	0	0
South Korea	4,512	3,943	4,767	5,116	5,173	4,784	4,760	0	0	0	0	0	0
Malaysia	0	0	0	0	0	0	0	0	0	0	0	0	0
Mongolia	0	0	0	0	0	0	0	0	0	0	0	0	0
Myanmar	0	0	0	0	0	0	0	0	0	0	0	0	0
Pakistan	0	0	0	0	0	0	0	0	0	0	0	0	0
Philippines	0	0	0	0	0	0	0	0	0	0	0	0	0
Singapore	0	0	0	0	0	0	0	0	0	0	0	0	0
Sri Lanka	0	0	0	0	0	0	0	0	0	0	0	0	0
Taiwan, China	1,710	1,545	1,569	1,520	1,570	1,520	1,570	0	0	0	0	0	0
Thailand	0	0	0	0	0	0	0	0	0	0	0	0	0
Vietnam	0	0	0	0	0	0	0	0	0	0	0	0	0
Total—Asia	72,911	69,415	77,808	76,376	78,140	74,888	73,045	0	0	0	0	0	0
Australia	606	525	610	574	612	616	665	0	0	0	0	0	0
New Zealand	70	69	72	73	75	72	71	0	0	0	0	0	0
Total—Oceania	676	594	682	647	687	688	736	0	0	0	0	0	0
Total countries	66	66	66	66	66	66	66	0	0	0	0	0	0
Total	113,441	108,235	122,196	120,497	124,567	118,346	114,794	0	0	0	0	0	0

Aycock had this to say about Iverson: "Ken was a very good leader, with an entrepreneurial spirit. He is easy to work with and has the courage to do things, to take lots of risks. Many things didn't work, but some worked very well." There is the old saying "failure to take risk is failure." This saying epitomizes a cultural value personified by the company's founder and reinforced by Iverson during his time at the helm. Nucor was very innovative in steel and joists. Their plant was years ahead in wire rod welding at Norfolk. In the late 1960s, they had one of the first computer inventory management systems and design/engineering programs. They were very sophisticated in purchasing, sales, and managing, and they beat their competition often by the speed of their design efforts.

By 1984 the bankrupt conglomerate became a leading U.S. steel company. It was a fairytale story. Tom Peters used Nucor's management style as an example of "excellence," while the barons of old steel ruled over creeping ghettos. NBC featured Nucor on television and *New Yorker* magazine serialized a book about how a relatively small American steel company built a team, which led the whole world into a new era of steelmaking. As the NBC program asked: "If Japan can, why can't we?" Nucor had! Iverson was rich, owning $10 million in stock, but with a salary that rarely reached $1 million, compared to some U.S. executives' $50 or $100 million. The 40-year-old manager of the South Carolina Vulcraft plant had become a millionaire. Stockholders chuckled and non-unionized hourly workers, who had never seen a layoff in 20 years, earned more than the unionized workers of old steel and more than 85 percent of the people in the states where they worked. Many employees were financially quite secure.

Nucor owed much of its success to its benchmark organizational style and the empowered division managers. There were two basic lines of business, the first being the six steel joist plants that made the steel frames seen in many buildings. The second line included four steel mills that utilized the innovative mini-mill technology to supply the joist plants at first and later outside customers. In 1984, Nucor was still only the seventh largest steel company in America but they had established the organization design, management philosophy, and incentive system, which lead to their continued success.

Nucor's Formula for Success 1964–1999

In the early 1990s, Nucor's 22 divisions, one for every plant, had a general manager, who was also a vice president of the corporation. The divisions were of three basic types: joist plants, steel mills, and miscellaneous plants. The corporate staff consisted of less than 25 people. In the beginning, Iverson had chosen Charlotte "as the new home base for what he had envisioned as a small cadre of executives who would guide a decentralized operation with liberal authority delegated to managers in the field," according to *South* magazine. The divisions did their own manufacturing, selling, accounting, engineering, and personnel management, and there were only four levels from top to bottom (see Exhibit 3 for structure in 1991).

Iverson gave his views on keeping a lean organization:

> Each division is a profit center and the division manager has control over the day-to-day decisions that make that particular division profitable or not profitable. We expect the division to provide contribution, which is earnings before corporate expenses. And we expect a division to earn 25 percent return on total assets employed, before corporate expenses, taxes, interest or profit sharing. And we have a saying in the company-if a manager doesn't provide that for a number of years, we are either going to get rid of the division or get rid of the general manager, and it's generally the division manager.

Nucor strengthened its position by developing strong alliances with outside parties. It did no internal research and development. Instead, they monitored others' work worldwide and attracted investors who brought them new technical applications at the earliest possible dates. Though Nucor was known for constructing new facilities at the lowest possible costs, their engineering and construction team consists of only three individuals. They did not attempt to specify exact equipment parameters, but asked the equipment supplier to provide this information and then held the manufacturer accountable. They had alliances with selected construction companies around the country who knew the kind of work Nucor wanted. Nucor bought 95 percent of its scrap steel from an independent broker who followed the market and made recommendations regarding scrap purchases. They did not have a corporate advertising department, corporate public relations department, or a corporate legal or environmental department. They had long-term relationships with outsiders to provide these services.

The steel industry had established a pattern of absorbing the cost of shipments, so regardless of the distance from the mill, all users paid the same delivered price. Nucor broke with this tradition and stopped equalizing freight. It offered all customers the same sales terms, price plus actual shipping costs. Nucor also gave no volume discounts, feeling that with modern computer systems there was no justification. Customers located next to the plant

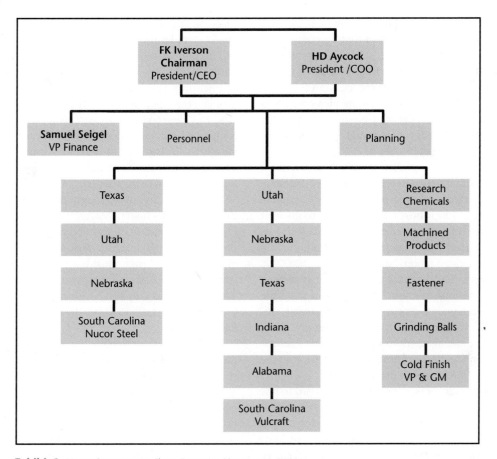

Exhibit 3   Nucor Organization Chart, Executive Management 1991

guaranteed themselves the lowest possible costs for steel purchases. Two tube manufacturers, two steel service centers, and a cold rolling facility were located adjacent to the Arkansas plant. These facilities accounted for 60 percent of the shipments from the mill. The plants were linked electronically to each other's production schedules, allowing them to function in a just-in-time inventory mode. All new mills were built on large enough tracts of land to accommodate collaborating businesses.

Iverson did not feel that greater centralization would be good for Nucor. Hamilton Lott, a Vulcraft plant manager, commented in 1997, "We're truly autonomous; we can duplicate efforts made in other parts of Nucor. We might develop the same computer program six times. But the advantages of local autonomy make it worth it." Joe Rutkowski, manager at Darlington Steel, agreed. "We're not constrained; headquarters doesn't restrict what I spend. I just have to make my profit contribution at the end of year."

South magazine observed that Iverson had established a characteristic organizational style described as "stripped down" and "no nonsense." "Jack Benny would like this company," observed Roland Underhill, an analyst with Crowell, Weedon and Company of Los Angeles, "so would Peter Drucker." Underhill pointed out that Nucor's thriftiness does not end with its "Spartan" office staff or modest offices. "There are no corporate perquisites," he recited. "No company planes. No country club memberships. No company cars."

Fortune noted: "Iverson takes the subway when he is in New York, a Wall Street analyst reports in a voice that suggests both admiration and amazement." The general managers reflected this style in the operation of their individual divisions. Their offices were more like plant offices or the offices of private companies built around manufacturing rather than for public appeal. They were simple, routine, and businesslike.

Division Managers

The corporate personnel manager described management relations as informal, trusting, and not "bureaucratic." He felt there was a minimum of paperwork, that a phone call was more common than memos and that no confirming memo was thought to be necessary.

A Vulcraft manager commented: "We have what I would call a very friendly spirit of competition from one plant to the next. And of course all of the vice presidents and general managers share the same bonus systems so we are in this together as a team even though we operate our divisions individually."

The divisions managed their activities with a minimum of contact with the corporate staff. Each day disbursements were reported to the corporate office. Payments flowed into regional lock-boxes. On a weekly basis, joist divisions reported total quotes, sales cancellations, backlog, and production. Steel mills reported tons rolled, outside shipments, orders, cancellations, and backlog.

Each month the divisions completed a two-page (11" × 70") "Operations Analysis" that was sent to all the managers. Its three main purposes were (1) financial consolidation, (2) sharing information among the divisions, and (3) corporate management examination. The summarized information and the performance statistics for all the divisions were then returned to the managers.

The general managers met three times a year. In late October, they presented preliminary budgets and capital requests. In late February, they met to finalize budgets and treat miscellaneous matters. Then, at a meeting in May, they handled personnel matters, such as wage increases and changes of policies or benefits. The general managers as a group considered the raises for the department heads, the next lower level of management for all the plants.

Vulcraft—The Joist Divisions

One of Nucor's major businesses was the manufacture and sale of open web steel joists and joist girders at Vulcraft divisions located in Florence, South Carolina; Norfolk, Nebraska; Ft. Payne, Alabama; Grapeland, Texas; St. Joe, Indiana; Brigham City, Utah; and Chemung, New York. Open web joists, in contrast to solid joists, were made of steel angle iron separated by round bars or smaller angle iron. These joists cost less, were of greater strength for many applications, and were used primarily as the roof support systems in larger buildings, such as warehouses and shopping malls.

The joist industry was characterized by high competition among many manufacturers for many small customers. With an estimated 40 percent of the market, Nucor was the largest supplier in the United States. It utilized national advertising campaigns and prepared competitive bids on 80–90 percent of the buildings using joists. Competition was based on price and delivery performance. Nucor had developed computer programs to prepare designs for customers and to compute bids based on current prices and labor standards. In addition, each Vulcraft plant maintained its own engineering department to help customers with design problems or specifications. The Florence manager commented, "Here on the East Coast we have six or seven major competitors; of course none of them are as large as we are." He added, "It has been said to us by some of our competitors that in this particular industry we have the finest selling organization in the country."

Nucor aggressively sought to be the lowest-cost producer in the industry. Materials and freight were two important elements of cost. Nucor maintained its own fleet of almost 150 trucks to ensure on-time delivery to all of the states, although most business was regional due to transportation costs. Plants were located in rural areas near the markets they served. Nucor's move into steel production was a move to lower the cost of steel used by the joist business.

On the basic assembly line used at the joist divisions, three or four of which might make up any one plant, about six tons of joists per hour would be assembled. In the first stage, eight people cut the angles to the right lengths or bent the round bars to the desired form. These were moved on a roller conveyer to six-man assembly stations, where the component parts would be tacked together for the next stage, welding. Drilling and miscellaneous work were done by three people between the lines. The nine-man welding station completed the welds before passing the joists on roller conveyers to two-man inspection teams. The last step before shipment was the painting.

The workers had control over and responsibility for quality. There was an independent quality control inspector who had the authority to reject the run of joists and cause them to be reworked. The quality control people were not under the incentive system and reported to the engineering department.

Daily production might vary widely, since each joist was made for a specific job. The wide range of joists made control of the workload at each station difficult; bottlenecks might arise anywhere along the line. Each workstation was responsible for identifying such bottlenecks so that the foreman could reassign people promptly to maintain productivity. Since workers knew most of the jobs on the line, including the more skilled welding job, they could be shifted as needed. Work on the line was described by one general manager as "not machine type but mostly physical labor." He said the important thing was to avoid bottlenecks.

There were four lines of about 28 people each on two shifts at the Florence division. The jobs on the line were rated on responsibility and assigned a base wage, from $11 to $13 per hour. In addition, a weekly bonus was paid on the total output of each line. Each worker received the same percent bonus on his base wage. The Texas plant was typical with the bonus running 225 percent, giving a wage of $27.00 an hour in 1999.

The amount of time required to make a joist had been established as a result of experience. As a job was bid, the cost of each joist was determined through the computer program. The time required depended on the length, number of panels, and depth of the joist. At the time of production, the labor value of production, the standard, was determined in a similar manner. The South Carolina general manager stated, "In the last nine or ten years we have not changed a standard." The Grapeland plant maintained a time chart, which was used to estimate the labor required on a job. The plant teams were measured against this time for bonus. The chart was based on the historical time required on the jobs. The production manager at Grapeland considered himself an example for the Nucor policy—"the sky is the limit." He had started in an entry position and risen to the head of this plant of 200 people.

Steel Divisions

Nucor moved into the steel business in 1968 to provide raw material for the Vulcraft plants. Iverson said, "We got into the steel business because we wanted to build a mill that could make steel as cheaply as we were buying it from foreign importers or from offshore mills." Thus, they entered the industry using the new mini-mill technology after they took a task force of four people around the world to investigate new technological advancements. A case writer from Harvard recounted the development of the steel divisions:

> By 1967 about 60% of each Vulcraft sales dollar was spent on materials, primarily steel. Thus, the goal of keeping costs low made it imperative to obtain steel economically. In addition, in 1967 Vulcraft bought about 60% of its steel from foreign sources. As the Vulcraft Division grew, Nucor became concerned about its ability to obtain an adequate economical supply of steel and in 1968 began construction of its first steel mill in Darlington, South Carolina. By 1972 the Florence, South Carolina, joist plant was purchasing over 90% of its steel from this mill. The Fort Payne, Alabama plant bought about 50% of its steel from Florence. Since the mill had excess capacity, Nucor began to market its steel products to outside customers. In 1972, 75% of the shipments of Nucor steel were to Vulcraft and 25% were to other customers.

Between 1973 and 1981, they constructed three more bar mills and their accompanying rolling mills to convert the billets into bars, flats, rounds, channels, and other products. Iverson explained in 1984:

> In constructing these mills we have experimented with new processes and new manufacturing techniques. We serve as our own general contractor and design and build much of our own equipment. In one or more of our mills we have built our own continuous casting unit, reheat furnaces, cooling beds and in Utah even our own mill stands. All of these to date have cost under $125 per ton of annual capacity—compared with projected costs for large integrated mills of $1,200–1,500 per ton of annual capacity, ten times our cost. Our mills have high productivity. We currently use less than four man hours to produce a ton of steel. Our total employment costs are less than $60 per ton compared with the average employment costs of the seven largest U.S. steel companies of close to $130 per ton. Our total labor costs are less than 20% of our sales price.

In 1987, Nucor was the first steel company in the world to begin to build a mini-mill to manufacture steel sheet, the raw material for the auto industry and other major manufacturers. This project opened up another 50 percent of the total steel market. The first plant in Crawfordsville, Indiana, was successful, and three additional sheet mills were constructed between 1989 and 1990. Through the years, these steel plants were significantly modernized and expanded until the total capacity was 3 million tons per year at a capital cost of less than $170 per ton by 1999. Nucor's total steel production capacity was 5.9 million tons per year at a cost of $300 per ton of annual capacity. The eight mills sold 80 percent of their output to outside customers and the balance to other Nucor divisions.

The Steel-Making Process

A steel mill's work is divided into two phases: preparation of steel of the proper "chemistry" and the forming of the steel into the desired products. The typical mini-mill utilized scrap steel, such as junk auto parts, instead of the iron ore, which would be used in larger, integrated steel mills. The typical bar mini-mill had an annual capacity of 200,000–600,000 tons, compared with the seven million tons of Bethlehem Steel's integrated plant at Sparrow's Point, Maryland.

In the bar mills, a charging bucket fed loads of scrap steel into electric arc furnaces. The melted load, called a heat, was poured into a ladle to be carried by an overhead crane to the casting machine. In the casting machine, the liquid steel was extruded as a continuous red-hot solid bar of steel and cut into lengths weighing some 900 pounds called "billets." In the typical plant, the billet, about four inches in cross section and about 20 feet long, was held temporarily in a pit where it was cooled to normal temperatures. Periodically billets were carried to the rolling mill and placed in a reheat oven to bring them up to 2,000° F, at which temperature they would be malleable. In the rolling mill, presses and dies progressively converted the billet into the desired round bars, angles, channels, flats, and other products. After cutting to standard lengths, they were moved to the warehouse.

Nucor's first steel mill, which employed more than 500 people, was located in Darlington, South Carolina. The mill, with its three electric arc furnaces, operated 24 hours per day, 5½ days per week. Nucor had made a number of improvements in the melting and casting operations. Thus, less time and lower capital investment were required at Darlington than other mini-mills at the time of its construction. The casting machines were "continuous casters," as opposed to the old batch method. All research projects had not been successful. The company spent approximately $2,000,000 in an unsuccessful effort to utilize resistance heating. They lost even more on an effort at induction melting. As Iverson told *Metal Producing*, "That costs us a lot of money. Time wise it was very expensive. But you have got to make mistakes and we've had lots of failures." The Darlington design became the basis for plants in Nebraska, Texas, and Utah. The Texas plant had cost under $80 per ton of annual capacity. Whereas the typical mini-mill at the time cost approximately $250 per ton, the average cost of Nucor's four mills was under $135. An integrated mill was expected to cost between $1,200 and $1,500 per ton.

The Darlington plant was organized into 12 natural groups for the purpose of incentive pay. Two mills each had two shifts with three groups—melting and casting, rolling mill, and finishing. In melting and casting, there were three or four different standards, depending on the material, established by the department manager years ago based on historical performance. The general manager stated, "We don't change the standards." The caster, key to the operation, was used at a 92 percent level—one greater than the claims of the manufacturer. For every good ton of billet above the standard hourly rate for the week, workers in the group received a 4 percent bonus. Workers received a 4 percent to 6 percent bonus for every good ton sheared per hour for the week over the computed standard. A manager stated: "Meltshop employees don't ask me how much it costs Chaparral or LTV to make a billet. They want to know what it costs Darlington, Norfolk, Jewitt to put a billet on

the ground—scrap costs, alloy costs, electrical costs, refractory, gas, etc. Everybody from Charlotte to Plymouth watches the nickels and dimes."

Management Philosophy

Aycock, while still the Darlington manager, stated:

The key to making a profit when selling a product with no aesthetic value, or a product that you really can't differentiate from your competitors, is cost. I don't look at us as a fantastic marketing organization, even though I think we are pretty good; but we don't try to overcome unreasonable costs by mass marketing. We maintain low costs by keeping the employee force at the level it should be, not doing things that aren't necessary to achieve our goals, and allowing people to function on their own and by judging them on their results.

To keep a cooperative and productive workforce you need, number one, to be completely honest about everything; number two, to allow each employee as much as possible to make decisions about that employee's work, to find easier and more productive ways to perform duties; and number three, to be as fair as possible to all employees. Most of the changes we make in work procedures and in equipment come from the employees. They really know the problems of their jobs better than anyone else.

To communicate with my employees, I try to spend time in the plant and at intervals have meetings with the employees. Usually if they have a question they just visit me. Recently a small group visited me in my office to discuss our vacation policy. They had some suggestions and, after listening to them, I had to agree that the ideas were good.

In discussing his philosophy for dealing with the workforce, the Florence manager stated:

I believe very strongly in the incentive system we have. We are a non-union shop and we all feel that the way to stay so is to take care of our people and show them we care. I think that's easily done because of our fewer layers of management... I spend a good part of my time in the plant, maybe an hour or so a day. If a man wants to know anything, for example an insurance question, I'm there and they walk right up to me and ask me questions, which I'll answer the best I know how.

We don't lay our people off and we make a point of telling our people this. In the slowdown of 1994, we scheduled our line for four days, but the men were allowed to come in the fifth day for maintenance work at base pay. The men in the plant on an average running *bonus might make $17 to $19 an hour. If their base pay is half that, on Friday they would only get $8–$9 an hour. Surprisingly, many of the men did not want to come in on Friday. They felt comfortable with just working four days a week. They are happy to have that extra day off. About 20% of the people took the 5th day at base rate, but still no one had been laid off, in an industry with a strong business cycle.*

In an earlier business cycle, the executive committee decided in view of economic conditions that a pay freeze was necessary. The employees normally received an increase in their base pay on the first of June. The decision was made at that time to freeze wages. The officers of the company, as a show of good faith, accepted a 5 percent pay cut. In addition to announcing this to the workers with a stuffer in their pay envelopes, meetings were held. Each production line, or incentive group of workers, met in the plant conference room with all supervision—foreman, plant production manager, and division manager. The economic crisis the company was facing was explained to the employees by the production manager and all of their questions were answered.

The Personnel Policies

The foremost characteristic of Nucor's personnel system was its incentive plan. Another major personnel policy was providing job security. Also all employees at Nucor received the same fringe benefits. There was only one group insurance plan. Holidays and vacations did not differ by job. Every child of every Nucor employee received up to $1,200 a year for four years if they chose to go on to higher education, including technical schools. The company had no executive dining rooms or restrooms, no fishing lodges, company cars, or reserved parking places.

Jim Coblin, Nucor's vice president of Human Resources at the time, described Nucor's systems for *HR Magazine* in a 1994 article, "No-frills HR at Nucor: a lean, bottom-line approach at this steel company empowers employees." Coblin, as benefits administrator, received part-time help from one of the corporate secretaries in the corporate office. The plants typically used someone from their finance department to handle compensation issues, although two plants had personnel generalists. Nucor plants did not have job descriptions finding they caused more problems than they solved, given the flexible workforce and non-union status of Nucor employees. Surprisingly, Coblin found performance appraisal a waste of time. If an employee was not performing well, the problem would be dealt with directly. The key, he believed, was not to put a maximum on what an employee could earn and pay them directly for productivity. Iverson firmly believed that the bonus should be direct and involve no discretion on part of a manager.

Employees were kept informed about the company. Charts showing the division's results in return-on-assets and bonus payoff were posted in prominent places in the plant. The personnel manager commented that as he traveled around to all the plants, he found that everyone in the company could tell him the level of profits in their division. The general managers held dinners at least once but usually twice a year with each of their employees. The dinners were held with 50 or 60 employees at a time, resulting in as many as 20 dinners per year. After introductory remarks, the floor was open for discussion of any work-related problems. There was a new employee orientation program and an employee handbook that contained personnel policies and rules. The corporate office sent all news releases to each division where they were posted on bulletin boards. Each employee in the company also received a copy of the annual report. For the last several years, the cover of the annual report had contained the names of all Nucor employees.

Absenteeism and tardiness were not a problem at Nucor. Each employee had four days of absences before pay was reduced. In addition to these, missing work was allowed for jury duty, military leave, or the death of close relatives. After this, a day's absence cost them bonus pay for that week and lateness of more than a half hour meant the loss of bonus for that day.

Safety was a concern of Nucor's critics. With 10 fatalities in the 1980s, Nucor was committed to doing better. Safety administrators had been appointed in each plant and safety had improved in the 1990s. The company also had a formal grievance procedure, although the Darlington manager could not recall the last grievance he had processed.

The average hourly worker's pay was over twice the average earnings paid by other manufacturing companies in the states where Nucor's plants were located. In many rural communities where Nucor had located, they provided better wages than most other manufacturers. The new plant in Hertford County illustrated this point as reported in a June 21, 1998, article in *The Charlotte Observer*, titled "Hope on the horizon: in Hertford County, poverty reigns and jobs are scarce." Here the author wrote, "In North Carolina's forgotten northeastern corner, where poverty rates run more than twice the state average, Nucor's $300 million steel mill is a dream realized." The plant on the banks of the Chowan River in North Carolina's coastal district would have their employees earning a rumored $60,000 a year, three times the local average manufacturing wage upon completion. Nucor had recently begun developing its plant sites with the expectation of other companies co-locating to save shipping costs. Four companies announced plans to locate close to Nucor's property, adding another 100–200 jobs. People could not believe such wages, but calls to the plant's chief financial officer got "we don't like to promise too much, but $60,000 might be a little low." The average wage for these jobs at Darlington was $70,000. The plant's CFO added that Nucor did not try to set pay "a buck over Wal-Mart" but went for the best workers. The article noted that steel work is hot and often dangerous and that turnover at the plant may be high as people adjust to this and Nucor's hard-driving team system. He added, "Slackers don't last." The State of North Carolina had given $155 million in tax credits over 25 years. The local preacher said "In 15 years, Baron (a local child) will be making $75,000 a year at Nucor, not in jail. I have a place now I can hold in front of him and say 'Look, right here. This is for you.'"

In the early 2009 crisis, Nucor's unique policies with its employees were evident. Performance in 2008 had been good and $40 million in bonuses were still distributed, with an extra bonus on top because of the extraordinary year. The company paid $270 million in March in the 2008 profit sharing. Gail Bruce, the new vice president of human resources, explained how Nucor had avoided the layoffs other plants experienced. First there was a history of open communications and a system designed to deal with the nature of the industry. Over the years there had been financial training for the workers explaining the cyclical nature of the industry. And if plants were idled, pay went automatically to a base pay, which was about half the usual total income with bonuses. No one was laid off and the well-paid workers could adapt, just like the company. He marveled, "The spirit in the operations is extraordinary." The cooperation extended to other solutions. *Business Week* reported: "Work that used to be done by contractors, such as making special parts, mowing the lawns, and even cleaning the bathrooms, is now handled by Nucor staff. The bathrooms, managers say, was an employee suggestion." *Business Week* reported that DiMicco and other managers received hundreds of cards and e-mails thanking them for caring about workers and their families.

The Incentive System

There were four incentive programs at Nucor, one each for (1) production workers, (2) department heads, (3) staff people, such as accountants, secretaries, or engineers, and (4) senior management, which included the division managers (vice presidents/general managers of each division). All of these programs were based on group performance.

Within the production program, groups ranged in size from 25 to 30 people and had definable and measurable operations. The company believed that a program should be simple and that bonuses should be paid promptly. "We don't have any discretionary bonuses—zero. It is all based on performance. Now we don't want anyone to sit in judgment, because it never is fair...," said Iverson. The personnel manager stated: "Their bonus is based on roughly 90% of historical time it takes to make a particular joist. If during a week they make joists at 60% less than the standard time, they receive a 60% bonus." The bonus was paid with the regular pay the following week. The complete paycheck amount, including overtime, was multiplied by the bonus factor. A bonus was not paid when equipment was not operating: "We have the philosophy that when equipment is not operating everybody suffers and the bonus for downtime is zero." The foremen are also part of the group and received the same bonus as the employees they supervised.

The second incentive program was for department heads in the various divisions. The incentive pay here was based on division contribution, defined as the division earnings before corporate expenses and profit sharing are determined. Bonuses were reported to run between 0 and 90 percent (averaging over 50 percent) of a person's base salary. The base salaries at this level were set at 75 percent of industry norms.

There was a third plan for people who were not production workers, department managers, or senior managers. Their bonuses were based on either the division return-on-assets or the corporate return-on-assets, depending on their unit. Bonuses were typically 30 percent or more of a person's base salary for corporate positions.

The fourth program was for the senior officers. This group had no employment contracts, pension or retirement plans, or other perquisites. Their base salaries were set at about 75 percent of what an individual doing similar work in other companies would receive. Once return-on-equity reached 9 percent (slightly below the average for manufacturing firms), 5 percent of net earnings before taxes went into a pool, which was divided among the officers based on their salaries. "Now if return-on-equity for the company reaches, say 20 percent, which it has, then we can wind up with as much as 190 percent of our base salaries and 115 percent on top of that in stock. We get both," the personnel director said half the bonus was paid in cash and half was deferred. Individual bonuses ranged from zero to several hundred percent, averaging 75–150 percent.

However, the opposite was true as well. In 1982, the return was 8 percent and the executives received no bonus. Iverson's pay in 1981 was approximately $300,000 but dropped the next year to $110,000. "I think that ranked by total compensation I was the lowest paid CEO in the Fortune 500. I was kind of proud of that, too." In his 1997 book, *Plain Talk: Lessons From a Business Maverick*, Iverson said, "Can management expect employees to be loyal if we lay them all off at every dip of the economy, while we go on padding our own pockets?" Even so by 1986, Iverson's stock was worth over $10 million and the former Vulcraft manager was a millionaire.

In lieu of a retirement plan, the company had a profit-sharing plan with a deferred trust. Each year 10 percent of pre-tax earnings was put into profit sharing for all people below the officer level. Twenty percent of this was set aside to be paid to employees in the following March as a cash bonus and the remainder was put into trust for each employee on the basis of percent of their earnings as a percent of total wages paid within the corporation. The employee was vested after the first year. Employees received a quarterly statement of their balance in profit sharing.

The company had an employer monthly stock investment plan to which Nucor added 10 percent to the amount the employee contributed on the purchase of any Nucor stock and paid the commission. After each five years of service with the company, the employee received a service award consisting of five shares of Nucor stock. Moreover, if profits were good, extraordinary bonus payments would be made to the employees. For example, in December 1998, each employee received an $800 payment. According to Iverson:

> I think the first obligation of the company is to the stockholder and to its employees. I find in this country too many cases where employees are underpaid and corporate management is making huge social donations for self-fulfillment. We regularly give donations, but we have a very interesting corporate policy. First, we give donations where our employees are. Second, we give donations that will benefit our employees, such as to the YMCA. It is a difficult area and it requires a lot of thought. There is certainly a strong social responsibility for a company, but it cannot be at the expense of the employees or the stockholders.

Having welcomed a parade of visitors over the years, Iverson had become concerned with the pattern apparent at other companies' steel plants: "They only do one or two of the things we do. It's not just incentives or the scholarship program; it's all those things put together that results in a unified philosophy for the company."

Building on Their Success

Throughout the 1980s and 1990s Nucor continued to take the initiative and be the prime mover in steel as well as the

industries vertically related to steel. For example, in 1984 Nucor broke with the industry pattern of basing the price of an order of steel on the quantity ordered. Iverson noted, "Some time ago we began to realize that with computer order entry and billing, the extra charge for smaller orders was not cost justified." In a seemingly risky move in 1986, Nucor began construction of a $25 million plant in Indiana to manufacture steel fasteners. Imports had grown to 90 percent of this market as U.S. companies failed to compete. Iverson said, "We're going to bring that business back; we can make bolts as cheaply as foreign producers." A second plant, in 1995, gave Nucor 20 percent of the U.S. market for steel fasteners. Nucor also acquired a steel bearings manufacturer in 1986, which Iverson called "a good fit with our business, our policies and our people."

In early 1986, Iverson announced plans for a revolutionary plant at Crawfordsville, Indiana, that would be the first mini-mill in the world to manufacture flat-rolled or sheet steel, the last bastion of the integrated manufacturers. This market alone was twice the size of the existing market for mini-mill products. It would be a quarter of a billion dollar gamble on a new technology. The plant was expected to halve the integrated manufacturer's $3 of labor per ton and save $50–$75 on a $400 a ton selling price. If it worked, the profit from this plant alone would come close to the profit of the whole corporation. *Forbes* commented, "If any mini-mill can meet the challenge, it's Nucor. But expect the going to be tougher this time around." If successful, Nucor had the licensing rights to the next two plants built in the world with this technology. Nucor had spent millions trying to develop the process when it heard of some promising developments at a German company. In the spring of 1986, Aycock flew to Germany to see the pilot machine at SMS Schloemann-Siemag AG. In December, the Germans came to Charlotte for the first of what they thought would be many meetings to hammer out a deal with Nucor. Iverson shocked them when he announced Nucor was ready to proceed to build the first plant of its kind.

Keith Busse was given the job of building the steel sheet plant at Crawfordsville, Indiana. The process of bringing this plant online was so exciting it became the basis for a best-selling book by Robert Preston, which was serialized in *New Yorker* magazine. Preston reported on a conversation at dinner during construction between Iverson and Busse. Thinking about the future, Busse is worried that Nucor might someday become like Big Steel. He asked, "How do we allow Nucor to grow without expanding the bureaucracy?" He commented on the vice presidents stacked on vice presidents, research departments, assistants to assistants and so on. Iverson agreed. Busse seriously suggested, "Maybe we're going to need group vice presidents." Iverson's heated response was, "Do you want to ruin the company?—that's the old Harvard Business School thinking. They would only get in the way, slow us down." He said the company could at least double, to $2 billion, before it added a new level of management. "I hope that by the time we have group vice presidents I'll be collecting social security."

The gamble on the new plant paid off and Busse, the general manager of the plant, became a key man within Nucor. The new mill began operations in August of 1989 and reached 15 percent of capacity by the end of the year. In June of 1990 it had its first profitable month, and Nucor announced the construction of a second plant in Arkansas.

The supply and cost of scrap steel to feed the mini-mills was an important future concern to Iverson. So at the first of 1993 Nucor announced the construction of the plant in Trinidad to supply its mills with iron carbide pellets. The innovative plant would cost $60 million and take a year and a half to complete. In 1994 the two existing sheet mills were expanded and a new $500 million, 1.8 million ton sheet mill in South Carolina was announced to begin operation in early 1997.

In 1987 in what the *New York Times* called its "most ambitious project yet," Nucor began a joint venture with Yamato Kogyo, Ltd., to make structural steel products in a mill on the Mississippi River in direct challenge to the Big Three integrated steel companies. He put John Correnti in charge of the operation. Correnti built and then became the general manager of Nucor-Yamato when it started up in 1988. In 1991 he surprised many people by deciding to double Nucor-Yamato's capacity by 1994. It became Nucor's largest division and the largest wide flange producer in the United States. By 1995, Bethlehem Steel was the only other wide flange producer of structural steel products left and had plans to leave the business.

Nucor started up its first facility to produce metal buildings in 1987. A second metal buildings facility began operations in late 1996 in South Carolina and a new steel deck facility, in Alabama, was announced for 1997. At the end of 1997 the Arkansas sheet mill was undergoing a $120 million expansion to include a galvanizing facility.

In 1995 Nucor became involved in its first international venture, an ambitious project with Brazil's Companhia Siderurgica National to build a $700 million steel mill in the state of Ceara. While other mini-mills were cutting deals to buy and sell abroad, Nucor was planning to ship iron from Brazil and process it in Trinidad.

Nucor set records for sales and net earnings in 1997. In the spring of 1998, as Iverson approached his 73rd birthday, he was commenting, "people ask me when I'm going to retire. I tell them our mandatory retirement age is 95, but

I may change that when I get there." It surprised the world when, in October 1998, Ken Iverson left the board. He retired as chairman at the end of the year. Although sales for 1998 decreased 1 percent and net earnings were down 10 percent, the management made a number of long-term investments and closed draining investments. Start-up began at the new South Carolina steam mill and at the Arkansas sheet mill expansion. The plans for a North Carolina steel plate mill in Hertford were announced. This would bring Nucor's total steel production capacity to 12 million tons per year. Moreover, the plant in Trinidad, which had proven much more expensive than was originally expected, was deemed unsuccessful and closed. Finally, directors approved the re-purchase of up to 5 million shares of Nucor stock.

Still, the downward trends at Nucor continued. Sales and earnings were down 3 percent and 7 percent, respectively, for 1999. However, these trends did not seem to affect the company's investments. Expansion was underway in the steel mills and a third building systems facility was under construction in Texas. Nucor was actively searching for a site for a joist plant in the Northeast. A letter of intent was signed with Australian and Japanese companies to form a joint venture to commercialize the strip casting technology. To understand the challenges facing Nucor, industry, technology, and environmental trends in the 1980s and 1990s had to be considered.

Evolution of the U.S. Steel Industry

The early 1980s had been the worst years in decades for the steel industry. Data from the American Iron and Steel Institute (AISI) showed shipments falling from 100 million tons in 1979 to the mid-80 levels in 1980 and 1981. A slackening in the economy, particularly in auto sales, led the decline. In 1986, when industry capacity was at 130 million tons, the outlook was for a continued decline in per capita consumption and movement toward capacity in the 90–100 million-ton range. The chairman of Armco saw "millions of tons chasing a market that's not there: excess capacity that must be eliminated."

The large, integrated steel firms, such as U.S. Steel and Armco, which made up the major part of the industry, were the hardest hit. The *Wall Street Journal* stated, "The decline has resulted from such problems as high labor and energy costs in mining and processing iron ore, a lack of profits and capital to modernize plants, and conservative management that has hesitated to take risks." These companies produced a wide range of steels, primarily from ore processed in blast furnaces. They had found it difficult to compete with imports, usually from Japan, and had given market share to imports. They sought the protection of import quotas.

Imported steel accounted for 20 percent of the U.S. steel consumption, up from 12 percent in the early 1970s. The U.S. share of world production of raw steel declined from 19 to 14 percent over the period. *Iron Age* stated that exports, as a percentage of shipments in 1985, were 34 percent for Nippon, 26 percent for British Steel, 30 percent for Krupp, 49 percent for USINOR of France, and less than 1 percent for every American producer on the list. The consensus of steel experts was that imports would average 23 percent of the market in the last half of the 1980s.

By the mid-1980s, the integrated mills were moving fast to get back into the game: they were restructuring, cutting capacity, dropping unprofitable lines, focusing products, and trying to become responsive to the market. The industry made a pronounced move toward segmentation. Integrated producers focused on mostly flat-rolled and structural grades, reorganized steel companies focused on a limited range of products, mini-mills dominated the bar and light structural product areas, and specialty steel firms sought niches. There was an accelerated shutdown of older plants, elimination of products by some firms, and the installation of new product lines with new technologies by others.

The road for the integrated mills was not easy. As *Purchasing* pointed out, tax laws and accounting rules slowed down the closing of inefficient plants. Shutting down a 10,000-person plant could require a firm to hold a cash reserve of $100 million to fund health, pension, and insurance liabilities. The chairman of Armco commented: "Liabilities associated with a planned shutdown are so large that they can quickly devastate a company's balance sheet."

Joint ventures had arisen to produce steel for a specific market or region. The chairman of USX called them "an important new wrinkle in steel's fight for survival" and stated, "If there had been more joint ventures like these two decades ago, the U.S. steel industry might have built only half of the dozen or so hot-strip mills it put up in that time and avoided today's overcapacity."

The AISI reported steel production in 1988 of 99.3 million tons, up from 89.2 in 1987, and the highest in seven years. As a result of modernization programs, 60.9 percent of production was from continuous casters. Exports for steel increased and imports fell. Some steel experts believed the United States was now cost competitive with Japan. However, 1989 proved to be a year of "waiting for the other shoe to drop," according to *Metal Center News*. U.S. steel production was hampered by a new recession, the expiration of the voluntary import restraints, and labor

negotiations in several companies. Declines in car production and consumer goods hit flat-rolled hard. AUJ Consultants told MCN, "The U.S. steel market has peaked. Steel consumption is tending down. By 1990, we expect total domestic demand to dip under 90 million tons."

The economic slowdown of the early 1990s did lead to a decline in the demand for steel through early 1993, but by 1995 America was in its best steel market in 20 years and many companies were building new flat-roll mini-mills. A *Business Week* article at the time described it as "the race of the Nucor look-alikes." Six years after Nucor pioneered the low-cost German technology in Crawfordsville, Indiana, the competition was finally gearing up to compete. Ten new projects were expected to add 20 million tons per year of the flat-rolled steel, raising U.S. capacity by as much as 40 percent by 1998. These mills opened in 1997 just as the industry was expected to move into a cyclical slump. It was no surprise that worldwide competition increased and companies that had previously focused on their home markets began a race to become global powerhouses. The foreign push was new for U.S. firms that had focused on defending their home markets. U.S. mini-mills focused their international expansion primarily in Asia and South America.

Meanwhile in 1994, U.S. Steel, North America's largest integrated steel producer, began a major business process re-engineering project to improve order fulfillment performance and customer satisfaction on the heels of a decade of restructuring. According to *Steel Times International*, "U.S. Steel had to completely change the way it did business. Cutting labor costs and increasing reliability and productivity took the company a long way toward improving profitability and competitiveness. However, it became clear that this leaner organization still had to implement new technologies and business processes if it was to maintain a competitive advantage." The goals of the business process re-engineering project included a sharp reduction in cycle time, greatly decreased levels of inventory, shorter order lead times, and the ability to offer real-time promise dates to customers. In 1995, they successfully installed integrated planning/production/order fulfillment software, and the results were very positive. U.S. Steel believed that the re-engineering project had positioned it for a future of increased competition, tighter markets, and raised customer expectations.

In late 1997 and again in 1998, the decline in demand prompted Nucor and other U.S. companies to slash prices in order to compete with the unprecedented surge of imports. By the last quarter of 1998, these imports had led to the filing of unfair trade complaints with U.S. trade regulators, causing steel prices in the spot market to drop sharply in August and September before they stabilized.

A press release by the U.S. Secretary of Commerce, William Daley, stated "I will not stand by and allow U.S. workers, communities and companies to bear the brunt of other nations' problematic policies and practices. We are the most open economy of the world. But we are not the world's dumpster."

The commerce department concluded in March 1999 that six countries had illegally dumped stainless steel in the United States at prices below production costs or home market prices. The commerce department found that Canada, South Korea, and Taiwan were guilty only of dumping, while Belgium, Italy, and South Africa also gave producers unfair subsidies that effectively lowered prices. However, on June 23, 1999, the *Wall Street Journal* reported that the Senate decisively shut off an attempt to restrict U.S. imports of steel despite industry complaints that a flood of cheap imports were driving them out of business. Advisors of President Clinton were reported to have said the president would likely veto the bill if it passed. Administrative officials opposed the bill because it would violate international trade law and leave the United States open to retaliation.

The AISI reported that in May 1999, U.S. steel mills shipped 8,330,000 net tons, a decrease of 6.7 percent from the 8,927,000 net tons shipped in May 1998. They also stated that for the first five months of 1999 shipments were 41,205,000 net tons, down 10 percent from the same period in 1998. AISI President and CEO Andrew Sharkey III said, "Once again, the May data show clearly that America's steel trade crisis continues. U.S. steel companies and employees continue to be injured by high levels of dumping and subsidized imports. . . . In addition, steel inventory levels remain excessive, and steel operating rates continue to be very low."

As the 1990s ended, Nucor was the second largest steel producer in the United States, behind USX. The company's market capitalization was about two times that of the next smaller competitor. Even in a tight industry, someone can win. Nucor was in the best position because the industry was very fragmented and there are many marginal competitors.

Steel Technology and the Mini-Mill

A new type of mill, the "mini-mill," had emerged in the United States during the 1970s to compete with the integrated mill. The mini-mill used electric arc furnaces initially to manufacture a narrow product line from scrap steel. The leading U.S. mini-mills in the 1980s were Nucor, Florida Steel, Georgetown Steel, North Star Steel, and Chaparral. Between the late 1970s and 1980s, the integrated mills' market share fell from about 90 percent to about 60 percent, with the integrated steel companies averaging a 7 percent return on equity, the mini-mills averaging 14 percent, and some, such as Nucor, achieving about 25 percent. In the 1990s, the integrated mills' market share fell to around 40 percent, while mini-mills' share rose to 23 percent, reconstructed mills increased their share from 11 to 28 percent, and specialized mills increased their share from 1 percent to 6 percent.

Some experts believed that a relatively new technology, the twin shell electric arc furnace, would help mini-mills increase production and lower costs and take market share. According to the *Pittsburgh Business Times*, "With a twin shell furnace, one shell—the chamber holding the scrap to be melted—is filled and heated. During the heating of the first shell, the second shell is filled. When the heating is finished on the first shell, the electrodes move to the second. The first shell is emptied and refilled before the second gets hot." This increased the production by 60 percent. Twin shell production had been widely adopted in the last few years. For example, Nucor Steel began running a twin shell furnace in November 1996 in Berkeley, South Carolina, and installed another in Norfolk, Nebraska, which began operations in 1997. "Everyone accepts twin shells as a good concept because there's a lot of flexibility of operation," said Rodney Mott, vice president and general manager of Nucor-Berkeley. However, this move toward twin shell furnaces could mean trouble in the area of scrap availability. According to an October 1997 quote in *Pittsburgh Business Times* by Ralph Smaller, vice president of process technology at Kvaerner, "Innovations that feed the electric furnaces' production of flat-rolled (steel) will increase the demand on high quality scrap and alternatives. The technological changes are just beginning and will accelerate over the next few years."

According to a September 1997 *Industry Week* article, steelmakers around the world were now closely monitoring the development of continuous "strip casting" technology, which may prove to be the next leap forward for the industry. "The objective of strip casting is to produce thin strips of steel (in the 1–4-mm range) as liquid steel flows from a tundish—the stationary vessel which received molten steel from the ladle. It would eliminate the slab-casting stage and all of the rolling that now takes place in a hot mill." Strip casting was reported to have some difficult technological challenges but companies in Germany, France, Japan, Australia, Italy, and Canada had strip-casting projects underway. In fact, all of the significant development work in strip casting was taking place outside the United States.

Larry Kavanaph, AISI vice president for manufacturing and technology, said "Steel is a very high-tech industry, but nobody knows it." Today's most productive steel-making facilities incorporated advanced metallurgical practices, sophisticated process-control sensors, state-of-the art computer controls, and the latest refinements in continuous casting and rolling mill technology. Michael Shot, vice president—manufacturing at Carpenter Technology Corporation, Reading, PA, a specialty steels and premium grade alloys, said "You don't survive in this industry unless you have the technology to make the best products in the world in the most efficient manner."

Management Evolution

Only five, not six, members of the board were in attendance during the board of directors meeting in the fall of 1998, due to the death of Jim Cunningham. Near its end, Aycock read a motion, drafted by Siegel, that Ken Iverson be removed as chairman. It was seconded by Hlavacek and passed. It was announced in October that Iverson would be a chairman emeritus and a director, but after disagreements Iverson left the company completely. It was agreed that Iverson would receive $500,000 a year for five years. Aycock left retirement to become chairman.

The details of Iverson's leaving did not become known until June of 1999 when John Correnti resigned after disagreements with the board and Aycock took his place. All of this was a complete surprise to investors and brought the stock price down 10 percent. Siegel commented "the board felt Correnti was not the right person to lead Nucor into the 21st century." Aycock assured everyone he would be happy to move back into retirement as soon as replacements could be found.

Aycock moved to increase the corporate office staff by adding a level of executive vice presidents over four areas of business and adding two specialist jobs in strategic planning and steel technology. When Siegel retired, Aycock promoted Terry Lisenby to CFO and treasurer and hired a Director of IT to report to Lisenby (see Exhibit 4 for the organization chart in 2000).

Jim Coblin, vice president of human resources, believed the additions to management were necessary, "It's not bad to get a little more like other companies." He noted that the various divisions did their business cards and plant signs differently; some did not even want a Nucor sign. Sometimes six different Nucor salesmen would call on the same customer. "There is no manager of human resources in the plants, so at least we needed to give additional training to the person who does most of that work at the plant," he stated. With these new additions there would be a director of information technology and two important committees, one for environmental issues and the second for audit.

He believed the old span of control of 20 might have worked well when there was less competition.

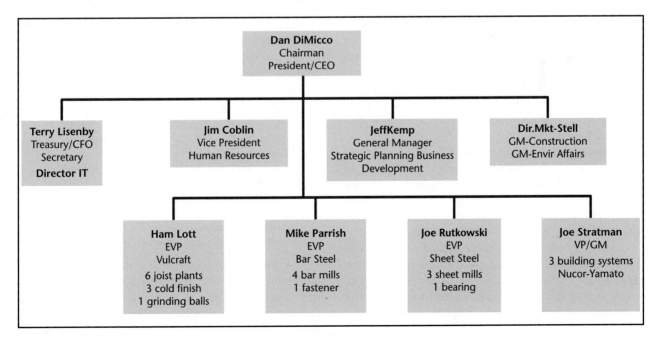

Exhibit 4   Nucor Organization Chart, Executive Management 2000

Aycock considered it "ridiculous." "It was not possible to properly manage, to know what was going own. The top managers have totally lost contact with the company." Coblin was optimistic that the use of executive vice presidents (EVPs) would improve management. The three meetings of the general managers had slowly increased from about 1½ days to about 2½ days and become more focused. The new EVP positions would bring a perspective above the level of the individual plants. Instead of 15 individual detailed presentations, each general manager would give a short, five-minute briefing and then there would be an in-depth presentation on the group, with team participation. After some training by Lisenby, the divisions had recently done a pretty good job with a strength, weakness, opportunities, threats (SWOT) analysis. Coblin thought these changes would make Nucor a stronger global player.

To Jeff Kemp, the new general manager of strategic planning and business development, the big issue was how to sustain earnings' growth. In the U.S. steel industry there were too many marginal competitors. The U.S. government had recently added to the problem by giving almost a billion dollars to nine mills, which simply allowed them to limp along and weaken the industry. He was looking for Nucor's opportunities within the steel industry. He asked why Nucor had bought a bearing company. His experience in the chemical industry suggested a need for Nucor to establish a position of superiority and grow globally, driving industry competition rather than reacting. He argued that a company should protect its overall market position, which could mean sacrifices for individual plants. Aycock liked Kemp's background in law and accounting and had specifically sought someone from outside the steel industry to head up Nucor's strategic planning. By June 2000 Kemp had conducted studies of other industries in the U.S. market and developed a working document which identified opportunities worthy of further analysis.

"Every company hits a plateau," Aycock observed "you can't just go out and build plants to grow. How do you step up to the next level? I wouldn't say it's a turning point but we have to get our strategic vision and strategic plans." He stated, "we are beginning Nucor's first ever strategic planning sessions, it was not necessary before."

Aycock believed that Nucor needed to be quick to recognize developing technology in all production areas. He noted the joint venture to develop a new "strip caster," which would cast the current flat-rolled material in a more finished form. The impact could be "explosive," allowing Nucor to build smaller plants closer to markets. This would be particularly helpful on the West Coast.

Nucor would own the U.S. and Brazilian rights, their partners the rest. He was also looking forward to the next generation of steel mills and wanted to own the rights, this time. He praised Iverson's skill at seeing technology and committing to it.

He was very interested in acquisitions, but "they must fit strategically." A bar mill in the upper central Midwest and a flat-rolled plant in the Northeast would be good. A significant opportunity existed in pre-engineered buildings. Aycock intended to concentrate on steel for the next five to six years, achieving an average growth rate of 15 percent per year. In about seven years, he would like to see Nucor ready to move into other areas. He said Nucor had already "picked the low hanging grapes" and must be careful in its next moves.

Daniel DiMicco assumed the role of Nucor's president and chief executive officer in September 2000, when David Aycock stepped down as planned. Peter Browning was elected chairman of the board of directors. Aycock retired from the board a year later.

Sales for 2000 increased 14 percent over 1999 to reach a record level. Earnings were also at record levels, 27 percent over 1999. The year had begun on a strong footing but had turned weak by the years' end. While Nucor remained profitable, other steel companies faced bankruptcy. A Vulcraft plant was under construction in New York. It was their first northeastern operation which expanded the geographical coverage into a new region. They were also attempting a breakthrough technological step in strip casting at Crawfordsville, the Castrip process. They sold their grinding ball process and the bearing products operation because they were not a part of their core business. In the company's annual report, DiMicco laid out their plans for 2000 and beyond:

> Our targets are to deliver an average annual earnings growth of 10–15 percent over the next 10 years, to deliver a return well in excess of our cost of capital, to maintain a minimum average return on equity of 14 percent and to deliver to return on sales a 8–10 percent. Our strategy will focus on Nucor becoming a "market leader" in every product group and business in which we compete. This calls for significant increases in market share for many of our core products and the maintenance of market share where we currently enjoyed a leadership position.

While pointing out that it would be impossible to obtain this success through the previous strategy of greenfield construction, he added, "there will now be a heavy focus on growth through acquisitions. We will also continue growing through the commercialization of new disruptive and leapfrog technologies."

Steel and Nucor in the Twenty-First Century

In late 2010, Dan reflected over his 10-year tenure as CEO of Nucor with pride. These had been some of the steel industry's rockiest times, and yet under his leadership Nucor had almost doubled its size, and even during the dark days of 2009 did not lay off any of its employees.

By October 2001 more than 20 steel companies in the United States, including Bethlehem Steel Corporation and LTV Corporation, the nation's third and fourth largest steel producers, respectively, had filed for bankruptcy protection. Over a dozen producers were operating under Chapter 11 Bankruptcy Law Protection, which allows them to maintain market share by selling steel cheaper than non-Chapter 11 steelmakers. On October 20, *The Economist* noted that of the 14 steel companies followed by Standard & Poor's, only Nucor was indisputably healthy. In the fall of 2001, 25 percent of domestic steel companies were in bankruptcy proceedings, although the United States was the largest importer of steel in the world. Experts believed that close to half of the U.S. steel industry might be forced to close before conditions improved.

In 2001 the world steel industry found itself in the middle of one of its most unprofitable and volatile periods ever, in part due to a glut of steel that had sent prices to 20-year lows. While domestic steel producers were mired in red ink, many foreign steelmakers desperately needed to continue to sell in the relatively open U.S. market to stay profitable. The industry was hovering around 75 percent capacity utilization, a level too low to be profitable for many companies. Three European companies—France's Usinor SA, Luxembourg's Arbed SA, and Spain's Aceralia Corporation—merged to form the world's largest steel company. Two Japanese companies—NKK Corporation and Kawasaki Steel Corporation—merged to form the world's second biggest steelmaker. These new mega steelmakers could outmuscle U.S. competitors, which were less efficient, smaller, and financially weaker than their competitors in Asia and Europe. At this time, the largest U.S. steelmaker, USX–U.S. Steel Group, was only the 11th largest producer in the world. Furthermore, while in 1990 mini-mills accounted for 36 percent of the domestic steel market, by 2000 the more efficient mini-mill had seized 50 percent of the market and the resulting competition had driven prices lower for integrated steel as well as mini-mills.

The year 2001 turned out to be one of the worst years ever for steel. There was 9/11, a recession, and a surge of imports. DiMicco broke with Nucor's traditional opposition to government intervention to make a major push for protective tariffs. He stated, "The need to enforce trade rules is similar to the need to enforce any other law. If two merchants have stores side by side, but one sells stolen merchandise at a vast discount, we know that it's time for the police to step in." In March 2002 President Bush, after an investigation and recommendation by the ITC, imposed anti-dumping tariffs under section 201 of the Trade Act of 1974. This restricted some imports of steel and placed quotas of up to 30 percent on others. The move was opposed by many, including steel users. Columnist George Will in his editorial on March 10, 2002, criticized Bush for abandoning free trade and pointed out that protection would hamper the necessary actions to restructure the steel industry in America by reducing excess capacity. The European Union immediately threatened reprisals and appealed to the World Trade Organization (WTO). In December China imposed its own three-year program of import duties. Steel prices rose 40 percent in 2002 after the tariffs. Within a year hot-rolled steel prices increased 50 percent to $260 per ton over the 20-year low of $210 during 2002. The price had been $361 in 1980. In November 2003, the WTO ruled against the tariffs and, under increasing pressure of retaliation, Bush withdrew the tariffs.

While many steel companies floundered, Nucor was able to take advantage of the weakened conditions. In March 2001, Nucor made its first acquisition in 10 years, purchasing a mini-mill in New York from Sumitomo Corporation. Nucor had hired about five people to help plan for future acquisitions. DiMicco commented "it's taken us three years before our team has felt this is the right thing to do and get started making acquisitions." In the challenged industry, he argued, it would be cheaper to buy than build plants. They purchased the assets of Auburn Steel, which gave them a merchant bar presence in the Northeast and helped the new Vulcraft facility in New York. They acquired ITEC Steel, a leader in the emerging load-bearing light gauge steel-framing market, and saw an opportunity to aggressively broaden its market. Nucor increased its sheet capacity by roughly one third when it acquired the assets of Trico Steel Company in Alabama for $120 million. In early 2002, they acquired the assets of Birmingham Steel Corporation. The $650 million purchase of four mini-mills was the largest acquisition in Nucor's history. However, 2002 also proved to be a difficult year for Nucor. While they increased their steelmaking capacity by more than 25 percent, revenue increased 11 percent, and earnings improved 43 percent over weak 2001, their other financial goals were not met.

The difficult times in the industry did not stop Nucor from continuing their expansion through acquisitions to increase their market share and capacity in steel and by actively working on new production processes that would provide them with technological advantages. They acquired the U.S. and Brazilian rights to the promising Castrip process for strip casting, the process of directly casting thin sheet steel. After development work on the process in Indiana, they began full-time production in May 2002 and produced 7,000 tons in the last 10 months of 2002. Moreover, in April, Nucor entered into a joint venture with a Brazilian mining company, CVRD, the world's largest producer of iron-ore pellets, to jointly develop low-cost iron-based products. Success with this effort would give them the ability to make steel by combining iron ore and coke rather than using scrap steel which was becoming less available.

During 2003 prices of steel rose in the United States and Asia as global demand outpaced supply. China, with its booming economy, drove the market. An article in *Wall Street Journal*, October 15, quoted Guy Dolle, chief executive of Arcelor SA of Luxembourg, the world's largest steelmaker in terms of steel product shipped, as saying, "China is the wild card in the balance between supply and demand." World prices did not soar dangerously because the steel industry continued to be plagued by overcapacity. Yet steel-hungry China and other fast-growing nations added to their steel capacity.

Imports of steel commodities into the United States fell in August 2003 by 22 percent. A weakened dollar, the growing demand from China, and tariffs imposed in 2002 by Bush limited imports. Domestic capacity declined as producers consolidated, idled plants, or went out of business, which increased capacity utilization from 77.2 to 93.4 percent. Prices for iron ore and energy rose, affecting integrated producers. Mini-mills saw their costs rise as worldwide demand for scrap rose. Thus, U.S. steelmakers boosted their prices. By February 2004, a growing coalition of U.S. steel producers and consumers were considering whether to petition to limit soaring exports of scrap steel from the United States, the world's largest producer of steel scrap. One result was that the International Steel Group (ISG) replaced Nucor as the most profitable U.S. steel producer. ISG was created when investor Wilbur Ross acquired the failing traditional steel producers in America, including LTV, Bethlehem, and Weirton. These mills used iron ore rather than scrap steel.

When 2003 ended, Nucor struck a positive note by reminding their investors that they had been profitable every single quarter since beginning operations in 1966. But while Nucor set records for both steel production and steel shipments, net earnings declined 61 percent. While the steel industry struggled, Nucor increased its market share and held on to profitability. They worked on expanding their business with the automotive industry, continued

their joint venture in Brazil to produce pig iron, and pursued a joint venture with the Japanese and Chinese to make iron without the usual raw materials. In February 2004 they were "optimistic about the prospects for obtaining commercialization" of their promising Castrip process for strip casting in the United States and Brazil. The mini-mills could not produce sheet steel, a large share of the market.

Global competition continued. According to the *Wall Street Journal*, Posco steelworks in Pohang, South Korea, enjoyed the highest profits in the global steel industry as of 2004. Moreover, *Business Week* reported that the company had developed a new technology called Finex, which turned coal and iron ore into iron without coking and sintering, and it was expected to cut production costs by nearly a fifth and harmful emissions by 90 percent. They had also expanded their 80 Korean plants by investing in 14 Chinese joint ventures. By December 2004, demand in China had slowed down and it had become a net steel exporter, sparking concerns of global oversupply.

Global consolidation also continued. In October 2004 London's Mittal family announced that they would merge their Ispat International NV with the LNM Group and ISG to create the world's largest steelmaker, with an estimated annual revenue of $31.5 billion and an output of 57 million tons. This would open a new chapter for the industry's consolidation, which had been mostly regional. Although the world's steel industry remains largely fragmented with the world's top 10 steelmakers supplying less than 30 percent of global production, Mittal Steel would have about 40 percent of the U.S. market in flat-rolled steel. Moreover Mittal, which had a history of using its scale to buy lower cost raw materials and import modern management techniques into previously inefficient state-run mills, was buying ISG, a U.S. company which already owned the lowest-cost, highest-profit mills in the United States.

In 2004 and 2005 Nucor continued its aggressive geographic expansion and introduction of new products. For example, Nuconsteel ("Nucon"), a wholly owned subsidiary of Nucor which specialized in load-bearing light gauge steel framing systems for commercial and residential construction markets, introduced two new low-cost automated fabrication systems for residential construction. And in March 2005, Nucor formed a joint venture with Lennar Corporation, named Nexframe, LP, to provide comprehensive light gauge steel framing for residential construction. Nucor's 25 percent joint venture with the Rio Tinto Group, Mitsubishi Corporation, and Chinese steelmaker Shougang Corporation for a Hlsmelt commercial plant in Kwinana, Western Australia, started up in 2005. In 2004 Nucor acquired assets of an idled direct-reduced iron (DRI) plant in Louisiana and moved them to

Trinidad. By December 2006 construction was completed and by 2008 Nu-Iron Unlimited produced 1,400,000 metric tons of DRI from Brazilian iron ore for the United States.

By 2005, Nucor had 16 steel facilities producing three times as much as in 1999. The number of bar mills had grown to nine mills with a capacity of 6,000,000 tons by the addition of Birmingham's four mills with 2,000,000 tons and Auburn's 400,000 tons. The sheet mills grew to four and increased capacity by one third with the acquisition of Trico. Nucor-Yamato's structural steel capacity was increased by half a million tons from the South Carolina plant. A new million ton plate mill, their second, had opened in North Carolina in 2000. Ninety-three percent of production was sold to outside customers.

By 2006 DiMicco had made many acquisitions while still managing to instill Nucor's unique culture in the new facilities. A *Business Week* article in May 2006 stated that Nucor's culture and compensation system had changed very little since the 1990s. Michael Arndt reported, "Nucor gave out more than $220 million in profit sharing and bonuses to the rank and file in 2005. The average Nucor steelworker took home nearly $79,000 last year. Add to that a $2,000 one-time bonus to mark the company's record earnings and almost $18,000, on average, in profit sharing." He also noted that executive pay was still geared toward team building as "the bonus of a plant manager, a department manager's boss, depends on the entire corporation's return on equity. So there's no glory in winning at your plant if the others are failing."

Globally steel mergers and acquisitions boomed during 2006–2008. For example, Arcelor SA took over Canadian steelmaker Dofasco, Inc., for $4.85 billion in March 2006, followed by their merger in June with Mittal Steel Company, NV, to create the world's largest steel company. In January 2007, Russian steelmaker Evraz SA acquired Oregon Steel Mills, a Portland-based producer of specialty steel, for $2.3 billion and in March, India-based Tata Steel, Ltd., completed its acquisition of UK-based Corus Group, Plc., for $12.4 billion. SSAB Svenskt Stal AB of Sweden completed its acquisition of IPSCO, Inc., of Lisle, Illinois, for $7.7 billion in July 2007 and in October Steel Dynamics completed the acquisition of privately held OmniSource Corporation, a scrap processor and trading company. In May 2008 OAO Severstal, a Russia-based steel company acquired ArcelorMittal's Sparrow Point steel plant in Maryland and in June they outbid Essar Steel Holdings Ltd., an India-based steel company for Esmark, Inc. Also in June 2008, Tangsham Iron & Steel Group merged with Handan Iron & Steel Group; the new company called Hebei Iron & Steel Group Company surpassed Baosteel Group Company as China's largest steel producer. Despite all the transactions in 2006, 2007, and 2008, the industry remained fragmented, both domestically and internationally, and more mergers were expected.

Future merger activity was expected to differ slightly as steel companies attempted to become more vertically integrated. Examples were integration forward with Esmark's service center's combination with Wheeling-Pittsburgh's steel production and integration backward into scrap with the takeover of OmniSource by Steel Dynamics in 2007 and Nucor's acquisition of David J. Joseph Company in 2008. These represented a trend toward becoming less dependent on outside vendors. This was due to the rising cost of scrap, which jumped from $185/ton in January 2006 to $635/ton in June 2008, and the highly concentrated nature of iron ore sources.

Nucor was also active in mergers. In March of 2007, Nucor acquired Harris Steel Group Inc. of Canada for $1.06 billion in cash, adding 770,000 tons of rebar fabrication capacity and over 350,000 tons of capacity in other downstream steel products. This acquisition showed that Nucor saw growth opportunities in finishing steel products for its customers and in distribution rather than additional steelmaking capacity. While many large steel companies were buying other primary steelmakers around the world, Nucor was focusing its investments largely in North America's manufacturing infrastructure such as reinforced steel bars, platform grating, and wire mesh for construction products ranging from bridges to airports and stadiums, which according to Dan DiMicco "significantly advances Nucor's downstream growth initiatives." Through the acquisition of Harris, Nucor also acquired a 75 percent interest in Novosteel SA, a Switzerland-based steel trading company which matched buyers and sellers of steel products on a global basis and offered its customers logistics support, material handling, quality certifications, and schedule management. The Harris team was operating as a growth platform within Nucor and had completed several acquisitions. Nucor made several other acquisitions, and some internal organic growth increased Nucor's cold finish and drawn products' capacity by over 75 percent from 490,000 tons in 2006 to 860,000 tons at the end of 2007.

Nucor had had a joint venture with Harris for the previous three years and already owned a 50 percent stake in the company. Harris kept its name, as a Nucor subsidiary, and was led by the previous Chairman and CEO John Harris. However, the Harris board consisted of Harris and three Nucor representatives. This was the first time Nucor had broken from its non-union tradition, as about half of Harris's 3,000 employees belonged to a mix of iron-workers, auto-workers, and steel-workers unions. As Timna Tanners, a steel analyst in New York said, "It's definitely a

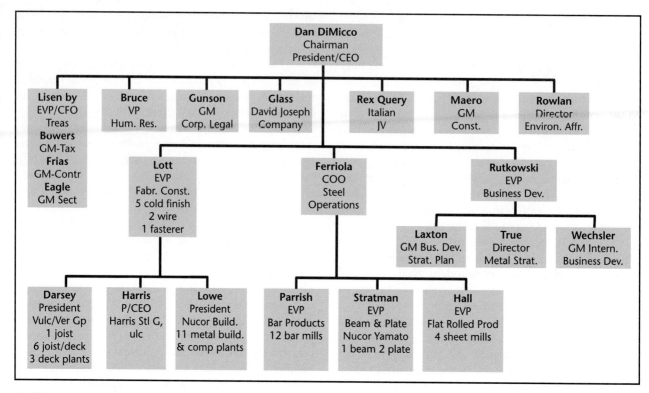

Exhibit 5   Nucor Organization Chart, Executive Management 2009

stretch for Nucor, culturally, since they have managed to keep its other operations non-union by offering higher salaries and production incentives. But there are not many non-union options left in North America when it comes to acquisitions and expansion."

Nucor continued to invest in other downstream and upstream businesses (see Exhibit 5 for the organization chart in 2009). In the third quarter of 2007, they completed the acquisition of Magnatrax Corporation, a leading provider of custom-engineering metal buildings, for $275.2 million in cash. The Magnatrax acquisition, when combined with their existing building systems divisions and a newly constructed buildings systems division in Brigham City, Utah, made Nucor the second largest metal-building producer in the United States, more than doubling their annual capacity to 480,000 tons of pre-engineered metal buildings.

In 2007, Nucor's seven Vulcraft facilities supplied more than 40 percent of total domestic buildings using steel joists and joist girders. In both 2006 and 2007, 99 percent of its steel requirements were obtained from Nucor bar mills. Nucor's nine steel-deck plants supplied almost 30 percent of total domestic sales in decking; six of these plants were constructed by Nucor adjacent to Vulcraft joist facilities and three were acquired in November 2006 as a wholly

owned subsidiary called Verco Decking. These decking plants obtained 99 percent of their steel requirements from Nucor sheet plants in 2006 but only 76 percent in 2007.

In March 2008, Nucor completed the acquisition of the David J. Joseph Company (DJJ), the largest broker of ferrous and non-ferrous scrap in the United States and one of the nation's largest processors of ferrous scrap for $1.44 billion. The company had been a supplier of scrap to Nucor since 1969. DJJ operated over 30 scrap-processing facilities. This acquisition expanded Nucor's scrap-processing capabilities to four million short tons from 500,000 and provided them additional steelmaking raw materials through their brokerage operations and rail services and logistics through its private fleet of some 2,000 scrap-related railcars. This allowed them to capture further margins in the steelmaking supply chain and to more closely control their raw material inputs. In May, they announced a plan to raise $3 billion for expansions and acquisitions, two-thirds to come from selling 25 million new shares. Nucor stopped making acquisitions in 2008 following their acquisition of 50 percent interest in a steel operation in Italy, due to the economic reversal that took place globally.

U.S. steelmakers saw a major transition in 2008. In the first quarter the combination of higher volume and increased prices led to a sizable gain in profits. At the end

Exhibit 6   Top 15 Global Steel Producers as of the End of 2009 According to the International Iron and Steel Institute.

Rank in 2009	Company	mmt in 2009	Rank in 2007	mmt in 2007	Rank in 2006	mmt in 2006
1	ArcelorMittal	77.5	1	116.4	1	117.2
2	Baosteel	31.3	5	28.6	6	22.5
3	POSCO	31.1	4	31.1	4	30.1
4	Nippon Steel (1)	26.5	2	35.7	2	34.7
5	JFE	25.8	3	34.0	3	32.0
6	Jiangsu Shagang (2)	20.5	8	22.9	17	14.6
7	Tata Steel (3)	20.5	6	26.5	45	6.4
8	Ansteel	20.1	—	—	—	—
9	Severstal	16.7	—	—	11	17.5
10	Evraz	15.3	—	—	13	16.1
11	U.S. Steel	15.2	10	21.5	7	21.2
12	Shougang (4)	15.1	—	—	26	10.5
13	Gerdau	14.2	—	—	14	15.6
14	Nucor	14.0	12	20.0	8	20.3
15	Wuhan	13.7	—	—	17	13.8

of July, major U.S. steelmakers' results were still supported by months of steel-price increases, which eased the burden of rising raw materials' prices, as demand from emerging markets kept global steel supplies tight. However, in September 2008 steelmakers in the United States experienced a sharp pullback from buyers who were concerned with the credit crisis and a slowdown in the automobile and construction markets. This caused inventories to rise and prices on some key products to drop 10 percent. The *Wall Street Journal* reported on November 17 that "metal prices fell 35 percent in just four weeks last month—the steepest decline ever recorded, according to Barclays Capital." They also reported that big steelmakers worldwide were cutting production as much as 35 percent and that U.S. Steel Corporation planned to lay off 2 percent of its workforce. Chinese demand also slowed. This was a swift reversal in an industry that saw its profits increase 20-fold in five years. The pricing volatility was intensified by the global financial crisis as many hedge funds, pension funds, and other investors desperate to raise cash rapidly sold their commodities holdings. Still, the article said that ultimately the industry's problems were rooted in weakened demand, particularly in China, rather than the financial crisis.

In 2009 the producer price index for steel products in the United States fell 25.1 percent. This was due to the decrease in demand for steel, resulting from the global financial crisis. Key markets (construction, industrial equipment, and durable consumer products) were hurt by the recession and fixed investment was hampered by tight credit conditions. Demand for certain steel products was propped up by some of the large public stimulus money for infrastructure. U.S. steel mills responded by cutting

production 36.4 percent between 2008 and 2009. The domestic price of steel had exhibited high volatility because of exposure to world steel prices and exchange rate fluctuations.

As 2010 began, a recovery was expected and U.S. steel prices rose as demand for steel increased. Companies ramped up production but prices fell again in July when demand did not materialize. Despite predictions that world steel prices would remain weak for the rest of 2010, by September they had begun to climb for several products. This was based on the expectation that China would cut production by 3 percent to 5 percent. However, some steelmakers doubted the cut in China would be widespread or sustained. Furthermore, some steel markets remained so weak that prices were not expected to rise at all. For example, sales of construction steel were so weak that Nucor, the largest maker of nonresidential construction steel in the United States, lowered its third-quarter outlook.

In 2010, five major competitors had nearly 63.5 percent of the U.S. market:

AcelorMittal (Luxembourg based) with 18 plants	20.5%
Nucor (United States) with 22 plants	19.9%
United States Steel Corporation (United States) with five plants	13.0%
AK Steel Holding Corporation (United States)	6.0%
Severstal North America, Inc. (Russia)	4.0%

In 2009 U.S. imports totaled 24.1 million metric tons, approximately 20 percent of the total market, while U.S. exports totaled only 8.8 million metric tons.

	Imports	Exports
China	17%	6%
Canada	15%	43%
Mexico	7%	18%
Brazil	7%	0.1%

According to the World Steel Association 115 million metric tons (mmt) of crude steel was produced by 66 countries in July 2010, up 9.6 percent from July 2009. Production was up 2.2 percent in China, 20.4 percent in Japan, 11.5 percent in Russia, and 32.9 percent in the United States (see Exhibit 7). However, the crude steel capacity utilization ratio of the 66 countries in July 2010 declined 5.3 percent in June 2010, but was 2.7 percent higher than in July 2009.

IBISWorld forecast that the producer price index for steel mill products would increase at an annualized rate of 2.7 percent over the five years from December 2010 to 2015. They predicted that world steel consumption would continue to be driven largely by developments in China. The Chinese economy was expected to continue to grow strongly and to account for over 50 percent of world steel consumption growth. However, during this period Chinese consumption growth was expected to slow and Indian consumptions were forecast to increase at a faster rate than Chinese consumption. India was expected to become the second largest consumer of steel by 2020 but was not expected to rival China, which currently consumed eight times more than India.

While steel production was expected to grow, there is a great deal of uncertainty as to who would benefit. With the growth expected in China and India over the next five years, the opportunities would appear to be going to those markets.

In the United States, concerns had emerged with the September announcement that Anshan Iron & Steel Group, a state-owned Chinese steel producer, would buy 14 percent of a new Mississippi-based Steel Development Company and invest in up to five U.S. mills. Some U.S. lawmakers opposing government-subsidized loans for the project worried that the advantages of the cleaner production technology to be developed would flow to China, and U.S. jobs would be lost. Other partners in the joint venture included U.S., Japanese, Italian, and German companies. John Correnti, chairman and CEO of Steel Development, played down the venture's impact.

In 2009, Nucor's sales were down 53 percent and earnings per share dropped 116 percent. Steel production decreased 32 percent. Vulcraft's production was down 46 percent. Nucor cut capital expenditures by 62 percent. Net earnings per share fell from a record $5.98 in 2008 to a low of $.94 in 2009. In addition to the collapse of sales, the company was hurt by commodity contracts based on the pre-recession prices. In their annual report, they said that "2009 was one of the most tumultuous and difficult periods in Nucor's history."

As 2010 began, they expressed concern with the government response, noting that Nucor, and others, received no help from the "stimulus" money. They were concerned about recent legislative and regulatory proposals related to climate change and new interpretations of existing laws. They worried that these might create new financial risks and competitive disadvantages for U.S. companies by increasing energy costs as well as the costs of compliance, capital investment, and operation. They noted the challenges at their Louisiana iron-making plant where they were trying to develop alternatives to scrap steel but had been delayed by extended permitting processes and proposed climate change legislation.

The United States, and much of the world, was facing the worst economic situation in almost a hundred years. Governments were responding by changing the basic rules that guided business, in ways no one fully understood. China, India, Brazil, and others were for the first time aspiring to world economic leadership. The future of the United States, the future of American business, and the future of Nucor were in question. Nucor's Dan DiMicco said, "Nucor has a long history of turning economic downturns into opportunities" and expected "to emerge stronger leaving the recession."

	Country	Production in 2009 (mmt)	Production in the First Half of 2010 (mmt)
1	China	567.8	323.17
2	Japan	87.5	54.58
3	India	62.8	32.43
4	Russia	60.0	32.69
5	United States	58.2	40.90

Exhibit 7   The World Steel Association's List of Top Steel-Producing Countries in 2009 and Aggregated Data for Their Production During the First Six Months of 2010

Case 2-3: The Levi's Personal Pair Proposal*

"I'll have my recommendation to you by the end of the week." Heidi Green hung up the phone and surveyed her calendar for appointments that could be pushed into the next week. It was a rainy afternoon in December of 1994 and she had yet to recover from the pre-holiday rush to get product out to retailers.

She had three days to prepare a presentation for the Executive Committee on a new concept called Personal Pair. Custom Clothing Technology Corporation (CCTC) had approached Levi Strauss with the joint venture proposal that would marry Levi's core products with the emerging technologies of mass customization. Jeans could be customized in style and fit to meet each customer's unique needs and taste. If CCTC was correct, this would reach the higher end of the jeans market, yielding stronger profit margins due to both the price premium and the streamlined production process involved.

On the other hand, the technology was new to Levi Strauss and the idea could turn out to be an expensive and time-consuming proposal that would come back later to haunt her, since she would have to manage the venture. The initial market studies seemed supportive, but there was no way to know how customers would respond to the program since there was nothing quite like it out there. She also was unsure whether the program would work as smoothly in practice as the plan suggested.

Company Background and History

Levi Strauss and Co. is a privately held company owned by the family of its founder, Levi Strauss. The Bavarian immigrant was the creator of durable work pants from cloth used for ships' sails, which were reinforced with his patented rivets. The now-famous "waist-overalls" were originally created over 130 years ago for use by California gold rush workers. These were later seen as utilitarian farm- or factory-wear. By the 1950s, Levi's jeans had acquired a Hollywood cachet, as the likes of Marilyn Monroe, James Dean, Marlon Brando, Elvis, and Bob Dylan proudly wore them, giving off an air of rebellious hipness.

The jeans would become a political statement and an American icon, as all jeans soon became known generically as "Levi's." The baby boomer generation next adopted the jeans as a fashion statement, and from 1964 to 1975, the company's annual sales grew tenfold, from $100 million to $1 billion.[2] By the late 1970s, Levi's had become synonymous with the terms, "authentic," "genuine," "original," and "real," and wearing them allowed the wearer to make a statement. According to some who recognize the brand's recognition even over that of Coke, Marlboro, Nike, or Microsoft, "Levi Strauss has been, and remains, both the largest brand-apparel company in the world and the number one purveyor of blue jeans in the world."

While blue jeans remain the company's mainstay, the San Francisco–based company also sells pants made of corduroy, twill and various other fabrics, as well as shorts, skirts, jackets, and outerwear. The company, with its highly recognizable brand name, holds a top position in many of its markets, and is sold in more than 80 countries. More than half of the company's revenue was from its U.S. sales; nevertheless, Europe and Asia are highly profitable markets. Latin America and Canada are secondary markets, with smaller contributions to overall profits. As the graphic (below) shows, apparel imports were increasing faster than exports during this period.

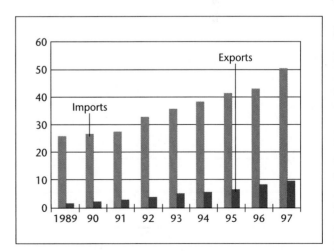

Import and Exports of Apparel (in billions of dollars)

Source: U.S. Department of Commerce.

* Used with permission of Professor Russell Coff and the Goizueta Business School.

The company's non-denim brand, Dockers, was introduced in 1986, and is sold in the U.S., Canada, Mexico, and Europe. While it is composed of both women's and men's clothing, the men's line of khaki pants occupies the leading position in U.S. sales of khaki trousers and sells well with baby boomers. Sales of Dockers have steadily increased with the rise in casual workplaces, and this line of non-denim products has helped in allowing Levi's to be less reliant on the denim industry.

Competition and the Denim Industry

Denim is "one of the fastest-growing apparel fabrics," and sales have been increasing approximately 10% per year. According to some surveys, an average American consumer owns 17 denim items, which includes 6 to 7 pairs of jeans.[3] Levi Strauss and Company held the largest market share in 1990, at 31 percent, followed by VF Corporation's Lee and Wrangler (17.9 percent), designer labels (6 percent), The Gap (3 percent), and department store private labels (3.2 percent). By 1995, women's jeans had grown to a $2 billion market, of which Levi's held first place.

However, at the same time, many jeans producers were starting to move production to low-cost overseas facilities, which allowed for cost (especially labor) advantages. As the graph (below) shows, this trend was represented throughout the apparel industry and is clearly visible in employment statistics. Indeed, JCPenney, one of Levi's long-time partners, had become a competitor by introducing a cheaper alternative, the Arizona label. They and other rivals had realized that by sourcing all

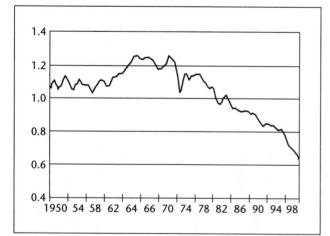

U.S. Apparel Industry Employment (production workers, in millions)

Source: Bureau of Labor Statistics.

production in cheap overseas facilities they could enter the business with a cost advantage over Levi Strauss.

Levi's, as a private company that viewed itself as having a strong "social conscience," wanted to avoid being seen as exploiting disadvantaged workers. Accordingly, they preferred to have their jeans "U.S.-made," and Levi Strauss was a leader in providing generous salary and benefits packages to its employees.

Accordingly, it did not relish the notion of entering into price-based competition with rivals committed to overseas production. Their delayed response led to some significant incursions by rivals into Levi's core product arenas.

Levi's also wanted to avoid price-based competition because they had a history of brand recognition and brand loyalty. They were accustomed to the Levi's brand carrying enough clout to justify a reasonable price premium. However, over the years, the brand name carried less cachet, and as hundreds of competitors with similar products dotted the landscape, it became necessary to create valued features that would help to differentiate the product in the eyes of consumers.

Levi Strauss' financial performance is summarized in Exhibit 1 for the period from 1990 to 1994. While the company was profitable throughout the period, revenue growth had clearly slowed and income growth was quite uneven. This is especially apparent for 1994, where net income dropped by 35 percent due to fierce competition for market share and narrowing margins.

Cost Structure

Exhibit 2 provides an estimate of the cost and margins on an average pair of jeans sold through Levi's two outlets. Much of their product was sold through wholesale channels, to be distributed by competing retailers. However, Levi's maintained a chain of Original Levi's Stores (OLS) primarily to help keep them closer to the customer. The profit per pair of jeans was about 30% lower in the wholesale channel ($2 as opposed to $3). This was driven by the 30% margin that accrued to the channel, and which was somewhat balanced by the higher costs of operating the OLS outlets (especially the additional SG&A costs for operating the stores).

Exhibit 2 also indicates the ongoing investment per pair of jeans. Once this is considered, the wholesale outlets are nearly twice as profitable—the pre-tax return on invested capital is 15 percent, as opposed to 8 percent. Here, the OLS outlets required additional investment in inventory ($8/pair), which was normally borne by the retailer, and the capital tied up in the retail stores ($20/pair).

Exhibit 1	Levi Strauss Financial Performance				
	1994	**1993**	**1992**	**1991**	**1990**
Income Statement					
Net sales	$6,074,321	$5,892,479	$5,570,290	$4,902,882	$4,247,150
Cost of goods	$3,632,406	$3,638,152	$3,431,469	$3,024,330	$2,651,338
Gross Profit	$2,441,915	$2,254,327	$2,138,821	$1,878,552	$1,595,812
Selling G&A Exp	$1,472,786	$1,394,170	$1,309,352	$1,147,465	$922,785
Non Operating Income	−$18,410	$8,300	−$142,045	$31,650	−$36,403
Interest Exp	$19,824	$37,144	$53,303	$71,384	$82,956
Income Before Taxes	$930,895	$831,313	$634,121	$691,353	$553,668
Taxes	$373,402	$338,902	$271,673	$324,812	$288,753
Net Inc Before Ext Items	$557,493	$492,411	$362,448	$366,541	$264,915
Ext Items	−$236,517	$0	−$1,611	−$9,875	−$13,746
Net Income	$320,976	$492,411	$360,837	$356,666	$251,169
Growth					
Sales Growth	3.1%	5.8%	13.6%	15.4%	
Net Income Growth	−34.8%	36.5%	1.2%	42.0%	
Key Financial Ratios					
Quick ratio	1.57	1.03	0.76	0.87	0.73
SG&A/Sales	24.25	23.66	23.51	23.4	21.73
Receivables Turnover	6.68	6.87	7.67	7.31	6.88
Inventories Turnover	7.76	7.44	7.64	7.5	7.29
Total Debt/Equity	2.57	10.57	34.39	71.82	22.21
Net inc/Sales	5.28	8.36	6.48	7.27	5.91
Net inc/Total assets	8.18	15.84	12.53	13.54	10.51

Mass Customization

Mass customization uses emerging communication and computer technologies to bypass the limitations of traditional mass production methods. From a strategic standpoint, the concept is based on the idea that "the ultimate niche is a market of one."[4] Previously, it was thought that highly-customized products were necessarily expensive to produce; however, with the advent of various information technologies, meeting the customer's needs for flexibility and greater choice in the marketplace is becoming more and more economical.

> "A silent revolution is stirring in the way things are made and services are delivered. Companies with millions of customers are starting to build products designed just for you. You can, of course, buy a Dell computer assembled to your exact specifications. . . . But you can also buy pills with the exact blend of vitamins, minerals, and herbs that you like, glasses molded to fit your face precisely, CD's with music tracks that you choose, cosmetics mixed to match your skin tone, textbooks whose chapters are picked out by your professor, a loan structured to meet your financial profile, or a night at a hotel where everyone knows your favorite wine. And if your child does not like any of Mattel's 125 different Barbie dolls, she will soon be able to design her own."[5]

There is, of course, a delicate balance between providing consumers enough flexibility to meet their needs without so much that the decision-making process becomes perplexing and the company's costs spiral out of control trying to meet the customers' phantom needs.

In the early 1990s, Levi Strauss found itself facing a dual set of competitors. There were the low-cost, high-volume producers with a distinct advantage over Levi's, and there were also the higher-cost producers of jeans that targeted the affluent end of the denim-buying public. As a high-volume producer with a cost disadvantage, Levi's increasingly found itself at a disadvantage in both the upper and lower ends of the apparel market.

Personal Pair Proposal

Proponents of the Personal Pair project envisioned a niche that would allow Levi's to avoid competing against the low-cost high-volume producers. Market research revealed

Exhibit 2   Profitability Analysis of Women's Jeans

	Wholesale Channel	Original Levi's Store Channel	Personal Pair?	Notes
Operations, per pair				
Gross Revenue	$35	$50		$50 retail price with a 30% channel margin.
Less markdowns	(3)	(5)		Avg. channel markdowns of $5; 60% born by mfg.
Net Revenue	32	45		
Costs				
Cotton	5	5		
Mfg. conversion	7	7		High labor content since all jeans hand-sewn.
				Wholly owned distribution network for OLS
Distribution	9	11		channel. Add $2 for warehouse to store.
Total	21	23		
COGS				
Gross Margin	11	22		
SG&A	9[1]	19[2]		
Profit Before	$2	$3		
Tax				
Investment, per pair				
Inventory	$4	$12		77 days for Levi's wholesale channel & 240 days
				for OLS stores to include retail inventory.
Less A/P	(1)	(1)		Reflects 27 days of Accounts Payable.
Accounts	4	0		51-day collection period for wholesale. Retail
				customers pay immediately.
Receivable				
Net working capital	7	11		
Factory PP&E	5	5		Reflects a sales to fixed asset turnover of 5.33.
Distribution PP&E	1	2		Doubled for OLS channel due to additional retail
				distribution investment (estimate).
Retail Store	0	20		$2.4M/OLS store for 120,000 pairs sold/yr (est.).
Total Investment	$13	$38		
Pre-tax return on invested capital	15%	8%		

[1]At $9, a little higher than Levi's overall 25% SG&A due to supply chain problems with women's jeans.

[2]The additional $10 reflects an average 22% store expense for retail clothiers (Compact Disclosure database).

Source: Adapted from Carr, 1998.

that only a quarter of women were truly happy with the fit of their jeans, and the company hoped to attract higher-income customers who would be willing to pay a little extra for a perfect fit.

In addition, a mass customization model could lower costs as well as provide the differentiation advantage since the re-engineered process is often more efficient once new technologies are applied. For example, the mass customization model, which operates on the "pull-driven" approach of having the customer drive the production process,

would lower distribution costs and inventories of unsold products.

Personal Pair was a jeans customization program made possible through a joint venture with Custom Clothing Technology Corporation (CCTC), in Newton, Massachusetts. CCTC approached Levi Strauss, described the potential of its technology, and suggested that, together, the two companies could enter the mass customization arena.

The Personal Pair proposal reflected a form of collaborative customization. This approach helps customers who find the array of choices in the marketplace overwhelming to narrow down their specific needs. The company enters into a dialogue with customers to help them understand what they need, and is then able to provide specialized products that meet that specific need. Collaborative customizers are able to keep inventories of finished products at a minimum, which brings new products to market faster. That is, they manufacture products in a "just-in-time" fashion to respond to specific customer requests.

How It Would Work.

Original Levi's Stores (OLS) would be equipped with networked PC's and Personal Pair kiosks. Trained sales clerks would measure customers' waist, hips, rise, and inseam, resulting in one of 4,224 possible size combinations—a dramatic increase over the 40 combinations normally available to customers. The computer would then generate a code number that corresponded to one of 400 prototype pairs of jeans kept in the kiosk. Within three tries, more measurements would be taken and a perfect fit would be obtained; the customer would then pay for the jeans and opt for Federal Express delivery ($5 extra) or store pickup, with a full money-back guarantee on every pair.

The order was then sent to CCTC in Boston via a Lotus Notes computer program. This program would "translate" the order and match it with a pre-existing pattern at the Tennessee manufacturing facility. The correct pattern would be pulled, "read," and transferred to the cut station, where each pair was cut individually. A sewing line composed of eight flexible team members would process the order, it would be sent to be laundered, and it would be inspected and packed for shipping. A bar code would be sewn into each pair to simplify reordering details, and the customer would have a custom-fit pair within three weeks.

Once the program was underway, the proposal suggested that about half of the orders would be from existing customers. Reordering would be simplified and encouraged by the bar code sewn into each pair. In addition, reorders could be handled through a web-based interface.

Pricing.

There was some question about how much of a price premium the new product would command. The proposal called for a $15 premium (over the standard $50/pair off the rack) and focus groups suggested that women, in particular, would consider this a fair price to pay for superior fit. However, other's argued that this price point was a bit optimistic, suggesting that $5 or $10 might be more realistic given the lower-priced alternatives.

Planned Scope.

The initial proposal was to equip four Original Levi's Stores (OLS) with Personal Pair kiosks and specialized PCs. Once the systems were worked out, this would be expanded to more than 60 kiosks across the United States and Canada. In addition, they envisioned opening kiosks in London where they estimated that the product would command a premium of £19 over the original £46 price for standard jeans. The jeans would still be produced in Tennessee and shipped via Federal Express.

Cost Impact.

Although the new process would require some investments in technology and process changes, many other costs were projected to drop. These are illustrated by the complex supply chain for the OLS channel (Exhibit 3) and the relatively simple supply chain for the proposed Personal Pair program (Exhibit 4).

- The most obvious ongoing cost savings would be in distribution. Here, the order is transmitted electronically and the final product is shipped directly to the customer at his/her expense. These costs would be nearly eliminated in the proposed program.
- Manufacturing and raw materials would not change much since all jeans are hand sewn and would use the same materials for the traditional and mass-customized processes.
- The portion of SG&A expenses attributable to retail operations would be reduced if 50% of the sales are reorders that do not incur incremental costs in the retail stores ($5/pair savings). However, CCTC would incur its own SG&A costs that would have to be considered (about $3/pair).
- Finally, no price adjustments would be needed in such a tight channel since there would be no inventory of finished product. In the retail channel, about one-third of jeans are sold at a discount to clear out aging stock (the discounts average 30 percent).[6]

Investment Impact.

While the factory PP&E was not projected to change much (they would continue to use the same facilities), a number of other factors would impact the invested capital tied up in a pair of jeans (both positively and negatively) under the proposed program:
Increases in invested capital:

- First, there would be an initial $3 million required to integrate the systems of CCTC with Levi's existing systems. This was relatively small since it was a matter of integrating existing systems in the two companies.
- CCTC would also require additional IT investments estimated at $10/pair to maintain the system and upgrade it regularly as scale requirements increased.

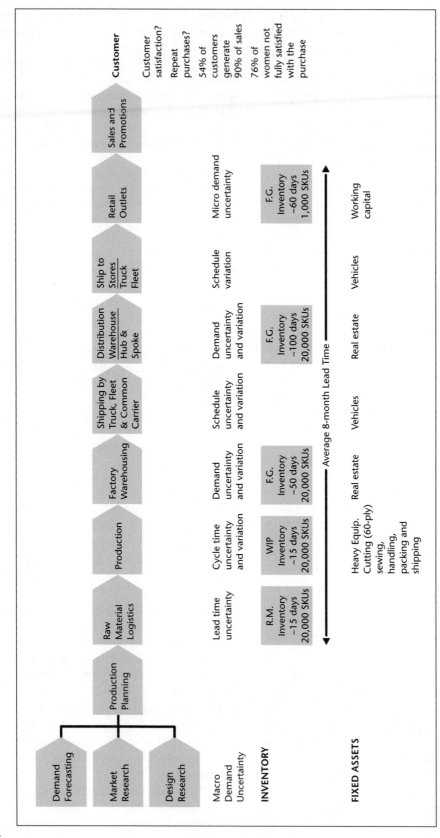

Exhibit 3 Traditional Original Levi's Store Supply Chain

Source: Adapted from Carr, 1998.

Exhibit 4 Personal Pair Value Chain

*Although this approach changes cutting from 60-ply to one, it does not otherwise change manufacturing since jeans were, and are, sewn one pair at a time.

Personal Pair kiosk in retail store → EDI link to manufacturing via CCTC → Raw material logistics → Manufacturing the one pair of jeans* → Pack pair for daily pickup at factory by FedEx → FedEx directly to customer

- In addition, the kiosks would take up about one-third of the space in the OLS retail stores (about $7/pair for retail space).

Decreases in invested capital:

- The required inventory was significantly lower under the proposed program. Recent estimates calculated Levi's average inventory at about eight months.[7] In contrast, the Personal Pair program called for no inventory of finished product and only a small inventory of raw materials (about $1/pair).
- Finally, the proposal suggested that accounts receivable would lead to a net gain of about $2/pair since customers would have paid about three weeks prior to receiving the product (similar to the Amazon.com model).

Cost-Efficient Mass Customization.   In order for a company to transform an existing product into one that is cost-efficient to mass produce, certain product modifications must be made. The Personal Pair proposal incorporated several of the key elements suggested as helpful for implementing successful mass-customization programs.[8]

First, it is important to introduce the differentiating component of the product (that which must be customized) as late in the production process as possible. For example, paint is not mixed by the manufacturer, but at the point of sale, after being demanded by individual customers. Unfortunately, the making of personalized jeans would not lend itself to a differentiating component late in the production process. Therefore, in this case, the customizing would have to take place at the beginning of the process.

Then, it is helpful if either the product or the process of manufacturing can be easily separated into production modules. Steps in the process can then be reassembled in a different order. For example, a sweater manufacturer might wait until the last possible moment to dye its products in different colors for each season, instead of dying the wool first and knitting the sweaters. This allows for much more flexibility and helps the manufacturer to keep up with fast moving fashion trends. The Personal Pair proposal suggested that the manufacturing process would be modified to allow for better flow—specifically teams would be used to allow for more flexibility and handling of custom products. Unfortunately, since elements in the jean manufacturing process do not always come together in the same way, it would be important that employees accumulate a large range of skills to accommodate idiosyncratic problems that cannot be anticipated.

Finally, it is helpful if either the products or the sub-processes in the manufacturing chain are standardized. This allows for more efficient production and inventory management, whether it be for different types of domestic uses or different markets (for example, international as well as domestic markets were served by a printer manufacturer that allowed all its printers to be adjusted for both 110/220-volt usage). Here, the Personal Pair proposal called for a complex computer program with computerized patterns that were then beamed directly to the cutting floor. This would help them to integrate some technology-enhanced sub-processes with existing standard labor-intensive manufacturing methods.

It also goes without saying that all the parts of the new mass customization process need to come together in an "instantaneous, costless, seamless and frictionless manner."[9]

The Decision.   As Heidi leaned back and gazed outside at the rain-soaked plaza, she considered the pros and cons to the proposal. The proposal carried several risks that she could not fully quantify. First, there was the ability of Levi Strauss to implement new technologies. Second, the cost savings in the proposal were based on CCTC's estimates in their proposal for the program. Would the program still be successful if the costs turned out to be very different? Third, market research indicated that women were not satisfied about fit. How much would they be willing to pay for a better fit?

On another level, she wondered about the competition. If the program were successful, would their low-cost rivals dive into this market as well? Did Levi's have any advantage here? What if they did not move forward with the proposal? Would one of their rivals partner with CCTC?

Bibliography

1. Aron, L. J. (1998). "From push to pull: The supply chain management shifts." *Apparel Industry Magazine*, 59(6), pp. 58–59.
2. (1999.) "Jeanswear gets squeezed: Plants close at Levi's." *Apparel Industry Magazine*, 60(3), p. 10.
3. Billington, J. 1997. "How to customize for the real world." *Harvard Management Update*, Reprint #U9704A.
4. Bounds, W. (1998.) "Inside Levi's race to restore a tarnished brand." *The Wall Street Journal*, August 4, p. B1.
5. Carr, L., W. Lawler, and J. Shank. (1998.) "Levi's Personal Pair cases A, B, and Teaching Note." F. W. Olin Graduate School of Business, Babson College, December, #BAB020, BAB021, and BAB520.
6. Chaplin, H. (1999.) "The truth hurts." *American Demographics*, 21(4), pp. 68–69.
7. Charlet, J-C., and E. Brynjolfsson. (1998.) "Broad vision." *Stanford University Graduate School of Business Case* #OIT-21, March.
8. Church, E. (1999.) "Personal pair didn't fit into Levi Strauss's plans." *The Globe and Mail*, May 27, p. B13.
9. Collett, S. (1999.) "Levi shuts plants, misses trends." *Computerworld*, March 1, p. 16.
10. (2001). "Keeping the customer satisfied." *The Economist*, July 14, pp. 9–10; and (2001). "Mass customization: A long march." *The Economist*, Special Report, July 14, pp. 63–65.
11. Ellison, S. (2001.) "Levi's is ironing some wrinkles out of its sales." *The Wall Street Journal*, February 12, p. B9.
12. Espen, H. (1999.) "Levi's blues." *New York Times Magazine*, March 21, p. 6.
13. Esquivel, J. R., and H. C. Belpedio. (2001). Textile and Apparel Suppliers Industry Overview, Morgan Stanley Dean Witter, March 14, pp. 1–72.
14. Feitzinger, E., and H. L. Lee. (1997). "Mass customization at Hewlett-Packard: The power of postponement." *Harvard Business Review*, January–February, Reprint #97101, pp. 116–121.
15. (2001). FITCH Company Reports, Levi Strauss and Co., February 15, www.fitchratings.com.
16. (2000). FITCH Company Reports, Levi Strauss and Co., October 31, www.fitchratings.com.
17. (1999.) FITCH Company Reports, Levi Strauss and Co., March 18, www.fitchratings.com.
18. Gilbert, C. (1998.) "Did modules fail Levi's or did Levi's fail modules?" *Apparel Industry Magazine*, 59(9), pp. 88–92.
19. Gilmore, J. H. (1997.) "The four faces of mass customization." *Harvard Business Review*, January–February, Reprint #97103, pp. 91–101.
20. Ginsberg, S. (1998.) "Ripped Levi's: Blunders, bad luck take toll." *San Francisco Business Times*, 13(18).
21. Hill, S. (1999.) "Levi Strauss and Co.: Icon in revolution." *Apparel Industry Magazine*, 60(1), pp. 66–69.
22. Hill, S. (1998.) "Levi Strauss puts a new spin on brand management." *Apparel Industry Magazine*, November, pp. 46–47.
23. Hofman, M. (1999.) "Searching for the mountain of youth." *Inc.*, 21(18), pp. 33–36.
24. Homer, E. (2001.) "Levi's zips up first ever private deal." *Private Placement Letter*, July 23.
25. Hunt, B. C., and M. O. Doehla. (1999.) *FirstUnion Industry Report*. Denim Industry, February 23.
26. Jastrow, D. (1999.) "Saying no to Web sales." *Computer Reseller News*, November 29, Issue 871, p. 73.
27. Johnson, G. (1998.) "Jeans war: Survival of the fittest." *Los Angeles Times*, December 3, p. C1.

28. King, R. T., Jr. (1998.) "Jeans therapy: Levi's factory workers are assigned to teams, and morale takes a hit." *The Wall Street Journal*, May 20, p. A1.
29. Laberis, B. (1999.) "Levi's shows it may not be driver it pretends to be." *Computerworld*, 33(15) p. 36.
30. Lee, J. (1999.) "Can Levi's ever be cool again?" *Marketing*, April 15, pp. 28-29.
31. Lee, L. (2000.) "Can Levi's be cool again?" *BusinessWeek*, March 13, pp. 144-148.
32. Levi Strauss and Company Promotional Materials.
33. Levine, B. (1999.) "Fashion fallout from the Levi Strauss layoffs." *Los Angeles Times*, March 1, p. 1.
34. Magretta, J. (1998.) "The power of virtual integration: An interview with Dell Computer's Michael Dell." *Harvard Business Review*, March–April, Reprint #98208, pp. 73-84.
35. Meadows, S. (2000.) "Levi shifts on-line strategy." *Bobbin*, 41(5), p. 8.
36. Merrill Lynch Company Report, Levi Strauss and Co., Global Securities Research and Economics Group. March 23, 2001.
37. Merrill Lynch Company Report, Levi Strauss and Co., Global Securities Research and Economics Group. January 11, 2001.
38. Merrill Lynch Company Report, Levi Strauss and Co., Global Securities Research and Economics Group. September 20, 2000.
39. Munk, N. (1999.) "How Levi's trashed a great American brand." *Fortune*, 139(7), pp. 82-90.
40. (1999.) "The view from outside: Levi's needs more than a patch." *The New York Times*, February 28, p. 4.
41. Pine, B. J. II. (1996). "Serve each customer efficiently and uniquely." *Network Transformation*, BCR, January, pp. 2-5.
42. Pine, B. J. II, B. V., and A. C. Boynton. (1993). "Making mass customization work." *Harvard Business Review*, September–October, Reprint #93509, pp. 108-116.
43. Pressler, M. W. (1998.) "Mending time at Levi's: Jeans maker struggles to recapture youth market, reshape its culture." *The Washington Post*, April 12, p. HO1.
44. Reidy, C. (1999.) "In marketplace, they're no longer such a great fit." *Boston Globe*, February 23, p. A1.
45. Reda, S. (1999.) "Internet channel conflicts." *Stores*, 81(12), pp. 24-28.
46. Robson, D. (1999.) "Levi showing new signs of fraying in San Francisco." *San Francisco Business Times*, 14(10), p. 1.
47. Rosenbush, S. (1998). "Personalizing service on Web." *USA Today*, November 16, p. 15E.
48. Schoenberger, K. (2000). "Tough jeans, a soft heart and frayed earnings." *The New York Times*, June 25, p. 3.
49. Schonfeld, E. (1998.) "The customized, digitized, have-it-your-way economy." *Fortune*, September 28.
50. Stoughton, S. (1999.) "Jeans market now a tight fit for Levi's; Denim leader missed marketing opportunities, failed to spot trends." *The Washington Post*, February 23, p. E1.
51. Trebay, G. (2001.) "What's stonewashed, ripped, mended and $2,222?" *The New York Times*, April 17, p. 10, col. 1.
52. Voight, J. (1999.) "Red, white, and blue: An American icon fades away." *Adweek*, 40(17), pp. 28-35.
53. Watson, R. T., S. Akselsen, and L. F. Pitt. (1998). "Attractors: Building mountains in the flat landscape of the World Wide Web." *California Management Review*, 40(2 Winter), pp. 36-54.
54. Zito, K. (2000.) "Levi reveals rare look at inner secrets." *San Francisco Chronicle*, May 6, p. B1.

End Notes

1. This case was prepared by Farah Mihoubi under the supervision of Associate Professor Russell Coff of the Goizueta Business School, as the basis for class discussion, rather than to illustrate either effective or ineffective management. Information assembled from published sources and interviews with company sources. Copyright 2001, by the Goizueta Business School, Case and Video Series, Atlanta, Georgia, 30322, U.S.A. All rights reserved.

2. Espen, H. (1999.) "Levi's blues." *New York Times Magazine*, March 21, p. 6.

3. Levine, B. (1999.) "Fashion fallout from the Levi Strauss layoffs." *Los Angeles Times*, March 1, p. 1.

4. Schonfeld, E. (1998.) "The customized, digitized, have-it-your-way economy." *Fortune*, September 28.

5. Ibid.

6. Carr, L., W. Lawler, and J. Shank. (1998.) "Levi's Personal Pair cases A, B, and Teaching Note." F. W. Olin Graduate School of Business, Babson College, December, #BAB020, BAB021, and BAB520.

7. Ibid.

8. Billington, J. (1997.) "How to customize for the real world" *Harvard Management Update*, Reprint #U9704A.

9. Pine, B. Joseph II. "Serve each customer efficiently and uniquely." *Network Transformation*, BCR, January 1996, pp. 2–5.

Case 2-4: Papa John's International, Inc.: Twenty-First Century Growth Challenges*

Papa John's International was a classic American success story. Founder John Schnatter had started selling pizza out of a makeshift kitchen in a small lounge in Indiana and in a little more than a decade had built a business that included more than 2,500 locations. Schnatter wanted to see Papa John's return to the days when it opened 200 to 300 stores a year. This ambition brought new challenges. The U.S. economy had changed over the two decades that Papa John's had been in business due to an aging population and to the severe economic crisis that faced the nation starting in 2008. The economy had been particularly challenging for firms serving food and drinks (see Exhibit 1). Though clearly profitable (see Exhibit 2), Papa John's had enjoyed only incremental growth in the new century. Despite the challenges, the leadership at Papa John's believed that the company had developed some important advantages that could be leveraged for high growth in either the U.S. or international markets or perhaps even in activities that went beyond pizza. The question facing Papa John's executives was which path would produce rapid but profitable growth.

Firm History and Background

Papa John's founder, John Schnatter, realized as a young person that he loved pizza more than most people, and this love was reflected in his early jobs. He started working for Rocky's Sub Pub in Jeffersonville, Indiana, as a 15-year-old high school student. While attending college, he worked for Greek's Pizzeria. Upon graduating from college in 1983, he returned home to Jeffersonville, Indiana, and began working for his father at Mick's Lounge. In 1984, Schnatter sold his prized 1972 Z28 Camaro and bought out the co-owner of Mick's Lounge. He knew that Mick's was not doing well financially, but believed that after getting Mick's to run at a profit, he might try selling pizza. Something was missing from national pizza chains, he had concluded—a superior-quality traditional pizza. After converting a broom closet in the back of Mick's Lounge to a kitchen with $1,600 worth of used restaurant

equipment, Schnatter began selling pizza to the tavern's customers.[1]

By using fresh dough and superior-quality ingredients, Schnatter believed that he could make a better pizza than others. The tavern's patrons would be brutally honest about the quality of his pizzas and provided rapid and candid feedback. Through trial and error, he created a pizza that the tavern customers loved. Once pizzas were selling well, Schnatter leased space next to Mick's Lounge and opened the first Papa John's restaurant in 1985. This was the beginning of Papa John's Pizza. Schnatter credited his father and grandfather with instilling in him the sense of pride in one's work, the importance of a strong work ethic, and the belief that a person should focus on what they do best and do it better than anyone else.[2]

When Schnatter opened his first Papa John's, his expectations were not very high. When asked about his strategy and plans for his business when he started his first Papa John's, he stated, "I never thought we'd get this big. It still baffles my mind. My original goal was to make $50,000 a year. In 1984, I dreamed of possibly owning 100 stores. I never imagined having the success we now have."[3] The first Papa John's was a sit-down restaurant. Schnatter learned that he wasn't very good at the sit-down restaurant when he tried to serve too many different items. He paid careful attention to what customers liked and did not like and adjusted his menu accordingly. Schnatter concluded "the Papa John's you know today is a function of what the customer told us they wanted. We simply listened to the customer. The customer wanted the pizza delivered. They did not want a sit-down pizza shop that served fifty other things."[4]

The company grew rapidly, opening eight stores during its first year of operation. Papa John's generated revenues of $500,000 in its first year.[5] In January 1986, Papa John's sold its first franchise. The company remained private until the initial public stock offering on June 8, 1993, under the symbol PZZA. Papa John's total revenues for the year ending in December 1992 were close to $50 million, having roughly doubled in size every year since 1986. After going public, the company experienced an accelerated domestic growth in the number of restaurants and opened its first international restaurant in 1998.

---

*This case is adapted from a report prepared by Rebekah Meier, Wade Okelberry, Odie Washington, Chad Witcher, and J. C. Woelich.

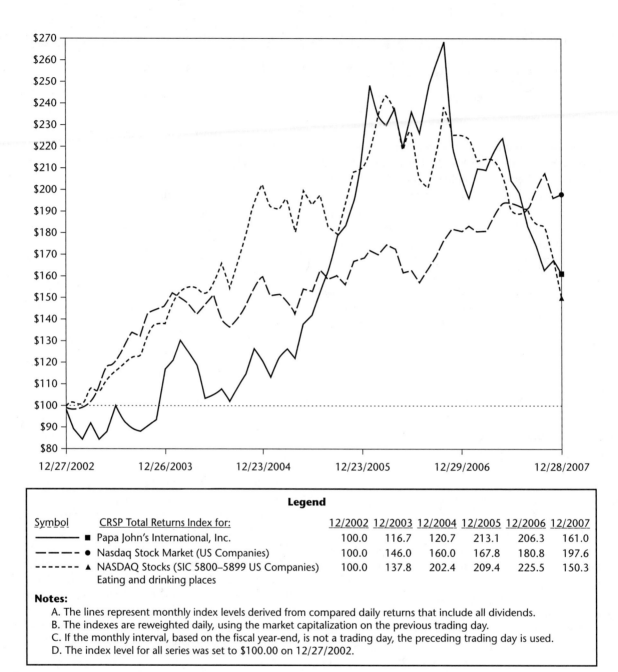

Legend

Symbol	CRSP Total Returns Index for:	12/2002	12/2003	12/2004	12/2005	12/2006	12/2007
——— ■	Papa John's International, Inc.	100.0	116.7	120.7	213.1	206.3	161.0
— — — ●	Nasdaq Stock Market (US Companies)	100.0	146.0	160.0	167.8	180.8	197.6
- - - - ▲	NASDAQ Stocks (SIC 5800–5899 US Companies) Eating and drinking places	100.0	137.8	202.4	209.4	225.5	150.3

Notes:

  A. The lines represent monthly index levels derived from compared daily returns that include all dividends.
  B. The indexes are reweighted daily, using the market capitalization on the previous trading day.
  C. If the monthly interval, based on the fiscal year-end, is not a trading day, the preceding trading day is used.
  D. The index level for all series was set to $100.00 on 12/27/2002.

Exhibit 1   Papa John's Stock Performance Compared to Peers and NASDAQ Index*
Source: Annual Report.

International growth was aided by the 205-unit acquisition of "Perfect Pizza," the quality leader for pizzas in the United Kingdom.

This domestic and international growth continued unabated until 2001, when it decreased dramatically leading to a one percent contraction in domestic growth in 2003. Since 2003, growth has been positive and relatively stable,

and Papa John's executives believed that there was significant opportunity for domestic unit growth. Papa John's was among the highest return on invested capital (ROIC) in the restaurant category. While domestic growth was anticipated to be stable, international opportunities were significantly large and promising. Papa John's had 350 domestic restaurants and 1,100 international restaurants that were

(in thousands, except per share data)	Year Ended (1)				
	Dec. 30, 2007	Dec. 31, 2006	Dec. 25, 2005	Dec. 26, 2004	Dec. 28, 2003
Income Statement Data	52 weeks	53 weeks	52 weeks	52 weeks	52 weeks
Domestic revenues:					
Company-owned restaurant sales	$ 504,330	$ 447,938	$434,525	$412,676	$ 416,049
Variable interest entities restaurant sales (2)	7,131	7,359	11,713	14,337	–
Franchise royalties (3)	55,285	56,374	52,289	50,292	49,851
Franchise and development fees	4,758	2,597	3,026	2,475	1,475
Commissary sales	399,099	413,075	398,372	376,642	369,825
Other sales	61,820	50,505	50,474	53,117	48,541
International revenues:					
Royalties and franchise and development fees (4)	10,314	7,551	6,529	5,010	3,810
Restaurant and commissary sales (5)	20,860	15,658	11,860	10,747	10,572
Total revenues	1,063,595	1,001,557	963,753	925,346	900,123
Operating income (6)	52,047	97,955	72,700	36,632	55,353
Investment income	1,446	1.682	1,248	639	672
Interest expense	(7,465)	(3,480)	(4,316)	(5,313)	(6,851)
Income from continuing operations before income taxes and cumulative effect of a change in accounting principle	46,028	96,157	69,632	32,058	49,174
Income tax expense	13,293	33,171	25,364	12,021	13,440
Income from continuing operations before income taxes and cumulative effect of a change in accounting principle	32,735	62,986	44,268	20,037	30,734
Income from discontinued operations, net of tax (7)	–	389	1,788	3,134	3,242
Cumulative effect of accounting change, net of tax (8)	–	–	–	–	(413)
Net income	$ 32,735	$ 63.375	$ 46.056	$ 23.221	$ 33,563
Basic earnings per common share:					
Income from continuing operations before cumulative effect of a change in accounting principle	$ 1.10	$ 1.95	$ 1.32	$ 0.58	$ 0.86
Income from discontinued operations, net of tax (7)	–	0.01	005	0.09	0.09
Cumulative effect of accounting change, net of tax (8)	–	–	–	–	(0.01)
Basic earnings per common share	$ 1.10	$ 1.96	$ 1.37	$ 0.67	$ 0.94
Earnings per common share—assuming dilution:					
Income from continuing operations before cumulative effect of a change in accounting principle	$ 1.09	$ 1.91	$ 1.29	$ 0.58	$ 0.85
Income from discontinued operations, net of tax (7)	–	0.01	0.05	0.09	0.09
Cumulative effect of accounting change, net of tax (8)	–	–	–	–	(0.01)
Earnings per common share—assuming dilution	$ 1.09	$ 1.92	$ 1.34	$ 0.67	$ 0.93
Basic weighted average shares outstanding	29,666	32,312	33,594	34,414	35,876
Diluted weighted average shares outstanding	30,017	33,046	34,316	34,810	36,074
Balance Sheet Data					
Total assets	$ 401,817	$ 379,639	$350,562	$374.437	$ 347,214
Total debt	142,706	97,036	55,116	94.230	61,250
Total stockholders' equity	126,003	146.168	161,279	139.223	159,272

Exhibit 2   Papa John's Financial Performance

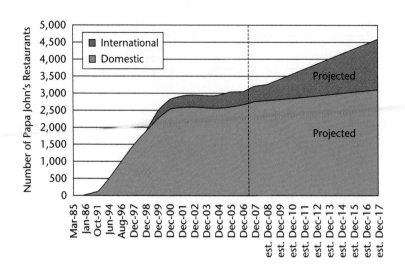

Exhibit 3 Papa John's Restaurant Growth with Projections to 2017

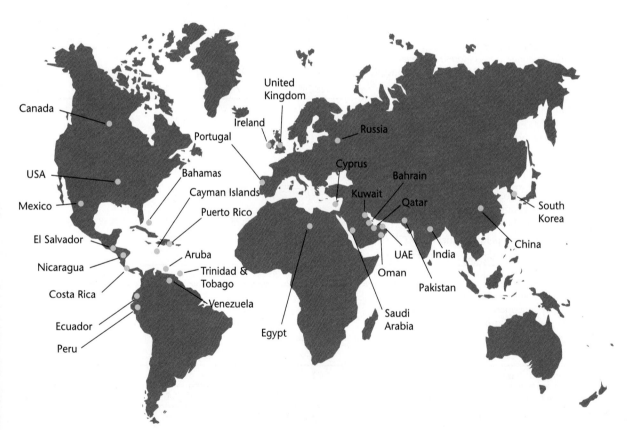

Exhibit 4 International Locations of Papa John's Restaurants

contractually scheduled to open over the next 10 years.[6] Exhibit 3 shows the historical growth of Papa John's restaurants including projected growth through 2017 and Exhibit 4 reports the current international locations of Papa John's Restaurants.

Business Structure

Papa John's had five major reportable segments of their business: domestic restaurants, domestic commissaries, domestic franchises, international operations, and variable

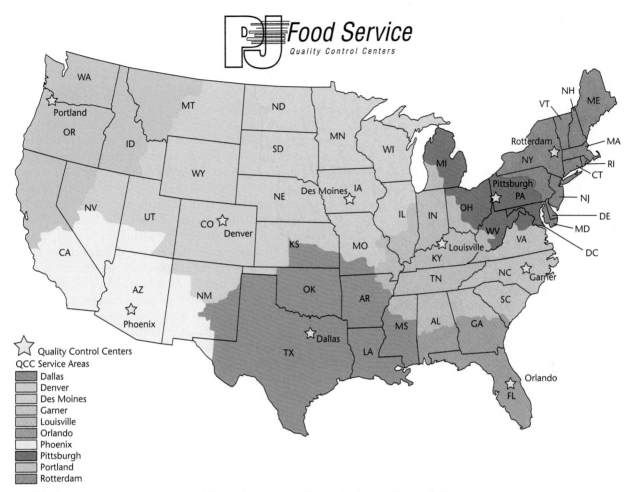

Exhibit 5   PJ Food Service Quality Control Centers Locations and Geographic Areas of Responsibility

interest entities. Domestic restaurants were restaurants that were wholly owned by Papa John's in the contiguous 48 states. Domestic franchises were restaurants in which Papa John's had licensed to franchisees for a franchise fee. These franchisee restaurants, as well as company-owned restaurants, were supported by domestic commissaries that supplied pizza dough, food products, paper products, small wares, and cleaning supplies twice weekly to each restaurant. There were 10 regional commissaries that supported domestic restaurants and franchises. The geographic locations and areas of responsibility can be seen in Exhibit 5.

An important part of Papa John's strategy revolved around the central commissary. It allowed Papa John's to exercise control over the quality and consistency of its products. When asked about the central commissary, Schnatter stated, "The commissary was added out of necessity. It did not start as a strategic decision to ensure quality. It started out of financial need. We simply did not have the money to put a mixer in every store. We had stores in Jeffersonville, Clarksville, and New Albany, so we just put a mixer in the middle store and made all the dough there. I can remember in 1987, we had a commissary, but we were doing it all by hand. We just grew into the commissary system. I wish I could say that it was a part of a grand plan that I envisioned from the time I started in the broom closet of Mick's Lounge, but it was not."[7]

The commissary system was frequently cited by industry analysts and company officials as a key factor in the success of Papa John's. The system not only reduced labor costs and reduced waste because the dough was premeasured, but it maintained control over the consistency of the product. The centralized production facility supplied all of the Papa John's stores with the same high-quality ingredients for their pizza. One of the most important aspects of this system is that it allowed Papa John's to start up more stores because they did not require additional expensive equipment to be purchased for each store. Part of the company's strategy was to expand into new markets only after a commissary had been built that could support the growth and geographical expansion of restaurants.[8]

John Schnatter stated, "Papa John's Mission Statement and Values represent the basic beliefs and purpose of the company. They are not just words printed on a piece of paper. They are truly what we believe and live here at Papa John's."[9]

Papa John's Mission Statement:

Customers: Papa John's will create superior brand loyalty, i.e. "raving fans", through (a) authentic, superior-quality products, (b) legendary customer service, and (c) exceptional community service.

Team Members: People are our most important asset. Papa John's will provide clear, consistent, strategic leadership and career opportunities for Team Members who (a) exhibit passion toward their work, (b) uphold our Core Values, (c) take pride of ownership in building the long-term value of the Papa John's brand, and (d) have ethical business practices.

Franchisees: We will partner with our franchisees to create a continued opportunity for outstanding financial returns to those franchisees who (a) adhere to Papa John's proven Core Values and systems, (b) exhibit passion in running their businesses, and (c) take pride of ownership in building the long-term value of the Papa John's brand.

Shareholders: We will produce superior long-term value for our shareholders. (www.papajohns.com)

Papa John's Core Values are the following:

Focus: We must keep The Main Thing, The Main Thing. We will consistently deliver a traditional Papa John's superior quality pizza.

Accountability: We do what we say we are going to do, when we say we are going to do it. We earn the right to hold others to a higher level of accountability by being accountable to ourselves, our customers, and our business partners.

Superiority: Our customer satisfaction must be consistent, quantifiable, and demonstrable. At Papa John's, we expect excellence—the "best in its class" in everything we do.

P.A.P.A: People Are Priority Always. Our success depends upon our ability, as a team, to work together to achieve our goals and expectations.

Attitude: If you think you can or you think you can't—you're right! The difference between winners and losers is a positive mental attitude. Our attitude is a reflection of

what we value: successful team members must be upbeat, proactive, and passionate about everything they do.

Constant Improvement: We never stop trying to surpass our previous best. We constantly "Raise the Bar." No matter how good we are, we will always get better. (www.papajohns.com)

According to Schnatter, "making a quality pizza using Better Ingredients has been the foundation of Papa John's for more than 20 years. You have my commitment that Papa John's will not stray from the foundation of quality and superiority upon which the company was built. We will always strive to be your Better Pizza Company."[10] This unwavering focus enabled Papa John's to be rated number one in customer satisfaction among all pizza chains in the American Customer Satisfaction Index for nine consecutive years from 1999 to 2008. As Schnatter had remarked in a 1997 interview, "We keep it simple, consistent, and focused. We don't keep changing what we are doing."[11] Papa John's president, USA, William Van Epps, echoed this emphasis, "While other national pizza chains have recently focused their national marketing efforts on deeply discounted or reduced-ingredients pizzas and other offerings such as pasta, I am proud of our system for remaining focused on delivering a superior-quality pizza."[12]

Papa John's core strategy was to sell a high-quality pizza for takeout or delivery. Their focus on using the highest-quality ingredients to produce a high-quality pizza was communicated in their motto: "Better Ingredients. Better Pizza." Schnatter considered it a sign of success when Pizza Hut sued Papa John's over the assertion that they had better ingredients and, therefore, a better pizza. Papa John's was ultimately successful in proving they used fresher ingredients and were, therefore, able to continue using their slogan. Papa John's stated goal was to build the strongest brand loyalty of all pizzerias internationally. Early on, Schnatter also introduced a signature bonus that served to signal the quality of the product: Each pizza was accompanied by a container of the company's special garlic sauce and two pepperoncinis.

Technology, Menu Enhancements, and Company Growth

Papa John's had long strived to be on the cutting edge of the use of technology. The company made ordering pizza even more convenient with the introduction of online ordering in 2001. It was the first pizza company to offer online ordering. Papa John's online sales grew exponentially between 2001 and 2007, with online sales growing

50 percent a year and nearly reaching $400 million in 2007. In November 2007, Papa John's led the way, once again, by offering text message ordering.[13] More than 20 percent of all Papa John's sales came online or via text. Papa John's was also using both the Internet and mobile technologies to make potential customers aware of current promotions and to allow them to easily order a pizza from virtually anywhere.

In October 2006, Papa John's introduced online ordering in Spanish in an attempt to meet growing customer needs and expectations. According to Javier Souto, Papa John's regional marketing director, "Papa John's has proven to be a technology leader in the pizza industry as the only national pizza chain to offer online ordering for all of its restaurants and now we are pleased to offer that service to our many Spanish-speaking customers."[14]

Papa John's also extended its menu. In January 2006, Papa John's announced that they were adding dessert pizzas to their carryout and delivery menus. "We created Papa's Sweetreats in direct response to consumer demand," said Catherine Hull, Papa John's vice president of strategy and brand marketing.[15] In July 2008, Papa John's introduced another permanent addition to its menu: Chocolate Pastry Delight.

Menu additions and new ways to order did not signal a change in strategy, according to company executives. Nigel Travis, president and CEO of Papa John's stated, in the company Annual Report 2007, "our stated strategy from a year ago remains unchanged. We will continue to focus on quality, growing the brand globally, and competing aggressively. It has proven the right course in a challenging economic time and has the opportunity to be even more successful as the economy rebounds." Papa John's 2007 annual report indicated that restaurants in the international arena were targeted as the company's primary source of long-term growth. Papa John's saw their use of innovative marketing, product offerings, and industry-leading technology as a major advantage over their competitors.[16]

Papa John's outlined their company strategy in their 2007 Annual Report as follows: "Our goal is to build the strongest brand loyalty of all pizzerias internationally. The key elements of our strategy include the following":

Menu. Domestic Papa John's restaurants offer a menu of high-quality pizza along with side items, including breadsticks, cheesesticks, chicken strips and wings, dessert pizza and canned or bottled soft drinks. Papa John's traditional crust pizza is prepared using fresh dough (never frozen). Papa John's pizzas are made from a proprietary blend of wheat flour, cheese made from 100% real mozzarella, fresh packed pizza sauce made from vine-ripened tomatoes (not from concentrate) and a proprietary mix of savory spices, and a choice of high-quality meat (100% beef, pork and chicken with no fillers) and vegetable toppings. Domestically, all ingredients and toppings can be purchased from our Quality Control Center ("QC Center") system, which delivers to individual restaurants twice weekly. (2007 Annual Report 1)

Internationally, the menu may be more diverse than in our domestic operations to meet local tastes and customs. In addition to our fresh dough, we offer a thin crust pizza and Papa's Perfect Pan Pizza, which features a square, thick buttery-tasting crust made with olive oil, and a zesty robusto pizza sauce with chunks of tomato and flavored with garlic, Italian herbs and spices. Both the thin and pan crusts are par-baked products produced by third-party vendors. Each traditional crust and pan pizza offers a container of our special garlic sauce and a pepperoncini pepper. Each thin crust pizza is served with a packet of special seasonings and a pepperoncini pepper. We will continue to test new product offerings both domestically and internationally. The new products can become a part of the permanent menu if they meet certain established guidelines. (2007 Annual Report 1-2)

Efficient Operating System. We believe our operating and distribution systems, restaurant layout and designated delivery areas result in lower restaurant operating costs and improved food quality, and promote superior customer service. Our domestic QC Center system takes advantage of volume purchasing of food and supplies, and provides consistency and efficiencies of scale in fresh dough production. This eliminates the need for each restaurant to order food from multiple vendors and commit substantial labor and other resources to dough preparation. (2007 Annual Report 2)

Commitment to Team Member Training and Development. We are committed to the development and motivation of our team members through training programs, incentive compensation and opportunities for advancement. Team member training programs are conducted for corporate team members, and offered to our franchisees at training locations across the United States and internationally. We offer performance-based financial incentives to corporate and restaurant team members at various levels. Our management compensation program is designed to attract and retain highly motivated people. (2007 Annual Report 2)

Marketing. Our marketing strategy consists of both national and local components. Our domestic national strategy includes national advertising on television, through print and direct mail and via the Internet. Seven national television campaigns aired in 2007 to support new product launches and DVD promotions. Our local restaurant-level marketing programs target *consumers within the delivery area of each restaurant, making extensive use of print materials including targeted direct mail and store-to-door couponing. Local marketing efforts also include a variety of community-oriented activities within schools, sports venues and other organizations. Local marketing efforts are supplemented with radio and television advertising, produced both locally and on a national basis. Additionally, we have developed joint cross-marketing plans with certain third-party companies. For example, we entered into marketing and partnership agreements with Six Flags theme parks and Live Nation amphitheaters, which provide for cross-marketing activities. We will continue to explore additional cross-marketing opportunities with third-party companies. In international markets, we target customers who live or work within a small radius of a Papa John's restaurant. Certain markets can effectively use television and radio as part of their marketing strategies. The majority of the marketing efforts include using print materials such as flyers, newspaper inserts and in-store marketing materials. Local marketing efforts, such as sponsoring or participating in community events, sporting events and school programs, are also used to build customer awareness. (2007Annual Report 2)*

Franchise System. *We are committed to maintaining and developing a strong franchise system by attracting experienced operators, supporting them to expand and grow their business and monitoring their compliance with our high standards. We seek to attract franchisees with experience in restaurant or retail operations and with the financial resources and management capability to open single or multiple locations. To ensure consistent food quality, each domestic franchisee is required to purchase dough and seasoned sauce from our QC Centers and to purchase all other supplies from our QC Centers or approved suppliers. QC Centers outside the U.S. or in remote areas may be operated by franchisees pursuant to license agreements or by other third parties. We devote significant resources to provide Papa John's franchisees with assistance in restaurant operations, management training, team member training, marketing, site selection and restaurant design. We also provide significant assistance to licensed international QC Centers in sourcing high-quality suppliers located in-country or regional suppliers to the extent possible. (2007Annual Report 2)*

Cost Management and Operational Support Systems

Papa John's Annual Report in 2007 lists net property and equipment value at $2.0 million, with most of the corporate and retail building spaces being leased. Lease payments for 2007 were $22.4 million. Papa John's subleased retail locations to franchise owners. Papa John's had expressed its intention to lower the number of corporate-owned stores by about five percent over the next few years. By selling the corporate-owned stores to franchisees, Papa John's was expected to lower its net lease payment from $24.0 million in 2008 to $9.4 million in 2012. Leasing building space gave Papa John's the flexibility to move locations quickly with minimal cost, should a profitable location turn bad.

Papa John's also leased the trailers used to distribute ingredients from the commissary centers to the retail locations, typically on an eight-year lease agreement. By leasing the trailers, it allowed Papa John's to manage their shipping logistics and costs in a structured manner while not requiring them to maintain the trailers as they aged.

As Papa John's Pizza started to grow, Schnatter recognized the importance of sharing his passion for pizza with others in his company. The Operation Support Service and Training (OSST) Center was created and was actively engaged in the training and development of "team" members. In order to instill his passion into his new franchisees and corporate employees, Schnatter had them complete a management training program at the OSST Center when they started with the company. The aim of this training was to help franchise owners be successful and to instill in them a firm understanding of the Papa John's culture. By making a franchisee feel like they were in a partnership with Papa John's, it facilitated a level of buy-in that the company believed was seldom found in restaurant chains.

Throughout Papa John's tremendous growth during its first 10 years of operation, its marketing programs targeted the delivery area of each restaurant, primarily through direct mailings and direct store-to-door couponing. In an effort to improve the marketing campaign, John Schnatter realized that he needed to find a printing company that could offer consistent high-quality service at a reasonable price. In the mid-1990s, Schnatter found a printer who met his expectations better than most. The decision to vertically integrate into the business of printing was made. The franchise owners were not required to use the in-house printing service. The in-house printing operation was required to earn the business of each franchisee. In an effort to keep costs low within the printing division, Papa John's regularly accepted outside print jobs. It was not uncommon to print a flyer for a real estate company between jobs for a Papa John's franchise. In additional efforts to keep costs low, the printing presses were operated 24 hours a day.

From its beginning, Papa John's had been active in community affairs, from supporting local sports teams with fund-raising opportunities, to offering college scholarships. Papa John's had awarded more than $5 million in college scholarships. Papa John's actively supported the National FFA, Cerebral Palsy K.I.D.S. Center, and Children's Miracle Network, to name only a few. Papa John's executives believed that giving back to the community was good business.

Papa John's had entered into numerous marketing partnerships over the years. For example, Papa John's aligned with Coca-Cola to offer only Coke products in their stores through 2011. When Papa John's added a pan pizza to its menu, they enlisted the aid of former Miami Dolphins quarterback Dan Marino. At the time, this was the most intensive new product launch ever undertaken by Papa John's. Another combined effort for Papa John's involved coordinating with eBay for a limited edition Superman pan pizza box. In Kentucky, Papa John's and Blockbuster video combined efforts in a "take dinner and a movie online" in which the customer would receive a free 30-day trial of Blockbuster online with an online pizza purchase at papajohns.com.

By using a combination of internal and external resources, Papa John's was determined to not compete with its competition on price. Focusing on a quality product, active participation in the local communities in which they operated, and product branding enabled Papa John's to hold its own with the other pizza chains. Papa John's has worked to create a product branded in such a way that customers came to expect the very best pizza; and they were willing to pay a premium price. Papa John's was committed to holding firm on the quality and prices of their pizzas.

The Restaurant Industry and Pizza Segment

The restaurant industry had historically been very attractive to entrepreneurs. Most of these new entrants opened single locations. The relatively low capital requirements made the restaurant business very attractive to small-scale entrepreneurs. Some of these businesses succeeded, but there was an intense amount of competition. There were relatively high fixed costs associated with entering into the restaurant business. These factors caused many of the new businesses to fail. However, for the businesses that succeeded, the payback on the investment could be quite high. After sales reached the break-even point, a relatively high percentage of incremental revenues became profit.

Restaurant analysts were generally amazed at how successfully Schnatter built Papa John's. Michael Fineman, a restaurant analyst with Raymond James in St. Petersburg, Florida, stated, "here's an industry that appears to be mature and saturated, and here comes John Schnatter with his company Papa John's. He has proven to be a fantastic visionary."[17]

Large restaurant chains, like Papa John's, were able to realize economies of scale that have made competition extremely difficult for small operators. Some of these advantages included purchasing power in negotiating food and packaging supply contracts, as well as real estate purchasing, location selection, menu development, and marketing.

Papa John's operated in the highly competitive pizza restaurant market, where the cost of entry was relatively low and product differentiation was difficult. Other pizza chains tried to compete in ways other than Papa John's emphasis. Some chains focused on being less expensive or having a broad menu. According to the *S&P Industry Surveys*, "in 2007, the pizza chain segment struggled to find the right balance of promotions and pricing to keep both customers and profits. The pizza category is also suffering from a longer-term trend, in which the growth of take-out food capabilities at full service restaurants and the creation of more diversified menus at fast-food competitors have given consumers other options. In response, competition among pizza chains has recently centered on new product offerings, such as pasta and desserts. The segment has also pulled back on heavily price-based promotions that have dominated the marketing messages in recent years." The meal options available for consumers were increasing both for convenience dining and at-home consumption. The quality of frozen pizza available at grocery stores had improved significantly in recent years. A broader trend was that restaurant and quick-service restaurant dinner occasions were declining, which was significant for pizza restaurants such as Papa John's, which gained 70 percent of its sales from dinner orders. Declining restaurant and quick-service restaurant dining was attributed to an increase in at-home dinner preparation, linked to a decline in the percentage of women in the workforce.[18]

The large number of restaurant types throughout North America made it unlikely that any firm would gain a competitive advantage by offering one style or type of cuisine. The one principle that made Papa John's rare in the restaurant industry was their ongoing passion to offer the perfect pizza. Many companies claimed to place quality at the forefront of their business, but often the commitment to quality went no deeper than public relations and was not a core value.

Papa John's commitment to the highest-quality ingredients created challenges in managing the supply of the foods that went into its pizza. The volatility in the price of cheese had been a major problem for Papa John's. Cheese material costs contribute approximately 35 to 40 percent of Papa John's restaurants' food costs. In order to reduce the cheese price volatility, Papa John's partnered with a third-party entity formed by franchisees, BIBP Commodities, Inc., whose sole purpose was to reduce cheese price volatility to domestic system wide restaurants. This allowed Papa John's to purchase cheese from BIBP at a fixed quarterly price. Profits and losses from BIBP were then passed on to Papa John's.[19]

Rising costs challenged pizza restaurants in multiple areas. According to the *S&P Industry Surveys*, labor costs, as well as food commodity costs, were rising in the industry. "Although restaurants are experiencing cost increases for labor, utilities, and transportation, perhaps no other factor has prompted restaurants to increase their prices in 2008 more than food commodity cost inflation." Food commodity prices increased in excess of 20 percent from June 2007 to June 2008. Rising energy costs had a dual impact on Papa John's and its competitors. Food prices of products related to corn were increasing even more rapidly because of corn's use as an alternative fuel. Additionally, in-store utility costs and delivery driver fuel costs had experienced dramatic increases in 2007 and 2008. Another area of rising costs stemmed from legislation at the federal level as well as many states that mandated a higher minimum wage.

Many companies, including Papa John's, engaged in forward pricing to stabilize food costs. "Forward pricing is a hedging strategy whereby a company negotiates with a supplier to purchase a certain amount of a product at a given price. Some supply contracts, signed by larger chains, can lock in less volatile food products for an entire year. Some of the products subject to the greatest variability, especially dairy products, can be locked in only for shorter periods."[20] Papa John's created a separate variable interest entity, BIBP Commodities, Inc., for the sole purpose of reducing cheese price volatility for its U.S. restaurants.

The *S&P Industry Survey* referred to 2007 and 2008 as a "perfect storm" of events in the industry. "Based on recent corporate actions taken in response to current weak industry conditions, we have a sense of growing crisis within the industry."[21] According to the survey, it is clear that there has been "deterioration from last fall, when we noted that the high price of gasoline and concerns about the U.S. housing market had forced many consumers to scale back the portion of the household budget allocated toward dining out. In addition to these still-serious issues, we must add an increasingly challenging outlook for restaurants' food and labor costs to the mix." Some analysts forecasted that 2009 would be the "most challenging environment ever faced by the modern restaurant industry."[22]

Analysts expected the weakest sales performances by the domestic restaurant industry in nearly four decades.

Another important factor that was affecting the restaurant industry was a decline in travel. In mid-2008, economists expected further declines in travel. With less travel, fewer people dined out while on vacation or on business trips.

Of the $200.3 billion restaurant market, the pizza segment currently held 6.7 percent of the market. Pizza Hut, a division of Yum! Brands, Inc., was the leader (U.S. sales of $5.4 billion in 2007), followed by Domino's Pizza, Inc. ($3.2 billion), Papa John's International, Inc. ($2.0 billion), and Little Caesars (a division of Ilitch Holdings, Inc., about $1.2 billion). Each was a large, nationally known pizza provider. These four accounted for 88 percent of the aggregate sales in the pizza chain restaurant segment; each was significantly larger than the #5 chain Chuck E. Cheese's (operated by CEC Entertainment, Inc., about $570 million).

Economic trends played an important role in the number of consumers that dined out. When asked about the tough economic times the country faced in late 2008 and the effect it would have on Papa John's, Schnatter stated, "it is a tough time for our country. In the 90s we were seeing really good growth in this industry; however, the industry has softened and it has gotten very competitive. I foresee some pizza casualties in the future and it may be hard for some to survive. I think if the trend continues that we have seen over the last eighteen months, it is going to be tough on everybody. I think there are going to be a lot of people out there closing up shop." Schnatter continued by saying, "I think it's going to be a real test for all the operators in our category to see who is up to the task and who is not. We are going to separate the men from the boys, really quickly."[23]

Papa John's Looking Forward

In May 2007, John Schnatter stepped down as the executive chairman of Papa John's to serve just as the head of the board of directors. In this new role, he planned to remain as spokesman for the company with no cash compensation, just stock options. Schnatter stated, "with Nigel Travis having led the company for the last two years as president and CEO, and the strength of our Board and the management team supporting him, the time is right for me to pull back a bit from the day-to-day operation of the company. I'm fine working for stock options alone—that way, I get compensated only if the rest of the shareholders win through a stock price increase."[24]

Schnatter was optimistic about the future of Papa John's. He wanted to see Papa John's get back on the path of opening 200 to 300 stores per year. Over the next five years, he wanted to see Papa John's reach the 4,000 store mark, and long term, he aspired to see 6,000 to 7,000 stores worldwide.[25] Papa John's also sought to reduce the number of company-run stores by turning them into franchising opportunities. At the end of 2007, Papa John's owned approximately 680 locations, while the rest were franchised. Franchising more of its current company-run stores offered Papa John's some important benefits. Franchise royalties were based on a percentage of sales and not on a percentage of profits, which allowed Papa John's to ensure a steady stream of revenue even in a difficult operating environment.

Papa John's had several options at its disposal. Among them were international market expansion, increased domestic market penetration, and related diversification (primarily via strategic acquisitions). The case for international expansion was based on the conclusion that the U.S. pizza industry (and quick-serve restaurant industry in general) had matured and that the most significant growth opportunities were beyond U.S. borders. Pizza Hut benefited from a first-mover advantage in several, if not most, attractive international markets. Historically, Papa John's international efforts centered in Mexico, Canada, the United Kingdom, the Middle East, and Asia. Some believed that Asian markets would generally favor quality-centered business models due to higher preferences for quality. Another favorable trend in these markets was a growing income base for the local population.

In building its international infrastructure, the company would need to cultivate new relationships and develop new skills. One critical element was the company's ability to continue to partner with local producers in order to maintain tight quality control and keep ingredients fresh. In terms of new skills, Papa John's needed to develop the ability to modify its standard smaller carry-out restaurant blueprint. Looking at the success of firms such as McDonald's or Yum! Brands, Inc.'s Kentucky Fried Chicken, there was persuasive evidence that international customers tended to view their eating-out experience as more of a formal dining event. Thus, the standard Papa John's takeout restaurant model would need to be expanded to accommodate a sit-down dining area for patrons.

In addition to expanding internationally, Papa John's sought to grow and maintain its domestic market share. Traditionally, restaurants did this by adding new menu items, or introducing a value selection such as McDonald's dollar menu, or Little Caesars' Hot-N-Ready $5 pizza offering. For Papa John's, these strategies presented the risk of overextending its menu and, consequently, reducing its overall brand quality, or ability to charge premium prices.

Extending the company's co-branding efforts was another possible avenue for domestic growth. For example, Papa John's partnered with firms such as Nestle to provide some of its dessert menu offerings. There were a vast number of co-branding opportunities that were, in theory at least, possible.

A third alternative for Papa John's involved diversifying from pizza. For example, Papa John's could develop or acquire an additional restaurant chain under a different brand. Such an approach would allow Papa John's to compete in another restaurant category without fear of diluting its quality brand. Other competitors in the industry had operated chains in multiple categories. McDonald's, for example, had invested in Chipotle Mexican Grill and Boston Market before disposing of its investments in 2006 and 2007, respectively. Yum! Brands, Inc. operated Pizza Hut, Taco Bell, Kentucky Fried Chicken, and A&W. With the growing influence of the Hispanic population and culture in the United States, some believed that a Hispanic/Mexican-themed restaurant would allow the company to benefit from this trend without impairing the Papa John's franchise.

End Notes

1. Interview with John Schnatter, October 2008.
2. Interview with John Schnatter, October 2008.
3. Ibid.
4. Ibid.
5. Hoover's Profiles. Papa John's International, Inc.
6. UBS London Investor Meeting on August 22, 2008.
7. Interview with John Schnatter, October 2008.
8. Hoover's Profiles. Papa John's International, Inc.
9. Interview with John Schnatter, October 2008.
10. Ibid.
11. Walkup, C. (1997.) "John Schnatter." *Food Industry*, January . . .

12. Papa John's Press Release, May 20, 2008.
13. (2007). *Pizza Today*, November 19.
14. (2006). *Pizza Today*, October 16.
15. (2006). *Pizza Today*, January 17.
16. Papa John's International, Inc. Annual Report 2007.
17. Walkup, C. (1997.) "John Schnatter." *Food Industry*, January.
18. UBS Investor Meeting on August 22, 2008.
19. Ibid.
20. Standard & Poor's Industry Surveys, September 4, 2008.
21. Ibid.
22. Ibid.
23. Interview with John Schnatter, October 2008.
24. Papa John's Press Release, May 14, 2007.
25. Interview with John Schnatter, October 2008.

3 CORPORATE STRATEGIES

6

Vertical Integration

After reading this chapter, you should be able to:

1. Define vertical integration, forward vertical integration, and backward vertical integration.

2. Discuss how vertical integration can create value by reducing the threat of opportunism.

3. Discuss how vertical integration can create value by enabling a firm to exploit its valuable, rare, and costly-to-imitate resources and capabilities.

4. Discuss how vertical integration can create value by enabling a firm to retain its flexibility.

5. Describe conditions under which vertical integration may be rare and costly to imitate.

6. Describe how the functional organization structure, management controls, and compensation policies are used to implement vertical integration.

Outsourcing Research

First it was simple manufacturing—toys, dog food, and the like—that was outsourced to Asia. This was OK, because even though manufacturing could be outsourced to China and India, the real value driver of the Western economy—services—could never be outsourced. Or at least that was what we thought.

And then firms started outsourcing call centers, and tax preparation, and travel planning, and a host of other services to India and the Philippines. Anything that could be done on a phone or online, it seemed, could be done cheaper in Asia. Sometimes, the quality of the service was compromised, but with training and additional technological development, maybe even these problems could be addressed. And this was OK, because the real value driver of the Western economy—research and intellectual property—could never be outsourced. Or at least that was what we thought.

Now, it turns out that some leading Western pharmaceutical firms—including Merck, Eli Lilly, and Johnson and Johnson—have begun outsourcing some critical aspects of the pharmaceutical research and development process to pharmaceutical firms in India. This seemed impossible just a few years ago.

In the 1970s, India announced that it would not honor pharmaceutical patents. This policy decision had at least two important implications for the pharmaceutical industry in India. First, it led to the founding of thousands of generic drug manufacturers there—firms that reverse engineered patented drugs produced by U.S. and Western European pharmaceutical companies and then sold them on world markets for a fraction of their original price. Second, virtually no pharmaceutical research and development took place in India. After all, why spend all the time and money needed to develop a new drug when generic drug firms would instantly reverse engineer your technology and undercut your ability to make a profit?

All this changed in 2003 when the Indian government reversed its policies and began honoring pharmaceutical patents. Now, for the first time in over two decades, Indian firms could tap into their pool of highly educated scientists and engineers and begin engaging in original research. But, developing the skills needed to do world-class pharmaceutical research on your own is difficult and time-consuming. So, Indian firms began searching for potential partners in the West.

In the beginning, Western pharmaceutical companies outsourced only very routine lab work to their new Indian

partners. But many of these firms found that their Indian partners were well managed, with potentially significant technical capability, and willing to do more research-oriented kinds of work. Since 2007, a surprisingly large number of Western pharmaceutical firms have begun outsourcing progressively more important parts of the research and development process to their Indian partners.

And what do the Western firms get out of this outsourcing? Not surprisingly—low costs. It costs about $250,000 per year to employ an outsourced Ph.D. chemist in the West. That same $250,000 buys five such scientists in India. Five times as many scientists means that pharmaceutical firms can develop and test more compounds faster by working with their Indian partners than they could do on their own. The mantra in the pharmaceutical industry—"fail fast and cheap"—is more easily realized when much of the early testing of potential drugs is done in India and not the West.

Of course, testing compounds developed by Western firms is not exactly doing basic research in pharmaceuticals. It will never be possible to outsource this central driver of the Western economy. Or will it?

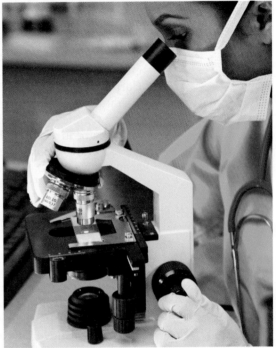

Sources: M. Kripalani and P. Engardio. (2003). "The rise of India." *BusinessWeek*, December 8, pp. 66 +; K. J. Delaney. (2003). "Outsourcing jobs—and workers—to India." *The Wall Street Journal*, October 13, pp. B1 +; B. Eihhorn. (2006). "A dragon in R&D." *BusinessWeek*, November 6, pp. 44 +; and P. Engardio and A. Weintraub. (2008). "Outsourcing the drug industry." *BusinessWeek*, September 5, 2008, pp. 48–52; Peter Arnold, Inc.

The decision to hire an offshore company to accomplish a specific business function is an example of a decision that determines the level of a firm's vertical integration. This is the case whether the company that is hired to perform these services is located in the United States or India.

What Is Corporate Strategy?

Vertical integration is the first corporate strategy examined in detail in this book. As suggested in Chapter 1, **business strategy** is a firm's theory of how to gain competitive advantage in a single business or industry. The two business strategies discussed in this book are cost leadership and product differentiation. **Corporate strategy** is a firm's theory of how to gain competitive advantage by operating in several businesses simultaneously. Decisions about whether to vertically integrate often determine whether a firm is operating in a single business or industry or in multiple businesses or industries. Other corporate strategies discussed in this book include strategic alliances, diversification, and mergers and acquisitions.

What Is Vertical Integration?

The concept of a firm's value chain was first introduced in Chapter 3. As a reminder, a **value chain** is that set of activities that must be accomplished to bring a product or service from raw materials to the point that it can be sold to a final customer. A simplified value chain of the oil and gas industry, originally presented in Figure 3.2, is reproduced in Figure 6.1.

A firm's level of **vertical integration** is simply the number of steps in this value chain that a firm accomplishes within its boundaries. Firms that are more vertically integrated accomplish more stages of the value chain within their boundaries than firms that are less vertically integrated. A more sophisticated approach to measuring the degree of a firm's vertical integration is presented in the Strategy in Depth feature.

A firm engages in **backward vertical integration** when it incorporates more stages of the value chain within its boundaries and those stages bring it closer to the beginning of the value chain; that is, closer to gaining access to raw materials. When computer companies developed all their own software, they were engaging in backward vertical integration, because these actions are close to the beginning of the value chain. When they began using independent companies operating in India to develop this software, they were less vertically integrated backward.

A firm engages in **forward vertical integration** when it incorporates more stages of the value chain within its boundaries and those stages bring it closer to the end of the value chain; that is, closer to interacting directly with final customers. When companies staffed and operated their own call centers in the United States, they were engaging in forward vertical integration, because these activities brought them closer to the ultimate customer. When they started using independent companies in India to staff and operate these centers, they were less vertically integrated forward.

Of course, in choosing how to organize its value chain, a firm has more choices than whether to vertically integrate or not vertically integrate. Indeed,

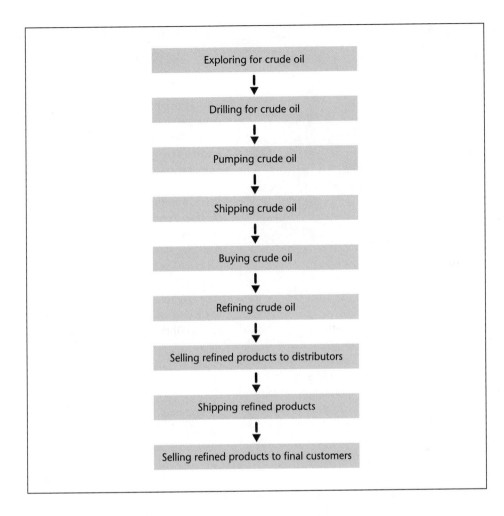

Figure 6.1 A Simplified Value Chain of Activities in the Oil and Gas Industry

between these two extremes a wide range of somewhat vertically integrated options exist. These alternatives include various types of strategic alliances and joint ventures, the primary topic of Chapter 9.

The Value of Vertical Integration

The question of vertical integration—which stages of the value chain should be included within a firm's boundaries and why—has been studied by many scholars for almost 100 years. The reason this question has been of such interest was first articulated by Nobel Prize–winning economist Ronald Coase. In a famous article originally published in 1937, Coase asked a simple question: Given how efficiently markets can be used to organize economic exchanges among thousands, even hundreds of thousands, of separate individuals, why would markets, as a method for managing economic exchanges, ever be replaced by firms? In markets, almost as if by magic, Adam Smith's "invisible hand" coordinates the quantity and quality of goods and services produced with the quantity and quality of goods and services demanded through the adjustment of prices—all without a centralized controlling authority. However, in firms, centralized bureaucrats

Strategy in Depth

It is sometimes possible to observe which stages of the value chain a firm is engaging in, and thus the level of that firm's vertical integration. Sometimes, however, it is more difficult to directly observe a firm's level of vertical integration. This is especially true when a firm believes that its level of vertical integration is a potential source of competitive advantage. In this case, the firm would not likely reveal this information freely to competitors.

In this situation, it is possible to get a sense of the degree of a firm's vertical integration—though not a complete list of the steps in the value chain integrated by the firm—from a close examination of the firm's **value added as a percentage of sales**. Valued added as a percentage of sales measures that percentage of a firm's sales that is generated by activities done within the boundaries of a firm. A firm

Measuring Vertical Integration

with a high ratio between value added and sales has brought many of the value-creating activities associated with its business inside its boundaries, consistent with a high level of vertical integration. A firm with a low ratio between value added and sales does not have, on average, as high a level of vertical integration.

Value added as a percentage of sales is computed using the following equation in Exhibit 1.

The sum of net income and income taxes is subtracted in both the numerator and the denominator in this equation to control for inflation and changes in the tax code over time. Net income, income taxes, and sales can all be taken directly from a firm's profit-and-loss statement. Value added can be calculated using the equation in Exhibit 2.

Again, most of the numbers needed to calculate value added can be found either in a firm's profit-and-loss statement or in its balance sheet.

Sources: A. Laffer. (1969). "Vertical integration by corporations: 1929–1965." *Review of Economics and Statistics,* 51, pp. 91–93; I. Tucker and R. P. Wilder. (1977). "Trends in vertical integration in the U.S. manufacturing sector." *Journal of Industrial Economics,* 26, pp. 81–94; and K. Harrigan. (1986). "Matching vertical integration strategies to competitive conditions." *Strategic Management Journal,* 7, pp. 535–555.

Exhibit 1

$$\text{vertical integration}_i = \frac{\text{value added}_i - (\text{net income}_i + \text{income taxes}_i)}{\text{sales}_i - (\text{net income}_i + \text{income taxes}_i)}$$

where,

$\text{vertical integration}_i$ = the level of vertical integration for firm$_i$

value added_i = the level of value added for firm$_i$

net inform_i = the level of net income for firm$_i$

income taxes_i = firm$_i$'s income taxes

sales_i = firm$_i$'s sales

Exhibit 2

value added = depreciation + amortization + fixed charges + interest expense + labor and related expenses + pension and retirement expenses + income taxes + net income (after taxes) + rental expense

monitor and control subordinates who, in turn, battle each other for "turf" and control of inefficient internal "fiefdoms." Why would the "beauty" of the invisible hand ever be replaced by the clumsy "visible hand" of the modern corporation?[1]

Coase began to answer his own question when he observed that sometimes the cost of using a market to manage an economic exchange must be higher than the cost of using vertical integration and bringing an exchange within the boundary of a firm. Over the years, efforts have focused on identifying the conditions under which this would be the case. The resulting work has described several different situations where vertical integration can either increase a firm's revenues or decrease its costs compared to not vertically integrating; that is, several situations where vertical integration can be valuable. The following sections present three of the most influential of these explanations of when vertical integration can create value for a firm.

Vertical Integration and the Threat of Opportunism

One of the best-known explanations of when vertical integration can be valuable focuses on using vertical integration to reduce the threat of opportunism.[2] **Opportunism** exists when a firm is unfairly exploited in an exchange. Examples of opportunism include when a party to an exchange expects a high level of quality in a product it is purchasing, only to discover it has received a lower level of quality than it expected; when a party to an exchange expects to receive a service by a particular point in time and that service is delivered late (or early); and when a party to an exchange expects to pay a price to complete this exchange and its exchange partner demands a higher price than what was previously agreed to.

Obviously, when one of its exchange partners behaves opportunistically, this reduces the economic value of a firm. One way to reduce the threat of opportunism is to bring an exchange within the boundary of a firm, that is, to vertically integrate into this exchange. This way, managers in a firm can monitor and control this exchange instead of relying on the market to manage it. If the exchange that is brought within the boundary of a firm brings a firm closer to its ultimate suppliers, it is an example of backward vertical integration. If the exchange that is brought within the boundary of a firm brings a firm closer to its ultimate customer, it is an example of forward vertical integration.

Of course, firms should only bring market exchanges within their boundaries when the cost of vertical integration is less than the cost of opportunism. If the cost of vertical integration is greater than the cost of opportunism, then firms should not vertically integrate into an exchange. This is the case for both backward and forward vertical integration decisions.

So, when will the threat of opportunism be large enough to warrant vertical integration? Research has shown that the threat of opportunism is greatest when a party to an exchange has made transaction-specific investments. A **transaction-specific investment** is any investment in an exchange that has significantly more value in the current exchange than it does in alternative exchanges. Perhaps the easiest way to understand the concept of a transaction-specific investment is through an example.

Consider the economic exchange between an oil refining company and an oil pipeline building company, which is depicted in Figure 6.2. As can be seen in the figure, this oil refinery is built on the edge of a deep-water bay. Because of this, the refinery has been receiving supplies of crude oil from large tanker ships. However, an oil field exists several miles distant from the refinery, but the only way to

Figure 6.2 The Exchange Between an Oil Refinery and an Oil Pipeline Company

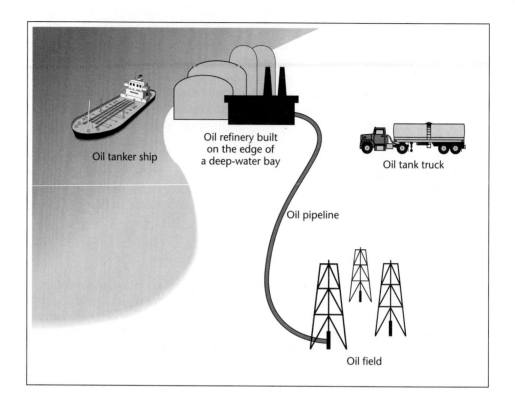

Oil tanker ship

Oil refinery built on the edge of a deep-water bay

Oil tank truck

Oil pipeline

Oil field

transport crude oil from the oil field to the refinery is with trucks—a very expensive way to move crude oil, especially compared to large tankers. But if the oil refining company could find a way to get crude oil from this field cheaply, it would probably make this refinery even more valuable.

Enter the pipeline company. Suppose this pipeline company approaches the refinery and offers to build a pipeline from the oil field to the refinery. In return, all the pipeline company expects is for the refinery to promise to buy a certain number of barrels of crude at an agreed-to price for some period of time, say, five years, through the pipeline. If reasonable prices can be negotiated, the oil refinery is likely to find this offer attractive, for the cost of crude oil carried by the pipeline is likely to be lower than the cost of crude oil delivered by ship or by truck. Based on this analysis, the refinery and the oil pipeline company are likely to cooperate and the pipeline is likely to be built.

Now, five years go by, and it is time to renegotiate the contract. Which of these two firms has made the largest transaction-specific investments? Remember that a transaction-specific investment is any investment in an exchange that is more valuable in that particular exchange than in alternative exchanges.

What specific investments has the refinery made? Well, how much is this refinery worth if this exchange with the pipeline company is not renewed? Its value would probably drop some, because oil through the pipeline is probably cheaper than oil through ships or trucks. So, if the refiner doesn't use the pipeline any longer, it will have to use these alternative supplies. This will reduce its value some—say, from $1 million to $900,000. This $100,000 difference is the size of the transaction-specific investment made by the refining company.

However, the transaction-specific investment made by the pipeline firm is probably much larger. Suppose the pipeline is worth $750,000 as long as it is pumping oil to the refinery. But if it is not pumping oil, how much is it worth? Not very much. An oil pipeline that is not pumping oil has limited alternative uses. It has value either as scrap or (perhaps) as the world's largest enclosed water slide. If the value of the pipeline is only $10,000 if it is not pumping oil to the refinery, then the level of transaction specific investment made by the pipeline firm is substantially larger than that made by the firm that owns the refinery: $750,000 − $10,000, or $740,000 for the pipeline company, versus $100,000 for the refining company.

So, which company is at greater risk of opportunism when the contract is renegotiated—the refinery or the pipeline company? Obviously, the pipeline company has more to lose. If it cannot come to an agreement with the oil refining company, it will lose $740,000. If the refinery cannot come to an agreement with the pipeline company, it will lose $100,000. Knowing this, the refining company can squeeze the pipeline company during the renegotiation by insisting on lower prices or more timely deliveries of higher-quality crude oil, and the pipeline company really cannot do much about it.

Of course, managers in the pipeline firm are not stupid. They know that after the first five years of their exchange with the refining company they will be in a very difficult bargaining position. So, in anticipation, they will insist on much higher prices for building the oil pipeline in the first place than would otherwise be the case. This will drive up the cost of building the pipeline, perhaps to the point that it is no longer cheaper than getting crude oil from ships. If this is the case, then the pipeline will not be built, even though if it could be built and the threat of opportunism eliminated both the refining company and the pipeline company would be better off.

One way to solve this problem is for the oil refining company to buy the oil pipeline company—that is, for the oil refinery to backward vertically integrate.[3] When this happens, the incentive for the oil refinery to exploit the vulnerability of the pipeline company will be reduced. After all, if the refinery business tries to rip off the pipeline business, it only hurts itself, because it owns the pipeline business.

This, then, is the essence of opportunism-based explanations of when vertical integration creates value: Transaction-specific investments make parties to an exchange vulnerable to opportunism, and vertical integration solves this vulnerability problem. Using language developed in Chapter 3, this approach suggests that vertical integration is valuable when it reduces threats from a firm's powerful suppliers or powerful buyers due to any transaction-specific investments a firm has made.

Vertical Integration and Firm Capabilities

A second approach to vertical integration decisions focuses on a firm's capabilities and its ability to generate sustained competitive advantages.[4] This approach has two broad implications. First, it suggests that firms should vertically integrate into those business activities where they possess valuable, rare, and costly-to-imitate resources and capabilities. This way, firms can appropriate at least some of the profits that using these capabilities to exploit environmental opportunities will create. Second, this approach also suggests that firms should not vertically integrate into business activities where they do not possess the resources necessary to gain competitive advantages. Such vertical integration decisions would not be a source of profits to a firm, because they do not possess any of the valuable, rare, or costly-to-imitate resources needed to gain competitive advantages in these business activities. Indeed, to the extent that some other firms have competitive advantages in these business activities, vertically integrating into them could put a firm at a competitive disadvantage.

This, then, is the essence of the capabilities approach to vertical integration: If a firm possesses valuable, rare, and costly-to-imitate resources in a business activity, it should vertically integrate into that activity; otherwise, no vertical integration. This perspective can sometimes lead to vertical integration decisions that conflict with decisions derived from opportunism-based explanations of vertical integration.

Consider, for example, firms acting as suppliers to Wal-Mart. Wal-Mart has a huge competitive advantage in the discount retail industry. In principle, firms that sell to Wal-Mart could vertically integrate forward into the discount retail market to sell their own products. That is, these firms could begin to compete against Wal-Mart. However, such efforts are not likely to be a source of competitive advantage for these firms. Wal-Mart's resources and capabilities are just too extensive and costly to imitate for most of these suppliers. So, instead of forward vertical integration, most of these firms sell their products through Wal-Mart.

Of course, the problem is that by relying so much on Wal-Mart, these firms are making significant transaction-specific investments. If they stop selling to Wal-Mart, they may go out of business. However, this decision will have a limited impact on Wal-Mart. Wal-Mart can go to any number of suppliers around the world who are willing to replace this failed firm. So, Wal-Mart's suppliers are at risk of opportunism in this exchange, and indeed, it is well known that Wal-Mart can squeeze its suppliers, in terms of the quality of the products it purchases, the price at which it purchases them, and the way in which these products are delivered.

So the tension between these two approaches to vertical integration becomes clear. Concerns about opportunism suggest that Wal-Mart's suppliers should vertically integrate forward. Concerns about having a competitive disadvantage if they do vertically integrate forward suggest that Wal-Mart's suppliers should not vertically integrate. So, should they or shouldn't they vertically integrate?

Not many of Wal-Mart's suppliers have been able to resolve this difficult problem. Most do not vertically integrate into the discount retail industry. However, they try to reduce the level of transaction-specific investment they make with Wal-Mart by supplying other discount retailers, both in the United States and abroad. They also try to use their special capabilities to differentiate their products so much that Wal-Mart's customers insist on Wal-Mart selling these products. And these firms constantly search for cheaper ways to make and distribute higher-quality products.

Vertical Integration and Flexibility

A third perspective on vertical integration focuses on the impact of this decision on a firm's flexibility. **Flexibility** refers to how costly it is for a firm to alter its strategic and organizational decisions. Flexibility is high when the cost of changing strategic choices is low; flexibility is low when the cost of changing strategic choices is high.

So, which is less flexible—vertical integration or no vertical integration? Research suggests that, in general, vertically integrating is less flexible than not vertically integrating.[5] This is because once a firm has vertically integrated, it has committed its organizational structure, its management controls, and its compensation policies to a particular vertically integrated way of doing business. Undoing this decision often means changing these aspects of an organization.

Suppose, for example, that a vertically integrated firm decides to get out of a particular business. To do so, the firm will have to sell or close its factories (actions that can adversely affect both the employees it has to lay off and those that remain), alter its supply relationships, hurt customers that have come to rely on it as a partner, and change its internal reporting structure. In contrast, if a non-vertically integrated firm decides to get out of a business, it simply stops. It cancels whatever contracts it might have had in place and ceases operations in that business. The cost of exiting a non-vertically integrated business is generally much lower than the cost of exiting a vertically integrated business.

Of course, flexibility is not always valuable. In fact, flexibility is only valuable when the decision-making setting a firm is facing is uncertain. A decision-making setting is **uncertain** when the future value of an exchange cannot be known when investments in that exchange are being made. In such settings, less vertical integration is better than more vertical integration. This is because vertically integrating into an exchange is less flexible than not vertically integrating into an exchange. If an exchange turns out not to be valuable, it is usually more costly for firms that have vertically integrated into an exchange to exit that exchange compared to those that have not vertically integrated.

Consider, for example, a pharmaceutical firm making investments in biotechnology. The outcome of biotechnology research is very uncertain. If a pharmaceutical company vertically integrates into a particular type of biotechnology research by hiring particular types of scientists, building an expensive laboratory, and developing the other skills necessary to do this particular type of biotechnology research, it has made a very large investment. Now suppose that this research turns out not to be profitable. This firm has made huge investments that now have little value. As important, it has failed to make investments in other areas of biotechnology that could turn out to be valuable.

A flexibility-based approach to vertical integration suggests that rather than vertically integrating into a business activity whose value is highly uncertain, firms should not vertically integrate and but should instead form a strategic alliance to manage this exchange. A strategic alliance is more flexible than vertical integration but still gives a firm enough information about an exchange to estimate its value over time.

An alliance has a second advantage in this setting. The downside risks associated with investing in a strategic alliance are known and fixed. They equal the cost of creating and maintaining the alliance. If an uncertain investment turns out not to be valuable, parties to this alliance know the maximum amount they can lose—an amount equal to the cost of creating and maintaining the alliance. On the other hand, if this exchange turns out to be very valuable, then maintaining an alliance can give a firm access to this huge upside potential. These aspects of strategic alliances will be discussed in more detail in Chapter 9.

Each of these explanations of vertical integration has received significant empirical attention in the academic literature. Some of these studies are described in the Research Made Relevant feature.

Applying the Theories to the Management of Call Centers

One of the most common business functions to be outsourced, and even off-shored, is a firm's call center activities. So, what do these three theories say about how call centers should be managed: When should they be brought within the boundaries of a firm, and when should they be outsourced? Each of these theories will be discussed in turn.

Research Made Relevant

Of the three explanations of vertical integration discussed here, opportunism-based explanations are the oldest and thus have received the greatest empirical support. One review of this empirical work, by Professor Joe Mahoney of the University of Illinois, observes that the core assertion of this approach—that high levels of transaction-specific investment lead to higher levels of vertical integration—receives consistent empirical support.

More recent work has begun to examine the trade-offs among these three explanations of vertical integration by examining their effects on vertical integration simultaneously. For example, Professor Tim Folta of Purdue University examined the opportunism and flexibility approaches to vertical integration simultaneously. His results show that the basic assertion of the opportunism approach still holds. However, when he incorporates uncertainty into his empirical analysis, he

Empirical Tests of Theories of Vertical Integration

finds that firms engage in less vertical integration than predicted by opportunism by itself. In other words, firms apparently worry not only about transaction-specific investments when they make vertical integration choices; they also worry about how costly it is to reverse those investments in the face of high uncertainty.

An even more recent study by Michael Leiblein from The Ohio State University and Doug Miller from the University of Illinois examines all three of these explanations of vertical integration simultaneously. These authors study vertical integration decisions in the semiconductor manufacturing industry and find that all three explanations hold. That is, firms in this industry worry about transaction-specific investment, the capabilities they possess, the capabilities they would like to possess, and the uncertainty of the markets within which they operate when they make vertical integration choices.

Sources: J. Mahoney. (1992). "The choice of organizational form: Vertical financial ownership versus other methods of vertical integration." *Strategic Management Journal*, 13, pp. 559–584; T. Folta. (1998). "Governance and uncertainty: The trade-off between administrative control and commitment." *Strategic Management Journal*, 19, pp. 1007–1028; and M. Leiblein and D. Miller. (2003). "An empirical examination of transaction- and firm-level influences on the vertical boundaries of the firm." *Strategic Management Journal*, 24(9), pp. 839–859.

Transaction-Specific Investments and Managing Call Centers

When applying opportunism-based explanations of vertical integration, start by looking for actual or potential transaction-specific investments that would need to be made in order to complete an exchange. High levels of such investments suggest the need for vertical integration; low levels of such investments suggest that vertically integrating this exchange is not necessary.

When the call-center approach to providing customer service was first developed in the 1980s, it required substantial levels of transaction-specific investment. First, a great deal of special-purpose equipment had to be purchased. And although this equipment could be used for any call center, it had little value except within a call center. Thus, this equipment was an example of a somewhat specific investment.

More important, in order to provide service in call centers, call-center employees would have to be fully aware of all the problems likely to emerge with the use of a firm's products. This requires a firm to study its products very closely and then to train call-center employees to be able to respond to any problems customers might have. This training was sometimes very complex and very time consuming and represented substantial transaction-specific investments on the part of call-center employees. Only employees that worked full-time for a large corporation—where job security was usually high for productive workers—would be willing to make these kinds of specific investments. Thus, vertical integration into call-center management made a great deal of sense.

However, as information technology improved, firms found it was possible to train call-center employees much faster. Now, all call-center employees had to do was follow scripts that were prewritten and preloaded onto their computers. By asking a few scripted questions, call-center employees could diagnose most problems. In addition, solutions to those problems were also included on an employee's computer. Only really unusual problems could not be handled by employees working off these computer scripts. Because the level of specific investment required to use these scripts was much lower, employees were willing to work for companies without the job security usually associated with large firms. Indeed, call centers became good part-time and temporary employment opportunities. Because the level of specific investment required to work in these call centers was much lower, not vertically integrating into call-center management made a great deal of sense.

Capabilities and Managing Call Centers

In opportunism-based explanations of vertical integration, you start by looking for transaction-specific investments and then make vertical integration decisions based on these investments. In capability-based approaches, you start by looking for valuable, rare, and costly-to-imitate resources and capabilities, and then make vertical integration decisions appropriately.

In the early days of call-center management, how well a firm operated its call centers could actually be a source of competitive advantage. During this time period, the technology was new, and the training required to answer a customer's questions was extensive. Firms that developed special capabilities in managing these processes could gain competitive advantages and thus would vertically integrate into call-center management.

However, over time, as more and more call-center management suppliers were created, and as the technology and training required to staff a call center became more widely available, the ability of a call center to be a source of competitive advantage for a firm dropped. That is, the ability to manage a call center was still valuable, but it was no longer rare or costly to imitate. In this setting, it is not surprising to see firms getting out of the call-center management business, outsourcing this business to low-cost specialist firms, and focusing on those business functions where they might be able to gain a sustained competitive advantage.

Flexibility and Managing Call Centers

Opportunism logic suggests starting with a search for transaction-specific investments; capabilities logic suggests starting with a search for valuable, rare, and costly-to-imitate resources and capabilities. Flexibility logic suggests starting by looking for sources of uncertainty in an exchange.

One of the biggest uncertainties in providing customer service through call centers is the question of whether the people staffing the phones actually help a firm's customers. This is a particularly troubling concern for firms that are selling complex products that can have numerous types of problems. A variety of technological solutions have been developed to try to address this uncertainty. But, if a firm vertically integrates into the call-center management business, it is committing to a particular technological solution. This solution may not work, or it may not work as well as some other solutions.

In the face of this uncertainty, maintaining relationships with several different call-center management companies—each of whom have adopted different technological solutions to the problem of how to use call-center employees to assist customers who are using very complex products—gives a firm technological flexibility that it would not otherwise have. Once a superior solution is identified, then a firm no longer needs this flexibility and may choose to vertically integrate into call-center management or not, depending on opportunism and capabilities considerations.

Integrating Different Theories of Vertical Integration

At first glance, having three different explanations about how vertical integration can create value seems troubling. After all, won't these explanations sometimes contradict each other?

The answer to this question is yes. We have already seen such a contradiction in the case of opportunism and capabilities explanations of whether Wal-Mart suppliers should forward vertically integrate into the discount retail industry.

However, more often than not, these three explanations are complementary in nature. That is, each approach generally leads to the same conclusion about how a firm should vertically integrate. Moreover, sometimes it is simply easier to apply one of these approaches to evaluate a firm's vertical integration choices than the other two. Having a "tool kit" that includes three explanations of vertical integration enables the analyst to choose the approach that is most likely to be a source of insight in a particular situation.

Even when these explanations make contradictory assertions about vertical integration, having multiple approaches can be helpful. In this context, having multiple explanations can highlight the trade-offs that a firm is making when choosing its vertical integration strategy. Thus, for example, if opportunism-based explanations suggest that vertical integration is necessary because of high transaction-specific investments, capabilities-based explanations caution about the cost of developing the resources and capabilities necessary to vertically integrate and flexibility concerns caution about the risks that committing to vertical integration imply, and the costs and benefits of whatever vertical integration decision is ultimately made can be understood very clearly.

Overall, having three explanations of vertical integration has several advantages for those looking to analyze the vertical integration choices of real firms. Of course, applying these explanations can create important ethical dilemmas for a firm, especially when it becomes clear that a firm needs to become less vertically integrated than it has historically been. Some of these dilemmas are discussed in the Ethics and Strategy feature.

Vertical Integration and Sustained Competitive Advantage

Of course, in order for vertical integration to be a source of sustained competitive advantage, not only must it be valuable (because it responds to threats of opportunism; enables a firm to exploit its own or other firms' valuable, rare, and costly-to-imitate resources; or because it gives a firm flexibility), it must also be rare and costly to imitate, and a firm must be organized to implement it correctly.

The Rarity of Vertical Integration

A firm's vertical integration strategy is rare when few competing firms are able to create value by vertically integrating in the same way. A firm's vertical integration strategy can be rare because it is one of a small number of competing firms that is able to vertically integrate efficiently or because it is one of a small number of firms that is able to adopt a non-vertically integrated approach to managing an exchange.

Rare Vertical Integration

A firm may be able to create value through vertical integration, when most of its competitors are not able to, for at least three reasons. Not surprisingly, these reasons parallel the three explanations of vertical integration presented in this chapter.

Ethics and Strategy

Imagine a firm that has successfully operated in a vertically integrated manner for decades. Employees come to work, they know their jobs, they know how to work together effectively, they know where to park. The job is not just the economic center of their lives; it has become the social center as well. Most of their friends work in the same company, in the same function, as they do. The future appears to be much as the past—stable employment and effective work, all aiming toward a comfortable and well-planned retirement. And then the firm adopts a new outsourcing strategy. It changes its vertical integration strategy by becoming less vertically integrated and purchasing services from outside suppliers that it used to obtain internally.

The economics of outsourcing can be compelling. Outsourcing can help firms reduce costs and focus their efforts on those business functions that are central to their competitive advantage. When done well, outsourcing creates value—value that firms can share with their owners, their stockholders.

The Ethics of Outsourcing

Indeed, outsourcing is becoming a trend in business. Some observers predict that by 2015, an additional 3.3 million jobs in the United States will be outsourced, many to operations overseas.

But what of the employees whose jobs are taken away? What of their lifetime of commitment, their steady and reliable work? What of their stable and secure retirement? Outsourcing often devastates lives, even as it creates economic value. Of course, some firms go out of their way to soften the impact of outsourcing on their employees. Those that are near

retirement age are often given an opportunity to retire early. Others receive severance payments in recognition of their years of service. Other firms hire "outplacement" companies—firms that specialize in placing suddenly unemployed people in new jobs and new careers.

But all these efforts to soften the blow do not make the blow go away. Many employees assume that they have an implicit contract with the firms they work for. That contract is: "As long as I do my job well, I will have a job." That contract is being replaced with: "As long as a firm wants to employ me, I will have a job." In such a world, it is not surprising that many employees now look first to maintain their employability in their current job—by receiving additional training and experiences that might be valuable at numerous other employers—and are concerned less with what they can do to improve the performance of the firm they work for.

Sources: S. Steele-Carlin. (2003). "Outsourcing poised for growth in 2002." *FreelanceJobsNews.com*, October 20; and (2003). "Who wins in offshoring?" *McKinseyQuarterly.com*, October 20.

Rare Transaction-Specific Investment and Vertical Integration. First, a firm may have developed a new technology, or a new approach to doing business, that requires its business partners to make substantial transaction-specific investments. Firms that engage in these activities will find it in their self-interest to vertically integrate, whereas firms that have not engaged in these activities will not find it in their self-interest to vertically integrate. If these activities are rare and costly to imitate, they can be a source of competitive advantage for a vertically integrating firm.

For example, the opening case in this chapter suggests that many firms in the computer industry are offshoring some of their key business functions. However, one firm, Dell, recently brought one of these functions—its technical call centers for corporate customers—back from India and re-vertically integrated into this business.[6] The problems faced by corporate customers are typically much more complicated than those faced by individual consumers. Thus, it is much more difficult to provide call-center employees with the training they need to address corporate problems. Moreover, because corporate technologies change more rapidly than many consumer technologies, keeping call-center employees up-to-date on how to service corporate customers is also more complicated than having call-center employees provide services to its noncorporate customers. Because Dell needs the people staffing its corporate call centers to make substantial specific investments in its technology and in understanding its customers, it has found it necessary to bring these individuals within the boundaries of the firm and to re-vertically integrate the operation of this particular type of service center.

If Dell, through this vertical integration decision, is able to satisfy its customers more effectively than its competitors, and if the cost of managing this call center is not too high, then this vertical integration decision is both valuable and rare and thus a source of at least a temporary competitive advantage for Dell.

Rare Capabilities and Vertical Integration. A firm such as Dell might also conclude that it has unusual skills, either in operating a call center or in providing the training that is needed to staff certain kinds of call centers. If those capabilities are valuable and rare, then vertically integrating into businesses that exploit these capabilities can enable a firm to gain at least a temporary competitive advantage. Indeed, the belief that a firm possesses valuable and rare capabilities is often a justification for rare vertical integration decisions in an industry.

Rare Uncertainty and Vertical Integration. Finally, a firm may be able to gain an advantage from vertically integrating when it resolves some uncertainty it faces sooner than its competition. Suppose, for example, that several firms in an industry all begin investing in a very uncertain technology. Flexibility logic suggests that, to the extent possible, these firms will prefer to not vertically integrate into the manufacturing of this technology until its designs and features stabilize and market demand for this technology is well established.

However, imagine that one of these firms is able to resolve these uncertainties before any other firm. This firm no longer needs to retain the flexibility that is so valuable under conditions of uncertainty. Instead, this firm might be able to, say, design special-purpose machines that can efficiently manufacture this technology. Such machines are not flexible, but they can be very efficient.

Of course, outside vendors would have to make substantial transaction-specific investments to use these machines. Outside vendors may be reluctant to make these investments. In this setting, this firm may find it necessary to vertically integrate to be able to use its machines to produce this technology. Thus, this firm, by resolving uncertainty faster than its competitors, is able to gain some of the advantages of vertical integration sooner than its competitors. Whereas the competition is still focusing on flexibility in the face of uncertainty, this firm gets to focus on production efficiency in meeting customers' product demands. This can obviously be a source of competitive advantage.

Rare Vertical Dis-Integration

Each of the examples of vertical integration and competitive advantage described so far have focused on a firm's ability to vertically integrate to create competitive advantage. However, firms can also gain competitive advantages through their decisions to vertically dis-integrate, that is, through the decision to outsource an activity that used to be within the boundaries of the firm. Whenever a firm is among the first in its industry to conclude that the level of specific investment required to manage an economic exchange is no longer high, or that a particular exchange is no longer rare or costly to imitate, or that the level of uncertainty about the value of an exchange has increased, it may be among the first in its industry to vertically dis-integrate this exchange. Such activities, to the extent they are valuable, will be rare, and thus a source of at least a temporary competitive advantage.

The Imitability of Vertical Integration

The extent to which these rare vertical integration decisions can be sources of sustained competitive advantage depends, as always, on the imitability of the rare resources that give a firm at least a temporary competitive advantage. Both direct duplication and substitution can be used to imitate another firm's valuable and rare vertical integration choices.

Direct Duplication of Vertical Integration

Direct duplication occurs when competitors develop or obtain the resources and capabilities that enable another firm to implement a valuable and rare vertical integration strategy. To the extent that these resources and capabilities are path dependent, socially complex, or causally ambiguous, they may be immune from direct duplication, and thus a source of sustained competitive advantage.

With respect to offshoring business functions, it seems that the very popularity of this strategy suggests that it is highly imitable. Indeed, this strategy is becoming so common that firms that move in the other direction by vertically integrating a call center and managing it in the United States (like Dell) make news.

But the fact that many firms are implementing this strategy does not mean that they are all equally successful in doing so. These differences in performance may reflect some subtle and complex capabilities that some of these outsourcing firms possess but others do not. These are the kinds of resources and capabilities that may be sources of sustained competitive advantage.

Some of the resources that might enable a firm to implement a valuable and rare vertical integration strategy may not be susceptible to direct duplication. These might include a firm's ability to analyze the attributes of its economic exchanges and its ability to conceive and implement vertical integration strategies. Both of these capabilities may be socially complex and path dependent— built up over years of experience.

Substitutes for Vertical Integration

The major substitute for vertical integration—strategic alliances—is the major topic of Chapter 9. An analysis of how strategic alliances can substitute for vertical integration will be delayed until then.

VRIO   # Organizing to Implement Vertical Integration

Organizing to implement vertical integration involves the same organizing tools as implementing any business or corporate strategy: organizational structure, management controls, and compensation policies.

Organizational Structure and Implementing Vertical Integration

The organizational structure that is used to implement a cost leadership and product differentiation strategy—the functional, or U-form, structure—is also used to implement a vertical integration strategy. Indeed, each of the exchanges included within the boundaries of a firm as a result of vertical integration decisions are incorporated into one of the functions in a functional organizational structure. Decisions about which manufacturing activities to vertically integrate into determine the range and responsibilities of the manufacturing function within a functionally organized firm; decisions about which marketing activities to vertically integrate into determine the range and responsibilities of the marketing function within a functionally organized firm; and so forth. Thus, in an important sense, vertical integration decisions made by a firm determine the structure of a functionally organized firm.

The Chief Executive Officer (CEO) in this vertically integrated, functionally organized firm has the same two responsibilities that were first identified in Chapter 4: strategy formulation and strategy implementation. However, these two responsibilities take on added dimensions when implementing vertical integration decisions. In particular, although the CEO must take the lead in making decisions about whether each individual function should be vertically integrated into a firm, this person must also work to resolve conflicts that naturally arise between vertically integrated functions. The approach of one reluctant CEO to this management challenge is described in the Strategy in the Emerging Enterprise feature.

Resolving Functional Conflicts in a Vertically Integrated Firm

From a CEO's perspective, coordinating functional specialists to implement a vertical integration strategy almost always involves conflict resolution. Conflicts among functional managers in a U-form organization are both expected and normal. Indeed, if there is no conflict among certain functional managers in a U-form organization, then some of these managers probably are not doing their jobs. The task facing the CEO is not to pretend this conflict does not exist or to ignore it, but to manage it in a way that facilitates strategy implementation.

Consider, for example, the relationship between manufacturing and sales managers. Typically, manufacturing managers prefer to manufacture a single product with long production runs. Sales managers, however, generally prefer to sell numerous customized products. Manufacturing managers generally do not like large inventories of finished products; sales managers generally prefer large inventories of finished products that facilitate rapid deliveries to customers. If these various interests of manufacturing and sales managers do not, at least sometimes, come into conflict in a vertically integrated U-form organization, then the manufacturing manager is not focusing enough on cost reduction and quality improvement in manufacturing or the sales manager is not focusing enough on meeting customer needs in a timely way, or both.

Numerous other conflicts arise among functional managers in a vertically integrated U-form organization. Accountants often focus on maximizing managerial accountability and close analysis of costs; research and development managers may fear that such accounting practices will interfere with innovation and creativity. Finance managers often focus on the relationship between a firm and its external capital markets; human resource managers are more concerned with the relationship between a firm and external labor markets.

In this context, the CEO's job is to help resolve conflicts in ways that facilitate the implementation of the firm's strategy. Functional managers do not have to "like" each other. However, if a firm's vertical integration strategy is correct, the reason that a function has been included within the boundaries of a firm is that

Strategy in the Emerging Enterprise

With a net worth over $1 billion, Oprah Winfrey heads one of the most successful multimedia companies in the United States. One of the businesses she owns—Harpo, Inc.—produces one of the most successful daytime television shows ever (with revenues of over $300 million a year); a magazine with the most successful launch ever and currently 2.5 million paid subscribers (more than *Vogue* and *Fortune*); and a movie production unit. One investment banker estimates that if Harpo, Inc. was a publicly traded firm, it would be valued at $575 million. Other properties Oprah owns—including investments, real estate, a stake in the cable television channel Oxygen, and stock options in Viacom—generate another $468 million in revenues per year.

And Oprah Winfrey does not consider herself to be a CEO.

Certainly, her decision-making style is not typical of most CEOs. She has been quoted as describing her business decision making as "leaps of faith" and "If I called a strategic planning meeting, there would be dead

Oprah, Inc.

silence, and then people would fall out of their chairs laughing."

However, she has made other decisions that put her firmly in control of her empire. For example, in 1987, she hired a tough Chicago entertainment attorney—Jeff Jacobs—as president of Harpo, Inc. Whereas Oprah's business decisions are made from her gut and from her heart, Jacobs makes sure that the numbers add up to more revenues and profits for Harpo. She has also been unwilling to license her name to other firms, unlike Martha Stewart, who licensed her name to

Kmart. Oprah has made strategic alliances with King World (to distribute her TV show), with ABC (to broadcast her movies), with Hearst (to distribute her magazine), and with Oxygen (to distribute some other television programs). But she has never given up control of her business. And she has not taken her firm public. She currently owns 90 percent of Harpo's stock. She was once quoted as saying, "If I lost control of my business, I'd lose myself—or at least the ability to be myself."

To help control this growing business, Oprah and Jacobs hired a chief operating officer (COO), Tim Bennett, who then created several functional departments, including accounting, legal, and human resources, to help manage the firm. With 221 employees, an office, and a real organization, Harpo is a real company, and Oprah is a real CEO—albeit a CEO with a slightly different approach to making business decisions.

Sources: P. Sellers. (2002). "The business of being Oprah." *Fortune*, April 1, pp. 50 +; Oprah.com; Hoovers.com; and (2003). "Harpo Inc." October 20.

this decision creates value for the firm. Allowing functional conflicts to get in the way of taking advantage of each of the functions within a firm's boundaries can destroy this potential value.

Management Controls and Implementing Vertical Integration

Although having the correct organizational structure is important for firms implementing their vertical integration strategies, that structure must be supported by a variety of management control processes. Among the most important of these processes are the budgeting process and the management committee oversight process, which can also help CEOs resolve the functional conflicts that are common within vertically integrated firms.

The Budgeting Process

Budgeting is one of the most important control mechanisms available to CEOs in vertically integrated U-form organizations. Indeed, in most U-form companies enormous management effort goes into the creation of budgets and the evaluation of performance relative to budgets. Budgets are developed for costs, revenues, and a variety of other activities performed by a firm's functional managers. Often, managerial compensation and promotion opportunities depend on the ability of a manager to meet budget expectations.

Although budgets are an important control tool, they can also have unintended negative consequences. For example, the use of budgets can lead functional managers to overemphasize short-term behavior that is easy to measure and underemphasize longer-term behavior that is more difficult to measure. Thus, for example, the strategically correct thing for a functional manager to do might be to increase expenditures for maintenance and management training, thereby ensuring that the function will have both the technology and the skilled people needed to do the job in the future. An overemphasis on meeting current budget requirements, however, might lead this manager to delay maintenance and training expenditures. By meeting short-term budgetary demands, this manager may be sacrificing the long-term viability of this function, compromising the long-term viability of the firm.

CEOs can do a variety of things to counter the "short-termism" effects of the budgeting process. For example, research suggests that evaluating a functional manager's performance relative to budgets can be an effective control device when (1) the process used in developing budgets is open and participative, (2) the process reflects the economic reality facing functional managers and the firm, and (3) quantitative evaluations of a functional manager's performance are augmented by qualitative evaluations of that performance. Adopting an open and participative process for setting budgets helps ensure that budget targets are realistic and that functional managers understand and accept them. Including qualitative criteria for evaluation reduces the chances that functional managers will engage in behaviors that are very harmful in the long run but enable them to make budget in the short run.[7]

The Management Committee Oversight Process

In addition to budgets, vertically integrated U-form organizations can use various internal management committees as management control devices. Two particularly common internal management committees are the **executive committee** and the **operations committee** (although these committees have many different names in different organizations).

The executive committee in a U-form organization typically consists of the CEO and two or three key functional senior managers. It normally meets weekly and reviews the performance of the firm on a short-term basis. Functions represented on this committee generally include accounting, legal, and other functions (such as manufacturing or sales) that are most central to the firm's short-term business success. The fundamental purpose of the executive committee is to track the short-term performance of the firm, to note and correct any budget variances for functional managers, and to respond to any crises that might emerge. Obviously, the executive committee can help avoid many functional conflicts in a vertically integrated firm before they arise.

In addition to the executive committee, another group of managers meets regularly to help control the operations of the firm. Often called the *operations committee*, this committee typically meets monthly and usually consists of the CEO and each of the heads of the functional areas included in the firm. The executive committee is a subset of the operations committee.

The primary objective of the operations committee is to track firm performance over time intervals slightly longer than the weekly interval of primary interest to the executive committee and to monitor longer-term strategic investments and activities. Such investments might include plant expansions, the introduction of new products, and the implementation of cost-reduction or quality improvement programs. The operations committee provides a forum in which senior functional managers can come together to share concerns and opportunities and to coordinate efforts to implement strategies. Obviously, the operations committee can help resolve functional conflicts in a vertically integrated firm after they arise.

In addition to these two standing committees, various other committees and task forces can be organized within the U-form organization to manage specific projects and tasks. These additional groups are typically chaired by a member of the executive or operations committee and report to one or both of these standing committees, as warranted.

Compensation in Implementing Vertical Integration Strategies

Organizational structure and management control systems can have an important impact on the ability of a firm to implement its vertical integration strategy. However, a firm's compensation policies can be important as well.

We have already seen how compensation can play a role in implementing cost leadership and product differentiation, and how compensation can be tied to budgets to help implement vertical integration. However, the three explanations of vertical integration presented in this chapter have important compensation implications as well. We will first discuss the compensation challenges these three explanations suggest and then discuss ways these challenges can be addressed.

Opportunism-Based Vertical Integration and Compensation Policy

Opportunism-based approaches to vertical integration suggest that employees who make firm-specific investments in their jobs will often be able to create more value for a firm than employees who do not. Firm-specific investments are a type of transaction-specific investment. Whereas transaction-specific investments are investments that have more value in a particular exchange than in alternative exchanges, **firm-specific investments** are investments made by employees that have more value in a particular firm than in alternative firms.[8]

Examples of firm-specific investments include an employee's understanding of a particular firm's culture, his or her personal relationships with others in the firm, and an employee's knowledge about a firm's unique business processes. All this knowledge can be used by an employee to create a great deal of value in a firm. However, this knowledge has almost no value in other firms. The effort to create this knowledge is thus a firm-specific investment.

Despite the value that an employee's firm-specific investments can create, opportunism-based explanations of vertical integration suggest that employees will often be reluctant to make these investments, because, once they do, they become vulnerable in their exchange with this firm. For example, an employee who has made very significant firm-specific investments may not be able to quit and go to work for another company, even if he or she is passed over for promotion, does not receive a raise, or is even actively discriminated against. This is because by quitting this firm, this employee loses all the investment he or she made in this particular firm. Because this employee has few employment options other than his or her current firm, this firm can treat this employee badly and the employee can do little about it. This is why employees are often reluctant to make firm-specific investments.

But the firm needs its employees to make such investments if it is to realize its full economic potential. Thus, one of the tasks of compensation policy is to create incentives for employees whose firm-specific investments could create great value to actually make those investments.

Capabilities and Compensation

Capability explanations of vertical integration also acknowledge the importance of firm-specific investments in creating value for a firm. Indeed, many of the valuable, rare, and costly-to-imitate resources and capabilities that can exist in a firm are a manifestation of firm-specific investments made by a firm's employees. However, whereas opportunism explanations of vertical integration tend to focus on firm-specific investments made by individual employees, capabilities explanations tend to focus on firm-specific investments made by groups of employees.[9]

In Chapter 3, it was suggested that one of the reasons that a firm's valuable and rare resources may be costly to imitate is that these resources are socially complex in nature. Socially complex resources reflect the teamwork, cooperation, and culture that have evolved within a firm—capabilities that can increase the value of a firm significantly, but capabilities that other firms will often find costly to imitate, at least in the short to medium term. Moreover, these are capabilities that exist because several employees—not just a single employee—have made specific investments in a firm.

From the point of view of designing a compensation policy, capabilities analysis suggests that not only should a firm's compensation policy encourage employees whose firm-specific investments could create value to actually make those investments; it also recognizes that these investments will often be collective in nature—that, for example, until all the members of a critical management team make firm-specific commitments to that team, that team's ability to create and sustain competitive advantages will be significantly limited.

		TABLE 6.1 Types of Compensation and Approaches to Making Vertical Integration Decisions
Opportunism explanations	Salary	
	Cash bonuses for individual performance	
	Stock grants for individual performance	
Capabilities explanations	Cash bonuses for corporate or group performance	
	Stock grants for corporate or group performance	
Flexibility explanations	Stock options for individual, corporate, or group performance	

Flexibility and Compensation

Flexibility explanations of vertical integration also have some important implications for compensation. In particular, because the creation of flexibility in a firm depends on employees being willing to engage in activities that have fixed and known downside risks and significant upside potential, it follows that compensation that has fixed and known downside risks and significant upside potential would encourage employees to choose and implement flexible vertical integration strategies.

Compensation Alternatives

Table 6.1 lists several compensation alternatives and how they are related to each of the three explanations of vertical integration discussed in this chapter. Not surprisingly, opportunism-based explanations suggest that compensation that focuses on individual employees and how they can make firm-specific investments will be important for firms implementing their vertical integration strategies. Such individual compensation includes an employee's salary, cash bonuses based on individual performance, and **stock grants**—or payments to employees in a firm's stock—based on individual performance.

Capabilities explanations of vertical integration suggest that compensation that focuses on groups of employees making firm-specific investments in valuable, rare, and costly-to-imitate resources and capabilities will be particularly important for firms implementing vertical integration strategies. Such collective compensation includes cash bonuses based on a firm's overall performance and stock grants based on a firm's overall performance.

Finally, flexibility logic suggests that compensation that has a fixed and known downside risk and significant upside potential is important for firms implementing vertical integration strategies. **Stock options**, whereby employees are given the right, but not the obligation, to purchase stock at predetermined prices, are a form of compensation that has these characteristics. Stock options can be granted based on an individual employee's performance or the performance of the firm as a whole.

The task facing CEOs looking to implement a vertical integration strategy through compensation policy is to determine what kinds of employee behavior they need to have for this strategy to create sustained competitive advantages and then to use the appropriate compensation policy. Not surprisingly, most CEOs find that all three explanations of vertical integration are important in their decision making. Thus, not surprisingly, many firms adopt compensation policies that feature a mix of the compensation policies listed in Table 6.1. Most firms use both individual and corporate-wide compensation schemes along with salaries, cash bonuses, stock grants, and stock options for employees who have the greatest impact on a firm's overall performance.

Summary

Vertical integration is defined as the number of stages in an industry's value chain that a firm has brought within its boundaries. Forward vertical integration brings a firm closer to its ultimate customer; backward vertical integration brings a firm closer to the sources of its raw materials. In making vertical integration decisions for a particular business activity, firms can choose to be not vertically integrated, somewhat vertically integrated, or vertically integrated.

Vertical integration can create value in three different ways: First, it can reduce opportunistic threats from a firm's buyers and suppliers due to transaction-specific investments the firm may have made. A transaction-specific investment is an investment that has more value in a particular exchange than in any alternative exchanges. Second, vertical integration can create value by enabling a firm to exploit its valuable, rare, and costly-to-imitate resources and capabilities. Firms should vertically integrate into activities in which they enjoy such advantages and should not vertically integrate into other activities. Third, vertical integration typically only creates value under conditions of low uncertainty. Under high uncertainty, vertical integration can commit a firm to a costly-to-reverse course of action and the flexibility of a non-vertically integrated approach may be preferred.

Often, all three approaches to vertical integration will generate similar conclusions. However, even when they suggest different vertical integration strategies, they can still be helpful to management.

The ability of valuable vertical integration strategies to generate a sustained competitive advantage depends on how rare and costly to imitate the strategies are. Vertical integration strategies can be rare in two ways: (1) when a firm is vertically integrated while most competing firms are not vertically integrated and (2) when a firm is not vertically integrated while most competing firms are. These rare vertical integration strategies are possible when firms vary in the extent to which the strategies they pursue require transaction-specific investments; they vary in the resources and capabilities they control; or they vary in the level of uncertainty they face.

The ability to directly duplicate a firm's vertical integration strategies depends on how costly it is to directly duplicate the resources and capabilities that enable a firm to pursue these strategies. The closest substitute for vertical integration—strategic alliances—is discussed in more detail in Chapter 9.

Organizing to implement vertical integration depends on a firm's organizational structure, its management controls, and its compensation policies. The organizational structure most commonly used to implement vertical integration is the functional, or U-form, organization, which involves cost leadership and product differentiation strategies. In a vertically integrated U-form organization, the CEO must focus not only on deciding which functions to vertically integrate into, but also how to resolve conflicts that inevitably arise in a functionally organized vertically integrated firm. Two management controls that can be used to help implement vertical integration strategies and resolve these functional conflicts are the budgeting process and management oversight committees.

Each of the three explanations of vertical integration suggests different kinds of compensation policies that a firm looking to implement vertical integration should pursue. Opportunism-based explanations suggest individual-based compensation—including salaries and cash bonus and stock grants based on individual performance; capabilities-based explanations suggest group-based compensation—including cash bonuses and stock grants based on corporate or group performance; and flexibility-based explanations suggest flexible compensation—including stock options based on individual, group, or corporate performance. Because all three approaches to vertical integration are often operating in a firm, it is not surprising that many firms employ all these devices in compensating employees whose actions are likely to have a significant impact on firm performance.

Challenge Questions

1. Some firms have engaged in backward vertical integration strategies in order to appropriate the economic profits that would have been earned by suppliers selling to them. How is this motivation for backward vertical integration related to the opportunism logic for vertical integration described in this chapter? (Hint: Compare the competitive conditions under which firms may earn economic profits to the competitive conditions under which firms will be motivated to avoid opportunism through vertical integration.)

2. You are about to purchase a used car. What kinds of threats do you face in this purchase? What can you do to protect yourself from these threats? How is buying a car like and unlike vertical integration decisions?

3. What are the competitive implications for firms if they assume that all potential exchange partners cannot be trusted?

4. Common conflicts between sales and manufacturing are mentioned in the text. What conflicts might exist between research and development and manufacturing? Between finance and manufacturing? Between marketing and sales? Between accounting and everyone else? What could a CEO do to help resolve these conflicts?

5. Under what conditions would you accept a lower-paying job over a higher-paying one? What implications does your answer have for your potential employer's compensation policy?

Problem Set

1. Which of the following two firms is more vertically integrated? How can you tell?

(a) Firm A has included manufacturing, sales, finance, and human resources within its boundaries and has outsourced legal and customer service.

(b) Firm B has included manufacturing, sales, legal, and customer service within its boundaries and has outsourced finance and human resources.

2. What is the level of transaction-specific investment for each firm in the following transactions? Who in these transactions is at greater risk of being taken unfair advantage of?

(a) Firm I has built a plant right next door to Firm II. Firm I's plant is worth $5 million if it supplies Firm II. It is worth $200,000 if it does not supply Firm II. Firm II has three alternative suppliers. If it receives supplies from Firm I, it is worth $10 million. If it does not receive supplies from Firm I, it is worth $9.8 million.

(b) Firm A has just purchased a new computer system that is only available from Firm B. Firm A has redesigned its entire production process around this new computer system. The old production process is worth $1 million, the new process is worth $12 million. Firm B has several hundred customers for its new computer system.

(c) Firm Alpha, a fast-food restaurant company, has a contract with Firm Beta, a movie studio. After negotiating with several other potential partners, Firm Alpha agreed to a contract that requires Firm Alpha to pay Firm Beta $5 million per year for the right to use characters from Firm Beta's movies in its packaged meals for children. Demand for children's movies has recently dropped.

(d) Firm I owns and runs a printing press. Firm J uses the services of a printing press. Historically, Firm I has sold its services to many customers. However, it was recently approached by Firm J to become its exclusive supplier of printing-press services. Currently, Firm I is worth $1 million. If it became the sole supplier to Firm J, it would be worth $8 million. To complete this deal, Firm I would have to stop supplying its current customers and modify its machines to meet Firm J's needs. No other firm needs the same services as Firm J. Firm J contacted several other suppliers who said they would be willing to become a sole supplier for Firm J before deciding to propose this arrangement with Firm I.

3. In each of the following situations, would you recommend vertical integration or no vertical integration? Explain.

(a) Firm A needs a new and unique technology for its product line. No substitute technologies are available. Should Firm A make this technology or buy it?

(b) Firm I has been selling its products through a distributor for some time. It has become the market share leader. Unfortunately, this distributor has not been able to keep up with the evolving technology and customers are complaining. No alternative distributors are available. Should Firm I keep its current distributor or should it begin distribution on its own?

(c) Firm Alpha has manufactured its own products for years. Recently, however, one of these products has become more and more like a commodity. Several firms are now able to manufacture this product at the same price and quality as Firm Alpha. However, they do not have Firm Alpha's brand name in the marketplace. Should Firm Alpha continue to manufacture this product or should it outsource it to one of these other firms?

(d) Firm I is convinced that a certain class of technologies holds real economic potential. However, it does not know, for sure, which particular version of this technology is going to dominate the market. There are eight competing versions of this technology currently, but ultimately, only one will dominate the market. Should Firm I invest in all eight of these technologies itself? Should it invest in just one of these technologies? Should it partner with other firms that are investing in these different technologies?

End Notes

1. Coase, R. (1937). "The nature of the firm." *Economica*, 4, pp. 386–405.
2. This explanation of vertical integration is known as transactions cost economics in the academic literature. See Williamson, O. (1975). *Markets and hierarchies: Analysis and antitrust implications.* New York: Free Press; Williamson, O. (1985). *The economic institutions of capitalism.* New York: Free Press; and Klein, B., R. Crawford, and A. Alchian. (1978). "Vertical integration, appropriable rents, and the competitive contracting process." *Journal of Law and Economics*, 21, pp. 297–326.
3. Another option—forming an alliance between these two firms—is discussed in more detail in Chapter 9.
4. This explanation of vertical integration is known as the capabilities-based theory of the firm in the academic literature. It draws heavily from the resource-based view described in Chapter 3. See Barney, J. B. (1991). "Firm resources and sustained competitive advantage." *Journal of Management*, 17, pp. 99–120; Barney, J. B. (1999). "How a firm's capabilities affect boundary decisions." *Sloan Management*

Review, 40(3); and Conner, K. R., and C. K. Prahalad. (1996). "A resource-based theory of the firm: Knowledge versus opportunism." *Organization Science*, 7, pp. 477–501.
5. This explanation of vertical integration is known as real-options theory in the academic literature. See Kogut, B. (1991). "Joint ventures and the option to expand and acquire." *Management Science*, 37, pp. 19–33.
6. Kripalani, M., and P. Engardio. (2003). "The rise of India." *BusinessWeek*, December 8, pp. 66 +.
7. See Gupta, A. K. (1987). "SBU strategies, corporate-SBU relations and SBU effectiveness in strategy implementation." *Academy of Management Journal*, 30(3), pp. 477–500.
8. Becker, G. S. (1993). *Human capital: A theoretical and empirical analysis, with special reference to education.* Chicago: University of Chicago Press.
9. Barney, J. B. (1991). "Firm resources and sustained competitive advantage." *Journal of Management*, 17, pp. 99–120.

7 Corporate Diversification

LEARNING OBJECTIVES

After reading this chapter, you should be able to:

1. Define corporate diversification and describe five types of corporate diversification.

2. Specify the two conditions that a corporate diversification strategy must meet in order to create economic value.

3. Define the concept of "economies of scope" and identify eight potential economies of scope a diversified firm might try to exploit.

4. Identify which of these economies of scope a firm's outside equity investors are able to realize on their own at low cost.

5. Specify the circumstances under which a firm's diversification strategy will be rare.

6. Indicate which of the economies of scope identified in this chapter are more likely to be subject to low-cost imitation and which are less likely to be subject to low-cost imitation.

7. Identify two potential substitutes for corporate diversification.

The Worldwide Leader

The breadth of ESPN's diversification has even caught the attention of Hollywood writers. In the 2004 movie *Dodgeball: A True Underdog Story*, the championship game between the underdog Average Joes and the bad guy Purple Cobras is broadcast on the fictitious cable channel ESPN8. Also known as "the Ocho," ESPN8's theme is "If it's almost a sport, we've got it."

Here's the irony: ESPN has way over eight networks currently in operation.

ESPN was founded in 1979 by Bill and Scott Rasmussen after the father and son duo was fired from positions with the New England Whalers, a National Hockey League team now playing in Raleigh, North Carolina. Their initial idea was to rent satellite space to broadcast sports from Connecticut—the University of Connecticut's basketball games, Whaler's hockey games, and so forth. But they found that it was cheaper to rent satellite space for 24 hours straight than to rent space a few hours during the week, and thus a 24-hour sports channel was born.

ESPN went on the air September 7, 1979. The first event broadcast was a slow-pitch softball game. Initially, the network broadcast sports that, at the time, were not widely known to U.S. consumers—Australian rules football, Davis Cup tennis, professional wrestling, minor league bowling. Early on, ESPN also gained the rights to broadcast early rounds of the NCAA basketball tournament. At the time, the major networks did not broadcast these early round games, even though we now know that some of these early games are among the most exciting in the entire tournament.

The longest-running ESPN program is, of course, *Sports Center*. Although the first *Sports Center* contained no highlights and a scheduled interview with the football coach at the University of Colorado was interrupted by technical difficulties, *Sports Center* and its familiar theme have become icons in American popular culture. The 25,000th episode of *Sports Center* was broadcast on August 25, 2002.

ESPN was "admitted" into the world of big-time sports in 1987 when it signed with the National Football League to broadcast Sunday Night Football. Since then, ESPN has broadcast Major League Baseball, the National Basketball Association, and, at various times, the National Hockey League. These professional sports have been augmented by college football, basketball, and baseball games.

ESPN's first expansion was modest—in 1993, it introduced ESPN2. Originally, this station played nothing but rock music and scrolled sports scores. Within a few months, however, ESPN2 was broadcasting a full program of sports.

After this initial slow expansion, ESPN began to diversify its businesses rapidly. In 1996, it added ESPN News (an all-sports news channel); in 1997, it acquired

a company and opened ESPN Classics (this channel shows old sporting events); and in 2005, it started ESPNU (a channel dedicated to college athletics).

However, these five ESPN channels represent only a fraction of ESPN's diverse business interests. In 1998, ESPN opened its first restaurant, the ESPN Zone. This chain has continued to expand around the world. Also, in 1998, it started a magazine to compete with the then-dominant *Sports Illustrated*. Called *ESPN The Magazine,* it now has over 2 million subscribers. In 2001, ESPN went into the entertainment production business when it founded ESPN Original Entertainment. In 2005, ESPN started ESPN De Portes, a Spanish-language 24-hour sports channel. And in 2006, it founded ESPN on ABC, a company that manages much of the sports content broadcast on ABC. (In 1984, ABC purchased ESPN. Subsequently, ABC was purchased by Capital Cities Entertainment, and most of Capital Cities Entertainment was then sold to Walt Disney Corporation. Currently, ESPN is a division of Disney.)

And none of this counts ESPN HD, ESPN2 HD, ESPN Pay Per View, ESPN Radio, and ESPN's retail operations on the Web—ESPN.com.

Of all the expansion and diversification efforts, so far ESPN has only stumbled once. In 2006, it founded Mobile ESPN, a mobile telephone service. Not only would this service provide its customers mobile telephone

Sam Aronov/Shutterstock

service, it would also provide them up-to-the-minute scoring updates and a variety of other sports information. ESPN spent over $40 million advertising its new service and over $150 million on the technology required to make this service available. Unfortunately, it never signed up more than 30,000 subscribers. The breakeven point was estimated to be 500,000 subscribers.

Despite this setback, ESPN has emerged from being that odd little cable channel that broadcast odd little games to a $5 billion company with operations around the world in cable and broadcast television, radio, restaurants, magazines, books, and movie and television production. Which of those numerous enterprises could be characterized as "the Ocho" is hard to tell.

Sources: T. Lowry. (2006). "ESPN's cell-phone fumble." *BusinessWeek*, October 30, pp. 26 +; http://en.wikipedia.org/wiki/ESPN; AP Wide World Photos.

ESPN is like most large firms in the United States and the world: It has diversified operations. Indeed, virtually all of the 500 largest firms in the United States and the 500 largest firms in the world are diversified, either by product or geographically. Large single-business firms are very unusual. However, like most of these large diversified firms, ESPN has diversified along some dimensions but not others.

What Is Corporate Diversification?

A firm implements a **corporate diversification strategy** when it operates in multiple industries or markets simultaneously. When a firm operates in multiple industries simultaneously, it is said to be implementing a **product diversification strategy**. When a firm operates in multiple geographic markets simultaneously, it is said to be implementing a **geographic market diversification strategy**. When a firm implements both types of diversification simultaneously, it is said to be implementing a **product-market diversification strategy**. Just how geographically diversified firms really are is examined in the Global Perspectives feature.

We have already seen glimpses of these diversification strategies in the discussion of vertical integration strategies in Chapter 6. Sometimes, when a firm vertically integrates backward or forward, it begins operations in a new product or geographic market. This happened to computer software firms when they began manning their own call centers. These firms moved from the "computer software development" business to the "call-center management" business when they vertically integrated forward. In this sense, when firms vertically integrate, they may also be implementing a diversification strategy. However, the critical difference between the diversification strategies studied here and vertical integration (discussed in Chapter 6) is that in this chapter, product-market diversification is the primary objective of these strategies, whereas in Chapter 6 such diversification was often a secondary consequence of pursuing a vertical integration strategy.

Types of Corporate Diversification

Firms vary in the extent to which they have diversified the mix of businesses they pursue. Perhaps the simplest way of characterizing differences in the level of corporate diversification focuses on the relatedness of the businesses pursued by a firm. As shown in Figure 7.1, firms can pursue a strategy of **limited corporate diversification**, of **related corporate diversification**, or of **unrelated corporate diversification**.

Limited Corporate Diversification

A firm has implemented a strategy of **limited corporate diversification** when all or most of its business activities fall within a single industry and geographic market (see Panel A of Figure 7.1). Two kinds of firms are included in this corporate diversification category: **single-business firms** (firms with greater than 95 percent of their total sales in a single-product market) and **dominant-business firms** (firms with between 70 and 95 percent of their total sales in a single-product market).

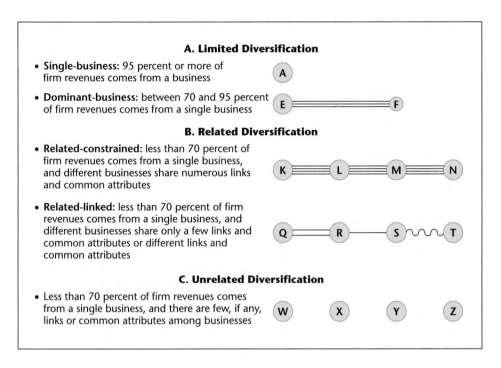

Figure 7.1   Levels and Types of Diversification

Differences between single-business and dominant-business firms are represented in Panel A of Figure 7.1. The firm pursuing a single-business corporate diversification strategy engages in only one business, Business A. An example of a single-business firm is the WD-40 Company of San Diego, California. This company manufactures and distributes only one product—the spray cleanser and lubricant WD-40. The dominant-business firm pursues two businesses, Business E and a smaller Business F that is tightly linked to Business E. An example of a dominant-business firm is Donato's Pizza. Donato's Pizza does the vast majority of its business in a single product—pizza—in a single market—the United States. However, Donato's has begun selling non-pizza food products, including sandwiches, and also owns a subsidiary that makes a machine that automatically slices and puts pepperoni on pizzas. Not only does Donato's use this machine in its own pizzerias, it also sells this machine to food manufacturers that make frozen pepperoni pizza.

In an important sense, firms pursuing a strategy of limited corporate diversification are not leveraging their resources and capabilities beyond a single product or market. Thus, the analysis of limited corporate diversification is logically equivalent to the analysis of business-level strategies (discussed in Part 2 of this book). Because these kinds of strategies have already been discussed, the remainder of this chapter focuses on corporate strategies that involve higher levels of diversification.

Related Corporate Diversification

As a firm begins to engage in businesses in more than one product or market, it moves away from being a single-business or dominant-business firm and begins to adopt higher levels of corporate diversification. When less than 70 percent of a firm's revenue comes from a single-product market and these multiple lines of business are linked, the firm has implemented a strategy of **related corporate diversification**.

The multiple businesses that a diversified firm pursues can be related in two ways (see Panel B in Figure 7.1). If all the businesses in which a firm operates share a significant number of inputs, production technologies, distribution channels, similar customers, and so forth, this corporate diversification strategy is called **related-constrained**. This strategy is *constrained* because corporate managers pursue business opportunities in new markets or industries only if those markets or industries share numerous resource and capability requirements with the businesses the firm is currently pursuing. Commonalities across businesses in a strategy of related-constrained diversification are represented by the linkages among Businesses K, L, M, and N in the related-constrained section of Figure 7.1.

PepsiCo is an example of a related-constrained diversified firm. Although PepsiCo operates in multiple businesses around the world, all of its businesses focus on providing snack-type products, either food or beverages. PepsiCo is not in the business of making or selling more traditional types of food—such as pasta, or cheese, or breakfast cereal. Moreover, PepsiCo attempts to use a single, firm-wide capability to gain competitive advantages in each of its businesses—its ability to develop and exploit well-known brand names. Whether it's Pepsi, Doritos, Mountain Dew, or Big Red, PepsiCo is all about building brand names. In fact, PepsiCo has 16 brands that generate $1 billion or more in revenues each year. That is more so-called "power brands" than Nestlé, Procter & Gamble, or Coca-Cola![1]

If the different businesses that a single firm pursues are linked on only a couple of dimensions, or if different sets of businesses are linked along very different dimensions, the corporate diversification strategy is called **related-linked**. For example, Business Q and Business R may share similar production technology, Business R and Business S may share similar customers, Business S and Business T may share similar suppliers, and Business Q and Business T may have no common attributes. This strategy is represented in the related-linked section of Figure 7.1 by businesses with relatively few links between them and with different kinds of links between them (i.e., straight lines and curved lines).

An example of a related-linked diversified firm is Disney. Disney has evolved from a single-business firm (when it did nothing but produce animated motion pictures), to a dominant business firm (when it produced family-oriented motion pictures and operated a theme park), to a related-constrained diversified firm (when it produced family-oriented motion pictures, operated multiple theme parks, and sold products through its Disney Stores). Recently, it has become so diversified that it has taken on the attributes of related-linked diversification. Although much of the Disney empire still builds on characters developed in its animated motion pictures, it also owns and operates businesses—including a movie studio that produces movies more appropriate for mature audiences, several hotels and resorts that have little or nothing to do with Disney characters, and a television network (ABC) that broadcasts non-Disney-produced content—that are less directly linked to these characters. This is not to suggest that Disney is pursuing an unrelated diversification strategy. After all, most of its businesses are in the entertainment industry, broadly defined. Rather, this is only to suggest that it is no longer possible to find a single thread—like a Mickey Mouse or a Lion King—that connects all of Disney's business enterprises. In this sense, Disney has become a related-linked diversified firm.[2]

Unrelated Corporate Diversification

Firms that pursue a strategy of related corporate diversification have some type of linkages among most, if not all, the different businesses they pursue. However, it is possible for firms to pursue numerous different businesses and for there to be *no* linkages among them (see Panel C of Figure 7.1). When less than 70 percent of a firm's revenues are generated in a single-product market, and when a firm's businesses share few, if any, common attributes, then that firm is pursuing a strategy of **unrelated corporate diversification**.

General Electric (GE) is an example of a firm pursuing an unrelated diversification strategy. GE's mix of businesses includes aviation products ($16.8 billion in 2007 revenues), aviation financial services ($4.6 billion in 2007 revenues), energy products ($21.8 billion in 2007 revenues), energy financial services ($2.4 billion in 2007 revenues), oil and gas products ($6.8 billion in 2007 revenues), transportation ($4.5 billion in 2007 revenues), capital solutions ($14.3 billion in 2007 revenues), real estate ($7 billion in 2007 revenues), GE Money ($25.1 billion in 2007 revenues), health care ($17 billion in 2007 revenues), consumer and industrial products ($13.3 billion in 2007 revenues), enterprise solutions ($4.5 billion in 2007 revenues), and NBC Universal ($16 billion in 2007 revenues). It is difficult to see how these businesses are closely related to each other. Indeed, GE tends to manage each of its businesses as if they were stand-alone entities—a management approach consistent with a firm implementing an unrelated diversified corporate strategy.[3]

The Value of Corporate Diversification

V R I O

For corporate diversification to be economically valuable, two conditions must hold. First, there must be some valuable economy of scope among the multiple businesses in which a firm is operating. Second, it must be less costly for managers in a firm to realize these economies of scope than for outside equity holders on their own. If outside investors could realize the value of a particular economy of scope on their own, and at low cost, then they would have few incentives to "hire" managers to realize this economy of scope for them. Each of these requirements for corporate diversification to add value for a firm will be considered below.

What Are Valuable Economies of Scope?

Economies of scope exist in a firm when the value of the products or services it sells increases as a function of the number of businesses in which that firm operates. In this definition, the term *scope* refers to the range of businesses in which a diversified firm operates. For this reason, only diversified firms can, by definition, exploit economies of scope. Economies of scope are valuable to the extent that they increase a firm's revenues or decrease its costs, compared to what would be the case if these economies of scope were not exploited.

A wide variety of potentially valuable sources of economies of scope have been identified in the literature. Some of the most important of these are listed in Table 7.1 and discussed in the following text. How valuable economies of scope actually are, on average, has been the subject of a great deal of research, which we summarize in the Research Made Relevant feature.

TABLE 7.1 Different Types of Economies of Scope

1. Operational economies of scope
   - Shared activities
   - Core competencies
2. Financial economies of scope
   - Internal capital allocation
   - Risk reduction
   - Tax advantages
3. Anticompetitive economies of scope
   - Multipoint competition
   - Exploiting market power
4. Employee and stakeholder incentives for diversification
   - Maximizing management compensation

Research Made Relevant

In 1994, Lang and Stulz published a sensational article that suggested that, on average, when a firm began implementing a corporate diversification strategy, it destroyed about 25 percent of its market value. Lang and Stulz came to this conclusion by comparing the market performance of firms pursuing a corporate diversification strategy with portfolios of firms pursuing a limited diversification strategy. Taken together, the market performance of a portfolio of firms that were pursuing a limited diversification strategy was about 25 percent higher than the market performance of a single diversified firm operating in all of the businesses included in this portfolio. These results suggested that not only were economies of scope not valuable, but, on average, efforts to realize these economies actually destroyed economic value. Similar results were published by Comment and Jarrell using different measures of firm performance.

How Valuable Are Economies of Scope, on Average?

Not surprisingly, these results generated quite a stir. If Lang and Stulz were correct, then diversified firms—no matter what kind of diversification strategy they engaged in—destroyed an enormous amount of economic value. This could lead to a fundamental restructuring of the U.S. economy.

However, several researchers questioned Lang and Stutz's conclusions. Two new findings suggest that, even if there is a 25 percent discount, diversification can still add value. First, Villalonga and others found that firms pursuing diversification strategies were generally performing more poorly before they began diversifying than firms that never pursued diversification strategies. Thus, although it might appear that diversification leads to a significant loss of economic value, in reality that loss of value occurred before these firms began implementing a diversification strategy. Indeed, some more recent research suggests that these relatively poor-performing firms may actually increase their market value over what would have been the case if they did not diversify.

Second, Miller found that firms that find it in their self-interest to diversify do so in a very predictable pattern. These firms tend to diversify

Diversification to Exploit Operational Economies of Scope

Sometimes, economies of scope may reflect operational links among the businesses in which a firm engages. **Operational economies of scope** typically take one of two forms: shared activities and shared core competencies.

Shared Activities.   In Chapter 3, it was suggested that value-chain analysis can be used to describe the specific business activities of a firm. This same value-chain analysis can also be used to describe the business activities that may be shared across several different businesses within a diversified firm. These **shared activities** are potential sources of operational economies of scope for diversified firms.

Consider, for example, the hypothetical firm presented in Figure 7.2. This diversified firm engages in three businesses: A, B, and C. However, these three businesses share a variety of activities throughout their value chains. For example, all three draw on the same technology development operation. Product design and manufacturing are shared in Businesses A and B and separate for Business C. All three businesses share a common marketing and service operation. Business A has its own distribution system.

into the most profitable new business first, the second most profitable business second, and so forth. Not surprisingly, the fiftieth diversification move made by these firms might not generate huge additional profits. However, these profits—it turns out—are still, on average, positive. Because multiple rounds of diversification increase profits at a decreasing rate, the overall average profitability of diversified firms will generally be less than the overall average profitability of firms that do not pursue a diversification strategy—thus, a substantial difference between the market value of nondiversified and diversified firms might exist. However, this discount, per se, does not mean that the diversified firm is destroying economic value. Rather, it may mean only that a diversifying firm is creating value in smaller increments as it continues to diversify.

However, some even more recent research suggests that Lang and

Stulz's original "diversification discount" finding may be reemerging. It turns out that all the papers that show that diversification does not, on average, destroy value, and that it sometimes can add value, fail to consider all the investment options open to firms. In particular, firms that are generating free cash flow but have limited growth opportunities in their current businesses—that is, the kinds of firms that Villalonga and Miller suggest will create value through diversification—have other investment options besides diversification. In particular, these firms can return their free cash to their equity holders, either through a direct cash dividend or through buying back stock.

Mackey and Barney show that firms that do not pay out to shareholders destroy value compared to firms that do pay out. In particular, firms that use their free cash flow to pay dividends and buy back stock create

value; firms that pay out and diversify destroy some value; and firms that just diversify destroy significant value.

Of course, these results are "on average." It is possible to identify firms that actually create value from diversification—about 17 percent of diversified firms in the United States create value from diversification. What distinguishes firms that destroy and create value from diversification is likely to be the subject of research for some time to come.

Sources: H. P. Lang and R. M. Stulz. (1994). "Tobin's *q*, corporate diversification, and firm performance." *Journal of Political Economy*, 102, pp. 1248–1280; R. Comment and G. Jarrell. (1995). "Corporate focus and stock returns." *Journal of Financial Economics*, 37, pp. 67–87; D. Miller. (2006). "Technological diversity, related diversification, and firm performance." *Strategic Management Journal*, 27(7), pp. 601–620; B. Villalonga. (2004). "Does diversification cause the 'diversification discount'?" *Financial Management*, 33(2), pp. 5–28; and T. Mackey and J. Barney. (2006). "Is there a diversification discount—really?" Unpublished, Department of Management and Human Resources, The Ohio State University.

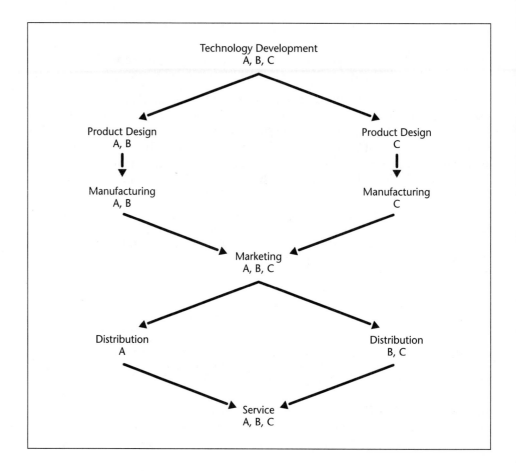

Figure 7.2 A Hypothetical Firm Sharing Activities Among Three Businesses

These kinds of shared activities are quite common among both related-constrained and related-linked diversified firms. At Texas Instruments, for example, a variety of electronics businesses share some research and development activities and many share common manufacturing locations. Procter & Gamble's numerous consumer products businesses often share common manufacturing locations and rely on a common distribution network (through retail grocery stores).[4] Some of the most common shared activities in diversified firms and their location in the value chain are summarized in Table 7.2.

Many of the shared activities listed in Table 7.2 can have the effect of reducing a diversified firm's costs. For example, if a diversified firm has a purchasing function that is common to several of its different businesses, it can often obtain volume discounts on its purchases that would otherwise not be possible. Also, by manufacturing products that are used as inputs into several of a diversified firm's businesses, the total costs of producing these products can be reduced. A single sales force representing the products or services of several different businesses within a diversified firm can reduce the cost of selling these products or services. Firms such as IBM, HP, and General Motors (GM) have all used shared activities to reduce their costs in these ways.

Failure to exploit shared activities across businesses can lead to out-of-control costs. For example, Kentucky Fried Chicken, when it was a division of PepsiCo, encouraged each of its regional business operations in North America to develop

Value Chain Activity	Shared Activities
Input activities	Common purchasing
	Common inventory control system
	Common warehousing facilities
	Common inventory delivery system
	Common quality assurance
	Common input requirements system
	Common suppliers
Production activities	Common product components
	Common product components manufacturing
	Common assembly facilities
	Common quality control system
	Common maintenance operation
	Common inventory control system
Warehousing and distribution	Common product delivery system
	Common warehouse facilities
Sales and marketing	Common advertising efforts
	Common promotional activities
	Cross-selling of products
	Common pricing systems
	Common marketing departments
	Common distribution channels
	Common sales forces
	Common sales offices
	Common order processing services
Dealer support and service	Common service network
	Common guarantees and warranties
	Common accounts receivable management systems
	Common dealer training
	Common dealer support services

Sources: Porter, M. E. (1985). *Competitive advantage*. New York: Free Press; Rumelt, R. P. (1974). *Strategy, structure, and economic performance*. Cambridge, MA: Harvard University Press; and Ansoff, H. I. (1965). *Corporate strategy*. New York: McGraw-Hill.

its own quality improvement plan. The result was enormous redundancy and at least three conflicting quality efforts—all leading to higher-than-necessary costs. In a similar way, Levi Strauss's unwillingness to centralize and coordinate order processing led to a situation where six separate order-processing computer systems operated simultaneously. This costly redundancy was ultimately replaced by a single, integrated ordering system shared across the entire corporation.[5]

Shared activities can also increase the revenues in diversified firms' businesses. This can happen in at least two ways. First, it may be that shared product development and sales activities may enable two or more businesses in a diversified firm to offer a bundled set of products to customers. Sometimes, the value of these "product bundles" is greater than the value of each product separately. This additional customer value can generate revenues greater than would have been the case if the businesses were not together and sharing activities in a diversified firm.

In the telecommunications industry, for example, separate firms sell telephones, access to telephone lines, equipment to route calls in an office, mobile telephones, and paging services. A customer that requires all these services could contact five different companies. Each of these five different firms would likely possess its own unique technological standards and software, making the development of an integrated telecommunications system for the customer difficult, at best. Alternatively, a single diversified firm sharing sales activities across these businesses could significantly reduce the search costs of potential customers. This one-stop shopping is likely to be valuable to customers, who might be willing to pay a slightly higher price for this convenience than they would pay if they purchased these services from five separate firms. Moreover, if this diversified firm also shares some technology development activities across its businesses, it might be able to offer an integrated telecommunications network to potential customers. The extra value of this integrated network for customers is very likely to be reflected in prices that are higher than would have been possible if each of these businesses were independent or if activities among these businesses were not shared. Most of the regional telephone operating companies in the United States are attempting to gain these economies of scope.[6]

Such product bundles are important in other firms as well. Many grocery stores now sell prepared foods alongside traditional grocery products in the belief that busy customers want access to all kinds of food products—in the same location.[7]

Second, shared activities can enhance business revenues by exploiting the strong, positive reputations of some of a firm's businesses in other of its businesses. For example, if one business has a strong positive reputation for high-quality manufacturing, other businesses sharing this manufacturing activity will gain some of the advantages of this reputation. And, if one business has a strong positive reputation for selling high-performance products, other businesses sharing sales and marketing activities with this business will gain some of the advantages of this reputation. In both cases, businesses that draw on the strong reputation of another business through shared activities with that business will have larger revenues than they would were they operating on their own.

The Limits of Activity Sharing.   Despite the potential of activity sharing to be the basis of a valuable corporate diversification strategy, this approach has three important limits.[8] First, substantial organizational issues are often associated with a diversified firm's learning how to manage cross-business relationships. Managing these relationships effectively can be very difficult, and failure can lead to excess bureaucracy, inefficiency, and organizational gridlock. These issues are discussed in detail in Chapter 8.

Second, sharing activities may limit the ability of a particular business to meet its specific customers' needs. For example, if two businesses share manufacturing activities, they may reduce their manufacturing costs. However, to gain these cost advantages, these businesses may need to build products using somewhat standardized components that do not fully meet their individual customers' needs. Businesses that share distribution activities may have lower overall distribution costs but be unable to distribute their products to all their customers. Businesses that share sales activities may have lower overall sales costs but be unable to provide the specialized selling required in each business.

One diversified firm that has struggled with the ability to meet the specialized needs of customers in its different divisions is GM. To exploit economies of scope in the design of new automobiles, GM shared the design process across several automobile divisions. The result through much of the 1990s was "cookie-cutter" cars—the traditional distinctiveness of several GM divisions, including Oldsmobile and Cadillac, was all but lost.[9]

Third, if one business in a diversified firm has a poor reputation, sharing activities with that business can reduce the quality of the reputation of other businesses in the firm.

Taken together, these limits on activity sharing can more than offset any possible gains. Indeed, over the past decade more and more diversified firms have been abandoning efforts at activity sharing in favor of managing each business's activities independently. For example, ABB, Inc. (a Swiss engineering firm) and CIBA-Geigy (a Swiss chemicals firm) have adopted explicit corporate policies that restrict almost all activity sharing across businesses.[10] Other diversified firms, including Nestlé and GE, restrict activity sharing to just one or two activities (such as research and development or management training). However, to the extent that a diversified firm can exploit shared activities while avoiding these problems, shared activities can add value to a firm.

Core Competencies.   Recently, a second operational linkage among the businesses of a diversified firm has been described. Unlike shared activities, this linkage is based on different businesses in a diversified firm sharing less tangible resources such as managerial and technical know-how, experience, and wisdom. This source of operational economy of scope has been called a firm's core competence.[11] **Core competence** has been defined by Prahalad and Hamel as "the collective learning in the organization, especially how to coordinate diverse production skills and integrate multiple streams of technologies." Core competencies are complex sets of resources and capabilities that link different businesses in a diversified firm through managerial and technical know-how, experience, and wisdom.[12]

Two firms that have well-developed core competencies are 3M and Johnson & Johnson (J&J). 3M has a core competence in substrates, adhesives, and coatings. Collectively, employees at 3M know more about developing and applying adhesives and coatings on different kinds of substrates than do employees in any other organization. Over the years, 3M has applied these resources and capabilities in a wide variety of products, including Post-it notes, magnetic tape, photographic film, pressure-sensitive tape, and coated abrasives. At first glance, these widely diversified products seem to have little or nothing in common. Yet they all draw on a single core set of resources and capabilities in substrates, adhesives, and coatings.

Johnson & Johnson has a core competence in developing or acquiring pharmaceutical and medical products and then marketing them to the public. Many of J&J's products are dominant in their market segments—J&J's in baby powder, Ethicon in surgical sutures, and Tylenol in pain relievers. And although these products range broadly from those sold directly to consumers (e.g., the Band-Aid brand of adhesive bandages) to highly sophisticated medical technologies sold only to doctors and hospitals (e.g., Ethicon sutures), all of J&J's products build on the same ability to identify, develop, acquire, and market products in the pharmaceutical and medical products industry.

To understand how core competencies can reduce a firm's costs or increase its revenues, consider how core competencies emerge over time. Most firms begin operations in a single business. Imagine that a firm has carefully evaluated all of its current business opportunities and has fully funded all of those with a positive net present value. Any of the above-normal returns that this firm has left over after fully funding all its current positive net present value opportunities can be thought of as **free cash flow**.[13] Firms can spend this free cash in a variety of ways: They can spend it on benefits for managers; they can give it to shareholders through dividends or by buying back a firm's stock; they can use it to invest in new businesses.

Suppose a firm chooses to use this cash to invest in a new business. In other words, suppose this firm chooses to implement a diversification strategy. If this firm is seeking to maximize the return from implementing this diversification strategy, which of all the possible businesses that it could invest in should it invest in? Obviously, a profit-maximizing firm will choose to begin operations in a business in which it has a competitive advantage. What kind of business is likely to generate this competitive advantage for this firm? The obvious answer is a business in which the same underlying resources and capabilities that gave this firm an advantage in its original business are still valuable, rare, and costly to imitate. Consequently, this first diversification move sees the firm investing in a business that is closely related to its original business, because both businesses will draw on a common set of underlying resources and capabilities that provide the firm with a competitive advantage.

Put another way, a firm that diversifies by exploiting its resource and capability advantages in its original business will have lower costs than those that begin a new business without these resource and capability advantages, or higher revenues than firms lacking these advantages, or both. As long as this firm organizes itself to take advantage of these resource and capability advantages in its new business, it should earn high profits in its new business, along with the profits it will still be earning in its original business.[14] This can be true for even relatively small firms, as described in the Strategy in the Emerging Enterprise feature.

Of course, over time this diversified firm is likely to develop new resources and capabilities through its operations in the new business. These new resources and capabilities enhance the entire set of skills that a firm might be able to bring to still another business. Using the profits it has obtained in its previous businesses, this firm is likely to enter another new business. Again, choosing from among all the new businesses it could enter, it is likely to begin operations in a business in which it can exploit its now-expanded resource and capability advantages to obtain a competitive advantage, and so forth.

After a firm has engaged in this diversification strategy several times, the resources and capabilities that enable it to operate successfully in several businesses become its core competencies. A firm develops these core competencies by transferring the technical and management knowledge, experience, and wisdom it developed in earlier businesses to its new businesses. A firm that has just begun this diversification process has implemented a dominant-business strategy. If all of a firm's businesses share the same core competencies, then that firm has implemented a strategy of related-constrained diversification. If different businesses exploit different sets of resources and capabilities, that firm has implemented a strategy of related-linked diversification. In any case, these core competencies enable firms to have lower costs or higher revenues as they include more businesses in their diversified portfolio, compared to firms without these competencies.

Of course, not all firms develop core competencies in this logical and rational manner. That is, sometimes a firm's core competencies are examples of the emergent strategies described in Chapter 1. Indeed, as described in Chapter 1, J&J is an example of a firm that has a core competence that emerged over time. However, no matter how a firm develops core competencies, to the extent that they enable a diversified firm to have lower costs or larger revenues in its

Strategy in the Emerging Enterprise

W. L. Gore & Associates is best known for manufacturing a waterproof and windproof, but breathable, fabric that is used to insulate winter coats, hiking boots, and a myriad of other outdoor apparel products. This fabric—known as Gore-Tex—has a brand name in its market niche every bit as strong as any of the brand names controlled by PepsiCo or Procter & Gamble. The "Gore-Tex" label attached to any outdoor garment promises waterproof comfort in even the harshest conditions.

But W. L. Gore & Associates did not start out in the outdoor fabric business. Indeed, for the first 10 years of its existence, W. L. Gore sold insulation for wires and similar industrial products using a molecular technology originally developed by DuPont—a technology most of us know as Teflon. Only 10 years after its initial founding did the founder's son, Bob Gore, discover that it was possible to stretch the Teflon molecule to form a strong and porous material that is chemically inert, has a low friction coefficient, functions within a wide temperature range, does not age, and is extremely strong. This is the material called Gore-Tex.

Gore-Tex and Guitar Strings

By extending its basic technology, W. L. Gore and Associates has been able to diversify well beyond its original wire insulation business. With over 8,000 employees and more than $2 billion in revenues, the company currently has operations in medical products (including synthetic blood vessels and patches for soft tissue regeneration), electronics products (including wiring board materials and computer chip components), industrial products (including filter bags for environmental protection and sealants for chemical manufacturing), and fabrics (including Gore-Tex fabric,

Wind-Stopper fabric, and CleanStream filters).

And Gore continues to discover new ways to exploit its competence in the Teflon molecule. In 1997, a team of Gore engineers developed a cable made out of the Teflon molecule to control puppets at Disney's theme parks. Unfortunately, these cables did not perform up to expectations and were not sold to Disney. However, some guitar players discovered these cables and began using them as strings for their guitars. They found out that these "Gore-Tex" strings sounded great and lasted five times as long as alternative guitar strings. So Gore entered yet another market—the $100 million fretted-stringed-instrument business—with its Elixir brand of guitar strings. Currently, W. L. Gore is the second-largest manufacturer in this market.

The flexibility of the Teflon molecule—and W. L. Gore's ability to explore and exploit that flexibility—has created a diversified company whose original objective was simply to sell insulation for wires.

Sources: www.gore.com; D. Sacks. (2003). "The Gore- Tex of guitar strings." *Fast Times*, December, p. 46.

business operations, these competencies can be thought of as sources of economies of scope.

Some diversified firms realize the value of these kinds of core competencies through shared activities. For example, as suggested earlier, 3M has a core competence in substrates, adhesives, and coatings. To exploit this, 3M has adopted a multitiered product innovation process. In addition to product innovations within each business unit separately, 3M also supports a corporate research and development lab that seeks to exploit and expand its core competence in substrates, adhesives, and coatings. Because the corporate research and development laboratory is shared by all of 3M's different businesses, it can be thought of as a shared activity.

However, other firms realize the value of their core competencies without shared activities. Although J&J has a core competence in developing, acquiring, and marketing pharmaceutical and medical products, it does not realize this core competence through shared activities. Indeed, each of J&J's businesses is run very independently. For example, although one of its most successful products is Tylenol, the fact that the company that manufactures and distributes Tylenol—McNeil—is actually a division of J&J is not printed on any Tylenol packaging. If you did not know that Tylenol was a J&J product, you could not tell from the bottles of Tylenol you buy.

Although J&J does not use shared activities to realize the value of its core competencies, it does engage in other activities to realize this value. For example, it is not uncommon for members of the senior management team of each of the businesses in J&J's portfolio to have obtained managerial experience in some other J&J business. That is, J&J identifies high-potential managers in one of its businesses and uses this knowledge by giving these managers additional responsibilities in another J&J business. This ability to leverage its management talent across multiple businesses is an example of a firm's core competence, although the realization of the value of that competence does not depend on the existence of a shared activity.

Sometimes, because a firm's core competence is not reflected in specific shared activities, it is easy to conclude that it is not exploiting any economies of scope in its diversification strategy. Diversified firms that are exploiting core competencies as an economy of scope but are not doing so with any shared activities are sometimes called **seemingly unrelated diversified firms**. They may appear to be unrelated diversified firms, but are, in fact, related diversified firms without any shared activities.

One example of a seemingly unrelated diversified firm is the British company Virgin Group. Operating in a wide variety of businesses—everything from record producing, music retailing, air and rail travel, soft drinks, spirits, mobile phones, cosmetics, retail bridal shops, financial services, and providing gas and electricity, to hot air ballooning—the Virgin Group is clearly diversified. The firm has few, if any, shared activities. However, at least two core competencies cut across all the business activities in the group—the brand name "Virgin" and the eccentric marketing and management approach of Virgin's founder, Richard Branson. Branson is the CEO who walked down a "catwalk" in a wedding gown to help publicize the opening of Virgin Brides—the Virgin Group's line of retail bridal shops. Branson is also the CEO who had all of Virgin Air's airplanes repainted with the British "Union Jack" and the slogan "Britain's Real Airline" when British Airways eliminated the British flag from its airplanes. Whether these two core competencies create sufficient value to justify the Virgin Group's continued existence and whether they will continue beyond Branson's affiliation with the group are still open questions.

Limits of Core Competencies.   Just as there are limits to the value of shared activities as sources of economies of scope, so there are limits to core competencies as sources of these economies. The first of these limitations stems from important organizational issues to be discussed in Chapter 8. The way that a diversified firm is organized can either facilitate the exploitation of core competencies or prevent this exploitation from occurring.

A second limitation of core competencies is a result of the intangible nature of these economies of scope. Whereas shared activities are reflected in tangible operations in a diversified firm, core competencies may be reflected only in shared knowledge, experience, and wisdom across businesses. The intangible character of these relationships is emphasized when they are described as a **dominant logic** in a firm, or a common way of thinking about strategy across different businesses.[15]

The intangibility of core competencies can lead diversified firms to make two kinds of errors in managing relatedness. First, intangible core competencies can be illusory inventions by creative managers who link even the most completely unrelated businesses and thereby justify their diversification strategy. A firm that manufactures airplanes and running shoes can rationalize this diversification by claiming to have a core competence in managing transportation businesses. A firm operating in the professional football business and the movie business can rationalize this diversification by claiming to have a core competence in managing entertainment businesses. Such **invented competencies** are not real sources of economies of scope.

Second, a diversified firm's businesses may be linked by a core competence, but this competence may affect these businesses' costs or revenues in a trivial way. Thus, for example, all of a firm's businesses may be affected by government actions, but the impact of these actions on costs and revenues in different businesses may be quite small. A firm may have a core competence in managing relationships with the government, but this core competence will not reduce costs or enhance revenues for these particular businesses very much. Also, each of a diversified firm's businesses may use some advertising. However, if advertising does not have a major impact on revenues for these businesses, core competencies in advertising are not likely to significantly reduce a firm's costs or increase its revenues. In this case, a core competence may be a source of economies of scope, but the value of those economies may be very small.

Diversification to Exploit Financial Economies of Scope

A second class of motivations for diversification shifts attention away from operational linkages among a firm's businesses and toward financial advantages associated with diversification. Three financial implications of diversification have been studied: diversification and capital allocation, diversification and risk reduction, and tax advantages of diversification.

Diversification and Capital Allocation.   Capital can be allocated to businesses in one of two ways. First, businesses operating as independent entities can compete for capital in the external capital market. They do this by providing a sufficiently high return to induce investors to purchase shares of their equity, by having a sufficiently high cash flow to repay principal and interest on debt, and in other ways. Alternatively, a business can be part of a diversified firm. That diversified firm competes in the external capital market and allocates capital among its various businesses. In a sense, diversification creates an **internal capital market** in which businesses in a diversified firm compete for corporate capital.[16]

For an internal capital market to create value for a diversified firm, it must offer some efficiency advantages over an external capital market. It has been suggested that a potential efficiency gain from internal capital markets depends on the greater amount and quality of information that a diversified firm possesses about the businesses it owns, compared with the information that external suppliers of capital possess. Owning a business gives a diversified firm access to detailed and accurate information about the actual performance of the business, its true future prospects, and thus the actual amount and cost of the capital that should be allocated to it. External sources of capital, in contrast, have relatively limited access to information and thus have a limited ability to judge the actual performance and future prospects of a business.

Some have questioned whether a diversified firm, as a source of capital, actually has more and better information about a business it owns, compared to external sources of capital. After all, independent businesses seeking capital have a strong incentive to provide sufficient information to external suppliers of capital to obtain required funds. However, a firm that owns a business may have at least two informational advantages over external sources of capital.

First, although an independent business has an incentive to provide information to external sources of capital, it also has an incentive to downplay or even not report any negative information about its performance and prospects. Such negative information would raise an independent firm's cost of capital. External sources of capital have limited ability to force a business to reveal all information about its performance and prospects and thus may provide capital at a lower cost than they would if they had full information. Ownership gives a firm the right to compel more complete disclosure, although even here full disclosure is not guaranteed. With this more complete information, a diversified firm can allocate just the right amount of capital, at the appropriate cost, to each business.

Second, an independent business may have an incentive not to reveal all the positive information about its performance and prospects. In Chapter 3, the ability of a firm to earn economic profits was shown to depend on the imitability of its resources and capabilities. An independent business that informs external sources of capital about all of its sources of competitive advantage is also informing its potential competitors about these sources of advantage. This information sharing increases the probability that these sources of advantage will be imitated. Because of the competitive implications of sharing this information, firms may choose not to share it, and external sources of capital may underestimate the true performance and prospects of a business.

A diversified firm, however, may gain access to this additional information about its businesses without revealing it to potential competitors. This information enables the diversified firm to make more informed decisions about how much capital to allocate to a business and about the cost of that capital, compared to the external capital market.[17]

Over time, there should be fewer errors in funding businesses through internal capital markets, compared to funding businesses through external capital markets. Fewer funding errors, over time, suggest a slight capital allocation advantage for a diversified firm, compared to an external capital market. This advantage should be reflected in somewhat higher rates of return on invested capital for the diversified firm, compared to the rates of return on invested capital for external sources of capital.

However, the businesses within a diversified firm do not always gain cost-of-capital advantages by being part of a diversified firm's portfolio. Several authors have argued that because a diversified firm has lower overall risk (see the following discussion), it will have a lower cost of capital, which it can pass along to the businesses within its portfolio. Although the lower risks associated with a diversified firm may lower the firm's cost of capital, the appropriate cost of capital to businesses within the firm depends on the performance and prospects of each of those businesses. The firm's advantages in evaluating its businesses' performances and prospects result in more appropriate capital allocation, not just in lower cost of capital for those businesses. Indeed, a business's cost of capital may be lower than it could have obtained in the external capital market (because the firm is able to more fully evaluate the positive aspects of that business), or it may be higher than it could have obtained in the external capital market (because the firm is able to more fully evaluate the negative aspects of that business).

Of course, if these businesses also have lower cost or higher revenue expectations because they are part of a diversified firm, then those cost/revenue advantages will be reflected in the appropriate cost of capital for these businesses. In this sense, any operational economies of scope for businesses in a diversified firm may be recognized by a diversified firm exploiting financial economies of scope.

Limits on Internal Capital Markets.   Although internal capital allocation has several potential advantages for a diversified firm, this process also has several limits. First, the level and type of diversification that a firm pursues can affect the efficiency of this allocation process. A firm that implements a strategy of unrelated diversification, whereby managers have to evaluate the performance and prospects of numerous very different businesses, puts a greater strain on the capital allocation skills of its managers than does a firm that implements related diversification. Indeed, in the extreme, the capital allocation efficiency of a firm pursuing broad-based unrelated diversification will probably not be superior to the capital allocation efficiency of the external capital market.

Second, the increased efficiency of internal capital allocation depends on managers in a diversified firm having better information for capital allocation than the information available to external sources. However, this higher-quality information is not guaranteed. The incentives that can lead managers to exaggerate their performance and prospects to external capital sources can also lead to this behavior within a diversified firm. Indeed, several examples of business managers falsifying performance records to gain access to more internal capital have been reported.[18] Research suggests that capital allocation requests by managers are routinely discounted in diversified firms in order to correct for these managers' inflated estimates of the performance and prospects of their businesses.[19]

Finally, not only do business managers have an incentive to inflate the performance and prospects of their business in a diversified firm, but managers in charge of capital allocation in these firms may have an incentive to continue investing in a business despite its poor performance and prospects. The reputation and status of these managers often depend on the success of these business investments, because often they initially approved them. These managers often continue throwing good money at these businesses in hope that they will someday improve, thereby justifying their original decision. Organizational psychologists call this process **escalation of commitment** and have presented numerous examples of managers' becoming irrationally committed to a particular investment.[20]

Indeed, research on the value of internal capital markets in diversified firms suggests that, on average, the limitations of these markets often outweigh their advantages. For example, even controlling for firm size, excessive investment in poorly performing businesses in a diversified firm reduces the market value of the average diversified firm.[21] However, the fact that many firms do not gain the advantages associated with internal capital markets does not necessarily imply that no firms gain these advantages. If only a few firms are able to obtain the advantages of internal capital markets while successfully avoiding their limitations, this financial economy of scope may be a source of at least a temporary competitive advantage.

Diversification and Risk Reduction.   Another possible financial economy of scope for a diversified firm has already been briefly mentioned—the riskiness of the cash flows of diversified firms is lower than the riskiness of the cash flows of undiversified firms. Consider, for example, the riskiness of two businesses operating separately compared to the risk of a diversified firm operating in those same two businesses simultaneously. If both these businesses are very risky on their own, and the cash flows from these businesses are not highly correlated over time, then combining these two businesses into a single firm will generate a lower level of overall risk for the diversified firm than for each of these businesses on their own.

This lower level of risk is due to the low correlation between the cash flows associated with these two businesses. If Business I is having a bad year, Business II might be having a good year, and a firm that operates in both of these businesses simultaneously can have moderate levels of performance. In another year, Business II might be off, while Business I is having a good year. Again, the firm operating in both these businesses can have moderate levels of performance. Firms that diversify to reduce risk will have relatively stable returns over time, especially as they diversify into many different businesses with cash flows that are not highly correlated over time.

Tax Advantages of Diversification.   Another financial economy of scope from diversification stems from possible tax advantages of this corporate strategy. These possible tax advantages reflect one or a combination of two effects. First, a diversified firm can use losses in some of its businesses to offset profits in others, thereby reducing its overall tax liability. Of course, substantial losses in some of its businesses may overwhelm profits in other businesses, forcing businesses that would have remained solvent if they were independent to cease operation. However, as long as business losses are not too large, a diversified firm's tax liability can be reduced. Empirical research suggests that diversified firms do, sometimes, offset profits in some businesses with losses in others, although the tax savings of these activities are usually small.[22]

Second, because diversification can reduce the riskiness of a firm's cash flows, it can also reduce the probability that a firm will declare bankruptcy. This can increase a firm's debt capacity. This effect on debt capacity is greatest when the cash flows of a diversified firm's businesses are perfectly and negatively correlated. However, even when these cash flows are perfectly and positively correlated, there can still be a (modest) increase in debt capacity.

Debt capacity is particularly important in tax environments where interest payments on debt are tax deductible. In this context, diversified firms can increase their leverage up to their debt capacity and reduce their tax liability accordingly. Of course, if interest payments are not tax deductible, or if the marginal corporate tax rate is relatively small, then the tax advantages of diversification can be quite small. Recent empirical work suggests that diversified firms do have greater debt capacity than undiversified firms. However, low marginal corporate tax rates, at least in the United States, make the accompanying tax savings on average relatively small.[23]

Diversification to Exploit Anticompetitive Economies of Scope

A third group of motivations for diversification is based on the relationship between diversification strategies and various anticompetitive activities by firms. Two specific examples of these activities are (1) multipoint competition to facilitate mutual forbearance and tacit collusion and (2) exploiting market power.

Multipoint Competition.   Multipoint competition exists when two or more diversified firms simultaneously compete in multiple markets. For example, HP and Dell compete in both the personal computer market and the market for

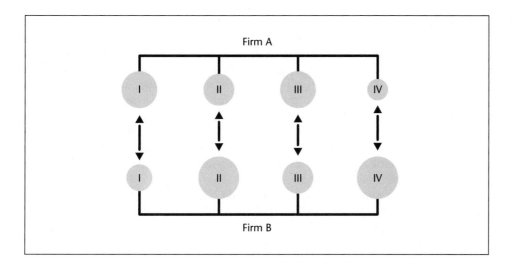

Figure 7.3 Multipoint Competition Between Hypothetical Firms A and B

computer printers. Michelin and Goodyear compete in both the U.S. automobile tire market and the European automobile tire market. Disney and AOL/Time Warner compete in both the movie production and book publishing businesses.

Multipoint competition can serve to facilitate a particular type of tacit collusion called **mutual forbearance**. Firms engage in **tacit collusion** when they cooperate to reduce rivalry below the level expected under perfect competition. Consider the situation facing two diversified firms, A and B. These two firms operate in the same businesses, I, II, III, and IV (see Figure 7.3). In this context, any decisions that Firm A might make to compete aggressively in Businesses I and III must take into account the possibility that Firm B will respond by competing aggressively in Businesses II and IV and vice versa. The potential loss that each of these firms may experience in some of its businesses must be compared to the potential gain that each might obtain if it exploits competitive advantages in other of its businesses. If the present value of gains does not outweigh the present value of losses from retaliation, then both firms will avoid competitive activity. Refraining from competition is mutual forbearance.[24]

Mutual forbearance as a result of multipoint competition has occurred in several industries. For example, this form of tacit collusion has been described as existing between Michelin and Goodyear, Maxwell House and Folger's, Caterpillar and John Deere, and BIC and Gillette.[25] Another clear example of such cooperation can be found in the airline industry. For example, America West began service into the Houston Intercontinental Airport with very low introductory fares. Continental Airlines, the dominant firm at Houston Intercontinental, rapidly responded to America West's low Houston fares by reducing the price of its flights from Phoenix, Arizona, to several cities in the United States. Phoenix is the home airport of America West. Within just a few weeks, America West withdrew its low introductory fares in the Houston market, and Continental withdrew its reduced prices in the Phoenix market. The threat of retaliation across markets apparently led America West and Continental to tacitly collude on prices.[26]

However, sometimes multipoint competition does not lead to mutual forbearance. Consider, for example, the conflict between The Walt Disney Company and Time Warner in the early 1990s. As mentioned earlier, Disney operates in the theme park, movie and television production, and television broadcasting industries. Time Warner operates in the theme park and movie and television production industries and also operates a very large magazine business (*Time, People, Sports Illustrated*, among others). From 1988 through 1993, Disney spent over $40 million in advertising its theme parks in Time Warner magazines. Despite this substantial revenue, Time Warner began an aggressive advertising campaign aimed at wooing customers away from Disney theme parks to its own. Disney retaliated by canceling all of its advertising in Time Warner magazines. Time Warner responded to Disney's actions by canceling a corporate meeting to be held in Florida at Disney World. Disney responded to Time Warner's meeting cancellation by refusing to broadcast Time Warner theme park advertisements on its Los Angeles television station.[27]

Some recent research investigates the conditions under which mutual for-bearance strategies are pursued, as well as conditions under which multipoint competition does not lead to mutual forbearance.[28] In general, the value of the threat of retaliation must be substantial for multipoint competition to lead to mutual forbearance. However, not only must the payoffs to mutual forbearance be substantial, but the firms pursuing this strategy must have strong strategic link-ages among their diversified businesses. This suggests that firms pursuing mutual forbearance strategies based on multipoint competition are usually pursuing a form of related diversification.

Diversification and Market Power.   Internal allocations of capital among a diversified firm's businesses may enable it to exploit in some of its businesses the market power advantages it enjoys in other of its businesses. For example, suppose that a firm is earning monopoly profits in a particular business. This firm can use some of these monopoly profits to subsidize the operations of another of its businesses. This cross-subsidization can take several forms, including **predatory pricing**—that is, setting prices so that they are less than the subsidized business's costs. The effect of this cross-subsidy may be to drive competitors out of the subsidized business and then to obtain monopoly profits in that subsidized business. In a sense, diversification enables a firm to apply its monopoly power in several different businesses. Economists call this a **deep-pockets model** of diversification.[29]

Diversified firms with operations in regulated monopolies have been criticized for this kind of cross-subsidization. For example, most of the regional telephone companies in the United States are engaging in diversification strate-gies. The consent decree that forced the breakup of the original AT&T expressly forbade cross-subsidies between these regional companies' telephone monopo-lies and other business activities, under the assumption that such subsidies would give these firms an unfair competitive advantage in their diversified business activities.[30]

Although these market power economies of scope, in principle, may exist, relatively little empirical work documents their existence. Indeed, research on reg-ulated utilities diversifying into nonregulated businesses in the 1980s suggests not that these firms use monopoly profits in their regulated businesses to unfairly subsidize nonregulated businesses, but that the poor management skills devel-oped in the regulated businesses tend to make diversification less profitable rather than more profitable.[31] Nevertheless, the potential that large diversified firms have to exercise market power and to behave in socially irresponsible ways has led some observers to call for actions to curtail both the economic and political power of these firms. These issues are discussed in the Ethics and Strategy feature.

Firm Size and Employee Incentives to Diversify

Employees may have incentives to diversify that are independent of any benefits from other sources of economies of scope. This is especially the case for employees in senior management positions and employees with long tenure in a particular firm. These employee incentives reflect the interest of employees to diversify because of the relationship between firm size and management compensation.

Research over the years demonstrates conclusively that the primary determinant of the compensation of top managers in a firm is not the economic performance of the firm but the size of the firm, usually measured in sales.[32] Thus, managers seeking to maximize their income should attempt to grow their firm. One of the easiest ways to grow a firm is through diversification, especially unrelated diversification through mergers and acquisitions. By making large acquisitions, a diversified firm can grow substantially in a short period of time, leading senior managers to earn higher incomes. All of this is independent of any economic profit that diversification may or may not generate. Senior managers need only worry about economic profit if the level of that profit is so low that unfriendly takeovers are a threat or so low that the board of directors may be forced to replace management.

Recently, the traditional relationship between firm size and management compensation has begun to break down. More and more, the compensation of senior managers is being tied to the firm's economic performance. In particular, the use of stock and other forms of deferred compensation makes it in management's best interest to be concerned with a firm's economic performance. These changes in compensation do not necessarily imply that firms will abandon all forms of diversification. However, they do suggest that firms will abandon those forms of diversification that do not generate real economies of scope.

Can Equity Holders Realize These Economies of Scope on Their Own?

Earlier in this chapter, it was suggested that for a firm's diversification strategies to create value, two conditions must hold. First, these strategies must exploit valuable economies of scope. Potentially valuable economies of scope were presented in Table 7.1 and discussed in the previous section. Second, it must be less costly for managers in a firm to realize these economies of scope than for outside equity holders on their own. If outside equity holders could realize a particular economy of scope on their own, without a firm's managers, at low cost, why would they want to hire managers to do this for them by investing in a firm and providing capital to managers to exploit an economy of scope?

Table 7.3 summarizes the discussion on the potential value of the different economies of scope listed in Table 7.1. It also suggests which of these economies of scope will be difficult for outside equity investors to exploit on their own and thus which bases of diversification are most likely to create positive returns for a firm's equity holders.

Most of the economies of scope listed in Table 7.3 cannot be realized by equity holders on their own. This is because most of them require activities that equity holders cannot engage in or information that equity holders do not possess. For example, shared activities, core competencies, multipoint competition, and exploiting market power all require the detailed coordination of business activities across multiple businesses in a firm. Although equity holders may own a portfolio of equities, they are not in a position to coordinate business activities across this portfolio. In a similar way, internal capital allocation requires information

Ethics and Strategy

In 1999, a loose coalition of union members, environmentalists, youth, indigenous peoples, human rights activists, and small farmers took to the streets of Seattle, Washington, to protest a meeting of the World Trade Organization (WTO) and to fight against the growing global power of corporations. Government officials and corporate officers alike were confused by these protests. After all, hadn't world trade increased 19 times from 1950 to 1995 ($0.4 trillion to $7.6 trillion in constant 2003 dollars), and hadn't the total economic output of the entire world gone from $6.4 trillion in 1950 to $60.7 trillion in 2005 (again, in constant 2003 dollars)? Why protest a global economic system—a system that was enhancing the level of free trade and facilitating global economic efficiency—that was so clearly improving the economic well-being of the world's population?

The protestors' message to government and big business was that these aggregate growth numbers masked more truth than they told. Yes, there has been economic growth. But that growth has benefited only a small percentage of the world's population. Most of the population still struggles to survive. The combined net worth of 358 U.S. billionaires in the early 1990s ($760 billion) was equal to the combined net worth of the 2.5 billion poorest people on the earth! Eighty-three percent of the world's total income goes to the richest fifth of the population while the poorest fifth of the world's population receives only 1.4 percent of the world's total income. Currently, 45 to 70 million people worldwide have had to leave

Globalization and the Threat of the Multinational Firm

their home countries to find work in foreign lands, and approximately 1.4 billion people around the world live on less than $1 a day. Even in relatively affluent societies such as the United States, people are finding it increasingly difficult to meet their financial obligations. Falling real wages, economic insecurity, and corporate downsizing have led many people to work longer hours or to hold two or three jobs. While the number of billionaires in the world continues to grow, the number of people facing mind-numbing and strength-robbing poverty grows even faster.

The causes of this apparent contradiction—global economic growth linked with growing global economic decay—are numerous and complex. However, one explanation focuses on the growing economic power of the diversified multinational corporation. The size of these institutions can be immense—many international diversified firms are larger than the entire economies of many nations. And these huge institutions, with a single-minded focus on maximizing their performance, can make profit-making decisions that adversely affect their suppliers, their customers, their employees, and the environment, all with relative impunity. Armed with the unspoken mantra that "Greed is good," these corporations can justify almost any action, as long as it increases the wealth of their shareholders.

Of course, even if one accepts this hypothesis—and it is far from being universally accepted—solutions to the growing power of internationally diversified firms are not obvious. The problem is that one way that firms become large and powerful is by being able to meet customer demands effectively. Thus, firm size, per se, is not necessarily an indication that a firm is behaving in ways inconsistent with the public good. Government efforts to restrict the size of firms simply because they are large could easily have the effect of making citizens worse off. However, once firms are large and powerful, they may very well be tempted to exercise that power in ways that benefit themselves at great cost to society.

Whatever the causes and solutions to these problems, the protests in Seattle in 1999 and at every WTO meeting since Seattle have at least one clear message—global growth for growth's sake is no longer universally accepted as the correct objective of international economic policy.

Sources: D. C. Korten. (2001). *When corporations rule the world*, 2nd ed. Bloomfield, CT: Kumarian Press; and H. Demsetz. (1973). "Industry structure, market rivalry, and public policy." *Journal of Law and Economics*, 16, pp. 1–9.

TABLE 7.3 The Competitive Implications of Different Economies of Scope

Type of Economy of Scope	Are They Valuable?	Can They Be Realized by Equity Holders on Their Own?	Positive Returns to Equity Holders?
1. *Operational economies of scope*			
Shared activities	Possible	No	Possible
Core competencies	Possible	No	Possible
2. *Financial economies of scope*			
Internal capital allocation	Possible	No	Possible
Risk reduction	Possible	Yes	No
Tax advantages	Possible—small	No	Possible—small
3. *Anticompetitive economies of scope*			
Multipoint competition	Possible	No	Possible
Exploiting market power	Possible	No	Possible
4. *Employee incentives for diversification*			
Maximizing management compensation	No	No	No

about a business's prospects that is simply not available to a firm's outside equity holders.

Indeed, the only two economies of scope listed in Table 7.3 that do not have the potential for generating positive returns for a firm's equity holders are diversification in order to maximize the size of a firm—because firm size, per se, is not valuable— and diversification to reduce risk—because equity holders can do this on their own at very low cost by simply investing in a diversified portfolio of stocks. Indeed, although risk reduction is often a published rationale for many diversification moves, this rationale, by itself, is not directly consistent with the interests of a firm's equity holders. However, some scholars have suggested that this strategy may directly benefit other of a firm's stakeholders and thus indirectly benefit its equity holders. This possibility is discussed in detail in the Strategy in Depth feature.

Overall, this analysis of possible bases of diversification suggests that related diversification is more likely to be consistent with the interests of a firm's equity holders than unrelated diversification. This is because the one economy of scope listed in Table 7.3 that is the easiest for outside equity holders to duplicate—risk reduction—is the only economy of scope that an unrelated diversified firm can try to realize. All the other economies of scope listed in Table 7.3 require coordination and information sharing across businesses in a diversified firm that are very difficult to realize in unrelated diversified firms. Indeed, the preponderance of empirical research suggests that related diversified firms outperform unrelated diversified firms.[33]

Corporate Diversification and Sustained Competitive Advantage

V R I O

Table 7.3 describes those economies of scope that are likely to create real economic value for diversifying firms. It also suggests that related diversification can be valuable, and unrelated diversification is usually not valuable. However, as we

Strategy in Depth

Although diversifying in order to reduce risk generally does not directly benefit outside equity investors in a firm, it can *indirectly* benefit outside equity investors through its impact on the willingness of other stakeholders in a firm to make firm-specific investments. A firm's **stakeholders** include all those groups and individuals who have an interest in how a firm performs. In this sense, a firm's equity investors are one of a firm's stakeholders. Other firm stakeholders include employees, suppliers, and customers.

Firm stakeholders make **firm-specific investments** when the value of the investments they make in a particular firm is much greater than the value of those same investments would be in other firms. Consider, for example, a firm's employees. An employee with a long tenure in a particular firm has generally made substantial **firm-specific human capital investments**. These investments include understanding a particular firm's culture, policies, and procedures; knowing the "right" people to contact to complete a task; and so forth. Such investments have significant value in the firm where they are made. Indeed, such firm-specific knowledge is generally necessary if an employee is to be able to help a firm

Risk-Reducing Diversification and a Firm's Other Stakeholders

conceive and implement valuable strategies. However, the specific investments that an employee makes in a particular firm have almost no value in other firms. If a firm were to cease operations, employees would instantly lose almost all the value of any of the firm-specific investments they had made in that firm.

Suppliers and customers can also make these firm-specific investments. Suppliers make these investments when they customize their products or services to the specific requirements of a particular customer. They also make firm-specific investments when they forgo opportunities to sell to other firms in order to sell to a particular firm. Customers make firm-

specific investments when they customize their operations to fully utilize the products or services of a particular firm. Also, by developing close relationships with a particular firm, customers may forgo the opportunity to develop relationships with other firms. These, too, are firm-specific investments made by customers. If a firm were to cease operations, suppliers and customers would instantly lose almost the entire value of the specific investments they have made in this firm.

Although the firm-specific investments made by employees, suppliers, and customers are risky—in the sense that almost their entire value is lost if the firm in which they are made ceases operations—they are extremely important if a firm is going to be able to generate economic profits. As was suggested in Chapter 3, valuable, rare, and costly-to-imitate resources and capabilities are more likely to be a source of sustained competitive advantage than resources and capabilities without these attributes. Firm-specific investments are more likely to have these attributes than non-firm-specific investments. Non-firm-specific investments are investments that can generate value in numerous different firms.

Thus, valuable, rare, and costly-to-imitate firm-specific investments made by a firm's employees, suppliers,

have seen with all the other strategies discussed in this book, the fact that a strategy is valuable does not necessarily imply that it will be a source of sustained competitive advantage. In order for diversification to be a source of sustained competitive advantage, it must be not only valuable but also rare and costly to imitate, and a firm must be organized to implement this strategy. The rarity and imitability of diversification are discussed in this section; organizational questions are deferred until the next.

and customers can be the source of economic profits. And because a firm's outside equity holders are residual claimants on the cash flows generated by a firm, these economic profits benefit equity holders. Thus, a firm's outside equity holders generally will want a firm's employees, suppliers, and customers to make specific investments in a firm because those investments are likely to be sources of economic wealth for outside equity holders.

However, given the riskiness of firm-specific investments, employees, suppliers, and customers will generally only be willing to make these investments if some of the riskiness associated with making them can be reduced. Outside equity holders have little difficulty managing the risks associated with investing in a particular firm, because they can always create a portfolio of stocks that fully diversifies this risk at very low cost. This is why diversification that reduces the riskiness of a firm's cash flows does not generally directly benefit a firm's outside equity holders. However, a firm's employees, suppliers, and customers usually do not have these low-cost diversification opportunities. Employees, for example, are rarely able to make firm-specific human capital investments in a large enough number of different firms to fully diversify the risks associated with

making them. And although suppliers and customers can diversify their firm-specific investments to a greater degree than employees—through selling to multiple customers and through buying from multiple suppliers—the cost of this diversification for suppliers and customers is usually greater than the costs that are born by outside equity holders in diversifying their risk.

Because it is often very costly for a firm's employees, suppliers, and customers to diversify the risks associated with making firm-specific investments on their own, these stakeholders will often prefer that a firm's managers help manage this risk for them. Managers in a firm can do this by diversifying the portfolio of businesses in which a firm operates. If a firm is unwilling to diversify its portfolio of businesses, then that firm's employees, suppliers, and customers will generally be unwilling to make specific investments in that firm. Moreover, because these firm-specific investments can generate economic profits, and because economic profits can directly benefit a firm's outside equity holders, equity holders have an indirect incentive to encourage a firm to pursue a diversification strategy, even though that strategy does not directly benefit them.

Put differently, a firm's diversification strategy can be thought of as

compensation for the firm-specific investments that a firm's employees, suppliers, and customers make in a firm. Outside equity holders have an incentive to encourage this compensation in return for access to some of the economic profits that these firm-specific investments can generate. In general, the greater the impact of the firm-specific investment made by a firm's employees, suppliers, and customers on the ability of a firm to generate economic profits, the more likely that pursuing a corporate diversification strategy is indirectly consistent with the interests of a firm's outside equity holders. In addition, the more limited the ability of a firm's employees, suppliers, and customers to diversify the risks associated with making firm-specific investments at low cost, the more that corporate diversification is consistent with the interests of outside equity investors.

Sources: J. B. Barney. (1991). "Firm resources and sustained competitive advantage." *Journal of Management*, 17, pp. 99–120; R. M. Stulz. (1996). "Rethinking risk management." *Journal of Applied Corporate Finance*, Fall, pp. 8–24; K. Miller. (1998). "Economic exposure and integrated risk management." *Strategic Management Journal*, 33, pp. 756–779; R. Amit and B. Wernerfelt. (1990). "Why do firms reduce business risk?" *Academy of Management Journal*, 33, pp. 520–533; and H. Wang and J. Barney. (2006), "Employee incentives to make firm specific investments: Implications for resource-based theories of diversification." *Academy of Management Review*, 31(2), pp. 466–476.

The Rarity of Diversification

At first glance, it seems clear that diversification per se is usually not a rare firm strategy. Most large firms have adopted some form of diversification, if only the limited diversification of a dominant-business firm. Even many small and medium-sized firms have adopted different levels of diversification strategy.

Less Costly-to-Duplicate Economies of Scope	Costly-to-Duplicate Economies of Scope
Shared activities	Core competencies
Risk reduction	Internal capital allocation
Tax advantages	Multipoint competition
Employee compensation	Exploiting market power

However, the rarity of diversification depends not on diversification per se but on how rare the particular economies of scope associated with that diversification are. If only a few competing firms have exploited a particular economy of scope, that economy of scope can be rare. If numerous firms have done so, it will be common and not a source of competitive advantage.

The Imitability of Diversification

Both forms of imitation—direct duplication and substitution—are relevant in evaluating the ability of diversification strategies to generate sustained competitive advantages, even if the economies of scope that they create are rare.

Direct Duplication of Diversification

The extent to which a valuable and rare corporate diversification strategy is immune from direct duplication depends on how costly it is for competing firms to realize this same economy of scope. As suggested in Table 7.4, some economies of scope are, in general, more costly to duplicate than others.

Shared activities, risk reduction, tax advantages, and employee compensation as bases for corporate diversification are usually relatively easy to duplicate. Because shared activities are based on tangible assets that a firm exploits across multiple businesses, such as common research and development labs, common sales forces, and common manufacturing, they are usually relatively easy to duplicate. The only duplication issues for shared activities concern developing the cooperative cross-business relationships that often facilitate the use of shared activities—issues discussed in the next chapter. Moreover, because risk reduction, tax advantages, and employee compensation motives for diversifying can be accomplished through both related and unrelated diversification, these motives for diversifying tend to be relatively easy to duplicate.

Other economies of scope are much more difficult to duplicate. These difficult-to-duplicate economies of scope include core competencies, internal capital allocation efficiencies, multipoint competition, and exploitation of market power. Because core competencies are more intangible, their direct duplication is often challenging. The realization of capital allocation economies of scope requires very substantial information-processing capabilities. These capabilities are often very difficult to develop. Multipoint competition requires very close coordination between the different businesses in which a firm operates. This kind of coordination is socially complex and thus often immune from direct duplication. Finally, exploitation of market power may be costly to duplicate because it requires that a firm must possess significant market power in one of its lines of business. A firm that does not have this market power advantage would have to obtain it. The cost of doing so, in most situations, would be prohibitive.

Substitutes for Diversification

Two obvious substitutes for diversification exist. First, instead of obtaining cost or revenue advantages from exploiting economies of scope *across* businesses in a diversified firm, a firm may decide to simply grow and develop each of its businesses separately. In this sense, a firm that successfully implements a cost leadership strategy or a product differentiation strategy in a single business can obtain the same cost or revenue advantages it could have obtained by exploiting economies of scope but without having to develop cross-business relations. Growing independent businesses within a diversified firm can be a substitute for exploiting economies of scope in a diversification strategy.

One firm that has chosen this strategy is Nestlé. Nestlé exploits few, if any, economies of scope among its different businesses. Rather, it has focused its efforts on growing each of its international operations to the point that they obtain cost or revenue advantages that could have otherwise been obtained in some form of related diversification. Thus, for example, Nestlé's operation in the United States is sufficiently large to exploit economies of scale in production, sales, and marketing, without reliance on economies of scope between U.S. operations and operations in other countries.[34]

A second substitute for exploiting economies of scope in diversification can be found in strategic alliances. By using a strategic alliance, a firm may be able to gain the economies of scope it could have obtained if it had carefully exploited economies of scope across its businesses. Thus, for example, instead of a firm exploiting research and development economies of scope between two businesses it owns, it could form a strategic alliance with a different firm and form a joint research and development lab. Instead of a firm exploiting sales economies of scope by linking its businesses through a common sales force, it might develop a sales agreement with another firm and obtain cost or revenue advantages in this way.

Summary

Firms implement corporate diversification strategies that range from limited diversification (single-business, dominant-business) to related diversification (related-constrained, related-linked) to unrelated diversification. In order to be valuable, corporate diversification strategies must reduce costs or increase revenues by exploiting economies of scope that outside equity holders cannot realize on their own at low cost.

Several motivations for implementing diversification strategies exist, including exploiting operational economies of scope (shared activities, core competencies), exploiting financial economies of scope (internal capital allocation, risk reduction, obtaining tax advantages), exploiting anticompetitive economies of scope (multipoint competition, market power advantages), and employee incentives to diversify (maximizing management compensation). All these reasons for diversifying, except diversifying to maximize management compensation, have the potential to create economic value for a firm. Moreover, a firm's outside equity holders will find it costly to realize all of these bases for diversification, except risk reduction. Thus, diversifying to maximize management compensation or diversifying to reduce risk is not consistent with the wealth-maximizing interests of a firm's equity holders. This analysis also suggests that, on average, related diversified firms will outperform unrelated diversified firms.

The ability of a diversification strategy to create sustained competitive advantages depends not only on the value of that strategy, but also on its rarity and imitability. The rarity of a diversification strategy depends on the number of competing firms that are exploiting the same economies of scope through diversification. Imitation can occur either through direct duplication or through substitutes. Costly-to-duplicate economies of scope include core competencies, internal capital allocation, multipoint competition, and exploitation of market power. Other economies of scope are usually less costly to duplicate. Important substitutes for diversification are when relevant economies are obtained through the independent actions of businesses within a firm and when relevant economies are obtained through strategic alliances.

This discussion set aside important organizational issues in implementing diversification strategies. These issues are examined in detail in the next chapter.

Challenge Questions

1. One simple way to think about relatedness is to look at the products or services a firm manufactures. The more similar these products or services are, the more related is the firm's diversification strategy. However, will firms that exploit core competencies in their diversification strategies always produce products or services that are similar to each other? Why or why not?

2. A firm implementing a diversification strategy has just acquired what it claims is a strategically related target firm but announces that it is not going to change this recently acquired firm in any way. Will this type of diversifying acquisition enable the firm to realize any valuable economies of scope that could not be duplicated by outside investors on their own? Why or why not?

3. One of the reasons why internal capital markets may be more efficient than external capital markets is that firms may not want to reveal full information about their sources of competitive advantage to external capital markets in order to reduce the threat of competitive imitation. This suggests that external capital markets may systematically undervalue firms with competitive advantages that are subject to imitation. Do you agree with this analysis? If yes, how could you trade on this information in your own investment activities? If no, why not?

4. A particular firm is owned by members of a single family. Most of the wealth of this family is derived from the operations of this firm, and the family does not want to "go public" with the firm by selling its equity position to outside investors. Will this firm pursue a highly related diversification strategy or a somewhat less related diversification strategy? Why?

5. Under what conditions will a related diversification strategy not be a source of competitive advantage for a firm?

Problem Set

1. Visit the corporate Web sites for the following firms. How would you characterize the corporate strategies of these companies? Are they following a strategy of limited diversification, related diversification, or unrelated diversification?
(a) Exxon Mobil
(b) Google
(c) General Motors
(d) JetBlue
(e) Citigroup
(f) Entertainment Arts
(g) IBM
(h) Dell
(i) Berkshire Hathaway

2. Consider the following list of strategies. In your view, which are examples of potential economies of scope underlying a corporate diversification strategy? For those strategies that are an economy of scope, which economy of scope are they? For those strategies that are not an economy of scope, why aren't they?
(a) The Coca-Cola Corporation replaces its old diet cola drink (Tab) with a new diet cola drink called Diet Coke.
(b) Apple introduces an iPod MP3 player with a larger memory.
(c) PepsiCo distributes Lay's Potato Chips to the same stores where it sells Pepsi.
(d) Kmart extends its licensing arrangement with Martha Stewart for four years.
(e) Wal-Mart uses the same distribution system to supply its Wal-Mart stores, its Wal-Mart Supercenters (Wal-Mart stores with grocery stores in them), and its Sam's Clubs.

(f) Head Ski Company introduces a line of tennis rackets.

(g) General Electric borrows money from BankAmerica at 3 percent interest and then makes capital available to its jet engine subsidiary at 8 percent interest.

(h) McDonald's acquires Boston Market and Chipotle (two restaurants where many customers sit in the restaurant to eat their meals).

(i) A venture capital firm invests in a firm in the biotechnology industry and a firm in the entertainment industry.

(j) Another venture capital firm invests in two firms in the biotechnology industry.

3. Consider the following facts. The standard deviation of the cash flows associated with Business I is 0.8. The larger this standard deviation, the riskier a business's future cash flows are likely to be. The standard deviation of the cash flows associated with Business II is 1.3. That is, Business II is riskier than Business I. Finally, the correlation between the cash flows of these two businesses over time is 0.8. This means that when Business I is up, Business II tends to be down, and vice versa. Suppose one firm owns both of these businesses.

(a) Assuming that Business I constitutes 40 percent of this firm's revenues and Business II constitutes 60 percent of its revenues, calculate the riskiness of this firm's total revenues using the following equation:

$$sd_{I,II} = \sqrt{w^2 sd_I^2 + (1-w)^2 sd_{II}^2 + 2w(1+w)\left(r_{I,II} sd_I sd_{II}\right)}$$

Where $w = 0.40$; $sd_I = 0.8$, $sd_{II} = 1.3$, and $r_{I, II} = -8$.

(b) Given this result, does it make sense for this firm to own both Business I and Business II? Why or why not?

End Notes

1. See Sellers, P. (2004). "The brand king's challenge." *Fortune*, April 5, pp. 192 +.
2. The Walt Disney Company. (1995). Harvard Business School Case No. 1-388-147.
3. Useem, J. (2004). "Another boss, another revolution." *Fortune*, April 5, pp. 112 +.
4. See Burrows, P. (1995). "Now, TI means 'taking initiative,'" *BusinessWeek*, May 15, pp. 120–121; Rogers, A. (1992). "It's the execution that counts." *Fortune*, November 30, pp. 80–83; Wallas, J., and J. Erickson. (1993). *Hard drive: Bill Gates and the making of the Microsoft empire*. New York: Harper Business; and Porter, M. E. (1981). "Disposable diaper industry in 1974." Harvard Business School Case No. 9-380-175. Whether or not Microsoft continues to share activities across operating systems and applications software was one of the key issues at stake in the Microsoft antitrust suit. A more general discussion of the value of shared activities can be found in St. John, C. H., and J. S. Harrison. (1999). "Manufacturing-based relatedness, synergy, and coordination." *Strategic Management Journal*, 20, pp. 129–145.
5. See Fuchsberg, G. (1992). "Decentralized management can have its drawbacks." *TheWall Street Journal*, December 9, p. B1.
6. See Crockett, R. (2000). "A Baby Bell's growth formula." *BusinessWeek*, March 6, pp. 50–52; and Crockett, R. (1999). "The last monopolist." *BusinessWeek*, April 12, p. 76.
7. de Lisser, E. (1993). "Catering to cooking-phobic customers, supermarkets stress carryout." *The Wall Street Journal*, April 5, p. B1.
8. See, for example, Davis, P., R. Robinson, J. Pearce, and S. Park. (1992). "Business unit relatedness and performance: A look at the pulp and paper industry." *Strategic Management Journal*, 13, pp. 349–361.
9. Loomis, C. J. (1993). "Dinosaurs?" *Fortune*, May 3, pp. 36–42.
10. Rapoport, C. (1992). "A tough Swede invades the U.S." *Fortune*, June 29, pp. 776–779.
11. Prahalad, C. K., and G. Hamel (1990). "The core competence of the organization." *Harvard Business Review*, 90, p. 82.
12. See also Grant, R. M. (1988). "On 'dominant logic' relatedness and the link between diversity and performance." *Strategic Management Journal*, 9, pp. 639–642; Chatterjee, S., and B. Wernerfelt. (1991). "The link between resources and type at diversification: Theory and evidence." *Strategic Management Journal*, 12, pp. 33–48; Markides, C., and P. J. Williamson. (1994). "Related diversification, core competencies, and corporate performance." *Strategic Management Journal*, 15, pp. 149–165; Montgomery, C. A., and B. Wernerfelt. (1991). "Sources of superior performance: Market share versus industry effects in the U.S. brewing industry." *Management Science*, 37, pp. 954–959; Liedtka, J. M. (1996). "Collaborating across lines of business for competitive advantage." *Academy of Management Executive*, 10(2), pp. 20–37; and Farjoun, M. (1998). "The independent and joint effects of the skill and physical bases of relatedness in diversification." *Strategic Management Journal*, 19, pp. 611–630.
13. Jensen, M. C. (1986). "Agency costs of free cash flow, corporate finance, and takeovers." *American Economic Review*, 76, pp. 323–329.
14. See Nayyar, P. (1990). "Information asymmetries: A source of competitive advantage for diversified service firms." *Strategic Management Journal*, 11, pp. 513–519; and Robins, J., and M. Wiersema. (1995). "A resource-based approach to the multibusiness firm: Empirical analysis of portfolio interrelationships and corporate financial performance." *Strategic Management Journal*, 16, pp. 277–299, for a discussion of the evolution of core competencies.
15. Prahalad, C. K., and R. A. Bettis. (1986). "The dominant logic: A new linkage between diversity and performance." *Strategic Management Journal*, 7(6), pp. 485–501.
16. See Williamson, O. E. (1975). *Markets and hierarchies: Analysis and antitrust implications*. New York: Free Press.

17. See Liebeskind, J. P. (1996). "Knowledge, strategy, and the theory of the firm." *Strategic Management Journal*, 17 (Winter Special Edition), pp. 93–107.

18. Perry, L. T., and J. B. Barney. (1981). "Performance lies are hazardous to organizational health." *Organizational Dynamics*, 9(3), pp. 68–80.

19. Bethel, J. E. (1990). *The capital allocation process and managerial mobility: A theoretical and empirical investigation.* Unpublished doctoral dissertation, University of California at Los Angles.

20. Staw, B. M. (1981). "The escalation of commitment to a course of action." *Academy of Management Review*, 6, pp. 577–587.

21. See Comment, R., and G. Jarrell. (1995). "Corporate focus and stock returns." *Journal of Financial Economics*, 37, pp. 67–87; Berger, P. G., and E. Ofek. (1995). "Diversification's effect on firm value." *Journal of Financial Economics*, 37, pp. 39–65; Maksimovic, V., and G. Phillips. (1999). "Do conglomerate firms allocate resources inefficiently?" Working paper, University of Maryland; Matsusaka, J. G., and V. Nanda. (1998). "Internal capital markets and corporate refocusing." Working paper, University of Southern California; Palia, D. (1998). "Division-level overinvestment and agency conflicts in diversified firms." Working paper, Columbia University; Rajan, R., H. Servaes, and L. Zingales. (1997). "The cost of diversity: The diversification discount and inefficient investment." Working paper, University of Chicago; Scharfstein, D. S. (1997). "The dark side of internal capital markets II: Evidence from diversified conglomerates." NBER [National Bureau of Economic Research]. Working paper; Shin, H. H., and R. M. Stulz. (1998). "Are internal capital markets efficient?" *The Quarterly Journal of Economics*, May, pp. 551–552. But Houston and James (1998) show that internal capital markets can create competitive advantages for firms: Houston, J., and C. James. (1998). "Some evidence that banks use internal capital markets to lower capital costs." *Journal of Applied Corporate Finance*, 11(2), pp. 70–78.

22. Scott, J. H. (1977). "On the theory of conglomerate mergers." *Journal of Finance*, 32, pp. 1235–1250.

23. See Brennan, M. (1979). "The pricing of contingent claims in discrete time models." *Journal of Finance*, 34, pp. 53–68; Cox, J., S. Ross, and M. Rubinstein. (1979). "Option pricing: A simplified approach." *Journal of Financial Economics*, 7, pp. 229–263; Stapleton, R. C. (1982). "Mergers, debt capacity, and the valuation of corporate loans." In M. Keenan and L. J. White. (eds.), *Mergers and acquisitions.* Lexington, MA: D. C. Heath, Chapter 2; and Galai, D., and R. W. Masulis. (1976). "The option pricing model and the risk factor of stock." *Journal of Financial Economics*, 3, pp. 53–82.

24. See Karnani, A., and B. Wernerfelt. (1985). "Multiple point competition." *Strategic Management Journal*, 6, pp. 87–96; Bernheim, R. D., and M. D. Whinston. (1990). "Multimarket contact and collusive behavior." *Rand Journal of Economics*, 12, pp. 605–617; Tirole, J. (1988). *The theory of industrial organization.* Cambridge, MA: MIT Press; Gimeno, J., and C. Y. Woo. (1999). "Multimarket contact, economies of scope, and firm performance." *Academy of Management Journal*, 43(3), pp. 239–259; Korn, H. J., and J. A. C. Baum. (1999). "Chance, imitative, and strategic antecedents to multimarket contact." *Academy of Management Journal*, 42(2), pp. 171–193; Baum, J. A. C., and H. J. Korn. (1999). "Dynamics of dyadic competitive interaction." *Strategic Management Journal*, 20, pp. 251–278; Gimeno, J. (1999). "Reciprocal threats in multimarket rivalry: Staking our 'spheres of influence' in the U.S. airline industry." *Strategic Management Journal*, 20, pp. 101–128; Gimeno, J., and C. Y. Woo. (1996). "Hypercompetition in a multimarket environment: The role of strategic similarity and multimarket contact in competitive de-escalation." *Organization Science*, 7(3), pp. 322–341; Ma, H. (1998). "Mutual forbearance in international business." *Journal of International Management*, 4(2), pp. 129–147; McGrath, R. G., and M.-J. Chen. (1998). "Multimarket maneuvering in uncertain spheres of influence: Resource diversion strategies." *Academy of Management Review*, 23(4), pp. 724–740; Chen, M.-J. (1996). "Competitor analysis and interfirm rivalry: Toward a theoretical integration." *Academy of Management Review*, 21(1), pp. 100–134; Chen, M.-J., and K. Stucker. (1997). "Multinational management and multimarket rivalry: Toward a theoretical development of global competition." *Academy of Management Proceedings 1997*, pp. 2–6; and Young, G., K. G. Smith, and C. M. Grimm. (1997). "Multimarket contact, resource heterogeneity, and rivalrous firm behavior." *Academy of Management Proceedings 1997*, pp. 55–59. This idea was originally proposed by Edwards, C. D. (1955). "Conglomerate bigness as a source of power." In *Business concentration and price policy.* NBER Conference Report. Princeton, NJ: Princeton University Press.

25. See Karnani, A., and B. Wernerfelt. (1985). "Multiple point competition." *Strategic Management Journal*, 6, pp. 87–96.

26. This is documented by Gimeno, J. (1994). "Multipoint competition, market rivalry and firm performance: A test of the mutual forbearance hypothesis in the United States airline industry, 1984–1988." Unpublished doctoral dissertation, Purdue University.

27. See Landro, L., P. M. Reilly, and R. Turner. (1993). "Cartoon clash: Disney relationship with Time Warner is a strained one." *The Wall Street Journal*, April 14, p. A1; and Reilly, P. M., and R. Turner. (1993). "Disney pulls ads in tiff with *Time*." *The Wall Street Journal*, April 2, p. B1. The growth and consolidation of the entertainment industry since the early 1990s has made Disney and Time Warner (especially after its merger with AOL) large entertainment conglomerates. It will be interesting to see if these two larger firms will be able to find ways to tacitly collude or will continue the competition begun in the early 1990s.

28. The best work in this area has been done by Gimeno, J. (1994). "Multipoint competition, market rivalry and firm performance: A test of the mutual forbearance hypothesis in the United States airline industry, 1984–1988." Unpublished doctoral dissertation, Purdue University. See also Smith, F., and R. Wilson. (1995). "The predictive validity of the Karnani and Wernerfelt model of multipoint competition." *Strategic Management Journal*, 16, pp. 143–160.

29. See Tirole, J. (1988). *The theory of industrial organization.* Cambridge, MA: MIT Press.

30. Carnevale, M. L. (1993). "Ring in the new: Telephone service seems on the brink of huge innovations." *The Wall Street Journal*, February 10, p. A1. SBC recently acquired the remaining assets of the original AT&T and renamed the newly merged company AT&T.

31. See Russo, M. V. (1992). "Power plays: Regulation, diversification, and backward integration in the electric utility industry." *Strategic Management Journal*, 13, pp. 13–27. Recent work by Jandik and Makhija indicates that when a regulated utility diversifies out of a regulated industry, it often earns a more positive return than when an unregulated firm does this [Jandik, T., and A. K. Makhija. (1999). "An Empirical Examination of the Atypical Diversification Practices of Electric Utilities: Internal Capital Markets and Regulation." Fisher College of Business, Ohio State University, working paper (September)]. This work shows that regulators have the effect of making a regulated firm's internal capital market more efficient. Differences between Russo's (1992) findings and Jandik and Makhija's (1999) findings may have to do with when this work was done. Russo's (1992) research may have focused on a time period before regulatory agencies had learned how to improve a firm's internal capital market. However, even though Jandik and Makhija (1999) report positive returns from regulated firms diversifying, these positive returns do not reflect the market power advantages of these firms.

32. Finkelstein, S., and D. C. Hambrick. (1989). "Chief executive compensation: A study of the intersection of markets and political processes." *Strategic Management Journal*, 10, pp. 121–134.

33. See William, J., B. L. Paez, and L. Sanders. (1988). "Conglomerates revisited." *Strategic Management Journal*, 9, pp. 403–414; Geringer, J. M., S. Tallman, and D. M. Olsen. (2000). "Product and international diversification among Japanese multinational firms." *Strategic Management Journal*, 21, pp. 51–80; Nail, L. A., W. L. Megginson, and C. Maquieira. (1998). "How stock-swap mergers affect shareholder (and bondholder) wealth: More evidence of the value of corporate 'focus.'" *Journal of Applied Corporate Finance*, 11(2), pp. 95–106; Carroll, G. R., L. S. Bigelow, M.-D. L. Seidel, and L. B. Tsai. (1966). "The fates of *De Novo* and *De Alio* producers in the American automobile industry 1885–1981." *Strategic Management Journal*, 17 (Special Summer Issue), pp. 117–138; Nguyen, T. H., A. Seror, and T. M. Devinney. (1990). "Diversification strategy and performance in Canadian manufacturing firms." *Strategic Management Journal*, 11, pp. 411–418; and Amit, R., and J. Livnat. (1988). "Diversification strategies, business cycles and economic performance." *Strategic Management Journal*, 9, pp. 99–110, for a discussion of corporate diversification in the economy over time.

34. The Nestlé story is summarized in Templeman, J. (1993). "Nestlé: A giant in a hurry." *BusinessWeek*, March 22, pp. 50–54.

Organizing to Implement Corporate Diversification

After reading this chapter, you should be able to:

1. Describe the multidivisional, or M-form, structure and how it is used to implement a corporate diversification strategy.

2. Describe the roles of the board of directors, institutional investors, the senior executive, corporate staff, division general managers, and shared activity managers in making the M-form structure work.

3. Describe how three management control processes—measuring divisional performance, allocating corporate capital, and transferring intermediate products—are used to help implement a corporate diversification strategy.

4. Describe the role of management compensation in helping to implement a corporate diversification strategy.

Tyco Ten Years On

For almost 10 years, now, Tyco International has been the poster child for managerial irresponsibility and fraud. Acquisitions gone wild, decadent corporate parties on exotic Italian islands, millions in unethical loans, all leading to one of the most notorious trials for corporate fraud in the last decade. After one hung jury, a second jury found Tyco's former Chief Executive Officer (CEO), Dennis Kozlowski, guilty of fraud and sentenced him to serve a term of 8 to 25 years in federal prison.

But, Tyco, the company, remained. Many of the businesses it owned continued operating—despite accounting malfeasance and creativity at the corporate level—largely untouched. Customers still bought their products, those products still required service, and the cash still had to be counted.

But, how do you manage the mess that Tyco—the corporation—had become without putting the businesses that Tyco still owned—many of which were very viable—at risk? This was the dilemma that Edward Breen, the new CEO at Tyco, has had to face.

In the short term, Breen put most of his energies into cleaning up Kozlowski's mess. This included replacing Tyco's entire board of directors and most of its senior corporate management team, settling most of its outstanding stockholder lawsuits, and reducing its level of indebtedness by three quarters. This emergency first aid allowed Tyco to gain some credibility among its shareholders, debt holders, and even among its own employees.

With these changes in place, Breen then turned his attention to rationalizing the mishmash portfolio of companies that Kozlowski—through some 600 acquisitions—had stitched together. Step One: Divide the company into three parts—the first focusing on health care–related activities; the second on electronic parts and products; the third focusing on Tyco's security, fire, and flow management businesses. Step Two: Sell off the first two parts of the business—the first known as Covidien, the second as Tyco Electronics—so that management could focus on the remaining businesses at Tyco. This restructuring work was done by late 2007.

While not nearly as diverse as it was, these actions still left Tyco in a wide range

of businesses, including ADT home security monitoring systems; a business that makes valves and pipes for the oil, gas, and water industries; a business that focuses on fire protection services; a business that manufactures materials for pipes, wiring, and razor fencing; and a business that makes video security and related products. Now a "mini-conglomerate," Tyco has shrunk from $40 billion in revenues—in the Kozlowski days—to a more modest $18 billion in revenues.

But, even as a "mini-conglomerate," Breen still needs to explain how his firm is managing this mix of businesses in a way that creates value in excess of what would be the case if each of these businesses were owned separately. So far, the market does not seem convinced by Breen's managerial efforts—Tyco's stock has fallen by 22 percent over the past few months. This does not compare favorably to the stock price of other conglomerates during the same time period, including Danaher, whose share price dropped just four percent, and Emerson Electric, whose share price went up six percent. Managing a diverse portfolio of businesses in a

Mike Flippo/Shutterstock

way that creates value is hard to do, even when your firm is no longer dragged down by fraud, and even when your portfolio is not as diverse as it once was.

Source: Brian Hindo (2008). "Solving Tyco's identity crisis." *BusinessWeek*, February 18, pp. 62–63; AP Wide World Photos.

This chapter is about how large diversified firms—like Tyco—are managed and governed efficiently. The chapter explains how these kinds of firms are managed in a way that is consistent with the interests of their owners—equity holders—as well as the interests of their other stakeholders. The three components of organizing to implement any strategy, which were first identified in Chapter 3—organizational structure, management controls, and compensation policy—are also important in implementing corporate diversification strategies.

VRIO

Organizational Structure and Implementing Corporate Diversification

The most common organizational structure for implementing a corporate diversification strategy is the **M-form**, or **multidivisional**, structure. A typical M-form structure, as it would appear in a firm's annual report, is presented in Figure 8.1. This same structure is redrawn in Figure 8.2 to emphasize the roles and responsibilities of each of the major components of the M-form organization.[1]

In the multidivisional structure, each business that the firm engages in is managed through a **division**. Different firms have different names for these divisions—strategic business units (SBUs), business groups, companies. Whatever their names, the divisions in an M-form organization are true **profit-and-loss centers**: Profits and losses are calculated at the level of the division in these firms.

Different firms use different criteria for defining the boundaries of profit-and-loss centers. For example, General Electric defines its divisions in terms of the types of products each one manufactures and sells (e.g., Energy Infrastructure, Technology Infrastructure, GE Capital, and NBC Universal). Nestlé defines its

Figure 8.1   An Example of M-Form Organizational Structure as Depicted in a Firm's Annual Report

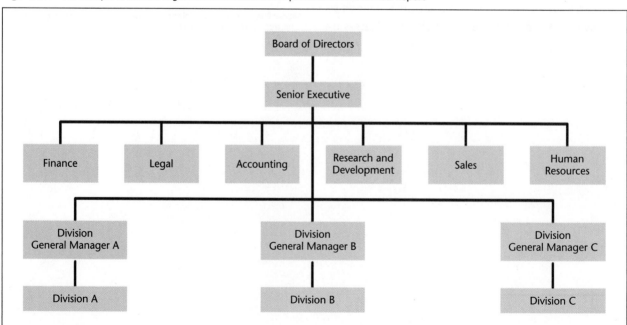

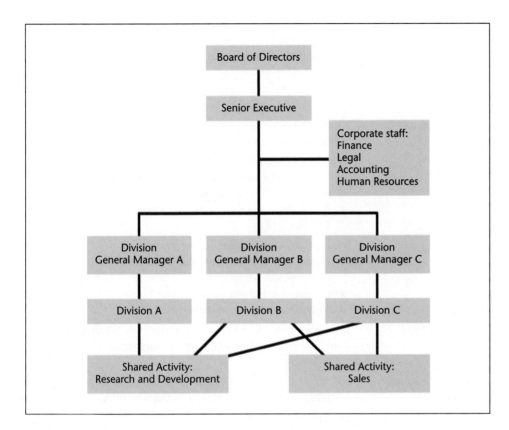

Figure 8.2 An M-Form Structure Redrawn to Emphasize Roles and Responsibilities

divisions with reference to the geographic scope of each of its businesses (North America, South America, and so forth). General Motors defines its divisions in terms of the brand names of its products (Cadillac, Chevrolet, and so forth). However they are defined, divisions in an M-form organization should be large enough to represent identifiable business entities but small enough so that each one can be managed effectively by a division general manager. Indeed, each division in an M-form organization typically adopts a U-form structure (see the discussion of the U-form structure in Chapters 4, 5, and 6), and the division general manager takes on the role of a U-form senior executive for his or her division.

The M-form structure is designed to create checks and balances for managers that increase the probability that a diversified firm will be managed in ways consistent with the interests of its equity holders. The roles of each of the major elements of the M-form structure in accomplishing this objective are summarized in Table 8.1 and discussed in the following text. Some of the conflicts of interest that might emerge between a firm's equity holders and its managers are described in the Strategy in Depth feature.

The Board of Directors

One of the major components of an M-form organization is a firm's **board of directors**. In principle, all of a firm's senior managers report to the board. The board's primary responsibility is to monitor decision making in the firm, ensuring that it is consistent with the interests of outside equity holders.

A board of directors typically consists of 10 to 15 individuals drawn from a firm's top management group and from individuals outside the firm. A firm's

TABLE 8.1 The Roles and
Responsibilities of Major
Components of the M-Form
Structure

Component	Activity
Board of directors	Monitor decision making in a firm to ensure that it is consistent with the interests of outside equity holders
Institutional investors	Monitor decision making to ensure that it is consistent with the interests of major institutional equity investors
Senior executives	Formulate corporate strategies consistent with equity holders' interests and assure strategy implementation
	Strategy formulation: ■ Decide the businesses in which the firm will operate ■ Decide how the firm should compete in those businesses ■ Specify the economies of scope around which the diversified firm will operate
	Strategy implementation: ■ Encourage cooperation across divisions to exploit economies of scope ■ Evaluate performance of divisions ■ Allocate capital across divisions
Corporate staff	Provides information to the senior executive about internal and external environments for strategy formulation and implementation
Division general managers	Formulate divisional strategies consistent with corporate strategies and assure strategy implementation
	Strategy formulation: ■ Decide how the division will compete in its business, given the corporate strategy
	Strategy implementation: ■ Coordinate the decisions and actions of functional managers reporting to the division general manager to implement divisional strategy ■ Compete for corporate capital allocations ■ Cooperate with other divisions to exploit corporate economies of scope
Shared activity managers	Support the operations of multiple divisions

senior executive (often identified by the title president or chief executive officer or CEO), its chief financial officer (CFO), and a few other senior managers are usually on the board—although managers on the board are typically outnumbered by outsiders. The firm's senior executive is often, but not always, the **chairman of the board** (a term used here to denote both female and male senior executives). The task of managerial board members—including the board chairman—is to provide other board members information and insights about critical decisions being made in the firm and the effect those decisions are likely to have on a firm's equity holders. The task of outsiders on the board is to evaluate the past, current, and future performance of the firm and of its senior managers to ensure that the actions taken in the firm are consistent with equity holders' interests.[2]

Strategy in Depth

In Chapter 7, it was suggested that sometimes it is in the best interest of equity holders to delegate to managers the day-to-day management of their equity investments in a firm. This will be the case when equity investors cannot realize a valuable economy of scope on their own, while managers *can* realize that economy of scope.

Several authors have suggested that whenever one party to an exchange delegates decision-making authority to a second party, an **agency relationship** has been created between these parties. The party delegating this decision-making authority is called the **principal**; the party to whom this authority is delegated is called the **agent**. In the context of corporate diversification, an agency relationship exists between a firm's outside equity holders (as principals) and its managers (as agents) to the extent that equity holders delegate the day-to-day management of their investment to those managers.

The agency relationship between equity holders and managers can be very effective as long as managers make investment decisions that are consistent with equity holders' interests. Thus, if equity holders are interested in maximizing the rate of return on their investment in a firm and if managers make their investment decisions with this objective in mind, then equity holders will have few concerns about delegating the day-to-day management of their investments to managers. Unfortunately, in numerous situations the interests of a firm's outside equity holders and its managers do not coincide. When parties in an agency relationship differ in their

Agency Conflicts Between Managers and Equity Holders

decision-making objectives, **agency problems** arise. Two common agency problems have been identified: investment in managerial perquisites and managerial risk aversion.

Managers may decide to take some of a firm's capital and invest it in **managerial perquisites** that do not add economic value to the firm but do directly benefit those managers. Examples of such investments include lavish offices, fleets of corporate jets, and corporate vacation homes. Dennis Kozlowski, former CEO of Tyco International, is accused of "stealing" $600 million in these kinds of managerial perquisites from his firm. The list of goods and services that Kozlowski lavished on himself and those close to him is truly astounding—a multimillion-dollar birthday party for his wife, a $6,000 wastebasket, a $15,000 umbrella stand, a $144,000 loan to a board member, toga-clad waiters at an event, and so on.

As outrageous as some of these managerial perquisites can be, the second source of agency problems—**managerial risk aversion**—is probably

more important in most diversified firms. As discussed in Chapter 7, equity holders can diversify their portfolio of investments at very low cost. Through their diversification efforts, they can eliminate all firm-specific risk in their portfolios. In this setting, equity holders would prefer that managers make more risky rather than less risky investments, because the expected return on risky investments is usually greater than the expected return on less risky investments.

Managers, in contrast, have limited ability to diversify their human capital investments in their firm. Some portion of these investments is specific to a particular firm and has limited value in alternative uses. The value of a manager's human capital investment in a firm depends critically on the continued existence of the firm. Thus, managers are *not* indifferent to the riskiness of investment opportunities in a firm. Very risky investments may jeopardize a firm's survival and thus eliminate the value of a manager's human capital investments. These incentives can make managers more risk averse in their decision making than equity holders would like them to be.

One of the purposes of the M-form structure, and indeed of all aspects of organizing to implement corporate diversification, is to reduce these agency problems.

Sources: M. C. Jensen and W. H. Meckling (1976). "Theory of the firm: Managerial behavior, agency costs, and ownership structure." *Journal of Financial Economics*, 3, pp. 305–360; J. Useem (2003). "The biggest show." *Fortune*, December 8, pp. 157 +; R. Lambert (1986). "Executive effort and selection of risky projects." *Rand Journal of Economics*, 13(2), pp. 369–378.

Research Made Relevant

A great deal of research has tried to determine when boards of directors are more or less effective in ensuring that firms are managed in ways consistent with the interests of equity holders. Three issues have received particular attention: (1) the roles of insiders (i.e., managers) and outsiders on the board, (2) whether the board chair and the senior executive should be the same or different people, and (3) whether the board should be active or passive.

With respect to insiders and outsiders on the board, in one way this seems like a simple problem. Because the primary role of the board of directors is to monitor managerial decisions to ensure that they are consistent with the interests of equity holders, it follows that the board should consist primarily of outsiders because they face no conflict of interest in evaluating managerial performance. Obviously, managers, as inside members of the board, face significant conflicts of interest in evaluating their own performance.

Research on outsider members of boards of directors tends to support this point of view. Outside directors, as compared to insiders, tend to focus

The Effectiveness of Boards of Directors

more on monitoring a firm's economic performance than on other measures of firm performance. Obviously, a firm's economic performance is most relevant to its equity investors. Outside board members are also more likely than inside members to dismiss CEOs for poor performance. Also, outside board members have a stronger incentive than inside members to maintain their reputations as effective monitors. This incentive by itself can lead to more effective monitoring by outside board members. Moreover, the

monitoring effectiveness of outside board members seems to be enhanced when they personally own a substantial amount of a firm's equity.

However, the fact that outside members face fewer conflicts of interest in evaluating managerial performance compared to management insiders on the board does not mean that there is no appropriate role for inside board members. Managers bring something to the board that cannot be easily duplicated by outsiders—detailed information about the decision-making activities inside the firm. This is precisely the information that outsiders need to effectively monitor the activities of a firm, and it is information available to them only if they work closely with insiders (managers). One way to gain access to this information is to include managers as members of the board of directors. Thus, while most research suggests that a board of directors should be composed primarily of outsiders, there is an important role for insiders/managers to play as members of a firm's board.

There is currently some debate about whether the roles of board

Boards of directors are typically organized into several subcommittees. An **audit committee** is responsible for ensuring the accuracy of accounting and financial statements. A **finance committee** maintains the relationship between the firm and external capital markets. A **nominating committee** nominates new board members. A **personnel and compensation committee** evaluates and compensates the performance of a firm's senior executive and other senior managers. Often, membership on these standing committees is reserved for external board members. Other standing committees reflect specific issues for a particular firm and are typically open to external and internal board members.[3]

Over the years, a great deal of research has been conducted about the effectiveness of boards of directors in ensuring that a firm's managers make decisions in ways consistent with the interests of its equity holders. Some of this work is summarized in the Research Made Relevant feature.

chairman and CEO should be combined or separated and, if separated, what kinds of people should occupy these positions. Some have argued that the roles of CEO and chairman of the board should definitely be separated and that the role of the chairman should be filled by an outside (nonmanagerial) member of the board of directors. These arguments are based on the assumption that only an outside member of the board can ensure the independent monitoring of managerial decision making. Others have argued that effective monitoring often requires more information than would be available to outsiders, and thus the roles of board chairman and CEO should be combined and filled by a firm's senior manager.

Empirical research on this question suggests that whether these roles of CEO and chairman should be combined or not depends on the complexity of the information analysis and monitoring task facing the CEO and chairman. Brian Boyd has found that combining the roles of CEO and chairman is positively correlated with firm performance when firms operate in slow-growth and simple competitive environments—

environments that do not overtax the cognitive capability of a single individual. This finding suggests that combining these roles does not necessarily increase conflicts between a firm and its equity holders. This research also found that separating the roles of CEO and board chairman is positively correlated with firm performance when firms operate in high-growth and very complex environments. In such environments, a single individual cannot fulfill all the responsibilities of both CEO and chairman, and thus the two roles need to be held by separate individuals.

Finally, with respect to active versus passive boards, historically the boards of major firms have been relatively passive and would take dramatic action, such as firing the senior executive, only if a firm's performance was significantly below expectations for long periods of time. However, more recently, boards have become more active proponents of equity holders' interests. This recent surge in board activity reflects a new economic reality: If a board does not become more active in monitoring firm performance, then other monitoring

mechanisms will. Consequently, the board of directors has become progressively more influential in representing the interests of a firm's equity holders.

However, board activity can go too far. To the extent that the board begins to operate a business on a day-to-day basis, it goes beyond its capabilities. Boards rarely have sufficient detailed information to manage a firm directly. When it is necessary to change a firm's senior executive, boards will usually not take on the responsibilities of that executive, but rather will rapidly identify a single individual—either an insider or outsider—to take over this position.

Sources: E. Zajac and J. Westphal (1994). "The costs and benefits of managerial incentives and monitoring in large U.S. corporations: When is more not better?" *Strategic Management Journal*, 15, pp. 121–142; P. Rechner and D. Dalton (1991). "CEO duality and organizational performance: A longitudinal analysis." *Strategic Management Journal*, 12, pp. 155–160; S. Finkelstein and R. D'Aveni (1994). "CEO duality as a double-edged sword: How boards of directors balance entrenchment avoidance and unity of command." *Academy of Management Journal*, 37, pp. 1079–1108; B. K. Boyd (1995). "CEO duality and firm performance: A contingency model." *Strategic Management Journal*, 16, pp. 301–312; and F. Kesner and R. B. Johnson (1990). "An investigation of the relationship between board composition and stockholder suits." *Strategic Management Journal*, 11, pp. 327–336.

Institutional Owners

Historically, the typical large diversified firm has had its equity owned in small blocks by millions of individual investors. The exception to this general rule was family-owned or -dominated firms, a phenomenon that is relatively more common outside the United States. When a firm's ownership is spread among millions of small investors, it is difficult for any one of these investors to have a large enough ownership position to influence management decisions directly. The only course of action open to such investors if they disagree with management decisions is to sell their stock.

However, the growth of institutional owners has changed the ownership structure of many large diversified firms over the last several years. **Institutional owners** are usually pension funds, mutual funds, insurance companies, or other groups of individual investors that have joined together to manage their investments. In 1970, institutions owned 32 percent of the equity traded in the United States. By 1990, institutions owned 48 percent of this equity. In 2005, they owned 59 percent of all equity traded in the United States and 69 percent of the equity of the 1,000 largest firms in the United States.[4]

Institutional investors can use their investment clout to insist that a firm's management behaves in ways consistent with the interests of equity holders. Observers who assume that institutional investors are interested more in maximizing the short-term value of their portfolios than in the long-term performance of firms in those portfolios fear that such power will force firms to make only short-term investments. Recent research in the United States and Japan, however, suggests that institutional investors are not unduly myopic. Rather, as suggested earlier, these investors use approximately the same logic equity investors use when evaluating the performance of a firm. For example, one group of researchers examined the impact of institutional ownership on research and development investments in Research and Development (R&D)–intensive industries. R&D investments tend to be longer term in orientation. If institutional investors are myopic, they should influence firms to invest in relatively less R&D in favor of investments that generate shorter-term profits. This research showed that high levels of institutional ownership did not adversely affect the level of R&D in a firm. These findings are consistent with the notion that institutional investors are not inappropriately concerned with the short term in their monitoring activities.[5]

More generally, other researchers have shown that high levels of institutional ownership lead firms to sell strategically unrelated businesses. This effect of institutional investors is enhanced if, in addition, outside directors on a firm's board have substantial equity investments in the firm. Given the discussion of the value of unrelated diversification in Chapter 7, it seems clear that these divestment actions are typically consistent with maximizing the present value of a firm.[6]

The Senior Executive

As suggested in Table 8.1, the senior executive (the president or CEO) in an M-form organization has two responsibilities: strategy formulation and strategy implementation. *Strategy formulation* entails deciding which set of businesses a diversified firm will operate in; *strategy implementation* focuses on encouraging behavior in a firm that is consistent with this strategy. Each of these responsibilities of the senior executive is discussed in turn.

Strategy Formulation

At the broadest level, deciding which businesses a diversified firm should operate in is equivalent to discovering and developing valuable economies of scope among a firm's current and potential businesses. If these economies of scope are also rare and costly to imitate, they can be a source of sustained competitive advantage for a diversified firm.

The senior executive is uniquely positioned to discover, develop, and nurture valuable economies of scope in a diversified firm. Every other manager in this kind of firm either has a divisional point of view (e.g., division general managers and shared activity managers) or is a functional specialist (e.g., corporate staff and functional managers within divisions). Only the senior executive has a truly corporate perspective. However, the senior executive in an M-form organization should involve numerous other divisional and functional managers in strategy formulation to ensure complete and accurate information as input to the process and a broad understanding of and commitment to that strategy once it has been formulated.

Strategy Implementation

As is the case for senior executives in a U-form structure, strategy implementation in an M-form structure almost always involves resolving conflicts among groups of managers. However, instead of simply resolving conflicts between functional managers (as is the case in a U-form), senior executives in M-form organizations must resolve conflicts within and between each of the major managerial components of the M-form structure: corporate staff, division general managers, and shared activity managers. Various corporate staff managers may disagree about the economic relevance of their staff functions, corporate staff may come into conflict with division general managers over various corporate programs and activities, division general managers may disagree with how capital is allocated across divisions, division general managers may come into conflict with shared activity managers about how shared activities should be managed, shared activity managers may disagree with corporate staff about their mutual roles and responsibilities, and so forth.

Obviously, the numerous and often conflicting relationships among groups of managers in an M-form organization can place significant strategy implementation burdens on the senior executive.[7] While resolving these numerous conflicts, however, the senior executive needs to keep in mind the reasons why the firm began pursuing a diversification strategy in the first place: to exploit real economies of scope that outside investors cannot realize on their own. Any strategy implementation decisions that jeopardize the realization of these real economies of scope are inconsistent with the underlying strategic objectives of a diversified firm. These issues are analyzed in detail later in this chapter, in the discussion of management control systems in the M-form organization.

The Office of the President: Chairman, CEO, and COO

It is often the case that the roles and responsibilities of the senior executive in an M-form organization are greater than can be reasonably managed by a single individual. This is especially likely if a firm is broadly diversified across numerous complex products and markets. In this situation, it is not uncommon for the tasks of the senior executive to be divided among two or three people: the **chairman of the board**, the **chief executive officer**, and the **chief operating officer (COO)**. The primary responsibilities of each of these roles in an M-form organization are listed in Table 8.2. Together, these roles are known as the **office of the president**. In general, as the tasks facing the office of the president become more demanding and complex, the more likely it is that the roles and responsibilities of this office will be divided among two or three people.

Corporate Staff

The primary responsibility of **corporate staff** is to provide information about the firm's external and internal environments to the firm's senior executive. This information is vital for both the strategy formulation and the strategy implementation

Chairman of the board	Supervision of the board of directors in its monitoring role	
Chief executive officer	Strategy formulation	
Chief operating officer	Strategy implementation	

TABLE 8.2 Responsibilities of Three Different Roles in the Office of the President

responsibilities of the senior executive. Corporate staff functions that provide information about a firm's external environment include finance, investor relations, legal affairs, regulatory affairs, and corporate advertising. Corporate staff functions that provide information about a firm's internal environment include accounting and corporate human resources. These corporate staff functions report directly to a firm's senior executive and are a conduit of information to that executive.

Corporate and Divisional Staff

Many organizations re-create some corporate staff functions within each division of the organization. This is particularly true for internally oriented corporate staff functions such as accounting and human resources. At the division level, divisional staff managers usually have a direct "solid-line" reporting relationship to their respective corporate staff functional managers and a less formal "dotted-line" reporting relationship to their division general manager. The reporting relationship between the divisional staff manager and the corporate staff manager is the link that enables the corporate staff manager to collect the information that the senior executive requires for strategy formulation and implementation. The senior executive can also use this corporate staff–division staff relationship to communicate corporate policies and procedures to the divisions, although these policies can also be communicated directly by the senior executive to division general managers.

Although divisional staff managers usually have a less formal relationship with their division general managers, in practice division general managers can have an important influence on the activities of divisional staff. After all, divisional staff managers may formally report to corporate staff managers, but they spend most of their time interacting with their division general managers and with the other functional managers who report to their division general managers. These divided loyalties can sometimes affect the timelines and accuracy of the information transmitted from divisional staff managers to corporate staff managers and thus affect the timeliness and accuracy of the information the senior executive uses for strategy formulation and implementation.

Nowhere are these divided loyalties potentially more problematic than in accounting staff functions. Obviously, it is vitally important for the senior executive in an M-form organization to receive timely and accurate information about divisional performance. If the timeliness and accuracy of that information are inappropriately affected by division general managers, the effectiveness of senior management can be adversely affected. Moreover, in some situations division general managers can have very strong incentives to affect the timeliness and accuracy of divisional performance information, especially if a division general manager's compensation depends on this information or if the capital allocated to a division depends on this information.

Efficient monitoring by the senior executive requires that corporate staff, and especially the accounting corporate staff function, remain organizationally independent of division general managers—thus, the importance of the solid-line relationship between divisional staff managers and corporate staff managers. Nevertheless, the ability of corporate staff to obtain accurate performance information from divisions also depends on close cooperative working relationships between corporate staff, divisional staff, and division general managers—hence, the importance of the dotted-line relationship between divisional staff managers and division general managers. How one maintains the balance between, on the one hand, the distance and objectivity needed to evaluate a division's performance and, on the other hand, the cooperation and teamwork needed to gain access to the information required to evaluate a division's performance distinguishes excellent from mediocre corporate staff managers.

Overinvolvement in Managing Division Operations

Over and above the failure to maintain a balance between objectivity and cooperation in evaluating divisional performance, the one sure way that corporate staff can fail in a multidivisional firm is to become too involved in the day-to-day operations of divisions. In an M-form structure, the management of such day-to-day operations is delegated to division general managers and to functional managers who report to division general managers. Corporate staff managers collect and transmit information; they do not manage divisional operations.

One way to ensure that corporate staff does not become too involved in managing the day-to-day operations of divisions is to keep corporate staff small. This is certainly true for some of the best-managed diversified firms in the world. For example, just 1.5 percent of Johnson & Johnson's 82,700 employees work at the firm's headquarters, and only some of those individuals are members of the corporate staff. Hanson Industries has in its U.S. headquarters 120 people who help manage a diversified firm with $8 billion in revenues. Clayton, Dubilier, and Rice, a management buyout firm, has only 11 headquarters staff members overseeing eight businesses with collective sales of over $6 billion.[8]

Division General Manager

Division general managers in an M-form organization have primary responsibility for managing a firm's businesses from day to day. Division general managers have full profit-and-loss responsibility and typically have multiple functional managers reporting to them. As general managers, they have both strategy formulation and strategy implementation responsibilities. On the strategy formulation side, division general managers choose strategies for their divisions, within the broader strategic context established by the senior executive of the firm. Many of the analytical tools described in Parts 1 and 2 of this book can be used by division general managers to make these strategy formulation decisions.

The strategy implementation responsibilities of division general managers in an M-form organization parallel the strategy implementation responsibilities of senior executives in U-form organizations. In particular, division general managers must be able to coordinate the activities of often-conflicting functional managers in order to implement a division's strategies.

In addition to their responsibilities as a U-form senior executive, division general managers in an M-form organization have two additional responsibilities: to compete for corporate capital and to cooperate with other divisions to exploit corporate economies of scope. Division general managers compete for corporate capital by promising high rates of return on capital invested by the corporation in their business. In most firms, divisions that have demonstrated the ability to generate high rates of return on earlier capital investments gain access to more capital or to lower-cost capital, compared to divisions that have not demonstrated a history of such performance.

Division general managers cooperate to exploit economies of scope by working with shared activity managers, corporate staff managers, and the senior executive in the firm to isolate, understand, and use the economies of scope around which the diversified firm was originally organized. Division general managers can even become involved in discovering new economies of scope that were not anticipated when the firm's diversification strategy was originally implemented but nevertheless may be both valuable and costly for outside investors to create on their own.

Of course, a careful reader will recognize a fundamental conflict between the last two responsibilities of division general managers in an M-form organization. These managers are required to compete for corporate capital and to cooperate to exploit economies of scope at the same time. Competition is important, because it leads division general managers to focus on generating high levels of economic performance from their divisions. If each division is generating high levels of economic performance, then the diversified firm as a whole is likely to do well also. However, cooperation is important to exploit economies of scope that are the economic justification for implementing a diversification strategy in the first place. If divisions do not cooperate in exploiting these economies, there are few, if any, justifications for implementing a corporate diversification strategy, and the diversified firm should be split into multiple independent entities. The need to simultaneously compete and cooperate puts significant managerial burdens on division general managers. It is likely that this ability is both rare and costly to imitate across most diversified firms.[9]

Shared Activity Managers

One of the potential economies of scope identified in Chapter 7 was shared activities. Divisions in an M-form organization exploit this economy of scope when one or more of the stages in their value chains are managed in common. Typical examples of activities shared across two or more divisions in a multidivisional firm include common sales forces, common distribution systems, common manufacturing facilities, and common research and development efforts (also see Table 7.2). The primary responsibility of the individuals who manage shared activities is to support the operations of the divisions that share the activity.

The way in which M-form structure is often depicted in company annual reports (as in Figure 8.1) tends to obscure the operational role of shared activities. In this version of the M-form organizational chart, no distinction is made between corporate staff functions and shared activity functions. Moreover, it appears that managers of shared activities report directly to a firm's senior executive, just like corporate staff. These ambiguities are resolved by redrawing the M-form organizational chart to emphasize the roles and responsibilities of different units within the M-form (as in Figure 8.2). In this more accurate representation of how an M-form actually functions, corporate staff groups are separated from shared activity managers, and each is shown reporting to its primary internal "customer." That "internal customer" is the senior executive for corporate staff groups and two or more division general managers for shared activity managers.

Shared Activities as Cost Centers

Shared activities are often managed as cost centers in an M-form structure. That is, rather than having profit-and-loss responsibility, **cost centers** are assigned a budget and manage their operations to that budget. When this is the case, shared activity managers do not attempt to create profits when they provide services to the divisions they support. Rather, these services are priced to internal customers in such a way that the shared activity just covers its cost of operating.

Because cost center shared activities do not have to generate profits from their operations, the cost of the services they provide to divisions can be less than the cost of similar services provided either by a division itself or by outside suppliers. If a shared activity is managed as a cost center, and the cost of services from this shared activity is *greater than* the cost of similar services provided by alternative sources, then either this shared activity is not being well managed or it was not a real economy of scope in the first place. However, when the cost of services from a shared activity is *less than* the cost of comparable services provided by a division itself or by an outside supplier, then division general managers have a strong incentive to use the services of shared activities, thereby exploiting an economy of scope that may have been one of the original reasons why a firm implemented a corporate diversification strategy.

Shared Activities as Profit Centers

Some diversified firms are beginning to manage shared activities as profit centers, rather than as cost centers. Moreover, rather than requiring divisions to use the services of shared activities, divisions retain the right to purchase services from internal shared activities or from outside suppliers or to provide services for themselves. In this setting, managers of shared activities are required to compete for their internal customers on the basis of the price and quality of the services they provide.[10]

One firm that has taken this profit-center approach to managing shared activities is ABB, Inc., a Swiss engineering firm. ABB eliminated almost all its corporate staff and reorganized its remaining staff functions into shared activities. Shared activities in ABB compete to provide services to ABB divisions. Not only do some traditional shared activities—such as research and development and sales—compete for internal customers, but many traditional corporate staff functions—such as human resources, marketing, and finance—do as well. ABB's approach to managing shared activities has resulted in a relatively small corporate staff and in increasingly specialized and customized shared activities.[11]

Of course, the greatest risk associated with treating shared activities as profit centers and letting them compete for divisional customers is that divisions may choose to obtain no services or support from shared activities. Although this course of action may be in the self-interest of each division, it may not be in the best interest of the corporation as a whole if, in fact, shared activities are an important economy of scope around which the diversified firm is organized.

In the end, the task facing the managers of shared activities is the same: to provide such highly customized and high-quality services to divisional customers at a reasonable cost that those internal customers will not want to seek alternative suppliers outside the firm or provide those services themselves. In an M-form organization, the best way to ensure that shared activity economies of scope are realized is for shared activity managers to satisfy their internal customers.

Management Controls and Implementing Corporate Diversification

The M-form structure presented in Figures 8.1 and 8.2 is complex and multifaceted. However, no organizational structure by itself is able to fully implement a corporate diversification strategy. The M-form structure must be supplemented with a variety of management controls. Three of the most important management controls in an M-form structure—systems for evaluating divisional performance, for allocating capital across divisions, and for transferring intermediate products between divisions—are discussed in this section.[12]

Evaluating Divisional Performance

Because divisions in an M-form structure are profit-and-loss centers, evaluating divisional performance should, in principle, be straightforward: Divisions that are very profitable should be evaluated more positively than divisions that are less profitable. In practice, this seemingly simple task is surprisingly complex. Two problems typically arise: (1) How should division profitability be measured? and (2) How should economy-of-scope linkages between divisions be factored into divisional performance measures?

Measuring Divisional Performance

Divisional performance can be measured in at least two ways. The first focuses on a division's accounting performance; the second on a division's economic performance.

Accounting Measures of Divisional Performance.   Both accounting and economic measures of performance can be used in measuring the performance of divisions within a diversified firm. Common accounting measures of divisional performance include the return on the assets controlled by a division, the return on a division's sales, and a division's sales growth. These accounting measures of divisional performance are then compared with some standard to see if a division's performance exceeds or falls short of that standard. Diversified firms use three different standards of comparison when evaluating the performance of a division: (1) a hurdle rate that is common across all the different business units in a firm, (2) a division's budgeted level of performance (which may vary by division), and (3) the average level of profitability of firms in a division's industry.

Each of these standards of comparison has its strengths and weaknesses. For example, if a corporation has a single hurdle rate of profitability that all divisions must meet or exceed, there is little ambiguity about the performance objectives of divisions. However, a single standard ignores important differences in performance that might exist across divisions.

Comparing a division's actual performance to its budgeted performance allows the performance expectations of different divisions to vary, but the budgeting process is time-consuming and fraught with political intrigue. One study showed that corporate managers routinely discount the sales projections and capital requests of division managers on the assumption that division managers are trying to "game" the budgeting system.[13] Moreover, division budgets are usually based on a single set of assumptions about how the economy is going to evolve, how competition in a division's industry is going to evolve, and what actions that division is going to take in its industry. When these assumptions no longer hold, budgets are redone—a costly and time-consuming process that has little to do with generating value in a firm.

Finally, although comparing a division's performance with the average level of profitability of firms in a division's industry also allows performance expectations to vary across divisions within a diversified firm, this approach lets other firms determine what is and is not excellent performance for a division within a diversified firm. This approach can also be manipulated: By choosing just the "right" firms with which to compare a division's performance, almost any division can be made to look like it's performing better than its industry average.[14]

No matter what standard of comparison is used to evaluate a division's accounting performance, most accounting measures of divisional performance have a common limitation. All these measures have a short-term bias. This short-term bias reflects the fact that all these measures treat investments in resources and capabilities that have the potential for generating value in the long run as costs during a particular year. In order to reduce costs in a given year, division managers may sometimes forgo investing in these resources and capabilities, even if they could be a source of sustained competitive advantage for a division in the long run.

Economic Measures of Divisional Performance.   Given the limitations of accounting measures of divisional performance, several firms have begun adopting economic methods of evaluating this performance. Economic methods build on accounting methods but adjust those methods to incorporate short-term investments that may generate long-term benefits. Economic methods also compare a division's performance with a firm's cost of capital (see Chapter 1). This avoids some of the gaming that can characterize the use of other standards of comparison in applying accounting measures of divisional performance.

Perhaps the most popular of these economically oriented measures of division performance is known as **economic value added (EVA)**.[15] EVA is calculated by subtracting the cost of capital employed in a division from that division's earnings in the following manner:

$$\text{EVA} = \text{adjusted accounting earnings}$$
$$(\text{weighted average cost of capital} \times \text{total capital employed by a division})$$

Several of the terms in the EVA formula require some discussion. For example, the calculation of economic value added begins with a division's "adjusted" accounting earnings. These are a division's traditional accounting earnings, adjusted so that they approximate a division's economic earnings. Several adjustments to a division's accounting statements have been described in the literature. For example, traditional accounting practices require R&D spending to be deducted each year from a division's earnings. This can lead division general managers to under-invest in longer-term R&D efforts. In the EVA measure of divisional performance, R&D spending is added back into a division's performance, and R&D is then treated as an asset and depreciated over some period of time.

One consulting firm (Stern Stewart) that specializes in implementing EVA-based divisional evaluation systems in multidivisional firms makes up to 40 "adjustments" to a division's standard accounting earnings so that they more closely approximate economic earnings. Many of these adjustments are proprietary to this consulting firm. However, the most important adjustments—such as how R&D should be treated—are broadly known.

The terms in parentheses in the EVA equation reflect the cost of investing in a division. Rather than using some alternative standard of comparison, EVA applies financial theory and multiplies the amount of money invested in a division by a firm's weighted average cost of capital. A firm's weighted average cost of capital is the amount of money a firm could earn if it invested in any of its other divisions. In this sense, a firm's weighted average cost of capital can be thought of as the opportunity cost of investing in a particular division, as opposed to investing in any other division in the firm.

By adjusting a division's earnings and accounting for the cost of investing in a division, EVA is a much more accurate estimate of a division's economic performance than are traditional accounting measures of performance. The number of diversified firms evaluating their divisions with EVA-based measures of divisional performance is impressive and growing. These firms include AT&T, Coca-Cola, Quaker Oats, CSX, Briggs and Stratton, and Allied Signal. At Allied Signal, divisions that do not earn their cost of capital are awarded the infamous "leaky bucket" award. If this performance is not improved, division general managers are replaced. The use of EVA has been touted as the key to creating economic wealth in a diversified corporation.[16]

Economies of Scope and the Ambiguity of Divisional Performance

Whether a firm uses accounting measures to evaluate the performance of a division or uses economic measures of performance such as EVA, divisional performance in a well-managed diversified firm can never be evaluated unambiguously. Consider a simple example.

Suppose that in a particular multidivisional firm there are only two divisions (Division A and Division B) and one shared activity (R&D). Also, suppose that the two divisions are managed as profit-and-loss centers and that the R&D shared activity is managed as a cost center. To support this R&D effort, each division pays $10 million per year and has been doing so for 10 years. Finally, suppose that after 10 years of effort (and investment) the R&D group develops a valuable new technology that perfectly addresses Division A's business needs.

Obviously, no matter how divisional performance is measured it is likely to be the case that Division A's performance will rise relative to Division B's performance. In this situation, what percentage of Division A's improved performance should be allocated to Division A, what percentage should be allocated to the R&D group, and what percentage should be allocated to Division B?

The managers in each part of this diversified firm can make compelling arguments in their favor. Division general manager A can reasonably argue that without Division A's efforts to exploit the new technology, the full value of the technology would never have been realized. The R&D manager can reasonably argue that, without the R&D effort, there would not have been a technology to exploit in the first place. Finally, division general manager B can reasonably argue that, without the dedicated long-term investment of Division B in R&D, there would have been no new technology and no performance increase for Division A.

That all three of these arguments can be made suggests that, to the extent that a firm exploits real economies of scope in implementing a diversification strategy, it will not be possible to unambiguously evaluate the performance of individual divisions in that firm. The fact that there are economies of scope in a diversified firm means that all of the businesses a firm operates in are more valuable bundled together than they would be if kept separate from one another. Efforts to evaluate the performance of these businesses as if they were separate from one another are futile.

One solution to this problem is to force businesses in a diversified firm to operate independently of each other. If each business operates independently, then it will be possible to unambiguously evaluate its performance. Of course, to the extent that this independence is enforced, the diversified firm is unlikely to be able to realize the very economies of scope that were the justification for the diversification strategy in the first place.

Divisional performance ambiguity is bad enough when shared activities are the primary economy of scope that a diversified firm is trying to exploit. This ambiguity increases dramatically when the economy of scope is based on intangible core competencies. In this situation, it is shared learning and experience that justify a firm's diversification efforts. The intangible nature of these economies of scope multiplies the difficulty of the divisional evaluation task.

Even firms that apply rigorous EVA measures of divisional performance are unable to fully resolve these performance ambiguity difficulties. For example, the Coca-Cola division of the Coca-Cola Company has made enormous investments in the Coke brand name over the years, and the Diet Coke division has exploited some of that brand name capital in its own marketing efforts. Of course, it is not clear that all of Diet Coke's success can be attributed to the Coke brand name. After all, Diet Coke has developed its own creative advertising, its own loyal group of customers, and so forth. How much of Diet Coke's success—as measured through that division's economic value added—should be allocated to the Coke brand name (an investment made long before Diet Coke was even conceived) and how much should be allocated to the Diet Coke division's efforts? EVA measures of divisional performance do not resolve ambiguities created when economies of scope exist across divisions.[17]

In the end, the quantitative evaluation of divisional performance—with either accounting or economic measures—must be supplemented by the experience and judgment of senior executives in a diversified firm. Only by evaluating a division's performance numbers in the context of a broader, more subjective evaluation of the division's performance can a true picture of divisional performance be developed.

Allocating Corporate Capital

Another potentially valuable economy of scope outlined in Chapter 7 (besides shared activities and core competencies) is internal capital allocation. In that discussion, it was suggested that for internal capital allocation to be a justification for diversification the information made available to senior executives allocating capital in a diversified firm must be superior, in both amount and quality, to the information available to external sources of capital in the external capital market. Both the quality and the quantity of the information available in an internal capital market depend on the organization of the diversified firm.

One of the primary limitations of internal capital markets is that division general managers have a strong incentive to overstate their division's prospects and understate its problems in order to gain access to more capital at lower costs. Having an independent corporate accounting function in a diversified firm can help address this problem. However, given the ambiguities inherent in evaluating divisional performance in a well-managed diversified firm, independent corporate accountants do not resolve all these informational problems.

In the face of these challenges, some firms use a process called **zero-based budgeting** to help allocate capital. In zero-based budgeting, corporate executives create a list of all capital allocation requests from divisions in a firm, rank them from "most important" to "least important," and then fund all the projects a firm can afford, given the amount of capital it has available. In principle, no project will receive funding for the future simply because it received funding in the past. Rather, each project has to stand on its own merits each year by being included among the important projects the firm can afford to fund.

Although zero-based budgeting has some attractive features, it has some important limitations as well. For example, evaluating and ranking all projects in a diversified firm from "most important" to "least important" is a very difficult task. It requires corporate executives to have a very complete understanding of the strategic role of each of the projects being proposed by a division, as well as an understanding of how these projects will affect the short-term performance of divisions.

In the end, no matter what process firms use to allocate capital, allocating capital inside a firm in a way that is more efficient than could be done by external capital markets requires the use of information that is not available to those external markets. Typically, that information will be intangible, tacit, and complex. Corporate managers looking to realize this economy of scope must find a way to use this kind of information effectively.[18] The difficulty of managing this process effectively may be one of the reasons why internal capital allocation often fails to qualify as a valuable economy of scope in diversified firms.[19]

Transferring Intermediate Products

The existence of economies of scope across multiple divisions in a diversified firm often means that products or services produced in one division are used as inputs for products or services produced by a second division. Such products or services are called **intermediate products or services**. Intermediate products or services can be transferred between any of the units in an M-form organization. This transfer is perhaps most important and problematic when it occurs between profit center divisions.

The transfer of intermediate products or services among divisions is usually managed through a **transfer-pricing system**: One division "sells" its product or service to a second division for a transfer price. Unlike a market price, which is typically determined by market forces of supply and demand, transfer prices are set by a firm's corporate management to accomplish corporate objectives.

Setting Optimal Transfer Prices

From an economic point of view, the rule for establishing the optimal transfer price in a diversified firm is quite simple: The transfer price should be the value of the opportunities forgone when one division's product or service is transferred to another division. Consider the following example. Division A's marginal cost of production is $5 per unit, but Division A can sell all of its output to outside customers for $6 per unit. If Division A can sell all of its output to outside customers for $6 per unit, the value of the opportunity forgone of transferring a unit of production from Division A to Division B is $6—the amount of money that Division A forgoes by transferring its production to Division B instead of selling it to the market.

However, if Division A is selling all the units it can to external customers for $6 per unit but still has some excess manufacturing capacity, the value of the opportunity forgone in transferring the product from Division A to Division B is only $5 per unit—Division A's marginal cost of production. Because the external market cannot absorb any more of Division A's product at $6 per unit, the value of the opportunity forgone when Division A transfers units of production to Division B is not $6 per unit (Division A can't get that price), but only $5 per unit.[20]

When transfer prices are set equal to opportunity costs, selling divisions will produce output up to the point that the marginal cost of the last unit produced equals the transfer price. Moreover, buying divisions will buy units from other divisions in the firm as long as the net revenues from doing so just cover the transfer price. These transfer prices will lead profit-maximizing divisions to optimize the diversified firm's profits.

Difficulties in Setting Optimal Transfer Prices

Setting transfer prices equal to opportunity costs sounds simple enough, but it is very difficult to do in real diversified firms. Establishing optimal transfer prices requires information about the value of the opportunities forgone by the "selling" division. This, in turn, requires information about this division's marginal costs, its manufacturing capacity, external demand for its products, and so forth. Much of this information is difficult to obtain. Moreover, it is rarely stable. As market conditions change, demand for a division's products can change, marginal costs can change, and the value of opportunities forgone can change. Also, to the extent that a selling division customizes the products or services it transfers to other divisions in a diversified firm, the value of the opportunities forgone by this selling division become even more difficult to calculate.

Even if this information could be obtained and updated rapidly, division general managers in selling divisions have strong incentives to manipulate the information in ways that increase the perceived value of the opportunities forgone by their division. These division general managers can thus increase the transfer price for the products or services they sell to internal customers and thereby appropriate for their division profits that should have been allocated to buying divisions.

Setting Transfer Prices in Practice

Because it is rarely possible for firms to establish an optimal transfer-pricing scheme, most diversified firms must adopt some form of transfer pricing that attempts to approximate optimal prices. Several of these transfer-pricing schemes are described in Table 8.3. However, no matter what particular scheme a firm uses, the transfer prices it generates will, at times, create inefficiencies and conflicts in a diversified firm. Some of these inefficiencies and conflicts are described in Table 8.4.[21]

The inefficiencies and conflicts created by transfer-pricing schemes that only approximate optimal transfer prices mean that few diversified firms are ever fully satisfied with how they set transfer prices. Indeed, one study found that as the

TABLE 8.3 Alternative Transfer-Pricing Schemes

Exchange autonomy	■ Buying and selling division general managers are free to negotiate transfer price without corporate involvement. ■ Transfer price is set equal to the selling division's price to external customers.
Mandated full cost	■ Transfer price is set equal to the selling division's actual cost of production. ■ Transfer price is set equal to the selling division's standard cost (i.e., the cost of production if the selling division were operating at maximum efficiency).
Mandated market based	■ Transfer price is set equal to the market price in the selling division's market.
Dual pricing	■ Transfer price for the buying division is set equal to the selling division's actual or standard costs. ■ Transfer price for the selling division is set equal to the price to external customers or to the market price in the selling division's market.

Source: Eccles, R. (1985). *The Transfer Pricing Problem: A Theory for Practice.* Lexington Books: Lexington, MA. Used with permission of Rowman and Littlefield Publishing Group.

TABLE 8.4 Weaknesses of Alternative Transfer-Pricing Schemes

1. Buying and selling divisions negotiate transfer price.
   - What about the negotiating and haggling costs?
   - The corporation risks not exploiting economies of scope if the right transfer price cannot be negotiated.
2. Transfer price is set equal to the selling division's price to external customers.
   - Which customers? Different selling division customers may get different prices.
   - Shouldn't the volume created by the buying division for a selling division be reflected in a lower transfer price?
   - The selling division doesn't have marketing expenses when selling to another division. Shouldn't that be reflected in a lower transfer price?
3. Transfer price is set equal to the selling division's actual costs.
   - What are those actual costs, and who gets to determine them?
   - *All* the selling division's costs, or only the costs relevant to the products being purchased by the buying division?
4. Transfer price is set equal to the selling division's standard costs.
   - Standard costs are the costs the selling division would incur if it were running at maximum efficiency. This hypothetical capacity subsidizes the buying division.
5. Transfer price is set equal to the market price.
   - If the product in question is highly differentiated, there is no simple "market price."
   - Shouldn't the volume created by the buying division for a selling division be reflected in a lower transfer price?
   - The selling division doesn't have marketing expenses when selling to a buying division. Shouldn't that be reflected in a lower transfer price?
6. Transfer price is set equal to actual costs for the selling division and to market price for the buying division.
   - This combination of schemes simply combines other problems of setting transfer prices.

level of resource sharing in a diversified firm increases (thereby increasing the importance of transfer-pricing mechanisms) the level of job satisfaction for division general managers decreases.[22]

It is not unusual for a diversified firm to change its transfer-pricing mechanisms every few years in an attempt to find the "right" transfer-pricing mechanism. Economic theory tells us what the "right" transfer-pricing mechanism is: Transfer prices should equal opportunity cost. However, this "correct" transfer-pricing mechanism cannot be implemented in most firms. Firms that continually change their transfer-pricing mechanisms generally find that all these systems have some weaknesses. In deciding which system to use, a firm should be less concerned about finding the right transfer-pricing mechanism and more concerned about choosing a transfer-pricing policy that creates the fewest management problems—or at least the kinds of problems that the firm can manage effectively. Indeed, some scholars have suggested that the search for optimal transfer pricing should be abandoned in favor of treating transfer pricing as a conflict-resolution process. Viewed in this way, transfer pricing highlights differences between divisions, and thus makes it possible to begin to resolve those differences in a mutually beneficial way.[23]

Overall, the three management control processes described here—measuring divisional performance, allocating corporate capital, and transferring intermediate products—suggest that the implementation of a corporate diversification strategy

Strategy in the Emerging Enterprise

A **corporate spin-off** exists when a large, typically diversified firm divests itself of a business in which it has historically been operating and the divested business operates as an independent entity. Thus, corporate spin-offs are different from asset divestitures, where a firm sells some of its assets, including perhaps a particular business, to another firm. Spin-offs are a way that new firms can enter into the economy.

Spin-offs can occur in numerous ways. For example, a business might be sold to its managers and employees who then manage and work in this independently operating firm. Alternatively, a business unit within a diversified firm may be sold to the public through an **initial public offering (IPO)**. Sometimes, the corporation spinning off a business unit will retain some ownership stake in the spin-off; other times, this corporation will sever all financial links with the spun-off firm.

In general, large diversified firms might spin off businesses they own for three reasons. First, the efficient management of these businesses may require very specific skills that are not available in a diversified firm. For example, suppose a diversified manufacturing firm finds itself operating in an R&D-intensive industry. The management skills required to manage manufacturing efficiently can be very different from the management skills required to manage R&D. If a diversified firm's skills do not match the skills required in a particular business, that business might be spun off.

Second, anticipated economies of scope between a business and the rest of a diversified firm may turn out

Transforming Big Business into Entrepreneurship

to not be valuable. For example, PepsiCo acquired Kentucky Fried Chicken, Pizza Hut, and Taco Bell, anticipating important marketing synergies between these fast-food restaurants and PepsiCo's soft drink business. Despite numerous efforts to realize these synergies, they were not forthcoming. Indeed, several of these fast-food restaurants began losing market share because they were forced to sell Pepsi rather than Coca-Cola products. After a few years, PepsiCo spun off its restaurants into a separate business.

Finally, it may be necessary to spin a business off in order to fund a firm's other businesses. Large diversified firms may face capital constraints due to, among other things, their high level of debt. In this setting, firms may need to spin off a business in order to raise capital to invest in other parts of the firm. Moreover, spinning off a part of the business that is particularly costly in terms of the capital it consumes may not only be a source of funds for other parts of this firm's business, it can also reduce the demand for that capital within a firm.

Research in corporate finance suggests that corporations are most likely to spin off businesses that are unrelated to a firm's corporate diversification strategy; those that are poorly performing compared to other businesses a firm operates in; and relatively small businesses. Also, the amount of merger and acquisition activity in a particular industry will determine which businesses are spun off. The greater the level of this activity in an industry, the more likely that a business owned by a corporation in such an industry will be spun off. This is because the level of merger and acquisition activity in an industry is an indicator of the number of people and firms that might be interested in purchasing a spun-off business. However, when there is not much merger and acquisition activity in an industry, businesses in that industry are less likely to be spun off, even if they are unrelated to a firm's corporate diversification strategy, are poorly performing, or are small. In such settings, large firms are not likely to obtain the full value associated with spinning off a business and thus are reluctant to do so.

Whatever the conditions that lead a large diversified firm to spin off one of its businesses, this process is important for creating new firms in the economy.

Sources: F. Schlingemann, R. M. Stulz, and R. Walkling (2002). "Divestitures and the liquidity of the market for corporate assets." *Journal of Financial Economics*, 64, pp. 117–144; G. Hite, J. Owens, and R. Rogers (1987). "The market for inter-firm asset sales: Partial sell-offs and total liquidations." *Journal of Financial Economics*, 18, pp. 229–252; and P. Berger and E. Ofek (1999). "Causes and consequences of corporate focusing programs." *Review of Financial Studies*, 12, pp. 311–345.

requires a great deal of management skill and experience. They also suggest that sometimes diversified firms may find themselves operating businesses that no longer fit with the firm's overall corporate strategy. What happens when a division no longer fits with a firm's corporate strategy is described in the Strategy in the Emerging Enterprise feature.

Compensation Policies and Implementing Corporate Diversification

A firm's compensation policies constitute a final set of tools for implementing diversification. Traditionally, the compensation of corporate managers in a diversified firm has been only loosely connected to the firm's economic performance. One important study examined the relationship between executive compensation and firm performance and found that differences in CEO cash compensation (salary plus cash bonus) are not very responsive to differences in firm performance.[24] In particular, this study showed that a CEO of a firm whose equity holders

Ethics and Strategy

Nothing gets as much negative press as CEO salaries. And the numbers *are* staggering. In 2007, the CEO of Countrywide Financial, Angelo Mozilo, was paid $103 million; Lloyd Blankfein, CEO of Goldman Sachs, was paid $74 million; Richard Fuld, CEO of Lehman Brothers, was paid $72 million; and John Mack, CEO of Morgan Stanley, was paid $41 million.

Of course, what is interesting about these particular compensation examples is that, despite the serious dollars that were paid out to these CEOs in 2007, by the end of 2008, all of these companies were in serious financial difficulty—either facing bankruptcy, acquired as a way to avoid bankruptcy, or reorganized to reduce the impact of severe economic losses. So, how can a CEO be "worth" millions of dollars in 2007 and then head up an economically depressed—nearly bankrupt—company less than 12 months later?

CEO Compensation and the Credit Crisis of 2008

Part of the explanation for this disconnect between CEO compensation and firm performance has to do with the unexpected and radical nature of the economic downturn associated with the credit crunch of 2008. All of these CEOs were working

in financial services companies in 2007 and 2008, a segment of the economy that was badly hurt by the credit crunch of 2008. It could be argued that the compensation these CEOs received in 2007 reflected the value they created in that year and had little to do with the performance of these organizations in 2008, a level of performance that—many have suggested—could not have been anticipated in 2007.

However, another view of this situation is that the compensation these CEOs received in 2007 was partly responsible for the credit crisis of 2008. In this view, CEO compensation is not just the benign result of market forces in the market for CEOs, but rather can shape firm strategies and actions in ways that can help—or hurt—economic activity in the long run. Consider the following.

Most CEOs receive compensation packages that consist of a base salary, a cash bonus, and various stock grants

lost, collectively, $400 million in a year earned average cash compensation worth $800,000, while a CEO of a firm whose equity holders gained, collectively, $400 million in a year earned average cash compensation worth $1,040,000. Thus, an $800 million difference in the performance of a firm only had, on average, a $204,000 impact on the size of a CEO's salary and cash bonus. Put differently, for every million dollars of improved firm performance, CEOs, on average, get paid an additional $255. After taxes, increasing a firm's performance by a million dollars is roughly equal in value to a good dinner at a nice restaurant.

However, this same study was able to show that if a substantial percentage of a CEO's compensation came in the form of stock and stock options in the firm, changes in compensation would be closely linked with changes in the firm performance. In particular, the $800 million difference in firm performance just described would be associated with a $1.2 million difference in the value of CEO compensation if CEO compensation included stock and stock options in addition to cash compensation. In this setting, an additional million dollars of firm performance increases a CEO's salary by $667.

These and similar findings reported elsewhere have led more and more diversified firms to include stock and stock options as part of the compensation

and stock options. When CEOs receive stock options, they obtain the right, but not the obligation, to buy the firm's stock at a particular price—usually the price at which the firm's stock is trading when the stock options are granted. If a firm's stock rises significantly, then CEOs can cash in their stock options—they are "in the money"—and purchase their company's stock at sometimes very significant discounts. This can represent a great deal of money to CEO—often millions, and even hundreds of millions of dollars, over time.

In the face of this huge upside potential, CEOs have a strong incentive to increase the price of their firm's stock. In general, these are actions that are consistent with the interests of a firm's shareholders. However, sometimes CEOs can engage in very risky activities to increase their share price. Investors in these firms may not fully understand the nature of these risks, and thus may not be fully protected from these risks through diversification and other investment strategies.

In particular, many financial services companies apparently engaged in these risky actions in the early 2000s—selling mortgages to people who could not afford them; packaging these mortgages in financial instruments that were then sold to financial institutions that didn't fully understand the risks they were taking on; purchasing "insurance" policies against any downsides associated with these investments, even though the nature of these risks were not well understood and the firms selling this insurance did not have the capital needed to offset any losses that were forthcoming. In short, in an effort to crank up the stock price as high as possible—and thereby pocket huge gains from cashing in stock options—CEOs in some financial services companies put the entire financial services industry at risk. And not just in the United States, but around the world as well.

Put differently, CEO compensation in the financial services industry in 2005, 2006, and 2007 may have had a negative consequence—what economists call a negative externality—for the entire economy in 2008. A measure of the size of this negative externality is the size of the government bailouts that were used to shore up the financial system during 2008—bailouts and subsidies that total several trillions of dollars around the world.

In the face of such substantial negative externalities, some have wondered whether or not CEO compensation should be regulated—to prevent future CEOs from engaging in actions that not only hurt their individual companies but also put the entire financial system at risk.

Sources: www.nytimes.com/interactive/2008/05/05/business/20080405_EXECCOMP; www.forbes.com/lists/2008/12/lead_bestbosses08_CEO-Compensation_Rank; www.forbes.com/leaderhip/2008/08/13/yahoo-memc-nvidia-lead-comp-cz_mk_0813.

package for the CEO. As important, many firms now extend this non-cash compensation to other senior managers in a diversified firm, including division general managers. For example, the top 1,300 managers at General Dynamics receive stock and stock options as part of their compensation package. Moreover, the cash bonuses of these managers also depend on General Dynamics' stock market performance. At Johnson & Johnson, all division general managers receive a five-component compensation package. The level of only one of those components, salary, does not vary with the economic profitability of the business over which a division general manager presides. The level of the other four components—a cash bonus, stock grants, stock options, and a deferred income package—varies with the economic performance of a particular division. Moreover, the value of some of these variable components of compensation also depends on Johnson & Johnson's long-term economic performance.[25]

To the extent that compensation in diversified firms gives managers incentives to make decisions consistent with stockholders' interests, they can be an important part of the process of implementing corporate diversification. However, the sheer size of the compensation paid to some CEOs raises ethical issues for some. These ethical issues are discussed in the Ethics and Strategy feature.

Summary

To be valuable, diversification strategies must exploit valuable economies of scope that cannot be duplicated by outside investors at low cost. However, to realize the value of these economies of scope, firms must organize themselves appropriately. A firm's organizational structure, its management control processes, and its compensation policies are all relevant in implementing a corporate diversification strategy.

The best organizational structure for implementing a diversification leveraging strategy is the multidivisional, or M-form, structure. The M-form structure has several critical components, including the board of directors, institutional investors, the senior executive, corporate staff, division general managers, and shared activity managers.

This organizational structure is supported by a variety of management control processes. Three critical management control processes for firms implementing diversification strategies are (1) evaluating the performance of divisions, (2) allocating capital across divisions, and (3) transferring intermediate products between divisions. The existence of economies of scope in firms implementing corporate diversification strategies significantly complicates the management of these processes.

Finally, a firm's compensation policies are also important for firms implementing a diversification strategy. Historically, management compensation has been only loosely connected to a firm's economic performance, but the last few years have seen the increased popularity of using stock and stock options to help compensate managers. Such compensation schemes help reduce conflicts between managers and outside investors, but the absolute level of CEO compensation is still very high, at least in the United States.

Challenge Questions

1. Agency theory has been criticized for assuming that managers, left on their own, will behave in ways that reduce the wealth of outside equity holders when, in fact, most managers are highly responsible stewards of the assets they control. This alternative view of managers has been called *stewardship theory*. Do you agree with this criticism of agency theory? Why or why not?

2. Suppose that the concept of the stewardship theory is correct and that most managers, most of the time, behave responsibly and make decisions that maximize the present value of the assets they control. What implications, if any, would this supposition have on organizing to implement diversification strategies?

3. The M-form structure enables firms to pursue complex corporate diversification strategies by delegating different management responsibilities to different individuals and groups within a firm. Will there come a time when a firm becomes too large and too complex to be managed even through an M-form structure? In other words, is there a natural limit to the efficient size of a diversified firm?

4. Most observers agree that centrally planned economies fail because it is impossible for bureaucrats in large government hierarchies to coordinate different sectors of an economy as efficiently as market mechanisms do. Many diversified firms, however, are as large as some economies and use private sector hierarchies to coordinate diverse business activities in a firm. Are these large, private sector hierarchies somehow different from the government hierarchies of centrally planned economies? If yes, in what way? If no, why do these large, private sector hierarchies continue to exist?

5. Suppose that the optimal transfer price between one business and all other business activities in a firm is the market price. What does this condition say about whether this firm should own this business?

Problem Set

1. Which elements of the M-form structure (the board of directors, the office of the CEO, corporate staff, division general managers, shared activity managers) should be involved in the following business activities? If more than one of these groups should be involved, indicate their relative level of involvement (e.g., 20 percent office of the CEO, 10 percent shared activity manager, 70 percent division general manager). Justify your answers.

(a) Determining the compensation of the CEO
(b) Determining the compensation of the corporate vice president of human resources
(c) Determining the compensation of a vice president of human resources in a particular business division
(d) Deciding to sell a business division
(e) Deciding to buy a relatively small firm whose activities are closely related to the activities of one of the firm's current divisions
(f) Deciding to buy a larger firm that is not closely related to the activities of any of a firm's current divisions
(g) Evaluating the performance of the vice president of sales, a manager whose sales staff sells the products of three divisions in the firm
(h) Evaluating the performance of the vice president of sales, a manager whose sales staff sells the products of only one division in the firm
(i) Determining how much money to invest in a corporate R&D function
(j) Deciding how much money to invest in an R&D function that supports the operations of two divisions within the firm
(k) Deciding whether to fire an R&D scientist
(l) Deciding whether to fire the vice president of accounting in a particular division

(m) Deciding whether to fire the corporation's vice president of accounting

(n) Deciding whether to take a firm public by selling stock in the firm to the general public for the first time

2. Consider the following facts. Division A in a firm has generated $847,000 of profits on $24 million worth of sales, using $32 million worth of dedicated assets. The cost of capital for this firm is 9 percent, and the firm has invested $7.3 million in this division.

(a) Calculate the Return on Sales (ROS) and Return on Total Assets (ROA) of Division A. If the hurdle rates for ROS and ROA in this firm are, respectively, 0.06 and 0.04, has this division performed well?

(b) Calculate the EVA of Division A (assuming that the reported profits have already been adjusted). Based on this EVA, has this division performed well?

(c) Suppose you were CEO of this firm. How would you choose between ROS/ROA and EVA for evaluating this division?

3. Suppose that Division A sells an intermediate product to Division B. Choose one of the ways of determining transfer prices described in this chapter (not setting transfer prices equal to the selling firm's opportunity costs) and show how Division Manager A can use this mechanism to justify a higher transfer price while Division Manager B can use this mechanism to justify a lower transfer price. Repeat this exercise with another approach to setting transfer prices described in the chapter.

End Notes

1. The structure and function of the multidimensional firm was first described by Chandler, A. (1962). *Strategy and structure: Chapters in the history of the industrial enterprise.* Cambridge, MA: MIT Press. The economic logic underlying the multidimensional firm was first described by Williamson, O. E. (1975). *Markets and hierarchies: Analysis and antitrust implications.* New York: Free Press. Empirical examinations of the impact of the M-form or firm performance include Armour, H. O., and D. J. Teece. (1980). "Vertical integration and technological innovation." *Review of Economics and Statistics,* 60, pp. 470–474. There continues to be some debate about the efficiency of the M-form structure. See Freeland, R. F. (1966). "The myth of the M-form? Governance, consent, and organizational change." *American Journal of Sociology,* 102(2), pp. 483–626; and Shanley, M. (1996). "Straw men and M-form myths: Comment on Freeland." *American Journal of Sociology,* 102(2), pp. 527–536.

2. See Finkelstein, S., and R. D'Aveni. (1994). "CEO duality as a double-edged sword: How boards of directors balance entrenchment avoidance and unity of command." *Academy of Management Journal,* 37, pp. 1079–1108.

3. Kesner, I. F. (1988). "Director's characteristics and committee membership: An investigation of type, occupation, tenure and gender." *Academy of Management Journal,* 31, pp. 66–84; and Zahra, S. A., and J. A. Pearce II. (1989). "Boards of directors and corporate financial performance: A review and integrative model." *Journal of Management,* 15, pp. 291–334.

4. Investor Relations Business. (2000). "Reversal of fortune: Institutional ownership is declining." *Investor Relations Business,* May 1, pp. 8–9; and Federal Reserve Board. (2006). "Flow of funds report." www.corpgov.net.

5. See Hansen, G. S., and C. W. L. Hill. (1991). "Are institutional investors myopic? A time-series study of four technology-driven industries." *Strategic Management Journal,* 12, pp. 1–16.

6. See Bergh, D. (1995). "Size and relatedness of units sold: An agency theory and resource-based perspective." *Strategic Management Journal,* 16, pp. 221–239; and Bethel, J., and J. Liebeskind (1993). "The effects of ownership structure on corporate restructuring." *Strategic Management Journal,* 14, pp. 15–31.

7. Burdens that are well described by Westley, F., and H. Mintzberg. (1989). "Visionary leadership and strategic management." *Strategic Management Journal,* 10, pp. 17–32.

8. See Dumaine, B. (1992). "Is big still good?" *Fortune,* April 20, pp. 50–60.

9. See Golden, B. (1992). "SBU strategy and performance: The moderating effects of the corporate–SBU relationship." *Strategic Management Journal,* 13, pp. 145–158; Berger, P., and E. Ofek. (1995). "Diversification effect on firm value." *Journal of Financial Economics,* 37, pp. 36–65; Lang, H. P., and R. M. Stulz. (1994). "Tobin's q, corporate diversification, and firm performance." *Journal of Political Economy,* 102, pp. 1248–1280; and Rumelt, R. (1991). "How much does industry matter?" *Strategic Management Journal,* 12, pp. 167–185.

10. See Halal, W. (1994). "From hierarchy to enterprise: Internal markets are the new foundation of management." *The Academy of Management Executive,* 8(4), pp. 69–83.

11. Bartlett, C., and S. Ghoshal. (1993). "Beyond the M-form: Toward a managerial theory of the firm." *Strategic Management Journal,* 14, pp. 23–46.

12. See Simons, R. (1994). "How new top managers use control systems as levers of strategic renewal." *Strategic Management Journal,* 15, pp. 169–189.

13. Bethel, J. E. (1990). "The capital allocation process and managerial mobility: A theoretical and empirical investigation." Unpublished doctoral dissertation, UCLA.

14. Some of these are described in Duffy, M. (1989). "ZBB, MBO, PPB, and their effectiveness within the planning/marketing process." *Strategic Management Journal,* 12, pp. 155–160.

15. See Stern, J., B. Stewart, and D. Chew. (1995). "The EVA financial management system." *Journal of Applied Corporate Finance,* 8, pp. 32–46; and Tully, S. (1993). "The real key to creating wealth." *Fortune,* September 20, pp. 38–50.

16. Applications of EVA are described in Tully, S. (1993). "The real key to creating wealth." *Fortune,* September 20, pp. 38–50; Tully, S. (1995). "So, Mr. Bossidy, we know you can cut. Now show us how to grow." *Fortune,* August 21, pp. 70–80; and Tully, S. (1995). "Can EVA deliver profits to the post office?" *Fortune,* July 10, p. 22.

17. A special issue of the *Journal of Applied Corporate Finance* in 1994 addressed many of these issues.

18. See Priem, R. (1990). "Top management team group factors, consensus, and firm performance." *Strategic Management Journal*, 11, pp. 469–478; and Wooldridge, B., and S. Floyd. (1990). "The strategy process, middle management involvement, and organizational performance." *Strategic Management Journal*, 11, pp. 231–241.

19. A point made by Westley, F. (1900). "Middle managers and strategy: Microdynamics of inclusion." *Strategic Management Journal*, 11, pp. 337–351; Lamont, O. (1997). "Cash flow and investment: Evidence from internal capital markets." *The Journal of Finance*, 52(1), pp. 83–109; Shin, H. H., and R. M. Stulz. (1998). "Are internal capital markets efficient?" *Quarterly Journal of Economics*, May, pp. 531–552; and Stein, J. C. (1997). "Internal capital markets and the competition for corporate resources." *The Journal of Finance*, 52(1), pp. 111–133.

20. See Brickley, J., C. Smith, and J. Zimmerman. (1996). *Organizational architecture and managerial economics approach*. Homewood, IL: Irwin; and Eccles, R. (1985). *The transfer pricing problem: A theory for practice*. Lexington, MA: Lexington Books.

21. See Cyert, R., and J. G. March. (1963). *A behavioral theory of the firm*. Upper Saddle River, NJ: Prentice Hall; Swieringa, R. J., and

J. H. Waterhouse. (1982). "Organizational views of transfer pricing." *Accounting, Organizations & Society*, 7(2), pp. 149–165; and Eccles, R. (1985). *The transfer pricing problem: A theory for practice*. Lexington, MA: Lexington Books.

22. Gupta, A. K., and V. Govindarajan. (1986). "Resource sharing among SBUs: Strategic antecedents and administrative implications." *Academy of Management Journal*, 29, pp. 695–714.

23. A point made by Swieringa, R. J., and J. H. Waterhouse. (1982). "Organizational views of transfer pricing." *Accounting, Organizations and Society*, 7(2), pp. 149–165.

24. Jensen, M. C., and K. J. Murphy. (1990). "Performance pay and top management incentives." *Journal of Political Economy*, 98, pp. 225–264.

25. See Dial, J., and K. J. Murphy. (1995). "Incentive, downsizing, and value creation at General Dynamics." *Journal of Financial Economics*, 37, pp. 261–314 on General Dynamics' compensation scheme; and Aguilar, F. J., and A. Bhambri. (1983). "Johnson & Johnson (A)." Harvard Business School Case No. 9-384-053 on Johnson & Johnson's compensation scheme.

Strategic Alliances

LEARNING OBJECTIVES

*After reading this chapter,
you should be able to:*

1. Define a strategic alliance
   and give three specific
   examples of strategic
   alliances.

2. Describe nine different
   ways that alliances can
   create value for firms and
   how these nine sources of
   value can be grouped into
   three large categories.

3. Describe how adverse
   selection, moral hazard,
   and holdup can threaten
   the ability of alliances to
   generate value.

4. Describe the conditions
   under which a strategic
   alliance can be rare and
   costly to duplicate.

5. Describe the conditions
   under which "going it
   alone" and acquisitions are
   not likely to be substitutes
   for alliances.

6. Describe how contracts,
   equity investments, firm
   reputations, joint ventures,
   and trust can all reduce the
   threat of cheating in
   strategic alliances.

Who Makes Video Games?

Video games are a large and growing market. Some video games—*Madden, FIFA Soccer, NBA Live*—are built around established sports franchises. Other video games—*Sims, Guitar Hero, Rock Band*—are built around their own unique concepts. And still other video games—*James Bond, Harry Potter, Toy Story*—build on characters and situations that were originally developed in motion pictures.

This last category of video games—those that build on motion picture content—may be in the process of radically changing the way that all video games are made.

In the early 1990s, several movie studios tried to develop their own video games based on the content of their own movies. But most of these firms quickly discovered that the technical skills required to develop the games were actually more important to their success than the creative story creating/character building skills they possessed as movie studios. And so, after several failed attempts, most movie studios outsourced video game development to video game specialists, firms like Electronic Arts, Activision, and THQ, to develop video games based on characters and situations in movies. THQ, for example, partnered with Pixar—before Pixar was acquired by Disney—and developed all the video games based on Pixar's animated characters. These games were then sold, and Disney/Pixar would get a licensing fee from each game sold.

Forming alliances with video game firms seemed to make a great deal of sense. But some problems began to emerge. First, some movie studios believed that the video game firms were not investing sufficient quality in their movie-based games, and instead, invested all their technical and creative talent on their own proprietary titles. That is, some studios thought that *Toy Story* video games were simply not getting the support that, say, *Guitar Hero* or *Halo* were getting.

Second, some video game firms began to complain about unrealistic development schedules—schedules that required video games to be released at the same time as the movies themselves. These tight schedules, the video game firms argued, increased their development costs and cut into their profits from selling the games.

Now, despite alliances that have lasted over a decade, some big media companies are thinking about getting back into the video game production business. One way to do this would be to buy some independent video game firms and incorporate them into these media companies. However, throughout 2007 and early 2008, the price of these stand-alone video game firms was very high—high enough to discourage most acquisitions. Those acquisitions that did occur were relatively small. For example, Warner Brother's bought TT games—maker of *Lego Star Wars* games—and Viacom bought

Harmonix Music Systems—developer of *Rock Band*—for $175 million.

Other firms, including Disney and Time Warner, are attempting to create their own video game development skills, in-house, without the benefit of an acquisition. Disney, for example, has 800 employees working in Disney Interactive Studios. However, until these firms successfully create state of the art video game development skills, they will still be forced to form alliances with video game specialists, especially in the development of technically more sophisticated games. For example, while Disney decided to develop the game for *Toy Story 3* in-house, it decided to use an alliance with a Canadian firm to develop the video game for *High School Musical*. The *Toy Story 3* game is a straightforward extension of previous *Toy Story* games, while the *High School Musical* game required more sophisticated "sing-along technology."

In the long run, whether they acquire these capabilities or create them in-house, large media companies are ultimately interested in doing more than just building video games based on their motion picture content. As box office revenues remain flat (up just 4 percent in 2007) and home video sales actually decline (down 3.2 percent in 2007), video game sales continue to grow

Barone Firenze/Shutterstock

(up 34 percent in 2007). So, many media firms see the development of all kinds of video games, not just those based on motion picture content, to be an important growth opportunity.

However, it remains to be seen if media firms have either the creative or technical abilities needed to develop video games that do not rely on motion picture content. These uncertainties could lead these media firms to retain alliances with video game specialist firms for some time to come.

Sources: M. Marr and N. Wingfield (2008). "Big media companies want back in the game." *The Wall Street Journal*, February 19, 2008, pp. B1 +; and C. Salter (2002). "Playing to win." *Fast Company*. December, pp. 80 +; Corbis/Reuters America LLC.

The use of strategic alliances to manage economic exchanges has grown substantially over the last several years. In the early 1990s, strategic alliances were relatively uncommon, except in a few industries. And not just in the video game industry. However, by the late 1990s they had become much more common in a wide variety of industries. Indeed, over 20,000 alliances were created worldwide in 2000 and 2001. In the computer-technology–based industries, over 2,200 alliances were created between 2001 and 2005. And in 2006, both General Motors (GM) and Ford were considering alliances as a way to help solve their economic problems.[1]

What Is a Strategic Alliance?

A **strategic alliance** exists whenever two or more independent organizations cooperate in the development, manufacture, or sale of products or services. As shown in Figure 9.1, strategic alliances can be grouped into three broad categories: nonequity alliances, equity alliances, and joint ventures.

In a **nonequity alliance**, cooperating firms agree to work together to develop, manufacture, or sell products or services, but they do not take equity positions in each other or form an independent organizational unit to manage their cooperative efforts. Rather, these cooperative relations are managed through the use of various contracts. **Licensing agreements** (where one firm allows others to use its brand name to sell products), **supply agreements** (where one firm agrees to supply others), and **distribution agreements** (where one firm agrees to distribute the products of others) are examples of nonequity strategic alliances. Most of the alliances between Tony Hawk and his partners take the form of nonequity licensing agreements.

In an **equity alliance**, cooperating firms supplement contracts with equity holdings in alliance partners. For example, when GM began importing small cars manufactured by Isuzu, not only did these partners have supply contracts in place, but GM purchased 34.2 percent of Isuzu's stock. Ford had a similar relationship with Mazda, and Chrysler had a similar relationship with Mitsubishi.[2] Equity alliances are also very common in the biotechnology industry. Large pharmaceutical firms such as Pfizer and Merck own equity positions in several start-up biotechnology companies.

Figure 9.1 Types of Strategic Alliances

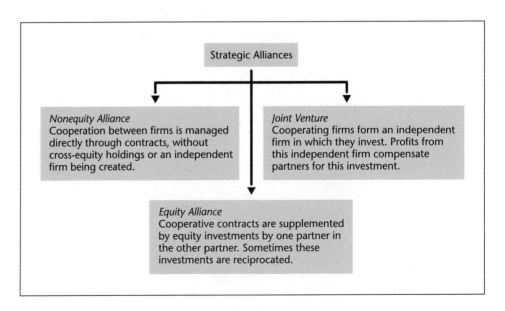

In a **joint venture**, cooperating firms create a legally independent firm in which they invest and from which they share any profits that are created. Some of these joint ventures can be very large. For example, Dow and Corning's joint venture, Dow-Corning, is a Fortune 500 company on its own. AT&T and BellSouth before they merged were co-owners of the joint venture Cingular, one of the largest wireless phone companies in the United States. And CFM—a joint venture between General Electric and SNECMA (a French Aerospace firm)—is one of the world's leading manufacturers of jet engines for commercial aircraft. If you have ever flown on a Boeing 737, then you have placed your life in the hands of this joint venture, because it manufactures the engines for virtually all of these aircraft.

How Do Strategic Alliances Create Value?

V R I O

Like all the strategies discussed in this book, strategic alliances create value by exploiting opportunities and neutralizing threats facing a firm. Some of the most important opportunities that can be exploited by strategic alliances are listed in Table 9.1. Threats to strategic alliances are discussed later in this chapter.

Strategic Alliance Opportunities

Opportunities associated with strategic alliances fall into three large categories. First, these alliances can be used by a firm to improve the performance of its current operations. Second, alliances can be used to create a competitive environment favorable to superior firm performance. Finally, they can be used to facilitate a firm's entry into or exit from new markets or industries.

Improving Current Operations

One way that firms can use strategic alliances to improve their current operations is to use alliances to realize economies of scale. The concept of economies of scale was first introduced in Chapter 2. **Economies of scale** exist when the per-unit cost of production falls as the volume of production increases. Thus, for example, although the per-unit cost of producing one Bic pen is very high, the per-unit cost of producing 50 million Bic pens is very low.

To realize economies of scale, firms have to have a large volume of production, or at least a volume of production large enough so that the cost advantages

Helping firms improve the performance of their current operations

1. Exploiting economies of scale
2. Learning from competitors
3. Managing risk and sharing costs
4. Creating a competitive environment favorable to superior performance
5. Facilitating the development of technology standards
6. Facilitating tacit collusion
7. Facilitating entry and exit
8. Low-cost entry into new industries and new industry segments
9. Low-cost exit from industries and industry segments
10. Managing uncertainty
11. Low-cost entry into new markets

TABLE 9.1 Ways Strategic Alliances Can Create Economic Value

associated with scale can be realized. Sometimes—as was described in Chapters 2 and 4—a firm can realize these economies of scale by itself; other times, it cannot. When a firm cannot realize the cost savings from economies of scale all by itself, it may join in a strategic alliance with other firms. Jointly, these firms may have sufficient volume to be able to gain the cost advantages of economies of scale.

But, why wouldn't a firm be able to realize these economies all by itself? A firm may have to turn to alliance partners to help realize economies of scale for a number of reasons. For example, if the volume of production required to realize these economies is very large, a single firm might have to dominate an entire industry in order to obtain these advantages. It is often very difficult for a single firm to obtain such a dominant position in an industry. And even if it does so, it may be subject to anti-monopoly regulation by the government. Also, although a particular part or technology may be very important to several firms, no one firm may generate sufficient demand for this part or technology to realize economies of scale in its development and production. In this setting as well, independent firms may join together to form an alliance to realize economies of scale in the development and production of the part or technology.

Firms can also use alliances to improve their current operations by learning from their competitors. As suggested in Chapter 3, different firms in an industry may have different resources and capabilities. These resources can give some firms competitive advantages over others. Firms that are at a competitive disadvantage may want to form alliances with the firms that have an advantage in order to learn about their resources and capabilities.

General Motors formed this kind of alliance with Toyota. In the early 1990s, GM and Toyota jointly invested in a previously closed GM plant in Fremont, California. This joint venture—called NUMI—was to build compact cars to be distributed through GM's distribution network. But why did GM decide to build these cars in an alliance with Toyota? Obviously, it could have built them in any of its own plants. However, GM was very interested in learning about how Toyota was able to manufacture high-quality small cars at a profit. Indeed, in the NUMI plant, Toyota agreed to take total responsibility for the manufacturing process, using former GM employees to install and operate the "lean manufacturing" system that had enabled Toyota to become the quality leader in the small-car segment of the automobile industry. However, Toyota also agreed to let GM managers work in the plant and directly observe how Toyota managed this production process. Since its inception, GM has rotated thousands of its managers from other GM plants through the NUMI plant so that they can be exposed to Toyota's lean manufacturing methods.

It is clear why GM would want this alliance with Toyota. But why would Toyota want this alliance with GM? Certainly, Toyota was not looking to learn about lean manufacturing, per se. However, because Toyota was contemplating entering the United States by building its own manufacturing facilities, it did need to learn how to implement lean manufacturing in the United States with U.S. employees. Thus, Toyota also had something to learn from this alliance.

When both parties to an alliance are seeking to learn something from that alliance, an interesting dynamic called a *learning race* can evolve. This dynamic is described in more detail in the Strategy in Depth feature.

Finally, firms can use alliances to improve their current operations through sharing costs and risks. For example, HBO produces most of its original programs in alliances with independent producers. Most of these alliances are created to share costs and risks. Producing new television shows can be costly. Development and production costs can run into the hundreds of millions of dollars, especially for long and complicated series like HBO's *Deadwood, Entourage,* and *The Sopranos.* And, despite audience testing and careful market analyses, the production of these new shows is also very risky. Even bankable stars like Dustin Hoffman and Warren Beatty and Ben Affleck and Jennifer Lopez—remember *Gigli*?—cannot guarantee success.

In this context, it is not surprising that HBO decides to not "go it alone" in its production efforts. If HBO was to be the sole producer of its original programming, not only would it have to absorb all the production costs, but it would also bear all the risk if a production turned out not to be successful. Of course, by getting other firms involved in its production efforts, HBO also has to share whatever profits a particular production generates. Apparently, HBO has concluded that sharing this upside potential is more than compensated for by sharing the costs and risks of these productions.

Creating a Favorable Competitive Environment

Firms can also use strategic alliances to create a competitive environment that is more conducive to superior performance. This can be done in at least two ways. First, firms can use alliances to help set technology standards in an industry. With these standards in place, technology-based products can be developed and consumers can be confident that the products they buy will be useful for some time to come.

Such technological standards are particularly important in what are called **network industries**. Such industries are characterized by **increasing returns to scale**. Consider, for example, fax machines. How valuable is one fax machine, all by itself? Obviously, not very valuable. Two fax machines that can talk to each other are a little more valuable, three that can talk to each other are still more valuable, and so forth. The value of each individual fax machine depends on the total number of fax machines in operation that can talk to each other. This is what is meant by increasing returns to scale—the value (or returns) on each product increases as the number of these products (or scale) increases.

If there are 100 million fax machines in operation but none of these machines can talk to each other, none of these machines has any value whatsoever—except as a large paperweight. For their full value to be realized, they must be able to talk to each other. And to talk to each other, they must all adopt the same—or at least compatible—communication standards. This is why setting technology standards is so important in network industries.

Standards can be set in two ways. First, different firms can introduce different standards, and consumers can decide which they prefer. This is how the standard for home videotapes was set. Sony sold one type of videotape machine—the Betamax—and Matsushita sold a second type of videotape machine—VHS. These two technologies were incompatible. Some consumers preferred Beta and purchased Sony's technology. Others preferred VHS and bought Matsushita's technology. However, because Matsushita licensed its VHS technology to numerous other firms, whereas Sony refused to do so, more and more consumers started buying VHS machines, until VHS became the de facto standard. This was the case even though most observers agreed that Beta was superior to VHS on several dimensions.

Of course, the biggest problem with letting customers and competition set technology standards is that customers may end up purchasing technologies that are incompatible with the standard that is ultimately set in the industry. What about all those consumers who purchased Beta products? For this reason, customers may be unwilling to invest in a new technology until the standards of that technology are established.

Strategy in Depth

A **learning race** exists in a strategic alliance when both parties to that alliance seek to learn from each other but the rate at which these two firms learn varies. In this setting, the first firm to learn what it wants to learn from an alliance has the option to begin to underinvest in, and perhaps even withdraw from, an alliance. In this way, the firm that learns faster is able to prevent the slower-learning firm from learning all it wanted from an alliance. If, outside of this alliance, these firms are competitors, winning a learning race can create a sustained competitive advantage for the faster-learning firm over the slower-learning firm.

Firms in an alliance may vary in the rate they learn from each other for a variety of reasons. First, they may be looking to learn different things, some of which are easier to learn than others. For example, in the GM–Toyota example, GM wanted to learn about how to use "lean manufacturing" to build high-quality small cars profitably. Toyota wanted to learn how to apply the "lean manufacturing" skills it already possessed in the United States. Which of these is easier to learn—"lean manufacturing" or how to apply "lean manufacturing" in the United States?

An argument can be made that GM's learning task was much more complicated than Toyota's. At the very least, in order for GM to apply knowledge about "lean manufacturing" gleaned from Toyota it would have to transfer that knowledge to several of its currently operating plants. Using this knowledge would require these plants to change their current operations—a difficult and time-consuming process. Toyota, however, only had to transfer

Winning Learning Races

its knowledge of how to operate a "lean manufacturing" operation in the United States to its other U.S. plants—plants that at the time this alliance was first created had yet to be built. Because GM's learning task was more complicated than Toyota's, it is very likely that Toyota's rate of learning was greater than GM's.

Second, firms may differ in terms of their ability to learn. This ability has been called a firm's **absorptive capacity**. Firms with high levels of absorptive capacity will learn at faster rates than firms with low levels of absorptive capacity, even if these two firms are trying to learn exactly the same things in an alliance. Absorptive capacity has been shown to be an important organizational capability in a wide variety of settings.

Third, firms can engage in activities to try to slow the rate of learning of their alliance partners. For example, although a firm might make its technology available to an alliance partner—thereby fulfilling the alliance agreement—it may not provide all the know-how necessary to exploit this technology. This can slow a partner's

learning. Also, a firm might withhold critical employees from an alliance, thereby slowing the learning of an alliance partner. All these actions, to the extent that they slow the rate of a partner's learning without also slowing the rate at which the firm engaging in these activities learns, can help this firm win a learning race.

Although learning race dynamics have been described in a wide variety of settings, they are particularly common in relations between entrepreneurial and large firms. In these alliances, entrepreneurial firms are often looking to learn about all the managerial functions required to bring a product to market, including manufacturing, sales, distribution, and so forth. This is a difficult learning task. Large firms in these alliances often are only looking to learn about the entrepreneurial firm's technology. This is a less difficult learning task. Because the learning task facing entrepreneurial firms is more challenging than that facing their large-firm partners, larger firms in these alliances typically win the learning race. Once these large firms learn what they want from their alliance partners, they often underinvest or even withdraw from these alliances. This is why, in one study, almost 80 percent of the managers in entrepreneurial firms felt unfairly exploited by their large-firm alliance partners.

Sources: S. A. Alvarez and J. B. Barney (2001). "How entrepreneurial firms can benefit from alliances with large partners." *Academy of Management Executive,* 15, pp. 139–148; G. Hamel (1991). "Competition for competence and inter-partner learning within international alliances." *Strategic Management Journal,* 12, pp. 83–103; and W. Cohen and D. Levinthal (1990). "Absorptive capacity: A new perspective on learning and innovation." *Administrative Science Quarterly,* 35, pp. 128–152.

This is where strategic alliances come in. Sometimes, firms form strategic alliances with the sole purpose of evaluating and then choosing a technology standard. With such a standard in place, technologies can be turned into products that customers are likely to be more willing to purchase, because they know that they will be compatible with industry standards for at least some period of time. Thus, in this setting, strategic alliances can be used to create a more favorable competitive environment.

Another incentive for cooperating in strategic alliances is that such activities may facilitate the development of tacit collusion. As explained in Chapter 3, **collusion** exists when two or more firms in an industry coordinate their strategic choices to reduce competition in an industry. This reduction in competition usually makes it easier for colluding firms to earn high levels of performance. A common example of collusion is when firms cooperate to reduce the quantity of products being produced in an industry in order to drive prices up. **Explicit collusion** exists when firms directly communicate with each other to coordinate their levels of production, their prices, and so forth. Explicit collusion is illegal in most countries.

Because managers that engage in explicit collusion can end up in jail, most collusion must be tacit in character. **Tacit collusion** exists when firms coordinate their production and pricing decisions, not by directly communicating with each other, but by exchanging signals with other firms about their intent to cooperate. Examples of such signals might include public announcements about price increases, public announcements about reductions in a firm's productive output, public announcements about decisions not to pursue a new technology, and so forth.

Sometimes, signals of intent to collude are very ambiguous. For example, when firms in an industry do not reduce their prices in response to a decrease in demand, they may be sending a signal that they want to collude, or they may be attempting to exploit their product differentiation to maintain high margins. When firms do not reduce their prices in response to reduced supply costs, they may be sending a signal that they want to collude, or they may be individually maximizing their economic performance. In both these cases, a firm's intent to collude or not, as implied by its activities, is ambiguous at best.

In this context, strategic alliances can facilitate tacit collusion. Separate firms, even if they are in the same industry, can form strategic alliances. Although communication between these firms cannot legally include sharing information about prices and costs for products or services that are produced outside the alliance, such interaction does help create the social setting within which tacit collusion may develop.[3] As suggested in the Research Made Relevant feature, most early research on strategic alliances focused on their implications for tacit collusion. More recently, research suggests that alliances do not usually facilitate tacit collusion.

Facilitating Entry and Exit

A final way that strategic alliances can be used to create value is by facilitating a firm's entry into a new market or industry or its exit from a market or industry. Strategic alliances are particularly valuable in this context when the value of market entry or exit is uncertain. Entry into an industry can require skills, abilities, and products that a potential entrant does not possess. Strategic alliances can help a firm enter a new industry by avoiding the high costs of creating these skills, abilities, and products.

For example, recently DuPont wanted to enter into the electronics industry. However, building the skills and abilities needed to develop competitive products in this industry can be very difficult and costly. Rather than absorb these costs, DuPont developed a strategic alliance (DuPont/Philips Optical) with an established electronics firm, Philips, to distribute some of Philips's products in the United States. In this way, DuPont was able to enter into a new industry (electronics) without having to absorb all the costs of creating electronics resources and abilities from the ground up.

Of course, for this joint venture to succeed, Philips must have had an incentive to cooperate with DuPont. Whereas DuPont was looking to reduce its cost of entry into a new industry, Philips was looking to reduce its cost of continued entry into a new market—the United States. Philips used its alliance with DuPont to sell in the United States the compact discs it already was selling in Europe.[4] The role of alliances in facilitating entry into new geographic markets will be discussed in more detail later in this chapter.

Alliances to facilitate entry into new industries can be valuable even when the skills needed in these industries are not as complex and difficult to learn as skills in the electronics industry. For example, rather than develop their own frozen novelty foods, Welch Foods, Inc., and Leaf, Inc. (maker of Heath candy bars) asked Eskimo Pie to formulate products for this industry. Eskimo Pie developed Welch's frozen grape juice bar and the Heath toffee ice cream bar. These firms then split the profits derived from these products.[5] As long as the cost of using an alliance to enter a new industry is less than the cost of learning new skills and capabilities, an alliance can be a valuable strategic opportunity.

Some firms use strategic alliances as a mechanism to withdraw from industries or industry segments in a low-cost way. Firms are motivated to withdraw from an industry or industry segment when their level of performance in that business is less than expected and when there are few prospects of it improving. When a firm desires to exit an industry or industry segment, often it will need to dispose of the assets it has developed to compete in that industry or industry segment. These assets often include tangible resources and capabilities, such as factories, distribution centers, and product technologies, and intangible resources and capabilities, such as brand name, relationships with suppliers and customers, a loyal and committed workforce, and so forth.

Firms will often have difficulty in obtaining the full economic value of these tangible and intangible assets as they exit an industry or industry segment. This reflects an important information asymmetry that exists between the firms that currently own these assets and firms that may want to purchase these assets. By forming an alliance with a firm that may want to purchase its assets, a firm is giving its partner an opportunity to directly observe how valuable those assets are. If those assets are actually valuable, then this "sneak preview" can lead the assets to be more appropriately priced and thereby facilitate the exit of the firm that is looking to sell its assets. These issues will be discussed in more detail in Chapter 10's discussion of mergers and acquisitions.

One firm that has used strategic alliances to facilitate its exit from an industry or industry segment is Corning. In the late 1980s, Corning entered the medical diagnostics industry. After several years, however, Corning concluded that its resources and capabilities could be more productively used in other businesses. For this reason, it began to extract itself from the medical diagnostics business. However, to ensure that it received the full value of the assets it had created in the medical diagnostics business upon exiting, it formed a strategic alliance with the Swiss specialty chemical company Ciba-Geigy. Ciba-Geigy paid $75 million to purchase half of Corning's medical diagnostics business. A couple of years later, Corning finished exiting from the medical diagnostics business by selling its remaining assets in this industry to Ciba-Geigy. However, whereas Ciba-Geigy

Research Made Relevant

Several authors have concluded that joint ventures, as a form of alliance, do increase the probability of tacit collusion in an industry. As reviewed in books by Scherer and Barney, one study found that joint ventures created two industrial groups, besides U.S. Steel, in the U.S. iron and steel industry in the early 1900s. In this sense, joint ventures in the steel industry were a substitute for U.S. Steel's vertical integration and had the effect of creating an oligopoly in what (without joint ventures) would have been a more competitive market. Other studies found that over 50 percent of joint venture parents belong to the same industry. After examining 885 joint venture bids for oil and gas leases, yet another study found only 16 instances where joint venture parents competed with one another on another tract in the same sale. These results suggest that joint ventures might encourage subsequent tacit collusion among firms in the same industry.

In a particularly influential study, Pfeffer and Nowak found that joint ventures were most likely in industries of moderate concentration. These authors argued that in highly concentrated

Do Strategic Alliances Facilitate Tacit Collusion?

industries—where there were only a small number of competing firms—joint ventures were not necessary to create conditions conducive to collusion. In highly fragmented industries, the high levels of industry concentration conducive to tacit collusion could not be created by joint ventures. Only when joint venture activity could effectively create concentrated industries—that is, only when industries were moderately concentrated—were joint ventures likely.

Scherer and Barney also review more recent work that disputes these findings. Joint ventures between firms in the same industry may be valuable for a variety of reasons that have little or nothing to do with collusion. Moreover, by using a lower level of aggregation, several authors have disputed the finding that joint ventures are most likely in moderately concentrated industries. The original study defined industries using very broad industry categories—"the electronics industry," "the automobile industry," and so forth. By defining industries less broadly—"consumer electronics" and "automobile part manufacturers"—subsequent work found that 73 percent of the joint ventures had parent firms coming from different industries. Although joint ventures between firms in the same industry (defined at this lower level of aggregation) may have collusive implications, subsequent work has shown that these kinds of joint ventures are relatively rare.

Sources: F. M. Scherer (1980). *Industrial market structure and economic performance.* Boston: Houghton Mifflin; J. B. Barney (2006). *Gaining and sustaining competitive advantage,* 3rd ed. Upper Saddle River, NJ: Prentice Hall; and J. Pfeffer and P. Nowak (1976). "Patterns of joint venture activity: Implications for anti-trust research." *Antitrust Bulletin,* 21, pp. 315–339.

---

had paid $75 million for the first half of Corning's assets, it paid $150 million for the second half. Corning's alliance with Ciba-Geigy had made it possible for Ciba-Geigy to fully value Corning's medical diagnostics capabilities. Any information asymmetry that might have existed was reduced, and Corning was able to get more of the full value of its assets upon exiting this industry.[6]

Finally, firms may use strategic alliances to manage **uncertainty**. Under conditions of high uncertainty, firms may not be able to tell at a particular point in time which of several different strategies they should pursue. Firms in this setting have an incentive to retain the flexibility to move quickly into a particular market or industry once the full value of that strategy is revealed. In this sense, strategic alliances enable a firm to maintain a point of entry into a market or industry, without incurring the costs associated with full-scale entry.

Based on this logic, strategic alliances have been analyzed as **real options**.[7] In this sense, a joint venture is an option that a firm buys, under conditions of uncertainty, to retain the ability to move quickly into a market or industry if valuable opportunities present themselves. One way in which firms can move quickly into a market is simply to buy out their partner(s) in the joint venture. Moreover, by investing in a joint venture a firm may gain access to the information it needs to evaluate full-scale entry into a market. In this approach to analyzing strategic alliances, firms that invest in alliances as options will acquire their alliance partners only after the market signals an unexpected increase in value of the venture; that is, only after uncertainty is reduced and the true, positive value of entering into a market is known. Empirical findings are consistent with these expectations.[8]

Given these observations, it is not surprising to see firms in new and uncertain environments develop numerous strategic alliances. This is one of the reasons that strategic alliances are so common in the biotechnology industry. Although there is relatively little uncertainty that at least some drugs created through biotechnology will ultimately prove to be very valuable, which specific drugs will turn out to be the most valuable is very uncertain. Rather than investing in a small number of biotechnology drugs on their own, pharmaceutical companies have invested in numerous strategic alliances with small biotechnology firms. Each of these smaller firms represents a particular "bet" about the value of biotechnology in a particular class of drugs. If one of these "bets" turns out to be valuable, then the large pharmaceutical firm that has invested in that firm has the right, but not the obligation, to purchase the rest of this company. In this sense, from the point of view of the pharmaceutical firms, alliances between large pharmaceutical firms and small biotechnology firms can be thought of as real options.

Alliance Threats: Incentives to Cheat on Strategic Alliances

Just as there are incentives to cooperate in strategic alliances, there are also incentives to cheat on these cooperative agreements. Indeed, research shows that as many as one-third of all strategic alliances do not meet the expectations of at least one alliance partner.[9] Although some of these alliance "failures" may be due to firms forming alliances that do not have the potential for creating value, some are also due to parties to an alliance cheating—that is, not cooperating in a way that maximizes the value of the alliance. Cheating can occur in at least the three different ways presented in Table 9.2: adverse selection, moral hazard, and holdup.[10]

Adverse Selection

Potential cooperative partners can misrepresent the skills, abilities, and other resources that they will bring to an alliance. This form of cheating, called **adverse selection**, exists when an alliance partner promises to bring to an alliance certain

TABLE 9.2 Ways to Cheat in Strategic Alliances

- *Adverse selection*: Potential partners misrepresent the value of the skills and abilities they bring to the alliance.
- *Moral hazard*: Partners provide to the alliance skills and abilities of lower quality than they promised.
- *Holdup*: Partners exploit the transaction-specific investments made by others in the alliance.

resources that it either does not control or cannot acquire. For example, a local firm engages in adverse selection when it promises to make available to alliance partners a local distribution network that does not currently exist. Firms that engage in adverse selection are not competent alliance partners.

Adverse selection in a strategic alliance is likely only when it is difficult or costly to observe the resources or capabilities that a partner brings to an alliance. If potential partners can easily see that a firm is misrepresenting the resources and capabilities it possesses, they will not create a strategic alliance with that firm. Armed with such understanding, they will seek a different alliance partner, develop the needed skills and resources internally, or perhaps forgo this particular business opportunity.

However, evaluating the veracity of the claims of potential alliance partners is often not easy. The ability to evaluate these claims depends on information that a firm may not possess. To fully evaluate claims about a potential partner's political contacts, for example, a firm needs its own political contacts; to fully evaluate claims about potential partners' market knowledge, a firm needs significant market knowledge. A firm that can completely, and at low cost, evaluate the resources and capabilities of potential alliance partners probably does not really need these partners in a strategic alliance. The fact that a firm is seeking an alliance partner is in some sense an indication that the firm has limited abilities to evaluate potential partners.

In general, the less tangible the resources and capabilities that are to be brought to a strategic alliance, the more costly it will be to estimate their value before an alliance is created, and the more likely it is that adverse selection will occur. Firms considering alliances with partners that bring intangible resources such as "knowledge of local conditions" or "contacts with key political figures" will need to guard against this form of cheating.

Moral Hazard

Partners in an alliance may possess high-quality resources and capabilities of significant value in an alliance but fail to make those resources and capabilities available to alliance partners. This form of cheating is called **moral hazard**. For example, a partner in an engineering strategic alliance may agree to send only its most talented and best-trained engineers to work in the alliance but then actually send less talented, poorly trained engineers. These less qualified engineers may not be able to contribute substantially to making the alliance successful, but they may be able to learn a great deal from the highly qualified engineers provided by other alliance partners. In this way, the less qualified engineers effectively transfer wealth from other alliance partners to their own firm.[11]

Often both parties in a failed alliance accuse each other of moral hazard. This was the case in the abandoned alliance between Disney and Pixar, described in the Strategy in the Emerging Enterprise feature.

The existence of moral hazard in a strategic alliance does not necessarily mean that any of the parties to that alliance are malicious or dishonest. Rather, what often happens is that market conditions change after an alliance is formed, requiring one or more partners to an alliance to change their strategies.

For example, in the early days of the personal computer industry Compaq Computer Corporation relied on a network of independent distributors to sell its computers. However, as competition in the personal computer industry increased, Internet, mail order, and so-called computer superstores became much more valuable distribution networks, and alliances between Compaq and its traditional distributors became strained. Over time, Compaq's traditional distributors were unable to obtain the inventory they wanted in a timely manner. Indeed, to satisfy the needs of large accounts, some traditional distributors actually purchased Compaq computers from local computer superstores and then shipped them to their customers. Compaq's shift from independent dealers to alternative distributors looked like moral hazard—at least from the point of view of the independent dealers. However, from Compaq's perspective, this change simply reflected economic realities in the personal computer industry.[12]

Holdup

Even if alliance partners do not engage in either adverse selection or moral hazard, another form of cheating may evolve. Once a strategic alliance has been created, partner firms may make investments that have value only in the context of that alliance and in no other economic exchanges. These are the transaction-specific investments mentioned in Chapter 6. For example, managers from one alliance partner may have to develop close, trusting relationships with managers from other alliance partners. These close relationships are very valuable in the context of the alliance, but they have limited economic value in other economic exchanges. Also, one partner may have to customize its manufacturing equipment, distribution network, and key organizational policies to cooperate with other partners. These modifications have significant value in the context of the alliance, but they do not help the firm, and may even hurt it, in economic exchanges outside the alliance. As was the case in Chapter 6, whenever an investment's value in its first-best use (in this case, within the alliance) is much greater than its value in its second-best use (in this case, outside the alliance), that investment is said to be **transaction specific**.[13]

When one firm makes more transaction-specific investments in a strategic alliance than partner firms make, that firm may be subject to the form of cheating called **holdup**. Holdup occurs when a firm that has not made significant transaction-specific investments demands returns from an alliance that are higher than the partners agreed to when they created the alliance.

For example, suppose two alliance partners agree to a 50–50 split of the costs and profits associated with an alliance. To make the alliance work, Firm A has to customize its production process. Firm B, however, does not have to modify itself to cooperate with Firm A. The value to Firm A of this customized production process, if it is used in the strategic alliance, is $5,000. However, outside the alliance, this customized process is only worth $200 (as scrap).

Obviously, Firm A has made a transaction-specific investment in this alliance and Firm B has not. Consequently, Firm A may be subject to holdup by Firm B. In particular, Firm B may threaten to leave the alliance unless Firm A agrees to give Firm B part of the $5,000 value that Firm A obtains by using the modified production process in the alliance. Rather than lose all the value that could be generated by its investment, Firm A may be willing to give up some of its $5,000 to avoid gaining only $200. Indeed, if Firm B extracts up to the value of Firm A's production process in its next-best use (here, only $200), Firm A will still be better off continuing in this relationship rather than dissolving it. Thus, even though Firm A and Firm B initially agreed on a 50–50 split from this strategic alliance, the agreement may be modified if one party to the alliance makes significant transaction-specific investments. Research on international joint ventures suggests that the existence of transaction-specific investments in these relationships often leads to holdup problems.[14]

Strategy in the Emerging Enterprise

In 1994, Pixar was a struggling start-up company in northern California that was trying to compete in an industry that really didn't yet exist—the computer graphics animated motion picture industry. Headed by the former founder of Apple Computer, Steven Jobs, Pixar was desperately looking for a partner that could help finance and distribute its new brand of animated movies. Who better, Pixar thought, than the world's leader in animated feature-length films: Disney. And thus, a strategic alliance between Pixar and Disney was formed.

In the alliance, Disney agreed to help finance and distribute Pixar's films. In return, they would share in any profits these films generated. Also, Disney would retain the right to produce any sequels to Pixar's films—after first offering Pixar the right to make these sequels. This agreement gave Disney a great deal of control over any characters that Pixar created in movies distributed through Pixar's alliance with Disney. Of course, at the time the alliance was originally formed there were no such characters. Indeed, Pixar had yet to produce any movies. So, because Pixar was a weak alliance partner, Disney was able to gain control of any characters Pixar developed in the future. Disney, after all, had the track record of success.

A funny thing happened over the next 10 years. Pixar produced blockbuster animated features such as *Toy Story* (total revenues of $419.9 million); *A Bug's Life* (total revenues of $358 million); *Toy Story 2* (total revenues of $629.9 million); *Monsters, Inc.* (total

Disney and Pixar

revenues of $903.1 million); *Finding Nemo* (total revenues of $1,281.4 million); *The Incredibles* (total revenues of $946.6 million); and *Cars* (total revenues of $331.9 million). And these revenue numbers do not include sales of merchandise associated with these films. During this same time period, Disney's traditional animated fare performed much more poorly—*Treasure Planet* generated only $112 million in revenues, *The Emperor's New Groove* only $169 million, and *Brother Bear* only $126 million. Disney's "big hit" during this time period was *Lilo & Stitch*, with revenues of $269 million—less than any of the movies produced by Pixar.

Oops! The firm with the "proven track record" of producing hit animated features—Disney—stumbled badly, and the upstart company with no track record—Pixar—had all the success. Because Disney did not have many of its own characters upon which to base sequels, it began to eye Pixar's characters.

Fast-forward to 2004. It's time to renew this alliance. But now Pixar has the upper hand, because it has the track record. Disney comes knocking and asks Pixar to redo the alliance. What does Pixar say, "Okay, but ... we want control of our characters, we want Disney to act just as a distributor"—in other words, "We want Disney out of our business!" Disney balks at these demands, and Pixar—well, Pixar just cancelled the alliance.

But Pixar still needed a distribution partner. Pixar simply does not produce enough films to justify the expense of building its own distribution system. After a several-month search, Pixar found what it considered to be its best distribution partner. The only problem was—it was Disney.

Reestablishing the alliance between Pixar and Disney seemed out of the question. After all, such an alliance would have all the same challenges as the previous alliance.

Instead, Disney decided to buy Pixar. On January 25, 2006, Disney announced that it was buying Pixar in a deal worth $7.4 billion. Steve Jobs became Disney's single largest investor and became a member of Disney's board of directors. John Lasseter—the creative force behind Pixar's success—became chief creative officer at Disney.

Sources: S. Levy and D. Jefferson (2004). "Hey Mickey, buzz off!" *BusinessWeek*, February 9, pp. 4; T. Lowry et al. (2004). "Megamedia mergers: How dangerous?" *BusinessWeek*, February 23, pp. 34 +; and http://money.cnn.com/2006/01/24/newscompanies/disney_pixar_deal.

Although holdup is a form of cheating in strategic alliances, the threat of holdup can also be a motivation for creating an alliance. Bauxite-smelting companies often join in joint ventures with mining companies in order to exploit economies of scale in mining. However, these firms have another option: They could choose to operate large and efficient mines by themselves and then sell the excess bauxite (over and above their needs for their own smelters) on the open market. Unfortunately, bauxite is not a homogeneous commodity. Moreover, different kinds of bauxite require different smelting technologies. In order for one firm to sell its excess bauxite on the market, other smelting firms would have to make enormous investments, the sole purpose of which would be to refine that particular firm's bauxite. These investments would be transaction specific and subject these other smelters to holdup problems.

In this context, a strategic alliance can be thought of as a way of reducing the threat of holdup by creating an explicit management framework for resolving holdup problems. In other words, although holdup problems might still exist in these strategic alliances, the alliance framework may still be a better way in which to manage these problems than attempting to manage them in arm's-length market relationships. Some of the ethical dimensions of adverse selection, moral hazard, and holdup are discussed in the Ethics and Strategy feature.

Strategic Alliances and Sustained Competitive Advantage

The ability of strategic alliances to be sources of sustained competitive advantage, like all the other strategies discussed in this book, can be analyzed with the VRIO framework developed in Chapter 3. An alliance is economically valuable when it exploits any of the opportunities listed in Table 9.1 but avoids the threats in Table 9.2. In addition, for a strategic alliance to be a source of sustained competitive advantage it must be rare and costly to imitate.

The Rarity of Strategic Alliances

The rarity of strategic alliances does not only depend on the number of competing firms that have already implemented an alliance. It also depends on whether the benefits that firms obtain from their alliances are common across firms competing in an industry.

Consider, for example, the U.S. automobile industry. Over the past several years, strategic alliances have become very common in this industry, especially with Japanese auto firms. General Motors developed an alliance with Toyota that has already been described; Ford developed an alliance with Mazda before it purchased this Japanese firm outright; and Chrysler developed an alliance with Mitsubishi. Given the frequency with which alliances have developed in this industry, it is tempting to conclude that strategic alliances are not rare and thus not a source of competitive advantage.

Closer examination, however, suggests that these alliances may have been created for different reasons. For example, until recently, GM and Toyota have cooperated only in building a single line of cars, the Chevrolet Nova. General Motors has been less interested in learning design skills from Toyota and has been more interested in learning about manufacturing high-quality small cars profitably. Ford and Mazda, in contrast, have worked closely together in designing new cars and have joint manufacturing operations. Indeed, Ford and Mazda have worked so closely together that Ford finally purchased Mazda. Mitsubishi has acted primarily as a supplier to Chrysler, and (until recently) there has been relatively little joint development or manufacturing. Thus, although all three U.S. firms have strategic alliances, the alliances serve different purposes, and therefore each may be rare.[15]

One of the reasons why the benefits that accrue from a particular strategic alliance may be rare is that relatively few firms may have the complementary resources and abilities needed to form an alliance. This is particularly likely when an alliance is formed to enter into a new market, especially a new foreign market. In many less-developed economies, only one local firm or very few local firms may exist with the local knowledge, contacts, and distribution network needed to facilitate entry into that market. Moreover, sometimes the government acts to limit the number of these local firms. Although several firms may seek entry into this market, only a very small number will be able to form a strategic alliance with the local entity and therefore the benefits that accrue to the allied firms will likely be rare.

The Imitability of Strategic Alliances

As discussed in Chapter 3, the resources and capabilities that enable firms to conceive and implement valuable strategies may be imitated in two ways: direct duplication and substitution. Both duplication and substitution are important considerations in analyzing the imitability of strategic alliances.

Direct Duplication of Strategic Alliances

Recent research suggests that successful strategic alliances are often based on socially complex relations among alliance partners.[16] In this sense, successful strategic alliances often go well beyond simple legal contracts and are characterized by socially complex phenomena such as a trusting relationship between alliance partners, friendship, and even (perhaps) a willingness to suspend narrow self-interest for the longer-term good of the relationship.

Some research has shown that the development of trusting relationships between alliance partners is both difficult and essential to the success of strategic alliances. In one study, the most common reason that alliances failed to meet the expectations of partner firms was the partners' inability to trust one another. Interpersonal communication, tolerance for cultural differences, patience, and willingness to sacrifice short-term profits for longer-term success were all important determinants of the level of trust among alliance partners.[17]

Of course, not all firms in an industry are likely to have the organizational and relationship-building skills required for successful alliance building. If these skills and abilities are rare among a set of competing firms and costly to develop, then firms that are able to exploit these abilities by creating alliances may gain competitive advantages. Examples of firms that have developed these specialized skills include Corning and Cisco, with several hundred strategic alliances each.[18]

Substitutes for Strategic Alliances

Even if the purpose and objectives of a strategic alliance are valuable and rare, and even if the relationships on which an alliance is created are socially complex and costly to imitate, that alliance will still not generate a sustained competitive advantage if low-cost substitutes are available. At least two possible substitutes for strategic alliances exist: "going it alone" and acquisitions.[19]

"Going It Alone."   Firms "go it alone" when they attempt to develop all the resources and capabilities they need to exploit market opportunities and neutralize market threats by themselves. Sometimes "going it alone" can create the same—or even more—value than using alliances to exploit opportunities and neutralize threats. In these settings, "going it alone" is a substitute for a strategic alliance. However, in

Ethics and Strategy

Firms in strategic alliances can cheat on their alliance partners by engaging in adverse selection, moral hazard, or holdup. These three activities all have at least one thing in common—they all involve one alliance partner lying to another. And these lies can often pay off big in the form of the lying firm appropriating more than its "fair share" of the value created in an alliance. Are alliances one place in the economy where the adage "cheaters never prosper" does not hold?

There is little doubt that, in the short run, firms that cheat on their alliance partners can gain some advantages. But research suggests that cheating does not pay in the long run, because firms that cheat on their alliance partners will find it difficult to form alliances with new partners and thus have many valuable exchange opportunities foreclosed to them.

One study that examined the long-term return to "cheaters" in strategic alliances analyzed alliances using a simple game called the "Prisoner's Dilemma." In a "Prisoner's Dilemma" game, firms have two options: to continue cooperating in a strategic alliance or to "cheat" on that alliance through adverse selection, moral hazard, or holdup. The payoffs to firms in this game depend on the decisions made by both firms. As shown in Table 9.3, if

When It Comes to Alliances, Do "Cheaters Never Prosper"?

both firms decide to cooperate, they each get a good size payoff from the alliance ($3,000 in Table 9.3); if they both decide to cheat on the alliance, they each get a very small payoff ($1,000 in Table 9.3); and if one decides to cheat while the other decides to cooperate, then the cheating firm gets a very big payoff ($5,000 in Table 9.3) while the cooperating firm gets a very small payoff ($0 in Table 9.3).

If Firm 1 and Firm 2 in this game are going to engage in only one strategic alliance, then they have a very strong incentive to "cheat." The worst that could happen if they cheat is that they earn a $1,000 payoff, but there is a possibility of a $5,000 payoff. However,

research has shown that if a firm is contemplating engaging in multiple strategic alliances over time, then the optimal strategy is to cooperate in all its alliances. This is true even if all these alliances are not with the same partner firm.

The specific "winning" strategy in repeated "Prisoner Dilemma" games is called a "tit-for-tat" strategy. "Tit-for-tat" means that Firm 1 will cooperate in an alliance as long as Firm 2 cooperates. However, as soon as Firm 2 cheats on an alliance, Firm 1 cheats as well. "Tit-for-tat" works well in this setting because adopting a cooperative posture in an alliance ensures that, most of the time, the alliance will generate a high payoff (of $3,000 in Table 9.3). However, by immediately responding to cheaters by cheating, the firm implementing a "tit-for-tat" strategy also minimizes the times when it will earn the lowest payoff in the table ($0). So, "tit-for-tat" maximizes the upside potential of an alliance while minimizing its downside.

All this analysis suggests that although cheating on an alliance can give a firm competitive advantages in the short to medium term, in the long run, "cheaters never prosper."

Sources: R. M. Axelrod (1984). *The evolution of cooperation.* New York: Basic Books; and D. Ernst and J. Bleeke (1993). *Collaborating to compete.* New York: Wiley.

TABLE 9.3 Returns from Cooperating and Cheating in a "Prisoner's Dilemma"

		Strategic Alliance	
Firm 1			
		Cooperates	Cheats
Firm 2	Cooperates	1: $3,000 2: $3,000	1: $5,000 2: $0
	Cheats	1: $0 2: $5,000	1: $1,000 2: $1,000

Alliances will be preferred over "going it alone" when: 1. The level of transaction-specific investment required to complete an exchange is moderate. 2. An exchange partner possesses valuable, rare, and costly-to-imitate resources and capabilities. 3. There is great uncertainty about the future value of an exchange.	**TABLE 9.4** When Alliances Will Be Preferred Over "Going It Alone"

other settings using an alliance can create substantially more value than "going it alone." In these settings, "going it alone" is not a substitute for a strategic alliance.

So, when will firms prefer an alliance over "going it alone"? Not surprisingly, the three explanations of vertical integration, discussed in Chapter 6, are relevant here as well. These three explanations focused on the threat of opportunism, the impact of firm resources and capabilities, and the role of uncertainty. If you need to review these three explanations, they are described in detail in Chapter 6. They are relevant here because "going it alone"—as a potential substitute for a strategic alliance—is an example of vertical integration. The implications of these three explanations for when strategic alliances will be preferred over "going it alone" are summarized in Table 9.4. If any of the conditions listed in Table 9.4 exist, then "going it alone" will not be a substitute for strategic alliances.

Recall from Chapter 6 that opportunism-based explanations of vertical integration suggest that firms will want to vertically integrate an economic exchange when they have made high levels of transaction-specific investment in that exchange. That is, using language developed in this chapter, firms will want to vertically integrate an economic exchange when using an alliance to manage that exchange could subject them to holdup. Extending this logic to strategic alliances suggests that strategic alliances will be preferred over "going it alone" and other alternatives when the level of transaction-specific investment required to complete an exchange is moderate. If the level of this specific investment is low, then market forms of exchange will be preferred; if the level of this specific investment is high, then "going it alone" in a vertically integrated way will be preferred; if the level of this specific investment is moderate, then some sort of strategic alliance will be preferred. Thus, when the level of specific exchange in a transaction is moderate, then "going it alone" is not a substitute for a strategic alliance.

Capabilities-based explanations suggest that an alliance will be preferred over "going it alone" when an exchange partner possesses valuable, rare, and costly-to-imitate resources and capabilities. A firm without these capabilities may find them to be too costly to develop on its own. If a firm must have access to capabilities it cannot develop on its own, it must use an alliance to gain access to those capabilities. In this setting, "going it alone" is not a substitute for a strategic alliance.[20]

Finally, it has already been suggested that, under conditions of high uncertainty, firms may be unwilling to commit to a particular course of action by engaging in an exchange within a firm. In such settings, firms may choose the strategic flexibility associated with alliances. As suggested earlier in this chapter, alliances can be thought of as real options that give a firm the right, but not the obligation, to invest further in an exchange—perhaps by bringing it within the boundaries of a firm—if that exchange turns out to be valuable sometime in the future. Thus, under conditions of high uncertainty, "going it alone" is not a substitute for strategic alliances.

Acquisitions.   The acquisition of other firms can also be a substitute for alliances. In this case, rather than developing a strategic alliance or attempting to develop and exploit the relevant resources by "going it alone," a firm seeking to exploit the

TABLE 9.5 Reasons Why Strategic Alliances May Be More Attractive Than Acquisitions to Realize Exchange Opportunities

Alliances will be preferred to acquisitions when:
1. There are legal constraints on acquisitions.
2. Acquisitions limit a firm's flexibility under conditions of high uncertainty.
3. There is substantial unwanted organizational "baggage" in an acquired firm.
4. The value of a firm's resources and capabilities depends on its independence.

opportunities listed in Table 9.1 may simply acquire another firm that already possesses the relevant resources and capabilities. However, such acquisitions have four characteristics that often limit the extent to which they can act as substitutes for strategic alliances. These are summarized in Table 9.5.[21]

First, there may be legal constraints on acquisitions. These are especially likely if firms are seeking advantages by combining with other firms in their own industry. Thus, for example, using acquisitions as a substitute for strategic alliances in the aluminum industry would lead to a very concentrated industry and subject some of these firms to serious antitrust liabilities. These firms have acquisitions foreclosed to them and must look elsewhere to gain advantages from cooperating with their competition.

Second, as has already been suggested, strategic alliances enable a firm to retain its flexibility either to enter or not to enter into a new business. Acquisitions limit that flexibility, because they represent a strong commitment to engage in a certain business activity. Consequently, under conditions of high uncertainty firms may choose strategic alliances over acquisitions as a way to exploit opportunities while maintaining the flexibility that alliances create.

Third, firms may choose strategic alliances over acquisitions because of the unwanted organizational baggage that often comes with an acquisition. Sometimes, the value created by combining firms depends on combining particular functions, divisions, or other assets in the firms. A strategic alliance can focus on exploiting the value of combining just those parts of firms that create the most value. Acquisitions, in contrast, generally include the entire organization, both the parts of a firm where value is likely to be created and parts of a firm where value is not likely to be created.

From the point of view of the acquiring firm, parts of a firm that do not create value are essentially unwanted baggage. These parts of the firm may be sold off subsequent to an acquisition. However, this sell-off may be costly and time consuming. If enough baggage exists, firms may determine that an acquisition is not a viable option, even though important economic value could be created between a firm and a potential acquisition target. To gain this value, an alternative approach—a strategic alliance—may be preferred. These issues will be explored in more detail in Chapter 10.

Finally, sometimes a firm's resources and capabilities are valuable because that firm is independent. In this setting, the act of acquiring a firm can actually reduce the value of a firm. When this is the case, any value between two firms is best realized through an alliance, not an acquisition. For example, the international growth of numerous marketing-oriented companies in the 1980s led to strong pressures for advertising agencies to develop global marketing capabilities. During the 1990s, many domestic-only advertising firms acquired nondomestic agencies to form a few large international advertising agencies. However, one firm that was reluctant to be acquired in order to be part of an international advertising network was the French advertising company Publicis. Over and above the personal interests of its owners to retain control of the company, Publicis wanted to remain an independent French agency in order to retain its stable of French and French-speaking clients—including Renault and Nestlé. These firms had indicated that they preferred working with a French advertising agency and that they would look for alternative suppliers if Publicis were acquired by a foreign firm. Because much of the value that Publicis created in a potential acquisition depended on obtaining access to its stable of clients, the act of acquiring Publicis would have had the effect of destroying the very thing that made the acquisition attractive. For this reason, rather than allowing itself to be acquired by foreign advertising agencies, Publicis developed a complex equity strategic alliance and joint venture with a U.S. advertising firm, Foote, Coyne, and Belding. Although, ultimately, this alliance was not successful in providing an international network for either of these two partner firms, an acquisition of Publicis by Foote, Coyne, and Belding would almost certainly have destroyed some of the economic value that Publicis enjoyed as a stand-alone company.

Organizing to Implement Strategic Alliances

V R I O

One of the most important determinants of the success of strategic alliances is their organization. The primary purpose of organizing a strategic alliance is to enable partners in the alliance to gain all the benefits associated with cooperation while minimizing the probability that cooperating firms will cheat on their cooperative agreements. The organizing skills required in managing alliances are, in many ways, unique. It often takes some time for firms to learn these skills and realize the full potential of their alliances. This is why some firms are able to gain competitive advantages from managing alliances more effectively than their competitors. Indeed, sometimes firms may have to choose alternatives to alliances—including "going it alone" and acquisitions—even when those alternatives are not preferred, simply because they do not have the skills required to organize and manage alliances.

A variety of tools and mechanisms can be used to help realize the value of alliances and minimize the threat of cheating. These include contracts, equity investments, firm reputations, joint ventures, and trust.

Explicit Contracts and Legal Sanctions

One way to avoid cheating in strategic alliances is for the parties to an alliance to anticipate the ways in which cheating may occur (including adverse selection, moral hazard, and holdup) and to write explicit contracts that define legal liability if cheating does occur. Writing these contracts, together with the close monitoring of contractual compliance and the threat of legal sanctions, can reduce the probability of cheating. Earlier in this chapter, such strategic alliances were called *nonequity alliances*.

However, contracts sometimes fail to anticipate all forms of cheating that might occur in a relationship—and firms may cheat on cooperative agreements in subtle ways that are difficult to evaluate in terms of contractual requirements. Thus, for example, a contract may require parties in a strategic alliance to make available to the alliance certain proprietary technologies or processes. However, it may be very difficult to communicate the subtleties of these technologies or processes to alliance partners. Does this failure in communication represent a clear violation of contractual requirements, or does it represent a good-faith effort by alliance partners? Moreover, how can one partner tell whether it is obtaining all the necessary information about a technology or process when it is unaware of all the information that exists in another firm? Hence, although contracts are an important component of most strategic alliances, they do not resolve all the problems associated with cheating.

TABLE 9.6 Common Clauses in Contracts Used to Govern Strategic Alliances

Establishment Issues

Shareholdings
> If an equity alliance or joint venture is to be formed, what percentage of equity is to be purchased by each firm involved in the alliance?

Voting rights
> The number of votes assigned to each partner in an alliance. May or may not be equal to shareholding percentages.

Dividend percentage
> How the profits from an alliance will be allocated among cooperating firms. May or may not be equal to shareholding percentages.

Minority protection
> Description of the kinds of decisions that can be vetoed by firms with a minority interest in an alliance.

Board of directors
> Initial board of directors, plus mechanisms for dismissing and appointing board members.

Articles of association
> Procedures for passing resolutions, share issuance, share disposal, etc.

Place of incorporation
> If a joint venture, geographic location of incorporation.

Advisors
> Lawyers, accountants, and other consultants to the alliance.

Identification of parties
> Legal entities directly involved in an alliance.

Operating Issues

Performance clauses
> Duties and obligations of alliance partners, including warranties and minimum performance levels expected.

Noncompete clauses
> Partners are restricted from entering the primary business of the alliance.

Nonsolicitation clauses
> Partners are restricted from recruiting employees from each other.

Confidentiality clauses
> Proprietary information from partners or from the alliance cannot be shared outside the alliance.

Although most contracts associated with strategic alliances are highly customized, these different contracts do have some common features. These common features are described in detail in Table 9.6. In general, firms contemplating a strategic alliance that will be at least partially governed by a contract will have to include clauses that address the issues presented in Table 9.6.

Equity Investments

The effectiveness of contracts can be enhanced by having partners in an alliance make equity investments in each other. When Firm A buys a substantial equity position in its alliance partner, Firm B, the market value of Firm A now depends,

Licensing intellectual property rights
Who owns the intellectual property created by an alliance and how this property is licensed to other firms.

Liability
Liability of the alliance and liability of cooperating partners.

Changes to the contract
Process by which the contract can be amended.

Dispute resolution
Process by which disputes among partners will be resolved.

Termination Issues
Preemption rights
If one partner wishes to sell its shares, it must first offer them to the other partner.

Variations on preemption rights
Partners are forbidden to ever discuss the sale of their shares to an outsider without first informing their partner of their intention to do so.

Call options
When one partner can force the other partner to sell its shares to it. Includes discussion on how these shares will be valued and the circumstances under which a call option can be exercised.

Put options
A partner has the right to force another partner to buy its alliance shares.

Drag-along rights
One partner can arrange a sale to an outside firm and force the other partner to sell shares as well.

Tag-along rights
A partner can prevent the sale of the second partner's shares to an outside firm unless that outside firm also buys the first partner's shares.

Initial public offering (IPO)
Circumstances under which an IPO will be pursued.

Termination
Conditions under which the contract can be terminated and consequences of termination for partners.

Source: Based on E. Campbell and J. Reuer (2001). "Note on the legal negotiation of strategic alliance agreements." Copyright © 2000 INSEAD.

to some extent, on the economic performance of that partner. The incentive of Firm A to cheat Firm B falls, for to do so would be to reduce the economic performance of Firm B and thus the value of Firm A's investment in its partner. These kinds of strategic alliances are called *equity alliances*.

Many firms use cross-equity investments to help manage their strategic alliances. These arrangements are particularly common in Japan, where a firm's largest equity holders often include several of its key suppliers, including its main banks. These equity investments, because they reduce the threat of cheating in alliances with suppliers, can reduce these firms' supply costs. In turn, not only do firms have equity positions in their suppliers, but suppliers often have substantial equity positions in the firms to which they sell.[22]

Firm Reputations

A third constraint on incentives to cheat in strategic alliances exists in the effect that a reputation for cheating has on a firm's future opportunities. Although it is often difficult to anticipate all the different ways in which an alliance partner may cheat, it is often easier to describe after the fact how an alliance partner has cheated. Information about an alliance partner that has cheated is likely to become widely known. A firm with a reputation as a cheater is not likely to be able to develop strategic alliances with other partners in the future, despite any special resources or capabilities that it might be able to bring to an alliance. In this way, cheating in a current alliance may foreclose opportunities for developing other valuable alliances. For this reason, firms may decide not to cheat in their current alliances.[23]

Substantial evidence suggests that the effect of reputation on future business opportunities is important. Firms go to great lengths to make sure that they do not develop a negative reputation. Nevertheless, this reputational control of cheating in strategic alliances does have several limitations.[24]

First, subtle cheating in a strategic alliance may not become public, and if it does become public, the responsibility for the failure of the strategic alliance may be very ambiguous. In one equity joint venture attempting to perfect the design of a new turbine for power generation, financial troubles made one partner considerably more anxious than the other partner to complete product development. The financially healthy, and thus patient, partner believed that if the alliance required an additional infusion of capital, the financially troubled partner would have to abandon the alliance and would have to sell its part of the alliance at a relatively low price. The patient partner thus encouraged alliance engineers to work slowly and carefully in the guise of developing the technology to reach its full potential. The financially troubled, and thus impatient, partner encouraged alliance engineers to work quickly, perhaps sacrificing some quality to develop the technology sooner. Eventually, the impatient partner ran out of money, sold its share of the alliance to the patient partner at a reduced price, and accused the patient partner of not acting in good faith to facilitate the rapid development of the new technology. The patient partner accused the other firm of pushing the technology too quickly, thereby sacrificing quality and, perhaps, worker safety. In some sense, both firms were cheating on their agreement to develop the new technology cooperatively. However, this cheating was subtle and difficult to spot and had relatively little impact on the reputation of either firm or on the ability of either firm to establish alliances in the future. It is likely that most observers would simply conclude that the patient partner obtained a windfall because of the impatient partner's bad luck.[25]

Second, although one partner to an alliance may be unambiguously cheating on the relationship, one or both of the firms may not be sufficiently connected into a network with other firms to make this information public. When information about cheating remains private, public reputations are not tarnished and future opportunities are not forgone. This is especially likely to happen if one or both alliance partners operate in less developed economies where information about partner behavior may not be rapidly diffused to other firms or to other countries.

Finally, the effect of a tarnished reputation, as long as cheating in an alliance is unambiguous and publicly known, may foreclose future opportunities for a firm, but it does little to address the current losses experienced by the firm that was cheated. Moreover, any of the forms of cheating discussed earlier—adverse selection, moral hazard, or holdup—can result in substantial losses for a firm currently in an alliance. Indeed, the wealth created by cheating in a current alliance may be large enough to make a firm willing to forgo future alliances. In this case, a tarnished reputation may be of minor consequence to a cheating firm.[26]

Joint Ventures

A fourth way to reduce the threat of cheating is for partners in a strategic alliance to invest in a joint venture. Creating a separate legal entity, in which alliance partners invest and from whose profits they earn returns on their investments, reduces some of the risks of cheating in strategic alliances. When a joint venture is created, the ability of partners to earn returns on their investments depends on the economic success of the joint venture. Partners in joint ventures have limited interests in behaving in ways that hurt the performance of the joint venture, because such behaviors end up hurting both partners. Moreover, unlike reputational consequences of cheating, cheating in a joint venture does not just foreclose future alliance opportunities; it can hurt the cheating firm in the current period as well.

Given the advantages of joint ventures in controlling cheating, it is not surprising that when the probability of cheating in a cooperative relationship is greatest, a joint venture is usually the preferred form of cooperation. For example, bauxite mining has some clear economies of scale. However, transaction-specific investments would lead to significant holdup problems in selling excess bauxite in the open market, and legal constraints prevent the acquisition of other smelter companies to create an intraorganizational demand for excess bauxite. Holdup problems would continue to exist in any mining strategic alliances that might be created. Nonequity alliances, equity alliances, and reputational effects are not likely to restrain cheating in this situation, because the returns on holdup, once transaction-specific investments are in place, can be very large. Thus, most of the strategic alliances created to mine bauxite take the form of joint ventures. Only this form of strategic alliance is likely to create incentives strong enough to significantly reduce the probability of cheating.[27]

Despite these strengths, joint ventures are not able to reduce all cheating in an alliance without cost. Sometimes the value of cheating in a joint venture is sufficiently large that a firm cheats even though doing so hurts the joint venture and forecloses future opportunities. For example, a particular firm may gain access to a technology through a joint venture that would be valuable if used in another of its lines of business. This firm may be tempted to transfer this technology to this other line of business even if it has agreed not to do so and even if doing so would limit the performance of its joint venture. Because the profits earned in this other line of business may have a greater value than the returns that could have been earned in the joint venture and the returns that could have been earned in the future with other strategic alliances, cheating may occur.

Trust

It is sometimes the case that alliance partners rely only on legalistic and narrowly economic approaches to manage their alliance. However, recent work seems to suggest that although successful alliance partners do not ignore legal and economic disincentives to cheating, they strongly support these narrower linkages with a rich set of interpersonal relations and trust. Trust, in combination with contracts, can help reduce the threat of cheating. More important, trust may enable partners to explore exchange opportunities that they could not explore if only legal and economic organizing mechanisms were in place.[28]

At first glance, this argument may seem far-fetched. However, some research offers support for this approach to managing strategic alliances, suggesting that successful alliance partners typically do not specify all the terms and conditions in their relationship in a legal contract and do not specify all possible forms of cheating and their consequences. Moreover, when joint ventures are formed, partners do not always insist on simple 50–50 splits of equity ownership and profit sharing. Rather, successful alliances involve trust, a willingness to be flexible, a willingness to learn, and a willingness to let the alliance develop in ways that the partners could not have anticipated.[29]

Commitment, coordination, and trust are all important determinants of alliance success. Put another way, a strategic alliance is a relationship that evolves over time. Allowing the lawyers and economists to too-rigorously define, a priori, the boundaries of that relationship may limit it and stunt its development.[30]

This "trust" approach also has implications for the extent to which strategic alliances may be sources of sustained competitive advantage for firms. The ability to move into strategic alliances in this trusting way may be very valuable over the long run. There is strong reason to believe that this ability is not uniformly distributed across all firms that might have an interest in forming strategic alliances and that this ability may be history-dependent and socially complex and thus costly to imitate. Firms with these skills may be able to gain sustained competitive advantages from their alliance relationships. The observation that just a few firms, including Corning and Cisco, are well known for their strategic alliance successes is consistent with the observation that these alliance management skills may be valuable, rare, and costly to imitate.

Summary

Strategic alliances exist whenever two or more organizations cooperate in the development, manufacture, or sale of products or services. Strategic alliances can be grouped into three large categories: nonequity alliances, equity alliances, and joint ventures.

Firms join in strategic alliances for three broad reasons: to improve the performance of their current operations, to improve the competitive environment within which they are operating, and to facilitate entry into or exit from markets and industries. Just as there are incentives to cooperate in strategic alliances, there are also incentives to cheat. Cheating generally takes one or a combination of three forms: adverse selection, moral hazard, or holdup.

Strategic alliances can be a source of sustained competitive advantage. The rarity of alliances depends not only on the number of competing firms that have developed an alliance, but also on the benefits that firms gain through their alliances.

Imitation through direct duplication of an alliance may be costly because of the socially complex relations that underlie an alliance; however, imitation through substitution is more likely. Two substitutes for alliances may be "going it alone," where firms develop and exploit the relevant sets of resources and capabilities on their own, and acquisitions. Opportunism, capabilities, and uncertainty all have an impact on when "going it alone" will be a substitute for a strategic alliance. Acquisitions may be a substitute for strategic alliances when there are no legal constraints, strategic flexibility is not an important consideration, when the acquired firm has relatively little unwanted "organizational baggage," and when the value of a firm's resources and capabilities does not depend on its remaining independent. However, when these conditions do not exist, acquisitions are not a substitute for alliances.

The key issue facing firms in organizing their alliances is to facilitate cooperation while avoiding the threat of cheating. Contracts, equity investments, firm reputations, joint ventures, and trust can all reduce the threat of cheating in different contexts.

Challenge Questions

1. One reason why firms might want to pursue a strategic alliance strategy is to exploit economies of scale. Exploiting economies of scale should reduce a firm's costs. Does this mean that a firm pursuing an alliance strategy to exploit economies of scale is actually pursuing a cost leadership strategy? Why or why not?

2. Consider the joint venture between GM and Toyota. General Motors has been interested in learning how to profitably manufacture high-quality small cars from its alliance with Toyota. Toyota has been interested in gaining access to GM's U.S. distribution network and in reducing the political liability associated with local content laws. Which of these firms do you think is more likely to accomplish its objectives, and why? What implications, if any, does your answer have for a possible "learning race" in this alliance?

3. Some researchers have argued that strategic alliances are one way in which firms can help facilitate the development of a tacit collusion strategy. In your view, what are the critical differences between tacit collusion strategies and strategic alliance strategies? How can one tell whether two firms are engaging in an alliance to facilitate collusion or are engaging in an alliance for other purposes?

4. Some researchers have argued that alliances can be used to help firms evaluate the economic potential of entering into a new industry or market. Under what conditions will a firm seeking to evaluate these opportunities need to invest in an alliance to accomplish this evaluation? Why couldn't such a firm simply hire some smart managers, consultants, and industry experts to evaluate the economic potential of entering into a new industry? What, if anything, about an alliance makes this a better way to evaluate entry opportunities than alternative methods?

5. If adverse selection, moral hazard, and holdup are such significant problems for firms pursuing alliance strategies, why do firms even bother with alliances? Why don't they instead adopt a "go it alone" strategy to replace strategic alliances?

Problem Set

1. Which of the following firms faces the greater threat of "cheating" in the alliances described, and why?

(a) Firm I and Firm II form a strategic alliance. As part of the alliance, Firm I agrees to build a new plant right next to Firm II's primary facility. In return, Firm II promises to buy most of the output of this new plant. Who is at risk, Firm I or Firm II?

(b) Firm A and Firm B form a strategic alliance. As part of the alliance, Firm A promises to begin selling products it already sells around the world in the home country of Firm B. In return, Firm B promises to provide Firm A with crucial contacts in its home country's government. These contacts are essential if Firm A is going to be able to sell in Firm B's home country. Who is at risk, Firm A or Firm B?

(c) Firm 1 and Firm 2 form a strategic alliance. As part of the alliance, Firm 1 promises to provide Firm 2 access to some new and untested technology that Firm 2 will use in its products. In return, Firm 2 will share some of the profits from its sales with Firm 1. Who is at risk, Firm 1 or Firm 2?

2. For each of the strategic alliances described in the above question, what actions could be taken to reduce the likelihood that partner firms will "cheat" in these alliances?

3. Examine the Web sites of the following strategic alliances and determine which of the sources of value presented in Table 9.1 are present:

(a) Dow-Corning (an alliance between Dow Chemical and Corning)
(b) CFM (an alliance between General Electric and SNECMA)
(c) Cingular (an alliance between SBC and BellSouth)

    (d) NCAA (an alliance among colleges and universities in the United States)

    (e) Visa (an alliance among banks in the United States)

    (f) The alliance among United, Delta, Singapore Airlines, AeroMexico, Alitalia, and Korean Air

End Notes

1. See www.pwc.com/extweb/exccps.nsf/docid; www.addme.com/issue208; McCracken, J. (2006). "Ford doubles reported loss for second quarter." *The Wall Street Journal*, August 3, pp. A3; and www.msnbc.msn.com/id/13753688.

2. Badaracco, J. L., and N. Hasegawa. (1988). "General Motors' Asian alliances." Harvard Business School Case No. 9-388-094.

3. See Burgers, W. P., C. W. L. Hill, and W. C. Kim. (1993). "A theory of global strategic alliances: The case of the global auto industry." *Strategic Management Journal*, 14, pp. 419–432.

4. See Freeman, A., and R. Hudson. (1980). "DuPont and Philips plan joint venture to make, market laser disc products." *The Wall Street Journal*, December 22, p. 10.

5. Teitelbaum, R. S. (1992). "Eskimo pie." *Fortune*, June 15, p. 123.

6. Nanda, A., and C. A. Bartlett. (1990). "Corning Incorporated: A network of alliances." Harvard Business School Case No. 9-391-102.

7. See Knight, F. H. (1965). *Risk, uncertainty, and profit.* New York: John Wiley & Sons, Inc., on uncertainty; Kogut, B. (1991). "Joint ventures and the option to expand and acquire." *Management Science*, 37, pp. 19–33; Burgers, W. P., C. W. L. Hill, and W. C. Kim. (1993). "A theory of global strategic alliances: The case of the global auto industry." *Strategic Management Journal*, 14, pp. 419–432; Noldeke, G., and K. M. Schmidt. (1998). "Sequential investments and options to own." *Rand Journal of Economics*, 29(4), pp. 633–653; and Folta, T. B. (1998). "Governance and uncertainty: The tradeoff between administrative control and commitment." *Strategic Management Journal*, 19, pp. 1007–1028.

8. See Kogut, B. (1991). "Joint ventures and the option to expand and acquire." *Management Science*, 37, pp. 19–33; and Balakrishnan, S., and M. Koza. (1993). "Information asymmetry, adverse selection and joint-ventures." *Journal of Economic Behavior & Organization*, 20, pp. 99–117.

9. See, for example, Ernst, D., and J. Bleeke. (1993). *Collaborating to compete: Using strategic alliances and acquisition in the global marketplace.* New York: John Wiley & Sons, Inc.

10. These terms are defined in Barney, J. B., and W. G. Ouchi. (1986). *Organizational economics.* San Francisco: Jossey-Bass; and Holmstrom, B. (1979). "Moral hazard and observability." *Bell Journal of Economics*, 10(1), pp. 74–91. Problems of cheating in economic exchanges, in general, and in alliances in particular, are discussed by Gulati, R., and H. Singh. (1998). "The architecture of cooperation: Managing coordination costs and appropriation concerns in strategic alliances." *Administrative Science Quarterly*, 43, pp. 781–814; Williamson, O. E. (1991). "Comparative economic organization: The analysis of discrete structural alternatives." *Administrative Science Quarterly*, 36, pp. 269–296; Osborn, R. N., and C. C. Baughn. (1990). "Forms of interorganizational governance for multinational alliances." *Academy of Management Journal*, 33(3), pp. 503–519; Hagedoorn, J., and R. Narula. (1996). "Choosing organizational modes of strategic technology partnering: International and sectoral differences." *Journal of International Business Studies*, second quarter, pp. 265–284; Hagedorn, J. (1996). "Trends and patterns in strategic technology partnering since the early seventies." *Review of Industrial Organization*, 11, pp. 601–616; Kent, D. H. (1991). "Joint ventures vs. non-joint ventures: An empirical investigation." *Strategic Management Journal*, 12, pp. 387–393; and Shane, S. A. (1998). "Making new franchise systems work." *Strategic Management Journal*, 19, pp. 697–707.

11. Such alliance difficulties are described in Ouchi, W. G. (1984). *The M-form society: How American teamwork can capture the competitive edge.* Reading, MA: Addison-Wesley; and Bresser, R. K. (1988). "Cooperative strategy." *Strategic Management Journal*, 9, pp. 475–492.

12. Pope, K. (1993). "Dealers accuse Compaq of jilting them." *The Wall Street Journal*, February 26, pp. 8, B1+.

13. Williamson, O. E. (1975). *Markets and hierarchies: Analysis and antitrust implications.* New York: Free Press; Klein, B., R. Crawford, and A. Alchian. (1978). "Vertical integration, appropriable rents, and the competitive contracting process." *Journal of Law and Economics*, 21, pp. 297–326.

14. See, for example, Yan, A., and B. Gray. (1994). "Bargaining power, management control, and performance in United States–China joint ventures: A comparative case study." *Academy of Management Journal*, 37, pp. 1478–1517.

15. See Badaracco, J. L., and N. Hasegawa. (1988). "General Motors' Asian alliances." Harvard Business School Case No. 9-388-094, on GM and Toyota; Patterson, G. A. (1991). "Mazda hopes to crack Japan's top tier." *The Wall Street Journal*, September 20, pp. B1 +; and Williams, M., and M. Kanabayashi. (1993). "Mazda and Ford drop proposal to build cars together in Europe." *The Wall Street Journal*, March 4, p. A14, on Ford and Mazda; and Ennis, P. (1991). "Mitsubishi group wary of deeper ties to Chrysler." *Tokyo Business Today*, 59, July, p. 10, on DaimlerChrysler and Mitsubishi.

16. See, for example, Ernst, D., and J. Bleeke. (1993). *Collaborating to compete: Using strategic alliances and acquisition in the global marketplace.* New York: John Wiley & Sons, Inc.; and Barney, J. B., and M. H. Hansen. (1994). "Trustworthiness as a source of competitive advantage." *Strategic Management Journal*, 15, winter (special issue), pp. 175–190.

17. Ernst, D., and J. Bleeke. (1993). *Collaborating to compete: Using strategic alliances and acquisition in the global marketplace.* New York: John Wiley & Sons, Inc.

18. Bartlett, C., and S. Ghoshal. (1993). "Beyond the M-form: Toward a managerial theory of the firm." *Strategic Management Journal*, 14, pp. 23–46.

19. See Nagarajan, A., and W. Mitchell. (1998). "Evolutionary diffusion: Internal and external methods used to acquire encompassing, complementary, and incremental technological changes in the lithotripsy industry." *Strategic Management Journal*, 19, pp. 1063–1077; Hagedoorn, J., and B. Sadowski. (1999). "The transition from strategic technology alliances to mergers and acquisitions: An exploratory study." *Journal of Management Studies*, 36(1), pp. 87–107; and Newbury, W., and Y. Zeira. (1997). "Generic differences between equity international joint ventures (EIJVs), international acquisitions (IAs) and International Greenfield investments (IGIs): Implications for parent companies." *Journal of World Business*, 32(2), pp. 87–102, on alliance substitutes.

20. Barney, J. B. (1999). "How a firm's capabilities affect boundary decisions." *Sloan Management Review*, 40(3), pp. 137–145.

21. See Hennart, J. F. (1988). "A transaction cost theory of equity joint ventures." *Strategic Management Journal*, 9, pp. 361–374; Kogut, B. (1988). "Joint ventures: Theoretical and empirical perspectives." *Strategic Management Journal*, 9, pp. 319–332; and Barney, J. B. (1999). "How a firm's capabilities affect boundary decisions." *Sloan Management Review*, 40(3), pp. 137–145, for a discussion of these limitations.

22. See Ouchi, W. G. (1984). *The M-form society: How American teamwork can capture the competitive edge.* Reading, MA: Addison-Wesley; and Barney, J. B. (1990). "Profit sharing bonuses and the cost of debt: Business finance and compensation policy in Japanese electronics firms." *Asia Pacific Journal of Management*, 7, pp. 49–64.

23. This is an argument developed by Barney, J. B., and M. H. Hansen. (1994). "Trustworthiness as a source of competitive advantage." *Strategic Management Journal*, 15, winter (special issue), pp. 175–190; Weigelt, K., and C. Camerer. (1988). "Reputation and corporate strategy: A review of recent theory and applications." *Strategic Management Journal*, 9, pp. 443–454; and Granovetter, M. (1985). "Economic action and social structure: The problem of embeddedness." *American Journal of Sociology*, 3, pp. 481–510.

24. See, for example, Eichenseher, J., and D. Shields. (1985). "Reputation and corporate strategy: A review of recent theory and applications." *Strategic Management Journal*, 9, pp. 443–454; Beatty, R., and R. Ritter. (1986). "Investment banking, reputation, and the underpricing of

initial public offerings." *Journal of Financial Economics*, 15, pp. 213–232; Kalleberg, A. L., and T. Reve. (1992). "Contracts and commitment: Economic and Sociological Perspectives on Employment Relations." *Human Relations*, 45(9), pp. 1103–1132; Larson, A. (1992). "Network dyads in entrepreneurial settings: A study of the governance of exchange relationships." *Administrative Science Quarterly*, March, pp. 76–104; Stuart, T. E., H. Hoang, and R. C. Hybels. (1999). "Interorganizational endorsements and the performance of entrepreneurial ventures." *Administrative Science Quarterly*, 44, pp. 315–349; Stuart, T. E. (1998). "Network positions and propensities to collaborate: An investigation of strategic alliance formation in a high-technology industry." *Administrative Science Quarterly*, 43(3), pp. 668–698; and Gulati, R. (1998). "Alliances and networks." *Strategic Management Journal*, 19, pp. 293–317.

25. Personal communication, April 8, 1986.

26. This same theoretic approach to firm reputation is discussed in Tirole, J. (1988). *The theory of industrial organization.* Cambridge, MA: MIT Press.

27. Scherer, F. M. (1980). *Industrial market structure and economic performance.* Boston: Houghton Mifflin.

28. See again, Ernst, D., and J. Bleeke. (1993). *Collaborating to compete: Using strategic alliances and acquisition in the global marketplace.* New York: John Wiley & Sons, Inc.; and Barney, J. B., and M. H. Hansen. (1994). "Trustworthiness as a source of competitive advantage." *Strategic Management Journal*, 15, winter (special issue), pp. 175–190. In fact, there is a great deal of literature on the role of trust in strategic alliances. Some of the most interesting of this work can be found in Holm, D. B., K. Eriksson, and J. Johanson. (1999). "Creating value through mutual commitment to business network relationships." *Strategic Management Journal*, 20, pp. 467–486; Lorenzoni, G., and A. Lipparini. (1999). "The leveraging of interfirm relationships as a distinctive organizational capability: A longitudinal study." *Strategic Management Journal*, 20(4), pp. 317–338; Blois, K. J. (1999). "Trust in business to business relationships: An evaluation of its status." *Journal of Management Studies*, 36(2), pp. 197–215; Chiles, T. H., and J. F. McMackin. (1996). "Integrating variable risk preferences, trust, and transaction cost economics." *Academy of Management Review*, 21(1), pp. 73–99; Larzelere, R. E., and T. L. Huston. (1980). "The dyadic trust scale: Toward understanding interpersonal trust in close relationships." *Journal of Marriage and the Family*, August, pp. 595–604; Butler, J. K., Jr. (1983). "Reciprocity of trust between professionals and their secretaries." *Psychological Reports*, 53, pp. 411–416; Zaheer, A., and N. Venkatraman. (1995). "Relational governance as an interorganizational strategy: An empirical test of the role of trust in economic exchange." *Strategic Management Journal*, 16, pp. 373–392; Butler, J. K., Jr., and R. S. Cantrell. (1984). "A behavioral decision theory approach to modeling dyadic trust in superiors and subordinates." *Psychological Reports*, 55, pp. 19–28; Carney, M. (1998). "The competitiveness of networked production: The role of trust and asset specificity." *Journal of Management Studies*, 35(4), pp. 457–479.

29. Ernst, D., and J. Bleeke. (1993). *Collaborating to compete: Using strategic alliances and acquisition in the global marketplace.* New York: John Wiley & Sons, Inc.

30. See Mohr, J., and R. Spekman. (1994). "Characteristics of partnership success: Partnership attributes, communication behavior, and conflict resolution techniques." *Strategic Management Journal*, 15, pp. 135–152; and Zaheer, A., and N. Venkatraman. (1995). "Relational governance as an interorganizational strategy: An empirical test of the role of trust in economic exchange." *Strategic Management Journal*, 16, pp. 373–392.

10 Mergers and Acquisitions

After reading this chapter, you should be able to:

1. Describe different types of mergers and acquisitions.

2. Estimate the return to the stockholders of bidding and target firms when there is no strategic relatedness between firms.

3. Describe different sources of relatedness between bidding and target firms.

4. Estimate the return to stockholders of bidding and target firms when there is strategic relatedness between firms.

5. Describe five reasons why bidding firms might still engage in acquisitions, even if, on average, they do not create value for a bidding firm's stockholders.

6. Describe three ways that bidding firms might be able to generate high returns for their equity holders through implementing mergers or acquisitions.

7. Describe the major challenges that firms integrating acquisitions are likely to face.

A Merger Mystery

It has all the intrigue and backstabbing of an episode of *Survivor*; all the tension and uncertainty of the final night of *American Idol*; all the lying and greed of a season of the *Bachelor*. And it wasn't even created for television.

It's Microsoft's attempted acquisition of Yahoo.

In some ways, Yahoo had to see this coming. Microsoft has struggled for years to establish itself on the Web. It built MSN; it acquired Hotmail; it gave many of its services away for free and cut rates to its advertisers. And still, despite all this effort, Microsoft commanded only five percent of the revenue coming from the U.S. online search market in 2007 (the ads listed on the results of Web searches). It has a stronger position in the display ad market (ads displayed on Web sites), but still captures only a small share of this market. Indeed, from 2005 to 2008, Microsoft lost $1.5 billion in its online businesses.

And a presence on the Web was very important to Microsoft. Its core businesses—its operating systems and applications software—were being threatened by free online software that accomplished the same tasks as Microsoft's products. If, in the long run, Microsoft would not be able to charge for its programs directly, it needed to be able to generate revenue from them indirectly, through advertising associated with selling its software. But Microsoft had limited experience with this business model and needed to learn about it in an area on the Web already dominated by revenue generated from ads—online searches.

The current winner in this market space is Google, with 77 percent market share. Indeed, Google has become so pervasive in the search market that its brand—a proper noun—was rapidly morphing into a verb—"to google," meaning to search for some piece of information in a complex setting, as in "I googled him to see if he had a criminal record."

And the dollars at stake here are not trivial. The ad revenue from the search market is expected to grow to $17.6 billion by 2012. Five percent of $17 billion is still a big chunk of change, but it is trivial compared to Google's 77 percent. The display market is expected to grow to $15.1 billion by that same year.

Enter Yahoo, the second largest presence in the search market. Yahoo has more online visitors than Microsoft, generates over twice as much revenue from online ads as Microsoft, and continues to build a stable of user-friendly and effective online applications—just ask eBay about Yahoo's online auction site. If Microsoft couldn't build its own profitable presence on the Web, well, it would buy that presence.

On February 1, 2008, Microsoft announced a $44 billion bid to buy Yahoo. Yahoo's CEO, Jerry Yang, immediately

responded by suggesting that Microsoft's bid undervalued Yahoo—despite the fact that at $31 per share, Microsoft's bid represented a 62 percent price premium for Yahoo's stock. Later, Microsoft raised the bid to $47.5 billion, or $33 per share. And still, Yang resisted.

In fact, Yang and the Yahoo board adopted a "poison pill"—a policy designed to increase the cost of acquiring Yahoo so much that Microsoft would withdraw its offer. The poison pill Yahoo adopted paid very high severance packages to any Yahoo employee laid off as a result of an acquisition. Estimates about the cost of this severance package ranged from $757 million to $2.4 billion, depending on the details of any acquisition that would have been completed.

Enter Carl Icahn—the well-known corporate raider and arbitrage specialist. As soon as Microsoft announced its offer and Yahoo its resistance, Icahn began buying Yahoo stock. Once he established his position as a major Yahoo shareholder, he began pressuring Yahoo to accept Microsoft's offer. In an open letter to other Yahoo shareholders and Yahoo's management team, Icahn called for Yang to resign, for the board to resign, and for negotiations with Microsoft to begin again. Icahn also filed suit against Yahoo's management, alleging that they were no longer behaving in ways consistent with the interests of Yahoo's stockholders.

And still, Jerry Yang resisted. Ultimately, Microsoft withdrew its offer and Yahoo's shareholders saw their

James M Phelps, Jr /Shutterstock

stock fall from the mid-twenties to the mid-teens. Most observers argue that both Microsoft and Yahoo are worse off for not having consummated this deal—Microsoft's weaknesses in online advertising are still unresolved and now widely understood; Yahoo's management is now widely mistrusted and the weaknesses of their ongoing business model are also now widely understood.

But, just like soap operas on television, this story just continues. On November 17, 2008, Jerry Yang announced that he would step down as CEO of Yahoo.

Sources: Jay Greene (2008). "Inside Microsoft's war against Google." *Business-Week*, May 19, 2008, pp. 36–40; "Icahn writes Yahoo again," *BusinessWeek* Online, June 9, 2008; Robert Hof (2008). "Why Yahoo's Yang keeps holding out." *BusinessWeek*, June 16, 2008, pp. 30; Robert Hof (2008). "Yahoo, Microsoft left searching." *BusinessWeek* Online, May 5, 2008; http://mashable.com/2008/11/17/jerry-yang-out-as-yahoo-ceo/; and Getty Images, Inc.– Agence France Presse.

Mergers and acquisitions are one very common way that a firm can accomplish its vertical integration and diversification objectives. However, although a firm may be able to accomplish its vertical integration and diversification objectives through mergers or acquisitions, it is sometimes difficult to generate real economic profit from doing so. Indeed, one of the strongest empirical findings in the fields of strategic management and finance is that, on average, the equity holders of target firms in mergers and acquisitions make money while the equity holders of bidding firms in these same mergers and acquisitions usually only "break even."

What Are Mergers and Acquisitions?

The terms *mergers* and *acquisitions* are often used interchangeably, even though they are not synonyms. A firm engages in an **acquisition** when it purchases a second firm. The form of this purchase can vary. For example, an acquiring firm can use cash it has generated from its ongoing businesses to purchase a target firm; it can go into debt to purchase a target firm; it can use its own equity to purchase a target firm; or it can use a mix of these mechanisms to purchase a target firm. Also, an acquiring firm can purchase all of a target firm's assets; it can purchase a majority of those assets (greater than 51 percent); or it can purchase a **controlling share** of those assets (i.e., enough assets so that the acquiring firm is able to make all the management and strategic decisions in the target firm).

Acquisitions also vary on several other dimensions. For example, **friendly acquisitions** occur when the management of the target firm wants the firm to be acquired. **Unfriendly acquisitions** occur when the management of the target firm does not want the firm to be acquired. Some unfriendly acquisitions are also known as **hostile takeovers**. Some acquisitions are accomplished through direct negotiations between an acquiring firm's managers and the managers of a target firm. This is especially common when a target firm is **privately held** (i.e., when it has not sold shares on the public stock market) or **closely held** (i.e., when it has not sold very many shares on the public stock market). Other acquisitions are accomplished by the acquiring firm publicly announcing that it is willing to purchase the outstanding shares of a potential target for a particular price. This price is normally greater than the current market price of the target firm's shares. The difference between the current market price of a target firm's shares and the price a potential acquirer offers to pay for those shares is known as an **acquisition premium**. This approach to purchasing a firm is called a **tender offer**. Tender offers can be made either with or without the support of the management of the target firm. Obviously, tender offers with the support of the target firm's management are typically friendly in character; those made without the support of the target firm's management are typically unfriendly.

It is usually the case that larger firms—in terms of sales or assets—acquire smaller firms. For example, Microsoft is a much larger company than its intended acquisition target, Yahoo. In contrast, when the assets of two similar-sized firms are combined, this transaction is called a **merger**. Mergers can be accomplished in many of the same ways as acquisitions, that is, using cash or stock to purchase a percentage of another firm's assets. Typically, however, mergers will not be unfriendly. In a merger, one firm purchases some percentage of a second firm's assets while the second firm simultaneously purchases some percentage of the first firm's assets. For example, DaimlerChrysler was created as a merger between Daimler-Benz (the maker of Mercedes-Benz) and Chrysler. Daimler-Benz invested some of its capital in Chrysler, and Chrysler invested some of its capital in Daimler-Benz. More recently, these merged companies split into two firms again.

Although mergers typically begin as a transaction between equals—that is, between firms of equal size and profitability—they often evolve after a merger such that one firm becomes more dominant in the management of the merged firm than the other. For example, most observers believe that Daimler (the German part of DaimlerChrysler) became more dominant in the management of the combined firm than Chrysler (the American part).[1] Put differently, although mergers usually start out as something different from acquisitions, they usually end up looking more like acquisitions than mergers.

The Value of Mergers and Acquisitions

That merger and acquisition strategies are an important strategic option open to firms pursuing diversification and vertical integration strategies can hardly be disputed. The number of firms that have used merger and acquisition strategies to become diversified over the last few years is staggering. This is the case even though the credit crunch crisis in 2008 reduced M&A activity somewhat. For the first 11 months of 2008, there were 8,190 acquisitions or mergers done in the United States, with a total value of $1.1 trillion. For this same time period in 2007, there were over 10,000 deals in the United States, valued at $1.7 trillion.[2]

The list of firms that have recently engaged in mergers or acquisitions is long and varied. For example, AT&T (recently acquired by SBC) acquired BellSouth for $85.6 billion, ConocoPhillips acquired Burlington Resources for $35 billion, Boston Scientific bought Guidant for $25.1 billion, Wachovia bought Golden West Financial for $24.2 billion, Thermo Electron bought Fisher Scientific for $11.1 billion, Duke Energy bought Cinergy for $9 billion, BASF bought Englehard for $4.8 billion, and Oshkosh Trucks bought JLG Industries for $2.9 billion. And the list goes on and on.[3]

That mergers and acquisitions are common is clear. What is less clear is that they actually generate value for firms implementing these strategies. Two cases will be examined here: mergers and acquisitions between strategically unrelated firms and mergers and acquisitions between strategically related firms.

Mergers and Acquisitions: The Unrelated Case

Imagine the following scenario: One firm (the target) is the object of an acquisition effort, and 10 firms (the bidders) are interested in making this acquisition. Suppose the **current market value** of the target firm is $10,000—that is, the price of each of this firm's shares times the number of shares outstanding equals $10,000. Also, suppose the current market value of each of the bidding firms is $15,000.[4] Finally, suppose there is no strategic relatedness between these bidding firms and the target. This means that the value of any one of these bidding firms when combined with the target firm exactly equals the sum of the value of these firms as separate entities. In this example, because the current market value of the target is $10,000 and the current market value of the bidding firms is $15,000, the value of this target when combined with any of these bidders would be

$25,000 ($10,000 + $15,000). Given this information, at what price will this target be acquired, and what are the economic performance implications for bidding and target firms at this price?

In this, and all acquisition situations, bidding firms will be willing to pay a price for a target up to the value that the target firm adds to the bidder once it is acquired. This price is simply the difference between the value of the two firms combined (in this case, $25,000) and the value of the bidding firm by itself (in this case, $15,000). Notice that this price does not depend on the value of the target firm acting as an independent business; rather, it depends on the value that the target firm creates when it is combined with the bidding firm. Any price for a target less than this value (i.e., less than $10,000) will be a source of economic profit for a bidding firm; any price equal to this value (i.e., equal to $10,000) will be a source of zero economic profits; and any price greater than this value (i.e., greater than $10,000) will be a source of economic losses for the bidding firm that acquires the target.

It is not hard to see that the price of this acquisition will quickly rise to $10,000, and that at this price the bidding firm that acquires the target will earn zero economic profits. The price of this acquisition will quickly rise to $10,000 because any bid less than $10,000 will generate economic profits for a successful bidder. These potential profits, in turn, will generate entry into the bidding war for a target. Because entry into the acquisition contest is very likely, the price of the acquisition will quickly rise to its value, and economic profits will not be created.

Moreover, at this $10,000 price the target firm's equity holders will also gain zero economic profits. Indeed, for them, all that has occurred is that the market value of the target firm has been capitalized in the form of a cash payment from the bidder to the target. The target was worth $10,000, and that is exactly what these equity holders will receive.

Mergers and Acquisitions: The Related Case

The conclusion that the acquisition of strategically unrelated targets will generate only zero economic profits for both the bidding and the target firms is not surprising. It is very consistent with the discussion of the economic consequences of unrelated diversification in Chapter 7. There it was argued that there is no economic justification for a corporate diversification strategy that does not build on some type of economy of scope across the businesses within which a firm operates, and therefore unrelated diversification is not an economically viable corporate strategy. So, if there is any hope that mergers and acquisitions will be a source of superior performance for bidding firms, it must be because of some sort of strategic relatedness or economy of scope between bidding and target firms.

Types of Strategic Relatedness

Of course, bidding and target firms can be strategically related in a wide variety of ways. Three particularly important lists of these potential linkages are discussed here.[5]

The Federal Trade Commission Categories.   Because mergers and acquisitions can have the effect of increasing (or decreasing) the level of concentration in an industry, the Federal Trade Commission (FTC) is charged with the responsibility of evaluating the competitive implications of proposed mergers or acquisitions. In principle, the FTC will disallow any acquisition involving firms with headquarters in the United States that could have the potential for generating

■ Vertical merger	A firm acquires former suppliers or customers.
■ Horizontal merger	A firm acquires a former competitor.
■ Product extension merger	A firm gains access to complementary products through an acquisition.
■ Market extension merger	A firm gains access to complementary markets through an acquisition.
■ Conglomerate merger	There is no strategic relatedness between a bidding and a target firm.

TABLE 10.1 Federal Trade Commission Categories of Mergers and Acquisitions

monopoly (or oligopoly) profits in an industry. To help in this regulatory effort, the FTC has developed a typology of mergers and acquisitions (see Table 10.1). Each category in this typology can be thought of as a different way in which a bidding firm and a target firm can be related in a merger or acquisition.

According to the FTC, a firm engages in a **vertical merger** when it vertically integrates, either forward or backward, through its acquisition efforts. Vertical mergers could include a firm purchasing critical suppliers of raw materials (backward vertical integration) or acquiring customers and distribution networks (forward vertical integration). eBay's acquisition of Skype is an example of a backward vertical integration as eBay tries to assemble all the resources to compete in the Internet telephone industry. Disney's acquisition of Capital Cities/ABC can be understood as an attempt by Disney to forward vertically integrate into the entertainment distribution industry, and its acquisition of ESPN can be seen as backward vertical integration into the entertainment production business.[6]

A firm engages in a **horizontal merger** when it acquires a former competitor; Adidas's acquisition of Reebok is an example of a horizontal merger, as the number 2 and number 3 sneaker manufacturers in the world combined their efforts. Obviously, the FTC is particularly concerned with the competitive implications of horizontal mergers because these strategies can have the most direct and obvious anticompetitive implications in an industry. For example, the FTC raised antitrust concerns in the $10 billion merger between Oracle and PeopleSoft, because these firms, collectively, dominated the enterprise software market. Similar concerns were raised in the $16.4 billion merger between ChevronTexaco and Unocal and the merger between Mobil and Exxon.

The third type of merger identified by the FTC is a **product extension merger**. In a product extension merger, firms acquire complementary products through their merger and acquisition activities. Examples include SBC's acquisition of AT&T and Verizon's acquisition of MCI.

The fourth type of merger identified by the FTC is a **market extension merger**. Here, the primary objective is to gain access to new geographic markets. Examples include SABMiller's acquisition of Bavaria Brewery Company in Columbia, South America.

The final type of merger or acquisition identified by the FTC is a **conglomerate merger**. For the FTC, conglomerate mergers are a residual category. If there are no vertical, horizontal, product extension, or market extension links between firms, the FTC defines the merger or acquisition activity between firms as a conglomerate merger. Given our earlier conclusion that mergers or acquisitions between strategically *unrelated* firms will not generate economic profits for either bidders or targets, it should not be surprising that there are currently relatively few examples of conglomerate mergers or acquisitions; however, at various times in history, they have been relatively common. In the 1960s, for example, many acquisitions took the form of conglomerate mergers. Research has shown that the fraction of single-business firms in the Fortune 500 dropped from 22.8 percent in 1959 to 14.8 percent in 1969, while the fraction of firms in the Fortune 500 pursuing unrelated diversification strategies rose from 7.3 to 18.7 percent during the same time period. These findings are consistent with an increase in the number of conglomerate mergers and acquisitions during the 1960s.[7]

Despite the popularity of conglomerate mergers in the 1960s, many mergers or acquisitions among strategically unrelated firms are divested shortly after they are completed. One study estimated that over one-third of the conglomerate mergers of the 1960s were divested by the early 1980s. Another study showed that over 50 percent of these acquisitions were subsequently divested. These results are all consistent with our earlier conclusion that mergers or acquisitions involving strategically unrelated firms are not a source of economic profits.[8]

Other Types of Strategic Relatedness.   Although the FTC categories of mergers and acquisitions provide some information about possible motives underlying these corporate strategies, they do not capture the full complexity of the links that might exist between bidding and target firms. Several authors have attempted to develop more complete lists of possible sources of relatedness between bidding and target firms. One of these lists, developed by Professor Michael Lubatkin, is summarized in Table 10.2. This list includes **technical economies** (in marketing, production, and similar forms of relatedness), **pecuniary economies** (market power), and **diversification economies** (in portfolio management and risk reduction) as possible bases of strategic relatedness between bidding and target firms.

A second important list of possible sources of strategic relatedness between bidding and target firms was developed by Michael Jensen and Richard Ruback after a comprehensive review of empirical research on the economic returns to mergers and acquisitions. This list is summarized in Table 10.3 and includes the following factors as possible sources of economic gains in mergers and acquisitions: potential reductions in production or distribution costs (from economies of

TABLE 10.2 Lubatkin's List of Potential Sources of Strategic Relatedness Between Bidding and Target Firms		
Technical economies		Scale economies that occur when the physical processes inside a firm are altered so that the same amounts of input produce a higher quantity of outputs. Sources of technical economies include marketing, production, experience, scheduling, banking, and compensation.
Pecuniary economies		Economies achieved by the ability of firms to dictate prices by exerting market power.
Diversification economies		Economies achieved by improving a firm's performance relative to its risk attributes or lowering its risk attributes relative to its performance. Sources of diversification economies include portfolio management and risk reduction.

Source: M. Lubatkin (1983). "Mergers and the performance of the acquiring firm." *Academy of Management Review*, 8, pp. 218–225. © 1983 by the Academy of Management. Reproduced with permission.

To reduce production or distribution costs:

1. Through economies of scale.
2. Through vertical integration.
3. Through the adoption of more efficient production or organizational technology.
4. Through the increased utilization of the bidder's management team.
5. Through a reduction of agency costs by bringing organization-specific assets under common ownership.

Financial motivations:

1. To gain access to underutilized tax shields.
2. To avoid bankruptcy costs.
3. To increase leverage opportunities.
4. To gain other tax advantages.
5. To gain market power in product markets.
6. To eliminate inefficient target management.

Source: Reprinted from Jensen, M. C., and R. S. Ruback "The Market for Corporate Control: The Scientific Evidence." *Journal of Financial Economics*, 11, pp. 5–50. Vol. II. Copyright © 1983, with permission from Elsevier.

TABLE 10.3 Jensen and Ruback's List of Reasons Why Bidding Firms Might Want to Engage in Merger and Acquisition Strategies

scale, vertical integration, reduction in agency costs, and so forth); the realization of financial opportunities (such as gaining access to underutilized tax shields, avoiding bankruptcy costs); the creation of market power; and the ability to eliminate inefficient management in the target firm.

To be economically valuable, links between bidding and target firms must meet the same criteria as diversification strategies (see Chapter 7). First, these links must build on real economies of scope between bidding and target firms. These economies of scope can reflect either cost savings or revenue enhancements that are created by combining firms. Second, not only must this economy of scope exist, but it must be less costly for the merged firm to realize than for outside equity holders to realize on their own. As is the case with corporate diversification strategies, by investing in a diversified portfolio of stocks, outside equity investors can gain many of the economies associated with a merger or acquisition on their own. Moreover, investors can realize some of these economies of scope at almost zero cost. In this situation, it makes little sense for investors to "hire" managers in firms to realize these economies of scope for them through a merger or acquisition. Rather, firms should pursue merger and acquisition strategies only to obtain valuable economies of scope that outside investors find too costly to create on their own.

Economic Profits in Related Acquisitions

If bidding and target firms are strategically related, then the economic value of these two firms combined is greater than their economic value as separate entities. To see how this changes returns to merger and acquisition strategies, consider the following scenario: As before, there is one target firm and 10 bidding firms. The market value of the target firm as a stand-alone entity is $10,000, and the market value of the bidding firms as stand-alone entities is $15,000. However, unlike the earlier scenario in this chapter, the bidding and target firms are strategically related. Any of the types of relatedness identified in Table 10.1, Table 10.2, or Table 10.3

could be the source of these economies of scope. They imply that when any of the bidding firms and the target are combined, the market value of this combined entity will be $32,000—note that $32,000 is greater than the sum of $15,000 and $10,000. At what price will this target firm be acquired, and what are the economic profit implications for bidding and target firms at this price?

As before, bidding firms will be willing to pay a price for a target up to the value that a target firm adds once it is acquired. Thus, the maximum price bidding firms are willing to pay is still the difference between the value of the combined entity (here, $32,000) and the value of a bidding firm on its own (here, $15,000), or $17,000.

As was the case for the strategically unrelated acquisition, it is not hard to see that the price for actually acquiring the target firm in this scenario will rapidly rise to $17,000, because any bid less than $17,000 has the potential for generating profits for a bidding firm. Suppose that one bidding firm offers $13,000 for the target. For this $13,000, the bidding firm gains access to a target that will generate $17,000 of value once it is acquired. Thus, to this bidding firm, the target is worth $17,000, and a bid of $13,000 will generate $4,000 economic profit. Of course, these potential profits will motivate entry into the competitive bidding process. Entry will continue until the price of this target equals $17,000. Any price greater than $17,000 would mean that a bidding firm is actually losing money on its acquisition.[9]

At this $17,000 price, the successful bidding firm earns zero economic profits. After all, this firm has acquired an asset that will generate $17,000 of value and has paid $17,000 to do so. However, the owners of the target firm will earn an economic profit worth $7,000. As a stand-alone firm, the target is worth $10,000; when combined with a bidding firm, it is worth $17,000. The difference between the value of the target as a stand-alone entity and its value in combination with a bidding firm is the value of the economic profit that can be appropriated by the owners of the target firm.

Thus, the existence of strategic relatedness between bidding and target firms is not a sufficient condition for the equity holders of bidding firms to earn economic profits from their acquisition strategies. If the economic potential of acquiring a particular target firm is widely known and if several potential bidding firms can all obtain this value by acquiring a target, the equity holders of bidding firms will, at best, earn only zero economic profits from implementing an acquisition strategy. In this setting, a "strategically related" merger or acquisition will create economic value, but this value will be distributed in the form of economic profits to the equity holders of acquired target firms.

Because so much of the value created in a merger or acquisition is appropriated by the stockholders of the target firm, it is not surprising that many small and entrepreneurial firms look to be acquired as one way to compensate their owners for taking the risks associated with founding these firms. This phenomenon is discussed in more detail in the Strategy in the Emerging Enterprise feature.

What Does Research Say About Returns to Mergers and Acquisitions?

The empirical implications of this discussion of returns to bidding and target firms in strategically related and strategically unrelated mergers and acquisitions have been examined in a variety of academic literatures. One study reviewed over 40 empirical merger and acquisition studies in the finance literature. This study

Strategy in the Emerging Enterprise

Imagine you are an entrepreneur. You have mortgaged your home, taken out loans, run up your credit cards, and put all you own on the line in order to help grow a small company. And finally, after years of effort, things start going well. Your product or service starts to sell, customers start to appreciate your unique value proposition, and you actually begin to pay yourself a reasonable salary. What do you do next to help grow your company?

Some entrepreneurs in this situation decide that maintaining control of the firm is very important. These entrepreneurs may compensate certain critical employees with equity in the firm, but typically limit the number of outsiders who make equity investments in their firm. To grow these closely held firms, these entrepreneurs must rely on capital generated from their ongoing operations (called **retained earnings**) and debt capital provided by banks, customers, and suppliers. Entrepreneurs who decide to maintain control of their companies are compensated for taking the risks associated with starting a firm through the salary they pay themselves.

Other entrepreneurs get more outside equity investors involved in providing the capital a firm needs to grow. These outside investors might include wealthy individuals—called **business angels**—looking to invest in entrepreneurial ventures or **venture capital firms**. Venture capital firms typically raise money from numerous

Cashing Out

smaller investors that they then invest in a portfolio of entrepreneurial firms. Over time, many of these firms decide to "go public" by engaging in what is called an **initial public offering (IPO)**. In an IPO, a firm, typically working with an investment banker, sells its equity to the public at large. Entrepreneurs who decide to sell equity in their firm are compensated for taking the risks associated with starting a firm through the sale of their equity on the public markets through an IPO. An entrepreneur who receives compensation for risk-taking in this manner is said to be **cashing out**.

Finally, still other entrepreneurs may decide to not use an IPO to cash out, but rather to have their firm acquired by another, typically larger firm. In this scenario, entrepreneurs are compensated by the acquiring firm for taking the risks associated with starting a firm. Indeed, because the demand for IPOs has been volatile since the

technology-bubble burst of 2000, more and more small and entrepreneurial firms are looking to be acquired as a way for their founders to cash out. Moreover, because the stockholders of target firms typically appropriate a large percentage of the total value created by an acquisition, and because the founders of these entrepreneurial firms are also often large stockholders, being acquired is often a source of great wealth for an entrepreneurial firm's founders.

The choice between keeping a firm private, going public, or being acquired is a difficult and multidimensional one. Issues such as the personal preferences of a firm's founders, demand for IPOs, how much capital a firm will need in order to continue to grow its business, and what other resources—besides capital—the firm will need to create additional value all play a role. In general, firms that do not need a great deal of money or other resources to grow will choose to remain private. Those that need only money to grow will choose IPOs, whereas those that need managerial or technical resources controlled by another firm to grow will typically be acquired. Of course, this changes if the entrepreneurs decide to maintain control of their firms because they want to.

Sources: R. Hennessey (2004). "Underwriters cut prices on IPOs as market softens." *The Wall Street Journal*, May 27, p. C4; and F. Vogelstein (2003). "Can Google grow up?" *Fortune*, December 8, pp. 102 +.

concluded that acquisitions, on average, increased the market value of target firms by about 25 percent and left the market value of bidding firms unchanged. The authors of this report concluded that "corporate takeovers generate positive gains, . . . target firm equity holders benefit, and . . . bidding firm equity holders do not lose."[10] The way these studies evaluate the return to acquisition strategies is discussed in the Strategy in Depth feature.

Strategy researchers have also attempted to examine in more detail the sources of value creation in mergers and acquisitions and the question of whether these sources of value creation affect whether bidders or targets appropriate this value. For example, two well-known studies examined the impact of the type and degree of strategic relatedness (defined using the FTC typology summarized in Table 10.1) between bidding and target firms on the economic consequences of mergers and acquisitions.[11] These studies found that the more strategically related bidding and target firms are, the more economic value mergers and acquisitions create. However, like the finance studies, this work found that this economic value was appropriated by the owners of the target firm, regardless of the type or degree of relatedness between the bidding and target firms. Bidding firms—even when they attempt to acquire strategically related targets—earn, on average, zero economic profits from their merger and acquisition strategies.

Why Are There So Many Mergers and Acquisitions?

Given the overwhelming empirical evidence that most of the economic value created in mergers and acquisitions is appropriated by the owners of the target firm most of the time, an important question becomes: "Why do managers of bidding firms continue to engage in merger and acquisition strategies?" Some possible explanations are summarized in Table 10.4 and discussed in this section.

To Ensure Survival

Even if mergers and acquisitions, on average, generate only zero economic profits for bidding firms, it may be necessary for bidding firms to engage in these activities to ensure their survival. In particular, if all of a bidding firm's competitors have been able to improve their efficiency and effectiveness through a particular type of acquisition, then failing to make such an acquisition may put a firm at a competitive disadvantage. Here, the purpose of a merger or acquisition is not to gain competitive advantages, but rather to gain competitive parity.

Many recent mergers among banks in the United States seem to have competitive parity and normal economic profits as an objective. Most bank managers recognize that changing bank regulations, increased competition from nonbanking financial institutions, and soft demand are likely to lead to a consolidation of the U.S. banking industry. To survive in this consolidated industry, many U.S. banks will have to merge. As the number of banks engaging in mergers and acquisitions goes up, the ability to earn superior profits from those strategies goes down. These lower returns from acquisitions have already reduced the economic value of some of the most aggressive acquiring banks. Despite these lower returns, acquisitions are likely to continue for the foreseeable future, as banks seek survival opportunities in a consolidated industry.[12]

TABLE 10.4 Possible Motivations to Engage in Mergers and Acquisitions Even Though They Usually Do Not Generate Profits for Bidding Firms

1. To ensure survival
2. Free cash flow
3. Agency problems
4. Managerial hubris
5. The potential for above-normal profits

Free Cash Flow

Another reason why firms may continue to invest in merger and acquisition strategies is that these strategies, on average, can be expected to generate at least competitive parity for bidding firms. This zero economic profit may be a more attractive investment for some firms than alternative strategic investments. This is particularly the case for firms that generate free cash flow.[13]

Free cash flow is simply the amount of cash a firm has to invest after all positive net present-value investments in its ongoing businesses have been funded. Free cash flow is created when a firm's ongoing business operations are very profitable but offer few opportunities for additional investment. One firm that seems to have generated a great deal of free cash flow over the last several years is Philip Morris. Philip Morris's retail tobacco operations are extremely profitable. However, regulatory constraints, health concerns, and slowing growth in demand limit investment opportunities in the tobacco industry. Thus, the amount of cash generated by Philip Morris's ongoing tobacco business has probably been larger than the sum of its positive net present-value investments in that business. This difference is free cash flow for Philip Morris.[14]

A firm that generates a great deal of free cash flow must decide what to do with this money. One obvious alternative would be to give it to stockholders in the form of dividends or stock buybacks. However, in some situations (e.g., when stockholders face high marginal tax rates), stockholders may prefer a firm to retain this cash flow and invest it for them. When this is the case, how should a firm invest its free cash flow?

Because (by definition) no positive net present-value investment opportunities in a firm's ongoing business operations are available, firms have only two investment options: to invest their free cash flow in strategies that generate competitive parity or in strategies that generate competitive disadvantages. In this context, merger and acquisition strategies are a viable option, because bidding firms, on average, can expect to generate at least competitive parity. Put differently, although mergers and acquisitions may not be a source of superior profits, there are worse things you could do with your free cash flow.

Agency Problems

Another reason why firms might continue to engage in mergers and acquisitions, despite earning only competitive parity from doing so, is that mergers and acquisitions benefit managers directly, independent of any value they may or may not create for a bidding firm's stockholders. As suggested in Chapter 8, these conflicts of interest are a manifestation of agency problems between a firm's managers and its stockholders.

Merger and acquisition strategies can benefit managers—even if they do not directly benefit a bidding firm's equity holders—in at least two ways. First, managers can use mergers and acquisitions to help diversify their human capital investments in their firm. As discussed in Chapter 7, managers have difficulty diversifying their firm-specific human capital investments when a firm operates in a narrow range of businesses. By acquiring firms with cash flows that are not perfectly correlated with the cash flows of a firm's current businesses, managers can reduce the probability of bankruptcy for their firm and thus partially diversify their human capital investments in their firm.

Second, managers can use mergers and acquisitions to quickly increase firm size, measured in either sales or assets. If management compensation is closely linked to firm size, managers who increase firm size are able to increase their compensation.

Strategy in Depth

By far, the most popular way to evaluate the performance effects of acquisitions for bidding firms is called **event study analysis.** Rooted in the field of financial economics, event study analysis compares the actual performance of a stock after an acquisition has been announced to the expected performance of that stock if no acquisition had been announced. Any performance greater (or less) than what was expected in a short period of time around when an acquisition is announced is attributed to that acquisition. This **cumulative abnormal return (CAR)** can be positive or negative depending on whether the stock in question performs better or worse than expected without an acquisition.

The CAR created by an acquisition is calculated in several stages. First, the expected performance of a stock, without an acquisition, is estimated with the following regression equation:

$$E(R_{j,t}) = a_j + b_j R_{m,t} + e_{j,t}$$

where $E(R_{j,t})$ is the expected return of stock j during time t; a_j is a constant (approximately equal to the rate of return on risk-free equities); b_j is an empirical estimate of the financial parameter β (equal to the covariance between the returns of a particular firm's stock and the average return of all stocks in the market, over time); $R_{m,t}$ is the actual average rate of return of all stocks in the market over time; and $e_{j,t}$ is an error term. The form of this equation is derived from the capital asset pricing model in finance. In this model, $E(R_{j,t})$ is simply the

Evaluating the Performance Effects of Acquisitions

expected performance of a stock, given the historical relationship between that stock and the overall performance of the stock market.

To calculate the unexpected performance of a stock, this expected level of performance is simply subtracted from the actual level of performance for a stock. This is done in the following equation:

$$XR_{j,t} = R_{j,t} - (a_j + b_j R_{m,t})$$

where $R_{j,t}$ is the actual performance of stock j during time t, and $XR_{j,t}$ is the unexpected performance of stock j during time t.

In calculating the CAR for a particular acquisition, it is necessary to sum the unexpected returns ($XR_{j,t}$) for a stock across the t periods when the stock market is responding to news about this acquisition. Most analyses of acquisitions examine the market's reaction one day before an acquisition is formally announced to three days after it is announced. The sum of these unexpected returns over this time period is the CAR attributable to this acquisition.

This methodology has been applied to literally thousands of acquisition episodes. For example, when Manulife Financial purchased John Hancock Financial, Manulife's CAR was −10 percent, whereas John Hancock's CAR was 6 percent; when Anthem acquired Wellpoint, Anthem's CAR was −10 percent, and Wellpoint's was 7 percent; when Bank of America acquired FleetBoston Financial, Bank of America's CAR was −9 percent, and FleetBoston's was 24 percent; and when UnitedHealth acquired Mid Atlantic Medical, UnitedHealth's CAR was −4 percent, and Mid Atlantic Medical's was 11 percent.

Although the event study method has been used widely, it does have some important limitations. First, it is based entirely on the capital asset pricing model, and there is some reason to believe that this model is not a particularly good predictor of a firm's expected stock price. Second, it assumes that a firm's equity holders can anticipate all the benefits associated with making an acquisition at the time that acquisition is made. Some scholars have argued that value creation continues long after an acquisition is announced as parties in this exchange discover value-creating opportunities that could not have been anticipated.

Sources: A. Arikan (2004). "Long-term returns to acquisitions: The case of purchasing tangible and intangible assets." Unpublished, Fisher College of Business, Ohio State University; S. J. Brown and J. B. Warner (1985). "Using daily stock returns: The case of event studies." *Journal of Financial Economics*, 14, pp. 3–31; and D. Henry, M. Der Hovanseian, and D. Foust (2003). "M&A deals: Show me." *BusinessWeek*, November 10, pp. 38 +.

Of all the ways to increase the size of a firm quickly, growth through mergers and acquisitions is perhaps the easiest. Even if there are no economies of scope between a bidding and a target firm, an acquisition ensures that the bidding firm will grow by the size of the target (measured in either sales or assets). If there are economies of scope between a bidding and a target firm, the size of the bidding firm can grow at an even faster rate, as can the value of management's compensation, even though, on average, acquisitions do not generate wealth for the owners of the bidding firm.

Managerial Hubris

Another reason why managers may choose to continue to invest in mergers and acquisitions, despite the fact that, on average, they gain no profits from doing so, is the existence of what has been called **managerial hubris**.[15] This is the unrealistic belief held by managers in bidding firms that they can manage the assets of a target firm more efficiently than the target firm's current management. This notion can lead bidding firms to engage in acquisition strategies even though there may not be positive economic profits from doing so.

The existence of managerial hubris suggests that the economic value of bidding firms will fall once they announce a merger or acquisition strategy. Although managers in bidding firms might truly believe that they can manage a target firm's assets more efficiently than the target firm's managers, investors in the capital markets are much less likely to be caught up in this hubris. In this context, a commitment to a merger or acquisition strategy is a strong signal that a bidding firm's management has deluded itself about its abilities to manage a target firm's assets. Such delusions will certainly adversely affect the economic value of the bidding firm.

Of course, empirical work on mergers and acquisitions discussed earlier in this chapter has concluded that although bidding firms do not obtain profits from their merger and acquisition strategies, they also do not, on average, reduce their economic value from implementing these strategies. This is inconsistent with the "hubris hypothesis." However, the fact that, on average, bidding firms do not lose economic value does not mean that some bidding firms do not lose economic value. Thus, although it is unlikely that all merger and acquisition strategies are motivated by managerial hubris, it is likely that at least some of them are.[16]

The Potential for Economic Profits

A final reason why managers might continue to pursue merger and acquisition strategies is the potential that these strategies offer for generating profits for at least some bidding firms. The empirical research on returns to bidding firms in mergers and acquisitions is very strong. On average, bidding firms do not gain profits from their merger and acquisition strategies. However, the fact that bidding firms, *on average*, do not earn profits on these strategies does not mean that *all* bidding firms will *always* fail to earn profits. In some situations, bidding firms may be able to gain competitive advantages from merger and acquisition activities. These situations are discussed in the following section.

Mergers and Acquisitions and Sustained Competitive Advantage

V R I O

We have already seen that the economies of scope that motivate mergers and acquisitions between strategically related bidding and target firms can be valuable. However, the ability of these economies to generate profits and competitive advantages for bidding firms depends not only on their economic value, but also on the competitiveness of the market for corporate control through which these valuable economies are realized. The **market for corporate control** is the market that is created when multiple firms actively seek to acquire one or several firms. Only when the market for corporate control is imperfectly competitive might it be possible for bidding firms to earn profits from implementing a merger or acquisition strategy. To see how the competitiveness of the market for corporate control can affect returns to merger and acquisition strategies, we will consider three scenarios involving bidding and target firms and examine their implications for the managers of these firms.[17]

Valuable, Rare, and Private Economies of Scope

An imperfectly competitive market for corporate control can exist when a target is worth more to one bidder than it is to any other bidders and when no other firms—including bidders and targets—are aware of this additional value. In this setting, the price of a target will rise to reflect public expectations about the value of the target. Once the target is acquired, however, the performance of the special bidder that acquires the target will be greater than generally expected, and this level of performance will generate profits for the equity holders of the bidding firm.

Consider a simple case. Suppose the market value of bidder Firm A combined with target firms is $12,000, whereas the market value of all other bidders combined with targets is $10,000. No other firms (bidders or targets) are aware of Firm A's unique relationship with these targets, but they are aware of the value of all other bidders combined with targets (i.e., $10,000). Suppose also that the market value of all bidding firms, as stand-alone entities, is $7,000. In this setting, Firm A will be willing to pay up to $5,000 to acquire a target ($12,000 − $7,000), and all other bidders will only be willing to pay up to $3,000 to acquire a target ($10,000 − $7,000).

Because publicly available information suggests that acquiring a target is worth $3,000 more than the target's stand-alone price, the price of targets will rapidly rise to this level, ensuring that, if bidding firms, apart from Firm A, acquire a target, they will obtain no profits. If there is only one target in this market for corporate control, then Firm A will be able to bid slightly more than $3,000 (perhaps $3,001) for this target. No other firms will bid higher than Firm A, because, from their point of view, the acquisition is simply not worth more than $3,000. At this $3,001 price, Firm A will earn a profit of $1,999—Firm A had to spend only $3,001 for a firm that brings $5,000 in value above its stand-alone market price. Alternatively, if there are multiple targets, then several bidding firms, including Firm A, will pay $3,000 for their targets. At this price, these bidding firms will all earn zero economic profits, except for Firm A, which will earn an economic profit equal to $2,000. That is, only Firm A will gain a competitive advantage from acquiring a target in this market.

In order for Firm A to obtain this profit, the value of Firm A's economy of scope with target firms must be greater than the value of any other bidding firms with that target. This special value will generally reflect unusual resources and capabilities possessed by Firm A—resources and capabilities that are more valuable in combination with target firms than are the resources and capabilities that other bidding firms possess. Put differently, to be a source of economic profits and competitive advantage, Firm A's link with targets must be based on resources and capabilities that are rare among those firms competing in this market for corporate control.

However, not only does Firm A have to possess valuable and rare links with bidding firms to gain economic profits and competitive advantages from its acquisition strategies, but information about these special economies of scope must not be known by other firms. If other bidding firms know about the additional value associated with acquiring a target, they are likely to try to duplicate this value for themselves. Typically, they would accomplish this by imitating the type of relatedness that exists between Firm A and its targets by developing the resources and capabilities that enabled Firm A to have its valuable economies of scope with targets. Once other bidders developed the resources and capabilities necessary to obtain this more valuable economy of scope, they would be able to enter into bidding, thereby increasing the likelihood that the equity holders of successful bidding firms would earn no economic profits.

Target firms must also be unaware of Firm A's special resources and capabilities if Firm A is to obtain competitive advantages from an acquisition. If target firms were aware of this extra value available to Firm A, along with the sources of this value, they could inform other bidding firms. These bidding firms could then adjust their bids to reflect this higher value, and competitive bidding would reduce profits to bidders. Target firms are likely to inform bidding firms in this way because increasing the number of bidders with more valuable economies of scope increases the likelihood that target firms will extract all the economic value created in a merger or acquisition.[18]

Valuable, Rare, and Costly-to-Imitate Economies of Scope

The existence of firms that have valuable, rare, and private economies of scope with targets is not the only way that the market for corporate control can be imperfectly competitive. If other bidders cannot imitate one bidder's valuable and rare economies with targets, then competition in this market for corporate control will be imperfect, and the equity holders of this special bidding firm will earn economic profits. In this case, the existence of valuable and rare economies does not need to be private, because other bidding firms cannot imitate these economies, and therefore bids that substantially reduce the profits for the equity holders of the special bidding firm are not forthcoming.

Typically, bidding firms will be unable to imitate one bidder's valuable and rare economies of scope with targets when the strategic relatedness between the special bidder and the targets stems from some rare and costly-to-imitate resources or capabilities controlled by the special bidding firm. Any of the costly-to-imitate resources and capabilities discussed in Chapter 3 could create costly-to-imitate economies of scope between a firm and a target. If, in addition, these economies are valuable and rare, they can be a source of profits to the equity holders of the special bidding firm. This can happen even if all firms in this market for corporate control are aware of the more valuable economies of scope available to this firm and its sources. Although information about this special economy of scope is publicly available, equity holders of special bidding firms will earn a profit when acquisition occurs. The equity holders of target firms will not obtain all of this profit, because competitive bidding dynamics cannot unfold when the sources of a more valuable economy of scope are costly to imitate.

Of course, it may be possible for a valuable, rare, and costly-to-imitate economy of scope between a bidding and a target firm to also be private. Indeed, it is often the case that those attributes of a firm that are costly to imitate are also difficult to describe and thus can be held as proprietary information. In that case, the analysis of profits associated with valuable, rare, and private economies of scope presented earlier applies.

Unexpected Valuable Economies of Scope Between Bidding and Target Firms

Thus far, this discussion has adopted, for convenience, the strong assumption that the present value of the strategic relatedness between bidders and targets is known with certainty by individual bidders. This is, in principle, possible, but certainly not likely. Most modern acquisitions and mergers are massively complex, involving numerous unknown and complicated relationships between firms. In these settings, unexpected events after an acquisition has been completed may make an acquisition or merger more valuable than bidders and targets anticipated it would be. The price that bidding firms will pay to acquire a target will equal the expected value of the target only when the target is combined with the bidder. The difference between the unexpected value of an acquisition actually obtained by a bidder and the price the bidder paid for the acquisition is a profit for the equity holders of the bidding firm.

Of course, by definition, bidding firms cannot expect to obtain unexpected value from an acquisition. Unexpected value, in this context, is a surprise, a manifestation of a bidding firm's good luck, not its skill in acquiring targets. For example, when the British advertising firm WPP acquired J. Walter Thompson for $550 million, it discovered some property owned by J. Walter Thomson in Tokyo. No one knew of this property when the firm was acquired. It turned out to be worth over $100 million after taxes, a financial windfall that helped offset the high cost of this acquisition. When asked, Martin Sorrel, president of WPP and the architect of this acquisition, admitted that this $100 million windfall was simply good luck.[19]

Implications for Bidding Firm Managers

The existence of valuable, rare, and private economies of scope between bidding and target firms and of valuable, rare, and costly-to-imitate economies of scope between bidding and target firms suggests that although, on average, most bidding firms do not generate competitive advantages from their acquisition strategies, in some special circumstances it may be possible for them to do so. Thus, the task facing managers in firms contemplating merger and acquisition strategies is to choose strategies that have the greatest likelihood of being able to generate profits for their equity holders. Several important managerial prescriptions can be derived from this discussion. These "rules" for bidding firm managers are summarized in Table 10.5.

TABLE 10.5 Rules for Bidding Firm Managers

1. Search for valuable and rare economies of scope.
2. Keep information away from other bidders.
3. Keep information away from targets.
4. Avoid winning bidding wars.
5. Close the deal quickly.
6. Operate in "thinly traded" acquisition markets.

Search for Rare Economies of Scope

One of the main reasons why bidding firms do not obtain competitive advantages from acquiring strategically related target firms is that several other bidding firms value the target firm in the same way. When multiple bidders all value a target in the same way, competitive bidding is likely. Competitive bidding, in turn, drives out the potential for superior performance. To avoid this problem, bidding firms should seek to acquire targets with which they enjoy valuable and rare linkages.

Operationally, the search for rare economies of scope suggests that managers in bidding firms need to consider not only the value of a target firm when combined with their own company, but also the value of a target firm when combined with other potential bidders. This is important, because it is the difference between the value of a particular bidding firm's relationship with a target and the value of other bidding firms' relationships with that target that defines the size of the potential economic profits from an acquisition.

In practice, the search for valuable and rare economies of scope is likely to become a search for valuable and rare resources already controlled by a firm that are synergistically related to a target. For example, if a bidding firm has a unique reputation in its product market, and if the target firm's products could benefit by association with that reputation, then the target firm may be more valuable to this particular bidder than to other bidders (firms that do not possess this special reputation). Also, if a particular bidder possesses the largest market share in its industry, the best distribution system, or restricted access to certain key raw materials, and if the target firm would benefit from being associated with these valuable and rare resources, then the acquisition of this target may be a source of economic profits.

The search for valuable and rare economies of scope as a basis of mergers and acquisitions tends to rule out certain interfirm linkages as sources of economic profits. For example, most acquisitions can lead to a reduction in overhead costs, because much of the corporate overhead associated with the target firm can be eliminated subsequent to acquisition. However, the ability to eliminate these overhead costs is not unique to any one bidder, and thus the value created by these reduced costs will usually be captured by the equity holders of the target firm.

Keep Information Away from Other Bidders

One of the keys to earning superior performance in an acquisition strategy is to avoid multiple bidders for a single target. One way to accomplish this is to keep information about the bidding process, and about the sources of economies of scope between a bidder and target that underlie this bidding process, as private as possible. In order for other firms to become involved in bidding for a target, they must be aware of the value of the economies of scope between themselves and that target. If only one bidding firm knows this information, and if this bidding firm can close the deal before the full value of the target is known, then it may gain a competitive advantage from completing this acquisition.

Of course, in many circumstances, keeping all this information private is difficult. Often, it is illegal. For example, when seeking to acquire a publicly traded firm, potential bidders must meet disclosure requirements that effectively reduce the amount of private information a bidder can retain. In these circumstances, unless a bidding firm has some valuable, rare, and costly-to-imitate economy of scope with a target firm, the possibility of economic profits coming from an acquisition is very low. It is not surprising that the research conducted on mergers and acquisitions of firms traded on public stock exchanges governed by the U.S. Securities and Exchange Commission (SEC) disclosure rules suggests that, most of the time, bidding firms do not earn economic profits from implementing their acquisition strategies.

However, not all potential targets are publicly traded. Privately held firms may be acquired in an information environment that can create opportunities for above-normal performance for bidding firms. Moreover, even when acquiring a publicly traded firm, a bidder does not have to release all the information it has about the potential value of that target in combination with itself. Indeed, if some of this value reflects a bidding firm's taken-for-granted "invisible" assets, it may not be possible to communicate this information. In this case, as well, there may be opportunities for competitive advantages for bidding firms.

Keep Information Away from Targets

Not only should bidding firms keep information about the value of their economy of scope with a target away from other bidders; they should also keep this information away from target firms. Suppose that the value of a target firm to a bidding firm is $8,000, but the bidding firm, in an attempt to earn economic profits, has bid only $5,000 for the target. If the target knows that it is actually worth $8,000, it is very likely to hold out for a higher bid. In fact, the target may contact other potential bidding firms and tell them of the opportunity created by the $5,000 bid. As the number of bidders goes up, the possibility of superior economic performance for bidders goes down. Therefore, to keep the possibility of these profits alive, bidding firms must not fully reveal the value of their economies of scope with a target firm. Again, in some circumstances, it is very difficult, or even illegal, to attempt to limit the flow of information to target firms. In these settings, superior economic performance for bidding firms is very unlikely.

Limiting the amount of information that flows to the target firm may have some other consequences as well. For example, it has been shown that a complete sharing of information, insights, and perspectives before an acquisition is completed increases the probability that economies of scope will actually be realized once it is completed.[20] By limiting the flow of information between itself and a target, a bidding firm may actually be increasing the cost of integrating the target into its ongoing business, thereby jeopardizing at least some of the superior economic performance that limiting information flow is designed to create. Bidding firms will need to carefully balance the economic benefits of limiting the information they share with the target firm against the costs that limiting information flow may create.

Avoid Winning Bidding Wars

It should be reasonably clear that if a number of firms bid for the same target, the probability that the firm that successfully acquires the target will gain competitive advantages is very low. Indeed, to ensure that competitive bidding occurs, target firms can actively encourage other bidding firms to enter into the bidding process. The implications of these arguments are clear: Bidding firms should generally avoid winning a bidding war. To "win" a bidding war, a bidding firm will often have to pay a price at least equal to the full value of the target. Many times, given the emotions of an intense bidding contest, the winning bid may actually be larger than the true value of the target. Completing this type of acquisition will certainly reduce the economic performance of the bidding firm.

The only time it might make sense to "win" a bidding war is when the winning firm possesses a rare and private or a rare and costly-to-imitate economy of scope with a target that is more valuable than the strategic relatedness that exists between any other bidders and that target. In this setting, the winning firm may be able to earn a profit if it is able to fully realize the value of its relationship with the target.

Close the Deal Quickly

Another rule of thumb for obtaining superior performance from implementing merger and acquisition strategies is to close the deal quickly. All the economic processes that make it difficult for bidding firms to earn economic profits from acquiring a strategically related target take time to unfold. It takes time for other bidders to become aware of the economic value associated with acquiring a target; it takes time for the target to recruit other bidders; information leakage becomes more of a problem over time; and so forth. A bidding firm that begins and ends the bidding process quickly may forestall some of these processes and thereby retain some superior performance for itself.

The admonition to close the deal quickly should not be taken to mean that bidding firms need to make their acquisition decisions quickly. Indeed, the search for valuable and rare economies of scope should be undertaken with great care. There should be little rush in isolating and evaluating acquisition candidates. However, once a target firm has been located and valued, bidding firms have a strong incentive to reduce the period of time between the first bid and the completion of the deal. The longer this period of negotiation, the less likely it is that the bidding firm will earn economic profits from the acquisition.

Complete Acquisitions in "Thinly Traded" Markets

Finally, an acquisition strategy can be a source of economic profits to bidding firms if these firms implement this corporate strategy in what could be described as "thinly traded markets." In general, a **thinly traded market** is a market where there are only a small number of buyers and sellers, where information about opportunities in this market is not widely known, and where interests besides purely maximizing the value of a firm can be important. In the context of mergers and acquisitions, thinly traded markets are markets where only a few (often only one) firms are implementing acquisition strategies. These unique firms may be the only firms that understand the full value of the acquisition opportunities in this market. Even target firm managers may not fully understand the value of the economic opportunities in these markets, and, if they do, they may have other interests besides maximizing the value of their firm if it becomes the object of a takeover.

In general, thinly traded merger and acquisition markets are highly fragmented. Competition in these markets occurs at the local level, as one small local firm competes with other small local firms for a common group of geographically defined customers. Most of these small firms are privately held. Many are sole proprietorships. Examples of these thinly traded markets have included, at various points in history, the printing industry, the fast-food industry, the used-car industry, the dry-cleaning industry, and the barber shop/hair salon industry.

As was suggested in Chapter 2, the major opportunity in all highly fragmented industries is consolidation. In the context of mergers and acquisitions, consolidation can occur by one firm (or a small number of firms) buying numerous independent firms to realize economies of scope in these industries. Often, these economies of scope reflect economies of scale in these industries—economies of scale that were not realized in a highly fragmented setting. As long as the number of firms implementing this consolidation strategy is small, then the market for corporate control in these markets will probably be less than perfectly competitive, and opportunities for profits from implementing an acquisition strategy may be possible.

More generally, if a merger or acquisition contest is played out through full-page ads in *The Wall Street Journal*, the ability of bidding firms to gain competitive advantages from their acquisitions is limited. Such highly public acquisitions are likely to lead to very competitive markets for corporate control. Competitive markets for corporate control, in turn, assure that the equity holders of the target firm will appropriate any value that could be created by an acquisition. However, if these contests occur in obscure, out-of-the-way industries, it is more likely that bidding firms will be able to earn profits from their acquisitions.

Service Corporation International: An Example

Empirical research on mergers and acquisitions suggests that it is not easy for bidding firms to earn economic profits from these strategies. However, it may be possible for some bidding firms, some of the time, to do so. One firm that has been successful in gaining competitive advantages from its merger and acquisition strategies is Service Corporation International (SCI). Service Corporation International is in the funeral home and cemetery business. It grew from a collection of five funeral homes in 1967 to being the largest owner of cemeteries and funeral homes in the United States today. It has done this through an aggressive and what was until recently a highly profitable acquisitions program in this historically fragmented industry.

The valuable and rare economy of scope that SCI brought to the funeral home industry is the application of traditional business practices in a highly fragmented and not often professionally managed industry. Service Corporation International–owned funeral homes operate with gross margins approaching 30 percent, nearly three times the gross margins of independently owned funeral homes. Among other things, higher margins reflected savings from centralized purchasing services, centralized embalming and professional services, and the sharing of underutilized resources (including hearses) among funeral homes within geographic regions. Service Corporation International's scale advantages made a particular funeral home more valuable to SCI than to one of SCI's smaller competitors, and more valuable than if a particular funeral home was left as a stand-alone business.

Moreover, the funeral homes that SCI targeted for acquisition were, typically, family owned and lacked heirs to continue the business. Many of the owners or operators of these funeral homes were not fully aware of the value of their operations to SCI (they are morticians more than business managers), nor were they just interested in maximizing the sale price of their funeral homes. Rather, they were often looking to maintain continuity of service in a community, secure employment for their loyal employees, and ensure a comfortable (if not lavish) retirement for themselves. Being acquired by SCI was likely to be the only alternative to closing the funeral home once an owner or operator retired. Extracting less than the full value of the funeral home when selling to SCI often seemed preferable to other alternatives.

Because SCI's acquisition of funeral homes exploited real and valuable economies of scope, this strategy had the potential for generating superior economic performance. Because SCI was, for many years, the only firm implementing this strategy in the funeral home industry, because the funeral homes that SCI acquired were generally not publicly traded, and because the owner or operators of these funeral homes often had interests besides simply maximizing the price of their operation when they sold it, it seems likely that SCI's acquisition strategy generated superior economic performance for many years. However, in the last several years, information about SCI's acquisition strategy has become widely known. This has led other funeral homes to begin bidding to acquire formerly independent funeral homes. Moreover, independent funeral home owners have become more aware of their full value to SCI. Although SCI's economy of scope with independent funeral homes is still valuable, it is no longer rare, and thus it is no longer a source of economic profits to SCI. Put differently, the imperfectly

TABLE 10.6 Rules for Target
Firm Managers

1. Seek information from bidders.
2. Invite other bidders to join the bidding competition.
3. Delay but do not stop the acquisition.

competitive market for corporate control that SCI was able to exploit for almost 10 years has become more perfectly competitive. Future acquisitions by SCI are not likely to be a source of sustained competitive advantage and economic profit. For these reasons, SCI is currently reevaluating its corporate strategy, attempting to discover a new way that it might be able to generate superior profits.[21]

Implications for Target Firm Managers

Although bidding firm managers can do several things to attempt to maximize the probability of earning economic profits from their merger and acquisition strategies, target firm managers can attempt to counter these efforts to ensure that the owners of target firms appropriate whatever value is created by a merger or acquisition. These "rules" for target firm managers are summarized in Table 10.6.

Seek Information from Bidders
One way a bidder can attempt to obtain superior performance from implementing an acquisition strategy is to keep information about the source and value of the strategic relatedness that exists between the bidder and target private. If that relationship is actually worth $12,000, but targets believe it is only worth $8,000, then a target might be willing to settle for a bid of $8,000 and, thereby, forgo the extra $4,000 it could have extracted from the bidder. Once the target knows that its true value to the bidder is $12,000, it is in a much better position to obtain this full value when the acquisition is completed. Therefore, not only should a bidding firm inform itself about the value of a target, target firms must inform themselves about their value to potential bidders. In this way, they can help obtain the full value of their assets.

Invite Other Bidders to Join the Bidding Competition
Once a target firm is fully aware of the nature and value of the economies of scope that exist between it and current bidding firms, it can exploit this information by seeking other firms that may have the same relationship with it and then informing these firms of a potential acquisition opportunity. By inviting other firms into the bidding process, the target firm increases the competitiveness of the market for corporate control, thereby increasing the probability that the value created by an acquisition will be fully captured by the target firm.

Delay, but Do Not Stop, the Acquisition
As suggested earlier, bidding firms have a strong incentive to expedite the acquisition process in order to prevent other bidders from becoming involved in an acquisition. Of course, the target firm wants other bidding firms to enter the process. To increase the probability of receiving more than one bid, target firms have a strong incentive to delay an acquisition.

The objective, however, should be to delay an acquisition to create a more competitive market for corporate control, not to stop an acquisition. If a valuable economy of scope exists between a bidding firm and a target firm, the merger of these two firms will create economic value. If the market for corporate control within which this merger occurs is competitive, then the equity holders of the target firm will appropriate the full value of this economy of scope. Preventing an acquisition in this setting can be very costly to the equity holders of the target firm.

Target firm managers can engage in a wide variety of activities to delay the completion of an acquisition. Some common responses of target firm management to takeover efforts, along with their economic implications for the equity holders of target firms, are discussed in the Research Made Relevant feature.

VRIO

Organizing to Implement a Merger or Acquisition

To realize the full value of any strategic relatedness that exists between a bidding firm and a target firm, the merged organizations must be organized appropriately. The realization of each of the types of strategic relatedness discussed earlier in this chapter requires at least some coordination and integration between the bidding and target firms after an acquisition has occurred. For example, to realize economies of scale from an acquisition, bidding and target firms must coordinate in the combined firm the functions that are sensitive to economies of scale. To realize the value of any technology that a bidding firm acquires from a target firm, the combined firm must use this technology in developing, manufacturing, or selling its products. To exploit underutilized leverage capacity in the target firm, the balance sheets of the bidding and target firms must be merged, and the resulting firm must then seek additional debt funding. To realize the opportunity of replacing the target firm's inefficient management with more efficient management from the bidding firm, these management changes must actually take place.

Post-acquisition coordination and integration is essential if bidding and target firms are to realize the full potential of the strategic relatedness that drove the acquisition in the first place. If a bidding firm decides not to coordinate or integrate any of its business activities with the activities of a target firm, then why was this target firm acquired? Just as corporate diversification requires the active management of linkages among different parts of a firm, mergers and acquisitions (as one way in which corporate diversification strategies can be created) require the active management of linkages between a bidding and a target firm.

Post-Merger Integration and Implementing a Diversification Strategy

Given that most merger and acquisition strategies are used to create corporate diversification strategies, the organizational approaches previously described for implementing diversification are relevant for implementing merger and acquisition strategies as well. Thus, mergers and acquisitions designed to create diversification strategies should be managed through the M-form structure. The management control systems and compensation policies associated with implementing diversification strategies should also be applied in organizing to implement merger and acquisition strategies. In contrast, mergers and acquisitions designed to create vertical integration strategies should be managed through the U-form structure and have management controls and compensation policies consistent with this strategy.

Special Challenges in Post-Merger Integration

Although, in general, organizing to implement merger and acquisition strategies can be seen as a special case of organizing to implement corporate diversification strategies or vertical integration strategies, implementing merger and acquisition strategies can create special problems. Most of these problems reflect the fact that

Research Made Relevant

Managers in potential target firms can respond to takeover attempts in a variety of ways. As suggested in Table 10.7, some of these responses increase the wealth of target firm shareholders, some have no impact on target firm shareholders, and others decrease the wealth of target firm shareholders.

Management responses that have the effect of reducing the value of target firms include greenmail, standstill agreements, and "poison pills." Each of these is an anti-takeover action that target firm managers can take to reduce the wealth of target firm equity holders. **Greenmail** is a maneuver in which a target firm's management purchases any of the target firm's stock owned by a bidder and does so for a price that is greater than the current market value of that stock. Greenmail effectively ends a bidding firm's effort to acquire a particular target and does so in a way that can greatly reduce the wealth of a target firm's equity holders. Not only do these equity holders not appropriate

The Wealth Effects of Management Responses to Takeover Attempts

any economic value that could have been created if an acquisition had been completed, but they have to bear the cost of the premium price that management pays to buy its stock back from the bidding firm.

Not surprisingly, target firms that resort to greenmail substantially reduce the economic wealth of their equity holders. One study found that

the value of target firms that pay greenmail drops, on average, 1.76 percent. Another study reported a 2.85 percent drop in the value of such firms. These reductions in value are greater if greenmail leads to the cancellation of a takeover effort. Indeed, this second study found that such episodes led to a 5.50 percent reduction in the value of target firms. These reductions in value as a response to greenmail activities stand in marked contrast to the generally positive market response to efforts by a firm to repurchase its own shares in nongreenmail situations.

Standstill agreements are often negotiated in conjunction with greenmail. A standstill agreement is a contract between a target and a bidding firm wherein the bidding firm agrees not to attempt to take over the target for some period of time. When a target firm negotiates a standstill agreement, it prevents the current acquisition effort from being completed, and it reduces the number of bidders that might become involved in future

---

1. Responses that reduce the wealth of target firm equity holders:
   - Greenmail
   - Standstill agreements
   - Poison pills

2. Responses that do not affect the wealth of target firm equity holders:
   - Shark repellents
   - Pac Man defense
   - Crown jewel sale
   - Lawsuits

3. Responses that increase the wealth of target firm equity holders:
   - Search for white knights
   - Creation of bidding auctions
   - Golden parachutes

TABLE 10.7 The Wealth Effects of Target Firm Management Responses to Acquisition Efforts

(Continued)

acquisition efforts. Thus, the equity holders of this target firm forgo any value that could have been created if the current acquisition had occurred, and they also lose some of the value that they could have appropriated in future acquisition episodes by the target's inviting multiple bidders into a market for corporate control.

Standstill agreements, either alone or in conjunction with greenmail, reduce the economic value of a target firm. One study found that standstill agreements that were unaccompanied by stock repurchase agreements reduced the value of a target firm by 4.05 percent. Such agreements, in combination with stock repurchases, reduced the value of a target firm by 4.52 percent.

So-called **poison pills** include any of a variety of actions that target firm managers can take to make the acquisition of the target prohibitively expensive. In one common poison-pill maneuver, a target firm issues rights to its current stockholders indicating that if the firm is acquired in an unfriendly takeover, it will distribute a special cash dividend to stockholders. This cash dividend effectively increases the cost of acquiring the target and can discourage otherwise interested bidding firms from attempting to acquire this target. Another poison-pill tactic substitutes the distribution of additional shares of a target firm's stock, at very low prices, for the special cash dividend. Issuing this low-price stock to current stockholders effectively undermines the value of a bidding firm's equity investment in a target and thus increases the cost of the acquisition. Other poison pills involve

granting current stockholders other rights—rights that effectively increase the cost of an unfriendly takeover.

Although poison pills are creative devices that target firms can use to prevent an acquisition, they generally have not been very effective. If a bidding firm and a target firm are strategically related, the value that can be created in an acquisition can be substantial, and most of this value will be appropriated by the stockholders of the target firm. Thus, target firm stockholders have a strong incentive to see that the target firm is acquired, and they are amenable to direct offers made by a bidding firm to them as individual investors; these are called **tender offers**. However, to the extent that poison pills actually do prevent mergers and acquisitions, they are usually bad for the equity holders of target firms.

Target firm management can also engage in a wide variety of actions that have little or no impact on the wealth of a target firm's equity holders. One class of these responses is known as shark repellents. **Shark repellents** include a variety of relatively minor corporate governance changes that, in principle, are supposed to make it somewhat more difficult to acquire a target firm. Common examples of shark repellents include **supermajority voting rules** (which specify that more than 50 percent of the target firm's board of directors must approve a takeover) and state incorporation laws (in some states, incorporation laws make it difficult to acquire a firm incorporated in that state). However, if the value created by an acquisition is sufficiently large, these shark repellents will neither slow

an acquisition attempt significantly nor prevent it from being completed.

Another response that does not affect the wealth of target firm equity holders is known as the **Pac Man defense**. Targets using this tactic fend off an acquisition by taking over the firm or firms bidding for them. Just as in the old video game, the hunted becomes the hunter; the target turns the tables on current and potential bidders. It should not be too surprising that the Pac Man defense does not, on average, either hurt or help the stockholders of target firms. In this defense, targets become bidders, and we know from empirical literature that, on average, bidding firms earn only zero economic profits from their acquisition efforts. Thus, one would expect that, on average, the Pac Man defense would generate only zero economic profits for the stockholders of target firms implementing it.

Another ineffective and inconsequential response is called a **crown jewel sale**. The idea behind a crown jewel sale is that sometimes a bidding firm is interested in just a few of the businesses currently being operated by the target firm. These businesses are the target firm's "crown jewels." To prevent an acquisition, the target firm can sell off these crown jewels, either directly to the bidding firm or by setting up a separate company to own and operate these businesses. In this way, the bidding firm is likely to be less interested in acquiring the target.

A final, relatively ineffective defense that most target firm managers pursue is filing lawsuits against bidding firms. Indeed, at least in the United States, the filing of a lawsuit has been almost automatic as soon as an acquisition effort is announced. These suits, however, usually do not delay or stop an acquisition or merger.

Finally, as suggested in Table 10.7, some of the actions that the management of target firms can take to delay (but not stop) an acquisition actually benefit target firm equity holders. The first of these is the search for a **white knight**—another bidding firm that agrees to acquire a particular target in the place of the original bidding firm. Target firm management may prefer to be acquired by some bidding firms more than by others. For example, it may be that some bidding firms possess much more valuable economies of scope with a target firm than other bidding firms. It may also be that some bidding firms will take a longer-term view in managing a target firm's assets than other bidding firms. In both cases, target firm managers are likely to prefer some bidding firms over others.

Whatever motivation a target firm's management has, inviting a white knight to bid on a target firm has the effect of increasing the number of firms bidding for a target by at least one. If there is currently only one bidder, inviting a white knight into the bidding competition doubles the number of firms bidding for a target. As the number of bidders increases, the competitiveness of the market for corporate control and the likelihood that the equity holders of the target firm will appropriate all the value created by an acquisition also increase. On average, the entrance of a white knight into a competitive bidding contest for a target firm increases the wealth of target firm equity holders by 17 percent.

If adding one firm into the competitive bidding process increases the wealth of target firm equity holders some, then adding more firms to the process is likely to increase this wealth even more. Target firms can accomplish this outcome by creating an **auction** among bidding firms. On average, the creation of an auction among multiple bidders increases the wealth of target firm equity holders by 20 percent.

A third action that the managers of a target firm can take to increase the wealth of their equity holders from an acquisition effort is the institution of **golden parachutes**. A golden parachute is a compensation arrangement between a firm and its senior management team that promises these individuals a substantial cash payment if their firm is acquired and they lose their jobs in the process. These cash payments can appear to be very large, but they are actually quite small in comparison to the total value that can be created if a merger or acquisition is completed. In this sense, golden parachutes are a small price to pay to give a potential target firm's top managers incentives not to stand in the way of completing a takeover of their firm. Put differently, golden parachutes reduce agency problems for the equity holders of a potential target firm by aligning the interests of top managers with the interests of that firm's stockholders. On average, when a firm announces golden parachute compensation packages for its top management team, the value of this potential target firm's equity increases by seven percent.

Overall, substantial evidence suggests that delaying an acquisition long enough to ensure that a competitive market for corporate control emerges can significantly benefit the equity holders of target firms. One study found that when target firms did not delay the completion of an acquisition, their equity holders experienced, on average, a 36 percent increase in the value of their stock once the acquisition was complete. If, however, target firms did delay the completion of the acquisition, this average increase in value jumped to 65 percent.

Of course, target firm managers can delay too long. Delaying too long can create opportunity costs for their firm's equity holders, because these individuals do not actually realize the gain from an acquisition until it has been completed. Also, long delays can jeopardize the completion of an acquisition, in which case the equity holders of the target firm do not realize any gains from the acquisition.

Sources: R. Walkling and M. Long' (1984). "Agency theory, managerial welfare, and takeover bid resistance." *Rand Journal of Economics*, 15(1), pp. 54–68; R. D. Kosnik (1987). "Greenmail: A study of board performance in corporate governance." *Administrative Science Quarterly*, 32, pp. 163–185; J. Walsh (1989). "Doing a deal: Merger and acquisition negotiations and their impact upon target company top management turnover." *Strategic Management Journal*, 10, pp. 307–322; L. Y. Dann and H. DeAngelo (1983). "Standstill agreements, privately negotiated stock repurchases, and the market for corporate control." *Journal of Financial Economics*, 11, pp. 275–300; M. Bradey and L. Wakeman (1983). "The wealth effects of targeted share repurchases." *Journal of Financial Economics*, 11, pp. 301–328; H. Singh and F. Haricento (1989). "Top management tenure, corporate ownership and the magnitude of golden parachutes." *Strategic Management Journal*, 10, pp. 143–156; and T. A. Turk (1987). "The determinants of management responses to interfirm tender offers and their effect on shareholder wealth." Unpublished doctoral dissertation, Graduate School of Management, University of California at Irvine.

operational, functional, strategic, and cultural differences between bidding and target firms involved in a merger or acquisition are likely to be much greater than these same differences between the different parts of a diversified or vertically integrated business that was not created through acquisition. The reason for this difference is that the firms involved in a merger or acquisition have had a separate existence, separate histories, separate management philosophies, and separate strategies.

Differences between bidding and target firms can manifest themselves in a wide variety of ways. For example, they may own and operate different computer systems, different telephone systems, and other conflicting technologies. These firms might have very different human resource policies and practices. One firm might have a very generous retirement and health care program; the other, a less generous program. One firm's compensation system might focus on high salaries; the other firm's compensation system might focus on large cash bonuses and stock options. Also, these firms might have very different relationships with customers. At one firm, customers might be thought of as business partners; in another, the relationship with customers might be more arm's-length in character. Integrating bidding and target firms may require the resolution of numerous differences.

Perhaps the most significant challenge in integrating bidding and target firms has to do with cultural differences.[22] In Chapter 3, it was suggested that it can often be difficult to change a firm's organizational culture. The fact that a firm has been acquired does not mean that the culture in that firm will rapidly change to become more like the culture of the bidding firm; cultural conflicts can last for very long periods of time. Indeed, the difference between the relative success of Renault's acquisition of Nissan and DaimlerChrysler's acquisition of Mitsubishi has largely been attributed to the inability of Mitsubishi to modify its traditional management culture.

Cultural differences were apparently an important part of the post-merger integration challenges in the merger between Bank One and First Chicago Bank. Bank One had many operations and offices in small and medium-sized cities in the Midwest. First Chicago was a more urban bank. Different kinds of employees may have been attracted to these different firms, leading to significant cultural clashes as these two firms sought to rationalize their combined operations.[23] Most reports suggest that First Chicago employees have come to dominate this "merger." Unlike the merger between Bank One and First Chicago, JP Morgan Chase clearly acquired Bank One in 2004.

Operational, functional, strategic, and cultural differences between bidding and target firms can all be compounded by the merger and acquisition process—especially if that process was unfriendly. Unfriendly takeovers can generate anger and animosity among the target firm management that is directed toward the management of the bidding firm. Research has shown that top management turnover is much higher in firms that have been taken over compared to firms not subject to takeovers, reflecting one approach to resolving these management conflicts.[24]

The difficulties often associated with organizing to implement a merger and acquisition strategy can be thought of as an additional cost of the acquisition process. Bidding firms, in addition to estimating the value of the strategic relatedness between themselves and a target firm, also need to estimate the cost of organizing to implement an acquisition. The value that a target firm brings to a bidding firm through an acquisition should be discounted by the cost of organizing to implement this strategy. In some circumstances, it may be the case that the cost of organizing to realize the value of strategic relatedness between a bidding firm and a target may be greater than the value of that strategic relatedness, in which case the acquisition should not occur. For this reason, many observers argue that potential economies of scope between bidding and target firms are often not fully realized. For example, despite the numerous multimedia mergers in the 1990s (Time Warner, Turner Broadcasting, and AOL; The Walt Disney Company, Capital Cities/ABC, and ESPN; General Electric and NBC; Westinghouse and CBS), few seem to have been able to realize any important economies of scope.[25]

Although organizing to implement mergers and acquisitions can be a source of significant cost, it can also be a source of value and opportunity. Some scholars have suggested that value creation can continue to occur in a merger or acquisition long after the formal acquisition is complete.[26] As bidding and target firms continue to coordinate and integrate their operations, unanticipated opportunities for value creation can be discovered. These sources of value could not have been anticipated at the time a firm was originally acquired (and thus are, at least partially, a manifestation of a bidding firm's good luck), but bidding firms can influence the probability of discovering these unanticipated sources of value by learning to cooperate effectively with target firms while organizing to implement a merger or acquisition strategy.

Summary

Firms can use mergers and acquisitions to create corporate diversification and vertical integration strategies. Mergers or acquisitions between strategically unrelated firms can be expected to generate only competitive parity for both bidders and targets. Thus, firms contemplating merger and acquisition strategies must search for strategically related targets.

Several sources of strategic relatedness have been discussed in literature. On average, the acquisition of strategically related targets does create economic value, but most of that value is captured by the equity holders of target firms. The equity holders of bidding firms generally gain competitive parity even when bidding firms acquire strategically related targets. Empirical research on mergers and acquisitions is consistent with these expectations. On average, acquisitions do create value, but that value is captured by target firms, and acquisitions do not hurt bidding firms.

Given that most mergers and acquisitions generate only zero economic profits for bidding firms, an important question becomes: "Why are there so many mergers and acquisitions?" Explanations include (1) the desire to ensure firm survival, (2) the existence of free cash flow, (3) agency problems between bidding firm managers and equity holders, (4) managerial hubris, and (5) the possibility that some bidding firms might earn economic profits from implementing merger and acquisition strategies.

To gain competitive advantages and economic profits from mergers or acquisitions, these strategies must be either valuable, rare, and private or valuable, rare, and costly to imitate. In addition, a bidding firm may exploit unanticipated sources of strategic relatedness with a target. These unanticipated sources of relatedness can also be a source of economic profits for a bidding firm. These observations have several implications for the managers of bidding and target firms.

Organizing to implement a merger or acquisition strategy can be seen as a special case of organizing to implement a corporate diversification or vertical integration strategy. However, historical differences between bidding and target firms may make the integration of different parts of a firm created through acquisitions more difficult than if a firm is not created through acquisitions. Cultural differences between bidding and target firms are particularly problematic. Bidding firms need to estimate the cost of organizing to implement a merger or acquisition strategy and discount the value of a target by that cost. However, organizing to implement a merger or acquisition can also be a way that bidding and target firms can discover unanticipated economies of scope.

Challenge Questions

1. Consider the following scenario: A firm acquires a strategically related target after successfully fending off four other bidding firms. Under what conditions, if any, can the firm that acquired this target expect to earn an economic profit from doing so?

2. Consider this scenario: A firm acquires a strategically related target; there were no other bidding firms. Is this acquisition situation necessarily different from the situation described in question 1? Under what conditions, if any, can the firm that acquired this target expect to earn an economic profit from doing so?

3. Some researchers have argued that the existence of free cash flow can lead managers in a firm to make inappropriate acquisition decisions. To avoid these problems, these authors have argued that firms should increase their debt-to-equity ratio and "soak up" free cash flow through interest and principal payments. Is free cash flow a significant problem for many firms? What are the strengths and weaknesses of increased leverage as a response to free cash flow problems in a firm?

4. The hubris hypothesis suggests that managers continue to engage in acquisitions, even though, on average, they do not generate economic profits, because of the unrealistic belief on the part of these managers that they can manage a target firm's assets more efficiently than that firm's current management. This type of systematic nonrationality usually does not last too long in competitive market conditions: Firms led by managers with these unrealistic beliefs change, are acquired, or go bankrupt in the long run. Are there any attributes of the market for corporate control that suggest that managerial hubris could exist in this market, despite its performance-reducing implications for bidding firms? If yes, what are these attributes? If no, can the hubris hypothesis be a legitimate explanation for continuing acquisition activity?

5. It has been shown that so-called poison pills rarely prevent a takeover from occurring. In fact, sometimes when a firm announces that it is instituting a poison pill, its stock price goes up. Why?

Problem Set

1. For each of the following scenarios, estimate how much value an acquisition will create, how much of that value will be appropriated by each of the bidding firms, and how much of that value will be appropriated by each of the target firms. In each of these scenarios, assume that firms do not face significant capital constraints.

(a) A bidding firm, A, is worth $27,000 as a stand-alone entity. A target firm, B, is worth $12,000 as a stand-alone entity, but $18,000 if it is acquired and integrated with Firm A. Several other firms are interested in acquiring Firm B, and Firm B is also worth $18,000 if it is acquired by these other firms. If Firm A acquired Firm B, would this acquisition create value? If yes, how much? How much of this value would the equity holders of Firm A receive? How much would the equity holders of Firm B receive?

(b) The same scenario as above except that the value of Firm B, if it is acquired by the other firms interested in it, is only $12,000.

(c) The same scenario in part (a), except that the value of Firm B, if it is acquired by the other firms interested in it, is $16,000.

(d) The same scenario as in part (b), except that Firm B contacts several other firms and explains to them how they can create the same value with Firm B that Firm A does.

(e) The same scenario as in part (b), except that Firm B sues Firm A. After suing Firm A, Firm B installs a "supermajority" rule in how its board of directors operates. After putting this new rule in place, Firm B offers to buy back any stock purchased by Firm A for 20 percent above the current market price.

End Notes

1. See Welch, D., and G. Edmondson. (2004). "A shaky automotive ménage à trois." *BusinessWeek*, May 10, pp. 40–41.
2. www.streetinsider.com/Press+Release/PricewaterhouseCoopers+outlook.
3. Money.cnn.com/magazines/fortune/fortune500/2007.
4. Here, and throughout this chapter, it is assumed that capital markets are semi-strong efficient, that is, all publicly available information about the value of a firm's assets is reflected in the market price of those assets. One implication of semi-strong efficiency is that firms will be able to gain access to the capital they need to pursue any strategy that generates positive present value. See Fama, E. F. (1970). "Efficient capital markets: A review of theory and empirical work." *Journal of Finance*, 25, pp. 383–417.
5. See Trautwein, I. (1990). "Merger motives and merger prescriptions." *Strategic Management Journal*, 11, pp. 283–295; and Walter, G., and J. B. Barney. (1990). "Management objectives in mergers and acquisitions." *Strategic Management Journal*, 11, pp. 79–86. The three lists of potential links between bidding and target firms were developed by the Federal Trade Commission; Lubatkin, M. (1983). "Mergers and the performance of the acquiring firm." *Academy of Management Review*, 8, pp. 218–225; and Jensen, M. C., and R. S. Ruback. (1983). "The market for corporate control: The scientific evidence." *Journal of Financial Economics*, 11, pp. 5–50.
6. See Huey, J. (1995). "Eisner explains everything." *Fortune*, April 17, pp. 44–68; and Lefton, T. (1996). "Fitting ABC and ESPN into Disney: Hands in glove." *Brandweek*, 37(18), April 29, pp. 30–40.
7. See Rumelt, R. (1974). *Strategy, structure, and economic performance.* Cambridge, MA: Harvard University Press.
8. The first study was by Ravenscraft, D. J., and F. M. Scherer. (1987). *Mergers, sell-offs, and economic efficiency.* Washington, DC: Brookings Institution. The second study was by Porter, M. E. (1987). "From competitive advantage to corporate strategy." *Harvard Business Review*, 3, pp. 43–59.
9. This is because if the combined firm is worth $32,000 the bidder firm is worth $15,000 on its own. If a bidder pays, say, $20,000 for this target, it will be paying $20,000 for a firm that can only add $17,000 in value. So, a $20,000 bid would lead to a $3,000 economic loss.
10. This is Jensen, M. C., and R. S. Ruback. (1983). "The market for corporate control: The scientific evidence." *Journal of Financial Economics*, 11, pp. 5–50.
11. See Lubatkin, M. (1987). "Merger strategies and stockholder value." *Strategic Management Journal*, 8, pp. 39–53; and Singh, H., and C. A. Montgomery. (1987). "Corporate acquisition strategies and economic performance." *Strategic Management Journal*, 8, pp. 377–386.
12. See Grant, L. (1995). "Here comes Hugh." *Fortune*, August 21, pp. 43–52; Serwer, A. E. (1995). "Why bank mergers are good for your savings account." *Fortune*, October 2, p. 32; and Deogun, N. (2000). "Europe catches merger fever as global volume sets record." *The Wall Street Journal*, January 3, p. R8.
13. The concept of free cash flow has been emphasized in Jensen, M. C. (1986). "Agency costs of free cash flow, corporate finance, and takeovers." *American Economic Review*, 76, pp. 323–329; and Jensen, M.

14. (1988). "Takeovers: Their causes and consequences." *Journal of Economic Perspectives*, 2, pp. 21–48.
14. See Miles, R. H., and K. S. Cameron. (1982). *Coffin nails and corporate strategies.* Upper Saddle River, NJ: Prentice Hall.
15. Roll, R. (1986). "The hubris hypothesis of corporate takeovers." *Journal of Business*, 59, pp. 205–216.
16. See Dodd, P. (1980). "Merger proposals, managerial discretion and stockholder wealth." *Journal of Financial Economics*, 8, pp. 105–138; Eger, C. E. (1983). "An empirical test of the redistribution effect in pure exchange mergers." *Journal of Financial and Quantitative Analysis*, 18, pp. 547–572; Firth, M. (1980). "Takeovers, shareholder returns, and the theory of the firm." *Quarterly Journal of Economics*, 94, pp. 235–260; Varaiya, N. (1985). "A test of Roll's hubris hypothesis of corporate takeovers." Working paper, Southern Methodist University, School of Business; Ruback, R. S., and W. H. Mikkelson. (1984). "Corporate investments in common stock." Working paper, Massachusetts Institute of Technology, Sloan School of Business; Ruback, R. S. (1982). "The Conoco takeover and stockholder returns." *Sloan Management Review*, 14, pp. 13–33.
17. This section of the chapter draws on Barney, J. B. (1988). "Returns to bidding firms in mergers and acquisitions: Reconsidering the relatedness hypothesis." *Strategic Management Journal*, 9, pp. 71–78.
18. See Turk, T. A. (1987). "The determinants of management responses to interfirm tender offers and their effect on shareholder wealth." Unpublished doctoral dissertation, Graduate School of Management, University of California at Irvine. In fact, this is an example of an anti-takeover action that can increase the value of a target firm. These anti-takeover actions are discussed later in this chapter.
19. See Bower, J. (1996). "WPP-integrating icons." Harvard Business School Case No. 9-396-249.
20. See Jemison, D. B., and S. B. Sitkin. (1986). "Corporate acquisitions: A process perspective." *Academy of Management Review*, 11, pp. 145–163.
21. Blackwell, R. D. (1998). "Service Corporation International." Presented to The Cullman Symposium, October, Columbus, OH.
22. Cartwright, S., and C. Cooper. (1993). "The role of culture compatibility in successful organizational marriage." *The Academy of Management Executive*, 7(2), pp. 57–70; and Chatterjee, S., M. Lubatkin, D. Schweiger, and Y. Weber. (1992). "Cultural differences and shareholder value in related mergers: Linking equity and human capital." *Strategic Management Journal*, 13, pp. 319–334.
23. See Deogun, N. (2000). "Europe catches merger fever as global volume sets record." *The Wall Street Journal*, January 3, p. R8.
24. See Walsh, J., and J. Ellwood. (1991). "Mergers, acquisitions, and the pruning of managerial deadwood." *Strategic Management Journal*, 12, pp. 201–217; and Walsh, J. (1988). "Top management turnover following mergers and acquisitions." *Strategic Management Journal*, 9, pp. 173–183.
25. Landro, L. (1995). "Giants talk synergy but few make it work." *The Wall Street Journal*, September 25, pp. B1 +. Indeed, one of these mergers was reversed when Viacom spun off CBS as a separate firm.
26. See Haspeslagh, P., and D. Jemison. (1991). *Managing acquisitions: Creating value through corporate renewal.* New York: Free Press.

11 International Strategies

After reading this chapter, you should be able to:

1. Define international strategy.

2. Describe the relationship between international strategy and other corporate strategies, including vertical integration and diversification.

3. Describe five ways that international strategies can create economic value.

4. Discuss the trade-off between local responsiveness and international integration, and transnational strategies as a way to manage this trade-off.

5. Discuss the political risks associated with international strategies and how they can be measured.

6. Discuss the rarity and imitability of international strategies.

7. Describe four different ways to organize to implement international strategies.

The Russians Are Coming

In the depths of the Cold War, some of the most monumental struggles between communism and capitalism did not take place in Vietnam, or Afghanistan, or Nicaragua, or Cuba, but on athletic fields of various shapes and sizes around the world. Like the basketball court in the 1976 Montreal Summer Olympics, where the men's team from the Soviet Union beat the U.S. team in three overtimes—in such controversial circumstances that members of the U.S. team didn't even show up to accept their medal. Or, like the 1980 Lake Placid Winter Olympics, where the U.S. men's ice hockey team upset the heavily favored team from the Soviet Union, on its way to winning the gold medal with the cheers of "USA, USA, USA" ringing throughout the rink. Or like the 1980 Moscow Summer Olympics, boycotted by much of the West in protest of the Soviet Union's invasion of Afghanistan, and the 1984 Los Angeles Summer Olympics boycotted by much of the Soviet block in retaliation for the Moscow boycott.

And so it went, until the fall of the Soviet empire in the early 1990s. Since then, teams and athletes from Russia have generally not fared well in international competitions—exemplified, perhaps, by Russia's embarrassing 7 to 1 World Cup qualifying loss to Portugal in 2004. The state apparatus that identified, housed, and trained budding world class athletes in the Soviet Union days simply did not survive the fall of the Soviet Union. By the early 2000s, the best Russian athletes—including, for example, Wimbledon tennis champion Maria Sharapova—were leaving Russia to live in the West, often in Florida.

All of that is beginning to change. Russia's current government leaders are apparently committed to rebuilding Russia's athletic prowess. This time, however, these efforts will not be sponsored by the state, but by wealthy private citizens, citizens who have a love of sport—and more money than they know what to do with.

When the Soviet Union fell, a small number of men were able to use the resulting chaos to gain control of several key industries. Later, when Russia was on the verge of financial collapse, these "oligarchs" rescued the state with loans, loans that ultimately increased their wealth even more. Currently, 22 men control over 40 percent of the Russian economy. Under the political slogan, "United Russia is an athletic Russia," the Russian government—under the leadership of its current Prime Minister (and former Leningrad city judo champion) Vladimir Putin—has asked these wealthy men to rebuild the Russian athletic system. Partly out of a sense of patriotism, an interest in sport, and a reluctance to not do what the Russian government has asked, these men have responded.

The early results suggest that Russia may once again emerge as a major figure in world sports. For example, some Russian businessmen have begun taking ownership

positions in well-known sports clubs around the world, including Chelsea and Arsenal, both members of the English Premier League. Several Russian businessmen have joined forces to create the Kontinental Hockey League (KHL) and successfully lured former New York Rangers captain Jaromir Jagr—for $14 million over two years, tax free—to play in a league designed to compete with the National Hockey League. Kobe Bryant—when asked if he would ever be willing to play in a European basketball league—joked by saying "$40 million a year, and I'm there." Within days, several Russians had put together a deal for this amount—which Kobe apparently politely refused. And in women's basketball, certain Russian businessmen have put together, arguably, the most powerful teams in the world. Women playing in the WNBA can increase their salaries by over ten times by playing in the WNBA off-season in Russia for teams like the Spartak Moscow Region. And Russia's national soccer team? It has gone from thirty-fourth in the world in November of 2004 to seventh in the world in November of 2008.

Stanislaw Tokarski/Shutterstock

These results, together with ongoing investments in junior training camps in soccer, basketball, and numerous other sports, suggest that Russia may be an important player on the world sports scene for some time to come.

Sources: Alexander Wolff. (2008). "To Russia with love." *Sports Illustrated*, December 15, 2008, pp. 58–67; Dick Pond (2006). *Inside the Olympics*. New York: Wiley; and Corbis/Sigma..

Just like in international sports, business competition can come from numerous sources around the world. In anticipation of these challenges, many firms proactively engage in international strategies.

Firms that operate in multiple countries simultaneously are implementing **international strategies**. International strategies are actually a special case of the corporate strategies already discussed in Part 3 of this book. That is, firms can vertically integrate, diversify, form strategic alliances, and implement mergers and acquisitions, all across national borders. Thus, the reasons why firms might want to pursue these corporate strategies identified in Chapters 6 through 10 also apply to firms pursuing international strategies. For this reason, this chapter emphasizes the unique characteristics of international strategies.

At some level, international strategies have existed since before the beginning of recorded time. Certainly, trade across country borders has been an important determinant of the wealth of individuals, companies, and countries throughout history. The search for trading opportunities and trade routes was a primary motivation for the exploration of much of the world. Therefore, it would be inappropriate to argue that international strategies are an invention of the late twentieth century.

Strategy in the Emerging Enterprise

Logitech is a leader in peripheral devices for personal computers and related digital technology. With 2008 sales of $2.4 billion, and profits of $286 million, Logitech sells computer pointing devices (e.g., computer mice and trackballs), regular and cordless computer keyboards, webcam cameras, PC headsets and VoIP (voice over Internet protocol) handsets, PC game controllers, and speakers and headphones for PCs in virtually every country in the world. Headquartered in Switzerland, and with offices in California, Switzerland, China, Hong Kong, Taiwan, and Japan, Logitech is a classic example of a firm pursuing an international strategy.

And it has always been this way. Not that Logitech had sales of $2.4 billion when it was first founded, in 1981. But Logitech was one of the first entrepreneurial firms that began its operations—way back in 1981—by pursuing an international strategy. At its founding, for example, Logitech had offices in Switzerland and the United States. Within two years of its

International Entrepreneurial Firms: The Case of Logitech

founding, it had research and development and manufacturing operations in Taiwan and Ireland. In short, Logitech was "born global."

Of course, not all entrepreneurial firms pursue international strategies from their inception. But this is less unusual for firms in high technology industries, where global technical standards make it possible for products made in one market to be sold as "plug and play" products in markets around the world. Because Logitech's pointing

devices and other peripherals could be used by any personal computer around the world, their market—from day one—was global in scope. Indeed, in one study of firms that were "born global," most of these firms were operating in high technology markets with well-developed technical standards.

More recently, entrepreneurial firms have begun exploiting international opportunities in sourcing the manufacturing of their products. The rise of low-cost manufacturing in China, Vietnam, and the Philippines—among other places—has led increased numbers of firms, including many small and entrepreneurial firms, to outsource their manufacturing operations to these countries. In this global environment, even the smallest entrepreneurial firms must become aware of and manage the challenges associated with implementing international strategies discussed in this chapter.

Sources: Logitech.com; Logitech 10 K Report, 2008; and B. Oviatt and P. McDougall (1995). "Global start-ups: Entrepreneurs on a worldwide stage." *Academy of Management Executive*, 9, pp. 30–44.

In the past, however, the implementation of international strategies was limited to relatively small numbers of risk-taking individuals and firms. Today these strategies are becoming remarkably common. For example, in 2008, 24.2 percent of WalMart's sales revenues came from outside the United States; only about a third of Exxon Mobile's profits came from its U.S. operations; 42 percent of General Motor's automobile sales came from outside the United States; and about half of General Electric's revenues came from non-U.S. operations. And it's not only U.S-based firms that have invested in non-U.S. operations. Numerous non-U.S. firms have invested around the world as well. For example, the U.S. market provides the largest percentage of the sales of such firms as Nestlé (a Swiss food company), Toyota (a Japanese car company), and Royal Dutch/Shell Group (an energy company headquartered in both the United Kingdom and the Netherlands). Moreover, as described in the Strategy in the Emerging Enterprise section, international strategies are not limited to just huge multinational companies.

The increased use of international strategies by both large and small firms suggests that the economic opportunities associated with operating in multiple geographic markets can be substantial. However, to be a source of sustained competitive advantages for firms, these strategies must exploit a firm's valuable, rare, and costly to imitate resources and capabilities. Moreover, a firm must be appropriately organized to realize the full competitive potential of these resources and capabilities. This chapter examines the conditions under which international strategies can create economic value, as well as the conditions under which they can be sources of sustained competitive advantages.

The Value of International Strategies

VR I O

As suggested earlier, international strategies are an example of corporate strategies. So to be economically valuable, they must meet the two value criteria originally introduced in Chapter 7: They must exploit real economics of scope, and it must be costly for outside investors to realize these economies of scope on their own. Many of the economies of scope discussed in the context of vertical integration, corporate diversification, strategic alliances, and merger and acquisition strategies can be created when firms operate across multiple businesses. These same economies can also be created when firms operate across multiple geographic markets.

More generally, like all the strategies discussed in this book, to be valuable, international strategies must enable a firm to exploit environmental opportunities or neutralize environmental threats. To the extent that international strategies enable a firm to respond to its environment, they will also enable a firm to reduce its costs or increase the willingness of its customers to pay compared to what would have been the case if that firm did not pursue these strategies. Several potentially valuable economies of scope particularly relevant for firms pursuing international strategies are summarized in Table 11.1.

1. To gain access to new customers for current products or services
2. To gain access to low-cost factors of production
3. To develop new core competencies
4. To leverage current core competencies in new ways
5. To manage corporate risk

TABLE 11.1 Potential Sources of Economies of Scope for Firms Pursuing International Strategies

To Gain Access to New Customers for Current Products or Services

The most obvious economy of scope that may motivate firms to pursue an international strategy is the potential new customers for a firm's current products or services that such a strategy might generate. To the extent that customers outside a firm's domestic market are willing and able to buy a firm's current products or services, implementing an international strategy can directly increase a firm's revenues.

Internationalization and Firm Revenues

If customers outside a firm's domestic market are willing and able to purchase its products or services, then selling into these markets will increase the firm's revenues. However, it is not always clear that the products and services that a firm sells in its domestic market will also sell in foreign markets.

Are Nondomestic Customers Willing to Buy?

It may be the case that customer preferences vary significantly in a firm's domestic and foreign markets. These different preferences may require firms seeking to internationalize their operations to substantially change their current products or services before nondomestic customers are willing to purchase them.

This challenge faced many U.S. home appliance manufacturers as they looked to expand their operations into Europe and Asia. In the United States, the physical size of most home appliances (washing machines, dryers, refrigerators, dishwashers, and so forth) has become standardized, and these standard sizes are built into new homes, condominiums, and apartments. Standard sizes have also emerged in Europe and Asia. However, these non-U.S. standard sizes are much smaller than the U.S. sizes, requiring U.S. manufacturers to substantially retool their manufacturing operations in order to build products that might be attractive to Asian and European customers.[1]

Different physical standards can require a firm pursuing international opportunities to change its current products or services to sell them into a nondomestic market. Physical standards, however, can easily be measured and described. Differences in tastes can be much more challenging for firms looking to sell their products or services outside the domestic market.

The inability to anticipate differences in tastes around the world has sometimes led to very unfortunate, and often humorous, marketing blunders. For example, General Motors once introduced the Chevrolet Nova to South America, even though "No va" in Spanish means "it won't go." When Coca-Cola was first introduced in China, it was translated into Ke-kou-ke-la, which turns out to mean either "bite the wax tadpole" or "female horse stuffed with wax," depending on which dialect one speaks. Coca-Cola reintroduced its product with the name Ke-kou-ko-le, which roughly translates into "happiness in the mouth."

Coca-Cola is not the only beverage firm to run into problems internationally. Pepsi's slogan "Come alive with the Pepsi generation" was translated into "Pepsi will bring your ancestors back from the dead" in Taiwan. In Italy, a marketing campaign for Schweppes tonic water was translated into Schweppes toilet water—not a terribly appealing drink. Bacardi developed a fruity drink called "Pavian." Unfortunately, "Pavian" means baboon in German. Coors used its "Turn it loose" slogan when selling beer in Spain and Latin America. Unfortunately, "Turn it loose" was translated into "Suffer from diarrhea."

Food companies have had similar problems. Kentucky Fried Chicken's slogan "Finger-lickin' good" translates into "eat your fingers off" in Chinese. In Arabic, the "Jolly Green Giant" translates into "Intimidating Green Ogre." Frank Perdue's famous catch phrase—"It takes a tough man to make a tender chicken"—takes on a slightly different meaning when translated into Spanish—"It takes a sexually stimulated man to make a chicken affectionate." And Gerber found that it was unable to sell its baby food in Africa—with pictures of cute babies on the jar—because the tradition in Africa is to put pictures of what is inside the jar on the label. Think about it.

Other marketing blunders include Colgate's decision to introduce Cue toothpaste in France, even though Cue is the name of a French pornographic magazine; an American T-shirt manufacturer who wanted to print T-shirts in Spanish that said "I saw the Pope" (el Papa) but instead printed T-shirts that said "I saw the potato" (la papa); and Salem cigarettes, whose slogan "Salem—feeling free" translated into Japanese as "When smoking Salem, you feel so refreshed that your mind seems to be free and empty." What were they smoking?

However, of all these blunders, perhaps none tops Electrolux—a Scandinavian vacuum cleaner manufacturer. While its marketing slogan for the U.S. market does rhyme—"Nothing sucks like an Electrolux"—it doesn't really communicate what the firm had in mind.[2]

It's not just these marketing blunders that can limit sales in nondomestic markets. For example, Yugo had difficulty selling its automobiles in the United States. Apparently, U.S. consumers were unwilling to accept poor-performing, poor-quality automobiles, despite their low price. Sony, despite its success in Japan, was unable to carve out significant market share in the U.S. video market with its Betamax technology. Most observers blame Sony's reluctance to license this technology to other manufacturers, together with the shorter recording time available on Betamax, for this product failure. The British retail giant Marks and Spencer's efforts to enter the Canadian and U.S. retail markets with its traditional mix of clothing and food stores also met with stiff consumer resistance.[3]

In order for the basis of an international strategy to attract new customers, those products or services must address the needs, wants, and preferences of customers in foreign markets at least as well as, if not better than, alternatives. Firms pursuing international opportunities may have to implement many of the cost-leadership and product differentiation business strategies discussed in Chapters 4 and 5, modified to address the specific market needs of a nondomestic market. Only then will customers in nondomestic markets be willing to buy a firm's current products or services.

Are Nondomestic Customers Able to Buy?

Customers in foreign markets might be willing to buy a firm's current products or services but be unable to buy them. This can occur for at least three reasons: inadequate distribution channels, trade barriers, and insufficient wealth to make purchases.

Inadequate distribution channels may make it difficult, if not impossible, for a firm to make its products or services available to customers outside its domestic market. In some international markets, adequate distribution networks exist but are tied up by firms already operating in these markets. Many European firms face this situation as they try to enter the U.S. market. In such a situation, firms pursuing international opportunities must either build their own distribution networks from scratch (a very costly endeavor) or work with a local partner to utilize the networks that are already in place.

However, the problem facing some firms pursuing international opportunities is not that distribution networks are tied up by firms already operating in a market. Rather, the problem is that distribution networks do not exist or operate in ways that are very different from the operation of the distribution networks in a firm's domestic market. This problem can be serious when firms seek to expand their operations into developing economies. Inadequate transportation, warehousing, and retail facilities can make it difficult to distribute a firm's products or services into a new geographic market. These kinds of problems have hampered investment in Russia, China, and India. For example, when Nestlé entered the Chinese dairy market, it had to build a network of gravel roads connecting the villages where dairy farmers produce milk and factory collection points. Obtaining the right to build this network of roads took 13 years of negotiations with Chinese government officials.[4]

Such distribution problems are not limited to developing economies. For example, Japanese retail distribution has historically been much more fragmented, and much less efficient, than the system that exists in either the United States or Western Europe. Rather than being dominated by large grocery stores, discount retail operations, and retail superstores, the Japanese retail distribution network has been dominated by numerous small, "mom-and-pop" operations. Many Western firms find this distribution network difficult to use because its operating principles are so different from what they have seen in their domestic markets. However, Proctor & Gamble and a few other firms have been able to crack open this Japanese distribution system and exploit significant sales opportunities in Japan.[5]

Even if distribution networks exist in nondomestic markets, and even if international firms can operate through those networks if they have access to them, it still might be the case that entry into these markets can be restricted by various tariff and nontariff trade barriers. A list of such trade barriers is presented in Table 11.2. Trade barriers, no matter what their specific form, have the effect of

TABLE 11.2 Tariffs, Quotas, and Nontariff Trade Barriers

Tariffs: Taxes levied on imported goods or services	Quotas: Quantity limits on the number of products or services that can be imported	Nontariff barriers: Rules, regulations, and policies that increase the cost of importing products or services
Import duties	Voluntary quotas	Government policies
Supplemental duties	Involuntary quotas	Government procurement policies
Variable levies	Restricted import licenses	Government-sponsored export
Subsidies	Minimum import limits	Domestic assistance programs
Border levies	Embargoes	Custom policies
Countervailing duties		Valuation systems
		Tariff classifications
		Documentation requirements
		Fees
		Quality standards
		Packaging standards
		Labeling standards

increasing the cost of selling a firm's current products or services in a new geographic market and thus make it difficult for a firm to realize this economy of scope from its international strategy.

Despite a worldwide movement toward free trade and reduction in trade barriers, trade barriers are still an important economic phenomenon for many firms seeking to implement an international strategy. Japanese automobile manufacturers have faced voluntary quotas and various other trade barriers as they have sought to expand their presence in the U.S. market; U.S. automobile firms have argued that Japan has used a series of tariff and nontariff trade barriers to restrict their entry into the Japanese market. Kodak once asked the U.S. government to begin negotiations to facilitate Kodak's entry into the Japanese photography market—a market that Kodak argued is controlled, through a government-sanctioned monopoly, by Fuji. Historically, beginning operations in India was hampered by a variety of tariff and nontariff trade barriers. Tariffs in India have averaged more than 80 percent; foreign firms have been restricted to a 40 percent ownership stake in their operations in India; and foreign imports have required government approvals and licenses that could take up to three years to obtain. Over the past several years, many of these trade barriers in India have been reduced but not eliminated. The same is true for the United States. The tariff on imported goods and services imposed by the U.S. government reached an all-time high of 60 percent in 1932. It averaged from 12 to 15 percent after the Second World War and now averages about 5 percent for most imports into the United States. Thus, U.S. trade barriers have been reduced but not eliminated.[6]

Governments create trade barriers for a wide variety of reasons: to raise government revenue, to protect local employment, to encourage local production to replace imports, to protect new industries from competition, to discourage foreign direct investment, and to promote export activity. However, for firms seeking to implement international strategies, trade barriers, no matter why they are erected, have the effect of increasing the cost of implementing these strategies. Indeed, trade barriers can be thought of as a special case of artificial barriers to entry, as discussed in Chapter 2. Such barriers to entry can turn what could have been economically viable strategies into nonviable strategies.

Finally, customers may be willing but unable to purchase a firm's current products or services even if distribution networks are in place and trade barriers are not making internationalization efforts too costly. If these customers lack the wealth, or sufficient hard currency, to make these purchases, then the potential value of this economy of scope can go unrealized.

Insufficient consumer wealth limits the ability of firms to sell products into a variety of markets. For example, per capita gross national product in Bangladesh is $270, $240 in Chad, and $110 in the Congo. In these countries, it is unlikely that there will be significant demand for many products or services originally designed for affluent Western economies. This situation also exists in India. The middle class in India is large and growing (164 million people with the highest 20 percent of income in 1998), but the income of this middle class is considerably lower than the income of the middle class in other economies. These income levels are sufficient to create demand for some consumer products. For example, Gillette estimates the market in India for its shaving products could include 240 million consumers, and Nestlé believes that the market in India for its noodles, ketchup, and instant coffee products could include over 100 million people. However, the potential market for higher-end products in India is somewhat smaller. For example, Bausch & Lomb believes that only about 30 million consumers in India can afford to purchase its high-end sunglasses and soft contact lenses. The level of consumer wealth is such an important determinant of the economic potential of beginning operations in a new country that McDonald's adjusts the number of restaurants it expects to build in a new market by the per capita income of people in that market.[7]

Even if there is sufficient wealth in a country to create market demand, lack of hard currency can hamper internationalization efforts. **Hard currencies** are currencies that are traded, and thus have value, on international money markets. When an international firm does business in a country with hard currency, the firm can take whatever after-tax profits it earns in that country and translate those profits into other hard currencies—including the currency of the country in which the firm has headquarters. Moreover, because the value of hard currencies can fluctuate in the world economy, firms can also manage their currency risk by engaging in various hedging strategies in world money markets.

When firms begin operations in countries without hard currency, they are able to obtain few of these advantages. Indeed, without hard currency, cash payments to these firms are made with a currency that has essentially no value outside the country where the payments are made. Although these payments can

Strategy in Depth

When international firms engage in countertrade, they receive payment for the products or services they sell into a country, but not in the form of currency. They receive payment in the form of other products or services that they can sell on the world market. Countertrade has been a particularly important way by which firms have tried to gain access to the markets in the former Soviet Union. For example, Marc Rich and Company (a Swiss commodity-trading firm) once put together the following deal: Marc Rich purchased 70,000 tons of raw sugar from Brazil on the open market; shipped this sugar to Ukraine, where it was refined; then transported 30,000 tons of refined sugar (after using some profits to pay the refineries) to Siberia, where it was sold for 130,000 tons of oil products that, in turn, were shipped to Mongolia in exchange for 35,000 tons of copper concentrate, which was moved to Kazakhstan, where it was refined into copper, and,

Countertrade

finally, sold on the world market to obtain hard currency. This complicated countertrade deal is typical of the kinds of actions that international firms must take if they are to engage in business in countries without hard currency and if they desire to extract their profits out of those countries. Indeed, countertrade in various forms is actually quite common. One estimate suggests that countertrade accounts for between 10 and 20 percent of world trade.

Although countertrade can enable a firm to begin operations in countries without hard currency, it can create difficulties as well. In particular, in order to do business, a firm must be willing to accept payment in the form of some good or commodity that it must sell in order to obtain hard currency. This is not likely to be a problem for a firm that specializes in buying and selling commodities. However, a firm that does not have this expertise may find itself taking possession of natural gas, sesame seeds, or rattan in order to sell its products or services in a country. If this firm has limited expertise in marketing these kinds of commodities, it may have to use brokers and other advisers to complete these transactions. This, of course, increases the cost of using countertrade as a way to facilitate international operations.

Source: See A. Ignatius (1993). "Commodity giant: Marc Rich & Co. does big deals at big risk in former U.S.S.R." *The Wall Street Journal*, May 13, p. A1; and D. Marin (1990). "Tying in trade: Evidence on countertrade." *World Economy*, 13(3), p. 445.

be used for additional investments inside that country, an international firm has limited ability to extract profits from countries without hard currencies and even less ability to hedge currency fluctuation risks in this context. The lack of hard currency has discouraged firms from entering a wide variety of countries at various points in time despite the substantial demand for products and services in those countries.[8] One solution to this problem, called **countertrade**, is discussed in the Strategy in Depth feature.

Internationalization and Product Life Cycles

Gaining access to new customers not only can directly increase a firm's revenues but also can enable a firm to manage its products or services through their life cycle. A typical **product life cycle** is depicted in Figure 11.1. Different stages in this life cycle are defined by different growth rates in demand for a product. Thus, in the first emerging stage (called **introduction** in the figure), relatively few firms are producing a product, there are relatively few customers, and the rate of growth in demand for the product is relatively low. In the second stage (**growth**) of the product life cycle, demand increases rapidly, and many new firms enter to begin producing the product or service. In the third phase of the product life cycle (**maturity**), the number of firms producing a product or service remains stable, demand growth levels off, and firms direct their investment efforts toward refining the process by which a product or service is created and away from developing entirely new products. In the final phase of the product life cycle (**decline**), demand drops off when a technologically superior product or service is introduced.[9]

From an international strategy perspective, the critical observation about product life cycles is that a product or service can be at different stages of its life cycle in different countries. Thus, a firm can use the resources and capabilities it developed during a particular stage of the life cycle in its domestic market during that same stage of the life cycle in a nondomestic market. This can substantially enhance a firm's economic performance.

One firm that has been very successful in managing its product life cycles through its international efforts is Crown Cork & Seal. This firm had a traditional

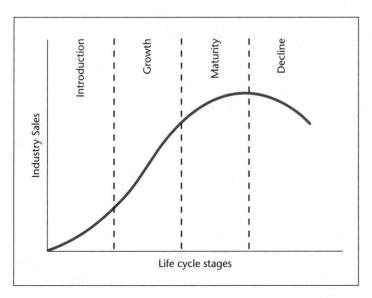

Figure 11.1 The Product Life Cycle.

strength in the manufacturing of three-piece metal containers, when the introduction of two-piece metal cans into the U.S. market rapidly made three-piece cans obsolete. However, rather than abandoning its three-piece manufacturing technology, Crown Cork & Seal moved many of its three-piece manufacturing operations overseas into developing countries where demand for three-piece cans was just emerging. In this way, Crown Cork & Seal was able to extend the effective life of its three-piece manufacturing operations and substantially enhance its economic performance.[10]

Internationalization and Cost Reduction

Gaining access to new customers for a firm's current products or services can increase a firm's sales. If aspects of a firm's production process are sensitive to economies of scale, this increased volume of sales can also reduce the firm's costs and enable the firm to gain cost advantages in both its nondomestic and its domestic markets.

Many firms in the worldwide automobile industry have attempted to realize manufacturing economies of scale through their international operations. According to one estimate, the minimum efficient scale of a single compact-car manufacturing plant is 400,000 units per year.[11] Such a plant would produce approximately 20 percent of all the automobiles sold in Britain, Italy, or France. Obviously, to exploit this 400,000 car-per-year manufacturing efficiency, European automobile firms have had to sell cars in more than just a single country market. Thus, the implementation of an international strategy has enabled these firms to realize an important manufacturing economy of scale.[12]

To Gain Access to Low-Cost Factors of Production

Just as gaining access to new customers can be an important economy of scope for firms pursuing international opportunities, so is gaining access to low-cost factors of production such as raw materials, labor, and technology.

Raw Materials

Gaining access to low-cost raw materials is, perhaps, the most traditional reason why firms begin international operations. For example, in 1600, the British East India Company was formed with an initial investment of $70,000 to manage trade between England and the Far East, including India. In 1601, the third British East India Company fleet sailed for the Indies to buy cloves, pepper, silk, coffee, saltpeter, and other products. This fleet generated a return on investment of 234 percent. These profits led to the formation of the Dutch East India Company in 1602 and the French East India Company in 1664. Similar firms were organized to manage trade in the New World. The Hudson Bay Company was chartered in 1670 to manage the fur trade, and the rival North West Company was organized in 1784 for the same purpose. All these organizations were created to gain access to low-cost raw materials that were available only in nondomestic markets.[13]

Labor

In addition to gaining access to low-cost raw materials, firms also begin international operations in order to gain access to low-cost labor. After World War II, Japan had some of the lowest labor costs, and highest labor productivity, in the

Ethics and Strategy

One of the most important productive inputs in almost all companies is labor. Getting differential low-cost access to labor can give a firm a cost advantage.

This search for low labor costs has led some firms to engage in an international "race to the bottom." It is well known that the wage rates of most U.S. and Western European workers are much higher than the wage rates of workers in other, less developed parts of the world. While a firm might have to pay its employees $20 per hour (in wages and benefits) to make sneakers and basketball shoes in the United States, that same firm may only have to pay an employee in the Philippines, or Malaysia, or China $1 to $2 per day to make the same sneakers and basketball shoes—shoes the firm might be able to sell for $150 a pair in the United States and Europe. Thus, many firms look to overseas manufacturing as a way to keep their labor cost low.

But this search for low labor cost has some important unintended consequences. First, the location of the lowest cost labor rates in the world changes over time. It used to be that Mexico had the lowest labor rates, then Korea and the Philippines, then Malaysia, then China. As the infrastructures of each of these countries evolve to the point that they

The Race to the Bottom

can support worldwide manufacturing, firms abandon their relationships with firms in prior countries in search of still lower costs in new countries. The only way former "low-cost centers" can compete is to drive their costs even lower.

This sometimes leads to a second unintended consequence of the "race to the bottom": horrendous working conditions and low wages in these low-cost manufacturing settings. Employees earning $1 for working a 10-hour day, 6 days a week, may look good on the corporate bottom line, but many observers are deeply concerned about the moral and ethical issues associated with this strategy. Indeed, several companies—including Nike and Kmart—have been forced to increase the wages and improve the

working conditions of many of their overseas employees.

An even more horrific result of this "race to the bottom" has been the reemergence of what amounts to slavery in some Western European countries and some parts of the United States. In search of the promise of a better life, illegal immigrants are sometimes brought to Western European countries or the United States and forced to work in illegal, underground factories. These illegal immigrants are sometimes forced to work as many as 20 hours a day, for little or no pay— supposedly to "pay off" the price of bringing them out of their less developed countries. And because of their illegal status and language barriers, they often do not feel empowered to go to the local authorities.

Of course, the people who create and manage these facilities are criminals and deserve contempt. But, what about the companies that purchase the services of these illegal and immoral manufacturing operations? Aren't they also culpable, both legally and morally?

Sources: R. DeGeorge (2000). "Ethics in international business—A contradiction in terms?" *Business Credit*, 102, pp. 50 +; G. Edmondson, K. Carlisle, I. Resch, K. Nickel Anhalt, and H. Dawley (2000). "Workers in bondage." *BusinessWeek*, November 27, pp. 146 +; and D. Winter (2000). "Facing globalization." *Ward's Auto World*, 36, pp. 7 +.

world. Over time, however, the improving Japanese economy and the increased value of the yen has had the effect of increasing labor costs in Japan, and South Korea, Taiwan, Singapore, and Malaysia all emerged as geographic areas with inexpensive and highly productive labor. More recently, China, Mexico, and Vietnam have taken this role in the world economy.[14]

Numerous firms have attempted to gain the advantages of low labor costs by moving their manufacturing operations. For example, Mineba, a Japanese ball-bearing and semiconductor manufacturer, attempted to exploit low labor costs by manufacturing ball bearings in Japan in the 1950s and early 1960s, in Singapore in the

1970s, and since 1980 has been manufacturing them in Thailand. Hewlett-Packard operates manufacturing and assembly operations in Malaysia and Mexico, Japan's Mitsubishi Motors recently opened an automobile assembly plant in Vietnam, General Motors operates assembly plants in Mexico, and Motorola has begun operations in China. All these investments were motivated, at least partly, by the availability of low-cost labor in these countries.[15] Some of the ethical issues associated with search for low-cost labor are discussed in the Ethics and Strategy feature.

Although gaining access to low-cost labor can be an important determinant of a firm's international efforts, this access by itself is usually not sufficient to motivate entry into particular countries. After all, relative labor costs can change over time. For example, South Korea used to be the country in which most sports shoes were manufactured. In 1990, Korean shoe manufacturers employed 130,000 workers in 302 factories. However, by 1993, only 80,000 Koreans were employed in the shoe industry, and only 244 factories (most employing fewer than 100 people) remained. A significant portion of the shoe-manufacturing industry had moved from Korea to China because of the labor-cost advantages of China (approximately $40 per employee per month) compared to Korea (approximately $800 per employee per month).[16]

Moreover, low labor costs are not beneficial if a country's workforce is not able to produce high-quality products efficiently. In the sport shoe industry, China's access to some of the manufacturing technology and supporting industries (for example, synthetic fabrics) to efficiently produce high-end sports shoes and high-technology hiking boots was delayed for several years. As a result, Korea was able to maintain a presence in the shoe-manufacturing industry—even though most of that industry had been outsourced to China.

One interesting example of firms gaining access to low-cost labor through their international strategies is maquiladoras—manufacturing plants that are owned by non-Mexican companies and operated in Mexico near the U.S. border. The primary driver behind maquiladora investments is lower labor costs than similar plants located in the United States. In addition, firms exporting from maquiladoras to the United States have to pay duties only on the value added that was created in Mexico; maquiladoras do not have to pay Mexican taxes on the goods processed in Mexico; and the cost of land on which plants are built in Mexico is substantially lower than would be the case in the United States. However, a study by the Banco de Mexico suggests that without the 20 percent cost-of-labor advantage, most maquildoras would not be profitable.[17]

Technology

Another factor of production that firms can gain low-cost access to through operations is technology. Historically, Japanese firms have tried to gain access to technology by partnering with non-Japanese firms. Although the non-Japanese firms have often been looking to gain access to new customers for their current products or services by operating in Japan, Japanese firms have used this entry into the Japanese market to gain access to foreign technology.[18]

To Develop New Core Competencies

One of the most compelling reasons for firms to begin operations outside their domestic markets is to refine their current core competencies and to develop new core competencies. By beginning operations outside their domestic markets, firms can gain a greater understanding of the strengths and weaknesses of their core competencies. By exposing these competencies to new competitive contexts, traditional competencies can be modified, and new competencies can be developed.

Of course, for international operations to affect a firm's core competencies, firms must learn from their experiences in nondomestic markets. Moreover, once these new core competencies are developed, they must be exploited in a firm's other operations in order to realize their full economic potential.

Learning from International Operations

Learning from international operations is anything but automatic. Many firms that begin operations in a nondomestic market encounter challenges and difficulties and then immediately withdraw from their international efforts. Other firms continue to try to operate internationally but are unable to learn how to modify and change their core competencies.

One study examined several strategic alliances in an effort to understand why some firms in these alliances were able to learn from their international operations, modify their core competencies, and develop new core competencies, while others were not. This study identified the intent to learn, the transparency of business partners, and receptivity to learning as determinants of a firm's ability to learn from its international operations (see Table 11.3).

The Intent to Learn

A firm that has a strong intent to learn from its international operations is more likely to learn than a firm without this intent. Moreover, this intent must be communicated to all those who work in a firm's international activities. Compare, for example, a quote from a manager whose firm failed to learn from its international operations with a quote from a manager whose firm was able to learn from these operations.[19]

> Our engineers were just as good as [our partner's]. In fact, theirs were narrower technically, but they had a much better understanding of what the company was trying to accomplish. They knew they were there to learn; our people didn't.
>
> We wanted to make learning an automatic discipline. We asked the staff every day, "What did you learn from [our partner] today?" Learning was carefully monitored and recorded.

Obviously, the second firm was in a much better position than the first to learn from its international operations and to modify its current core competencies and develop new core competencies. Learning from international operations takes place by design, not by default.

1. The intent to learn
2. The transparency of business partners
3. Receptivity to learning

Source: G. Hamel (1991). "Competition for competence and inter-partner learning within international strategic alliances." *Strategic Management Journal,* 12, pp. 83–103.

TABLE 11.3 Determinants of the Ability of a Firm to Learn from Its International Operations

Transparency and Learning

It has also been shown that firms were more likely to learn from their international operations when they interacted with what have been called **transparent business partners**. Some international business partners are more open and accessible than others. This variance in accessibility can reflect different organizational philosophies, practices, and procedures, as well as differences in the culture of a firm's home country. For example, knowledge in Japanese and most other Asian cultures tends to be context specific and deeply embedded in the broader social system. This makes it difficult for many Western managers to understand and appreciate the subtlety of Japanese business practices and Japanese culture. This, in turn, limits the ability of Western managers to learn from their operations in the Japanese market or from their Japanese partners.[20]

In contrast, knowledge in most Western cultures tends to be less context specific, less deeply embedded in the broader social system. Such knowledge can be written down, can be taught in classes, and can be transmitted, all at a relatively low cost. Japanese managers working in Western economies are more likely to be able to appreciate and understand Western business practices and thus are more able to learn from their operations in the West and from their Western partners.

Receptivity to Learning

Firms also vary in their receptiveness to learning. A firm's receptiveness to learning is affected by its culture, its operating procedures, and its history. Research on organizational learning suggests that, before firms can learn from their international operations, they must be prepared to unlearn. **Unlearning** requires a firm to modify or abandon traditional ways of engaging in business. Unlearning can be difficult, especially if a firm has a long history of success using old patterns of behavior and if those old patterns of behavior are reflected in a firm's organizational structure, its management control systems, and its compensation policies.[21]

Even if unlearning is possible, a firm may not have the resources it needs to learn. If a firm is using all of its available managerial time and talent, capital, and technology just to compete on a day-to-day business, the additional task of learning from international operations can go undone. Although managers in this situation often acknowledge the importance of learning from their international operations in order to modify their current core competencies or build new ones, they simply may not have the time or energy to do so.[22]

The ability to learn from operations can also be hampered if managers perceive that there is too much to be learned. It is often difficult for a firm to understand how it can evolve from its current state to a position where it operates with new and more valuable core competencies. This difficulty is exacerbated when the distance between where a firm is and where it needs to be is large. One Western manager who perceived this large learning gap after visiting a state-of-the-art manufacturing facility operated by a Japanese partner was quoted as saying:[23]

> It's no good for us to simply observe where they are today, what we have to find out is how they got from where we are to where they are. We need to experiment and learn with intermediate technologies before duplicating what they've done.

Leveraging New Core Competencies in Additional Markets

Once a firm has been able to learn from its international operations and modify its traditional core competencies or develop new core competencies, it must then leverage those competencies across its operations, both domestic and international, in order to realize their full value. Failure to leverage these "lessons learned" can substantially reduce the return associated with implementing an international strategy.

To Leverage Current Core Competencies in New Ways

International operations can also create opportunities for firms to leverage their traditional core competencies in new ways. This ability is related to, though different from, using international operations to gain access to new customers for a firm's current products or services. When firms gain access to new customers for their current products, they often leverage their domestic core competencies across country boundaries. When they leverage core competencies in *new* ways, they not only extend operations across country boundaries but also leverage their competencies across products and services in ways that would not be economically viable in their domestic market.

Consider, for example, Honda. There is widespread agreement that Honda has developed core competencies in the design and manufacture of power trains. Honda has used this core competence to facilitate entry into a variety of product markets—including motorcycles, automobiles, and snow blowers—both in its domestic Japanese market and in nondomestic markets such as the United States. However, Honda has begun to explore some competence-leverage opportunities in the United States that are not available in the Japanese market. For example, Honda has begun to design and manufacture lawn mowers of various sizes for the home in the U.S. market—lawn mowers clearly build on Honda's traditional power train competence. However, given the crowded living conditions in Japan, consumer demand for lawn mowers in that country has never been very great. Lawns in the United States, however, can be very large, and consumer demand for high-quality lawn mowers in that market is substantial. The opportunity for Honda to begin to leverage its power train competencies in the sale of lawn mowers to U.S. homeowners exists only because Honda operates outside its Japanese home market.

To Manage Corporate Risk

The value of risk reduction for firms pursuing a corporate diversification strategy was evaluated previously. It was suggested that, although diversified operations across businesses with imperfectly correlated cash flows can reduce a firm's risk, outside equity holders can manage this risk more efficiently on their own by investing in a diversified portfolio of stocks. Consequently equity holders have little direct interest in hiring managers to operate a diversified portfolio of businesses, the sole purpose of which is risk diversification.

Similar conclusions apply to firms pursuing international strategies—with two qualifications. First, in some circumstances, it may be difficult for equity holders in one market to diversify their portfolio of investments across multiple markets. To the extent that such barriers to diversification exist for individual equity holders but not for firms pursuing international strategies, risk reduction can directly benefit equity holders. In general, whenever barriers to international capital flows exist, individual investors may not be able to diversify their portfolios

Research Made Relevant

Firms whose ownership is dominated by a single family are surprisingly common around the world. In the United States, for example, Marriott, Walgreens, Wrigley, Alberto-Culver, Campbell Soup, Dell, and Wal-Mart are all family dominated. However, only 4 of the 20 largest firms in the United States are family dominated, and only 1 of the 20 largest firms in the United Kingdom is family dominated.

Though not uncommon in the United States and the United Kingdom, family-dominated firms are the rule, not the exception, in most economies around the world. For example, in New Zealand, 9 of the 20 largest firms are family dominated; in Argentina, 13 of the 20 largest firms are family dominated; and in Mexico, all 20 of the 20 largest firms are family dominated. In many countries, including Argentina, Belgium, Canada, Denmark, Greece, Hong Kong, Israel, Mexico, New Zealand, Portugal, Singapore, South Korea, Sweden, and Switzerland, over one-third of the largest 20 firms are dominated by family owners.

A variety of explanations of why family-dominated firms continue to be an important part of the world economy have been proposed. For example, some researchers have argued that family owners obtain private benefits of ownership—over and above the financial benefits they might receive. Such private benefits include high social status in their countries. Other researchers have argued that family

Family Firms in the Global Economy

ownership helps guarantee that family members will be able to control their property in countries with less well-developed property rights. And still others have argued that concentrated family owners help a firm gain political clout in its negotiations with the government.

On the positive side, family ownership may reduce conflicts that might otherwise arise between a firm's managers and its outside equity holders—the agency costs discussed in the Strategy in Depth feature in Chapter 8. Managers of family firms are "playing with" their own money, not "other people's money," and thus are less likely to pursue strategies that benefit themselves but hurt the firm's owners, since they are the firm's owners.

On the negative side, family firms may become starved for capital, and especially equity capital. Non-family members will often be reluctant

to invest in family firms since the interests of the family are often likely to take precedence over the interests of outsiders. Also, family firms must limit their search for senior leadership to family members. It may well be the case that the best leaders of a family firm are not members of the family, but family ownership can prevent a firm from gaining access to the entire labor market. Finally, for reasons explained in the text, family firms may need to pursue a broad diversification strategy in order to reduce the risk borne by their family owners. As suggested in Chapter 8, such unrelated diversification strategies can sometimes be difficult to manage.

From a broader perspective, the importance of family-dominated firms throughout the world suggests that the "standard" model of corporate governance—with numerous anonymous stockholders, an independent board of directors, and senior managers chosen only for their ability to lead and create economic value—may not apply that broadly. This approach to corporate governance, so dominant in the United States and the United Kingdom, may actually be the exception, not the rule.

Sources: R. Morck and B. Yeung (2004). "Family control and the rent-seeking society." *Entrepreneurship: Theory and Practice,* Summer, pp. 391–409; R. LaPorta, F. Lopez-de-salina, A. Shleifer, and R. Vishny (1999). "Corporate ownership around the world." *Journal of Finance,* 54, pp. 471–520; and J. Weber, L. Lavelle, T. Lowry, W. Zellner, and A. Barrett (2003). "Family, Inc.," *BusinessWeek,* November 10, pp. 100 +.

across country boundaries optimally. In this context, individual investors can indirectly diversify their portfolio of investments by purchasing shares in diversified multinationals.[24]

Second, large privately held firms may find it in their wealth maximizing interests to broadly diversify to reduce risk. In order to gain the risk reduction advantages of diversifying their investments by owning a portfolio of stocks, the owners of these firms would have to "cash out" their ownership position in their firm—by, for example, taking their firm public—and then use this cash to invest in a portfolio of stocks. However, these individuals may gain other advantages from owning their firms and may not want to cash out. In this setting, the only way that owners can gain the risk-reducing benefits of broad diversification is for the firm that they own to broadly diversify.

This justification of diversification for risk reduction purposes is particularly relevant in the international context because, as described in the Research Made Relevant feature, many of the economies of countries around the world are dominated by private companies owned by large families. Not surprisingly, these family-owned firms tend to be much more diversified than the publicly traded firms that are more common in the United States and the United Kingdom.

The Local Responsiveness/International Integration Trade-Off

As firms pursue the economies of scope listed in Table 11.1, they constantly face a trade-off between the advantages of being responsive to market conditions in their nondomestic markets and the advantages of integrating their operations across the multiple markets in which they operate.

On the one hand, **local responsiveness** can help firms be successful in addressing the local needs of nondomestic customers, thereby increasing demand for a firm's current products or services. Moreover, local responsiveness enables a firm to expose its traditional core competencies to new competitive situations, thereby increasing the chances that those core competencies will be improved or will be augmented by new core competencies. Finally, detailed local knowledge is essential if firms are going to leverage their traditional competencies in new ways in their nondomestic markets. Honda was able to begin exploiting its power train competencies in the U.S. lawn mower market only because of its detailed knowledge of, and responsiveness to, that market.

On the other hand, the full exploitation of the economies of scale that can be created by selling a firm's current products or services in a nondomestic market often can occur only if there is tight integration across all the markets in which a firm operates. Gaining access to low-cost factors of production can not only help a firm succeed in a nondomestic market but also help it succeed in all its markets— as long as those factors of production are used by many parts of the international firm. Developing new core competencies and using traditional core competencies in new ways can certainly be beneficial in a particular domestic market. However, the full value of these economies of scope is realized only when they are transferred from a particular domestic market into the operations of a firm in all its other markets.

Traditionally, it has been thought that firms have to choose between local responsiveness and international integration. For example, firms like CIBA-Geigy (a Swiss chemical company), Nestlé (a Swiss food company), and Phillips (a Dutch consumer electronics firm) have chosen to emphasize local responsiveness. Nestlé, for example, owns nearly 8,000 brand names worldwide. However, of those 8,000 brands, only 750 are registered in more than 1 country, and only 80 are registered in more than 10 countries. Nestlé adjusts its product attributes to the needs of local consumers, adopts brand names that resonate with those consumers, and builds its brands for long-run profitability by country. For example, in the United States, Nestlé's condensed milk carries the brand name "Carnation" (obtained through the acquisition of the Carnation Company); in Asia, this same product carries the brand name "Bear Brand." Nestlé delegates brand management authority to country managers, who can (and do) adjust traditional marketing and manufacturing strategies in accordance with local tastes and preferences. For example, Nestlé's Thailand management group dropped traditional coffee-marketing efforts that focused on taste, aroma, and stimulation and instead began selling coffee as a drink that promotes relaxation and romance. This marketing strategy resonated with Thais experiencing urban stress, and it prompted Nestlé coffee sales in Thailand to jump from $25 million to $100 million 4 years later.[25]

Of course, all this local responsiveness comes at a cost. Firms that emphasize local responsiveness are often unable to realize the full value of the economies of scope and scale that they could realize if their operations across country borders were more integrated. Numerous firms have focused on appropriating this economic value and have pursued a more integrated international strategy. Examples of such firms include IBM, General Electric, Toyota Motor Corporation, and most major pharmaceutical firms, to name just a few.

Internationally integrated firms locate business functions and activities in countries that have a comparative advantage in these functions or activities. For example, the production of components for most consumer electronics is research intensive, capital intensive, and subject to significant economies of scale. To manage component manufacturing successfully, most internationally integrated consumer electronics firms have located their component operations in technologically advanced countries like the United States and Japan. Because the assembly of these components into consumer products is labor intensive, most internationally integrated consumer electronics firms have located their assembly operations in countries with relatively low labor costs, including Mexico and China.

Of course, one of the costs of locating different business functions and activities in different geographic locations is that these different functions and activities must be coordinated and integrated. Operations in one country might very efficiently manufacture certain components. However, if the wrong components are shipped to the assembly location, or if the right components are shipped at the wrong time, any advantages that could have been obtained from exploiting the comparative advantages of different countries can be lost. Shipping costs can also reduce the return on international integration.

To ensure that the different operations in an internationally integrated firm are appropriately coordinated, these firms typically manufacture more standardized products, using more standardized components, than do locally responsive firms. Standardization enables these firms to realize substantial economies of scale and scope, but it can limit their ability to respond to the specific needs of individual markets. When international product standards exist, as in the personal computer industry and the semiconductor chip industry, such standardization is not problematic. Also, when local responsiveness requires only a few modifications of a standardized product (for example, changing the shape of the electric plug or changing the color of a product), international integration can be very effective. However, when local responsiveness requires a great deal of local knowledge and product modifications, international integration can create problems for a firm pursuing an international strategy.

The Transnational Strategy

Recently, it has been suggested that the traditional trade-off between international integration and local responsiveness can be replaced by a **transnational strategy** that exploits all the advantages of both international integration and local responsiveness.[26] Firms implementing a transnational strategy treat their international operations as an integrated network of distributed and interdependent resources and capabilities. In this context, a firm's operations in each country are not simply independent activities attempting to respond to local market needs; they are also repositories of ideas, technologies, and management approaches that the firm might be able to use and apply in its other international operations. Put differently, operations in different countries can be thought of as "experiments" in the creation of new core competencies. Some of these experiments will work and generate important new core competencies; others will fail to have such benefits for a firm.

When a particular country operation develops a competence in manufacturing a particular product, providing a particular service, or engaging in a particular activity that can be used by other country operations, the country operation with this competence can achieve international economies of scale by becoming the firm's primary supplier of this product, service, or activity. In this way, local responsiveness is retained as country managers constantly search for new competencies that enable them to maximize profits in their particular markets, and international integration and economies are realized as country operations that have developed unique competencies become suppliers for all other country operations.

Managing a firm that is attempting to be both locally responsive and internationally integrated is not an easy task. Some of these organizational challenges are discussed later in this chapter.

Financial and Political Risks in Pursuing International Strategies

There is little doubt that the realization of the economies of scope listed in Table 11.1 can be a source of economic value for firms pursuing international strategies. However, the nature of international strategies can create significant risks that these economies of scope will never be realized. Beyond the implementation problems (to be discussed later in this chapter), both financial circumstances and political events can significantly reduce the value of international strategies.

Financial Risks: Currency Fluctuation and Inflation

As firms begin to pursue international strategies, they may begin to expose themselves to financial risks that are less obvious within a single domestic market. In particular, currency fluctuations can significantly affect the value of a firm's international investments. Such fluctuations can turn what had been a losing investment into a profitable investment (the good news). They can also turn what had been a profitable investment into a losing investment (the bad news). In addition to currency fluctuations, different rates of inflation across countries can require very different managerial approaches, business strategies, and accounting practices. Certainly, when a firm first begins international operations, these financial risks can seem daunting.

Fortunately, it is now possible for firms to hedge most of these risks through the use of a variety of financial instruments and strategies. The development of money markets, together with growing experience in operating in high-inflation economies, has substantially reduced the threat of these financial risks for firms pursuing international strategies. Of course, the benefits of these financial tools and experience in high-inflation environments do not accrue to firms automatically. Firms seeking to implement international strategies must develop the resources and capabilities they will need to manage these financial risks. Moreover, these hedging strategies can do nothing to reduce the business risks that firms assume when they enter into nondomestic markets. For example, it may be the case that consumers in a nondomestic market simply do not want to purchase a firm's products or services, in which case this economy of scope cannot be realized. Moreover, these financial strategies cannot manage political risks that can exist for firms pursuing an international strategy.

Political Risks

The political environment is an important consideration in all strategic decisions. Changes in the political rules of the game can have the effect of increasing some environmental threats and reducing others, thereby changing the value of a firm's resources and capabilities. However, the political environment can be even more problematic as firms pursue international strategies.

Types of Political Risks

Politics can affect the value of a firm's international strategies at the macro and micro levels. At the macro level, broad changes in the political situation in a country can change the value of an investment. For example, after the Second World War, nationalist governments came to power in many countries in the Middle East. These governments expropriated for little or no compensation many of the assets of oil and gas companies located in their countries. Expropriation of foreign company assets also occurred when the Shah of Iran was overthrown, when a communist government was elected in Chile, and when new governments came to power in Angola, Ethiopia, Peru, Zambia, and more recently, in Venezuela and Bolivia.[27]

Government upheaval and the attendant risks to international firms are facts of life in some countries. Consider, for example, oil-rich Nigeria. Since its independence in 1960, Nigeria has experienced several successful coups d'états, one civil war, two civil governments, and six military regimes.[28] The prudent course of action for firms engaging in business activities in Nigeria is to expect the current government to change and to plan accordingly.

Quantifying Political Risks

Political scientists have attempted to quantify the political risk that firms seeking to implement international strategies are likely to face in different countries. Although different studies vary in detail, the country attributes listed in Table 11.4 summarize most of the important determinants of political risk for firms pursuing international strategies.[29] Firms can apply the criteria listed in the table by evaluating the political and economic conditions in a country and by adding up the scores associated with these conditions. For example, a country that has a very unstable political system (14 points), a great deal of control of the economic system (9 points), and significant import restrictions (10 points) represents more political risk than a country that does not have these attributes.

TABLE 11.4 Quantifying Political Risks from International Operations

Increments to Country		
Risk if Risk Factor Is:	**Low**	**High**
The political economic environment		
1. Stability of the political system	3	14
2. Imminent internal conflicts	0	14
3. External threats to stability	0	12
4. Degree of control of the economic system	5	9
5. Reliability of country as a trade partner	4	12
6. Constitutional guarantees	2	12
7. Effectiveness of public administration	3	12
8. Labor relations and social peace	3	15
Domestic economic conditions		
1. Size of the population	4	8
2. Per capita income	2	10
3. Economic growth over the past five years	2	7
4. Potential growth over the next three years	3	10
5. Inflation over the past two years	2	10
6. Availability of domestic capital markets to outsiders	3	7
7. Availability of high-quality local labor force	2	8
8. Possibility of employing foreign nationals	2	8
9. Availability of energy resources	2	14
10. Environmental pollution legal requirements	4	8
11. Transportation and communication infrastructure	2	14
External economic relations		
1. Import restrictions	2	10
2. Export restrictions	2	10
3. Restrictions on foreign investments	3	9
4. Freedom to set up or engage in partnerships	3	9
5. Legal protection for brands and products	3	9
6. Restrictions on monetary transfers	2	8
7. Revaluation of currency in the past five years	2	7
8. Balance-of-payments situation	2	9
9. Drain on hard currency through energy imports	3	14
10. Financial standing	3	8
11. Restrictions on the exchange of local and foreign currencies	2	8

Source: Adapted from E. Dichtl and H. G. Koeglmayr (1986). "Country Risk Ratings." *Management Review,* 26(4), pp. 2–10. Reprinted with permission.

Managing Political Risk

Unlike financial risks, there are relatively few tools for managing the political risks associated with pursuing an international strategy. Obviously, one option would be to pursue international opportunities only in countries where political risk is very small. However, it is often the case that significant business opportunities exist in politically risky countries precisely because they are politically risky. Alternatively, firms can limit their investment in politically risky environments. However, these limited investments may not enable a firm to take full advantage of whatever economies of scope might exist by engaging in business in that country.

Another approach to managing political risk is to see each of the determinants of political risk, listed in Table 11.4, as negotiation points as a firm enters into a new country market. In many circumstances, those in a nondomestic market have just as much an interest in seeing a firm begin doing business in a new market as does the firm contemplating entry. International firms can sometimes use this bargaining power to negotiate entry conditions that reduce, or even neutralize, some of the sources of political risk in a country. Of course, no matter how skilled a firm is in negotiating these entry conditions, a change of government or changes in laws can quickly nullify any agreements.

A third approach to managing political risk is to turn this risk from a threat into an opportunity. One firm that has been successful in this way is Schlumberger, an international oil services company. Schlumberger has headquarters in New York, Paris, and the Caribbean; it is a truly international company. Schlumberger management has adopted a policy of strict neutrality in interactions with governments in the developing world. Because of this policy, Schlumberger has been able to avoid political entanglements and continues to do business where many firms find the political risks too great. Put differently, Schlumberger has developed valuable, rare, and costly-to-imitate resources and capabilities in managing political risks and is using these resources to generate high levels of economic performance.[30]

Research on the Value of International Strategies

Overall, research on the economic consequences of implementing international strategies is mixed. Some research has found that the performance of firms pursuing international strategies is superior to the performance of firms operating only in domestic markets.[31] However, most of this work has not examined the particular economies of scope that a firm is attempting to realize through its internationalization efforts. Moreover, several of these studies have attempted to evaluate the impact of international strategies on firm performance by using accounting measures of performance. Other research has found that the risk-adjusted performance of firms pursuing an international strategy is not different from the risk-adjusted performance of firms pursuing purely domestic strategies.[32]

These ambivalent findings are not surprising, since the economic value of international strategies depends on whether a firm pursues valuable economies of scope when implementing this strategy. Most of this empirical work fails to examine the economies of scope that a firm's international strategy might be based on. Moreover, even if a firm is able to realize real economies of scope from its international strategies, to be a source of sustained competitive advantage, this economy of scope must also be rare and costly to imitate, and the firm must be organized to fully realize it.

International Strategies and Sustained Competitive Advantage

As suggested earlier in this chapter, much of the discussion of rarity and imitability in strategic alliance, diversification, and merger and acquisition strategies also applies to international strategies. However, some aspects of rarity and imitability are unique to international strategies.

The Rarity of International Strategies

In many ways, it seems likely that international strategies are becoming less rare among most competing firms. Consider, for example, the increasingly international strategies of many telephone companies around the world. Through much of the 1980s, telecommunications remained a highly regulated industry around the world. Phone companies rarely ventured beyond their country borders and had few, if any, international aspirations. However, as government restrictions on telecommunications firms around the world began to be lifted, these firms began exploring new business alternatives. For many firms, this originally meant exploring new telecommunications businesses in their domestic markets. Thus, for example, many formerly regulated telecommunications firms in the United States began to explore business opportunities in less regulated segments of the U.S. telecommunications market, including cellular telephones and paging. Over time, these same firms began to explore business opportunities overseas.

In the past several years, the telecommunications industry has begun to consolidate on a worldwide basis. For example, in the early 1990s, Southwestern Bell (now AT&T) purchased a controlling interest in Mexico's government-owned telecommunications company. Ameritech (now a division of AT&T), Bell Atlantic, U.S. West, BellSouth, and Pacific Telesis (now a division of AT&T) also engaged in various international operations. In the late 1990s, MCI (a U.S. firm) and British Telecom (a British company) merged. In 1999, the Vodafone Group (a British-headquartered telecommunications company) purchased AirTouch Cellular (a U.S. firm) for $60.29 billion, formed a strategic alliance with U.S. West (another U.S. firm), purchased Mannesman (a German telecommunications firm) for $127.76 billion, and increased its ownership interest in several smaller telecommunications companies around the world. Also, in 1999, Olivetti (the Italian electronics firm) successfully beat back Deutsche Telephone's effort to acquire ItaliaTelecom (the Italian telephone company). Obviously, international strategies are no longer rare among telecommunications companies.[33]

There are, of course, several reasons for the increased popularity of international strategies. Not the least of these are the substantial economies of scope that internationalizing firms can realize. In addition, several changes in the organization of the international economy have facilitated the growth in popularity of international strategies. For example, the General Agreement on Tariff and Trade (GATT) treaty, in conjunction with the development of the European Community (EC), the Andean Common Market (ANCOM), the Association of Southeast Asian Nations (ASEAN), the North American Free Trade Agreement (NAFTA), and other free-trade zones, has substantially reduced both tariff and nontariff barriers to trade. These changes have helped facilitate trade among countries included in an agreement; they have also spurred firms that wish to take advantage of these opportunities to expand their operations into these countries.

Improvements in the technological infrastructure of business are also important contributors to the growth in the number of firms pursuing international strategies. Transportation (especially air travel) and communication (via computers, fax, telephones, pagers, cellular telephones, and so forth) have evolved to the point where it is now much easier for firms to monitor and integrate their international operations than it was just a few years ago. This infrastructure helps reduce the cost of implementing an international strategy and thus increases the probability that firms will pursue these opportunities.

Finally, the emergence of various communication, technical, and accounting standards is facilitating international strategies. For example, there is currently a de facto world standard in personal computers. Moreover, most of the software that runs off these computers is flexible and interchangeable. Someone can write a report on a PC in India and print that report out on a PC in France with no real difficulties. There is also a world de facto standard business language—English. Although fully understanding a non-English–speaking culture requires managers to learn the native tongue, it is nevertheless possible to manage international business operations by using English.

Even though it seems that more and more firms are pursuing international strategies, it does not follow that these strategies will never be rare among a set of competing firms. Rare international strategies can exist in at least two ways. Given the enormous range of business opportunities that exist around the globe, it may very well be the case that huge numbers of firms can implement international strategies and still not compete head to head when implementing these strategies.

Even if several firms are competing to exploit the same international opportunity, the rarity criterion can still be met if the resources and capabilities that a particular firm brings to this international competition are themselves rare. Examples of these rare resources and capabilities might include unusual marketing skills, highly differentiated products, special technology, superior management talent, and economies of scale.[34] To the extent that a firm pursues one of the economies of scope listed in Table 11.1 using resources and capabilities that are rare among competing firms, that firm can gain at least a temporary competitive advantage, even if its international strategy, per se, is not rare.

VRIO

The Imitability of International Strategies

Like all the strategies discussed in this book, both the direct duplication of and substitutes for international strategies are important in evaluating the imitability of these actions.

Direct Duplication of International Strategies

In evaluating the possibility of the direct duplication of international strategies, two questions must be asked: (1) Will firms try to duplicate valuable and rare international strategies? and (2) Will firms be able to duplicate these valuable and rare strategies?

There seems little doubt that, in the absence of artificial barriers, the profits generated by one firm's valuable and rare international strategies will motivate other firms to try to imitate the resources and capabilities required to implement these strategies. This is what has occurred in the international telecommunications industry. This rush to internationalization has occurred in numerous other industries as well. For example, the processed-food industry at one time had a strong home-market orientation. However, because of the success of Nestlé and Proctor & Gamble worldwide, most processed-food companies now engage in at least some international operations.

However, simply because competing firms often try to duplicate a successful firm's international strategy does not mean that they are always able to do so. To the extent that a successful firm exploits resources or capabilities that are path dependent, uncertain, or socially complex in its internationalization efforts, direct duplication may be too costly, and thus international strategies can be a source of sustained competitive advantage. Indeed, there is some reason to believe that at least some of the resources and capabilities that enable a firm to pursue an international strategy are likely to be costly to imitate.

For example, the ability to develop detailed local knowledge of nondomestic markets may require firms to have management teams with a great deal of foreign experience. Some firms may have this kind of experience in their top management teams; other firms may not. One survey of 433 chief executive officers from around the world reported that 14 percent of U.S. Chief Executive Officers (CEOs) had no foreign experience and that the foreign experience of 56 percent of U.S. CEOs was limited to vacation travel. Another survey showed that only 22 percent of the CEOs of multinational companies have extensive international experience.[35] Of course, it can take a great deal of time for a firm that does not have much foreign experience in its management team to develop that experience. Firms that lack this kind of experience will have to bring managers in from outside the organization, invest in developing this experience internally, or both. Of course, these activities are costly. The cost of creating this experience base in a firm's management team can be thought of as one of the costs of direct duplication.

Substitutes for International Strategies

Even if direct duplication of a firm's international strategies is costly, substitutes might still exist that limit the ability of that strategy to generate sustained competitive advantages. In particular, because international strategies are just a special case of corporate strategies in general, any of the other corporate strategies discussed in this book—including some types of strategic alliances, diversification, and mergers and acquisitions—can be at least partial substitutes for international strategies.

For example, it may be possible for a firm to gain at least some of the economies of scope listed in Table 11.1 by implementing a corporate diversification strategy within a single country market, especially if that market is large and geographically diverse. One such market, of course, is the United States. A firm that originally conducted business in the northeastern United States can gain many of the benefits of internationalization by beginning business operations in the southern United States, on the West Coast, or in the Pacific Northwest. In this sense, geographic diversification within the United States is at least a partial substitute for internationalization and is one reason why many U.S. firms have lagged behind European and Asian firms in their international efforts.

There are, however, some economies of scope listed in Table 11.1 that can be gained only through international operations. For example, because there are usually few limits on capital flows within most countries, risk management is directly valuable to a firm's equity holders only for firms pursuing business opportunities across countries where barriers to capital flow exist.

The Organization of International Strategies

VRIO

To realize the full economic potential of a valuable, rare, and costly-to-imitate international strategy, firms must be appropriately organized.

Becoming International: Organizational Options

A firm implements an international strategy when it diversifies its business operations across country boundaries. However, firms can organize their international business operations in a wide variety of ways. Some of the most common, ranging

TABLE 11.5 Organizing Options for Firms Pursuing International Strategies

Market Governance	Intermediate Market Governance	Hierarchical Governance
Exporting	Licensing	Mergers
	Non-equity alliances	Acquisitions
	Equity alliances	Wholly owned subsidiaries
	Joint ventures	

from market forms of governance to manage simple export operations to the use of wholly owned subsidiaries to manage **foreign direct investment**, are listed in Table 11.5.

Market Exchanges and International Strategies

Firms can maintain traditional arm's-length market relationships between themselves and their nondomestic customers and still implement international strategies. They do this by simply exporting their products or services to nondomestic markets and limiting any foreign direct investment into nondomestic markets. Of course, exporting firms generally have to work with some partner or partners to receive, market, and distribute their products in a nondomestic setting. However, it is possible for exporting firms to use contracts to manage their relationship with these foreign partners and thereby maintain arm's-length relationships with them—all the time engaging in international operations.

The advantages of adopting exporting as a way to manage an international strategy include its relatively low cost and the limited risk exposure that firms pursuing international opportunities in this manner face. Firms that are just beginning to consider international strategies can use market-based exporting to test international waters—to find out if there is demand for their current products or services, to develop some experience operating in nondomestic markets, or to begin to develop relationships that could be valuable in subsequent international strategy efforts. If firms discover that there is not much demand for their products or services in a nondomestic market, or if they discover that they do not have the resources and capabilities to effectively compete in those markets, they can simply cease their exporting operations. The direct cost of ceasing export operations can be quite low, especially if a firm's volume of exports is small and the firm has not invested in plant and equipment designed to facilitate exporting. Certainly, if a firm has limited its foreign direct investment, it does not risk losing this investment if it ceases export operations.

However, the opportunity costs associated with restricting a firm's international operations to exporting can be significant. Of the economies of scope listed in Table 11.1, only gaining access to new customers for a firm's current products or services can be realized through exporting. Other economies of scope that hold some potential for firms exploring international business operations are out of the reach of firms that restrict their international operations to exporting. For some firms, realizing economies from gaining access to new customers is sufficient, and exporting is a long-run viable strategy. However, to the extent that other economies of scope might exist for a firm, limiting international operations to exporting can limit the firm's economic profit.

Intermediate Market Exchanges and International Strategies

If a firm decides to move beyond exporting in pursuing international strategies, a wide range of **strategic alliances** are available. These alliances range from simple licensing arrangements, where a domestic firm grants a firm in a nondomestic market the right to use its products and brand names to sell products in that nondomestic market, to full-blown joint ventures, where a domestic firm and a nondomestic firm create an independent organizational entity to manage international efforts. As suggested in Chapter 9, the recent growth in the number of firms pursuing strategic alliance strategies is a direct result of the growth in popularity of international strategies. Strategic alliances are one of the most common ways that firms manage their international efforts.

Most of the discussion of the value, rarity, imitability, and organization of strategic alliances in Chapter 9 applies to the analysis of strategic alliances to implement an international strategy. However, many of the opportunities and challenges of managing strategic alliances as cooperative strategies, discussed in Chapter 9, are exacerbated in the context of international strategic alliances.

For example, it was suggested that opportunistic behavior (in the form of adverse selection, moral hazard, or holdup) can threaten the stability of strategic alliances domestically. Opportunistic behavior is a problem because partners in a strategic alliance find it costly to observe and evaluate the performance of alliance partners. Obviously, the costs and difficulty of evaluating the performance of an alliance partner in an international alliance are greater than the costs and difficulty of evaluating the performance of an alliance partner in a purely domestic alliance. Geographic distance, differences in traditional business practices, language barriers, and cultural differences can make it very difficult for firms to accurately evaluate the performance and intentions of international alliance partners.

These challenges can manifest themselves at multiple levels in an international strategic alliance. For example, one study has shown that managers in U.S. organizations, on average, have a negotiation style very different from that of managers in Chinese organizations. Chinese managers tend to interrupt each other and ask many more questions during negotiations than do U.S. managers. As U.S. and Chinese firms begin to negotiate collaborative agreements, it will be difficult for U.S. managers to judge whether the Chinese negotiation style reflects Chinese managers' fundamental distrust of U.S. managers or is simply a manifestation of traditional Chinese business practices and culture.[36]

Similar management style differences have been noted between Western and Japanese managers. One Western manager was quoted:[37]

> *Whenever I made a presentation [to our partner], I was one person against 10 or 12. They'd put me in front of a flip chart, and then stop me while they went into a conversation in Japanese for 10 minutes. If I asked them a question they would break into Japanese to first decide what I wanted to know, and then would discuss options in terms of what they might tell me, and finally would come back with an answer.*

During those 10-minute breaks in the conversation, it would be very difficult for this manager to know whether the Japanese managers were trying to develop a complete and accurate answer to his question or scheming to provide an incomplete and misleading answer. In this ambiguous setting, to prevent potential opportunism, Western managers might demand greater levels of governance than were actually necessary. In fact, one study has shown that differences in the perceived trustworthiness of international partners have an impact on the kind of governance mechanisms that are put into place when firms begin international operations. If partners are not perceived as being trustworthy, then elaborate governance devices, including joint ventures, are created even if the partners are in fact trustworthy.[38]

Cultural and style conflicts leading to perceived opportunism problems are not restricted to alliances between Asian and Western organizations. U.S. firms operating with Mexican partners often discover numerous subtle and complex cultural differences. For example, a U.S. firm operating a steel conveyor plant in Puebla, Mexico, implemented a three-stage employee grievance policy. An employee who had a grievance first went to the immediate supervisor and then continued up the chain of command until the grievance was resolved one way or another. United States managers were satisfied with this system and pleased that no grievances had been registered—until the day the entire plant walked out on strike. It turns out that there had been numerous grievances, but Mexican workers had felt uncomfortable directly confronting their supervisors with these problems. Such confrontations are considered antisocial in Mexican culture.[39]

Although significant challenges are associated with managing strategic alliances across country boundaries, there are significant opportunities as well. Strategic alliances can enable a firm pursuing an international strategy to realize any of the economies of scope listed in Table 11.1. Moreover, if a firm is able to develop valuable, rare, and costly to imitate resources and capabilities in managing strategic alliances, the use of alliances in an international context can be a source of sustained competitive advantage.

Hierarchical Governance and International Strategies

Firms may decide to integrate their international operations into their organizational hierarchies by acquiring a firm in a nondomestic market or by forming a new wholly owned subsidiary to manage their operations in a nondomestic market. Obviously, both of these international investments involve substantial direct foreign investment by a firm over long periods of time. These investments are subject to both political and economic risks and should be undertaken only if the economy of scope that can be realized through international operations is significant and other ways of realizing this economy of scope are not effective or efficient.

Although full integration in international operations can be expensive and risky, it can have some important advantages for internationalizing firms. First, like strategic alliances, this approach to internationalization can enable a firm to realize any of the economies of scope listed in Table 11.1. Moreover, integration enables managers to use a wider range of organizational controls to limit the threat of opportunism that are normally not available in market forms of international governance or intermediate market forms of international governance. Finally, unlike strategic alliances, where any profits from international operations must be shared with international partners, integrating into international operations enables firms to capture all the economic profits from their international operations.

Managing the Internationally Diversified Firm

Not surprisingly, the management of international operations can be thought of as a special case of managing a diversified firm. Thus, many of the issues discussed in Chapter 8 apply here. However, managing an internationally diversified firm does create some unique challenges and opportunities.

Decentralized federation	Strategic and operational decisions are delegated to divisions/country companies.
Coordinated federation	Operational decisions are delegated to divisions/country companies; strategic decisions are retained at corporate headquarters.
Centralized hub	Strategic and operational decisions are retained at corporate headquarters.
Transnational structure	Strategic and operational decisions are delegated to those operational entities that maximize responsiveness to local conditions and international integration.

TABLE 11.6 Structural Options for Firms Pursuing International Strategies

Source: C. A. Bartlett and S. Ghoshal (1989). *Managing Across Borders: The Transnational Solution.* Boston: Harvard Business School Press.

Organizational Structure. Firms pursuing an international strategy have four basic organizational structural alternatives, listed in Table 11.6 and discussed later. Although each of these structures has some special features, they are all special cases of the multidivisional structure first introduced in Chapter 8.[40]

Some firms organize their international operations as a **decentralized federation**. In this organizational structure, each country in which a firm operates is organized as a full profit-and-loss division headed by a division general manager who is typically the president of the company in a particular country. In a decentralized federation, there are very few shared activities or other relationships among different divisions/country companies, and corporate headquarters plays a limited strategic role. Corporate staff functions are generally limited to the collection of accounting and other performance information from divisions/country companies and to reporting this aggregate information to appropriate government officials and to the financial markets. Both strategic and operational decision making are delegated to division general managers/country company presidents in a decentralized federation organizational structure. There are relatively few examples of pure decentralized federations in today's world economy, but firms like Nestlé, CIBA-Geigy, and Electrolux have many of the attributes of this type of structure.[41]

A second structural option for international firms is the **coordinated federation**. In a coordinated federation, each country operation is organized as a full profit-and-loss center, and division general managers can be presidents of country companies. However, unlike the case in a decentralized federation, strategic and operational decisions are not fully delegated to division general managers. Operational decisions are delegated to division general managers/country presidents, but broader strategic decisions are made at corporate headquarters. Moreover, coordinated federations attempt to exploit various shared activities and other relationships among their divisions/country companies. It is not uncommon for coordinated federations to have corporately sponsored central research and development laboratories, corporately sponsored manufacturing and technology development initiatives, and corporately sponsored management training and development operations. There are numerous examples of coordinated federations in today's world economy, including General Electric, General Motors, IBM, and Coca-Cola.

A third structural option for international firms is the **centralized hub**. In centralized hubs, operations in different companies may be organized into profit-and-loss centers, and division general managers may be country company presidents. However, most of the strategic and operational decision making in these firms takes place at the corporate center. The role of divisions/country companies in centralized hubs is simply to implement the strategies, tactics, and policies that have been chosen at headquarters. Of course, divisions/country companies are also a source of information for headquarters staff when these decisions are being made. However, in centralized hubs, strategic and operational decision rights are retained at the corporate center. Many Japanese and Korean firms are managed as centralized hubs, including Toyota, Mitsubishi, and NEC (in Japan) and Goldstar, Daewoo, and Hyundai (in Korea).[42]

A fourth structural option for international firms is the **transnational structure**. This structure is most appropriate for implementing the transnational strategy described earlier in this chapter. In many ways, the transnational structure is similar to the coordinated federation. In both, strategic decision-making responsibility is largely retained at the corporate center, and operational decision making is largely delegated to division general managers/country presidents. However, important differences also exist.

In a coordinated federation structure, shared activities and other cross-divisional/cross-country economies of scope are managed by the corporate center. Thus, for many of these firms, if research and development is seen as a potentially valuable economy of scope, a central research and development laboratory is created and managed by the corporate center. In the transnational structure, these centers of corporate economies of scope may be managed by the corporate center. However, they are more likely to be managed by specific divisions/country companies within the corporation. Thus, for example, if one division/country company develops valuable, rare, and costly-to-imitate research-and-development capabilities in its ongoing business activities in a particular country, that division/country company could become the center of research-and-development activity for the entire corporation. If one division/country company develops valuable, rare, and costly-to-imitate manufacturing technology development skills in its ongoing business activities in a particular country, that division/country company could become the center for manufacturing technology development for the entire corporation.

The role of corporate headquarters in a transnational structure is to constantly scan business operations across different countries for resources and capabilities that might be a source of competitive advantage for other divisions/country companies in the firm. Once these special skills are located, corporate staff must then determine the best way to exploit these economies of scope—whether they should be developed within a single division/country company (to gain economies of scale) and then transferred to other divisions/country companies, or developed through an alliance between two or more divisions/country companies (gain economies of scale) and then transferred to other divisions/country companies, or developed for the entire firm at corporate headquarters. These options are not available to decentralized federations (which always let individual divisions/country companies develop their own competencies), coordinated federations, or centralized hubs (which always develop corporate-wide economies of scope at the corporate level). Firms that have been successful in adopting this transnational structure include Ford (Ford Europe has become a leader for automobile design in all of the Ford Motor Company) and Ericson (Ericson's Australian subsidiary developed this Swedish company's first electronic telecommunication switch, and corporate headquarters was able to help transfer this technology to other Ericson subsidiaries).[43]

Organizational Structure, Local Responsiveness, and International Integration. It should be clear that the choice among these four approaches to managing international strategies depends on the trade-offs that firms are willing to make between local responsiveness and international integration. Firms that seek to maximize their local responsiveness will tend to choose a decentralized federation structure. Firms that seek to maximize international integration in their operations will typically opt for centralized hub structures. Firms that seek to balance the need for local responsiveness and international integration will typically choose centralized federations. Firms that attempt to optimize both local responsiveness and international integration will choose a transnational organizational structure.

Management Control Systems and Compensation Policies. Like the multidivisional structure discussed in Chapter 8, none of the organizational structures described in Table 11.5 can stand alone without the support of a variety of management control systems and management compensation policies. All the management control processes discussed in Chapter 8, including evaluating the performance of divisions, allocating capital, and managing the exchange of intermediate products among divisions, are also important for firms organizing to implement an international strategy. Moreover, the same management compensation challenges and opportunities discussed in that chapter apply in the organization of international strategies as well.

However, as is often the case when organizing processes originally developed to manage diversification within a domestic market are extended to the management of international diversification, many of the management challenges highlighted in Chapter 8 are exacerbated in an international context. This puts an even greater burden on senior managers in an internationally diversified firm to choose control systems and compensation policies that create incentives for division general managers/country presidents to appropriately cooperate to realize the economies of scope that originally motivated the implementation of an international strategy.

Summary

International strategies can be seen as a special case of diversification strategies. Firms implement international strategies when they pursue business opportunities that cross country borders. Like all diversification strategies, international strategies must exploit real economies of scope that outside investors find too costly to exploit on their own in order to be valuable. Five potentially valuable economies of scope in international strategies are (1) to gain access to new customers for a firm's current products or services, (2) to gain access to low-cost factors of production, (3) to develop new core competencies, (4) to leverage current core competencies in new ways, and (5) to manage corporate risk.

As firms pursue these economies of scope, they must evaluate the extent to which they can be responsive to local market needs and obtain the advantages of international integration. Firms that attempt to accomplish both these objectives are said to be implementing a transnational strategy. Both economic and political risks can affect the value of a firm's international strategies.

To be a source of sustained competitive advantage, a firm's international strategies must be valuable, rare, and costly to imitate, and the firm must be organized to realize the full potential of its international strategies. Even though more and more firms are pursuing international strategies, these strategies can still be rare, for at least two reasons: (1) Given the broad range of international opportunities, firms may not compete head to head with other firms pursuing the same international strategies that they are pursuing; and (2) firms may bring valuable and rare resources and capabilities to the international strategies they pursue. Both direct duplication and substitution can affect the imitability of a firm's international strategy. Direct duplication is not likely when firms bring valuable, rare, and costly to imitate resources and capabilities to bear in their international strategies. Several substitutes for international strategies exist, including some strategic alliances, vertical integration, diversification, and mergers and acquisitions, especially if these strategies are pursued in a large and diverse single country market. However, some potential economies of scope from international strategies can be exploited only by operating across country borders.

Firms have several organizational options as they pursue international strategies, including market forms of exchange (for example, exports), strategic alliances, and vertical integration (for example, wholly owned subsidiaries). Four alternative structures, all special cases of the multidivisional structure introduced in Chapter 8, can be used to manage these international operations: a decentralized federation structure, a coordinated federation structure, a centralized hub structure, and a transnational structure. These structures need to be consistent with a firm's emphasis on being responsive to local markets, on exploiting international integration opportunities, or both.

Challenge Questions

1. Are international strategies always just a special case of diversification strategies that a firm might pursue? What, if anything, is different about international strategies and diversification strategies?

2. In your view, is gaining access to low-cost labor a sufficient reason for a firm to pursue an international strategy? Why or why not? In your view, is gaining access to special tax breaks a sufficient reason for a firm to pursue an international strategy? Why or why not?

3. The transnational strategy is often seen as one way in which firms can avoid the limitations inherent in the local responsiveness/international integration trade-off. However, given the obvious advantages of being both locally responsive and internationally integrated, why are apparently only a relatively few firms implementing a transnational strategy? What implications does your analysis have for the ability of a transnational strategy to be a source of sustained competitive advantage for a firm?

4. On average, is the threat of adverse selection and moral hazard in strategic alliances greater for firms pursuing an international strategy or a domestic strategy? Why?

5. How are the organizational options for implementing an international strategy related to the M-form structure described in Chapter 8? Are these international organizational options just special cases of the M-form structure, with slightly different emphases, or are these international organizational options fundamentally different from the M-form structure?

Problem Set

1. In which country is it riskiest to begin international operations: Mexico, Argentina, or Poland? Justify your conclusions.

2. Your firm has decided to begin selling its mining machinery products in Ghana. Unfortunately, there is not a highly developed trading market for currency in Ghana. However, Ghana does have significant exports of cocoa. Describe a process by which you would be able to sell your machines in Ghana and still translate your earnings into a tradable currency (e.g., dollars or euros).

3. Match the actions of these firms with their sources of potential value.

(a) Tata Motors (India) acquires Jaguar (U.K.).
(b) Microsoft (U.S.) opens four research and development centers in Europe.
(c) Disney opens Disney–Hong Kong.
(d) Merck forms a research and development alliance with an Indian pharmaceutical firm.
(e) Lenovo purchases IBM's laptop computer business.
(f) Honda Motor Company opens an automobile manufacturing plant in southern China. Most of the cars it produces are sold in China.
(g) Honda starts exporting cars made in its China plant to Japan.
(h) A Canadian gold mining company acquires an Australian opal mining company.

1. Managing corporate risk
2. New core competencies
3. Leveraging current core competencies in new ways
4. Gaining access to low-cost factors of production
5. New customers for current products or services

End Notes

1. See Yoshino, M., S. Hall, and T. Malnight. (1991). "Whirlpool Corp.," Harvard Business School Case no. 9-391-089.
2. http://258marketing.wordpress.com/2008/02/27/bad-ads-nothing-sucks-like-an-electrolux/. Accessed June 17, 2009.
3. See Perry, N. J. (1991). "Will Sony make it in Hollywood?" *Fortune*, September 9, pp. 158–166; and Montgomery, C. (1993). "Marks and Spencer Ltd. (A)," Harvard Business School Case no. 9-391-089.
4. See Rapoport, C. (1994). "Nestlé's brand building machine." *Fortune*, September 19, pp. 147–156.
5. See Yoshino, M. Y., and P. Stoneham. (1992). "Proctor & Gamble Japan (A)," Harvard Business School Case no. 9-793-035.
6. See Davis, B. (1995). "U.S. expects goals in pact with Japan to be met even without overt backing," *The Wall Street Journal*, June 30, p. A3; Bounds, W., and B. Davis. (1995). "U.S. to launch new case against Japan over Kodak," *The Wall Street Journal*, June 30, p. A3; Jacob, R. (1992). "India is opening for business," *Fortune*, November 16, pp. 128–130; and Rugman, A., and R. Hodgetts. (1995). *Business: A Strategic Management Approach*. New York: McGraw-Hill.
7. See Jacob, R. (1992). "India is opening for business," *Fortune*, November 16, pp. 128–130; Serwer, A. E. (1994). "McDonald's conquers the world," *Fortune*, October 17, pp. 103–116; and World Bank (1999). *World Development Report*, Oxford: Oxford University Press.
8. See Jacob, R. (1992). "India is opening for business," *Fortune*, November 16, pp. 128–130; Ignatius, A. (1993). "Commodity giant: Marc Rich & Co. does big deals at big risk in former U.S.S.R.," *The Wall Street Journal*, May 13, p. A1; and Kraar, L. (1995). "The risks are rising in China," *Fortune*, March 6, pp. 179–180.
9. The life cycle is described in Utterback, J. M., and W. J. Abernathy. (1975). "A dynamic model of process and product innovation," *Omega*, 3, pp. 639–656; Abernathy, W. J., and J. M. Utterback. (1978). "Patterns of technological innovation," *Technology Review*, 80, pp. 40–47; and Grant, R. M. (1991a). *Contemporary Strategy Analysis*. Cambridge, MA: Basil Blackwell.
10. See Bradley, S. P., and S. Cavanaugh. (1994). "Crown Cork and Seal in 1989," Harvard Business School Case no. 9-793-035; and Hamermesh, R. G., and R. S. Rosenbloom. (1989). "Crown Cork and Seal Co., Inc.," Harvard Business School Case no. 9-388-096. Of course, this strategy works only until nondomestic markets mature. This occurred for Crown Cork and Seal during the 1990s. Since then, they have had to search elsewhere for growth opportunities.
11. Porter, M. E. (1986). "Competition in international industries: A conceptual framework," in M. E. Porter (ed.), *Competition in International Industries*. Boston: Harvard Business School Press, p. 43; and Ghoshal, S. (1987). "Global strategy: An organizing framework," *Strategic Management Journal*, 8, p. 436.
12. See Kobrin, S. (1991). "An empirical analysis of the determinants of global integration," *Strategic Management Journal*, 12, pp. 17–31.
13. See Trager, J. (1992). *The People's Chronology*. New York: Henry Holt.
14. Kraar, L. (1992). "Korea's tigers keep roaring," *Fortune*, May 4, pp. 108–110.
15. See Collis, D. J. (1991). "A resource-based analysis of international competition: The case of the bearing industry," *Strategic Management Journal*, 12 (Summer Special Issue), pp. 49–68; and Engardio, P. (1993). "Motorola in China: A great leap forward," *Business Week*, May 17, pp. 58–59.
16. Gain, S. (1993). "Korea is overthrown as sneaker champ," *The Wall Street Journal*, October 7, p. A14.
17. See Reibstein, L., and M. Levinson. (1991). "A Mexican miracle?" *Newsweek*, May 20, p. 42; and de Forest, M. E. (1994). "Thinking of a plant in Mexico?" *Academy of Management Executive*, 8(1), pp. 33–40.
18. See Zimmerman, M. (1985). *How to Do Business with the Japanese*. New York: Random House; and Osborn, R. N., and C. C. Baughn. (1987). "New patterns in the formation of US/Japan cooperative ventures: The role of technology," *Columbia Journal of World Business*, 22, pp. 57–65.
19. Ibid.
20. See Benedict, R. (1946). *The Chrysanthemum and the Sword*. New York: New American Library; Peterson, R. B., and H. F. Schwind. (1977). "A comparative study of personnel problems in companies and joint ventures in Japan," *Journal of Business Studies*, 8(1), pp. 45–55; Peterson, R. B., and J. Y. Shimada. (1978). "Sources of management problems in Japanese-American joint ventures," *Academy of Management Review*, 3, pp. 796–804; and Hamel, G. (1991). "Competition for competence and

inter-partner learning within strategic alliances," *Strategic Management Journal*, 12, pp. 83–103.
21. See Burgleman, R. A. (1983). "A process model of internal corporate venturing in the diversified major firm," *Administrative Science Quarterly*, 28(2), pp. 223–244; Hedberg, B. L. T. (1981). "How organizations learn and unlearn," in P. C. Nystrom and W. H. Starbuck (eds.), *Handbook of Organizational Design*. London: Oxford University Press; Nystrom, P. C., and W. H. Starbuck. (1984). "To avoid organizational crisis, unlearn," *Organizational Dynamics*, 12(4), pp. 53–65; and Argyris, C., and D. A. Schon. (1978). *Organizational Learning*. Reading, MA: Addison-Wesley.
22. A problem described in Burgleman, R. A. (1983b). "A process model of internal corporate venturing in the diversified major firm," *Administrative Science Quarterly*, 28(2), pp. 223–244.
23. Quoted in Hamel, G. (1991). "Competition for competence and inter-partner learning within strategic alliances," *Strategic Management Journal*, 12, p. 97.
24. See Agmon, T., and D. R. Lessard. (1977). "Investor recognition of corporate diversification," *The Journal of Finance*, 32, pp. 1049–1056.
25. Rapoport, C. (1994). "Nestlé's brand building machine," *Fortune*, September 19, pp. 147–156.
26. See Bartlett, C. A., and S. Ghoshal. (1989). *Managing across Borders: The Transnational Solution*. Boston, MA: Harvard Business School Press.
27. See Rugman, A., and R. Hodgetts. (1995). *International Business: A Strategic Management Approach*. New York: McGraw-Hill.
28. Glynn, M. A. (1993). "Strategic planning in Nigeria versus U.S.: A case of anticipating the (next) coup," *Academy of Management Executive*, 7(3), pp. 82–83.
29. Dichtl, E., and H. G. Koeglmayr. (1986). "Country risk ratings," *Management International Review*, 26(4), pp. 2–10.
30. See Auletta, K. (1983). "A certain poetry—Parts I and II," *The New Yorker*, June 6, pp. 46–109; and June 13, pp. 50–91.
31. See, for example, Leftwich, R. B. (1974). "U.S. Multinational companies: Profitability, financial leverage and effective income tax rates," *Survey of Current Business*, 54, May, pp. 27–36; Dunning, J. H. (1973). "The determinants of production," *Oxford Economic Papers*, 25, November, pp. 289–336; Errunza, V., and L. W. Senbet. (1981). "The effects of international operations on the market value of the firm: Theory and evidence," *The Journal of Finance*, 36, pp. 401–418; Grant, R. M. (1987). "Multinationality and performance among British manufacturing companies," *Journal of International Business Studies*, 18, (Fall), pp. 78–89; and Rugman, A. (1979). *International Diversification and the Multinational Enterprise*. Lexington, MA: Lexington Books.
32. See, for example, Brewer, H. L. (1981). "Investor benefits from corporate international diversification," *Journal of Financial and Quantitative Analysis*, 16, March, pp. 113–126; and Michel, A., and I. Shaked. (1986). "Multinational corporations vs. domestic corporations: Financial performance and characteristics," *Journal of Business*, 17, (Fall), pp. 89–100.
33. Kirkpatrick, D. (1993). "Could AT&T rule the world?" *Fortune*, May 17, pp. 54–56; Deogun, N. (2000). "Europe Catches Merger Fever As International Volume Sets Record," *The Wall Street Journal*, January 3, p. R8.
34. See Caves, R. E. (1971). "International corporations: The industrial economics of foreign investment," *Economica*, 38, Feb. pp. 1–28; Dunning, J. H. (1973). "The determinants of production," *Oxford Economic Papers*, 25, Nov., pp. 289–336; Hymer, S. (1976). *The International Operations of National Firms: A Study of Direct Foreign Investment*. The MIT Press, Cambridge, MA; Errunza, V., and L. W. Senbet. (1981). "The effects of international operations on the market value of the firm: Theory and evidence," *The Journal of Finance*, 36, pp. 401–418.
35. Anders, G. (1989). "Going global: Vision vs. reality," *The Wall Street Journal*, September 22, p. R21; and Carpenter, M., G. Sanders, and H. Gregerson. (2000). "Building Human Capital with Organizational Context: The Impact of Assignment Experience on Multinational Firm Performance and CEO Pay," *Academy of Management Journal*, forthcoming.
36. Adler, N., J. R. Brahm, and J. L. Graham. (1992). "Strategy implementation: A comparison of face-to-face negotiations in the People's Republic of China and the United States," *Strategic Management Journal*, 13, pp. 449–466.

37. Hamel, G. (1991). "Competition for competence and inter-partner learning within international strategic alliances," *Strategic Management Journal*, 12, p. 95.

38. Shane, S. (1994). "The effect of national culture on the choice between licensing and direct foreign investment," *Strategic Management Journal*, 15, pp. 627–642.

39. See de Forest, M. E. (1994). "Thinking of a plant in Mexico?" *Academy of Management Executive*, 8(1), pp. 33–40.

40. See Bartlett, C. A. (1986). "Building and managing the transnational: The new organizational challenge," in M. E. Porter (ed.), *Competition in International Industries*. Boston: Harvard Business School Press; pp. 367–401; and Bartlett, C. A., and S. Ghoshal. (1989). *Managing across Borders; The Transnational Solution*. Boston: Harvard Business School Press.

41. See Baden-Fuller, C. W. F., and J. M. Stopford. (1991). "Globalization frustrated: The case of white goods," *Strategic Management Journal*, 12, pp. 493–507.

42. See Kraar, L. (1992). "Korea's tigers keep roaring," *Fortune*, May 4, pp. 108–110.

43. Bartlett, C. A., and S. Ghoshal. (1989). *Managing across Borders: The Transnational Solution*. Boston: Harvard Business School Press; and Grant, R. M. (1991a). *Contemporary Strategy Analysis*. Cambridge, MA: Basil Blackwell.

Case 3–1: eBay Customer Support Outsourcing*

"If we are to continue outsourcing, and even consider expanding it, why should we keep paying someone else to do what we can do for ourselves?"

Kathy Dalton leaned forward in her chair. She read the message on her computer screen and let the words sink in. Why had she not anticipated that? After all, she was adept at asking insightful questions. She felt her heart rate quicken.

She would have stared out her office window and pondered this question, but she didn't have an office. In keeping with a well-established Silicon Valley tradition, everyone at eBay, including CEO Meg Whitman, occupied a cubicle. Dalton, an attractive, 38-year-old executive, had joined eBay in late 2002 after years of call center experience for major long distance carriers. Now, nearly two years later, she couldn't think of doing business any other way. She liked being in the center of the action. Sitting in a transparent cube, surrounded by hundreds of service representatives, added to her already high level of energy, and kept her in touch with eBay's internal and external customers.

Dalton reflected on the e-mail she had just received from her boss, Wendy Moss, Vice President of Global Customer Support. She knew she would pick up the phone soon, call Moss, and ask her clarifying questions about her e-mail. Her mind raced through the details of the proposed outsourcing strategy she had submitted to Moss last week. She quizzed herself:

- "Did my team and I make a strong enough case for proposing almost a 100% increase in the amount of volume to be outsourced?"
- "Will eBay management concur with our recommendation to begin outsourcing potentially sensitive risk-related inquires for the first time?"
- "How will senior management react to the addition of a second outsourcing vendor?"
- "Did we cover adequately the types of proposed volumes targeted and how these would be transitioned to the outsourcing vendors?"
- "In the event of a major vendor problem, systems issue, or natural disaster, how executable is our back-out plan?"
- "Will the data in our proposal allay the growing concerns among executives about offshore outsourcing altogether?"

She wondered, "How would eBay senior management react to our proposal to reorganize and expand outsourcing in a new three-tiered approach?" "And, would they even consider expansion in light of recent headlines about companies reducing the amount of work outsourced to India because of quality issues?"

This last question had perplexed her for several months. Not only was it a personal issue for Dalton—she felt her job security at eBay depended largely on the company's continuing commitment to offshore outsourcing—but one she recognized as a business practice whose time perhaps had come and gone. Several leading consultants were claiming that offshoring had lost much of its cachet in recent years as companies were coming to grips with the real costs, logistics, management commitment and service quality associated with third-party partners in India, the

*Professors Scott Newman, Gary Grikscheit, Rohit Verma and Research Assistant Vivek Malapati prepared this case solely as the basis for class discussion. The information presented in this case is based on publicly available information and insights gained through numerous interactions between University of Utah MBA students, their faculty advisors, and local eBay managers during a field study project (sponsored by the University of Utah and approved by the eBay Salt Lake City Service Center). The case contains writer-compiled, disguised information and is not intended to endorse and/or illustrate effective or ineffective service management practices. Certain sections of the case study have been fabricated based on current service management and customer service literature to provide a realistic and stimulating classroom experience. The numbers in the case are available from public information, or estimates, or are fictitious. This case was the winner of the 2006 CIBER-Production and Operations Management Society International Case Competition.

Philippines, and elsewhere. In her proposal, Dalton had reinforced the benefits to eBay of continuing to outsource outside the United States and to weave into her new strategy more "nearshoring" alternatives as well.

Dalton was scheduled to fly to San Jose in just two weeks to present her outsourcing strategy to Whitman and her executive staff. Now, here's Moss' e-mail, questioning why she had not addressed the option of cutting out the middleman and building eBay-owned outsourcing locations in other countries.

A Little History

eBay called itself "The World's Online Marketplace." For the sale of goods and services by a diverse community of individuals and small businesses no venue was more appropriate. eBay's mission was to provide a robust trading platform where practically anyone could trade practically anything. Sellers included individual collectors of the rare and eclectic, as well as major corporations like Microsoft and IBM. Items sold on eBay ranged from collectibles like trading cards, antiques, dolls and housewares to everyday items like used cars, clothing, books, CDs and electronics. With 11 million or more items available on eBay at any one time, it was the largest and most popular person-to-person trading community on the Internet.

eBay came a long way from being a pet project for founder Pierre Omidyar and holding its first auction on Labor Day in September of 1995. Omidyar developed a program and launched it on a Web site called Auction Web. According to eBay legend, he was trying to help his wife find other people with whom she could trade Pez dispensers. Omidyar found he was continually adding storage space to handle the amount of e-mail generated, reflecting the pent-up demand for an online meeting place for sellers and buyers. The site soon began to outgrow his personal Internet account.

Realizing the potential this web service could have, he quit his job as a services development engineer at General Magic, a San Jose based software company, and devoted full time attention managing Auction Web. As traffic increased, he also began charging a fee of $0.25 per listing to compensate for the cost involved in maintaining a business Internet account.

In 1996, Jeff Skoll, a Stanford Business School graduate and friend of Omidyar's joined him to further develop Auction Web. They changed the name to eBay, short for East Bay Technologies. In mid-1997, a Menlo Park based venture capital firm invested $5 million for a 22 percent stake in eBay. Omidyar knew that the venture capital

would be critical in building infrastructure and attracting top-tier management to the company.

In early 1998, Omidyar and Skoll realized eBay needed an experienced CEO to lead and develop an effective management team, as well as to solidify the company's financial position with an IPO. In March of that year, Whitman accepted the position of president and CEO. A graduate of the Harvard Business School, Whitman had learned the importance of branding at companies such as Hasbro and Walt Disney. She hired senior staff from companies like Pepsico and Disney. She built a management team with an average of 20 years of business experience per executive and developed a strong vision for the company. Whitman immediately understood that the eBay community of users was the foundation of the company's business model. A central tenant of eBay's culture was captured in the phrase "The community was not built for eBay, but eBay was built by and for the community." It was not about just selling things on the Internet; it was about bonding people through the Web site.

Business Model and Market Share

Unlike many companies that were born before the Internet and then had to scramble to get online, eBay was born with the net. Its transaction-based business model was perfectly suited for the Internet. Sellers "listed" items for sale on the Web site. Interested buyers could either bid higher than the previous bid in an auction format, or use the "Buy It Now" feature and pay a predetermined price. The seller and buyer worked out the shipping method. Payment was usually made through PayPal, the world's leading online payment company, which eBay acquired in 2002. Because eBay never handled the items being sold, it did not incur warehousing expense and, of course, did not hold any inventory. For a company with almost $8 billion in assets, not a single dollar was invested in inventory (Exhibit 1).

In 2004, eBay reported revenue of nearly $3.3 billion. Revenue was mainly generated from two categories. The first, called the Listing Fee, involved a nominal fee incurred by the seller in posting an item for sale. This fee ranged from $0.25 to $2.00. The second, the Final Value Fee, was charged to the seller as a percentage of the final price when a sale was made. This amounted to between 1.25 percent and 5 percent of the selling price, depending on the price of the item. The Final Value Fee on a $4.00 Beanie Baby would be $0.20, representing a 5 percent fee. The same fee on a mainframe computer selling for $400,000.00 would be 1.25 percent, or $5,000.00.

Being first-to-market in the e-commerce world was frequently an insurmountable competitive edge. eBay

Exhibit 1   Income Statement and Balance Sheet, abridged

eBay's Income Statement (in 000s Dollars)	12/31/2004	12/31/2003	12/31/2002
Net revenues	$ 3,271,309	$ 2,165,096	$ 1,214,100
Cost of net revenues	614,415	416,058	213,876
Gross profit (loss)	2,656,894	1,749,038	1,000,224
Sales & marketing expenses	857,874	567,565	349,650
Product development expenses	240,647	159,315	104,636
General & administrative expenses	415,725	302,703	171,785
Patent litigation expense		29,965	
Payroll expense on employee stock options	17,479	9,590	4,015
Amortization of acquired intangible assets	65,927	50,659	15,941
Total operating expenses	1,597,652	1,119,797	646,027
Income (loss) from operations	1,059,242	629,241	354,197
Interest & other income, net	77,867	37,803	49,209
Interest expense	8,879	4,314	1,492
Impairment of certain equity investments		−1,230	−3,781
Income before income tax—United States	820,892		
Income before Income tax—international	307,338		
Net income (loss)	778,223	441,771	249,891
Net income (loss) per share-diluted	0.57	0.335	0.213
Net income (loss)	778,223	441,771	249,891
Cumulative effect of accounting change		5,413	
Provision for doubtful accounts & auth cred	90,942	46,049	25,455
Provision for transaction losses	50,459	36,401	7,832
Depreciation & amortization	253,690	159,003	76,576
Stock-based compensation		5,492	5,953
Amortization of unearned stock-based compens	5,832		
Tax benefit on the exer of employ stock opts	261,983	130,638	91,237
Impairment of certain equity investments		1,230	3,781
Minority interests	6,122		
Minority interest & other net income adj		7,784	1,324
Gain (loss) on sale of assets			−21,378
Accounts receivable	−105,540	−153,373	−54,583
Funds receivable from customers	−44,751	−38,879	−11,819
Other current assets	−312,756	−13,133	10,716
Other non-current assets	−308	−4,111	−1,195
Deferred tax assets, net		69,770	8,134
Deferred tax liabilities, net	28,652		
Accounts payable	−33,975	17,348	14,631
Net cash flows from investing activities	−2,013,220	−1,319,542	−157,759
Proceeds from issuance of common stock, net	650,638	700,817	252,181
Proceeds (principal pmts) on long-term obligs	−2,969	−11,951	−64
Partnership distributions			−50
Net cash flows from financing activities	647,669	688,866	252,067
Eff of exch rate change on cash & cash equivs	28,768	28,757	11,133
Net incr (decr) in cash & cash equivalents	−51,468	272,200	585,344
Cash & cash equivalents, beginning of year	1,381,513	1,109,313	523,969
Cash & cash equivalents, end of year	1,330,045	1,381,513	1,109,313
Cash paid for interest	8,234	3,237	1,492

Source: Case writers' estimates, compilations, and public records

capitalized on being the first online auction house. Early competition came from companies like OnSale, Auction Universe, Amazon, Yahoo!, and Classified2000. These companies battled eBay on a number of fronts, mainly pricing, advertising online, and on attempting to lure key eBay employees away to join their ranks. eBay's biggest and most formidable competitive threat came from Amazon.com when it spent over $12 million launching its person-to-person auction service in 1999. eBay withstood all of these challenges. Amazon's efforts ultimately failed because it could

Exhibit 2   Online Auction Market Share

	2001		2002		2003		2004	
	U.S.	Int'l	U.S.	Int'l	U.S.	Int'l	U.S.	Int'l
eBay	83%	41%	87%	50%	90%	65%	92%	74%
Yahoo	7%	28%	6%	25%	4%	16%	3%	11%
Amazon	6%	10%	4%	8%	2%	5%	1%	2%
Overstock	N/A	N/A	1%	1%	2%	2%	2%	2%
uBid	1%	1%	1%	1%	1%	N/A	1%	N/A
All others	3%	20%	1%	15%	1%	12%	1%	11%

Source: Case writers' estimates, compilations, and public records

not generate enough site traffic. Auction buyers went where the most items were available for sale, and sellers went where the most buyers were found for their products. eBay had more buyers, more sellers, and more items—more than 1.4 billion items were listed on the site in 2004! These numbers dwarfed the nearest competitor by a factor of over 50. eBay enjoyed a dominant 92 percent market share of the domestic online auction business, and a 74 percent share of the international market (Exhibit 2).

eBay's Customer Support Organization

In December 2004, Dalton was an operations director in eBay's Customer Support organization. She had several major responsibilities; the most critical one was customer support outsourcing, both domestic and offshore (Exhibit 3). This role occupied approximately 80 percent of her time. Upon joining the company, she had relocated to Salt Lake

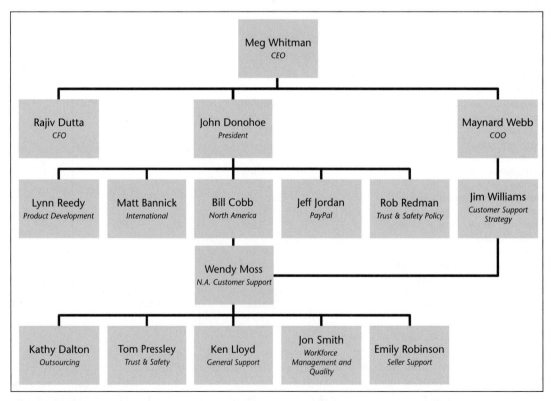

Exhibit 3 eBay Organization Chart

Source: Case writers' compilations and public records

City, Utah, the site of eBay's largest customer service center. Utah's four seasons and mountainous terrain suited her. She loved to ski knee-deep powder in the winter and navigate forest trails on her mountain bike in summer. While thoughts of early season skiing had entered her mind, she had in fact spent the last three weekends in her cube and in conference rooms with her managers hammering out the strategy she had passed on to Moss for review.

Worldwide, eBay's Customer Support staff consisted of an estimated 3,000 FTE, comprising roughly two-thirds of the corporate work force. eBay operated major service centers in Salt Lake City, Omaha, Vancouver, Berlin, and Dublin. Smaller company-owned Customer Support groups were located in Sydney, Hong Kong, London, and Seoul. The majority of these employees spent their workdays responding to customer e-mails. In 2004, eBay answered over 30 million customer inquiries, covering everything from questions about selling, bidding, product categories, billing, and pricing to thornier issues involving illegal or prohibited listings and auction security (Exhibit 4).

The Customer Support organization was made up of two major units—1) General Support and 2) Trust and Safety. Historically, most of the customer contacts were handled by the General Support unit. The communications consisted of questions regarding bidding on auctions, listing and selling items, and account adjustments. By mid-2004, however, nearly 45 percent of inquiries were directed toward the Trust and Safety function. Here, hundreds of employees were responsible for ensuring that the items listed on eBay were legitimate, legal, did not infringe on

copyrighted, patented, or original material, and that they fell within the company's policies, (i.e., no firearms, tobacco or alcohol, human body parts, etc.). It also enforced eBay's guidelines for proper member behavior by policing activities such as shill bidding, merchandise misrepresentation, and outright fraud.

PowerSellers

Approximately 94 percent of eBay's customer service volume was e-mail-based. However, live chat and phone inquiries were growing as the company opened up these channels to more customers, based on their profitability. Live chat volume was predicted to increase to 1.5 million communications in 2005, up 50 percent over 2004. Phone calls handled in 2005 were anticipated to reach 1.4 million, almost double the number in the previous year. This phone volume was expected to come primarily from "PowerSellers," who represented less than 7 percent of eBay users, but, due to the volume of merchandise they traded on the site, accounted for nearly 90 percent of the company's profit.

Phone and live chat access to Customer Support was designed to enlarge the pool of PowerSellers. Dedicated service representatives received additional training in upsell, cross-sell, and auction display techniques to share with sellers to increase the number of items they sold and qualify them for higher PowerSeller monthly sales volume thresholds (Bronze, Silver, Gold, Platinum, Titanium). Once attained, these thresholds qualified sellers for dedicated phone and chat support, as well as for the coveted PowerSeller logo (Exhibit 5).

Trust and Safety

No other company was able to harness the ubiquity of the Web and marry it to the auction concept as successfully as eBay. At the same time, eBay had to confront challenges never faced before, particularly in the arena of auction security and fraud prevention. Caveat emptor, "let the buyer beware," had been a rule in the auction world since the middle ages. With the advent of eBay, buyers had to deal with unknown sellers over the Internet, sight unseen, often in a totally different country, without the ability to personally examine the goods, and with little information about the seller except some written feedback from other buyers who had previously done business with him or her. It was absolutely critical for eBay's survival to create and nurture an environment of trust where millions of people around the globe could feel secure in trading online. The Trust and Safety Department was given this task. Procedural

Exhibit 4	eBay Customer Support Volumes by Channel (in millions)			
	2001	**2002**	**2003**	**2004**
General Support				
E-mail	8.1	12.1	14.6	16.1
Phone	0.1	0.3	0.4	0.8
Chat	NA	NA	0.4	0.4
Total	8.2	12.4	15.4	17.3
Trust & Safety				
E-mail	4	6.8	9.8	12.6
Phone	0	0	0	0
Chat	NA	NA	0.1	0.6
Total	4	6.8	9.9	13.2
Combined GS and T&S				
E-mail	12.1	18.9	24.4	28.7
Phone	0.1	0.3	0.4	0.8
Chat	NA	NA	0.5	1
Total	12.2	19.2	25.3	30.5

Source: Case writers' estimates, compilations, and public records

---

Exhibit 5   PowerSeller Criteria

To qualify, members must:

- Uphold the eBay community values, including honesty, timeliness, and mutual respect
- Average a minimum of $1,000 in sales per month, for three consecutive months
- Achieve an overall Feedback rating of 100, of which 98 percent or more is positive
- Have been an active member for 90 days
- Have an account in good financial standing
- Not violate any severe policies in a 60-day period
- Not violate three or more of **any** eBay policies in a 60-day period
- Maintain a minimum of four average monthly listings for the past three months

PowerSeller program eligibility is reviewed every month. To remain PowerSellers, members must:

- Uphold eBay community values, including honesty, timeliness, and mutual respect
- Maintain the minimum average monthly sales amount for your PowerSeller level
- Maintain a 98 percent positive total feedback rating
- Maintain an account in good financial standing
- Comply with all eBay listing and marketplace *policies*—Not violate any severe policies in a 60-day period and not violate three or more of **any** eBay policies in a 60-day period

PowerSeller Levels

There are five tiers that distinguish PowerSellers, based on their gross monthly sales. Some benefits and services vary with each tier. eBay automatically calculates eligibility each month and notifies qualified sellers via e-mail.

Gross Sales Criteria for each PowerSeller tier

Bronze	Silver	Gold	Platinum	Titanium
$1,000	$3,000	$10,000	$25,000	$150,000

Source: eBay Web site, case writers' estimates, compilations, and public records

---

complexities, the differing legal environments and customs between countries, and the sophistication of online identity theft scams combined to make Trust and Safety a challenging business unit to manage.

Dalton wrestled with a number of questions related to Trust and Safety and its potential for outsourcing:

- "What kind of Trust and Safety volume could be safely outsourced?
- "What kind of Trust and Safety volume could not be outsourced?"
- "How could she and eBay determine the credibility and quality of the potential outsourcing vendors?"
- "How could she guarantee the vendors' ability to safeguard the eBay information entrusted to them?"

A number of eBay's executives had expressed concern and outright hostility to the idea of outsourcing any Trust and Safety volume. Rob Redman headed up the Trust and Safety Policy group in San Jose. He and other executives worried about outside vendors handling the sensitive type of customer inquiries common to this unit, especially when personal information such as Social Security numbers and credit card account numbers could be accessed. In addition, many of the jobs within Trust and Safety required direct and ongoing contact with local, national, and international law enforcement agencies in the hunt for and prosecution of fraudsters. Redman believed outsourcing vendors would never be as skilled at developing and nurturing these key liaisons as eBay's own personnel, and he had made this known to Whitman, Moss, and Dalton on numerous occasions.

Underneath her confident exterior, Dalton worried about these issues as well. She did not have any hands-on background in Trust and Safety herself. Still, she was intrigued by the possibility that several categories of inquiries within the department might be outsourced without undue risk.

Outsourcing Beginnings

By late 1999, eBay had enrolled four million registered members, nearly all in the United States. Five years later, the eBay community had burgeoned to over 135 million members, living in every country in the world. If eBay were its own country, it would have been the ninth largest on earth, behind Russia.

To stay abreast of the growth of its customer base, eBay significantly increased the resources dedicated to its Customer Support group. In the very early days of 1995–1996, founder Omidyar would reserve part of his Saturday afternoons in a local San Jose park to respond directly to member questions. He soon could not manage the volume himself so the first customer service staff was organized. A measure of the power of the eBay community was the fact that these first service staffers were not employees at all, but members who had shown a penchant for helping other eBayers. These people worked on a contract basis out of their homes responding to customers' e-mails. At one time, there were close to 75 such employees, called "remotes," living in 17 different states across the country, handling an average of 5 e-mails per hour at all hours of the day and night, often while sitting in their pajamas!

In early 1998, eBay Customer Support took another step to simplify management and improve the consistency and quality of service. The company hired a small corps of "in-house" customer service personnel in the San Jose, California, headquarters to supplement its remote contractors. The "remotes" had been a creative solution for a time, but one that could not be scaled as the technology, logistics, and training requirements of the Customer Support group increased in sophistication.

Kana

One such technological advancement occurred when eBay purchased the Kana e-mail management system later that year to provide service personnel with a variety of "canned" responses and performance statistics similar to an Automatic Call Distributor. Kana allowed representatives to answer common questions, such as "How do I list an item for sale?", "How do I leave feedback?" or "What do I do with an item I received that is damaged in shipment?" with a few quick keystrokes to input the code number of a pre-scripted e-mail reply. The representatives then took a moment to personalize the e-mail with their name and the recipients' names.

The Kana technology enabled service employees to be trained more quickly and effectively. Most importantly, it reduced response time to customer inquiries and increased the accuracy of information the customer received. It doubled the service representatives' e-mail productivity from 5 responses per hour to 10 and over. Without Kana, there was no way that eBay could have ever considered outsourcing even a portion of its overall Customer Support volume, let alone, as Dalton's new strategy proposed, increasing it to over 50 percent.

By early 1999, nearly twice as many in-house representatives were employed as compared to the "remotes." This staffing strategy had paid off in improved productivity and in the rising customer satisfaction scores received from the hundreds of customers polled by mail each month (Exhibit 6). More in-house staff was needed, and a search was begun to build a dedicated center for Customer Support outside of California in a more cost-efficient locale. Three potential sites were considered—Salt Lake City, Tucson, and Albuquerque. In the end, the Utah location was selected due to the availability of a ready-made facility, as well as a communications infrastructure, generous incentives offered by the state, and the educational level, work ethic, and foreign language capabilities of the potential employees.

Designed originally for around 300 personnel, the Salt Lake facility was enlarged to accommodate over 1,000 by year-end 2000. In addition, a staff of 125 was added in both the newly opened Berlin and the Sydney locations to handle customer service inquiries. Still, with the worldwide popularity of eBay growing at a rate of 250,000 new members each month, it was apparent by 2001 that eBay could hire only so many of its own service personnel and build only so much of its own brick and mortar contact centers, and that even trying to do so would not keep up with the demand (Exhibit 7). Alternatives like outsourcing had to be explored.

Exhibit 6   eBay Customer Support Productivity and Quality

	1998	1999	2000	2001	2002	2003	2004
E-mails Productivity/Hr	4.7	9.5	11.1	13.8	15.3	16	16.1
E-mails per FTE/Month	571	1254	1475	1980	2078	2225	2280
E-mail Quality %	N/A	83%	89%	91%	94%	95%	94%
Customer Satisfaction %	N/A	N/A	84%	86%	87%	88%	88%

Source: Case writers' estimates, compilations, and public records

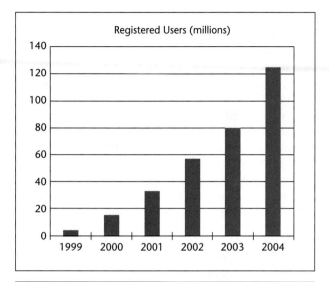

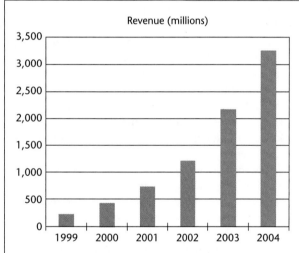

Exhibit 7   Growth in eBay Users and Revenues

Source: Case writers' estimates, compilations, and public records

Outsourcing Pilot

eBay had made headlines for years for its innovation in the online auction space, its market leadership, its product and technological ingenuity, such as member feedback, the Buy-It-Now feature, item search capabilities, Kana, and for its irresistible pace and can-do attitude. eBay did not manage itself by "the seat of its pants," contrary to what others may consider to be a trademark of dotcoms. Far from it, the company was thoughtfully led, financially disciplined, and extremely customer conscious. These were the underpinnings of its tremendous success. eBay let others serve as lab mice, test and bleed, stub their toe, and work out the

wrinkles. Then, and only then, it stepped in and adopted the "latest and greatest" business practices.

Such was the case with outsourcing the elementary portions of its Customer Support operation. Leading companies like American Express, GE, and Citibank had been outsourcing some of their customer service functions for 10 to 15 years domestically, and for at least half that time offshore before eBay felt comfortable in considering outsourcing. By mid-2001, outsourcing surfaced as a viable way for eBay Customer Support to scale to demand, avoid capital outlays, reduce unit costs, and leverage its investment in technology and management talent.

But, the senior staff in San Jose, including Whitman, was concerned about the potential reaction of the eBay community. If you traded on eBay, you were not a customer. You were a member of a passionate and vocal community of users, who felt strongly (and rightly so) that eBay's success was directly attributable more to them than to any business savvy of headquarters staff in San Jose. How would the community react to knowing that some customer support inquiries were answered by staff not employed by eBay, or not even residing within the United States?

Another concern at headquarters was the lack of talent inside eBay who had experience with outsourcing. For eBay to uphold its philosophy of "prudent adoption," it needed a team of managers who could thoroughly investigate how other companies had successfully outsourced, and then actually run the day-to-day operation.

In December 2001, eBay hired Jim Williams, an Executive Vice President from Precision Response Corporation (PRC), one of the country's top echelon outsourcing vendors, and gave him responsibility for customer service worldwide. Williams brought instant credibility to the outsourcing initiative. His knowledge of the industry from the providers' point of view reinforced the research already compiled on other companies that had been successfully outsourcing elements of customer service in India and the Philippines for years. Furthermore, his intimate association with PRC, its management team, and its training and technological capabilities made Whitman and her executives comfortable utilizing PRC as eBay's first global outsourcing partner.

When it came to the issue of how the eBay community would react to the new venture, Williams had an answer for that, too. He proposed rather than launch a pilot in India, to begin with a small test near PRC's domestic headquarters in Fort Lauderdale. He essentially hand picked the most talented customer service representatives at PRC to handle the eBay business. By February 2002, all preparations for the pilot were completed, and eBay's first ever outsourcing effort was launched (Exhibit 8).

1995: Beginning of auction web

1996: First remote service representative hired

1997: eBay name introduced

1998: "Number of remotes" exceeds 75
First in-house reps hired in San Jose
Kana system introduced
eBay goes public

1999: Trust and safety launched
Salt Lake City service center opens
Customer support staff exceeds 200

2000: San Jose service center absorbed into Salt Lake City
Salt Lake City service center grows to over 800 employees

2001: First outsourcing strategy devised
Jim Williams hired

2002: Domestic outsourcing piloted at PRC in Florida
First e-mails sent to India for handling
Kathy Dalton joins eBay
Customer support staff grows to over 1,200 with purchase of PayPal

2003: Outsourced monthly volume exceeds 250,000 e-mails
Outsourcing pilot launched in Philippines for phone volume

2004: Outsourced volume exceeds 30 percent of total inquiries
Customer service staff exceeds 3,000 serving 19 counties
Dalton proposes to expand outsourcing to 50 percent of
total volume.

Exhibit 8   eBay Customer Support Timeline

Source: Case writers' estimates, compilations, and public records

Expansion of Outsourcing

Dalton reflected on the progress made in outsourcing over the past several years. The outsourcing pilot program begun in Fort Lauderdale in 2002 had been relatively seamless. The plan had been to run the pilot for six months before attempting to route volume offshore to one of PRC's service centers in Bangalore, India. Yet, the service quality and e-mail productivity results from the vendor were on par with eBay's own staff after only three months. Williams and his Customer Support team decided to cut the pilot short and sent the first e-mails to India in June 2002.

The eBay community's reaction to outsourcing portions of its customer service was essentially only a small ripple in a big pond. There had been some issues with the written English of the agents in India. A handful of complaints found their way to Whitman's desk. Still, the service quality and productivity metrics of the outsource providers, both domestic and foreign, rivaled and frequently surpassed the same measurements of eBay's own employees (Exhibit 9).

And who could argue with the cost differential? While eBay honored its community, it was also a publicly-traded company with shareholders who were accustomed to a compounded annual growth rate in revenues of over 65 percent. The domestic outsourcing cost per contact for the volume handled in Fort Lauderdale was not that much less than eBay's own staff results. This was perfectly acceptable, because a significant driver for outsourcing to another location within the United States had been, in addition to initially testing the outsourcing model, to avoid the capital outlay of building more plant and equipment for Customer Support.

The unit cost for the e-mail volume being sent to India was another matter. It was literally half the cost per contact handled in the United States. An occasional complaint letter

Exhibit 9   Metric Comparison for eBay In-house and Outsourcing Vendors (Comparison for similar volume types)

	Jul-02		Dec-02		Jul-03		Dec-03		Jul-04		Dec-04	
	In	Out	In	Out	In	Out	In	Out	In	Out	In	Out
E-mails Productivity/Hr	14.8	13.1	15.2	14.7	15.5	15.4	15.7	16.1	15.8	16.3	15.8	16.3
E-mails per FTE/Month	2050	1963	2181	2095	2202	2189	2240	2255	2250	2291	2250	2285
E-mail Quality %	94%	88%	95%	94%	95%	95%	94%	95%	93%	95%	93%	96%
Customer Satisfaction %	87%	83%	87%	86%	87%	88%	88%	88%	87%	88%	87%	89%
E-mail Unit Cost ($)	1.59	0.87	1.55	0.86	1.56	0.85	1.49	0.82	1.48	0.81	1.48	0.81

Source: Case writers' estimates, compilations, and public records

to Whitman about the way an e-mail response was worded by one of the service reps in India was not taken lightly, but it was still considered a small price to pay for the level of operational savings. No question about it, after both the domestic and offshore outsourcing performance of 2002, eBay executives were satisfied that outsourcing would remain a component of its customer support strategy. Dalton wondered, "What are the limits?"

Throughout 2003 and most of 2004, eBay had increased the volume of customer service sent offshore. Through analyses of e-mail complexity and available canned responses in Kana, about 40 percent of the General Support volume, representing close to 500,000 e-mails a month, had been earmarked as "outsourceable." As additional service staff was hired and uptrained in India, the throttle was opened and more e-mail was directed overseas for handling.

Dalton grabbed the hard copy of the strategy document she had submitted to Moss the previous week. She focused on several pages that highlighted the outsourcing expansion since her arrival at eBay. In a business as fluid as eBay's, it was realistic to expect that the original outsourcing strategy devised in 2002 would change over time. Indeed, even with eBay's penchant for hindsight learning from others' mishaps, Dalton's three-tiered strategy had only evolved after some operational missteps and plenty of analysis of test results.

Customer Relationship Management

One such misstep occurred in late 2003, when eBay conducted an outsourcing pilot in the Philippines for phone volumes. Less than two percent of eBay's volume arrived via telephone, but it was an expensive piece. The hope had been to cut eBay's phone unit cost in half, to just around $2.00. It did not play out that well in reality. During the pilot, both the accents of the Philippino agents and their

language comprehension were issues. Logistical issues with phone lines and data servers plagued the start-up. The biggest concern, however, was that eBay at the same time was taking its first major steps into Customer Relationship Management (CRM).

The company's marketing group had just completed a thorough segmentation analysis of its community members and saw potential opportunities in building deeper service relationships with its more profitable customer segments. Over 40 distinct customer segments were identified, and strategies for increasing profitability were then prepared for each segment. One of the proposed strategies was to offer dedicated live phone support to certain segments, particularly PowerSellers and potential PowerSellers.

With its focus on optimizing the phone touch point to generate revenue, senior management wanted to keep its phone support group in-house, rather than outsource it to third parties offshore. Management reasoned that this not only allowed for more efficient roll out of profit enhancing marketing programs, but also provided job enrichment and new career paths to eBay's own employees. In line with being more accessible by phone to high value customers, Customer Support shut down its phone outsourcing pilot in the Philippines in early 2004. Whether the pilot could have eventually been successful was unclear.

The same logic was used for eBay's live chat channel, which represented 2 percent of total volume or about 45,000 chat sessions a month. The original plan was to outsource this volume overseas as well. However, with the vision of using the chat channel to cross sell products and increase seller volume, it was determined to service chat line customers in-house too. These CRM-led constraints for the phone and chat channels helped fashion the new outsourcing strategy that Dalton had proposed to her boss last week and that she was scheduled to present to Whitman.

New Outsourcing Strategy

When she was given the responsibility for outsourcing in July of 2004, Dalton dug deeply into the existing operation to understand the issues as well as the opportunities and threats facing the department. She identified three major opportunities for improvement. She needed to figure out how to analyze each one and implement programs within 12 months, which was the timeframe she and Moss had agreed was feasible.

The first opportunity she saw was to increase the percentage of outsourcing from 30 percent of overall volume to at least 50 percent. She calculated that this would save an incremental $3.9 million a year. What made this endeavor particularly difficult, however, was the CRM initiative that required her to keep the growing phone and chat volume with in-house service representatives only.

The second opportunity would help her to accomplish the first. It was to target for the first time specific volume types within Trust and Safety and demonstrate that these could be successfully handled by a third party outsourcer. Several within Whitman's executive team felt strongly that it was too risky to outsource any of this volume and Dalton knew she would be in for a fight. She deemed it a worthwhile fight because, according to her analysis, between 20 percent and 25 percent of Trust and Safety's monthly volume was straightforward enough to be included in the outsourceable pool.

The third area of opportunity was to seek an outsourcing partner in addition to PRC with which to contract. Dalton was concerned that eBay had for two years used only one outsourcing vendor. She reasoned that adding a second one would benefit eBay by instilling competition both in pricing and performance metrics between the two vendors, as well as providing a measure of redundancy in the event of system outages.

She and her staff had wrestled with these three problems over the ensuing months. Selecting a second vendor that could meet eBay's criteria proved challenging. The candidate company had to have both domestic and international presence, had to have a proven track record in servicing large quantities of phone, chat and e-mail inquiries, and be willing to rival PRC's already attractive per unit pricing. Finding a vendor that had sufficient e-mail experience proved the toughest challenge. Dalton and her team finally settled on I-Sky, a medium-sized vendor, but one that could deliver impressive e-mail results out of its several service centers located in more rural parts of Canada.

Three Tiers

In order to increase the outsourcing to 50 percent of total volume, while at the same time taking advantage of the opportunity for including Trust and Safety volume in the mix, Dalton had devised a strategy comprising three levels or tiers. Each tier represented a progressively more complex type of work, both in terms of the nature of the customer inquiry and the channel through which it accessed Customer Support (Exhibit 10).

- **TIER ONE**—Was comprised of e-mail-only volume involving the most basic of General Support type questions. These were typically simple bidding and selling questions that could be answered using a template of responses from Kana. Since these were less complex customer inquiries, training for the service representatives was less demanding and could be conducted over a three-week period. Most of eBay's Tier One volume was already being handled by PRC's two outsourcing facilities in India. Dalton analyzed all remaining inquiry types to find an additional 260,000+ e-mails per month that

Exhibit 10 Proposed Outsourced Volume and Unit Cost by Tiers

	Current (Dec. 2004)			Proposed (Dec. 2004)		
	Monthly Volume	% of Total Volume	Unit Cost	Monthly Volume	% of Total Volume	Unit Cost
Tier One						
Gen'l Support	510000	21.30%	$0.81	775000	32.40%	$0.72
Tier Two						
Gen'l Support	68000	2.80%	$1.45	186000	7.80%	$1.15
Tier Three						
Gen'l Support	20000	0.80%	$1.48	25000	1.04%	$1.33
Trust & Safety	NA	NA	NA	210000	8.80%	$1.33
Total	598000	24.20%		1196000	50.00%	

Source: Case writers' estimates, compilations, and public records

could be safely off-loaded to India as well. If these volumes could be found, she thought she might be able to negotiate with the vendor for a price reduction from $0.81 to $0.72 per e-mail.

- **TIER TWO**—Was designated for General Support e-mail volume that was considered a bit more complex than Tier One work. This accounted for more billing-related and account adjustment questions, where more in-depth training was needed for the service representatives. eBay had outsourced a small portion of this volume, but only to PRC's Florida center, where English was the native language. Now, utilizing I-Sky's locations in Canada, Dalton proposed another option for handling this volume. These locations could satisfy the native English requirement and prove very effective from a cost standpoint. Though not as low cost an environment as India, the Canadian Tier Two locations were on average 22 percent more economical in cost per e-mail than PRC's domestic facilities and eBay's wholly owned service centers.

- **TIER THREE**—Was reserved for more complex General Support questions, those that required flexibility and some judgment on the part of the service employees. Also, it was in this tier that Dalton proposed that some simple Trust & Safety inquiries be handled. She was careful not to select work that was overly sensitive in terms of customers' personal information or that necessitated detailed investigative work. Types of inquires that qualified included reports from eBay users on spam or potential scam sites, and on listing violations or member misbehavior, such as not paying for items received, and shill bidding. This tier consisted mainly of e-mail volume, yet Dalton designed it so that some simple phone and chat inquiries were included as well. While this was contrary to eBay's CRM philosophy that phone calls and chat sessions be kept in-house with experienced eBay service agents, she asserted that top reps at both PRC and I-Sky could be taught to service this volume just as adeptly as eBay's own.

Tier Three was to be handled by outsourcing centers exclusively in the United States, located in close proximity to eBay's own contact centers. This "nearshoring" arrangement ensured that no language barrier existed, and that Dalton and her managers were within close proximity if the outsourcer needed extra support and training.

In her recommendations to Moss last week, Dalton had made sure her boss understood that the arrangement for Tier Three volume would save the company only about $500,000 per year from a pure cost reduction standpoint, but that it did pay off in keeping Customer Support from having to invest in additional plant and equipment, as well as reducing the risk of spreading its management talent too thin. Plus, it opened the door to outsourcing approximately 20 percent of Trust and Safety work types, which was essential to meeting the goal of offloading upward of 50 percent of eBay's entire support volume.

Moss had readily acknowledged and appreciated Dalton's explanation on her team's strategy behind the logic for Tiers Two and Three. She was more inquisitive, however, about the Tier One work being serviced in India. The payoffs there in reduced operating expense were impressive, saving the company almost $3 million annually, and Dalton had sensed right away Moss's interest in bringing more dollars to the bottom line. Moss had quizzed her in detail last week on PRC's Indian-based operations and I-Sky. How experienced, how financially muscled, how well led, how competitively positioned, how quick to market were these two companies? What kind of presence did Customer Support have in these centers? Were eBay managers always on site in India training new hires, sampling e-mails, admonishing the "eBay way"?

As she recounted these queries in her mind from last week's meeting, Dalton admitted that the question her boss had posed in her e-mail was really no surprise at all. Customer Support was heavily invested in making the Indian operation a long-term service and financial win. But, why line someone else's pockets along the way? What Moss wanted to know, and what she had anticipated that Whitman and her staff would likewise want to know, was the feasibility of doing exactly what Dalton's outsourcing group was doing in India, but doing it without the middleman. "Imagine if Customer Support was saving approximately 45% per email by offshore outsourcing, how much more could be saved by running our own sites in India?" Moss's e-mail concluded.

To BOT or Not to BOT

Fortunately, Dalton had done research on the subject of developing eBay-owned and managed sites offshore, though not in real depth. She had figured that opportunities would exist for her and her staff to still work out the minor kinks with the present outsourcing strategy. "Chalk up another one to the exhilarating eBay pace," she thought to herself.

She wanted to call Moss in San Jose and discuss her e-mail and the next steps in preparing for the upcoming presentation to Whitman. But, first she opened her file drawer and pulled out a folder labeled across the top with the letters "BOT." It had been several months since she gathered the contents. Before she knew it, an hour elapsed

Exhibit 11   Dalton's Spreadsheet

		Cost/Hr/Seat (250 seats)	Cost/Hr/Seat (500 seats)	Cost/Hr/Seat (1,000 seats)	Avg. Initial Investment/Seat (one-time cost)	Avg. Transfer Cost/Seat (one-time cost)
Scenario #1: Outsourcing to 3rd party vendors	*e-mail, phone, chat*	$ 10.17	$ 9.56	$ 8.60	N/A	N/A
	e-mail only	$ 6.24	$ 5.38	$ 4.66	N/A	N/A
Scenario #2: Build eBay owned center	*e-mail, phone, chat*	$ 9.73	$ 8.85	$ 7.77	$ 12,000	N/A
	e-mail only	$ 5.30	$ 4.68	$ 4.14	$ 11,000	N/A
Scenario #3: Build, Operate, Transfer (BOT)	*e-mail, phone, chat*	$ 9.88	$ 9.03	$ 8.10	N/A	$ 3,500
	e-mail only	$ 5.34	$ 4.96	$ 4.40	N/A	$ 2,900

Source: Case writers' estimates, compilations, and public records

and she remained focused on sifting through the packet of information, occasionally pausing to run several scenarios through a quickly composed Excel spreadsheet.

After another 45 minutes of analysis she was ready. She printed the spreadsheet and quickly surveyed it for clarity. It was not as detailed as it would need to be in the coming days, but it would help her frame a conversation with Moss about the question she asked in her e-mail, the one she asked on behalf of Whitman:

"Why should we keep paying someone else to do what we can do for ourselves?"

In her spreadsheet, Dalton outlined and quantified three alternatives (Exhibit 11). The first alternative was the Tier One of her proposed three tiered strategy—maintain the relationships with eBay's offshore outsourcing partners, continue to improve the operation in India, and identify incremental volume to outsource in order to drive e-mail costs lower. She viewed this scenario as the least risky of the three alternatives.

The second alternative was to eliminate the outsourcing vendors altogether. In this option, she proposed that Customer Support not renew its contracts with the vendors, and instead purchase or lease land or an already established facility in India and build its own operation. Dalton knew this alternative presented the most risks to eBay, including capital outlay, real estate commitments, governmental compliance, communications infrastructure, and in-country management resources. Yet, according to

her spreadsheet assumptions, this alternative promised the biggest potential payoff long-term in unit cost reduction, something that eBay's Executive Staff prized highly.

She believed her third alternative, called "Build, Operate, and Transfer," or "BOT" for short, was the most creative and represented a hybrid of the first two. She recommended that eBay contract with a third party vendor that would acquire or build an operations center, staff and manage it, and then after a specified period of time of perhaps a year or two, transfer full ownership to eBay. This option appealed to her more than the second one because the vendor would bear the initial risks for the start-up phase, which she considered the most challenging and expensive. eBay could limit its cost exposure up front until the operation was ramped up and running. She planned to tell Moss that the most critical points of the BOT alternative were to negotiate the appropriate level of management fees with the outsourcing vendor and to work out the intricacies of the actual transfer of ownership down the road.

Dalton's biggest concern, however, was the fact that to date she had not been able to find any example of a domestic company utilizing a BOT approach with a vendor in India. To her knowledge, eBay would be the first customer service operation attempting such a strategy. As she prepared to pick up the phone and dial Moss's number, she was haunted by eBay's well entrenched mantra of not being on the "bleeding edge" with any new unproven experiments.

Case 3–2: Nucleon, Inc.*

Robert Moore, a recent graduate of a top-ranked M.B.A. program, now realized what it was like to be on the other side of a case study. It was December 1990, and Nucleon, the young biotechnology start-up at which he had recently become project manager, faced critical manufacturing choices. Moore and Jeff Hurst, the firm's CEO, had met to discuss the situation, and within the next few weeks, Hurst needed to present the company's manufacturing strategy to the board of directors. In the meantime, he asked Moore to evaluate in detail Nucleon's options and give his own recommendation.

Nucleon's first potential product, "cell regulating ein-1" (CRP-1), had been undergoing extensive experimentation and analysis in the company's R&D laboratories for several years. The next major hurdle was human clinical trials, which also typically took place over several years. However, before Nucleon could launch clinical trials, it had to decide how and where CRP-1 would be manufactured. To ensure participants' safety, the U.S. Food and Drug Administration (FDA) imposed strict guidelines; products being tested in humans had to be made in facilities certified for "clinical grade" production.[1]

Since CRP-1 was the company's first product to go into the clinic, Nucleon had no manufacturing facilities which met FDA requirements. It was faced with three options for supplying CRP-1 to the clinic: The first was to build a new 5,000-square-foot pilot plant with enough capacity to supply all the CRP-1 needed for Phases I and II of clinical trials. The second option was to contract clinical manufacturing to an outside firm. And a third option was to license the manufacturing to another biotechnology company or to a pharmaceutical firm. Under this third option, the licensee would be responsible for all manufacturing, clinical development, and eventual marketing of CRP-1.

Definite risks and rewards were attached to each option, and Moore knew that the one ultimately chosen by Hurst would have long-term consequences for Nucleon's survival in the intensively competitive and high-stakes drug industry.

Background

Nucleon was founded in 1985 by Dr. Alan Ball, an internationally respected researcher at the Children's Hospital and an Associate Professor of Clinical Medicine at the Greaves Medical Center, to develop pharmaceutical products based on a class of proteins known as cell regulating factors. From 1985 to 1988, Dr. Ball and a small group of scientists who joined Nucleon researched ways of producing CRP-1 outside the human body. Although CRP-1 was a naturally occurring protein contained in human blood plasma, the amount that could be extracted was far too small to be of any commercial use.

Scientists first isolated a small amount of naturally occurring CRP-1 and determined the gene that instructed human cells how to produce CRP-1. The gene was then cloned. While this laboratory process for producing CRP-1 was still very small scale, it generated enough material to send to academic collaborators who were exploring the potential therapeutic uses of CRP-1. Although an actual product was still several years and millions of dollars away, early research indicated that CRP-1 had potential as a treatment for burns and for kidney failure.

*Professor Gary Pisano wrote this case as the basis for class discussion rather than to illustrate either effective or ineffective handling of an administrative situation.

Data and names have been altered for purposes of confidentiality.

Reprinted by permission of Harvard School Press from Nucleon, Inc. by Professor Gary Pisano. Copyright © 1991 by the President and Fellows of Harvard College. To order copies or request permission to reproduce materials, call 1-800-545-7685, write Harvard Business School Publishing, Boston, MA 02163, or go to http://www.hbsp.harvard.edu. No part of this publication may be reproduced, stored in a retrieval system, used in a spreadsheet, or transmitted in any form or by any means—electronic, mechanical photocopying, recording, or otherwise—without the permission of Harvard Business School.

Strategy and Competition

Nucleon was one of over 200 firms founded since the mid-1970s to develop pharmaceutical technologies based on recent advances in molecular biology and immunology. This new field of R&D, commonly called "biotechnology," also attracted the attention of established companies. By 1989, most of the world's largest pharmaceutical enterprises, such as Eli Lilly, Merck, and Hoffman LaRoche, had extensive in-house biotechnology R&D programs as well as collaborative ties with many of the new entrants.

Competition was intense. Scientists at both start-up and established companies were racing to be the first to clone certain genes and establish proprietary positions for their firms in emerging areas such as cell regulating factors. Establishing a strong patent position was particularly important for small companies such as Nucleon. Moore explained: "Given the enormous costs of developing and commercializing a new drug, potential investors want to see a strong proprietary position before they commit serious capital. Just one strong patent on the right molecule can ensure survival for years by allowing you to attract capital."

Biotechnology patent law, however, was as new and uncertain as the technology itself. Indeed, the legality of patenting a genetically engineered microorganism was only established in 1980 by a landmark U.S. Supreme Court decision, and the ensuing decade saw many legal battles over the scope and efficacy of specific patents. In some cases, two or more companies had claims on different proprietary elements of the same molecule. For example, one company might claim ownership of the molecule itself while another of the genetic sequence used to synthesize the molecule. Further, it was extremely difficult to patent the process technology used to obtain a biologically important molecule, even though the starting material and the resulting molecule were considered original enough to be patented. Given the lack of precedent, it was always difficult to predict how the courts would rule in any given situation.

Moreover, the U.S. Patent Office might take several years to process an application. And while few companies could afford to wait until a patent was granted before continuing development, there were big risks in going ahead with development before the granting of a patent. A company could spend tens of millions of dollars in clinical trials and manufacturing facilities yet wind up not having a proprietary position if the patent office denied the application. Even if patents were granted, it was always possible for a competitor to challenge them in court. While Nucleon believed it had a strong patent position on the CRP-1 molecule, its rights to other necessary proprietary components (such as the genetic sequence) were less certain.

Nucleon management believed that several factors were critical to the company's survival. As Hurst commented:

Given how small we are, it's absolutely essential that we pick the right projects. We can't hedge our bets with a big portfolio of projects, like the big pharmaceutical companies can. We've got to pick winners the first time.

Gordon Banks, Nucleon's vice president of R&D, and one of the leading scientists in the field of cell regulating factors, added:

That's why it's so important for us to be at the leading edge of scientific research. This means not only attracting the best in-house scientists, but also maintaining close contact with universities. If someone at a university clones the genes for a new cell regulating factor, we want to know about it.

Nucleon management believed that it had found an attractive niche: relatively few firms were working on cell regulating proteins. Banks believed that the company's distinctive technical capability lay in its ability to identify potentially therapeutic cell regulating factors. Although Nucleon was a leader in cell regulating factors, the company was not free from competition. Other companies were developing drugs using somewhat similar technology. Also, many companies were using alternative technologies to develop drugs for some of the same diseases for which cell regulating factors were being developed. As Hurst commented, "We're a leader, but we're not alone. It's important for us to get our products into the clinic before others do."

Biotechnology firms were using different strategies for developing and commercializing their technologies. Virtually all the biotechnology companies started, like Nucleon, as specialized R&D laboratories. Over time, some vertically integrated into production, and a few of the oldest companies, like Genentech, were even vertically integrating into marketing. Nucleon was presently contemplating its manufacturing strategy. Its marketing strategy, however, was clear. Nucleon management believed that the company could not afford to market its products on its own. Instead, it planned to link up with established pharmaceutical companies, with strong distribution capabilities, to market its products. Hurst, who once worked in marketing for a large pharmaceutical company, noted:

Companies like Merck have hundreds of salespeople. They can reach every doctor's office in the country within one week. It would be crazy for a company like us to go up against them in marketing. Besides, our products are likely to be targeted at a variety of therapeutic markets. We would need a few hundred salespeople to market all these products directly. We're much better off linking up with the best company in each therapeutic market.

By December 1990, the privately held company had grown to 22 employees, 18 of whom were engaged in R&D; of these about one-third had Ph.D.s from scientific disciplines such as biochemistry, molecular biology, protein chemistry, and immunology. Most of the R&D staff had been recruited from leading university research laboratories and were strongly attracted to cutting-edge, product-oriented research. Nucleon's size and entrepreneurial spirit created an academic atmosphere in R&D and tight links to the academic/scientific community.

Since its founding, Nucleon had raised approximately $6 million in venture capital and received research grants from the U.S. Department of Agriculture totaling $600,000.

Drug Development: From Research to Market

Establishing the safety and efficacy of products like CRP-1 that were based upon novel genetic engineering technology was enormously complex, time-consuming, and expensive. Nucleon's drug development process, divided into several distinct phases, is discussed below.

Research

Before launching a research project to develop a new drug, Nucleon management considered several factors in evaluating a project's profit potential. First, there had to be a chance of achieving a dominant proprietary position. Second, the market had to be large enough to justify the R&D investment. Finally, Nucleon wanted to develop drugs where no alternative treatments were available. During the research phase, Nucleon's scientists sought to identify and purify from human plasma minute quantities of cell regulating proteins that might have therapeutic value. Some critical information to pursue this research was obtained by perusing scientific literature or by consulting with leading academic researchers. Much necessary information, however, was still undiscovered and came only from in-house research and experimentation, which seldom moved in a straight-forward, logical manner but from one obstacle to the next. This could entail abandoning one strategy and starting over again.

Cloning and Purification

Products like CRP-1 and others that Nucleon intended to develop were fundamentally different from most drugs developed by pharmaceutical companies, which traditionally were synthetic chemicals. Chemical synthesis was effective for relatively small and simple molecules, but proteins like CRP-1 were simply too big and complex to be synthesized that way and instead were produced by genetic engineering.

Through genetic engineering, the scientist created a microscopic protein factory. The gene for the protein was identified, isolated, and cloned, then inserted into different strains of the bacterium *E. coli*. In theory, the genetically engineered bacteria could then produce the protein in a test tube or shake flask. However, since genetic engineering was still a relatively new scientific discipline, it was not always easy to either identify the relevant genes or to get "host" (genetically altered) bacteria to produce a specific protein. In practice, it was usually necessary to try different types of host cells to find one or more capable of producing the protein in quantities that could be scaled-up to an economically feasible process.

Only a few milligrams of protein could be produced from genetically engineered cells grown in shake flasks. Thus, an extensive amount of work then had to go into developing the processes for making each of these proteins in large quantity.

Pre-Clinical Research

Before a pharmaceutical was tested in humans it underwent pre-clinical evaluation, consisting of experiments in animals to evaluate its efficacy. Over six to eight months, increasing doses were administered to animals with and without the simulated disease. Another six months might be needed to evaluate the data.

By this point, the company might have spent $6 to $10 million in R&D and preparation of regulatory documents. Only after completing all the requisite animal tests, and having a suitable production process, could the company file for permission with the FDA to commence clinical trials in humans. Though Nucleon had not begun human clinical trials, management expected to file an application with the FDA to begin human trials for CRP-1 as a burn wound treatment in 1992. The company was also doing research to determine if CRP-1 might have other therapeutic applications. There was some preliminary data suggesting that it might treat kidney failure. Moore estimated that about another two years and $3 million of work were needed before the kidney failure application could be tested in the clinic.

Human Clinical Trials

Most governments required every new pharmaceutical product to undergo extensive clinical testing before it could be marketed widely, and the FDA regulations were considered the most stringent in the world. To meet them, any new drug, or any approved drug being modified for a different therapeutic application, had to undergo three phases of clinical trials.

Phase I trials assessed basic safety. During these trials, the drug was administered to a small group of healthy volunteers and any adverse reactions (such as fevers, dizziness, or nausea) were noted.[2] This phase usually required between 6 and 12 months. As long as there were no serious side effects, the product moved to phase II trials where it was administered to a small group of patients having the disease the drug was presumed to treat. The patients were monitored to determine whether their condition improved as a result of the drug and whether they suffered any adverse side effects. It was during phase II trials that appropriate dosages were determined. This phase typically required between one and two years to complete. If Phase II trials succeeded, the product then moved to Phase III trials.

Phase III trials assessed the product's efficacy with a relatively large sample of patients on a statistically rigorous basis. Typically, these trials involved multiple hospitals and could require from two to five years to complete. Because of the large number of patients, doctors, and hospitals involved, this stage was by far the most expensive. The costs of manufacturing the drug, administering it to patients, monitoring results, analyzing data, and preparing the requisite regulatory paperwork could run between $30 million to $100 million. It was imperative for regulatory reasons to manufacture the product with the same process that would be used when the product was marketed commercially. Any change in manufacturing would mean repeating human clinical trials to prove that the deviation did not alter the product's safety and efficacy. This also added significantly to the costs of running Phase III clinical trials.

The CRP-1 Project: Current Applications

Since Nucleon's founding, its main development project had been CRP-1 and most of the company's R&D resources had been focused on the CRP-1 projects. While CRP-1's commercialization was still a few years away, Nucleon's scientists and investors were optimistic about its potential. Exhibit 1 depicts the expected time for FDA approval. Initial research focused on developing two major therapeu-

Exhibit 1   Approximate Time Frame for CRP-1 Project

April 1992	Begin Phase I Clinical Trials
December 1992	Begin Phase II Clinical Trials
December 1993	End Phase II Clinical Trials
June 1994	Begin Phase III Clinical Trials
December 1996	Complete Phase III Clinical Trials; File data with FDA
January 1998	Expected FDA approval and commencement of sales

tic applications—one for topical treatment of burn wounds, the other for acute kidney failure. Both the burn wound and kidney failure markets were estimated to be similar in size. Furthermore, in 1988, the company had also begun investigating two new cell regulating factors, still in the early stages of research. Dr. Banks estimated that these could be ready for clinical trials in about four years if the company spent $10 million on each one.

One of the most critical activities currently taking place on the CRP-1 project was the development of a larger scale production process, with sufficient capacity to meet all clinical trial requirements. Every step of the process had to be carefully documented and validated to ensure that it could produce identical product from batch to batch.

Process Development and Manufacturing

CRP-1 production would require four basic process steps: 1) fermentation, 2) purification, 3) formulation, 4) filling and packaging (see Exhibit 2).

Fermentation.   Fermentation initially focused on growing the genetically engineered E. coli in small laboratory flasks; the process was then scaled up to successively larger vessels. Unfortunately, the process used to grow cells in a 1-liter glass bottle might not work when attempted in a 10-liter glass chamber or a 100-liter stainless steel tank (also known as a fermentor or bioreactor), given differences in heat exchange, tank aeration, and fermentor geometry. The kinds of nutrients cells were fed, bioreactor temperature, acidity level, oxygen flow rate into the bioreactor, and dozens of other process parameters were all determined during fermentation process development.

While crude fermentation processes existed for over 6,000 years, fermentation using genetically engineered cells dated to the early 1980s. Many biotechnology firms encountered major difficulties when trying to run pilot and

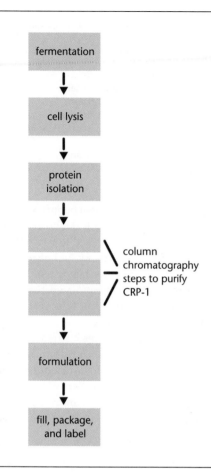

Fermentation: A process in which organisms such as bacteria or yeast are suspended in a nutrient growth medium, consisting of sugars, salts, and amino acids (protein building blocks), at an appropriate temperature and aeration level (oxygen and other gases) in order to promote these organisms' growth and metabolism. The desired products of the organisms' metabolism may be the whole organism itself, metabolic products, modified compounds, or in this case proteins.

Cell Lysis: In cases where the protein of interest is not excreted by the cell into the surrounding medium but remains inside, the cell needs to be broken open to obtain the protein. This process is know as cell lysis. Lysis can be done mechanically or chemically.

Isolation and Purification: After cells are lysed, the protein of interest must be isolated and purified from among all of the other contents of the cell. Initially, methods such as centrifugation (using centrifugal force to separate heavy and light debris) and chemical precipitation can be used to concentrate the mixture.

After a series of initial separation steps have been performed, finer, more precise separation techniques can be employed to isolate the protein of interest from other similar protein molecules. For example, chromatography isolated substances based upon their ability to separate between a liquid and a solid.

Formulation: In drug formulation, the protein of interest is put into an appropriate medium for administration as a therapeutic drug. The protein may be dissolved in purified water or another pure solvent such as ethanol for injection. In some cases, a protein must be formulated to be applied in a topical form such as a cream or put in an aerosol suspension. The challenge is to ensure the drug's safety and efficacy.

Filling: The therapeutic is then placed in an appropriate container under sterile conditions and is packaged and labeled.

Exhibit 2   Process Flow for CRP-1[1]

[1]Diagram does not include holding points where work-in-process is stored between operations. The diagram also does not include quality control steps that are conducted after every operation.

commercial scale fermentation processes for the first time, as Dr. Ann Dawson, Nucleon's director of process science, explained:

There are so many unknowns and so many things which can go wrong. If a virus gets into your bioreactor, you could be shut down for weeks. Incredibly tight process control is an absolute must, and even then, you may still run into troubles.

For regulatory reasons, it was absolutely critical to run the process exactly as specified. Such strict adherence to process specifications was necessary because even minor process deviations could impact product quality. In addition, the efficiency of the process could be severely affected by changes in any one of the key process parameters.

Because such production methods were new, process development required a great deal of trial-and-error and close collaboration between research scientists and process development scientists early on in the project. Research scientists had to design a process that worked in a test tube as well as on a larger scale, and process development scientists had to be aware of and understand the details of the product and its host cell. Some genetically engineered cell lines, for example, were extremely difficult to grow large-scale. Dr. Dawson noted:

Ideally, we want the research scientists to work with only those cell lines which we know can be scaled-up. While I think they agree with this in principle, they really don't want to be constrained, particularly if they're having trouble getting expression with one of our "preferred" cell lines.

While much progress had been made over the past decade, many people considered the biotechnology production process very much an art. It was not unheard of for a process to work well in one facility but fail completely when transferred to another. One Nucleon researcher who had experience with such transfers explained:

You would be surprised at all the little things that could be done differently from one organization to another. Most of these things are so minor you would not even think of writing them down. But they make the difference between a successful and unsuccessful process.

Currently, Nucleon had scaled up the process for making CRP-1 to 10 liters, enough to supply material for its own biochemical studies, academic collaborators, and potential joint venture partners who wanted to evaluate the product. Early phase clinical trials were likely to require a 100-liter process, and commercial production a much larger scale process.

As complex as it was, bacterial fermentation was considered one of the more efficient ways of producing proteins like CRP-1. In some cases, product characteristics could be enhanced if a mammalian cell (e.g., from a mouse or human) rather than a bacterial cell was used as a host. Mammalian cell processes, while desirable from the product side, were much more complex than bacterial processes, not well understood, and much more expensive to maintain. Mammalian cells had to be fed more expensive nutrients, and they grew much more slowly than bacterial cells. They required different bioreactors, and even stricter adherence to original process specifications than bacterial cells. Dr. Dawson explained, "With bacterial cells, a one degree Centigrade temperature change can slow the growth rate and increase your costs, whereas mammalian cells might just die altogether."

Although most biotechnology companies had some experience with bacterial cell processes, many fewer had mammalian cell capabilities. Fortunately, CRP-1 could be produced using bacterial cells. The company's R&D lab, however, was already working on second generation CRP-1 molecules produced in mammalian cells. And biotechnology companies overall were unsure whether existing process development technology would be viable in the future to produce biological products.[3]

Purification. After fermentation, the cells would be broken apart and the CRP-1 protein separated from all other proteins and cell debris contained in the fermentation tank. A series of fractionation and centrifugation steps would isolate the cell protein from carbohydrates, fatty acids, and DNA. The CRP-1 containing protein mixture would then be purified in three additional steps using a filtration procedure known as column chromatography. Like fermentation, the purification process specified during process development had to be strictly followed during manufacturing. After purification, the material would be subjected to extensive quality testing to ensure that the product met the FDA's extremely high purity standards.

Formulation. Purification process yielded nearly pure quantities of the protein of interest, for example CRP-1. At this stage, the product was made into the intended dosage form (e.g., oral, topical, injectable) and subjected to extensive quality testing. For burn treatment, CRP-1 would be formulated into a topical dosage form.

Filling and Packaging. During the final step, bulk quantities of the formulated product were put into tubes, bottles, or other vessels required for administration to patients. The sealed vessels were then inserted into packages, which were also sealed.

The Financial Environment

A critical issue affecting Nucleon was capital availability. The situation had changed dramatically since the late 1970s and early 1980s when investors lined up to provide capital to brand new biotechnology companies. By the mid- to late 1980s, private and public equity markets grew tighter, and venture capitalists, who expected investment returns of 30 percent, became more selective. The state of the public equity markets in 1990 made "going public" virtually impossible for a company like Nucleon; furthermore, potential corporate partners, who had been disappointed by previous biotechnology relationships, were unwilling to fund early stage projects. As Hurst described it:

In the early 1980s, a company like ours could have gotten corporate funding with just our idea. By the mid-1980s, we probably would have needed to have started some lab work and have had some preliminary experimental data. Now, it's hard to get a large pharmaceutical company to talk to you unless you've got some solid Phase I and Phase II clinical results and can demonstrate that you've got a stable manufacturing process. And even then, they'll cut some pretty tough terms with you. When it comes to raising capital today, it's a buyers' market.

Nucleon was just about to receive another $6 million infusion from its venture capitalist. This funding, combined with existing cash on-hand, revenues, interest, and grants, would give Nucleon about $6.5 million. Furthermore, if CRP-1 showed promise in pre-clinical trials, Hurst felt that

Nucleon could raise enough money to pursue Phase I and II clinical trials. Some analysts were predicting that by 1991 or 1992, Wall Street would once again find biotechnology stocks attractive and there would be opportunities for smaller companies to raise money by selling stock to the public. Others thought the capital situation would stay tight for at least several more years. The possibility that a long awaited "shake-out" was about to hit the biotechnology industry was making many investors cautious. One promising sign was that large corporations again seemed willing to fund some selected projects at very early stages of research. As Moore noted, "Today, some brand new start-ups in new fields, like antisense, are cutting some deals on projects which are still years away from the clinic."

Manufacturing Options for Phase I and Phase II CRP-1 Development

Nucleon management contemplated three options to produce clinical grade CRP-1: 1) build a new pilot facility, 2) contract CRP-1 production to a third-party, or 3) license manufacturing and marketing rights to another biotechnology company or pharmaceutical firm in exchange for up front cash payments and royalties on future product sales. Each option is described below.

The New Pilot Plant

Nucleon commissioned an engineering consulting firm to study the physical requirements and costs of a new pilot plant (Exhibit 3). The proposed 5,000-square-foot plant would be fully equipped with all the state-of-the-art processing equipment and environmental controls necessary to meet clinical production standards. Planned capacity would meet Nucleon's requirements for Phase I and Phase II clinical trials. The pilot facility, however, could not be used to produce CRP-1 for Phase III trials, because it would

not meet FDA manufacturing standards for those trials. It was beyond Nucleon's financial capability to build such a plant at this time.

The main advantage in building a pilot plant, as Moore saw it, was that it would enable the firm to develop the nucleus of a future larger-scale, in-house manufacturing capability. Because most of Nucleon's employees were Ph.D. scientists engaged in R&D, it currently lacked supervisors and technicians who could carry out the maintenance, procurement, quality assurance, technical support, logistics, and other functions to operate even a small manufacturing plant. Recruiting people with the appropriate skills and getting the manufacturing organization to work effectively would take time. Supplying clinical trials would allow manufacturing time to accumulate experience dealing with many complicated technical and regulatory issues. Moore noted:

> If Nucleon waits until Phase III trials to bring manufacturing in-house, we might find ourselves with a "green" manufacturing organization just when the stakes are highest. By starting now, we'll have the basic manufacturing skills in-house and ready to go when we are really going to need them. The second big advantage of the pilot facility is that it would keep control over process and quality procedures firmly in Nucleon's hands.

Dawson added, "Scaling up will be much easier if we have our own pilot plant to experiment in."

Of course, building a pilot plant was risky. Moore knew that despite its promise in laboratory experiments, it was uncertain at this point how well CRP-1 would work when tested in humans. Indeed, if the history of the pharmaceutical industry was any guide, most drugs that entered clinical trials never reached the market. This high risk of failure was offset somewhat by the fact that CRP-1 had several potential therapeutic applications. If clinical trials for burn wounds were not promising, it might be used in other applications. Nevertheless, Nucleon management had to consider the possibility of the pilot plant being

Exhibit 3   Time and Cost to Obtain Phase II Data for CRP-1 (Burn Treatment) Using a New Pilot Facility for Clinical-Grade Production of CRP-1. Midrange Estimate ($000)

Pilot Facility	1991	1992	1993	Total Thru 12/93
Construction and Equipment Costs	3,100	0	0	3,100
Variable Production Expenses and Overhead	0	800	1,204	2,004
Pre-Clinical Development	250	0	0	250
Clinical Trials (Phase I/II)	0	1,040	1,000	2,040
Total	3,350	1,840	2,204	7,394

idled if CRP-1 performed poorly in the clinic. Other products under development were still years away from requiring pilot manufacturing capabilities.

Another major risk involved process uncertainty. The pilot plant would be designed to produce products using bacterial fermentation, but the company was already in the early stages of developing a version in mammalian cells, which would require vastly different process development capabilities.

Some board members believed that Nucleon should focus all of its financial, managerial, and technical resources on R&D. Manufacturing, they felt, would only distract the company from its main mission of exploiting its unique scientific capabilities in the discovery of cell regulating proteins. According to Hurst:

> Our venture capitalists are asking us where we, as a company, add the most value. As a small research-intensive company, we can be the "fastest guns on the block" when it comes to drug discovery. But that means funneling our limited resources into R&D. Some of our investors are concerned that we could get bogged down in manufacturing. On the other hand, it's getting to the point where anyone can clone a gene. I keep wondering whether we can still differentiate ourselves on R&D alone.

Contract Manufacturing

Contracting manufacturing was a second option for Phase I and Phase II CRP-1 development. The biggest advantage of this option was that it required no major capital investments on Nucleon's part. If CRP-1 failed, the contract could be easily terminated. Aside from relatively small termination penalties, the company would have little else at risk. Another advantage was that companies supplying contract manufacturing services had facilities and personnel in place.

Contract production was not inexpensive (see Exhibit 4). There were very few U.S. companies capable and willing to contract manufacture pharmaceuticals from bacteria. Nucleon management was meeting with several potential contractors. These included other biotechnology companies who had excess capacity. In recent years, many biotechnology companies had built GMP plants in anticipation of future products. When product approvals were delayed or even rejected by the FDA, these companies found themselves with tremendous excess manufacturing capacity. Because of mounting financial pressures, some of these companies were providing contract manufacturing services. Some industry experts believed that excess manufacturing capacity would continue to accumulate during the next few years.

One of contract manufacturing's biggest risks was confidential information disclosure. It was virtually impossible for any contractor to provide reliable time and cost estimates without knowing many proprietary product details. Moreover, the complexity of the products and processes made estimates of time and cost painstaking; reaching an agreement could take many months. Even after a contract was signed, technology transfer and scale-up might take another nine months. Moore noted, "It will take about as much time to negotiate an agreement and transfer and validate the process as it will for us to build a pilot plant."

Although production contracts typically were negotiated for fixed quantities (e.g., 100grams of CRP-1 over 10 months), in contract negotiations, a balance needed to be struck. On one hand, it was risky to commit to large quantities of material—which might not be required if product specifications changed or the product was pulled from the clinic. On the other hand, short-term contracts usually involved a higher price to offset fixed costs of scale-up and batch set-ups.

Under either the pilot plant or the contract manufacturing option, Nucleon would retain ownership of the product rights at least until the commencement of Phase III clinical trials. At that point, the company would enter into licensing and marketing with a large corporate partner. The options for Phase III trials and beyond are discussed later.

Exhibit 4   Time and Cost to Obtain Phase II Clinical Trial Data for CRP-1 (Burn Treatment) Using Contract Production for Clinical-Grade CRP-1

	1991	1992	1993	Total Thru 12/93
Contract Production and Related Expense	0	955	1,550	2,505
Pre-Clinical Development	250	0	0	250
Clinical Trials (Phase I/II)	0	1,040	1,000	2,040
Total	250	1,995	2,550	4,795

Licensing the Product to Another Company

Rather than waiting until Phase III trials to enter a licensing deal, Nucleon could license the product immediately in exchange for fixed payments and future royalties. Under this option, the licensed partner, not Nucleon, would make all the requisite expenditures in clinical development, clinical manufacturing, regulatory filings, and commercial manufacturing and marketing. The partner would have the right to market CRP-1 to treat burn wounds. Nucleon would retain the right to develop CRP-1 for other therapeutic applications. Nucleon also would receive an up-front, fixed licensing fee and reimbursement for any additional development work it performed on the project. If and when CRP-1 was commercialized, Nucleon would receive royalties as a percentage of sales.

This licensing option had the chief benefit of generating cash immediately; it also spared Nucleon from making large capital investments in clinical development and manufacturing, and allowed the company to concentrate all of its financial and human resources on R&D. Of course, if the product turned out to be successful, Nucleon would receive far lower revenues than if it had made all of these investments itself. Some Nucleon employees viewed this option as "mortgaging away" the company's future.

Whether this option would mortgage the company's future depended upon the exact terms of the agreement that Nucleon could negotiate. While it was virtually impossible to know for sure what kind of deal could be struck, Nucleon management had conducted preliminary discussions with several firms. From these and consultations with the company's venture capitalists, Moore determined that Nucleon could expect to reach an agreement with the following terms:

Upon signing the contract Nucleon would get a $3 million payment. After the FDA approved CRP-1 for burn wounds, Nucleon would receive annual royalty payments from the partner equivalent to five percent of gross sales (see Exhibit 5).

Manufacturing Options for Phase III and Commercialization

One of the chief advantages of either in-house pilot manufacturing or contract manufacturing over immediate licensing was that it gave Nucleon more options if the project survived Phase I and Phase II trials. As noted earlier, under these two options, Nucleon intended to line up with a partner who would be responsible for conducting Phase III trials, handling regulatory filings, and marketing the product.

Exhibit 5	Estimated Gross Sales of CRP-1 (as topical burn wound treatment)

Year	Sales ($000)
1998	53,700
1999	99,500
2000	125,000
2001	130,000
2002	150,000

After the year 2000, sales of CRP-1 as a burn wound treatment were expected to grow at approximately 5 percent per year, assuming no introduction of a substitute product.

However, under such an arrangement, Nucleon could either retain commercial manufacturing responsibilities or license these to the partner. Each of these approaches are discussed below.

Vertically Integrate into Commercial Manufacturing

Before Phase III trials began, Nucleon could invest in a full-scale commercial manufacturing facility that met the FDA guidelines for Good Manufacturing Practice (see Exhibit 6). The FDA required that Phase III trials be supplied largely by the plant that would be used to supply the commercial market. Thus it would be necessary to commence construction in mid-1993 so that the plant could be fully validated and operational by the scheduled commencement of Phase III trials.

Moore estimated that the costs of such a facility would be about $20 million, and another $1 million in development resources would be required to perform scale-up. He and Nucleon's financial advisors believed that once the project cleared Phase II trials, it would have little difficulty raising the needed funds to build the plant. The company would also have to hire at least 20 people to handle such functions as procurement, quality control, maintenance, technical support, and logistics.[4]

It was difficult to know exactly what terms could be reached. If Nucleon built a commercial plant, it would be the sole supplier of CRP-1 to its marketing partner. Judging by what other firms in the industry were receiving for similar products, Nucleon management estimated that the company could negotiate a combined supply contract and royalty agreement with the following terms: Nucleon would receive a $5 million payment upon FDA approval of CRP-1, plus royalties equal to 40 percent of the partner's gross sales of the product. Nucleon would sell CRP-1 to the partner at cost.[5]

Exhibit 6   Good Manufacturing Practices (GMPs)

The following are some of the major concepts behind "Good Manufacturing Practices" (GMPs):

- A facility must have an uncluttered fermentation area, precautions for fermentation spills, and surfaces that are easily cleaned.
- Adequate air systems to prevent cross-contamination of the product from other research products or micro-organisms in the facility. Closed system fermenters. Steps must be performed in a controlled environment. (A controlled environment is defined as being adequate to control air pressure, humidity, temperature, microorganisms, and particulate matter.) An environmental monitoring system is necessary for all manufacturing areas.
- The water used in the downstream manufacturing steps should be of high quality and, again, there should be a monitoring system in place.
- A trained Quality Assurance department is required to oversee and assure GMP manufacturing and control.
- A documentation system is required for the process or support systems.
- Uni-directional production flow is required.

- Validated processes to demonstrate removal of major contaminants are required.
- Validated cleaning procedures to demonstrate those in place are adequate for multi-use of equipment are required.
- A uni-directional flow of raw material, product, and personnel is required with product moving from less clean and controlled areas (fermentation) to very clean areas (formulation and filling). There should be positive air pressure differentials between clean and less clean areas.
- Space should be designated for raw material and final product storage. The area should be designed to allow for separate areas for quarantine, released, and rejected material and there should be adequate security.
- Space should be designated for media/reagent preparation with a controlled environment.
- There should be adequate space for glassware washing and autoclaving.
- There should be gowning areas for very clean areas (formulation/filling) and possibly the fermentation area.
- Find out now what other microorganisms are being used in the facility and keep track of any new organisms which may be used in the future.

Licensing Out Manufacturing and Marketing Rights at Phase III

A second option at the beginning of Phase III trials would be to license out both the manufacturing and marketing rights to a partner. This option would be similar to that discussed above, except, in this case, the partner would also be responsible for Phase III and commercial manufacturing. Nucleon therefore would not have to invest the $20 million in a commercial plant. Under this option, Nucleon could expect to receive a $7 million payment if and when CRP-1 was approved by the FDA. After that, Nucleon would receive a royalty equivalent to 10 percent of the partner's gross sales of CRP-1.

Moore recognized that Hurst leaned towards manufacturing CRP-1 in-house. He had said, "I keep asking myself, 'How many times will we get to the plate?' If I thought that this were our only chance, I'd go for the home run and take the risks of manufacturing." For his part, Moore decided to review Nucleon's options another time before making a recommendation.

End Notes

1. "Clinical grade" indicates the minimum conditions under which drugs must be produced for use in human clinical trials.
2. For some very serious diseases, Phase I trials were performed on afflicted patients.
3. On the horizon was a hybrid of biotechnology and synthetic chemical techniques that could alter or replace existing process technologies. These hybrid companies used molecular biology techniques to clone and produce small amounts of biologically important proteins. The protein was studied to learn the chemical and physical structure of its therapeutically active site and then, using computer-aided modeling techniques, the active site of the protein could be constructed synthetically.
4. This assumes the company already has a pilot plant with a staff of six.
5. All costs, except depreciation, would be reflected in the transfer price.

Case 3-3: Danaher Corporation

Early in the morning on January 24, 2008, Danaher Corporation's Chief Executive Officer Larry Culp leafed through some slides at his desk. He was about to begin a year-end conference call with analysts and investors to review the firm's performance over the past year. Culp had joined Danaher after graduating from Harvard Business School in 1990, and was appointed CEO in 2001 at the age of 38. He had taken over a company that had generated compound annual stock returns of over 25% since its founding in 1985. During the first five years of Culp's leadership, Danaher's performance continued unabated. Danaher's revenues and net income more than doubled, the firm consummated over 50 acquisitions, and its stock price continued to outperform its peers by impressive margins[1] (see Exhibit 1). Indeed, 2007 had been yet another record year for the Washington, D.C.-based industrial conglomerate.

Culp was wary of the term "conglomerate," instead referring to Danaher as a family of strategic growth platforms. Management defined a strategic growth platform as "a multi-billion-dollar market in which Danaher can generate $1 billion or more in revenue while being No. 1 or No. 2 in the market."[2] In 2007, Danaher's portfolio comprised six such platforms, representing over 80% of its total revenue. In addition, the firm, operated in seven focused niche businesses—a "business operating in a fragmented or small market in which Danaher has sufficient market share and acceptable margins and returns"[3] (see Exhibit 2 for Danaher's reporting structure).

The company's portfolio had evolved over the years. Once a cyclical industrial company, Danaher had in recent years become a value-added instrumentation provider that competed in less cyclical markets.[4] This evolution was most apparent in the firm's four core growth platforms: Electronic Test, Environmental, Medical Technologies and

Product ID.[5] By 2007, Danaher boasted leading market positions in a number of their business areas (see Exhibit 3). Many of these companies were the result of successful acquisitions executed in the past 10 years.

Culp had earned widespread praise for being a "hands-on" CEO. Culp believed that "the role of the CEO is to ensure the company has a clear and well articulated strategy coupled with the right people to execute that strategy."[6] For Danaher, a central pillar of that strategy was the Danaher Business System, or DBS (Exhibit 4 illustrates the system's core tenets). As one analyst described, "the DBS process system is the soul of Danaher. The system guides planning, deployment and execution."[7] Culp affirmed the significance of the company's philosophy of "kaizen," or continuous improvement, in his first letter to shareholders in the 2001 annual report: "The bedrock of our company is the Danaher Business System (DBS). DBS tools give all of our operating executives the means with which to strive for world-class quality, delivery, and cost benchmarks and deliver superior customer satisfaction and profitable growth."

Danaher's successful implementation of DBS across its acquisitions had resulted in rapid growth. Indeed, Danaher's management team had an impressive track record of expanding the operating margins of acquired companies (see Exhibit 5). One equity research firm also noted that they "were pretty amazed at the number of new product introductions across the portfolio."[8] By early 2007, Danaher remained poised for further success.

However, despite its tremendous success, Danaher still faced a number of challenges. First, as the company grew to over $12 billion in revenues with strong cash flow, could it continue to identify and execute attractive, value-added acquisitions? Second, although the cyclicality in the portfolio was significantly reduced, some parts were still exposed to vertical markets with demand volatility. Third, Danaher like many others was exposed to a slowing U.S. economy with signs of a broader global slowdown. Last, some observers wondered how long the model of "continuous improvement" could continue.

During Culp's 17-year tenure with Danaher, he had seen the company rise to numerous challenges before. He was quietly confident that the firm would do so again.

Professors Bharat Anand and David J. Collis and Research Associate Sophie Hood prepared this case. HBS cases are developed solely as the basis for class discussion. Cases are not intended to serve as endorsements, sources of primary data, or illustrations of effective or ineffective management.

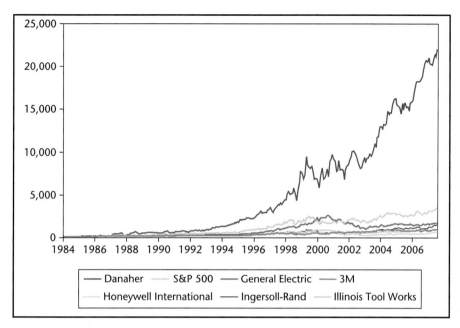

Exhibit 1   Danaher Share Price versus S&P and Competitors, 1984–2007 (indexed to 100)

Source: Created by casewriters using data from Thomson Financial, October 2007.

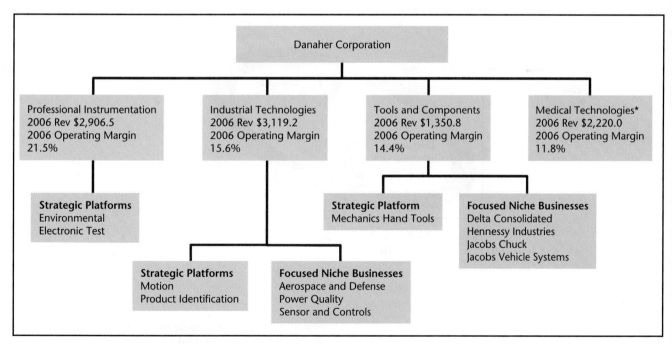

Exhibit 2   Danaher's Operating Segments, from a Reporting Perspective ($ in billions)

Source: Adapted by casewriters from company reports and Friedman, Billings, Ramsey Research.

*Medical Technologies is both a segment and a strategic platform.

Exhibit 3   Leading Brands in the Danaher Portfolio

Platform	Key Brands	Position	Global Share
Electronic Test	Fluke, Fluke Networks	#1	25%
Environmental			
Water Quality	Hach, Lange, Trojan	#1	2%
Retail Petroleum Solutions	Gilbarco Veeder-Root	#1	30%
Medical Technology			
Dental Equipment	KaVo, Gendex, Pelton & Crane	#1	20%
Critical Care Diagnostics	Radiometer	#1	35%
Life Sciences	Leica Microsystems	#2	35%
Motion	Kollmorgen, Portescap, Dover	#2	8%
Product Identification	Videojet, Accusort	#1	15%
Mechanics Hand Tools	Craftsman, Matco	#1	30%

Source: Adapted by casewriters from company Investor Presentation, December 2005.

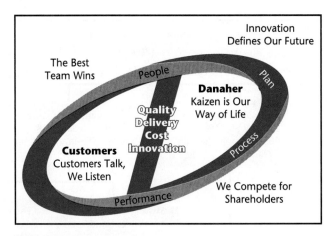

Exhibit 4   The Danaher Business System Image
Source: Company materials.

Corporate History

Origins

Steven and Mitchell Rales were two of four brothers who grew up in Bethesda, Maryland. In 1980 they formed their initial investment vehicle, Equity Group Holdings, with an objective to acquire businesses with the following characteristics: (i) understandable operations in a reasonably defined niche, (ii) predictable earnings that generate cash profits, and (iii) experienced management with an entrepreneurial orientation. In 1981, they acquired Master Shield, Inc., a Texas-based vinyl siding manufacturer. Then, they acquired Mohawk Rubber Company of Hudson, Ohio, using $2 million of their own money, and borrowing $90 million.

Soon after, a real estate investment trust (REIT) called DMG, Inc. came to the attention of several investor groups,

Exhibit 5   Operating Margin Expansion of Acquired Companies

		Op Margin Year Prior to Purchase	Current Margins	Improvement
1998	FLUKE.	HSD	20%+	+1200 bps
1999	HACH	Mid Teens	20%+	+700 bps
2000	DANAHER MOTION	HSD	Low DD	+400 bps
2002	GILBARCO	MSD	Low DD	+700 bps
2002	VIDEOJET.	Mid Teens	20%+	+700 bps

Source: Company Investor Presentation, December 2005.

including the Rales. DMG had not posted a profit since 1975, but it had more than $130 million in tax-loss carry forwards.[9] In 1983, the brothers gained control of publicly traded DMG, and sold the company's real estate holdings the following year. They then folded both Master Shield and Mohawk Rubber Company into the REIT, sheltering the manufacturing earnings under the tax credits.[10] They also changed the company's name to Danaher, after a favorite fly-fishing locale in western Montana. The Danaher River traced its name to the Celtic root "Dana," or "swift flowing."[11]

From then on, the brothers used the newly tailored Danaher as an acquisition vehicle. Using a considerable amount of debt, Danaher launched a series of both friendly and hostile takeovers. They focused on low-profile industrial firms, and purchased 12 additional companies within two years of Danaher's debut. Early acquisitions included various manufacturers of tools, controls, precision components and plastics. In such mergers, Danaher's focus was on cutting costs and paying down debt through the divestiture of underperforming assets. By 1986, Danaher was listed as a Fortune 500 company with revenues of $456 million. The 14 subsidiaries were at that time organized into four business units: automotive/transportation, instrumentation, precision components, and extruded products.

Despite their rate of growth, Danaher's acquisitive strategy was far from indiscriminate. As outlined in the 1986 annual report: "As we pursue our objective of becoming the most-innovative and lowest-cost manufacturer of the products we offer, we are seeking a market position with each product line that is either first, second or within a very distinctive market niche."[12] At least 12 of their 14 subsidiaries were market leaders. Danaher considered its strategy distinct among the numerous serial acquirers of the mid 1980s: "If there's one thing that distinguishes us from the other players in the M&A field, it's that we stay in touch with the companies," commented Steven Rales in 1986. After all, he added, "we're reasonably young fellows with long time horizons."[13]

Continuous Improvement.   Around 1988, the Rales brothers shifted tack in three noteworthy areas. First, they turned an eye inward—both to the subsidiaries' operations, and the operations of the overall corporate entity. The managers of Jacobs Vehicle Systems, one of Danaher's divisions, had studied Toyota Motor Corp.'s lean manufacturing with great success. Before long, the brothers implemented the system companywide. The move bespoke what certain Danaher managers later described as their "near-instinctive affinity for lean manufacturing."[14] This penchant for lean manufacturing was the first aspect of a broader philosophy of kaizen, or continuous improvement—an approach that would ultimately become known as DBS, one of Danaher's hallmarks.

Second, the Rales brothers noticed early warning signs in the junk-bond market, prompting them to reduce their debt. As a result, they were able to successfully weather the recession of the early 1990s.[15] Finally, Steven and Mitchell chose to retire their positions as chief executive and president. Although the brothers stayed on as chairman of the board and chairman of the executive committee, they looked to someone else to take the day-to-day helm.

The Sherman Years

In February 1990, Danaher appointed George M. Sherman as president and chief executive officer. Sherman was 48 at the time of his appointment, an engineer by training who also had an M.B.A. He joined Danaher from the Black & Decker Corporation, where he had been a corporate executive vice president and president of the Power Tools and Home Improvement Group. Sherman was known as a highly effective leader; one analyst commented that he was "the highest-energy CEO I've met. He is exhausting to be around."[16] At Black & Decker, he was widely credited with the turnaround of the Power Tools businesses, which grew twice as fast as the market during his tenure. Prior to that, Sherman had been at General Electric and Emerson Electric.

Sherman commented upon joining Danaher that he hoped "to add strategic planning with a market-driven emphasis to enhance the admirable position of Danaher's companies."[17] In addition, he looked to reposition the portfolio towards more attractive, less cyclical businesses. The company began to "look at international opportunities for expansion both in terms of selling our products overseas and selective acquisitions."[18] It also began divesting those companies making tires, tools and components for the auto industry, as Danaher had neither the brand identity nor the sufficient scale to withstand pricing pressures affecting the industry. Beyond this, Danaher invested in new "platforms," re-focusing the firm's acquisition approach and generating economies of scale not only in production but in distribution. Initial platforms included environmental controls, electronic test instrumentation, and precision motors. Last, Sherman concentrated on "making fewer but larger acquisitions, many of them family-owned firms with good products and respectable market shares that were underperforming financially."[19]

In 1986, Danaher had 16 operating companies. By 1995, it had 24 operating companies and by 2000 it had 51 operating companies.[20] As Danaher moved into electronic test instruments, water quality instruments, temperature and pressure sensors for food and pharmaceutical manufacturing, and hardware for utility companies and other businesses,"[21] their management team "proved to be adept at integrating these companies into their existing operations."[22] The acquisitions also solidified the shift in the company's business mix that Sherman had jumpstarted in 1990. In 1985, 86% of revenue came from tires and rubber goods; in 1991, 78% of sales came instead from tools and automotive equipment. By 2001, over half of all revenues came from the Environmental, Electronic Test and Motion Control platforms[23] (see Exhibit 6 for percentages of revenue and profit by segment and geographic area from 2004–2006).

During Sherman's tenure, Danaher's sales increased from $750 million to $3.8 billion.[24] The last five years of Sherman's leadership saw Danaher achieve a compound annual growth rate in earnings of over 20% and revenue growth of about 15% per year.[25] Danaher also worked to expand and ingrain the continuous quality improvement techniques the founders had introduced. DBS came to be understood as the keystone of the firm's continual success. An analyst in 1997 commented that Danaher was growing both "internally and by acquisition. . . . It's a nice balance."[26] The investment community praised Sherman's leadership, opining that between 1990 and 2001, Danaher had emerged "from midcap company status to become the premier large-cap industrial company."[27]

Danaher, 2001–Present

Portfolio

During its early years, Danaher pursued a financial orientation towards its choice of businesses, making resource allocation decisions on the basis of return on invested capital (ROIC). Starting in the mid-nineties, Culp noted, the company's portfolio evolved towards "fewer, better businesses"[28] by creating "platforms" based on a lead company with a strong position in an attractive market around which add-on acquisitions could be made. Danaher's purchase of Fluke in 1998 was the first substantial acquisition that demonstrated the value in this approach.

Business selection was driven by a belief that "the market comes first, the company second." In this, the firm adhered to Warren Buffet's famous epithet that "when an industry with a reputation for difficult economics meets a manager with a reputation for excellence, it is usually the industry that keeps its reputation intact." Rather than identify potential targets and then assess their market potential, Danaher conducted a top-down analysis that progressed from market analysis to company evaluation to diligence, valuation, negotiation, and finally, integration.[29]

Industries were screened according to certain desirable criteria. "First, the market size should exceed $1 billion. Second, core market growth should be at least 5%–7% and without undue cyclicality or volatility. This excludes Rust Belt and Silicon Valley businesses for us. Third, we look for fragmented industries with a long tail of participants that have $25–$100 million in sales, and that can be acquired for their products without necessarily needing their overheads. Fourth, we try to avoid outstanding competitors such as

Exhibit 6   Breakdown of Total Revenue and Operating Income/Loss by Segment

	2004	2005	2006
Revenue by Business Segment			
Professional Instrumentation	33.2%	32.6%	30.3%
Medical Technologies	9.8%	14.8%	23.1%
Industrial Technologies	38.0%	36.4%	32.5%
Tools and Components	19.0%	16.2%	14.1%
Revenue by Geographic Segment			
United States	64.8%	57.5%	54.4%
Germany	11.2%	14.5%	15.2%
United Kingdom	3.6%	4.2%	3.8%
Denmark	3.8%	NA	NA
All Other	16.6%	23.7%	26.5%
Operating Income/Loss by Business Segment			
Professional Instrumentation	43.3%	42.6%	41.2%
Medical Technologies	6.9%	11.0%	17.2%
Industrial Technologies	34.7%	33.7%	32.0%
Tools and Components	17.9%	15.8%	12.8%
Other	−2.8%	−3.0%	−3.2%

Source: Compiled by casewriters using data provided by OneSource® Business Browser[SM], an online business information product of OneSource Information Services, Inc. ("OneSource").

Toyota or Microsoft. Fifth, the target arena should present a good opportunity for applying the DBS so that we can leverage our Danaher skill sets. Last, we look for tangible product-centric businesses. This rules out, for example, financial services. Broadly, this set of criteria is rooted in a simple premise: we look for markets of size and where we can win."

Acquisitions that followed these criteria fell into three categories based upon the target's relation to existing businesses:

- **New Platforms** As the classification suggested, a new platform acquisition represented a significant expansion of Danaher's portfolio into new markets and products. Such an entry point could be a division of a larger corporation, a stand-alone public firm or a private company. "Platform-establishing acquisitions," explained the 2001 annual report, "bring in 'Danaher-like' businesses where our skills and abilities can create value."[30] Summarizing their importance, Culp remarked that "it was tough to build a string of pearls from later add-on acquisitions without a center of gravity on which to

build." Targets tended to be large and in sectors of strategic importance. Danaher's recent expansion into the medical sector was one instance of platform entry into an attractive market where, by 2006, the firm had "invested over $2.6 billion in acquisitions with a focus on building our Medical Technologies platform, which is now approaching 25% of total revenues and is reported as a segment."[31]

- **Bolt-Ons** Bolt-ons were smaller transactions that sought synergies between existing Danaher businesses and new targets. Acquired companies were comprehensively integrated into the core business in terms of management, organization, and distribution. In 2004, for example, Danaher acquired various product lines from Harris Corporation for $50 million, bolting them on to the Electronic Test Platform.

- **Adjacencies** Unlike bolt-ons, adjacencies tended to function as predominantly stand-alone businesses after acquisition, despite their connection to a particular platform. For instance, Danaher acquired Trojan Technologies in 2004 for $191 million. While Trojan operated within the Environmental platform, their water treatment products occupied a particular niche and the business continued to function post-acquisition as a more or less distinct organization.

Although Danaher was on a pace of one acquisition per month by 2007, platform acquisitions were rare. A list of target industries was maintained by a corporate group that included the CEO, CFO, head of Strategy Development, and head of M&A, and this list was reviewed regularly by the board. Often, Danaher would already know something about a business that it became interested in. For example, Culp noted that "American Sigma (acquired in 1995) was familiar to us as we had used its waste water sampling products at Veeder Root. Similarly, Gilbarco (acquired in 2002) had been my first customer back in 1990." But the firm also searched broadly to find the right business opportunity. The idea of entering the dental market, for example, was identified as early as 2002.

In identifying appropriate targets, Danaher was "willing to accept that an entry-point firm might not have a great leadership team, a key facility, or a terrific infrastructure in place. The only deal killer is when we cannot identify management to fill any anticipated gaps." If a suitable company was not available Danaher was prepared to wait. Yet, Culp believed that "because of our preparation, we are tactically advantaged when it comes to entering a new platform business. For example, we were decisive in the bid for KaVo in 2004 since the dental market had already been investigated by us and approved as a target by our board in 2002–2003."

Smaller bolt-on acquisitions to existing platform businesses were more common than entering new business areas. Bolt-on acquisitions were the responsibility of the operating companies with legal, pricing, and deal expertise contributed by the corporate M&A group. Implementation of such acquisitions would typically involve folding the target's structure and operations into the existing platform. Such deal opportunities were reviewed monthly with each business although the company walked away from far more deals than it ultimately consummated.

Distinguishing between various types of acquisitions informed the merger process from start to finish. Indeed, even post-acquisition benchmarks were determined by the type of add-on, as explained in the 2001 annual report: "[W]e scrutinize return on invested capital (ROIC) on all acquisitions. Our minimum hurdle rate is 10% after-tax ROIC within three years on average with bolt-ons frequently reaching this threshold more quickly and platform-establishing transactions taking a little longer, but not exceeding five years."[32]

Reshaping the portfolio since the mid-nineties had occurred without any large divestitures. Instead, trimming had mainly occurred around the edges.

Danaher's acquisition strategy had not gone unnoticed. As one strategy consultant favorably commented in *BusinessWeek*, "those guys have a very well-defined model of how to do M&A."[33] Over the prior decade Danaher had expanded into Western and Eastern Europe, Asia, Latin America, and the Middle East. Initial expansion was fueled by adding small European companies to an existing U.S. operation in order to access international markets. More recently, as the firm's international experience grew, it used certain European acquisitions (such as Radiometer in Denmark or Leica in Germany) as its core entry points into desirable sectors. Indeed, Culp viewed the German "Mittelstand"—medium-sized, often family-owned, German-engineering companies—as ideal territory in which Danaher might make acquisitions since they included companies that had a broad geographic footprint but were typically "capable of more." Culp believed that the Danaher operating model had been shown to effectively transfer overseas: "It might take a bit longer to change things, but if you accommodate the system to the new context and are always respectful of stakeholders' needs and requirements, it can be done." To date, Danaher had pursued fewer acquisitions in Asia, seeing companies there as too small to be valuable additions, and instead emphasized building businesses organically through their growth platforms. For example, by 2008, Danaher's sales in China were rapidly approaching $1 billion.

By 2007, Danaher comprised six strategic platforms, grouped into four business segments: Professional Instrumentation, Industrial Technologies, Tools & Components, and Medical Technologies (see Exhibit 7 for detailed descriptions of the platforms, and see Exhibit 8 for acquisitions within various platforms over the years). Culp broadly sketched future possibilities: "We don't believe that Danaher's operating model itself imposes any constraints on the size of the company. While our current platforms are primarily in B2B industries, we believe that we can potentially compete in a wide range of industries."

Organization

Danaher was headquartered in; Washington D.C. in an unassuming office building six blocks north of the White House. The company's name was not on the front of the building, nor was it even listed inside. Offices for the 45 or so corporate employees featured plain décor. Corporate functions represented in Washington included finance, accounting, legal, tax, treasury, HR, and M&A deal making.

Exhibit 7 Danaher Strategic Platform Overview

	Market Size	Market Growth	Sales	Operating Margins	Geographic Mix	Key Customers	Growth Drivers	Key Brands
Medical Technologies								
Dental	$16 billion	5–7%	$1.6 billion	Mid teens	NA 45%, EU 40%, ROW 15%	General Practitioners, Endodontists, Orthodontists, Lab technicians	Favorable demographic trends, patient demand for aesthetics, improved care in emerging markets, productivity enhancing branded products at premium price points, further consolidation opportunities	KaVo, Gendex, Dexis, Pelton & Crane, Imaging Sciences International, Ormco, Kerr
Life Sciences	$4 billion	5–7%	$900 million	>10%	NA 30%, EU 35%, ROW 35%	Life science research labs, hospitals, universities, histopathology labs	Public & private funding of life science research (e.g., live cell/stem cell), industrial markets micro/nano technologies, healthcare expenditures in emerging markets, drive towards more advanced cancer diagnostics, digital imaging & quantitative analysis	Leica Microsystems
Radiometer	$1.2 billion	4–6%	$400 million	~25%	NA 20%, EU 55%, ROW 25%	Critical Care departments in hospitals; central labs, operating rooms, emergency departments	Point-of-care (POC) segments, emerging markets (China, India, Brazil, Russia and Middle East), New clinical guidelines in cardiology, laboratory and emergency medicine	Radiometer
Environmental								
Retail Petroleum, Environmental and Automation Technology	$2.5 billion	3–5%	$1 billion	High teens	NA 45%, EU 33%, ROW 22%	Global major and national oil companies, big box and supermarkets, convenience stores	Environmental regulations (air, water), Point-of-sale & payment system upgrades, geographic expansion, NA/Europe retrofit opportunities	Gilbarco, Veeder-Root

(continued)

Exhibit 7 Danaher Strategic Platform Overview (*continued*)

	Market Size	Market Growth	Sales	Operating Margins	Geographic Mix	Key Customers	Growth Drivers	Key Brands
Water Quality	$6.5 billion	4–6%	$1.1 billion	20%+	NA 65%, EU 20%, ROW 15%	Municipal water facilities, Ultra Pure industrial; beverage, electronics, biopharm, power, environmental agencies, industrial boiler cooler facilities	Water/waste water infrastructure opportunities in emerging markets, increasing regulatory requirements, water treatment process optimization	Hach, Lange, ChemTreat, Trojan
Test & Measurement								
Fluke	$4.5 billion	5–7%	$1.3 billion	20%+	NA 50%, EU 30%, ROW 20%	Industrial/Electrical, Calibration/Metrology, Hospitals/Field Service, Communications/Datacomm	Emerging market opportunities, High Vitality/Innovation, Leverage strong brand	Fluke, Fluke Networks
Tektronix	$12 billion	5–7%	$1.1 billion	>10%	NA 38%, EU 27%, Asia/Pacific 20%, Japan 15%	Computer, Communications; Consumer, Education, Gov. and Semiconductor	Proliferation of wireless, higher performance requirements, growth of Next Gen networks, emerging market opportunities	Tektronix
Motion	$14 billion	5–7%	$1 billion	Mid teens	NA 50%, Europe 40%, ROW 10%	90% OEMs (original equipment manufacturers)	Targeted vertical markets, continued conversion opportunities, Asia expansion led by strength in China, developing clean energy market	Kollmorgen, Dover, Thomson, Portescap
Product Identification	$5.1 billion	~5%	$900 million	High teens	NA 40%, EU 35%, ROW 25%	Consumer packaged goods, Pharmaceuticals, electronics, automotive; letter and parcel distribution	Emerging markets, New regulations (e.g., traceability, environmental), new applications (e.g., product decoration), new verticals (e.g., textile printing, graphics)	Videojet, Accu-Sort Systems, Linx Printing Technologies
Mechanics' Hand Tools	US: ~$4.5 billion Global: ~$9 billion	2–3% globally, China growth low double digit	$900 million	Mid teens	NA 90%, EU 5%, ROW 5%	Retail, Industrial, Professional	Innovative New Products: ergonomics, electronic torque measurement, industrial ratcheting wrenches; Emerging markets	Craftsman, Matco Tools, Sata, GearWrench

In addition to the six strategic platforms, Danaher has seven focused niche businesses: Aerospace & Defense, Danaher Industrial Controls Group, Delta Consolidated Industries, Hennessy Industries, Jacobs Chuck Manufacturing, Jacobs Vehicle Systems and Power Quality. *Source:* Compiled by casewriters from company materials.

Strategic Platforms

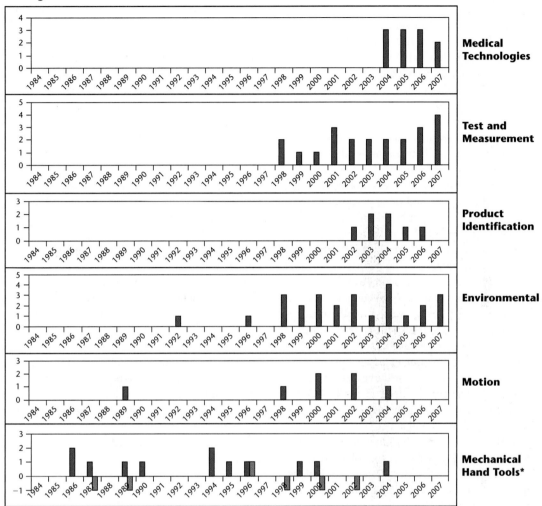

Focused Niche Businesses

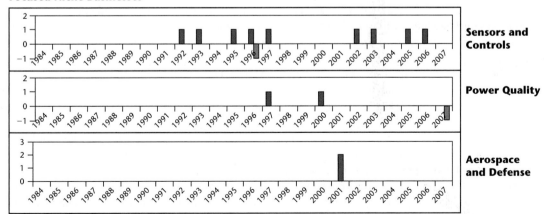

Exhibit 8 Historical Acquisitions and Diverstitures by Platform

Source: Created by casewriters from Thomson data and company information.

Note: Rubber and Related Automotive Products and Vinyl/Plastic Consumer Good and Real Estate were segments in Danaher's early years.

*Mechanics' Hand Tools was the Strategic Platform designation as of summer 2007; it also includes subsidiaries once mapped to the "Tools and Components" segment.

By 2008, Danaher was active in dozens of different businesses, and had grown to over $12 billion in sales. It operated with 45–55 separate business P&Ls, but only three segment EVPs reported to the CEO. Danaher liked fewer reporting units and, unlike other conglomerates such as Dover and Illinois Tool Works that split units when they got large, Danaher invariably looked to combine smaller units into one operating entity.

Culp himself spent about half a day a week on external affairs (investor relations), between one and a half and two days a week on strategic or M&A issues, and the remaining time—more than half the week—on operational and HR matters. Although he and other corporate executives had run a number of Danaher businesses effectively in the past, he noted that "today, I don't make many operating decisions directly. Everything I do is really organization and people related. It's all about influencing people and helping frame the conversation in a developmental way."

The other important corporate function at Danaher was the DBS Office (DBSO) that comprised 15–20 executives who were physically located in the businesses rather than at headquarters. Individuals worked in the DBSO for a limited time as it was seen as a developmental role, but the basic requirement for the position was to have been a senior operating executive. The current head of the DBSO, for example, was the former President of a Danaher company. The DBSO's role was to train managers, both in acquired companies and existing Danaher operations, in the Danaher Business System (DBS). The DBSO was involved with the initial training and *kaizen* sessions for all new acquisitions. For existing businesses, its services were in most cases invited by the business itself although, on occasion, it was told to assist a particular business. The DBSO was intentionally kept small because it was not intended to supersede the authority of line managers who were expected to ultimately implement DBS themselves.

Corporate HR was run by a former company president. Individual businesses were responsible for managing their own people, but there was also a talent funnel from which to fill senior positions. Procedurally, however, corporate HR was intimately involved in executive careers. Any new job opportunity was run through an approximately 2,000-person corporate talent funnel, and all important moves were reviewed by the CEO and head of HR. A talent review was a key part of every operating company review. While Danaher believed in developing an expertise in a function within a single business, the bias was to promote and retain executives within Danaher. As a result, approximately three out of every four senior promotions were filled internally and roughly one-fifth of the senior managers were promoted to a new position every year.

Opportunities included both promotions within a business as well as opportunities in another Danaher business. An assignment did not have a predetermined length, and further promotions would be considered and planned as part of the talent review process when an employee mastered required competencies within the assignment and performed at or above expectations. Senior managers were expected to continuously develop, performance manage, and upgrade their team members. However, no bottom performer reduction targets were set. Rather, individuals were assessed based on their performance and fit with DBS values.

Hiring into the firm included a psychological assessment as well as more typical interview procedures. Candidates were expected to "want to win with a team and demonstrate personal humility, while having a passion and energy for creative change." Executives hired from outside were put through a rigorous 8–12 week immersion program to learn about DBS, the tools and culture. During this period, new executives focused exclusively on immersion and did not perform the job for which they were hired. Hires at an undergraduate level came primarily from schools like University of Illinois and Virginia Tech. At the MBA level, Danaher recruited at top-tier schools like Darden, Harvard Business School, Kellogg, Stanford, IMD, and Insead, with a focus on long-term leadership potential. New hires were given job rotations, but were expected to run parts of a Danaher operation at an early stage, whether as shift leader for a manufacturing cell or as a regional sales manager.

Corporate M&A consisted of a small team of dealmakers. The team worked extensively with Business Development in each of the platforms as well as with Strategy Development on all transactions. The businesses were encouraged to identify and cultivate potential targets within their industry as well as adjacencies whereas Strategy Development focused most of their energy on potential new platforms. During each of the last four years, Danaher had acquired 8–12 companies.

Compensation for senior managers included base salary, a bonus, and equity participation. Base pay was set to be competitive within function and industry, and was not standardized across Danaher, although at the very senior levels (presidents and their reports) base pay levels did converge. The bonus was equal to one quarter to half of base pay, with the mix shifting to the bonus as seniority increased. Bonuses were paid according to performance of the business and the individual's own goals for the year. The latter were set to specific objectives, such as revenue growth in China, or the number and success of new product launches, or how many potential president candidates had been developed. Long-term equity compensation was intended for long-term wealth creation of executives. Given Danaher's stock performance, wealth creation for executives at Danaher had outpaced compensation for executives at peer companies.

Danaher Business System (DBS)

At the core of Danaher's operating model and acquisition strategy was the Danaher Business System (DBS). The firm's investor presentations described DBS as "defining our high-performance culture. DBS is who we are and how we do what we do." Outsiders noted that DBS "is a set of management tools borrowed liberally from the famed Toyota Production System. In essence it requires every employee, from the janitor to the president, to find ways every day to improve the way works get done."[34] While such programs were "de rigeur for manufacturers for years, the difference at Danaher (was) the company started lean in 1987, one of the earliest U.S. companies to do so, and it has maintained a cultish devotion to making it pay off."[35] The lean approach replaced a traditional "batch-and-queue" manufacturing system with a "single-piece flow" that minimized in-process time and so reduced inventory and other overhead costs. "In a typical Danaher factory, floors are covered with strips of tape indicating where everything should be, from the biggest machine to the humblest trash can. Managers determine the most efficient place for everything, so a worker won't have to walk an extra few yards to pick up a tool, for instance."[36]

Over time, DBS came to represent a broader approach than simply lean manufacturing, and had taken these same principles to transactional processes. More recently, Danaher had been expanding DBS to include "Ideas to Execution"—which expanded DBS tools and capabilities into innovation, new product development, marketing, and sales.

The DBS approach embodied "four P's—people, plan, process, and performance." These four elements were applied rigorously and unemotionally both to current businesses and new acquisitions.

People. Talent assessment was a major component of acquisition due diligence as well as of ongoing reviews of existing businesses. Managerial retention rates differed across acquisitions, but Danaher typically transitioned out between zero and 50% of senior management within a couple of years of ownership. For an acquisition like Videojet, replacing the management team might have been seen as part of the value-creation opportunity. In other deals, like Radiometer, no one was asked to leave. Personnel decisions were made not only on the basis of interviews during the due-diligence process but after observing managers in operation, and were made as quickly as possible to sort among executives who were either unlikely to succeed or unlikely to fit in the Danaher culture. As Culp noted, "you get a different view of someone when you spend a week or a month working with them, than in a three- or four-hour interview." If, before completing the deal, it was known that certain key personnel would leave, a plan to replace them, either with a pre-identified internal candidate or an outsider (preferably a Danaher proven manager) would have been developed.

Plan. The second element of DBS was creating a strategic plan for every business (existing or acquired) that would address two questions: "What game are we playing?" and "How do we win?" Although Danaher executives obtained some idea of a preferred strategy for an acquisition target during the due-diligence process, Culp noted that "it was only *after* the deal was completed, and the bankers and lawyers are out of the room, that we can have an honest strategic conversation with management. At that point, we throw out the 180-page strategy manuals and create a plan for the new acquisition that is due within 100 days of purchase that is intended to produce a shared long-term vision. No sacred cows are left unchallenged, and our due-diligence findings are shared with the company. This entire conversation is usually very important." The Danaher team involved in this process included the CEO, EVP of the segment, head of HR, CFO and two members of the M&A deal team. The intent was to encourage managers to realize that substantial improvement in performance was possible, and to challenge them to identify the gaps that were preventing them from reaching such a stretch target.

Process. A key element of the integration process was introducing DBS to new managers. This first occurred through "one week of a training session for executives followed by a one-week kaizen event." Danaher's CEO himself taught a full day in the training program, with the DBSO teaching the remainder. The week-long "kaizen" event usually took place in one of the target's manufacturing facilities and was designed to improve the process flow of a single piece, as in the Toyota Production System. The goal for such an exercise would be set high, such as halving the floor space required, but managers found they typically exceeded even that aggressive goal. Culp noted that "we really don't care if it's manufacturing focused or not, the goal is to get newcomers to appreciate elements like single piece flow, visual maps, and so on. It is action learning. Furthermore, having the president of the company put on jeans and work boots and get involved with a broom on the shop floor can be powerful in setting expectations. It is an opportunity to touch a lot of people quickly."

Since the Leica acquisition in 2005, Danaher had added an additional step in the training process that took roughly 12 mid-level managers away from their jobs on a three-month Danaher world tour to immerse them in DBS and drive cultural integration. This immersion exercise involved several kaizen events and managers were expected to "get the mindset" if not yet become experts in certain Danaher tools, like accelerated product development.

After the initial training period, the process shifted into a "maniacal focus on DBS which seeks to drive sustainable improvement over an indefinite time period." This involved both an operating philosophy and ongoing management development. The intent was to create a culture where every executive was continually looking for opportunities to improve any and every aspect of the business. While specific tools (such as value-stream mapping, and "kaizen" events, where a team dedicated a week to developing and implementing a solution to an identified problem) were the most visible manifestations of DBS, Danaher believed that building a managerial mindset of continuous improvement was ultimately the most important result of the process.

Performance. Once the strategy for a business was agreed upon, a policy deployment (PD) tool was used to drive and monitor its implementation (see Exhibit 9 for a Top-Level Policy Deployment Chart). The core of this system was the Policy Deployment Review (PD), "a literal but perhaps awkward translation of the Japanese term

---

Exhibit 9   Top-Level Policy Deployment Chart

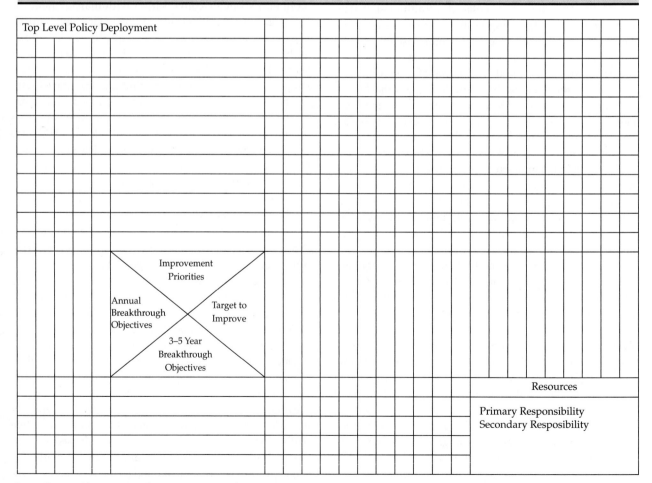

Source: Recreated by casewriters from company materials.

'Hoshin Kanri' which really means *guiding lights.*"[37] PD reviews took place once a month for every business and PD objectives were directly linked to the strategic plan. First were a series of three to five year objectives that would dramatically improve firm performance. Next were annual objectives that had to be met in order to keep the strategy on path, particularly those objectives that tracked the breakthrough initiatives essential to achieving a step change in performance. In turn, these objectives triggered a series of process improvements that were needed, and whose performance was tracked against specific output measures. HR, for example, would end up with targets for items such as "time to fill a vacant position" or "internal fill rate of positions," rather than input measures, such as completing the design of a talent development plan. Culp offered additional detail on the nature of the monthly reviews:

First, there are the financial variables we focus on: profit/loss, balance sheet, and cash, with particular emphasis placed on achieving a target ROIC in the case of a new acquisition. In addition, there are key performance indicators for each business—on-time delivery, yield, etc.—which number around 15 for each business and are derived from the plan. Then there are the elements driving breakthroughs. Last,

there are the intangibles we examine by walking through the shop floor, or having skip-level lunches. These meetings are hands-on. They are designed to ensure that the numbers are real, as well as to build process and organization for the longer term.

PDs don't just involve senior managers but are cascaded through the organization. For example, if a business level objective were the doubling of R&D productivity, one PD goal might be to improve the product development process. In turn, that objective would trigger a series of objectives for other parts of the R&D organization [see Exhibit 10 for an Improvement Priorities Cascade Slide].

We capture the PD review objectives on a single piece of paper. Progress against goals is color coded: red if off-track, green if on-track, yellow if questionable. Red numbers receive the most attention naturally, but we don't always start with these—we may talk through the greens first . . . to ensure that they are really greens. For the red indicators, we do a root cause analysis of the failure, asking the "five why's" in order to understand what needs to be corrected and to propose a series of countermeasures. The number of red metrics in a business is not by itself important, but neither is it acceptable for a red metric to continue for long.

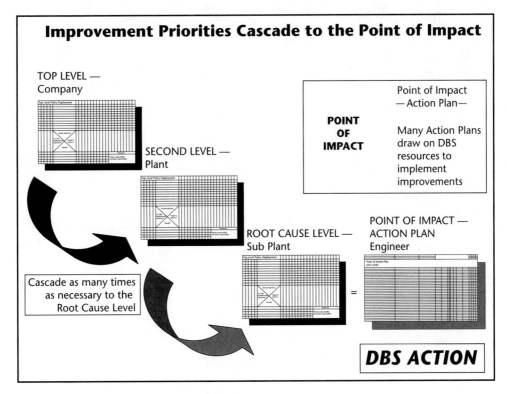

Exhibit 10 Improvement Priorities Cascade Slide

Source: Recreated by casewriters from company materials, as cited by Janney Montgomery Scott.

Analysts noted how DBS arose from a firm belief at Danaher that "everything is measurable." At the same time, Culp noted that:

> PD reviews are not simply "managing by the numbers," as some people think. We iteratively start with the numbers, then talk through process, then cycle back to the numbers. Performance is not just painting by numbers, it's understanding how those numbers were achieved that is important. We may be as focused on the numbers as any company but we combine this with a Toyota-like drive around operational improvements. Indeed, what is critical about PD reviews is that tools and processes are being deployed to address the metrics. As a result, red metrics can be good since it is through these that we build processes for the longer term. Conversely, there would be as much concern if all the metrics are green because it would indicate that there was no further potential for improvement.

Over time, Danaher had internally developed a series of over 50 tools (see Exhibit 11 for a sample) that covered processes from general management, human resources, growth tools (ideas to execution, or I2E), operating lean within your own four walls (manufacturing), problem solving (six sigma) and working through suppliers (supply chain). This set of tools had evolved over time with a conscious effort to develop processes that were applicable beyond manufacturing as well. Use of the particular tool was left up to managers who were expected to choose the tool that helped solve their problem, rather than just to check the boxes ("I've done six sigma").

Culp concluded by summarizing the role of PD reviews in DBS more broadly:

> Our objective is a blameless culture: we try to attack the problem, not the person. At the same time, these conversations can be intense. But that is how we build muscle and culture in the organization. Indeed, if there were only one DBS tool to use, it would be PD. This is at the root of sustained performance improvement since it does not accept a low bar as sufficient. We set very high expectations and have a bias for action while maintaining a competitive sense of winning. It demands that management have experience

Exhibit 11   DBS Training Modules

Business Process	Lean, Supply Chain, Variation Reduction Tools		12E & Growth Tools	Associate Development	Leadership Development
Strategic Planning	5S Visual Management	(DMP) Danaher Materials Process	(VOC) Voice of the Customer	Introduction to DBS	DBS Immersion
Policy Deployment	Value Stream Mapping	Materials Assessment Tool	Value Selling	DBS Tool Certification MBB Process	ECO
Daily Management	Standard Work	(PSI) Product Sales Inventory	Customer Segmentation	DBSL Boot Camp	DBS Leadership Training
Kaizen Event Basics	Model Cell	Lean Supply Chain	Accelerated Product Development	Training & Facilitation Techniques	Crucial Conversations
Acquisition Integration	(SMED) Set-up Reduction	Sourcing Workshop	Product Life Cycle Management	Root Cause/Counter Measure	Interview & Selection Training
JIT Accounting	(3P) Production Prep. Process	Supply Base Management	Project Management	Change Management	Danaher Leadership Program
Accounts Receivable Benchmarking	(TPM) Total Productive Mfg	Commodity Management	Ideation	DBSL Continuing Education Workshop	DBS Zealotry Boot Camp
Financial Acumen	Flow/5S/Standard Work	(VRK) Variation Reduction Kaizen	TG-2 Kaizen		
(IPP) Intellectual Property Process	Lean Conversion Boot Camp	(MSA) Measurement System Analysis	Open Innovation		
	(TPI) Transactional Process Improvement	(FMEA) Failure Mode & Effective Analysis	Pricing Margin Management		
	Heijunka	Six Sigma	Sales Force Initiative		
	Lean Conversion Roadmap	Supply Chain & Logistics Best Practices	Breakthrough Ideation		
			Lean Software Design		

Source: Company materials.

and commitment to DBS to lead from the front, as well as the confidence and the thick skin required to truly stretch the organization.

DBS in Action: The Radiometer Acquisition

In January 2005 Danaher acquired Radiometer, a Danish firm that had been family controlled since its founding in 1935 and publicly traded since 1984. Radiometer made instruments for testing and measuring blood gases (oxygen and carbon dioxide) for acute care patients, and was the world leader in a $1 billion global niche market. During the previous five years, sales had grown at 6.5% per year, and return on sales had grown to almost 20%. Peter Kurstein, CEO of Radiometer, also recalled that "the management team had an average tenure of 16 years in the company. We loved the company, but also thought we were pretty good and were skeptical that anybody, without detailed knowledge about our niche, could make us any better. There were may bidders for our company, including private equity. They all worked through the 'data room' as did Danaher's M&A team. The only real difference between the buyers was that two Danaher executives asked for a three-hour walk through one of our plants in order to understand its potential for, 'lean manufacturing.'"[38] Kurstein continued:

> *The first key event, that took place four weeks after the acquisition, was the Executive Champion Orientation (or ECO). That was a positive, teambuilding eye-opener. Having the top 40 managers at Radiometer split into six groups to do a value-stream mapping and seeing the absolutely obvious improvement opportunities from simple changes was very powerful. In our group, we discovered that a little plastic part which took 18 days to move from raw material to shipping actually took only 1,447 seconds of operating time to produce. We came up with improvements that reduced that in-process time to less than two days by creating a one-piece work flow and eliminating the planning department and IT infrastructure that had previously managed work scheduling. Similarly, the head of R&D came to me a couple of days after the ECO and said "We can use the same way of thinking in R&D. I suggest that we set the goal of reducing development time by 33%." What more can you ask for—a commitment from the person who is in charge, and the tools readily available to get started. The experience has been the same since.*
>
> *The next major event was the "strat plan"— two months after the acquisition. It was really not a new strat plan, it was our existing information, analysis, and strategy. But what came through for us was that Danaher really wanted to understand our market and why we have succeeded. Danaher was not going to tell us what to do differently, rather they were*

> *going to challenge us on whether we are getting enough out of our opportunities. For example, in some segments Radiometer has more than 40% market share, which we thought was pretty good. But Danaher management challenged us and asked: why do 60% prefer other products? We gave them our standard answer which is that the remaining 60% are really not attractive customers. They buy at low prices, don't care about quality, and are not really competent. Well, they weren't really happy with our answer, and asked when was the last time we had systematically asked these 60% why they buy something different. Well, the answer was pretty weak, for certain segments we might have done something 3–4 years ago, for most we were pretty blank. Through the strat plan discussions, it became clear to us that we probably knew our own existing customers very well, but we did not know our competitors' customers. And once you realize this, you also see that you don't have a growth strategy because converting the competitors' accounts is where the growth is. So rather than protecting the leading segment share and profitability, the strat plan discussion got us thinking about how we can further win in the market.*

With the strategic plan in place, an organizational review allowed Danaher to identify necessary organizational and personnel changes. At Radiometer, two executives were brought in from Danaher—the head of U.S. sales and the vice president of marketing—otherwise it received the equivalent of 3–4 FTEs of time from Danaher personnel in the transition, including a week that several senior team members spent with Peter Kurstein working to "kaizen" the shop floor of a Michigan plant. In return, Kurstein was obliged to spend one week a year involved in a kaizen project at another Danaher company.

Kurstein believed that Policy Deployment was perhaps the biggest and most important change at Radiometer after the acquisition. Indeed, he had previously been looking "to employ some way to improve execution of strategy through the application of a systematic process, like the Balanced Scorecard." He went on to note that:

> *Radiometer used to make three-year strategic plans every year. Lots of work went into it and they were always strictly confidential documents which ended up well protected in some closets, secrets also from our own employees. Frankly, those plans were not bad but it is awfully difficult to execute a secret plan. Policy deployment is pure logic, pushing consistent execution of the breakthrough priorities from the overall strategic level to the factory floor. I did not see it at first, and it took me a while to understand the finer mechanics of this tool.*
>
> *We started by cascading the five to seven strategic priorities needed to radically move the needle on the company's performance (such as entering a new segment) into a series of one-year goals. The next step*

was to identify the processes that needed change, such as accelerating product development or introducing value selling into the sales force. For each process change required, one or two metrics were defined that would effectively monitor progress towards those goals and monthly targets identified for each. These targets were posted on a single piece of paper outside the CEO's office and other locations, such as the lunchroom, and tracked monthly for all to see progress. Level one goals for the organization as a whole were then translated into level two goals for each department, and then into individual action plans, each of which had its own sheet attached to individuals' doors.

Policy deployment does not happen automatically. It takes a lot of hard work in the beginning to set it up; it takes several iterations and a lot of discipline to establish throughout level one, two and three and most importantly to get the right action plans developed. If you do it half way, it does not work well. If sloppily done, it just becomes a paper game with no improvement. For me the monthly PD meetings became the key. If these monthly meetings become inquisitions where we try to find somebody to blame for the misses, PD will start working against you. You have to be intent to use the meetings to direct the relevant resources to where they matter the most. Catch the misses early and hit them hard. And when misses are discussed, it is imperative that root causes and countermeasures are defined by those who really know what is going on. . . . Today, I am not in doubt: PD is the most powerful execution tool around, and you get it for free—except for the initial investment in setting it up and keeping the discipline.

Not every PD initiative succeeded: for example, dividing the manufacturing floor into 47 cells had been undertaken too quickly and had disrupted purchasing to the extent that production halted on several occasions. But three years after the acquisition, Kurstein noted the results: "Danaher has been able to help us improve not by a little, but by a lot. You can look at almost any aspect of the business, strategy, execution, growth, market share, working capital, inventory—improvements have been accelerated in all areas. Most importantly we have been able to improve our growth from low single digits to high single digits and our operating margin by another 4%, while at the same time increasing our R&D spending for further growth by 2%." Despite these successes, Kurstein felt that "only half the potential improvement has actually been achieved. We have not used at least half of the tools available through the Tool Box since we only use them when they are relevant."

Building on the success of Radiometer, Danaher expanded into Dental and Life-Sciences. In 2007, revenues from Medical Technology were $3 billion or 25% of the total, growing at high single digits.

Performance

Between 1986 and 2006, Danaher's revenues grew from $296 million to $9.6 billion, an annual percentage growth rate of nearly 50% (see Exhibit 12). Profitability also increased: Danaher's net margins grew from 3.5% in 1986 to 11.7% in 2006 (see Exhibit 13 for Revenue, Operating Profit and Capital Expenditure Year over Year). For the decade 1996–2006, operating cash flows increased from $217 million to $1.5 billion. Between 1987 and 2007, the compound annual growth rate in Danaher's share price was 23%.

Danaher's performance since 2001 was similarly impressive. Between 2001 and 2006, Danaher's revenues increased from $3.8 billion to $9.6 billion—an annual percentage growth rate of over 20%.[39] Operating cash flows increased by nearly $1 billion between 2001 and 2006, and Danaher's share price increased by 180% between May 2001 and September 2007 (see Exhibit 14 for Annual Balance Sheet from 2002–2006). In 2007, Danaher's trailing twelve month gross margin was 45%, approximately 10% higher than the average for its peer group (see Exhibit 15 for Annual Ratio Report). One business journalist dubbed Danaher "probably the best-run conglomerate in America," pointing out that over the previous 20 years the firm had returned a "remarkable 25% to shareholders annually, far better than GE (16%), Berkshire Hathaway (21%), or the Standard & Poor's 500-stock index."[40] Another analyst simply noted that Danaher had "made process improvement an art."[41]

Going Forward

Between 2001 and 2007, Danaher had undergone various changes. More than 50% of its revenues now came from markets outside the U.S., with a significant presence in emerging economies. Over $3 billion in revenues came from its Medical Technologies platform that enjoyed high single digit constant currency growth in 2007. Danaher had seen a significant expansion in its leadership positions in Water, Test, and Measurement, and Product Identification. And, the Danaher Business System continued to evolve and extend, from the manufacturing floor to innovation, marketing, R&D, sales, and the back office. Cumulative returns on Danaher's stock from 2001–2007 exceeded 150%, in comparison with S&P 500 returns of about 25%. Indeed, when managers of other large broadly diversified firms were asked "'Which company do you emulate?' the consistent reply was, 'Danaher.'"[42]

Despite this success, Danaher faced a number of challenges.

	1985	1986	1987	1988	1989	1990	1991	1992	1993	1994	1995	1996	1997	1998	1999	2000	2001	2002	2003	2004	2005	2006
Sales (Net)	295.9	446.3	616.1	714.6	749.1	843.8	836.3	954.1	1,073.6	1,288.7	1,486.8	1,811.9	2,051.0	2,910.0	3,197.2	3,777.8	3,782.4	4,577.2	5,293.9	6,889.3	7,984.7	9,596.4
Cost of Goods Sold	240.2	342.4	406.4	462.0	499.1	580.6	611.9	679.3	758.0	889.8	981.1	1,171.2	1,306.4	1,712.4	1,834.4	2,166.0	2,159.6	2,661.6	3,021.4	3,840.5	4,362.7	5,353.0
Selling, General, and Administrative Expense	31.6	61.3	110.6	130.4	136.9	165.5	161.6	177.1	180.2	208.5	266.9	345.9	401.6	722.1	778.4	909.9	872.7	1,097.4	1,316.4	1,795.7	2,175.8	2,741.8
Operating Income Before Depreciation	24.1	42.6	99.0	122.2	113.1	97.7	62.8	97.7	135.4	190.4	238.8	294.8	343.0	475.5	584.4	701.9	750.1	818.3	956.1	1,253.1	1,446.2	1,788.4
Depreciation and Amortization	6.3	9.3	13.5	17.6	19.1	18.3	23.1	28.1	35.8	44.6	58.5	68.6	76.1	108.7	126.4	149.7	178.4	129.6	133.4	156.1	177.0	217.2
Operating Income After Depreciation	17.8	33.4	85.6	104.6	93.9	79.3	39.7	69.6	99.5	145.8	180.3	226.1	266.9	366.8	458.0	552.1	571.7	688.7	822.7	1,097.0	1,269.3	1,518.0
Interest Expense	15.9	31.1	48.1	37.3	27.9	25.6	14.5	10.9	10.3	9.3	7.2	16.4	13.1	24.9	16.7	29.2	25.7	43.7	59.0	55.0	44.9	79.8
Interest Income	3.2	7.7	5.1	4.6	5.7	6.8	0.0	0.0	0.0	0.0	0.0	0.0	0.0	0.0	0.0	0.0	0.0	0.0	10.1	7.6	14.7	8.0
Pretax Income	14.0	17.7	43.4	73.0	79.1	62.1	26.3	56.7	91.1	136.5	173.1	209.8	253.8	301.1	429.6	522.9	476.3	657.5	797.0	1,057.7	1,234.4	1,446.2
Net Income (Loss)	13.5	15.4	19.0	44.0	61.1	35.7	13.3	31.6	17.7	81.7	108.3	207.8	154.8	182.9	261.6	324.2	297.7	290.4	536.8	746.0	897.8	1,122.0

Source: Standard & Poor's Compustat® data and Company SEC filings.

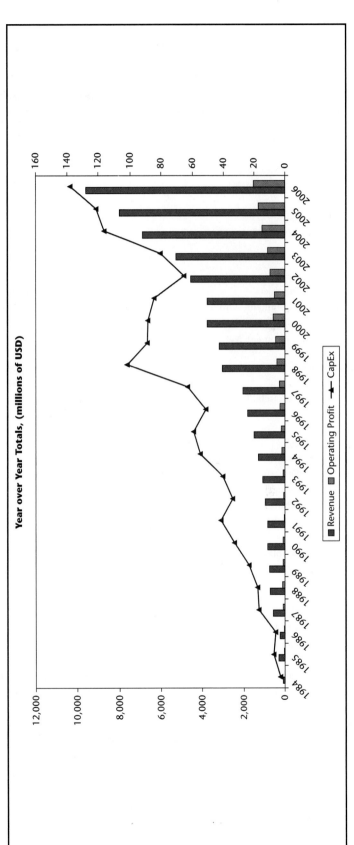

Year over Year Totals, (millions of USD)

Legend: ■ Revenue ■ Operating Profit ▲ CapEx

Exhibit 13 Total Revenue, Operating Profit, and Capital Expenditure, 1984–2006

Source: Created by casewriters using data provided by OneSource® Business Browser^SM, an online business information product of OneSource Information Services, Inc. ("OneSource").

Exhibit 14   Danaher Annual Balance Sheet, 2002–2006 (numbers in USD millions)

	2006	2005	2004	2003	2002
Cash and Short-Term Investments	317.8	315.6	609.1	1,230.20	810.5
Total Receivables, Net	1,675.00	1,407.90	1,231.10	868.1	759
Inventories—Finished Goods	427.8	314.8	281.3	191.5	165.1
Inventories—Work In Progress	186.2	178.6	138.3	121.8	119.9
Inventories—Raw Materials	391.4	331.9	284.4	223	200.7
Total Inventory	1,005.40	825.3	704	536.2	485.6
Prepaid Expenses	396.8	396.3	374.5	307.7	332.2
Total Current Assets	3,394.90	2,945.00	2,918.70	2,942.20	2,387.30
Buildings	549.1	474.4	451.7	326.1	350.3
Land/Improvements	73.9	66.7	55.7	44	37.8
Machinery/Equipment	1,531.30	1,337.90	1,260.60	1,142.90	1,041.20
Property/Plant/Equipment—Gross	2,154.40	1,879.00	1,768.00	1,513.00	1,429.30
Accumulated Depreciation	−1,280.00	−1,130.80	−1,015.00	−939.6	−831.9
Property/Plant/Equipment, Net	874.4	748.2	753	573.4	597.4
Goodwill, Net	6,596.10	4,475.00	3,970.30	3,064.10	2,776.80
Intangibles, Net	1,698.30	834.1	760.3	277.9	230.9
Other Long-Term Assets, Total	300.4	160.8	91.7	32.6	36.8
Total Assets	12,864.20	9,163.10	8,493.90	6,890.10	6,029.10
Accounts Payable	952.3	782.9	612.1	473	366.6
Accrued Expenses	1,496.40	1,301.80	1,165.50	892.6	786.2
Notes Payable/Short-Term Debt	0	0	0	0	0
Current Portion Long-Term Debt/Capital Leases	10.9	184	424.8	14.4	112.5
Total Current Liabilities	2,459.60	2,268.60	2,202.30	1,380.00	1,265.30
Total Long-Term Debt	2,422.90	857.8	925.5	1,284.50	1,197.40
Total Debt	2,433.70	1,041.70	1,350.30	1,298.90	1,310.00
Other Liabilities, Total	1,337.10	956.4	746.4	578.8	556.8
Total Liabilities	6,219.50	4,082.80	3,874.20	3,243.30	3,019.50
Common Stock	3.4	3.4	3.4	1.7	1.7
Additional Paid-in Capital	1,027.50	861.9	1,052.20	999.8	915.6
Retained Earnings (Accumulated Deficit)	5,421.80	4,324.40	3,448.10	2,719.90	2,198.30
Other Equity, Total	192	−109.3	116	−74.6	−106
Total Equity	6,644.70	5,080.40	4,619.70	3,646.70	3,009.60
Total Liabilities and Shareholders' Equity	12,864.20	9,163.10	8,493.90	6,890.10	6,029.10
Total Common Shares Outstanding	308.2	305.6	308.9	307.4	305.1
Treasury Shares—Common Primary Issue	33	33	28	28	28

Source: Data provided by OneSource® Business Browser[SM], an online business information product of OneSource Information Services, Inc. ("OneSource").

Exhibit 15   Danaher Annual Ratio Report, 2002–2006

	2006	2005	2004	2003	2002
Liquidity Ratios					
Current Ratio	1.4	1.3	1.3	2.1	1.9
Quick Ratio	0.8	0.8	0.8	1.5	1.2
—Working Capital[a]	935.3	676.4	716.4	1,562.1	1,122.0
Operating Ratios					
Asset Turnover	0.9	0.9	0.9	0.8	0.8
Inventory Turnover	5.8	5.9	6.4	6.2	6.2
Receivables Turnover	6.2	6.1	6.6	6.5	6.8
Profitability Ratios					
Gross Margin	44.2%	43.1%	42.0%	40.4%	39.0%
Operating Margin	15.6%	15.9%	16.0%	16.0%	15.3%
EBITDA Margin	17.9%	18.1%	18.3%	18.7%	18.4%
EBIT Margin	15.6%	15.9%	16.0%	16.2%	15.5%
Pretax Margin	11.7%	11.2%	10.8%	10.1%	6.3%
Profit Margin	11.7%	11.2%	10.8%	10.1%	9.5%
Return on Equity	19.1%	18.5%	18.0%	16.1%	11.1%
Return on Assets	10.2%	10.2%	9.7%	8.3%	5.4%
SG&A Expense/Sales	28.6%	27.2%	26.1%	24.9%	24.0%
Leverage Ratios					
Long-Term Debt/Equity	0.4	0.2	0.2	0.4	0.4
Total Debt/Equity	0.4	0.2	0.3	0.4	0.4
Long-Term Debt/Total Capitalization	0.3	0.1	0.2	0.3	0.3
Total Debt/Total Capitalization	0.3	0.2	0.2	0.3	0.3
—Tax Rate	22.4%	27.3%	29.5%	32.6%	34.0%
—Total Capital[a]	9,078.4	6,122.1	5,970.0	4,945.6	4,319.6
Valuation Ratios					
Free Cash Flow/Share	$4.57	$3.54	$2.97	$2.54	$2.11
Operating Cash Flow/Share	$5.02	$3.94	$3.34	$2.80	$2.33

Source: Data provided by OneSource® Business Browser[SM], an online business information product of OneSource Information Services, Inc. ("OneSource").

[a]Millions of U.S. dollars.

Growth

Danaher's historical revenue growth had been largely driven by acquisition (see Exhibit 16). From 1992 to 2006, the compound annual organic growth rate was approximately 5%, versus total growth of 18%. Maintaining its high growth rates required that Danaher confront certain challenges. First, it would have to continue to put its strong cash flow to work with attractive value-added acquisitions. Second, a slowing U.S. economy, together with some signs of a weakening world economy, placed natural limits on organic revenue growth. Third, while cyclicality had been reduced, parts of Danaher's portfolio were still exposed to swings in end-markets.

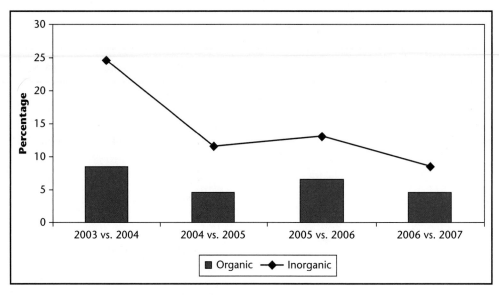

Exhibit 16   Organic (core) versus Inorganic (acquisition) Growth, 2003–2007

Source: Created by casewriters from company materials.

Some of Danaher's platforms were poised for organic expansion in 2007: for example, analysts predicted that the environmental and medical platforms would benefit from expanding end-user markets. However, other Danaher businesses, such as Mechanics' Hand Tools, served more mature markets. One analyst acknowledged that even though the Hand Tools business had a "decade-plus track record of outpacing the market, [. . .] the "underlying market growth projections [ran] in the less-than-inspiring 2%–3% range."[43]

Growth in acquisitions presented other challenges. As Danaher continued to be active in its search for new targets, it faced the prospect of going head-to-head with a different type of competitor: private equity firms. In October 2006, the *Wall Street Journal* characterized private equity firms as "on a tear," noting that 15 of the top 20 buyouts on record had been announced in the previous year and a half by players such as Kohlberg, Kravis, and Roberts, Bain Capital, and the Blackstone Group.[44] As recently as 2005, the largest fund was worth $6 billion, but by 2007 Blackstone's fund was worth some $20 billion,[45] and its initial public offering was widely covered even in non-financial media outlets.[46] Large buy-out firms were increasingly being referred to as the "new conglomerates," and observers began to question the role of the old ones. The *Financial Times* summarized this view: "The conglomerate business model, which looked so visionary in the deal fever of the 1980s, appears more and more endangered. . . . Many [conglomerates] are either disappearing or struggling to justify their existence. Their predicament is made all the more serious by the rise of nimbler predators—private-equity groups."[47]

In the second-quarter 2007 earnings results conference call, Culp fielded a specific question regarding private equity, replying that:

> . . . obviously there is a lot of private equity money out there with some smart people looking to put it to work. They tend, I think . . . to focus on properties that aren't necessarily high on our list. When we take the long view—because we're building businesses and we're not buying to sell—when we look at our synergies and the other things that we would bring to a transaction, we tend to see, frankly, other strategic as really the relevant competitive set, much more so than private equity. Not that they won't be there, but we find they, more often than not, are going to set a floor in a process as opposed to be a finalist in a sale process with a company like Danaher, particularly around properties that we covet.[48]

In addition to the challenges posed by a more heated market for acquisitions was the risk of acquiring bigger targets. A recent *BusinessWeek* article cautioned that "as M&A gets more expensive, Danaher must either increase the pace of its deals or swallow bigger fish. And it may be more difficult to convert bigger companies with established traditions, entrenched cultures, and larger workforces to its fervent brand of lean manufacturing."[49] Some analysts noted the potential to bolster Danaher's acquisition prospects through the infusion of cash that could come through divestment. Yet Danaher's divestments had been infrequent: between January 1984 and July 2007, Danaher consummated 79 acquisitions, with only 12 divestitures (see Exhibit 17 for a chart of Danaher's acquisitions over time). Despite this,

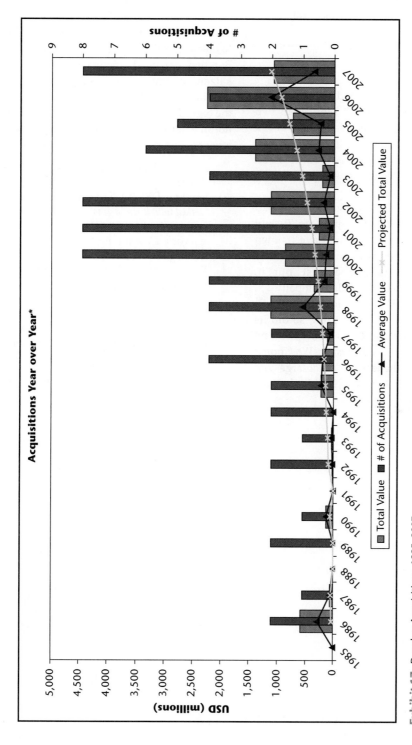

Exhibit 17 Danaher Acquisitions, 1985–2007

Source: Created by casewriters from Thomson data, August 2007.

*Undisclosed data excluded from acquisition value, both total and average.

Danaher management maintained in 2007 that the conglomerate had plenty of free cash flow to sustain forthcoming deals, and that the acquisition pipeline remained full.

Sustaining the Culture

The success of DBS, and Danaher, had been built on mantra of "continuous improvement." More than two decades after the firm's founding, it was natural to ask how long this platform could sustain itself. Was it feasible for a firm like Danaher to continue to add value on an ongoing basis? Indeed, could "continuous improvement" continue indefinitely?

In addition, despite all its success, Danaher had remained remarkably unfamiliar to the public eye. Twenty years after its founding, Danaher did not have its own public relations staff, and senior managers granted only the occasional interview.[50] As one analyst put it, "[Danaher] is kind of a . . . below-the-radar company. . . . They don't look for publicity. They just do a great job."[51] But, as Danaher's market capitalization grew, so did its coverage. In 1992, 10 analysts had covered the firm; by 2007, 23 analysts followed it. Indeed, *BusinessWeek* noted that "a continued ascent into the rarefied air of large conglomerates carries one big risk: It makes [Danaher] all the more conspicuous for their success."[52] With coverage came attempts at emulation.

Danaher's senior management team recognized that evolving and sustaining the culture of DBS was necessary to ensure continued high value add across all businesses. But, they remained quietly confident that the core value of kaizen, or continuous, improvement, would continue to provide strong performance. Indeed, Culp believed that the biggest threat to sustained performance at Danaher lay not in external factors, but in the firm's ability to create a large enough pool of managerial talent internally:

> DBS is basically just applied common sense, but it will succeed only if we are staffed by leaders who live and breathe it. DBS is a differentiator that those who have worked with it really grasp. Bringing outsiders into the system is hard since they have to learn a new culture and approach. Therefore, practice, making mistakes, and learning how to use DBS are critical to their success. For this reason, we believe that the real value of Danaher lies in the accumulated experience of operating with DBS that enables leaders to understand the interrelationships between the hard and soft elements of our system. Time is hard to buy . . . no one else has had 20 years of experience with our system.

As Culp ended the earnings call he pondered what the company should do in the months ahead.

Appendix

Strategic Platforms[*]

Medical Technologies

The medical technologies business was Danaher's newest strategic platform comprising businesses with leading positions in dental technologies, life sciences, and acute care diagnostics. It was also created with a series of platform-establishing transactions, beginning in 2004 with the acquisitions of Radiometer, the Gendex business of Dentsply International Inc., and Kaltenbach & Voigt GmbH & Co KG (KaVo). In 2005 Leica Microsystems was added to the growing portfolio, and in 2006 Sybron Dental Specialties and Vision Systems Limited were acquired

Danaher was a global leader in dental technologies and consumables including treatment units, hand pieces, dental imaging and diagnostic systems, dental materials, orthodontic systems, and infection control products. These products were marketed primarily under the KaVo, Gendex, Dexis, Pelton & Crane, Kerr, Ormco, and ISI brands.

Danaher's acute care diagnostics business began in 2004 with the acquisition of Radiometer. While two subsequent acquisitions expanded their involvement in the market, most products were still marketed under the Radiometer brand. The business primarily produced critical care applications for blood gas analysis and related services in hospitals and point-of-care locations.

Entry into life sciences instrumentation came in 2005 with the addition of Leica Microsystems to the platform's portfolio, and was expanded the next year with the acquisition of Vision Systems Limited (which was combined with a division of Leica Microsystems to create Leica Biosystems). These businesses made high precision optimal instruments, solutions and related consumables for life sciences and medical applications, pathology diagnostics products, laboratory and surgical microscopes, and workflow solutions for clinical histopathology laboratories.

The investment community responded favorably to Danaher's expansion into the medical technologies industry, and to their concerted growth of the business. While rising healthcare costs became a much discussed issue throughout 2006 and 2007, most agreed that the healthcare market would continue to balloon as the United Stated underwent demographic shifts and saw an increase in the application of innovative medical technology.[53]

Professional Instrumentation

Test and Measurement. In 2007, Danaher acquired Tektronix, a global leader in Test & Measurement (T&M), doubling the size of one of its strongest platforms. They entered the T&M market with the acquisition of Fluke Corporation in 1998. Additional acquisitions bolstered the business, which produced and serviced compact professional test tools and calibration equipment for electrical, industrial, and electronic applications. Test products measured voltage, current, resistance, power quality, frequency, temperature, pressure, and air quality. Additionally, the Fluke Networks business provided both software and hardware for the testing, analysis, and monitoring of local and wide area networks. This business area expanded in 2006 with the acquisition of Visual Networks.

Environmental. The environmental businesses operated primarily in water quality analytical disinfection, and treatment systems/solutions and petroleum. Danaher entered the water quality market via a series of acquisitions, starting with American Sigma in 1996 and recently with ChemTreat in 2007. Operations in these businesses provided a range of instruments, consumables and services that detected, measured, and treated various water characteristics. Users generally included municipal drinking water and water treatment plants, industrial plants, environmental monitoring and regulatory agencies, and third-party testing laboratories. The company had numerous established water quality brands, including Hach-Lange, Hach Ultra Analytics, Trojan UV, ChemTreat, Buhler Montec, and McCrometer.

Danaher's retail and commercial petroleum business, by contrast, had been in operation since the mid 1980s, and consisted of a smaller collection of businesses and brands. The Gilbarco Veeder-Root business products included monitoring and lead detection systems, vapor recovery equipment, fuel dispensers, point-of-sale and merchandising systems, and submersible turbine pumps. Service offerings included outsourced fuel management, compliance, fuel system maintenance, and inventory planning and supply chain support. Users of such products and services included independent and company-owned retail

---

Source: Danaher's 2006 Annual Report and "Danaher Company Profile," Datamonitor Research Report, February 2007.

petroleum stations, high-volume retailers, convenience stores, supermarkets, and commercial vehicle fleets.

Industrial Technologies

Product Identification. Danaher acquired Videojet (previously Marconi Data Systems) in 2002, thus entering the product identification business. Subsequent acquisitions rapidly expanded the platform, which produced a variety of equipment used to print and read bar, date, and lot codes, as well as other information on primary and secondary packaging. Customers typically included food and beverage manufacturers, pharmaceutical manufacturers, retailers, commercial printing and mailing operations, and package and parcel delivery-companies, including the United States Postal Service. Danaher's Videojet, Linx, Accu-Sort, and Alltec were all well-known brands within the industry.

Motion. Danaher entered the motion control industry in 1998 with the acquisition of Pacific Scientific Company. Subsequent acquisitions further expanded the business's footprint and product lines, which grew to include controls, drives, motors, and mechanical components. Such products were sold in various precision motion markets such as packaging, medical, or circuit board assembly equipment; robotics; elevators; and electric vehicles (such as lift trucks). Key brands included Kollmorgen, Thomson, Dover, Portescap, and Pacific Scientific.

Tools and Components

Mechanics' Hand Tools. Danaher's Hand Tools platform was primarily made up of the Danaher Tool Group (DTG) and Matco Tools. Danaher was one of the largest global producers of general-purpose tools, including ratchets, sockets, and wrenches. These products were used throughout the retail, automotive, and industrial sectors. Danaher's position was well-established in what most analysts believed to be a mature market. DTG, for example, had been the principal manufacturer of Sears Holdings Corporation's Craftsman line of tools for over 60 years. Matco manufactured and distributed professional tools and equipment. Beyond DTG and Matco, Danaher marketed under the Allen, Armstrong Tools, GearWrench, Holo-Krome, Iseli, K-D Tools, NAPA, Sata, and Lowes brands.

Source: Casewriters.

Endnotes

1. George Anders, "The Best Acquisitions Start With a CEO Who Charms Sellers," *The Wall Street Journal,* August 21, 2006, p. B1.
2. Ned Armstrong and Ian Fleischer, "Danaher Corporation: Outperform," Friedman, Billings, Ramsey & Co., Inc. Equity Research Report, September 14, 2006.
3. Ibid.
4. Nicole M. Parent, Andrew Noorigian, and Russell W. Lane, "Danaher Corporation: Company Update," Credit Suisse Equity Research, December 14, 2006.
5. Ibid.
6. James C. Lucas, "Danaher Corporation: Kaizen and the Art of Value Creation," Janney Montgomery Scott Equity Research Report, February 22, 2006.
7. Richard C. Eastman, Robert W. Mason, "Danaher Corporation: Analyst Meeting Update, CY-07 Outlook Favorable, Maintain Outperform Rating," Baird Equity Research Report, December 14, 2006.
8. Parent, Noorigian and Lane.
9. Wendy Cooper and Erik Ipsen, "The new generation of corporate raiders," *Institutional Investor,* January 1986.
10. Ibid.
11. Danaher Corporate website accessed online July 13, 2007.
12. Danaher Annual Report, 1986.
13. Cooper and Ipsen.
14. Ibid.
15. Steven Pearlstein, "The Power Behind a Washington Presence," *The Washington Post,* April 26, 2004, p. E03.
16. Cliff Ransom of NatWest Securities, as quoted by Angela Paik, "Danaher master of takeover," *The News & Observer Raleigh, NC,* August 3,1997.
17. "Sherman Appointed President and CEO of Danaher," *PR Newswire,* February 8, 1990.
18. "Danaher President Looks to Overseas Market," *Reuters News,* February 8, 1990.
19. Ibid.

20. Danaher's 2006 10-K S.E.C. filing and Bob Drummond, "Rales Brothers Eclipse Buffet as Danaher Shares Soar," bloomberg.com, March 31, 2004.
21. Drummond.
22. Mead, as quoted by Paik.
23. Drummond, and Danaher's 2001 10-K S.E.C. filing.
24. Tim Lemke, "Danaher seen 'weathering' economic slump; Analysts cite restructuring, strategy," *The Washington Times,* June 24, 2002.
25. John Moye, "Danaher: Adding Weight," *Forbes,* January 8, 2001.
26. Ransom, as quoted by Paik.
27. Thomas D'Amore of First Union Securities, as quoted by Moye.
28. Interview with Larry Culp, April 2007. Except where otherwise noted, quotes are likewise from this interview.
29. Discussion of acquisition categorization and processes draws heavily from James C. Lucas's Report, "Danaher Corporation: Buy; Kaizen and the Art of Value Creation," Janney Montgomery Scott, February 22, 2006.
30. Danaher, 2001 Annual Report (Washington, DC: Danaher, 2001). p. 4, http://www.danaher.com/investors/annualreports.htm, accessed September 2007.
31. Danaher, 2006 Annual Report (Washington, DC: Danaher, 2006). p. 14, http://www.danaher.com/investors/annualreports.htm.
32. Danaher, 2001 Annual Report (Washington, DC: Danaher, 2001). p. 5, http://www.danaher.com/investors/annualreports.htm.
33. Jim McTaggart, founder of strategy consulting firm Marakon Associates, as quoted by Brian Hindo, "A Dynamo Called Danaher," *Business Week,* February 19, 2007.
34. Hindo, p. 58.
35. Ibid.
36. Ibid, p. 59.
37. Interview with Larry Culp, April 2007.
38. Interview with Peter Kurstein, April 2007.
39. Hindo.
40. Ibid.
41. Wendy B. Caplan, Julie Russo, Allison Poliniak and Kelly P. McClintock, "Danaher Corporation: DHR: Anywhere, USA = Shanghai, China; Postcard from the Chinese Road," Wachovia Equity Research Report, August 27, 2007.
42. Caplan, Russo, Poliniak and McClintock.
43. Lucas, February 22, 2006.
44. Jason Singer and Henny Sender, "Growing Funds Fuel Buyout Boom—Already Biggest, Blackstone Pool Will Raise Additional $4.4 Billion As Firms Seek Larger Targets," *The Wall Street Journal,* October 26, 2006, accessed via http://global.factiva.com, September 2007.
45. "The uneasy crown: Private Equity," *The Economist (London),* vol. 382, iss. 8515, February 10, 2007, p. 82.
46. Andrew Ross Sorkin (editor), "How Low Can Blackstone Go?" nytimes.com Dealbook, September 7, 2007, accessed online at http://dealbook.blogs.nytimes.com/2007/09/07/how-low-can-blackstone-go/
47. Francesco Guerrera, "Less than the sum of its parts? Decline sets in at the conglomerate industry: After half a century in vogue, diversified business groups are increasingly seen as redundant but some may still have a role," *Financial Times (London Edition),* February 5, 2007, p. 15.
48. "Q2 2007 Danaher Earnings Conference Call—Final," Voxant FD Wire, July 19, 2007, accessed online via http://global.factiva.com, September 2007.
49. Hindo.
50. Drummond.
51. Robert Mitchell of Northern Trust, as quoted by Drummond.
52. Hindo.
53. Jim Lucas, "Danaher Corporation (DHR-$78.61), Consistency is not a Fluke; NEUTRAL but Warming Up," Janney Montgomery Scott Research Report, July 20, 2007, p. 4.

Case 3-4: LVMH: Managing the Multi-Brand Conglomerate

The mission of the LVMH group is to represent the most refined qualities of Western "Art de Vivre" around the world. LVMH must continue to be synonymous with both elegance and creativity. Our products, and the cultural values they embody, blend tradition and innovation, and kindle dream and fantasy.*

On March 4, 2004, 54-year-old Bernard Arnault stood under his Picasso painting at the LVMH headquarters in Paris and pondered about the future of his fashion empire. He had just announced a 30% rise in net income for 2003; with improved profits in all sectors of the business except watches and jewelry. Margins for the flagship leather goods brand Louis Vuitton topped 45% due to increased publicity spending featuring the actress Jennifer Lopez in its latest global ad campaign.

As the chief shareholder in LVMH Moët Hennessy Louis Vuitton, plus ownership stakes in the high-profile labels of Christian Dior, Givenchy, Christian Lacroix, Kenzo, Céline, Emilio Pucci, Fendi, Loewe, Donna Karan, and a substantial investment in Marc Jacobs, Arnault held much of the future of world fashion in his hands. His properties also include Tag Heuer watches, Moët and Chandon champagne, and a chain of duty-free shops in many international airports. The fashion conglomerate's leadership in the luxury sector has been sustained by new product launches, store openings and an increased investment in communications. The group continued new launches and initiatives in 2004, including the new leather goods Damier Geant line, the Théda bags, an entire new jewelry line at Louis Vuitton, a new perfume for women at Dior, a new fragrance for men at Guerlain, an array of watch and jewelry creations, and the new Ellipse Cognac from Hennessy.

LVMH also continued to develop its worldwide distribution network. The Louis Vuitton brand, which celebrated its 150th anniversary, opened its largest store in the world in New York. Advancements in markets with significant potential for luxury products, such as Asia, also bolstered the group's performance. Future focus would likely be on new

The case was written by Ashok Som, Associate Professor, Management Department at ESSEC Business School, Paris. It is intended to be used as a basis for class discussion rather than to illustrate either effective or ineffective handling of a business situation. The author gratefully acknowledges Lilly Liu, Deepak Yachamaneni, ESSEC MBA Exchange students and Boris Gbahoue, ESSEC MBA student for their research help. The case was compiled from published sources and general experience.
* www.lvmh.com.

growth markets and regions such as China, a market with considerable potential for cognac, fashion and perfumes; Russia with its promise for Sephora, which had already shown promise in several Central and Eastern European countries; and India, where Louis Vuitton opened its first store in 2003.

However, the $12 billion fashion and liquor conglomerate controlled by Bernard Arnault was not without worries. Wall Street continued to question whether the company's multi-brand strategy could be sustained. Arnault had to consider the increasing importance of succession as he approached the legal retirement age and would soon need to plan for his successor who could replace him at the helm of his group.

Company Background

History

Established in 1987, LVMH was created by the fusion of two fashion houses: Louis Vuitton, a leather goods specialist founded in 1834, and Moët-Hennessy, a wine and spirits group created in 1971. The luxury group grew through key acquisitions and the development of new products. Under the leadership of Bernard Arnault, the 1990s saw a period of great expansion with the purchase of large stakes in the company's subsidiaries. In recent years, the luxury group had begun to shed-some of its portfolio, with the strategy of focusing on its *"star"* brands, defined by Arnault as *"timeless modern, fast-growing, and highly profitable"* brands (see Exhibit 1 for a list of the recent acquisitions and divestitures). Observers commented that;

> *"This collection of global brands was the stepping stone for realizing lucrative synergies in the fashion business, which would add to the bottom line."*

With over 56,000 employees and approximately €12 billion in revenue during the fiscal year 2003, the LVMH group operated in 5 primary sectors: wines and spirits, fashion and leather goods, perfumes and cosmetics,

---

Exhibit 1   LVMH Conglomerate in a Glance

Wines & Spirits	Watches & Jewelry	Fashion & Leather	Selective Retailing	Perfumes & Cosmetics
Moët & Chandon*	TAG Heuer*	Louis Vuitton*	DFS*	Parfums Christian Dior*
Dom Pérignon		Loewe*	Miami Cruiseline Services*	Guerlain*
Veuve Clicquot*	Zenith*	Céline*	Sephora*	Parfums Givenchy*
Krug	Christian Dior Watches*	Berluti*	Le Bon Marché*	Kenzo Parfums*
Mercier	Fred*	Kenzo*	La Samaritaine*	Laflachère*
Ruinart	Chaumet*	Givenchy*		Bliss*
Château d'Yquem*	OMAS*	Christian Lacroix*		BeneFit Cosmetics*
Chandon Estates*		Marc Jacobs*		Fresh*
Hennessy*		Fendi*		Make Up For Ever*
Cloudy Bay		StefanoBi		Acqua di Parma*
Cape Mentelle		Emilio Pucci*		Perfumes Loewe*
Newton		Thomas Pink*		
MountAdam		Donna Karan*		

Acquisitions:

1987   Fashion house Céline

1988   Fashion house Givenchy

1991   Champagne brand Pommery

1993   Fashion house Kenzo

1994   Perfume company Kenzo, cosmetics company Guerlain

1995   Jeweler Fred

1996   Leather goods specialist Loewe

1997   DFS, the luxury goods distribution network

1998   Sephora, the fragrance and cosmetics retail chain

1999   Champagne producer Krug and the watch manufacturer TAG Heuer, a 34% minority stake in the Italian luxury goods maker, Gucci

2000   LVMH purchased the US start-up, Urban Decay, and Donna Karan apparel line

2001   La Samaritaine department store, Acqua di Parma perfumes, a stake in Fendi

2002   Millennium & Company, prestige wines and alcohol

New business creations:

1987   Christian Lacroix in 1987

2001   Newton and MountAdam vineyards

         Marketing De Beers diamond jewelry in a 50-50 joint venture

Divestitures:

2001   Sale of stake in Gucci to Pinault Printemps Redoute

2002   Pommery champagne brand, Hard Candy and Urban Decay

2003   Canard-Duchene to the Alain Thienot Group

         Final stake of 27.5% in Phillips, de Pury & Luxembourg, an auction house

         Minority stake in Michael Kors, including cosmetics and fragrance licenses

         Marc Jacobs and Kenneth Cole fragrance divisions

         Bliss spa line & Ebel watches

* Indicates company status.

watches and jewelry, and selective retailing. LVMH today controls more than 60 luxury brands across its product lines. The acquisition strategy at LVMH focused on brands that had strong brand power, resulting in the company reaching leadership positions in almost every segment it served. Each division functioned as a strategic business unit with its own general manager and a top management team. These divisions also managed overseas sales of their respective lines.

Wines & Spirits

Wines and spirits contributed 18% of sales and 36% of operating profit in 2003. LVMH, through Hennessy, holds 40% of the cognac market and between 20%–25% of the overall champagne market. In the premium champagne segment, LVMH has a dominant 50% share built around exclusive brands such as Moët Chandon and Veuve Clicquot. It also ventured outside the traditional wine belts in France and Italy to acquire high-end wine producers in California and Australia. Given the rising prominence of both California and Australia in the wine business, these moves allowed the company to market a truly global selection of wines and champagnes. However, considering the total liquor market, LVMH was not in the top 10 due to the absence of its drinks in the "Popular segment" like beers, whisky and vodka. However this is in line with LVMH's strategy to focus only on high margin activities. Analysts have suggested spinning off the wines and spirits businesses as a separate unit as they consider it to be non-core to LVMH's fashion image. For example, the sale of Pommery, a profitable champagne brand in 2001, was a strategic move by LVMH. The brand was bought for the vast lands it owned in the champagne region, as high quality land is limited in this region, LVMH wanted more land to produce more grapes for its Moët and Veuve brands of champagne. When Pommery was purchased, its land was also acquired but when it was sold, the land was retained and only the brand was sold.

Fashion & Leather Goods

The fashion and leather goods contributed 35% of sales and 60% of operating profit in 2003 and had an operating margin of 32%. Much of the sales of this division was concentrated in the Asia-Pacific region, particularly Japan, which accounts for 33% of sales, which in this segment are directly attributable to the Louis Vuitton brand. This label grew by leaps and bounds under the leadership of its legendary designer, Marc Jacobs. Demand for Louis Vuitton products often exceeded supply, requiring customers to go on a waiting list that often took several months to clear. The Louis Vuitton label, combined with the strength of the LVMH group, provided opportunities for expanding into new brands and products. Using this as a launching pad, the company engaged in significant brand expansion efforts to reach a wider audience. These efforts were well supported by fashion buyers.

The company leveraged synergies across its fashion brands. For example, its Kenzo production facility was transformed into a logistics platform for men's ready-to-wear products serving other brands such as Givenchy and Christian Lacroix. Given the historically lower profit margins in the ready-to-wear market, synergies resulting in cost savings boosted profitability. As Muriel Zingraff, Harrods' fashion and beauty director, observed,

> "What I will say is that we may have more patience with smaller brands if they are owned by a parent company, such as LVMH or the Gucci Group."

Perfumes & Cosmetics

The perfumes and cosmetics (P&C) unit contributed 18% of sales and 8% of operating profit in 2003. This division had an enviable collection of brands such as Christian Dior, Guerlain, Kenzo and Givenchy. The company recently acquired popular U.S. brands such as Bliss, Hard Candy, Urban Decay and Fresh geared toward a younger clientele. These acquisitions were an integral part of the drive to internationalize LVMH's perfumes and cosmetics offerings. Europe is the largest market for perfumes perhaps due to the heritage of the brands the company offered. The P&C division was able to leverage R&D synergies across brands, while its R&D expenditure remained in line with industry norms, LVMH was able to generate twice the average growth rate in the industry. It is believed that the R&D skills would help boost sales of the acquired companies. As part of a larger drive to consolidate margins in this division, the company integrated R&D, production, distribution, sourcing and other back-office operations across brands, moves that proved beneficial. For example, integrating the purchasing function across brands resulted in cost savings in raw materials of 20%. Analysts believed the division was well positioned to reap the spillover benefits arising from the co-branding strategy under which many of the brands were linked directly to ready-to-wear apparel brands, a unique avenue of differentiation at LVMH.

Watches & Jewelry

The latest portfolio addition at LVMH, watches and jewelry, contributed 4% of sales and −2% of operating profit in 2003. In the watches section, the company owned prestigious brands that included Tag Heuer, Ebel and Zenith. In jewelry, the company's brands included Fred Joallier and Chaumet. The purchase of the Zenith brand was crucial to LVMH's strategy to expand its watches operations. Most watches have an identical manufacturing process and brands reflect minor differences in quality. According to industry sources, there are only 3 manufacturers in the world from whom all the luxury watchmakers source their products. It is noteworthy that Zenith is the only manufacturer in the world of a certain component used in every watch. LVMH wanted a platform to sell more watches by utilizing its design experience and production know-how of Zenith. Watches could be one of the most lucrative segments at LVMH with margins as high as 80%.

Unlike its constellation of brands in other divisions, many think that the company does not have the same star power in watches and jewelry. Competitors such as Richemont, Hermès and Bulgari seem to have more recognizable brands and more upscale products in this category. However, tangible synergies appear to be a definite possibility because the division could centralize the manufacturing and utilize Tag Heuer's expertise in retail distribution across all brands. The jewelry business is also extremely competitive due to the presence of leading brands such as Cartier and Van Cleef & Arpels. Despite the Place Vendôme heritage of both Chaumet and Fred Joallier, neither of them is currently profitable.

Selective Retailing

Selective retailing contributed 25% of sales and 5% of operating profit in 2003. The vertical integration strategy of LVMH came to fruition when the selective retailing arm was established. The division manages LVMH investments in Sephora, DFS Galleria and Miami Cruiseline Services. While this division contributed 26% of company sales in 2002, it had not made a profit in the previous three years. DFS Galleria, with 150 duty-free and general merchandise stores, is the world's largest travel retailer. Acquired in 1996, the business was a victim of poor timing since the Asian financial crisis hit soon thereafter. LVMH since instituted several good management practices, including the execution of a strategy that would reduce DFS' reliance on Asian airports, selective closing of underperforming stores and the creation of DFS Galleria stores in large metropolitan areas. Despite these changes, Japanese travelers remained the company's most important and loyal customers and any economic development that hurt Japanese travel would invariably find its way to DFS' bottom line.

Miami Cruiseline Services (MCS) was acquired in January 2000. It offers retail services on cruise ships and accounts for 76% of the world's major cruise lines (over 100 ships) as its customers. Conceived as an extension of the DFS concept, Miami Cruiseline focused primarily (90%) on North American passengers, thus counterbalancing the over-reliance on Japanese tourists. It also managed duty-free operations at the Miami International Airport, the gateway to Latin America, opening possibilities of strengthening LVMH's brands in a region of the world where they have been underrepresented.

In addition to these distribution based assets, LVMH acquired La Samaritaine, the prestigious Paris department store. The company also entered the retailing end of the made-to-order tailoring business with the acquisition of Thomas Pink, the legendary Mayfair tailoring house that has a worldwide reputation for excellence in shirts. Thomas Pink has retail outlets in the United States as well. LVMH also took a minority stake in the 200-year-old U.K. fashion retailer, Asprey & Garrard that has global aspirations of its own.

Functioning of the Group

LVMH's five product groups are decentralised into production and distribution subsidiaries. Some of the major brands have their own national subsidiaries. Overlaying this, there is a regional structure, with corporate headquarters in Paris, New York, Tokyo, and Amsterdam. The wine and spirits operations of Moët Hennessy has its own headquarters, with main offices in France and regional headquarters in Singapore.

Depending on the geographic region, LVMH has different organizational setups. In France, the hub of LVMH has individual headquarters for every brand, with an LVMH headquarters handling some centralized activities. In contrast, in New York, the central LVMH office houses the LVMH and Givenchy brands, while Dior and Fendi have their own US offices. Tokyo centralizes the human resources function, and each brand operates independently on all aspects of business.

The Group's decentralised organizational structure helps the Company to foster efficiency productivity, and creativity. LVMH strives to create a highly motivating and dynamic atmosphere for its employees, emphasizing individual initiative and offers real responsibilities—often early on in one's career. LVMH gives each brand almost complete freedom to pursue its creative vision. However, it does realize synergies through almost 20% discount in advertising by negotiating in bulk for all its brands.

The challenge of this structure is that it requires highly entrepreneurial executive teams in each company within the Group. This entrepreneurial spirit requires a healthy dose of common sense from managers, as well as hard work, pragmatism, efficiency, and the ability to motivate people in the pursuit of ambitious goals.

Bernard Arnault: "The Pope of Fashion"

Dubbed "the Pope of Fashion," Bernard Arnault spent the past 15 years building LVMH from a small, clothing manufacturer to a conglomerate comprising approximately 50 of the world's most powerful brands. Trained as an engineer at the Ecole Polytechnique in France, Arnault joined his family's construction business where he worked for 13 years, before becoming president of the company in 1978. In 1984, he left his family business to reorganize a French state-owned holding company, Boussac, which owned Christian Dior. In the late 1980s, Bernard Arnault took control of LVMH. With growing success in his business, Bernard Arnault acquired Givenchy (1988) and Kenzo (1993). Today, through a complex web of partnerships, Bernard Arnault owns at least 33 percent of the company's stock.

Bernard Arnault is deeply involved in the creative process, far more than his peers. He believes that in the creative and highly seasonal fashion business, the ability to match effective CEOs with temperamental designers can make the difference between a star and a failure. He believes that *"to have the right DNA in a team is very rare. It's almost like a miracle."* Deemed the *"Billionaire Matchmaker,"* in the past 15 years he has formed close creative bonds with designer John Galliano, whose collections for Christian Dior have been hailed by fashion critics. His selection of Hedi Slimane did wonders for Dior Homme, and his pairing of Marc Jacobs with Louis Vuitton was a critical and financial success. His vision of the luxury and fashion industry as he states is:

> *"This link to creativity, it's not far from art, and I like it very much. You must like to be with designers and creators. You have to like an image. That's also a key to success. And at the same time, you must be able to organize a business worldwide."*

Industry Background

> *Luxury is not the opposite of poverty. It is the opposite of vulgarity*—Coco Chanel

> *We are in the business of selling dreams. The strength of a brand depends on how many dreams it inspires*—Chanel

The luxury products industry has been estimated to be worth $58 billion, excluding automobiles and travel. The breakdown by sector is shown in Exhibit 2.

Major players in the global luxury goods market include: LVMH Moët Hennessey Louis Vuitton, Richemont, Christian Dior, Gucci, Tiffany, Hermes, Swatch and Bulgari. Traditionally, the luxury sector has been highly fragmented, characterized by a large number of family-owned and medium-sized enterprises. In the past two decades, it has been increasingly dominated by multi-brand luxury conglomerates. Although smaller companies still thrive in this environment by serving niche markets, larger luxury goods companies have acquired or overtaken many of their smaller competitors (see Exhibit 3 for luxury market growth, by sector).

Survival of the Multi-Brand Strategy?

LVMH and France's biggest retail-to-luxury group Pinault-Printemps-Redoute (PPR), which controls Gucci, led the consolidation spree in the luxury industry in the late 1990s. More luxury conglomerates have emerged through acquisitions and many separate brands have united under a holding company structure intended to spread best practices and impose commercial and financial discipline. The goal is to allow firms to grow strongly without over-exploiting a particular brand and killing exclusivity.

However, Michael Zaoui, Morgan Stanley's head of mergers and acquisitions in Europe, doubts the viability of the multi-brand model, citing the slump in luxury M&A activity since 1999. *"It's a hotly debated issue . . . but is the multi-brand model holding up?"* asks Zaoui, whose investment bank has been involved in every Gucci acquisition since 1999 as well as the initial public offerings of Bulgari SpA and Burberry PLC.

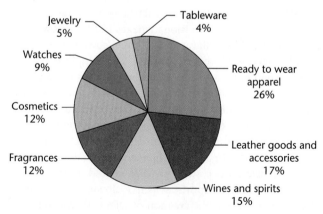

Exhibit 2 Breakdown of Luxury Goods Industry
Sources: Merrill Lynch Research.

Exhibit 3   Luxury Market Growth, by Sector

Sectors of the Luxury Products Industry	Annual sales growth, 1998–2002
Home fashions	>10%
Ready to wear	10
Accessories	10
Leather goods	<10
Watches and jewelry	8
Perfume and cosmetics	6
Crystal and silverware	5
Shoes	4

Source: Eurostat.

According to Zaoui, M&A in luxury goods slumped to $800 million in 2002 from $10 billion in 1999, and the rate of return on capital employed in the sector dropped to 20% in 2001 from 32% in 1997. As companies seek to stretch their brands to target new customers, some 1,400 new luxury goods stores have opened since 1999, the equivalent of strategic investments worth $4.5 billion. Large advertising budgets are required to attract people to the new stores. According to Zaoui, the 10 leading luxury companies spent $1.1 billion on advertising in 2001, which is equivalent to 8% of sales, compared with 6% of revenue in 1995. *"This expansion trend increases the inflexibility of the cost base . . . it can reduce margins if the growth's not there."*

"Luxury for the Masses"

There has been a systemic change in the luxury products market. In the past decade, Gucci sunglasses, Prada handbags and Louis Vuitton suitcases have become must-have items for many thousands of middle-class buyers. According to Boston Consulting Group's newly released book, *Trading Up: The Transforming Power of New Luxury*, the trend in the market is toward mass elitism. While traditional luxury brands such as Louis Vuitton, Rolls-Royce and Hermes remain items for the elite, luxury has been democratized for all. According to BCG, "new luxury" ranges from a Starbucks frappuccino to a Porsche and can be extended across categories like personal care, home wares and appliances, oral care, toys, restaurants and wines.

Consumers are in a "state of heightened emotionalism" and often address feelings of being overworked, isolated, lonely, worried and unhappy by shopping for premium-priced products. "New" luxury is the idea that middle-class consumers trade up to premium products because of emotional needs, to give them a sense of indulgence and personal fulfillment. They spend a disproportionate amount of their income on such goods and trade down in other categories perceived to be less important. For example, a consumer might visit a Dior boutique to spend several hundred dollars on a Gucci handbag, then go to Wal-Mart or Carrefour to buy cotton socks.

This new middle class market for luxury products creates a wide range of challenges for luxury conglomerates like Gucci and Louis Vuitton, as they have to understand and cater to a different target consumer.

Market Trends

In 2003, the luxury retail market segment was adversely affected by SARS (Severe Acute Respiratory Syndrome) in Asia, the United States led a war against Iraq, the Euro was strengthening and a weak "feel good factor" was spreading worldwide. SARS in Asia—which represents 30% of sales in the luxury retail market segment—led to a general decline in travel and spending. Consumers in the United States spent less in 2003 due to the war in Iraq and a weak economy. According to a study by Cotton Inc., published by Women's Wear Daily, consumers put 39% of their disposable income into savings and 14% to pay down debt in 2003. The strengthening of the Euro led to a drop in tourism, which translated into lower sales in the luxury retail segment since a significant portion of luxury retail sales is generated by Japanese tourists. A strong Euro also means equal sales in foreign currencies appear as less Euro revenues. All of these events contributed to the weak "feel good factor" in 2003.

The luxury sector is cyclical and partially correlates to economic conditions. The luxury retail market segment appeared to be rebounding in 2004 after two years of lackluster performance. Mr. Arnault predicted that the coming years would be *"very good for luxury because the world economy is doing well. The U.S. is booming, interest rates are very low and there is a lot of optimism, Japan recovering, and China and the Far East are growing fast."* Consumers dug into their pockets during the 2003/2004 holiday season to purchase more of the finer things in life. This turnaround in the luxury retail market segment ended the slump that plagued the market since the September 11, 2001, terrorist attacks.

However, signs of a turnaround in the luxury retail market were surfacing as consumer confidence improved and spending increased. In addition, performance in the luxury retail market segment was expected to improve throughout 2004. According to Mike Niemira, chief economist for the New York-based International Council of Shopping Centers,

"2004 will be a year of transition. Luxury items are strong and I think they are going to continue to be strong." Consumer spending in the United States was propelled by the rebounding stock markets, President Bush's $350 billion tax cut plan and improving employment rates. Consumer spending in Asia also recovered after the SARS epidemic.

In the long term, growth opportunities for the luxury retail market remained positive. The luxury retail market was driven by Japan, Europe and the United States; however, the market would go on to include other parts of Asia such as China and Eastern Europe as the regions became richer.

Competition

Traditionally, the luxury goods sector has been very fragmented and dominated by small and medium size companies, which have over the years developed an expertise in a particular product. But since the late 1990s, the boom years, the sector was governed by multi-product and multi-brand conglomerates. Growth by acquisitions was an important strategy for all major players in the industry. Conglomerates tried to preempt each other in acquiring brands that had managed to survive successfully. The race changed the dynamics of the industry from "creativity focused" to more "financially focused." The years since 2000 seriously dampened spirits as sales stagnated and the conglomerates paid a heavy price for their acquisition spree.

As the luxury goods industry looked to move beyond the three turbulent years, the independent and family-controlled companies that yielded the spotlight to sprawling conglomerates during the boom years were claiming a measure of vindication. Leaders of several of the world's leading fashion houses said their strategy of resisting corporate advances had worked. It gave them better control over product direction at a time when consumers were showing signs of weariness with the glitz and type of some of fashion's biggest names. *"Never be exploited; don't give up control of design,"* says Giorgio Armani, head of the company he owns.

While keeping it in the family made sense from a brand-development standpoint, it had limitations. During the past three years, a weak global economy tested the financial resources of a number of family-owned luxury goods houses. There was also the question of what would happen to companies that became associated with the name, charisma and creativity of a larger-than-life founder. While Armani himself steadfastly resisted the idea of offering shares to the public, he refused to rule out the option of bringing in a big strategic investor, expressing willingness to partner with LVMH or PPR.

Selling to a bigger holding company does not always mean that a formerly privately controlled designer had to compromise on identity. When Phillips-Van Heusen bought Calvin Klein to help the biggest U.S. shirt maker compete against department stores, industry insiders were skeptical that Klein would be able to retain complete design control over his empire. Finances at one of the world's most recognizable brands were dismal. The designer had reportedly been losing up to $25 million a year on its couture collection and millions more on retail operations. Rather than clamping down on Klein's creativity, Phillips spun the label into two new midrange sportswear lines and pledged to cut costs while keeping Klein's 100 designers. Klein continues to play an important role in the image-making of the company. This is an example that shows how designers can funnel their creative energies and coexist with large conglomerates that offer substantial financial support—as both parties have adopted a middle path in the quest for control.

GUCCI-PPR: What after Tom Ford?

Originally a reseller of luggage imported from Germany, Gucci took advantage of the economic expansion following World War I. Since then, the company displayed an innovative streak, improvising leather alternatives. After World War II, Gucci began its global expansion strategy with a store in New York in 1953. The company suffered setbacks in the 1970s and 1980s after scandals and murder plots. There was intense fighting within the Gucci family that resulted in poor strategy and dilution of valuable brand equity. In the late 1980s, Investcorp bought 50% of the company. The revival of Gucci commenced with the appointment of Domenico De Sole as the CEO, who hired Tom Ford, a highly acclaimed designer who revamped Gucci's product designs. The company took firmer control of the brand, its products and the distribution. Investcorp sold its holdings through an IPO in 1996, making a five-fold return on its original investment. This was followed by a bitter battle for control of Gucci by LVMH and PPR. Finally, after poison pill measures taken by Gucci management failed to deter LVMH, PPR raised its offer and took control of the group. The move was welcomed by Domenico De Sole and Tom Ford, who preferred PPR to LVMH for fear of losing their "creative license" if LVMH took over Gucci.

Gucci started a multi-brand model later than LVMH. It acquired Yves Saint Laurent's fragrance and ready-to-wear apparel lines and added the renowned shoemaker, Sergio Rossi, to its umbrella of brands. The multi-brand strategy was expected to deliver important synergies. Unfortunately, the benefits were never realized and all YSL pulled down the group's earnings year after year. In the meantime Gucci continued its aggressive ascent choreographed by De Sole and Ford. The brand is strong in North America today and its strategy of portraying Gucci as a youthful and sensuous brand has appealed immensely to Americans.

After the PPR group acquired a majority control of Gucci, it started infringing on the independence enjoyed by the creative duo of De Sole and Ford. It is ironic that the very same group that was supposedly chosen to protect the creative freedom was curtailing it. Tensions with the chairman of PPR group, Pinault, led to both De Sole and Ford refusing to renew their contracts after 2004.

According to analysts, *"The decade old revival of Gucci from almost a dead brand to one of the most promising ones today made Mr. Tom Ford a bigger name than Gucci and PPR would have immense trouble replacing him."* Adding to PPR's woes, in September 2003 a US court started investigations against Pinault for fraud in an unrelated acquisition in the 1990s. These drawbacks indeed have put a question mark on whether Gucci and PPR can continue their growth in future after Ford exits.

A nagging concern for the PPR group is whether Ford is going to be hired by rival LVMH group. Bernard Arnault was openly critical of Pinault and De Sole but refrained from saying anything against Ford, since the Gucci episode in 2000. He was quoted as crediting Ford as *"one of the best designers of his time."* This could reflect Arnault's intention to hire Ford after his exit from Gucci, which would significantly affect the dynamics at LVMH. Sources familiar with the situation feel that Ford is more likely to join a smaller company or launch his own label than join LVMH. The reason for his quitting is the constraint over his freedom, and given the temperament of Mr. Arnault, Ford might not want an association with LVMH.

This has created a buzz in the industry as to where Ford is headed and also whom PPR would recruit to replace him. It seems particularly interesting as the new job profile for the position of Head of Gucci is a person out of the luxury industry. It remains to be seen if this proves a good option to recruit a person from outside the luxury industry for the top position and how a key figure in this industry can make, break or manage a conglomerate.

Managing a Multi-Brand Conglomerate

Creativity and innovation are synonymous with success in the fashion business. As two analysts recently observed, *"Luxury brands must foster an appreciation and tolerance for creativity that is unconstrained by commercial or production constraints."* In almost all its acquisitions, LVMH main-tained the creative talent as an independent pool without attempting to generate synergies across product lines or brands. Lately though, the sourcing has slowly been centralized to gain synergies and cost savings with centralized purchasing mechanism.

Bernard Arnault believes that, *"If you think and act like a typical manager around creative people—with rules, policies, data on customer preferences, and so forth—you will quickly kill their talent."* The company has been decentralized by design and has a very small cadre of managers.

However, industry insiders cite that all is not well with a financial man like Bernard Arnault at the helm. His management style is described as providing "constrained freedom." For example, a manager for Céline could recruit a person himself, independent of the central LVMH human resources department, but he must send a copy of the CV of the person he hired so the head office is aware of the new development. Though his managers are given autonomy, they know they are being watched and who has the final word in case of any conflict.

Another concern is the ruthless pursuit toward the bottom line. LVMH believes in running businesses profitably. Managers are supported as long as they make money over the stipulated minimum. *"You have the freedom as long as you exceed your targets. Once you do not . . . there is no freedom anymore."* The emphasis is on profit and if any division or company did not deliver, it would promptly be sold off. This approach contrasts with the traditional and creative view of Haute Couture, which though loses money on different sets of collections, waits for the market to accept its designs over a period of time.

Managing "Star Brands"

The core pillar of LVMH's current business strategy is "star brands," coupled with innovation and quality. More specifically, Bernard Arnault describes the group's stellar financial performance in 2003 *as "a consequence of the priority placed on internal growth and profitability, the development of brands around the dual goals of innovation and quality, and the conquest of new markets"* (see Exhibit 4 for key financials). According to Bernard Arnault, a star brand is:

> *"timeless modern, fast-growing, and highly profitable. . . . There are fewer than 10 star brands in the luxury world, because it is very hard to balance all four characteristics at once—after all, fast growth is often at odds with high profitability—but that is what makes them stars. If you have star brand, then basi-cally you can be sure you have mastered a paradox."*

According to him, star brands are born only when a company manages to make products that *"speak to the ages"*

Exhibit 4   Consolidated Group Performance (in € millions)

	2002	2001	2000	1999	1998	5 Yr. Growth
Total Current Assets	7 168	8 260	8 280	6 887	5 414	32,40%
Total Current Liabilities	6 890	8 017	9 829	8 615	6 328	8,88%
Total Assets	20 658	22 540	21 124	19 671	16 008	29,05%
Total Liabilities	12 864	15 122	14 947	13 194	9 408	36,73%
Total Common Equity	6 022	5 618	4 696	5 400	5 736	4,99%
Income Statement	**2002**	**2001**	**2000**	**1999**	**1998**	**5 Yr. Growth**
Sales	12 693	12 229	11 581	8 547	6 936	83,00%
Cost of Goods Sold	3 806	3 466	3 821	2 698	2 197	73,25%
Net Income	556	10	705	636	429	29,65%

Source: Thomson Analytics Financial Database.

but the feel is intensely modern. Such products are designed to sell fast, raking in profits for the fashion empire. This is a paradox and he confides that *"mastering the paradox of star brands is very difficult and rare."*

Bernard Arnault has never specified what those 10 "star brands" were, but using his criteria, the following luxury labels could be considered star brands: Christian Dior, Louis Vuitton, Hermes, Cartier, Giorgio Armani, Gucci, Chanel and Prada (see Exhibit 5). Of these, LVMH controls just two—Dior and Vuitton, of which he says:

"If you take Vuitton, which has existed for more than 150 years, I think, today, it is also modern. Dior has been there for 50 years, but also I think it is the most hip fashion brand today."

Innovation. Bernard Arnault believes that innovation *"is the ultimate driver, of growth and profitability. Our whole business is based on giving our artists and designers complete freedom to invent without limits."* He has acknowledged past mistakes, including the rapid expansion of the Sephora

Exhibit 5   Representative Primary Competitors, by Business Unit

Product Sector	LVMH Businesses	Primary Competitors
Fashion and Leather Goods	Louis Vuitton, Loewe, Céline, Berluti, Kenzo, Christian Lacroix, Givenchy, Marc Jacobs, Fendi, StefanoBi, Emilio Pucci, Thomas Pink, Donna Karan	Prada, Versace, Armani, Saint-Laurent, Chanel, Ralph Lauren, MaxMara, Burberry, Ferragamo, Hugo Boss, Gucci, Hermès, Bulgari, Lancel, etc.
Jewelry and Watches	TAG Heuer, Zenith, Dior Watches, FRED, Chaumet, OMAS*	Oméga, Breitling, Vendôme-Cartier, Cartier, Van Cleef & Arpels, Rolex, Baume et Mercier
Perfume and Cosmetics	Parfums Christian Dior, Guerlain, Parfums Givenchy, Kenzo Parfums, Laflachère, BeneFit Cosmetics, Fresh, Make Up For Ever, Acqua di Parma, Perfumes Loewe*	Many brands, including Lancôme, Lanvin et Armani, all brands under L'Oréal, Chanel, Yves Saint-Laurent, Gautier, Calvin Klein, Ralph Lauren, Estée Lauder, Shiseido, Hard Candy*, Bliss*, specialty perfumeries, etc.
Wines and Spirits	Moët & Chandon, Dom Pérignon, Veuve Clicquot, Krug, Mercier, Ruinart, Château d'Yquem, Chandon Estates, Hennessy, Cloudy Bay, Cape Mentelle, Newton, MountAdam	Pommery*, Marne et Champagne, Laurent Perrier, Seagram, Johnny Walker, Smirnoff, Rémy Cointreau, Remy Martin, Courvoisier, etc.
Distribution	DFS, Le Bon Marché, La Samaritaine, Sephora, sephora.com, Miami Cruiseline Services	Many stores and retailing franchises

*Indicates former LVMH businesses.

Exhibit 6a   Net Sales by Business Group

(EUR million)	2001	(1)	2002	(1)	2003	(1)
Wines & Spirits	2 232	18%	2 266	18%	2 116	18%
Fashion & Leather Goods	3 612	30%	4 207	33%	4 149	35%
Perfumes & Cosmetics	2 231	18%	2 336	18%	2 181	18%
Watches & Jewelry	548	4%	552	4%	503	4%
Selective Retailing	3 493	29%	3 337	26%	3 039	25%
Other businesses and eliminations	113	1%	−5	0%	−25	0%
Total	**12 229**		**12 693**		**11 963**	

(1) As a % of total sales.

Source: LVMH 2003 Annual Report.

Exhibit 6b   Income from Operations by Business Group

(EUR million)	2001	(1)	(2)	2002	(1)	(2)	2003	(1)	(2)
Wines & Spirits	676	43%	30%	750	37%	33%	796	36%	38%
Fashion & Leather Goods	1 274	82%	35%	1 280	64%	30%	1 311	60%	32%
Perfumes & Cosmetics	149	10%	7%	161	8%	7%	178	8%	8%
Watches & Jewelry	27	2%	5%	−13	−1%	N/S	−48	−2%	N/S
Selective Retailing	−213	−14%	N/S	20	1%	1%	106	5%	3%
Other businesses and eliminations	−353	−23%	N/S	−190	−9%	N/S	−161	−7%	N/S
Total	**1 560**			**2 008**			**2 182**		

(1) As a % of total sales.
(2) Operating Margin.
Source: LVMH 2003 Annual Report.

beauty and fragrance supermarkets, for which he said LVMH paid too much. After expanding too quickly in the United States, the company had to close stores and reposition the unit. In a business based on giving artists and designers the freedom to create without limits, LVHM allows each brand to run itself, headed by a creative director. Only 250 out of the 56,000 employees are based in the Paris headquarters; the essence of the business is to identify the right creative people to stimulate new and cutting edge ideas and trusting their instincts.

Quality. In the luxury products business, quality is essential in production as well as in product development. This is also an essential element in LVMH's success strategy. For example, to exercise the utmost control over the quality of its Louis Vuitton "star brand," the company owns manufacturing facilities employing more than 4,000 in France, Spain and in the United States, among other countries. While LVMH produces its Louis Vuitton brand in-house, the firm outsources part of the production of its other fashion labels, such as Céline and Fendi. *"For all of our brands, we manufacture part of the overall production within our facilities to be sure that there is a consistency between what is done by external sub-contractors and what we do,"* explained Jean-Paul Vivier, executive vice president of the LVMH Fashion Group.

Managing People

Human resources and management of talent are critical for the luxury conglomerate. When Arnault first began his consolidation, the group was full of problems and only a few of the companies were profitable. HR Director Concetta Lanciaux confided that his primary concern

2002

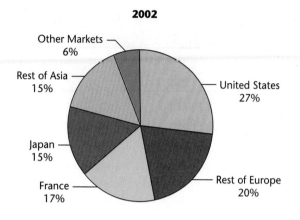

2003

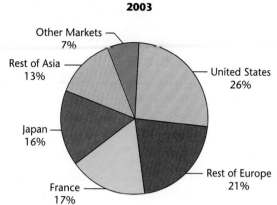

Exhibit 7   Net Sales by Geographic Region

Source: LVMH 2003 Annual Report.

was to *"have the best managers."* Lanciaux's challenge was particularly difficult because there was a scarcity of executives in luxury goods at the time. Most firms were small, family-owned companies, without graduates or succession planning LVMH had to recruit and develop talent from different fields. Regarding the mobilization of LVMH's resources Bernard Arnault said:

> *"In a global context, progress of LVMH in 2003 will be based above all on the excellence of the fundamentals and its capacity to mobilize its internal resources. We can rely on our traditional strengths, namely the talent of our managers and employees and their determination to make the difference, the appeal of our major brands, the certain values—more than ever in a difficult period, the creativity and excellence of our products and the power of our distribution networks.*
>
> *We are continuing to deploy the organic growth strategy[. . .] while still carrying out the sale of non-strategic assets, we will maintain strict management focus, enabling us to reinvest the cost savings achieved in the driving forces of our growth."*

LVMH encouraged and passed on the know-how, skills, the spirit of excellence and the ethic that conveys, through its creations and products, an exceptional art of living, which is appreciated worldwide. The awakening and education of young people to these values has always constituted an essential part of the Group's goal. LVMH carried out various original initiatives for young people in France and abroad. It is through these initiatives that primary school children, high school students, art students, young artists and designers, as well as those closer to the Group's new work opportunities such as

college and higher education students, can benefit. In 1991, for example, LVMH partnered with Paris-based business school ESSEC to launch the luxury brand marketing LVMH ESSEC chair, funded with FF10 million. Further partnerships have since been launched in Asia as well.

The company had to hire people with experience in other industries, such as consumer goods, and select people with "good taste." Lanciaux cited engineering and business schools as specific sources of talent. LVMH also instituted strong company-wide induction and training program as well as on-the-job training to introduce the world of luxury to its capable, bright novices to the industry. Lanciaux explained:

> *"With some 40 brands potentially competing against each other in the group, recruitment and everyday business becomes complex. In the case of our group, what builds value and profits is the ability to act in*

Exhibit 8 LVMH Global Reach (Number of Stores in 2003)	
North America	344
Latin America	16
France	277
Europe	401
Africa & Middle East	6
Asia	287
Japan	232
Pacific Region	29

Source: LVMH 2003 Annual Report.

Exhibit 9   Benchmarking Louis Vuitton vs. Other Luxury Brands

Brand	2003 Sales (Billions)	Percent Change*	Operating Margin
Louis Vuitton	$3.80b	16%	45.0%
Prada	$1.95b	0.0%	13.0%
Gucci**	$1.85b	−1.0%	27.0%
Hermes	$1.57b	+7.7%	25.4%
Coach	$1.20b	+34.0%	29.9%

*At constant rate of exchange.
**Gucci division of Gucci Group.
Source: Company reports, BusinessWeek.

an autonomous way and create new products. The business is built on the number of innovative products that come out every year—20% to 30% of the turnover is based on new products. Therefore our companies' senior executives have to have a large dose of autonomy and creative capacity. People use these as aspirational products, so we need people who manage and dream—and make others dream."

Despite the group's aggressive growth through acquisition, LVMH tried to treat such moves sensitively, with a vision of integration. Lanciaux commented:

"First of all, it was about respecting, identifying and then preserving all of the assets of the Company—not changing everything at once. One of the mistakes that companies in this situation make is that they want to change everything and bring in their own culture. When we buy these brands, we buy them to develop them. To develop the brand, the first thing you need to know is what makes that brand. Very often it's a number of people who are behind it, often invisible. . . . You have to find them, make them visible. This means that we have been able to preserve the integrity of these brands. Our style is not to go in there and replace everybody—never."

Jean-Paul Vivier, executive vice president of the LVMH, agrees that the group seeks to foster creativity not just among its design teams but also with professionals throughout the business. He compares the process to mixing the perfect cocktail—LVMH tries to build a work environment that promotes creativity and at the same time adheres to strict business disciplines.

Integration, training and top management seminars designed to support business strategies played an essential role in the professional development of the LVMH Group. Since 2001, it steadily increased the number of training days for all personnel categories within the Group and in centers located in Paris, New York, Hong Kong and Tokyo. The total number of training days in 2001 was 103,585 worldwide. Each of the companies developed a specific training program that reflects its own vision of excellence and strategic objectives. At Louis Vuitton, which operates in 44 countries, vendors from all over the world participate in "brand immersion" seminars organized in Asnières, the company's birthplace and communications center. They tour the workshops built in 1859 and the Louis Vuitton travel museum. These sites are filled with the spirit of the company, which has remained constant even as it adapts to changing fashions and trends—a spirit embodied in the skills of the craftsmen, the details, and a unique talent for anticipating, analyzing and meeting the requirements of the contemporary world. In 1999, Hennesy developed a teaching game called "Strateco" that takes place over two days. It is designed to make all non-managerial employees more aware of economic influences affecting the companies and their operating realities. Another program, *"Decompartimentalizing people and their jobs,"* presents the mission, organization and business of each department to the company's managers and brings together participants from the various departments. Finally, the inter-company seminars offered to all of the Group's manager's focus on topics of mutual interest and are primarily designed to develop or perfect management, communication and leadership skills.

American designer Michael Kors joined LVMH and successfully revived Céline, a dusty brand. However, it didn't seem that anyone at LVMH noticed. During Kors' six and a half year tenure at Céline, the position of chief executive officer turned five times, from Nan Legeai, to Bernard Divisia, Yves Carcelle, Thierry Andretta and, finally, to Jean-Marc Loubier. At the same time, Bernard

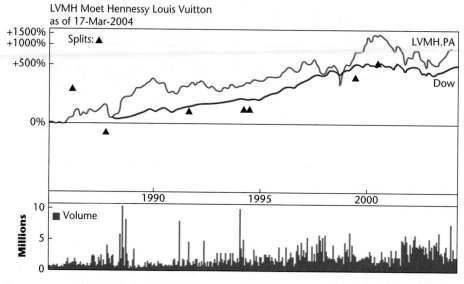

Exhibit 10   LVMH Stock Performance, 1985 to March 2004

© 2003 Yahoo! Inc. http://uk.finance.yahoo.com

Arnault attended only two of Kors' fashion shows for Céline. In total, Kors estimated that he spent a total of three hours in Bernard Arnault's company, including the two shows and two "hellos" when he ran into Arnault at the Dior store in Paris. Kors said:

> "Was I mistreated? No. Was I neglected? Yes. I never felt as though there was a strategy at LVMH as far as pitting the designers against each other or the brands against each other. It's just that I never felt anyone was watching the smaller companies at all, but everybody was spending their time on the two first-born children—Louis Vuitton and Christian Dior. In a way, if you're a nice kid, no one pays attention to you. If you are a bad kid, you get spoiled."

Interesting is the case of Marc Jacobs. In 1997, Marc Jacobs was struggling to keep his namesake brand afloat.

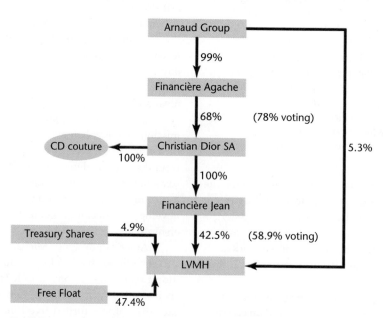

Exhibit 11 LVMH Group Shareholder Structure

Source: Company data, UBS Warbung.

Exhibit 12   The 15 Leadership Factors

Identified by 450 LVMH Group senior executives during LVMH House sessions (October 2001)

Creativity
Comes up with a lot of new and unique ideas; easily makes connections among previously unrelated notions; tends to be seen as original and value-added in brainstorming sessions.

Strategic Agility
Sees ahead clearly; can anticipate future consequences and trends accurately; has broad knowledge and perspective; is future oriented; can articulately paint credible pictures and visions of possibilities and likelihood; can create competitive and breakthrough strategies and plans.

Innovation Management
Is good at bringing the creative ideas of others to market; has good judgment about the creative process of others; can facilitate effective brainstorming; can project how potential ideas may play out in the market place.

Managing Vision & Purpose
Communicates a compelling and inspired vision or sense of core purpose; talks beyond today; talks about possibilities; is optimistic; creates mileposts and symbols to rally support behind the vision; makes the vision sharable by everyone; can inspire and motivate entire units or organizations.

Customer Focus
Is dedicated to meeting the expectations and requirements of internal and external customers; gets first-hand customer information and uses it for improvements in products and services; acts with customers in mind; establishes and maintains effective relationships with customers and gains their trust and respect.

Priority Setting
Spends his/her time and the time of others on what's important; quickly zeros in on the critical few and puts the trivial many aside; can quickly sense what will help or hinder accomplishing a goal; eliminates roadblocks; creates focus.

Building Effective Teams
Blends people into teams when needed; creates strong morale and spirit in his/her team; shares wins and successes; fosters open dialogue; lets people finish and be responsible for their work; defines success in terms of the whole team; creates a feeling of belonging in the team.

Action Oriented
Enjoys working hard; is action oriented and full of energy for the things he/she sees as challenging; not fearful of acting with a minimum of planning; seizes more opportunities than others.

Drive for Results
Can be counted on to exceed goals successfully; is constantly and consistently one of the top performers; very bottom-line oriented; steadfastly pushes self and others for results.

Hiring and Staffing
Has a nose for talent; hires the best people available from inside or outside; is not afraid of selecting strong people; assembles talented staffs.

Motivating Others
Creates a climate in which people want to do their best; can motivate many kinds of direct reports and team or project members; can assess each person's hot button and use it to get the best out of him/her; pushes tasks and decisions down; empowers others; invites input from each person and shares ownership and visibility; makes each individual feel his/her work is important; is someone people like working for and with.

Business Acumen
Knows how businesses work; knowledgeable in current and possible future policies, practices, trends, and information affecting his/her business and organization; knows the competition; is aware of how strategies and tactics work in the market place.

Integrity and Trust
Is widely trusted; is seen as a direct, truthful individual; can present the unvarnished truth in an appropriate and helpful manner; keeps confidences; admits mistakes; doesn't misrepresent him/herself for personal gain.

Learning on the Fly
Learns quickly when facing new problems; a relentless and versatile learner; open to change; analyzes both successes and failures for clues to improvement; experiments and will try anything to find solutions; enjoys the challenge of unfamiliar tasks; quickly grasps the essence and the underlying structure of anything.

Delegation
Clearly and comfortably delegates both routine and important tasks and decisions; broadly shares both responsibility and accountability; tends to trust people to perform; lets direct reports finish their own work.

Bernard Arnault approached him with an irresistible offer to lend his creative flair to the venerable but stodgy Louis Vuitton label in return for LVMH underwriting his beleaguered design firm.

Jacobs' designs helped boost sales and buzz around the $3.8 billion Louis Vuitton brand, which accounts for 60% of LVMH's operating profit. His multicolored Murakami handbag alone drove more than $300 million in sales. The 41-year-old designer also developed his own Marc Jacobs label, which soared to about $75 million in sales in 2003, helped by a $50 million investment from LVMH.

However, tensions arose between the designer and the company. Jacobs believes his ambitions to develop his own brand were hindered by LVMH. He complained that the French conglomerate hadn't invested enough in the Marc Jacobs business and locked him out of critical decisions about the operations at his own line. For example, in May 2003, LVMH, while closing its U.S. fragrance division, sold the Marc Jacobs perfume too to Coty Inc. without informing or consulting the designer. None of the proceeds went to Jacobs, instead went directly to LVMH.

Due to its heavy dependence on creative and modern designs, the departure of key creative personnel would be devastating to Vuitton. There was speculation that Jacobs might leave unless LVMH gave more backing to his clothing line. As seen in the example of Tom Ford and Domenico De Sole's departures from luxury rival Gucci, losing its young star designer could spell trouble for the Louis Vuitton brand.

In May, 2004 a spokesman in Paris confirmed that Moët Hennessy Louis Vuitton SA had resolved a year-long dispute with New York designer Marc Jacobs, the artistic director of Loius Vuitton, and his business partner Robert Duffy, president of Marc Jacobs, by signing them to 10-year employment contracts and committing to invest in the partners' Marc Jacobs International fashion house. Under the new agreement Marc Jacobs and Robert Duffy received salary raises—and for the first time—stock options. According to Robert Duffy,

"Now Marc and I can achieve our dream of turning Marc Jacobs into a global powerhouse."

The Future

While the Louis Vuitton brand remains enormously profitable, none of the other labels have rivaled its level of commercial success. With its current dependence on star designers such as John Galliano and Marc Jacobs, the group's success is highly correlated to the whim of the creative. Given the current internal politics and recent departure of Michael Kors, will consumers remain loyal to the brand or the designer? The bigger question is, can LVMH oversee so many luxury brands, make them all profitable and maintain the highest standards of creativity? How will this "loose" conglomerate that Bernard Arnault created in the last decade be integrated and managed effectively?

Case 3–5: Aegis Analytical Corporation's Strategic Alliances

Paul Olk

Joan Winn

—***University of Denver***

As Gretchen Jahn, cofounder and executive vice president of Corporate Development of Aegis Analytical Corporation, looked over the financial statements for the first half of 2003, she tried to muster the enthusiasm she had had the previous spring when Aegis entered into alliances with two leading pharmaceutical manufacturing distributors. Jahn had expected that the increased visibility in the market would buoy Aegis's lagging sales. Meanwhile, Justin Neway, cofounder of the company, carefully prepared a presentation to potential investors, as they both knew that this round of funding was needed to support Aegis's growth plan and achieve positive cash flow in late 2004.

Gretchen L. Jahn and Justin O. Neway formed Aegis Analytical Corporation in 1995 to provide process manufacturing software and consulting services to pharmaceutical and biotech manufacturers. The product, called "Discoverant," helped managers see what was happening during the manufacturing process. It allowed users to connect to multiple databases simultaneously—including electronic data formats and manual inputs taken from paper records—and assemble the data. The user could then develop models to evaluate the performance of specific manufacturing processes. The product greatly reduced the time and effort needed to identify problems in a company's manufacturing processes.

In March 2002, Aegis formed an alliance with Honeywell POMS that made POMS a reseller of the Aegis Discoverant product. As an add-on product to the POMS software that monitored manufacturing plant activities, Honeywell agreed to sell the product under the name "POMS Explorer, powered by Aegis." Jahn and Neway believed that combining the products would enhance the sales of each, and that Honeywell's name recognition in the pharmaceutical market would help Aegis gain credibility and visibility.

Later that spring, Aegis entered into an agreement with Rockwell Automation to market Aegis's Discoverant with Rockwell's ProPack Data manufacturing software, designed to help companies monitor production operations. Again, because a customer could use the ProPack Data system with Discoverant, both companies hoped the collaboration would increase the sales of each product.

Neither relationship had yet produced a single sale, and Aegis began questioning the wisdom of this strategy. Strategic alliances were integral to the company's sales efforts, and after Jahn reflected upon the disappointments of the past year, she and Neway debated what actions the much smaller Aegis should take to improve these alliances with the larger companies.

History of Aegis Analytical

In 1995, Gretchen Jahn and Justin Neway cofounded Aegis Analytical Corporation in Lafayette, Colorado. Jahn had 20 years of experience in information technology and integrated resources management prior to starting Aegis. She had recently sold her software consulting company and was working as an independent information technology and management consultant. Neway, a biochemist, had 20 years of experience in pharmaceutical and biotechnology manufacturing. He had moved to Colorado from California in 1990 and taken a job as director of manufacturing for Somatogen, a biotech research company. (Exhibit 1 shows management team profiles.) Both had worked closely with the regulatory, quality-control, and operational issues that plagued pharmaceutical manufacturing processes.

The authors wish to thank Gretchen Jahn, Justin Neway, and the employees of the Aegis Analytical Corporation for their cooperation in the preparation of this case. The authors also thank Chooch Jewel and Brian Swenson for research assistance and insights. This case is intended to stimulate class discussion rather than to illustrate the effective or ineffective handling of a managerial situation. All events and individuals in this case are real.

Exhibit 1   Aegis Management Team, 2003

Gretchen L. Jahn, Cofounder, Executive Vice President, Corporate Development, has over 20 years' experience in IT. Ms. Jahn most recently led the turnaround of the software development of a CEO-less venture-backed start-up company. Previously, Ms. Jahn was a principal and vice president at Mile-High Information Services, a consulting, software development, and product sales company. She has prior experience as a data processing manager and a software specialist for Digital Equipment Corporation. Ms. Jahn received her BA in 1973 from Lawrence University and her MA in 1975 from the University of Colorado.

Justin O. Neway, Ph.D., Cofounder, Executive Vice President, and Chief Science Officer, has over 19 years of experience in pharmaceutical and biotechnology manufacturing, and in software marketing and applications. Prior to joining Aegis, Dr. Neway was director of fermentation R&D at Somatogen, a biotechnology manufacturer. He was the project leader for several technical teams, one of which developed a demonstration system for data analysis and visualization of batch process information. Dr. Neway received his B.Sc. (microbiology, 1975) and M.Sc. (biochemistry, 1977) from the University of Calgary, and his Ph.D. in biochemistry from the University of Illinois in 1982.

John M. Darcy, President and CEO, has over 25 years in proven management and leadership in *Fortune* 50 companies, turnarounds, and start-ups. Mr. Darcy has been an advisor to Aegis, and is providing significant marketing assistance for the Discoverant product launch as director of marketing. Most recently he built three separate start-up companies in the food, agricultural chemicals, and Web imaging businesses. Prior to this, Mr. Darcy was president and

chief operating officer at Avis Enterprises, a $2B private investment company with majority equity positions in several industries including automobile rentals and dealerships, and has held management positions at Carnation/Nestlé and Pillsbury. Mr. Darcy received his BA in 1967 and his MA in 1969 from the University of California, Los Angeles.

Geri L. Studebaker, Vice President, Marketing, has over 12 years of experience in software marketing and applications. Prior to Aegis, Ms. Studebaker was senior director of worldwide marketing for Webb Interactive, an e-business software provider for small to medium-size business. There she successfully managed overall product redesign and company positioning efforts. Prior to Webb, Ms. Studebaker held several positions with JD Edwarc's, the most recent being senior marketing manager.

Cheryl M. Boeckman, Vice President, Sales, has over 17 years of experience in executive-level sales. Ms. Boeckman was vice president of sales with SoftBrands Manufacturing/Fourth Shift, where she managed a team selling enterprise resource planning and supply chain management software to tier-one through tier-three manufacturing companies focusing on multiple industries including medical device and pharmaceuticals.

Steve C. Sills, Director, Business Development, has over 10 years of experience in software marketing and business development. Mr. Sills joins Aegis with a broad range of experience in the software industry. Prior to joining Aegis, he was a business development manager with Vitria Technology, a leading enterprise application integration (EAI) vendor.

Finding Development Partners

Jahn, a self-described "serial entrepreneur," had started two companies before Aegis. She had experience with software development and implementation, and understood the importance of manufacturing efficiencies and process improvements in getting drugs through the regulatory process. Neway's experiences in biotech and pharmaceutical manufacturing gave him an in-depth understanding of the difficulties in accessing data from a variety of sources and across many different products and then putting them into a unified format. Originally, Jahn and Neway had hoped to use Somatogen's name as a launching pad for their product. However, when Somatogen began negotiations for its eventual sale to the pharmaceutical company Baxter, they recognized they would need to find an alternative. Neway focused his efforts on courting potential development partners. Jahn recalled,

We spent several years working out of our respective basements, using our own funds to make invited

technical presentations. We made 23 presentations in the United States and Europe to major pharmaceutical companies to demonstrate our product and to get feedback to improve the product and also to see if we could find someone who would be an initial development partner. Eventually Aventis gave us a contract worth $1.3 million to jointly develop our software product with them. This was in 1999. In May and July of 1999, we received our first funding—seed investments of $400,000 and $500,000—from angel investors and Sandlot Capital. We were three people at that time.

So we built this first version and we got office space and then graduated to other office space once we were all sitting on top of each other. And we hired people and subcontracted all kinds of nifty stuff and then we went out for the next round of funding. We closed on that in 2000—right around 4½ million—from GlaxoSmithKline's investment arm, SR One, and Aventis's investment arm, Future Capital, which is in Frankfurt, Germany, as well as Viscardi Ventures, a financial investment firm in Munich, Germany.

Growing the Organization

Aegis had been successful in getting enough financing to develop and test its manufacturing software product, set up a team of applications and technical specialists, a management team, and an advisory board of industry and regulatory experts. It had organized research seminars and conferences with leaders in biotech research and application, and successfully sold and implemented its first product in July 2000. Jahn continued,

> Our next funding in 2001 just about destroyed me. We brought in $14.5 million in October 2001, after the bubble had burst. What's funny is that Aegis is not a dot-com. So during the boom we were discounted because we weren't a dot-com. After the boom, we were discounted because every software company was. The Friday before September 11 (2001), I turned down $4 million because our valuation was so low. Then September 11th happened. We were supposed to have a board meeting on the 14th over in Munich, which we ended up having over the phone, and I said, "Look guys, we don't know what is going to happen . . . we just better get through this." We were one of the few people whose funding got bigger. Everybody else that I talked to that was raising money at that time had their investors dry up and go away.

By 2002, the company had grown to 35 employees. Aegis had entered into sales agreements with eight corporate customers and had 25 sales in the pipeline by the end of that year. Exhibit 2 reports Aegis's financial performance over the last several years. Also in 2002, Jahn hired John M. Darcy, former Avis CEO, as president and CEO to reposition the company with a sales and marketing focus rather than a development focus. Jahn moved into a corporate development role to pursue new markets for the product, and develop alliances and market awareness. Because of its small size, Aegis was able to share information within the organization quickly and did not need to spend a lot of time making decisions. Aegis also prided itself on having an organization that emphasized precision in its work as well as honesty and integrity when dealing with others. Management believed that understanding and concern for customers would be a key to Aegis's success.

The Discoverant Product

Aegis positioned Discoverant as a manufacturing performance management software system that fulfilled three critical requirements: practical data access, useful data analysis, and ability to communicate results to nonexperts.

Aegis's Discoverant enabled manufacturing employees and managers to analyze specific manufacturing processes that crossed database boundaries. Exhibit 3 shows the relationship of Discoverant to disparate data sources and to analysis and results reporting. The software did not require that every piece of corporate data be stored and controlled in a single location. In developing Discoverant, Aegis's developers had incorporated existing software engines, both as a cost savings and implementation aid, building only those parts of the product that were needed to fill the gap and integrate the various systems. Jahn and Neway explained that companies without Aegis's product would have to go through a lot of time and effort to get the same information. Without Discoverant, it was common for a company's information technology (IT) department to spend two to four weeks to get appropriate data from multiple systems. After company employees collected the data, it would take them another week to interpret and analyze the data. Discoverant took minutes to perform the same steps. The cost savings became significant when a company that manufactured a defective product or ran invalid experiments searched for the errors in the manufacturing process.

The company emphasized Discoverant's ability to "easily access millions of data values from diverse sources, drill down on any operation, make informed proactive decisions by identifying critical process parameters, and enable manufacturing enterprise compliance strategies." A simple point-and-click feature allowed the user to select the relevant data and produce desired statistical analyses, charts, or graphs. A major advantage was the fact that the person running the analyses and reports did not have to have a programming background. Aegis would help the company install the system and develop the data models. Aegis's implementation process required staff from the client company to be active participants. Aegis provided a two-day user-training session for its customers so that they understood the product's basic functions and tools, and how to use it to evaluate the various manufacturing systems. This included a basic course on statistics so nonstatisticians could use the software. Postimplementation customer support was provided via phone, fax, e-mail, and Internet. Aegis wanted to make sure that everyone in the company who used the software had a complete understanding of Discoverant.

Aegis also offered additional consulting services, including follow-up, validation, and advanced technical and user training. These services were offered to companies who needed more assistance or wanted additional advice for improving their manufacturing systems.

Exhibit 2   Five-Year Financial Performance, 1998–2003[a]

Income Statement Summaries

Calendar Year Ending:	1998	1999	2000	2001	2002	2003 Jan–June	Cumulative 1998–2003
Revenues	$8,053	$814,001	$670,754	$562,741	$2,513,267	$352,847	$4,921,663
Operating Expenses	152,189	1,239,510	3,417,575	5,128,508	7,779,047	3,446,349	21,163,178
Net Operating Income	(144,136)	(425,509)	(2,746,821)	(4,565,767)	(5,265,780)	(3,093,502)	(16,241,515)

Consolidated Balance Sheet Summaries (at December 31)

	1998	1999	2000	2001	2002
ASSETS					
Current Assets					
Cash Equivalent	$ 2,732	$ 193,481	$1,393,732	$12,268,918	$ 6,210,001
Accounts Receivable	3,774	248,267	397,581	158,381	364,613
Other Current Assets		25,151	122,732	146,494	406,589
Total Current Assets	6,506	466,899	1,914,045	12,573,793	6,981,203
Long-Term Assets					
Furniture and Equipment (net)[b]	15,103	102,960	340,679	523,743	378,162
Capitalized Lease and Improvements	182,468	38,261	40,061	40,061	
Other Assets (Net)[c]	1,632	227,524	533,581	661,249	297,832
Total Long-Term Assets	16,735	512,952	912,521	1,225,053	716,055
Total Assets	23,241	979,851	2,826,566	13,798,846	7,697,258
LIABILITIES AND EQUITY					
Liabilities					
Accounts Payable	89,941	360,716	255,024	491,971	572,740
Deferred Revenue			291,700	1,580,040	799,000
Capitalized Lease obligation	4,808	173,760	225,318	252,837	111,753
Total Liabilities	94,749	534,476	772,042	2,324,848	1,483,493
Equity					
Stock and Paid-In Capital	104,313	1,053,474	5,495,757	20,498,977	28,095,497
Retained Earnings	(38,840)	(183,017)	(694,412)	(4,459,213)	(16,615,952)
Net Income	(136,981)	(425,509)	(2,746,821)	(4,565,767)	(5,265,780)
Total Equity	(71,508)	444,948	2,054,524	11,473,997	6,213,765
Total Liabilities and Equity	$ 23,241	$ 979,424	$2,826,566	$13,798,845	$ 7,697,258

[a] Some figures may be disguised.
[b] Furniture and Equipment is net of depreciation.
[c] Other Assets includes trademarks and patent costs, capitalized software development costs, and Web site development.

Source: Aegis Analytical Corporation documents, 2003.

Sales Efforts

The keys to selling such a sophisticated product were having a simple way to communicate the benefits of the product, a knowledgeable sales force, and skilled consultants to implement the software for the client. Neway understood that his audience—research scientists who used mathematics and statistics but were not programmers themselves—needed an image of the numeric processes. He worked to put together a visual representation that showed the manufacturing data in a three-dimensional image. This eventually became Aegis's "visual process signature" used for both sales presentations and actual data tracking.

To help convey the Discoverant product, Aegis developed a short video clip based on a case study. Aegis management made the video available to potential customers via a CD-ROM and posted it on the company's Web site. The scenario depicted a manager preparing for a meeting the next day where she would need to explain to her superiors why there were batch failures in a drug's tablet dissolution rate. Even though she had all the data she had requested on the manufacturing processes, she did not have weeks to analyze

Exhibit 3 The Discoverant
Connectivity Link Between
Disparate Data Sources and
Reports

Source: Adapted from Aegis
material.

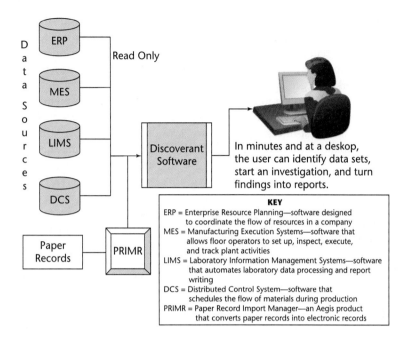

the data and expected than she would have to spend more time collecting additional data. What she needed was immediate access to all of the company's manufacturing data and a program that would help with the analysis. A colleague introduces her to Discoverant. With this program, she has direct access to the raw data stored in the various databases (e.g., Laboratory Information Management Systems [LIMS], enterprise resource planning [ERP]) and can begin analyzing the manufacturing conditions associated with the batch failures. Discoverant revealed that the failures appeared to be related to the drying process—particularly, to lower dryer air temperature. Through Discoverant's statistical tools, she is able to analyze the relationship and reveal that it is highly significant. Discoverant's reporting tools—including the visual process signature—then enable her to illustrate the relationship between temperature variations and batch variations. Within minutes she has her answer and feels very prepared for the next day's meeting.

Beyond these promotional efforts, Aegis set up sales teams to provide long-term consultative relationships that would help customize the product for each customer. A sales account manager led a specialized team of applications and technical specialists organized for each sales and market effort and was responsible for the relationship with each customer. Full installation and implementation of the product was expected to take between six and nine months. The standard purchase cycle for enterprise software within the pharmaceutical industry started with an evaluation in one facility or production line followed by expansion to other facilities on a global scale. A contract

often was negotiated for the full expansion up front in the purchase process. Specific sites were identified and a timeline established. This enabled Aegis to understand the total potential value of a customer at the time of initial phase.

The sales cycle itself varied from seven months to more than two years. The delay was due to the multiple sales cycles involved in selling the product. In its initial efforts, Aegis sales teams quickly found that there were really three selling cycles, each requiring multiple visits. Aegis thought it would only have to make the first sale, to the individuals in the company who would actually use the product. The sales team typically started with the head of manufacturing but also spoke with the head of quality and process scientists. Although this effort often took from three to nine months, the product was generally well received, particularly by the IT departments, because it eliminated their having to write numerous queries. After getting commitment by these users, however, Aegis discovered two more cycles. First, Aegis had to help convince upper management to purchase the software. Aegis found that upper management would spend as much time conducting due diligence on the decision to spend an estimated $0.5 to $1.5 million on Discoverant as they would on a $15 million software installation. This cycle typically took between three months and a year. After getting approval from upper management, Aegis would then have to work with the company's purchasing and legal department to complete the sale, which could take another one to six months. This lengthy three-tier sales cycle process increased the amount of time and effort required by Aegis's sales team.

Aegis planned to set up direct sales teams in key geographic areas where there were high concentrations of potential customers. Aegis had already set up a team in Frankfurt, Germany, to provide sales and marketing support for the European market. In geographic areas of lower customer concentration, Aegis planned to use sales agents and alliances to leverage the direct sales force and to provide local coverage and first-line support. Strategic partners would help expand sales and implementation capabilities.

Demand for Manufacturing Process Software in the Pharmaceutical Industry

To succeed in a global context, pharmaceutical companies continually needed to reduce costs while increasing efficiency, responsiveness, and customer satisfaction. Improving profitability in the manufacturing process depended on reducing the cost of raw materials, energy, and capital, and on increasing the yield from their assets. Profitability also depended upon demonstrating that they could meet quality standards in producing the drug. To meet such regulations, manufacturers made significant investments in software systems to collect information that revealed where, if any, manufacturing problems existed and, after correcting the problems, demonstrated compliance to the regulators. Initially, production processes were automated through distributed control systems (DCS) that used hardware, software, and industrial instruments to measure, record, and automatically control process variables. More recently, process manufacturers had begun to automate key business processes by implementing ERP and manufacturing execution system (MES) software solutions to enhance the flow of business information across the enterprise, as well as other software programs such as LIMS (Exhibit 3).

The implementation of each of these systems led to an accumulation of large amounts of raw data that recorded in detail the performance of each manufacturing process at full commercial scale over extended periods of time. The proliferation of software products resulted in companies having mountains of data scattered across numerous disparate data sources. Collectively, these held a great deal of information about how to improve manufacturing performance. Prior to 2000, there was no simple way to access all the data and extract the big picture about the manufacturing process. Aegis wanted to become the recognized leader in process manufacturing technology by providing software that could be used to integrate all major functions and provide system-wide information.

The demand for Aegis's product was not driven solely by pharmaceutical companies' interest in reducing costs. Increasing pressure from consumer groups and the federal government's Food and Drug Administration (FDA) led Aegis to believe that this market would be highly receptive to any product that shortened and improved the product-to-market cycle time. In 2002 alone, the FDA had issued 755 warning letters about product quality—an increase of more than 40 percent from 1998. The FDA had also increased the number and severity of penalties levied against pharmaceutical manufacturers, including criminal convictions and fines as high as $500 million.

Discoverant had no direct competitors. Other companies had products that performed parts of what Discoverant did, but no one besides Aegis had a product that did it all. In 2003, there were several commercial vendors of general statistical and visualization tools such as Mathsoft, Statistica, MatLab, IMSL, SAS, Visual Numerics, and AVS. These tools permitted the analysis of already collected data but did not help in accessing the various databases. Other software companies, such as Aspen Technology, OSI, and Lighthammer, provided process manufacturing software that captured shop floor data for process control and data management, but typically the data had to be inside a single database. These products could not combine data from dissimilar databases. Finally, Spotfire and Aspen Technology had recently announced an alliance to develop data analysis capabilities for manufacturing systems, but the product was not yet available. Although some large pharmaceutical and food production companies had custom in-house systems developed by internal IT departments or third-party consultants, most companies' systems were limited in use and required a team of experts to interpret the disparate data that the systems generated. Someone who was not a programmer could use Discoverant.

Aegis had identified a number of pharmaceutical manufacturing companies that would benefit by an integrated manufacturing information system. Though many pharmaceutical manufacturing companies in 2002 were quite small, with annual revenues under $250 million, targeting only those pharmaceutical companies with annual revenues over $250 million would give Aegis access to a potential market of $604 million in license, service, and maintenance fees. Pharmaceutical manufacturers with annual revenues in excess of $1 billion had the largest IT budget and were therefore most likely to implement manufacturing enterprise software solutions like Discoverant. Importantly, companies

Exhibit 4   Market Projections for 2003

(dollar values are in thousands)

Annual Revenues	Number of Companies	Mfg. Sites	Total Cells	Licenses $250K	Services at 50%	Maint. at 15%	TOTAL VALUE
$1 Billion +	52	225	1,125	281,250	140,065	42,188	$464,063
$500M–$1B	41	62	186	46,500	23,350	6,975	76,225
$250M–$500M	71	77	154	38,500	19,250	5,775	63,225
Opportunity	164	364	1,465	$366,250	$183,125	$54,938	$604,313

Note: The standard purchase cycle for enterprise software within the pharmaceutical industry starts with an evaluation in one facility or production line followed by expansion to other facilities on a global scale. A contract often is negotiated for the full expansion up front in the purchase process. Specific sites are identified and a timeline established. Therefore, Aegis understands the total potential value of a customer at the time of initial phase. Even under current (sluggish) market conditions, Aegis believes that sales to new pharma accounts can be expected to result in large total sales in the same accounts in the next 18 to 24 months as the initial projects show good results and decisions are made to proceed with wider deployments.

Source: Aegis Analytical Corporation documents, 2003.

of this size accounted for approximately 77 percent, or $464 million, of the total potential market for Aegis's products (Exhibit 4).

Aegis's Alliance Strategy

Jahn and Neway understood the power of brand recognition and company reputation in reaching their target market. They developed research partnerships with top-tier pharmaceutical manufacturing companies such as Merck, Genentech, and Aventis and invited representatives from Abbott, Amgen, Aventis, Merck, Novartis, GlaxoSmithKline, Eli Lilly, Roche, and Wyeth to join discussions at Aegis-hosted conferences in Colorado. Contacts at the University of Newcastle and University College London, two of the top universities in the world known for software technology applicable to manufacturing processes, joined Aegis's Scientific Advisory Board. These relationships fostered an exchange of technical information and ideas, and gave Aegis professional connections and sales leads.

In their initial efforts to sell Discoverant, Neway and a small team of sales and technical people made direct calls to large pharmaceutical and biotech manufacturers. Believing that alliances with well-known service providers would give them credibility and visibility in the marketplace, and also permit them to reach more companies than they could alone, Aegis's growth strategy focused on finding partners. Aegis's first partners were client-investors, pharmaceutical companies like Merck and GlaxoSmithKline in California and Hoechst Marion Roussel in Kansas City. Having big company names as successful users of Aegis's Discoverant product provided important testimonials for

Discoverant's features. This networking helped form the research and technical partnerships that Aegis used to get its first contracts and secure venture funding.

The focus in 2002 was on creating alliances that would enhance sales. Although Aegis had made some sales of Discoverant, as top managers began to understand that the three-part sales process was the norm, they realized they did not have enough internal resources. Their sales staff could continue to pursue direct sales, but sales might benefit from partners who could help convince top management to purchase Discoverant. These alliances were considered an integral part of the sales force. In choosing sales partners, then, Aegis sought out companies that had complementary products and would agree to promote the Discoverant brand using the Aegis name to distinguish it from perceived competition. While it had started screening potential candidates, in 2002, Aegis was approached by two companies that seemed to be the best candidates with which to partner. In that year, Aegis formed a relationship with Honeywell POMS and another with Rockwell Automation.

Honeywell POMS Alliance

In 1999, Honeywell acquired the POMS Corporation, a leader in providing manufacturing execution systems (MES) for the pharmaceutical as well as for other industries. POMS had sold over 70 systems to nine of the top 10 pharmaceutical companies in the world. POMS employed 150 people and was headquartered in Herndon, Virginia. Prior to the acquisition, POMS was strictly a reseller of software and, according to an Aegis manager, had a spotty record of implementing and supporting its software offerings.

On March 13, 2002, Aegis formed an alliance with Honeywell POMS that made it a reseller of the Aegis Discoverant product in combination with POMS's manufacturing system. Honeywell approached Aegis after a potential customer asked if POMS was compatible with Discoverant. This interest helped Aegis during negotiations. Although Honeywell initially requested an exclusive relationship, Aegis thought that it was not in the company's best interests. Eventually the two sides did come to an agreement that Aegis's product would be packaged and resold under the name "POMS Explorer, powered by Aegis." According to Chris Lyden, vice president and general manager of Honeywell's Industry Solutions Business for Chemicals, Life Sciences, and Consumer Goods,

> By combining Aegis's Discoverant with our the flagship POMS MES product, we will be able to provide added benefits to our customers and further enhance the way they manage their manufacturing systems. Honeywell's new POMS Explorer module, powered by Aegis, can save significant cost for our customers by reducing batch failures, stabilizing the manufacturing operations, and getting products to market faster.

Both companies recognized the mutual benefits from the alliance. Aegis believed this alliance was a significant step toward gaining both credibility and visibility within the Life Sciences market. With Honeywell, Aegis aligned itself with an organization that had $24 billion in sales, over 120,000 employees, and operations in 95 countries throughout the world.

Aegis was banking on POMS's name recognition and reputation to build market awareness for Aegis and Discoverant. Honeywell POMS, located in the Automation and Control Solutions division, one of four major strategic business units in Honeywell (besides Aerospace, Specialty Materials and Transportation, and Power Systems), viewed Discoverant as an additional software offering that would expand the capability of its MES product. The Aegis software provided POMS customers with the software needed to visually see and analyze the manufacturing data. To help reach these expectations, the two companies put together a relatively standard contract that included the following:

- Honeywell POMS had a nonexclusive, nontransferable, non-sublicensable license to resell Aegis's product.
- The agreement would initially run for 2 years with an additional 1-year automatic renewal, unless either party wished to terminate the agreement at least 90 days before the end of the 2-year period.
- Aegis and Honeywell POMS agreed to appoint one sales professional to act as the primary representative to the other. The agreement specified that the representatives

shall meet in person at least once per calendar quarter to discuss the status of the sales effort and other questions about selling the software. These meetings will alternate between Aegis's and Honeywell POMS's facilities, unless both parties agree to talk telephonically or at another location.

- Aegis would provide training sessions for Honeywell POMS sales personnel within 90 days of the start date of the contract.
- Honeywell POMS was responsible for the point-of-contact sales support for users. If Honeywell POMS was not able to solve the problem, they would contact Aegis for support. Provisions were provided for the time by which Aegis had to respond.
- The parties agreed to prepare mutually agreed press releases to promote the relationship. They also agreed to collaborate on marketing events, on distributing promotional materials, and on promotion of the other's product on its Web sites.
- Honeywell POMS would receive a discount on the licensing fees Aegis charged. This was a reduced price on what Aegis would charge Honeywell POMS to resell Discoverant. The more sales Honeywell POMS recorded, the greater the discount.
- Termination clauses permitted each party to end the relationship if the other went out of business or if there was a breach of any provisions within the agreement.

In considering the agreement, Jahn acknowledged that it had provisions for Honeywell to "make sure that their sales reps would get enough of a commission so that they would be motivated to sell it and also that our sales reps would not be disadvantaged by selling through our partner instead of selling direct. . . . There are lots of ways of arranging [sales incentives plans] and we had lots of conversation with Honeywell to determine what would work best in this particular environment." Aegis's VP of sales also was involved in making sure both sides were aware of the selling message and pricing structures and were present at the training sessions. He had numerous face-to-face meetings with his Honeywell counterparts to discuss the product. They focused on building a relationship first and did that successfully. Further, the Honeywell relationships benefited from Jahn having personal contact with Honeywell's director of business development.

However, from her experience in larger companies, Jahn was concerned about Honeywell's commitment to promoting the Discoverant product, and the VP of sales spent much of his time convincing his counterparts of the value of this add-on product. "For Honeywell, we're a line item in their sales catalogue," Jahn later observed. "When the market fell out, their sales reps were concentrating on how to get people to buy their own products, much less other things in the catalogue."

Rockwell Automation Agreement

Rockwell Automation purchased ProPack Data in April 2002. ProPack Data, a German company established in 1984, was a market leader of MES and electronic batch record systems (EBRS) for the pharmaceutical and other regulated industries. The company employed 230 people and became a part of Rockwell's Process Solutions business. Rockwell Automation had revenues of $4.3 billion, employed 23,000 individuals, and had operations in 80 different countries.

Aegis had been approached by ProPack—and had already begun negotiations with them—before the Rockwell acquisition. The ProPack Data manufacturing execution system PMX was designed to help customers reduce operating costs, shorten cycle times, and improve product quality in production operations. The software solution provided by Aegis provided connectivity and visibility to the manufacturing processes that PMX was managing.

As with the Honeywell alliance, the relationship with ProPack was designed to make Aegis visible to much larger organizations. The addition of Rockwell into the ProPack equation was a double-edged sword for Aegis's management team. On one hand they were excited by the large size of Rockwell and the possibility to leverage that size to their advantage. However, Jahn was concerned that those advantages might be offset by increased bureaucracy and added delays.

Aegis and ProPack Data set up a sales and marketing agreement for lead generation that was simpler than the Honeywell POMS agreement. If a company's referral led to a sale for the partner, the company would receive a finder's fee. The agreement's primary function was to increase access to new sales territory. Aegis hoped to increase the number of sales leads, thus generating a higher number of sales opportunities. According to Bernhard Thurnbauer, senior vice president of strategic marketing of ProPack Data,

> We are excited about this agreement with Aegis. We feel that this [arrangement] will give ProPack Data a significant edge in providing a true value added solution. Aegis's Discoverant Manufacturing Informatics system meets the need of leading pharmaceutical manufacturers to analyze and visualize all their data in a multitude of disparate sources. Using Discoverant, manufacturers can find and control the key process drivers across their entire manufacturing processes, all the way from raw materials to final product.

Each company intended to use the partner's strengths to build interest in its own products and services and committed its sales representatives to prospect for the partner. Once opportunities were identified, various strategies would be employed to close the sale. The sales opportunity itself would dictate how the two companies would work together and who would take the dominant role in the sales process. Each sale would be governed by a separate agreement, which would include a finder's fee for the partner that developed the sale. Additional highlights of the agreement included:

- The agreement committed both Aegis and Propack Data to explore mutually beneficial ways in which they could complement one another's sales and marketing activities.

- Both Aegis and Propack Data agreed this was an important relationship and would seek to communicate ideas for improving the relationship.

- Each party would assign a person to act as the primary liaison to the other party.

- Each party would independently market its respective products and services, but the two companies would prepare mutually agreed press releases to promote the relationship, provide marketing and sales support to each other, and spread the word about the relationship within their respective organizations.

- The liaisons were to attend quarterly meetings to discuss comarketing of their products and customer leads. The location of the meetings would alternate between Aegis and Propack Data facilities.

- Unless there was a sale, there would be no commissions or other type of remuneration owed by one party to the other.

- Upon request, each party agreed to provide on-site product training to the other party's employees up to once a year.

- A separate agreement would be written up when both parties decided to pursue jointly a product installation and implementation.

- The agreement could be terminated at any time without cause with 90 days' written notification.

Effectiveness of the Partnerships

When, by 2003, neither the Honeywell nor Rockwell relationship had produced a single sale, Jahn began to question the value of these alliances. With sales as the major focus in the alliances, and the primary criterion for evaluating the success of the alliance, Jahn tried to understand possible reasons for the lack of sales. It was easy to blame lagging sales on the struggling economy. With the drug manufacturing industry not experiencing consistent growth, companies were not able to spend money on improving their processes, upgrading software, or revamping production. Budgets cuts and purchasing managers following orders to reduce expenses led to a shrinking market. Unfortunately, the products that Aegis and its alliance partners were selling fell into the category of items that were not essential to current operations. In fact, Honeywell's POMS division, while having some success with other software products, overall had low sales and had recently laid off 25 percent of its sales force, including individuals with whom Aegis had worked. Aegis had also lost some its original sales team. During lean times, the companies that normally would be interested in purchasing Aegis software solutions were looking internally to make incremental improvements.

Another reason for the absence of sales might have been the characteristics of the relationships and the partner communication systems and performance metrics that were set up. Effective communication between alliance partners was essential. Was Aegis effectively communicating with either alliance partner? Although there were contractual specifications about how often they had to meet, communication appeared to be confined to situations when either side had a question or needed clarification on an issue. Communications between Honeywell POMS and ProPack Data had been cordial, but there was no evidence that the partners had a free flow of communication beyond the "need to know" when problems arose.

For Honeywell POMS, the Aegis director of business development handled all direct communications. The current agreement allowed the companies to set agendas and develop sales opportunities at a level that met the alliance's needs. Group phone calls, sales calls, and bi-yearly face-to-face meetings were designed to keep the companies in contact with each other. Though initially there was contact between engineers to make sure the technologies were compatible, most communication occurred between the companies' sales teams and corporate management. Communication between sales teams occurred when they were working the same sales together, which they had done on several occasions; then, there was frequent communication. The loss of key personnel in both companies required the new managers to begin to rebuild the communication level and the overall interest in the relationship. At the corporate level, they communicated weekly. Though more frequent communication would perhaps be better, Jahn believed the current level allowed the companies to set agendas and develop sales opportunities at a level that

met the alliance's needs. As the alliance developed, Aegis realized it had a good cultural fit with Honeywell POMS and noted very few communication problems. Aegis believed it could share information with Honeywell.

The Aegis and ProPack Data agreement was hindered when Aegis's primary contact left ProPack Data, handing off responsibility to someone who did not take an active role, thereby frustrating the Aegis team. On both sides, communication had not extended beyond the contact persons, and the relationship suffered. The two companies had been trying to move beyond these events and had taken steps to improve the channels of communication between the firms.

A Difficult Decision

As Jahn reflected upon the development of the company and these relationships, she wondered about Aegis's alliance strategy and what actions to take. Perhaps it was too early to make changes—these were difficult economic times and Aegis might not have given the relationships enough time to produce sales. Jahn and Neway knew that communication and trust were important to keeping a relationship going through troubled times. Their comfort level and trust increased with each partner as time went on. On the other hand, one could argue that these relationships had already had sufficient time to prove themselves and it did not appear that either would be successful. If Aegis terminated one or both of these relationships, it would need to focus its time and energy on more productive sales options. But what would these be?

Relationships with other partners large enough to get the attention of main pharmaceutical companies would likely have some of the same problems as these two relationships and would take time to develop. Rather than terminate these alliances, a more reasonable solution might be to restructure the relationships. This could include changes in the contract with either Rockwell or Honeywell, or in their interactions with one another. Believing they had put together contracts with appropriate incentives to encourage sales, their thoughts turned to improving the relationships with each company. But how would a company of fewer than 40 employees influence either of these large corporations? Further, as a small company between rounds of financing, Aegis did not have a lot of extra financial or staffing resources. Any solution would have to be a low-cost one. Each path was filled with risk and difficulties in implementation, but Jahn and Neway knew that for Aegis to attract investments and to succeed would require a quick but thoughtful decision.

Case 3-6: The Activision Blizzard Merger*

Activision Inc., a leading developer and publisher for video game software for platforms such as Xbox, PlayStation, and Nintendo as well as personal computers, was considering a merger with Vivendi Games in 2007. Activision was a market leader in console games such as *Guitar Hero* and *Call of Duty*, while Vivendi Games was the creator of *World of Warcraft*, the largest massive multi-player online game (MMOG) in the world. At first glance, a merger combining leaders in two different segments of the market appeared attractive. Yet, some observers questioned the wisdom of the merger. The two companies relied on substantively different business models, with Vivendi focusing on subscriber revenue versus the production of hit sequels for Activision. Other questions about the merger remained as well. Would the proposed merger produce sufficient synergies to justify the cost of merging? Would the proposed governance structure help the two firms maximize their value?

Industry

The first video game was created in 1958 and consisted of little more than green lines and dashes on a TV screen. Since then, the video game software industry had grown to $9.5 billion in domestic sales by 2007, becoming the fastest-growing sector in the overall entertainment industry. Video games were played primarily on two types of hardware platforms: gaming consoles such as Xbox, Nintendo, and PlayStation, and computers. By 2007, the "next-generation" gaming consoles consisting of Xbox 360, Nintendo Wii, and PlayStation3 had redefined the video game industry by introducing controllers that were easier to use and manipulate. The increased ease of use attracted a wider demographic of players. Video games were also played on handheld, portable devices such as the Nintendo DS and the PlayStation Portable (PSP). Of the $9.5 billion spent on

video game software in 2007, $6.6 billion (153.9 million units) was spent on video game console software, $0.91 billion (36.4 million units) on personal computer (PC) games, and $2.0 billion (77.5 million units) on portable software.

Software for video games was initially developed by the companies that wrote the complex coding for the games. These companies were known as developers. Developers frequently partnered with publishing companies to sell and distribute their games. Most publishing companies, in addition to partnering with third-party developers, had their own in-house developing division. Some publishers depended heavily on their partnerships with third-party developers, while other publishers relied primarily on their own developers.

Publishing companies enjoyed several sources of revenue. Traditionally, publishers gained revenue through the sale of games designed for independent play. These were games that could be loaded onto a hardware platform and played without any further cost to the player. With the development of gaming consoles that were able to connect online, however, players were now able to purchase additional features related to online play. They could download additional environments for their characters to interact in, acquire newly released songs to play along with the games, or even purchase upgraded in-game items. In recent years, video games such as *World of Warcraft* had been developed that relied entirely on an online gaming experience. These games were referred to as MMOGs, and were primarily played on computer platforms. People wishing to play these games were required to first pay for the game itself and then pay a recurring monthly subscription fee to continue to play. In addition, these games also gained revenue through the sales of expansion packs that most serious gamers considered a necessary purchase to continue their gaming experience.

With sales of $9.5 billion at the end of 2007, the industry realized a 28 percent growth over the previous year. The video game software industry was rapidly becoming a significant portion of the entertainment sector. In comparison, the movie industry grew only 1.8 percent from 2006, and the music industry shrank by 10 percent. Several factors contributed to this explosive growth. Two groups of players, females and individuals over the age of 35, had been

*This case is adapted from a report prepared by Dane Falkner, Melinda Keng, Armando Lujan, Kota Mineshima, Nathan Page, Brittney Sinquefield, and Christian Timothy for the University of Utah Investment Fund under the supervision of Professor Elizabeth Tashjian.

purchasing games in higher proportions than ever before. Females made up 38 percent of the game player population, and the average game player age had risen to 33 years old by 2008. This constituted a significant shift from the stereotypical teenage boy gamer to a middle-aged worker with higher disposable income. In addition, innovations in gaming practices, such as the development of the easy-to-learn Nintendo Wii, contributed to this growth in nontraditional gaming demographics. Furthermore, family-oriented games grew from 9.1 percent of gaming sales in 2006 to 17.2 percent in 2007. Games rated "Everyone" or "Everyone 10+" dominated sales with 56 percent of sales, while those rated "Teen" held 28 percent of games. Only 15 percent of gaming sales were attributed to "Mature" games. These trends clearly contradicted the image that the industry was dominated by controversial graphic content.[1]

Growth expectations were strong for the video gaming software industry. Domestically, it was expected that the industry would grow at an average of 6.7 percent over the next five years, from $9.5 billion in 2007 to approximately $12.5 billion in 2011. Most of the growth was anticipated in international markets, however, with a strong emphasis on Asian countries. Projections were for an international average growth of 9.1 percent over the next 5 years, going from $37.5 billion to $48.9 billion. For the Asian markets specifically, a 10 percent average increase per year was expected.[2]

Competitors

Multiple companies of varying sizes and strategies competed in the video game software industry. Some conglomerates, such as Sony and Microsoft, had an in-house software development division that produced games exclusively for their gaming consoles. Although the games themselves competed directly with the products produced by Activision and Vivendi Games, the companies were not comparable because of their drastic differences in size and business strategy. However, a few companies were somewhat comparable such as THQ, EA Games, and Take-Two (see Appendix A).

THQ Inc. (THQI)

THQ was a $1.48 billion company that distributed primarily in North America, Europe, and the Asia-Pacific region through mass merchandisers and third-party retail chains. The company's game titles included action, adventures, fighting, racing, sports, and strategy games. The company was founded in 1989 and was based in Agoura Hills, California.[3]

THQ had collaborated with Disney's Pixar to produce video games based on its movie titles such as *Toy Story* and *A Bug's Life*. While these games generated modest revenue, THQ's limitations in its licensing rights confined its player demographics to a primarily younger target audience. It was not able to market to the older, more profitable gamers as Activision did. In addition, THQ's simple games were not as appealing to the Asian market, which preferred games that were more difficult and complicated to play.

Electronic Arts Inc. (ERTS)

EA marketed its products under several different brands, highlighted by the EA Sports brand, which was an industry leader in the sporting games arena. The company also gained revenue by selling advertising in its games and distributing software games that were developed and published by other companies. The company was founded in 1982 and was headquartered in Redwood City, California.[4]

Although EA had a strong presence in the sports games genre, Activision Blizzard's lineup of games had strength in a variety of arenas, particularly in the MMOG arena with *World of Warcraft* and in the highly interactive arena with *Guitar Hero*. EA, with its focus on the sports genre, lacked the wide diversity and appeal of Activision Blizzard's products.

Take-Two Interactive Software Inc. (TTWO)

Take-Two was comprised of two main segments, publishing and distribution. Take-Two Interactive was founded in 1993 and was headquartered in New York, New York. The publishing segment's products consisted of several different brands, most notably Rockstar Games, 2K Games, and 2K Sports. Rockstar Games' most popular title was the *Grand Theft Auto* series, with the fourth version of the series set for release on April 29, 2008. 2K Sports, although not as popular as the EA Sports brand, was EA's most direct and strong competition in the sporting games market. The distribution segment operated primarily in North America and Europe, and saw revenue growth in the distribution of third-party software and hardware products (in addition to TTWO's own proprietary software titles). The company served "mass merchandisers; video, electronic, and toy stores; national and regional drug stores; supermarket and discount store chains; and specialty retailers."[5]

Although Take-Two possessed one of the strongest games in the industry (*Grand Theft Auto*), Activision Blizzard possessed several strong games of its own (*Starcraft*, *Diablo*, *Call of Duty*, *World of Warcraft*, and *Guitar Hero*). Also, Activision had a strong presence in the rapidly growing Asian markets, whereas Take-Two had very little presence and relied heavily on North American sales for the majority of its revenue. These weaknesses, in addition to the fact that Activision had several more blockbuster games than Take-Two, suggested that Activision would be a stronger performer (see Appendix B).

Activision, Inc (NASDAQ: ATVI)

Company Background

Activision, Inc. was a leading developer and publisher of interactive software for various game platforms including PlayStation3, Nintendo Wii, Xbox 360, and various hand-held devices. Activision started in 1979 and was influential in popularizing the concept of video games by developing hit titles for the Atari 2600. By 2007, it had grown into an $8 billion company, publishing and distributing some of the most popular video game titles on the market such as *Guitar Hero*, *Call of Duty*, and *Tony Hawk*. The company experienced its greatest success with games designed for gaming consoles, with weaker performance in computer-based games.

Activision generated $1.51 billion in revenues in 2007, up 3.4 percent from $1.46 billion in 2006. Although this represented a small increase in revenue, net income increased 115 percent over the same period, from $40 million in 2006 to $86 million in 2007. This was due mostly to Activision's ability to produce successful sequels with lower developmental costs.

Domestically, Activision's products were primarily sold on a direct basis to mass-market retailers, consumer electronic stores, and game specialty stores. Wal-Mart and GameStop were its two largest customers, accounting for 22 percent and 8 percent of sales, respectively. Internationally, the company's products were sold to retailers and directly to the customers through Activision's wholly owned European subsidiaries and through third-party distribution arrangements.

Activision employed 2,125 employees as of March 2007. Of these, approximately 1,300 were in product development, 200 in North American publishing, 175 in international publishing, 150 in operations and administration, and 300 in European distribution activities.[6] For detailed information on the company's executive management, please see Appendix C.

Activision was headquartered in Santa Monica, California. It had operating divisions in the United States, Canada, the United Kingdom, France, Germany, Italy, Japan, Australia, Sweden, Spain, the Netherlands, and South Korea.

Strategy

Activision followed a strategy of acquiring strong brands with sustainable franchising opportunities and developing strategic alliances with companies with profitable intellectual properties. In selecting its product line, it utilized a rigorous quality control process to develop high-quality games in search of high unit sales. In addition, Activision strived to create a diverse product line that appealed to all player demographics, and which could be played on all gaming console platforms. This strategy helped Activision achieve its objective "to be a worldwide leader in the development, publishing and distribution of quality interactive entertainment software and peripheral products that deliver a highly satisfying consumer entertainment experience."[7]

Acquisitions. Activision's strategy included acquiring and maintaining strong brands that "have the potential to become franchise properties with sustainable consumer appeal and brand recognition."[8] Durable franchise brands have the potential for sequels, prequels, and related new products that can be released over an extended period of time and provide predictable and recurring revenues. Since its inception, Activision acquired numerous software developers and interactive entertainment product distributors. Its most successful acquisition in recent years had been completed in May 2006 with the acquisition of video game publisher RedOctane Inc., the publisher of the popular *Guitar Hero* franchise (see Appendix D for a timeline of Activision's major acquisitions).

Partnerships. Activision also sought to foster and maintain strategic relationships with the owners and developers of significant intellectual property through license agreements. Licenses allowed Activision to create and publish video games based on popular franchises. Some of the company's more popular titles included well-known brands owned by Marvel such as *Spider-Man* and *X-Men*, and movie titles released by DreamWorks Animation including *Shrek 2*, *A Shark's Tale*, *Madagascar*, and *Over the Hedge*. The company also had an exclusive agreement with professional skateboarder Tony Hawk to publish video games through 2015. Through December 31, 2007, Activision published nine Tony Hawk titles that generated net revenues of $1.3 billion (Cite: 10Q 11-Feb 2008). The company also maintained partnerships with MGM Interactive and EON Productions Ltd. for the rights to the James Bond franchise, Hasbro Properties Group for rights to the Transformers brand, and Harrah's Entertainment, Inc., for rights to develop video games based on the popular World Series of Poker Tournament.

Quality Control.   Activision had historically placed a strong emphasis on developing high-quality games. It used a rigorous "Greenlight process" to carefully scrutinize each product at four different stages throughout the product development process. By doing this, Activision ensured that each product created a high-quality experience for the user, encouraging high-volume sales for each game released. In addition, Activision strived to create the potential for successor games that could generate future sales.

Product Diversity.   Activision sought to create and maintain a diverse product mix in order to reduce the risks associated with developing video game software. The company maintained a diverse product mix by publishing games over a wide span of genres including action/adventure, action sports, racing, role-playing, simulation, first-person action, and strategy. This product mix was intended to appeal to a wide range of player demographics, ranging from children to adults, and casual to serious players. Additionally, Activision published games that operated on a variety of hardware platforms such as Sony PlayStation3, PlayStation2, Microsoft Xbox 360, NintendoWii, various handheld devices, and the PC (see Appendix E).

Profitability

Tony Hawk.   *Tony Hawk* was a first-person game that allowed players to manipulate and experience the motions of a skateboarder. Activision partnered with the famous skateboarder Tony Hawk to obtain exclusive licensing rights to his name. Neversoft, the developer of the *Tony Hawk* franchise, was acquired by Activision in 1999 by issuing 698,835 Activision shares.[9] Based on the closing price, Neversoft was valued at roughly $1.7 million. The *Tony Hawk* franchise had been the leader in skateboarding games since 1999. Since the release of *Tony Hawk*, the franchise had generated over $1 billion in sales worldwide, with the tenth version of the game due out during fall 2008.[10]

Call of Duty.   *Call of Duty* was a first-person shooter game that allowed players to mimic the actions and strategies of warfare fighting. Infinity Ward was the original developer of *Call of Duty*, in which Activision had owned a 30 percent share since 2002. After the successful release of *Call of Duty*, Activision acquired the remainder of the company for $3.5 million.[11] The most recent release in the franchise, *Call of Duty 4*, sold over seven million copies in its first three months. At $59.99 a copy this translated into approximately $420 million in retail sales.

Guitar Hero.   *Guitar Hero* involved a simulated concert environment where players used a wireless guitar to play along to songs dictated on the screen. *Guitar Hero* was originally developed by Harmonix Music Systems and published by RedOctane, Inc. and was first released in 2005. RedOctane was acquired by Activision in 2006 and along with it, the *Guitar Hero* series, for $99.9 million. The transaction included $30.9 million in cash, $30 million in Activision stock, and an additional $39 million in stock to be "issued within two years of the closing date."[12] *Guitar Hero* went on to release four additional games in the series, with more planned to be released in 2008 including *Guitar Hero: Aerosmith*, *Guitar Hero IV*, and *Guitar Hero: On Tour* for the Nintendo DS.

The Activision Blizzard merger promised to propel the creation of PC versions of *Guitar Hero*. *Guitar Hero* was considered a "cultural phenomenon" with bars holding "*Guitar Hero* nights" and concert tours holding *Guitar Hero* contests. *Guitar Hero* helped revive the music industry by helping bands gain or regain popularity by featuring their songs, leading to an increased demand in digital downloads. Activision and iTunes established a partnership in providing customers with over 1,300 *Guitar Hero*–related songs to capitalize on this potential market. In addition, *Guitar Hero* helped sell more than five million downloadable songs through Xbox Live, Microsoft's online portal for its Xbox console.[13] *Guitar Hero III: Legends of Rock* surpassed $1 billion in sales in 2007.[14]

Overall, these acquisitions gave Activision a leading position in first-person shooters, skateboarding games, and the emerging music-oriented video games. Activision's management sought to continue its acquisition growth strategy by entering into a merger with Vivendi's video game subdivision, Vivendi Games. If completed, the merged company would form the largest company in the video game industry.

Vivendi Games

Vivendi was a French conglomerate, listed on the Paris stock exchange, involved in multiple sectors within the entertainment industry. It had subdivisions in music, TV, mobile telecommunications, and video games. Vivendi Games, the subdivision of Vivendi that created and published video game software, was formed when Vivendi acquired Sierra and Blizzard, both video game developers, in 1998. In 2007, Vivendi Games consisted of four divisions: Sierra Entertainment, Sierra Online, Vivendi Game Mobile, and Blizzard Entertainment.[15] Vivendi employed approximately 4,000 employees.

Blizzard Entertainment was the developer and publisher of the best-selling franchises *Warcraft*, *Starcraft*, *Diablo*, and *World of Warcraft*. In 2007, Vivendi Games reported record revenues in excess of €1 billion, EBITA growth of 57.4 percent over 2006 at €181 million, and operating margins of 17.8 percent. Sierra Entertainment, Vivendi Games Mobile, and Sierra Online ended the year with a loss of €80 million. However, Blizzard's phenomenal success more than made up for the other division's losses by a wide margin. In 2007, Blizzard was estimated to generate €702.2 million in revenues and reported actual EBITA performance of €345 million, up 37 percent from 2006, and operating margins greater than 40 percent.[16]

Blizzard

Blizzard Entertainment was formed in 1991 by three UCLA graduates as Silicon & Synapse. After going through a series of name changes and acquisitions, Blizzard was finally obtained by Vivendi Games. Blizzard's main focus was on the development of PC games. Blizzard was widely considered the "crown jewel" of the PC-gaming industry leader, with operating margins in excess of 40 percent. Blizzard Entertainment was credited with developing and publishing four of the five best-selling PC games of all time: *Diablo*, *Warcraft*, *StarCraft*, and *World of Warcraft*.

World of Warcraft.   *World of Warcraft* experienced phenomenal success worldwide as the leading PC game in the MMORPG sector, with 10 million subscribed players and an overall market share of 62 percent. In 2005 and 2006, it was the best-selling PC game worldwide, and in 2007, was ranked second in sales due only to the popularity of the release of its first expansion pack. This expansion pack, entitled *World of Warcraft: The Burning Crusades*, was the fastest-selling computer game of all time, selling 2.4 million copies, or $143.8 million in sales, within 24 hours.[17]

World of Warcraft was released in 2004 after several years of extensive product development and marketing publicity. The game was designed as an online, first-person version of the widely popular *Warcraft* games, utilizing the same characters, storyline, and graphical quality. Players were required to pay a monthly subscription fee in order to continue play. Because of its strategic release and popular in-game elements, it quickly became, indisputably, the most popular MMOG worldwide. In 2007, it had 2.5 million subscribed players in North America, 2 million in Europe, and 5.5 million in Asia. *World of Warcraft* was the only game created by a U.S. or European developer that successfully penetrated the Asian market. The subscription-based revenue model generated approximately $1 billion in 2007, creating operating margins of over 40 percent.[18] In

2007, Blizzard had a number of promising products being developed for future release, which included *StarCraft 2*, *World of Warcraft: Wrath of the Lich King*, and a live-action *Warcraft* movie.[19]

Activision Blizzard: Transaction Details

Activision, Inc., and Vivendi Games were expected to complete the combination of the two companies within the first half of 2008. According to the terms of the proposal, Vivendi would contribute its gaming division, Vivendi Games, to Activision Inc. in exchange for 295.3 million newly issued ATVI shares. The newly formed Activision Blizzard would retain its original stock ticker of ATVI. In addition, Vivendi would contribute $1.7 billion in cash for an additional 62.9 million newly issued shares. In total, Vivendi would own 358.2 million ATVI shares, representing a 52 percent ownership in Activision Blizzard. Both companies agreed to value ATVI shares at $27.50, which represented a 31 percent premium to the 20-day average as of the date of the announcement. Within 5 days of closing, Activision Blizzard pledged to initiate a $4 billion all-cash tender offer to purchase 146.5 million fully diluted Activision Blizzard common shares at $27.50. At the time of the tender offer, Vivendi agreed to acquire additional newly issued shares worth $700 million (at the $27.50 price). If the tender offer was fully subscribed, Vivendi would own 68 percent of Activision Blizzard. The tender offer would be funded by Activision's current cash on hand (roughly $0.9 billion), the $1.7 billion from Vivendi, the $0.7 billion from Vivendi's additional purchase, and short-term borrowing not to exceed $0.8 billion. The transaction was expected to be immediately accretive in the first year post-closing for Activision shareholders ($0.20 per share).

If Activision shares exceeded the price of $27.50 at the time of the tender offer, Activision Blizzard would look for alternative strategic uses for the large amount of cash on hand. One of the alternatives was to offer more than $2 billion to purchase all outstanding shares of Take-Two, a software developer that had recently received a $2 billion hostile tender offer from Electronic Arts. If there were no attractive alternatives, management made it clear that it would maximize shareholder value by returning excess cash up to $2.8 billion to shareholders.[20] If the management decided to pay out all of their cash on hand, each share would receive a $3.79 dividend. Several different scenarios were considered to ensure this investment would create positive net present value.

Activision Blizzard Governance

Activision Blizzard's board of directors would be made up of eleven members—six directors that would be designated by Vivendi, two Activision management directors, and three independent directors who served on Activision's board at the time. The new management team would include: Robert Kotick, the chairman and CEO of Activision, as president and CEO of Activision Blizzard; Rene Penisson of Vivendi as chairman of the board; Bruce Hack, CEO of Vivendi Games as vice chairman and chief corporate officer; Brian Kelly of Activision as co-chairman; Thomas Tippl of Activision as chief financial officer of Activision Blizzard; Jean-Francois Grollemund of Vivendi Games as chief accounting officer; Mike Griffith of Activision as CEO and president of Activision Publishing; and Michael Morhaime of Vivendi Games as CEO and president of Blizzard Entertainment. (A list of Activision's management appears in Appendix C.) It was believed that the new management would align the interests of Vivendi with Activision shareholders. In addition, the separation of chairman and CEO roles was expected to promote better corporate governance.

Activision Blizzard Rationale

The most important rationale offered behind the creation of Activision Blizzard was the resulting complementary nature of its portfolio of games. Activision's licensed content with the potential of hit sequels and Blizzard's *World of Warcraft* and its subscription base would provide consistent revenues year over year. Licensed content was vulnerable to competition and by expanding its portfolio, Activision Blizzard would reduce its dependence on content owners. In addition, Western publishers including Activision had long struggled to sell games in Asia. Activision Blizzard would be able to capitalize on Blizzard's expertise in this market. Its subscription-based revenue model and penetration experience into Asian markets combined with Activision's best-selling franchises would create a dominant player in the industry. Activision Blizzard would have leading market positions in all areas of the interactive entertainment industry.

Transaction Synergies

Activision Inc. as a stand-alone was expected to earn between $1.00 to $1.14 EPS in fiscal year (FY) 2009.[21] The newly created Activision Blizzard anticipated FY 2009 EPS of $1.20—an increase due to combined revenues and some operational synergies. Analysts expected these synergies to be between $50 and $100 million per year, which were expected to improve operating margins from the mid-teens in 2008 to the mid-twenties by 2012, and gross profit margins from Activision's current level of 35 percent to 45 percent.[22] These expectations were based on the assumption of lower manufacturing and distribution costs, and the more profitable nature of *World of Warcraft*'s subscription business and Activision's internally developed *Call of Duty* and *Guitar Hero*.[23] In addition, Activision Blizzard planned to apply Activision's focused management (or "Greenlight process") to Vivendi's *Sierra* games in order to reduce operating losses. In this process, Activision Blizzard looked for the same competitive qualities that it expected of its own games: global appeal, ability to be developed on multiple platforms, sequel potential, and high margin potential.

APPENDIX A Ratio Analysis for Video Game Competitors

	Activision $7.8 Billion			Electronic Arts $15.81 Billion			THQ Interactive $1.45 Billion			Take-Two Interactive $1.95 Billion		
Market cap	9 months 31-Dec-07	FYE 31-Mar-07	FYE 31-Mar-06	9 months 31-Dec-07	FYE 31-Mar-07	FYE 31-Mar-06	9 months 31-Dec-07	FYE 31-Mar-07	FYE 31-Mar-06	9 months 31-Dec-07	FYE 31-Mar-07	FYE 31-Mar-06
Profitability												
Gross Margin	43%	35%	36%	47%	61%	60%	32%	40%	40%	24%	25%	20%
Operating Margin	18%	5%	1%	−17%	1%	11%	−4%	8%	4%	−11%	−12%	−18%
Return on Equity	15%	7%	3%	−9%	2%	7%	1%	10%	5%	−22%	−27%	−29%
Liquidity												
Current	4.52	4.10	5.75	3.54	3.51	3.47	3.21	3.85	4.07	1.75	1.59	2.06
Quick	3.24	3.83	5.43	3.45	3.45	3.40	3.07	3.71	3.88	1.30	1.27	1.70
Turnover												
Inventory Turnover*	12.21	12.81	17.17	15.13	19.70	19.20	18.94	22.01	18.49	7.05	7.13	7.17
Market Value												
P/E**	32.52	67.64	98.50	N/A	186.52	65.93	97.20	29.99	39.83	N/A	N/A	N/A

*average inventory over last four quarters.
**ending price.

APPENDIX B   Analysis of a Potential Merger of Electronic Arts and Take-Two Interactive

The video game industry, which was spawned by the release of *Pong* by Atari in 1972, had been around for almost 40 years. Some observers believed that video games were fairly mature in industry stage.[24] Nevertheless, there were still numerous independent companies who created, manufactured, and distributed video games. Also, for an industry considered mature, it had extraordinary projected growth of between 12 and 17 percent. The combination of EA and Take-Two promised EA increased economies of scale and scope.

EA, through its EA Sports brand, held a very large portion of the sporting games market including titles through official licenses to the biggest sports leagues around the world, including the NBA, NFL, NHL, MLB, FIFA, and the NCAA. More importantly, EA owned the sole rights to the NFL, through a contract with the NFL Player's Union, and, therefore, was the only video game maker that could use real-life NFL players in its games. Other game makers, like Take-Two, had to use fictional names and players in their football titles. This exclusivity, along with the

production of a solid game, had allowed EA to cash in on the great success of the *Madden Football* (*NFL*) series. On the other hand, Take-Two, through its brand *Rockstar Games*, owned one of the industry's most profitable action video games: *Grand Theft Auto* (*GTA*). With the fourth version on the verge of release, Take-Two executives were optimistic about the revenue that *GTA IV* would bring. With over 60 million copies of *GTA III* and *GTA: Vice City* sold since 2001, Take-Two had reason to be optimistic.

In addition to the increased market share that Take-Two would bring to EA, the company would have access to greater distribution channels throughout the world, and potentially be able to consolidate production and manufacturing to create vast economies of scale. A newly combined EA and Take-Two would provide a serious threat to Activision and other competitors.

In spite of the potential dangers that a takeover of Take-Two posed to Activision, the possibility of the acquisition occurring was considered to be slim unless EA increased its bid for Take-Two by a significant margin.

APPENDIX C   Activision Executive Management

Robert Kotick, Chairman of the Board and Chief Executive Officer, Activision Inc.
Robert Kotick had been a director, chairman, and chief executive officer of Activision, Inc. since February 1991. Since March 2003, Mr. Kotick had served on the board of directors of Yahoo! Inc. as Internet content and service provider and as a member of that board's nominating and corporate governance committee. He was also member of the board of trustees at The Center for Early Education and is chairman of the committee of trustees at the Los Angeles County Museum of Art.

Michael Griffith, President and Chief Executive Officer, Activision Publishing, Inc.
Michael J. Griffith had been president and chief executive officer of Activision Publishing Inc. and principal executive officer of Activision, Inc. since June 2005. Prior to joining Activision, Mr. Griffith served in a number of executive level positions at the Proctor and Gamble Company, a manufacturer of consumer goods products, from 1981 to 2005, including president of the Proctor and Gable Company's Global Beverage Division from 2002 to 2005. Mr. Griffith held a BA degree from Albion College and an MBA from the University of Michigan.

Thomas Tippl, Chief Financial Officer, Activision Publishing, Inc.
Thomas Tippl has been chief financial officer of Activision Publishing Inc. since October 2005 and principal financial and accounting officer of Activision, Inc., since January 2006. Prior to joining Activision, Mr. Tippl served as head of Investor Relations

and Shareholders Services at Procter and Gamble from 2004 to 2005. Mr. Tippl held a master's degree in economics and social sciences from the Vienna University of Economics and Business Administration.

Ronald Doornink, Director and Senior Advisor, Activision, Inc.
Ronald Doornink had served as a director of the company since April 2003 and a senior advisor to the company since December 31, 2005. He was president of the company from 1998 until December 31, 2005. He was also chairman of Activision Publishing Inc., the company's only direct operating subsidiary and the holding company for all other active subsidiaries, from June 15, 2005, until December 31, 2005, and was chief executive officer of Activision Publishing, Inc., from March 28, 2002, through June 14, 2005. Mr. Doornink joined Activision in 1998 from ConAgra Foods, Inc. where for three years he served as president of the Hunt-Wesson snack food division. Mr. Doornink held an MBA degree from Columbia University and an undergraduate degree in economics.

Brian Kelly, Co-Chairman and Director, Activision Publishing Inc.
Brian Kelly had held various positions of responsibility with Activision, Inc. since 1991, including serving as a director of the company since July 1995 and co-chairman of the company since October 1998. Mr. Kelly received a BA degree in accounting from Rutgers University and a JD degree from Fordham University School of Law.

APPENDIX D   Activision Timeline

1979: Founded October 1, Activision produced games for the Atari 2600 console.

1982: Activision had its first big hit with the release of *Pitfall!*

1983: Activision completed an IPO.

1988: Diversification into other areas led the company to change its name to Mediagenic.

1992: Mediagenic filed chapter 11 bankruptcy, changed name back to Activision upon emerging from bankruptcy.

1997: Activision acquired *Raven Software, HeXen II, Heretic II, Soldier of Fortune 1* and *2*, and *Quake 4*.

1998: Activision signed several deals with big names in 1998 including Marvel, Disney, and Tony Hawk. 1998 marked the beginning of a long-term relationship with Marvel; over time this alliance provided Activision with rights to create games based on *X-MEN, Spiderman, Blade, Fantastic Four, Iron Man,* and *Spider-Man 3*. Disney signed a deal allowing Activision to publish games based on Disney's animated films. Tony Hawk signed an agreement allowing Activision to create a series of games based on the skateboarding champion.

1999: Activision acquired Neversoft Entertainment, the developer of the *Tony Hawk* franchise.

2000: Activision made an equity investment with Gray Matter Interactive to develop *Return to Castle Wolfenstein*, the sequel to the hit *Wolfenstein 3D*. Activision acquired Gray Matter in 2002.

2001: Activision acquired the rights to create a game based on Columbia Pictures' box office hit *Spider-Man*.

2002: Activision made an equity investment in Infinity Ward, the developer of *Medal of Honor Allied Assault* and the *Call of Duty* franchise. Activision acquired Infinity Ward in 2003. Activision also acquired Luxoflux, developer of *Star Wars Demolition*, and Z-Axis Ltd., creator of the *Dave Mirra Freestyle BMX* franchise.

2003: A multi-year partnership between Activision and DreamWorks SKG was established initially giving Activision rights to publish games based on *Sharkslayer, Madagascar,* and *Over the Hedge*. As the partnership progressed, further rights have been granted to create games based on *Shrek 2, Kung Fu Panda, Rex Havoc,* and *How to Train Your Dragon*.

2006: Activision acquired the rights to develop games based on *TRANSFORMERS* from Hasbro, and MGM Interactive and EON Productions Ltd. awarded Activision rights to create games based on James Bond through 2014. The biggest event of 2006 occurred with the acquisition of RedOctane, Inc., publisher of the *Guitar Hero* franchise.

2007: The Activision and Vivendi Games merger was announced in December 2007. Vivendi Games consisted of Sierra, Sierra Online, Vivendi Games Mobile, and Blizzard Entertainment. Sierra was well known for its *King's Quest, Space Quest, Gabriel Knight,* and *Leisure Suit Larry* games, while Blizzard was known for its *Warcraft, Starcraft, Diablo,* and *World of Warcraft* games. The deal was expected to close during the first half of 2008 and the new company would be called Activision Blizzard.

APPENDIX E   Activision Sales by Gaming Console

Publishing Net Revenues	Year Ended March 31, 2007	% of Publishing Net Revs	Year Ended March 31, 2006	% of Publishing Net Revs	Increase/ (Decrease)	Percent Change
PC	$ 78,886	7%	$ 183,457	16 %	$ (104,571)	(57)%
Console						
Sony PlayStation 3	53,842	5%	—	—%	53,842	n/a
Sony PlayStation 2	500,927	45%	422,239	36%	78,688	19%
Microsoft Xbox360	200,394	18%	102,809	9%	97,585	95%
Microsoft Xbox	54,232	5%	205,864	18%	(151,632)	(74)%
Nintendo Wii	54,636	5%	—	—%	54,636	n/a
Nintendo GameCube	22,761	2%	80,964	7%	(58,203)	(72)%
Other	3	—%	469	—%	(466)	(99)%
Total console	886,795	80%	812,345	70%	74,450	9%
Hand-held						
Game Boy Advance	48,478	4%	79,738	7%	(31,260)	(39)%
PlayStation Portable	49,931	4%	52,016	5%	(2,085)	(4)%
Nintendo Dual Screen	54,948	5%	27,107	2%	27,841	103%
Total hand-held	153,357	13%	158,861	14%	(5,504)	(3)%
Total publishing net revenues	1,119,038	100%	1,154,663	100%	(35,625)	(3)%

APPENDIX F   Activision, Inc. and Subsidiaries Consolidated Balance Sheets
(in thousands, except share data) for Quarterly Period Ended December 31, 2007

	December 31, 2007 (Unaudited)	March 31, 2007
Assets		
Current assets:		
Cash and cash equivalents	$648,659	$384,409
Short-term investments	539,914	570,440
Accounts receivable, net of allowances of $177,533 and $91,418 at December 31, 2007, and March 31, 2007, respectively	704,075	148,694
Inventories	153,423	91,231
Software development	68,240	107,779
Intellectual property licenses	16,686	27,784
Deferred income taxes	20,552	51,564
Other current assets	25,812	19,332
Total current assets	2,177,361	1,401,233
Software development	31,555	23,143
Intellectual property licenses	60,940	72,490
Property and equipment, net	54,203	46,540
Deferred income taxes	119	48,791
Other assets	9,639	6,376
Goodwill	279,297	195,374
Total assets	$2,613,114	$1,793,947
Liabilities and Shareholders' Equity		
Current liabilities:		
Accounts payable	$243,338	$136,517
Accrued expenses and other liabilities	482,367	204,652
Total current liabilities	725,705	341,169
Other liabilities	21,009	41,246
Total liabilities	746,714	382,415
Commitments and contingencies		
Shareholders' equity:		
Preferred stock, $0.000001 par value, 3,750,000 shares authorized, no shares issued at December 31, 2007, and March 31, 2007	—	—
Series A Junior Preferred stock, $.000001 par value, 1,250,000 shares authorized, no shares issued at December 31, 2007, and March 31, 2007	—	—
Common stock, $.000001 par value, 450,000,000 shares authorized, 293,720,682 and 283,310,734 shares issued and outstanding at December 31, 2007, and March 31, 2007, respectively	—	—
Additional paid-in capital	1,113,963	963,553
Retained earnings	728,497	427,777
Accumulated other comprehensive income	23,940	20,202
Total shareholders' equity	1,866,400	1,411,532
Total liabilities and shareholders' equity	$2,613,114	$1,793,947

APPENDIX G   Activision, Inc. and Subsidiaries Consolidated Statements of Operations
(Unaudited) (in thousands, except per share data) for Quarterly Period Ended December 31, 2007

	For the Three Months Ended December 31,		For the Nine Months Ended December 31,	
	2007	2006	2007	2006
Net revenues	$1,482,484	$824,259	$2,295,685	$1,200,500
Costs and expenses:				
Cost of sales—product costs	597,046	382,165	966,271	618,162
Cost of sales—software royalties and amortization	125,614	77,449	242,293	106,058
Cost of sales—intellectual property licenses	39,630	23,566	86,642	37,838
Product development	124,501	37,162	190,483	88,395
Sales and marketing	120,090	87,410	240,670	156,139
General and administrative	71,069	43,387	144,245	91,647
Total costs and expenses	1,077,950	651,139	1,870,604	1,098,239
Operating income	404,534	173,120	425,081	102,261
Investment income, net	12,018	9,724	35,712	26,031
Income before income tax provision	416,552	182,844	460,793	128,292
Income tax provision	144,356	40,024	160,073	28,083
Net income	$272,196	$142,820	$300,720	$100,209
Basic earnings per share	$0.93	$0.51	$1.05	$0.36
Weighted average common shares outstanding	291,176	282,512	287,439	280,499
Diluted earnings per share	$0.86	$0.46	$0.96	$0.33
Weighted average common shares outstanding assuming dilution	316,472	307,175	313,546	304,317

End Notes

1. www.theesa.com.
2. http://www.businessandgames.com/blog/2007/06/serious_games_a_sizeable_marke.html.
3. THQ Inc., Profile, Yahoo! Finance, http://finance.yahoo.com/q/pr?s=THQI.
4. Electronic Arts, Inc., Profile, Yahoo! Finance, http://finance.yahoo.com/q/pr?s=ERTS.
5. Take-Two Interactive Software Inc., Profile, Yahoo! Finance, http://finance.yahoo.com/q/pr?s=TTWO.
6. Activision 10-K Annual Report 2007.
7. http://investor.activision.com/background.cfm.
8. http://investor.activision.com/background.cfm.
9. http://files.shareholder.com/downloads/ACTI/276273427x0x25712/C585BB17-26EA-4F0A-A206-5F3B43CE1A1A/ar_2000.pdf.
10. http://videogames.yahoo.com/celebrity-byte/tony-hawk/522182.
11. http://files.shareholder.com/downloads/ACTI/276273427x0x25716/FA04C4A7-7347-47E3-9D7A-D3DD1B54F31A/ar_2004.pdf 2004 annual report pg 36.
12. http://www.joystiq.com/2006/08/09/activision-paid-nearly-100-million-for-redoctane/.
13. http://www.kotaku.com.au/games/2008/02/activision_take_money_money_make_money_money_money-2.html.
14. http://en.wikipedia.org/wiki/Guitar_Hero_%28series%29.
15. http://en.wikipedia.org/wiki/Vivendi_Games.

16. http://www.foxbusiness.com/markets/industries/media/article/vivendi-announces-excellent-2007-results_500851_15.html.
17. http://www.gamespot.com/news/6164555.html.
18. http://www.activisionblizzard.com/webcastsPresentations/ActivisionBlizzard_Final.pdf pg 9.
19. http://www.activisionblizzard.com/webcastsPresentations/ActivisionBlizzard_Final.pdf pg 8.
20. http://investor.activision.com; Activision Q3 2008 Earnings Release Conference Call.
21. EPS of $1.00 in FY 2009 is conservative. Many analysts have revised earnings expectations for FY 2009 to be near $1.14. This is according to Standard and Poor's and Argus Research Company.
22. See Activision, Inc. Analyst Research Reports from Morningstar and Standard and Poor's.
23. Activision's lower gross profit margins are largely due to the license fees it must pay to content owners.
24. *Video Game*, Wikipedia.com, http://en.wikipedia.org/wiki/Video_games.

Case 3–7: McDonald's and KFC: Recipes for Success in China

Quick Service Restaurant Giants in the Middle Kingdom

In 2008, McDonald's and KFC were the two largest quick-service restaurants (QSR) in the world, with 31,999 and 15,580 outlets, respectively.[1] Both chains were renowned for their broad spectrum of consumers on a global basis.

McDonald's appeared to be a clear winner in international expansion. It had over 17,500 international outlets and was the first corporation to set up a solid foundation for international franchising. It spearheaded global expansion with its first overseas outlet in Canada in 1967, and entered Japan in 1971.[2] McDonald's outlets had tremendous success in Japan—despite the difference in culture—with record-breaking daily sales and speed of expansion in the initial stage.[3]

KFC also started international expansion early, opening its first overseas outlet in England in 1964. However, it was given a bumpy ride when it began to penetrate the market in Asia. The Japanese outlets were far less successful than McDonald's and only started to make a profit in 1976, six years after KFC entered Japan. KFC outlets opened in Hong Kong in 1973 but were all closed down within two years. The company would eventually win the confidence of Hong Kong customers ten years after its first entry. In Taiwan it experienced relatively smoother development, although KFC headquarters was to spend a huge amount of money and effort in order

This case was written by Gabriel Szulanski, Professor of Strategy at INSEAD, Weiru Chen, Assistant Professor of Strategy, and Jennifer Lee, Research Associate. It is intended to be used as a basis for class discussion rather than to illustrate either effective or ineffective handling of an administrative situation. The authors gratefully acknowledge funding from INSEAD R&D.

to get the ownership back from its joint venture partners at a later stage.[4]

It was a totally different picture in China. In the 'Middle Kingdom,' KFC was not only recognised as the leader in foreign quick-service restaurants but was also a significant player in the Chinese restaurant industry as a whole, alone contributing 1% of the country's total food and beverage industry revenues in 2005.[5] In 2005, KFC's outlets in China recorded an average of US$1.2 million in annual sales per store, compared with just US$900,000 for similar stores in the US.[6] According to the 2008 figures, KFC had over 2,300 outlets in China, with an average profit margin of nearly 20.1%.[7]

In contrast, at 1,000 outlets, McDonald's presence in China was less than half of KFC's, with an estimated profit margin significantly below that of its leading competitor. Many people attributed KFC's success in China to its early entry—three years earlier than McDonald's—and its natural advantage in menu selection which corresponded to the typical consumer's preference for chicken over beef. However, were these reasons enough to explain KFC's continued growth and the extension of its lead over its rival? How could McDonald's as a latecomer and the second-largest QSR player in China, capitalize upon its global dominance and resources to catch up with KFC?

Replicate or Adapt?

The Inherent Challenge for International Franchisors

International franchising is frequently associated with service firms, such as hotels, retail outlets and quick service restaurants. These firms often have strongly identifiable trademarks and try to guarantee the customer a uniform and consistent level of service and product quality across different locations and over time. However, the high degree of standardised operations makes the replication of the format across diverse markets difficult. Differences in things such as ingredients, labour and physical space can mean significant modifications to the service formula. Consequently, the basic service may be similar to that of the home country, but details in the delivery of the service are often altered.[8]

Many foreign enterprises found China very different in culture and consumer behaviour. Franchise restaurants faced several major hurdles, including a different labour force structure, difficulty in recruiting technically competent and culturally sensitive managers, tough technological problems and a less than satisfactory legal environment and enforcement.[9] So the challenge for international franchisors like McDonald's and KFC was to decide whether to comply strictly with their original models, and if adaptation was required, when and how to make adaptations in order to deliver globally consistent standards while catering to local consumer needs.

Potential of China's Restaurant Industry

Chinese consumers' spending on eating out had increased tremendously along with the country's economic boom in the past decade. Retail revenues of the restaurant industry increased from 5.2% in 1991 to 14% in 2007 as a portion of total retail revenues from consumer goods.[10] According to annual statistics from the Ministry of Commerce of the People's Republic of China, the retail revenue of the hotel and restaurant industry reached 1,235.2 billion RMB in 2007, representing 19.4% growth over the previous year; foreign franchises were the main driver of food and beverage revenue growth as foreign direct investment in the hotel and restaurant industry totaled US$10.4 billion, an increase of 25.8% on the previous year.[11] China was the world's largest consumer of meat. The Economist Intelligence Unit forecast that annual meat consumption in China would jump from 59 kg per head in 2005 to 74 kg per head in 2009.[12] With US meat consumption at 128 kg a head, there seemed plenty of scope for the Western fast-food industry to expand in China.[13]

Foreign quick service restaurants played a significant role in China's restaurant industry. The share of fast food in the retail industry was expected to reach 9.3% by 2011 from 74% in 2007. China's fast-food industry was expected to grow at a CAGR of around 25% during 2008–2011.[14]

The first comprehensive franchising regulations, which came into effect in February 2005, made it easier for foreign fast-food operators to open branches and roll out the franchising model, which had proven to be such a sure path for fast-track growth in the US and Europe.[15] The new Law on Franchise Regulations, passed in February 2007, helped clear up the ambiguity surrounding franchisor's disclosure duty.[16] Thenceforth, the rights of both franchisors and franchisees were better protected.

Quick Service Restaurant Chains: A New Experience for China

Foreign quick service restaurants began to surface in China with the opening of KFC's first store in 1987, followed by McDonald's entry three years later. The timing was propitious for foreign enterprises as it had been nine years since China embarked upon a policy of opening up and reform in 1978 and Chinese curiosity about the West was at a peak.

Although GDP growth in China had averaged well over 9% per year since 1978, per capita GDP at the time of KFC's entry was a mere US$621.05.[17] Given the 120 to 130 yuan monthly salary of Beijing urban residents at that time, KFC prices were unaffordable to most, but many still flocked to the store to purchase the 12-yuan KFC hamburger or 8-yuan fried chicken. The most frequent customers were foreigners living in China. Despite the attractiveness of fast food chains, local consumers in those early days could seldom afford to eat at KFC, McDonald's or Pizza Hut. Dining at these establishments was considered such a luxury that some couples chose to hold their wedding banquets there.[18]

Behind the 'dream market' with a vast land area and 1.3 billion people, the complexity of China's population, geography and history presented major challenges for foreign players. Population density, economic development and wealth distribution varied greatly from east to west and from south to north. Foreign invested enterprises usually focused on the populous, more affluent eastern China. The western regions were beyond the reach of even domestic businesses without an effective national transportation system.

Chinese-style fast food had existed prior to the entry of western quick service restaurants but represented a totally different concept and ambience compared with modern chains. Most of the catering units for Chinese fast food were small in scale, serving pre-made appetizers such as congee, buns and fritters of twisted dough (yiu-tiao). They lacked funding, trained employees and a well-maintained dining environment.[19] As restaurant staff required at least five years of experience, western food chains could not find a sufficient number of internal candidates to meet growth-driven demand and had to import skilled managers from neighbouring markets such as Taiwan and Hong Kong, and even from headquarters in the US.

KFC in China

The Very First Western Restaurant Chain

Yum!'s KFC brand was the first foreign quick-service restaurant chain to enter China.[20] On 12 November 1987, the first KFC in China was officially opened at Beijing Qianmen, within walking distance of Tiananmen. In 2002, KFC opened the first ever drive-through restaurant in the country. In 2004, the 1,000th KFC restaurant was opened in China (Beijing), only a few kilometres from the site of its first restaurant. From the beginning of 2005, the Yum! China Division (including Mainland China, Thailand and KFC Taiwan), based in Shanghai, reported directly to Yum! headquarter instead of to its international division, reflecting China's market size, unique strength and importance.[21] From 1987 to 2005, the number of KFC outlets in China grew by 50% annually, growth which was considered exponential outside its parent market in the US,[22] particularly in a country known for its culinary sophistication developed over thousands of years. Today, KFC is the number one quick-service restaurant brand in China. Yum! China has more than 2,300 KFC restaurants in nearly 500 cities in Mainland China (Q3 2008).[23]

Initial Stage—Replication with Localisation in Mind

In 1987, KFC set up a joint venture, B-KFC, with Beijing Animal Production Company and Beijing Tourism Board in order to gain access to better product supply and F&B management authority. Sim Kay Soon, a Singaporean who had held area manager and training officer positions within KFC system since the 1980s, was appointed to be its the first general manager, responsible for day-to-day operations.[24] Positions below (and including) assistant managers were all held by Chinese nationals. The company started using local food ingredients from day one. Chicken was purchased from Beijing Animal Production, and potatoes, cabbage and carrots were all purchased locally. However, cooking equipment was mostly imported, such as blenders, heating racks and even cash registers.

The first Beijing outlet represented KFC's largest restaurant worldwide with 1,400 square metres of space allowing for a capacity of 500 seats and considerable office space for B-KFC staff. Only four months after opening, the Beijing restaurant had become the highest-selling single KFC store in the world.

The response to B-KFC's recruitment was overwhelming as the base salary offered was set at 140 RMB per month, about 40% more than could be earned by associate professors at the country's universities at that time. So

attractive was the compensation package that a ratio of 20 to 1 people applied for every opening. In the end, B-KFC hired those applicants who were high school graduates, could speak some English, did not have previous restaurant work experience, and had demonstrated a willingness to work hard.[25]

A Management Team Familiar with Local Culture

From the beginning, KFC hired elites from overseas—Hong Kong, Taiwan and other Asian countries—some with decades of experiences in the QSR industry, and most with a deep understanding of the language, culture, habits and customs of China. As many of the management team members were associated with Taiwan, they were nicknamed the "Taiwanese gang."[26]

Other than the top management team which was composed of almost all overseas Chinese, KFC was keen on developing local talent from day one. The company paid well to hire highly educated and motivated restaurant staff, and used its training system to develop those staff into future restaurant managers or even district general managers. 80% of China KFC's district general managers were university graduates, some from top schools. This strategy paid off when the company decided to expand aggressively after 10 years in China. Joseph Han, Operating Vice President of Yum! Brands in greater China from 1996 to 2003, described KFC China's people strategy:

> . . . in China, KFC understands the importance of people's talent. . . . In the United States, in the fast-food chains, it is very difficult to hire very high-quality people, especially on the cook labour side. So in China, KFC built very aggressive talent recruitment projects. It went to universities to hire university students. KFC hired management trainees with very qualified university graduates. . . . There are a total of 22 branch offices for Yum! Brands in China and the general managers are now already 90% localised. Those people actually, 20 years ago, started at the restaurants as the cook person, or as a management trainee. This talent pool has become their great asset for the future development.[27]

Takeoff during Time of Crisis

KFC chose to put down roots in big eastern cities along the coast in the 1980s and to go west in the 1990s. Like many foreign enterprises, KFC's expansion route was from east to west, from cities to towns, and blanketed China with wider coverage by linking outlet presence in cities and towns. Within 10 years of its entry into China, KFC has basically covered the main cities in the populated areas, with only the sparsely populated and low purchasing-powered south-western and north-western districts yet to be penetrated.

During the Asia economic downturn in 1997, KFC faced the challenge of a thinning bottom line. It had two alternatives, either to cut costs or to increase sales. It chose to aggressively expand the number of outlets at a time when most competitors were holding back. The same strategy was applied in other times of crisis, for example, during the SARS epidemic in 2003—that year KFC added more than 300 new outlets, even more than in the previous year.[28]

Self-Developed Logistic and Distribution System

Along with the aggressive expansion plan, a well-connected supply chain was needed before any new KFC outlet could be opened in any city. KFC expected to establish a logistics system to supply neighbouring KFC outlets. If it took more than one day to reach any new KFC restaurant, the logistics team would start finding a new warehouse closer to the outlet.

What was different about the global KFC system was that Yum! Brands established its own logistics system by working closely with local partners rather than simply outsourcing its supply to a third party. KFC established the "STAR System" for its China partners, and suppliers who passed the STAR test could also easily achieve national ISO9002 and HACCP[29] certification. Yum! Brands later consolidated a separate supply system in China—which saved the company nearly 100 million RMB in costs in 1998.[30] It set up Asia's largest logistics and distribution centre in Beijing in October 2004 for its groups of restaurants in China, a move that was the first and only for Yum! Brands Global companies, and which allowed another 10% cost reduction.[31] Warren K. Liu, Vice President of Yum! Brands Greater China from 1997 to 2000, later recalled that he was challenged again and again by headquarters on the decision to invest in its own warehouse, logistics and distribution system, which didn't exist in other parts of the world where Yum! Brands was present:

> What we faced in China were an inefficient and frag-mented distribution network, an inadequate highway system, local protectionism that lead to fragmentation in the supply chain, and inter-provincial trade barriers such as excessive tolls. In such an infrastructure-deficient market environment, direct control over supply storage and distribution complements KFC's rapid growth strategy; allowing KFC to penetrate new markets further, sooner, faster, at lower unit cost than its competitors.[32]

Menu Selection—an American Brand with Chinese Characteristics

KFC has followed the principle of menu localization, striving to become an 'American brand with Chinese character-istics' since its entry.[33] Even in the earliest days, KFC China's most popular items were the spicy chicken wings and spicy chicken thigh burger, rather than its signature Colonel Sanders Original Recipe chicken.

Large-scale menu localisation started in 1998[34] when a local food R&D team and a test kitchen were set up in Shanghai. Since then, KFC has introduced many Chinese items onto their menus. Preserved Sichuan pickle and shredded pork soup was one of the first. The soup proved a success, and mushroom rice, tomato and egg soup, and Dragon Twister (traditional Peking chicken roll) were soon added to the menu. KFC also serves packets of Happy French Fry Shakes that contain beef, orange and Uygur barbecue spices.[35] Chinese consumers received those localised food items very well. While some global companies might have second thoughts about launching a food item containing bones for family consumers, as it might potentially create food safety concerns, KFC's chicken kebab is made of soft bones and meat (see Exhibit 1), and has become one of the most popular items among children and teenagers. Chinese consumers can find preserved egg with pork porridge, egg and pork floss roll, and Hong Kong milk tea for breakfast, egg and vegetable soup as a side dish, Dragon Twister for a main meal, and Portuguese egg tart for dessert on the menu.

In an interview, Joseph Han talked about why KFC China was determined to provide a localised menu, one of the keys to successfully penetrating into fourth and fifth tier cities in rural areas:

> I think McDonald's and KFC do bring in the dining environment, and they bring in their working concept to change people's lifestyle. But product-wise, you can see Chinese are still Chinese. When Chinese students go to the United States to study, they still choose the kind of food they feel is close to their life. Even though they admire the Western lifestyle, I think they still need time to change their dietary habits. Especially breakfast. In the three meals, breakfast is usually cooked by your mother. Your mother always cooks traditional food. So that's why now even McDonald's in China created its own breakfast menu. Everywhere in the world you don't change, but when you came to China and India, I can guarantee you have to change, because maybe you can change younger people's lifestyle, but you cannot change some of their dietary habits.[36]

China
KFC China Print Advertisement

Chicken Kebab—*"Bone and flesh Relations"*

KFC China TV Advertisement

Exhibit 1 KFC Advertisement

Franchised or Not?

KFC's aggressive expansion through franchising did not get off to a good start in China. In 1993, it signed its first regional franchise agreement for the Xian area in the northwest of China with a Taiwanese entrepreneur.[37] This served the purpose at that time for KFC China headquarters to focus on more strategically important coastal cities. However, due to a slower-than-expected development pace in Xian, KFC China had to go down the same path as in Taiwan during the 1990s, launch new outlets separately and

independently from those operated by the franchisee, and finally bought back restaurant ownership in Xian.

The KFC team in China decided not to authorise any franchise agreements with entrepreneurs in any city or region to avoid making the same mistake as in Taiwan or Xian, no matter how small or remote that city or region might be. In August 2000, KFC authorised the first individual franchisee in Changzhou. By paying a one-time transfer fee of 8 million RMB, the franchisee could own an operating KFC outlet which was already in profit. The franchising strategy was limited to townships with a population of between

150,000 and 400,000, and which achieved more than 6,000 RMB in per capita annual consumption.[38] By the end of 2007, there were 228 franchised KFC outlets, 8.7% of its total number of outlets in China.[39]

McDonald's in China

Entry into China

On 8th October 1990, nearly three years after KFC set up its first outlet near Tiananmen Square, McDonald's opened its first outlet in China in Shenzhen[40] and it was warmly welcomed by the local consumers. It continued to extend in the southern cities of China, and in April 1992, the Golden Arches could finally be seen in McDonald's Wangfujing outlet in Beijing. This outlet was formed with an unlisted investment unit of the Beijing municipal government. Overtaking the Moscow outlet in size, it became the largest McDonald's restaurant in the world, attracting 13,000 customers on its very first day.[41]

By September 2003, McDonald's had 566 outlets in 94 cities across 19 provinces and China had become McDonald's third largest Asian market behind Japan and Australia. In 2004, China became one of its top ten markets—making the country McDonald's Corp's fastest-growing market worldwide.[42]

However, although the number of McDonald's outlets was on a par with that of KFC in the first six years after its entry, it had started to lag behind KFC since 1997. While KFC celebrated the opening of its 1,500th outlet in China (Shanghai) in 2005, McDonald's had around 600.[43] What had McDonald's done differently in China to explain this?

Consistent Global Supply Chain Partners

McDonald's developed its supply chain partners along with its global business growth. HAVI Food, its global logistics partner, would enter any new market to invest and set up the logistics system even before the first McDonald's outlet opened in that market. In China, HAVI Food also established a logistics centre exclusively for McDonald's, and there were three major distribution centres in Beijing, Shanghai, Guangzhou, and satellite dispatch centres in other smaller cities.

McDonald's also tried to work with its global food suppliers as much as possible. There were 43 suppliers for McDonald's in China, 70% of which were its global partners. For example, J.R. Simplot Co., which supplied frozen French fries to McDonald's, had founded a joint venture company in Beijing in 1993, surveying the varieties of potatoes before McDonald's entry; McDonald's vegetable supplier set up a branch in Guangzhou in 1997 in order to satisfy McDonald's intention to source locally, and 100% of its facility and equipment were imported from overseas. Likewise, the global suppliers of McDonald's buns and seasonings had all set up branches in China to strengthen the supply chain network for McDonald's in China.[44]

Why did McDonald's insist on bringing their global partners to China? Peter Tan, former Senior Vice President and President of McDonald's Greater China, summed it up:

> McDonald's in China today reflects the attitude that they are a global brand, hence the need to set standards that are globally consistent, be it in Oakbrook, USA, or Xian, China . . . McDonald's is saying that 'we are in this emerging country, but because we are a global brand, we need to give them first world standards . . .' McDonald's had fewer than five chicken suppliers up in the northeast, and the reason for this is that McDonald's is very concerned about quality consistency.[45]

Catching Up with Cautiously Aggressive Expansion

Although McDonald's came in late, its expansion in China was still aggressive, especially in the earlier years. Its strategy was to start in the foreign influenced and economically affluent southern cities and then expand to cities in north and central China.

However, compared with KFC, McDonald's did not successfully penetrate as many third and fourth tier cities as its rival (see Exhibits 2 and 3). By September 2003, McDonald's had 566 outlets in 94 cities across 19 provinces. The bulk of the restaurants were concentrated in over 40 cities on China's east coast where incomes were higher. The bulk of McDonald's sales in China came through its restaurants in Beijing, Shanghai, Shenzhen and Guangzhou. In

Exhibit 2 KFC's penetration in China in the first ten years	

Year of Entry	Coverage
1987	Beijing
1989	Shanghai
1992	Nanjing
1993	Suzhou, Hangzhou, Wuxi, Guangzhou, Qingdao, Xian (franchised)
1994	Fuzhou, Tianjin, Shenyang
1995	Chendu, Dalian, Wuhan
1996	Shenzhen, Xiamen
1997	Changsha, Chongqing

Source: Warren K. Liu, *KFC in China—Secret Recipe for Success,* John Wiley & Sons (Asia) Pte Ltd., 2008.

Exhibit 3	McDonald's penetration in China in the first 10 years

Year of Entry	Coverage
1990	Shenzhen
1992	Beijing
1993	Guangzhou
1994	Tianjin, Shanghai, Nangjing, Wuhan, Chendu, Chongqing
2001	Xian

Source: McDonald's and KFC edited by B.Q. Chen, China Economy Publishing, 2005.

September 2003, it was reported that McDonald's planned to open 100 new stores per year in China over the next couple of years. A majority of the proposed outlets would be opened in developed markets such as Beijing, Shanghai and Guangzhou. The remainder would be located in Inner Mongolia and other less developed regions of China. The company also planned to expand in Western China.[46] By January 2007, McDonald's had penetrated into more than 120 cities across China,[47] and in November 2008, it finally crossed the 1,000 outlets threshold, with plans to add another 175 in 2009.[48]

However, unlike KFC, McDonald's did not take bold steps in expanding its territory in China. The number of outlets in China began to dwindle from 2002 onwards. In order to strengthen its foothold in China, McDonald's moved its Asia headquarters from Hong Kong to Shanghai in January 2005, signaling its determination to intensify its aggressive expansion in China.

Standardised Global Menu with Local Selections

McDonald's was known for its quality of food and consistency in food preparation processes. In order to maintain quality and consistency, McDonald's imposed standardisation in three domains—ingredient procurement, food preparation and food quality. The same consistency could be seen in their food menu; Big Mac remained their signature product, although chicken varieties were added to suit local consumers' tastes and accounted for an estimated 60% of food sales in McDonald's China.[49]

The McDonald's menu in China was essentially the same as in the US. Its use of local food selection was apparently not as varied as KFC's. However, not content to lag behind KFC, McDonald's introduced Vegetable and Seafood Soup and Corn Soup in 2004,[50] and other Chinese-style menu items such as red bean sundaes and taro pies, which also became popular. McDonald's gradually recognised the importance of catering to local consumers' tastes. Jeffrey Schwartz, newly-appointed President of McDonald's China in 2005, said that 80% of the menu in China would be the same and the other 20% would be allowed to be different in order to reflect regional tastes. He also said that McDonald's would open outlets in more areas in the future to make McDonald's food accessible to more customers.[51]

McDonald's detail-oriented approach was also extended to their China operations. Every aspect of food preparation was done according to the operating manual. Packaging such as Happy Meal boxes and apple pie wrappers were produced to exactly the same global standards. In an interview, Peter Tan commented on the balance between production innovation and global consistency:

> For a global brand to maintain brand consistency, it is important to ensure that the icon products remain an integral part of the menu offering. But then the question arises as to how you penetrate into emerging countries where you need to balance between what the brand stands for versus local tastes. That's where I think product innovation done strategically plays a vital role.[52]

Today, McDonald's menu in China has grown to include foods tweaked for local tastes to satisfy consumers, such as spicy chicken fillet and pineapple sundae. Some of the menu ideas, such as the corn cup developed in China, have been exported to other markets around the world. However, according to CEO Jeffrey Schwartz, the hamburger and fries Western-style are still at the heart of the Chinese menus.[53]

Franchised or Not?

McDonald's has always been a franchising company and franchisees have played a significant role in its success. About three-quarters of McDonald's outlets worldwide have been franchised.[54] However, due to ambiguity in China's legal environment, up until 2003 McDonald's China had established all of its 566 outlets by joint venture or sole proprietor, rather than using its global franchising model. It announced in 2003 that it would open ten franchised outlets in China by June 2006, with a loyalty fee of 2.5 to 3.2 million RMB. The requirements that individuals must meet before being granted a franchise were the same in China as they are worldwide. The first pilot franchise was launched in Tianjin in September 2003. The licence was awarded to Meng Sun on the basis of her business acumen and understanding of the Tianjin market.[55] In 2007, McDonald's had fewer than 0.5% outlets in China that were franchised[56] while the percentage was 78% worldwide.[57]

The Challenges Ahead

McDonald's

2004 was a year of tragedy and loss for the company. The CEO who had put McDonald's on the road to revitalization, Jim Cantalupo, died on the eve of the company's global convention. His successor, Charlie Bell, was diagnosed with cancer soon after taking the helm. He resigned in November of that same year, and passed away in January 2005.[58] The China management team saw a high level of turnover: McDonald's Greater China President, Peter Tan, left in June 2005. His post was filled by Guy Russo, who was originally President of McDonald's Australia. In October the same year, the Managing Director of McDonald's North region and the General Manager of McDonald's Beijing both left the company.[59]

Despite the general perception that McDonald's would try to catch up with KFC in China using franchising, a report in 2007 revealed that they were cautious about franchises. China Vice President, Gary Rosen, commented: "The franchise business requires a lot of effort and right now we have other priorities in China." The company would open at least 100 new stores in the country annually and half of them would be wholly owned drive-through outlets.[60] McDonald's took a strategic move to link with China's SinoPec in 2006, giving McDonald's the rights to build drive-through outlets at the oil company's 30,000 gas stations.[61] Up until November 2008, it owned 81 drive-through restaurants in China. Another expansion direction for McDonald's China was to convert its restaurants into 24-hour operations. By the end of 2008, 80% of its 1,000 outlets in China already provided service round the clock.[62] All these efforts were consistent with its global strategy of making McDonald's a convenient choice for customers.[63]

> *We have a business model of getting better versus getting bigger. It's not about how many restaurants you have, it's about how many restaurants that serve your customers well. It's not about how big, it's about how good and how you run your business.*[64]
>
> —Jeffrey Schwartz, CEO, McDonald's China, 2008

KFC

Despite its success in China, KFC Global was struggling to overcome weak performance in the homeland. Data showed that in 2008 Yum's overall second-quarter profit rose 4%; it achieved 38% growth in operating profit in its China division and 18% growth in its international division. These figures offset a 12% drop in US operating profit for that quarter. Yum! CEO, David C. Novak, singled out KFC in the US as "our only major soft spot."[65]

On the road of aggressive expansion, KFC China ran up against the issue of consumer confidence in its food safety standards. Sudan I, a red chemical dye thought to cause cancer, was discovered in two products sold in China: KFC's New Orleans Roast Chicken Wings and New Orleans Roast Chicken Legs.[66] KFC took the dishes off the menu, but Chinese consumers were still angry because a large amount of the consumption was made by children.[67]

Other Competition

Burger King, the second-largest United States hamburger chain, entered China in 2005, planning to open ten stores in China in 12 months with a view to participating in the large and fast-growing eating out market.[68] It signed a regional franchisee agreement with a company in Fujian, a populous province in southern China, in order to expand its territory.

Faced with increasing competition, how could McDonald's strengthen its position in China? Should it aggressively increase its number of outlets by taking bold steps like KFC, or gradually expand its presence by strictly following its global strategy and procedures? Could KFC sustain its leading edge while ensuring expansion and quality at the same time? Would the success of China KFC be carried over to its US base and bring changes to the business model in order to compete with McDonald's Global?

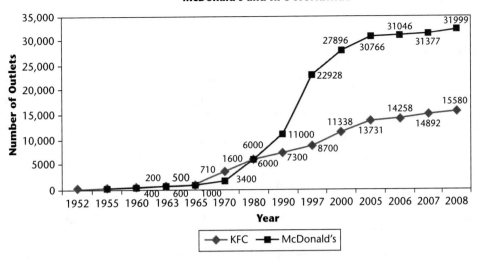

McDonald's and KFC Worldwide

Exhibit 4 Historical Store Count

Source: McDonald's and Yum website. Various press releases and web articles.

Exhibit 5   KFC Top 25 Markets by Unit Count

For Full Year 2007

2007 Top 25 Markets	KFC
United States	**5,273**
China Mainland	2,140
Japan	1,152
Canada	720
Great Britain	664
Australia	559
South Africa	479
Malaysia	402
Mexico	323
Thailand	314
Indonesia	300
Philippines	165
Korea	158
Taiwan	138
Saudi Arabia	97
New Zealand	95
Puerto Rico	86
Poland	83
Egypt	81
Singapore	70
Hong Kong	69
France	57
Germany	51
Spain	47
India	31

Source: www.yum.com

Exhibit 6   Yum Worldwide System Units

Year end	2008	2007	2006	2005	2004	2003
Company Owned	7,568	7,625	7,736	7,587	7,743	7,854
Franchisees	25,911	24,297	23,516	22,666	21,858	21,471
Licensees	2,168	2,109	2,137	2,376	2,345	2,362
Total (a)	36,292	35,345	34,595	34,277	33,608	33,199

Year end	2008	2007	2006	2005	2004	2003
United States						
KFC	5,253	5,358	5,394	5,443	5,525	5,524
Pizza Hut	7,564	7,515	7,532	7,566	7,500	7,523
Taco Bell	5,588	5,580	5,608	5,845	5,900	5,989
Long John Silver's	1,022	1,081	1,121	1,169	1,200	1,204
A & W	363	371	406	449	485	576
Total Us	19,790	19,905	20,061	20,472	20,610	20,822

International	2008	2007	2006	2005	2004	2003
KFC	7,347	6,942	6,606	6,307	6,084	5,944
Pizza Hut	5,026	4,882	4,788	4,701	4,528	4,357
Taco Bell	245	238	236	243	237	247
Long John Silver's	38	38	35	34	34	31
A & W	264	254	238	229	210	183
Total International	12,920	12,354	11,903	11,514	11,093	10,762

China	2008	2007	2006	2005	2004	2003
KFC	2,980	2,592	2,258	1,981	1,657	1,410
Pizza Hut	585	480	365	305	246	204
Taco Bell	0	2	2	2	1	1
A & W	0	0	0	0	0	0
Total China (b)	3,582	3,086	2,631	2,291	1,905	1,615

(a) Includes unconsolidated affiliates.

(b) Includes East Dawning units for China.

Source: www.yum.com

Exhibit 7 Yum China Division Operating Results (in millions)

	2001	2002	2003	2004	2005	2006	2007
Company sales	$569	$722	$871	$1,082	$1,255	$1,587	$2,075
Franchise and licence fees	18	22	30	38	41	51	69
Revenues	587	744	901	1,120	1,296	1,638	2,144
Food and paper	244	289	331	401	454	562	756
Payroll and employee benefits	61	77	93	125	167	205	273
Occupancy and other operating expenses	179	217	275	337	415	497	629
Company restaurant expenses	484	583	699	863	1,036	1,264	1,658
General and administrative expenses	46	51	62	80	92	119	151
Franchise and licence expenses	-	-	-	-	-	-	-
Closures and impairment expenses	6	6	6	4	7	6	7
Other (income) expenses	(12)	(16)	(27)	(32)	(50)	(41)	(47)
	524	624	740	915	1,085	1,348	1,769
Operating profit	$63	$120	$161	$205	$211	$290	$375
Company sales	100%	100%	100%	100%	100%	100%	100%
Food and paper	42.9	40.0	38.0	37.1	36.2	35.4	36.4
Payroll and employee benefits	10.7	10.6	10.7	11.5	13.3	12.9	13.2
Occupancy and other operating expenses	31.5	30.1	31.5	31.1	33.1	31.3	30.3
Restaurant margin	14.9%	19.3%	19.8%	20.3%	17.4%	20.4%	20.1%
	$	$	$	$	$	$	$
Company sales	569	722	871	1,082	1,255	1,587	2,075
Franchisee sales	328	397	510	619	665	840	1,098
System sales growth							
Local currency	17%	25%	23%	23%	11%	23%	24%
US dollars	14%	25%	23%	23%	13%	26%	31%

Source: www.yum.com

Exhibit 8   Yum U.S. Division Operating Results (in millions)

	2001	2002	2003	2004	2005	2006	2007
Company sales	$4,287	$4,778	$5,081	$5,163	$5,294	$4,952	$4,518
Franchise and licence fees	540	569	574	600	635	651	679
Revenues	4,827	5,347	5,655	5,763	5,929	5,603	5,197
Food and paper	1,225	1,346	1,463	1,546	1,576	1,399	1,317
Payroll and employee benefits	1,313	1,479	1,576	1,573	1,600	1,489	1,377
Occupancy and other operating expenses	1,100	1,189	1,303	1,333	1,385	1,340	1,221
Company restaurant expenses	3,638	4,014	4,342	4,452	4,561	4,228	3,915
General and administrative expenses	418	469	469	501	536	546	510
Franchise and licence expenses	49	39	16	19	26	23	29
Closures and impairment expenses	27	23	16	14	46	37	14
Other income	-	-	-	-	-	6	(10)
	4,132	4,545	4,843	4,986	5,169	4,840	4,458
Operating profit	$695	$802	$812	$777	$760	$763	$739
Company sales	100%	100%	100%	100%	100%	100%	100%
Food and paper	28.6	28.2	28.8	29.9	29.8	28.2	29.2
Payroll and employee benefits	30.6	30.9	31.0	30.5	30.2	30.1	30.5
Occupancy and other operating expenses	25.6	24.9	25.6	25.8	26.2	27.1	27.0
Restaurant margin	15.2%	16.0%	14.6%	13.8%	13.8%	14.6%	13.3%
Company same store sales growth	1%	2%	0%	3%	4%	0%	(3)%
Company sales	$4,287	$4,778	$5,081	$5,163	$5,294	$4,952	$4,518
Franchise sales	10,309	11,061	11,257	11,724	12,428	12,804	13,304

Source: www.yum.com

Exhibit 9   Yum Division Historical Sales Growth (in %)

CHINA DIVISION
(Mainland China, Thailand, KFC Taiwan)

	2008	2007	2006	2005	2004
1st Quarter	28%	19%	14%	26%	17%
2nd Quarter	28%	19%	29%	2%	34%
3rd Quarter		23%	25%	11%	20%
4th Quarter		30%	23%	6%	21%
Full Year		24%	23%	10%	23%

INTERNATIONAL DIVISION
(Excludes China Division)

	2008	2007	2006	2005	2004
1st Quarter	9%	10%	6%	7%	5%
2nd Quarter	8%	11%	8%	6%	6%
3rd Quarter		11%	9%	4%	9%
4th Quarter		9%	11%	4%	6%
Full Year		10%	9%	5%	6%

U.S. COMPANY SAME-STORE

	2008	2007	2006	2005	2004
1st Quarter	3%	−6%	4%	4%	3%
2nd Quarter	4%	−3%	0	5%	2%
3rd Quarter		−1%	−2%	4%	4%
4th Quarter		−1%	−2%	4%	2%
Full Year		−3%	0	4%	3%

Source: www.yum.com

Exhibit 10   McDonald's Number of Restaurants Top 25 Market by unit count

(at year-end 2007 and 2002)	2007	2002
Total	31,377	31,108
United States	13,862	13,491
Japan	3,746	3,891
Canada	1,401	1,304
Germany	1,302	1,211
United Kingdom	1,191	1,231
France	1,108	973
England	1,019	1,055
China Mainland	876	546
Australia	761	726
Brazil*	551	584
Spain	378	333
Mexico*	364	261
Italy	361	329
Taiwan	348	350
Philippines*	273	236
South Korea	233	357
Sweden	230	245
Netherlands	220	220
Poland	213	200
Hong Kong	207	216
Russia	189	94
Argentina*	183	203
Malaysia	176	149
Austria	163	157

*Developmental Licensee market as of December 31, 2007.

Source: www.mcdonalds.com.

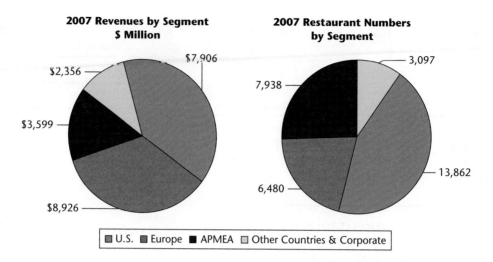

2007 Revenues by Segment $ Million

$7,906
$2,356
$3,599
$8,926

2007 Restaurant Numbers by Segment

3,097
7,938
13,862
6,480

☐ U.S. ▨ Europe ■ APMEA ☐ Other Countries & Corporate

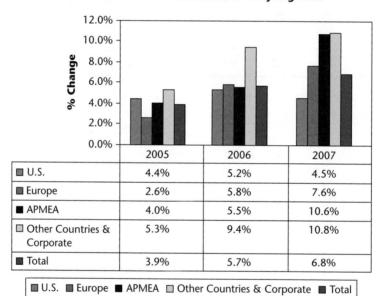

Sales Increase % by Segment

	2005	2006	2007
▨ U.S.	4.4%	5.2%	4.5%
▨ Europe	2.6%	5.8%	7.6%
■ APMEA	4.0%	5.5%	10.6%
☐ Other Countries & Corporate	5.3%	9.4%	10.8%
■ Total	3.9%	5.7%	6.8%

☐ U.S. ▨ Europe ■ APMEA ☐ Other Countries & Corporate ■ Total

Exhibit 11 McDonald's Financial Results by Segment
APMEA: Asia/Pacific, Middle East and Africa.

Source: www.mcdonalds.com

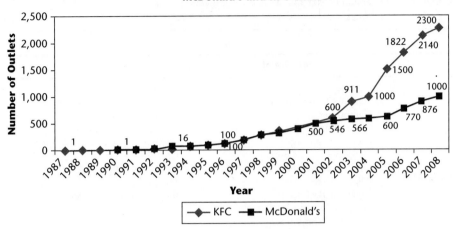

Exhibit 12 Historical Store Count

Source: McDonald's and Yum website. Various press releases and web articles.

Exhibit 13   Comparsion of McDonald's and KFC in-store Menu

	China	
	McDonald's	**KFC**
Main Meal	Big Mac Double Cheese Burger Hamburger Cheese Burger Beef 'N' Egg Burger McSpicy Chicken Burger McChicken Burger Fillet-O-Fish Vegetable Beef Burger McSpicy Chicken Twister Curry Chicken Burger Teriyaki Chicken Burger Double Mala Chicken Burger Spicy Teriyaki Chicken Burger	Buckets of Chicken New Orleans BBQ Chicken Burger Spicy Chicken Burger Crispy Chicken Burger Garden Crispy Chicken Burger Cod Fish Burger Mexican Chicken Twister Dragon Twister Spicy 'Saliva' Chicken Burger
Side Dishes/ Light Snacks	McNugget McSpicy Chicken Wings Sweet Corn in a Cup French Fries	Corn on a cob Mashed Potato Egg 'N' Vegetable Soup Vegetable Salad Corn Salad Carrot Bread Roll Chicken Kebab French Fries Chicken Nuggets Popcorn Chicken New Orleans BBQ Chicken Wings Original Recipe Chicken Spicy Chicken Wings Cod Fish Sticks
Breakfast	Big Breakfast Pancake Cheese'N'Egg Burger Pork McMuffin Orange Juice Fresh Milk	Crispy Chicken Burger (with egg) Cheese'N' Egg Burger Pork'N' Egg Burger Beef'N' Egg Porridge Chicken'N' Mushroom Porridge Preserved Egg'N' Lean Pork Porridge Egg'N' Pork Floss Twister Egg'N' Pork Twister Shrimp'N' Egg Twister Hong Kong Milk Tea Shrimp Spring Roll Orange Juice
Dessert	Sundae (Chocolate/Pineapple/Strawberry) Ice Cream Cone (Vanilla/Chocolate/Mixed/Crunchy) Milkshake (Chocolate/Strawberry)	Portuguese Egg Tart Sundae Ice Cream Cone Coffee/Irish Coffee Lemon Cola Pomelo Honey Tea

Shaded areas: local specialities.

Source: McDonald's and KFC China websites.

**China
McDonald's China Print Advertisement**

I just love not having a backbone

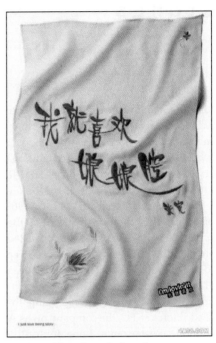

I just love being sissy

I just love fighting my teacher

McDonald's China TV Advertisement

Exhibit 14 McDonald's Advertisement

Appendix: KFC and McDonald's Global Milestones

KFC

At the start of the Great Depression in 1930, Harland Sanders opened his first restaurant in the small front room of a gas station in Corbin, Kentucky. He was made an honorary Kentucky colonel six years later in recognition of his contribution to the state's cuisine. The Original Recipe chicken, which was deep fried in a pressure cooker with 11 herbs and spices, was created in 1940. In 1969, the Kentucky Fried Chicken Corporation was listed on the New York Stock Exchange. In 1986, PepsiCo, Inc. acquired KFC from RJR Nabisco, Inc., and 11 years later, in 1997, PepsiCo, Inc. announced the spin-off of its quick service restaurants—KFC, Taco Bell and Pizza Hut. In 2002, the world's largest restaurant company changed its corporate name to Yum! Brands, Inc. In addition to KFC, the company owns A&W® All-American Food® Restaurants, Long John Silver's®, Pizza Hut® and Taco Bell® restaurants.

Management Philosophy

KFC's parent company, Yum! Brands, runs a multi-brand strategy and is proud of its customer focus approach. Its restaurant management philosophy is summarized by the acronym "CHAMPS"—cleanness, hospitality, accuracy, maintenance, product quality, and speed. After the first successful ten years, Yum! began looking to sustain long-term growth, especially on an international level. According to the Yum! 2008 management presentation, its four key growth strategies are to build leading brands in China in every significant category; drive aggressive international expansion and build strong brands everywhere; dramatically improve US brand positions, consistency and returns, and drive industry-leading, long-term shareholder and franchisee value.[69]

International Expansion

KFC's penetration of Asia started with Japan in 1970. In 1984, it entered Taiwan, awarding the franchise to a joint venture company formed by two Japanese companies and a local entity. A year later, it re-entered Hong Kong after a 10-year gap, by giving franchise rights to Birdland, which later acquired the franchisee in Taiwan. From 1996 to 2001,

Yum! Brands tried to win back ownership in the Greater China area by launching new KFC outlets in Taiwan in tandem with Birdland's operations, until finally in 2001, Birdland agreed to sell its KFC outlets in Taiwan to Yum! Brands. These experiences in Asian markets prepared Yum! Brands for its entry in 1987 into the largest and most exciting market in the world—China.[70]

McDonald's

The McDonald's concept was introduced in Southern California by Dick and Mac McDonald in 1937. In 1953, the McDonald brothers franchised their restaurant to Neil Fox, the first franchisee. The second McDonald's opened in Fresno, California—the first to feature the Golden Arches design. The fast-food idea was modified and expanded by their business partner Ray Kroc, of Oak Park, Illinois, who later bought out business interest of the McDonald brothers in the concept and went on to found McDonald's Corporation in 1955. In 1965, McDonald's went public with the company's first offering on the stock exchange. Twenty years later, in 1985, McDonald's was added to the 30-company Dow Jones Industrial Average.

The signature product, the Big Mac, was added to the product line in 1968 and was the brainchild of Jim Delligatti, one of Ray Kroc's earliest franchisees. Another popular product—the Happy Meal—has been making children's visits special since 1979.[71] McDonald's has become a global phenomenon, with more than 31,000 outlets operating in over 100 countries today.

Management Philosophy

Like KFC, McDonald's values were consumer driven. Its principles were summarized by QSCV. Quality, Service, Cleanness and Value. McDonald's was also known for the consistency of its procedures and quality, and its powerful global marketing campaigns. Its recent advertising campaign "i'm lovin' it",™ launched in every country in the world by September 2005, featured sports, entertainment, music, and fashion. Pop icons such as Justin Timberlake, Destiny's Child, and Wang Lee Hom for Asia were central to the campaign.

McDonald's was also known for its detail-oriented insistence on food preparation. Fred Turner, Senior Chairman of McDonald's, developed the first operations manual in 1957. By 1991, it counted 750 detailed pages, setting out exact cooking times, proper temperature settings, and precise portions for all food items. For example, French fries were to be 9/32 of an inch; to ensure quality and taste, no products were to be held more than 10 minutes in the transfer bin.[72]

Peter Tan, former Senior Vice President and President of McDonald's Corporation Greater China, attributed McDonald's success to the fact that it provided consistency, convenience in terms of location, and good pricing. Great advertising, great taste in signature products such as Big Mac and French fries, and retail excitement such as Happy Meal promotions also played important roles.[73]

International Expansion

In 1967, the first McDonald's restaurant outside the United States opened in Richmond, British Columbia. In 1971, the first Asian McDonald's opened in Japan, in Tokyo's Ginza district. Although McDonald's opened its first outlet in greater China in Hong Kong as early as 1975, and Taiwan opened its first McDonald's in 1984, the first Mainland China McDonald's outlet was only introduced in October 1990 in Shenzhen. On 23 April 1992, the world's largest McDonald's opened in Beijing, China with over 700 seats.[74] In 1994, McDonald's made an historical debut in Kuwait City, and in 1996 the fast-food giant entered India.

Bibliography

1. *Transcript: Interview with Joseph Han, former Operating Vice President of Yum! Brands, greater China*, 2 November, 2007.
2. *Transcript: Interview with Peter Tan, former Senior Vice President and President of McDonald's Corporation*, Greater China, 20 March 2008 and 18 July 2008.
3. *KFC in China Secret Recipe for Success*, by Warren K. Liu, 2008, John Wiley & Sons (Asia) Pte Ltd.
4. *McDonald's and KFC*, edited by B.Q. Chen, China Economy Publishing, 2005.
5. *Globalization of Services: Some Implications for Theory and Practice*, Yair Aharoni, Lilach Nachum. Routledge, 2000.
6. *Kentucky Fried Chicken in China*, Professor Allen J. Morrison and Paul W. Beamish, Richard Ivey School of Business, The University of Western Ontario, Version(A) 1993-08-18.
7. www.mcdonalds.com.
8. www.yum.com.
9. *Shantel Wong; McDonald's China Development Co.*, Advertising Age, January, 2004.
10. *KFC and McDonald's—a model of blended culture*, China Today, June 2004.
11. *Hamburger heaven*, Economist, February 2005.
12. *McDonald's China Development Co.*, Advertising Age, 00018899, 1/26/2004, Vol. 75, Issue 4.
13. *McDonald's considers reform to adapt to Chinese tastes*, Xinhuanet, November 9, 2005.
14. *Fast Food Domination*, Chinese International Business, April 2007.
15. *Adapt Franchise to China's Soil: China's Regulations on Franchise in the Past Ten Years*, The Illinois Business Law Journal, 29 March 2007.
16. *McDonald's in China*, ICFAI Business School, 2003.
17. *McDonald's enter into puzzledom, what's its outlet?* December 2005, Chinese and Foreign Corporate Culture.
18. *McDonald's*, Harvard Business School Review: April 3, 2008.
19. *SW China begins dialogues with UK on food safety*, People's Daily online, March 23, 2005.
20. *Franchising Opportunities in China for American Fast Food Restaurants*, Zerong Yu, Karl Titz, Asia Pacific Journal of Tourism Research, Volume 5 Issue 1, 2000.
21. *2007 National Economic and Social Development Statistic Report*, Ministry of Commerce, People's Republic of China, http://provincedata.mofcom.gov.cn/communique/disp.asp?pid=43705.
22. *Rivals to feel bite from Burger King*, Janet Ong, June 28, 2005, Bloomberg.
23. *McDonald's Corporation (Abridged)*, Harvard Business School, Rev: June 16, 2005.

24. *Yum Brands CEO says poor performance at KFC, higher costs have taken 'fun' from US business*, Bruce Schreiner, July 17, 2008, Canadian Business Online.
25. *China Fast Food Analysis*, Just-food.com, Aroq Ltd., 2007.
26. *McDonald's opens 100th China store, sees 175 more in 2009*, http://www.forbes.com/feeds/afx/2008/ll/14/afx5693724.html.
27. *McDonald's Growing in China*, Liu Jie, China Daily, 2008-09-08 10:27, http://www.chinadaily.com.cn/bizchina/2008-09/08/content_7007412.htm.
28. Fast food nation, Ding Qing-Fen, China Daily, 30th June 2008.

End Notes

1. www.mcdonalds.com, www.yum.com, end of 2008 data.
2. www.mcdonalds.com.
3. McDonald's and KFC, edited by B.Q. Chen, China Economy Publishing, 2005.
4. Warren K. Liu, KFC in China—Secret Recipe for Success, John Wiley & Sons (Asia) pte Ltd., 2008.
5. Ibid.
6. Hamburger heaven, *Economist*, February 2005.
7. www.yum.com, Q3 2008.
8. Yair Aharoni, Lilach Nachum. Routledge, *Globalization of Services: Some Implication for Theory and Practice*, 2000.
9. Zerong Yu, Karl Titz, Franchising Opportunities in China for American Fast Food Restaurant, *Asia Pacific Journal of Tourism Research*, Volume 5 Issue 1, 2000.
10. China National Statistics Bureau, 2007.
11. 2007 National Economic and Social Development Statistics Report. Ministry of Commerce, People's Republic of China, http://provincedata.mofcom.gov.cn/communique/disp.asp?pid=43705.
12. Op Cit. Hamburger heaven.
13. Ibid.
14. China Fast Food Analysis, Just-food.com, Aroq.Ltd., 2007.
15. Fast Food Domination, *Chinese International Business*, April 2007.
16. Adapt Franchise to China's Soil: China's Regulations on Franchise in the Past Ten Years, *The Illinois Business Law Journal*, 29th March 2007.
17. International Monetary Fund—2008 World Economic Outlook.
18. Fast food nation, Ding Qing-Fen, *China Daily*, 30th June 2008.
19. Op Cit. KFC in China—Secret Recipe for Success.
20. Ibid.
21. www.yum.com.
22. Op Cit. KFC in China—Secret Recipe for Success.
23. www.yum.com.
24. Kentucky Fried Chicken in China, Professor Allen J. Morrison and Paul W. Beamish, Richard Ivey School of Business, The University of Western Ontario, 1993.
25. Op Cit. Kentucky Fried Chicken in China.
26. Op Cit. KFC in China—Secret Recipe for Success.
27. Interview with Joseph Han, former operating Vice President of Yum! Brands, Greater China, 2 November, 2007.
28. Op Cit. KFC China—Secret Recipe for Success.
29. Hazard Analysis and Critical Control Points, a systematic preventive approach to food safety and pharmaceutical safety. The Food and Drug Administration (FDA) and the United States Department of Agriculture (USDA) use mandatory juice, seafood, meat and poultry HACCP programmes as an effective approach to food safety and protecting public health.
30. Op Cit. KFC in China—Secret Recipe for Success.
31. Ibid.

32. Interview with Warren Liu, former Vice President of Yum! Brands, Greater China, 30 January, 2009.
33. Op Cit. KFC in China—Secret Recipe for Success.
34. Ibid.
35. Op Cit. KFC and McDonald's—a model of blended culture.
36. Op Cit. Interview with Joseph Han.
37. Op Cit. KFC in China—Secret Recipe for Success.
38. Op Cit. McDonald's and KFC.
39. www.yum.com.
40. Op Cit. McDonald's and KFC.
41. Op Cit. McDonald's in China.
42. Shantel Wong; McDonald's China Development Co., *Advertising Age*, January 2004.
43. McDonald's enters into puzzledom, what's its outlet? December 2005, Chinese and Foreign Corporate Culture.
44. Op Cit. McDonald's and KFC.
45. Interview with Peter Tan, former senior vice president and president of McDonald's Corporation, Greater China, 20 March 2008.
46. Op Cit. McDonald's in China.
47. McD's Preps for China Drive-Thru Boom, The Associated Press, January 19, 2007.
48. McDonald's opens 1,000th China store, sees 175 more in 2009, Thomson Financial News, http://www.forbes.com/feeds/afx/2008/11/14/afx5693724.html.
49. Op Cit. McDonald's in China.
50. Op Cit. KFC and McDonald's—a model of blended culture.
51. McDonald's considers reform to adapt to Chinese tastes, *Xinhuanet*, November 9, 2005.
52. Op Cit. Interview with Peter Tan.
53. McDonald's Growing in China, Liu Jie, *China Daily*, September 8, 2008, http://www.chinadaily.com.cn/bizchina/2008-09/08/content_7007412.htm.
54. Op Cit. McDonald's in China.
55. Ibid.
56. McDonalds's goes slow in China franchising, *International Herald Tribune*. February 7, 2007.
57. McDonald's Corporation Annual Report 2007.
58. McDonald's, Harvard Business School, Rev: April 3, 2008.
59. Op Cit. McDonald's enters into puzzledom, what's its outlet?
60. McDonald's to issue franchise licenses slowly, *Shenzhen Daily*, February 9, 2007.
61. McDonald's Press Release, December 10, 2005.
62. http://www.mcdonalds.com.cn/news/news_content.aspx?id=123.
63. McDonald's Corporation Annual Report 2007.
64. McDonald's growing in China, *China Daily*, September 8, 2008.
65. Yum Brands CEO says poor performance at KFC, higher costs have taken "fun" from US business, Bruce Schreiner, July 17, 2008, *Canadian Business Online*.
66. Stricter standards needed, Liu Jie, *China Daily*, 2006-03-16 http://www.chinadaily.com.cn/bizchina/2006-03/16/content_539721.htm.
67. SW China begins dialogues with UK on food safety, *People's Daily Online*, March 23, 2005.
68. Rivals to feel bite from Burger King, Janet Ong, June 28, 2005, Bloomberg.
69. Presentations for Investor and Analysts Conference, May 2008, www.yum.com.
70. Op Cit. KFC in China—Secret Recipe for Success.
71. www.mcdonalds.com.
72. McDonald's Corporation (Abridged), Harvard Business School Review: June 16, 2005.
73. Interview with Peter Tan, former senior vice president and president of McDonald's Corporation, Greater China, 20 March 2008.
74. McDonald's In China, ICFAI Business School, Case Development Center.

Appendix

Analyzing Cases and Preparing for Class Discussions

This book, properly understood, is really about how to analyze cases. Just reading the book, however, is no more likely to fully develop one's skills as a strategist than reading a book about golf will make one a golfer. Practice in applying the concepts and tools is essential. Cases provide the opportunity for this necessary practice.

Why the Case Method?

The core of many strategic management courses is the case method of instruction. Under the case method, you will study and discuss the real-world challenges and dilemmas that face managers in firms. Cases are typically accounts of situations that a firm or manager has faced at a given point in time. By necessity, cases do not possess the same degree of complexity that a manager faces in the real world, but they do provide a concrete set of facts that suggest challenges and opportunities that real managers have faced. Very few cases have clear answers. The case method encourages you to engage problems directly and propose solutions or strategies in the face of incomplete information. To succeed at the case method, you must develop the capability to analyze and synthesize data that are sometimes ambiguous and conflicting. You must be able to prioritize issues and opportunities and make decisions in the face of ambiguous and incomplete information. Finally, you must be able to persuade others to adopt your point of view.

In an applied field like strategic management, the real test of learning is how well you can apply knowledge to real-world situations. Strategic management cases offer you the opportunity to develop judgment and wisdom in applying your conceptual knowledge. By applying the concepts you have learned to the relatively unstructured information in a case, you develop judgment in applying concepts. Alfred North Whitehead discussed the importance of application to knowledge:

> *This discussion rejects the doctrine that students should first learn passively, and then, having learned, should apply knowledge. . . . For the very meaning of the things known is wrapped up in their relationship beyond themselves. This unapplied knowledge is knowledge shorn of its meaning.*

Alfred North Whitehead (1947). *Essays in Science and Philosophy.* New York: Philosophical Library, Inc. pp. 218–219.

Thus, you gain knowledge as you apply concepts. With the case method, you do not passively absorb wisdom imparted from your instructor, but actively develop it as you wrestle with the real-world situations described in the cases.

How to Analyze Cases

Before discussing how to analyze a case, it may be useful to comment on how *not* to prepare a case. We see two common failings in case preparation that often go hand-in-hand. First, students often do not apply conceptual frameworks in a rigorous and systematic manner. Second, many students do not devote sufficient time to reading, analyzing, and discussing a case before class. Many students succumb to the temptation to quickly read a case and latch on to the most visible issues that present themselves. Thus, they come to class prepared to make only a few superficial observations about a case. Often, they entirely miss the deeper issues around why a firm is in the situation that it is in and how it can better its performance. Applying the frameworks systematically may take more time and effort in the beginning, but it will generally lead to deeper insights about the cases and a more profound understanding of the concepts in the chapters. As you gain experience in this systematic approach to analyzing cases, many of you will find that your preparation time will decrease. This appendix offers a framework that will assist you as you analyze cases. The framework is important, but no framework can substitute for hard work. There are no great shortcuts to analyzing cases, and there is no single right method for preparing a case. The following approach, however, may help you develop your ability to analyze cases.

1. **Skim through the case very quickly.** Pay particular attention to the exhibits. The objective in this step is to gain familiarity with the broad facts of the case. What apparent challenges or opportunities does the company face? What information is provided? You may find it especially useful to focus on the first and last few paragraphs of the case in this step.

2. **Read the case more carefully and make notes, underline, etc.** What appear to be important facts? The conceptual frameworks in the chapters will be essential in helping you identify the key facts. Throughout the course, you will want to address central questions such as the following:
   - What is the firm's performance?
   - What is the firm's mission? strategy? goals?
   - What are the resources involved in the firm's value chain? How do they compare to competitors on cost and differentiation?
   - Does the firm have a competitive advantage?
   - Are the firm's advantages and disadvantages temporary or sustainable?
   - What is the value of the firm's resources?
   - Are the firm's resources rare?
   - Are the firm's resources costly to imitate?
   - Is the firm organized sufficiently to exploit its resources?

   Depending on the case, you may also want to consider other frameworks and questions, where appropriate. Each chapter provides concepts and frameworks that you may want to consider. For example:
   - What are the five forces? How do they influence industry opportunities and threats? (Chapter 2)
   - What are the sources of cost differences in an industry? (Chapter 4)
   - What are the bases and potential bases for product differentiation in an industry? (Chapter 5)

Each chapter suggests more specific questions and concepts than those above. You will want to consider these concepts in detail. In some cases, the instructor may offer direction about which concepts to apply to a given case. In other instances, you may be left to use your judgment in choosing which concepts to focus on in analyzing a case.

3. **Define the basic issues.** This is perhaps the most important step and also the stage of analysis that requires the most wisdom and judgment. Cases are rarely like tidy problem sets where the issues or problems are explicitly stated and the tools needed to address those issues are prescribed. Generally, you need to determine what the key issues are. In doing this, it may help for you to begin by asking: What are the fundamental issues in the case? Which concepts matter most in providing insight into those issues? One trap to avoid in defining basic issues is doing what some decision-making scholars label "plunging-in," which is drawing conclusions without first thinking about the crux of the issues involved in a decision.[1] Many students have a tendency to seize the first issues that are prominently mentioned in a case. As an antidote to this trap, you may want to consider a case from the perspective of different conceptual frames.

4. **Develop and elaborate your analysis of the key issues.** As with all of the steps, there is no substitute for painstaking work in this stage. You need to take the key issues you have defined in Step 3, examine the facts that you have noted in Step 2, and assess what are the key facts. What does quantitative analysis reveal? Here it is not just ratio analysis that we are concerned with. Just as body temperature, blood pressure, and pulse rate may reveal something about a person's health but little about the causes of a sickness, ratio analysis typically tells us more about the health of a company than the causes of its performance. You should assemble facts and analysis to support your point of view. Opinions unsupported by factual evidence and analysis are generally not persuasive. This stage of the analysis involves organizing the facts in the case. You will want to develop specific hypotheses about what factors relate to success in a particular setting. Often, you will find it helpful to draw diagrams to clarify your thinking.

5. **Draw conclusions and formulate a set of recommendations.** You may be uncomfortable drawing conclusions and making recommendations because you do not have complete information. This is an eternal dilemma for managers. Managers who wait for complete information to do something, however, usually act too late. Nevertheless, you should strive to do the most complete analysis that you can under reasonable time constraints. Recommendations should also flow naturally from your analysis. Too often, students formulate their recommendations in an ad hoc way. In formulating recommendations, you should be clear about priorities and the sequence of actions that you recommend.

6. **Prepare for class discussion.** Students who diligently work through the first five steps and rigorously examine a case should be well prepared for class discussion. You may find it helpful to make some notes and bring them to class. Over the years, we have observed that many of the students who are low contributors to class discussions bring few or no notes to class. Once in class, a case discussion usually begins with a provocative question from the instructor.

---

[1] J. E. Russo and P. J. H. Schoemaker (1989). *Decision Traps: The Ten Barriers to Brilliant Decision-Making and How to Overcome Them.* New York: Fireside.

Many instructors will "cold call"—direct a question to a specific student who has not been forewarned. Students who have thoroughly analyzed and discussed the case before coming to class will be much better prepared for these surprise calls. They will also be better prepared to contribute to the analysis, argument, and persuasion that will take place in the class discussion. Discussions can move rapidly. You will hear new insights from fellow students. Preparation helps you to absorb, learn, and contribute to the insights that emerge from class discussion.

Summary

Students who embark in the case method soon learn that analyzing cases is a complex process. Having a clear conceptual approach such as the VRIO framework does not eliminate the complexity. This systematic approach, however, does allow the analyst to manage the complexity of real-world business situations. In the end, though, neither cases nor real-world businesses conclude their analyses with tidy solutions that resolve all the uncertainties and ambiguities a business faces. However, the case method coupled with a good theory such as the VRIO approach and hard work do make it more likely that you will generate valuable insights into the strategic challenges of firms and develop the strategic skills needed to lead a firm.

Glossary

above average accounting performance when a firm's accounting performance is greater than the industry average

above normal economic performance when a firm earns above its cost of capital

absorptive capacity the ability of firms to learn

accounting performance a measure of a firm's competitive advantage; calculated from information in the firm's published profit-and-loss and balance sheet statements

accounting ratios numbers taken from a firm's financial statements that are manipulated in ways that describe various aspects of the firm's performance

acquisition a firm purchases another firm

acquisition premium the difference between the current market price of a target firm's shares and the price a potential acquirer offers to pay for those shares

activity ratios accounting ratios that focus on the level of activity in a firm's business

adverse selection an alliance partner promises to bring to an alliance certain resources that it either does not control or cannot acquire

agency problems parties in an agency relationship differ in their decision-making objectives

agency relationship one party to an exchange delegates decision-making authority to a second party

agent a party to whom decision-making authority is delegated

architectural competence the ability of a firm to use organizational structure and other organizing mechanisms to facilitate coordination among scientific disciplines to conduct research

auction in mergers and acquisitions, a mechanism for establishing the price of an asset when multiple firms bid for a single target firm

audit committee sub-group of the board of directors responsible for ensuring the accuracy of accounting and financial statements

average accounting performance when a firm's accounting performance is equal to the industry average

backward vertical integration a firm incorporates more stages of the value chain within its boundaries and those stages bring it closer to gaining access to raw materials

barriers to entry attributes of an industry's structure that increase the cost of entry

below average accounting performance when a firm's accounting performance is less than the industry average

below normal economic performance when a firm earns less than its cost of capital

board of directors a group of 10 to 15 individuals drawn from a firm's top management and from people outside the firm whose primary responsibilities are to monitor decisions made in the firm and to ensure that they are consistent with the interests of outside equity holders

business angels wealthy individuals who act as outside investors typically in an entrepreneurial firm

business cycle the alternating pattern of prosperity followed by recession followed by prosperity

business-level strategies actions firms take to gain competitive advantages in a single market or industry

business plan a document that summarizes how an entrepreneur will organize a firm to exploit an opportunity, along with the economic implications of exploiting that opportunity

business strategy a firm's theory of how to gain competitive advantage in a single business or industry

buyers those who purchase a firm's products or services

capabilities a subset of a firm's resources, defined as tangible and intangible assets, that enable a firm to take full advantage of other resources it controls

cashing out the compensation paid to an entrepreneur for risk-taking associated with starting a firm

causally ambiguous imitating firms do not understand the relationship between the resources and capabilities controlled by a firm and that firm's competitive advantage

centralized hub each country in which a firm operates is organized as a full profit-and-loss division headed by a division general manager; strategic and operational decisions are retained at headquarters

chairman of the board the person who presides over the board of directors; may or may not be the same person as a firm's senior executive

chief executive officer (CEO) person to whom all functional managers report in a U-form organization; the person to whom all divisional personal and corporate staff report to in an M-form organization

chief executive officer (CEO) (duties of) strategy formulation and implementation

chief operating officer (COO) (duties of) strategy implementation

closely held firm a firm that has not sold many of its shares on the public stock market

collusion two or more firms in an industry coordinate their strategic choices to reduce competition in that industry

compensation policies the ways that firms pay employees

competitive advantage a firm creates more economic value than rival firms

competitive disadvantage   a firm generates less economic value than rival firms

competitive dynamics   how one firm responds to the strategic actions of competing firms

competitive parity   a firm creates the same economic value as rival firms

competitor   any firm, group, or individual trying to reduce a firm's competitive advantage

complementary resources and capabilities   resources and capabilities that have limited ability to generate competitive advantage in isolation but in combination with other resources can enable a firm to realize its full potential for competitive advantage

complementor   the value of a firm's products increases in the presence of another firm's products

conglomerate merger   a merger or acquisition where there are no vertical, horizontal, product extension, or market extension links between the firms

consolidation strategy   strategy that reduces the number of firms in an industry by exploiting economies of scale

controlling share   when an acquiring firm purchases enough of a target firm's assets to be able to make all the management and strategic decisions in the target firm

coordinated federation   each country in which a firm operates is organized as a full profit-and-loss division headed by a division general manager; operational decisions are delegated to these divisions or countries, but strategic decisions are retained at headquarters

core competence   the collective learning in an organization, especially how to coordinate diverse production skills and integrate multiple streams of technologies

corporate diversification strategy   when a firm operates in multiple industries or markets simultaneously

corporate-level strategies   actions firms take to gain competitive advantages by operating in multiple markets or industries simultaneously

corporate spin-off   exists when a large, typically diversified firm divests itself of a business in which it has historically been operating and the divested business operates as an independent entity

corporate staff   upper level managers who provide information about a firm's external and internal environments to the firm's senior executive

corporate strategy   a firm's theory of how to gain competitive advantage by operating in several businesses simultaneously

cost centers   divisions are assigned a budget and manage their operations to that budget

cost leadership business strategy   focuses on gaining advantages by reducing costs below those of competitors

cost of capital   the rate of return that a firm promises to pay its suppliers of capital to induce them to invest in a firm

cost of debt   the interest that a firm must pay its debt holders to induce them to lend money to the firm

cost of equity   the rate of return a firm must promise its equity holders to induce them to invest in the firm

countertrade   international firms receiving payment for the products or services they sell into a country, not in the form of currency, but in the form of other products or services that they can sell on the world market

crown jewel sale   a bidding firm is interested in just a few of the most highly regarded businesses being operated by the target firm, known as its *crown jewels*, and the target firm sells these businesses

culture   the values, beliefs, and norms that guide behavior in a society and in a firm

cumulative abnormal return (CAR)   performance that is greater (or less) than what was expected in a short period of time around when an acquisition is announced

current market value   the price of each of a firm's shares multiplied by the number of shares outstanding

customer-switching costs   customers make investments in order to use a firm's particular products or services that are not useful in using other firms' products

debt   capital from banks and bondholders

decentralized federation   each country in which a firm operates is organized as a full profit-and-loss division headed by a division general manager and strategic and operational decisions are delegated to these country managers

decline   the final phase of the product life cycle during which demand drops off when a technologically superior product or service is introduced

declining industry   an industry that has experienced an absolute decline in unit sales over a sustained period of time

deep-pockets model   a firm that takes advantage of its monopoly power in one business to subsidize several different businesses

demographics   the distribution of individuals in a society in terms of age, sex, marital status, income, ethnicity, and other personal attributes that may determine their buying patterns

depression   a severe recession that lasts for several years

direct duplication   the attempt to imitate other firms by developing resources that have the same strategic effects as the resources controlled by those other firms

diseconomies of scale   a firm's costs begin to rise as a function of the volume of production

distinctive competence   a valuable and rare resource or capability

distribution agreement   one firm agrees to distribute the products of others

diversification economies   sources of relatedness in a diversified firm

divestment   a firm sells a business in which it had been operating

division   each business that a firm engages in, also called strategic business units (SBUs) or business group

dominant-business firms   firms with between 70 percent and 95 percent of their total sales in a single product market

dominant logic   common theory of how to gain competitive advantages shared by each business in a diversified firm

economic climate   the overall health of the economic systems within which a firm operates

economic measures of competitive advantage   measures that compare a firm's level of return to its cost of capital instead of to the average level of return in the industry

economic value   the difference between the perceived benefits gained by a customer who purchases a firm's products or services and the full economic cost of these products or services

economic value added (EVA)   worth calculated by subtracting the cost of the capital employed in a division from that division's earnings

economies of scale   the per unit cost of production falls as the volume of production increases

economies of scope   the value of a firm's products or services increases as a function of the number of different businesses in which that firm operates

emerging industries   newly created or newly re-created industries formed by technological innovations, change in demand, or the emergence of new customer needs

emergent strategies   theories of how to gain competitive advantage in an industry that emerge over time or have been radically reshaped once they are initially implemented

environmental threat   any individual, group, or organization outside a firm that seeks to reduce the level of that firm's performance

equity   capital from individuals and institutions that purchase a firm's stocks

equity alliance   cooperating firms supplement contracts with equity holdings in alliance partners

escalation of commitment   an increased commitment by managers to an incorrect course of action, even as its limitations become manifest

event study analysis   evaluates the performance effects of acquisitions for bidding firms

executive committee   typically consists of the CEO and two or three functional senior managers

explicit collusion   firms directly communicate with each other to coordinate levels of production, prices, and so forth (illegal in most countries)

external analysis   identification and examination of the critical threats and opportunities in a firm's competitive environment

finance committee   subgroup of the board of directors that maintains the relationship between the firm and external capital markets

financial resources   all the money, from whatever source, that firms use to conceive and implement strategies

firm-specific human capital investments   investments made by employees in a particular firm over time, including understanding the culture, policies, and procedures and knowing the people to contact to complete a task, that have limited value in other firms

firm-specific investments   the value of stakeholders' investments in a particular firm is much greater than the value those same investments would be in other firms

first-mover advantages   advantages that come to firms that make important strategic and technological decisions early in the development of an industry

five forces framework   identifies the five most common threats faced by firms in their local competitive environments and the conditions under which these threats are more or less likely to be present; these forces are the threat of entry, of rivalry, of substitutes, of buyers, and of suppliers

flexibility   how costly it is for a firm to alter its strategic and organizational decisions

foreign direct investment   investing in operations located in a foreign country

formal management controls   a firm's budgeting and reporting activities that keep people higher up in a firm's organizational chart informed about the actions taken by people lower down in the organizational chart

formal reporting structure   a description of who in the organization reports to whom

forward vertical integration   a firm incorporates more stages of the value chain within its boundaries and those stages bring it closer to interacting directly with final customers

fragmented industries   industries in which a large number of small or medium-sized firms operate and no small set of firms has dominant market share or creates dominant technologies

free cash flow   the amount of cash a firm has to invest after all positive net present-value investments in its ongoing businesses have been funded

friendly acquisition   the management of a target firm wants the firm to be acquired

functional manager   a manager who leads a particular function within a firm, such as manufacturing, marketing, finance, accounting, or sales

functional organizational structure   the structure a firm uses to implement business-level strategies it might pursue where each function in the firm reports to the CEO

general environment   broad trends in the context within which a firm operates that can have an impact on a firm's strategic choices

generic business strategies   another name for business-level strategies, which are cost leadership and product differentiation

geographic market diversification strategy   when a firm operates in multiple geographic markets simultaneously

golden parachutes   incentive compensation paid to senior managers if the firm they manage is acquired

greenmail a target firm's management purchases any of the target firm's stock owned by a bidder for a price that is greater than its current market value

growth the second stage of the product life cycle during which demand increases rapidly, and many new firms enter to begin producing the product or service

hard currencies currencies that are traded globally, and thus have value on international money markets

harvest strategy a firm engages in a long, systematic, phased withdrawal from a declining industry, extracting as much value as possible

hedonic price that part of the price of a product or service that is attributable to a particular characteristic of that product or service

holdup one firm makes more transaction-specific investments in an exchange than partner firms make and the firm that has not made these investments tries to exploit the firm that has made the investments

horizontal merger a firm acquires a former competitor

hostile takeover the management of a target firm does not want the firm to be acquired

human capital resources the training, experience, judgment, intelligence, relationships, and insight of individual managers and workers in a firm

human resources includes the training, experience, judgment, intelligence, relationships, and insight of *individual* managers and workers in a firm

imperfectly imitable resources and capabilities that are more costly for other firms to imitate, compared to firms that already possess them

increasing returns to scale in network industries, the value of a product or service increases as the number of people using those products or services increases

inelastic in supply the quantity of supply is fixed and does not respond to price increases, such as the total supply of land, which is relatively fixed and cannot be significantly increased in response to higher demand and prices

informal management controls include a firm's culture and the willingness of employees to monitor each others' behavior

initial public offering (IPO) the initial sale of stock of a privately held firm or a division of a corporation to the general public

institutional owners pension funds, corporations, and others that invest other peoples' money in firm equities

intermediate products or services products or services produced in one division that are used as inputs for products or services produced by a second division

internal analysis identification of a firm's organizational strengths and weaknesses and of the resources and capabilities that are likely to be sources of competitive advantage

internal capital market when businesses in a diversified firm compete for corporate capital

international strategies operations in multiple geographic markets: vertical integration, diversification, the formation of strategic alliances, or implementation of mergers and acquisitions, all across national borders

introduction the first stage of a product's life cycle when relatively few firms are producing a product, there are relatively few customers, and the rate of growth in demand for the product is relatively low

invented competencies illusory inventions by creative managers to justify poor diversification moves by linking intangible core competencies to completely unrelated businesses

joint venture cooperating firms create a legally independent firm in which they invest and from which they share any profits that are created

learning curve a concept that formalizes the relationship between cumulative volumes of production and falling per unit costs

learning race both parties to an alliance seek to learn from each other, but the rate at which these two firms learn varies; the first party to learn "wins" the race and may withdraw from the alliance

legal and political conditions the laws and the legal system's impact on business, together with the general nature of the relationship between government and business

leverage ratios accounting ratios that focus on the level of a firm's financial flexibility

licensing agreement one firm allows others to use its brand name to sell products in return for some fee or percentage of profits

limited corporate diversification all or most of a firm's business activities fall within a single industry and geographic market

liquidity ratios accounting ratios that focus on the ability of a firm to meet its short-term financial obligations

local responsiveness in an international strategy, the ability a firm has to respond to the consumer preferences in a particular geographic market

management control systems a range of formal and informal mechanisms to ensure that managers are behaving in ways consistent with a firm's strategies

managerial hubris the unrealistic belief held by managers in bidding firms that they can manage the assets of a target firm more efficiently than the target firm's current management

managerial know-how the often taken-for-granted knowledge and information that are needed to compete in an industry on a day-to-day basis

managerial perquisites activities that do not add economic value to the firm but directly benefit the managers who make them

managerial risk aversion   managers unable to diversify their firm-specific human capital investments may engage in less risky business decisions than what would be preferred by equity holders

market extension merger   firms make acquisitions in new geographical markets

market for corporate control   the market that is created when multiple firms actively seek to acquire one or several firms

market leader   the firm with the largest market share in an industry

matrix structures   one employee reports to two or more people

mature industries   an industry in which, over time, ways of doing business have become widely understood, technologies have diffused through competitors, and the rate of innovation in new products and technologies drops

maturity   third phase of the product life cycle during which the number of firms producing a product or service remains stable, demand growth levels off, and firms direct their investment efforts toward refining the process by which a product or service is created and away from developing entirely new products

merger   the assets of two similar-sized firms are combined

M-form   an organizational structure for implementing a corporate diversification strategy whereby each business a firm engages in is managed through a separate profit-and-loss division

mission   a firm's long-term purpose

mission statement   written statement defining both what a firm aspires to be in the long run and what it wants to avoid in the meantime

monopolistic competition   a market structure where within the market niche defined by a firm's differentiated product, a firm possesses a monopoly

monopolistic industries   industries that consist of only a single firm

monopolistically competitive industries   industries in which there are large numbers of competing firms and low-cost entry and exit, but products are not homogeneous with respect to cost or product attributes; firms are said to enjoy a "monopoly" in that part of the market they dominate

moral hazard   partners in an exchange possess high-quality resources and capabilities of significant value to the exchange but fail to make them available to the other partners

multinational opportunities   opportunities for a firm to operate simultaneously in several national or regional markets but the operations are independent of each other

mutual forbearance   a form of tacit collusion whereby firms tacitly agree to not compete in one industry in order to avoid competition in a second industry

network industries   industries in which a single technical standard and increasing returns to scale tend to dominate; competition in these industries tends to focus on which of several competing standards will be chosen

new entrants   firms that have either recently begun operations in an industry or that threaten to begin operations in an industry soon

niche strategy   a firm reduces its scope of operations and focuses on narrow segments of a declining industry

nominating committee   sub-group of the board of directors that nominates new board members

nonequity alliance   cooperating firms agree to work together to develop, manufacture, or sell products or services, but they do not take equity positions in each other or form an independent organizational unit to manage the cooperative efforts

normal economic performance   a firm earns its cost of capital

objectives   specific, measurable targets a firm can use to evaluate the extent to which it is realizing its mission

office of the president   together, the roles of chairman of the board, CEO, and COO

oligopolies   industries characterized by a small number of competing firms, by homogeneous products, and by costly entry and exit

operational economies of scope   shared activities and shared core competencies in a diversified firm

operations committee   typically meets monthly and usually consists of the CEO and each of the heads of the functional areas included in the firm

opportunism   a firm is unfairly exploited in an exchange

organizational chart   a depiction of the formal reporting structure within a firm

organizational resources   a firm's formal reporting structure; its formal and informal planning, controlling, and coordinating systems; its culture and reputation; and informal relations among groups within a firm and between a firm and those in its environment

Pac Man defense   fending off an acquisition by a firm acquiring the firm or firms bidding for it

path dependence   events early in the evolution of a process have significant effects on subsequent events

pecuniary economies   sources of relatedness in market power between bidding and target firms

perfectly competitive industry   when there are large numbers of competing firms, the products being sold are homogeneous with respect to cost and product attributes, and entry and exit are very low cost

personnel and compensation committee   sub-group of the board of directors that evaluates and compensates the performance of a firm's senior executive and other senior managers

physical resources   all the physical technology used in a firm

poison pills a variety of actions that target firm managers can take to make the acquisition of the target prohibitively expensive

policy choices choices firms make about the kinds of products or services they will sell—choices that have an impact on relative cost and product differentiation position

policy of experimentation exists when firms are committed to engage in several related product differentiation efforts simultaneously

predatory pricing setting prices so that they are less than a business's costs

price takers where the price of the products or services a firm sells is determined by market conditions and not by the decisions of firms

principal the party who delegates the decision-making authority

privately held a firm that has stock that is not traded on public stock markets and that is not a division of a larger company

processes the activities a firm engages in to design, produce, and sell its products or services

process innovation a firm's effort to refine and improve its current processes

process manufacturing when manufacturing is accomplished in a continuous system; examples include manufacturing in chemical, oil refining, and paper and pulp industries

product differentiation a business strategy whereby firms attempt to gain a competitive advantage by increasing the perceived value of their products or services relative to the perceived value of other firms' products or services

product diversification strategy a firm operates in multiple industries simultaneously

product extension merger firms acquire complementary products through merger and acquisition activities

product life cycle naturally occurring process that occurs when firms begin offering a product or service; the stages consist of introduction, growth, maturity, and decline

productive inputs any supplies used by a firm in conducting its business activities, such as labor, capital, land, and raw materials, among others

product-market diversification strategy a firm implements both product and geographic market diversification simultaneously

profitability ratios accounting ratios with some measure of profit in the numerator and some measure of firm size or assets in the denominator

profit-and-loss centers profits and losses are calculated at the level of the division in a firm

proprietary technology secret or patented technology that gives incumbent firms important advantages over potential entrants

question of imitability "Do firms without a resource or capability face a cost disadvantage in obtaining or developing it compared to firms that already possess it?"

question of organization "Is a firm organized to exploit the full competitive potential of its resources and capabilities?"

question of rarity "How many competing firms already possess particular valuable resources and capabilities?"

question of value "Does a resource enable a firm to exploit an external opportunity or neutralize an external threat?"

real options investments in real assets that create the opportunity for additional investments in the future

recession a period of relatively low prosperity; demand for goods and services is low and unemployment is high

related-constrained diversification all the businesses in which a firm operates share a significant number of inputs, product technologies, distribution channels, similar customers, and so forth

related corporate diversification less than 70 percent of a firm's revenue comes from a single product market and its multiple lines of business are linked

related-linked diversification strategy the different businesses that a single firm pursues are linked on only a couple of dimensions or different sets of businesses are linked along very different dimensions

reputation beliefs customers hold about a firm

resource-based view (RBV) a model of firm performance that focuses on the resources and capabilities controlled by a firm as sources of competitive advantage

resource heterogeneity for a given business activity, some firms may be more skilled in accomplishing the activity than other firms

resource immobility resources controlled by some firms may not diffuse to other firms

resources the tangible and intangible assets that a firm controls, which it can use to conceive and implement its strategies

retained earnings capital generated from a firm's ongoing operations that is retained by a firm

rivalry the intensity of competition among a firm's direct competitors

seemingly unrelated diversified diversified firms that exploit core competencies as an economy of scope, but are not doing so with any shared activities

senior executive the president or CEO of a firm

shakeout period period during which the total supply in an industry is reduced by bankruptcies, acquisitions, and business closings

shared activities potential sources of operational economies of scope for diversified firms

shark repellents a variety of relatively minor corporate governance changes that, in principle, are supposed to make it somewhat more difficult to acquire a target firm

single-business firms firms with greater than 95 percent of their total sales in a single product market

"skunk works" temporary teams whose creative efforts are intensive and focused

socially complex   resources and capabilities that involve interpersonal, social, or cultural links among individuals

social welfare   the overall good of society

specific international events   events such as civil wars, political coups, terrorism, wars between countries, famines, and country or regional economic recessions, all of which can have an enormous impact on the ability of a firm's strategies to generate competitive advantage

specific tariff   a tariff that is calculated as a percentage of the weight or volume of the goods being imported, regardless of the market value

stakeholders   all groups and individuals who have an interest in how a firm performs

standstill agreements   contract between a target and a bidding firm wherein the bidding firm agrees not to attempt to take over the target for some period of time

stock grants   payments to employees in a firm's stock

stock options   employees are given the right, but not the obligation, to purchase a firm's stock at predetermined prices

strategic alliance   whenever two or more independent organizations cooperate in the development, manufacture, or sale of products or services; a form of exchange governance between market exchanges and hierarchical exchanges; examples include licensing arrangements, manufacturing agreements, and joint ventures

strategic management process   a sequential set of analyses that can increase the likelihood of a firm's choosing a strategy that generates competitive advantages

strategically valuable assets   resources required to successfully compete in an industry, including access to raw materials, particularly favorable geographic locations, and particularly valuable product market positions

strategy   a firm's theory about how to gain competitive advantage

strategy implementation   a firm adopting organizational policies and practices that are consistent with its strategy

structure-conduct-performance model (S-C-P)   theory suggesting that industry structure determines a firm's conduct, which in turn determines its performance

substitutes   products or services that meet approximately the same customer needs but do so in different ways

substitution   developing or acquiring strategically equivalent, but different, resources as a competing firm

supermajority voting rules   an example of a shark repellent that specifies that more than 50 percent of the target firm's board of directors must approve a takeover

suppliers   firms that make a wide variety of raw materials, labor, and other critical assets available to firms

supply agreements   one firm agrees to supply others

sustainable distinctive competencies   valuable, rare, and costly to imitate resources or capabilities

sustained competitive advantage   a competitive advantage that lasts for a long period of time; an advantage that is not competed away through strategic imitation

tacit collusion   firms coordinate their production and pricing decisions not by directly communicating with each other, but by exchanging signals with other firms about their intent to cooperate; special case of tacit cooperation

tacit cooperation   actions a firm takes that have the effect of reducing the level of rivalry in an industry and that do not require firms in an industry to directly communicate or negotiate with each other

tactics   the specific actions a firm takes to implement its strategies

tax haven   a country that charges little or no corporate tax

technical economies   sources of relatedness in marketing, production, and similar activities between bidding and target firms

technological hardware   the machines and other hardware used by firms

technological leadership strategy   firms make early investments in particular technologies in an industry

technological strategy   in an international strategy, the ability a firm has to respond to the consumer preferences in a particular geographic market

technological software   the quality of labor–management relations, an organization's culture, and the quality of managerial controls in a firm

temporary competitive advantage   a competitive advantage that lasts for a short period of time

tender offer   a bidding firm offers to purchase the shares of a target firm directly by offering a higher than market price for those shares to current shareholders

thinly traded market   a market where there are only a small number of buyers and sellers, where information about opportunities in this market is not widely known, and where interests besides purely maximizing the value of a firm can be important

transaction specific investment   the value of an investment in its first-best use is much greater than its value in its second-best use; any investment in an exchange that has significantly more value in the current exchange than it does in alternative exchanges

transfer-pricing system   using internally administered "prices" to manage the movement of intermediate products or services among divisions within a firm

transnational strategy   actions in which a firm engages to gain competitive advantages by investing in technology across borders

transnational structure   each country in which a firm operates is organized as a full profit-and-loss division headed by a division general manager and strategic and operational decisions are delegated to operational entities that maximize local responsiveness and international integration

transparent business partners   international business partners that are open and accessible

U-form structure   organization where different functional heads report directly to CEO; used to implement business-level strategies

uncertainty   the future value of an exchange cannot be known when investments in that exchange are being made

unfriendly acquisition   the management of the target firm does not want the firm to be acquired

unrelated corporate diversification   less than 70 percent of a firm's revenues is generated in a single product market and a firm's businesses share few, if any, common attributes

value added as a percentage of sales   measures the percentage of a firm's sales that are generated by activities done within the boundaries of a firm; a measure of vertical integration

value chain   that set of activities that must be accomplished to bring a product or service from raw materials to the point that it can be sold to a final customer

venture capital firms   outside investment firms looking to invest in entrepreneurial ventures

vertical integration   the number of steps in the value chain that a firm accomplishes within its boundaries

vertical merger   when a firm vertically integrates, either forward or backward, through its acquisition efforts

visionary firms   firms whose mission is central to all they do

VRIO framework   four questions that must be asked about a resource or capability to determine its competitive potential: the questions of value, rarity, imitability, and organization

weighted average cost of capital (WACC)   the percentage of a firm's total capital that is debt multiplied by the cost of debt plus the percentage of a firm's total capital that is equity times the cost of equity

white knight   another bidding firm that agrees to acquire a particular target in place of the original bidding firm

zero-based budgeting   corporate executives create a list of all capital allocation requests from divisions in a firm, rank them from most important to least important, and then fund all the projects the firm can afford, given the amount of capital it has available

Company Index

In the page references, the number after "n" refers to the number of the end note in which the name is cited.

A

ABB, Inc., 199, 233
ABC, 179, 189, 305n6
Activision Inc., 248
Adidas, 281
AirTouch, 329
AirTran Airlines, 86, 102
Alberto-Culver, 322
Allegiant Airlines, 86
Allied Signal, 236
Amazon.com
  buyers, 46
  evaluating firm's capabilities, 64, 99n17
  innovation, 151
  rivalry, 42
  strategic management process, 2–3
  substitutes, 44
  threat of entry, 36
America West Airlines, 207
American Airlines, 97
American Express, 7
Ameritech, 329
Anheuser Busch, 40, 62n18, 111
AOL/Time Warner, 70, 98n7, 303
Apple Computer
  accounting performance, 15–16
  corporate diversification, 217
  evaluating firm's capabilities, 67
  innovation, 151
  strategic management process, 2–3
Applebee's, 55
Ashland Chemical, 97
AT&T
  corporate diversification, 208, 219n30
  economic measures of divisional
    performance, 236
  international strategies, 329
  mergers and acquisitions, 279, 281
  strategic alliances, 251
Atlanta Braves, 97

B

Bank of America, 288
Bank One, 302
Barnes & Noble.com, 36, 42, 44
BASF, 279
Bausch & Lomb, 313
Bavaria Brewery Company, 281
Bell Atlantic, 329
BellSouth, 251, 279, 329
Ben & Jerry's Ice Cream, 7–8, 27n7
Berkshire Hathaway, 217
Best Buy, 2
BIC
  corporate diversification, 207
  cost leadership strategy, 104–106,
    119
  product differentiation, 134
  strategic alliances, 251

BMW, 31
Boeing, 7, 87
Borders.com, 36, 42, 44
Boston Beer Company, 132
Boston Scientific, 279
Briggs and Stratton, 236
British Airways (BA), 153, 160n22, 202
British East India Company, 316
British Telecom, 329
Budweiser, 40
Burger King, 43, 54
Burlington Resources, 279

C

California Angels, 122
Campbell Soup Company, 47, 322
Canada Dry Mott's Inc, 137
Capital Cities/ABC, 281, 303
Cartoon Network, 137
Casio, 87, 99n30, 104, 132
Caterpillar, 207
CBS, 32, 42, 303, 305n25
CFM, 251, 273
Chaparral Steel, 126
Charles Schwab, 112, 153
ChevronTexaco, 281
Chicago Cubs, 122
Chili's, 55
Chrysler, 56, 145, 250, 262, 279
CIBA-Geigy, 199, 256–257, 323, 335
Cinergy, 279
Cingular, 273
Cisco, 151
Citigroup, 7, 217
City of Hope National Medical Center, 41
Clayton, Dubilier, and Rice, 231
CNN, 44
Coca-Cola Company
  changing tactics, 89
  corporate diversification, 192, 217
  economic measures of divisional
    performance, 236
  economies of scope and ambiguity of
    divisional performance, 237
  implementing corporate diversification,
    241
  international strategies, 310, 335
  PepsiCo vs., 160n12, 192
  product differentiation, 137, 160n12
Colgate, 311
Compaq Computer Corporation, 259–260
ConocoPhillips, 279
Continental Airlines, 85, 207
Coors, 40, 310
Corning, 256–257
Countrywide Financial, 242
Craig's List, 64
Cross, 134
Crown Cork & Seal Co. Inc.

cost leadership strategy, 108, 129n5
evaluating external environment, 63n35
international strategies, 315–316,
  340n10
CSX, 236
CW network, 32

D

Daewoo, 336
Daimler-Benz, 279
DaimlerChrysler, 279
Dairy Queen, 54
Dallas Cowboys, 97
Dell Computer
  competitive advantages in unattractive
    industries, 87
  corporate diversification, 206, 217
  cost leadership strategy, 121
  exercises/questions, 97
  innovation, 151
  international strategies, 322
  mission statement, 6
  vertical integration and firm's
    capabilities, 176
Deutsche Telephone, 329
Devanlay SA, 142
Digital, 41
DirecTV, 48–49
Dish Network, 48
Disney. *See* Walt Disney Company
Donato's Pizza, 191
Dow-Corning, 251, 273
Dr Pepper/Seven Up, Inc., 137
Duke Energy, 279
DuPont, 52, 201
Dupont, 255–256
Dutch East India Company, 316

E

E. & J. Gallo Winery, 40, 62n19
Eastman Kodak, 41, 137, 313, 340n6
eBay
  evaluating firm's internal capabilities,
    64–67
  mergers and acquisitions, 281
Electrolux, 311, 335
Electronic Arts, 248
Eli Lilly, 162
Englehard, 279
Enron, 5, 27n4
Entertainment Arts, 217
Eolas, 41
Ericson, 336
ESPN
  buyers, 46
  consumer marketing, 136
  corporate diversification, 188–190
  evaluating external environment, 62n13
  evaluating firm's capabilities, 77–78

Name Index

In the page references, the number after "n" refers to the number of the end note in which the name is cited.

359

Subject Index

In the page references, the number after "n" refers to the number of the end note in which the name is cited.